Irene C. Fountas
Gay Su Pinnell

The **Fountas&Pinnell**
Literacy Continuum

A Tool for Assessment, Planning, and Teaching

Expanded EDITION

HEINEMANN
Portsmouth, NH

Heinemann

361 Hanover Street

Portsmouth, NH 03801-3912

www.heinemann.com

Offices and agents throughout the world

The authors have dedicated a great deal of time and effort to writing the content of this book, and their written expression is protected by copyright law. We respectfully ask that you do not adapt, reuse, or copy anything on third-party (whether for-profit or not-for-profit) lesson-sharing websites. As always, we're happy to answer any questions you may have.

—**Heinemann Publishers**

"Dedicated to Teachers" is a trademark of Greenwood Publishing Group, Inc.

Acknowledgments for borrowed material begin on page 669.

Library of Congress Cataloging-in-Publication Data

Names: Fountas, Irene C., author. | Pinnell, Gay Su, author.

Title: The Fountas & Pinnell literacy continuum : a tool for assessment, planning, and teaching / Irene C. Fountas and Gay Su Pinnell.

Other titles: Fountas and Pinnell literacy continuum

Description: Expanded edition. | Portsmouth, NH : Heinemann, 2016. | Includes bibliographical references.

Identifiers: LCCN 2016014033 | ISBN 9780325060781 (pbk. : alk. paper)

Subjects: LCSH: Language arts (Elementary)—Handbooks, manuals, etc. | Language arts (Middle school)—Handbooks, manuals, etc. | Reading (Elementary)—Handbooks, manuals, etc. | Reading (Middle school)—Handbooks, manuals, etc. | Creative writing (Elementary education)—Handbooks, manuals, etc. | Creative writing (Middle school)—Handbooks, manuals, etc.

Classification: LCC LB1576 .F663 2016 | DDC 372.6—dc23

LC record available at https://lccn.loc.gov/2016014033

Editor: David Pence

Production: Lynne Costa, Angel Lepore

Cover design: Monica Ann Crigler and Suzanne Heiser

Interior design: Monica Ann Crigler

Typesetter: Technologies 'N Typography, Inc.

Manufacturing: Deanna Richardson

Printed in the United States of America on acid-free paper

6 7 8 9 10   WC   23 22 21 20 19

January 2019 Printing

CONTENTS

ACKNOWLEDGMENTS

The expanded publication of *The Fountas & Pinnell Literacy Continuum* represents a massive effort accomplished over several years. Many individuals have contributed to this effort, which involved meticulous, item-by-item, line-by-line analysis and the consultation of many expert sources.

We are indebted to Katie Wood Ray and Cynthia Downend for the insightful and thoughtful feedback they provided on the Writing continuum. Katie Wood Ray's work always makes us think in a deeper way. We also are grateful to Kerry Crosby, who provided suggestions for the Interactive Read-Aloud and the Writing About Reading continua. Susan Cusack and Troy Hicks were generous in their expert work on the Technology continuum. We especially thank Kathy Ha, who helped us with the Oral and Visual Communication continuum as well as, over time, giving us her special insights into working with English language learners.

The Heinemann team who supported us in this effort are truly exceptional. Editing this continuum was a unique and monumental task. We are especially grateful to David Pence for his extraordinary leadership, creativity, analysis, and hard work, as well as Betsy Sawyer-Melodia, Kathy Mormile, and the editorial team including Jill Backman, Laura Woollett, Deborah Doorack, Kimberly Capriola, Alana Jeralds, and Courtney Jordan.

Production, too, offered unique challenges. As always, we appreciate Michael Cirone's leadership in production; as well, we thank the expert production staff, Lynne Costa and Angel Lepore. We thank Lisa Fowler, Monica Crigler, and Suzanne Heiser for the brilliant cover and interior design. All of the Heinemann team have worked together with enthusiasm to make the continuum a useful tool for teachers.

We could not have produced this volume without the expert assistance of Cheryl Wasserstrom, Sharon Freeman, and Andrea Lelievre. We particularly appreciate their willingness to be flexible and to put in extra effort when needed.

To our publisher, Mary Lou Mackin, we are truly indebted. She is the person who keeps all systems going in the right direction. And, we realize that fully implementing this continuum will take professional support for teachers. We thank Cherie Bartlett, Mim Easton, and their team of high-level professional developers who will carry this forward. We also thank Samantha Garon for her brilliant and creative suggestions and advice as we thought about presenting this work to educators.

Finally, we are grateful to the many teachers, literacy coaches, and administrators who have used the original edition of the continuum over time and who helped us understand what was needed in terms of streamlining and ease of use.

INTRODUCTION

INTRODUCTION

This edition of *The Fountas & Pinnell Literacy Continuum* is labeled "expanded" because every part of it has been refined and at the same time elaborated. The basic descriptions of text characteristics and behaviors and understandings to notice, teach, and support are essentially the same. After all, reading, writing, and oral language are still the processes we have worked with for many years. But the descriptions are more precise. Our intention was to create a document that holds these precise details in a way that serves as a reference for teaching. In this way it serves as a curriculum guide to use in observation, planning, teaching, and reflecting, always asking, "What are my students showing that they know and can do?"

The continuum describes text characteristics and behavioral goals for prekindergarten through middle school, across the areas pertinent to the language arts. Taken together, the eight continua present a broad picture of the learning that takes place during the important years of school. The progress of learners across these continua, or even within each of them, is not an even, step-by-step process. Students learn as they have opportunities and give attention in different ways. A learner might make tremendous gains in one area while seeming to almost "stand still' in another. It's our job to provide these learning opportunities and guide their attention so that learning in one area informs and supports learning in others. Looking across the continua, we can see patterns of progress over time. Learners progress in their individual ways, but they ultimately reach the same goal—a complex and flexible literacy processing system.

In creating and now refining the continuum, we have consulted current research on the reading process, learning literacy, and English language learners. We have examined many sets of standards to determine how policy makers are looking at progress at the district, state, and national levels. You are probably working towards a set of standards that your district or school has adopted; we are confident that this continuum will not only be consistent with language and literacy standards but also will present descriptions of learning that are more detailed. We have attempted to describe the evidence of literacy learning that you will see in your students' behavior.

In this edition, you will notice more organization within categories as well as a red bullet to show new text characteristics or new behaviors that you expect to see evidence of at this grade or this level. You will also notice that behaviors evidencing "thinking within the text" are identified with a round bullet, behaviors evidencing "thinking beyond the text" with a diamond bullet, and behaviors evidencing "thinking about the text" with a square bullet.

Content of the Continuum

Across the eight continua included in this volume, several principles are important to consider:

- *Students learn by talking.* Talking represents the student's thinking. We engage students in conversation that is grounded in a variety of texts—those that students read, hear read aloud, or write—and that expands their ability to comprehend ideas and use language to share thinking.
- *Students need to process a large amount of written language.* A dynamic language and literacy curriculum provides many daily opportunities for students to read books of their choice independently, to read more challenging instructional material with teacher guidance, and to hear teacher-selected and grade-appropriate texts read aloud.
- *The ability to read and comprehend texts is expanded through talking and writing.* Students need to acquire a wide range of ways to write about their reading and also to talk about texts with the teacher and other students.
- *Learning deepens when students engage in reading, talking, and writing about texts across many different instructional contexts.* Each mode of communication provides a new way to process the ideas learned from oral and written texts and from each other.

This continuum provides a way to look for specific evidence of learning from prekindergarten through grade eight, and across eight curricular areas. To create it, we examined a wide range of research on language and literacy learning, and we asked teachers and researchers for feedback. We also examined the curriculum standards of many states. Some guiding principles were:

- Learning does not occur in stages but is a continually evolving process.
- The same concepts are acquired and then elaborated over time.
- Many complex literacy understandings take years to develop.
- Students learn by applying what they know to the reading and writing of increasingly complex texts.
- Learning does not automatically happen; most students need expert teaching to develop high levels of reading and writing expertise.
- Learning is different but interrelated across different kinds of language and literacy activities; one kind of learning enhances and reinforces others.

In this volume, we include eight different learning continua (see Figure I–1). Each of these continua focuses on a different aspect of our language and literacy instructional framework (*Guided Reading: Responsive Teaching Across the Grades,* Fountas and Pinnell 2017); and each contributes substantially, in different but complementary ways, to students' development of reading, writing, and language processes. Each of the continua is described in more detail in a separate introduction, but we briefly introduce them here.

FIGURE I–1 *The Fountas & Pinnell Literacy Continuum*

	INSTRUCTIONAL CONTEXT	BRIEF DEFINITION	DESCRIPTION OF THE CONTINUUM
1	**Interactive Read-Aloud and Literature Discussion**	Students engage in discussion with one another about a text that they have heard read aloud or one they have read independently.	• Year by year, grades PreK–8 • Genres appropriate to grades PreK–8 • Specific behaviors and understandings that are evidence of thinking within, beyond, and about the text
2	**Shared and Performance Reading**	Students read together or take roles in reading a shared text. They reflect the meaning of the text with their voices.	• Year by year, grades PreK–8 • Genres appropriate to grades PreK–8 • Specific behaviors and understandings that are evidence of thinking within, beyond, and about the text
3	**Writing About Reading**	Students extend their understanding of a text through a variety of writing genres and sometimes with illustrations.	• Year by year, grades PreK–8 • Genres/forms for writing about reading appropriate to grades PreK–8 • Specific evidence in the writing that reflects thinking within, beyond, and about the text
4	**Writing**	Students compose and write their own examples of a variety of genres, written for varying purposes and audiences.	• Year by year, grades PreK–8 • Genres/forms for writing appropriate to grades PreK–8 • Aspects of craft, conventions, and process that are evident in students' writing, grades PreK–8
5	**Oral and Visual Communication**	Students present their ideas through oral discussion and presentation.	• Year by year, grades PreK-8 • Specific behaviors and understandings related to listening and speaking, presentation
6	**Technological Communication**	Students learn effective ways of communicating and searching for information through technology; they learn to think critically about information and sources.	• Year by year, grades PreK-8 • Specific behaviors and understandings related to effective and ethical uses of technology
7	**Phonics, Spelling, and Word Study**	Students learn about the relationships of letters to sounds as well as the structure and meaning of words to help them in reading and spelling.	• Year by year, grades PreK-8 • Specific behaviors and understandings related to nine areas of understanding related to letters, sounds, and words, and how they work in reading and spelling
8	**Guided Reading**	Students read a teacher-selected text in a small group; the teacher provides explicit teaching and support for reading increasingly challenging texts.	• Level by level, A to Z • Genres appropriate to grades PreK-8 • Specific behaviors and understandings that are evidence of thinking within, beyond, and about the text • Specific suggestions for word work (drawn from the phonics and word analysis continuum)

Reading Process: Systems of Strategic Actions

Four of the continua specifically address reading: interactive read-aloud and literature discussion, shared and performance reading, guided reading, and writing about reading. Here we focus on strategic actions for thinking:

- ▶ *Within the text* (literal understanding achieved through searching for and using information, monitoring and self-correcting, solving words, maintaining fluency, adjusting, and summarizing for purposes and genre of text)
- ▶ *Beyond the text* (predicting; making connections with personal experience, content knowledge, and other texts; synthesizing new information; and inferring what is implied but not stated)
- ▶ *About the text* (analyzing or critiquing the text)

You can refer to the Systems of Strategic Actions chart on the inside front cover. Notice that readers are expected to engage in all systems simultaneously as they process texts. You can gain evidence of their control of the behaviors and understandings through observing oral reading, talk, or writing about reading.

Interactive read-aloud and literature discussion offer students an opportunity to extend their understandings through talk. In interactive read-aloud you have the opportunity to engage students with texts that are usually more complex than they can read for themselves. You can take strategic moments to stop for quick discussion during the reading and continue talking after the end. Students' talk provides evidence of their thinking.

Shared and performance reading offer an authentic reason for reading aloud. As they read in unison or read parts in readers' theater, students need to read in phrases, notice punctuation and dialogue, and think about the meaning of the text. All of these actions provide evidence that they are understanding the text and processing it effectively. On these familiar texts, you have the opportunity to support and extend students' understandings.

Guided reading offers small-group support and explicit teaching to help students take on more challenging texts. As they read texts that are organized along a gradient of difficulty, students expand their systems of strategic actions by meeting the demands of increasingly complex texts. They provide evidence of their thinking through oral reading and talk, and they extend understanding through writing. The Guided Reading continuum is related to text reading levels rather than grade levels because we envision continuous progress along these levels. In the introduction to the Guided Reading continuum, you will find a chart indicating a range of levels that approximately correlates with goals for each grade level.

In addition to specific evidence of thinking within, beyond, and about a text, each of these three continua lists genres of texts that are appropriate for use at each grade level or text level.

Writing about reading, which often includes drawing, is another way for students to extend their understanding and provide evidence of thinking. Writing about reading may be used in connection with interactive read-aloud and literature discussion or guided reading.

As you work with the continua related to reading, you will see a gradual increase in the complexity of the kinds of thinking that readers do. Most of the principles of learning cannot be pinpointed at one point in time or even one year. You will usually see the same kind of principle (behavior or understanding) repeated across grades or across levels of text; each time remember that the learner is applying the principle in a more complex way to read harder texts.

Oral and Visual, Technological, and Written Communication

Writing is a way of experimenting with and deepening understanding of genres students have read. Although writing about reading is an excellent approach to help students extend their thinking and support discussion, it does not take the place of specific instruction devoted to helping students develop as writers. Through the writing workshop, teachers help writers continually expand their learning of the craft, conventions, and process of writing to communicate meaning to an audience. The Writing continuum in this book lists specific understandings for each grade level related to craft, conventions, and process. It also suggests purposes and genres for students to consider and choose as they write at each grade level. You can refer to the chart, A Processing System for Writing, on the inside back cover to notice the complex dimensions in a processing system for writing.

Oral and visual communication are integral to all literacy processes; you'll see their presence in all other continua. This continuum singles out particular behaviors and understandings for intentional instruction.

Technological communication is essential for citizens of today's society. This continuum describes specific goals for helping students find effective ways to use technology effectively for learning, communication, and research. With the burgeoning role of technology in all of the contexts for communication, students need to build complex ways of thinking that will allow them to think critically about technology and to use it in effective and ethical ways.

Phonics, Spelling, and Word Study

As the eighth continuum, we include phonics, spelling, and word study. This grade-by-grade continuum is drawn from the longer continuum published in *The Fountas & Pinnell Comprehensive Phonics, Spelling, and Word Study Guide* (2017). For each grade, you will find specific principles related to the nine areas of learning that are important for grades PreK–8: early literacy concepts, phonological awareness, letter knowledge, letter-sound relationships, spelling patterns, high-frequency words, word meaning/vocabulary, word structure, and word-solving actions. Here you will find specific understandings related to spelling, which interface with the section on conventions provided in the Writing continuum.

Some Cautions

In preparing these continua we considered the typical range of students that can be found in PreK through grade eight classrooms. We also consulted teachers about their expectations and vision as to appropriate instruction at each grade level. We examined the district and state standards. We need to have a vision of expected levels of learning because it helps in making effective instructional decisions; and even more important, it helps us to identify students who need intervention.

At the same time, we would not want to apply these expectations in an inflexible way. We need to recognize that students vary widely in their progress—sometimes moving quickly and sometimes getting bogged down. They may make faster progress in one area than another. The continua should help you intervene in more precise ways to help students. But it is also important to remember that learners may not necessarily meet *every* expectation at all points in time. Nor should any one of the understandings and behaviors included in this document be used as criteria for promotion to the next grade. Educators can look thoughtfully across the full range of grade-level expectations as they make decisions about individual students.

It is also important to recognize that just because grade-level expectations exist, not all teaching will be pitched at that level. Through assessment, you may learn that your class only partially matches the behaviors and understandings on the continuum. Almost all teachers find that they need to consult the material at lower and higher levels (one reason that the Guided Reading continuum is not graded).

Ways to Use the Continuum

We see many different uses for this continuum, including the following.

Foundation for Teaching

As you think about, plan for, and reflect on the effectiveness of providing individual, small-group, and whole-group instruction, you may consult different areas of the continuum. For example, if you are working with students in guided reading at a particular level, use the lists of behaviors and understandings to plan text introductions, guide observations and interactions with individuals, and shape teaching decisions. The Word Work section gives you specific suggestions for principles to explore at the end of the guided reading lessons. You can plan specific teaching moves as you examine the section on interactive read-aloud and literature discussion. The interactive read-aloud as well as the Writing continuum and the Phonics, Spelling, and Word Study continuum will be useful in planning explicit minilessons. When you and your colleagues teach for the same behaviors and understandings, your students will benefit from the coherence.

Guide for Curriculum Planning

The continuum can also be used by a grade-level team or school staff to plan the language and literacy curriculum. It offers a starting point for thinking very specifically about goals and expectations. Your team may adapt the continuum to meet your own goals and district expectations.

Linking Assessment to Instruction

Sometimes assessment is administered and the results recorded, but then the process stops. Teachers are unsure what to do with the data or where to go next in their teaching. This continuum can be used as a bridge between assessment data and the specific teaching that students need. With assessment, you learn what students know; the continuum will help you think about what they need to know next.

Evaluation and Grading

The continuum can also serve as a guide for evaluating student progress over time. You can evaluate whether students are meeting grade-level standards. Remember that no student would be expected to demonstrate every single competency to be considered on grade level. *Grade level* is always a term that encompasses a range of levels of understanding at any given time.

Reporting to Parents

We would not recommend that you show parents such an overwhelming document as this continuum. It would get in the way of good conversation. However, you can use the continuum as a resource for the kind of specific information you need to provide to parents, but shape it into easy-to-understand language.

Guide to Intervention

Many students will need extra support in order to achieve the school's goals for learning. Assessment and observation will help you identify the specific areas in which students need help. Use the continuum to find the specific understandings that can guide intervention.

Organization of the Continuum

Eight continua are included in this document. They are arranged in the following way.

Grade-by-Grade

Seven of the continua are organized by grade level. Within each grade, you will find the continua for: (1) interactive read-aloud and literature discussion; (2) shared and performance reading; (3) writing about reading; (4) writing; (5) oral and visual communication; (6) technological communication; and (7) phonics, spelling, and word study. These seven continua are presented at each grade level, PreK through grade eight. You can turn to the section for your grade level and find all seven. If you have many students working below grade level, you can consult the next lower grade continuum in the area of interest; if you have students working above grade level, you can consult the continuum for the grade above for ideas.

Level-by-Level

The Guided Reading continuum is organized according to the Fountas & Pinnell text gradient levels A to Z (see Figure I–2). These levels typically correlate to grades K–8, but students may vary along them in their instructional levels. It is important for all students to receive guided reading instruction at a level that allows them to process texts successfully with teacher support.

Additional Resources

As an appendix for your reference, we have included a chart detailing standard "rules" for grammar and usage. This chart provides behaviors, principles, and examples that, in general, describe the kind of "standard" English that is expected in formal communication. As a speaker of this kind of English, sometimes called "media English," you follow almost all of these rules in your workplace without being able to state them explicitly, and that is how it should be. Language users have internalized these rules, and so they use them in an unconscious way, giving direct attention only when unsure. You will want to immerse students in language through hearing written language read aloud and through talk that is grounded in texts. Because you will be presenting them daily with many models of formal language and will also be creating a safe talking place for students, you may need to refer to this chart from time to time. We include it not so you can "correct" students or spend a great deal of time engaging them in exercises related to grammar; those actions don't really work. But as you observe students as they talk and write over time, you will want to look for evidence that they are expanding in their ability to use formal English. More information is provided at the beginning of the appendix.

FIGURE I–2 *Text Gradient*

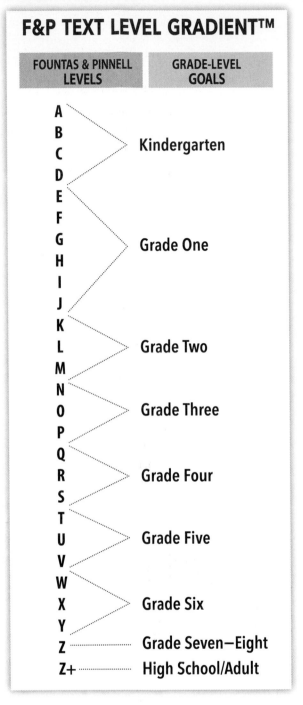

Ways Administrators or Staff Developers Can Use the Continuum

As a staff developer or an administrator, this document will give you a comprehensive view of language and literacy learning and how it changes and develops over time. The continuum is intended to provide teachers with a conceptual tool that they can use to think constructively about their work. We want to support them in crafting instruction that will link their observations and deep knowledge of their own students with learning over time. Administrators and staff developers are the key to teachers' support systems as they grow in conceptual understanding of their work.

Foundation for Setting School and/or District Goals

Since this continuum is a detailed description of every aspect of the language arts, you may want to adopt the continuum as your goals for instruction. Alternatively, you may want to review the document to select goals for your school or district. Remember, too, that these grade-level expectations are consistent with state and national standards in general. Depending on local priorities, you may want to adjust them lower or higher.

Link to State and National Standards

This continuum was checked against numerous examples of state and national standards to assure consistency and comprehensiveness. In general, you will find *The Fountas & Pinnell Literacy Continuum* to be much more detailed and in many cases more rigorous than state standards; so, it offers a way to make your state goals more specific as a basis for instruction. What really matters is for educators in each school to take ownership of the goals, share them with colleagues, and make them an integral part of teaching.

Helping Administrators and Teachers Achieve a Common Vision

Examining the continuum together, administrators and teachers can discuss their common expectations for students' achievement in each curriculum area, grade by grade. They can compare current expectations with the document and focus on goals that they want their students to achieve. For example, a principal and teachers in an elementary school or middle school can work together over a few weeks or months. In grade-level groups they can examine one instructional area at a time and then share their perspectives with teachers of other grades. Looking across the grades will help them to understand a long continuum of learning, as well as to work more effectively with students who are below or above their own grade levels. Working intensively with the continuum at their own grade levels (and perhaps the level below), they can make specific plans for instruction in the particular area.

A Basis for Instructional Coaching

An instructional coach (often called a literacy coach) can use the continuum as a foundation for coaching conversations. It will be useful for coaches to help teachers become able to access information quickly in their copies of the continuum as part of their reflection on lessons they have taught and on their planning. In other words, the coach can help teachers really get to know the continuum as a tool so that they can access information easily on their own. Typically, the coach and teacher would use the continuum as a reference before, during, and after the observation of a lesson. The continuum enables the coach to focus the conversation on critical areas of teaching and learning—behaviors to notice, teach, and support to help students read, write, and talk proficiently. It is also an excellent tool for discussing and analyzing texts in a variety of genres and at a variety of levels. The continuum will add specificity to the conversation that will extend teachers' understandings of learning processes and development over time.

Pre-Observation Conference

▶ The coach and teacher think about and analyze students' strengths, as well as their learning needs, referring to the continuum as appropriate.

▶ They may examine data from student assessment or the teacher's ongoing observation, again, using the continuum expectations as a reference.

▶ They may look at lesson artifacts—texts they are using or student writing—and consider them in the light of text characteristics for the particular area, thinking about the learning opportunities for students.

Observation of Lessons

▶ The continuum is not designed to be used as a checklist. Rather it is a foundation for discussing critical areas of development.

▶ The continuum offers a way of sharpening observation. During observation, coaches can keep in mind the evidence of student understanding and shifts in learning. This foundational knowledge will help the coach gather specific evidence of student learning that can be discussed later with the teacher.

Post-Observation Conference

▶ The continuum will provide a guide as to the appropriateness of texts or tasks in terms of students' current understandings and what they need to learn next.

▶ The coach and teacher can use the continuum to analyze the teaching and its effectiveness in meeting the goals discussed in the pre-observation conference.

▶ They can discuss examples of behaviors that provide evidence of student understanding or lack of understanding.

▶ They can also discuss teaching interactions that supported or extended student understanding, as well as potential interactions for working with the students in the next lesson.

▶ Together the coach and teacher can use the continuum to help set new learning goals for the students and to begin to plan for teaching.

The ultimate goals of every coaching interaction are to help the teacher expand knowledge of language and literacy learning and to analyze the effectiveness of the teaching. By talking about the ideas in the continuum and observing students carefully, teachers will come to understand more about the processes of learning language, reading, writing, and technology. The continuum serves as a guide that becomes internalized through its consistent use. Teachers who use it over time find that the understandings recorded in the continuum become part of their thinking and their teaching decisions.

Interactive Read-Aloud
and
Literature Discussion

Interactive Read-Aloud and Literature Discussion Continuum

In selecting curriculum goals for an interactive read-aloud, consider the text and opportunities for new learning. At all grade levels, students need to listen to and comprehend age-appropriate texts in a variety of genres and increasingly complex texts within those genres. Story problems, characters, content, and topics should be matched to the particular age group, with consideration of students' background, language, culture, experience, and interests. Also consider a variety of text formats and types of texts.

Beyond text selection, it is important to think about how to support readers' thinking within, beyond, and about a text. Before, during, and after listening to a text read-aloud, notice evidence of students' literal understanding. Did they pick up important information? Could they follow the plot? Could they remember important details? Students need to think beyond the text, making predictions and important connections. Look for evidence that they can notice and incorporate new information into their own understandings, as well as make inferences based on the available information. Finally, students need to form opinions about their reading and develop their own reading preferences. Look for evidence that they can think analytically about texts, noticing the writer's craft and style. It is also important for them to think critically about the quality, content, and accuracy of texts.

Interactive read-aloud is a powerful setting for teaching students to use academic language to talk about texts. The ability to use academic language is acquired over time—from talking about the book's title, author, and illustrator to using the highly sophisticated language that we expect in higher education, like *plot structure, character development,* and *expository text structures.* Daily, students experience high quality texts and are guided in rich discussion. You introduce and demonstrate academic language, and it becomes integral to the process of talking about texts.

Interactive read-aloud also offers you an opportunity to draw students' attention to significant features of the *peritext* (a space outside the body of the text). The peritext may include titles and subtitles, authors' names, prefaces, forewords, introductions, acknowledgments, epigraphs, glossaries, notes, illustrations, and design features that add to the aesthetic appeal and may have cultural significance or symbolic meaning. Elements of the peritext add meaning, communicate mood, and help readers interpret the text. It is part of the whole artistic creation that is the text. As you read aloud, you can point out these features and prompt students to notice them in the books they read independently and in guided reading lessons.

When students are actively listening to and discussing a text, all of the strategic actions for comprehending are in operation. (See Guided Reading continuum, pp. 399–630 and the inside front cover of this book.) In an interactive read-aloud, the listener is freed from decoding and is supported by the oral reader's fluency, phrasing, and stress—all elements of what we sometimes call *expression.* The scene is set for a high level of comprehending and engaging in thinking and talking about texts.

Interactive Read-Aloud and Literature Discussion

From prekindergarten through eighth grade, meaningful discussion is a part of interactive read-aloud and book clubs (see Fountas and Pinnell 2001, 2006). We advocate intentional teaching through interactive read-aloud. Enjoyment and engagement are necessary, and you will find these goals easy to achieve as you select high-quality texts and read them to students. At the same time, take an active approach that allows you to teach for comprehension at a pace that comes *before* students can process texts at this level of complexity. They may not be able to read all of the words or parse the sentences, but they can think, talk, and write about the ideas, the stories, and the content of the texts you select. A structure for interactive read-aloud is shown in Figure I-1.

FIGURE I-1 *Structure of Interactive Read-Aloud*

Selection and Preparation	• *Select the text based on your observations of students and your curriculum goals for developing readers.* • *Prepare for the session by reading and analyzing the text and planning for embedded teaching.*
Opening	• *Say a few words about the text to engage students' interest and clarify some points on any aspect of the text (e.g., setting, background information necessary to understanding the text).*
Reading Aloud **Embedded Teaching** **Text Talk**	• *Read the text aloud to students.* • *Stop for a brief (preplanned) conversation at several places in the text.* • *Invite students to engage in talk that is grounded in the text.*
Discussion and Self-Evaluation	• *Have a discussion of the book.* • *Ask students to self-evaluate what they learned and what they contributed.*
Record of Reading	• *Write the title and author of the book on a "Books We Have Shared" chart displayed in the classroom.*
Written or Artistic Response (Optional)	• *Ask students to write or draw in response to the text.*

Texts for interactive read-aloud are very carefully selected, and often you will want to make a plan and sequence the texts over several weeks. Through a superb sequence of read-aloud texts, you can help your students

  ▶ become acquainted with literary language and elements, sharpening their ability to notice and think analytically about them;

  ▶ get to know authors and illustrators;

  ▶ explore topics related to social studies, the environment, and people of the world;

  ▶ examine a range of social issues that become increasingly important to them as they grow toward the teenage years;

  ▶ explore many different cultures and kinds of family life;

  ▶ become immersed in the study of genre;

▶ learn about human problems;

▶ learn about history;

▶ expand vocabulary and the ability to use academic language to talk about texts.

We have recommended the use of "text sets" that establish such sequences. It is very effective when teachers work together to assemble them (always changing in response to students' interests and needs).

Before you read a text aloud to students, read it yourself and analyze it. What is there to learn in the text? What good examples appear in the text? What is the central message of the text? The text characteristics for each grade will be helpful here. Then, make a plan for using the text. How will you open the session? Where in the text should you plan to stop for a brief discussion? Place sticky notes with comments or questions so that they will be right there when you need them.

You can open the session with a very brief introduction to the book. The primary purpose of these remarks is to get the students interested in the book, but your analysis might also reveal something students should know "going in," for example, a little bit about the period of history or other background information. You can share the names of the author and illustrator, connecting to any other books students know.

Then, move into the reading. (This is, perhaps, the most enjoyable time of the day.) Your reading doesn't have to be dramatic, but remember that one thing you are doing is showing the students a model of excellent oral reading. Stop at your preplanned spots for a very brief discussion. (Don't go into long discussions or students will lose meaning and engagement.) Also, at those same spots, encourage students to use the routine "turn and talk," which you can teach them during their first week of read-aloud sessions. During this time, all students have the opportunity to express their own ideas about the text, building up expertise for the final discussion.

When the reading is over, invite an open discussion of the text. You may have some key ideas to bring to students' attention, as well as some questions or thoughts of your own to express. You may ask students to clarify their statements or to question each other. Finally, ask them to self-evaluate. What did they learn from this story or informational text that is interesting or helpful? Ask them to think about their own contributions and how they helped the group.

Write the title and author of the text on a posted chart in the classroom. This chart will help students remember the book if they want to write about it in a Reader's Notebook or to read the text again. Also, well-selected texts become *mentor texts* on which you base reading and writing minilessons. You can look across the shared texts to talk about a writer's message or how characters are revealed. Students can use them as resources as they write pieces in the same genre.

The opportunity is always there to write or draw about the text, but you may occasionally want to take a more structured approach and ask students to address a particular question or write analytically about the text in some way. Don't follow every read-aloud session with writing, because it may detract from the enjoyment and dynamic nature of this instructional context.

Text-based talk is the central tool in learning in this instructional context. Students discuss the book as a whole class, but they also need to be engaged in more intimate routines like "turn and talk" (focused on any aspect of text). For a minute or two a few times within the larger discussion, these routines provide opportunities for individuals to engage in more talk than would otherwise be possible in a whole-group discussion.

Inserting such routines into your interactive read-aloud lesson will make whole-group discussions more lively and give all students the opportunity for active participation. After students have spent some time talking in pairs, triads, or small circles, they will become skilled in small-group discussion. After students have had a great deal of experience using the routines, you may decide they are ready for a more extended discussion with their peers in book clubs. You can find extensive information about these instructional approaches in *Teaching for Comprehending and Fluency: Thinking, Talking, and Writing About Reading, K–8* (Fountas and Pinnell, Heinemann 2006).

Interactive read-aloud and literature discussion abound with *text talk*—shared talk in which students examine ideas and think about narrative, expository, or poetic texts. Every engagement gives students opportunities for thinking about texts in new ways. The more they have a chance to do it, the better they get at the academic language used for text talk. As students work together in groups, they develop a backlog of shared meanings that increasingly deepens their talk.

Interactive read-aloud and literature discussion are placed together in this continuum because in both settings we seek age-appropriate, grade-appropriate reading materials that have the potential to extend students' thinking and their ability to talk about texts. For prekindergarten students, literature discussion will take place during interactive read-aloud. But, as children gain more experience through turn-and-talk routines, they can begin to prepare for and engage in small-group discussions. For small-group literature discussion, students usually choose from several texts that you have preselected. If they can read the selection independently, they read at home or during the reading workshop. If they cannot read the text easily on their own, make an audio recording of it available. Sometimes, you will engage students in book clubs based on texts that you have read aloud to the entire class. Thus, in selecting and using books for interactive read-aloud and literature discussion, you do not need to consider a specific level, but you will want to think about the text characteristics as well as texts that are age and grade appropriate.

Framework for the Continuum of Learning

The continuum that follows is a guide for setting goals and creating instructional plans for interactive read-aloud and literature discussion. This continuum provides grade-by-grade information that includes

- ▶ characteristics of texts (descriptions of ten text factors to keep in mind when selecting and reading aloud texts);
- ▶ curriculum goals (descriptions of behaviors and understandings to notice and support to help readers think within, beyond, and about the text you have selected).

Characteristics of Texts for Interactive Read-Aloud and Literature Discussion

Ten text factors are important to consider when selecting texts for any kind of reading instruction. Figure I–2 provides descriptions of all ten text factors, with a focus on interactive read-aloud. As you use interactive read-aloud daily across the year, students accumulate a rich resource of texts that they hold in common. These texts can be used as examples for reading or writing minilessons. By reading aloud, you bring excellent writers into your classroom. When selecting texts for interactive read-aloud, consider the high level of support you need to provide to students to help them process and think about the text. It is important to ensure that the vocabulary in the text is understandable to listeners, although you will always be expanding their understanding of new words. You don't need to worry about word-solving difficulty since you will be doing the decoding.

FIGURE I-2 *Ten Text Characteristics for Interactive Read-Aloud and Literature Discussion*

Genre	We have listed a variety of types of texts that are appropriate at each grade level. For the most part, you will want to use the full range of genres suggested for every grade level, but be selective about the particular examples you choose.
Text Structure	The structure of a text refers to the way it is organized. Fiction texts are generally organized in a narrative structure, with a problem and a sequence of events that leads to the resolution of the problem. Interactive read-aloud is a context in which listeners can internalize plot structure and learn how stories work. Nonfiction texts may also be narrative; biographies, for example, usually tell the stories like fiction texts do. But most informational texts are organized categorically by subtopic with underlying structures such as description; temporal sequence; chronological sequence; comparison and contrast; cause and effect; and problem and solution. Often these structures are used in combination. Interactive read-aloud and literature discussion provide a setting within which you can teach students to recognize and understand text structures.
Content	The subject matter of the text should be accessible and interesting to listeners. Over time, the sophistication and complexity of content can be increased. Although direct experiences are always necessary for learning, students can acquire a great deal of content knowledge from hearing written language read aloud. Content is helpful to listeners when they already have some prior knowledge to bring to understanding new information.
Themes and Ideas	The major ideas of the books you choose to read aloud should be appropriate for all students' age and background experience. Interactive read-aloud is an ideal way to stretch students' knowledge, but they must be able to make connections to their existing knowledge. They can extend their own understanding of the themes and ideas as they discuss them with others.
Language and Literary Features	The way the writer uses language creates the literary quality of a text. It is important to select texts that students can understand in terms of language and literary features. Interactive read-aloud and literature discussion provide opportunities to expand your students' ability to process literary language, including dialogue and figurative language. Other literary features include the development of elements such as setting, plot, and characters.
Sentence Complexity	The syntactic complexity of sentences–their length, word order, and the number of embedded phrases and clauses–is another key factor. Through the grades, students can generally understand sentences that are more complex than those they can read. Interactive read-aloud provides a way to help them gradually internalize many examples of more complex sentences. Discussion with others will help students unpack complex sentences and understand them better.
Vocabulary	Vocabulary refers to the words that an individual knows and understands in both oral and written language. The words that the writer has selected may present a challenge to readers. Written texts usually include many words that are not in our everyday oral vocabulary; we constantly expand vocabulary by reading or hearing written language read aloud. Through interactive read-aloud and literature discussion, students begin to use new vocabulary in their talk. Students can greatly expand their listening and speaking vocabulary.

Words	When selecting books for students to read for themselves, we always consider the challenges the words present: length, number of syllables, inflectional endings, and general ease of solving. In interactive read-aloud, however, the teacher processes the print, so word solving is not a factor in text selection. Also, for literature discussion, students may use audio recordings of texts that they are not yet ready to read independently. Attention to vocabulary will take into account word complexity.
Illustrations	Illustrations (or other forms of art) provide a great deal of information to readers and listeners. A high-quality picture book is a coherent form of literary art. Think of a picture book as a short story with beautiful illustrations. Picture books are appropriate for a wide range of ages and all genres. For students of all ages, illustrations increase engagement and enjoyment. They add to the mood of a text. Illustrations for younger students provide a great deal of information; for older students they help create mood. Informational texts (and increasingly some fiction texts) also include graphics in the form of maps, diagrams, and drawings. These graphics may provide information that is additional to the body of the text. Some graphics may be large enough for students to see and discuss during interactive read-aloud, but students may attend to them during small-group discussion.
Book and Print Features	When selecting books for interactive read-aloud, you consider the physical aspects of the text, such as length, size, and layout. Book and print features also include organizational tools like the table of contents, glossary, pronunciation guide, indexes, sidebars, and headings. They also include features outside the body of the text such as endpapers, dedication, author's note, referred to as *peritext*. All of these features may be pointed out and discussed during interactive read-aloud or literature discussion.

Curriculum Goals

We have stated curriculum goals in terms of behaviors and understandings to notice, teach, and support at each level. These systems of strategic actions are further divided into evidence that the reader is thinking *within, beyond,* and *about* the text. (See Guided Reading continuum, pp. 399–630 and the inside front cover of this book.)

▶ *Within the Text.* To effectively and efficiently process a text and derive the literal meaning, readers must solve the words and monitor and self-correct their reading. In interactive read-aloud, readers are relieved of the task of decoding and they hear fluent, phrased reading; but they must self-monitor their own understanding, remember information in summary form, and adjust their thinking to the understanding of different fiction and nonfiction genres.

▶ *Beyond the Text.* Readers make predictions and connections to previous knowledge and their own lives. They also make connections between and among texts. They bring background knowledge to listening to a text, synthesize new information by incorporating it into their own understandings. They think about what the writer has not stated but implied. Readers may infer the feelings and motivations of characters in fiction texts or the implications of the writer's statements in nonfiction. Interactive read-aloud provides many opportunities to support students' thinking beyond the literal meaning. By engaging students in discussion before and after reading, you can demonstrate how to think beyond the text and help them expand their own ability to do so. You can also stop at selected intervals while reading aloud to discuss text elements that prompt expanded thinking.

▶ *About the Text.* Readers think analytically about the text as an object, noticing and appreciating elements of the writer's craft, such as use of language, characterization, organization, and structure. Reading like a writer helps students notice aspects of craft and more fully enjoy a text, sometimes revisiting it. Readers also think critically about texts, evaluating the quality and considering the writer's accuracy or objectivity. Interactive read-aloud time is ideal time for demonstrating the kind of sophisticated thinking that effective readers do. It provides the opportunity for students to engage in analytic thinking about texts. In addition, the books you read aloud become a collection of shared texts that can be turned to again and again to notice more about the writer's craft.

Organization

This continuum is organized by grade level. For each grade level, the first part, Selecting Texts, describes text characteristics for the books you read aloud. The items are organized according to the ten text characteristics listed in Figure I-2. You are reading the books, of course, so you can make available texts that students cannot yet read for themselves. But you will still want to consider

- ▶ the complexity and challenge of the genre;
- ▶ the vocabulary that students can stretch to understand;
- ▶ the age-appropriateness of the content and concepts;
- ▶ the appeal to students at this age.

In other words, the books must be appropriate for the age of your students. Use this continuum as a guide in selecting texts and to help you analyze the challenges and learning opportunities in them.

In the next section for each grade, Selecting Goals, we list goals that are categorized for thinking *within, beyond,* and *about* texts. The goals for using fiction and nonfiction texts are categorized by areas of understanding. The shape of the bullet designates the behavior as thinking within the text [●], beyond the text [◆], or about the text [■]. These goals are stated in the form of specific behaviors and understandings students need to develop in order to understand and learn from the texts that are being read.

For the text characteristics and goals, new items for the grade level are marked with a red bullet. This will help you find the new challenges quickly. But don't forget that *all* of the text characteristics and goals are important. In other words, the behavior or understanding may be the same, but students are challenged to *apply* it to more complex texts at each grade level.

Using the Interactive Read-Aloud and Literature Discussion Continuum

You can use this guide to set overall curriculum goals for grades PreK–8, or you can refer to it as you plan for interactive read-aloud. However, the continuum does not reference specific texts, topics, or content areas. Using the text characteristics, select a variety of high-quality texts with content that engages your students' interests, emotions, and intellectual curiosity. Consider topics of study in science and social studies for your grade level. You can apply the continuum's goals in connection with your district or state requirements and standards.

We use the term *intentional conversation* to describe the instructional moves you make during the conversation surrounding books in interactive read-aloud or in small-group literature discussion. Your first goals when reading aloud to your students and engaging them in small-group discussions are to engage their interest and intellect, to make the occasion enjoyable, and to guide them in active conversation. Interactive read-aloud and literature discussion give students opportunities to share their own ideas, to express their own meanings, and to contribute to deeper understanding of the text. Through the text examples, students develop understandings about their physical and social world. Conversation must be genuine. You are always keeping in mind your curriculum goals, and that is what makes the conversation intentional.

Without being heavy handed or stifling students' comments, you can guide the conversation so that students are constantly expanding their thinking. During the interactive read-aloud and literature discussion, the teacher

- keeps in mind the systems of strategic actions that readers must use;
- knows the text deeply and understands its demands and the opportunities it provides for new learning;
- provides conversational leads to focus students' attention;
- models and demonstrates behaviors that help students achieve better understanding;
- asks students to share their thinking in a focused way;
- prompts students to listen to and respond to one another rather than always being the center of the conversation;
- keeps the conversation grounded in the text;
- turns the conversation back to students, asking for deeper thinking;
- requires students to be accountable for their comments, asking for more than opinion and asking for evidence from the text or personal experience;
- gives feedback to students on what they are learning and the kinds of thinking they are doing;
- asks students to self-evaluate their conversation about the text.

You will find that interactive read-aloud and literature discussion provide rich opportunities for every student to expand background knowledge, experience age-appropriate and grade-appropriate text, and learn a variety of ways to think deeply and use academic language to talk about an engaging text.

Selecting Texts Characteristics of Texts for Reading Aloud and Discussion

Interactive Read-Aloud and Literature Discussion

GENRE

▶ **Fiction**
- Realistic fiction
- Folktale
- Simple animal fantasy

▶ **Nonfiction**
- Simple factual texts
- Memoir (personal memory story)
- Simple procedural texts

FORMS
- Picture books
- Wordless picture books
- Label books
- Short poems
- Nursery rhymes, rhymes, and songs
- Concept books
- ABC books
- Counting books
- Books with texture, padding, pop-ups, unusual features that promote interaction

TEXT STRUCTURE
- Simple narrative with beginning, series of episodes, and ending
- Many texts with repeating episodes
- Some texts with nonnarrative structure
- Most texts focusing on a single topic, usually one idea per page
- Underlying structural patterns: simple description, some temporal sequence, some question and answer

CONTENT
- Content that is appropriate for children's cognitive development, social and emotional maturity, and life experience
- Content that engages children's intellectual curiosity and emotions
- Language and word play: e.g., rhymes, nonsense, alliteration, and alphabet
- Content that reflects early conceptual understandings: e.g., colors, shapes, counting, sorting, size, alphabet, position
- Everyday actions familiar to young children: e.g., playing, making things, eating, getting dressed, bathing, cooking, shopping

- Familiar topics that are authentic and relevant: e.g., animals, pets, families, friends, growing and health, school, neighborhood, weather and seasons, food, plants
- Humor that is easy to grasp: e.g., silly characters, funny situations
- Content that reinforces and expands a child's experience and knowledge of self and the world
- A few topics that may be beyond children's immediate experiences
- Content that reflects a wide range of settings and cultures
- Realistic characters, settings, and events that occur in realistic fiction
- Imaginary characters, events (some nonsensical and funny), and settings that occur in fantasy
- Content that reflects beginning understanding of the physical and social world

THEMES AND IDEAS
- Themes reflecting everyday life: e.g., self, family relationships, home, friendship, community, diversity, first responsibilities, imagination, fears, courage, nature
- Clear, simple ideas easy to identify
- Ideas close to children's experience: e.g., taking care of self, staying healthy, expressing feelings, sharing with others, caring for others, helping your family, going to school, caring for your world, valuing differences, being part of a community

LANGUAGE AND LITERARY FEATURES
- A few simple elements of fantasy: e.g., talking animals
- Predictable story outcomes typical of traditional literature: e.g., cleverness overcomes physical strength, good defeats evil
- Familiar settings close to children's experience
- Both realistic and fantastic settings, events, and characters
- Memorable characters that are straightforward, uncomplicated, and predictable

- Characters with one or two simple traits: e.g., kind, generous, sly, brave, silly, wise, greedy
- Characters that do not change or that change in simple ways for clear reasons
- Characters' actions related to clear consequences: e.g., reward for trying hard
- Predictable sequence of events
- Language used to make comparisons
- Some poetic language, often using notable sound devices: e.g., rhythm, rhyme, repetition, refrain, onomatopoeia
- Simple dialogue and dialogue with pronouns (assigned by *said* in many texts) easily attributed to characters
- Some repetitive dialogue
- Some literary language typical of traditional literature: e.g., *once upon a time, long ago and far away, happily ever after*

SENTENCE COMPLEXITY
- Sentences that are easy for children to follow, though more complex than children generally use in oral language
- Simple sentences with subject and predicate
- Variety of language structures
- Sentences with clauses and phrases
- Sentences that are questions
- Sentences with adjectives, adverbs, and prepositional phrases

VOCABULARY
- A few interesting words that are new to children but easy to understand in context
- Some memorable words that children can take on as language play
- All words that are in common oral vocabulary for young children (Tier 1)
- Many simple adjectives describing people, places, or things
- A few simple adverbs that describe action
- Common (simple) connectives that are frequently used in oral language (words, phrases that clarify relationships ideas): e.g., *and, but, so, because, before, after*

Selecting Texts Characteristics of Texts for Reading Aloud and Discussion *(cont.)*

Interactive Read-Aloud and Literature Discussion

ILLUSTRATIONS

- Large, clear, colorful illustrations in a variety of media that fully support meaning
- Illustrations that add meaning to the text
- Very simple illustrations with no distracting detail
- Some illustrations with labels

BOOK AND PRINT FEATURES

LENGTH

- Short picture books that can be read in one sitting

PRINT AND LAYOUT

- Some picture books with print large enough for children to see during read-aloud
- Some print in speech bubbles or thought bubbles
- Some books with special features that engage interest and make texts interactive: e.g., pop-ups, pop-outs, flaps, pull-tabs, see-though holes, sound effects
- Some books with decorative or informative illustrations, engaging designs that catch the attention, and/or print or illustrations outside the body of the text (peritext)

PUNCTUATION

- Simple punctuation: e.g., period, question mark, exclamation mark

ORGANIZATIONAL TOOLS

- Title, author, and illustrator listed on cover and on title page

TEXT RESOURCES

- Some books with dedication, author's note, about the author and/or illustrator

Selecting Goals Behaviors and Understandings to Notice, Teach, and Support

Interactive Read-Aloud and Literature Discussion

FICTION TEXTS

General

- Ask questions to deepen understanding of a text
- Notice and ask questions when meaning is lost or understanding is interrupted
- Refer to important information and details
- Understand that the teacher reads the print, not the pictures
- Understand that the teacher must hold the book right side up
- Mimic the teacher's expression and word stress when reenacting a text or joining in
- Use hand and body movements to show understanding of the meaning or meanings of pictures and words in a text
- Join in on refrains or repeated words, phrases, and sentences after hearing them several times
- Gain new information from both pictures and print
- Recognize simple problems that occur in everyday life
- Give reasons (either text-based or from personal experience) to support thinking
- Relate texts to their own lives
- Use background knowledge to understand settings, problems, and characters
- Recognize and understand that stories may be about different kinds of people and different places
- Make connections (e.g., content, topic, theme) across texts that are read aloud
- Recognize that an author or illustrator may write or illustrate several books
- Express opinions about a text: e.g., interesting, funny, exciting
- Articulate why they like a text

Genre

- Understand that there are different types of books and that you can notice different things about them
- Understand when a story could happen in real life (realistic fiction) and when it could not happen in real life (folktales, animal fantasy)
- Notice story outcomes typical of traditional literature: e.g., cleverness overcomes physical strength, good defeats evil

Messages and Themes

- Infer the "lesson" in traditional literature
- Infer meanings in a story using understandings and experiences from their own lives: e.g., taking care of self, staying healthy, expressing feelings, sharing with others, caring for others, helping your family, going to school, caring for your world, valuing differences
- Understand that a fiction text can have different meanings for different people
- Understand that a book can have more than one message or big idea
- Notice when a writer or storyteller is "teaching a lesson"

Setting

- Recognize and understand that texts may have settings related to different places and different people

Plot

- Follow the events in simple narratives
- Notice and understand a simple plot with problem and solution
- Check on understanding of the plot of the story and ask questions if meaning is lost
- Tell the important events of a story using the pictures (after hearing the text read several times)
- Tell the problem in a story and how it is resolved
- Predict what will happen next in a story
- Predict story outcomes

Character

- Notice and remember characters in simple narratives
- Infer a character's feelings using text and pictures
- Notice when a character changes or learns a lesson
- Express opinions about characters in a story: e.g., funny, bad, silly, nice, friendly
- Learn from vicarious experiences with characters in stories
- Understand that animals in stories sometimes act like people (animal fantasy)
- Understand that the same type of characters may appear over and over again in traditional literature: e.g., sly, brave, silly, wise, greedy

● Thinking *Within* the Text   ◆ Thinking *Beyond* the Text   ■ Thinking *About* the Text

Selecting Goals Behaviors and Understandings to Notice, Teach, and Support *(cont.)*

Interactive Read-Aloud and Literature Discussion

FICTION TEXTS *(continued)*

Style and Language

- Play with words or language orally: e.g., nonsense words or refrains from texts that are read aloud
- Understand sentences that are simple but may be different from oral language
- Follow and understand simple dialogue with a clear idea about who is speaking
- Notice a writer's use of repetition, refrains, and rhythm
- Notice a writer's use of playful or poetic language: e.g., nonsense words, rhythm, rhyme, repetition, onomatopoeia, alliteration
- Recognize a writer's use of humor
- Understand the meaning of some literary language (the language of books in contrast to typical oral language)
- Notice and remember literary language patterns that are characteristic of traditional literature: e.g., *once upon a time, long ago and far away, happily ever after*

Vocabulary

- Notice and acquire understanding of new vocabulary from read-aloud content
- Understand the meaning of simple nouns, verbs, adjectives, adverbs, prepositions, and simple connectives (when listening to a story)
- Use new vocabulary in discussion of a text
- Use some academic language to talk about texts: e.g., *ABC book, poem, song, cover, title, author, illustrator, page, text, illustration, photograph, beginning, ending, problem*

Illustrations

- Tell the important events of a story using the pictures (after hearing the text read several times)
- Tell stories in response to pictures
- Understand that illustrations can have different meanings for different people
- Understand that an illustrator created the pictures in the book

Book and Print Features

- Notice letters, words, simple phrases, or sentences that are large enough to see, especially when they are repeated
- Enjoy special features such as pop-ups, pop-outs, flaps, pull-tabs, see-through holes, sound effects

---

● Thinking *Within* the Text   ◆ Thinking *Beyond* the Text   ■ Thinking *About* the Text

Selecting Goals Behaviors and Understandings to Notice, Teach, and Support *(cont.)*

Interactive Read-Aloud and Literature Discussion

NONFICTION TEXTS

General

- Ask questions to deepen understanding of a text
- Notice and ask questions when meaning is lost or understanding is interrupted
- Refer to important information and details
- Use hand and body movements to show understanding of the meaning or meanings of pictures and words in a text
- Understand and talk about everyday activities: e.g., playing, making things, eating, getting dressed, bathing, cooking, shopping
- Understand content that reflects beginning understanding of physical world and social world: e.g., mathematics, social studies, science, health, arts
- Understand that the teacher reads the print, not the pictures
- Understand that the teacher must hold the book right side up
- Mimic the teacher's expression and word stress when reenacting a text or joining in
- Use hand and body movements to show understanding of the meaning or meanings of pictures and words in a text
- Join in on refrains or repeated words, phrases, and sentences after hearing them several times
- Gain new information from both pictures and print
- Understand simple problems that occur in everyday life
- Give reasons (either text-based or from personal experience) to support thinking
- Use background knowledge to understand texts that are read aloud
- Relate texts to their own lives
- Recognize and understand that texts may be about different kinds of people and different places
- Recognize that an author or illustrator may write or illustrate several books
- Identify and discuss interesting information in a text
- Express opinions about a text: e.g., interesting, funny, exciting
- Articulate why they like a text

Genre

- Understand that there are different types of books and that you can notice different things about them
- Notice when a book is nonfiction (true information)
- Notice characteristics of some specific nonfiction genres: e.g., simple factual text, memoir (personal memory story)

Organization

- Understand that some nonfiction texts are like a story (narrative structure)
- Understand that some nonfiction texts tell information and are not like a story (nonnarrative structure)
- Notice simple text organization in nonnarrative texts: e.g., ABC, bigger to smaller, smaller to bigger
- Understand that a writer can tell about something that usually happens in the same order (temporal sequence)
- Notice when a writer is telling information in order (a sequence)
- Notice when a writer uses structural patterns such as simple description, temporal sequence, question and answer
- Identify a nonfiction writer's use of time order or other established sequences such as numbers, time of day, days of the week, seasons

Topic

- Understand and talk about familiar topics: e.g., animals, pets, families, friends, the five senses, growing and health, school, neighborhood, weather and seasons, food, plants
- Show curiosity about a topic
- Infer the importance of a topic
- Understand that a writer is presenting facts about a single topic
- Understand that a writer has a purpose in writing about a topic

● Thinking *Within* the Text   ◆ Thinking *Beyond* the Text   ■ Thinking *About* the Text

Selecting Goals Behaviors and Understandings to Notice, Teach, and Support *(cont.)*

Interactive Read-Aloud and Literature Discussion

NONFICTION TEXTS *(continued)*

Messages and Main Ideas

- ◆ Understand that a nonfiction text can have different meanings for different people
- ◆ Make connections among the content and ideas (e.g., taking care of self, staying healthy, expressing feelings, sharing with others, caring for others, helping your family, going to school, caring for your world, valuing differences) across texts that are read aloud
- ■ Understand that a writer can have more than one message or big idea

Style and Language

- ● Understand sentences that are simple but may be different from oral language
- ● Understand sentences with phrases and clauses when they are read aloud
- ■ Notice a writer's use of rhythm, refrain, and repetition
- ■ Notice a writer's use of playful or poetic language: e.g., nonsense words, onomatopoeia, alliteration, rhythm, rhyme

Vocabulary

- ● Notice and acquire understanding of new vocabulary from read-aloud content
- ● Use new vocabulary in discussion of a text
- ● Understand the meaning of simple nouns, verbs, adjectives, adverbs, prepositions, and simple connectives when listening to a nonfiction text read aloud
- ■ Use some academic language to talk about texts: e.g., *ABC book, poem, song, cover, title, author, illustrator, page, text, illustration, photograph, beginning, ending, problem*

Illustrations/Graphics

- ● Gain new understanding from illustrations
- ◆ Understand that illustrations can have different meanings for different people
- ■ Understand that an illustrator created the pictures in the book

Book and Print Features

- ● Notice letters, words, simple phrases, or sentences that are large enough to see, especially when they are repeated
- ● Enjoy special features such as pop-ups, pop-outs, flaps, pull-tabs, see-through holes, sound effects

---

- ● Thinking *Within* the Text
- ◆ Thinking *Beyond* the Text
- ■ Thinking *About* the Text

Selecting Texts Characteristics of Texts for Reading Aloud and Discussion

Interactive Read-Aloud and Literature Discussion

GENRE

▶ **Fiction**
- Realistic fiction
- Folktale
- Simple animal fantasy

▶ **Nonfiction**
- Simple factual texts
- Memoir (personal memory story)
- Procedural texts

FORMS
- Picture books
- Wordless picture books
- Label books
- Short poems
- Nursery rhymes, rhymes, and songs
- Poetry collections
- Concept books
- ABC books
- Counting books

TEXT STRUCTURE
- Simple narrative with beginning, middle, several episodes, and ending
- Many texts with repeating episodes or patterns
- Some texts with nonnarrative structure
- Stories with simple plot (problem and solution)
- Most informational texts focusing on a single topic, usually one idea per page
- Underlying structural patterns: description, temporal sequence, question and answer

CONTENT
- Content that is appropriate for children's cognitive development, social and emotional maturity, and life experience
- Content that engages children's intellectual curiosity and emotions
- Language and word play: e.g., rhymes, nonsense, alliteration, and alphabet
- Content that reflects early conceptual understandings: e.g., colors, shapes, counting, sorting, size, alphabet, position

- Everyday actions familiar to young children: e.g., playing, making things, eating, getting dressed, bathing, cooking, shopping
- Familiar topics that are authentic and relevant: e.g., animals, pets, families, friends, the five senses, growing and health, school, neighborhood, weather and seasons, food, plants
- Humor that is easy to grasp: e.g., silly characters, funny situations
- Content that reinforces and expands a child's experience and knowledge of self and the world
- A few topics that may be beyond children's immediate experiences
- Content that reflects a wide range of settings, languages, and cultures
- Some content linked to specific areas of study as described by the school curriculum or standards
- Realistic characters, settings, and events that occur in realistic fiction
- Imaginary characters, events (some nonsensical and funny), and settings that occur in fantasy
- Content that reflects beginning understanding of the physical and social world

THEMES AND IDEAS
- Themes reflecting everyday life: e.g., self, family relationships, home, friendship, community, diversity, first responsibilities, imagination, fears, courage, nature
- Clear, simple ideas easy to identify
- Ideas close to children's experience: e.g., taking care of self, staying healthy, expressing feelings, sharing with others, caring for others, helping your family, going to school, caring for your world, valuing differences, being part of a community

LANGUAGE AND LITERARY FEATURES
- A few simple elements of fantasy: e.g., talking animals
- Predictable story outcomes typical of traditional literature: e.g., cleverness overcomes physical strength, good defeats evil

- Familiar settings close to children's experience
- Both realistic and fantastic settings, events, and characters
- Memorable characters that are straightforward, uncomplicated, and predictable
- Characters with one or two simple traits: e.g., kind, generous, sly, brave, silly, wise, greedy
- Characters that do not change or that change in simple ways for clear reasons
- Characters' actions related to clear consequences: e.g., reward for trying hard
- Predictable sequence of events
- Simple plot with problem and solution
- Language used to make comparisons
- Descriptive language, including made-up words and other playful forms
- Some poetic language, often using notable sound devices: e.g., rhythm, rhyme, repetition, refrain, onomatopoeia
- Simple dialogue and dialogue with pronouns (assigned by *said* in many texts) easily attributed to characters
- Some repetitive dialogue
- Some simple procedural language
- Some literary language typical of traditional literature: e.g., *once upon a time, long ago and far away, happily ever after*

SENTENCE COMPLEXITY
- Sentences that are easy for children to follow, though more complex than children generally use in oral language
- Simple sentences with subject and predicate
- Variety of language structures
- Sentences with clauses and phrases
- Sentences that are questions
- Sentences with adjectives, adverbs, and prepositional phrases

VOCABULARY
- A few interesting words that are new to children but easy to understand in context
- A few new content words related to concepts that are easy to understand
- Some memorable words that children can take on as language play

Selecting Texts Characteristics of Texts for Reading Aloud and Discussion *(cont.)*

Interactive Read-Aloud and Literature Discussion

- Almost all words that are in common oral vocabulary for young children (Tier 1)
- Many simple adjectives describing people, places, or things
- A few simple adverbs that describe action
- Common (simple) connectives that are frequently used in oral language (words, phrases that clarify relationships ideas): e.g., *and, but, so, because, before, after*

ILLUSTRATIONS

- Large, clear, colorful illustrations in a variety of media that fully support meaning
- Illustrations that add meaning to the text
- Very simple graphics with no distracting detail
- Some drawings with labels

BOOK AND PRINT FEATURES

LENGTH

- Short picture books that can be read in one sitting

PRINT AND LAYOUT

- Some picture books with print large enough for children to see during read-aloud
- Some print in speech bubbles or thought bubbles
- Some books with special features that engage interest and make texts interactive: e.g., pop-ups, pop-outs, flaps, pull-tabs, see-though holes, sound effects
- Some books with decorative or informative illustrations, engaging designs that catch the attention, and/or print or illustrations outside the body of the text (peritext)

ORGANIZATIONAL TOOLS

- Title, author, and illustrator listed on cover and on title page

TEXT RESOURCES

- Some books with dedication, author's note

Selecting Goals Behaviors and Understandings to Notice, Teach, and Support

Interactive Read-Aloud and Literature Discussion

FICTION TEXTS

General

- Ask questions to deepen understanding of a text
- Notice and ask questions when meaning is lost or understanding is interrupted
- Refer to important information and details
- Understand that the teacher reads the print, not the pictures.
- Understand that the teacher must hold the book right side up
- Mimic the teacher's expression and word stress when reenacting a text or joining in
- Use hand and body movements to show understanding of the meaning or meanings of pictures and words in a text
- Join in on refrains or repeated words, phrases, and sentences after hearing them several times
- Tell what happened in a text after hearing it read
- Gain new information from both pictures and print
- Recognize and understand simple problems that occur in everyday life
- Give reasons (either text-based or from personal experience) to support thinking
- Relate texts to their own lives
- Use background knowledge to understand settings, problems, and characters
- Recognize and understand that stories may be about different kinds of people and different places
- Make connections (e.g., content, topic, theme) across fiction texts that are read aloud
- Use evidence from the text to support statements about the text
- Understand that a writer has a purpose in writing a fiction text
- Identify a fiction writer's use of time order or other established sequences such as numbers, time of day, days of the week, seasons
- Recognize that an author or illustrator may write or illustrate several books
- Connect texts by obvious categories: e.g., author, character, topic, genre, illustrator
- Express opinions about a text: e.g., interesting, funny, exciting
- Articulate why they like a text

Genre

- Understand that there are different types of books and that you can notice different things about them
- Notice and understand the characteristics of some specific fiction genres: e.g., realistic fiction, folktale, animal fantasy
- Understand that fiction stories are imagined

- Understand when a story could happen in real life (realistic fiction) and when it could not happen in real life (folktales, animal fantasy)
- Notice story outcomes typical of traditional literature: e.g., cleverness overcomes physical strength, good defeats evil
- Notice and understand texts that take the form of poems, nursery rhymes, rhymes, and songs

Messages and Themes

- Infer the "lesson" in traditional literature
- Understand that the "lesson" in fantasy or traditional literature can be applied to their own lives
- Infer simple messages in a work of fiction
- Notice and infer the importance of ideas relevant to their world: e.g., sharing, caring for others, doing your job, helping your family, taking care of self, staying healthy, caring for the world or environment, valuing differences, expressing feelings
- Understand that a fiction text can have different meanings for different people
- Notice and understand obvious themes: e.g., imagination, courage, fear, friendship, family, relationships, self, home, nature, growing, behavior, community, first responsibilities, diversity, feelings
- Understand that a book can have more than one message or big idea
- Notice when a fiction writer is "teaching a lesson"
- Notice recurring themes or motifs in traditional literature and fantasy: e.g., talking animals, magic, good and bad characters

Setting

- Recall important details about setting after a story is read
- Recognize and understand that texts may have settings related to different places and people

Plot

- Follow the events in simple narratives
- Notice and understand a simple plot with problem and solution
- Check understanding of the plot of the story and ask questions if meaning is lost
- Tell the important events of a story using the pictures (after hearing the text read several times)
- Include the problem and its resolution in telling what happed in a text
- Predict what will happen next in a story
- Predict story outcomes

● Thinking **Within** the Text   ◆ Thinking **Beyond** the Text   ■ Thinking **About** the Text

Selecting Goals Behaviors and Understandings to Notice, Teach, and Support *(cont.)*

Interactive Read-Aloud and Literature Discussion

FICTION TEXTS *(continued)*

Character

- Notice and remember characters in simple narratives
- Understand that animals in stories sometimes act like people (animal fantasy)
- Recall important details about characters after a story is read
- ◆ Infer a character's traits from story events
- ◆ Infer a character's traits from the physical details the illustrations include about them
- ◆ Infer characters' intentions, feelings, and motivations using text and pictures
- ◆ Notice when a character changes or learns a lesson
- ◆ Express opinions about characters and their behavior: e.g., funny, bad, silly, nice, friendly
- ◆ Learn from vicarious experiences with characters in stories
- ■ Understand that the same types of characters may appear over and over again in traditional literature: e.g., sly, brave, silly, wise, greedy

Style and Language

- Play with words or language orally: e.g., nonsense words or refrains from texts that are read aloud
- Understand sentences that are simple but may be different from oral language
- Follow and understand simple, assigned dialogue with a clear idea about who is speaking
- ■ Notice when a book has repeating episodes or language patterns
- ■ Notice a writer's use of playful or poetic language: e.g., nonsense words, rhythm, rhyme, repetition, onomatopoeia, alliteration
- ■ Notice a writer's use of descriptive language including invented words and other playful forms
- ■ Recognize a writer's use of humor
- ■ Understand the meaning of some literary language (language of books as opposed to typical oral language)
- ■ Notice and remember literary language patterns that are characteristic of traditional literature: e.g., *once upon a time, long ago and far away, happily ever after*

Vocabulary

- Notice and acquire understanding of new vocabulary from read-aloud content
- Use new vocabulary in discussion of a text
- Acquire new content words from texts and graphics, including labels for familiar objects, familiar animals, some new animals, and human activities
- ■ Use some academic language to talk about fiction genres: e.g., *fiction, folktale*
- ■ Use some academic language to talk about forms: e.g., *picture book, wordless picture book, label book, ABC book, poem, poetry, nursery rhyme, rhyme, song*
- ■ Use some academic language to talk about literary features: e.g., *beginning, ending, problem, character*
- ■ Use some academic language to talk about book and print features: e.g., *front cover, back cover, title, author, illustrator, page, text, illustration, photograph, label*

Illustrations

- Understand that an illustrator created the pictures in the book
- Tell the important events of a story using the pictures (after hearing the text read several times)
- Tell stories in response to pictures
- ◆ Understand that illustrations can have different meanings for different people
- ◆ Think about what characters are feeling from their facial expressions or gestures
- ◆ Notice that the background details in pictures often reveal characters' feelings or traits

Book and Print Features

- Notice letters, words, simple phrases, or sentences that are large enough to see especially when they are repeated
- Enjoy special features such as pop-ups, pop-outs, flaps, pull-tabs, see-though holes, sound effects
- Notice a book's title and its author and illustrator on the cover and title page
- Notice text resources outside the body (peritext): e.g., dedication, author's note, endpapers
- ■ Understand the purpose of some organizational tools: e.g., title, table of contents
- ■ Understand the purpose of some text resources: e.g., dedication, author's note

---

● Thinking *Within* the Text   ◆ Thinking *Beyond* the Text   ■ Thinking *About* the Text

Selecting Goals Behaviors and Understandings to Notice, Teach, and Support *(cont.)*

Interactive Read-Aloud and Literature Discussion

NONFICTION TEXTS

General

- ● Understand that the teacher reads the print, not the pictures
- ● Understand that the teacher must hold the book right side up
- ● Ask questions to deepen understanding of a text
- ● Notice and ask questions when meaning is lost or understanding is interrupted
- ● Refer to important information and details
- ● Understand and talk about everyday activities: e.g., playing, making things, eating, getting dressed, bathing, cooking, shopping
- ● Understand content that reflects beginning understandings of physical world and social world: e.g., health, social studies, science, mathematics, arts
- ● Mimic the teacher's expression and word stress when reenacting a text or joining in
- ● Use hand and body movements to show understanding of the meaning or meanings of pictures and words in a text
- ● Join in on refrains or repeated words, phrases, and sentences after hearing them several times
- ● Tell the important information in a text after hearing it read
- ◆ Gain new information from both pictures and print
- ◆ Understand simple problems that occur in everyday life
- ◆ Give reasons (either text-based or from personal experience) to support thinking
- ◆ Use background knowledge to understand texts that are read aloud
- ◆ Relate texts to their own lives
- ◆ Recognize and understand that nonfiction texts may be about different kinds of people and different places
- ◆ Use evidence from the text to support statements about the text
- ◆ Use basic conceptual understandings to understand a nonfiction text: e.g., colors, shapes, counting, sorting, size, alphabet, positions, textures
- ■ Recognize that an author or illustrator may write or illustrate several books
- ■ Identify and discuss interesting information in a text
- ■ Express opinions about a text: e.g., interesting, funny, and exciting
- ■ Articulate why they like a text
- ■ Connect texts by obvious categories: e.g., author, character, topic, genre, illustrator

Genre

- ● Understand that there are different types of texts and that you can notice different things about them
- ■ Understand when a book is nonfiction (true information)
- ■ Notice and understand the characteristics of some specific nonfiction genres: e.g., simple factual text, memoir (personal memory story), procedural text
- ■ Notice and understand texts that take the form of poems, nursery rhymes, rhymes, and songs

Organization

- ■ Understand that some nonfiction books are like a story (narrative structure)
- ■ Understand that some nonfiction books tell information and are not like a story (nonnarrative structure)
- ■ Notice simple text organization: e.g., ABC, bigger to smaller, smaller to bigger
- ■ Notice when a writer uses a question-and-answer structure
- ■ Identify the organization of a text: e.g., time order or established sequences such as numbers, time of day, days of the week, or seasons
- ■ Notice when a writer is telling information in order (a sequence)
- ■ Understand that a writer can tell about something that usually happens in the same order (temporal sequence)
- ■ Notice that a nonfiction writer puts together information related to the same topic (category)

Topic

- ● Understand and talk about familiar topics: e.g., animals, families, pets, food, plants, school, friends, growing, the five senses, neighborhood, weather and seasons, health
- ◆ Show curiosity about topics
- ◆ Infer the importance of a topic
- ◆ Infer the writer's attitude toward a topic (how the writer "feels")
- ■ Understand that a writer is presenting facts about a single topic
- ■ Understand that a writer has a purpose in writing about a topic
- ■ Understand that a writer may be telling about something that happened in his life (memoir)

- ● Thinking *Within* the Text
- ◆ Thinking *Beyond* the Text
- ■ Thinking *About* the Text

Selecting Goals Behaviors and Understandings to Notice, Teach, and Support *(cont.)*

Interactive Read-Aloud and Literature Discussion

NONFICTION TEXTS *(continued)*

Messages and Main Ideas

◆ Understand that a nonfiction text can have different meanings for different people

◆ Make connections among the content and ideas across texts that are read aloud: e.g., animals, pets, families, the five senses, growing and health, school, neighborhood, weather and seasons, food, plants

◆ Connect the information in nonfiction books to curriculum areas studied at school

◆ Infer the significance of nonfiction content to their own lives

■ Understand that a writer can have more than one message or big idea

Style and Language

● Understand sentences that are simple but may be different from oral language

● Understand sentences with embedded clauses and phrases

■ Notice a writer's use of rhythm, refrain, and repetition

■ Notice when a text has repeating episodes or language patterns

■ Notice a writer's use of playful or poetic language

■ Recognize some authors by the topics they choose or the style of their illustrations

Vocabulary

● Notice and acquire understanding of new vocabulary from read-aloud content

● Acquire new content words from texts and graphics, including those for familiar objects, familiar animals, some new animals, and human activities

● Use new vocabulary in discussion of a text

● Understand the meaning of simple nouns, verbs, adjectives, adverbs, prepositions, and simple connectives when listening to a nonfiction text read aloud

■ Use some academic language to talk about nonfiction genres: e.g., *nonfiction, personal memory story*

■ Use some academic language to talk about forms: e.g., *picture book, wordless picture book, label book, ABC book, counting book, poem, poetry, nursery rhyme, rhyme, song*

■ Use some academic language to talk about literary features: e.g., *beginning, ending, problem*

■ Use some academic language to talk about book and print features: e.g., *front cover, back cover, title, author, illustrator, page, text, illustration, photograph, label*

Illustrations/Graphics

● Gain new understanding from illustrations

● Notice and search for information in simple graphics: e.g., drawing with label

◆ Understand that illustrations can have different meanings for different people

■ Understand that an illustrator created the pictures in the book

Book and Print Features

● Notice letters, words, simple phrases, labels, or sentences that are large enough to see especially when they are repeated

● Enjoy special features such as pop-ups, pop-outs, flaps, pull-tabs, see-though holes, sound effects

● Notice a book's title and its author and illustrator on the cover and title page

● Notice some text resources outside the body (peritext): e.g., dedication, author's note, endpapers

■ Understand the purpose of some organizational tools: e.g., title, table of contents

■ Understand the purpose of some text resources: e.g., dedication, author's note

---

● Thinking *Within* the Text　　　◆ Thinking *Beyond* the Text　　　■ Thinking *About* the Text

Selecting Texts Characteristics of Texts for Reading Aloud and Discussion

Interactive Read-Aloud and Literature Discussion

GENRE

▶ **Fiction**

- Realistic fiction
- Traditional literature: e.g., folktale, fairy tale, fable
- Animal fantasy

▶ **Nonfiction**

- Simple expository texts
- Simple narrative nonfiction
- Simple biography
- Memoir
- Procedural texts
- Simple persuasive texts

FORMS

- Series books
- Picture books
- Wordless picture books
- A few beginning chapter books
- Label books
- Poems
- Nursery rhymes, rhymes, and songs
- Poetry collections
- Plays
- Concept books
- ABC books
- Counting books

TEXT STRUCTURE

- Simple narrative with straightforward structure (beginning, middle, several episodes, and ending), but more episodes included
- Many texts with repeating episodes or patterns
- Some texts with nonnarrative structure
- Stories with simple plot (problem and solution)
- Underlying structural patterns: description, temporal sequence, question and answer
- Informational texts with clearly defined overall structure and simple categories

CONTENT

- Content that is appropriate for children's cognitive development, social and emotional maturity, and life experience
- Content that engages children's intellectual curiosity and emotions
- Language and word play: e.g., rhymes, nonsense, alliteration, alphabet
- Content that reflects early conceptual understandings: e.g., colors, shapes, counting, sorting, size, alphabet, position
- Everyday actions familiar to young children: e.g., playing, making things, eating, cooking, shopping
- Familiar topics that are authentic and relevant: e.g., animals, pets, families, friends, the five senses, health and illness prevention, systems of the human body, school, neighborhood, weather and seasons, food, plants
- Humor that is easy to grasp: e.g., silly characters, funny situations, jokes, word play
- Content that reinforces and expands a child's experience and knowledge of self and the world
- Some topics that may be beyond most children's immediate experiences: e.g., nutrition, wild animals, environments such as ocean and desert, space
- Content that reflects a wide range of settings, languages, and cultures
- Some content linked to specific areas of study as described by the school curriculum or standards
- Realistic characters, settings, and events that occur in realistic fiction
- Imaginary characters, events (some nonsensical and funny), settings that occur in fantasy
- Content that reflects increasing understanding of the physical and social world

THEMES AND IDEAS

- Themes reflecting everyday life: e.g., self, family relationships, home, friendship, community, diversity, first responsibilities, imagination, fears, courage, nature
- Clear, simple ideas easy to identify
- Ideas close to children's experience: e.g., taking care of self, staying healthy, expressing feelings, sharing with others, caring for others, helping your family, doing your job, caring for your world, valuing differences, being part of a community

LANGUAGE AND LITERARY FEATURES

- Elements of traditional literature and modern fantasy: e.g., the supernatural, talking animals
- Basic motifs of traditional literature and modern fantasy: e.g., struggle between good and evil, magic, fantastic or magical objects, wishes, trickery, transformations
- Predictable story outcomes typical of traditional literature: e.g., cleverness overcomes physical strength, good defeats evil
- Familiar settings close to children's experience
- Both realistic and fantastic settings, events, and characters
- Memorable characters that are straightforward, uncomplicated, and predictable
- Characters with one or two simple traits: e.g., kind, generous, sly, brave, silly, wise, greedy
- Characters that do not change or that change in simple ways for clear reasons
- Characters' actions related to clear consequences: e.g., reward for trying hard
- Main characters and supporting characters
- Predictable sequence of events
- Simple plot with problem and solution
- Language used to make comparisons
- Descriptive language, including made-up words and other playful forms
- Some figurative language: e.g., metaphor, simile
- Some poetic language, often using notable sound devices: e.g., rhythm, rhyme, repetition, refrain, onomatopoeia
- Simple dialogue and dialogue with pronouns (assigned by *said* in many texts) easily attributed to characters
- Some repetitive dialogue
- Persuasive language
- Procedural language: e.g., step-by-step, directions, how-to
- Some literary language typical of traditional literature: e.g., *once upon a time, long ago and far away, happily ever after*

Selecting Texts Characteristics of Texts for Reading Aloud and Discussion *(cont.)*

Interactive Read-Aloud and Literature Discussion

SENTENCE COMPLEXITY

- Sentences that are easy for children to follow, though more complex than children generally use in oral language
- Variation in placement of subject, verb, adjectives, and adverbs
- Sentences beginning with phrases or subordinate clauses
- Sentences with multiple adjectives, adverbs, and prepositional phrases
- Sentences with common (simple) connectives
- Complex sentences with variety in order of clauses

VOCABULARY

- A few interesting words that are new to children but easy to understand in context
- A few new content words related to concepts that are easy to understand
- Some memorable words that children can take on as language play
- Almost all words that are in common oral vocabulary for younger children (Tier 1)
- A few words that appear in the vocabulary of mature language users (Tier 2)
- Many simple adjectives describing people, places, or things
- A few simple adverbs that describe action
- Common (simple) connectives that are frequently used in oral language (words, phrases that clarify relationships ideas): e.g., *and, but, so, because, before, after*

ILLUSTRATIONS

- Large, clear, colorful illustrations in a variety of media that fully support meaning
- Illustrations that enhance and extend meaning in the text
- Illustrations that support interpretation, enhance enjoyment, or set mood but that are not necessary for understanding
- Simple illustrations in a variety of forms: e.g., drawing with label or caption, photograph with label or caption, map with legend, diagram

BOOK AND PRINT FEATURES

LENGTH

- Short picture books that can be read in one sitting

PRINT AND LAYOUT

- Some picture books with print large enough for children to see during read-aloud
- Some print in speech bubbles or thought bubbles
- Some books with special features that engage interest and make texts interactive: e.g., pop-ups, pop-outs, flaps, pull-tabs, see-though holes, sound effects
- Some books with decorative or informative illustrations, engaging designs that catch the attention, and/or print or illustrations outside the body of the text (peritext)

ORGANIZATIONAL TOOLS

- Title, author, and illustrator listed on cover and on title page
- Table of contents, heading, sidebar

TEXT RESOURCES

- Some books with dedication, acknowledgments, author's note, special endpapers (peritext)

Selecting Goals Behaviors and Understandings to Notice, Teach, and Support

Interactive Read-Aloud and Literature Discussion

FICTION TEXTS

General

- Ask questions to deepen understanding of a text
- Notice and ask questions when meaning is lost or understanding is interrupted
- Refer to important information and details and use as evidence in discussion to support opinions and statements
- Mimic the teacher's expression and word stress when reenacting a text or joining in
- Use hand and body movements to show understanding of the meaning or meanings of pictures and words in a text
- Join in on refrains or repeated words, phrases, and sentences after hearing them several times
- Notice and respond to stress and tone of voice while listening and afterward
- Tell what happened in a text after hearing it read
- Gain new information from both pictures and print
- Understand simple problems that occur in everyday life
- Give reasons (either text-based or from personal experience) to support thinking
- Relate texts to their own lives
- Use background knowledge to understand settings, problems, and characters
- Use background knowledge of content to understand the problems and events of fiction texts
- Make connections (e.g., content, topic, theme) across fiction texts that are read aloud
- Make connections (similarities and differences) among texts that have the same author/illustrator, setting, characters, or theme
- Use evidence from the text to support statements about the text
- Use evidence from the text to support predictions (*I think . . . because . . .*)
- Understand that a writer has a purpose in writing a fiction or nonfiction text
- Identify the organization of a text: e.g., time order or established sequences such as numbers, time of day, days of the week, or seasons
- Recognize that an author or illustrator may write or illustrate several books
- Connect texts by obvious categories: e.g., author, character, topic, genre, illustrator
- Express opinions about a text (e.g., interesting, funny, exciting) and support with evidence
- Articulate why they like a text

- Form opinions about authors and illustrators and state the basis for those opinions

Genre

- Understand that there are different types of texts and that you can notice different things about them
- Notice and understand the characteristics of some specific fiction genres: e.g., realistic fiction, folktale, fairy tale, fable, animal fantasy
- Understand that fiction stories are imagined
- Understand when a story could happen in real life (realistic fiction) and when it could not happen in real life (traditional literature, animal fantasy)
- Notice story outcomes that are typical of traditional literature: e.g., cleverness overcomes power, good defeats evil
- Notice and understand texts that take the form of poems, nursery rhymes, rhymes, and songs

Messages and Themes

- Infer the "lesson" in traditional literature
- Understand that the "lesson" in fantasy or traditional literature can be applied to their own lives
- Infer the messages in a work of fiction
- Notice and infer the importance of ideas relevant to their world: e.g., sharing, caring for others, doing your job, helping your family, taking care of self, staying healthy, caring for the world or environment, valuing differences, expressing feelings, empathizing with others
- Understand that there can be different interpretations of the meaning of a text
- Notice and understand obvious themes: e.g., imagination, courage, fears, friendship, family, relationships, self, home, nature, growing up, behavior, community, first responsibilities, diversity, feelings
- Notice that a book may have more than one message or big idea
- Notice when a fiction writer is "teaching a lesson"
- Notice recurring themes or motifs in traditional literature and fantasy: e.g., struggle between good and evil, magic, fantastic or magical objects, wishes, trickery, transformations

Setting

- Recall important details about setting after a story is read
- Recognize and understand that a wide variety of fiction texts may be set in different places and that customs and people's behavior may reflect those settings
- Understand the setting for a story and infer why it is important

● Thinking **Within** the Text　　◆ Thinking **Beyond** the Text　　■ Thinking **About** the Text

Selecting Goals Behaviors and Understandings to Notice, Teach, and Support *(cont.)*

Interactive Read-Aloud and Literature Discussion

FICTION TEXTS *(continued)*

Plot

- Notice and understand a simple plot with problem and solution
- Follow a plot with multiple events
- Check understanding of the plot of the story and ask questions if meaning is lost
- Tell the important events of a story using the pictures (after hearing the text read several times)
- Notice and understand when a problem is solved
- Include the problem and its resolution in telling what happened in a text
- Predict what will happen next in a story
- Predict story outcomes

Character

- Recall important details about characters after a story is read
- Follow multiple characters in the same story
- Recognize characters and report important details about them after reading
- Infer a character's traits from story events
- Infer a character's traits from the physical details the illustrations include about them
- Infer characters' intentions, feelings, and motivations using text and pictures
- Notice when a character changes or learns a lesson
- Express opinions about characters and their behavior: e.g., funny, bad, silly, nice, friendly
- Learn from vicarious experiences with characters in stories
- Understand that the same types of characters may appear over and over again in traditional literature: e.g., sly, brave, silly, wise, greedy, clever
- Understand the difference between realistic characters and those that appear in fantasy

Style and Language

- Play with words or language orally: e.g., nonsense words or refrains from texts that are read aloud
- Understand sentences that are simple but may be different from oral language
- Follow and understand simple, assigned dialogue with a clear idea about who is speaking

- Notice when a book has repeating episodes or language patterns
- Notice a writer's use of playful or poetic language and sound devices: e.g., nonsense words, rhythm, rhyme, repetition, refrain, onomatopoeia
- Notice a writer's use of descriptive language, including invented words and other playful forms
- Notice a writer's choice of interesting words
- Recognize a writer's use of humor
- Understand the meaning of some literary language (language of books as opposed to typical oral language)
- Notice and remember literary language patterns that are characteristic of traditional literature: e.g., *once upon a time, long ago and far away, happily ever after*

Vocabulary

- Notice and acquire understanding of new vocabulary from read-aloud content
- Use new vocabulary in discussion of a text
- Acquire new content words from texts and graphics
- Understand the meaning of words representing all parts of speech when listening to a story
- Understand common (simple) connectives that link and clarify meaning and are frequently used in oral language when listening to a story (*and, but, so, because, before, after*)
- Use some academic language to talk about fiction genres: e.g., *fiction, folktale, fairy tale, fable*
- Use some academic language to talk about forms: e.g., *picture book, wordless picture book, label book, ABC book, poem, poetry, nursery rhyme, rhyme, song, series book, chapter book, play*
- Use some academic language to talk about literary features: e.g., *beginning, ending, problem, character, solution, main character*
- Use some academic language to talk about book and print features: e.g., *front cover, back cover, title, author, illustrator, page, text, illustration, photograph, label, table of contents, acknowledgments, chapter, section, heading, drawing, caption, map*

● Thinking ***Within*** the Text   ◆ Thinking ***Beyond*** the Text   ■ Thinking ***About*** the Text

Selecting Goals Behaviors and Understandings to Notice, Teach, and Support *(cont.)*

Interactive Read-Aloud and Literature Discussion

FICTION TEXTS *(continued)*

Illustrations

- Understand that an illustrator created the pictures in the book
- Tell the important events of a story using the pictures (after hearing the text read several times)
- Tell stories in response to pictures
- Understand that illustrations can have different meanings for different people
- Use details from illustrations and text to support points made in discussion
- Think about what characters are feeling from their facial expressions or gestures
- Notice that the background details in pictures often reveal characters' feelings or traits
- Notice how an illustrator creates the illusion of sound and motion in pictures
- Notice how an illustrator shows the passage of time through illustrations (use of light, weather)
- Notice how the tone of a book is created by the illustrator's choice of colors
- Notice how the tone of a book is impacted by the use of background color

- Notice how the tone of a book changes when the illustrator shifts the color
- Notice how the placement, size, and color of the print can convey meaning
- Notice the placement of words on a page in relation to the illustrations
- Notice how illustrators create perspective in their pictures (using images close up, far away, creating distance in between, etc.)

Book and Print Features

- Notice letters, words, simple phrases, or sentences that are large enough to see especially when they are repeated
- Enjoy special features such as pop-ups, pop-outs, flaps, pull-tabs, see-though holes, sound effects
- Notice a book's title and its author and illustrator on the cover and title page
- Notice some text resources outside the body (peritext): e.g., dedication, acknowledgments, author's note, endpapers
- Understand the purpose of some organizational tools: e.g., title, table of contents
- Understand the purpose of some text resources: e.g., dedication, acknowledgments, author's note

● Thinking **Within** the Text ◆ Thinking **Beyond** the Text ■ Thinking **About** the Text

Selecting Goals Behaviors and Understandings to Notice, Teach, and Support *(cont.)*

Interactive Read-Aloud and Literature Discussion

NONFICTION TEXTS

General

- Ask questions to deepen understanding of a text
- Notice and ask questions when meaning is lost or understanding is interrupted
- Refer to important information and details and use as evidence in discussion to support opinions and statements
- Understand and talk about everyday activities: e.g., playing, making things, eating, getting dressed, bathing, cooking, shopping
- Understand content that reflects beginning understandings of physical world and social world: e.g., health, social studies, science, mathematics, arts
- Notice and respond to stress and tone of voice while listening and afterward
- Join in on refrains or repeated words, phrases, and sentences after hearing them several times
- Tell the important information in a text after hearing it read
- Gain new information from both pictures and print
- Understand simple problems that occur in everyday life
- Give reasons (either text-based or from personal experience) to support thinking
- Use background knowledge of content to understand nonfiction topics
- Relate texts to their own lives
- Recognize and understand that nonfiction texts may be about a variety of places and that customs and people's behavior may reflect those places
- Use evidence from the text to support statements about the text
- Use evidence from the text to support predictions
- Use basic conceptual understandings to understand a nonfiction text: e.g., colors, shapes, counting, sorting, size, alphabet, positions, textures
- Recognize that an author or illustrator may write or illustrate several books
- Identify and discuss interesting information in a text
- Express opinions about a text: e.g., interesting, funny, and exciting

- Articulate why they like a text
- Form opinions about authors and illustrators and state the basis for those opinions
- Connect texts by obvious categories: e.g., author, character, topic, genre, illustrator

Genre

- Understand that there are different types of texts and that you can notice different things about them
- Notice and understand when a book is nonfiction (true information)
- Notice and understand the characteristics of some specific nonfiction genres: e.g., expository text, narrative nonfiction, biography, memoir, procedural text, persuasive text
- Notice and understand texts that take the form of poems, nursery rhymes, rhymes, and songs
- Notice when a writer is describing a step-by-step procedure
- Notice when a writer is trying to persuade readers
- Recognize informational texts with some examples of simple argument and persuasion

Organization

- Follow and understand nonfiction texts with clearly defined overall structure and simple categories
- Understand that some nonfiction books are like a story (narrative structure)
- Notice that some nonfiction books tell information and are not like a story (nonnarrative structure)
- Notice when a writer uses a question-and-answer structure
- Identify the organization of a text: e.g., time order or established sequences such as numbers, time of day, days of the week, or seasons
- Notice when a writer is telling information in order (a sequence)
- Understand that a writer can tell about something that usually happens in the same order (temporal sequence)
- Notice that a nonfiction writer puts together information related to the same topic (category)

● Thinking **Within** the Text   ◆ Thinking **Beyond** the Text   ■ Thinking **About** the Text

Selecting Goals Behaviors and Understandings to Notice, Teach, and Support *(cont.)*

Interactive Read-Aloud and Literature Discussion

NONFICTION TEXTS *(continued)*

Topic

- ● Understand and talk about familiar topics: e.g., animals, families, pets, food, plants, school, friends, growing, senses, neighborhood, weather and seasons, health
- ◆ Show curiosity about topics encountered in nonfiction texts and actively work to learn more about them
- ◆ Infer the importance of a topic
- ◆ Infer the writer's attitude toward a topic (how the writer "feels")
- ■ Understand that a writer is presenting facts about a single topic
- ■ Understand that a writer has a purpose in writing about a topic
- ■ Understand that a writer may be telling about something that happened in his life (memoir)

Messages and Main Ideas

- ● Follow arguments in a persuasive text
- ◆ Understand that a nonfiction text can have different meanings for different people
- ◆ Make connections among the content and ideas across texts that are read aloud: e.g., animals, pets, families, the five senses, growing, health and illness prevention, human body systems, school, neighborhood, weather and seasons, food, plants
- ◆ Connect the information in nonfiction books to curriculum areas studied at school

- ◆ Infer the significance of nonfiction content to their own lives
- ■ Understand that a book can have more than one message or big idea

Style and Language

- ● Understand sentences that are simple but may be different from oral language
- ● Understand sentences with embedded clauses and phrases
- ■ Notice a writer's use of rhythm, refrain, and repetition
- ■ Notice a writer's choice of interesting words
- ■ Notice when a text has repeating episodes or language patterns
- ■ Notice a writer's use of playful or poetic language
- ■ Recognize some authors by the topics they choose or the style of their illustrations

Vocabulary

- ● Notice and acquire understanding of new vocabulary from read-aloud content
- ● Understand the meaning of words representing all parts of speech when listening to a nonfiction text read aloud
- ● Understand (simple) connectives that link ideas and clarify meaning and are frequently used in oral language when listening to a nonfiction text read aloud: e.g., *and, but, so, because, before, after*

● Thinking **Within** the Text   ◆ Thinking **Beyond** the Text   ■ Thinking **About** the Text

Selecting Goals Behaviors and Understandings to Notice, Teach, and Support *(cont.)*

Interactive Read-Aloud and Literature Discussion

NONFICTION TEXTS *(continued)*

- Acquire new content words from texts and graphics, including those for familiar objects, familiar animals, some new animals, and human activities
- Use new vocabulary in discussion of a text
- Use some academic language to talk about nonfiction genres: e.g., *nonfiction, personal memory story, informational text, informational book, factual text, biography, how-to book*
- Use some academic language to talk about forms: e.g., *picture book, wordless picture book, label book, ABC book, counting book, poem, poetry, nursery rhyme, rhyme, song, series book, play*
- Use some academic language to talk about literary features: e.g., *beginning, ending, problem, question and answer, solution, topic*
- Use some academic language to talk about book and print features: e.g., *front cover, back cover, title, author, illustrator, page, text, illustration, photograph, label, table of contents, acknowledgments, chapter, section, heading, drawing, caption, map*

Illustrations/Graphics

- Gain new understandings from illustrations
- Notice and search for information in a variety of graphics: e.g., drawing with label or caption, photograph with label or caption, diagram, map with legend

- Understand that illustrations can have different meanings for different people
- Use details from illustrations to support points made in discussion
- Understand the purpose of various graphics: e.g., drawing with label or caption, photograph with label or caption, map, timeline, chart, diagram

Book and Print Features

- Notice letters, words, simple phrases, labels, or sentences that are large enough to see especially when they are repeated
- Enjoy special features such as pop-ups, pop-outs, flaps, pull-tabs, see-though holes, sound effects
- Notice a book's title and its author and illustrator on the cover and title page
- Notice some text resources outside the body (peritext): e.g., dedication, acknowledgments, author's note, endpapers
- Notice and use organizational tools: e.g., table of contents, heading, sidebar
- Understand the purpose of some organizational tools: e.g., table of contents, heading, sidebar
- Understand the purpose of some text resources (peritext): e.g., dedication, acknowledgments, author's note, illustrator's note, endpapers, book flap

---

- Thinking **Within** the Text
- Thinking **Beyond** the Text
- Thinking **About** the Text

Selecting Texts Characteristics of Texts for Reading Aloud and Discussion

Interactive Read-Aloud and Literature Discussion

GENRE

▶ Fiction

- Realistic fiction
- Traditional literature: e.g., folktale, tall tale, fairy tale, fable
- Fantasy
- Hybrid texts
- Special types of fiction: e.g., adventure story; animal story; family, friends, and school story; humorous story

▶ Nonfiction

- Simple expository nonfiction
- Simple narrative nonfiction
- Simple biography
- Memoir
- Procedural texts
- Persuasive texts
- Hybrid texts

FORMS

- Series books
- Picture books
- Chapter books
- Poems
- Nursery rhymes, rhymes, and songs
- Poetry collections
- Plays
- Types of poetry: lyrical poetry, free verse, limerick, haiku
- Letters

TEXT STRUCTURE

- Simple narratives with straightforward structure (beginning, middle, several episodes, and ending) but more episodes included
- Many texts with repeating episodes or patterns
- Stories with simple plot (problem and solution)
- Informational texts related to a larger topic, sometimes with subtopics
- Underlying structural patterns: description, cause and effect, chronological sequence, temporal sequence (e.g., life cycles, how-to books), compare and contrast
- Informational texts with clearly defined overall structure and simple categories

- Simple biographical and historical texts with narrative structure
- Informational texts with some examples of simple argument and persuasion

CONTENT

- Content that is appropriate for children's cognitive development, social and emotional maturity, and life experience
- Content that engages children's intellectual curiosity and emotions
- Language and word play related to concepts, parts of speech, and sound devices such as alliteration, assonance, onomatopoeia
- Familiar topics that are authentic and relevant: e.g., animals, pets, families, friends, sports, the five senses, nutrition and food, school, neighborhood, weather and seasons, machines, plants
- Humor that is easy to grasp: e.g., silly characters, funny situations, jokes, word play
- Content that reinforces and expands a child's experience and knowledge of self and the world
- Some topics that may be beyond most children's immediate experiences: e.g., wild animals, environments such as ocean and desert, space, events from various places and historical periods
- Content that reflects a wide range of settings, languages, and cultures
- Some content linked to specific areas of study as described by the school curriculum or standards
- Realistic characters, settings, and events that occur in realistic fiction
- Imaginary characters, events (some nonsensical and funny), settings that occur in fantasy
- Content that reflects increasing understanding of the physical and social world

THEMES AND IDEAS

- Themes reflecting everyday life: e.g., self, family relationships, home, friendship, belonging, community, diversity, responsibility, imagination, fear, loss, courage, nature
- Some books with multiple ideas that are easy to understand

- Ideas close to children's experience: e.g., taking care of self, staying healthy, expressing feelings, sharing with others, caring for others, empathizing with others, helping your family, doing your job, caring for your world, problem solving, learning about life's challenges, valuing differences, being part of a community

LANGUAGE AND LITERARY FEATURES

- Elements of traditional literature and modern fantasy: e.g., the supernatural, imaginary and otherworldly creatures, gods and goddesses, talking animals
- Basic motifs of traditional literature and modern fantasy: e.g., struggle between good and evil, magic, the hero's quest, special character types, fantastic or magical objects, wishes, trickery, transformations
- Predictable story outcomes typical of traditional literature: e.g., good overcomes evil
- Some literary language typical of traditional literature: e.g., *once upon a time, long ago and far away, happily ever after*
- A few texts with settings distant in time and place from children's own experiences
- Main characters and supporting characters, some with multiple dimensions
- Multiple characters, each with unique traits
- Character development as a result of plot events
- Character dimensions (attributes) and relationships revealed through dialogue and behavior
- Variety in presentation of dialogue among multiple characters
- Predictable and static characters with simple traits typical of traditional literature
- Simple plot with problem and resolution
- Plot with a few episodes
- Most texts told from a single point of view
- Most texts written in first- or third-person narrative
- Language used to make comparisons
- Descriptive language conveying a range of human feelings: e.g., joy, sadness, anger, eagerness
- Descriptive language conveying sensory experiences (imagery)
- Poetic language

Selecting Texts Characteristics of Texts for Reading Aloud and Discussion (cont.)

Interactive Read-Aloud and Literature Discussion

- Some figurative language
- Some procedural texts written in second person
- Mostly assigned dialogue
- Procedural language: e.g., step-by-step, directions, how-to
- Persuasive language

SENTENCE COMPLEXITY

- Sentences that are easy for children to follow, though more complex than children generally use in oral language
- Some long and complex sentences that require attention to follow
- Variation in placement of subject, verb, adjectives, and adverbs
- Sentences beginning with phrases or subordinate clauses
- Sentences with multiple adjectives, adverbs, and prepositional phrases
- Sentences with common (simple) connectives
- Complex sentences with variety in order of clauses

VOCABULARY

- A few interesting words that may be new
- A few new content words related to concepts that children are learning
- Some memorable words that children can take on as language play
- Almost all words that are in common oral vocabulary for younger children (Tier 1)
- Some words that appear in the vocabulary of mature language users (Tier 2)
- Many adjectives describing people, places, or things
- Adverbs that describe action
- Common (simple) connectives that are frequently used in oral language (words, phrases that clarify relationships ideas): e.g., *and, but, so, because, before, after*
- Technical vocabulary

ILLUSTRATIONS

- Large, clear, colorful illustrations in a variety of media that fully support meaning
- Illustrations that enhance and extend meaning in the text
- Illustrations that support interpretation or enhance enjoyment but that are not necessary for understanding
- Books with illustrations that represent a coherent artistic vision
- Some texts with minimal illustrations
- Some books with black-and-white illustrations
- Illustrations that convey complex emotions
- Books with illustrations that reflect the theme
- Simple illustrations in a variety of forms: drawing with label or caption, photograph with label or caption, map with legend, diagram, infographic

BOOK AND PRINT FEATURES

LENGTH

- Short picture books that can be read in one sitting

PRINT AND LAYOUT

- Some picture books with print large enough for children to see during read-aloud
- Some print in speech bubbles or thought bubbles
- Some books with decorative or informative illustrations, engaging designs that communicate meaning, and/or print or illustrations outside the body of the text (peritext)

ORGANIZATIONAL TOOLS

- Title, author, and illustrator listed on cover and on title page
- Table of contents, heading, sidebar
- Some simple chapter books (used occasionally) with chapter titles

TEXT RESOURCES

- Some books with dedication, acknowledgments, author's note, special endpapers (peritext)

Selecting Goals Behaviors and Understandings to Notice, Teach, and Support

Interactive Read-Aloud and Literature Discussion

FICTION TEXTS

General

- Ask questions to deepen understanding of a text
- Notice and ask questions when meaning is lost or understanding is interrupted
- Refer to important information and details and use as evidence to support opinions and statements during discussion
- Notice and respond to stress and tone of voice while listening and afterward
- Tell what happened in a text after hearing it read
- Sustain attention to listen to some books that take more than one read-aloud session
- Relate texts to their own lives
- Use background knowledge to understand settings, problems, and characters
- Gain new information from both pictures and print
- Learn (synthesize) new concepts and ideas from listening to fiction texts
- Understand simple problems that occur in everyday life
- Give reasons (either text-based or from personal experience) to support thinking
- Use background knowledge of content to understand the problems and events of fiction texts
- Make connections (e.g., content, theme) across fiction texts that are read aloud
- Make connections (similarities and differences) among texts that have the same author/illustrator, setting, characters, or theme
- Use evidence from the text to support statements about the text
- Use evidence from the text to support predictions (*I think . . . because . . .*)
- Relate important ideas in the text to each other and to other texts
- Understand that a writer has a purpose in writing a fiction or nonfiction text
- Connect texts by a range of categories: e.g., author, character, topic, genre, illustrator
- Express opinions about a text and support with evidence: e.g., interesting, funny, exciting
- Form and state the basis for opinions about authors and illustrators
- Form opinions about authors and illustrators and state the basis for those opinions

Genre

- Understand that there are different types of texts and that they have different characteristics

- Notice and understand the characteristics of some specific fiction genres: e.g., realistic fiction, folktale, fairy tale, fable, fantasy
- Understand that fiction stories are imagined
- Understand when a story could happen in real life (realistic fiction) and when it could not happen in real life (traditional literature, fantasy)
- Notice story outcomes that are typical of traditional literature
- Recognize hybrid texts and distinguish which sections are fiction and nonfiction
- Notice and understand some special types of fiction: e.g., mystery; adventure story; animal story; family, friends, and school story
- Notice and understand texts that take the form of poems, nursery rhymes, rhymes, and songs
- Recognize and understand some specific types of poetry: rhyming poetry, lyrical poetry, free verse, limerick, haiku
- Notice and understand some elements of poetry: e.g., figurative language, rhyme, repetition, onomatopoeia, layout/line breaks (shape)

Messages and Themes

- Infer the "lesson" in traditional literature
- Understand that the "lesson" in fantasy or traditional literature can be applied to their own lives
- Infer the messages in a work of fiction
- Notice and infer the importance of ideas relevant to their world: e.g., sharing, caring for others, doing your job, helping your family, taking care of self, staying healthy, caring for the world or environment, valuing differences, expressing feelings, empathizing with others, problem solving, learning about life's challenges
- Understand that there can be different interpretations of the meaning of a text
- Notice and understand themes that are close to their experience: e.g., imagination, courage, fear, sharing, friendship, family relationships, self, nature, behavior, community, responsibilities, diversity, belonging, peer relationships, loss
- Think across texts to derive larger messages, themes, or ideas
- Notice that a book may have more than one message or big (main) idea
- Notice when a fiction writer is "teaching a lesson"
- Notice recurring themes or motifs in traditional literature and fantasy: e.g., struggle between good and evil, magic, the hero's quest, fantastic or magical objects, wishes, trickery, transformations

● Thinking *Within* the Text   ◆ Thinking *Beyond* the Text   ■ Thinking *About* the Text

Selecting Goals Behaviors and Understandings to Notice, Teach, and Support *(cont.)*

Interactive Read-Aloud and Literature Discussion

FICTION TEXTS *(continued)*

Setting

- Recall important details about setting after a story is read
- ◆ Recognize and understand that fiction texts may have settings that reflect a wide range of diverse places, languages, and cultures
- ◆ Notice and understand settings that are distant in time and place from students' own experiences
- ◆ Infer the importance of the setting to the plot of the story in realistic fiction and in fantasy

Plot

- Follow a plot with multiple events or episodes
- Notice and understand a simple plot with problem and solution
- ● Notice and remember the important events of a text in sequence
- Check understanding of plots with multiple events and ask questions if meaning is lost
- Tell the important events of a story using the pictures (after hearing the text read several times)
- Notice and understand when a problem is solved
- Include the problem and its resolution in telling what happened in a text
- ◆ Predict what will happen next in a story
- ◆ Predict story outcomes
- ◆ Infer the significance of events in a plot
- ■ Give opinions about whether a problem seems real
- ■ Recognize and discuss aspects of narrative structure: beginning, series of events, high point of the story, problem resolution, ending

Character

- Recall important details about characters after a story is read
- Follow multiple characters, each with unique traits, in the same story
- ● Recognize that characters can have multiple dimensions: e.g., can be good but make mistakes, can change
- ◆ Infer characters' traits as revealed through thought, dialogue, behavior, and what others say or think about them and use evidence from the text to describe them
- ◆ Infer the character's traits from the physical details the illustrations include about them

- ◆ Infer characters' intentions, feelings, and motivations as revealed through thought, dialogue, behavior, and what others say or think about them
- ◆ Make predictions about what a character is likely to do and use evidence from the text to support predictions
- ◆ Notice character change and infer reasons from events of the plot
- ◆ Learn from vicarious experiences with characters in stories
- ◆ Notice predictable or static characters (characters that do not change) as typical in traditional literature
- ◆ Infer relationships between characters as revealed through dialogue and behavior
- ◆ Express opinions about the characters in a story (e.g., evil, dishonest, clever, sly, greedy, brave, loyal) and support with evidence
- ■ Understand that the same types of characters may appear over and over again in traditional literature: e.g., sly, brave, silly, wise, greedy, clever
- ■ Understand the difference between realistic characters and those that appear in fantasy
- ■ Express opinions about whether a character seems real

Style and Language

- Play with words or language orally: e.g., nonsense words or refrains from texts that are read aloud
- ● Follow and understand assigned and unassigned dialogue among multiple characters with a clear idea about who is speaking
- ■ Notice when a book has repeating episodes or language patterns
- ■ Notice a writer's choice of interesting words and language
- ■ Notice when a fiction writer uses poetic or descriptive language to show the setting, appeal to the five senses, or to convey human feelings such as loss, relief, or anger
- ■ Recognize how a writer creates humor
- ■ Understand the meaning of some literary language (language of books as opposed to typical oral language)
- ■ Notice and understand how the author uses literary language, including some figurative language
- ■ Notice and remember literary language patterns that are characteristic of traditional literature: e.g., *once upon a time, long ago and far away, happily ever after*
- ■ Recognize some authors by the style of their illustrations, characters they use, or typical plots

---

● Thinking ***Within*** the Text   ◆ Thinking ***Beyond*** the Text   ■ Thinking ***About*** the Text

INTERACTIVE READ-ALOUD AND LITERATURE DISCUSSION

Selecting Goals Behaviors and Understandings to Notice, Teach, and Support *(cont.)*

Interactive Read-Aloud and Literature Discussion

FICTION TEXTS *(continued)*

Vocabulary

- Continue to build vocabulary as a foundation for recognizing words in print
- Notice and acquire understanding of new vocabulary from read-aloud content
- Use new vocabulary in discussion of a text
- Acquire new content words from texts and graphics
- Learn some words that do not appear frequently in oral conversation but are used in writing (Tier 2)
- Derive the meaning of words from the context of a paragraph or the whole story
- Understand the meaning of words representing all parts of speech when listening to a story
- Understand common (simple) connectives that link and clarify meaning and are frequently used in oral language when listening to a story (*and, but, so, because, before, after*)
- Use some academic language to talk about fiction genres: e.g., *fiction, folktale, fairy tale, fable, tall tale*
- Use some academic language to talk about special types of fiction: e.g., *adventure story; animal story; family, friends, and school story; humorous story*
- Use some academic language to talk about forms: e.g., *picture book, wordless picture book, label book, ABC book, poem, poetry, nursery rhyme, rhyme, song, series book, chapter book, play, letter, poetry collection*
- Use some academic language to talk about literary features: e.g., *beginning, ending, problem, character, solution, main character, time and place, events, character change, message, dialogue*
- Use some academic language to talk about book and print features: e.g., *front cover, back cover, title, author, illustrator, page, text, illustration, photograph, label, table of contents, acknowledgments, chapter, section, heading, drawing, caption, map, chapter title, dedication, author's note, illustrator's note, endpapers*

Illustrations

- Notice and remember the important events of a story using the pictures (after hearing the text read several times)
- Think about what characters are feeling from their facial expressions or gestures
- Notice that the background details in pictures often reveal characters' feelings or traits
- Use details from illustrations and text to support points made in discussion
- Notice how an illustrator creates the illusion of sound and motion in pictures
- Notice how an illustrator shows the passage of time through illustrations (use of light, weather)
- Notice how the tone of a book is created by the illustrator's choice of colors
- Notice how the tone of a book is impacted by the use of background color
- Notice how the tone of a book changes when the illustrator shifts the color
- Notice how the placement, size, and color of the print can convey meaning
- Notice the placement of words on a page in relation to the illustrations
- Notice how illustrators create perspective in their pictures (using images close up, far away, creating distance in between, etc.)
- Notice how illustrations and graphics go together with the text in a meaningful way
- Notice how illustrations and graphics help to communicate the writer's message

Book and Print Features

- Notice and use and understand the purpose of some organizational tools: e.g., title, table of contents, chapter title, heading
- Notice and use and understand the purpose of some text resources outside the body (peritext): e.g., dedication, acknowledgments, author's note, illustrator's note, endpapers, book flap

● Thinking *Within* the Text   ◆ Thinking *Beyond* the Text   ■ Thinking *About* the Text

Selecting Goals Behaviors and Understandings to Notice, Teach, and Support *(cont.)*

Interactive Read-Aloud and Literature Discussion

NONFICTION TEXTS

General

- Ask questions to deepen understanding of a text
- Notice and ask questions when meaning is lost or understanding is interrupted
- Refer to important information and details and use as evidence in discussion to support opinions and statements
- Understand and talk about everyday activities
- Understand content that reflects beginning understandings of physical world and social world: e.g., health, social studies, science, mathematics, arts
- Notice and respond to stress and tone of voice while listening and afterward
- Join in on refrains or repeated words, phrases, and sentences after hearing them several times
- Notice and remember the important information in a text
- Notice and remember the important events or steps of a text in temporal or chronological sequence
- Tell the important information in a text after hearing it read
- Sustain attention to listen to some books that take more than one read-aloud session
- Gain new information from both pictures and print
- Learn (synthesize) new concepts and ideas from listening to nonfiction texts
- Understand simple problems and solutions
- Give reasons (either text-based or from personal experience) to support thinking
- Use background knowledge of content to understand nonfiction topics
- Use background knowledge of history to understand simple biography
- Relate texts to their own lives
- Recognize and understand that nonfiction texts may be set in a variety of places and that customs and people's behavior may reflect those places
- Use evidence from the text to support statements about the text

- Use evidence from the text to support predictions (*I think . . . because . . .*)
- Relate important information and concepts in one text and connect to information and concepts in other texts
- Identify and discuss interesting and important information in a text
- Express opinions about a text: e.g., interesting, funny, and exciting and tell reasons
- Form opinions about authors and illustrators and state the basis for those opinions
- Connect texts by a range of categories: e.g., content, message, genre, author/illustrator, special form, text structure, or organization

Genre

- Infer the importance of a subject's accomplishments (biography)
- Understand that there are different types of texts and that they have different characteristics
- Notice and understand the characteristics of some specific nonfiction genres: e.g., expository nonfiction, narrative nonfiction, biography, memoir, procedural text, persuasive text, hybrid text
- Understand that a biography is the story of a person's life written by someone else
- Understand that biographies are often set in the past
- Understand that a memoir is an account of a memory or set of memories written by the person who experienced it
- Recognize some types of poetry (e.g., rhyming, lyrical, free verse) when they appear in nonfiction (rare)
- Notice and understand some elements of poetry when they appear in nonfiction: e.g., figurative language, rhyme, repetition, onomatopoeia, layout/line breaks (shape)
- Notice when a writer is describing a step-by-step procedure
- Notice when a writer is trying to persuade readers
- Recognize informational texts with some examples of simple argument and persuasion
- Recognize hybrid texts and distinguish which sections are nonfiction and fiction

● Thinking *Within* the Text　　◆ Thinking *Beyond* the Text　　■ Thinking *About* the Text

INTERACTIVE READ-ALOUD AND LITERATURE DISCUSSION

Selecting Goals Behaviors and Understandings to Notice, Teach, and Support *(cont.)*

Interactive Read-Aloud and Literature Discussion

NONFICTION TEXTS *(continued)*

Organization

- Follow and understand nonfiction texts with clearly defined overall structure and simple categories
- Understand that biographies and memoirs have a narrative structure
- Understand that some nonfiction books tell information and are not like a story (nonnarrative structure)
- Notice when a writer uses a question-and-answer structure
- Identify the organization of a text: e.g., chronological sequence, temporal and established sequences, categories
- Understand when a writer is telling information in a sequence (chronological order)
- Understand that a writer can tell about something that usually happens in the same order (temporal sequence)
- Notice that a nonfiction writer puts together information related to the same topic (category)

Topic

- Understand and talk about familiar topics: e.g., animals, pets, families, friends, sports, the five senses, nutrition and food, school, neighborhood, weather and seasons, machines, plants
- Show curiosity about topics encountered in nonfiction texts and actively work to learn more about them
- Infer the importance of a topic of a nonfiction text
- Infer the writer's attitude toward a topic (how the writer "feels")
- Understand that a writer has a purpose in writing about a topic
- Understand that a writer may be telling about something that happened in his life (memoir)
- Understand that a writer is presenting facts about a single topic
- Notice the main topic of a nonfiction text and subtopics

Messages and Main Ideas

- Follow arguments in a persuasive text

- Understand that a nonfiction text can have different meanings for different people
- Make connections among the content and ideas in nonfiction texts: e.g., animals, pets, families, sports, the five senses, nutrition and food, school, neighborhood, weather and seasons, machines, plants
- Connect the information in nonfiction books to curriculum areas studied at school
- Infer the significance of nonfiction content to their own lives
- Understand that a book can have more than one message or big idea

Style and Language

- Understand sentences with embedded clauses and phrases
- Notice a writer's choice of interesting words
- Notice when a text has repeating episodes or language patterns
- Notice a writer's use of playful or poetic language
- Recognize some authors by the topics they choose or the style of their illustrations

Vocabulary

- Notice and acquire understanding of new vocabulary from read-aloud content
- Understand the meaning of words representing all parts of speech when listening to a nonfiction text read aloud
- Understand the meaning of common (simple) connectives and some sophisticated connectives when listening to a nonfiction text
- Acquire new content words from texts and graphics, including those for familiar objects, familiar animals, some new animals, and human activities
- Use new vocabulary in discussion of a text
- Learn some words that do not appear frequently in oral conversation but are used in writing (Tier 2)

● Thinking ***Within*** the Text   ◆ Thinking ***Beyond*** the Text   ■ Thinking ***About*** the Text

Selecting Goals Behaviors and Understandings to Notice, Teach, and Support *(cont.)*

Interactive Read-Aloud and Literature Discussion

NONFICTION TEXTS *(continued)*

- Derive the meaning of words from the context of a paragraph or the whole text
- Use some academic language to talk about nonfiction genres: e.g., *nonfiction, personal memory story, informational text, informational book, factual text, biography, how-to book*
- Use some academic language to talk about forms: e.g., *picture book, wordless picture book, label book, ABC book, counting book, poem, poetry, nursery rhyme, rhyme, song, series book, play, letter, poetry collection*
- Use some academic language to talk about literary features: e.g., *beginning, ending, problem, question and answer, solution, topic, description, time order, problem and solution, time and place, message, dialogue*
- Use some academic language to talk about book and print features: e.g., *front cover, back cover, title, author, illustrator, page, text, illustration, photograph, label, table of contents, acknowledgments, chapter, section, heading, drawing, caption, map, chapter title, dedication, author's note, illustrator's note, section, diagram, glossary, endpapers*

Illustrations/Graphics

- Understand that graphics provide important information
- Recognize and use information in a variety of graphics: e.g., photo and/or drawing with label or caption, diagram, map with legend, infographic
- Understand that illustrations can have different meanings for different people

- Use details from illustrations to support points made in discussion
- Notice how illustrations and graphics help to communicate the writer's message
- Understand that graphics and text are carefully placed in a nonfiction text so that ideas are communicated clearly

Book and Print Features

- Notice a text's title and the name of its author and illustrator on the cover and title page
- Notice and use and understand the purpose of some organizational tools: e.g., title, table of contents, chapter title, heading
- Notice and use and understand the purpose of some text resources outside the body (peritext): e.g., dedication, acknowledgments, author's note, illustrator's note, endpapers, book flap

---

● Thinking ***Within*** the Text   ◆ Thinking ***Beyond*** the Text   ■ Thinking ***About*** the Text

Selecting Texts Characteristics of Texts for Reading Aloud and Discussion

Interactive Read-Aloud and Literature Discussion

GENRE

▶ **Fiction**

- Realistic fiction
- Historical fiction
- Traditional literature: e.g., folktale, tall tale, fairy tale, fable
- Fantasy
- Hybrid text
- Special types of fiction: e.g., mystery; adventure story; animal story; family, friends, and school story; humorous story

▶ **Nonfiction**

- Expository nonfiction
- Narrative nonfiction
- Biography
- Autobiography
- Memoir
- Procedural text
- Persuasive text
- Hybrid text

FORMS

- Series books
- Picture books
- Chapter books
- Poems
- Poetry collections
- Plays
- Types of poetry: lyrical poetry, free verse, limerick, haiku, narrative poetry, ballads
- Letters, diary and journal entries

TEXT STRUCTURE

- Narratives with straightforward structure but multiple episodes
- Stories with complex plot and multiple problems
- A few texts with variations in structure (story-within-a-story, flashback) that are easily followed
- Informational texts related to a larger topic, many with subtopics
- Underlying structural patterns: description, cause and effect, chronological sequence, temporal sequence (e.g., life cycles, how-to books), compare and contrast, problem and solution, question and answer

- Informational texts with clearly defined structure and categories and subcategories, some defined by headings and sections
- Simple biographical and historical texts with narrative structure
- Informational texts with some examples of simple argument and persuasion

CONTENT

- Content that is appropriate for students' cognitive development, social and emotional maturity, and life experience
- Content that engages students' intellectual curiosity and emotions
- Content that promotes inquiry and investigation
- Language and word play related to concepts, parts of speech, and sound devices such as alliteration, assonance, onomatopoeia
- Familiar topics that are authentic and relevant: e.g., animals, pets, families, friends, sports, nutrition and food, school, neighborhood, weather and seasons, machines, maps, plants
- Humor that is easy to grasp: e.g., silly characters, funny situations, jokes, word play, some subtle humor
- Content that reinforces and expands a student's experience and knowledge of self and the world
- Topics that may be beyond most students' immediate experiences: e.g., systems of the human body (digestive, excretory, muscular, skeletal, nervous); domestic and wild animals; environments such as ocean, desert, rainforest, mountains, village, city, farm; customs and beliefs in different cultures; events from various places and historical periods
- Content that reflects a wide range of settings, languages, and cultures
- Some content linked to specific areas of study as described by the school curriculum or standards
- Characters, settings, and events that could exist in contemporary life or in another historical period
- Imaginary characters, events, settings that occur in fantasy

- Content that reflects increasing understanding of the physical and social world: e.g., health, social studies, science, mathematics, arts

THEMES AND IDEAS

- More sophisticated presentation of themes reflecting everyday life: e.g., self, family relationships, home, friendship, community, diversity, responsibility, fairness, imagination, fears, loss, courage, nature
- Many books with multiple ideas that are mostly easy to understand
- Ideas close to children's experience: e.g., taking care of self, staying healthy, expressing feelings, sharing with others, caring for others, empathizing with others, helping your family, doing your job, caring for your world, problem solving, learning about life's challenges, valuing differences

LANGUAGE AND LITERARY FEATURES

- Elements of traditional literature and modern fantasy: e.g., the supernatural; imaginary and otherworldly creatures; gods and goddesses; talking animals, toys, and dolls; heroic characters; technology or scientific advances; time travel; aliens or outer space
- Basic motifs of traditional literature and modern fantasy: e.g., struggle between good and evil, magic, secondary or alternative worlds, the hero's quest, special character types, fantastic or magical objects, wishes, trickery, transformations
- Predictable story outcomes typical of traditional literature: e.g., clever overcomes power, good defeats evil
- A few texts with settings distant in time and place from students' own experiences
- Main characters and supporting characters
- Many multidimensional characters
- Multiple characters, each with unique traits
- Character development as a result of plot events
- Character dimensions (attributes) and relationships revealed through dialogue and behavior
- Predictable and static characters with simple traits typical of traditional literature

Selecting Texts Characteristics of Texts for Reading Aloud and Discussion *(cont.)*

Interactive Read-Aloud and Literature Discussion

- Plot with problem and clear, satisfying resolution
- Plot with multiple episodes
- Some longer texts with one or more subplots
- Most texts told from a single point of view
- Most texts written in first- or third-person narrative
- Language and events that convey an emotional atmosphere (mood) in a text, affecting how the reader feels: e.g., tension, sadness, whimsicality, joy
- Language used to make comparisons
- Descriptive language conveying a range of human feelings: e.g., joy, sadness, anger, eagerness
- Descriptive language conveying sensory experiences
- Some literary language typical of traditional literature: e.g., *once upon a time, long ago and far away, therefore, finally, at long last, happily ever after*
- Both assigned and unassigned dialogue
- Variety in presentation of dialogue among multiple characters
- Procedural language: e.g., step-by-step, directions, how-to
- Persuasive language
- Some procedural texts written in second person

SENTENCE COMPLEXITY

- Some long and complex sentences that require attention to follow
- Variation in placement of subject, verb, and multiple adjectives, adverbs, and prepositional phrases
- Many sentences with embedded clauses and phrases
- Complex sentences with variety in order of phrases and clauses
- Sentences with common (simple) connectives
- Some sentences with sophisticated connectives
- Extended dialogue that increases sentence complexity

- Some texts with long sentences divided into numbered or bulleted lists
- Sentence structure adapted to fit purpose and form of book and print features: e.g., heading, subheading, label, caption, legend

VOCABULARY

- Some interesting words that may be new
- New content words related to concepts that children are learning
- Most words that are in common oral vocabulary for children (Tier 1)
- Some words that appear in the vocabulary of mature language users (Tier 2)
- Occasional use of words that are particular to a discipline (Tier 3)
- Common (simple) connectives that are frequently used in oral language (words, phrases that clarify relationships ideas): e.g., *and, but, so, because, before, after*
- A few sophisticated connectives (words that link ideas and clarify meaning) that are used in written texts but do not appear often in everyday oral language: e.g., *although, however, meantime, meanwhile, moreover, otherwise, therefore, though, unless, until, whenever, yet*
- Many adjectives describing people, places, or things
- Adverbs that describe action
- Technical vocabulary

ILLUSTRATIONS

- Illustrations in a variety of media that fully support meaning
- Illustrations that enhance and extend meaning in the text
- Complex illustrations with many details, some needing description by the teacher during reading
- Books with illustrations that represent a coherent artistic vision
- Some texts with minimal illustrations
- Chapter books with just a few black-and-white illustrations
- Illustrations that convey mood

- Books with illustrations that reflect the theme
- Simple illustrations in a variety of forms: drawing with label or caption, photograph with label or caption, map with legend, diagram (cutaway), infographic

BOOK AND PRINT FEATURES

LENGTH

- Short picture books that can be read in one sitting
- Some long illustrated texts with sections that may be selected and read

PRINT AND LAYOUT

- Some books with decorative or informative illustrations, engaging designs that communicate meaning, and/or print outside the body of the text (peritext)

ORGANIZATIONAL TOOLS

- Title, author, and illustrator listed on cover and on title page
- Table of contents, chapter title, heading, sidebar

TEXT RESOURCES

- Some books with dedication, acknowledgments, author's note, glossary, special endpapers (peritext)

Selecting Goals Behaviors and Understandings to Notice, Teach, and Support

Interactive Read-Aloud and Literature Discussion

FICTION TEXTS

General

- Ask questions to deepen understanding of a text
- Notice and ask questions when meaning is lost or understanding is interrupted
- Refer to important information and details and use as evidence to support opinions and statements during discussion
- Notice and respond to stress and tone of voice while listening and afterward
- Tell a summary of a text after hearing it read
- Sustain attention to listen to some books that take more than one read-aloud session
- ◆ Learn new concepts and ideas from listening to fiction texts
- ◆ Synthesize new information and ideas and revise thinking in response to it
- ◆ Understand the problems that occur in daily life, including some complex problems that can be related to readers' lives
- ◆ Give reasons (either text-based or from personal experience) to support thinking
- ◆ Use background knowledge to understand settings, problems, and characters
- ◆ Use background knowledge of content to understand the problems and events of fiction texts
- ◆ Use background knowledge of history to understand historical fiction
- ◆ Make connections (e.g., content, theme) across fiction texts that are read aloud
- ◆ Make connections (similarities and differences) among texts that have the same author/illustrator, setting, characters, or theme
- ◆ Use evidence from the text to support statements about the text
- ◆ Use evidence from the text to support a wide range of predictions (*I think . . . because . . .*)
- ◆ Relate important ideas in the text to each other and to ideas in other texts
- ■ Understand that a writer has a purpose in writing a fiction or nonfiction text
- ■ Connect texts by a range of categories: e.g., author, character, topic, genre, illustrator
- ■ Form and express opinions about a text and support with rationale and evidence
- ■ Form and state the basis for opinions about authors and illustrators

Genre

- ◆ Understand that there are different types of texts and that they have different characteristics
- ■ Notice and understand the characteristics of some specific fiction genres: e.g., realistic fiction, historical fiction, folktale, fairy tale, fable, fantasy, hybrid text
- ■ Understand when a story could happen in real life (realistic fiction) and when it could not happen in real life (traditional literature, fantasy)
- ■ Notice story outcomes that are typical of traditional literature
- ■ Recognize hybrid texts and distinguish which sections are fiction and nonfiction
- ■ Notice and understand some special types of fiction: e.g., mystery; adventure story; animal story; family, friends, and school story
- ■ Recognize and understand some specific types of poetry: e.g., lyrical poetry, free verse, limerick, haiku, narrative poetry, ballad
- ■ Notice and understand some elements of poetry: e.g., figurative language, rhyme, repetition, onomatopoeia, layout/line breaks (shape), imagery, alliteration, assonance

Messages and Themes

- ◆ Notice that a book may have more than one message or big (main) idea
- ◆ Infer the "lesson" in traditional literature
- ◆ Understand that the "lesson" in fantasy or traditional literature can be applied to their own lives
- ◆ Infer the messages in a work of fiction
- ◆ Notice and infer the importance of ideas relevant to their world: e.g., sharing, caring for others, doing your job, helping your family, taking care of self, staying healthy, caring for the world or environment, valuing differences, expressing feelings, empathizing with others, problem solving, learning about life's challenges, social justice
- ◆ Understand that there can be different interpretations of the meaning of a fiction text
- ◆ Notice and understand themes that are close to their experience: e.g., imagination, courage, fear, sharing, friendship, family relationships, self, nature, behavior, community, responsibility, fairness, diversity, belonging, peer relationships, loss
- ◆ Think across texts to derive larger messages, themes, or ideas
- ■ Notice when a fiction writer is communicating a moral lesson
- ■ Notice recurring themes or motifs in traditional literature and fantasy: e.g., struggle between good and evil

---

● Thinking **Within** the Text   ◆ Thinking **Beyond** the Text   ■ Thinking **About** the Text

Selecting Goals Behaviors and Understandings to Notice, Teach, and Support *(cont.)*

Interactive Read-Aloud and Literature Discussion

FICTION TEXTS *(continued)*

Setting

- Recall important details about setting after a story is read
- Recognize and understand that fiction texts may have settings that reflect a wide range of diverse places, languages, and cultures, and that characters' behavior may reflect those settings
- Notice and understand settings that are distant in time and place from students' own experiences
- Infer the importance of the setting to the plot of the story in realistic and historical fiction and fantasy

Plot

- Follow a plot with multiple events or episodes
- Notice and remember the important events of a text in sequence
- Check understanding of plots with multiple events and ask questions if meaning is lost
- Tell the important events of a story using the pictures (after hearing the text read several times)
- Notice and understand when a problem is solved
- Include the problem and its resolution in a summary of a text
- Follow a text with a complex plot and multiple problems (longer stories)
- Understand how one episode builds on another and use information from the beginning of a story to interpret later episodes
- Predict what will happen next in a story and outcomes of the plot
- Infer the significance of events in a plot
- Give opinions about whether a problem seems real
- Recognize and discuss aspects of narrative structure: e.g., beginning, series of events, high point of the story, problem resolution, ending)

Character

- Recall important details about characters after a story is read
- Follow multiple characters, each with unique traits, in the same story
- Recognize that characters can have multiple dimensions: e.g., can be good but make mistakes, can change
- Infer characters' traits as revealed through thought, dialogue, behavior, and what others say or think about them and use evidence from the text to describe them
- Infer the character's traits from the physical details the illustrations include about them
- Infer characters' intentions, feelings, and motivations as revealed through thought, dialogue, behavior, and what others say or think about them

- Make predictions about what a character is likely to do and use evidence from the text to support predictions
- Notice character change and infer reasons from events of the plot
- Learn from vicarious experiences with characters in stories
- Notice predictable or static characters (characters that do not change) as typical in traditional literature
- Infer relationships between characters as revealed through dialogue and behavior
- Express opinions about the characters in a story (evil, dishonest, clever, sly, greedy, brave, loyal), and support with evidence.
- Understand that the same types of characters may appear over and over again in traditional literature: e.g., sly, brave, silly, wise, greedy, clever
- Understand the difference between realistic characters and those that appear in fantasy
- Express opinions about whether a character seems real
- Notice how the writer reveals characters and makes them seem real

Style and Language

- Follow and understand assigned and unassigned dialogue among multiple characters with a clear idea about who is speaking
- Notice that words have special qualities, such as musical or pleasing sound, dramatic impact, or humor
- Notice and think critically about a writer's word choice
- Notice a writer's use of playful or poetic language and sound devices: e.g., rhythm, repetition, rhymes, refrains, onomatopoeia, alliteration, assonance
- Notice when a fiction writer uses poetic or descriptive language to show the setting, appeal to the five senses, or to convey human feelings such as loss, relief, or anger
- Recognize how a writer creates humor
- Notice language that conveys an emotional atmosphere (mood) in a text, affecting how the reader feels: e.g., tension, sadness, whimsicality, joy
- Notice and remember literary language patterns that are characteristic of traditional literature: e.g., *once upon a time, long ago and far away, therefore, finally, at long last, happily ever after*
- Notice and understand how the author uses literary language, including some figurative language and symbolism
- Analyze texts to determine aspects of a writer's style: e.g., use of language, choice of setting, plot, characters, themes and ideas
- Recognize some authors by the style of their illustrations, their topics, characters they use, or typical plots

● Thinking **Within** the Text   ◆ Thinking **Beyond** the Text   ■ Thinking **About** the Text

Selecting Goals Behaviors and Understandings to Notice, Teach, and Support *(cont.)*

Interactive Read-Aloud and Literature Discussion

FICTION TEXTS *(continued)*

Vocabulary

- Continue to build vocabulary as a foundation for recognizing words in print
- Notice and acquire understanding of new vocabulary from read-aloud content
- Acquire new content words from texts and graphics
- Use new vocabulary in discussion of a text
- Learn some words that do not appear frequently in oral conversation but are used in writing (Tier 2)
- Derive the meaning of words from the context of a sentence, paragraph, or the whole story
- Understand the meaning of words representing all parts of speech when listening to a story
- Understand common (simple) connectives that link and clarify meaning and are frequently used in oral language when listening to a story (*and, but, so, because, before, after*)
- Understand (when listening) some sophisticated connectives (words that link ideas and clarify meaning) that are used in written texts but do not appear often in everyday oral language: e.g., *although, however, meantime, meanwhile, moreover, otherwise, therefore, though, unless, until, whenever, yet*
- Use some academic language to talk about fiction genres: e.g., *fiction, folktale, fairy tale, fable, tall tale, realistic fiction*
- Use some academic language to talk about special types of fiction: e.g., *adventure story; animal story; family, friends, and school story; humorous story; mystery*
- Use some academic language to talk about forms: e.g., *picture book, wordless picture book, label book, ABC book, poem, poetry, nursery rhyme, rhyme, song, series book, chapter book, play, letter, poetry collection*
- Use some academic language to talk about literary features: e.g., *beginning, ending, problem, character, solution, main character, events, character change, message, dialogue, setting*
- Use some academic language to talk about book and print features: e.g., *front cover, back cover, title, author, illustrator, page, text, illustration, photograph, label, table of contents, acknowledgments, chapter, section, heading, drawing, caption, map, chapter title, dedication, author's note, illustrator's note, endpapers, book jacket*

Illustrations

- Notice and remember the important events of a story using the pictures (after hearing the text read several times)
- Think about what characters are feeling from their facial expressions or gestures
- Notice that the background details in pictures often reveal characters' feelings or traits
- Use details from illustrations and text to support points made in discussion
- Notice how an illustrator creates the illusion of sound and motion in pictures
- Notice how an illustrator shows the passage of time through illustrations (use of light, weather)
- Notice how the tone of a book is created by the illustrator's choice of colors
- Notice how the tone of a book is impacted by the use of background color
- Notice how the tone of a book changes when the illustrator shifts the color
- Notice how illustrators create perspective in their pictures (using images close up, far away, creating distance in between, etc.)
- Notice how illustrations and graphics go together with the text in a meaningful way
- Notice how illustrations and graphics can reflect the theme in a text
- Notice and infer how illustrations contribute to mood in a text

Book and Print Features

- Notice and use and understand the purpose of some organizational tools: e.g., title, table of contents, chapter title
- Notice and use and understand the purpose of some other text resources: e.g., glossary
- Notice and use and understand the purpose of some text resources outside the body (peritext): e.g., dedication, acknowledgments, author's note, illustrator's note, endpapers
- Notice and understand other features of the peritext that have symbolic value, add to aesthetic enjoyment, or add meaning

---

● Thinking *Within* the Text   ◆ Thinking *Beyond* the Text   ■ Thinking *About* the Text

Selecting Goals Behaviors and Understandings to Notice, Teach, and Support *(cont.)*

Interactive Read-Aloud and Literature Discussion

NONFICTION TEXTS

General

- ● Ask questions to deepen understanding of a text
- ● Notice and ask questions when meaning is lost or understanding is interrupted
- ● Refer to important information and details and use as evidence in discussion to support opinions and statements
- ● Understand content that reflects beginning understandings of physical world and social world: e.g., health, social studies, science, mathematics, arts
- ● Notice and respond to stress and tone of voice while listening and afterward
- ● Notice and remember the important information in a text
- ● Notice and remember the important events or steps in temporal or chronological sequence and tell them in order
- ● Tell a summary of a text after hearing it read
- ● Sustain attention to listen to some books that take more than one read-aloud session
- ◆ Synthesize new information and ideas and revise thinking in response to it
- ◆ Understand simple problems and solutions, including those that may relate to readers' lives
- ◆ Give reasons (either text-based or from personal experience) to support thinking
- ◆ Use background knowledge of content to understand nonfiction topics
- ◆ Use background knowledge of history to understand simple biography, autobiography, and memoir
- ◆ Recognize and understand that informational texts may reflect a wide range of diverse settings, languages, and cultures
- ◆ Use evidence from the text to support statements about the text
- ◆ Use evidence from the text to support predictions (*I think . . . because . . .*)
- ◆ Relate important information and concepts in one text and connect to information and concepts in other texts
- ◆ Relate the messages in a nonfiction text to one's own life
- ■ Identify and discuss interesting, surprising, and important information in a text
- ■ Form and express opinions about a text and support with rationale and evidence
- ■ Form and state the basis for opinions about authors and illustrators
- ■ Connect texts by a range of categories: e.g., content, message, genre, author/illustrator, text structure, or organization

Genre

- ◆ Infer the importance of a subject's accomplishments (biography)
- ■ Notice and understand the characteristics of some specific nonfiction genres: e.g., informational book, procedural and persuasive texts, biography, autobiography, memoir, hybrid text
- ■ Understand that a biography is the story of a person's life written by someone else
- ■ Understand that biographies are often set in the past
- ■ Understand that an autobiography is an account of a person's life written by that person
- ■ Understand that a memoir is an account of a memory or set of memories written by the person who experienced it
- ■ Notice when a writer is describing a step-by-step procedure
- ■ Notice a writer's use of argument and persuasion
- ■ Recognize hybrid texts and distinguish which sections are nonfiction and fiction
- ■ Recognize and understand some specific forms of nonfiction: e.g., series books; picture books; letters, diaries, and journals entries
- ■ Recognize and understand some specific types of poetry when they appear in nonfiction: e.g., lyrical poetry, free verse, limerick, haiku, narrative poetry, ballad
- ■ Notice and understand some elements of poetry when they appear in nonfiction: e.g., figurative language, rhyme, repetition, onomatopoeia, layout/line breaks (shape), imagery, alliteration, assonance

Organization

- ● Follow and understand nonfiction texts with clearly defined overall structure and simple categories
- ● Be aware when the teacher is reading bulleted or numbered lists
- ■ Understand that a nonfiction text can be expository or narrative in structure
- ■ Notice a nonfiction writer's use of narrative text structure in biography and narrative nonfiction
- ■ Notice when a writer uses a question-and-answer structure
- ■ Identify the organization of a text: e.g., chronological sequence, temporal and established sequences, categories
- ■ Understand when a writer is telling information in a sequence (chronological order)
- ■ Understand that a writer can tell about something that usually happens in the same order (temporal sequence)
- ■ Notice that a nonfiction writer puts together information related to the same topic or subtopic (category)

● Thinking **Within** the Text   ◆ Thinking **Beyond** the Text   ■ Thinking **About** the Text

Selecting Goals Behaviors and Understandings to Notice, Teach, and Support *(cont.)*

Interactive Read-Aloud and Literature Discussion

NONFICTION TEXTS *(continued)*

Topic

- Understand and talk about both familiar topics and those that offer new and surprising information and ideas
- Show curiosity about topics encountered in nonfiction texts and actively work to learn more about them
- Think across nonfiction texts to construct knowledge of a topic
- Infer the importance of a topic of a nonfiction text
- Infer the writer's attitude toward a topic
- Recognize that a variety of informational texts may be about a wide range of diverse places, languages, and cultures
- Infer a writer's purpose in writing a nonfiction text
- Understand that a writer is presenting related facts about a single topic
- Notice the topic of a nonfiction text and that subtopics are related to the main topic

Messages and Main Ideas

- Follow arguments in a persuasive text
- Understand that there can be different interpretations of the meanings of a text
- Make connections among the content and ideas in nonfiction texts: e.g., animals, pets, families, sports, the five senses, nutrition and food, school, neighborhood, weather and seasons, machines, plants
- Connect the information in nonfiction books to disciplinary studies
- Infer the significance of nonfiction content to their own lives
- Infer the larger ideas and messages in a nonfiction text
- Understand that a book can have more than one message or big idea

Style and Language

- Understand sentences with embedded clauses and phrases
- Understand sentence structure that varies according to purpose: e.g., headings, captions, labels, numbered and bulleted lists
- Notice and think critically about a writer's word choice
- Notice language that conveys an emotional atmosphere (mood) in a text, affecting how the reader feels: e.g., tension, sadness, whimsicality, joy
- Recognize a writer's use of the techniques for persuasion in a persuasive text
- Recognize some authors by the topics they choose or the style of their illustrations

Accuracy

- Examine the quality or accuracy of the text, citing evidence for opinions

Vocabulary

- Notice and acquire understanding of new vocabulary from read-aloud content
- Understand the meaning of words representing all parts of speech when listening to a nonfiction text read aloud
- Understand the meaning of common (simple) connectives and some sophisticated connectives when listening to a nonfiction text
- Acquire new content words from texts and graphics
- Use new vocabulary in discussion of a text
- Learn some words that do not appear frequently in oral conversation but are used in writing (Tier 2)
- Notice and understand the meaning of a few easy, domain-specific words (Tier 3)
- Derive the meaning of words from the context of a paragraph or the whole text
- Use some academic language to talk about nonfiction genres: e.g., *nonfiction, personal memory story, informational text, informational book, factual text, biography, how-to book, autobiography*
- Use some academic language to talk about forms: e.g., *picture book, wordless picture book, label book, ABC book, counting book, poem, poetry, nursery rhyme, rhyme, song, series book, play, letter, poetry collection*
- Use some academic language to talk about literary features: e.g., *beginning, ending, problem, question and answer, solution, topic, description, time order, problem and solution, message, dialogue, main idea, comparison and contrast, setting*
- Use some academic language to talk about book and print features: e.g., *front cover, back cover, title, author, illustrator, page, text, illustration, photograph, label, table of contents, acknowledgments, chapter, section, heading, drawing, caption, map, chapter title, dedication, author's note, illustrator's note, section, diagram, glossary, endpapers, sidebar, book jacket*

● Thinking *Within* the Text   ◆ Thinking *Beyond* the Text   ■ Thinking *About* the Text

Selecting Goals Behaviors and Understandings to Notice, Teach, and Support *(cont.)*

Interactive Read-Aloud and Literature Discussion

NONFICTION TEXTS *(continued)*

Illustrations/Graphics

- ● Understand that graphics provide important information
- ◆ Recognize and use information in a variety of graphics: e.g., photo and/or drawing with label or caption, diagram, cutaway, map with legend, infographic
- ◆ Use details from illustrations to support points made in discussion
- ■ Notice how illustrations and graphics help to communicate the writer's message
- ■ Understand that graphics and text are carefully placed in a nonfiction text so that ideas are communicated clearly

Book and Print Features

- ● Notice a text's title and the name of its author and illustrator on the cover and title page
- ◆ Gain new understandings from searching for and using information found in text body, sidebars, and graphics
- ■ Notice and use and understand the purpose of some organizational tools: e.g., title, table of contents, chapter title, heading, subheading
- ■ Notice and use and understand the purpose of some other text resources: e.g., glossary, index
- ■ Notice and use and understand the purpose of some text resources outside the body (peritext): e.g., dedication, acknowledgments, author's note, illustrator's note, endpapers
- ■ Notice and understand other features of the peritext that have symbolic value, add to aesthetic enjoyment, or add meaning

● Thinking *Within* the Text   ◆ Thinking *Beyond* the Text   ■ Thinking *About* the Text

Selecting Texts Characteristics of Texts for Reading Aloud and Discussion

Interactive Read-Aloud and Literature Discussion

GENRE

▶ Fiction

- Realistic fiction
- Historical fiction
- Traditional literature: e.g., folktale, tall tale, fairy tale (including fractured fairy tale), fable
- More complex fantasy including science fiction
- Hybrid text
- Special types of fiction: e.g., mystery; adventure story; animal story; family, friends, and school story; humorous story; sports story

▶ Nonfiction

- Expository nonfiction
- Narrative nonfiction
- Biography
- Autobiography
- Memoir
- Procedural text
- Persuasive text
- Hybrid text

FORMS

- Series books
- Picture books
- Chapter books, some with sequels
- Poems
- Poetry collections
- Plays
- Types of poetry: lyrical poetry, free verse, limerick, haiku, narrative poetry, ballad, epic/saga, concrete poetry
- Letters, diary and journal entries
- Short stories
- Photo essays, news articles, and feature articles

TEXT STRUCTURE

- Narratives with straightforward structure and multiple episodes that may be more elaborated
- Stories with complex plot and multiple problems
- Some texts with variations in structure: e.g., story-within-a-story, flashback
- Longer stories with multiple plots

- Some books with chapters connected to a single plot
- Some collections of short stories related to an overarching theme and with plots that intertwine
- Informational texts related to a larger topic with subtopics
- Underlying structural patterns: description, cause and effect, chronological sequence, temporal sequence (e.g., life cycles, how-to books), categorization, compare and contrast, problem and solution, question and answer
- Informational texts with clearly defined structure and categories and subcategories, some defined by headings and sections
- Simple biographical and historical texts with narrative structure
- Informational texts with some examples of simple argument and persuasion

CONTENT

- Content that is appropriate for students' cognitive development, social and emotional maturity, and life experience
- Content that engages students' intellectual curiosity and emotions
- Content that promotes inquiry and investigation
- Content that requires prior knowledge and invites extended discussion
- Familiar topics that are authentic and relevant: e.g., animals, family relationships, friendship, sports, music, neighborhoods, nutrition, weather and seasons, maps, plants
- More sophisticated, subtle humor: e.g., characters with humorous traits, surprising outcomes, humorous comparisons
- Content that reinforces and expands a student's experience and knowledge of self and the world
- Topics that may be beyond most students' immediate experiences: e.g., systems of the human body (circulatory, respiratory, endocrine); domestic and wild animals; environments such as ocean, desert, rainforest, mountains, village, city, farm; rocks and minerals; energy; magnetism; customs and beliefs in different cultures; government; economics
- Content that reflects a wide range of settings, languages, and cultures

- Content related to historical periods, circumstances, and places
- Some content linked to specific areas of study as described by the school curriculum or standards
- Characters, settings, and events that could exist in contemporary life or in another historical period
- More complex characters, settings, and events that occur in fantasy
- Content that reflects increasing understanding of the physical and social world: e.g., health, social studies, science, mathematics, arts

THEMES AND IDEAS

- Themes reflecting important human challenges and social issues: e.g., self and self-esteem, popularity, bullying, sportsmanship, transition to adolescence, life cycles, survival, interconnectedness of humans and the environment, social justice, social awareness and responsibility
- Many books with multiple ideas, some requiring inference to understand
- Ideas close to students' experience: e.g., becoming independent, family relationships, peer relationships, valuing change in self and others, empathizing with others, valuing differences, working with others to accomplish goals, connecting past and future, recognizing individual responsibility for the environment, overcoming challenges

LANGUAGE AND LITERARY FEATURES

- Elements of traditional literature and modern fantasy: e.g., the supernatural; imaginary and otherworldly creatures; gods and goddesses; talking animals, toys, and dolls; heroic characters; technology or scientific advances; time travel; aliens or outer space
- Basic motifs of traditional literature and modern fantasy: e.g., struggle between good and evil, magic, secondary or alternative worlds, the hero's quest, special character types, fantastic or magical objects, wishes, trickery, transformations
- Predictable story outcomes typical of traditional literature: e.g., clever overcomes power, good defeats evil

Selecting Texts Characteristics of Texts for Reading Aloud and Discussion *(cont.)*

Interactive Read-Aloud and Literature Discussion

- Some texts with settings distant in time and place from students' own experiences
- Main characters and supporting characters
- Memorable characters, many with multiple dimensions revealed by what they say, think, and do and what others say and think about them
- Characters that are complex and change over time in longer texts
- Predictable and static characters with simple traits typical of traditional literature
- Plot with problem and clear, satisfying resolution
- Plot with multiple episodes
- Some longer texts with one or more subplots
- Some texts told from multiple points of view
- Most texts written in first- or third-person narrative with some procedural texts in second-person
- Some texts with basic or obvious symbolism
- Language used to make comparisons
- Descriptive language conveying sensory experiences and a range of human feelings: e.g., joy, sadness, anger, eagerness
- Poetic language and other literary language
- Language and events that convey an emotional atmosphere (mood) in a text, affecting how the reader feels: e.g., tension, sadness, whimsicality, joy
- Descriptive and figurative language that is important to understanding the text: e.g., imagery, metaphor, simile
- Descriptive and figurative language that is important to understanding the content: e.g., imagery, metaphor, simile, personification, hyperbole
- Some literary language typical of traditional literature: e.g., *once upon a time, long ago and far away, therefore, finally, at long last, happily ever after*
- Both assigned and unassigned dialogue, including some strings of unassigned dialogue for which speakers must be inferred
- Procedural language: e.g., step-by-step, directions, how-to
- Persuasive language

SENTENCE COMPLEXITY

- Some long and complex sentences that require attention to follow

- Variation in placement of subject, verb, and multiple adjectives, adverbs, and prepositional phrases
- Many sentences with embedded clauses and phrases
- Complex sentences with variety in order of phrases and clauses
- Sentences with common (simple) connectives
- Sentences with sophisticated connectives
- Extended dialogue that increases sentence complexity
- Some texts with long sentences divided into bulleted or numbered lists
- Sentence structure adapted to fit purpose and form of book and print features: e.g., heading, subheading, label, caption, labels, legend

VOCABULARY

- Some interesting words that may be new
- New content words related to concepts that students are learning
- Many words that are in students' common oral vocabulary (Tier 1)
- Many words that appear in the vocabulary of mature language users (Tier 2)
- Some words that are particular to a discipline (Tier 3)
- Common (simple) connectives that are frequently used in oral language (words, phrases that clarify relationships ideas): e.g., *and, but, so, because, before, after*
- A few sophisticated connectives (words that link ideas and clarify meaning) that are used in written texts but do not appear often in everyday oral language: e.g., *although, however, meantime, meanwhile, moreover, otherwise, therefore, though, unless, until, whenever, yet*
- Many words with multiple meanings
- Many words with figurative meaning
- Some idioms
- Some words with connotative meanings that are essential to understanding the text
- A few words used ironically
- Some words from regional or historical dialects
- Some words from languages other than English
- Technical vocabulary

ILLUSTRATIONS

- Illustrations in a variety of media that fully support meaning
- Illustrations that enhance and extend meaning in the text
- Complex illustrations with many details, some needing description by the teacher during reading
- Books with illustrations that represent a coherent artistic vision
- Chapter books with just a few black and white illustrations
- Some texts with no illustrations other than decorative elements such as vignettes
- Some complex, nuanced illustrations that convey mood to match or extend the text
- Books with illustrations that reflect the theme
- Simple illustrations in a variety of forms: drawing with label or caption, photograph with label or caption, map with legend and scale, diagram (cutaway), infographic, chart, graph, timeline

BOOK AND PRINT FEATURES

LENGTH

- Short picture books that can be read in one sitting
- Long illustrated texts with sections that may be selected and read
- Some long illustrated texts that require several days to complete

PRINT AND LAYOUT

- Some books with decorative or informative illustrations and/or print outside the body of the text (peritext)
- Texts with engaging designs that add aesthetic value and have symbolic and/or cultural value (peritext)

ORGANIZATIONAL TOOLS

- Title, author, and illustrator listed on cover and on title page
- Table of contents, chapter title, heading, subheading, sidebar

TEXT RESOURCES

- Some books with dedication, acknowledgments, author's note, glossary, special endpapers (peritext), index

Selecting Goals Behaviors and Understandings to Notice, Teach, and Support

Interactive Read-Aloud and Literature Discussion

FICTION TEXTS

General

- Ask questions to deepen understanding of a text
- Notice and ask questions when meaning is lost or understanding is interrupted
- Refer to important information and details and use as evidence to support opinions and statements during discussion
- Notice and respond to stress and tone of voice while listening to read-aloud and afterward
- Tell a summary of a text after hearing it read
- Sustain attention for some longer texts that may require several days to finish
- Recall important details about setting, problem and resolution, and characters after a story is read
- Learn new concepts and ideas from listening to fiction texts
- Synthesize new information and ideas and revise thinking in response to it
- Understand complex problems that can be related to readers' lives
- Learn more about social issues, both local and global, as revealed through character, plot, and setting
- Give reasons (either text-based or from personal experience) to support thinking
- Use background knowledge to understand settings, problems, and characters
- Use background knowledge to extend understanding of historical fiction and science fiction
- Infer a writer's purpose in writing a fiction text
- Make connections (e.g., content, theme) across fiction texts that are read aloud
- Use evidence from the text to support statements about the text
- Make connections (similarities and differences) among texts that have the same author/illustrator, setting, characters, or theme
- Use evidence from the text to support a wide range of predictions
- Relate important ideas in the text to each other and to ideas in other texts
- Understand that a writer has a purpose in writing a fiction text
- Connect texts by a range of categories: e.g., content, theme, message, genre, author/illustrator, character, setting, special forms, text structure, or organization
- Form and express opinions about a text and support with rationale and evidence
- Form and state the basis for opinions about authors and illustrators

Genre

- Understand that there are different types of texts and that they have different characteristics
- Apply background knowledge to extend understanding of historical fiction
- Use scientific or technical knowledge to understand science fiction
- Notice and understand the characteristics of some specific fiction genres: e.g., realistic fiction, historical fiction, folktale, fairy tale, fractured fairy tale, fable, myth, legend, epic, ballad, fantasy including science fiction, hybrid text
- Understand when a story could happen in real life (realistic fiction) and when it could not happen in real life (traditional literature, fantasy)
- Notice story outcomes that are typical of traditional literature
- Identify elements of traditional literature and modern fantasy: e.g., the supernatural; imaginary and otherworldly creatures; gods and goddesses; talking animals, toys, and dolls; heroic characters; technology or scientific advances; time travel; aliens or outer space
- Identify some elements of science fiction: e.g., technology or scientific advances, futuristic setting, time travel, aliens and outer space
- Recognize hybrid texts and distinguish which sections are fiction and nonfiction
- Notice and understand some special types of fiction: e.g., mystery; adventure story; animal story; family, friends, and school story; humorous story; sports story
- Recognize and understand some specific types of poetry: e.g., lyrical poetry, free verse, limerick, haiku, narrative poetry, ballad, epic/saga, concrete poetry
- Notice and understand some elements of poetry: e.g., figurative language, rhyme, repetition, onomatopoeia, layout/line breaks (shape), imagery, alliteration, assonance

Messages and Themes

- Notice that a book may have more than one message or big (main) idea
- Understand that the messages or big ideas in fiction texts can be applied to their own lives or to other people and society
- Infer the messages in a work of fiction
- Infer and understand the moral lesson or cultural teaching in traditional literature

---

● Thinking **Within** the Text   ◆ Thinking **Beyond** the Text   ■ Thinking **About** the Text

Selecting Goals Behaviors and Understandings to Notice, Teach, and Support *(cont.)*

Interactive Read-Aloud and Literature Discussion

FICTION TEXTS *(continued)*

- ◆ Notice and infer the importance of ideas relevant to their world: e.g., becoming independent, family relationships, peer relationships, valuing change in self and others, empathizing with others, valuing differences, working with others to accomplish goals, connecting past and future, recognizing individual responsibility for the environment, overcoming challenges
- ◆ Extend understanding to fiction content that is beyond most students' immediate experience: e.g., customs and beliefs in different cultures, a wide range of settings
- ◆ Understand that there can be different interpretations of the meaning of a fiction text
- ◆ Notice and understand themes reflecting important human challenges and social issues: e.g., self and self-esteem, popularity, bullying, sportsmanship, transition to adolescence, life cycles, survival, interconnectedness of humans and the environment, social justice, social awareness and responsibility
- ◆ Think across texts to derive larger messages, themes, or ideas
- ◆ Understand themes and ideas that are mature issues and require experience to interpret
- ■ Notice when a fiction writer is communicating a moral lesson
- ■ Notice recurring themes or motifs in traditional literature and fantasy: e.g., struggle between good and evil, the hero's quest

Setting

- ● Recall important details about setting after a story is read
- ◆ Recognize and understand that fiction texts may have settings that reflect a wide range of places, languages, and cultures, and that characters' behavior may reflect those settings
- ◆ Notice and understand settings that are distant in time and place from students' own experiences
- ◆ Infer the importance of the setting to the plot of the story in realistic and historical fiction and fantasy

Plot

- ● Follow a complex plot with multiple events, episodes, or problems
- ● Notice and remember the important events of a text in sequence
- ● Check understanding of the plot of the story and ask questions if meaning is lost
- ● Tell the important events of a story using the pictures (after hearing the text read several times)

- ● Notice and understand when a problem is solved
- ● Include the problem and its resolution in a summary of a text
- ● Follow a text with short stories related to an overarching theme and with plots that intertwine
- ● Follow a text with multiple plots (longer stories)
- ● Understand how one episode builds on another and use information from the beginning of a story to interpret later episodes
- ◆ Predict what will happen next in a story and outcomes of the plot
- ◆ Infer the significance of events in a plot
- ■ Give opinions about whether a problem seems real
- ■ Recognize and discuss aspects of narrative structure (beginning, series of events, high point of the story, problem resolution, ending)
- ■ Notice a writer's use of multiple narratives to reveal the plot and relationships among characters
- ■ Recognize the text structure when the writer uses literary devices: e.g., flashback, story-within-a-story
- ■ Evaluate the logic and believability of the plot and its resolution

Character

- ● Follow multiple characters, each with unique traits, in the same story
- ● Recognize that characters can have multiple dimensions: e.g., can be good but make mistakes, can change
- ◆ Infer characters' traits as revealed through thought, dialogue, behavior, and what others say or think about them, and use evidence from the text to describe them
- ◆ Infer characters' intentions, feelings, and motivations as revealed through thought, dialogue, behavior, and what others say or think about them
- ◆ Make predictions about what a character is likely to do next and use evidence from the text to support predictions
- ◆ Notice character change and infer reasons from events of the plot
- ◆ Learn from vicarious experiences with characters in stories
- ◆ Express opinions about the characters in a story: e.g., evil, dishonest, clever, sly, greedy, brave, loyal, and support with evidence.
- ◆ Notice predictable or static characters (characters that do not change) as typical in traditional literature

● Thinking *Within* the Text   ◆ Thinking *Beyond* the Text   ■ Thinking *About* the Text

Selecting Goals Behaviors and Understandings to Notice, Teach, and Support *(cont.)*

Interactive Read-Aloud and Literature Discussion

FICTION TEXTS *(continued)*

Character *(continued)*

- ◆ Infer relationships between characters as revealed through dialogue and behavior
- ■ Understand that the same types of characters may appear over and over again in traditional literature: e.g., sly, brave, silly, wise, greedy, clever
- ■ Understand the difference between realistic characters and those that appear in fantasy
- ■ Express opinions about whether a character seems real
- ■ Notice how a writer reveals characters and makes them seem real
- ■ Notice how an author creates characters that are complex and change over many events of a plot
- ■ Think critically about the logic of a character's actions (causes and effects)
- ■ Think critically about the authenticity and believability of characters and their behavior, dialogue, and development
- ■ Assess the extent to which a writer makes readers feel empathy or identify with characters
- ■ Evaluate the consistency of characters' actions within a particular setting

Style and Language

- ● Follow and understand assigned and unassigned dialogue among multiple characters with a clear idea about who is speaking
- ● Notice that words have special qualities, such as musical or pleasing sound, dramatic impact, or humor
- ● Internalize complex and literary language structures from hearing them read aloud
- ■ Notice and think critically about a writer's word choice
- ■ Notice a writer's use of poetic language and sound devices: e.g., rhythm, rhyme, repetition, refrain, onomatopoeia, alliteration, assonance
- ■ Recognize how a writer creates humor
- ■ Appreciate or critique fiction texts that utilize subtle or whimsical humor
- ■ Notice when a fiction writer uses poetic or descriptive language to show the setting, appeal to the five senses, or to convey human feelings such as loss, relief, or anger
- ■ Notice and understand long stretches of descriptive language important to understanding setting and characters
- ■ Notice language that conveys an emotional atmosphere (mood) in a text, affecting how the reader feels: e.g., tension, sadness, whimsicality, joy

- ■ Notice and remember literary language patterns that are characteristic of traditional literature: e.g., *once upon a time, long ago and far away, therefore, finally, at long last, happily ever after*
- ■ Notice and understand how the author uses idioms and literary language, including metaphor, simile, symbolism, and personification
- ■ Notice a writer's use of some words from languages other than English
- ■ Notice the narrator of a text and notice a change in narrator and perspective
- ■ Think critically about the authenticity and appeal of a narrator's voice
- ■ Notice a writer's intentional use of language that violates conventional grammar to provide authentic dialogue to achieve the writer's voice
- ■ Analyze texts to determine aspects of a writer's style: e.g., use of language, choice of setting, plot, characters, themes and ideas
- ■ Recognize some authors by the style of their illustrations, their topics, characters they use, or typical plots

Vocabulary

- ● Continue to build vocabulary as a foundation for recognizing words in print
- ● Notice and acquire understanding of new vocabulary from read-aloud content
- ● Acquire new content words from texts and graphics
- ● Use new vocabulary in discussion of a text
- ● Learn many words that do not appear frequently in oral conversation but are used in writing (Tier 2)
- ● Derive the meaning of words from the context of a sentence, paragraph, or the whole story
- ● Understand the meaning of words representing all parts of speech when listening to a story
- ● Understand common (simple) connectives that link and clarify meaning and are frequently used in oral language when listening to a story (*and, but, so, because, before, after*)
- ● Understand (when listening) some sophisticated connectives (words that link ideas and clarify meaning) that are used in written texts but do not appear often in everyday oral language: e.g., *although, however, meantime, meanwhile, moreover, otherwise, therefore, though, unless, until, whenever, yet*

- ● Thinking ***Within*** the Text
- ◆ Thinking ***Beyond*** the Text
- ■ Thinking ***About*** the Text

Selecting Goals Behaviors and Understandings to Notice, Teach, and Support *(cont.)*

Interactive Read-Aloud and Literature Discussion

FICTION TEXTS *(continued)*

- Understand (when listening) some academic connectives (words that link ideas and clarify meaning that appear in written texts): e.g., *alternatively, consequently, despite, conversely, eventually, finally, in contrast, initially, nevertheless, nonetheless, previously, specifically, ultimately, whereas, whereby*

- Understand the connotative meanings of words that are essential to understanding the text

- Understand the meaning of idioms

- Understand the meaning of figurative words that are essential to understanding the text

- Understand the meaning of some words that are used ironically in a way that changes surface meaning

- Understand words with multiple meanings within the same text, often signaling subtly different meanings

- Understand words from regional or historical dialects

- Use some academic language to talk about fiction genres: e.g., *fiction, folktale, fairy tale, fractured fairy tale, fable, tall tale, realistic fiction, historical fiction, fantasy*

- Use some academic language to talk about special types of fiction: e.g., *adventure story; animal story; family, friends, and school story; humorous story; mystery; sports story*

- Use some academic language to talk about forms: e.g., *picture book, wordless picture book, label book, ABC book, poem, poetry, nursery rhyme, rhyme, song, series book, chapter book, play, letter, poetry collection, sequel, limerick, haiku, concrete poetry, short story, diary entry, journal entry*

- Use some academic language to talk about literary features: e.g., *beginning, ending, character, main character, events, character change, message, dialogue, setting, flashback, conflict, resolution, theme, descriptive language, simile*

- Use some academic language to talk about book and print features: e.g., *front cover, back cover, title, author, illustrator, page, text, illustration, photograph, label, table of contents, acknowledgments, chapter, section, heading, drawing, caption, map, chapter title, dedication, author's note, illustrator's note, endpapers, book jacket*

Illustrations

- Notice and remember the important events of a story using the pictures (after hearing the text read several times)

- Follow and understand some texts that have no illustrations

- Understand that there can be different interpretations of the meaning of an illustration

- Use details from illustrations and text to support points made in discussion

- Notice how the tone of a book is created by the illustrator's choice of colors

- Notice how illustrators create perspective in their pictures (using images close up, far away, creating distance in between, etc.)

- Notice how illustrations and graphics go together with the text in a meaningful way

- Notice how illustrations and graphics help to communicate the writer's message

- Notice and infer how illustrations contribute to mood in a fiction text

Book and Print Features

- Notice and use and understand the purpose of some organizational tools: e.g., title, table of contents, chapter title

- Notice and use and understand the purpose of some other text resources: e.g., glossary

- Notice and use and understand the purpose of some text resources outside the body (peritext): e.g., dedication, acknowledgments, author's note, illustrator's note, endpapers

- Notice and understand other features of the peritext that have symbolic or cultural significance or add to aesthetic enjoyment

- Infer the cultural or symbolic significance of the peritext (for example, design features)

- Appreciate artistry in text design: e.g., book jacket, cover, end pages, title page

● Thinking *Within* the Text   ◆ Thinking *Beyond* the Text   ■ Thinking *About* the Text

INTERACTIVE READ-ALOUD
AND LITERATURE DISCUSSION

Selecting Goals Behaviors and Understandings to Notice, Teach, and Support *(cont.)*

Interactive Read-Aloud and Literature Discussion

NONFICTION TEXTS

General

- Ask questions to deepen understanding of a text
- Notice and ask questions when meaning is lost or understanding is interrupted
- Refer to important information and details and use as evidence in discussion to support opinions and statements
- Understand content that reflects beginning understandings of physical world and social world: e.g., health, social studies, science, mathematics, arts
- Notice and respond to stress and tone of voice while listening and afterward
- Notice and remember the important events of a text in temporal or chronological sequence and tell them in order
- Notice and remember the important information in a text
- Tell a summary of a text after hearing it read
- Sustain attention for some longer texts that may require several days to complete
- Synthesize new information and ideas and revise thinking in response to hearing a text read
- Understand the problems that occur in everyday life, including some complex problems that may relate to readers' lives
- Give reasons (either text-based or from personal experience) to support thinking
- Use background knowledge of content to understand nonfiction topics
- Use background knowledge of history to understand simple biography, autobiography, and memoir
- Recognize and understand that informational texts may reflect a wide range of diverse settings, languages, and cultures
- Use evidence from the text to support statements about the text
- Use evidence from the text to support predictions
- Relate the messages in a nonfiction text to one's own life
- Relate important information and concepts in one text and connect to information and concepts in other texts
- Understand texts that require the application of knowledge of academic disciplines (sciences, history, humanities)
- Identify and discuss interesting, surprising, and important information in a text

- Form and express opinions about a text and support with rationale and evidence
- Form and state the basis for opinions about authors and illustrators
- Connect texts by a range of categories: e.g., content, message, genre, author/illustrator, special form, text structure, or organization

Genre

- Infer the importance of a subject's accomplishments (biography)
- Distinguish between fact and opinion in a text in order to reach new understanding
- Notice and understand the characteristics of some specific nonfiction genres: e.g., expository, narrative, procedural and persuasive texts, biography, autobiography, memoir, hybrid text
- Understand that a biography is the story of a person's life written by someone else
- Understand that biographies are often set in the past
- Understand that an autobiography is an account of a person's life written by that person
- Understand that a memoir is an account of a memory or set of memories written by the person who experienced it
- Notice when a writer is describing a step-by-step procedure
- Notice a writer's use of argument and persuasion
- Notice counterarguments and evidence against those counterarguments in a text
- Recognize hybrid texts and distinguish which sections are nonfiction and fiction
- Recognize and understand some specific forms of nonfiction: e.g., series books; picture books; letters, diaries, and journals entries; photo essays and news articles
- Recognize and understand some specific types of poetry when they appear in nonfiction: e.g., lyrical poetry, free verse, haiku, narrative poetry, ballad, epic/saga, concrete poetry
- Notice and understand some elements of poetry when they appear in nonfiction: e.g., figurative language, rhyme, repetition, onomatopoeia, layout/line breaks (shape), imagery, alliteration, assonance

---

● Thinking *Within* the Text   ◆ Thinking *Beyond* the Text   ■ Thinking *About* the Text

Selecting Goals Behaviors and Understandings to Notice, Teach, and Support *(cont.)*

Interactive Read-Aloud and Literature Discussion

NONFICTION TEXTS *(continued)*

Organization

- Follow and understand nonfiction texts with clearly defined overall structure and simple categories
- Be aware when the teacher is reading bulleted or numbered lists
- Notice and understand information in texts that are organized in categories (expository)
- Understand the use of headings and subheadings
- Use headings and subheadings to search for and use information
- Notice primary and secondary sources of information when embedded in a text
- Understand that a nonfiction text can be expository or narrative in structure
- Notice the organization of a nonfiction text, distinguishing between expository and narrative structure
- Notice a nonfiction writer's use of narrative text structure in biography and narrative nonfiction
- Recognize and understand a writer's use of underlying text structures: e.g., categorical, description, sequence (chronological, temporal), compare and contrast, cause and effect, problem and solution, question and answer, combination
- Notice a nonfiction writer's use of categories and subcategories to organize an informational text
- Understand when a writer is telling information in a sequence (chronological order)
- Understand that a writer can tell about something that usually happens in the same order (temporal sequence) and something that happens in time order (chronological sequence)
- Notice a nonfiction writer's use of organizational tools: e.g., title, table of contents, heading, subheading, sidebar

Topic

- Show curiosity about topics encountered in nonfiction texts and actively work to learn more about them
- Think across nonfiction texts to construct knowledge of a topic
- Think across texts to compare and expand understanding of content and ideas from academic disciplines: e.g., social responsibility, environment, climate, history, social and geological history, cultural groups

- Infer the importance of a topic of a nonfiction text
- Infer the writer's attitude toward a topic
- Recognize that a wide variety of informational texts may be about a wide range of diverse places, languages, and cultures
- Recognize that informational texts may present a larger topic with many subtopics
- Infer a writer's purpose in a nonfiction text
- Extend understanding to nonfiction topics and content that are beyond most students' immediate experience: e.g., systems of the human body (circulatory, respiratory, endocrine); domestic and wild animals; environments such as ocean, desert, rainforest, mountains, village, city, farm; rocks and minerals; energy; magnetism; customs and beliefs in different cultures; government; economics
- Understand that a writer is presenting related facts about a single topic
- Hypothesize the writer's reasons for choosing a topic and infer how the writer feels about a topic

Messages and Main Ideas

- Follow arguments in a persuasive text
- Understand that there can be different interpretations of the meanings of a text
- Make connections among the content and ideas in nonfiction texts: e.g., animals, pets, families, sports, the five senses, nutrition and food, school, neighborhood, weather and seasons, machines, plants
- Understand the relationships among ideas and content in an expository nonfiction text (larger topic with subtopics)
- Connect the information in nonfiction books to disciplinary studies
- Infer the significance of nonfiction content to their own lives
- Infer the larger ideas and messages in a nonfiction text
- Understand themes and ideas that are mature issues and require experience to interpret
- Understand that a nonfiction writer has one or more messages or big (main) ideas
- Distinguish fact from opinion

● Thinking **Within** the Text   ◆ Thinking **Beyond** the Text   ■ Thinking **About** the Text

INTERACTIVE READ-ALOUD AND LITERATURE DISCUSSION

Selecting Goals Behaviors and Understandings to Notice, Teach, and Support *(cont.)*

Interactive Read-Aloud and Literature Discussion

NONFICTION TEXTS *(continued)*

Style and Language

- Understand sentence structure that varies according to purpose (e.g., headings, captions, labels, numbered and bulleted lists) in nonfiction
- Internalize complex and literary language structures from hearing texts read aloud
- Notice and think critically about a writer's word choice
- Notice language that conveys an emotional atmosphere (mood) in a text, affecting how the reader feels: e.g., tension, sadness, whimsicality, joy
- Notice how the writer reveals the setting in a biographical or historical text
- Notice and understand multiple points of view on the same topic
- Recognize a writer's use of the techniques for persuasion in a persuasive text
- Recognize some authors by the topics they choose or the style of their illustrations

Accuracy

- Critically examine the quality or accuracy of the text, citing evidence for opinions
- Notice and evaluate the accuracy of the information presented in the text and across texts

Vocabulary

- Notice and acquire understanding of new vocabulary from read-aloud content
- Understand the meaning of words representing all parts of speech when listening to a nonfiction text read aloud
- Understand the meaning of common (simple) connectives and some sophisticated connectives when listening to a nonfiction text
- Acquire new content words from texts and graphics

- Use new vocabulary in discussion of a text
- Learn many words that do not appear frequently in oral conversation but are used in writing (Tier 2)
- Derive the meaning of words from the context of a sentence, paragraph, or the whole text
- Notice and understand the meaning of some domain-specific words (Tier 3)
- Understand the connotative meanings of words that are essential to understanding the text
- Understand the meaning of figurative words that are essential to understanding the text
- Use some academic language to talk about nonfiction genres: e.g., *nonfiction, personal memory story, informational text, informational book, factual text, biography, autobiography, narrative nonfiction, memoir, procedural text, persuasive text, hybrid text*
- Use some academic language to talk about forms: e.g., *picture book, wordless picture book, label book, ABC book, counting book, poem, poetry, nursery rhyme, rhyme, song, series book, play, letter, poetry collection, sequel, limerick, haiku, concrete poetry, diary entry, journal entry, news article, feature article*
- Use some academic language to talk about literary features: e.g., *beginning, ending, problem, question and answer, solution, topic, description, time order, problem and solution, message, dialogue, main idea, comparison and contrast, setting, cause and effect, categorization, descriptive language, figurative language, metaphor, simile, persuasive language*
- Use some academic language to talk about book and print features: e.g., *front cover, back cover, title, author, illustrator, page, text, illustration, photograph, label, table of contents, acknowledgments, chapter, section, heading, drawing, caption, map, chapter title, dedication, author's note, illustrator's note, section, diagram, glossary, endpapers, sidebar, book jacket, subheading, chart, graph, timeline, index*

● Thinking **Within** the Text ◆ Thinking **Beyond** the Text ■ Thinking **About** the Text

Selecting Goals Behaviors and Understandings to Notice, Teach, and Support *(cont.)*

Interactive Read-Aloud and Literature Discussion

NONFICTION TEXTS *(continued)*

Illustrations/Graphics

- Understand that graphics provide important information
- Follow and understand some texts that have no graphics or illustrations
- ◆ Recognize and use information in a variety of graphics: e.g., photo and/or drawing with label or caption, diagram, cutaway, map with legend and scale, infographic
- ◆ Use details from illustrations to support points made in discussion
- ■ Notice how illustrations and graphics help to communicate the writer's message
- ■ Understand that graphics and text are carefully placed in a nonfiction text so that ideas are communicated clearly

Book and Print Features

- Notice a text's title and the name of its author and illustrator on the cover and title page
- ◆ Gain new understandings from searching for and using information found in text body, sidebars, and graphics
- ■ Notice and use and understand the purpose of some organizational tools: e.g., title, table of contents, chapter title, heading, subheading
- ■ Notice and use and understand the purpose of some other text resources: e.g., glossary, index
- ■ Notice and use and understand the purpose of some text resources outside the body (peritext): e.g., dedication, acknowledgments, author's note, illustrator's note, endpapers
- ■ Notice and understand other features of the peritext that have symbolic value, add to aesthetic enjoyment, or add meaning
- ■ Appreciate artistry in text design: e.g,. book jacket, cover, end pages, title page (peritext)
- ■ Evaluate the effectiveness of page layout and design of a text

● Thinking *Within* the Text   ◆ Thinking *Beyond* the Text   ■ Thinking *About* the Text

Selecting Texts Characteristics of Texts for Reading Aloud and Discussion

Interactive Read-Aloud and Literature Discussion

GENRE

▶ Fiction

- Realistic fiction
- Historical fiction
- Traditional literature: e.g., folktale, tall tale, fairy tale (including fractured fairy tale), fable, myth, legend, ballad
- Complex fantasy (all types)
- Hybrid text
- Special types of fiction: e.g., mystery; adventure story; animal story; family, friends, and school story; humorous story; sports story

▶ Nonfiction

- Expository nonfiction
- Narrative nonfiction
- Biography
- Autobiography
- Memoir
- Procedural text
- Persuasive text
- Hybrid text

FORMS

- Series books
- Picture books
- Chapter books, some with sequels
- Poems
- Poetry collections
- Plays
- Types of poetry: lyrical poetry, free verse, limerick, haiku, narrative poetry, ballad, epic/saga, concrete poetry
- Letters, diary, and journal entries
- Short stories
- Photo essays, news articles, and feature articles
- Speeches

TEXT STRUCTURE

- Narratives with multiple episodes that are elaborated with many details
- Some longer texts with main plot and subplots, each with a conflict
- Texts with variations in structure: e.g., story-within-a-story, flashback, flash-forward, time-lapse
- Some books with chapters connected to a single plot
- Collections of short stories related to an overarching theme and with plots that intertwine
- A few texts with circular plots or with parallel plots
- Informational texts related to a larger topic with subtopics
- Underlying structural patterns: description, cause and effect, chronological sequence, temporal sequence, categorization, compare and contrast, problem and solution, question and answer
- Informational texts with clearly defined structure and categories and subcategories, some defined by headings, sections, and some subsections
- Biographical and historical texts with narrative structure
- Informational texts with examples of simple argument and persuasion

CONTENT

- Content that is appropriate for students' cognitive development, social and emotional maturity, and life experience
- Content that engages students' intellectual curiosity and emotions
- Content that promotes inquiry and investigation
- Content that requires analytical and critical thinking: e.g., to judge the authenticity of informational texts or historical fiction
- Texts with heavy content load that requires prior knowledge and invites extended discussion
- Familiar topics that are authentic and relevant: e.g., animals, family relationships, friendship, sports, music, neighborhoods, nutrition, weather and seasons, maps
- More sophisticated, subtle humor: e.g., characters with humorous traits, surprising outcomes, humorous comparisons
- Content that reinforces and expands a student's experience and knowledge of self and the world
- Topics that may be beyond most students' immediate experiences: e.g., systems of the human body; water; matter; energy; plant structures; the solar system; citizenship; periods of history; civilizations
- Content that reflects a wide range of settings, languages, and cultures
- Content related to historical periods, circumstances, and places
- Content linked to specific areas of study as described by the school curriculum or standards
- Characters, settings, and events that could exist in contemporary life or in another historical period
- More complex characters, settings, and events that occur in fantasy
- Content that reflects increasing understanding of the physical and social world: e.g., health, social studies, science, mathematics, arts

THEMES AND IDEAS

- Texts with deeper meanings applicable to important human challenges and social issues: e.g., life cycles, survival, interconnectedness of humans and the environment, social responsibility, poverty, justice, racism, war
- Themes and ideas that require a perspective not familiar to the reader or understanding of cultural diversity
- Themes and ideas that involve the problems of preadolescents and adolescents: self and self-esteem, gender differences, peer relationships and popularity, bullying, family relationships
- Many books with multiple ideas, most requiring inference and synthesis to understand
- Ideas close to students' experience: e.g., becoming independent; valuing change in self and others; empathizing with others; valuing differences; connecting past, present, and future; overcoming challenges; following your dreams; learning from the lives of others; exploring artistic expression and appreciation
- Themes that evoke different, sometimes conflicting interpretations

Selecting Texts Characteristics of Texts for Reading Aloud and Discussion *(cont.)*

Interactive Read-Aloud and Literature Discussion

LANGUAGE AND LITERARY FEATURES

- Elements of traditional literature and modern fantasy: e.g., the supernatural; imaginary and otherworldly creatures; gods and goddesses; talking animals, toys, and dolls; heroic characters; technology or scientific advances; time travel; aliens or outer space
- Basic motifs of traditional literature and modern fantasy: e.g., struggle between good and evil, magic, secondary or alternative worlds, the hero's quest, special character types, fantastic or magical objects, wishes, trickery, transformations
- Predictable story outcomes typical of traditional literature: e.g., clever overcomes power, good defeats evil
- Settings important to the plot, many distant in time and place from students' own experiences
- Main characters and supporting characters
- Many memorable characters with multiple dimensions revealed by what they say, think, and do and what others say and think about them
- "Round" characters that have a complex range of good and bad attributes and that change during the course of the plot, and "flat" characters that do not change but may play an important role in the plot
- Characters that are complex and change over time in longer texts
- Predictable and static characters with simple traits typical of traditional literature
- Plots with multiple episodes and problems and clear, satisfying resolutions, some left to inference
- Some longer texts with one or more subplots
- Some texts with ambiguous endings
- Most texts written in first- or third-person narrative with some procedural texts in second-person
- Some texts told from multiple points of view

- Language and events that convey an emotional atmosphere (mood) in a text, affecting how the reader feels: e.g., tension, sadness, whimsicality, joy, dread
- Language that expresses the author's attitude or feelings toward a subject reflected in the style of writing (tone): e.g., lighthearted, ironic, earnest, affectionate, formal
- Some texts with symbolism
- Descriptive language and imagery conveying sensory experiences and a range of human feelings: e.g., joy, sadness, anger, eagerness
- Poetic language and other literary language
- Descriptive and figurative language that is important to understanding the content: e.g., imagery, metaphor, simile, personification, hyperbole
- Some long stretches of descriptive language important to understanding setting, plot, characters, themes
- Both assigned and unassigned dialogue, including some strings of unassigned dialogue for which speakers must be inferred
- Procedural language: e.g., step-by-step, directions, how-to
- Persuasive language

SENTENCE COMPLEXITY

- Some long and complex sentences that require attention to follow
- Long sentences joined by semicolons or colons
- Variation in placement of subject, verb, and multiple adjectives, adverbs, and prepositional phrases
- Many sentences with embedded clauses and phrases
- Complex sentences with variety in order of phrases and clauses
- Sentences with common (simple) connectives
- Sentences with sophisticated connectives
- Extended dialogue that increases sentence complexity

- Some texts with long sentences divided into bulleted or numbered lists
- Sentence structure adapted to fit purpose and form of book and print features: e.g., heading, subheading, label, caption, labels, legend

VOCABULARY

- New content words related to concepts that students are learning
- Many words that appear in the vocabulary of mature language users (Tier 2)
- Many words that are particular to a discipline (Tier 3)
- Common (simple) connectives that are frequently used in oral language (words, phrases that clarify relationships ideas): e.g., *and, but, so, because, before, after*
- Sophisticated connectives (words that link ideas and clarify meaning) that are used in written texts but do not appear often in everyday oral language: e.g., *although, however, meantime, meanwhile, moreover, otherwise, therefore, though, unless, until, whenever, yet*
- Some academic connectives (words that link ideas and clarify meaning that appear in written texts): e.g., *alternatively, consequently, despite, conversely, eventually, finally, in contrast, initially, nevertheless, nonetheless, previously, specifically, ultimately, whereas, whereby*
- Many words with multiple meanings, some with subtle shadings of meaning
- Many words with figurative meaning
- Some idioms
- Many words with connotative meanings that are essential to understanding the text
- A few words used ironically
- Some words from regional or historical dialects
- Some words from languages other than English
- Some words (including slang) used informally by particular groups of people
- Wide variety of technical vocabulary

Selecting Texts Characteristics of Texts for Reading Aloud and Discussion *(cont.)*

Interactive Read-Aloud and Literature Discussion

ILLUSTRATIONS

- Illustrations in a variety of media that offer examples of notable artistic technique
- Illustrations that enhance and extend meaning in the text
- Complex illustrations with many details, some needing description by the teacher during reading
- Books with illustrations that represent a coherent artistic vision
- Chapter books with few illustrations
- Some texts with no illustrations other than decorative elements such as vignettes
- Some complex, nuanced illustrations that convey mood to match or extend the text
- Books with illustrations that reflect the theme and the writer's tone
- Some illustrations with figurative and symbolic characteristics requiring interpretation
- Simple illustrations in a variety of forms: e.g., drawing with label or caption, photograph with label or caption, map with legend and scale, diagram (cutaway), infographic, chart, graph, timeline

BOOK AND PRINT FEATURES

LENGTH

- Many short picture books that can be read in one sitting
- Long illustrated texts with sections that may be selected and read
- Long illustrated texts that require several days to complete

PRINT AND LAYOUT

- Some books with decorative or informative illustrations and/or print outside the body of the text (peritext)
- Texts with engaging designs that add aesthetic value and have symbolic and cultural meaning

ORGANIZATIONAL TOOLS

- Title, author, and illustrator listed on cover and on title page
- Table of contents, chapter title, heading, subheading, sidebar

TEXT RESOURCES

- Some books with dedication, acknowledgments, author's note, glossary, special endpapers (peritext), index
- Additional information provided by foreword, prologue, pronunciation guide, footnote, epilogue, appendix, endnote, references

Selecting Goals Behaviors and Understandings to Notice, Teach, and Support

Interactive Read-Aloud and Literature Discussion

FICTION TEXTS

General

- Ask questions to deepen understanding of a text
- Notice and ask questions when meaning is lost or understanding is interrupted
- Refer to important information and details and use as evidence to support opinions and statements during discussion
- Refer to the location of some important details in the text (setting, time order, problem, resolution)
- Notice and respond to stress and tone of voice while listening to read-aloud and afterward
- Tell a summary of a text after hearing it read
- Sustain attention for some longer texts that may require several days to finish
- Recall important details about setting, problem and resolution, and characters after a story is read
- Learn new concepts and ideas from listening to fiction texts
- Synthesize new information and ideas and revise thinking in response to it
- Form implicit and explicit questions about the content and concepts in a fiction text
- Understand complex problems that can be related to readers' lives
- Learn more about social issues, both local and global, as revealed through character, plot, and setting
- Give reasons (either text-based or from personal experience) to support thinking
- Use background knowledge to understand settings, problems, and characters
- Apply background knowledge to extend understanding of historical fiction and science fiction
- Infer a writer's purpose in writing a fiction text
- Make connections (e.g., content, theme) across fiction texts that are read aloud
- Use evidence from the text to support statements about it
- Make connections (similarities and differences) among texts that have the same author/illustrator, setting, characters, or theme
- Use evidence from the text to support a wide range of predictions
- Relate important ideas in the text to each other and to ideas in other texts
- Understand that a writer has a purpose in writing a fiction text
- Connect texts by a range of categories: e.g., content, theme, message, genre, author/illustrator, character, setting, special forms, text structure, or organization
- Form and express opinions about a text and support with rationale and evidence

- Form and state the basis for opinions about authors and illustrators
- Think critically about the authenticity of a text: e.g., characterization, plot, setting, social values

Genre

- Understand that there are different types of texts and that they have different characteristics
- Apply background knowledge to extend understanding of historical fiction
- Use scientific or technical knowledge to understand science fiction
- Notice and understand the characteristics of some specific fiction genres: e.g., realistic fiction, historical fiction, folktale, fairy tale, fractured fairy tale, fable, myth, legend, epic, ballad, fantasy including science fiction, hybrid text
- Understand when a story could happen in real life (realistic fiction) and when it could not happen in real life (traditional literature, fantasy)
- Notice story outcomes that are typical of traditional literature
- Identify elements of traditional literature and fantasy: e.g., the supernatural; imaginary and otherworldly creatures; gods and goddesses; talking animals, toys, and dolls; heroic characters; technology or scientific advances; time travel; aliens or outer space
- Identify some elements of science fiction: e.g., technology or scientific advances, futuristic setting, time travel, aliens and outer space
- Recognize hybrid texts and distinguish which sections are fiction and nonfiction
- Notice and understand some special types of fiction: e.g., mystery; adventure story; animal story; family, friends, and school story; humorous story; sports story
- Recognize and understand some specific types of poetry: e.g., lyrical poetry, free verse, limerick, haiku, narrative poetry, ballad, epic/saga, concrete poetry
- Notice and understand some elements of poetry: e.g., figurative language, rhyme, repetition, onomatopoeia, layout/line breaks (shape), imagery, alliteration, assonance

Messages and Themes

- Notice that a book may have more than one message or big (main) idea
- Understand that the messages or big ideas in fiction texts can be applied to their own lives or to other people and society
- Infer the messages in a work of fiction
- Infer and understand the moral lesson or cultural teaching in traditional literature

---

- Thinking **Within** the Text   ◆ Thinking **Beyond** the Text   ■ Thinking **About** the Text

Selecting Texts Characteristics of Texts for Reading Aloud and Discussion

Interactive Read-Aloud and Literature Discussion

GENRE

▶ Fiction

- Realistic fiction
- Historical fiction
- Traditional literature: e.g., folktale, tall tale, fairy tale (including fractured fairy tale), fable, myth, legend, ballad
- Complex fantasy (all types)
- Hybrid text
- Special types of fiction: e.g., mystery; adventure story; animal story; family, friends, and school story; humorous story; sports story

▶ Nonfiction

- Expository nonfiction
- Narrative nonfiction
- Biography
- Autobiography
- Memoir
- Procedural text
- Persuasive text
- Hybrid text

FORMS

- Series books
- Picture books
- Chapter books, some with sequels
- Sections of longer chapter books
- Poems
- Poetry collections
- Plays
- Types of poetry: lyrical poetry, free verse, limerick, haiku, narrative poetry, ballad, epic/saga, concrete poetry
- Letters, diary and journal entries
- Short stories
- Photo essays, news articles, and feature articles
- Speeches

TEXT STRUCTURE

- Longer narratives with main plot and subplots, each with a conflict
- Texts with variations in structure: e.g., story-within-a-story, flashback, flash-forward, time-lapse
- Some books with chapters connected to a single plot

- Collections of short stories related to an overarching theme and with plots that intertwine
- Texts with circular plots or with parallel plots
- Informational texts related to a larger topic with many subtopics
- Underlying structural patterns: description, cause and effect, chronological sequence, temporal sequence, categorization, compare and contrast, problem and solution, question and answer
- Informational texts with clearly defined structure and categories and subcategories, some defined by headings, sections, and subsections
- Biographical and historical texts with narrative structure
- Informational texts with examples of simple argument and persuasion

CONTENT

- Content that is appropriate for students' cognitive development, social and emotional maturity, and life experience
- Relevant content that engages students' intellectual curiosity and emotions
- Content that promotes inquiry and investigation
- Content that requires analytical and critical thinking: e.g., to judge the authenticity and relevance of informational texts or historical fiction
- Many texts with heavy content load that requires prior knowledge and invites extended discussion
- Sophisticated, subtle humor including irony: e.g., characters with unusual or humorous traits, surprising outcomes, humorous comparisons
- Content that reinforces and expands a student's experience and knowledge of self and the world
- Many topics that may be beyond most students' immediate experiences: e.g., elements and compounds; forces and motion; matter; energy use; climate and weather; countries and cultures of Africa, Asia, Australia, the Pacific, Europe, North and South America
- Content that reflects a wide range of settings, languages, and cultures and that requires some knowledge of diverse cultures

- Content that requires content knowledge related to historical periods, circumstances, and places
- Content that requires the student to appreciate or identify with diverse perspectives relating to culture, race, gender, etc.
- Content linked to specific areas of study as described by the school curriculum or standards
- More complex characters, settings, events, and conflicts that could exist in contemporary life or in another historical period
- More complex characters, settings, events, and conflicts that occur in fantasy
- Content that reflects increasing understanding of the physical and social world: e.g., health, social studies, science, mathematics, arts
- Some texts with dense presentation of facts and ideas

THEMES AND IDEAS

- Texts with deeper meanings applicable to important human challenges and social issues: e.g., life cycles, survival, interconnectedness of humans and the environment, social responsibility, poverty, justice, racism, war
- Themes and ideas that build social awareness and reveal insights into the human condition
- Themes and ideas that require a perspective not familiar to the reader or understanding of cultural diversity
- Themes and ideas that involve the problems of preadolescents and adolescents: e.g., self-esteem; gender differences; physical, emotional, and social self-awareness; individuality; peer relationships and popularity; bullying; family relationships
- Many books with multiple ideas, most requiring inference and synthesis to understand
- Ideas close to students' experience: e.g., empathizing with others; valuing differences; connecting past, present, and future; overcoming challenges; following your dreams; learning from the lives of others; exploring artistic expression and appreciation

Selecting Texts Characteristics of Texts for Reading Aloud and Discussion *(cont.)*

Interactive Read-Aloud and Literature Discussion

- Themes that evoke different, sometimes conflicting interpretations
- Texts that present multiple themes that may be understood in layers
- Themes related to conflict involving a person struggling against the forces of nature, against another person, against society, or against himself or herself
- Themes involving a symbolic representation of good vs. evil

LANGUAGE AND LITERARY FEATURES

- Elements of traditional literature and modern fantasy: e.g., the supernatural; imaginary and otherworldly creatures; gods and goddesses; talking animals, toys, and dolls; heroic characters; technology or scientific advances; time travel; aliens or outer space
- Basic motifs of traditional literature and modern fantasy: e.g., struggle between good and evil, magic, secondary or alternative worlds, the hero's quest, special character types, fantastic or magical objects, wishes, trickery, transformations
- Predictable story outcomes typical of traditional literature: e.g., clever overcomes power, good defeats evil
- Settings important to the plot, many distant in time and place from students' own experiences
- Characters with multiple dimensions revealed by what they say, think, and do and what others say and think about them
- Main character(s) centrally involved in the conflict and resolution, and supporting characters, some of which may be important to the plot
- "Round" characters that have a complex range of good and bad attributes and that change during the course of the plot, and "flat" characters that do not change but may play an important role in the plot
- Predictable and static characters with simple traits typical of traditional literature
- Plot with multiple episodes and conflicts and clear, satisfying resolutions, some left to inference
- Some longer texts with one or more subplots, each with a conflict

- Some texts with ambiguous endings
- Some texts with conflict involving a person struggling against the forces of nature, against another person, against society, or against himself or herself
- Most texts written in first- or third-person narrative with some procedural texts in second-person
- Texts told from multiple points of view
- Language and events that convey an emotional atmosphere (mood) in a text, affecting how the reader feels: e.g., tension, sadness, whimsicality, joy, dread
- Language that expresses the author's attitude or feelings toward a subject reflected in the style of writing (tone): e.g., lighthearted, ironic, earnest, affectionate, formal
- Many texts with symbolism
- Descriptive language and imagery conveying sensory experiences and a range of human feelings: e.g., joy, sadness, anger, eagerness
- Poetic language and other literary language
- Language that violates conventional rules of grammar and usage in order to provide colloquial speech or to achieve the writer's distinctive voice
- Descriptive and figurative language that is important to understanding the content: e.g., imagery, metaphor, simile, personification, hyperbole
- Some long stretches of descriptive language important to understanding setting, plot, characters, themes
- Both assigned and unassigned dialogue, including some strings of unassigned dialogue for which speakers must be inferred, and occasional use of monologue
- Procedural language: e.g., step-by-step, directions, how-to
- Persuasive language

SENTENCE COMPLEXITY

- Many long and complex sentences that require attention to follow
- Long sentences joined by semicolons or colons

- Variation in placement of subject, verb, and multiple adjectives, adverbs, and prepositional phrases
- Many sentences with multiple embedded clauses and phrases
- Complex sentences with variety in order of phrases and clauses
- Sentences with common (simple) connectives
- Sentences with sophisticated connectives
- Sentences with academic connectives
- Extended dialogue that increases sentence complexity
- Some texts with long sentences divided into bulleted or numbered lists
- Sentence structure adapted to fit purpose and form of book and print features: e.g., heading, subheading, label, caption, labels, legend

VOCABULARY

- New content words related to concepts that students are learning
- Many words that appear in the vocabulary of mature language users (Tier 2)
- Many words that are particular to a discipline (Tier 3)
- Common (simple) connectives that are frequently used in oral language (words, phrases that clarify relationships ideas): e.g., *and, but, so, because, before, after*
- Sophisticated connectives (words that link ideas and clarify meaning) that are used in written texts but do not appear often in everyday oral language: e.g., *although, however, meantime, meanwhile, moreover, otherwise, therefore, though, unless, until, whenever, yet*
- Academic connectives (words that link ideas and clarify meaning that appear in written texts): e.g., *alternatively, consequently, despite, conversely, eventually, finally, in contrast, initially, nevertheless, nonetheless, previously, specifically, ultimately, whereas, whereby*
- Many words with multiple meanings, some with subtle shadings of meaning
- Many words with figurative meaning
- Idioms as appropriate to genre

Selecting Texts Characteristics of Texts for Reading Aloud and Discussion *(cont.)*

Interactive Read-Aloud and Literature Discussion

VOCABULARY *(continued)*

- Many words with connotative meanings that are essential to understanding the text
- A few words used ironically
- Some words from regional or historical dialects
- Some words from languages other than English
- Some words (including slang) used informally by particular groups of people
- Some archaic words
- Wide variety of technical vocabulary

ILLUSTRATIONS

- Illustrations in a variety of media that offer examples of notable artistic technique
- Illustrations that enhance and extend meaning in the text
- Complex illustrations with many details, some needing description by the teacher during reading
- Books with illustrations that represent a coherent artistic vision
- Chapter books with few or no illustrations
- Some texts with decorative elements such as vignettes
- Some complex, nuanced illustrations that convey mood to match or extend the text
- Books with illustrations that reflect the theme and the writer's tone
- Some illustrations with figurative and symbolic characteristics requiring interpretation
- Simple illustrations in a variety of forms: drawing with label or caption, photograph with label or caption, map with legend and scale, diagram (cutaway), infographic, chart, graph, timeline

BOOK AND PRINT FEATURES

LENGTH

- Many short picture books that can be read in one sitting
- Long illustrated texts with sections that may be selected and read
- Long illustrated texts that require several days to complete

PRINT AND LAYOUT

- Some books with decorative or informative illustrations and/or print outside the body of the text (peritext)
- Texts with engaging designs that add aesthetic value and have symbolic and cultural meaning

ORGANIZATIONAL TOOLS

- Title, author, and illustrator listed on cover and on title page
- Table of contents, chapter title, heading, subheading, sidebar

TEXT RESOURCES

- Some books with dedication, acknowledgments, author's note, glossary, special endpapers (peritext), index
- Additional information provided by foreword, prologue, pronunciation guide, footnote, epilogue, appendix, endnote, references, bibliography

Selecting Goals Behaviors and Understandings to Notice, Teach, and Support

Interactive Read-Aloud and Literature Discussion

FICTION TEXTS

General

- Ask questions to deepen understanding of a text
- Notice and ask questions when meaning is lost or understanding is interrupted
- Refer to important information and details and use as evidence to support opinions and statements during discussion
- Notice and respond to dimensions of fluency (intonation, stress, pausing, phrasing) while listening and after a story is read
- Provide a concise, logically organized summary of a text after hearing it read
- Sustain attention for some longer texts that may require several days to finish
- Refer to the location of some important details in the text (setting, time order, problem, resolution)
- Recall important details about setting, problem and resolution, and characters after a story is read
- Learn new concepts and ideas from listening to fiction texts
- Synthesize new information and ideas and revise thinking in response to it
- Form implicit and explicit questions about the content and concepts in a fiction text
- Understand complex problems that can be related to readers' lives
- Learn more about social issues, both local and global, as revealed through character, plot, and setting
- Make connections to their own lives and contemporary issues and problems across all genres
- Give reasons/evidence (either text-based or from personal experience) to support thinking
- Apply background knowledge to extend understanding of historical fiction and science fiction
- Infer a writer's purpose in writing a fiction text
- Make connections (e.g., content, theme) across fiction texts that are read aloud, and where appropriate, connect to nonfiction texts
- Use evidence from the text to support statements about it
- Make connections (similarities and differences) among texts that have the same author/illustrator, setting, characters, or theme
- Use evidence from the text to support a wide range of predictions

- Relate important ideas in the text to each other and to ideas in other texts
- Change opinions based on new information or insights gained from fiction texts
- Understand that a writer has a purpose in writing a fiction text
- Connect texts by a range of categories: e.g., content, theme, message, genre, author/illustrator, character, setting, special forms, text structure, or organization
- Form and express opinions about a text and support with rationale and evidence
- Form and state the basis for opinions about authors and illustrators
- Think critically about the authenticity of a text: e.g., characterization, plot, setting, social values
- Critique a fiction text in terms of authenticity of characters, accurate portrayal of current or past issues, voice, tone, accuracy of setting

Genre

- Understand that there are different types of fiction and nonfiction texts and that they have different characteristics
- Apply background knowledge to extend understanding of historical fiction and science fiction
- Notice and understand the characteristics of some specific fiction genres: e.g., realistic fiction, historical fiction, folktale, fairy tale, fractured fairy tale, fable, myth, legend, epic, ballad, fantasy including science fiction, hybrid text
- Understand when a story could happen in real life (realistic fiction) and when it could not happen in real life (traditional literature, fantasy)
- Identify elements of traditional literature and fantasy: e.g., the supernatural; imaginary and otherworldly creatures; gods and goddesses; talking animals, toys, and dolls; heroic characters; technology or scientific advances; time travel; aliens or outer space
- Notice story outcomes that are typical of traditional literature
- Notice and understand basic motifs of traditional literature and fantasy: e.g., struggle between good and evil, magic, secondary or alternative worlds, the hero's quest, special character types, fantastic or magical objects, wishes, trickery, transformations
- Identify some elements of science fiction: e.g., technology or scientific advances, futuristic setting, time travel, aliens and outer space

---

● Thinking **Within** the Text   ◆ Thinking **Beyond** the Text   ■ Thinking **About** the Text

Selecting Goals Behaviors and Understandings to Notice, Teach, and Support *(cont.)*

Interactive Read-Aloud and Literature Discussion

FICTION TEXTS *(continued)*

Genre *(continued)*

- Recognize hybrid texts, distinguish which sections are fiction and nonfiction, and notice how the writer blends the two genres
- Notice and appreciate forms and genres embedded in another form or genre
- Notice and understand some special types of fiction: e.g., mystery; adventure story; animal story; family, friends, and school story; humorous story; sports story
- Recognize and understand some specific types of poetry: e.g., lyrical poetry, free verse, limerick, haiku, narrative poetry, ballad, epic/saga, concrete poetry
- Notice and understand some elements of poetry: e.g., figurative language, rhyme, repetition, onomatopoeia, layout/line breaks (shape), imagery, alliteration, assonance

Messages and Themes

- Notice that a book may have more than one message or big (main) idea
- Understand that the messages or big ideas in fiction texts can be applied to their own lives or to other people and society
- Infer the messages in a work of fiction
- Infer and understand the moral lesson or cultural teaching in traditional literature
- Notice and infer the importance of ideas relevant to their world: e.g., becoming independent; valuing change in self and others; empathizing with others; valuing differences; connecting past, present, and future; overcoming challenges; following your dreams; learning from the lives of others; social justice; exploring artistic expression and appreciation
- Notice and understand themes that are close to their own experiences and also themes that are beyond them: e.g., imagination, courage, fears, sharing, friendship, family relationships, self, nature, growing, behavior, community, responsibilities, diversity, belonging, peer relationships, loss
- Notice and understand themes reflecting important human challenges and social issues: e.g., self and self-esteem, popularity, bullying, sportsmanship, transition to adolescence, life cycles, survival, interconnectedness of humans and the environment, social awareness and responsibility, poverty, justice, racism, war

- Understand that there can be different interpretations of the meaning of a text
- Think across texts to derive larger messages, themes, or ideas
- Make connections to their own lives and to contemporary issues and problems across all genres
- Understand themes and ideas that are mature issues and require experience and/or prior reading to interpret
- Notice when a fiction writer is communicating a moral lesson
- Notice recurring themes or motifs in traditional literature and fantasy: e.g., struggle between good and evil, the hero's quest
- Recognize and understand symbolism in a text and illustrations
- Think across texts to compare the perspectives of different writers on the same problem, theme, or character types
- Notice how a writer reveals the underlying theme or messages of a text through a character's voice, the narrator's voice, or events of the plot

Setting

- Recognize and understand that fiction texts may have settings that reflect a wide range of diverse places, languages, and cultures, and that characters' behavior may reflect those settings
- Notice and understand settings that are distant in time and place from students' own experiences
- Infer the importance of the setting to the plot of the story in realistic and historical fiction and fantasy
- Form implicit and explicit questions in response to the characteristics of a setting
- Notice science fiction and fantasy settings: e.g., alternative or secondary world, futuristic setting, alternative histories, animal kingdom, fictional planet, pseudo-medieval setting
- Evaluate the significance of the setting in the story
- Evaluate the authenticity of the writer's presentation of the setting

---

● Thinking *Within* the Text   ◆ Thinking *Beyond* the Text   ■ Thinking *About* the Text

Selecting Goals Behaviors and Understandings to Notice, Teach, and Support *(cont.)*

Interactive Read-Aloud and Literature Discussion

FICTION TEXTS *(continued)*

Plot

- Follow a complex plot with multiple events, episodes, or problems
- Notice and remember the important events of a text in sequence
- Check understanding of complex plots and problems and raise questions if meaning is lost
- Tell the important events of a story using the pictures (after hearing the text read several times)
- Notice and understand when a problem is solved
- Include the problem and its resolution in a summary of a text
- Understand the problem in basic plots: e.g., overcoming evil, poverty and wealth, the quest, journey and return, comedy, tragedy, villain repents
- Understand how one episode builds on another and use information from the beginning of a story to interpret later episodes
- Follow and understand narratives with complex structure: e.g., multiple storylines, multiple points of view, subplots, circular plots, parallel plots, flashback, flash-forward, story-within-a-story, many kinds of conflict
- Make predictions on an ongoing basis during and after reading (based on progress of the plot, characteristics of the setting, attributes of the characters, actions of the characters)
- Infer the significance of events in a plot
- Form implicit and explicit questions in response to the events of a plot
- Give opinions about whether a problem seems real
- Recognize and discuss aspects of narrative structure: e.g., beginning, series of events, climax (turning point) of the story, problem resolution, ending
- Notice a writer's use of multiple narratives to reveal the plot and relationships among characters
- Recognize when the writer uses literary devices such as flashback, story-within-a-story, flash-forward, or parallel plot lines to structure the text
- Recognize a writer's use of plots and subplots
- Evaluate the logic and believability of the plot and its resolution

Character

- Follow multiple characters, each with unique traits, in the same story
- Recognize that characters can have multiple dimensions: e.g., can be good yet have flaws, can make mistakes based on confusion or misunderstanding, can do bad things but change for the better, can have contradicting feelings, can learn from mistakes, can have good intentions but do evil things
- Infer a character's traits, feelings, motivations, and intentions as revealed through what they say, think, or do and what others say or think about them, and use evidence from the text to describe them
- Make predictions about what a character is likely to do next or after the story ends, and use evidence from the text to support predictions
- Notice character change and infer reasons from events of the plot
- Learn from vicarious experiences with characters in stories
- Express opinions about the characters in a story and support those opinions with evidence
- Notice predictable or static characters (characters that do not change) as typical in traditional literature
- Infer relationships between characters as revealed through dialogue and behavior
- Infer the significance of heroic or larger-than-life characters in fantasy, who represent the symbolic struggle of good and evil
- Notice how a writer reveals predictable characters typical of traditional literature: e.g., sly, wise, greedy, clever, heroic, evil, devious, humorous
- Express opinions about whether a character seems real
- Notice how a writer reveals characters and makes them seem real
- Notice how an author creates characters that are complex and change over many events of a plot
- Think critically about the logic of a character's actions (causes and effects)
- Think critically about the authenticity and believability of characters and their behavior, dialogue, and development
- Assess the extent to which a writer makes readers feel empathy or identify with characters
- Evaluate the consistency of characters' actions within a particular setting

● Thinking **Within** the Text   ◆ Thinking **Beyond** the Text   ■ Thinking **About** the Text

Selecting Goals Behaviors and Understandings to Notice, Teach, and Support *(cont.)*

Interactive Read-Aloud and Literature Discussion

INTERACTIVE READ-ALOUD AND LITERATURE DISCUSSION

FICTION TEXTS *(continued)*

Style and Language

● Follow and understand assigned and unassigned dialogue among multiple characters with a clear idea about who is speaking

● Notice that words have special qualities, such as musical or pleasing sound, dramatic impact, or humor

● Internalize complex and literary language structures from hearing them read aloud

● Understand the meaning of author-created words, especially in fantasy and science fiction

● Understand the meaning of archaic words, used for authenticity

◆ Infer the mood by noticing aspects of a text, such as word choice

◆ Infer the writer's tone in a fiction text by noticing the language

■ Notice and think critically about a writer's word choice

■ Notice a writer's use of poetic language and sound devices: e.g., rhythm, rhyme, repetition, refrain, onomatopoeia, alliteration, assonance

■ Recognize how a writer creates humor: e.g., dialogue; effective descriptions of characters' actions, words, behavior, and feelings; surprising metaphors and similes; ironic expressions

■ Appreciate or critique fiction texts that utilize subtle or whimsical humor

■ Notice when a fiction writer uses poetic or descriptive language to show the setting, appeal to the five senses, or to convey human feelings such as loss, relief, or anger

■ Notice and understand long stretches of descriptive language important to understanding setting and characters

■ Notice language that conveys an emotional atmosphere (mood) in a text, affecting how the reader feels: e.g., tension, sadness, whimsicality, joy

■ Notice language that expresses the author's attitude or feelings toward a subject reflected in the style of writing (tone): e.g., lighthearted, ironic, earnest, affectionate, formal

■ Notice and remember literary language patterns that are characteristic of traditional literature: e.g., *once upon a time, long ago and far away, therefore, finally, at long last, happily ever after*

■ Notice and understand how the author uses idioms and literary language, including metaphor, simile, symbolism, and personification

■ Notice a writer's use of contradiction: e.g., paradox, figurative language, malaprop, oxymoron ("a silent roar")

■ Notice a writer's use of regional or historical vocabulary or features of dialect included for literary effect

■ Notice a writer's use of some words from languages other than English

■ Notice the narrator of a text, identify the narrative point of view (e.g., first-person narrative, second-person narrative, omniscient third-person narrative), and talk about why the writer chose this perspective

■ Notice a combination of narrative points of view within a single text

■ Think critically about the authenticity and appeal of a narrator's voice

■ Notice a writer's intentional use of language that violates conventional grammar to provide authentic dialogue to achieve the writer's voice

■ Recognize and appreciate an ambiguous ending of a fiction text

■ Analyze texts to determine aspects of a writer's style: e.g., use of language, choice of setting, plot, characters, themes and ideas

■ Recognize some authors by the style of their illustrations, their topics, characters they use, or typical plots

■ Assess the effectiveness of the writer's use of language

Vocabulary

● Continue to build vocabulary as a foundation for recognizing words in print

● Notice and acquire understanding of new vocabulary from read-aloud content

● Acquire new content words from texts and graphics

● Use new vocabulary in discussion of a text

● Learn many words that do not appear frequently in oral conversation but are used in writing (Tier 2)

● Understand words that appear in the academic disciplines (Tier 3)

● Understand the meaning of words representing all parts of speech when listening to a story

● Understand (when listening) common (simple) connectives that link and clarify meaning and are frequently used in oral language when listening to a story (*and, but, so, because, before, after*)

● Understand (when listening) some sophisticated connectives (words that link ideas and clarify meaning) that are used in written texts but do not appear often in everyday oral language: e.g., *although, however, meantime, meanwhile, moreover, otherwise, therefore, though, unless, until, whenever, yet*

● Thinking **Within** the Text   ◆ Thinking **Beyond** the Text   ■ Thinking **About** the Text

Selecting Goals Behaviors and Understandings to Notice, Teach, and Support *(cont.)*

Interactive Read-Aloud and Literature Discussion

FICTION TEXTS *(continued)*

- Understand (when listening) some academic connectives (words that link ideas and clarify meaning that appear in written texts): e.g., *alternatively, consequently, despite, conversely, eventually, finally, in contrast, initially, nevertheless, nonetheless, previously, specifically, ultimately, whereas, whereby*

- Derive the meaning of words from the context of a sentence, paragraph, or the whole story

- Understand the connotative meanings of words that are essential to understanding the text

- Understand words with multiple meanings within the same text–often signaling subtly different meanings

- Understand the figurative meaning of words that are essential to understanding the text

- Understand the meaning of idioms

- Understand words from regional or historical dialects

- Understand the meaning of words that are used ironically in a way that changes surface meaning

- Use some academic language to talk about fiction genres: e.g., *fiction, folktale, fairy tale, fractured fairy tale, fable, tall tale, realistic fiction, historical fiction, fantasy, traditional literature, hybrid text, myth, legend, ballad, science fiction*

- Use some academic language to talk about special types of fiction: e.g., *adventure story; animal story; family, friends, and school story; humorous story; mystery; sports story*

- Use some academic language to talk about forms: e.g., *picture book, wordless picture book, label book, ABC book, poem, poetry, nursery rhyme, rhyme, song, series book, chapter book, play, letter, poetry collection, sequel, limerick, haiku, concrete poetry, short story, diary entry, journal entry, narrative poetry, lyrical poetry, free verse, ballad*

- Use some academic language to talk about literary features: e.g., *beginning, ending, character, main character, events, message, dialogue, setting, flashback, conflict, resolution, theme, descriptive language, simile, plot, subplot, flash-forward, character development, supporting character, point of view, figurative language, metaphor, episode, climax, rising action, falling action, time-lapse, story-within-a-story, mood, personification, symbol, symbolism, first-person narrative, third-person narrative*

- Use some academic language to talk about book and print features: e.g., *front cover, back cover, title, author, illustrator, page, text, illustration, photograph, label, table of contents, acknowledgments, chapter, section, heading, drawing, caption, map, chapter title, dedication, author's note, illustrator's note, endpapers, book jacket, foreword, prologue, pronunciation guide, footnote, epilogue, endnote, stage directions*

Illustrations

- Notice and remember the important events of a story using the pictures (after hearing the text read several times)

- Follow and understand some texts that have no illustrations

- Understand that there can be different interpretations of the meaning of an illustration

- Use details from illustrations and text to support points made in discussion

- Interpret some illustrations with symbolic characteristics: e.g., use of color or symbols

- Notice how illustrations and graphics go together with the text in a meaningful way

- Notice how illustrations and graphics can reflect the theme or the writer's tone

- Notice and infer how illustrations contribute to mood in a fiction text

Book and Print Features

- Notice and use and understand the purpose of some organizational tools: e.g., title, table of contents, chapter title

- Notice and use and understand the purpose of some other text resources: e.g., glossary

- Notice and use and understand the purpose of some text resources outside the body (peritext): e.g., dedication, acknowledgments, author's note, illustrator's note, endpapers, foreword, prologue, pronunciation guide, footnote, epilogue, appendix, endnote, references

- Notice and understand other features of the peritext that have symbolic or cultural significance or add to aesthetic enjoyment

- Infer the cultural or symbolic significance of the peritext (for example, design features)

- Appreciate artistry in text design: e.g. book jacket, cover, end pages, title page, margins, chapter headings, illumination

- Evaluate what some text resources contribute to the meaning of a text

---

● Thinking *Within* the Text ◆ Thinking *Beyond* the Text ■ Thinking *About* the Text

Selecting Goals Behaviors and Understandings to Notice, Teach, and Support *(cont.)*

Interactive Read-Aloud and Literature Discussion

NONFICTION TEXTS

General

- Ask questions to deepen understanding of a text
- Notice and ask questions when meaning is lost or understanding is interrupted
- Refer to important information and details and use as evidence to support opinions and statements during discussion
- Understand content that reflects beginning understandings of physical world and social world: e.g., health, social studies, science, mathematics, arts)
- Notice and respond to stress and tone of voice while listening and afterward
- Notice and remember the important events of a text when temporal or chronological sequence is used
- Notice and remember the important information in a text
- Notice and understand information provided from primary sources that are embedded in the text
- Provide a concise and logically organized summary of a text after hearing it read
- Sustain attention for some longer texts that may require several days to complete
- Synthesize new information and ideas and revise thinking in response to it
- Form explicit and implicit questions about the content and concepts in a text
- Understand the problems that occur in everyday life, including some complex problems that may relate to readers' lives
- Make connections to their own lives and contemporary issues and problems across all genres
- Give reasons (either text-based or from personal experience) to support thinking
- Use background knowledge of content to understand nonfiction topics
- Use background knowledge of history to understand simple biography, autobiography, and memoir
- Recognize and understand that nonfiction texts may reflect a wide range of diverse settings, languages, and cultures
- Use evidence from the text to support statements about it
- Use evidence from the text to support predictions
- Relate the messages in a nonfiction test to one's own life
- Change opinions based on new information or insights gained from nonfiction texts

- Relate important information and concepts in one text and connect to information and concepts in other texts
- Understand texts that require the application of knowledge of academic disciplines (sciences, history, humanities)
- Draw information from secondary sources and other sources that may be in a nonfiction text
- Identify and discuss interesting, surprising, and important information in a text
- Form and express opinions about a text and support with rationale and evidence
- Form and state the basis for opinions about authors and illustrators
- Connect texts by a range of categories: e.g., content, message, genre, author/illustrator, special form, text structure, or organization
- Think critically about the quality of a nonfiction text: e.g., quality of writing contribution of illustration and other graphic design, accuracy

Genre

- Infer the importance of a subject's accomplishments (biography)
- Distinguish between fact and opinion in a text in order to reach new understanding
- Notice and understand the characteristics of some specific nonfiction genres: e.g., expository, narrative, procedural and persuasive texts, biography, autobiography, memoir, hybrid text
- Understand that a biography is the story of a person's life written by someone else
- Understand that biographies are often set in the past
- Understand that all autobiography is an account of a person's life written by that person
- Understand that a memoir is an account of a memory or set of memories written by the person who experienced it
- Notice when a writer is describing a step-by-step procedure
- Notice a writer's use of argument and persuasion
- Notice counterarguments and evidence against those counterarguments in a text
- Recognize hybrid texts and distinguish which sections are nonfiction and fiction
- Notice and appreciate forms and genres embedded in the main form or genre

---

● Thinking *Within* the Text   ◆ Thinking *Beyond* the Text   ■ Thinking *About* the Text

Selecting Goals Behaviors and Understandings to Notice, Teach, and Support *(cont.)*

Interactive Read-Aloud and Literature Discussion

NONFICTION TEXTS *(continued)*

- Recognize and understand some specific forms of nonfiction: e.g., series books; picture books; letters, diaries, and journals entries; photo essays and news articles
- Recognize and understand some specific types of poetry when they appear in nonfiction: e.g., lyrical poetry, free verse, limerick, haiku, narrative poetry, ballad, epic/saga, concrete poetry
- Notice and understand some elements of poetry when they appear in nonfiction: e.g., figurative language, rhyme, repetition, onomatopoeia, layout/line breaks (shape), imagery, alliteration, assonance

Organization

- Follow and understand nonfiction texts with clearly defined overall structure, categories, and subcategories and connect the structure to the table of contents
- Be aware of when the teacher is reading bulleted or numbered lists
- Understand the use of headings and subheadings
- Use headings and subheadings to search for and use information
- Refer to the location of some important information (category of information, supporting details, main ideas)
- Understand that a nonfiction text can be expository or narrative in structure and that the writer selects the structure for a specific purpose
- Notice the organization of a nonfiction text, distinguishing between expository and narrative structure
- Notice a nonfiction writer's use of narrative text structure in biography, memoir, autobiography, and other types of narrative nonfiction
- Notice a writer's use of primary and secondary sources as integral parts of a text
- Recognize and use a writer's use of underlying text structures: e.g., description, cause and effect, sequence (chronological, temporal), compare and contrast, problem and solution, question and answer, combination
- Notice a nonfiction writer's use of categories and subcategories to organize an informational text (expository)

- Understand that a writer can tell about something that usually happens in the same order (temporal sequence) and something that happens in time order (chronological order)
- Notice a writer's use of organizational tools: e.g., title, table of contents, chapter title, heading, subheading, sidebar
- Think critically about the way a writer has organized information (clear presentation, logic, appropriate to purpose)

Topic

- Show curiosity about topics encountered in nonfiction texts and actively work to learn more about them
- Think across texts to construct knowledge of a topic
- Think across texts to compare and expand understanding of content and ideas from academic disciplines: e.g., social responsibility, environment, climate, history, social and geological history, cultural groups
- Infer the importance of a topic of a nonfiction text
- Infer the writer's attitude toward a topic
- Infer a writer's purpose in a nonfiction text
- Infer a writer's stance (position, argument, or thesis) toward a topic or the subject of a biography
- Recognize that a wide variety of informational texts may be about different places and that customs and people's behavior may reflect those settings
- Recognize that informational texts may present a larger topic with many subtopics
- Extend understanding to nonfiction topics and content that are beyond most students' immediate experience: e.g., elements and compounds; forces and motion; matter; energy use; climate and weather; countries and cultures of Africa, Latin America, Asia, Australia, the Pacific, and Europe
- Understand that a writer is presenting facts about a single topic
- Notice the topic of a text and that subtopics are related to the main topic
- Hypothesize the writer's reasons for choosing a topic and infer how the writer feels about a topic
- Evaluate the writer's qualifications for writing on a topic

---

● Thinking *Within* the Text   ◆ Thinking *Beyond* the Text   ■ Thinking *About* the Text

Selecting Goals Behaviors and Understandings to Notice, Teach, and Support *(cont.)*

Interactive Read-Aloud and Literature Discussion

NONFICTION TEXTS *(continued)*

Messages and Main Ideas

- ● Follow arguments in a persuasive text
- ◆ Understand that there can be different interpretations of the meanings of a text
- ◆ Think across texts to compare and expand understanding of content and ideas from academic disciplines: e.g., social responsibility, environment, climate, history, social and geological history, cultural groups
- ◆ Understand the relationships among ideas and content in an expository nonfiction text (larger topic with subtopics)
- ◆ Connect the information in nonfiction books to disciplinary studies
- ◆ Infer the significance of nonfiction content for their own lives
- ◆ Infer the larger (main) ideas or messages in a nonfiction text
- ◆ Understand themes and ideas that are mature issues and require experience to interpret
- ■ Understand that a nonfiction text can have more than one message or big (main) idea
- ■ Distinguish fact from opinion

Style and Language

- ● Understand sentence structure that varies according to purpose (e.g., headings, captions, labels, numbered and bulleted lists) in nonfiction
- ■ Notice and think critically about a writer's word choice
- ■ Notice language that conveys an emotional atmosphere (mood) in a text, affecting how the reader feels: e.g., tension, sadness, whimsicality, joy
- ■ Notice language that expresses the author's attitude or feelings toward a subject reflected in the style of writing (tone): e.g., lighthearted, ironic, earnest, affectionate, formal
- ■ Notice how the writer reveals the setting in a biographical, historical, or other narrative nonfiction text
- ■ Notice and understand multiple points of view on the same topic
- ■ Think critically about the way a writer reveals different viewpoints or perspectives
- ■ Assess the objectivity with which a nonfiction topic is presented
- ■ Recognize bias and be able to identify evidence of it
- ■ Recognize a writer's use of the techniques for persuasion in a persuasive text
- ■ Notice and critique how a writer uses logical reasoning and specific evidence to support argument

- ■ Identify and critique specific language a writer uses to persuade
- ■ Recognize some authors by the topics they choose or the style of their illustrations

Accuracy

- ■ Critically examine the quality or accuracy of the text, citing evidence for opinions
- ■ Notice and evaluate the accuracy of the information presented in the text and across texts
- ■ Evaluate the way the writer of an argument supports statements with evidence

Vocabulary

- ● Continue to build vocabulary as a foundation for recognizing words in print
- ● Notice and acquire understanding of new vocabulary from read-aloud content
- ● Acquire new content words from texts and graphics
- ● Use new vocabulary in discussion of a text and in writing about reading
- ● Derive the meaning of words from the context of a sentence, paragraph, or the whole text
- ● Learn many words that do not appear frequently in oral conversation but are used in writing (Tier 2)
- ● Acquire vocabulary that is specialized and related to scientific domains (Tier 3)
- ● Understand the meaning of words representing all parts of speech when listening to a nonfiction text read aloud
- ● Understand the meaning of common (simple), sophisticated, and academic connectives when listening to a nonfiction text read aloud
- ● Notice and understand the meaning of technical words particular to academic disciplines
- ● Understand the connotative meanings of words that are essential to understanding the text
- ● Understand the meaning of figurative words that are essential to understanding the text
- ● Understand words with multiple meanings within the same text, often signaling subtly different meanings
- ■ Use some academic language to talk about nonfiction genres: e.g., *nonfiction, personal memory story, informational text, informational book, factual text, biography, autobiography, narrative nonfiction, memoir, procedural text, persuasive text, hybrid text, expository text*

- ● Thinking **Within** the Text   ◆ Thinking **Beyond** the Text   ■ Thinking **About** the Text

Selecting Goals Behaviors and Understandings to Notice, Teach, and Support *(cont.)*

Interactive Read-Aloud and Literature Discussion

NONFICTION TEXTS *(continued)*

- Use some academic language to talk about forms: e.g., *picture book, wordless picture book, label book, ABC book, counting book, poem, poetry, nursery rhyme, rhyme, song, series book, play, letter, poetry collection, sequel, limerick, haiku, concrete poetry, diary entry, journal entry, news article, feature article, narrative poetry, photo essay, speech, lyrical poetry, free verse, ballad*
- Use some academic language to talk about literary features: e.g., *beginning, ending, problem, question and answer, solution, topic, description, problem and solution, message, dialogue, main idea, comparison and contrast, setting, cause and effect, categorization, descriptive language, figurative language, metaphor, simile, persuasive language, temporal sequence, chronological sequence, subject, argument, personification, symbol, symbolism, second-person narrative*
- Use some academic language to talk about book and print features: e.g., *front cover, back cover, title, author, illustrator, page, text, illustration, photograph, label, table of contents, acknowledgments, chapter, section, heading, drawing, caption, map, chapter title, dedication, author's note, illustrator's note, section, diagram, glossary, endpapers, sidebar, book jacket, subheading, chart, graph, timeline, index, cutaway, foreword, prologue, pronunciation guide, footnote, epilogue, endnote, appendix, references, stage directions, bibliography*

Illustrations/Graphics
- Understand that graphics provide important information
- Follow and understand some texts that have no graphics or illustrations
- Recognize and use information in a variety of graphics: e.g., photo and/or drawing with label or caption, diagram, cutaway, map with legend and scale, infographic
- Use details from illustrations to support points made in discussion
- Notice how illustrations and graphics help to communicate the writer's message
- Understand that graphics and text are carefully placed in a nonfiction text so that ideas are communicated clearly

Book and Print Features
- Notice a text's title and the name of its author and illustrator on the cover and title page
- Gain new understandings from searching for and using information found in text body, sidebars, and graphics
- Notice and use and understand the purpose of some organizational tools: e.g., title, table of contents, chapter title, heading, subheading
- Notice and use and understand the purpose of some other text resources: e.g., glossary, index
- Notice and use and understand the purpose of some text resources outside the body (peritext): e.g., dedication, acknowledgments, author's note, illustrator's note, endpapers, foreword, prologue, pronunciation guide, footnote, epilogue, appendix, endnote, references
- Notice and understand other features of the peritext that have symbolic value, add to aesthetic enjoyment, or add meaning
- Appreciate artistry in text design: e.g., book jacket, cover, end pages, title page (peritext)
- Evaluate the effectiveness of page layout and design of a text and connect it to the culture represented or the main ideas
- Evaluate what some text resources contribute to the meaning of a text

● Thinking *Within* the Text   ◆ Thinking *Beyond* the Text   ■ Thinking *About* the Text

Selecting Texts Characteristics of Texts for Reading Aloud and Discussion

Interactive Read-Aloud and Literature Discussion

GENRE

▶ Fiction

- Realistic fiction
- Historical fiction
- Traditional literature: e.g., folktale, tall tale, fairy tale, (including fractured fairy tale), fable, myth, legend, epic, ballad
- Complex fantasy (all types)
- Hybrid text
- Special types of fiction: e.g., mystery; adventure story; animal story; family, friends, and school story; humorous story; sports story; satire/parody; horror; romance

▶ Nonfiction

- Expository nonfiction
- Narrative nonfiction
- Biography
- Autobiography
- Memoir
- Procedural text
- Persuasive text
- Hybrid text

FORMS

- Series books
- Picture books
- Chapter books, some with sequels
- Sections of longer chapter books
- Novellas
- Poems
- Poetry collections
- Plays
- Types of poetry: lyrical poetry, free verse, limerick, haiku, narrative poetry, ballad, epic/saga, concrete poetry
- Letters, diary and journal entries
- Short stories
- Photo essays, news articles, and feature articles
- Speeches

TEXT STRUCTURE

- Longer narratives with main plot and subplots, each with a conflict
- Texts with variations in structure: e.g., story-within-a-story, flashback, flash-forward, time-lapse
- Some books with chapters connected to a single plot
- Collections of short stories related to an overarching theme and with plots that intertwine or build across separate stories
- Texts with circular plots or with parallel plots
- Informational texts related to a larger topic with many subtopics
- Underlying structural patterns: description, cause and effect, chronological sequence, temporal sequence, categorization, compare and contrast, problem and solution, question and answer
- Informational texts with clearly defined structure and categories and subcategories, some defined by headings, sections, and subsections
- Biographical and historical texts with narrative structure
- Informational texts with examples of simple argument and persuasion

CONTENT

- Content that is appropriate for students' cognitive development, social and emotional maturity, and life experience
- Relevant content that engages students' intellectual curiosity and emotions
- Content that promotes inquiry and investigation
- Content that requires analytical and critical thinking: e.g., to judge the authenticity and relevance of informational texts or historical fiction
- Many texts with heavy content load that requires prior knowledge and invites extended discussion
- Sophisticated, subtle humor including irony: e.g., characters with unusual or humorous traits, surprising outcomes, humorous comparisons, whimsical settings
- Content that reinforces and expands a student's experience and knowledge of self and the world
- Many topics that may be beyond most students' immediate experiences: e.g., living organisms; reproduction and heredity; ecology; land forms and topography; astronomy; events and periods in United States history (colonization, independence, the Constitution, etc.), world history, ecological systems
- Content that reflects a wide range of settings, languages, and cultures and that requires some knowledge of diverse cultures
- Content that requires content knowledge related to historical periods, circumstances, and places
- Content that requires the student to appreciate or identify with diverse perspectives relating to culture, race, gender, etc.
- Content linked to specific areas of study as described by the school curriculum or standards
- More complex characters, settings, events, and conflicts that could exist in contemporary life or in another historical period
- More complex characters, settings, events, and conflicts that occur in fantasy
- Content that reflects increasing understanding of the physical and social world: e.g., health, social studies, science, mathematics, arts
- Some texts with dense presentation of facts and ideas

THEMES AND IDEAS

- Texts with deeper meanings applicable to important human challenges and social issues: e.g., life cycles, survival, interconnectedness of humans and the environment, social responsibility, poverty, justice, racism, war
- Themes and ideas that build social awareness and reveal insights into the human condition
- Themes and ideas that require a perspective not familiar to the reader or understanding of cultural diversity
- Themes and ideas that involve the problems of preadolescents and adolescents: e.g., self-esteem; gender differences; physical, emotional, and social self-awareness; individuality; peer relationships and popularity; bullying; family relationships
- Many books with multiple ideas, most requiring inference and synthesis to understand

Selecting Texts Characteristics of Texts for Reading Aloud and Discussion *(cont.)*

Interactive Read-Aloud and Literature Discussion

- Ideas close to students' experience: e.g., empathizing with others; valuing differences; connecting past, present, and future; overcoming challenges; following your dreams; learning from the lives of others; exploring artistic expression and appreciation
- Themes that evoke different, sometimes conflicting, interpretations
- Texts that present multiple themes that may be understood in layers
- Themes related to conflict involving a person struggling against the forces of nature, against another person, against society, or against himself or herself
- Themes involving a symbolic representation of good vs. evil

LANGUAGE AND LITERARY FEATURES

- Elements of traditional literature and modern fantasy: e.g., the supernatural; imaginary and otherworldly creatures; gods and goddesses; talking animals, toys, and dolls; heroic characters; technology or scientific advances; time travel; aliens or outer space
- Basic motifs of traditional literature and modern fantasy: e.g., struggle between good and evil, magic, secondary or alternative worlds, the hero's quest, special character types, fantastic or magical objects, wishes, trickery, transformations
- Predictable story outcomes typical of traditional literature: e.g., clever overcomes power, good defeats evil
- Settings important to the plot, many distant in time and place from students' own experiences
- Characters with multiple dimensions revealed by what they say, think, and do and what others say and think about them
- Main character(s) that are centrally involved in the conflict and resolution, and supporting characters, some of which may be important to the plot
- "Round" characters that have a complex range of good and bad attributes and that change during the course of the plot, and "flat" characters that do not change but may play an important role in the plot

- Predictable and static characters with simple traits typical of traditional literature
- Plot with multiple episodes and conflicts and clear, satisfying resolutions, some left to inference
- Some longer texts with one or more subplots, each with a conflict
- Some texts with conflict involving a person struggling against the forces of nature (or of the supernatural), against another person, against society, or against himself or herself
- Some texts with ambiguous endings
- Most texts written in first- or third-person narrative with some procedural texts in second-person
- Texts told from multiple points of view
- Language that expresses the author's attitude or feelings toward a subject reflected in the style of writing (tone): e.g., lighthearted, ironic, earnest, affectionate, formal
- Language that violates conventional rules of grammar and usage in order to provide colloquial speech, or to achieve the writer's distinctive voice
- Descriptive language and imagery conveying sensory experiences and a range of human feelings: e.g., joy, sadness, anger, eagerness
- Poetic language and other literary language
- Language and events that convey an emotional atmosphere (mood) in a text, affecting how the reader feels: e.g., tension, sadness, whimsicality, joy, dread
- Descriptive and figurative language that is important to understanding the content: e.g., imagery, metaphor, simile, personification, hyperbole
- Some long stretches of descriptive language important to understanding setting, plot, characters, themes
- Many texts with subtle and/or complex use of symbolism, including allegory
- Allegorical language
- Both assigned and unassigned dialogue, including some strings of unassigned dialogue for which speakers must be inferred
- Occasional use of monologue
- Dialect

- Archaic language
- Procedural language: e.g., step-by-step, directions, how-to
- Persuasive language

SENTENCE COMPLEXITY

- Many long and complex sentences that require attention to follow
- Long sentences joined by semicolons or colons
- Variation in placement of subject, verb, and multiple adjectives, adverbs, and prepositional phrases
- Many sentences with multiple embedded clauses and phrases
- Complex sentences with variety in order of phrases and clauses
- Sentences with common (simple) and sophisticated connectives
- Sentences with academic connectives
- Extended dialogue that increases sentence complexity
- Some texts with long sentences divided into bulleted or numbered lists
- Sentence structure adapted to fit purpose and form of book and print features: e.g., heading, subheading, label, caption, labels, legend

VOCABULARY

- New content words related to concepts that students are learning
- Many words that appear in the vocabulary of mature language users (Tier 2)
- Many words that are particular to a discipline (Tier 3)
- Common (simple) connectives that are frequently used in oral language (words, phrases that clarify relationships ideas): e.g., *and, but, so, because, before, after*
- Sophisticated connectives (words that link ideas and clarify meaning) that are used in written texts but do not appear often in everyday oral language: e.g., *although, however, meantime, meanwhile, moreover, otherwise, therefore, though, unless, until, whenever, yet*

Selecting Texts Characteristics of Texts for Reading Aloud and Discussion *(cont.)*

Interactive Read-Aloud and Literature Discussion

VOCABULARY *(continued)*

- Academic connectives (words that link ideas and clarify meaning that appear in written texts): e.g., *alternatively, consequently, despite, conversely, eventually, finally, in contrast, initially, nevertheless, nonetheless, previously, specifically, ultimately, whereas, whereby*
- Many words with multiple meanings, some with subtle shadings of meaning
- Many words with figurative meaning
- Idioms as appropriate to genre
- Many words with connotative meanings that are essential to understanding the text
- A few words used ironically or satirically
- Some words from regional or historical dialects
- Some words from languages other than English
- Some words (including slang) used informally by particular groups of people
- Archaic words
- Words that have meaning within specific dialects
- Wide variety of technical vocabulary

ILLUSTRATIONS

- Illustrations in a variety of media that offer examples of notable artistic technique
- Illustrations that enhance and extend meaning in the text
- Complex illustrations with many details, some needing description by the teacher during reading
- Books with illustrations that represent a coherent artistic vision
- Chapter books with few or no illustrations
- Some texts with decorative elements such as vignettes
- Some complex, nuanced illustrations that convey mood to match or extend the text
- Books with illustrations that reflect the theme and the writer's tone
- Some illustrations with figurative and symbolic characteristics requiring interpretation
- Simple illustrations in a variety of forms: drawing with label or caption, photograph with label or caption, map with legend and scale, diagram (cutaway), infographic, chart, graph, timeline

BOOK AND PRINT FEATURES

LENGTH

- Many short picture books that can be read in one sitting
- Long illustrated texts with sections that may be selected and read
- Long illustrated texts that require several days to complete

PRINT AND LAYOUT

- Some books with decorative or informative illustrations and/or print outside the body of the text (peritext)
- Texts with engaging designs that add aesthetic value and have symbolic and cultural meaning

ORGANIZATIONAL TOOLS

- Title, author, and illustrator listed on cover and on title page
- Table of contents, chapter title, heading, subheading, sidebar

TEXT RESOURCES

- Some books with dedication, acknowledgments, author's note, glossary, special endpapers (peritext), index
- Additional information provided by foreword, prologue, pronunciation guide, footnote, epilogue, appendix, endnote, references, bibliography

Selecting Goals Behaviors and Understandings to Notice, Teach, and Support

Interactive Read-Aloud and Literature Discussion

FICTION TEXTS

General

- Ask questions to deepen understanding of a text
- Notice and ask questions when meaning is lost or understanding is interrupted
- Refer to important information and details and use as evidence to support opinions and statements during discussion
- Notice and respond to dimensions of fluency (intonation, stress, pausing, phrasing) while listening and after a story is read
- Sustain attention for some longer texts that may require several days to finish
- Provide a concise, logically organized summary of a text after hearing it read
- Refer to the location of some important details in the text (setting, time order, problem, resolution)
- Recall important details about setting, problem and resolution, and characters after a story is read
- Learn new concepts and ideas from listening to fiction texts
- Synthesize new information and ideas and revise thinking in response to it
- Form implicit and explicit questions about the content and concepts in a fiction text
- Understand complex problems that can be related to readers' lives
- Learn more about social issues, both local and global, as revealed through character, plot, and setting
- Make connections to their own lives and contemporary issues and problems across all genres
- Give reasons/evidence (either text-based or from personal experience) to support thinking
- Use background knowledge to understand settings, problems, and characters
- Apply background knowledge to extend understanding of historical fiction and science fiction
- Infer a writer's purpose in writing a fiction text
- Make connections (e.g., content, theme) across fiction texts that are read aloud, and where appropriate, connect to nonfiction texts
- Use evidence from the text to support statements about it
- Make connections (similarities and differences) among texts that have the same author/illustrator, setting, characters, or theme
- Use evidence from the text to support a wide range of predictions (I think . . . because . . .)
- Relate important ideas in the text to each other and to ideas in other texts

- Change opinions based on new information or insights gained from fiction texts
- Understand that a writer has a purpose in writing a fiction text
- Connect texts by a range of categories: e.g., content, theme, message, genre, author/illustrator, character, setting, special forms, text structure, or organization
- Form and express opinions about a text and support with rationale and evidence
- Form and state the basis for opinions about authors and illustrators
- Critique the text in terms of quality of writing, organization, clarity, authenticity
- Critique the text in terms of bias, stereotypes, prejudice, misrepresentation, sexism, racism
- Think critically about the authenticity of a text: e.g., characterization, plot, setting, social values

Genre

- Understand that there are different types of fiction and nonfiction texts and that they have different characteristics
- Identify and understand the historical period, people, and events
- Apply background knowledge to extend understanding of historical fiction and science fiction
- Notice and understand the characteristics of some specific fiction genres: e.g., realistic fiction, historical fiction, folktale, fairy tale, fractured fairy tale, fable, myth, legend, epic, ballad, fantasy including science fiction, hybrid text
- Understand when a story could happen in real life (realistic fiction) and when it could not happen in real life (traditional literature, fantasy)
- Examine how different sources address the same topic
- Question the validity of the information presented in the text about the past
- Challenge the text as historical artifact
- Draw conclusions about the author's unique experiences and how they might have influenced the text
- Identify elements of traditional literature and fantasy: e.g., the supernatural; imaginary and otherworldly creatures; gods and goddesses; talking animals, toys, and dolls; heroic characters; technology or scientific advances; time travel; aliens or outer space
- Notice and understand basic motifs of traditional literature and fantasy: e.g., struggle between good and evil, magic, secondary or alternative worlds, the hero's quest, special character types, fantastic or magical objects, wishes, trickery, transformations

● Thinking **Within** the Text   ◆ Thinking **Beyond** the Text   ■ Thinking **About** the Text

Selecting Goals Behaviors and Understandings to Notice, Teach, and Support *(cont.)*

Interactive Read-Aloud and Literature Discussion

FICTION TEXTS *(continued)*

Genre *(continued)*

- Notice story outcomes that are typical of traditional literature
- Identify some elements of science fiction: e.g., technology or scientific advances, futuristic setting, time travel, aliens and outer space
- Recognize hybrid texts, distinguish which sections are fiction and nonfiction, and notice how the writer blends the two genres
- Notice and appreciate forms and genres embedded in another form or genre
- Notice and understand some special types of fiction: e.g., mystery; adventure story; animal story; family, friends, and school story; humorous story; sports story; satire/parody; horror; romance
- Recognize and understand some specific types of poetry: e.g., lyrical poetry, free verse, limerick, haiku, narrative poetry, ballad, epic/saga, concrete poetry
- Notice and understand some elements of poetry: e.g., figurative language, rhyme, repetition, onomatopoeia, layout/line breaks (shape), imagery, alliteration, assonance

Messages and Themes

- Notice that a book may have more than one message or big (main) idea
- Understand that the messages or big ideas in fiction texts can be applied to their own lives or to other people and society
- Infer the messages in a work of fiction
- Infer and understand the moral lesson or cultural teaching in traditional literature
- Notice and infer the importance of ideas relevant to their world: e.g., becoming independent; valuing change in self and others; empathizing with others; valuing differences; connecting past, present, and future; overcoming challenges; following your dreams; learning from the lives of others; social justice; exploring artistic expression and appreciation
- Notice and understand themes that are close to their own experiences and also themes that are beyond them: e.g., imagination, courage, fears, sharing, friendship, family relationships, self, nature, growing, behavior, community, responsibilities, diversity, belonging, peer relationships, loss
- Notice and understand themes reflecting important human challenges and social issues: e.g., self and self-esteem, popularity, bullying, sportsmanship, transition to adolescence, life cycles, survival, interconnectedness of humans and the environment, social awareness and responsibility, poverty, justice, racism, war
- Use background knowledge (experiential and academic) to understand sophisticated and mature content that is beyond most students' experiences

- Notice and understand themes reflecting important human challenges and social issues: e.g., life cycles, survival, interconnectedness of humans and the environment, social responsibility, poverty, justice, racism, war
- Understand that there can be different interpretations of the meanings in a text
- Think across texts to derive larger messages, themes, or ideas
- Make connections to their own lives and to contemporary issues and problems across all genres
- Recognize conflicting messages within a text
- Understand themes and ideas that are mature issues and require experience and/or prior reading to interpret
- Recognize underlying political messages in fiction and nonfiction texts
- Notice when a fiction writer is communicating a moral lesson
- Notice recurring themes or motifs in traditional literature and fantasy: e.g., struggle between good and evil, the hero's quest
- Recognize and understand symbolism in a text and illustrations
- Think across texts to compare the perspectives of different writers on the same problem, theme, or character types
- Notice how a writer reveals the underlying theme or message of a text through a character's voice, the narrator's voice, or events of the plot

Setting

- Recognize and understand that fiction texts may have settings that reflect a wide range of diverse places, languages, and cultures, and that characters' behavior may reflect those settings
- Notice and understand settings that are distant in time and place from students' own experiences
- Infer the importance of the setting to the plot of the story in realistic and historical fiction and fantasy
- Form implicit and explicit questions in response to the characteristics of a setting
- Notice science fiction and fantasy settings: e.g., alternative or secondary world, futuristic setting, alternative histories, animal kingdom, fictional planet, pseudo-medieval setting
- Evaluate the significance of the setting in the story
- Evaluate the authenticity of the writer's presentation of the setting

Plot

- Follow a complex plot with multiple events, episodes, or problems
- Notice and remember the important events of a text in sequence
- Check understanding of complex plots and problems and raise questions if meaning is lost

---

● Thinking *Within* the Text   ◆ Thinking *Beyond* the Text   ■ Thinking *About* the Text

Selecting Goals Behaviors and Understandings to Notice, Teach, and Support *(cont.)*

Interactive Read-Aloud and Literature Discussion

FICTION TEXTS *(continued)*

- Tell the important events of a story using the pictures (after hearing the text read several times)
- Notice and understand when a problem is solved
- Include the problem and its resolution in a summary of a text
- Understand the problem in basic plots: e.g., overcoming evil, poverty and wealth, the quest, journey and return, comedy, tragedy, villain repents
- Understand how one episode builds on another and use information from the beginning of a story to interpret later episodes
- Follow and understand narratives with complex structure: e.g., multiple storylines, multiple perspectives, subplots, flashback, flash-forward, time-lapse, story-within-a-story, many kinds of conflict
- Follow and understand narratives with complex structure: e.g., multiple storylines, multiple points of view, subplots, circular plots, parallel plots, flashback, flash-forward, story-within-a-story, many kinds of conflict
- Make predictions on an ongoing basis during and after reading (based on progress of the plot, characteristics of the setting, attributes of the characters, actions of the characters)
- Infer the significance of events in a plot
- Form implicit and explicit questions in response to the events of a plot
- Give opinions about whether a problem seems real
- Recognize and discuss aspects of narrative structure: e.g., beginning, series of events, climax (turning point) of the story, problem resolution, ending, denouement
- Recognize when the writer uses literary devices such as flashback, story-within-a-story, flash-forward, or parallel plot lines to structure the text
- Recognize a writer's use of plots and subplots
- Notice a writer's use of multiple narratives to reveal the plot and relationships among characters
- Evaluate the logic and believability of the plot and its resolution
- Recognize and critique writers' selection of plot structure: e.g., linear narration, flashbacks, stream of consciousness, parallel structures involving two narratives, frame stories/embedded narratives, circular narratives

Character

- Follow multiple characters, each with unique traits, in the same story
- Recognize that characters can have multiple dimensions: e.g., can be good yet have flaws, can make mistakes based on confusion or misunderstanding, can do bad things but change for the better, can have contradicting feelings, can learn from mistakes, can have good intentions but do evil things

- Infer a character's traits, feelings, motivations, and intentions as revealed through what they say, think, or do and what others say or think about them, and use evidence from the text to describe them
- Infer relationships between characters as revealed through dialogue and behavior
- Infer attributes of fully developed (round) characters that have multiple dimensions and change over time
- Infer attributes of characters that are one dimensional or not fully developed (flat) and do not change over time, but may be important to the problem resolution
- Make predictions about what a character is likely to do next or after the story ends, and use evidence from the text to support predictions
- Notice character change and infer reasons from events of the plot
- Learn from vicarious experiences with characters in stories
- Express opinions about the characters in a story and support with evidence
- Notice predictable or static characters (characters that do not change) as typical in traditional literature
- Infer the significance of heroic or larger-than-life characters in fantasy, who represent the symbolic struggle of good and evil
- Notice how a writer reveals predictable characters typical of traditional literature: e.g., sly, wise, greedy, clever, heroic, evil, devious, humorous
- Express opinions about whether a character seems real
- Notice how a writer reveals characters and makes them seem real
- Notice how a writer reveals round characters (fully developed that have multiple dimensions and change)
- Notice how a writer reveals static characters, as typical in traditional literature, who do not change yet contribute to the plot
- Think critically about the logic of a character's actions (causes and effects)
- Think critically about the authenticity and believability of characters and their behavior, dialogue, and development
- Assess the extent to which a writer makes readers feel empathy or identify with characters
- Evaluate the consistency of characters' actions within a particular setting

Style and Language

- Understand long and highly complex sentences with multiple phrases and clauses

● Thinking ***Within*** the Text   ◆ Thinking ***Beyond*** the Text   ■ Thinking ***About*** the Text

Selecting Goals Behaviors and Understandings to Notice, Teach, and Support *(cont.)*

Interactive Read-Aloud and Literature Discussion

FICTION TEXTS *(continued)*

Style and Language *(continued)*

- Follow and understand assigned and unassigned dialogue among multiple characters with a clear idea about who is speaking
- Notice that words have special qualities, such as musical or pleasing sound, dramatic impact, or humor
- Internalize complex and literary language structures from hearing them read aloud
- Understand the meaning of slang and author-invented words that add authenticity to a text
- Understand the meaning of archaic words, used for authenticity
- Infer the mood by noticing aspects of a text, such as word choice
- Infer the writer's tone in a fiction text by noticing the language
- ◆ Infer the writer's perspective (angle)
- ◆ Infer symbolic meaning and/or ironic meaning in a text
- ◆ Infer the meaning of satirical texts: e.g., identify what is being satirized and discuss its significance
- ■ Notice and think critically about a writer's word choice
- ■ Notice a writer's use of poetic language and sound devices: e.g., rhythm, rhyme, repetition, refrain, onomatopoeia, alliteration, assonance
- ■ Recognize how a writer creates humor: e.g., dialogue; effective descriptions of characters' actions, words, behavior, and feelings; surprising metaphors and similes; ironic expressions
- ■ Appreciate or critique fiction texts that utilize subtle or whimsical humor
- ■ Notice when a fiction writer uses poetic or descriptive language to show the setting, appeal to the five senses, or to convey human feelings such as loss, relief, or anger
- ■ Notice and understand long stretches of descriptive language important to understanding setting and characters
- ■ Notice language that conveys an emotional atmosphere (mood) in a text, affecting how the reader feels: e.g., tension, sadness, whimsicality, joy
- ■ Critique the way the writer communicates the mood of the story
- ■ Notice language that expresses the author's attitude or feelings toward a subject reflected in the style of writing (tone): e.g., lighthearted, ironic, earnest, affectionate, formal
- ■ Notice and remember literary language patterns that are characteristic of traditional literature: e.g., *once upon a time, long ago and far away, therefore, finally, at long last, happily ever after*
- ■ Notice and understand how the author uses idioms and literary language, including metaphor, simile, symbolism, and personification

- ■ Notice a writer's use of satire to change the surface meaning of words
- ■ Notice language that conveys irony or satirizes an idea or character
- ■ Notice a writer's use of contradiction: e.g., paradox, figurative language, malaprop, oxymoron ("a silent roar")
- ■ Notice a writer's use of regional or historical vocabulary or features of dialect included for literary effect
- ■ Notice a writer's use of some words from languages other than English
- ■ Notice the narrator of a text, identify the narrative point of view (e.g., first-person narrative, second-person narrative, omniscient third-person narrative), and talk about why the writer chose this perspective
- ■ Notice a combination of narrative points of view within a single text
- ■ Think critically about the authenticity and appeal of a narrator's voice
- ■ Notice a writer's intentional use of language that violates conventional grammar to provide authentic dialogue to achieve the writer's voice
- ■ Notice a writer's use of dialect to convey different cultures
- ■ Recognize and appreciate an ambiguous ending of a fiction text
- ■ Analyze texts to determine aspects of a writer's style: e.g., use of language, choice of setting, plot, characters, themes and ideas
- ■ Recognize some authors by the style of their illustrations, their topics, characters they use, or typical plots
- ■ Assess the effectiveness of the writer's use of language

Vocabulary

- Continue to build vocabulary as a foundation for recognizing words in print
- Notice and acquire understanding of new vocabulary from read-aloud content
- Acquire new content words from texts and graphics
- Use new vocabulary in discussion of a text and in writing about reading
- Learn many words that do not appear frequently in oral conversation but are used in writing (Tier 2)
- Understand words that appear in the academic disciplines (Tier 3)
- Understand the meaning of words representing all parts of speech when listening to a story
- Understand (when listening) common (simple) connectives that link and clarify meaning and are frequently used in oral language when listening to a story (*and, but, so, because, before, after*)

● Thinking *Within* the Text   ◆ Thinking *Beyond* the Text   ■ Thinking *About* the Text

The Fountas & Pinnell Literacy Continuum, Grades PreK–8

Selecting Goals Behaviors and Understandings to Notice, Teach, and Support *(cont.)*

Interactive Read-Aloud and Literature Discussion

FICTION TEXTS *(continued)*

- Understand (when listening) some sophisticated connectives (words that link ideas and clarify meaning) that are used in written texts but do not appear often in everyday oral language: e.g., *although, however, meantime, meanwhile, moreover, otherwise, therefore, though, unless, until, whenever, yet*

- Understand (when listening) some academic connectives (words that link ideas and clarify meaning that appear in written texts): e.g., *alternatively, consequently, despite, conversely, eventually, finally, in contrast, initially, nevertheless, nonetheless, previously, specifically, ultimately, whereas, whereby*

- Understand common (simple), sophisticated, and academic connectives when listening to a nonfiction text

- Derive the meaning of words from the context of a sentence, paragraph, or the whole story

- Understand the connotative meanings of words that are essential to understanding the text

- Understand words with multiple meanings within the same text–often signaling subtly different meanings

- Understand the figurative meaning of words that are essential to understanding the text

- Understand the meaning of idioms

- Understand words from regional or historical dialects

- Understand the meaning of words that are used satirically or ironically in a way that changes surface meaning

- Use some academic language to talk about fiction genres: e.g., *fiction, folktale, fairy tale, fable, tall tale, realistic fiction, historical fiction, fantasy, traditional literature, hybrid text, myth, legend, ballad, science fiction, epic*

- Use some academic language to talk about special types of fiction: e.g., *adventure story; animal story; family, friends, and school story; humorous story; mystery; sports story; satire/ parody; horror story; romance story*

- Use some academic language to talk about forms: e.g., *picture book, wordless picture book, label book, ABC book, poem, poetry, nursery rhyme, rhyme, song, series book, chapter book, play, letter, poetry collection, sequel, limerick, haiku, concrete poetry, short story, fractured fairy tale, diary entry, journal entry, narrative poetry, lyrical poetry, free verse, ballad, epic/saga*

- Use some academic language to talk about literary features: e.g., *beginning, ending, character, main character, events, message, dialogue, setting, flashback, conflict, resolution, theme, descriptive language, simile, plot, subplot, flash-forward, character development, supporting character, point of view, figurative language, metaphor, episode, climax, rising action, falling action, time-lapse, story-within-a-story, mood, personification, symbol, symbolism, first-person narrative, third-person narrative, circular plot, parallel plots, protagonist, antagonist, tone, irony, round and flat characters, monologue*

- Use some academic language to talk about book and print features: e.g., *front cover, back cover, title, author, illustrator, page, text, illustration, photograph, label, table of contents, acknowledgments, chapter, section, heading, drawing, caption, map, chapter title, dedication, author's note, illustrator's note, endpapers, book jacket, foreword, prologue, pronunciation guide, footnote, epilogue, endnote, stage directions*

Illustrations

- Notice and remember the important events of a story using the pictures (after hearing the text read several times)

- Follow and understand some texts that have no illustrations

- Understand that there can be different interpretations of the meaning of an illustration

- Use details from illustrations and text to support points made in discussion

- Interpret some illustrations with symbolic characteristics: e.g., use of color or symbols

- Notice how illustrations and graphics go together with the text in a meaningful way

- Notice how illustrations and graphics can reflect the theme or the writer's tone

- Notice and infer how illustrations contribute to mood in a fiction text

- Recognize how illustrations relate to the use of symbolism

Book and Print Features

- Notice and use and understand the purpose of some organizational tools: e.g., title, table of contents, chapter title

- Notice and use and understand the purpose of some other text resources: e.g., glossary

- Notice and use and understand the purpose of some text resources outside the body (peritext): e.g., dedication, acknowledgments, author's note, illustrator's note, endpapers, foreword, prologue, pronunciation guide, footnote, epilogue, appendix, endnote, references

- Notice and understand other features of the peritext that have symbolic or cultural significance or add to aesthetic enjoyment

- Infer the cultural or symbolic significance of the peritext (for example, design features)

- Appreciate artistry in text design: e.g., book jacket, cover, end pages, title page, margins, chapter headings, illumination

- Evaluate what some text resources contribute to the meaning of a text

---

● Thinking *Within* the Text   ◆ Thinking *Beyond* the Text   ■ Thinking *About* the Text

Selecting Goals Behaviors and Understandings to Notice, Teach, and Support *(cont.)*

Interactive Read-Aloud and Literature Discussion

NONFICTION TEXTS

General

- ● Ask questions to deepen understanding of a text
- ● Notice and ask questions when meaning is lost or understanding is interrupted
- ● Refer to important information and details and use as evidence to support opinions and statements during discussion
- ● Understand content that reflects beginning understandings of physical world and social world: e.g., health, social studies, science, mathematics, arts
- ● Notice and respond to stress and tone of voice while listening and afterward
- ● Notice and remember the important events of a text when a writer uses temporal or chronological sequence
- ● Notice and remember the important information in a text
- ● Notice and understand information provided from primary sources that are embedded in the text
- ● Provide a concise and logically organized summary of a text after hearing it read
- ● Sustain attention for some longer texts that may require several days to complete
- ◆ Synthesize new information and ideas and revise thinking in response to it
- ◆ Form explicit and implicit questions about the content and concepts in a text
- ◆ Understand the problems that occur in everyday life, including some complex problems that may relate to readers' lives
- ◆ Make connections to their own lives and contemporary issues and problems across all genres
- ◆ Give reasons (either text-based or from personal experience) to support thinking
- ◆ Use background knowledge of content to understand nonfiction topics
- ◆ Use background knowledge of history to understand simple biography, autobiography, and memoir
- ◆ Recognize and understand that nonfiction texts may reflect a wide range of diverse settings, languages, and cultures
- ◆ Use evidence from the text to support statements about it
- ◆ Use evidence from the text to support predictions
- ◆ Relate the messages in a nonfiction text to one's own life
- ◆ Change opinions based on new information or insights gained from nonfiction texts

- ◆ Relate important information and concepts in one text and connect to information and concepts in other texts
- ◆ Understand texts that require the application of knowledge of academic disciplines (sciences, history, humanities)
- ◆ Draw information from secondary sources and other sources that may be in a nonfiction text
- ■ Identify and discuss interesting, surprising, and important information in a text
- ■ Form and express opinions about a text and support with rationale and evidence
- ■ Form and state the basis for opinions about authors and illustrators
- ■ Connect texts by a range of categories: e.g., content, message, genre, author/illustrator, special form, text structure, or organization
- ■ Think critically about the quality of a nonfiction text: e.g., quality of writing contribution of illustration and other graphic design, accuracy
- ■ Critique the text in terms of quality of writing, organization, clarity, authenticity
- ■ Critique the text in terms of bias, stereotypes, prejudice, misrepresentation, sexism, racism

Genre

- ◆ Infer the importance of a subject's accomplishments (biography)
- ◆ Distinguish between fact and opinion in a text in order to reach new understanding
- ■ Notice and understand the characteristics of some specific nonfiction genres: e.g., expository, narrative, procedural and persuasive texts, biography, autobiography, memoir, hybrid text
- ■ Understand that a biography is the story of a person's life written by someone else
- ■ Understand that biographies are often set in the past
- ■ Understand that all autobiography is an account of a person's life written by that person
- ■ Understand that a memoir is an account of a memory or set of memories written by the person who experienced it
- ■ Notice when a writer is describing a step-by-step procedure
- ■ Notice a writer's use of argument and persuasion
- ■ Notice counterarguments and evidence against those counterarguments in a text
- ■ Recognize hybrid texts and distinguish which sections are nonfiction and fiction

---

● Thinking *Within* the Text   ◆ Thinking *Beyond* the Text   ■ Thinking *About* the Text

Selecting Goals Behaviors and Understandings to Notice, Teach, and Support *(cont.)*

Interactive Read-Aloud and Literature Discussion

NONFICTION TEXTS *(continued)*

- ■ Notice and appreciate forms and genres embedded in the main form or genre
- ■ Recognize and understand some specific forms of nonfiction: e.g., series books; picture books; letters, diaries, and journals entries; photo essays and news articles
- ■ Recognize and understand some specific types of poetry when they appear in nonfiction: e.g., lyrical poetry, free verse, limerick, haiku, narrative poetry, ballad, epic/saga, concrete poetry
- ■ Notice and understand some elements of poetry when they appear in nonfiction: e.g., figurative language, rhyme, repetition, onomatopoeia, layout/line breaks (shape), imagery, alliteration, assonance

Organization

- ● Follow and understand nonfiction texts with clearly defined overall structure, categories, and subcategories and connect the structure to the table of contents
- ● Be aware of when the teacher is reading bulleted or numbered lists
- ● Understand the use of headings and subheadings
- ● Use headings and subheadings to search for and use information
- ● Refer to the location of some important information (category of information, supporting details, main ideas)
- ● Understand and search for information in nonfiction texts that are organized in a variety of ways (e.g., problem/solution, cause/effect, compare/contrast, description/list, time order sequence, categorical)
- ■ Understand that a nonfiction text can be expository or narrative in structure and that the writer selects the structure for a specific purpose
- ■ Notice the organization of a nonfiction text, distinguishing between expository and narrative structure
- ■ Notice a nonfiction writer's use of narrative text structure in biography, memoir, autobiography, and other types of narrative nonfiction
- ■ Notice a writer's use of primary and secondary sources as integral parts of a text
- ■ Recognize and understand a writer's use of underlying text structures: e.g., description, cause and effect, sequence (chronological, temporal), categorization, compare and contrast, problem and solution, question and answer, combination

- ■ Notice a nonfiction writer's use of categories and subcategories to organize an informational text (expository)
- ■ Understand that a writer can tell about something that usually happens in the same order (temporal sequence) and something that happens in time order (chronological order)
- ■ Think critically about the way a writer has organized information (clear presentation, logic, appropriate to purpose)

Topic

- ◆ Show curiosity about topics encountered in nonfiction texts and actively work to learn more about them
- ◆ Think across texts to construct knowledge of a topic
- ◆ Think across texts to compare and expand understanding of content and ideas from academic disciplines: e.g., social responsibility, environment, climate, history, social and geological history, cultural groups
- ◆ Infer the importance of a topic of a nonfiction text
- ◆ Infer the writer's attitude toward a topic
- ◆ Infer a writer's purpose in a nonfiction text
- ◆ Infer a writer's stance (position, argument, or thesis) toward a topic or the subject of a biography
- ◆ Infer the writer's perspective (the angle or viewpoint)
- ◆ Recognize that a wide variety of informational texts may be about different places and that customs and people's behavior may reflect those settings
- ◆ Recognize that informational texts may present a larger topic with many subtopics
- ◆ Extend understanding to nonfiction topics and content that are beyond most students' immediate experience: e.g., living organisms; reproduction and heredity; ecology; land forms and topography; astronomy; events and periods in United States history
- ■ Understand that a writer is presenting facts about a single topic
- ■ Notice the topic of a text and that subtopics are related to the main topic
- ■ Think across texts to compare the stance of two or more writers on the same topic
- ■ Hypothesize the writer's reasons for choosing a topic and infer how the writer feels about a topic
- ■ Evaluate the writer's qualifications for writing on a topic
- ■ Evaluate the significance of a nonfiction topic

● Thinking *Within* the Text   ◆ Thinking *Beyond* the Text   ■ Thinking *About* the Text

Selecting Goals Behaviors and Understandings to Notice, Teach, and Support *(cont.)*

Interactive Read-Aloud and Literature Discussion

NONFICTION TEXTS *(continued)*

Messages and Main Ideas

- ● Follow arguments in a persuasive text
- ◆ Understand that there can be different interpretations of the meanings of a text
- ◆ Think across texts to compare and expand understanding of content and ideas from academic disciplines: social responsibility, environment, climate, history, social and geological history, cultural groups
- ◆ Understand the relationships among ideas and content in an expository nonfiction text (larger topic with subtopics)
- ◆ Connect the information in nonfiction books to disciplinary studies
- ◆ Infer the significance of nonfiction content for their own lives
- ◆ Infer the larger (main) ideas or messages in a nonfiction text
- ◆ Understand themes and ideas that are mature issues and require experience to interpret
- ◆ Recognize underlying political messages in nonfiction texts
- ■ Understand that a nonfiction text can have more than one message or big (main) idea
- ■ Distinguish fact from opinion
- ■ Identify contradictions (statements that disagree with each other) in a nonfiction text
- ■ Derive and critique the moral lesson in a nonfiction text

Style and Language

- ● Understand sentence structure that varies according to purpose (e.g., headings, captions, labels, numbered and bulleted lists) in nonfiction
- ◆ Infer the writer's perspective (angle)
- ◆ Infer the writer's tone in a nonfiction text by noticing selection of information, word choice, and language
- ■ Notice and think critically about a writer's word choice
- ■ Notice language that conveys an emotional atmosphere (mood) in a text, affecting how the reader feels: e.g., tension, sadness, whimsicality, joy
- ■ Notice language that expresses the author's attitude or feelings toward a subject reflected in the style of writing (tone): e.g., lighthearted, ironic, earnest, affectionate, formal
- ■ Notice how the writer reveals the setting in a biographical, historical, or other narrative nonfiction text
- ■ Notice and understand multiple points of view on the same topic
- ■ Think critically about the way a writer reveals different viewpoints or perspectives
- ■ Assess the objectivity with which a nonfiction topic is presented
- ■ Recognize bias and be able to identify evidence of it

- ■ Recognize a writer's use of the techniques for persuasion in a persuasive text
- ■ Notice and critique how a writer uses logical reasoning and specific evidence to support argument
- ■ Identify and critique specific language a writer uses to persuade
- ■ Analyze several texts to determine aspects of an individual writer's style: e.g., use of language, choice of topic, expression of ideas
- ■ Recognize some authors by the topics they choose or the style of their illustrations

Accuracy

- ■ Critically examine the quality or accuracy of the text, citing evidence for opinions
- ■ Notice and evaluate the accuracy of the information presented in the text and across texts
- ■ Evaluate the way the writer of an argument supports statements with evidence

Vocabulary

- ● Continue to build vocabulary as a foundation for recognizing words in print
- ● Notice and acquire understanding of new vocabulary from read-aloud content
- ● Acquire new content words from texts and graphics
- ● Use new vocabulary in discussion of a text and in writing about reading
- ● Derive the meaning of words from the context of a sentence, paragraph, or the whole text
- ● Learn many words that do not appear frequently in oral conversation but are used in writing (Tier 2)
- ● Understand the meaning of words representing all parts of speech when listening to a nonfiction text read aloud
- ● Understand the meaning of common (simple), sophisticated, and academic connectives when listening to a nonfiction text read aloud
- ● Acquire vocabulary that is specialized and related to scientific domains (Tier 3) especially in nonfiction
- ● Notice and understand the meaning of technical words particular to academic disciplines
- ● Understand the connotative meanings of words that are essential to understanding the text
- ● Understand the meaning of figurative words that are essential to understanding the text
- ● Understand words with multiple meanings within the same text, often signaling subtly different meanings

---

- ● Thinking *Within* the Text
- ◆ Thinking *Beyond* the Text
- ■ Thinking *About* the Text

Selecting Goals Behaviors and Understandings to Notice, Teach, and Support *(cont.)*

Interactive Read-Aloud and Literature Discussion

NONFICTION TEXTS *(continued)*

- ■ Use some academic language to talk about nonfiction genres: e.g., *nonfiction, personal memory story, informational text, informational book, factual text, biography, autobiography, narrative nonfiction, memoir, procedural text, persuasive text, hybrid text, expository text*

- ■ Use some academic language to talk about forms: e.g., *picture book, wordless picture book, label book, ABC book, counting book, poem, poetry, nursery rhyme, rhyme, song, series book, play, letter, poetry collection, sequel, limerick, haiku, concrete poetry, diary entry, journal entry, news article, feature article, narrative poetry, photo essay, speech, lyrical poetry, free verse, ballad, epic/saga*

- ■ Use some academic language to talk about literary features: e.g., *beginning, ending, problem, question and answer, solution, topic, description, problem and solution, message, dialogue, main idea, comparison and contrast, setting, cause and effect, categorization, descriptive language, figurative language, metaphor, simile, persuasive language, temporal sequence, chronological sequence, subject, argument, personification, symbol, symbolism, second-person narrative, tone, irony, monologue*

- ■ Use some academic language to talk about book and print features: e.g., *front cover, back cover, title, author, illustrator, page, text, illustration, photograph, label, table of contents, acknowledgments, chapter, section, heading, drawing, caption, map, chapter title, dedication, author's note, illustrator's note, section, diagram, glossary, endpapers, sidebar, book jacket, subheading, chart, graph, timeline, index, cutaway, foreword, prologue, pronunciation guide, footnote, epilogue, endnote, appendix, references, stage directions, bibliography*

Illustrations/Graphics

- ● Understand that graphics provide important information
- ● Follow and understand some texts that have no graphics or illustrations

- ◆ Recognize and use information in a variety of graphics: e.g., photo and/or drawing with label or caption, diagram, cutaway, infographic, map with legend and scale
- ◆ Use details from illustrations to support points made in discussion
- ■ Notice how illustrations and graphics help to communicate the writer's message
- ■ Understand that graphics and text are carefully placed in a nonfiction text so that ideas are communicated clearly

Book and Print Features

- ● Notice a text's title and the name of its author and illustrator on the cover and title page
- ◆ Gain new understandings from searching for and using information found in text body, sidebars, and graphics
- ■ Notice and use and understand the purpose of some organizational tools: e.g., title, table of contents, chapter title, heading, subheading
- ■ Notice and use and understand the purpose of some other text resources: e.g., glossary, index
- ■ Notice and use and understand the purpose of some text resources outside the body (peritext): e.g., dedication, acknowledgments, author's note, illustrator's note, endpapers, foreword, prologue, pronunciation guide, footnote, epilogue, appendix, endnote, references
- ■ Notice and understand other features of the peritext that have symbolic value, add to aesthetic enjoyment, or add meaning
- ■ Appreciate artistry in text design: e.g., book jacket, cover, end pages, title page (peritext)
- ■ Evaluate the effectiveness of page layout and design of a text and connect if to the culture represented or the main ideas
- ■ Evaluate what some text resources contribute to the meaning of a text

---

● Thinking **Within** the Text   ◆ Thinking **Beyond** the Text   ■ Thinking **About** the Text

Shared and Performance Reading

Shared and Performance Reading Continuum

Shared reading and performance reading have many of the same goals as interactive read-aloud, but they go beyond active listening and discussion: Students actually participate in the reading in some way. We define shared reading and performance reading as instructional contexts that involve reading aloud for the pleasure of oneself and others. All forms of performed reading involve:

- processing print in continuous text;
- working in a group (usually);
- oral reading of a common text;
- using the voice to interpret the meaning of a text;
- reading in unison with others, although there may be parts or solos; and
- opportunities to learn more about the reading process.

Shared reading has an important role in extending students' ability to process and understand texts across the grades. In the early years, shared reading gives children a high level of support in reading beginning texts. They learn how print "works" and develop a strong early reading process. Your support and the support of the group help them as they process texts that are more complex than their current abilities. It gives them a "step up" in the development of the reading process. Across the grades, even after readers have a well-established reading process, they need to continue to expand their abilities in many ways, and shared reading can play an important role in that. Through shared reading, intermediate and advanced readers can further develop their competencies in word analysis, vocabulary, fluency, and comprehension. They consider the text in new ways as they represent it through the voice in readers' theater, and they engage in close analysis of a text or a piece of a text that they all share.

Materials for beginning shared reading are listed in the text characteristics of this continuum, and you will notice a gradual change across the grades. Shared reading might start with big books and enlarged simple poems and progress to readers' theater scripts, plays, or just about any text that you want to enlarge and have all students consider. For early readers the basic components of a shared reading lesson are:

1. Introduce the text: You say a few words about the text and invite some conversation that is directed toward reading it.

2. Model reading of the text: The first reading of the text is by the teacher, and it is followed by a brief discussion.

3. Read the text together: You invite the students to join in with you on the second reading.

4. Discuss the text: You guide the conversation about the meaning of the text, inviting students to share their thinking.

5. Teach for specific strategic actions: You select a specific part of the text to visit to make a teaching point (or make the point during a subsequent reading).

6. Do repeated readings: You revisit the text to read it several more times on subsequent days, each time engaging students in discussion or making a teaching point (for example, locating words or word parts, noticing interesting words, practicing tricky language phrases).

7. Invite independent reading: Here, you give students the opportunity to read the text independently or with a partner using the big book or poem or a small individual version.

8. Provide extended language and literacy opportunities: You engage students in further exploration of the text if there is interest and need.

Intermediate students, too, can benefit from delving into complex texts in shared reading. For example, a text may have not only words that students can read with accuracy but also significant challenges in comprehension and/or literary elements that you want students to consider at a closer level. Discussing a text in preparation for readers' theater or choral reading is a great opportunity. It offers an authentic reason to read aloud and also involves students in a community-building effort. The transition from early to later ways of implementing shared reading is not abrupt; rather, it is gradual, as this continuum describes.

In *Teaching for Comprehending and Fluency: Thinking, Talking, and Writing About Reading, K–8* (Fountas and Pinnell, Heinemann 2006), we described three contexts for shared and performance reading.

1. *Shared reading* usually refers to students reading from a common enlarged text, either a large-print book, a chart, or a projected text. Alternately, students may have their own copies. The teacher leads the group, pointing to words or phrases. Reading is usually in unison, although there are adaptations, such as groups alternating lines or individuals reading some lines.

2. *Choral reading* usually refers to any group of people reading from a common text, which may be printed on a chart, projected on a screen, or provided as individual copies. The text is usually longer and/or more complex than one used for shared reading. The emphasis is on interpreting the text with the voice. Some reading is in unison by the whole group or subgroups, and there may be solos or duets.

3. *Readers' theater* usually refers to the enactment of a text in which readers assume individual or group roles. Readers' theater is similar to traditional play production, but the text is generally not memorized and props are rarely used. The emphasis is on vocal interpretation. Usually individuals read parts although groups may read some roles. Readers' theater scripts can be constructed from all kinds of texts—novels, short stories, poems, speeches, screenplays, but not from original plays.

In selecting and using books and other written texts for shared and performance reading, you need to consider some of the same kinds of factors that you would for guided and independent reading; after all, students do need to be able to read and understand them. However, since you will be providing a high level of support and students will be reading texts many times, it is not necessary to use the A–Z levels (see Guided Reading continuum in this book, pages 399–630). Instead, consider features such as interesting language, rhyme and rhythm, language play, poetic language, emotional appeal to students, and other aspects of texts that make them a good basis for performance.

Characteristics of Texts for Shared and Performance Reading

In thinking about texts for shared and performance reading, we again consider the ten text factors. As with interactive read-aloud, consider whether the vocabulary in the text is understandable to listeners, but word solving is a relatively minor issue. Students can easily pronounce and appreciate words like *fantabulous* or *humongous* in humorous poems or words like *somber* or *ponderous* from readers' theater once they are taught the meaning of the words. In fact, shared and performance reading is a great way to expand vocabulary.

The most important characteristic of texts you elect for shared and performance reading is that *they must be engaging and pleasurable enough* to be worthy of spending whole-class or small-group time on them and/or for students to read them again and again. This makes shared reading texts fundamentally different from those that students are interested in enough to read once. Another characteristic to keep in mind is that texts for shared reading are short. They may be:

- big books (14¼″ x 18 to 15″ x 20″) that are published for the purpose of shared reading and that are sixteen to about thirty-two pages;
- posters;
- enlarged charts (both published and handwritten) that can have poems, songs, chants, class-composed stories or records, and lists;
- individual copies of poems, songs, or chants;
- individual copies of readers' theater scripts, which may be drawn from longer texts that students have read; or
- excerpts from longer texts students have read or you have read to them that are enlarged for the class to see.

An exception might be a play that students read, but even here, you will usually select one-act plays or excerpts from plays.

Even in these shorter texts, students can experience a wide variety of genre and text characteristics. So, in the continuum that follows, we use the ten text characteristics (see Figure I-4) of texts to describe texts for shared and performance reading; however, keep in mind that we are referring to short texts or excerpts from longer texts. Figure I–4 provides descriptions of all ten text characteristics, in terms of shared and performance reading.

Curriculum Goals

We have stated curriculum goals in terms of behaviors and understandings to notice and support at each level. These systems of strategic actions are further divided into evidence that the reader is thinking *within, beyond,* or *about* the text.

- *Within the Text.* To effectively and efficiently process a text and derive the literal meaning, readers must solve the words and monitor and self-correct their reading. During shared and performance reading, students need to follow what the text is saying, picking up important information that will help them reflect that meaning in their voices. They must self-monitor their own understanding, remember information in summary form, and sometimes adjust their reading to reflect the genre. One of the major benefits of shared and performance reading is that students are producing a fluent, phrased, and expressive oral reading of a text or version of a text. This instructional setting provides a great deal of practice, group support, and an authentic reason to read aloud (not simply to let the teacher check on you).

▶ *Beyond the Text.* Readers make predictions and connections based on previous knowledge and their own lives. They also make connections between and among texts. They bring background knowledge to the reading of a text, synthesize new information by incorporating it into their own understandings, and think about what the writer has not stated but implied. Readers may infer the feelings and motivations of characters in fiction texts or the implications of the writer's statements in nonfiction. To interpret with voice, readers must actively seek meaning and even consider alternative meanings for a text. Shared reading, choral reading, and readers' theater all provide many opportunities for thinking beyond the text. To read with a character's voice, for example, you need to think deeply about how that character feels. Reading a speech requires inferring the passion of a speaker. Reading pro and con arguments means inferring the logic of each and presenting them dynamically.

▶ *About the Text.* Readers think analytically about the text as an object, noticing and appreciating elements of the writer's craft, such as use of language, characterization, organization, and structure. Reading like a writer helps students notice aspects of craft and more fully enjoy a text, sometimes prompting them to revisit it. Readers also think critically about texts, evaluating the quality and considering the writer's accuracy or objectivity. Texts are selected and created for shared and performance reading based on the quality of the writing and the power of the ideas. When students perform parts of a text or a readers' theater script made from a text, they have the opportunity to get to know the language. They may internalize and sometimes even memorize some powerful language. Through shared and performance reading you and your students can build a large repertoire of shared texts that can be revisited often to notice more about the writer's craft.

Organization

This continuum is organized by grade level. For each grade level, the first part, Selecting Texts, describes text characteristics for the books you read aloud. The items are organized according to the ten text characteristics listed in Figure I-1 on pages 108–109. You are reading the books, of course, so you can make available texts that students cannot yet read for themselves. But you will still want to consider:

▶ the complexity and challenge of the genre;

▶ the vocabulary that students can stretch to understand;

▶ the age-appropriateness of the content and concepts;

▶ the appeal to students at this age;

▶ the appropriateness of the text for use in shared reading.

In the next section for each grade, Selecting Goals, we list goals that are categorized for thinking *within, beyond,* and *about* texts. The goals for using fiction and nonfiction texts are categorized by areas of understanding. The shape of the bullet designates the behavior as thinking within the text [●], beyond the text [◆], or about the text [■]. These goals are stated in the form of specific behaviors and understandings students need to develop in order to understand and learn from the texts that are being read.

For the text characteristics and goals, new items for the grade level are marked with a red bullet. This will help you find the new challenges quickly. But don't forget that *all* of the text characteristics and goals are important. In other words, the behavior or understanding may be the same, but students are challenged to *apply* it to more complex texts at each grade level.

Using the Shared and Performance Reading Continuum

The continuum does not reference specific texts, topics, or content areas. You can apply the continuum's goals in connection with your district or state requirements. You can use this guide to set overall curriculum goals for grades PreK–8, or you can refer to it as you plan for and assess your teaching of shared and performance reading.

FIGURE I-1 *Ten Characteristics of Texts for Shared and Performance Reading*

Genre	We have listed a variety of types of texts that are appropriate at each grade level. We include poetry, songs, and chants. For the most part, you will want to use the full range of genres at every grade level, but be selective about the particular examples you choose. Use both fiction and nonfiction texts for shared and performance reading. Often, a narrative text is turned into a play or poetic text to create readers' theater scripts.
Text Structure	The structure of a text refers to the way it is organized. Fiction texts are generally organized as *narratives* with a problem and a sequence of events that lead to the resolution of the problem. Younger students generally read short texts that have humor or rhyme. Traditional tales are an excellent resource. When longer texts are turned into plays or readers' theater scripts, they are generally shortened: Students present a particular moment in time, perform the essence of the plot, or show the main character's feelings or point of view. Nonfiction texts may also be narrative; biographies, for example, are relatively easy to turn into readers' theater scripts, and so are narrative nonfiction texts. A narrative fiction or nonfiction text can be turned into a poem and remain a narrative, or it can take another structure. Many informational texts are organized categorically by subtopic with underlying structures such as description; temporal sequence; comparison and contrast; cause and effect; and problem and solution. Often these structures are used in combination. Through shared or performance reading, your students can highlight some of the underlying structures, and they will enjoy turning some content area learning (for example, a text on environmental pollution or a period of history) into readers' theater.
Content	The subject matter of the text should be accessible and interesting to listeners. Content is helpful to listeners when they already have some prior knowledge to bring to understanding new information. Through shared and performance reading, particularly of biography, students can think deeply about many different topics.
Themes and Ideas	Choose texts for shared and performance reading with ideas and themes that are appropriate for all students' age and experience. Students can extend their understanding of the themes and ideas as they discuss how texts should be read or performed.
Language and Literary Features	The way the writer uses language creates the literary quality of a text. It is important to select texts that students can understand in terms of language and literary features. Shared reading and performance reading provide an ideal setting in which to "try on" different interpretations of a text through changes in the voice.
Sentence Complexity	The structure of the sentences–their length and the number of embedded phrases and clauses–is another key factor. Through the primary and elementary grades, students can generally understand sentences that are more complex than those they can read independently. Practicing sentences for performance helps students internalize various sentence structures and also process longer and more complex sentences than they can read independently or write.

Vocabulary	Vocabulary refers to the words that an individual knows and understands in both oral and written language. Working with a text in shared or performance reading, students have the opportunity to meet new words many times and thus expand their vocabularies. It is important that students understand the text used in shared and performance reading; they will not enjoy the activity if they do not understand the words. Nonetheless, shared reading supports them in using many complex and unusual words that will delight them.
Words	You will be offering high support for word solving, and students will be reading selections several times, so words are not a major factor in choosing texts. You will want to select texts with words that students understand and can pronounce with your help. Shared and performance reading offer an excellent context within which students can learn more about how words work. As repeated readings make a text familiar, students will gradually add to the core of high-frequency words they know. They will also begin to notice beginnings, endings, and other parts of words and make connections between words.
Illustrations	Many texts used as a basis for shared and performance reading in the early grades are full of illustrations that help students interpret them. Along with the teacher support inherent in shared and performance reading, illustrations enable early readers to read higher-level big books together. For intermediate/middle students, too, performance reading may be based on picture books (fiction and nonfiction) that have illustrations contributing to the mood. Sometimes, students may perform their reading in conjunction with a slide show of some important illustrations. For other texts, however, illustrations may not be a factor. If you have enlarged text with graphics and other text features, you can use them effectively in shared reading to provide a powerful demonstration of how readers process and use this information. This setting, too, gives readers an opportunity to use academic vocabulary to talk about text features. At higher grades, teachers sometimes enlarge a page of a text to help students look at a common example.
Book and Print Features	When early readers are engaged in shared reading of enlarged texts (books and poems), print features such as length, layout, clarity of font, and number of lines on a page affect their ability to participate. In general, students can read more complex texts in shared reading than they can in guided or independent reading, but you will not want to overload them. Even intermediate/middle readers might find it difficult to read a long and complex poem in unison from an overhead transparency. For readers' theater, you may want to retype sections of a text so students can highlight their parts. We address book and print features for shared reading in kindergarten through grade three. Organizational tools like the table of contents, glossary, pronunciation guide, indexes, sidebars, and headings are not included here since they would only occasionally be a focus of shared reading. Shared and performance reading is a good context, however, for students to learn varying formats for print, for example, plays and other scripts, debates, speeches, poems, newscasts, etc.

Selecting Texts Characteristics of Texts for Sharing and Performing

Shared and Performance Reading

GENRE

▶ **Fiction**

- Realistic fiction
- Folktale
- Simple animal fantasy

▶ **Nonfiction**

- Simple factual texts
- Memoir (personal memory story)
- Simple procedural texts

FORMS

- Short poems
- Nursery rhymes, rhymes, and songs
- Enlarged poems, nursery rhymes, rhymes, and songs
- Picture books
- Wordless picture books
- Enlarged picture books
- Label books
- Concept books
- ABC books
- Counting books
- Books with texture, padding, popups, see-through holes, unusual features that promote interaction
- Texts produced through interactive and shared writing: e.g., lists, name charts, directions, sequences of actions, stories, poems, descriptions, dialogue from stories

TEXT STRUCTURE

- Simple narratives with beginning, series of episodes, and ending
- Many books with repeating episodes or patterns
- Some texts with nonnarrative structure
- Most texts focusing on a single topic, usually one idea per page
- Underlying structural patterns: simple description, some temporal sequence, some question and answer

CONTENT

- Content that is appropriate for children's cognitive development, emotional maturity, and life experience
- Content that engages children's intellectual curiosity and emotions
- Content that nurtures children's imaginations
- Language and word play: e.g., rhymes, nonsense, alliteration, and alphabet
- Content appropriate for preschool that reflects early conceptual understandings: e.g., colors, shapes, counting, sorting, size, alphabet, position
- Everyday actions familiar to young children: e.g., playing, making t hings, eating, getting dressed, bathing, cooking, shopping
- Familiar topics (e.g., animals, pets, families, friends, the five senses, growing and health, school, neighborhood, weather and seasons, food, plants) that are authentic and relevant
- Humor that is easy to grasp: e.g., silly characters, funny situations
- Content that reinforces and expands a child's experience and knowledge of self and the world
- A few topics that may be beyond some children's immediate experiences (farm, zoo)
- Content that reflects a wide range of settings, languages, and cultures
- Characters, settings, and events that could exist in real life
- Imaginary characters, events (some nonsensical and funny), and settings that occur in fantasy
- Content that reflects beginning understanding of the physical and social world
- Content focused on one simple topic

THEMES AND IDEAS

- Themes reflecting everyday life: e.g., self, family relationships, friendship, imagination, feelings, bravery, cleverness, wisdom, nature, cultural sensitivity
- Clear, simple ideas easy to identify
- Ideas close to children's experience: e.g., expressing feelings, sharing with others, valuing differences, cooperating, helping, belonging, problem solving, working hard, being clever or wise, appreciating the sounds of language

LANGUAGE AND LITERARY FEATURES

- Poetic language
- Rhymes
- Rhythm and repetition of words and language patterns
- Many refrains
- Language that promotes and involves movement
- Predictable sequence of events and outcomes
- Both realistic and fantastic settings, events, and characters
- Simple plot with problem and solution that are easy to understand
- Multiple characters, each predictable and easy to understand
- Characters' actions related to clear consequences: e.g., reward for trying hard
- Simple dialogue easily attributed to characters
- Repetitive dialogue

SENTENCE COMPLEXITY

- Sentences written in natural language that is close to oral language
- Short, simple sentences that are easy for children to understand and remember
- Sentences with a limited number of adjectives
- Sentences with repeated clauses and phrases
- Sentences that are questions
- Sentences with dialogue, sometimes repeated
- Sentences with common (simple) connectives

VOCABULARY

- A few interesting words that are new to children but easy to understand in context
- A few content words (labels) related to concepts that children can understand
- Some memorable words of high interest and novelty: e.g., *huffed and puffed*
- All words that are in common oral vocabulary for young children (Tier 1)

Selecting Texts Characteristics of Texts for Sharing and Performing *(cont.)*

Shared and Performance Reading

- Some simple onomatopoetic words
- Some common (simple) connectives that are frequently used in oral language (words, phrases that clarify relationships and ideas): e.g., *and, but, so*

WORDS

- Many very simple high-frequency words
- Mostly one- or two-syllable words with a few interesting three-syllable words
- Mostly CVC and CVCE words
- Words that have the same rime: e.g., *bit, sit*
- Alliterative sequences
- Simple plurals using *-s* or *-es*
- Some complex plurals that are in children's oral vocabulary: e.g., *children, sheep*
- Some words with endings that are in children's oral vocabularies (e.g., *running, painted*) or that are easy to understand

ILLUSTRATIONS

- Large, clear, colorful illustrations in a variety of media that fully support meaning
- Details that add interest rather than overwhelm or distract
- Many pieces of shared and interactive writing with art created by children
- Some illustrations and photographs with labels

BOOK AND PRINT FEATURES

LENGTH

- Short books or poems, songs, chants that can be read in one sitting

PRINT AND LAYOUT

- All texts enlarged, big books and charts
- Print large enough for the whole group (or a small group) to see clearly
- Clear spaces between words and between lines
- Limited number of lines on a page (usually one or two), except in the case of a well-known short poem or song
- Very consistent layout across pages
- Layout that supports phrasing by presenting word groups
- Some words in boldface or varying font sizes
- Occasional variety in color of print

- Some print in speech bubbles or thought bubbles
- Some books with special features: e.g., flaps, see-through holes
- Page numbers

PUNCTUATION

- Simple punctuation: e.g., period, question mark, exclamation mark

ORGANIZATIONAL TOOLS

- Title, author, and illustrator on cover and on title page

Selecting Goals Behaviors and Understandings to Notice, Teach, and Support

Shared and Performance Reading

FICTION AND NONFICTION TEXTS

General

- Notice and talk about the important information in a text
- After reading an enlarged text with others, discuss what it is about
- ◆ Connect classroom experiences (e.g., lists, directions, recipes recorded in shared/interactive writing) with the oral reading of enlarged texts (charts, big books they created)
- ◆ Understand and learn new content by reading fiction and nonfiction texts with others
- ■ Express opinions about texts that are read in unison

Early Literacy Concepts

- Locate one's own name in print
- Read name chart (first and last name) with teacher support
- Begin to notice some letters in print
- Connect some letters in print to one's own name or a known word
- Begin to notice some features of words (i.e., some letters)
- Begin to notice aspects of print to help in tracking words when reading in chorus
- Begin to notice that a word is defined by space on either side
- Use left-to-right directionality, word-by-word matching, and return sweep to monitor reading with teacher support
- Demonstrate awareness of some print conventions: e.g., turning pages, reading top to bottom, distinguishing print from pictures

- Follow the teacher's pointer with the eyes (left to right with return sweep to the next level) to read enlarged texts of one, two, or three lines
- Begin using features of print in enlarged texts to search for and use visual information: e.g., letters, words, "first" and "last" word, period
- Begin to search print for visual information

Letters

- Read a simple alphabet chart with high level of teacher support
- Notice letters in an enlarged text

Words

- Discuss words with others

Language Structure (Syntax)

- Use memory of repeating language patterns to monitor accuracy
- Search for information when processing simple sentences during choral reading: e.g., short, natural language; limited number of adjectives and adverbs; repeated clauses
- ◆ Understand when language in a story sounds like someone is talking
- ◆ Use language syntax and repeating language patterns to anticipate the text: e.g., next word, next phrase, or sentences

Vocabulary

- Understand the meaning of new words encountered in print
- Notice and use words that add action or emotion to a text: e.g., words that stand for sounds, some expressions

---

● Thinking ***Within*** the Text   ◆ Thinking ***Beyond*** the Text   ■ Thinking ***About*** the Text

SHARED AND PERFORMANCE READING

Selecting Goals Behaviors and Understandings to Notice, Teach, and Support *(cont.)*

Shared and Performance Reading

FICTION AND NONFICTION TEXTS *(continued)*

- Understand the meaning of simple plurals
- Understand the meaning of words in one's own oral vocabulary
- Remember and use new language (e.g., specific words, refrains, expressions) from reading enlarged texts in chorus
- ◆ Understand some common (simple) connectives that link ideas and clarify meaning and are frequently used in oral language: e.g., *and, but, so*

Fluency

- Assisted by unison reading, use phrasing, pausing, word stress, and intonation
- When reading in unison, remember and use repeating phrases with intonation
- When reading in unison, recognize dialogue and adjust the voice to reflect it

Performance

- Mimic the teacher's expression when reading enlarged print texts in chorus

Messages and Themes

- Follow and understand the ideas in simple poems and rhymes in enlarged texts
- ◆ Infer a "lesson" from reading a very simple version of a folktale or other text in unison with others
- ◆ Understand a simple theme in a text: e.g., friendship, families, relationships, self, nature, feelings, cleverness

Literary Elements

- Follow and understand simple plots in enlarged fiction texts
- ◆ Use the events of the story (and memory from previous readings) to predict what will happen next
- ◆ Anticipate exciting places or the ending of a story by remembering previous readings
- ◆ Talk about personal connections made to content, characters, or events in a shared text
- ◆ Infer the feelings of characters in stories and poems
- ■ Notice and discuss similar stories, poems, rhymes, and songs
- ■ Notice and talk about how enlarged texts are alike or different
- ■ Notice a writer's use of rhyme and rhythm
- ■ Notice and use rhyme and rhythm to anticipate language in a poem or song
- ■ Use some academic language to talk about texts: e.g., *ABC book, poem, song, cover, title, author, illustrator, page, text, illustration, photograph, beginning, ending, problem*

Book and Print Features

- Begin to notice visual aspects of print to help monitor and correct: e.g., lines, words, and features of print such as letters, spaces between words, and simple punctuation
- ◆ Make connections between the body of the text and illustrations

---

- Thinking *Within* the Text
- ◆ Thinking *Beyond* the Text
- ■ Thinking *About* the Text

Selecting Texts Characteristics of Texts for Sharing and Performing

Shared and Performance Reading

GENRE

▶ **Fiction**

- Realistic fiction
- Folktale
- Simple animal fantasy

▶ **Nonfiction**

- Simple factual texts
- Memoir (personal memory story)
- Procedural texts

FORMS

- Short poems
- Nursery rhymes, rhymes, and songs
- Enlarged poems, nursery rhymes, rhymes, and songs
- Poetry collections
- Picture books
- Wordless picture books
- Enlarged picture books
- Label books
- Concept books
- ABC books
- Counting books
- Books with texture, padding, popups, unusual features that promote interaction
- Texts produced through interactive and shared writing: e.g., lists, name charts, directions, sequences of actions, stories, poems, descriptions, dialogue from stories

TEXT STRUCTURE

- Simple narratives with beginning, series of episodes, and ending
- Many books with repeating episodes or patterns
- Some texts with nonnarrative structure
- Stories with simple plot (problem and solution)
- Most texts focusing on a single topic, usually one idea per page
- Underlying structural patterns: description, temporal sequence, question and answer

CONTENT

- Content that is appropriate for children's cognitive development, emotional maturity, and life experience
- Content that engages children's intellectual curiosity and emotions
- Content that nurtures children's imaginations
- Language and word play: e.g., rhymes, nonsense, alliteration, and alphabet
- Appropriate content that reflects early conceptual understandings: e.g., colors, shapes, counting, sorting, size, alphabet, position
- Everyday actions familiar to young children: e.g., playing, making things, eating, getting dressed, bathing, cooking, shopping
- Familiar topics (e.g., animals, pets, families, friends, the five senses, growing and health, school, neighborhood, weather and seasons, food, plants) that are authentic and relevant
- Humor that is easy to grasp: e.g., silly characters, funny situations
- Content that reinforces and expands a child's experience and knowledge of self and the world
- A few topics that may be beyond some children's immediate experiences (farm, zoo, beach)
- Content that reflects a wide range of settings, languages, and cultures
- Characters, settings, and events that could exist in real life
- Imaginary characters, events (some nonsensical and funny), and settings that occur in fantasy
- Content that reflects beginning understanding of the physical and social world
- Content focused on one simple topic

THEMES AND IDEAS

- Themes reflecting everyday life: e.g., self, family relationships, friendship, imagination, feelings, bravery, cleverness, wisdom, nature, cultural sensitivity
- Clear, simple ideas easy to identify and understand

- Ideas close to children's experience: e.g., expressing feelings, sharing with others, valuing differences, cooperating, helping, belonging, problem solving, working hard, being clever or wise, appreciating the sounds of language

LANGUAGE AND LITERARY FEATURES

- Playful descriptive language, including made-up words and onomatopoetic words
- Poetic language
- Rhymes
- Rhythm and repetition of words and language patterns
- Many refrains
- Language that promotes and involves movement
- Predictable sequence of events and outcomes
- Both realistic and fantastic settings, events, and characters
- Simple plot with problem and solution that is easy to understand
- Multiple characters, each predictable and easy to understand
- Characters' actions related to clear consequences: e.g., reward for trying hard and good behavior, punishment for bad behavior
- Simple dialogue easily attributed to characters
- Repetitive dialogue
- Simple, straightforward procedural language

SENTENCE COMPLEXITY

- Sentences written in natural language that is close to oral language
- Short, simple sentences that are easy for children to understand and remember
- Sentences with a limited number of adjectives
- Sentences with repeated clauses and phrases
- Sentences that are questions
- Some sentences with adjectives, adverbs, and prepositions
- Sentences with dialogue, sometimes repeated

Selecting Texts Characteristics of Texts for Sharing and Performing *(cont.)*

Shared and Performance Reading

VOCABULARY

- Sentences with common (simple) connectives
- A few interesting words that are new to children but easy to understand in context
- A few content words (labels) related to concepts that children can understand
- A few new content words related to concepts that are easy to understand
- Some memorable words of high interest and novelty: e.g., *huffed and puffed*
- Almost all words that are in common oral vocabulary for young children (Tier 1)
- Some simple onomatopoetic words
- Common (simple) connectives that are frequently used in oral language (words, phrases that clarify relationships and ideas): e.g., *and, but, so, because, before, after*

WORDS

- Many very simple high-frequency words
- Mostly one- or two-syllable words with a few interesting three-syllable words
- Mostly CVC and CVCe words
- Words that have the same rime: e.g., *bit, sit*
- Many pairs or sets of rhyming words
- Alliterative sequences
- Simple plurals using *-s* or *-es*
- Some complex plurals that are in children's oral vocabulary: e.g., *children, sheep*
- Some words with endings that are in children's oral vocabularies (e.g., *running, painted*) or that are easy to understand
- Some simple contractions using some letters from words including *not, am,* and *are*

ILLUSTRATIONS

- Large, clear, colorful illustrations in a variety of media that fully support meaning
- Details that add interest rather than overwhelm or distract
- Many pieces of shared and interactive writing with art created by children
- Some illustrations and photographs with labels

BOOK AND PRINT FEATURES

LENGTH

- Short books or poems, songs, or chants that can be read in one sitting

PRINT AND LAYOUT

- All texts enlarged, big books and charts
- Print large enough for the whole group (or a small group) to see clearly
- Clear spaces between words and between lines
- Limited number of lines on a page (usually one or two), except in the case of a well-known short poem or song
- Very consistent layout across pages
- Layout that supports phrasing by presenting word groups
- Some words in boldface or varying font sizes
- Occasional variety in color of print
- Some print in speech bubbles or thought bubbles
- Some books with special features: e.g., flaps, see-through holes
- Page numbers

PUNCTUATION

- Simple punctuation: e.g., period, question mark, exclamation mark, comma, quotation marks

ORGANIZATIONAL TOOLS

- Title, author, and illustrator listed on cover and on title page

TEXT RESOURCES

- Some books with dedication, author's note

Selecting Goals Behaviors and Understandings to Notice, Teach, and Support

Shared and Performance Reading

FICTION AND NONFICTION TEXTS

General

- ● Notice and talk about the important information in a text
- ● After reading an enlarged text and/or a small, individual version with others, discuss what it is about
- ● Tell the major events of a story after reading it with others
- ● Tell facts, a sequence of events, or directions after reading a nonfiction text with others
- ◆ Connect classroom experiences (e.g., lists, directions, recipes recorded in shared/interactive writing) with the oral reading of enlarged texts (charts, class-made big books)
- ◆ Understand and learn new content by reading fiction and nonfiction texts (including those produced through interactive writing)
- ■ Express opinions about texts that are read in unison
- ■ Talk about what is interesting in a photograph or illustration
- ■ Talk about whether a text is interesting or enjoyable and why

Early Literacy Concepts

- ● Locate one's own name and names of others in print
- ● Read name chart (first and last name) with teacher support
- ● Notice and identify letters in print during and after reading with others
- ● Connect letters in enlarged print texts to one's own name and names of friends and family or a known word
- ● Notice features of words: e.g., letters, beginnings, endings, uppercase and lowercase letters
- ● Use features of print to track words when reading texts in chorus
- ● Understand that a word is defined by space on either side
- ● Demonstrate beginning control of early reading behaviors: e.g., left-to-right directionality, return sweep, word-by-word matching, simple punctuation, distinguishing word and letter
- ● Read left to right, with return sweep when reading with teacher and group support
- ● Use left-to-right directionality, word-by-word matching, and return sweep to monitor reading with teacher support
- ● Follow the teacher's pointer with the eyes (left to right with return sweep to the next level) to read enlarged print texts of two to six lines
- ● With teacher support, use features of print in enlarged texts to search for and use visual information: e.g., letters, words, "first" and "last" word, period
- ● Begin to search print for visual information

Letters

- ● Read a simple alphabet chart with teacher support
- ● Notice letters in an enlarged text

Letter-Sound Relationships

- ● Locate a word by predicting the first letter

Words

- ● Discuss words with others
- ● Begin to notice and connect features and parts of words: e.g., phonograms, first letter, word endings
- ● Recognize at least twenty-five high-frequency words in context with the support of teacher and group training
- ● Recognize most of the twenty-five high-frequency words in isolation
- ● When reading texts individually and in unison with teacher support, use return sweep and read with word-by-word matching of one- and two-syllable words
- ● Recognize some simple plurals, words that have the same rime (e.g., *bit, sit*), and simple contractions
- ● Notice syllables in words and count them by clapping
- ● Notice word endings that are in one's own oral vocabulary: e.g., *running, painted*
- ● Locate known high-frequency words in print

Language Structure (Syntax)

- ● Use memory of repeating language patterns to monitor accuracy
- ● Search for information when processing simple sentences during choral reading: e.g., short, natural language; limited number of adjectives and adverbs; repeated clauses
- ◆ Understand when language in a story sounds like talking (simple dialogue)
- ◆ Use language syntax and repeating language patterns to anticipate the text: e.g., next word, next phrase, or sentences

Vocabulary

- ● Understand the meaning of new words after reading and talking about them
- ● Notice and use words that add action or emotion to a text: e.g., words that represent sounds, some expressions
- ● Recognize and understand the meaning of simple plurals
- ● Understand the meaning of words that are in one's own oral vocabulary
- ● Understand the meaning of words used in common oral language (Tier 1)
- ● Notice and understand words that are of high interest and novelty: e.g., *huffed and puffed*
- ● Understand the meaning of words that represent sounds: e.g., *buzz*
- ● Understand the meaning of a few new content words that are supported by the text, pictures, the teacher, and choral reading

---

● Thinking **Within** the Text   ◆ Thinking **Beyond** the Text   ■ Thinking **About** the Text

Selecting Goals Behaviors and Understandings to Notice, Teach, and Support *(cont.)*

Shared and Performance Reading

FICTION AND NONFICTION TEXTS *(continued)*

- ◆ Understand some common (simple) connectives that link ideas and clarify meaning and are frequently used in oral language: e.g., *and, but, so, because, before, after*
- ◆ Remember and use new language (e.g., specific words, refrains, expressions) from reading enlarged texts in unison

Fluency

- ● Use phrasing, pausing, and word stress with intonation when reading in unison
- ● When reading in unison, remember and use repeating phrases with intonation
- ● Use line breaks to guide phrasing when reading in chorus
- ● Adjust the voice to reflect dialogue in the body of the text and in speech bubbles or thought bubbles

Performance

- ● Mimic the teacher's expression when reading enlarged texts in chorus
- ● Recognize and reflect some simple punctuation with the voice (e.g., period, question mark, exclamation mark) when reading in chorus or individually
- ● Recognize and reflect variations in print with the voice (e.g., italics, bold type, special treatments, font size) when reading in chorus or individually
- ● When reading individually or in unison with others (with teacher support), adjust the voice to reflect emotional aspects of the text: e.g., humor, surprise, suspense, sadness

Messages and Themes

- ● Follow and understand the ideas in simple poems and rhymes in enlarged texts
- ◆ Infer a "lesson" from reading a very simple version of a folktale or other text in unison with others
- ◆ Infer an important idea from reading a personal memory story
- ◆ Understand a simple theme in a text: e.g., friendship, families, relationships, self, nature, feelings, cleverness

Literary Elements

- ● Follow and understand a simple plot in an enlarged fiction text
- ◆ Use the events of the story (and memory from previous readings) to predict what will happen next
- ◆ Anticipate exciting places in the text or the ending of a story by remembering previous readings
- ◆ Make predictions based on the kinds of characters that appear in fiction texts
- ◆ Talk about personal connections made to content, characters, or events in a shared text

- ◆ Make connections among texts by noting similarities: e.g., characters, story patterns, language patterns, use of dialogue, words or phrases, type of text
- ◆ Infer the feelings of characters in stories and poems
- ◆ Infer humor in a text
- ◆ Infer the reasons for characters' actions and feelings in a story
- ■ Notice and discuss similar stories, poems, rhymes, and songs read with others as enlarged texts and heard in read-aloud
- ■ Notice and talk about how texts read in shared reading are alike or different
- ■ Notice whether a book tells a story or gives information
- ■ Notice how aspects of a text like humor or interesting characters make it fun to read
- ■ Notice what simple dialogue is like and use understandings to decide how dialogue should be read
- ■ Notice a writer's use of rhyme and rhythm
- ■ Notice and use rhyme and rhythm to anticipate language in a poem or song
- ■ Notice how aspects of a text like rhyme, rhythm, and repetition make it fun to read
- ■ Use some academic language to talk about genres: e.g., *fiction, folktale; nonfiction, personal memory story*
- ■ Use some academic language to talk about forms: e.g., *picture book, wordless picture book, label book, ABC book, counting book, poem, poetry, nursery rhyme, rhyme, song, poetry collection*
- ■ Use some academic language to talk about literary features: e.g., *beginning, ending, problem, character*
- ■ Use some academic language to talk about book and print features: e.g., *front cover, back cover, title, author, illustrator, page, text, illustration, photograph, label*

Book and Print Features

- ● Notice visual aspects of print to help monitor and track: e.g., lines, words, features of print like letter, spaces between words, punctuation
- ● Search for and use information in the body of a text as well as in labels for pictures, titles and headings, and special features such as speech bubbles or thought bubbles
- ◆ Make connections between the body of the text and illustrations
- ◆ Make connections between the body of the text and features such as captions, labels that appear in the illustrations

---

● Thinking ***Within*** the Text   ◆ Thinking ***Beyond*** the Text   ■ Thinking ***About*** the Text

Selecting Goals Behaviors and Understandings to Notice, Teach, and Support

Shared and Performance Reading

SHARED AND PERFORMANCE READING

FICTION AND NONFICTION TEXTS

General

- Notice and talk about the important information in a text
- After reading an enlarged text and/or a small, individual version with others, discuss what it is about
- Tell the major events of a story after reading it with others
- Tell facts, a sequence of events, or directions after reading a nonfiction text with others
- Tell what happens in a readers' theater script or a play
- Search for and use information in a readers' theater script: e.g., lines, stage directions, punctuation, titles, headings
- Follow and understand content to derive facts from a nonfiction text
- ◆ Connect classroom experiences (e.g., lists, directions, recipes recorded in shared/interactive writing) with the oral reading of enlarged texts (charts, class-made big books)
- ◆ Understand and learn new content by reading fiction and nonfiction texts (including those produced through interactive writing)
- ◆ Synthesize new content related to familiar topics and some topics that may be new
- ◆ Identify what is known and what is new to the student in a nonfiction text
- ■ Express opinions about texts that are read in unison
- ■ Talk about what is interesting in a photograph or illustration
- ■ Talk about whether a text is interesting or enjoyable and why

Early Literacy Concepts

- Locate one's own name and names of others in print
- Read name chart (first and last name) with teacher support
- Notice and identify letters in print during and after reading enlarged and individual texts with others
- Connect letters and letter clusters in enlarged print texts to one's own name and names of friends and family or a known word
- Notice features of words: e.g., letters, beginnings, endings, uppercase and lowercase letters
- Use features of print to track words when reading texts individually and with others

- Demonstrate full control of early reading behaviors: e.g., left-to-right directionality, word-by-word matching and return sweep, use of simple punctuation
- Use left-to-right directionality, word-by-word matching, and return sweep to monitor reading with teacher support
- Use eyes to track print with minimal support from the pointer such as sweeping under print (as students gain experience in shared reading)
- Read left to right across words
- Follow the teacher's pointer with the eyes (left to right with return sweep to the next level) to read enlarged texts of two to eight lines
- With teacher support, read without pointer
- With teacher support, use features of print in enlarged texts to search for and use visual information: e.g., letters, words, "first" and "last" word, period

Letters

- Read a simple alphabet chart with teacher support as needed
- Notice letters in an enlarged text

Letter-Sound Relationships

- Locate a word in a text read individually and with others by predicting the first letter

Words

- Locate words with particular features: e.g., beginning letters, endings, phonogram
- Discuss words with others
- When reading texts individually and with others, notice and connect features and parts of words: e.g., phonograms, first letter, word endings
- Recognize at least 100 high-frequency words in context with the support of teacher and group reading
- Recognize most of the 100 high-frequency words in isolation
- When reading texts individually and with others and teacher support, read with word-by-word matching of one- and two-syllable words

---

● Thinking **Within** the Text   ◆ Thinking **Beyond** the Text   ■ Thinking **About** the Text

Selecting Goals Behaviors and Understandings to Notice, Teach, and Support *(cont.)*

Shared and Performance Reading

FICTION AND NONFICTION TEXTS *(continued)*

- ● Recognize some simple plurals, words that have the same rime (e.g., *bit, sit*), and simple contractions
- ● Notice syllables in words and count them by clapping
- ● Notice word endings that are in one's own oral vocabulary: e.g., *running, painted*
- ● Locate known high-frequency words in print
- ● Connect words that have similar features: e.g., phonogram patterns, letter clusters, beginnings and endings

Language Structure (Syntax)

- ● Use memory of repeating language patterns to monitor accuracy and self-correct
- ● Search for information when processing simple sentences during choral reading: e.g., short, natural language; limited number of adjectives and adverbs; repeated clauses
- ◆ Understand when language in a story sounds like talking (simple dialogue)
- ◆ When reading in unison, use language syntax and repeating language patterns to anticipate the text: e.g., next word, next phrase, or sentences

Vocabulary

- ● Understand the meaning of new words after reading and talking about them
- ● Notice and use words that add action or emotion to a text: e.g., words that represent sounds, some expressions
- ● Recognize and understand the meaning of simple plurals
- ● Understand the meaning of words that are in one's own oral vocabulary
- ● Understand the meaning of words that are in common oral language (Tier 1)
- ● Use contextual information to understand the meaning of new words
- ● Notice and understand words that are of high interest and novelty
- ● Understand the meaning of words that represent sounds: e.g., *buzz, pop*
- ● Understand the meaning of a few new content words that are supported by the text, pictures, the teacher, and choral reading

- ● Understand simple connectives
- ◆ Understand some common (simple) connectives that link ideas and clarify meaning and are frequently used in oral language: e.g., *and, but, so, because, before, after*
- ◆ Remember and use new language (e.g., specific words, refrains, expressions) from reading enlarged texts in unison

Fluency

- ● Read some words quickly and automatically
- ● Use phrasing, pausing, word stress with intonation when reading in unison
- ● When reading in unison and individually, remember and use repeating phrases with intonation
- ● Use line breaks to guide phrasing when reading poetry in chorus or individually
- ● Adjust the voice to recognize dialogue in the body of the text and in speech bubbles or unspoken thoughts in thought bubbles
- ● With group support, read orally with integration of all dimensions of fluency: e.g., pausing, phrasing, word stress, intonation, and rate

Performance

- ● Mimic the teacher's expression when reading texts in chorus, and reflect that expression when reading the same text individually
- ● Recognize and reflect some simple punctuation with the voice (e.g., period, question mark, exclamation mark) when reading in chorus or individually
- ● Recognize and reflect variations in print with the voice (e.g., italics, bold type, special treatments, font size) when reading in chorus or individually
- ● When reading individually or in unison with others (with teacher support), adjust the voice to reflect aspects of the text: e.g., humor, surprise, suspense, sadness
- ● Read a part in a brief play or readers' theater script in a way that reflects the dialogue and the attributes and emotions of characters

---

● Thinking *Within* the Text   ◆ Thinking *Beyond* the Text   ■ Thinking *About* the Text

Selecting Goals Behaviors and Understandings to Notice, Teach, and Support *(cont.)*

Shared and Performance Reading

SHARED AND
PERFORMANCE READING

FICTION AND NONFICTION TEXTS *(continued)*

Messages and Themes

- Follow and understand the ideas in simple poems and rhymes in enlarged texts
- Infer a "lesson" from reading a very simple version of a traditional tale in unison or in parts with others
- Infer an important idea from reading a personal memory story
- Infer the writer's purpose and message
- Understand a simple theme in a text: e.g., friendship, families, relationships, self, nature, feelings, cleverness, bravery

Literary Elements

- Follow and understand a simple plot in an enlarged fiction text
- Use the events of the story (and memory from previous readings) to predict what will happen next
- Anticipate exciting places in the text or the ending of a story by remembering previous readings
- Make predictions based on the kinds of characters that appear in fiction texts
- Talk about personal connections made to content, characters, or events in a shared text
- Make connections among texts by noting similarities: e.g., characters, story patterns, language patterns, use of dialogue, words or phrases, type of text
- Infer the feelings of characters in stories and poems
- Infer humor in a text
- Infer the reasons for characters' actions and feelings in a story
- Notice and discuss similar stories, poems, rhymes, and songs read with others as enlarged texts and heard in read-aloud
- Notice and talk about how texts read in shared reading are alike or different
- Distinguish between a story and a script
- Notice whether a book, play, or readers' theater script tells a story or gives information

- Recognize some characteristics of genres of fiction (e.g., realistic fiction, traditional literature, animal fantasy) and nonfiction (e.g., simple factual text) in easy, brief plays and readers' theater scripts
- Notice the different ways that an author tells a story in a fiction text (e.g., simple narrative structure, repeating episodes or language patterns, cumulative patterns) and how that affects understanding and enjoyment
- Notice how aspects of a text like humor or interesting characters make it fun to read
- Notice what simple dialogue is like and use understandings to decide how dialogue should be read
- Notice a writer's use of rhyme and rhythm
- Notice and use rhyme and rhythm to anticipate language in a poem or song
- Notice how aspects of a text like rhyme, rhythm, and repetition make it fun to read
- Notice and identify language that adds humor
- Notice interesting and playful language including made-up words and onomatopoetic words
- Use some academic language to talk about genres: e.g., *fiction, folktale, fairy tale, fable; nonfiction, informational text, informational book, factual text, personal memory story, how-to book*
- Use some academic language to talk about forms: e.g., *picture book, wordless picture book, label book, ABC book, counting book, poem, poetry, nursery rhyme, rhyme, song, poetry collection, series book, chapter book, play*
- Use some academic language to talk about literary features: e.g., *beginning, ending, problem, character, solution, main character, question and answer, topic*
- Use some academic language to talk about book and print features: e.g., *front cover, back cover, title, author, illustrator, page, text, illustration, photograph, label, table of contents, acknowledgments, chapter, section, heading, drawing, caption, map*

- Thinking **Within** the Text   ◆ Thinking **Beyond** the Text   ■ Thinking **About** the Text

Selecting Goals Behaviors and Understandings to Notice, Teach, and Support *(cont.)*

Shared and Performance Reading

FICTION AND NONFICTION TEXTS *(continued)*

Book and Print Features

- ● Notice visual aspects of print to help monitor and track: e.g., lines, words, spaces between words, punctuation
- ● Search for and use information in the body of a text as well as in labels for pictures, titles, headings, sidebars, and special features such as speech bubbles or thought bubbles
- ● Search for information in illustrations and in book and print features in a nonfiction text: e.g., drawing, photograph, map, diagram; table of contents, heading, sidebar
- ● Become aware that in a nonfiction text, information may be provided in several different formats and places on a page: e.g., body text; drawing, photograph, map, diagram; label, caption, legend

- ◆ Make connections between the body of the text and illustrations
- ◆ Make connections between text, illustrations, and book and print features: e.g., body text; drawing, photograph, map, diagram; label, caption, legend; table of contents, heading, sidebar
- ◆ Infer information from nonfiction illustrations and book and print features
- ■ Talk about illustrations and book and print features and evaluate whether they help readers understand information and add interest

---

● Thinking **Within** the Text   ◆ Thinking **Beyond** the Text   ■ Thinking **About** the Text

Selecting Texts Characteristics of Texts for Sharing and Performing

Shared and Performance Reading

GENRE

▶ Fiction

- Realistic fiction
- Traditional literature: e.g., folktale, tall tale, fairy tale, fable
- Fantasy
- Hybrid texts
- Special types of fiction: e.g., adventure story; animal story; family, friends, and school story; humorous story

▶ Nonfiction

- Expository texts
- Narrative nonfiction
- Memoir (personal memory story)
- Procedural texts
- Persuasive texts
- Hybrid texts

FORMS

- Longer poems of various types including free verse, lyrical poetry
- Nursery rhymes, rhymes, and songs from many cultures
- Enlarged poems, nursery rhymes, rhymes, and songs
- Poetry collections
- Plays
- Readers' theater scripts
- Picture books
- Enlarged picture books
- Enlarged informational texts
- Some sophisticated ABC books
- Texts produced through shared writing: e.g., lists, directions, sequences of actions, stories, poems, descriptions, dialogue from stories

TEXT STRUCTURE

- Simple narratives with straightforward structure (beginning, middle, several episodes, and ending) but more episodes included
- Some books with repeating episodes or patterns

- Some texts with nonnarrative structure
- Some stories with repeating refrains suitable for reading in unison
- Stories with simple plot (problem and solution)
- Some biographical and historical texts with narrative structure
- Most texts focusing on a single topic, usually one idea per page
- Informational texts with some examples of simple argument and persuasion
- Underlying structural patterns: description, temporal sequence, question and answer, cause and effect, chronological sequence, compare and contrast
- Informational texts with clearly defined overall structures and categories sometimes marked with headings

CONTENT

- Content that is appropriate for children's cognitive development, emotional maturity, and life experience
- Content that engages intellectual curiosity and emotions
- Content that nurtures the imagination
- Language and word play related to concepts or sounds of speech: e.g., alliteration, assonance, onomatopoetic words
- Familiar topics (e.g., animals, families, friends, human relationships, school, neighborhood, community, sports, weather and seasons, plants) that are authentic and relevant
- Humor that is easy to grasp: e.g., silly characters, funny situations, surprise endings
- Content that reinforces and expands a child's experience and knowledge of self and the world
- A few topics that may be beyond some children's immediate experiences (farm, beach, big city, forms of transportation)
- Content that reflects a wide range of settings, languages, and cultures
- Some content linked to specific areas of study as described by the school curriculum or standards
- Characters, settings, and events that could exist in real life

- Imaginary characters, events (some nonsensical and funny), and settings that occur in fantasy
- Content that reflects beginning understanding of the physical and social world

THEMES AND IDEAS

- Themes reflecting everyday life: e.g., self, family relationships, friendship, imagination, feelings, bravery, cleverness, wisdom, wonders of nature, cultural sensitivity, multiple and diverse views
- Clear, simple ideas easy to identify and understand
- Ideas close to children's experience: e.g., expressing feelings, sharing with others, valuing differences, taking different perspectives, cooperating, helping, belonging, problem solving, working hard, being clever or wise, appreciating the sounds of language, noticing and appreciating nature

LANGUAGE AND LITERARY FEATURES

- Playful descriptive language, including made-up words and onomatopoetic words
- Descriptive language conveying a range of human feelings: e.g., joy, sadness, anger, eagerness
- Descriptive language conveying sensory experiences (imagery)
- Poetic language
- Figurative language: metaphor, simile
- Rhythm and repetition of words and language patterns, as well as rhymes
- A few texts with settings distant in time and place from children's own experiences
- Predictable sequence of events and outcomes
- Both realistic and fantastic settings, events, and characters
- Simple plot with problem and solution and a few episodes
- Main characters and supporting characters
- Multiple characters, each with unique traits
- Characters' actions related to clear consequences: e.g., reward for trying hard and good behavior, punishment for bad behavior

Selecting Texts Characteristics of Texts for Sharing and Performing *(cont.)*

Shared and Performance Reading

- Mostly assigned dialogue
- Most texts told from a single point of view
- Most texts written in first- or third-person narrative
- Simple, straightforward procedural language
- Some procedural texts written in second-person

SENTENCE COMPLEXITY

- Sentences more complex than oral language
- A combination of short and longer sentences
- Variation in placement of subject, verb, adjectives, and adverbs
- Sentences with common (simple) connectives
- Some long and complex sentences that require close attention to follow
- Sentences with multiple adjectives, adverbs, and prepositions
- Sentences with multiple clauses (independent and dependent) and phrases
- Many sentences with dialogue, sometimes repeated for literary effect
- Poetic texts that include some nonstandard sentences
- Variation of tense that changes text complexity: e.g., *goes, was going, will be going*

VOCABULARY

- A few interesting words that are new to children but easy to understand in context
- A few content words (labels) related to concepts that students can understand
- Some memorable words of high interest and novelty: e.g., *huffed and puffed*
- Almost all words that are in common oral vocabulary for younger children (Tier 1)
- A few words that appear in the vocabulary of mature language users (Tier 2)
- Some simple onomatopoetic words
- Some words that guide readers in interpretation of the text
- Common (simple) connectives that are frequently used in oral language (words, phrases that clarify relationships and ideas): e.g., *and, but, so, because, before, after*

- Words to assign dialogue that guide readers in interpretation of the text: e.g., *cried, shouted, whispered*
- Some technical vocabulary

WORDS

- Many high-frequency words
- Mostly one-, two-, three-syllable words with occasional use of longer words
- Simple phonograms and words with vowel combinations (VC, CVC, VCe, VCC, VVC, CVCe)
- Words that have the same rime: e.g., *ring, sing; fight, might*
- Many pairs or sets of rhyming words
- A full range of plurals
- Words with suffixes and prefixes
- Contractions using some letters from words including *not, am, are, is, has, will, have,* and *would*

ILLUSTRATIONS

- Large, clear, colorful illustrations in a variety of media
- Illustrations that provide high support for comprehending language
- Details that add interest
- Many pieces of shared writing created by children, some without pictures
- Some poems, songs, or chants without pictures
- Illustrations that convey emotion
- Illustrations that reflect the theme
- Illustrations and photographs with labels or callouts
- Illustrations in a variety of forms: e.g., drawing with label or caption, photograph with label or caption, map with legend, diagram, infographic

BOOK AND PRINT FEATURES

LENGTH

- Short texts that can be read in one sitting

PRINT AND LAYOUT

- All texts enlarged (big books, charts) with print large enough for the whole group (or a small group) to see clearly
- Some individual copies of poems, books, scripts, or plays

- Clear spaces between words and between lines
- Limited number of lines on a page (usually five to ten), except in the case of a well-known short poem or song
- Variation in layout across pages, with layout that supports phrasing by presenting word groups
- Some words in boldface, italics, or varying font sizes, with occasional variety in color of print
- Page numbers

PUNCTUATION

- Simple punctuation: e.g., period, question mark, exclamation mark, comma, quotation marks, ellipses

ORGANIZATIONAL TOOLS

- Title, author, and illustrator listed on cover and on title page
- Table of contents, chapter title, section heading, sidebar

TEXT RESOURCES

- Some books with dedication, acknowledgments, author's note, illustrator's note

Selecting Goals Behaviors and Understandings to Notice, Teach, and Support

Shared and Performance Reading

FICTION AND NONFICTION TEXTS

General

- Tell facts, a sequence of events, or directions after reading a nonfiction text with others
- Tell what happens in a readers' theater script or a play
- Provide an oral summary of a story, play, or nonfiction text
- Search for and use information in a readers' theater script: e.g., lines, stage directions, punctuation, titles, headings
- Follow and understand content to derive facts from a nonfiction text
- Use content knowledge to monitor and correct while reading a fiction text
- Notice when understanding is lost, and take steps to make a text make sense (monitor)
- Connect classroom experiences (e.g., lists, directions, recipes recorded in shared/interactive writing) with the oral reading of enlarged texts (charts, class-made books)
- Understand and learn new content by reading fiction and nonfiction texts (including those produced through interactive writing)
- Synthesize new content related to familiar topics and topics that may be new
- Identify what is known and what is new in a nonfiction text
- Express opinions about a text and justify with evidence
- Express opinions about what is interesting in a photographs or illustration
- Talk about whether a text is interesting or enjoyable and why

Early Literacy Concepts

- Use the eyes to track from left to right with minimal or no support from the pointer, sweep back to the left to begin a new line, and match word by word
- Read left to right across words
- Follow the text to read enlarged print of five to twelve lines
- Search for and use visual information in print: e.g., words, word parts, letters, punctuation

Letters

- Read lists or charts in unison with others: e.g., letter cluster chart, lists of words with the same phonogram, plurals

Words

- Locate words with particular features: e.g., beginning letters, phonograms, letter clusters, syllables, prefixes, suffixes, endings, proper nouns, high-frequency words, content words
- Discuss words with others
- Use multiple sources of information to monitor, search, and self-correct in solving words
- Solve words by using letters and sounds, letter clusters, and word parts like syllables and endings
- Recognize approximately 200 high-frequency words
- Recognize simple regular plurals and some irregular plurals
- Recognize simple contractions
- Connect words that have similar features: e.g., syllables, prefixes, suffixes, base words, parts of speech

Language Structure (Syntax)

- Use sentence structure to monitor and correct reading
- Use awareness of rhyme and rhythm in poetry to monitor, correct, and anticipate the text
- Notice when sentence structure does not match knowledge of syntax and reread to correct (self-monitor)
- Search for information across sentences, using language structure (syntax)
- Search for information across some complex sentences
- Use language syntax to anticipate the text: e.g., next word, next phrase, sentences

Vocabulary

- Add new words from a text to oral and reading vocabulary
- Notice and use words that add action or emotion to a text: e.g., words that represent sounds, strong verbs, some expressions

● Thinking **Within** the Text   ◆ Thinking **Beyond** the Text   ■ Thinking **About** the Text

Selecting Goals Behaviors and Understandings to Notice, Teach, and Support *(cont.)*

Shared and Performance Reading

FICTION AND NONFICTION TEXTS *(continued)*

- Recognize and understand the meaning of plurals in various forms
- Understand the meaning of words that are in one's own oral vocabulary
- Understand the meaning of words that are in common oral language (Tier 1), some of which will be new
- Use contextual information to understand the meaning of new words
- Notice and understand words that are of high interest and novelty
- Understand the meaning of words that represent sounds: e.g., *buzz, hiss, pop*
- Understand the meaning of content words supported by the pictures in a nonfiction text
- Understand simple connectives
- ◆ Understand some common (simple) connectives that link ideas and clarify meaning and are frequently used in oral language: e.g., *and, but, so, because, before, after*
- ◆ Remember and use new language (e.g., specific words, refrains, expressions) from reading enlarged texts in unison

Fluency

- Read a growing number of words quickly and automatically
- Use line breaks to guide phrasing when reading poetry in unison or individually
- Adjust the voice to reflect dialogue in the body of the text
- Read orally with integration of all dimensions of fluency: e.g., pausing, phrasing, word stress, intonation, and rate

Performance

- Recognize and reflect punctuation with the voice (e.g., period, question mark, exclamation mark, comma, quotation marks, ellipses) when reading in chorus or individually
- Recognize and reflect variations in print with the voice (e.g., italics, bold type, special treatments, font size) when reading in chorus or individually

- When reading individually or in unison with others, adjust the voice to reflect aspects of the text: e.g., humor, surprise, suspense, sadness, humor
- Understand the role of the voice in communicating meaning in readers' theater, choral reading, songs, and poetry
- Read a part in a play or a readers' theater script in a way that reflects the dialogue and the attributes and emotions of characters
- Maintain appropriate volume when performing in readers' theater, plays, and choral performances
- Adjust volume and tone of voice to reflect stage directions (e.g., *quietly, shouted, with a laugh*) and to read a script with fluency and expression

Messages and Themes

- Follow and understand the ideas in poetry and rhymes
- ◆ Infer a "lesson" from reading a simple version of a traditional tale in chorus or in parts with others
- ◆ Infer important ideas from reading a narrative nonfiction text
- ◆ Infer the writer's purpose
- ◆ Infer the writer's message or theme in a text
- ◆ Understand a simple theme in a text: e.g., friendship, families, relationships, self, the wonders of nature, feelings, cleverness, bravery, wisdom
- ■ Talk about whether the message or theme of a text is important and justify opinion with evidence

Literary Elements

- Follow and understand simple plots in stories and readers' theater or plays
- Use understanding of types and elements of poetry to adjust reading
- Use a poem's layout and punctuation to monitor and correct while reading
- Use understanding of narrative structure in a fiction text to monitor and correct reading

---

● Thinking *Within* the Text   ◆ Thinking *Beyond* the Text   ■ Thinking *About* the Text

Selecting Goals Behaviors and Understandings to Notice, Teach, and Support *(cont.)*

Shared and Performance Reading

FICTION AND NONFICTION TEXTS *(continued)*

Literary Elements *(continued)*

- ● Use understanding of text structure (expository or narrative) to monitor and correct reading
- ◆ Use the events of a story or play to anticipate exciting places in a text or to predict what will happen next
- ◆ Make predictions based on the kinds of characters that appear in fiction texts
- ◆ Make predictions based on understanding of text structure in fiction and nonfiction texts
- ◆ Talk about personal connections with content, characters, or events in a shared text, poem, play, or readers' theater script
- ◆ Notice and talk about how shared texts are alike or different
- ◆ Make connections among texts by noting similarities: e.g., characters, story patterns, language patterns, use of dialogue, words or phrases, type of text
- ◆ Infer the feelings of characters in stories and poems
- ◆ Infer humor in a text
- ◆ Infer the reasons for characters' actions and feelings in a story or play
- ■ Distinguish between a story, a poem, and a readers' theater script or play
- ■ Notice whether a book, play, choral reading, or readers' theater script tells a story or gives information
- ■ Recognize some characteristics of fiction and nonfiction genres in plays and readers' theater scripts

- ■ Notice the different ways that a writer tells a story in a fiction text (e.g., simple narrative structure, repeating episodes or language patterns, cumulative patterns) and how that affects understanding and enjoyment
- ■ Notice underlying structural patterns in a nonfiction text: e.g., description, temporal sequence, question and answer, cause and effect, chronological sequence, compare and contrast
- ■ Notice how aspects of a text like humor or interesting characters affect appreciation and enjoyment
- ■ Notice aspects of simple dialogue and use those aspects to decide how dialogue should be read
- ■ Notice a writer's use of rhyme and rhythm and identify language that shares these features
- ■ Notice and use rhyme and rhythm to anticipate language in a poem or song
- ■ Notice how aspects of a text like rhyme, rhythm, and repetition affect appreciation or enjoyment
- ■ Notice and identify language that adds humor
- ■ Notice interesting and playful language including made up words and onomatopoeic words
- ■ Notice how a writer uses language to build tension or to describe action
- ■ Use some academic language to talk about genres: e.g., *fiction, folktale, fairy tale, fable, tall tale, adventure story, animal story, family, friends, and school story, humorous story; nonfiction, informational text, informational book, factual text, personal memory story, how-to book*

● Thinking *Within* the Text　　　◆ Thinking *Beyond* the Text　　　■ Thinking *About* the Text

Selecting Goals Behaviors and Understandings to Notice, Teach, and Support *(cont.)*

Shared and Performance Reading

FICTION AND NONFICTION TEXTS *(continued)*

- Use some academic language to talk about forms: e.g., *picture book, wordless picture book, label book, ABC book, counting book, poem, poetry, nursery rhyme, rhyme, song, poetry collection, series book, chapter book, play, letter*
- Use some academic language to talk about literary features: e.g., *beginning, ending, problem, character, solution, main character, question and answer, topic, time and place, events, character change, message, dialogue, description, time order, problem and solution*
- Use some academic language to talk about book and print features: e.g., *front cover, back cover, title, author, illustrator, page, text, illustration, photograph, label, table of contents, acknowledgments, chapter, section, heading, drawing, caption, map, chapter title, dedication, author's note, illustrator's note, section, diagram, glossary, endpapers*

Book and Print Features

- Use visual information in print (e.g., lines, words, spaces between words, punctuation) to monitor and correct while reading
- Search for information in illustrations and in book and print features in a nonfiction text: e.g., drawing, photograph, map, diagram, infographic; table of contents, heading, sidebar

- Become aware that in a nonfiction text, information may be provided in several different formats and places on a page: e.g., body text; drawing, photograph, map, diagram, infographic; label, caption, legend
- Use illustrations (when applicable) to monitor and correct reading
- Shift attention from one part of a page layout to another to gather information: e.g., body text; drawing, photograph, map, diagram, infographic; label, caption, legend
- Make connections between the body of the text and illustrations
- Make connections between text, illustrations, and book and print features: e.g., body text; drawing, photograph, map, diagram; label, caption, legend; table of contents, heading, sidebar, infographic
- Notice and learn new ways to present information in nonfiction texts using illustrations and book and print features
- Infer information from nonfiction illustrations and book and print features
- Talk about illustrations and book and print features and evaluate whether they help readers understand information and add interest

● Thinking ***Within*** the Text   ◆ Thinking ***Beyond*** the Text   ■ Thinking ***About*** the Text

Selecting Texts Characteristics of Texts for Sharing and Performing

Shared and Performance Reading

GENRE

▶ **Fiction**

- Realistic fiction
- Historical fiction
- Traditional literature: e.g., folktale, tall tale, fairy tale, fable
- Fantasy
- Hybrid texts
- Special types of fiction: e.g., mystery; adventure story; animal story; family, friends, and school story; humorous story

▶ **Nonfiction**

- Expository nonfiction
- Narrative nonfiction
- Biography
- Autobiography
- Memoir
- Procedural texts
- Persuasive texts
- Hybrid texts

FORMS

- Longer poems of various types: e.g., lyrical poetry, free verse, narrative poetry, limerick, haiku
- Rhymes and songs from many cultures
- Enlarged poems, rhymes, and songs
- Enlarged informational texts
- Individual poetry collections
- Plays
- Readers' theater scripts
- Picture books
- Excerpts from chapter books, series books
- Letters, diaries, and journal entries
- Texts produced through shared writing

TEXT STRUCTURE

- Narratives with straightforward structure but multiple episodes
- Excerpts that highlight particular literary features: e.g., description, turning point in a narrative, figurative language, dialogue, persuasive language
- Stories with complex plot and multiple problems
- A few fiction texts with variations in narrative structure: e.g., story-within-a-story, flashback

- Some biographical and historical texts (or excerpts from them) with narrative structure
- Informational texts related to a larger topic, sometimes with subtopics
- Informational texts with some examples of simple argument and persuasion
- Underlying structural patterns: description, temporal sequence, question and answer, cause and effect, chronological sequence, compare and contrast, problem and solution
- Poems that may have narrative structure or reflect the patterns of various types of poetry

CONTENT

- Content that is appropriate for students' cognitive development, emotional maturity, and life experience
- Content that engages intellectual curiosity and emotions
- Content that nurtures the imagination
- Language and word play related to concepts or sounds of speech: e.g., alliteration, assonance, onomatopoetic words
- Humor that is easy to grasp: e.g., silly characters, funny situations, surprise endings, jokes, play with words
- Content that reinforces and expands a student's experience and knowledge of self and the world
- A few topics that may be beyond students' immediate experiences
- Content that reflects a wide range of settings, languages, and cultures
- Some content linked to specific areas of study as described by the school curriculum or standards
- Characters, settings, and events that could exist in contemporary life or in history
- Characters and settings that occur in fantasy
- Content that reflects understanding of the physical and social world

THEMES AND IDEAS

- More sophisticated presentation of themes reflecting everyday life: e.g., self, family relationships, friendship, imagination, feelings, bravery, cleverness, wisdom, wonders of nature, cultural sensitivity, multiple and diverse views
- Themes, emotions, sensory experiences, and ideas expressed through poetry

- Clear, simple ideas easy to identify and understand
- More sophisticated presentation of ideas close to students' experience: e.g., expressing feelings, sharing with others, valuing differences, taking different perspectives, cooperating, helping, belonging, problem solving, working hard, being clever or wise, appreciating the sounds of language, noticing and appreciating nature

LANGUAGE AND LITERARY FEATURES

- Playful descriptive language, including made-up words and onomatopoetic words
- Descriptive language conveying sensory experiences (imagery) and a range of human feelings: e.g., joy, sadness, anger, eagerness
- Poetic language
- Sensory imagery expressed in poetry
- Figurative language: metaphor, simile, personification
- Rhythm and repetition of words and language patterns, as well as rhymes
- A few texts with settings distant in time and place from student's own experiences
- Predictable sequence of events and outcomes
- Language and events that convey an emotional atmosphere (mood) in a text, affecting how the reader feels
- Both realistic and fantastic settings, events, and characters
- Simple plot with problem and solution, a few episodes, and predictable story outcomes
- Excerpts from some longer texts with one or more subplots
- Main characters and supporting characters
- Characters with multiple dimensions
- Multiple characters, each with unique traits
- Character dimensions and relationships revealed through dialogue and behavior
- Characters' actions related to clear consequences: e.g., reward for trying hard and good behavior, punishment for bad behavior
- Both assigned and unassigned dialogue
- Most texts told from a single point of view

Selecting Texts Characteristics of Texts for Sharing and Performing *(cont.)*

Shared and Performance Reading

- Most texts written in first- or third-person narrative
- Simple, straightforward procedural language
- Some procedural texts written in second-person

SENTENCE COMPLEXITY

- Some long and complex sentences that require attention to follow
- Variation in placement of subject, verb, multiple adjectives, adverbs, and prepositions
- Sentences with embedded clauses (independent and dependent) and phrases
- Sentences with common (simple) connectives
- Extended dialogue that increases sentence complexity
- Poetic texts that include some nonstandard sentences
- Variation of tense that changes text complexity: e.g., *goes, was going, will be going*
- Some texts with long sentences divided into bulleted or numbered lists
- Sentence structure adapted to fit purpose and form of book and print features: e.g., heading, subheading, label, caption, legend

VOCABULARY

- A few interesting words that are new to students but easy to understand in context
- Some memorable words of high interest and novelty: e.g., *huffed and puffed*
- Almost all words that are in common oral vocabulary for children (Tier 1)
- A few words that appear in the vocabulary of mature language users (Tier 2)
- A few content words (labels) related to concepts that students can understand
- Some simple onomatopoetic words
- Some words that guide readers in interpretation of the text
- Common (simple) connectives that are frequently used in oral language (words, phrases that clarify relationships and ideas): e.g., *and, but, so, because, before, after*

- A few sophisticated connectives (words that link ideas and clarify meaning) and that are used in written texts but do not appear often in everyday oral language: e.g., *although, however, meantime, meanwhile, moreover, otherwise, therefore, though, unless, until, whenever, yet*
- Words to assign dialogue that guide readers in interpretation of the text: e.g., *chattered, begged, sharply*
- Some technical vocabulary

WORDS

- Many high-frequency words
- Many multisyllable words
- A full range of plurals in single-syllable and multisyllable words
- Words with affixes (prefixes and suffixes) attached to a base word or root
- Contractions using some letters from words including *not, am, are, is, has, will, have,* and *would*

ILLUSTRATIONS

- Illustrations in a variety of media that provide high support for comprehending language
- Some pieces of shared writing with no illustrations
- Many poems and other texts with decorative illustrations or vignettes
- Some poems without illustrations
- Some books with black-and-white illustrations
- Illustrations that convey mood
- Illustrations that reflect the theme
- Illustrations in a variety of forms: e.g., drawing with label or caption, photograph with label or caption, map with legend, diagram, infographic

BOOK AND PRINT FEATURES

LENGTH

- Short texts that can be read in one sitting

PRINT AND LAYOUT

- Some texts enlarged, some on charts made by students and/or teacher, with print large enough for the whole group (or a small group) to see clearly
- Individual copies of poems, books, scripts, or plays
- Clear spaces between words and between lines
- Limited number of lines on a page (usually five to ten), except in the case of a well-known short poem or song
- Variation in layout across pages, with layout that supports phrasing by presenting word groups
- Dialogue presented in script format in plays and scripts (no quotation marks)
- Some words in boldface, italics, or varying font sizes, with occasional variety in color of print and/or highlighting
- Page numbers

PUNCTUATION

- Wide range of punctuation: e.g., period, question mark, exclamation mark, comma, quotation marks, ellipses, dash, parentheses, colon (in some scripts)

ORGANIZATIONAL TOOLS

- Title, author, and illustrator listed on cover and on title page
- Table of contents, chapter title, list of characters, section heading, subheading, sidebar

TEXT RESOURCES

- Some books with dedication, acknowledgments, author's note, illustrator's note, glossary

Selecting Goals Behaviors and Understandings to Notice, Teach, and Support

Shared and Performance Reading

SHARED AND PERFORMANCE READING

FICTION AND NONFICTION TEXTS

General

- Tell what happens in a readers' theater script or a play
- Provide an oral summary of the story or play
- Search for and use information in readers' theater scripts: e.g., lines, stage directions, punctuation, titles, headings
- Follow and understand content to derive facts from a nonfiction text
- Use content knowledge to monitor and correct while reading fiction
- Notice when understanding is lost and take steps to make a text make sense (monitor)
- ◆ Acquire new ideas, information, perspectives, and attitudes from reading parts in scripts and poems
- ◆ Make connections between historical and current events and the scripts in plays and other readings
- ◆ Make connections between texts and readers' theater scripts that are made from them and understand the differences
- ◆ Infer reasons for selection of material to include in scripts (for readers' theater based on a longer narrative or expository text)
- ■ Express opinions about texts and justify with evidence
- ■ Talk about whether a readers' theater script or play is interesting or enjoyable and why
- ■ Talk about what makes dialogue effective in a play or readers' theater script: e.g., authenticity, rhythm
- ■ Notice use of language and print conventions (e.g., sentence and paragraph structure, punctuation, tense agreement and change) by looking at an enlarged page with the group

Words

- Locate many words in print: e.g., proper nouns, high-frequency words, content words
- Use multiple sources of information to monitor, search, and self-correct in solving words
- Solve words by using letters and sounds, letter clusters, and word parts like syllables and endings
- Solve words using a flexible range of strategies to access different sources of information

- Recognize many multisyllable words or take apart as needed to solve them
- Automatically read approximately 500 high-frequency words
- Recognize plurals and possessives
- Recognize words with affixes (prefixes and suffixes)
- Connect words that have similar features: e.g., affixes and other word parts, base words, parts of speech

Language Structure (Syntax)

- Use sentence structure to monitor and correct reading
- Use awareness of rhyme, rhythm, and the syntax of various types of poetry to monitor, correct, anticipate, and interpret a poem
- Notice when sentence structure does not match knowledge of syntax and reread to correct (self-monitor)
- Search for information across sentences, using language structure (syntax)
- Search for information across complex sentences
- Use language structure (syntax), meaning, and visual information in print to monitor and correct reading

Vocabulary

- Add new words from texts to vocabulary constantly
- Notice and use words that add action or emotion to a text: e.g., words that represent sounds, strong verbs, adjectives, and adverbs, some expressions
- Recognize and understand the meaning of plurals in various forms
- Understand the meaning of words that are in one's own oral vocabulary
- Understand the meaning of words that are common for oral language (Tier 1)
- Understand words used by mature language users (Tier 2)
- Use contextual information to solve the meaning of new words
- Notice and understand words that are of high interest and novelty

---

● Thinking *Within* the Text   ◆ Thinking *Beyond* the Text   ■ Thinking *About* the Text

Selecting Goals Behaviors and Understandings to Notice, Teach, and Support *(cont.)*

Shared and Performance Reading

FICTION AND NONFICTION TEXTS *(continued)*

- Understand the meaning of words that represent sounds: e.g., *buzz, hiss, pop, clang*
- Understand the meaning of content words supported by the pictures in a nonfiction text
- Understand common (simple) connectives and a few sophisticated connectives

Fluency

- Read a large number of words quickly and automatically
- Use line breaks to guide phrasing when reading poetry in unison or individually
- Adjust the voice to reflect dialogue in the body of the text
- Read orally with integration of all dimensions of fluency: e.g., pausing, phrasing, word stress, intonation, and rate

Performance

- Recognize and reflect punctuation with the voice: e.g., period, question mark, exclamation point, dash, comma, ellipses, when reading in chorus or individually
- Recognize and reflect variations in print with the voice (e.g., italics, bold type, special treatments, font size) when reading in chorus or individually
- When reading individually or in unison with others, adjust the voice to reflect the mood of the text: e.g., sadness, tension, joy, humor
- Understand the role of the voice in communicating meaning in readers' theater, choral reading, songs, and poetry
- Read a part in a play or readers' theater script in a way that reflects the dialogue and the attributes and emotions of characters
- Maintain appropriate volume when performing in readers' theater, plays, and choral performances
- Adjust volume and tone of voice to reflect stage directions (e.g., *quietly, shouted, with a laugh*) and to read a script with fluency and expression
- Discuss with others how a script or poem should be read and state reasons based on plot, characters, meaning

Messages and Themes

- Follow and understand the ideas in poetry
- Identify the main ideas or messages in readers' theater scripts or poems used for choral reading
- Provide a concise statement summarizing a readers' theater script, choral reading, or poem, including the important information and the major themes or ideas
- Infer important ideas from reading a narrative nonfiction text
- Infer the writer's purpose
- Infer the writers' message or theme in a text
- Infer the significance of themes: e.g., friendship, families, relationships, self, the wonders of nature, feelings, cleverness, bravery, wisdom, appreciation of the sounds of language, cultural sensitivity
- Talk about whether the message of a poem is important and justify opinion with evidence

Literary Elements

- Follow and understand simple plots in stories and readers' theater or plays
- Use understanding of types and elements of poetry to adjust reading
- Use a poem's layout and punctuation to monitor and correct while reading
- Use understanding of narrative structure in a fiction text to monitor and correct reading
- Use understanding of text structure in a nonfiction text (expository or narrative) to monitor and correct reading
- Make connections among texts by noting similarities: e.g., genre, form, text structure, characters, literary language, use of dialogue
- Notice and talk about how shared texts are alike or different
- Talk about personal connections with content, characters, or events in a shared text, poem, play, or readers' theater script

- Thinking *Within* the Text   ◆ Thinking *Beyond* the Text   ■ Thinking *About* the Text

Selecting Goals Behaviors and Understandings to Notice, Teach, and Support *(cont.)*

Shared and Performance Reading

FICTION AND NONFICTION TEXTS *(continued)*

Literary Elements *(continued)*

◆ Use the events of a story or play to anticipate exciting places in a text or to predict what will happen next

◆ Make predictions based on understanding of text structure in fiction and nonfiction texts

◆ Make predictions based on understanding of characters and character motivation

◆ Infer characters' feelings and motivations and the relationships between characters from reading dialogue in a script

◆ Gain insight into perspectives of characters in fiction and real historical characters

◆ Gain insight into historical events from reflecting them in the reading of a script or poem

◆ Infer humor in a text

■ Distinguish between a story, a poem, and a readers' theater script or play

■ Notice whether a book, play, choral reading, or readers' theater script tells a story or gives information

■ Recognize some characteristics of fiction and nonfiction genres in plays and readers' theater scripts

■ Notice the different ways that a writer tells a story in a fiction text (e.g., simple narrative structure, repeating episodes or language patterns, cumulative patterns, flashback, story-within-a-story) and how that affects understanding and enjoyment

■ Notice underlying structural patterns in a nonfiction text: e.g., description, temporal sequence, question and answer, cause and effect, chronological sequence, compare and contrast, problem and solution

■ Notice how aspects of a text like rhyme, rhythm, and repetition affect appreciation or enjoyment

■ Notice aspects of simple dialogue and use those aspects to decide how dialogue should be read

■ Notice a writer's use of rhyme and rhythm and identify language that shares these features

■ Notice and use rhyme and rhythm to anticipate language in a poem or song

■ Notice how aspects of a text like humor or interesting characters affect appreciation and enjoyment

■ Notice and identify language that adds humor

■ Notice interesting and playful language including made up words and onomatopoeic words

■ Notice how a writer uses language to convey a mood

■ Notice how a writer uses language to build tension or to describe action

■ Notice aspects of the writer's craft by looking at an enlarged page with the group

---

● Thinking *Within* the Text   ◆ Thinking *Beyond* the Text   ■ Thinking *About* the Text

Selecting Goals Behaviors and Understandings to Notice, Teach, and Support *(cont.)*

Shared and Performance Reading

FICTION AND NONFICTION TEXTS *(continued)*

- Use some academic language to talk about genres: e.g., *fiction, folktale, fairy tale, fable, tall tale, adventure story, animal story, family, friends, and school story, humorous story, realistic fiction, traditional literature; nonfiction, informational text, informational book, factual text, personal memory story, biography, how-to book, autobiography*

- Use some academic language to talk about forms: e.g., *picture book, wordless picture book, label book, ABC book, counting book, poem, poetry, nursery rhyme, rhyme, song, poetry collection, series book, chapter book, play, letter*

- Use some academic language to talk about literary features: e.g., *beginning, ending, problem, character, solution, main character, question and answer, topic, events, character change, message, dialogue, description, time order, problem and solution, setting, main idea, comparison and contrast*

- Use some academic language to talk about plays and performance: e.g., *line, speech, scene, act, actor, actress, role, part, hero, villain, playwright*

- Use some academic language to talk about book and print features: e.g., *front cover, back cover, title, author, illustrator, page, text, illustration, photograph, label, table of contents, acknowledgments, chapter, section, heading, drawing, caption, map, chapter title, dedication, author's note, illustrator's note, section, diagram, glossary, endpapers, sidebar, book jacket*

Book and Print Features

- Search for information in illustrations and in book and print features in a nonfiction text: e.g., drawing, photograph, map, diagram, infographic; table of contents, heading, sidebar

- Use illustrations (when applicable) to monitor and correct reading

- Shift attention from one part of a page layout to another to gather information: e.g., body text; drawing, photograph, map, diagram, infographic; label, caption, legend

- Make connections between the body of the text and illustrations

- Make connections between text, illustrations, and book and print features: e.g., body text; drawing, photograph, map, diagram, infographic; label, caption, legend; table of contents, heading, sidebar

- Notice and learn new ways to present information in nonfiction texts using illustrations and book and print features

- Infer information from nonfiction illustrations and book and print features

- Talk about illustrations and book and print features and evaluate whether they help readers understand information and add interest

● Thinking *Within* the Text   ◆ Thinking *Beyond* the Text   ■ Thinking *About* the Text

Selecting Texts Characteristics of Texts for Sharing and Performing

Shared and Performance Reading

GENRE

▶ Fiction

- Realistic fiction
- Historical fiction
- Traditional literature: e.g., folktale, tall tale, fairy tale, fractured fairy tale, fable
- More complex fantasy including science fiction
- Hybrid texts
- Special types of fiction: e.g., mystery; adventure story; animal story; family, friends, and school story; humorous story; sports story

▶ Nonfiction

- Expository nonfiction
- Narrative nonfiction
- Biography
- Autobiography
- Memoir
- Procedural texts
- Persuasive texts
- Hybrid texts

FORMS

- Poetry (much unrhymed) on many topics of various types: e.g., lyrical poetry, free verse, narrative poetry, limerick, haiku, ballad, concrete poetry
- Rhymes and songs from many cultures
- Individual poetry collections
- Plays
- Readers' theater scripts, some designed by students
- Picture books
- Excerpts from chapter books, series books
- Letters, diaries, and journal entries
- Texts produced through shared writing
- Short stories
- Photo essays, news articles, and feature articles

TEXT STRUCTURE

- Narratives with straightforward structure but multiple episodes
- Excerpts that highlight particular literary features: e.g., description, turning point in a narrative, figurative language, dialogue, persuasive language

- A few fiction texts with variations in narrative structure: e.g., story-within-a-story, flashback
- Informational texts with examples of simple argument and persuasion
- Short excerpts or scripts drawn from longer texts in a variety of genres and text structures
- Underlying structural patterns: description, temporal sequence, question and answer, cause and effect, chronological sequence, compare and contrast, problem and solution, categorization
- Poems that may have narrative structure or reflect the organizational patterns of various types of poetry

CONTENT

- Content that is appropriate for students' cognitive development, emotional maturity, and life experience
- Content that engages intellectual curiosity and emotions
- Content that nurtures the imagination
- Topics important to preadolescents: e.g., sibling rivalry, friendship, growing up, family problems, and conflicts
- Language and word play related to concepts or parts of speech: e.g., alliteration, assonance, onomatopoetic words
- Humor conveyed through playful or created language
- Content that reinforces and expands a student's experience and knowledge of self and the world
- A few topics that may be beyond students' immediate experiences
- Content that reflects a wide range of settings, languages, and cultures
- Some content linked to specific areas of study as described by the school curriculum or standards
- Characters, settings, and events that could exist in contemporary life or in history
- Characters and settings that occur in fantasy
- People, settings, and events in biographical texts that could exist in contemporary life or in history
- Content that reflects understanding of the physical and social world

THEMES AND IDEAS

- More sophisticated interpretation of themes reflecting everyday life: e.g., self, family relationships, friendship, imagination, feelings, bravery, cleverness, wisdom, wonders of nature, cultural sensitivity, multiple and diverse views, how things are made, how things work
- Themes, emotions, sensory experiences, inspiring ideas expressed through poetry
- More complex ideas requiring inference, sometimes expressed through the language of poetry
- More sophisticated interpretation of ideas close to students' experience: e.g., expressing feelings, sharing with others, valuing differences, taking different perspectives, cooperating, helping, caring for others, standing up for what is right, belonging, problem solving, working hard, being brave or clever or wise, appreciating the sounds of language, noticing and appreciating nature, caring for the world

LANGUAGE AND LITERARY FEATURES

- Descriptive language conveying sensory experiences and a range of human feelings
- Descriptive and figurative language that is important to understanding the content: imagery, metaphor, simile, personification, hyperbole
- Some texts and poems with basic or obvious symbolism used to convey larger meaning
- Poetic language
- Sensory imagery expressed in poetry
- Rhythm and repetition of words and language patterns, as well as rhymes
- Settings distant in time and place from students' own experiences
- Language and events that convey an emotional atmosphere (mood) in a text, affecting how the reader feels
- Both realistic and fantastic settings, events, and characters
- Excerpts from some longer texts with one or more subplots
- Main characters and supporting characters, some with multiple dimensions, especially in plays
- Characters revealed through dialogue and behavior, especially in plays

Selecting Texts Characteristics of Texts for Sharing and Performing (cont.)

Shared and Performance Reading

- Characters that are complex and change over time in longer texts
- Both assigned and unassigned dialogue, including some strings of unassigned dialogue for which speakers must be inferred
- Description of actions, appearance, behavior of characters given in stage directions in script
- Some texts told from multiple points of view
- Most texts written in first- or third-person narrative

SENTENCE COMPLEXITY

- Some long and complex sentences that require attention to follow
- Variation in placement of subject, verb, multiple adjectives, adverbs, and prepositions
- Sentences with embedded clauses (independent and dependent) and phrases
- Sentences with common (simple) connectives
- Extended dialogue that increases sentence complexity
- Poetic texts that include some nonstandard sentences
- Variation of tense that changes text complexity: e.g., *goes, was going, will be going*
- Some texts with long sentences divided into bulleted or numbered lists
- Sentence structure adapted to fit purpose and form of book and print features: e.g., heading, subheading, label, caption, legend

VOCABULARY

- Some interesting words that may be new to students
- New content words related to concepts that students are learning
- Almost all words that are in students' common oral vocabulary (Tier 1)
- Many words that appear in the vocabulary of mature language users (Tier 2)
- A few words that are particular to a discipline (Tier 3), especially in nonfiction
- A few content words (labels) related to concepts that students can understand

- Simple connectives (words, phrases that clarify relationships and ideas that are used frequently in oral language): e.g., *and, but, so, but, because, before, after*
- A few sophisticated connectives (words that link ideas and clarify meaning and that are used in written texts but do not appear often in everyday oral language): e.g., *although, however, meantime, meanwhile, moreover, otherwise, therefore, though, unless, until, whenever, yet*
- Words to assign dialogue that guide readers in interpretation of the text: e.g., *muttered, snarled, gratefully*
- Some words with multiple meanings, requiring interpretation to be conveyed through the voice
- Some words with connotative meanings, requiring interpretation to be conveyed through the voice
- Some idioms and other words with figurative meaning
- Some words from regional or historical dialects
- Some words from languages other than English
- Some technical vocabulary

WORDS

- Many high-frequency words
- Many multisyllable words
- Some multisyllable words with complex letter-sound relationships
- A full range of plurals in single-syllable and multisyllable words
- Compound words
- Words with affixes (prefixes and suffixes) attached to a base word or root
- Wide range of contractions and possessives
- Some words divided (hyphenated) across lines
- Words that offer decoding challenges because they come from regional dialect or are from languages other than English

ILLUSTRATIONS

- Illustrations in a variety of media that provide high support for comprehending language
- Some pieces of shared writing with no illustrations

- Many texts with decorative illustrations or vignettes
- Some books with black-and-white illustrations
- Some texts with no illustrations other than decorative elements such as illuminated letters or border designs (vignettes)
- Individual scripts with decorative illustrations
- Illustrations that convey mood
- Illustrations that reflect the theme
- Illustrations in a variety of forms: e.g., drawing with label or caption, photograph with label or caption, map with legend, diagram, infographic, chart, graph, timeline

BOOK AND PRINT FEATURES

LENGTH

- Short texts that can be read in one sitting

PRINT AND LAYOUT

- Some texts with enlarged print (poems, charts)
- Individual copies of scripts or plays
- Varied number of lines on a page
- Variation in layout across pages
- Dialogue presented in script format in plays and scripts
- Some words in boldface, italics, or varying font sizes, with occasional variety in color of print and/or highlighting

PUNCTUATION

- Wide range of punctuation: e.g., period, question mark, exclamation mark, comma, quotation marks, ellipses, dash, parentheses, hyphen, colon

ORGANIZATIONAL TOOLS

- Title, author, and illustrator listed on cover and on title page
- Table of contents, chapter title, list of characters, heading, subheading, sidebar

TEXT RESOURCES

- Some books with dedication, acknowledgments, author's note, glossary, index

Selecting Goals Behaviors and Understandings to Notice, Teach, and Support

Shared and Performance Reading

SHARED AND PERFORMANCE READING

FICTION AND NONFICTION TEXTS

General

- Tell what happens in a readers' theater script or a play
- Provide a logically organized oral summary of the story or play
- Provide an oral summary that includes the important information in a nonfiction text
- Search for and use information in readers' theater scripts: e.g., lines, stage directions, punctuation, titles, headings
- Follow and understand content to derive facts from a nonfiction text
- Use content knowledge to monitor and correct while reading fiction
- Notice when understanding is lost and take steps to make a text make sense (monitor)
- Acquire new ideas, information, perspectives, and attitudes from reading parts in scripts and poems
- Make connections between historical and current events and the scripts in plays and other readings
- Make connections between texts and readers' theater scripts that are made from them and understand the differences
- Infer reasons for selection of material to include in scripts (for readers' theater based on a longer narrative or expository text)
- Express opinions about texts and justify with evidence
- Express an opinion about the suitability of a text to be read aloud or performed and justify with evidence: e.g., language, messages, purpose, characters
- Think critically and discuss the relationship between the voice (rate, volume, word stress, pausing, phrasing, intonation) and the meaning of the script or poem
- Talk about whether a readers' theater script or play is interesting or enjoyable and why
- Talk about what makes dialogue effective in a play or readers' theater script: e.g., authenticity, rhythm

- Notice use of language and print conventions (e.g., sentence and paragraph structure, punctuation, tense agreement and change) by looking at an enlarged page with the group

Words

- Solve words using a flexible range of strategies to access different sources of information
- Recognize many multisyllable words or take apart as needed to solve them
- Recognize words with affixes (prefixes and suffixes) as well as base words

Language Structure (Syntax)

- Search for information across sentences, using language structure or syntax, meaning, and visual information in print
- Search for information across complex sentences
- Adjust to read phrases and sentences with unusual syntax to reflect rhythm or poetic language
- Adjust to read a variety of types of poetry

Vocabulary

- Add new words from texts to vocabulary constantly
- Notice and use words that add action or emotion to a text: e.g., words that represent sounds, strong verbs, adjectives, and adverbs, some expressions
- Recognize and understand the meaning of plurals in various forms
- Understand the meaning of words that are common for oral language (Tier 1)
- Understand the meaning of words (Tier 2) that appear often in literature but go beyond oral vocabulary, many poetic or literary
- Understand the meaning of a few words from the scientific domain (Tier 3)
- Use contextual information to solve the meaning of new words

● Thinking *Within* the Text   ◆ Thinking *Beyond* the Text   ■ Thinking *About* the Text

Selecting Goals Behaviors and Understandings to Notice, Teach, and Support *(cont.)*

Shared and Performance Reading

FICTION AND NONFICTION TEXTS *(continued)*

- Notice and understand words that are of high interest and novelty
- Understand the meaning of words that represent sounds: e.g., *buzz, hiss, pop, clang, plop*
- Understand the meaning of words used figuratively
- Use background information, illustrations, and reference tools to understand the meaning of content words
- Understand common (simple) connectives and a few sophisticated connectives

Fluency

- After practice, read all words quickly and automatically
- Use line breaks to guide phrasing when reading poetry in chorus or individually
- Adjust the voice to reflect dialogue in the body of the text
- Read orally with integration of all dimensions of fluency (e.g., pausing, phrasing, word stress, intonation, and rate) alone and while maintaining unison with others

Performance

- Recognize and reflect punctuation with the voice: e.g., period, question mark, exclamation point, dash, comma, ellipses, when reading in chorus or individually
- Recognize and reflect variations in print with the voice (e.g., italics, bold type, special treatments, font size) when reading in chorus or individually
- When reading individually or in unison with others, adjust the voice to reflect the mood of the text: e.g., sadness, tension, joy, humor
- Understand the role of the voice in communicating meaning in readers' theater, choral reading, songs, and poetry
- Read a part in a play or readers' theater script in a way that reflects the dialogue and the attributes and emotions of characters

- Maintain appropriate volume when performing in readers' theater, plays, and choral performances
- Adjust volume and tone of voice to reflect stage directions (e.g., *quietly, shouted, with a laugh*) and to read a script with fluency and expression
- Discuss with others how a script or poem should be read and state reasons based on plot, characters, meaning

Messages and Themes

- Follow and understand the ideas in poetry
- Identify the main ideas or messages in readers' theater scripts or poems used for choral reading
- Provide a concise statement summarizing a readers' theater script, choral reading, or poem, including the important information and the major themes or ideas
- Infer important ideas from reading a narrative nonfiction text
- Infer the writer's purpose
- Infer the writers' message or theme in a text
- Infer the significance of themes: e.g., friendship, families, relationships, self, the wonders of nature, feelings, cleverness, bravery, wisdom, appreciation of the sounds of language, cultural sensitivity
- Notice how the writer communicates the messages in a story, poem, or the dialogue of a script
- Talk about whether the message of a poem is important and justify opinion with evidence

Literary Elements

- Use understanding of genre and forms to monitor and correct reading
- Follow and understand simple plots in stories and readers' theater or plays
- Use understanding of types and elements of poetry to adjust reading

---

- Thinking **Within** the Text   ◆ Thinking **Beyond** the Text   ■ Thinking **About** the Text

Selecting Goals Behaviors and Understandings to Notice, Teach, and Support *(cont.)*

Shared and Performance Reading

FICTION AND NONFICTION TEXTS *(continued)*

Literary Elements *(continued)*

- Use the layout and punctuation of poems, readers' theater scripts, choral reading scripts, and plays to monitor and correct reading
- Use understanding of narrative structure in a fiction text to monitor and correct reading
- Use understanding of text structure in a nonfiction text (expository or narrative) to monitor and correct reading
- Make connections among texts by noting similarities: e.g., genre, form, text structure, characters, literary language, use of dialogue
- Talk about personal connections with content, characters, or events in a shared text, poem, play, or readers' theater script
- Use the events of a story or play to anticipate exciting places in a text or to predict what will happen next
- Make predictions based on understanding of text structure in fiction and nonfiction texts
- Make predictions based on understanding of characters and character motivation
- Infer characters' feelings and motivations and the relationships between characters from reading dialogue in a script
- Gain insight into perspectives of characters in fiction and real historical characters
- Gain insight into historical events from reflecting them in the reading of a script or poem
- Infer humor in a text
- Distinguish among various forms of manuscript used for performance: e.g., poems, readers' theater scripts, choral reading scripts, plays, letters, diaries, journal entries, short stories

- Notice whether a book, play, choral reading, or readers' theater script tells a story or gives information
- Recognize some characteristics of fiction and nonfiction genres in plays and readers' theater scripts
- Notice underlying structural patterns in a nonfiction text: e.g., description, temporal sequence, question and answer, cause and effect, chronological sequence, compare and contrast, problem and solution, categorization
- Notice the different ways that a writer tells a story in a fiction text (e.g., simple narrative structure, repeating episodes or language patterns, cumulative patterns, flashback, story-within-a-story) and how that affects understanding and enjoyment
- Notice how aspects of a text like rhyme, rhythm, and repetition affect appreciation or enjoyment
- Notice aspects of simple dialogue and use those aspects to decide how dialogue should be read
- Notice a writer's use of humor and identify what makes a script funny: e.g., characters, situation, language
- Notice interesting and playful language including made up words and onomatopoeic words
- Notice how a writer uses language to convey a mood
- Notice how a writer uses language to build tension or to describe action
- Notice a writer's use of strong and/or literary language in presenting an argument or idea in a nonfiction text
- Notice aspects of the writer's craft by looking at an enlarged page with the group

- Thinking **Within** the Text   ◆ Thinking **Beyond** the Text   ■ Thinking **About** the Text

Selecting Goals Behaviors and Understandings to Notice, Teach, and Support *(cont.)*

Shared and Performance Reading

FICTION AND NONFICTION TEXTS *(continued)*

- Use some academic language to talk about genres: e.g., *fiction, folktale, fairy tale, fractured fairy tale, fable, tall tale, adventure story, animal story, family, friends, and school story, humorous story, realistic fiction, traditional literature, historical fiction, fantasy; nonfiction, informational text, informational book, factual text, personal memory story, biography, autobiography, narrative nonfiction, memoir, procedural text, persuasive text*

- Use some academic language to talk about forms: e.g., *picture book, wordless picture book, label book, ABC book, counting book, poem, poetry, nursery rhyme, rhyme, song, poetry collection, series book, chapter book, play, letter, sequel, limerick, haiku, concrete poetry, short story, diary entry, journal entry, news article, feature article*

- Use some academic language to talk about literary features: e.g., *beginning, ending, problem, character, solution, main character, question and answer, topic, events, character change, message, dialogue, description, time order, setting, main idea, comparison and contrast, flashback, conflict, resolution, theme, descriptive language, simile, cause and effect, categorization, persuasive language*

- Use some academic language to talk about plays and performance: e.g., *line, speech, scene, act, actor, actress, role, part, hero, villain, playwright*

- Use some academic language to talk about book and print features: e.g., *front cover, back cover, title, author, illustrator, page, text, illustration, photograph, label, table of contents, acknowledgments, chapter, section, heading, drawing, caption, map, chapter title, dedication, author's note, illustrator's note, section, diagram, glossary, endpapers, sidebar, book jacket, subheading, chart, graph, timeline, index*

Book and Print Features

- Search for information in illustrations and in book and print features in an enlargement of a nonfiction text: e.g., drawing, photograph, map with legend or key, scale, diagram, infographic, cutaway; title, table of contents, chapter title, heading, subheading, sidebar, call-out

- Use illustrations (when applicable) to monitor and correct reading

- Shift attention from one part of a page layout to another to gather information: e.g., body text; drawing, photograph, map, diagram, infographic; label, caption, legend, key, scale, cutaway, sidebar, call-out

- Make connections between the body of the text and illustrations

- Make connections between text, illustrations, and book and print features: e.g., body text; drawing, photograph, map, diagram, infographic; label, caption, legend, key, scale, cutaway; title, table of contents, chapter title, heading, subheading, sidebar, call-out

- Notice and learn new ways to present information in nonfiction texts using illustrations and book and print features

- Infer information from nonfiction illustrations and book and print features

- Talk about illustrations and book and print features and evaluate whether they help readers understand information and add interest

---

● Thinking **Within** the Text   ◆ Thinking **Beyond** the Text   ■ Thinking **About** the Text

Selecting Texts Characteristics of Texts for Sharing and Performing

Shared and Performance Reading

GENRE

▶ Fiction

- Realistic fiction
- Historical fiction
- Traditional literature: e.g., folktale, tall tale, fairy tale, fractured fairy tale, fable, myth, legend
- More complex fantasy including science fiction
- Hybrid texts
- Special types of fiction: e.g., mystery; adventure story; animal story; family, friends, and school story; humorous story; sports story

▶ Nonfiction

- Expository nonfiction
- Narrative nonfiction
- Biography
- Autobiography
- Memoir
- Procedural texts
- Persuasive texts
- Hybrid texts

FORMS

- Poetry (much unrhymed) on many topics of various types: e.g., lyrical poetry, free verse, narrative poetry, limerick, haiku, ballad, concrete poetry
- Individual poetry collections
- Plays
- Readers' theater scripts, some designed by students
- Picture books
- Excerpts from chapter books, series books
- Letters, diaries, and journal entries
- Texts produced through shared writing
- Short stories
- Photo essays, news articles, and feature articles
- Speeches

TEXT STRUCTURE

- Narratives with straightforward structure but multiple episodes
- Excerpts that highlight particular literary features

- A few fiction texts with variations in narrative structure: e.g., story-within-a-story, flashback, flash-forward, time-lapse, circular plot, parallel plots
- Short excerpts or scripts drawn from longer texts in a variety of genres and text structures
- Informational texts with examples of argument and persuasion
- Underlying structural patterns: description, temporal sequence, question and answer, cause and effect, chronological sequence, compare and contrast, problem and solution, categorization
- Poems that may have narrative structure or reflect the organizational patterns of various types of poetry

CONTENT

- Content that is appropriate for students' cognitive development, emotional maturity, and life experience
- Content that engages intellectual curiosity and emotions
- Content that nurtures the imagination
- Topics important to preadolescents: e.g., sibling rivalry, friendship, growing up, family problems, and conflicts
- Poetic language related to concepts or parts of speech: e.g., alliteration, assonance, onomatopoetic words
- Humor conveyed through playful or created language
- Content that reinforces and expands a student's experience and knowledge of self and the world
- Many topics that may be beyond students' immediate experiences
- Content that reflects a wide range of settings, languages, and cultures
- Many texts requiring knowledge of cultural diversity around the world
- Some content linked to specific areas of study as described by the school curriculum or standards
- Texts that require critical thinking to judge the authenticity of facts and information
- Characters, settings, and events that could exist in contemporary life or in history
- Characters, settings, and events that occur in fantasy

- People, settings, and events in biographical texts that could exist in contemporary life or in history
- Content that reflects understanding of the physical and social world

THEMES AND IDEAS

- More sophisticated interpretation of themes: e.g., self-esteem, transition to adolescence, gender identity, family problems, peer relationships, belonging, popularity, bullying, courage, social awareness and responsibility, social justice, importance of historical events and people, life cycles, artistic expression and appreciation, poverty, racism, war, survival, interconnectedness of humans and the environment
- Themes, emotions, sensory experiences, inspiring ideas expressed through poetry
- Complex ideas requiring inference, sometimes expressed through the language of poetry
- More sophisticated interpretation of ideas close to students' experience: e.g., becoming independent; facing fears; overcoming challenges; expressing self through creativity; following dreams; appreciating differences; empathizing with others; learning from the lives of others; valuing change in self and others; taking care of the environment; connecting past, present, and future; appreciating nature

LANGUAGE AND LITERARY FEATURES

- Descriptive language conveying sensory experiences and a range of human feelings
- Descriptive and figurative language that is important to understanding the content: imagery, metaphor, simile, personification, hyperbole
- Some texts and poems with basic or obvious symbolism used to convey larger meaning
- Poetic language
- Sensory imagery expressed in poetry
- Rhythm and repetition of words and language patterns, as well as rhymes
- Language and events that convey an emotional atmosphere (mood) in a text, affecting how the reader feels

Selecting Texts Characteristics of Texts for Sharing and Performing *(cont.)*

Shared and Performance Reading

- Language that expresses the author's or speaker's attitude or feelings toward a subject reflected in the style of writing (tone)
- Settings important to the plot, many distant in time and place from students' own experiences
- Excerpts from some longer texts with one or more subplots
- Main characters and supporting characters, some with multiple dimensions, especially in plays
- Characters with distinct attributes revealed through dialogue and behavior, especially in plays
- Characters that are complex and change over time
- Both assigned and unassigned dialogue, including some strings of unassigned dialogue for which speakers must be inferred
- Description of actions, appearance, behavior of characters given in stage directions in script
- Some texts told from multiple points of view
- Most texts written in first- or third-person narrative

SENTENCE COMPLEXITY

- Some long and complex sentences that require attention to follow
- Long sentences joined by semicolons or colons
- Variation in placement of subject, verb, multiple adjectives, adverbs, and prepositions
- Sentences with embedded clauses (independent and dependent) and phrases
- Sentences with common (simple) connectives
- Extended dialogue that increases sentence complexity
- Poetic texts that include some nonstandard sentences
- Variation of tense that changes text complexity: e.g., *goes, was going, will be going*
- Some texts with long sentences divided into bulleted or numbered lists

- Sentence structure adapted to fit purpose and form of book and print features: e.g., heading, subheading, label, caption, legend

VOCABULARY

- Some interesting words that may be new to students
- New content words related to concepts that students are learning
- Sophisticated connectives (words that link ideas and clarify meaning that are used in written texts but do not appear often in everyday oral language): e.g., *although, however, meantime, meanwhile, moreover, otherwise, therefore, though, unless, until, whenever, yet*
- Many words that appear in the vocabulary of mature language users (Tier 2)
- Some words that are particular to a scientific discipline (Tier 3), especially in nonfiction
- A few content words (labels) related to concepts that students can understand
- Words to assign dialogue that guide readers in interpretation of the text: e.g., *confessed, instructed, modestly*
- Some words with multiple meanings, requiring interpretation to be conveyed through the voice
- Some words with connotative meanings, requiring interpretation to be conveyed through the voice
- Some idioms and other words with figurative meaning
- Some words (including slang) used informally by particular groups of people
- Some words from regional or historical dialects
- Some words from languages other than English
- Some technical vocabulary

WORDS

- Many multisyllable words, some technical or scientific
- Some multisyllable words with complex letter-sound relationships
- A full range of plurals in single-syllable and multisyllable words
- Full range of compound words
- Words with affixes (prefixes and suffixes) attached to a base word or root

- Wide range of contractions and possessives
- Some words divided (hyphenated) across lines
- Words that offer decoding challenges because they come from regional dialect or are from languages other than English

ILLUSTRATIONS

- Illustrations in a variety of media that provide high support for comprehending language
- Some pieces of shared writing with no illustrations
- Many texts with decorative illustrations (vignettes)
- Some books with black-and-white illustrations
- Some texts with no illustrations other than decorative elements such as illuminated letters or border decoration (vignettes)
- Individual scripts with decorative illustrations
- Student-created illustrations and decorations designed to enhance performance
- Illustrations that convey mood
- Illustrations that reflect the theme
- Some illustrations with figurative and symbolic characteristics requiring interpretation
- Illustrations in a variety of forms: e.g., drawing with label or caption, photograph with label or caption, map with legend, diagram, infographic, chart, graph, timeline

BOOK AND PRINT FEATURES

LENGTH

- Short texts that can be read in one sitting

PRINT AND LAYOUT

- Some texts with enlarged print (poems, charts)
- Individual copies of scripts or plays
- Varied number of lines on a page
- Variation in layout across pages
- Dialogue presented in script format in plays and scripts
- Some words in boldface, italics, or varying font sizes

Selecting Texts Characteristics of Texts for Sharing and Performing (cont.)

Shared and Performance Reading

BOOK AND PRINT FEATURES
(continued)

PUNCTUATION

■ Wide range of punctuation: e.g., period, question mark, exclamation mark, comma, quotation marks, ellipses, dash, parentheses, hyphen, colon

ORGANIZATIONAL TOOLS

■ Title, author, and illustrator listed on cover and on title page
■ Table of contents, chapter title, list of characters, section heading, subheading, sidebar

TEXT RESOURCES

■ Some books with dedication, acknowledgments, author's note, foreword, prologue, pronunciation guide, footnote, epilogue, appendix, endnote, glossary, references, index

Selecting Goals Behaviors and Understandings to Notice, Teach, and Support

Shared and Performance Reading

FICTION AND NONFICTION TEXTS

General

- ● Tell what happens in a readers' theater script or a play
- ● Provide a logically organized oral summary of the story or play
- ● Provide an oral summary that includes the important information in a nonfiction text
- ● Search for and use information in readers' theater scripts: e.g., lines, stage directions, punctuation, titles, headings
- ● Follow and understand content to derive facts from a nonfiction text
- ● Use content knowledge to monitor and correct while reading fiction
- ● Notice when understanding is lost and take steps to make a text make sense (monitor)
- ◆ Acquire new ideas, information, perspectives, and attitudes from reading parts in scripts and poems
- ◆ Make connections between historical and current events and the scripts in plays and other readings
- ◆ Infer the significance of a scene or vignette selected from a play for readers' theater
- ◆ Make connections between texts and readers' theater scripts that are made from them and understand the differences
- ◆ Infer reasons for selection of material to include in scripts (for readers' theater based on a longer narrative or expository text)
- ■ Express opinions about texts and justify with evidence
- ■ Express an opinion about the suitability of a text to be read aloud or performed and justify with evidence: e.g., language, messages, purpose, characters
- ■ Think critically and discuss the relationship between nonverbal behavior, the voice, and the meaning of the script, poem, or play
- ■ Talk about whether a readers' theater script or play is interesting or enjoyable and why
- ■ Talk about what makes dialogue effective in a play or readers' theater script: e.g., authenticity, rhythm
- ■ Notice use of language and print conventions (e.g., sentence and paragraph structure, punctuation, tense agreement and change) by looking at an enlarged page with the group

Words

- ● Solve words using a flexible range of strategies to access different sources of information
- ● Recognize plurals and possessives as well as words with affixes (prefixes and suffixes)

Language Structure (Syntax)

- ● Search for information across sentences, using language structure or syntax, meaning, and visual information in print
- ● Search for information across complex sentences
- ● Adjust to read phrases and sentences with unusual syntax to reflect rhythm or poetic language
- ● Adjust to read a variety of types of poetry

Vocabulary

- ● Add new words from texts to vocabulary constantly
- ● Notice and use words that add action or emotion to a text: e.g., words that represent sounds, strong verbs, adjectives, and adverbs, some expressions
- ● Recognize and understand the meaning of plurals in various forms
- ● Understand the meaning of words that are common for oral language (Tier 1)
- ● Understand the meaning of words (Tier 2) that appear often in literature but go beyond oral vocabulary, many poetic or literary
- ● Understand the meaning of some words particular to a discipline (Tier 3), including some scientific words used in a literary way: e.g., *magnetic personality*
- ● Use contextual information to solve the meaning of new words
- ● Notice and understand words that are of high interest and novelty
- ● Understand the meaning of words that represent sounds: e.g., *buzz, hiss, pop, clang, plop, quack*
- ● Understand the writer's meaning when words are used in figures of speech or idioms
- ● Understand the connotative meaning of words and how they add to the overall meaning of a script or poem
- ● Use background information, illustrations, and reference tools to understand the meaning of content words
- ● Understand common (simple) and sophisticated connectives

Fluency

- ● After practice, read all words quickly and automatically
- ● Use line breaks and white space to guide phrasing when reading poetry in unison or individually
- ● Adjust the voice to reflect dialogue in the body of the text
- ● Read orally with integration of all dimensions of fluency (e.g., pausing, phrasing, word stress, intonation, and rate) alone and while maintaining unison with others

---

● Thinking **Within** the Text   ◆ Thinking **Beyond** the Text   ■ Thinking **About** the Text

Selecting Goals Behaviors and Understandings to Notice, Teach, and Support *(cont.)*

Shared and Performance Reading

FICTION AND NONFICTION TEXTS *(continued)*

Performance

- Recognize and reflect punctuation with the voice: e.g., period, question mark, exclamation point, dash, comma, ellipses, when reading in chorus or individually
- Recognize and reflect variations in print with the voice (e.g., italics, bold type, special treatments, font size) when reading in chorus or individually
- When reading individually or in unison with others, adjust the voice to reflect the mood of the text: e.g., sadness, tension, joy, humor
- Understand the role of the voice in communicating meaning in readers' theater, choral reading, songs, and poetry
- Read a part in a play or readers' theater script in a way that reflects the dialogue and the attributes and emotions of characters
- Adjust the voice to communicate the attitudes of the original speaker when reading a speech aloud
- Maintain appropriate volume when performing in readers' theater, plays, and choral performances
- Adjust volume and tone of voice to reflect stage directions (e.g., *quietly, shouted, with a laugh*) and to read a script with fluency and expression
- ◆ Make decisions about how a role in a play should be read based on character attributes and the events of the plot
- ■ Discuss with others how a script or poem should be read and state reasons based on plot, characters, meaning

Messages and Themes

- Follow and understand the ideas in poetry
- Identify the main ideas or messages in readers' theater scripts or poems used for choral reading
- Provide a concise statement summarizing a readers' theater script, choral reading, or poem, including the important information and the major themes or ideas
- ◆ Infer important ideas from reading a narrative nonfiction text
- ◆ Infer the writer's purpose
- ◆ Infer the poet's message in a poem and use inferences as a basis for interpretation in performance
- ◆ Infer the significance of themes: e.g., friendship, families, relationships, self, the wonders of nature, feelings, cleverness, bravery, wisdom, appreciation of the sounds of language, cultural sensitivity, loss, patriotism, war, death
- ■ Notice how the writer communicates the messages in a story, poem, or the dialogue of a script
- ■ Talk about whether the message of a poem is important and justify opinion with evidence

Literary Elements

- Use understanding of genre and forms to monitor and correct reading
- Follow and understand plots in stories, poems, readers' theater, or plays
- Use understanding of types and elements of poetry to adjust reading
- Use the layout and punctuation of poems, readers' theater scripts, choral reading scripts, and plays to monitor and correct reading
- Use understanding of narrative structure in a fiction text to monitor and correct reading
- Use understanding of text structure in a nonfiction text (expository or narrative) to monitor and correct reading
- ◆ Make connections among texts by noting similarities: e.g., genre, form, text structure, characters, literary language, use of dialogue
- ◆ Talk about personal connections with content, characters, or events in a shared text, poem, play, short story, or readers' theater script
- ◆ Use the events of a text to predict what will happen next
- ◆ Make predictions based on understanding of text structure in fiction and nonfiction texts
- ◆ Make predictions based on understanding of characters and character motivation
- ◆ Infer feelings and motivations of people from history and characters in realistic fiction from reading dialogue in a script and performing in a play or readers' theater
- ◆ Infer the feelings, motivations, and messages of historical and living public figures through reading and performing their speeches and interviews
- ◆ Gain insight into perspectives and ideas of characters in fiction and real historical characters through reenacting their roles in scripts, speeches, or interviews
- ◆ Gain insight into historical or living individuals based on reading and reenacting their speeches or reenacting interviews
- ◆ Gain insight into historical events from reflecting them in the reading of a script or poem
- ■ Understand that all texts used for shared reading may be classified as prose or poetry and further classified by genre

---

● Thinking **Within** the Text   ◆ Thinking **Beyond** the Text   ■ Thinking **About** the Text

SHARED AND PERFORMANCE READING

Selecting Goals Behaviors and Understandings to Notice, Teach, and Support (cont.)

Shared and Performance Reading

FICTION AND NONFICTION TEXTS (continued)

- Distinguish among various forms of manuscript used for performance: e.g., poems, readers' theater scripts, choral reading scripts, plays, letters, diaries, journal entries, short stories, speeches
- Notice whether a book, play, choral reading, or readers' theater script tells a story or gives information
- Recognize some characteristics of fiction and nonfiction genres in plays and readers' theater scripts
- Notice underlying structural patterns in a nonfiction text: e.g., description, temporal sequence, question and answer, cause and effect, chronological sequence, compare and contrast, problem and solution, categorization
- Notice aspects of dialogue and use those aspects to decide how dialogue should be read
- Notice a writer's use of humor and identify what makes a script funny: e.g., characters, situation, language
- Notice how a writer uses language to convey a mood
- Notice how a writer uses language to build tension or to describe action
- Notice a writer's use of strong and/or literary language in presenting an argument or idea in a nonfiction text
- Notice aspects of the writer's craft when looking at an enlarged page with the group
- Notice the different ways that a writer tells a story in a fiction text (e.g., simple narrative structure, cumulative patterns, flashback, story-within-a-story, flash-forward, time-lapse, circular plot, parallel plots) and how that affects understanding and enjoyment
- Use some academic language to talk about genres: e.g., *fiction, folktale, fairy tale, fractured fairy tale, fable, tall tale, adventure story, animal story, family, friends, and school story, humorous story, realistic fiction, traditional literature, historical fiction, fantasy, myth, legend, ballad, science fiction, hybrid text; nonfiction, informational text, informational book, factual text, personal memory story, biography, autobiography, narrative nonfiction, memoir, procedural text, persuasive text, expository text*
- Use some academic language to talk about forms: e.g., *picture book, wordless picture book, label book, ABC book, counting book, poem, poetry, nursery rhyme, rhyme, song, poetry collection, series book, chapter book, play, letter, sequel, limerick, haiku, concrete poetry, short story, diary entry, journal entry, news article, feature article, narrative poetry, photo essay, speech*

- Use some academic language to talk about literary features: e.g., *beginning, ending, problem, character, solution, main character, question and answer, topic, events, message, dialogue, description, setting, main idea, comparison and contrast, flashback, conflict, resolution, theme, descriptive language, simile, figurative language, metaphor, cause and effect, categorization, persuasive language, plot, subplot, flash-forward, character development, supporting character, point of view, temporal sequence, chronological sequence, subject, argument*
- Use some academic language to talk about plays and performance: e.g., *line, speech, scene, act, actor, actress, role, part, hero, villain, playwright, enter, exit, skit, vignette, dramatization, pace, tempo, timing*
- Use some academic language to talk about book and print features: e.g., *front cover, back cover, title, author, illustrator, page, text, illustration, photograph, label, table of contents, acknowledgments, chapter, section, heading, drawing, caption, map, chapter title, dedication, author's note, illustrator's note, section, diagram, glossary, endpapers, sidebar, book jacket, subheading, chart, graph, timeline, index*

Book and Print Features

- Search for information in illustrations and in book and print features in an enlargement of a nonfiction text: e.g., drawing, photograph, map with legend or key, scale, diagram, infographic, cutaway; title, table of contents, chapter title, heading, subheading, sidebar, call-out
- Use illustrations (when applicable) to monitor and correct reading
- Shift attention from one part of a page layout to another to gather information: e.g., body text; drawing, photograph, map, diagram, infographic; label, caption, legend, key, scale, cutaway, sidebar, call-out
- Make connections between the body of the text and illustrations
- Make connections between text, illustrations, and book and print features: e.g., body text; drawing, photograph, map, diagram, infographic; label, caption, legend, key, scale, cutaway; title, table of contents, chapter title, heading, subheading, sidebar, call-out
- Notice and learn new ways to present information in nonfiction texts using illustrations and book and print features
- Infer information from nonfiction illustrations and book and print features
- Talk about illustrations and book and print features and evaluate whether they help readers understand information and add interest

---

- Thinking *Within* the Text   ◆ Thinking *Beyond* the Text   ■ Thinking *About* the Text

Selecting Texts Characteristics of Texts for Sharing and Performing

Shared and Performance Reading

GENRE

▶ **Fiction**

- Realistic fiction
- Historical fiction
- Traditional literature: e.g., folktale, tall tale, fairy tale, fractured fairy tale, fable, myth, legend
- More complex fantasy including science fiction
- Hybrid texts
- Special types of fiction: e.g., mystery; adventure story; animal story; family, friends, and school story; humorous story; sports story

▶ **Nonfiction**

- Expository nonfiction
- Narrative nonfiction
- Biography
- Autobiography
- Memoir
- Procedural texts
- Persuasive texts
- Hybrid texts

FORMS

- Poetry (much unrhymed) on many topics of various types: e.g., lyrical poetry, free verse, narrative poetry, limerick, haiku, ballad, concrete poetry
- Individual poetry collections
- Plays
- Readers' theater scripts, some designed by students
- Picture books
- Sections of longer chapter books and series books that can be adapted to choral reading or readers' theater scripts
- Letters, diaries, and journal entries
- Texts produced through shared writing
- Short stories
- Photo essays, news articles, and feature articles
- Speeches
- Newscasts, documentaries, other informational texts that can be adapted to choral reading or readers' theater scripts

TEXT STRUCTURE

- Narratives with straightforward structure but multiple episodes
- Excerpts that highlight particular literary features
- A few fiction texts with variations in narrative structure: e.g., story-within-a-story, flashback, flash-forward, time-lapse, circular plot, parallel plots
- Short excerpts or scripts drawn from longer texts in a variety of genres and text structures
- Informational text with examples of argument and persuasion
- Underlying structural patterns: description, temporal sequence, question and answer, cause and effect, chronological sequence, compare and contrast, problem and solution, categorization
- Poems that may have narrative structure or reflect the organizational patterns of various types of poetry

CONTENT

- Content that is appropriate for students' cognitive development, emotional maturity, and life experience
- Content that engages intellectual curiosity and emotions
- Content that nurtures the imagination
- Topics of interest to adolescents: e.g., personal and societal issues such as friendship, growing up, sexism, racism, oppression, poverty
- Poetic language related to concepts or parts of speech: e.g., alliteration, assonance, onomatopoetic words
- Humor conveyed through playful or created language
- Content that reinforces and expands a student's experience and knowledge of self and the world
- Many topics that may be beyond students' immediate experiences
- Content that reflects a wide range of settings, languages, and cultures
- Many texts requiring knowledge of cultural diversity around the world
- Some content linked to specific areas of study as described by the school curriculum or standards

- Texts that require critical thinking to judge the authenticity of facts and information
- Characters, settings, and events that could exist in contemporary life or in history
- Characters, settings, and events that occur in fantasy
- People, settings, and events in biographical texts that could exist in contemporary life or in history
- Content that reflects understanding of the physical and social world

THEMES AND IDEAS

- Universal themes appropriate to adolescence: e.g., self-esteem; physical, social, and emotional self-awareness; gender identity; family; peer relationships; popularity; bullying; courage; social awareness and responsibility; social justice; importance of historical events and people; life cycles; artistic expression and appreciation; political and social issues including human rights, racism, poverty, war; interconnectedness of humans and the environment
- Themes, emotions, sensory experiences, inspiring ideas expressed through poetry
- Complex ideas requiring inference, sometimes expressed through the language of poetry
- More sophisticated interpretation of ideas close to students' experience: e.g., becoming independent; facing fears; overcoming challenges; expressing self through creativity; coping with physical, emotional, and social changes; following dreams; appreciating differences; empathizing with others; learning from the lives of others; valuing change in self and others; taking care of the environment; connecting past, present, and future; appreciating nature

LANGUAGE AND LITERARY FEATURES

- Descriptive language conveying sensory experiences and a range of human feelings
- Descriptive and figurative language that is important to understanding the content: imagery, metaphor, simile, personification, hyperbole
- Texts with symbolism used to convey larger meaning

Selecting Texts Characteristics of Texts for Sharing and Performing *(cont.)*

Shared and Performance Reading

- Poetic and literary language
- Rhythm and repetition of words and language patterns, as well as rhymes
- Language and events that convey an emotional atmosphere (mood) in a text, affecting how the reader feels
- Language that expresses the author's attitude or feelings toward a subject reflected in the style of writing (tone)
- Settings important to the plot, many distant in time and place from students' own experiences
- Excerpts from some longer texts with one or more subplots
- Main characters and supporting characters, some with multiple dimensions, especially in plays
- Characters with distinct attributes revealed through dialogue (sometimes with unconventional use of language) and behavior, especially in plays
- Characters that are complex and change over time
- Both assigned and unassigned dialogue, including some strings of unassigned dialogue for which speakers must be inferred, and occasional use of monologue
- Description of actions, appearance, behavior of characters given in stage directions in script
- Some texts told from multiple points of view
- Most texts written in first- or third-person narrative

SENTENCE COMPLEXITY

- Some long and complex sentences that require attention to follow
- Long sentences joined by semicolons or colons
- Variation in placement of subject, verb, multiple adjectives, adverbs, and prepositions
- Sentences with embedded clauses (independent and dependent) and phrases
- Sentences with common (simple) connectives, sophisticated connectives, and academic connectives
- Extended dialogue or monologue that increases sentence complexity
- Poetic texts that include some nonstandard sentences

- Variation of tense that changes text complexity: e.g., *goes, was going, will be going*
- Some texts with long sentences divided into bulleted or numbered lists
- Sentence structure adapted to fit purpose and form of book and print features: e.g., heading, subheading, label, caption, legend

VOCABULARY

- Some interesting words that may be new to students
- New content words related to concepts that students are learning
- Sophisticated connectives (words that link ideas and clarify meaning and that are used in written texts but do not appear often in everyday oral language): e.g., *although, however, meantime, meanwhile, moreover, otherwise, therefore, though, unless, until, whenever, yet*
- Academic connectives (words that link ideas and clarify meaning and that appear in written texts): e.g., *alternatively, consequently, despite, conversely, eventually, finally, in contrast, initially, likewise, nevertheless, nonetheless, previously, specifically, ultimately, whereas, whereby*
- Many words that appear in the vocabulary of mature language users (Tier 2)
- Some words that are particular to a discipline (Tier 3), especially in nonfiction
- A few content words (labels) related to concepts that students can understand
- Words to assign dialogue that guide readers in interpretation of the text: e.g., *fumbled, informed, sensibly*
- Some words with multiple meanings, requiring interpretation to be conveyed through the voice
- Some words with connotative meanings, requiring interpretation to be conveyed through the voice
- Some idioms and other words with figurative meaning
- Some words (including slang) used informally by particular groups of people
- Some words from regional or historical dialects
- Some archaic words

- Some words from languages other than English
- Technical vocabulary

WORDS

- Many multisyllable words, some technical or scientific
- Some multisyllable words with complex letter-sound relationships
- A full range of plurals in single-syllable and multisyllable words
- Full range of compound words
- Words with affixes (prefixes and suffixes) attached to a base word or root
- Wide range of contractions and possessives
- Some words divided (hyphenated) across lines
- Words that offer decoding challenges because they are archaic, come from regional dialect, or are from languages other than English

ILLUSTRATIONS

- Illustrations in a variety of media that provide high support for comprehending language
- Some pieces of shared writing with no illustrations
- Many texts with decorative illustrations
- Some books with black-and-white illustrations
- Some texts with no illustrations other than decorative elements such as illuminated letters or border decoration
- Individual scripts with decorative illustrations
- Student-created illustrations and decorations designed to enhance performance
- Illustrations that convey mood
- Illustrations that reflect the theme
- Some illustrations with figurative and symbolic characteristics requiring interpretation
- Illustrations in a variety of forms: e.g., drawing with label or caption, photograph with label or caption, map with legend, diagram, infographic, chart, graph, timeline

Selecting Texts Characteristics of Texts for Sharing and Performing *(cont.)*

Shared and Performance Reading

SHARED AND
PERFORMANCE READING

BOOK AND PRINT FEATURES

LENGTH

- Short texts that can be read in one sitting

PRINT AND LAYOUT

- Individual copies of scripts or plays
- Variation in layout across pages
- Dialogue presented in script format in plays and scripts
- Some words in boldface, italics, or varying font sizes
- Page numbers

PUNCTUATION

- Wide range of punctuation: e.g., period, question mark, exclamation mark, comma, quotation marks, ellipses, dash, parentheses, hyphen, colon

ORGANIZATIONAL TOOLS

- Title, author, and illustrator listed on cover and on title page
- Table of contents, chapter title, list of characters, section heading, subheading, sidebar

TEXT RESOURCES

- Some books with dedication, acknowledgments, author's note, foreword, prologue, pronunciation guide, footnote, epilogue, appendix, endnote, glossary, references, index, bibliography

Selecting Goals Behaviors and Understandings to Notice, Teach, and Support

Shared and Performance Reading

FICTION AND NONFICTION TEXTS

General

- Tell what happens in a readers' theater script or a play
- Provide an oral summary of the story or play
- Provide an oral summary that includes the important information in a nonfiction text
- Provide a concise oral summary of a work of fiction (play, choral reading, poem) that includes all essential literary elements and the main idea
- Search for and use information in readers' theater scripts: e.g., lines, stage directions, punctuation, titles, headings
- Follow and understand content to derive facts from a nonfiction text
- Use content knowledge to monitor and correct while reading fiction
- Notice when understanding is lost and take steps to make a text make sense (monitor)
- Acquire new information, ideas, and perspectives from reading scripts for plays and readers' theater, poems, and speeches, and vignettes from biographies and memoirs
- Make connections between historical and current events and the scripts in plays and other readings
- Infer the significance of a scene or vignette selected from a play for readers' theater
- Make connections between texts and readers' theater scripts that are made from them and understand the differences
- Infer reasons for selection of material to include in scripts (for readers' theater based on a longer narrative or expository text)
- Express opinions about texts and justify with evidence
- Express an opinion about the suitability of a text to be read aloud or performed and justify with evidence: e.g., language, messages, purpose, characters
- Think critically and discuss the relationship between nonverbal behavior, the voice, and the meaning of the script, poem, or play
- Talk about whether a readers' theater script or play is interesting or enjoyable and why
- Talk about what makes dialogue and monologue effective in a play or readers' theater script: e.g., authenticity, rhythm
- Notice use of language and print conventions (e.g., sentence and paragraph structure, punctuation, tense agreement and change) by looking at an enlarged page with the group
- Critique the writer's stance toward a topic, idea, emotion, or situation in a script, poem, or speech

Words

- Solve words using a flexible range of strategies to access different sources of information
- Automatically read approximately 500+ high-frequency words
- Recognize plurals and possessives
- Recognize words with affixes (prefixes and suffixes)

Language Structure (Syntax)

- Search for information across sentences, using language structure or syntax, meaning, and visual information in print
- Search for information across complex sentences
- Adjust to read phrases and sentences with unusual syntax to reflect rhythm or poetic language
- Adjust to read a variety of types of poetry

Vocabulary

- Add new words from texts to vocabulary constantly
- Notice and use words that add action or emotion to a text: e.g., words that represent sounds, strong verbs, adjectives, and adverbs, some expressions
- Recognize and understand the meaning of plurals in various forms
- Understand the meaning of words (Tier 2) that appear often in literature but go beyond oral vocabulary, many poetic or literary
- Understand the meaning of some words particular to a discipline (Tier 3), especially when used figuratively or in scientific argument
- Use contextual information to solve the meaning of new words
- Notice and understand words that are of high interest and novelty
- Understand the meaning of words that represent sounds: e.g., *buzz, hiss, pop, clang, plop, quack, thump*
- Understand the writer's meaning when words are used in figures of speech or idioms
- Understand the connotative meaning of words and how they add to the overall meaning of a script or poem
- Use background information, illustrations, and reference tools to understand the meaning of content words
- Rapidly and automatically use a range of strategies (e.g., syllables, morphology, base words and affixes, Greek and Latin word roots) for deriving the meaning of words
- Understand common (simple) connectives, sophisticated connectives, and some academic connectives

Fluency

- After practice, read all words quickly and automatically
- Use line breaks and white space to guide phrasing when reading poetry in unison or individually
- Adjust the voice to reflect dialogue and monologue in the body of the text
- Read orally with integration of all dimensions of fluency (e.g., pausing, phrasing, word stress, intonation, and rate) alone and while maintaining unison with others
- After practice, give dramatic and interpretive oral reading of a script

---

- Thinking *Within* the Text   ◆ Thinking *Beyond* the Text   ■ Thinking *About* the Text

Selecting Goals Behaviors and Understandings to Notice, Teach, and Support *(cont.)*

Shared and Performance Reading

FICTION AND NONFICTION TEXTS *(continued)*

Performance

- Recognize and reflect punctuation with the voice: e.g., period, question mark, exclamation point, dash, comma, ellipses, when reading in chorus or individually
- Recognize and reflect variations in print with the voice (e.g., italics, bold type, special treatments, font size) when reading in chorus or individually
- When reading individually or in unison with others, adjust the voice to reflect the mood of the text: e.g., sadness, tension, joy, humor
- Understand the role of the voice in communicating meaning in readers' theater, choral reading, songs, and poetry
- Read a part in a play or readers' theater script in a way that reflects the dialogue and monologue and the attributes and emotions of characters
- Use the voice to communicate an individual interpretation of a role in a play or readers' theater script
- Understand the original intent of a speech or public discourse and reflect the appropriate tone when reading aloud
- Maintain appropriate volume when performing in readers' theater, plays, and choral performances
- Adjust volume and tone of voice to reflect stage directions (e.g., *quietly, shouted, with a laugh*) and to read a script with fluency and expression
- ◆ Make decisions about how a role in a play should be read based on character attributes and the events of the plot
- ◆ Make decisions about how the characters in a play should sound based on knowledge of history and culture
- ◆ Make decisions about how to read a speech based on knowledge of history or understanding of current events and issues
- ■ Discuss with others how a script or poem should be read and state reasons based on plot, characters, meaning

Messages and Themes

- Follow and understand the ideas in poetry
- Identify the main ideas or messages in readers' theater scripts or poems used for choral reading
- ◆ Infer important ideas from reading a narrative nonfiction text
- ◆ Infer the writer's purpose
- ◆ Infer the poet's message in a poem and use inferences as a basis for interpretation in performance
- ◆ Use inferences as a basis for interpretation of characters in plays or readers' theater or of the speaker in public discourse
- ◆ Infer the significance of themes: e.g., friendship, families, relationships, self, the wonders of nature, feelings, cleverness, bravery, wisdom, appreciation of the sounds of language, cultural sensitivity, loss, patriotism, war, death
- ■ Notice how the writer communicates the messages in a story, poem, or the dialogue of a script

- ■ Talk about whether the message of a poem is important and justify opinion with evidence

Literary Elements

- Use understanding of genre and forms to monitor and correct reading
- Follow and understand plots in stories, poems, readers' theater, or plays
- Use understanding of types and elements of poetry to adjust reading
- Use the layout and punctuation of poems, readers' theater scripts, choral reading scripts, and plays to monitor and correct reading
- Use understanding of narrative structure in a fiction text to monitor and correct reading
- Use understanding of text structure in a nonfiction text (expository or narrative) to monitor and correct reading
- ◆ Make connections among texts by noting similarities: e.g., genre, form, text structure, characters, literary language, use of dialogue and monologue
- ◆ Talk about personal connections with content, characters, or events in a shared text, poem, play, short story, or readers' theater script
- ◆ Use the events of a text to predict what will happen next
- ◆ Make predictions based on understanding of text structure in fiction and nonfiction texts
- ◆ Make predictions based on understanding of characters and character motivation
- ◆ Infer feelings and motivations of people from history and characters in realistic fiction from reading dialogue and monologue in a script and performing in a play or readers' theater
- ◆ Infer the feelings, motivations, and messages of historical and living public figures through reading and performing their speeches and interviews
- ◆ Gain insight into perspectives and ideas of characters in fiction and real historical characters through reenacting their roles in scripts, speeches, and interviews
- ◆ Gain insight into historical and cultural perspectives by reading and performing fiction and nonfiction texts
- ◆ Infer the writer's stance toward the theme, topic, or main idea of script, poem, or speech and use it to guide interpretation
- ■ Understand that all texts used for shared reading may be classified as prose or poetry and further classified by genre
- ■ Distinguish among various forms of manuscript used for performance: e.g., poems, readers' theater scripts, choral reading scripts, plays, letters, diaries, journal entries, short stories, speeches
- ■ Notice whether a book, play, choral reading, or readers' theater script tells a story or gives information

- ● Thinking **Within** the Text   ◆ Thinking **Beyond** the Text   ■ Thinking **About** the Text

Selecting Goals Behaviors and Understandings to Notice, Teach, and Support *(cont.)*

Shared and Performance Reading

FICTION AND NONFICTION TEXTS *(continued)*

- Recognize some characteristics of fiction and nonfiction genres in plays and readers' theater scripts
- Notice underlying structural patterns in a nonfiction text: e.g., description, temporal sequence, question and answer, cause and effect, chronological sequence, compare and contrast, problem and solution, categorization
- Notice aspects of dialogue and monologue and use those aspects to decide how dialogue and monologue should be read
- Discuss various interpretations of the attributes and motives of characters in plays and readers' theater scripts
- Notice a writer's use of humor and identify what makes a script funny: e.g., characters, situation, language
- Notice how a writer uses language to convey a mood
- Notice how a writer uses language to build tension or to describe action
- Notice a writer's use of strong and/or literary language in presenting an argument or idea in a nonfiction text
- Use some academic language to talk about genres: e.g., *fiction, folktale, fairy tale, fractured fairy tale, fable, tall tale, adventure story, animal story, family, friends, and school story, humorous story, realistic fiction, traditional literature, historical fiction, fantasy, myth, legend, ballad, science fiction, hybrid text; nonfiction, informational text, informational book, factual text, personal memory story, biography, autobiography, narrative nonfiction, memoir, procedural text, persuasive text, expository text*
- Use some academic language to talk about forms: e.g., *picture book, wordless picture book, label book, ABC book, counting book, poem, poetry, nursery rhyme, rhyme, song, poetry collection, series book, chapter book, play, letter, sequel, limerick, haiku, concrete poetry, short story, diary entry, journal entry, news article, feature article, narrative poetry, photo essay, speech, lyrical poetry, free verse, ballad*
- Use some academic language to talk about literary features: e.g., *beginning, ending, problem, character, solution, main character, question and answer, topic, events, message, dialogue, description, setting, main idea, comparison and contrast, flashback, conflict, resolution, theme, descriptive language, simile, figurative language, metaphor, cause and effect, categorization, persuasive language, plot, subplot, flash-forward, character development, supporting character, point of view, temporal sequence, chronological sequence, subject, argument, episode, climax, rising action, falling action, time-lapse, story-within-a-story, mood, personification, symbol, symbolism, first-person narrative, third-person narrative, second-person narrative*

- Use academic language to discuss the characteristics of poetry used for performance: e.g., *rhythm, refrain, rhyme, repetition, stress, verse, onomatopoeia, alliteration, assonance, consonance, couplet, imagery, figurative language, metaphor, simile, personification*
- Use some academic language to talk about plays and performance: e.g., *line, speech, scene, act, actor, actress, role, part, hero, villain, playwright, enter, exit, skit, vignette, dramatization, pace, tempo, timing, director, stage manager, producer, performer, designer, properties (props), lighting design, sound design*
- Use some academic language to talk about book and print features: e.g., *front cover, back cover, title, author, illustrator, page, text, illustration, photograph, label, table of contents, acknowledgments, chapter, section, heading, drawing, caption, map, chapter title, dedication, author's note, illustrator's note, section, diagram, glossary, endpapers, sidebar, book jacket, subheading, chart, graph, timeline, index*
- Notice aspects of the writer's craft when looking at an enlarged page with the group
- Notice the different ways that a writer tells a story in a fiction text (e.g., simple narrative structure, cumulative patterns, flashback, story-within-a-story, flash-forward, time-lapse, circular plot, parallel plots) and how that affects understanding and enjoyment

Book and Print Features

- Search for an enlargement of information in illustrations and in book and print features in an enlargement of a nonfiction text: e.g., drawing, photograph, map with legend or key, scale, diagram, infographic, cutaway; title, table of contents, chapter title, heading, subheading, sidebar, call-out
- Use illustrations (when applicable) to monitor and correct reading
- Shift attention from one part of a page layout to another to gather information: e.g., body text; drawing, photograph, map, diagram, infographic; label, caption, legend, key, scale, cutaway, sidebar, call-out
- Make connections between the body of the text and illustrations
- Make connections between text, illustrations, and book and print features: e.g., body text; drawing, photograph, map, diagram, infographic; label, caption, legend, key, scale, cutaway; title, table of contents, chapter title, heading, subheading, sidebar, call-out
- Notice and learn new ways to present information in nonfiction texts using illustrations and book and print features
- Infer information from nonfiction illustrations and book and print features
- Talk about illustrations and book and print features and evaluate whether they help readers understand information and add interest

● Thinking *Within* the Text ◆ Thinking *Beyond* the Text ■ Thinking *About* the Text

Selecting Texts Characteristics of Texts for Sharing and Performing

Shared and Performance Reading

GENRE

▶ **Fiction**

- Realistic fiction
- Historical fiction
- Traditional literature: e.g., folktale, tall tale, fairy tale, fractured fairy tale, fable, myth, legend, epic, ballad
- More complex fantasy including science fiction
- Hybrid texts
- Special types of fiction: e.g., mystery; adventure story; animal story; family, friends, and school story; humorous story; sports story; satire/parody; horror story; romance story

▶ **Nonfiction**

- Expository nonfiction
- Narrative nonfiction
- Biography
- Autobiography
- Memoir
- Procedural texts
- Persuasive texts
- Hybrid texts

FORMS

- Poetry (much unrhymed) on many topics of various types: e.g., lyrical poetry, free verse, narrative poetry, limerick, haiku, ballad, concrete poetry
- Individual poetry collections
- Plays
- Readers' theater scripts, some designed by students
- Picture books
- Sections of longer chapter books and series books that can be adapted to choral reading or readers' theater scripts
- Letters, diaries, and journal entries
- Texts produced through shared writing
- Short stories
- Photo essays, news articles, and feature articles
- Speeches
- Newscasts, documentaries, other informational texts that can be adapted to choral reading or readers' theater scripts

TEXT STRUCTURE

- Narratives with straightforward structure but multiple episodes
- Excerpts that highlight particular literary features
- A few fiction texts with variations in narrative structure: e.g., story-within-a-story, flashback, flash-forward, time-lapse, circular plot, parallel plots
- Short excerpts or scripts drawn from longer texts in a variety of genres and text structures
- Informational text with examples of argument and persuasion
- Underlying structural patterns: description, temporal sequence, question and answer, cause and effect, chronological sequence, compare and contrast, problem and solution, categorization
- Poems that may have narrative structure or reflect the organizational patterns of various types of poetry

CONTENT

- Content that is appropriate for a students' cognitive development, emotional maturity, and life experience
- Content that engages intellectual curiosity and emotions
- Content that nurtures the imagination
- Topics of interest to adolescents: e.g., personal and societal issues such as friendship, growing up, romance, sexism, racism, oppression, poverty, death, war
- Poetic language related to concepts or parts of speech: e.g., alliteration, assonance, onomatopoetic words
- Humor conveyed through playful or created language
- Content that reinforces and expands a student's experience and knowledge of self and the world
- Many topics that may be beyond students' immediate experiences
- Content that reflects a wide range of settings, languages, and cultures
- Many texts requiring knowledge of cultural diversity around the world
- Some content linked to specific areas of study as described by the school curriculum or standards

- Texts that require critical thinking to judge the authenticity of facts and information
- Characters, settings, and events that could exist in contemporary life or in history
- Characters, settings, and events that occur in fantasy
- People, settings, and events in biographical texts that could exist in contemporary life or in history
- Content that reflects understanding of the physical and social world

THEMES AND IDEAS

- Universal themes appropriate to adolescence: e.g., self-esteem; physical, social, and emotional self-awareness; gender identity; family; peer relationships; popularity; bullying; courage; social awareness and responsibility; social justice; importance of historical events and people; life cycles; artistic expression and appreciation; political and social issues including human rights, racism, poverty, war; interconnectedness of humans and the environment
- Themes, emotions, sensory experiences, inspiring ideas expressed through poetry
- Complex ideas requiring inference, sometimes expressed through the language of poetry
- More sophisticated interpretation of ideas close to students' experience: e.g., becoming independent; facing fears; overcoming challenges; expressing self through creativity; coping with physical, emotional, and social changes; following dreams; appreciating differences; empathizing with others; learning from the lives of others; valuing change in self and others; taking care of the environment; connecting past, present, and future; appreciating nature

LANGUAGE AND LITERARY FEATURES

- Descriptive language conveying sensory experiences and a range of human feelings
- Descriptive and figurative language that is important to understanding the content: imagery, metaphor, simile, personification, hyperbole
- Texts with subtle and/or complex use of symbolism, including allegory
- Poetic and literary language

Selecting Texts Characteristics of Texts for Sharing and Performing *(cont.)*

Shared and Performance Reading

- Rhythm and repetition of words and language patterns, as well as rhymes
- Language (including archaic language) and events that convey an emotional atmosphere (mood) in a text, affecting how the reader feels
- Language used to convey satire or irony
- Language that expresses the author's attitude or feelings toward a subject reflected in the style of writing (tone)
- Settings important to the plot, many distant in time and place from children's own experiences
- Excerpts from some longer texts with one or more subplots
- Main characters and supporting characters, some with multiple dimensions, especially in plays
- Characters with distinct attributes revealed through dialogue (sometimes with unconventional use of language) and behavior, especially in plays
- Characters that are complex and change over time
- Both assigned and unassigned dialogue, including some strings of unassigned dialogue for which speakers must be inferred, and occasional use of monologue
- Description of actions, appearance, behavior of characters given in stage directions in script
- Some texts told from multiple points of view
- Most texts written in first- or third-person narrative

SENTENCE COMPLEXITY

- Some long and complex sentences that require attention to follow
- Long sentences joined by semicolons or colons
- Variation in placement of subject, verb, multiple adjectives, adverbs, and prepositions
- Sentences with embedded clauses (independent and dependent) and phrases
- Sentences with common (simple) connectives, sophisticated connectives, and academic connectives
- Extended dialogue or monologue that increases sentence complexity
- Some dialogue or monologue with full range of complex language structures

- Poetic texts that include some nonstandard sentences
- Variation of tense that changes text complexity: e.g., *goes, was going, will be going*
- Some texts with long sentences divided into bulleted or numbered lists
- Sentence structure adapted to fit purpose and form of book and print features: e.g., heading, subheading, label, caption, legend

VOCABULARY

- Some interesting words that may be new to students
- New content words related to concepts that students are learning
- Sophisticated connectives (words that link ideas and clarify meaning and that are used in written texts but do not appear often in everyday oral language): e.g., *although, however, meantime, meanwhile, moreover, otherwise, therefore, though, unless, until, whenever, yet*
- Academic connectives (words that link ideas and clarify meaning and that appear in written texts but do not appear often in oral language): e.g., *alternatively, consequently, despite, conversely, eventually, finally, in contrast, initially, likewise, nevertheless, nonetheless, previously, specifically, ultimately, whereas, whereby*
- Many words that appear in the vocabulary of mature language users (Tier 2)
- Some words that are particular to a discipline (Tier 3), especially in nonfiction
- A few content words (labels) related to concepts that students can understand
- Words to assign dialogue that guide readers in interpretation of the text: e.g., *persisted, erupted, bashfully*
- Some words with multiple meanings, requiring interpretation to be conveyed through the voice
- Some words with connotative meanings, requiring interpretation to be conveyed through the voice
- Some words used to create irony, requiring interpretation to be conveyed through the voice
- Some idioms and other words with figurative meaning
- Some words (including slang) used informally by particular groups of people

- Some words from regional or historical dialects
- Some archaic words
- Some words from languages other than English
- Technical vocabulary

WORDS

- Many multisyllable words, some technical or scientific
- Some multisyllable words with complex letter-sound relationships
- A full range of plurals in single-syllable and multisyllable words
- Full range of compound words
- Base words with multiple affixes (prefixes and suffixes)
- Wide range of contractions and possessives
- Some words divided (hyphenated) across lines
- Words that offer decoding challenges because they are archaic, come from regional dialect, or are from languages other than English

ILLUSTRATIONS

- Illustrations in a variety of media that provide high support for comprehending language
- Some pieces of shared writing with no illustrations
- Many texts with decorative illustrations
- Some books with black-and-white illustrations
- Some texts with no illustrations other than decorative elements such as illuminated letters or border decoration
- Individual scripts with decorative illustrations
- Student-created illustrations and decorations designed to enhance performance
- Illustrations that convey mood
- Illustrations that reflect the theme
- Some illustrations with figurative and symbolic characteristics requiring interpretation
- Illustrations in a variety of forms: e.g., drawing with label or caption, photograph with label or caption, map with legend, diagram, infographic, chart, graph, timeline

Selecting Texts Characteristics of Texts for Sharing and Performing *(cont.)*

Shared and Performance Reading

BOOK AND PRINT FEATURES

LENGTH

- Short texts that can be read in one sitting

PRINT AND LAYOUT

- Some individual copies of scripts or plays
- Variation in layout across pages
- Dialogue presented in script form in plays and scripts
- Some words in boldface, italics, or varying font sizes
- Page numbers

PUNCTUATION

- Wide range of punctuation: e.g., period, question mark, exclamation mark, comma, quotation marks, ellipses, dash, parentheses, hyphen

ORGANIZATIONAL TOOLS

- Title, author, and illustrator listed on cover and on title page
- Table of contents, chapter title, list of characters, section heading, subheading, sidebar

TEXT RESOURCES

- Some books with dedication, acknowledgments, author's note, foreword, prologue, pronunciation guide, footnote, epilogue, appendix, endnote, glossary, references, index, bibliography

Selecting Goals Behaviors and Understandings to Notice, Teach, and Support

Shared and Performance Reading

FICTION AND NONFICTION TEXTS

General

- Tell what happens in a readers' theater script or a play
- Provide a logically organized oral summary of the story or play
- Provide an oral summary that includes the important information in a nonfiction text
- Provide a concise oral summary of a work of fiction (play, choral reading, poem) that includes all essential literary elements and the main idea
- Search for and use information in readers' theater scripts: e.g., lines, stage directions, punctuation, titles, headings
- Follow and understand content to derive facts from a nonfiction text
- Use content knowledge to monitor and correct while reading fiction
- Notice when understanding is lost and take steps to make a text make sense (monitor)
- Acquire new information, ideas, and perspectives from reading scripts for plays and readers' theater, poems, and speeches, and vignettes from biographies and memoirs
- Make connections between historical and current events and the scripts in plays and other readings
- Infer the significance of a scene or vignette selected from a play for readers' theater
- Make connections between texts and readers' theater scripts that are made from them and understand the differences
- Infer reasons for selection of material to include in scripts (for readers' theater based on a longer narrative or expository text)
- Express opinions about texts and justify with evidence
- Express an opinion about the suitability of a text to be read aloud or performed and justify with evidence: e.g., language, messages, purpose, characters
- Think critically and discuss the relationship between nonverbal behavior, the voice, and the meaning of the script, poem, or play
- Talk about whether a readers' theater script or play is interesting or enjoyable and why
- Talk about what makes dialogue effective in a play or readers' theater script: e.g., authenticity, rhythm
- Notice use of language and print conventions (e.g., sentence and paragraph structure, punctuation, tense agreement and change) by looking at an enlarged page with the group
- Critique the writer's stance toward a topic, idea, emotion, or situation in a script, poem, or speech

Words

- Solve words using a flexible range of strategies to access different sources of information
- Automatically read approximately 500+ high-frequency words
- Recognize plurals and possessives
- Recognize words with affixes (prefixes and suffixes)

Language Structure (Syntax)

- Search for information across sentences, using language structure or syntax, meaning, and visual information in print
- Search for information across complex sentences
- Adjust to read phrases and sentences with unusual syntax to reflect rhythm or poetic language
- Adjust to read a variety of types of poetry

Vocabulary

- Add new words from texts to vocabulary constantly
- Notice and use words that add action or emotion to a text: e.g., words that represent sounds, strong verbs, adjectives, and adverbs, some expressions
- Recognize and understand the meaning of plurals in various forms
- Understand the meaning of words (Tier 2) that appear often in literature but go beyond oral vocabulary, many poetic or literary
- Understand the meaning of some words particular to a discipline (Tier 3), especially when used figuratively or in scientific argument
- Use contextual information to solve the meaning of new words
- Notice and understand words that are of high interest and novelty
- Understand the meaning of words that represent sounds: e.g., *buzz, hiss, pop, clang, plop, quack, thump*
- Understand the writer's meaning when words are used in figures of speech or idioms
- Understand the connotative meaning of words and how they add to the overall meaning of a script or poem
- Use background information, illustrations, and reference tools to understand the meaning of content words
- Rapidly and automatically use a range of strategies (e.g., syllables, morphology, base words and affixes, Greek and Latin word roots) for deriving the meaning of words
- Understand sophisticated connectives and some academic connectives

---

● Thinking **Within** the Text   ◆ Thinking **Beyond** the Text   ■ Thinking **About** the Text

Selecting Goals Behaviors and Understandings to Notice, Teach, and Support *(cont.)*

Shared and Performance Reading

FICTION AND NONFICTION TEXTS *(continued)*

Fluency

- After practice, read all words quickly and automatically
- Use line breaks and white space to guide phrasing when reading poetry in unison or individually
- Adjust the voice to reflect dialogue in the body of the text
- Read orally with integration of all dimensions of fluency (e.g., pausing, phrasing, word stress, intonation, and rate) alone and while maintaining unison with others
- After practice, give dramatic and interpretive oral reading of a script

Performance

- Recognize and reflect punctuation with the voice: e.g., period, question mark, exclamation point, dash, comma, ellipses, when reading in chorus or individually
- Recognize and reflect variations in print with the voice (e.g., italics, bold type, special treatments, font size) when reading in chorus or individually
- When reading individually or in unison with others, adjust the voice to reflect the mood of the text: e.g., sadness, tension, joy, humor
- Understand the role of the voice in communicating meaning in readers' theater, choral reading, songs, and poetry
- Read a part in a play or readers' theater script in a way that reflects the dialogue and the attributes and emotions of characters
- Use the voice to communicate an individual interpretation of a role in a play or readers' theater script
- Understand the original intent of a speech or public discourse and reflect the appropriate tone when reading aloud
- Maintain appropriate volume when performing in readers' theater, plays, and choral performances
- Adjust volume and tone of voice to reflect stage directions (e.g., *quietly, shouted, with a laugh*) and to read a script with fluency and expression
- ◆ Make decisions about how a role in a play should be read based on character attributes and the events of the plot
- ◆ Make decisions about how the characters in a play should sound based on knowledge of history and culture

- ◆ Make decisions about how to read a speech based on knowledge of history or understanding of current events and issues
- ■ Discuss with others how a script or poem should be read and state reasons based on plot, characters, meaning

Messages and Themes

- Follow and understand the ideas in poetry
- Identify the main ideas or messages in readers' theater scripts or poems used for choral reading
- ◆ Infer important ideas from reading a narrative nonfiction text
- ◆ Infer the writer's purpose
- ◆ Infer the poet's message in a poem and use inferences as a basis for interpretation in performance
- ◆ Use inferences as a basis for interpretation of characters in plays or readers' theater or of the speaker in public discourse
- ◆ Infer the significance of themes: e.g., friendship, families, relationships, self, the wonders of nature, feelings, cleverness, bravery, wisdom, appreciation of the sounds of language, cultural sensitivity, loss, patriotism, war, death
- ■ Notice how the writer communicates the messages in a story, poem, or the dialogue of a script
- ■ Talk about whether the message of a poem is important and justify opinion with evidence

Literary Elements

- Use understanding of genre and forms to monitor and correct reading
- Follow and understand plots in stories, poems, readers' theater, or plays
- Use understanding of types and elements of poetry to adjust reading
- Use the layout and punctuation of poems, readers' theater scripts, choral reading scripts, and plays to monitor and correct reading
- Use understanding of narrative structure in a fiction text to monitor and correct reading
- Use understanding of text structure in a nonfiction text (expository or narrative) to monitor and correct reading

● Thinking **Within** the Text   ◆ Thinking **Beyond** the Text   ■ Thinking **About** the Text

Selecting Goals Behaviors and Understandings to Notice, Teach, and Support *(cont.)*

Shared and Performance Reading

FICTION AND NONFICTION TEXTS *(continued)*

- ◆ Make connections among texts by noting similarities: e.g., genre, form, text structure, characters, literary language, use of dialogue and monologue
- ◆ Talk about personal connections with content, characters, or events in a shared text, poem, play, short story, or readers' theater script
- ◆ Use the events of a text to predict what will happen next
- ◆ Make predictions based on understanding of text structure in fiction and nonfiction texts
- ◆ Make predictions based on understanding of characters and character motivation
- ◆ Infer feelings and motivations of people from history and characters in realistic fiction from reading dialogue and monologue in a script and performing in a play or readers' theater
- ◆ Infer the feelings, motivations, and messages of historical and living public figures through reading and performing their speeches and interviews
- ◆ Gain insight into perspectives of characters in fiction and real historical characters through reenacting their roles in scripts, speeches, and interviews
- ◆ Gain insight into historical and cultural perspectives by reading and performing fiction and nonfiction texts
- ◆ Infer the writer's stance toward the theme, topic, or main idea of script, poem, or speech and use it to guide interpretation
- ■ Understand that all texts used for shared reading may be classified as prose or poetry and further classified by genre
- ■ Distinguish among various forms of manuscript used for performance: e.g., poems, readers' theater scripts, choral reading scripts, plays, novellas, letters, diaries, journal entries, short stories, speeches

- ■ Notice whether a book, play, choral reading, or readers' theater script tells a story or gives information
- ■ Recognize some characteristics of fiction and nonfiction genres in plays and readers' theater scripts
- ■ Notice underlying structural patterns in a nonfiction text: e.g., description, temporal sequence, question and answer, cause and effect, chronological sequence, compare and contrast, problem and solution, categorization
- ■ Notice aspects of dialogue and monologue and use those aspects to decide how dialogue and monologue should be read
- ■ Discuss various interpretations of the attributes and motives of characters in plays and readers' theater scripts
- ■ Notice a writer's use of humor and identify what makes a script funny: e.g., characters, situation, language
- ■ Notice how a writer uses language to convey a mood
- ■ Notice how a writer uses language to build tension or to describe action
- ■ Notice a writer's use of strong and/or literary language in presenting an argument or idea in a nonfiction text
- ■ Use academic language to talk about genres: e.g., *fiction, folktale, fairy tale, fractured fairy tale, fable, tall tale, adventure story, animal story, family, friends, and school story, humorous story, realistic fiction, traditional literature, historical fiction, fantasy, myth, legend, ballad, science fiction, hybrid text, epic, satire/parody, horror story, romance story; nonfiction, informational text, informational book, factual text, personal memory story, biography, autobiography, narrative nonfiction, memoir, procedural text, persuasive text, expository text*

● Thinking **Within** the Text   ◆ Thinking **Beyond** the Text   ■ Thinking **About** the Text

Selecting Goals Behaviors and Understandings to Notice, Teach, and Support *(cont.)*

Shared and Performance Reading

FICTION AND NONFICTION TEXTS *(continued)*

Literary Elements *(continued)*

- Use academic language to talk about forms: e.g., *picture book, wordless picture book, label book, ABC book, counting book, poem, poetry, nursery rhyme, rhyme, song, poetry collection, series book, chapter book, play, letter, sequel, limerick, haiku, concrete poetry, short story, diary entry, journal entry, news article, feature article, narrative poetry, photo essay, speech, lyrical poetry, free verse, ballad, epic/saga*

- Use academic language to talk about literary features: e.g., *beginning, ending, problem, character, solution, main character, question and answer, topic, events, message, dialogue, description, setting, main idea, comparison and contrast, flashback, conflict, resolution, theme, descriptive language, simile, figurative language, metaphor, cause and effect, categorization, persuasive language, plot, subplot, flash-forward, character development, supporting character, point of view, temporal sequence, chronological sequence, subject, argument, episode, climax, rising action, falling action, time-lapse, story-within-a-story, mood, personification, symbol, symbolism, first-person narrative, third-person narrative, second-person narrative, circular plot, parallel plots, protagonist, antagonist, tone, irony, round and flat characters*

- Use academic language to discuss various aspects of poetry used for performance: e.g., *blank verse, elegy, epic, ode, pastoral sonnet, tamica, senryu, canzone, elegy, enjambment, envoy, epigram, epithalamium, idyll, lay, carpe diem, rhythm, refrain, rhyme, repetition, stress, verse, onomatopoeia, alliteration, assonance, consonance, accent, antithesis, apostrophe, caesura, classicism, conceit, feminine and masculine rhyme, hexameter, couplet, heroic couplet, litotes, metonymy, pentameter, quatrain, stanza, torchee, trope, imagery, figurative language, metaphor, simile, personification*

- Use academic language to talk about plays and performance: e.g., *line, speech, scene, act, actor, actress, role, part, hero, villain, playwright, enter, exit, skit, vignette, dramatization, pace, tempo, timing, director, stage manager, producer, performer, designer, properties (props), lighting design, sound design, monologue, comedy, folk drama, melodrama, tragedy, social drama, farce, script, improvisation*

- Use academic language to talk about book and print features: e.g., *front cover, back cover, title, author, illustrator, page, text, illustration, photograph, label, table of contents, acknowledgments, chapter, section, heading, drawing, caption, map, chapter title, dedication, author's note, illustrator's note, section, diagram, glossary, endpapers, sidebar, book jacket, subheading, chart, graph, timeline, index*

- Notice aspects of the writer's craft when looking at an enlarged page with the group

- Notice the different ways that a writer tells a story in a fiction text (e.g., simple narrative structure, cumulative patterns, flashback, story-within-a-story, flash-forward, time-lapse, circular plot, parallel plots) and how that affects understanding and enjoyment

Book and Print Features

- Search for information in illustrations and in book and print features in an enlargement of a nonfiction text: e.g., drawing, photograph, map with legend or key, scale, diagram, infographic, cutaway; title, table of contents, chapter title, heading, subheading, sidebar, call-out

- Use illustrations (when applicable) to monitor and correct reading

- Shift attention from one part of a page layout to another to gather information: e.g., body text; drawing, photograph, map, diagram, infographic; label, caption, legend, key, scale, cutaway, sidebar, call-out

- Make connections between the body of the text and illustrations

- Make connections between text, illustrations, and book and print features: e.g., body text; drawing, photograph, map, diagram, infographic; label, caption, legend, key, scale, cutaway; title, table of contents, chapter title, heading, subheading, sidebar, call-out

- Notice and learn new ways to present information in nonfiction texts using illustrations and book and print features

- Infer information from nonfiction illustrations and book and print features

- Talk about illustrations and book and print features and evaluate whether they help readers understand information and add interest

---

- Thinking **Within** the Text   ◆ Thinking **Beyond** the Text   ■ Thinking **About** the Text

Writing About Reading

WRITING ABOUT READING

Writing About Reading Continuum

Students' written responses to what they have read provide evidence of their thinking. When we examine writing in response to reading, we can make hypotheses about how well readers have understood a text. But there are more reasons to make writing an integral part of your reading instruction. Through writing—and drawing as well—readers can express and expand their thinking and improve their ability to reflect on and think analytically about a text. They can also communicate their thinking about texts to a variety of audiences for a variety of purposes. By helping students examine effective examples of writing about reading, they learn the characteristics of each kind of writing and can "try it out" for themselves. The models serve as mentor texts that students can refer to as they use different kinds of writing to reflect on reading.

▶ In *modeled writing,* the teacher writes a text and then reads it to the students. If appropriate, shared reading can be used to reread the text. The goal is to give students a clear, easy-to-understand model for the kind of writing about reading that is required. Modeled writing can be used for any kind of writing about reading.

▶ In *shared writing,* the teacher and students compose a text together. The teacher is the scribe. You may work on a chart displayed on an easel, on a smart board, or computer with screen display. Students participate in the composition of the text, word by word, and reread it many times. Sometimes, especially with younger students, the teacher asks students to say the word slowly or to divide it into syllables as they think about how a word is spelled. At other times, the teacher (with student input) writes a word quickly on the chart. The text becomes a model, example, or reference for student writing and discussion. (See McCarrier, Fountas, and Pinnell 2000.) Shared writing can be used with older students as a demonstration of any kind of writing about reading—summaries, reviews, graphic organizers, letters, character analyses, lists of important ideas or messages, comparisons of texts, etc. Shared writing can be used to demonstrate the four kinds of writing about reading we use as categories in this continuum. Be sure students participate in the composing process as you write.

▶ *Interactive writing,* an approach for use with young students, is identical to and proceeds in the same way as shared writing, with one exception: Occasionally the teacher, while making teaching points that help students attend to various features of letters and words, will invite a student to come up to the easel and contribute a letter, a word, or part of a word. (See McCarrier, Fountas, and Pinnell 2000.) Typically, interactive writing is used in grades prekindergarten through one, but it is also frequently used with small groups of writers who need instructional support in other grades. Student contributions to the writing are carefully selected for their instructional value. You will find an extensive discussion of shared and interactive writing in *Interactive Writing* by McCarrier, Pinnell, and Fountas (2000).

▶ After older students are confident with a kind of writing through the analysis of effective examples, whole- or small-group discussion can support their *independent writing* about reading. Discussion reminds writers of key characteristics of the text and the author's or illustrator's craft.

In this continuum, we describe many different forms of writing about reading in four categories: functional writing, narrative writing, informational writing, and poetic writing. The goal is for students to read many examples in each category, identify the specific characteristics, and have opportunities to apply their understandings in independent writing.

Functional Writing

Functional writing is undertaken for communication or to "get a job done." During literacy time, a great deal of functional writing takes place around reading as students use writing as a tool to think about and share their understandings about a text. Students make notes to themselves about written texts that they can use as a basis for an oral discussion or presentation or to support writing of more extended pieces. They may diagram or outline in an attempt to better understand how written texts are organized. Or they may write notes or letters to others to communicate their thinking. A key tool for learning is the Reader's Notebook, in which students reflect on their reading in various forms, including dialogue letters that are answered by the teacher. Some examples of functional writing about reading are:

- notes and sketches—words, phrases, or sketches on sticky notes or in a notebook
- Short Writes—a few sentences or paragraphs produced quickly in a notebook or on a large sticky note that is then placed in a notebook
- graphic organizers—words, phrases, sketches, or sentences in tables or diagrams
- letters—letters written to other readers or to the author or illustrator of a book
- diary entries—an entry or series of entries in a journal or diary from the perspective of a biographical subject or character, focusing on the setting, issues, or relationships
- notes or summaries with illustrations and text use of graphic features such as sidebars charts, labels, fills, graphs, and legends
- double-column entries—written responses in two columns, with a phrase, sentence, or quote from the text or a question about the text in the left column and room for the reader's thinking on the right
- quote and response—a written response to a memorable sentence or group of sentences in a text
- grid—an open-ended table or chart that provides a framework for analyzing and comparing elements of a text
- poster/advertisement—a visual image with art and writing that tells about the text in a way that is attention-getting or persuasive

Narrative Writing

Narrative writing tells a story. Students' narrative writing about reading might retell some or all of a plot or recount significant events in the life of a biographical subject. Or students might tell about an experience of their own that is similar to the one in a text or has a similar theme. Some examples of narrative writing about reading are:

- summary—a few sentences that tell the most important information in a text
- plot summary—a brief statement of what happens in a text

- readers' theater script—a scene with parts assigned to a narrator or specific characters
- cartoon/storyboarding—a succession of graphics or stick figures that presents a story or information (short versions of graphic novels)
- longer responses—longer pieces (often including sketches) that elaborate on thinking about one or several texts

Informational Writing

Informational writing organizes facts into a coherent whole. To compose an informational piece, the writer organizes data into categories and may use underlying structures such as description; comparison and contrast; cause and effect; time sequence; and problem and solution. Some examples of informational writing about reading are:

- outline—a list of headings and phrases that visually shows the organization and relationship of the main ideas, subpoint, and sub-subpoints in a text
- author study—a piece of writing that provides information about an author and his or her craft as exemplified in several specified works
- illustrator study—a piece of writing that provides information on an illustrator and his or her craft as exemplified in several specified works
- literary essay—a coherent, longer piece of writing that analyzes one or more texts
- interview (with an author or expert)—a series of questions and responses designed to provide information about an author or expert on a topic
- "how-to" article—an explanation of how something is made or done
- "all-about" book—factual information presented in an organized way
- photo or picture essay/digital slide presentation—a series of photographs, drawings, or digital images and video that explains a topic or event
- report—factual information presented in an organized way
- news or feature article—factual information written to inform readers about and share interest in a topic
- published article—a more formal response to a text or texts that is shared publicly
- editorials/op-ed pieces—ideas organized and presented in writing to communicate information or a specific opinion on a topic or issue
- biographical sketch—a short article about a person's life and accomplishments
- review or recommendation—an article evaluating a book, topic, product, or place
- project—a creative body of work that presents ideas and opinions about texts or topics in an organized way

Persuasive Writing

It is sometimes said that the most demanding use of language is argument. We tend to agree. When you construct an oral or written argument, you must simultaneously think from two or more perspectives, and only one is your own. You need to organize lan-

Selecting Genres and Forms

Writing About Reading

Most writing for preschool children is generated through very simple modeled, shared, or interactive writing. The genres and forms are likewise demonstrated in these ways. Often, teachers label pictures or children's drawings as a demonstration of writing. Preschool children's independent writing largely consists of drawing or painting accompanied by the use of whatever they have noticed about writing. They may write their names (or parts of them); they may use letter-like forms mixed with some known letters. They may use the letters they know over and over again in strings. It is helpful for teachers to invite children to talk about their drawings (or stories or just labels). Teachers may write a simple sentence or two that the child dictates. Some children can remember and "read" this sentence. Simple texts that are produced through shared/interactive writing are always reread as shared reading. Keep in mind that these genres and behaviors are for the end of PreK.

FUNCTIONAL WRITING

▶ **Notes and Sketches**

- Drawings or paintings that reflect something in a story or the subject of an informational book
- Lists based on shared books: e.g., things we like from books, things we see in books, ideas from books
- Labels for photographs or drawings related to a story or informational text

▶ **Graphic Organizers**

- Grids showing relationships among different kinds of information from a text or across texts
- Two columns comparing texts (for example, characters in two versions of *The Gingerbread Man* or *The Three Bears*)

▶ **Letters About Reading**

- Notes, messages, and simple letters about the subject of an informational book or about something in a story

▶ **Short Writes**

- Child-dictated labels or short sentences describing a drawing related to a book or story
- Child-dictated sentences retelling a familiar story or telling about a part of a story (after drawing a picture)

NARRATIVE WRITING

▶ **Summaries**

- Simple sentence summarizing or telling the end of a story

▶ **Cartoons/Storyboards**

- Drawings such as a story map showing the sequence of events in a story
- Speech bubbles showing dialogue or thought bubbles showing thoughts in the form of a word, phrase, or simple sentence

INFORMATIONAL WRITING

▶ **Reports**

- Drawings with labels showing information (e.g., what we learned) from a book
- Simple sentence telling an interesting fact (e.g., what we learned) from a book

▶ **How-to Articles**

- Representations through writing and drawing of a sequence of actions or directions from a text

POETIC WRITING

- Insertion of children's names or other words in a poem where appropriate

Selecting Goals Behaviors and Understandings to Notice, Teach, and Support

Writing About Reading

FICTION TEXTS

General

- Attempt to use vocabulary from a text to label drawings using dictation, temporary spelling, and letter-like forms
- Use names of authors and illustrators in interactive and shared writing
- Tell important information about a text
- Draw (or use other art media) to represent information from a text
- Use vocabulary common to everyday oral language to talk or dictate writing about reading (Tier 1)
- Label drawings to represent information from a dictated text using temporary spelling or letter-like forms
- Represent a sequence of events from a text using drawing or writing
- Reread (through shared reading) to remember something from a text in order to draw or write about it
- ◆ Draw and sometimes label or have children dictate sentences about something in their lives prompted by characters or events in a story
- ◆ Draw or write predictions for story outcomes
- ◆ Write about predictions of what might happen next in a story
- ◆ Write about predictions based on evidence from the text
- ■ Use class-written texts or poems as a resource for words, phrases, and ideas for writing
- ■ Use some academic language to talk about texts: e.g., *cover, page, title, writer, author, illustrator, page, text, illustration, beginning, ending, problem*
- ■ Express an opinion about or characterize a text (*interesting, funny, exciting*)
- ■ Record and write about different versions of the same story (for example, using two columns)
- ■ Write a short version of a familiar story

Plot

- Tell about the important events of a story, after hearing it read several times and using the pictures in the text
- Produce simple graphic representations of a story such as story maps or timelines
- Write a summary that includes the story problem and how it is resolved
- ■ Draw and write to make story maps showing beginning understanding of basic narrative structure: beginning, series of episodes, and ending

Characters

- ◆ Draw or write about feelings such as empathy for a character
- ◆ Discuss a problem in a story and draw and label how characters should act
- ◆ Draw or write predictions about what a character might do next in a story
- ◆ Label drawings using temporary spellings to show what a character might be saying
- ◆ Draw or write about how a character might feel
- ◆ Draw or write about the relationship between a character's actions and the consequences
- ■ List characters that have predictable character traits typical of traditional literature (e.g., sly, brave, silly, wise, greedy, clever)
- ■ Insert students' names into a poem that has been read many times

Messages and Themes

- ◆ Write about the lesson inferred from traditional literature
- ■ Notice and write about when a fiction writer is "teaching a lesson"

Style and Language

- ◆ Show the funny parts in fiction texts by drawing and writing
- ■ Recognize and use onomatopoetic words (which imitate sounds, as in *buzz* and *hiss*) in drawing or writing about a text

Illustrations

- Tell stories in response to pictures
- ■ Write about the details found in illustrations

● Thinking **Within** the Text　　◆ Thinking **Beyond** the Text　　■ Thinking **About** the Text

Selecting Goals Behaviors and Understandings to Notice, Teach, and Support

Writing About Reading

FICTION TEXTS

General

- Attempt to use new vocabulary from texts when writing to label drawings, using dictation, temporary spelling, and letter-like forms
- Use names of authors and illustrators in interactive and shared writing
- Attempt to independently record text titles and authors in Reader's Notebook (may be drawings)
- Tell important information about a text
- Draw (or use other art media) independently to represent information from a text
- Use vocabulary typical of everyday oral language to talk and write about reading (Tier 1)
- Use common (simple) connectives that are frequently used in oral language (words, phrases that clarify relationships and ideas): e.g., *and, but, so, because, before, after*
- Represent a sequence of events from a text through drawing or writing
- Remember information or details from a text to produce lists, simple sequences of action

- Compose notes, lists, letters, or statements to remember important information about a text
- Reread (through shared reading) to remember something from a text in order to draw or write about it
- Reread interactive or shared writing to check meaning, language structure, and appropriate word use
- Draw or write about connections between the ideas in texts and children's own life experience
- Draw and sometimes label or dictate sentences about something in children's lives prompted by characters or events in a story
- Draw or write predictions for story outcomes
- Write predictions of what might happen next in a story
- Write about predictions based on evidence from the text
- Reflect both prior knowledge and new knowledge from a text
- Use a text as a resource for words, phrases, and ideas for writing
- Express why an author might choose to write a story or write about a topic
- Note in interactive or shared writing when a writer uses repeating episodes or patterns

A kindergartener writes about his study of birds

- Thinking **Within** the Text   ◆ Thinking **Beyond** the Text   ■ Thinking **About** the Text

WRITING ABOUT READING

Selecting Goals Behaviors and Understandings to Notice, Teach, and Support *(cont.)*

Writing About Reading

FICTION TEXTS *(continued)*

- Use some academic language to talk about texts: e.g., *front cover, back cover, page, title, writer, author, illustrator, page, text, illustration, beginning, ending, problem*
- Express opinions (interesting, funny, exciting) about texts
- Identify and record different versions of the same story using interactive or shared writing
- Compose innovations on very familiar texts by changing the ending, the series of events, characters, or the setting

Setting
- Write a summary that includes important details about setting

Plot
- Tell about the important events of a story, after hearing it read several times and using the pictures in the text
- Produce simple graphic representations of a story such as story maps or timelines
- List events in a story
- Write a summary that includes the story problem and how it is resolved
- Draw and write to make story maps showing understanding of basic narrative structure: beginning, series of episodes, and ending

Characters
- Identify characters in a story with labels (after drawing)
- Write a summary that includes important details about characters
- Draw or write about feelings such as empathy for a character
- Discuss a problem in a story and draw and label how characters act

- Predict what a character might do next in a story by drawing or writing
- Label drawings to show what a character might be saying
- Draw or write about how a character might feel
- Draw or write about how a character might have changed or learned a lesson
- Draw or write about the relationship between a character's actions and the consequences
- List characters that have predictable character traits (e.g., sly, brave, silly, wise, greedy, clever) typical of traditional literature

Messages and Themes
- Write about the lesson inferred from traditional literature
- Notice and write about when a fiction writer is "teaching a lesson"

Style and Language
- Show the humor in fiction texts by drawing or using interactive or shared writing
- Tell what a writer does to be funny by drawing and writing
- Notice a fiction writer's use of onomatopoetic words (which imitate sounds, as in *buzz* and *hiss*) and use them in drawing or writing about the story
- Borrow a writer's style or use some words or expressions from the text

Illustrations
- Tell stories in response to pictures
- Draw or write about everyday actions noticed in a text: playing, making things, eating, getting dressed, bathing, cooking, shopping
- Draw or write about the details found in illustrations

● Thinking *Within* the Text   ◆ Thinking *Beyond* the Text   ■ Thinking *About* the Text

WRITING ABOUT READING

Selecting Goals Behaviors and Understandings to Notice, Teach, and Support *(cont.)*

Writing About Reading

NONFICTION TEXTS

General

- Use new vocabulary from texts when writing to label drawings
- Use names of authors and illustrators
- Record text titles and authors in a Reader's Notebook (and use drawings)
- Tell important information about a text
- Represent information from a text by drawing (or using other art media) or writing
- Represent a sequence of events from a text through drawing or writing
- Remember information or details from a text to produce lists, simple sequences of action, and directions
- Compose notes, lists, letters, or statements to remember important information about a text
- Reread (through shared reading) to remember something from a text for the purpose of drawing or writing about it
- Reread interactive or shared writing to check meaning, language structure, and appropriate word use
- Draw or write about connections between the ideas in texts and children's own life experiences
- Write predictions based on evidence from the text
- Express opinions about facts or information learned
- Reflect both prior knowledge and new knowledge from a text
- Use a text as a resource for words, phrases, and ideas for writing

- Express why an author might choose to write a story or to write about a topic
- Make lists differentiating between fiction and nonfiction texts
- Describe how ideas within a nonfiction text are alike and different by drawing or writing
- Use some academic language to talk about texts: e.g., *front cover, back cover, page, title, writer, author, illustrator, page, text, illustration, photograph, beginning, ending, problem*
- Express opinions (interesting, funny, exciting) about texts

Topic

- Using drawing or writing, ask questions to show curiosity about topics encountered in nonfiction texts and actively work to learn more about them

Messages and Main Ideas

- Draw or write about the author's message
- Make connections among ideas in nonfiction texts: animals, pets, families, food, plants, school, friends, growing, senses, neighborhood, weather and seasons, health, etc.

Illustrations/Graphics

- Draw and/or write about information found in simple graphics: labeled drawings, photographs, maps

Style and Language

- Show the humor in nonfiction text by drawing or writing

- Thinking **Within** the Text
- Thinking **Beyond** the Text
- Thinking **About** the Text

Selecting Genres and Forms

Writing About Reading

Genres and forms for writing about reading are demonstrated through interactive, shared, or modeled writing, often with close attention to mentor texts. Children learn how to respond to different forms and for a variety of purposes and audiences. After they learn about the forms in a supported experience, they use them independently as they respond to books they read. In independent writing children use temporary spellings—whatever they can do to represent a word. At the beginning of grade one, most children can write simple stories with temporary spellings. If they are not able, they will soon take on the action as they write and draw every day. Keep in mind that these behaviors represent goals for the year's instruction. You will continue to use modeled, shared, or interactive writing to demonstrate more complex examples than children can produce themselves. Also the shared/interactive/modeled writing provides clear conventional spelling texts for shared reading.

FUNCTIONAL WRITING

▶ Notes and Sketches

- Sketches or drawings that reflect content of a text
- Notes to support memory (e.g., events in a story, characters) for later use in discussion or writing
- Labels for photographs or drawings related to a text
- Lists of interesting words or phrases from a text
- Lists of books read with titles and authors
- Lists of favorite book titles
- Lists of favorite characters [fiction]
- Lists of favorite topics [nonfiction]

▶ Graphic Organizers

- Simple charts showing sequence of events
- Grids showing relationships among different kinds of information from a text or across texts
- Two columns to represent comparison (characters, problems, or different versions of the same tale)
- Web showing character traits
- Circle or flowcharts showing temporal sequence (life cycle, process for making something)

▶ Letters About Reading

- Simple letters to other readers or to authors and illustrators including dialogue letters in a Reader's Notebook

▶ Short Writes

- Short sentences stating a prediction, an opinion, or an interesting aspect of a text

NARRATIVE WRITING

▶ Summaries

- Simple statements summarizing a text
- Simple statements telling the sequence of events

▶ Cartoons/Storyboards

- Drawings showing the sequence of events in a text, sometimes with speech bubbles to show dialogue or thought bubbles to show thoughts as in a story map
- Innovations on known texts such as a new ending or a similar plot with different characters
- Graphic representations of stories such as story maps or timelines

INFORMATIONAL WRITING

▶ Reports

- Drawings with labels that represent interesting information from a text
- Short sentences and/or drawings reporting some interesting information from a text
- Lists of facts from a text supported by illustrations
- A few simple sentences with information about an author or illustrator

▶ Outlines

- Summaries of information learned from a text with headings that show sections

▶ How-to Articles

- Representations through writing and drawing of a sequence of actions or directions from a text

PERSUASIVE WRITING

- Posters or advertisements that tell about a text in an attention-getting or persuasive way
- Book recommendations

POETIC WRITING

- Poetic texts written in response to a prose text
- Insertion of children's names or other words in a poem where appropriate
- Innovations on a poem or song using the same language structure

Selecting Goals Behaviors and Understandings to Notice, Teach, and Support

Writing About Reading

FICTION TEXTS

General

- Use new vocabulary from texts when writing to appropriately reflect meaning
- Use names of authors and illustrators in interactive and shared writing
- Independently record in Reader's Notebook the titles, authors, and illustrators of texts
- Tell important information about a text through interactive or shared writing
- Draw (or use other art media) independently to represent information from a text
- Use vocabulary typical of everyday oral language to talk and write about reading (Tier 1)
- Use common (simple) connectives that are frequently used in oral language (words, phrases that clarify relationships and ideas): e.g., *and, but, so, because, before, after*
- Label drawings about texts using teacher writing or students' temporary spellings
- Draw and write about everyday actions noticed in a text: playing, making things, eating, getting dressed, bathing, cooking, shopping
- Represent a sequence of events from a text through drawing or writing
- Remember information or details from a text to independently produce lists, simple sequences of action, and directions through interactive or shared writing
- Compose notes, lists, letters, or statements based on a text using interactive, shared, or independent writing
- Reread to remember something from a text in order to draw or write about it
- Reread writing about reading to check meaning, language structure, and appropriate word use
- ◆ Draw and write about connections between the ideas in texts and children's own life experiences
- ◆ Draw and write about connections among texts by topic, ideas, authors, characters
- ◆ Draw and sometimes label or dictate sentences about something in children's lives prompted by characters or events in a story
- ◆ Provide evidence from the text or from personal experience to support written statements about a text
- ◆ Write predictions based on evidence from the text
- ◆ Write predictions for story outcomes
- ◆ Write predictions of what might happen next in a story
- ◆ Reflect both prior knowledge and new knowledge from a text

- ■ Form and record questions in response to events of a plot or to important information
- ■ Use a text as a resource for words, phrases, and ideas for writing
- ■ Express why an author might choose to write a story or write about a topic
- ■ Write the repeating episodes or patterns in a book
- ■ Make lists differentiating between fiction and nonfiction texts
- ■ Use some academic language to talk about genres: e.g., *fiction, folktale, fairy tale, fable*
- ■ Use some academic language to talk about forms: e.g., *picture book, wordless picture book, poem, poetry, nursery rhyme, rhyme, song*
- ■ Use some academic language to talk about literary features: e.g., *beginning, ending, problem, character, solution*
- ■ Use some academic language to talk about book and print features: e.g., *front cover, back cover, title, author, illustrator, page, text, illustration, label, table of contents, acknowledgments, drawing*
- ■ Express opinions (interesting, funny, exciting) about texts
- ■ Formulate opinions about authors and illustrators and use writing to state why
- ■ Compare different versions of the same story, rhyme, or traditional tale
- ■ Compose innovations on very familiar texts by changing the ending, the series of events, characters, and/or the setting

Setting

- Write summaries that include important details about setting
- ◆ Identify the setting for a story and why it is important

Plot

- Tell about the important events of a story, after hearing it read several times and using the pictures in the text
- Identify events in a story using labels
- Produce simple graphic representations of a story such as story maps or timelines
- Write summaries that include the story problem and how it is resolved
- ■ Compare the problems in different versions of the same story, rhyme, or traditional tale

Characters

- Identify characters in a story using labels and temporary spelling
- Write a summary that includes important details about character
- ◆ Draw and write to express opinions about the characters in a story (funny, bad, silly, nice, friendly)
- ◆ Draw and write about feelings for a character, such as empathy for a character

---

- ● Thinking **Within** the Text   ◆ Thinking **Beyond** the Text   ■ Thinking **About** the Text

Selecting Goals Behaviors and Understandings to Notice, Teach, and Support *(cont.)*

Writing About Reading

FICTION TEXTS *(continued)*

◆ Discuss a problem in a story and express opinions on how characters act using shared or interactive writing

◆ Predict what a character might do next in a story by drawing or writing

◆ Label drawings to show what a character might be saying

◆ Infer and describe a character's intentions, feelings, and motivations by drawing or writing

◆ Show when characters change or learn a lesson in a story by drawing or writing

◆ Draw and write about the relationships between a character's actions and their consequences

■ Using a graphic organizer and interactive or shared writing, list characters that have predictable character traits (e.g., sly, brave, silly, wise, greedy, clever) typical of traditional literature

Messages and Themes

◆ Draw and write about the author's message

◆ Write the lesson inferred from traditional literature

■ Notice and write a fiction writer's "lesson"

Style and Language

◆ Recognize and write about the humor in fiction texts

■ Notice and write about elements of the writer's craft: word choice, use of literary elements

■ Notice and record a fiction writer's choices of interesting words

■ Notice and write a fiction writer's use of repetition, refrains, rhythm using interactive or shared writing

■ Notice a fiction writer's use of onomatopoetic words (words for sounds) and use them in drawing or writing about the story

■ Notice and remember some interesting language from a text, sometimes using it to dictate stories or talk about drawings

■ Borrow the style or some words or expressions from a writer in writing about a text

Illustrations

● Write about the details found in illustrations

● Write about the characteristics (medium, style) of some illustrators

A first grader's writing about what she has learned about dinosaurs

● Thinking *Within* the Text ◆ Thinking *Beyond* the Text ■ Thinking *About* the Text

Selecting Goals Behaviors and Understandings to Notice, Teach, and Support

Writing About Reading

FICTION TEXTS

General

- Use new vocabulary from texts when writing to appropriately reflect meaning
- Record the titles and authors of favorite fiction books
- Record in Reader's Notebook the titles, authors, illustrators, and genre of texts read
- Draw (or use other art media) independently to represent information from a text
- Label drawings about a text
- Draw and write about everyday actions noticed in a text: playing, making things, eating, getting dressed, bathing, cooking, shopping
- Use vocabulary typical of everyday oral language to talk and write about reading (Tier 1)

- Use common (simple) connectives that are frequently used in oral language (words, phrases that clarify relationships and ideas): e.g., *and, but, so, because, before, after*
- Represent a sequence of events from a text through drawing or writing
- Remember information or details from a text to independently produce lists, simple sequences of action, and directions
- Compose notes, lists, letters, or statements to remember important information about a text
- Write or jot questions when meaning is lost or understanding is interrupted
- Reread to remember something from a text in order to draw or write about it
- Reread writing about reading to check meaning, language structure, and appropriate word use

A second grader writes about what she has learned about cats

- ● Thinking **Within** the Text   ◆ Thinking **Beyond** the Text   ■ Thinking **About** the Text

Selecting Goals Behaviors and Understandings to Notice, Teach, and Support *(cont.)*

Writing About Reading

FICTION TEXTS *(continued)*

- ● Write summaries that reflect literal understanding of a text
- ◆ Show connections between the setting, characters, and events of a text and the reader's own personal experiences
- ◆ Draw and write to relate important information/ideas within a text or to other texts
- ◆ Draw and write about connections among texts by topic, ideas, authors, characters
- ◆ Draw and write a few sentences about something in children's lives prompted by characters or events in a story
- ◆ Notice and write about the importance of ideas relevant to their world: sharing, caring for others, doing your job, helping your family, taking care of self, staying healthy, caring for the world or environment, valuing differences, expressing feelings, empathizing with others
- ◆ Provide evidence from the text or from personal experience to support written statements about a text
- ◆ Write about a wide range of predictions based on evidence from a text
- ◆ Write predictions for story outcomes and support with evidence from a text
- ◆ Write predictions of what might happen next in a story and support those predictions with evidence
- ◆ Reflect in writing both prior knowledge and new knowledge from a text
- ■ Form and record questions in response to events of a plot or to important information
- ■ Use a text as a resource for words, phrases, and ideas for writing
- ■ Notice and note decorative or informative illustrations and/or print outside the body of the text (peritext)
- ■ Write why an author might choose to write a story or write about a topic
- ■ Write the repeating episodes or patterns in a text
- ■ Identify and record whether a text is fiction or nonfiction as well as any known genres within those categories
- ■ Make lists of stories that could happen in real life, as in realistic fiction, and stories that could not happen in real life, as in fantasy
- ■ Notice and write about the characteristics of fiction genres: e.g., realistic fiction, folktale, tall tale, fairy tale, fable, fantasy
- ■ Use some academic language to talk about genres: e.g., *fiction, folktale, fairy tale, fable, tall tale, adventure story, animal story, family, friends, and school story, humorous story*

- ■ Use some academic language to talk about forms: e.g., *picture book, wordless picture book, poem, poetry, nursery rhyme, rhyme, song, poetry collection, series book, chapter book, play, letter*
- ■ Use some academic language to talk about literary features: e.g., *beginning, ending, problem, character, solution, main character, time and place, events, character change, message, dialogue*
- ■ Use some academic language to talk about book and print features: e.g., *front cover, back cover, title, author, illustrator, page, text, illustration, label, table of contents, acknowledgments, chapter, drawing, chapter title, dedication, author's note, illustrator's note*
- ■ Express opinions (e.g., interesting, funny, exciting) about a text in writing and support those opinions with evidence
- ■ Formulate opinions about authors and illustrators and state in writing the basis for those opinions
- ■ Compare in writing different versions of the same story, rhyme, or traditional tale
- ■ Compose innovations on very familiar texts by changing the ending, the series of events, characters, and/or the setting

Setting
- ● Make notes or write descriptions to help remember important details about setting
- ■ Write about the importance of setting to the plot of the story

Plot
- ● Make notes or write descriptions to help remember important details about plot
- ● Write summaries that include the story's main problem and how it is resolved
- ◆ Write about the significance of events in a plot
- ■ Recognize and write about or represent in diagrams or flowcharts aspects of narrative structure: beginning, series of episodes, events in sequential order, most exciting point in a story, and ending
- ■ Compare the problems in different versions of the same story, rhyme, traditional tale

---

● Thinking **Within** the Text   ◆ Thinking **Beyond** the Text   ■ Thinking **About** the Text

Selecting Goals Behaviors and Understandings to Notice, Teach, and Support *(cont.)*

Writing About Reading

NONFICTION TEXTS *(continued)*

Topic

◆ Using drawing and/or writing, show curiosity about topics encountered in texts and actively work to learn more about them

■ Notice and show in writing how a text is organized by main topics and subtopics

■ Use graphic organizers such as webs to show how a writer puts together information related to the same topic

Organization

● Write an outline by providing summaries of information learned using headings and subheadings that reflect a text's overall structure and simple categories

■ Draw or write to show how a text is organized: time order or established sequences such as numbers, time of day, days of the week, or seasons

Messages and Main Ideas

● List the significant events or ideas in an expository or biographical text

◆ Draw and write about the author's message

◆ Write about connections among ideas in a text: animals, pets, families, food, plants, school, friends, growing, senses, neighborhood, weather and seasons, health, etc.

Illustrations/Graphics

● Notice and write about information found in simple graphics such as photo and drawing with label or caption, diagram, map

● Reference book and print features in writing about reading: title, table of contents, chapter title, heading, sidebar; author's note, pronunciation guide, glossary

■ Notice and write to describe how the graphics in a text help explain information so ideas are clearly communicated

Style and Language

◆ Recognize and write about the humor in a text

■ Notice and write about elements of the writer's craft: word choice, use of literary elements

■ Notice and record a writer's choices of interesting words

● Thinking **Within** the Text   ◆ Thinking **Beyond** the Text   ■ Thinking **About** the Text

Selecting Genres and Forms

Writing About Reading

Students learn different ways to share their thinking about reading in explicit minilessons. Often, the teacher and students read several examples of a form, identify its characteristics, and try out the type of response. When you expect students to express new understandings or do it in new form, it is important to engage them in productive talk first. That means students need to *say* it first—not just hear the teacher. Then, use modeled/shared writing to demonstrate how to use the form (for example, a graphic organizer or description of a character) or articulate a new understanding. Remember that for every behavior or understanding listed here, writers have a choice of the form. You can demonstrate the form and/or suggest it. Then, students can select from the range of possible forms when responding to reading (usually in a Reader's Notebook). Keep in mind that these behaviors represent instructional goals for the year.

FUNCTIONAL WRITING

▶ Notes and Sketches

- Sketches or drawings that assist in remembering a text, interpreting an event or character, or representing the content of a text
- Notes (about setting, events in a story, characters, memorable words or phrases) on sticky notes, Thinkmarks, and in a Reader's Notebook to support memory for later use in discussion or writing
- Notes that record interesting information, details, language, or examples of the writer's craft as shown by quotes from a text
- Labels and legends for illustrations such as drawings, photographs, and maps related to a text
- Lists of books (completed or abandoned) with title, author, genre, and dates read
- Lists of favorite titles, authors, characters, or topics

▶ Graphic Organizers

- Webs that connect information within a text or across texts (organization, character traits, settings)
- Charts that show the way a text is organized: description, temporal sequence, question and answer, cause and effect, chronological sequence, compare and contrast, problem and solution
- Story maps that record title, author, setting, plot events, characters, problem, and resolution
- Graphic organizers showing embedded genres within hybrid texts
- Grids showing relationships among different kinds of information from a text or across texts
- Two columns to represent comparison (characters, problems, settings, different versions of the same tale)

▶ Letters About Reading

- Letters to the teacher, to other readers, or to authors and illustrators including dialogue letters in a Reader's Notebook

▶ Short Writes

- Short sentences stating a prediction, an opinion, or any interesting aspect of the text
- Draft of character sketch

▶ Longer Responses

- Double-column entry with a phrase, sentence, quote from a text, or question in left column and room for reader's thinking on the right
- Longer responses in a Reader's Notebook expanding on thinking from notes, sketches, Short Writes, or graphic organizers

NARRATIVE WRITING

▶ Summaries

- Plot summaries containing a brief statement of the central topic, theme, or message of a text
- Story maps that record title, author, setting, plot events, characters, problem, and resolution

▶ Writing for Dramatic Purposes

- Scripts for readers' theater

▶ Cartoons/Storyboards

- Graphic representations of stories such as story maps or timelines
- Cartoons or comics that present a story or information
- Storyboards that represent significant events in a text

INFORMATIONAL WRITING

▶ Reports

- Short reports giving information from one or more texts

- Lists of facts from a text supported by illustrations
- A few sentences with information about an author or illustrator
- Reports of information from a text that reflects use of illustrations (e.g., photo and/or drawing with label or caption, diagram, map with legend), organizational tools (e.g., title, table of contents, chapter title, heading, subheading, sidebar), and text resources (e.g., author's note, glossary)

▶ Outlines

- Lists of headings and subheadings that reflect the organization of the text
- Outline of main points and subpoints in a text with no headings

▶ How-to Articles

- Directions sometimes illustrated with drawings showing a sequence of actions based on a text

▶ Author and Illustrator Studies

- Author studies involving a response to one or more books by an author and/or using biographical information
- Illustrator studies involving a response to one or more books by an artist and/or using biographical information

PERSUASIVE WRITING

- Posters or advertisements that tell about a text in an attention-getting or persuasive way
- Book recommendations

POETIC WRITING

- Innovations on a poem or song using the same language structure
- Poetic texts written in response to poems and using the same topic, mood, and style

Selecting Goals Behaviors and Understandings to Notice, Teach, and Support *(cont.)*

Writing About Reading

NONFICTION TEXTS

General

- Use new vocabulary from texts when writing to appropriately reflect meaning
- Explore definitions of new words from texts by writing about them
- Use vocabulary typical of everyday oral language to talk and write about reading (Tier 1) and understand some words that appear in the language of mature users and in written texts (Tier 2)
- Use common (simple) connectives that are frequently used in oral language (words, phrases that clarify relationships and ideas): e.g., *and, but, so, because, before, after*
- Use some sophisticated connectives (words that link ideas and clarify meaning) that are used in written texts but do not appear often in everyday oral language: e.g., *although, however, meantime, meanwhile, moreover, otherwise, therefore, though, unless, until, whenever, yet*
- Use some Tier 3 vocabulary that is specialized and related to scientific domains in writing about reading
- Understand and note the purpose of the dedication, author's note, and acknowledgments
- Record the titles, authors, and genres of books to recommend
- Record in Reader's Notebook the titles, authors, illustrators, and genre of texts read and dates read
- Draw or sketch to assist in remembering a text or to represent its content
- Remember information or details from a text to independently produce lists, simple sequences of action, and directions
- Compose notes, lists, letters, or statements to remember important information about a text
- Write questions or notes about confusions to address during discussion
- Refer to notes about a text for evidence in discussion and writing to support opinions and statements
- Represent a longer series of events from a text through drawing and writing
- Write summaries that reflect literal understanding of a text
- Select and include appropriate and important details when writing a summary of a text
- Reference page numbers from text in writing about important information
- Revisit texts for ideas or to check details when writing or drawing
- Reread writing to check on meaning, accuracy, and clarity of expression
- Write about content from texts that reflects beginning understandings of the physical and social world: health, social studies, science, mathematics, arts
- ◆ Write about how nonfiction content is relevant to students' lives
- ◆ Relate important information/ideas within a text or to other texts

- ◆ Write about the important information and concepts in one text and connect it to information and concepts in other text
- ◆ Write about connections among texts by topic, theme, major ideas, authors' styles, and genres
- ◆ Connect the information in nonfiction books to disciplinary studies
- ◆ Express opinions about facts or information learned
- ◆ Provide evidence from the text or from personal experience to support written statements about a text
- ◆ Notice and write about the importance of ideas relevant to students' world: sharing, caring for others, doing your job, helping your family, taking care of self, staying healthy, caring for the world or environment, valuing differences, expressing feelings, empathizing with others
- ◆ Write predictions based on evidence from the text
- ◆ Make notes and write longer responses to indicate acquisition of new information and ideas from a text
- ◆ Reflect both prior knowledge and new knowledge from the text in writing or drawing
- ■ Use texts as resources for words, phrases, and ideas for writing
- ■ Write statements that reflect understanding of both the text body and the graphics or illustrations and how the two are integrated
- ■ Write about the meaning of a text's dedication, author's note, acknowledgments, and footnotes or endnotes
- ■ Notice and note decorative or informative illustrations or designs outside the body of the text (peritext)
- ■ Write about why an author might choose to write a story or to write about a topic
- ■ Write to explore the writer's purpose and stance toward a topic
- ■ Notice and write about the characteristics of certain nonfiction genres: expository nonfiction, narrative nonfiction, biography, autobiography, memoir, procedural texts, persuasive texts
- ■ Use names of specific genres accurately when writing about them
- ■ Write about hybrid texts distinguishing between fiction and nonfiction sections
- ■ Understand that biographies and historical picture books are set in the past and provide evidence of understanding in writing
- ■ Recognize and comment on how the writer's use of different forms of nonfiction such as diaries, logs, and letters affects the reader
- ■ Use some academic language to talk about genres: e.g., *nonfiction, informational text, informational book, factual text, personal memory story, biography, autobiography, narrative nonfiction, memoir, procedural text, persuasive text*
- ■ Use some academic language to talk about forms: e.g., *picture book, poem, poetry, nursery rhyme, rhyme, song, poetry collection, series book, play, letter, sequel, limerick, haiku, concrete poetry, diary entry, journal entry, news article, feature article*

- ● Thinking **Within** the Text
- ◆ Thinking **Beyond** the Text
- ■ Thinking **About** the Text

Selecting Goals Behaviors and Understandings to Notice, Teach, and Support *(cont.)*

Writing About Reading

NONFICTION TEXTS *(continued)*

- Use some academic language to talk about literary features: e.g., *beginning, ending, problem, solution, question and answer, topic, events, message, dialogue, description, time order, setting, main idea, comparison and contrast, descriptive language, simile, cause and effect, categorization, persuasive language*

- Use some academic language to talk about book and print features: e.g., *front cover, back cover, title, author, illustrator, page, text, illustration, photograph, label, table of contents, acknowledgments, section, heading, drawing, caption, map, dedication, author's note, illustrator's note, diagram, glossary, sidebar, book jacket, subheading, chart, graph, timeline, index*

- Form and express opinions about a text and/or an author or illustrator in writing and support those opinions with rationales and evidence

- Recognize and write about examples of argument and persuasion in informational texts

- Describe and critique a writer's use of persuasion

- Write about or critique a writer's use of nonfiction text features: titles, table of contents, headings, subheadings, sidebars, labels, legends, captions

Topic

- ◆ Using drawing and/or writing, show curiosity about topics encountered in nonfiction texts and actively work to learn more about them

- Outline the main topic of a book and its subtopics

- Use graphic organizers such as webs to show how a nonfiction writer puts together information related to the same topic or subtopic

- Write about how graphics and text are carefully placed in a nonfiction text to effectively communicate ideas

- Describe the relationship between ideas and content (larger topic and subtopics) in an expository nonfiction text

Organization

- ● Write an outline by providing summaries of information learned using headings and subheadings that reflect a text's overall structure and simple categories

- Draw, write, or diagram to show how a text is organized: time order or established sequences such as numbers, time of day, days of the week, or seasons

- Notice and write about the organization of a nonfiction text, distinguishing between expository and narrative structure

- Notice and write about an author's use of underlying structural patterns to organize information and sometimes apply the same structure to writing nonfiction texts: description, temporal sequence, question and answer, cause and effect, chronological sequence, compare and contrast, problem and solution, categorization

- Notice and write about a nonfiction writer's use of narrative text structure in biography and narrative nonfiction and its effect on the reader

- Clearly explain the steps in a process or an event (for a text with chronological or temporal sequence or a procedural text)

Messages and Main Ideas

- ● List the significant events or ideas in an informational or biographical text

- ◆ Write about connections among ideas in nonfiction texts: animals, pets, families, food, plants, school, friends, growing, senses, neighborhood, weather and seasons, health, etc.

- ◆ Write to compare and expand understanding of content and ideas from academic disciplines across texts

- ◆ Infer and write about the larger messages or main ideas

- ◆ Infer and write about moral lessons

- Write about how illustrations and graphics help communicate the writer's message

Accuracy

- Critically examine the quality or accuracy of the text, providing evidence in writing for opinions

Illustrations/Graphics

- ● Understand and note important information provided in graphics: photographs, paintings, drawings, captions, labels, insets, charts, diagrams, tables, graphs, maps, timelines, sidebars

- ● Notice and make note of significant information from illustrations

- ● Reference organizational tools and text resources in writing about reading: table of contents, chapter title, heading, subheading, sidebar; dedication, acknowledgments, author's note, glossary, index

- ● Write summaries reflecting understanding of graphic features: labels, headings, subheadings, sidebars, legends

- Write about how the information in the body of the text and graphics go together

- Write about how graphics and text are carefully placed in a nonfiction text to effectively communicate ideas

- Notice artistry in illustrations

- Write about the characteristics (medium, style) of the work of some illustrators

Style and Language

- ◆ Recognize and write about the humor in nonfiction texts

- Notice and write about elements of the writer's craft: word choice, use of literary elements

- Notice and record language that reveals the author's attitude (tone) toward the character, subject, or topic: serious, humorous, respectful, affectionate

---

● Thinking *Within* the Text   ◆ Thinking *Beyond* the Text   ■ Thinking *About* the Text

WRITING ABOUT READING

Selecting Genres and Forms

Writing About Reading

In grade five, many students may be working at a high level in writing about reading, but others may be new to articulating their thinking in writing. The diversity is wide at this level, and it depends on previous opportunities and teaching. If writing about reading is new to them, they will need strong teaching. Also, all of your students will need demonstrations of your expectations when they are asked to use a new form of writing about reading or to express more sophisticated thinking. Use minilessons to engage them in conversation; they will do more effective writing if they have a chance to rehearse what they are going to say by talking to a partner or the group. Use shared or modeled writing to demonstrate a higher level of understanding of anything on this continuum; such demonstration will be particularly needed for new behaviors or understandings. Also, you will need to use modeled or shared writing (on a chart, smart board, or computer) to show a good example of a new form of writing. Then, students can use the form or articulate the understanding independently. Some students will need several demonstrations, and it is also helpful for students to work with a partner. The major goal of writing about reading is to help students express and organize their thinking so that they can show it in writing. They are working toward a time when they will be expected to show a high level of thinking about texts and to display academic language. Keep in mind the behaviors listed here represent instructional goals for a year of writing about reading.

FUNCTIONAL WRITING

▶ Notes and Sketches

- Sketches or drawings that represent a text and provide a basis for discussion or writing
- Notes (about setting, events in a story, characters, memorable words or phrases) on sticky notes, Thinkmarks, and in a Reader's Notebook to support memory for later use in discussion or writing
- Notes that record interesting information, details, language, or examples of the writer's craft as shown by quotes from a text
- Labels and legends for illustrations such as drawings, photographs, and maps related to a text
- Lists of books (completed or abandoned) with title, author, genre, one-word responses in reaction to the book, and dates read

▶ Graphic Organizers

- Webs that connect information within a text or across texts (organization, character traits, settings, problems)
- Webs that represent the organization of a text
- Charts that show the way a text is organized: description, temporal sequence, question and answer, cause and effect, chronological sequence, compare and contrast, problem and solution

- Story maps that record title, author, setting, plot events, characters, problem, and resolution
- Graphic organizers supporting genre study including examples of books, noticings from inquiry, and working definitions of genres
- Graphic organizers showing embedded genres within hybrid texts
- Grids or columns that show analysis of a text

▶ Letters About Reading

- Letters to other readers or to authors and illustrators including dialogue letters in a Reader's Notebook

▶ Short Writes

- Short Writes giving personal response, interpretation, character analysis, description, or critique, focusing on any aspect of craft

▶ Longer Responses

- Double-column entry with a phrase, sentence, quote from a text, or question in left column and room for reader's thinking on the right
- Diary entries from the perspective of a biographical subject or a character focusing on the setting, issues, or relationships
- Longer responses in a Reader's Notebook expanding on thinking from notes, sketches, Short Writes, or graphic organizers

NARRATIVE WRITING

▶ Summaries

- Plot summaries containing a brief statement of the setting, characters, plot, important events, problem resolution, message
- Story maps that record title, author, setting, plot events, characters, problem, and resolution

▶ Writing for Dramatic Purposes

- Scripts for readers' theater
- Scripts for choral reading (some turning prose into poetry)

▪ Cartoons/Storyboards

- Cartoons or comics that present a story or information
- Storyboards that represent significant events in a text

INFORMATIONAL WRITING

▶ Reports

- Reports including text and graphic organizers that present information drawn from texts

Selecting Genres and Forms *(cont.)*

Writing About Reading

- Reports using illustrations (e.g., photo and/or drawing with label or caption; diagram, cutaway; map with legend or key, scale), organizational tools (e.g., title, table of contents, chapter title, heading, subheading, sidebar, callout), and text resources (e.g., copyright information, acknowledgments, author's note, pronunciation guide, glossary, references)

▶ **Outlines**

- Outlines that include headings, subheadings, and sub-subheadings that reflect the organization of a text

▶ **How-to Articles**

- Directions sometimes illustrated with drawings showing a sequence of actions based on a text
- How-to articles requiring research

▶ **Author and Illustrator Studies**

- Author studies involving a response to one or more books by an author and/or using biographical information
- Illustrator studies involving a response to one or more books by an artist and/or using biographical information

▶ **Biographical Sketches**

- Biographical sketches on an author or the subject of a biography (and sometimes a character in fiction)

▶ **Projects and Multimedia Presentations**

- Projects that present ideas and opinions about topics or texts in an organized way using text and visual images

▶ **Interviews**

- Write interviews with an author or expert (questions and responses designed to provide information)

▶ **News or Feature Articles**

- Write news or feature articles based on reading one or more texts

PERSUASIVE WRITING

- Posters or advertisements that tell about a text in an attention-getting or persuasive way
- Book reviews or recommendations

POETIC WRITING

- Poetic texts written in response to a prose text
- Poetic texts written in response to poems and applying the same topic, mood, and style

Selecting Goals Behaviors and Understandings to Notice, Teach, and Support

Writing About Reading

FICTION TEXTS

General

- ● Notice, comment on, and actively work to acquire new vocabulary, including technical, complex, and specialized words, and intentionally use it in writing about reading
- ● Explore definitions of new words from texts, including figurative and connotative uses, by writing about them
- ● Understand some words that appear in the language of mature users and in written texts (Tier 2) and a few words that appear in the scientific disciplines and are more likely to appear in writing (Tier 3)
- ● Use common (simple) connectives and sophisticated connectives (words that link ideas and clarify meaning) that are used in written texts but do not appear often in everyday oral language: e.g., *although, however, meantime, meanwhile*
- ● Use some academic connectives (words that link ideas and clarify meaning that appear in written texts): e.g., *alternatively, consequently, despite, conversely, eventually, finally, in contrast, initially, likewise, nevertheless, nonetheless, previously, specifically, ultimately, whereas, whereby*
- ● Understand and draw information for writing from the purpose of the dedication, author's note, and acknowledgments
- ● Record the titles, authors, and genres of books to recommend
- ● Record in Reader's Notebook the titles, authors, illustrators, genre of texts read independently, and dates read
- ● Draw or sketch to represent or remember the content of a text and provide a basis for discussion or writing
- ● Remember information or details from a text to independently produce lists, simple sequences of action, and directions
- ● Compose notes, lists, letters, or statements to remember important information about a text
- ● Make notes about the need to clarify information (questions, confusions)
- ● Record notes to navigate long and complex texts when checking opinions and theories in preparation for writing longer pieces
- ● Make notes about a text for evidence to support opinions and statements in discussion and writing
- ● Revisit texts for ideas or to check details when writing or drawing
- ● Provide evidence from the text or from personal experience to support written statements about that text
- ● Represent a longer series of events from a text through drawing and writing
- ● Write summaries that reflect literal understanding of a text
- ● Select and include appropriate and important details when writing a summary of a text
- ● Reference page numbers from text in writing about important information
- ● Continuously check evidence in the text to ensure that writing reflects understanding

- ◆ Reread writing to check on meaning, accuracy, and clarity of expression
- ◆ Draw and write about connections between the ideas in texts and students' own life experiences
- ◆ Draw and write about something in their own lives prompted by characters or events in a story
- ◆ Relate important information or ideas within a text or to other texts
- ◆ Write about connections among texts by topic, theme, major ideas, authors' styles, and genres
- ◆ Notice and write about the importance of ideas relevant to their world: sharing, caring for others, doing your job, helping your family, taking care of self, staying healthy, caring for the world or environment, valuing differences, expressing feelings, empathizing with others
- ◆ Provide evidence from the text or from personal experience to support written statements about a text
- ◆ Predict what will happen next in a story or after the story ends and support with evidence from the text
- ◆ Write about a wide range of predictions based on evidence from the text
- ◆ Demonstrate how background knowledge impacts understanding of historical fiction and science fiction
- ◆ Provide details that are important to understanding how a story's plot, setting, and character traits are related
- ◆ Write about changes in opinions based on new information or insights gained from fiction or nonfiction texts
- ◆ Write an interpretation of a story, a nonfiction text, or illustrations understanding that there can be more than one interpretation
- ◆ Infer and write about moral lessons derived from inferring across several fiction and nonfiction texts
- ◆ Make notes and write longer responses to indicate acquisition of new information and ideas from a text
- ■ Use texts as resources for words, phrases, and ideas for writing
- ■ Write statements that reflect understanding of both the text body and the graphics or illustrations and how the two are integrated
- ■ Notice and note decorative or informative illustrations and/or print outside the body of the text (peritext)
- ■ Write about the connections among pieces of information in various parts of a text: foreword, prologue, body, epilogue, appendix
- ■ Write about the meaning of a text's dedication, author's note, and acknowledgments
- ■ Write about why an author might choose to write a story or to write about a topic
- ■ Write to explore the writer's purpose and stance toward a story
- ■ Identify and record the specific genre of a book based on its characteristics

---

- ● Thinking **Within** the Text   ◆ Thinking **Beyond** the Text   ■ Thinking **About** the Text

Selecting Goals Behaviors and Understandings to Notice, Teach, and Support *(cont.)*

Writing About Reading

FICTION TEXTS *(continued)*

- Notice and write about the characteristics of fiction genres: e.g., realistic fiction, historical fiction, folktale, tall tale, fairy tale, fable, myth, legend, ballad, fantasy, science fiction, and some special types of fiction (adventure story, animal story, humorous story, family, friends, and school story)

- Write about hybrid texts distinguishing between fiction and nonfiction sections

- Appreciate and write about forms embedded within the main text

- Appreciate and write about the value of embedded primary and secondary sources within a text

- Use some academic language to talk about genres: e.g., *fiction, folktale, fairy tale, fable, tall tale, adventure story, animal story, family, friends, and school story, humorous story, realistic fiction, traditional literature, historical fiction, fantasy, myth, legend, ballad, science fiction, hybrid text*

- Use some academic language to talk about forms: e.g., *picture book, wordless picture book, poem, poetry, nursery rhyme, rhyme, song, poetry collection, series book, chapter book, play, letter, sequel, limerick, haiku, concrete poetry, short story, fractured fairy tale, diary entry, journal entry, narrative poetry, speech*

- Use some academic language to talk about literary features: e.g., *beginning, ending, problem, character, solution, main character, events, character change, message, dialogue, setting, flashback, conflict, resolution, theme, descriptive language, simile, figurative language, metaphor, plot, subplot, flash-forward, character development, supporting character, point of view*

- Use some academic language to talk about book and print features: e.g., *front cover, back cover, title, author, illustrator, page, text, illustration, label, table of contents, acknowledgments, chapter, drawing, caption, chapter title, dedication, author's note, illustrator's note, book jacket*

- Form and record questions in response to events of a plot or to important information

- Form and express opinions about a text in writing and support those opinions with rationales and evidence

- Formulate opinions about authors and illustrators and state in writing the basis for those opinions

- Notice and write to identify multiple points of view in a text

- Compose innovations on very familiar texts by changing the ending, the series of events, characters, and/or the setting

Setting

- Write summaries that include important details about setting

- Make notes or write descriptions to help remember important details about setting

- Write about the importance of setting to the plot in realistic and historical fiction and in fantasy

Plot

- Write summaries that include the story's main problem and how it is resolved

- Make notes or write descriptions to help remember important details about plot

- Write about the significance of events in a plot

- Recognize and write about aspects of narrative structure: beginning, series of events, problem, resolution, ending

- Write about a text's organization: time order or established sequences such as numbers, time of day, days of the week, or seasons

- Recognize and write about an author's use of plots and subplots

Characters

- Write summaries that include important details about characters

- Make notes or write descriptions to help remember important details about characters

- Recognize and begin to write about characters' multiple dimensions: can be good yet have flaws, can make mistakes based on confusion or misunderstanding, can do bad things but change for the better

- Express feelings such as empathy for or dislike of a character

- Discuss a problem in a story and write opinions on how characters should act

- Predict what a character is likely to do next or after the story ends and support with evidence from the text

- Describe character attributes as revealed through thought, dialogue, behavior, and what others say or think about them, and support with evidence

- Describe characters' intentions, feelings, and motivations as revealed through thought, dialogue, behavior, and what others say or think about them and support with evidence

- Describe relationships between characters as revealed through dialogue and behavior

- Notice and write about character change related to events of the plot

- Express opinions in writing about the characters in a story (e.g., evil, dishonest, clever, sly, greedy, brave, loyal) and support with evidence

- Write about the attributes of predictable or static characters (characters that do not change, as typical in traditional literature) vs. dynamic characters

- Differentiate in writing between the main character(s) and the supporting characters in a story

- Write about the relationships between a character's actions and their consequences

- Describe the significance of heroic or larger-than-life characters in fantasy that represent the symbolic struggle of good and evil

- Notice and write about characters that have predictable character traits typical of traditional literature: sly, brave, silly, wise, greedy, clever

---

● Thinking *Within* the Text   ◆ Thinking *Beyond* the Text   ■ Thinking *About* the Text

Selecting Goals Behaviors and Understandings to Notice, Teach, and Support *(cont.)*

Writing About Reading

FICTION TEXTS *(continued)*

Messages and Themes

- ◆ Infer and write about the larger messages of fiction texts
- ◆ Write about the lesson inferred from traditional literature
- ◆ Write about how the lesson in a story can be applied to their own lives and to other people's lives
- ◆ Infer and write about moral lessons
- ◆ Write about themes that are close to students' experiences: imagination, courage, fears, sharing, friendship, family relationships, self, nature, growing, behavior, community, responsibilities, diversity, belonging, peer relationships, loss
- ◆ Understand and write about themes and ideas that are mature issues and require experience and/or prior reading to interpret
- ■ Write about why a writer might tell a story and what messages to readers it might contain
- ■ Write about how illustrations and graphics help communicate the writer's message

Style and Language

- ◆ Recognize and write about symbolism in a text and its illustrations
- ■ Recognize and write about humor in a fiction text
- ■ Notice and write about elements of the writer's craft: word choice, use of literary elements
- ■ Appreciate and write about a fiction writer's use of sensory imagery to evoke mood
- ■ Notice and record language that reveals the author's attitude (tone) toward a character: serious, humorous, respectful, affectionate

- ■ Notice and record language that evokes feelings on the part of readers (mood)
- ■ Notice and write about the narrator of a text and how and when the narrator changes (if applicable)
- ■ Notice and write about how the author uses literary language, including some use of metaphor and simile as well as description
- ■ Recognize and write about what a writer does to create humor in a text
- ■ Appreciate and write critiques of fiction texts by noticing characteristics of style (interesting language, humor, suspense, depiction of characters)
- ■ Borrow the style or some words or expressions from a writer in writing about a text

Illustrations

- ● Notice and make note of significant information from illustrations or graphics
- ◆ Write interpretations of some illustrations that have symbolic characteristics
- ■ Write about the details found in illustrations
- ■ Notice artistry in illustrations
- ■ Write about how illustrations and graphics help communicate the writer's message
- ■ Write about the characteristics (medium, style) of some illustrators

---

Dear Mrs D,

This week I had some fun reading selections. I finished Walk Two Moons, read P.S Longer Letter Later, and started The Mother Daughter Book Club Dear Pen Pal.

First about Walk Two Moons. You were right!!! I ended up really liking it. It definitely had a twist in the ending. Until the end I had no idea why her mom never came back. Even though Sal was probably disappointed to realize that her mom would never come home, I think in the end it was good that her mom died, because I didn't think she was coming home. I read a similar book called Semi Precious. It was about a girl whose mom dropped her and her sister off at her poor aunt Julia's house. Garnet and Opal don't realize their mom is lying when she says once she's settled in Nashville as a country singer she'll come back, then her dad gets hurt in a fire so he can't come get Garnet and Opal. Garnet decides to run away and find her mother. When she's there she uncovers some horrible but true secrets.

I also read P.S Longer Letter Later it was pretty good, a quick read. It was about a girl named Tara*Starr (she always writes her name with a star), who moves away but keeps in touch with her friend Elizabeth, through letters. Surprisingly it was really sad.

The book I'm reading now is Dear Pen Pal and it is the third in my favorite book series The Mother Daughter Book Club. The book is about a book club, in Concord Massachusetts. In the book club is Jess Delaney and her mom. Jess just got a scholarship to a very good boarding school in their town. Her roommate Savannah Sinclair got kicked out of her old boarding school because of her low grades and only got accepted at Jess's boarding school because her father is the governor of Georgia. Savannah always teases Jess.

Daddy Long Legs the mean girl is named Julia. Megan Wong and her mom are also in the book club. Megan's grandma Gigi is living with them for a while but her mom doesn't get along with her because Megan's mom is a VERY healthy eater, she makes all tofu and spinach brownies, and whenever book club is at her house no one eats the food. Also, she only wears sweatpants and t-shirts with anti meat things like a turkey with a red line through it for thanksgiving. Unlike her, Megan and Gigi who are into fashion, Megan wants to be a fashion designer and Gigi goes to Paris every spring for fashion week. Also Gigi always cook delicious Chinese food and everyone loves it. I think Mrs. Wong is jealous of her mother. Cassidy and her mom are in the book club too. Cassidy loves hockey and sports, she is the opposite of her mother who used to be a model and is very girly. Becca and her mom are also in the book club. Becca used to be mean to the book club until she joined the book club, because her mom made her. Becca's mom is crazy, she wears crazy clothes like a leopard print jumpsuit. She is also loud and obnoxious. Emma, and her mom are in the book club too. They both love books and to write, Emma wants to be an author. Each chapter of the book is in a different girls point of view. The book club just finished "Daddy Long Legs" and is reading "Just Patty". The book is called "Dear Pen Pal" because they are pen pals with a book club in Wyoming.

Next week I plan to finish Dear Pen Pal and start a new book. I wonder if there will be another Mother Daughter book club book? I hope so. Have a good week!

Sincerely,

Dana Ward

A fifth grader's writing about recent reading experiences

● Thinking **Within** the Text   ◆ Thinking **Beyond** the Text   ■ Thinking **About** the Text

Selecting Goals Behaviors and Understandings to Notice, Teach, and Support *(cont.)*

Writing About Reading

NONFICTION TEXTS

General

- Use new vocabulary from texts when writing to appropriately reflect meaning
- Explore definitions of new words from texts by writing about them
- Understand some words that appear in the language of mature users and in written texts (Tier 2) and a few words that appear in the scientific disciplines and are more likely to appear in writing (Tier 3)
- Use common (simple) connectives and sophisticated connectives (words that link ideas and clarify meaning) that are used in written texts but do not appear often in everyday oral language: e.g., *although, however, meantime, meanwhile*
- Use some academic connectives (words that link ideas and clarify meaning that appear in written texts): e.g., *alternatively, consequently, despite, conversely, eventually, finally, in contrast, initially, likewise, nevertheless, nonetheless, previously, specifically, ultimately, whereas, whereby*
- Understand and note the purpose of the dedication, author's note, and acknowledgments
- Record the titles, authors, and genres of books to recommend
- Record in Reader's Notebook the titles, authors, illustrators, genre of texts read independently, and dates read
- Draw or sketch to help remember a text or to represent its content
- Remember information or details from a text to independently produce lists, simple sequences of action, and directions
- Compose notes, lists, letters, or statements to remember important information about a text
- Write questions or notes about confusions to address during discussion
- Refer to notes about a text for evidence to support opinions and statements in discussion and writing
- Represent a longer series of events from a text through drawing and writing
- Write summaries that reflect literal understanding of a text
- Select and include appropriate and important details when writing a summary of a text
- Reference page numbers from text in writing about important information
- Continuously check evidence in a text to ensure that writing reflects understanding
- Revisit texts for ideas or to check details when writing or drawing
- Reread writing to check on meaning, accuracy, and clarity of expression

- Write about content from texts that reflects beginning understandings of the physical and social world: health, social studies, science, mathematics, arts
- Write about how nonfiction content is relevant to their lives
- Relate important information and ideas within a text or to other texts
- Write about the important information and concepts in one text and connect it to information and concepts in other texts
- Write about connections among texts by topic, theme, major ideas, authors' styles, and genres
- Connect the information in nonfiction books to disciplinary studies
- Express opinions about facts or information learned
- Provide evidence from the text or from personal experience to support written statements about a text
- Notice and write about the importance of ideas relevant to their own world: sharing, caring for others, doing your job, helping your family, taking care of self, staying healthy, caring for the world or environment, valuing differences, expressing feelings, empathizing with others
- Write about a wide range of predictions based on evidence from the text
- Write short and long responses to indicate acquisition of new information and ideas from a text
- Reflect both prior knowledge and new knowledge from the text in writing or drawing
- ■ Use texts as resources for words, phrases, and ideas for writing
- ■ Write statements that reflect understanding of both the text body and the graphics or illustrations and how the two are integrated
- ■ Write about the meaning of a text's dedication, author's note, acknowledgments, and footnotes or endnotes
- ■ Notice and note decorative or informative illustrations or designs outside the body of the text (peritext)
- ■ Write about why an author might choose to write a story or to write about a topic
- ■ Write to explore the writer's purpose and stance toward a topic
- ■ Identify and record the specific genre of a book based on its characteristics
- ■ Notice and write about the characteristics of nonfiction genres: e.g., informational books, expository nonfiction, narrative nonfiction, biography, autobiography, memoir, persuasive texts, procedural texts
- ■ Use names of specific genres accurately in writing about reading
- ■ Write about hybrid texts, distinguishing between fiction and nonfiction sections

● Thinking **Within** the Text   ◆ Thinking **Beyond** the Text   ■ Thinking **About** the Text

WRITING ABOUT READING

Selecting Goals Behaviors and Understandings to Notice, Teach, and Support *(cont.)*

Writing About Reading

NONFICTION TEXTS *(continued)*

General *(continued)*

- Recognize and comment on how the writer's use of different forms of nonfiction such as diaries, logs, and letters affects the reader
- Write to describe how ideas and content within a nonfiction text are alike and different
- Demonstrate in writing the ability to distinguish between statements of fact supported by evidence and opinions
- Use some academic language to talk about genres: e.g., *nonfiction, informational text, informational book, factual text, personal memory story, biography, autobiography, narrative nonfiction, memoir, procedural text, persuasive text, expository text*
- Use some academic language to talk about forms: e.g., *picture book, poem, poetry, nursery rhyme, rhyme, song, poetry collection, series book, play, letter, sequel, limerick, haiku, concrete poetry, diary entry, journal entry, news article, feature article, narrative poetry, photo essay, speech*
- Use some academic language to talk about literary features: e.g., *beginning, ending, problem, solution, question and answer, topic, events, message, dialogue, description, time order, setting, main idea, comparison and contrast, descriptive language, simile, cause and effect, categorization, persuasive language, temporal sequence, chronological sequence, subject, argument*
- Use some academic language to talk about book and print features: e.g., *front cover, back cover, title, author, illustrator, page, text, illustration, photograph, label, table of contents, acknowledgments, section, heading, drawing, caption, map, dedication, author's note, illustrator's note, diagram, glossary, sidebar, book jacket, subheading, chart, graph, timeline, index*
- Form and express opinions about a text in writing and support those opinions with rationales and evidence
- Formulate opinions about authors and illustrators and state in writing the basis for those opinions

- Notice and write about how a writer reveals the setting in a biographical or historical text
- Recognize and write about examples of argument and persuasion in informational texts
- Describe and critique a writer's use of persuasion
- Write about or critique a writer's use of nonfiction text features: titles, table of contents, headings, subheadings, sidebars, labels, legends, captions
- Think and write critically about the authenticity of a nonfiction text based on facts, scientific evidence, author qualifications, supported statements and arguments, etc.

Topic

- ◆ Using drawing and/or writing, show curiosity about topics encountered in nonfiction texts and actively work to learn more about them
- Outline the main topic of a book and its subplots
- Use graphic organizers such as webs to show how a nonfiction writer puts together information related to the same topic or subtopic
- Write about how graphics and text are carefully placed in a nonfiction text to effectively communicate ideas
- Describe the relationship between ideas and content (larger topic with subtopics) in an expository nonfiction text

Organization

- ● Write an outline by providing summaries of information learned using headings and subheadings that reflect a text's overall structure and simple categories
- Draw, write, or diagram to show how a text is organized: time order or established sequences such as numbers, time of day, days of the week, or seasons
- Notice and write about the organization of a nonfiction text distinguishing between expository and narrative structure

WRITING ABOUT READING

Selecting Goals Behaviors and Understandings to Notice, Teach, and Support *(cont.)*

Writing About Reading

NONFICTION TEXTS *(continued)*

- Notice and write about an author's use of underlying structural patterns to organize information and sometimes apply the same structure to writing nonfiction texts: description, temporal sequence, question and answer, cause and effect, chronological sequence, compare and contrast, problem and solution, categorization
- Notice and write about a nonfiction writer's use of narrative text structure in biography and narrative nonfiction and its effect on the reader
- Clearly explain the steps in a process or an event (for a text with chronological or temporal sequence or a procedural text)

Messages and Main Ideas

- List the significant events or ideas in an informational or biographical text
- Write about connections among ideas in nonfiction texts: animals, pets, families, food, plants, school, friends, growing, senses, neighborhood, weather and seasons, health, etc.
- Write to compare and expand understanding of content and ideas from academic disciplines across texts
- Infer and write about the larger messages or main ideas in a nonfiction text
- Infer and write about moral lessons in a nonfiction text
- Write about how illustrations and graphics help communicate the writer's message

Accuracy

- Critically examine the quality or accuracy of the text, providing evidence in writing for opinions
- Write critically about how a writer uses evidence to support an argument

Illustrations/Graphics

- Understand and note important information provided in graphics: photographs, paintings, drawings, captions, labels, insets, charts, diagrams, tables, graphs, maps, timelines, sidebars
- Reference organizational tools and text resources in writing about reading: table of contents, chapter title, heading, subheading, sidebar; dedication, acknowledgments, author's note, glossary, index, foreword, prologue, pronunciation guide, footnote, epilogue, appendix, endnote, references
- Write summaries reflecting understanding of graphic features: labels, headings, subheadings, sidebars, legends
- Write about how the information in the body of the text and graphics go together
- Write about how graphics and text are carefully placed in a nonfiction text to effectively communicate ideas
- Notice artistry in illustrations
- Write about the characteristics (medium, style) of the work of some illustrators
- Write about how illustrations and graphics help communicate the writer's message

Style and Language

- Recognize and write about humor in nonfiction texts
- Notice and write about elements of the writer's craft: word choice, use of literary elements
- Notice and record language that reveals the author's attitude (tone) toward the character, subject, or topic: serious, humorous, respectful, affectionate
- Write and think critically about a writer's word choice

● Thinking *Within* the Text   ◆ Thinking *Beyond* the Text   ■ Thinking *About* the Text

Selecting Genres and Forms

Writing About Reading

Students at this level are expected to be able to write coherent summaries, reviews, literary essays, arguments, and analyses. They are expected to use academic language and words particular to the disciplines. But many students have little experience in accomplishing these tasks. The diversity in your class is probably very wide, but almost all students will need strong teaching to reach these high levels of thinking and using literacy. Most students need the advantage of good demonstrations so that they develop models in their heads. Use minilessons to engage them in conversation; they will do more effective writing if they have a chance to rehearse what they are going to say by talking to a partner or the group. Demonstrate new ways of thinking and writing about thinking. Prepare a piece of your own writing and have students read it and think analytically about it. Use shared writing to create a cooperatively composed example with student input. Write about a text you have read aloud so that they all share it. You will need to use modeled or shared writing—on a chart, smart board, or computer—to show a good example of a new form of writing. Then students can use the form or articulate the understanding independently. Some students will need several demonstrations, and it is also helpful for students to work with a partner. The major goal of writing about reading is to help students express and organize their thinking so that they can show it in writing. Keep in mind that the behaviors listed here represent the instructional goals for the year.

FUNCTIONAL WRITING

▶ Notes and Sketches

- Sketches or drawings that represent a text and provide a basis for discussion or writing
- Notes (about setting, events in a story, characters, memorable words or phrases) on sticky notes, Thinkmarks, and in a Reader's Notebook to support memory for later use in discussion or writing
- Notes that record interesting information, details, language, or examples of the writer's craft as shown by quotes from a text
- Labels and legends for illustrations such as drawings, photographs, and maps related to a text
- Graphic representations of structures such as parallel and circular plots
- Lists of books (completed or abandoned) with title, author, genre, one-word responses to the book, and dates read

▶ Graphic Organizers

- Webs that connect information within a text or across texts (organization, character traits, settings, problems)
- Charts that show the way a text is organized: description, temporal sequence, question and answer, cause and effect, chronological sequence, compare and contrast, problem and solution

- Story maps that record title, author, setting, plot events, characters, problem, and resolution
- Graphic organizers supporting genre study including examples of books, noticings from inquiry, and working definitions of genres
- Graphic organizers showing embedded genres within hybrid texts
- Grids or columns that show analysis of a text

▶ Letters About Reading

- Letters to other readers or to authors and illustrators including dialogue letters in a Reader's Notebook
- Letters to newspaper or magazine editors in response to articles

▶ Short Writes

- Short Writes giving a personal response, interpretation, character analysis, description, or critique, focusing on any aspect of craft

▶ Longer Responses

- Double-column entry with a phrase, sentence, quote from the text, or question in left column and room for reader's thinking on the right
- Diary entries from the perspective of a biographical subject or a character focusing on the setting, issues, or relationships

- Longer responses in a Reader's Notebook expanding on thinking from notes, sketches, Short Writes, or graphic organizers

NARRATIVE WRITING

▶ Summaries

- Plot summaries containing a brief statement of the setting, characters, plot, important events, turning point, character change, problem resolution, message
- Story maps that include setting, characters, and the rising and falling action of a basic narrative structure: plot events, problem, episodes, climax, and resolution

▶ Writing for Dramatic Purposes

- Scripts for readers' theater
- Scripts for choral reading (some turning prose into poetry)

▶ Cartoons/Storyboards

- Cartoons or comics that present a story or information
- Storyboards that represent significant events in a text

INFORMATIONAL WRITING

▶ Reports

- Reports including text and graphic organizers that present information drawn from texts

Selecting Genres and Forms (cont.)

Writing About Reading

- Reports using illustrations (e.g., photo and/or drawing with label or caption; diagram, cutaway; map with legend or key, scale), organizational tools (e.g., title, table of contents, chapter title, heading, subheading, sidebar, callout), and text resources (e.g., copyright information, acknowledgments, author's note, pronunciation guide, glossary, references)

▶ Outlines

- Outlines that include headings, subheadings, and sub-subheadings that reflect the organization of a text

▶ How-to Articles

- Directions or how-to pieces, sometimes illustrated with drawings showing a sequence of actions based on a text
- How-to articles requiring research

▶ Author and Illustrator Studies

- Author studies involving a response to one or more books by an author and/or using biographical information
- Illustrator studies involving a response to one or more books by an artist and/or using biographical information

▶ Biographical Sketches

- Biographical sketches on an author or the subject of a biography (and sometimes a character in fiction)

▶ Projects and Multimedia Presentations

- Projects that present ideas and opinions about topics or texts in an organized way using text and visual images

▶ Interviews

- Write interviews with an author or expert (questions and responses designed to provide information)

▶ News or Feature Articles

- News or feature articles based on reading one or more texts

PERSUASIVE WRITING

- Posters or advertisements that tell about a text in an attention-getting or persuasive way
- Book reviews
- Literary essays that present ideas about a text and may include examples and a summary of the text

POETIC WRITING

- Poetic texts written in response to a prose text
- Poetic texts written in response to poems and applying the same topic, mood, and style

Selecting Goals Behaviors and Understandings to Notice, Teach, and Support

Writing About Reading

FICTION TEXTS

General

- ● Notice, comment on, and actively work to acquire new vocabulary, including technical, complex, and specialized words, and intentionally use it in writing about reading

- ● Explore definitions of new words from texts, including figurative and connotative uses, by writing about them

- ● Understand some words that appear in the language of mature users and in written texts (Tier 2) and some words that appear in the scientific disciplines and are more likely to appear in writing (Tier 3)

- ● Use common (simple) connectives and sophisticated connectives (words that link ideas and clarify meaning) that are used in written texts but do not appear often in everyday oral language: e.g., *although, however, meantime, meanwhile*

- ● Use some academic connectives (words that link ideas and clarify meaning that appear in written texts): e.g., *alternatively, consequently, despite, conversely, eventually, finally, in contrast, initially, likewise, nevertheless, nonetheless, previously, specifically, ultimately, whereas, whereby*

- ● Understand and draw information for writing from the purpose of the dedication, author's note, and acknowledgments

- ● Record the titles, authors, and genres of books to recommend

- ● Record in Reader's Notebook the titles, authors, illustrators, genre of texts read independently, and dates read

- ● Draw or sketch to represent or remember the content of a text and provide a basis for discussion or writing

- ● Remember information or details from a text to independently produce lists, simple sequences of action, and directions

- ● Compose notes, lists, letters, or statements to remember important information about a text

- ● Make notes about the need to clarify information (questions, confusions)

- ● Record notes to navigate long and complex texts when checking opinions and theories in preparation for writing longer pieces

- ● Refer to notes about a text for evidence to support opinions and statements in discussion and writing

- ● Revisit texts for ideas or to check details when writing or drawing

- ● Provide evidence from the text or from personal experience to support written statements about that text

- ● Represent a longer series of events from a text through drawing and writing

- ● Write logically organized summaries that include the important information in a nonfiction text, the conclusions, and the larger message

- ● Select and include appropriate and important details when writing a summary of a text

- ● Reference page numbers from text in writing about important information

- ● Continuously check evidence in a text to ensure that writing reflect understanding

- ◆ Reread writing to check on meaning, accuracy, and clarity of expression

- ◆ Draw and write about connections between the ideas in texts and their own life experiences

- ◆ Draw and write about connections from their own lives to contemporary issues and problems across all genres

- ◆ Relate important information/ideas within a text or to other texts

- ◆ Write about connections among texts by topic, theme, major ideas, authors' styles, and genres

- ◆ Notice and write about the importance of ideas relevant to their world: sharing, caring for others, doing your job, helping your family, taking care of self, staying healthy, caring for the world or environment, valuing differences, expressing feelings, empathizing with others

- ◆ Provide evidence from the text or from personal experience to support written statements about that text

- ◆ Predict what will happen next in a story or after the story ends and support with evidence from the text

- ◆ Regularly write predictions during and after reading that are based on progress of the plot, characteristics of the setting, attributes of the characters, actions of the characters

- ◆ Demonstrate how background knowledge impacts understanding of historical fiction and science fiction

- ◆ Provide details that are important to understanding how a story's plot, setting, and character traits are related

- ◆ Write about changes in opinions based on new information or insights gained from fiction or nonfiction texts

- ◆ Write an interpretation of a story, a nonfiction text, or of illustrations understanding that there can be more than one interpretation

- ◆ Infer and write about moral lessons derived from inferring across several fiction and nonfiction texts

- ◆ Make notes and write longer responses to indicate acquisition of new information and ideas from a text

- ■ Use texts as resources for words, phrases, and ideas for writing

- ■ Write statements that reflect understanding of both the text body and the graphics or illustrations and how the two are integrated

- ■ Notice and note decorative or informative illustrations and/or print outside the body of the text (peritext)

- ■ Write about the connections among the information in various parts of a text: the body, prologue, epilogue, appendix, foreword, afterword, author's note, endnotes, footnotes, acknowledgments

- ■ Write to explore the writer's purpose and stance toward a story

- ■ Identify and record the specific genre of a book based on its characteristics

---

● Thinking *Within* the Text   ◆ Thinking *Beyond* the Text   ■ Thinking *About* the Text

Selecting Goals Behaviors and Understandings to Notice, Teach, and Support *(cont.)*

Writing About Reading

FICTION TEXTS *(continued)*

- Notice and write about the characteristics of fiction genres: e.g., realistic fiction, historical fiction, folktale, tall tale, fairy tale, fable, myth, legend, ballad, fantasy, science fiction, and some special types of fiction (adventure story, animal story, humorous story, family, friends, and school story)
- Write about hybrid texts, distinguishing between fiction and nonfiction sections and noticing how the writer blends the two genres
- Appreciate and write about forms embedded within the main text
- Appreciate and write about the value of embedded primary and secondary sources within a text
- Use some academic language to talk about genres: e.g., *fiction, folktale, fairy tale, fable, tall tale, adventure story, animal story, family, friends, and school story, humorous story, realistic fiction, traditional literature, historical fiction, fantasy, myth, legend, ballad, science fiction, hybrid text*
- Use some academic language to talk about forms: e.g., *picture book, wordless picture book, poem, poetry, nursery rhyme, rhyme, song, poetry collection, series book, chapter book, play, letter, sequel, limerick, haiku, concrete poetry, short story, fractured fairy tale, diary entry, journal entry, narrative poetry, speech, lyrical poetry, free verse, ballad*
- Use some academic language to talk about literary features: e.g., *beginning, ending, problem, character, solution, main character, events, character change, message, dialogue, setting, flashback, conflict, resolution, theme, descriptive language, simile, figurative language, metaphor, plot, subplot, flash-forward, character development, supporting character, point of view, episode, climax, rising action, falling action, time-lapse, story-within-a-story, mood, personification, symbol, symbolism, first-person narrative, third-person narrative*
- Use some academic language to talk about book and print features: e.g., *front cover, back cover, title, author, illustrator, page, text, illustration, label, table of contents, acknowledgments, chapter, drawing, caption, chapter title, dedication, author's note, illustrator's note, book jacket*
- Form and record questions in response to events of a plot or to important information
- Form and express opinions about a text in writing and support those opinions with rationales and evidence
- Formulate opinions about authors and illustrators and state in writing the basis for those opinions
- Notice and write to identify multiple points of view in a text as well as how the writer reveals them
- Recognize and write analytically about an ambiguous ending of a fiction text
- Write critiques of fiction texts, focusing on authenticity of characters, portrayal of current or past issues, voice, tone, accuracy of setting

Setting

- ● Write summaries that include important details about setting
- ● Makes notes or write descriptions to help remember important details about setting
- ■ Write about the importance of setting to the plot in realistic and historical fiction and in fantasy

Plot

- ● Write summaries that include the story's main problem and how it is resolved
- ● Make notes or write descriptions to help remember important details about plot
- ◆ Write about the significance of events in a plot
- ■ Recognize and write about aspects of narrative structure: beginning, series of events, climax (turning point), problem and resolution, ending
- ■ Recognize and write about an author's use of plots and subplots
- ■ Recognize and write analytically about complex narrative structures: multiple storylines, perspectives, subplots, flashbacks, flash forwards, story-within-a-story, many kinds of conflict

Characters

- ● Write summaries that include important details about characters
- ● Make notes or write descriptions to help remember important details about characters
- ● Recognize and begin to write about characters' multiple dimensions: can be good yet have flaws, can make mistakes based on confusion or misunderstanding, can do bad things but change for the better
- ◆ Express feelings such as empathy for or dislike of a character
- ◆ Discuss a problem in a story and write opinions on how characters should act
- ◆ Predict what a character is likely to do next or after the story ends and support predictions with evidence from the text
- ◆ Describe character attributes as revealed through thought, dialogue, behavior, and what others say or think about them, and support with evidence
- ◆ Describe characters' intentions, feelings, and motivations as revealed through thought, dialogue, behavior, and what others say or think about them and support with evidence
- ◆ Describe relationships between characters as revealed through dialogue and behavior
- ◆ Write about character development and infer reasons
- ◆ Differentiate in writing between the main character(s) and the supporting characters in a story
- ◆ Express opinions in writing about the characters in a story (e.g., evil, dishonest, clever, sly, greedy, brave, loyal) and support with evidence

---

● Thinking ***Within*** the Text   ◆ Thinking ***Beyond*** the Text   ■ Thinking ***About*** the Text

Selecting Goals Behaviors and Understandings to Notice, Teach, and Support *(cont.)*

Writing About Reading

FICTION TEXTS *(continued)*

- ◆ Write about the attributes of predictable or static characters (characters that do not change, as typical in traditional literature) vs. dynamic characters
- ◆ Write about the relationship between a character's actions and their consequences
- ◆ Describe the significance of heroic or larger-than-life characters in fantasy that represent the symbolic struggle of good and evil
- ■ Notice and write about characters that have predictable character traits typical of traditional literature: sly, brave, silly, wise, greedy, clever

Messages and Themes

- ◆ Infer and write the larger messages and sometimes moral lessons of fiction texts
- ◆ Write about the lesson inferred from traditional literature
- ◆ Write about how the lesson in a story can be applied to their own lives and others' lives
- ◆ Write about themes that are close to their experiences: imagination, courage, fears, sharing, friendship, family relationships, self, nature, growing, behavior, community, responsibilities, diversity, belonging, peer relationships, loss
- ◆ Understand and write about themes and ideas that are mature issues and require experience and/or prior reading to interpret
- ◆ Notice and write about theme based on various forms of conflict in a narrative: character vs. character, character vs. self, character vs. nature, character vs. society, character vs. supernatural

- ■ Write about why a writer might tell a story and what messages to readers it might contain
- ■ Write about how illustrations and graphics help communicate the writer's message

Style and Language

- ◆ Recognize and write about humor in a fiction text
- ■ Recognize and write about symbolism in a text and its illustrations
- ■ Notice and write about elements of the writer's craft: word choice, use of literary elements
- ■ Appreciate and write about a fiction writer's use of sensory imagery to evoke mood
- ■ Write about a text's organization: time order or established sequences such as numbers, time of day, days of the week, or seasons
- ■ Appreciate and write about the value of embedded primary and secondary sources
- ■ Notice language (serious, humorous, respectful, affectionate) that evokes strong feelings (mood) such as fear, suspense, sadness, and humor, in the reader or listener
- ■ Notice and record language that reveals the author's attitude (tone) toward a story or character: serious, humorous, respectful, affectionate

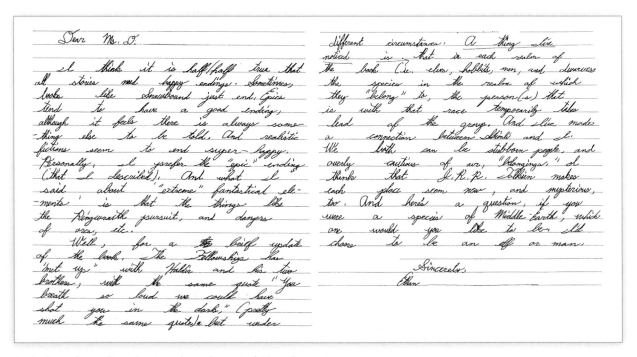

A sixth grader writes about various characteristics of a text

- ● Thinking **Within** the Text
- ◆ Thinking **Beyond** the Text
- ■ Thinking **About** the Text

WRITING ABOUT READING

Selecting Goals Behaviors and Understandings to Notice, Teach, and Support *(cont.)*

Writing About Reading

FICTION TEXTS *(continued)*

- Notice and record language that evokes feelings in the reading (mood)
- Distinguish among narrative styles: first-person narrative, third-person narrative, multiple narrators
- Write about how an author uses subtext (implication) to say one thing but mean another.
- Recognize and write about a fiction writer's use of irony
- Notice and write about an author's intentional use of language that violates conventional grammar to provide authentic dialogue and achieve the desired voice
- Notice and write about how the author uses literary language, including some use of metaphor and simile as well as description
- Recognize and write about what a writer does to create humor in a text

- Appreciate and write critiques of fiction texts by noticing characteristics of style (interesting language, humor, suspense, depiction of characters, imagery)
- Borrow the style or some words or expressions from a writer in writing about a text

Illustrations

- ◆ Write interpretations of some illustrations that have symbolic characteristics
- Write about the details found in illustrations
- Notice artistry in illustrations
- Write about how illustrations and graphics help communicate the writer's message and the mood of the text
- Write about how the illustrations contribute to the impact of the writer's message

NONFICTION TEXTS

General

- Use new vocabulary from texts when writing to appropriately reflect meaning
- Explore definitions of new words from texts by writing about them
- Understand some words that appear in the language of mature users and in written texts (Tier 2) and some words that appear in the scientific disciplines and are more likely to appear in writing (Tier 3)
- Use common (simple) connectives and sophisticated connectives (words that link ideas and clarify meaning) that are used in written texts but do not appear often in everyday oral language: e.g., *although, however, meantime, meanwhile*
- Use some academic connectives (words that link ideas and clarify meaning that appear in written texts): e.g., *alternatively, consequently, despite, conversely, eventually, finally, in contrast, initially, likewise, nevertheless, nonetheless, previously, specifically, ultimately, whereas, whereby*
- Understand and note the purpose of the dedication, author's note, and acknowledgments
- Record the titles, authors, and genres of books to recommend
- Record in Reader's Notebook the titles, authors, illustrators, and genre of texts read independently, and dates read
- Draw or sketch to help remember a text or to represent its content
- Remember information or details from a text to independently produce lists, simple sequences of action, and directions
- Compose notes, lists, letters, or statements to remember important information about a text

- Write questions or notes about confusions to address during discussion
- Provide evidence from the text or from personal experience to support written statements about that text
- Record notes to navigate long and complex texts when checking opinions and theories in preparation for writing longer pieces
- Refer to notes about a text for evidence to support opinions and statements in discussion and writing
- Represent a longer series of events from a text through drawing and writing
- Write summaries that reflect literal understanding of a text
- Select and include appropriate and important details when writing a summary of a text
- Reference page numbers from text in writing about important information
- Continuously check the evidence in a text to ensure that writing reflects understanding
- Revisit texts for ideas or to check details when writing or drawing
- Reread writing to check on meaning, accuracy, and clarity of expression
- Write about content from texts that reflects beginning understandings of the physical and social world: health, social studies, science, mathematics, arts
- ◆ Write about how nonfiction content is relevant to their lives
- ◆ Relate important information/ideas within a text or to other texts
- ◆ Write about the important information and concepts in one text and connect it to information and concepts in other texts

---

● Thinking *Within* the Text   ◆ Thinking *Beyond* the Text   ■ Thinking *About* the Text

Selecting Goals Behaviors and Understandings to Notice, Teach, and Support *(cont.)*

Writing About Reading

NONFICTION TEXTS *(continued)*

General *(continued)*

- ◆ Write about connections among texts by topic, theme, major ideas, authors' styles, and genres
- ◆ Connect the information in nonfiction books to disciplinary studies
- ◆ Express opinions about facts or information learned
- ◆ Provide evidence from the text or from personal experience to support written statements about a text
- ◆ Notice and write about the importance of ideas relevant to their own world: sharing, caring for others, doing your job, helping your family, taking care of self, staying healthy, caring for the world or environment, valuing differences, expressing feelings, empathizing with others
- ◆ Write about a wide range of predictions based on evidence from the text
- ◆ Reflect both prior knowledge and new knowledge from the text in writing or drawing
- ◆ Write about changes in opinions based on new information or insights gained from fiction or nonfiction texts
- ◆ Write an interpretation of a story, a nonfiction text, or of illustrations with the understanding that there can be more than one interpretation
- ◆ Write about moral lessons derived from inferring across several nonfiction texts
- ◆ Make notes and write longer responses to indicate acquisition of new information and ideas from a text
- ■ Use texts as resources for words, phrases, and ideas for writing
- ■ Write statements that reflect understanding of both the text body and the graphics or illustrations and how the two are integrated
- ■ Write about the meaning of the text's dedication, author's note, acknowledgments, prologue, footnotes, endnotes
- ■ Notice and note decorative or informative illustrations and/or design outside the body of the text (peritext)
- ■ Write to explore the writer's purpose and stance toward a topic
- ■ Notice and write about the characteristics of nonfiction genres: e.g., informational books, expository nonfiction, narrative nonfiction, biography, autobiography, memoir, persuasive texts, procedural texts
- ■ Use names of specific genres accurately in writing about reading
- ■ Record and categorize texts by content, genre, author, or other criteria
- ■ Write about hybrid texts distinguishing between fiction and nonfiction sections
- ■ Recognize and comment on how a writer's use of different forms of nonfiction, such as diaries, logs, or letters, may affect the reader

- ■ Appreciate and write about forms embedded within the main text
- ■ Describe how ideas and content within a nonfiction text are alike and different
- ■ Use graphic organizers, outlines, notes, reader-response letters, or Short Writes to distinguish in writing between fact and opinion in a nonfiction text
- ■ Appreciate and write about the value of embedded primary and secondary sources within a text
- ■ Use some academic language to talk about genres: e.g., nonfiction, informational text, informational book, factual text, personal memory story, biography, autobiography, narrative nonfiction, memoir, procedural text, persuasive text, expository text
- ■ Use some academic language to talk about forms: e.g., *picture book, poem, poetry, nursery rhyme, rhyme, song, poetry collection, series book, play, letter, sequel, limerick, haiku, concrete poetry, diary entry, journal entry, news article, feature article, narrative poetry, photo essay, speech, lyrical poetry, free verse, ballad*
- ■ Use some academic language to talk about literary features: e.g., *beginning, ending, problem, solution, question and answer, topic, events, message, dialogue, description, time order, setting, main idea, comparison and contrast, descriptive language, simile, cause and effect, categorization, persuasive language, temporal sequence, chronological sequence, subject, argument, mood, personification, symbol, symbolism, first-person narrative, third-person narrative, second-person narrative*
- ■ Use some academic language to talk about book and print features: e.g., *front cover, back cover, title, author, illustrator, page, text, illustration, photograph, label, table of contents, acknowledgments, section, heading, drawing, caption, map, dedication, author's note, illustrator's note, diagram, glossary, sidebar, book jacket, subheading, chart, graph, timeline, index*
- ■ Form and express opinions about a text in writing and support those opinions with rationales and evidence
- ■ Formulate opinions about authors and illustrators and state in writing the basis for those opinions
- ■ Notice and write about how a writer reveals the setting in a biographical or historical text
- ■ Recognize and write about examples of argument and persuasion in informational texts
- ■ Describe a writer's use of persuasion and how the writer supports arguments with evidence
- ■ Critique a text's quality of writing, organization, clarity, and authenticity
- ■ Critique a writer's use of nonfiction text features: titles, table of contents, headings, subheadings, sidebars, labels, legends, captions

● Thinking **Within** the Text   ◆ Thinking **Beyond** the Text   ■ Thinking **About** the Text

Selecting Goals Behaviors and Understandings to Notice, Teach, and Support *(cont.)*

Writing About Reading

NONFICTION TEXTS *(continued)*

- ■ Write critically about the authenticity of a nonfiction text based on facts, scientific evidence, author qualifications, supported statements and arguments, etc.
- ■ Write about how layout contributes to the meaning and quality of a nonfiction text

Topic

- ◆ Using drawing and/or writing, show curiosity about topics encountered in nonfiction texts and actively work to learn more about them
- ◆ Integrate information from several texts on the same topic in order to write about the topic
- ■ Use graphic organizers such as webs to show how a nonfiction writer puts together information related to the same topic or subtopic
- ■ Write about how graphics and text are carefully placed in a nonfiction text to effectively communicate ideas.
- ■ Understand how headings and subheadings are used to define topics and subtopics
- ■ Describe the relationship between ideas and content (larger topic and subtopics) in an expository nonfiction text

Organization

- ● Write an outline by providing summaries of information learned using headings and subheadings that reflect a text's overall structure and simple categories
- ■ Draw, write, or diagram to show how a text is organized: time order or established sequences such as numbers, time of day, days of the week, or seasons
- ■ Notice the organization of a nonfiction text, distinguishing between expository and narrative structure, and write about how the organization affects the reader
- ■ Notice and write about an author's use of underlying structural patterns to organize information and sometimes apply the same structure to writing nonfiction texts: description, temporal sequence, question and answer, cause and effect, chronological sequence, compare and contrast, problem and solution, categorization
- ■ Notice and write about a nonfiction writer's use of narrative text structure in biography, memoir, autobiography, and narrative nonfiction and its effect on the reader
- ■ Clearly explain the steps in a process or an event (for a text with chronological or temporal sequence or a procedural text)

Messages and Main Ideas

- ● List the significant events or ideas in an informational or biographical text
- ◆ Write about connections among ideas in nonfiction texts: animals, pets, families, food, plants, school, friends, growing, senses, neighborhood, weather and seasons, health, etc.

- ◆ Write to compare and expand understanding of content and ideas from academic disciplines across texts
- ◆ Infer and write about the larger messages or main ideas in a nonfiction text
- ◆ Infer and write about moral lessons in a nonfiction text
- ■ Write about how illustrations and graphics help communicate the writer's message

Accuracy

- ■ Critically examine the quality or accuracy of a text, providing evidence in writing for opinions
- ■ Write critically about how a writer uses evidence to support an argument

Illustrations/Graphics

- ● Understand and note important information provided in graphics: photographs, paintings, drawings, captions, labels, insets, charts, diagrams, tables, graphs, maps, timelines, sidebars
- ● Reference organizational tools and text resources in writing about reading: table of contents, chapter title, heading, subheading, sidebar; dedication, acknowledgments, author's note, glossary, index, foreword, prologue, pronunciation guide, footnote, epilogue, appendix, endnote, references
- ● Write summaries reflecting understanding of graphic features: labels, headings, subheadings, sidebars, legends
- ■ Write about how the information, illustrations, and other graphics provide an integrated set of ideas
- ■ Write about how graphics and text are carefully placed in a nonfiction text to effectively communicate ideas
- ■ Notice artistry in illustrations
- ■ Write about the characteristics (medium, style) of the work of some illustrators
- ■ Write about how illustrations and graphics help communicate the writer's message

Style and Language

- ■ Recognize and write about humor in nonfiction texts
- ■ Notice and write about elements of the writer's craft: word choice, use of literary elements
- ■ Notice and record language that reveals the author's attitude (tone) toward the character, subject, or topic: serious, humorous, respectful, affectionate
- ■ Write and think critically about a writer's word choice

● Thinking *Within* the Text   ◆ Thinking *Beyond* the Text   ■ Thinking *About* the Text

Selecting Genres and Forms

Writing About Reading

Students at this level are entering a new phase in their schooling. At this point, without explicit instruction in reading, they are expected to respond in writing to demonstrate their thinking about reading. As skilled users of oral and written language, they are expected to be able to write coherent summaries, reviews, literary essays, arguments, and analyses and to reflect their understanding in academic language. As they enter high school, they are expected to use disciplinary knowledge and vocabulary. But often, they have received little explicit instruction on how to prepare these written pieces and don't have good models in their heads. This level of writing about reading takes a long time and many demonstrations to acquire. Engage them in conversation; they will do more effective writing if they have a chance to rehearse what they are going to say by talking to a partner or the group. In minilessons, explicitly demonstrate new ways of thinking and writing about thinking. To express a new way of thinking or to use a new form, show your own writing in an enlarged way and have students read it and think analytically about it. Use shared writing to create a cooperatively composed example with student input. (Write about a text you have read aloud so that they all share it.) Draw explicit attention to academic language and discuss its precise use. Then students can use the form or articulate the understanding independently. Some students will need several demonstrations, and it is also helpful for students to work with a partner. The major goal of writing about reading is to help students express and organize their thinking so that they can show it in writing. Keep in mind that the behaviors listed here represent the instructional goals for the year.

FUNCTIONAL WRITING

▶ **Notes and Sketches**

- Sketches or drawings that represent a text and provide a basis for discussion or writing
- Notes (about setting, events in a story, characters, memorable words or phrases) on sticky notes, Thinkmarks, and in a Reader's Notebook to support memory for later use in discussion or writing
- Notes that record interesting information, details, language, or examples of the writer's craft as shown by quotes from a text
- Labels and legends for illustrations such as drawings, photographs, and maps related to a text
- Graphic representations of structures such as parallel and circular plots
- Lists of books (completed or abandoned) with title, author, genre, one-word responses to the book, and dates read

▶ **Graphic Organizers**

- Webs that connect information within a text or across texts (organization, character traits, settings, problems)
- Charts that show the way a text is organized: description, temporal sequence, question and answer, cause and effect, chronological sequence, compare and contrast, problem and solution

- Story maps that record title, author, setting, plot events, characters, problem, and resolution
- Graphic organizers supporting genre study including examples of books, noticings from inquiry, and working definitions of genres
- Graphic organizers showing embedded genres within hybrid texts
- Grids or columns that show analysis of a text

▶ **Letters About Reading**

- Letters to other readers or to authors and illustrators including dialogue letters in a Reader's Notebook
- Letters to newspaper or magazine editors in response to articles
- Letter-essays that include a structured, multiparagraph, personal response featuring an in-depth analysis of one book

▶ **Short Writes**

- Short Writes giving a personal response, interpretation, character analysis, description, or critique, focusing on any aspect of craft

▶ **Longer Responses**

- Double-column entry with a phrase, sentence, quote from the text, or question in left column and room for reader's thinking on the right

- Diary entries from the perspective of a biographical subject or a character focusing on the setting, issues, or relationships
- Longer responses in a Reader's Notebook expanding on thinking from notes, sketches, Short Writes, or graphic organizers

NARRATIVE WRITING

▶ **Summaries**

- Plot summaries containing a brief statement of the setting, characters, plot, important events, turning point, character change, problem resolution, message
- Story maps that include setting, characters, and the rising and falling action of a basic narrative structure: plot events, problem, episodes, climax, and resolution

▶ **Writing for Dramatic Purposes**

- Scripts for readers' theater
- Scripts for choral reading (some turning prose into poetry)

▶ **Cartoons/Storyboards**

- Cartoons or comics that present a story or information
- Storyboards that represent significant events in a text

Selecting Genres and Forms *(cont.)*

Writing About Reading

INFORMATIONAL WRITING

▶ Reports

- Reports including text and graphic organizers that present information drawn from texts
- Reports using of illustrations (e.g., photo and/or drawing with label or caption; diagram, cutaway; map with legend or key, scale), organizational tools (e.g., title, table of contents, chapter title, heading, subheading, sidebar, callout), and text resources (e.g., copyright information, acknowledgments, author's note, pronunciation guide, glossary, references, index)

▶ Outlines

- Outlines that include headings, subheadings, and sub-subheadings that reflect the organization of the text

▶ How-to Articles

- Directions or how-to pieces, sometimes illustrated with drawings showing a sequence of actions based on a text
- How-to articles requiring research

▶ Author and Illustrator Studies

- Author studies involving a response to one or more books by an author and/or using biographical information
- Illustrator studies involving a response to one or more books by an artist and/or using biographical information

▶ Biographical Sketches

- Biographical sketches on an author or the subject of a biography (and sometimes a character In fiction)

▶ Projects and Multimedia Presentations

- Projects that present ideas and opinions about topics or texts in an organized way using text and visual images
- Photo essays or picture essays explaining a topic or representing a setting or plot

▶ Interviews

- Write interviews with an author or expert (questions and responses designed to provide information)

▶ News or Feature Articles

- News or feature articles based on reading one or more texts

PERSUASIVE WRITING

- Posters or advertisements that tell about a text in an attention-getting or persuasive way
- Book reviews
- Critiques or analyses of informational articles
- Literary essays that present ideas about a text and may include examples and a summary of the text

POETIC WRITING

- Poetic texts written in response to a prose text
- Poetic texts written in response to poems and applying the same topic, mood, and style

Selecting Goals Behaviors and Understandings to Notice, Teach, and Support

Writing About Reading

FICTION TEXTS

General

- Consistently and automatically notice new vocabulary words and use them appropriately in writing about reading
- Explore definitions of new words from texts, including figurative and connotative uses, by writing about them
- Understand some words that appear in the language of mature users and in written texts (Tier 2) and some words that appear in the scientific disciplines and are more likely to appear in writing (Tier 3)
- Use words that link ideas and clarify meaning–common (simple connectives); sophisticated connectives that are used in written texts but do not appear often in everyday oral language: e.g., *although, however, meantime, meanwhile;* and academic connectives that appear in written texts: e.g., *alternatively, consequently, despite, conversely, eventually, finally, in contrast, initially, likewise, nevertheless, nonetheless, previously, specifically, ultimately, whereas, whereby*
- Use slang or author-invented words in writing about reading that demonstrates understanding of these words
- Understand and draw information for writing from the purpose of the dedication, author's note, and acknowledgments
- Record the titles, authors, and genres of books to recommend
- Record in Reader's Notebook the titles, authors, illustrators, genre of texts read independently, and dates read
- Draw or sketch to represent or remember the content of a text and provide a basis for discussion or writing
- Remember information or details from a text to independently produce lists, simple sequences of action, and directions
- Compose notes, lists, letters, or statements to remember important information about a text
- Write question or notes about confusions to address in the discussion
- Record notes to navigate long and complex texts when checking opinions and theories in preparation for writing longer pieces
- Refer to notes about a text for evidence in discussion and writing to support opinions and statements
- Revisit texts for ideas or to check details when writing or drawing
- Provide evidence from the text or from personal experience to support written statements about a text
- Represent a longer series of events from a text through drawing and writing
- Write logically organized summaries that include the important in a nonfiction text, the conclusions, and the larger message
- Select and include appropriate and important details when writing a summary of a text
- Reference page numbers from text in writing about important information

- Continuously check the evidence in a text to ensure that writing reflects understanding
- Reread writing to check on meaning, accuracy, and clarity of expression
- Draw and write about connections from their own lives to contemporary issues and problems across all genres
- Draw and write about connections between the ideas in texts and one's own life experiences
- Relate important information/ideas within a text or to other texts
- Write about connections among texts by topic, theme, major ideas, authors' styles, and genres
- Notice and write about the importance of ideas relevant to their world: sharing, caring for others, doing your job, helping your family, taking care of self, staying healthy, caring for the world or environment, valuing differences, expressing feelings, empathizing with others
- Provide evidence from the text or from personal experience to support written statements about a text
- Predict what will happen next in a story or after the end of a story and support the prediction with evidence
- Regularly write predictions during and after reading that are based on progress of the plot, characteristics of the setting, attributes of the characters, actions of the characters
- Demonstrate how background knowledge impacts understanding of historical fiction and science fiction
- Provide details that are important to understanding how a story's plot, setting, and character traits are related
- Write about changes in opinions based on new information or insights gained from a text
- Write an interpretation of a text or an illustration, understanding that there can be more than one interpretation
- Infer and write about moral lessons derived from inferring across several texts
- Make notes and write longer responses to indicate acquisition of new information and ideas from a text
- Use texts as resources for words, phrases, and ideas for writing
- Write statements that reflect understanding of both the text body and the graphics or illustrations and how the two are integrated
- Notice book and print features and write to explore their meaning: title and subtitle, author's name and pen portrait, preface, foreword, introduction, acknowledgments, dedication, cover blurb, endorsement, quotations from reviews, letters from readers, dateline, table of contents, epigraph, glossary, notes, epilogue, illustrations, decorative borders, end papers, dust cover, author's note, appendix
- Write to explore the writer's purpose and stance toward a story

---

- Thinking ***Within*** the Text   ◆ Thinking ***Beyond*** the Text   ■ Thinking ***About*** the Text

Selecting Goals Behaviors and Understandings to Notice, Teach, and Support *(cont.)*

Writing About Reading

FICTION TEXTS *(continued)*

- Identify and record the specific genre of a book based on its characteristics
- Notice and write about the characteristics of fiction genres: e.g., realistic fiction, historical fiction, folktale, tall tale, fairy tale, fable, myth, legend, ballad, fantasy, science fiction, epic, and some special types of fiction (adventure story, animal story, humorous story, family, friends, and school story, satire/parody, horror story, romance story)
- Write about hybrid texts distinguishing between fiction and nonfiction sections and noticing how the writer blends the two genres
- Appreciate and write about forms embedded within the main text
- Appreciate and write about the value of embedded primary and secondary sources within a text
- Record and categorize texts by theme, content, genre, author, or other criteria
- Use some academic language to talk about genres: e.g., *fiction, folktale, fairy tale, fable, tall tale, adventure story, animal story, family, friends, and school story, humorous story, realistic fiction, traditional literature, historical fiction, fantasy, myth, legend, ballad, science fiction, hybrid text, epic, satire/parody, horror story, romance story*
- Use some academic language to talk about forms: e.g., *picture book, wordless picture book, poem, poetry, nursery rhyme, rhyme, song, poetry collection, series book, chapter book, play, letter, sequel, limerick, haiku, concrete poetry, short story, fractured fairy tale, diary entry, journal entry, narrative poetry, speech, lyrical poetry, free verse, ballad, epic/saga*
- Use some academic language to talk about literary features: e.g., *beginning, ending, problem, character, solution, main character, events, character change, message, dialogue, setting, flashback, conflict, resolution, theme, descriptive language, simile, figurative language, metaphor, plot, subplot, flash-forward, character development, supporting character, point of view, episode, climax, rising action, falling action, time-lapse, story-within-a-story, mood, personification, symbol, symbolism, first-person narrative, third-person narrative, circular plot, parallel plots, protagonist, antagonist, tone, irony, round and flat characters*
- Use some academic language to talk about book and print features: e.g., *front cover, back cover, title, author, illustrator, page, text, illustration, label, table of contents, acknowledgments, chapter, drawing, caption, chapter title, dedication, author's note, illustrator's note, book jacket*
- Form and record questions in response to events of a plot or to important information
- Form and express opinions about a text in writing and support those opinions with rationales and evidence

- Formulate opinions about authors and illustrators and state in writing the basis for those opinions
- Notice and write to identify multiple points of view in a text as well as how the writer reveals them
- Recognize and appreciate an ambiguous ending of a fiction text
- Write critiques of fiction texts focusing on quality of writing, organization, clarity, authenticity
- Write about the significance of satirical texts identifying what is being satirized and discussing its significance
- Recognize and write analytically about a fiction writer's use of satire, parody
- Recognize and write about bias and identify a writer's point of view
- Write critiques of bias, stereotypes, prejudice, misrepresentation, sexism, and racism found in texts
- Appreciate and comment on how artistic and symbolic design features (e.g., margins, chapter headings, illumination) contribute to the meaning, effectiveness, and artistic qualities of texts

Setting
- Write summaries that include important details about setting
- Make notes or write descriptions to help remember important details about setting
- Write about the importance of setting to the plot in realistic and historical fiction and in fantasy

Plot
- Write summaries that include the story's main problem and how it is resolved
- Make notes or write descriptions to help remember important details about plot
- Write about the significance of events in a plot
- Recognize and write about aspects of narrative structure: beginning, series of events, climax (turning point), problem and resolution, ending
- Recognize and write about an author's use of plots and subplots
- Recognize and write analytically about complex narrative structures: multiple storylines, perspectives, subplots, flashbacks, flash forwards, story-within-a-story, many kinds of conflict

Characters
- Include important details about characters in a summary
- Make notes or write descriptions to help remember important details about characters

---

● Thinking **Within** the Text   ◆ Thinking **Beyond** the Text   ■ Thinking **About** the Text

Selecting Goals Behaviors and Understandings to Notice, Teach, and Support *(cont.)*

Writing About Reading

FICTION TEXTS *(continued)*

Characters *(continued)*

- Recognize and begin to write about characters' multiple dimensions: can be good yet have flaws, can make mistakes based on confusion or misunderstanding, can do bad things but change for the better

- Discuss a problem in a story and write opinions on how characters should act

- Write about what a character is likely to do next or after the story ends and use evidence from the text to support predictions

- Describe character attributes as revealed through thought, dialogue, behavior, and what others say or think about them, and support with evidence

- Describe characters' intentions, feelings, and motivations as revealed through thought, dialogue, behavior, and what others say or think about them and support with evidence

- Describe relationships between characters as revealed through dialogue and behavior

- Write about character development and infer reasons

- Differentiate in writing between the main character(s) and the supporting characters in a story

- Express opinions in writing about the characters in a story (evil, dishonest, clever, sly, greedy, brave, loyal) and support with evidence

- Write about the attributes of characters that are flat (do not change over time) but may be important to the conflict resolution

- Write about the attributes of fully developed (round) characters that have multiple dimensions and change over time

- Write about the relationship between a character's actions and their consequences

- Describe the significance of heroic or larger-than-life characters in fantasy that represent the symbolic struggle of good and evil

- Notice and write about characters with predictable character traits typical of traditional liaterature: sly, brave, silly, wise, greedy, clever

Messages and Themes

- Infer and write the larger messages and sometimes moral lessons of fiction texts

- Write about the lesson inferred from traditional literature

- Write about how the lesson in a story can be applied to their own lives and others' lives

- Write about themes that are close to their experiences: imagination, courage, fears, sharing, friendship, family relationships, self, nature, growing, behavior, community, responsibilities, diversity, belonging, peer relationships, loss

- Infer and write about moral lessons

- Understand and write about themes and ideas that are mature issues and require experience and/or prior reading to interpret

- Write about underlying political messages in fiction texts

- Write meaningfully and deeply about social issues, both local and global, as revealed through character, plot, and setting

- Notice and write about different forms of conflict in a narrative: character vs. character, character vs. self, character vs. nature, character vs. society, character vs. supernatural

- Write about why a writer might tell a story and what messages to readers it might contain

- Write about how illustrations and graphics help communicate the writer's message

Style and Language

- Recognize and write about subtle humor, satire, and parody in a text

- Recognize and write about symbolism in a text and its illustrations

- Write interpretations of dialogue, including language with double meaning (satire)

- Recognize and write about a writer's use of allegory or monologue in a text

- Write the meaning of a monologue

- Notice and write about elements of the writer's craft: word choice, use of literary elements

- Recognize and write about a fiction writer's use of sensory imagery to evoke mood

- Write about a text's organization: time order or established sequences such as numbers, time of day, days of the week, or seasons

- Appreciate and write analytically about the value of embedded primary and secondary sources

- Notice language (serious, humorous, respectful, affectionate) that evokes strong feelings (mood) such as fear, suspense, sadness, and humor, in the reader or listener

---

● Thinking *Within* the Text ◆ Thinking *Beyond* the Text ■ Thinking *About* the Text

Selecting Goals Behaviors and Understandings to Notice, Teach, and Support *(cont.)*

Writing About Reading

- Notice and record language that reveals the author's attitude (tone) toward a story or character: serious, humorous, respectful, affectionate

- Notice and record language that evokes feelings in the reading (mood)

- Notice the narrator of a text and distinguish among narrative styles: first-person narrative, third-person narrative, multiple narrators, alternating first- and third-person narrators

- Write about how an author uses subtext (implication) to say one thing but mean another.

- Notice and write about an author's intentional use of language that violates conventional grammar to provide authentic dialogue and achieve the desired voice

- Notice and write about how the author uses literary language, including some use of metaphor and simile as well as description

- Recognize and write about what a writer does to create humor in a text

- Appreciate and write critiques of fiction texts by noticing characteristics of style (interesting language, humor, suspense, depiction of characters, imagery)

- Borrow the style or some words or expressions from a writer in writing about a text

Illustrations

- ◆ Write interpretations of some illustrations that have symbolic characteristics

- Write about the details found in illustrations

- Notice artistry in illustrations

- Write about how illustrations and graphics help communicate the writer's message and the mood of the text

- Write about how the illustrations contribute to the impact of the writer's message

---

THE KITE RUNNER
By Khaled Hosseini
324 pp. New York:
Riverhead Books

In his debut novel, Khaled Hosseini offers a gripping, unique look into modern Afghanistan. The essence of the book is the build-up of a friendship between Amir, an upper class boy, and Hassan, his servant, age-mate and friend, and the subsequent feelings that Amir experiences when he abandons Hassan as he is brutally attacked and raped.

The first third of the book takes place in Afghanistan thirty years ago, before the Russian invasion. Things have a warm and safe feeling, as Amir and Hassan play and grow up together. There is an underlying tension as plot elements foretell the conflict ahead. As Amir and his father escape the Russians, Hosseini's depiction of the trip, under cramped and hot conditions and with terrifying anxiety, is reminiscent of Elie Weisel's account of his train ride to Auschwitz in Night. In the dramatic conclusion, Amir returns to Afghanistan to look for Hassan.

In The Kite Runner, Hosseini brilliantly weaves fiction and current events. These interlace so well that one forgets this is fiction and not autobiographical. Unlike most writers today, he does not candy-coat reality, accurately portraying the horrors of modern-day Afghanistan.

This first attempt is a real page turner. It provides a heart-wrenching window into the struggles of the Afghan people.

A seventh grader writes about a novel set in modern Afghanistan

---

Dear Ms D

Now I'm also finished, Behind the Bedroom Wall by Laura E. Williams. This is a breathtaking book that is based in the time of the Nazis.

Before, Korrina shunned Jews and loved Hitler, the man who would make the Fatherland stronger. But now Korrina realizes that Jews are nothing to despise, and the Fuhrer is the man to hate.

This book is historical fiction. It takes place during and around World War 2, and many of these sorts of events did take place during history. But this book is fictional because the names and story were fake, even though similar things happened to other families.

I think that Korrina made the right choice by not turning her parents in, and opening her eyes to see what's really going on. She shouldn't have trusted Rita, even though she was her best friend. During that time period, you should never tell anyone who is involved in being a "loyal German" that you like Jews, or feel sorry for them, unless you are completely certain they have the same feelings about it (like Korrina's parents.)

Happy Reading,
Kirstie

An eighth grader writes about a historical fiction text

- ◆ Thinking *Within* the Text   ◆ Thinking *Beyond* the Text   ■ Thinking *About* the Text

Selecting Goals Behaviors and Understandings to Notice, Teach, and Support *(cont.)*

Writing About Reading

NONFICTION TEXTS

General

- Use new vocabulary from texts when writing to appropriately reflect meaning
- Explore definitions of new words from texts by writing about them
- Understand some words that appear in the language of mature users and in written texts (Tier 2) and some words that appear in the scientific disciplines and are more likely to appear in writing (Tier 3)
- Use words that link ideas and clarify meaning–common (simple connectives); sophisticated connectives that are used in written texts but do not appear often in everyday oral language: e.g., *although, however, meantime, meanwhile*; and academic connectives that appear in written texts: e.g., *alternatively, consequently, despite, conversely, eventually, finally, in contrast, initially, likewise, nevertheless, nonetheless, previously, specifically, ultimately, whereas, whereby*
- Understand and note the purpose of the dedication, author's note, and acknowledgments
- Record the titles, authors, and genres of books to recommend
- Record in Reader's Notebook the titles, authors, illustrators and genre of texts read independently, and dates read
- Draw or sketch to represent or remember the content of a text and provide a basis for discussion or writing
- Remember information or details from a text to produce lists, simple sequence of actions, and directions independently
- Compose notes, lists, letters, or statements to remember important information about a text
- Write questions or notes about confusions to address during discussion
- Provide evidence from the text or from personal experience to support written statements about a text
- Record notes to navigate long and complex texts when checking opinions and theories in preparation for writing longer pieces
- Refer to notes about a text for evidence in discussion and writing to support opinions and statements
- Represent a longer series of events from a text through drawing and writing
- Write summaries that reflect literal understanding of a text
- Select and include appropriate and important details when writing a summary of a text
- Reference page numbers from text in writing about important information
- Continuously check the evidence in a text to ensure that writing reflects understanding

- Revisit texts for ideas or to check details when writing or drawing
- Reread writing to check meaning, accuracy, and clarity of expression
- Write about content from texts that reflects beginning understandings of the physical and social world: health, social studies, science, mathematics, arts
- ◆ Write about how nonfiction content is relevant to their lives
- ◆ Relate important information/ideas within a text
- ◆ Write about the important information and concepts in one text and connect it to information and concepts in other texts
- ◆ Write about connections among texts by topic, theme, major ideas, authors' styles, and genres
- ◆ Connect the information in nonfiction books to disciplinary studies
- ◆ Express opinions about facts or information learned
- ◆ Provide evidence from the text or from personal experience to support written statements about a text
- ◆ Notice and write about the importance of ideas relevant to their own world: sharing, caring for others, doing your job, helping your family, taking care of self, staying healthy, caring for the world or environment, valuing differences, expressing feelings, empathizing with others
- ◆ Write about a wide range of predictions based on evidence from the text
- ◆ Reflect both prior knowledge and new knowledge from the text in writing or drawing
- ◆ Write about changes in opinions based on new information or insights gained from a text
- ◆ Write an interpretation of a text or an illustration, understanding that there can be more than one interpretation
- ◆ Write about moral lessons derived from inferring across several texts
- ◆ Make notes and write longer responses to indicate acquisition of new information and ideas from a text
- ■ Use texts as resources for words, phrases, and ideas for writing
- ■ Write statements that reflect understanding of both the text body and the graphics or illustrations and how the two are integrated
- ■ Notice book and print features and write to explore their meaning and refer to them in writing as appropriate: e.g., title and subtitle, author's name and pen portrait, preface, foreword, introduction, acknowledgments, dedication, cover blurb, endorsement, quotations from reviews, letters from readers, dateline, table of contents, epigraph, glossary, notes, epilogue, illustrations, decorative borders, end papers, dust cover, author's note, appendix

● Thinking *Within* the Text   ◆ Thinking *Beyond* the Text   ■ Thinking *About* the Text

Selecting Goals Behaviors and Understandings to Notice, Teach, and Support *(cont.)*

Writing About Reading

NONFICTION TEXTS *(continued)*

- Write to explore the writer's purpose and stance toward a topic
- Notice and write about the characteristics of nonfiction genres: e.g., informational books, expository nonfiction, narrative nonfiction, biography, autobiography, memoir, persuasive texts, procedural texts
- Use names of specific genres accurately in writing about reading
- Record and categorize texts by theme, content, genre, author, or other criteria
- Write about hybrid texts distinguishing between fiction and nonfiction sections and noticing how the writer blends the two genres
- Appreciate and write about forms embedded within the main text
- Describe how ideas and content within a nonfiction text are alike and different
- Use graphic organizers, outlines, notes, reader-response letters, or Short Writes to distinguish in writing between fact supported by evidence and opinion in a nonfiction text
- Appreciate and write about the value of embedded primary and secondary sources within a text
- Use some academic language to talk about genres: e.g., *nonfiction, informational text, informational book, factual text, personal memory story, biography, autobiography, narrative nonfiction, memoir, procedural text, persuasive text, expository text*
- Use some academic language to talk about forms: e.g., *picture book, poem, poetry, nursery rhyme, rhyme, song, poetry collection, series book, play, letter, sequel, limerick, haiku, concrete poetry, diary entry, journal entry, news article, feature article, narrative poetry, photo essay, speech, lyrical poetry, free verse, ballad, epic/saga*
- Use some academic language to talk about literary features: e.g., *beginning, ending, problem, solution, question and answer, topic, events, message, dialogue, description, time order, setting, main idea, comparison and contrast, descriptive language, simile, cause and effect, categorization, persuasive language, temporal sequence, chronological sequence, subject, argument, mood, personification, symbol, symbolism, first-person narrative, third-person narrative, second-person narrative*
- Use some academic language to talk about book and print features: e.g., front cover, back cover, title, author, illustrator, page, text, illustration, photograph, label, table of contents, acknowledgments, section, heading, drawing, caption, map, dedication, author's note, illustrator's note, diagram, glossary, sidebar, book jacket, subheading, chart, graph, timeline, index
- Form and record questions in response to important information

- Form and express opinions about a text in writing and support those opinions with rationales and evidence
- Formulate opinions about authors and illustrators and state in writing the basis for those opinions
- Notice and write about how a writer reveals the setting in a biographical, historical, or narrative nonfiction text
- Recognize and write about examples of argument and persuasion in an informational text
- Describe and critique a writer's use of persuasion and how the writer supports arguments with evidence
- Identify and write about contradictions (statements that disagree with each other) in a nonfiction text
- Critique a text's quality of writing, organization, clarity, and authenticity
- Critique a writer's use of nonfiction text features: titles, table of contents, headings, subheadings, sidebars, labels, legends, captions
- Write critically about the authenticity of a nonfiction text based on facts, scientific evidence, author qualifications, supported statements and arguments, etc.
- Recognize and write about bias in a nonfiction text and identify the writer's point of view
- Write critiques of nonfiction texts, focusing on bias, stereotypes, prejudice, misrepresentation, sexism, or racism, and identifying the author's point of view
- Write about how layout contributes to the meaning and quality of a nonfiction text
- Appreciate and comment on how artistic and symbolic design features (e.g. margins, chapter headings, illumination) contribute to the meaning, effectiveness, and artistic qualities of texts

Topic

- ◆ Using drawing and/or writing, show curiosity about topics encountered in nonfiction texts and actively work to learn more about them
- ◆ Integrate information from several texts on the same topic in order to write about it
- Use graphic organizers such as webs to show how a writer puts together information related to the same topic or subtopic
- Understand how headings and subheadings are used to define topics and subtopics
- Describe the relationship between ideas and content (larger topic and subtopics) in an expository nonfiction text
- Write about how graphics and text are carefully placed in a nonfiction text to effectively communicate ideas

---

● Thinking **Within** the Text　　◆ Thinking **Beyond** the Text　　■ Thinking **About** the Text

Selecting Goals Behaviors and Understandings to Notice, Teach, and Support *(cont.)*

Writing About Reading

NONFICTION TEXTS *(continued)*

Organization

- ● Write an outline by providing summaries of information learned using headings and subheadings that reflect a text's overall structure and simple categories

- ■ Draw, write, or diagram to show how a text is organized: time order or established sequences such as numbers, time of day, days of the week, or seasons

- ■ Notice the organization of a nonfiction text, distinguishing between expository and narrative structure, and write about how the organization affects the reader

- ■ Notice and write about an author's use of underlying structural patterns to organize information and sometimes apply the same structure to writing nonfiction texts: description, temporal sequence, question and answer, cause and effect, chronological sequence, compare and contrast, problem and solution, categorization

- ■ Notice and write about a nonfiction writer's use of narrative text structure in biography, memoir, autobiography, and narrative nonfiction and its effect on the reader

- ■ Explore through writing alternative ways to organize an informational text

- ■ Clearly explain the steps in a process or series of events (for a text with chronological or temporal sequence or a procedural text)

Messages and Main Ideas

- ● List the significant events or ideas in an informational or biographical text

- ◆ Write about connections among ideas in nonfiction texts: animals, pets, families, food, plants, school, friends, growing, senses, neighborhood, weather and seasons, health, etc

- ◆ Write to compare and expand understanding of content and ideas from academic disciplines across texts

- ◆ Infer and write about the larger messages or main ideas in a nonfiction text

- ◆ Infer and write about moral lessons in a nonfiction text

- ◆ Write an in-depth analysis of social issues, both local and global, as revealed through facts, arguments, conclusions, and opinions

- ■ Write about how illustrations and graphics help communicate the writer's message

Accuracy

- ■ Critically examine the quality or accuracy of the text providing evidence for opinions in writing

- ■ Write critically about how a writer uses evidence to support an argument

Illustrations/Graphics

- ● Understand and note important information provided in graphics: photographs, paintings, drawings, captions, labels, insets, charts, diagrams, tables, graphs, maps, timelines, sidebars

- ● Reference organizational tools and text resources in writing about reading: table of contents, chapter title, heading, subheading, sidebar; dedication, acknowledgments, author's note, glossary, index, foreword, prologue, pronunciation guide, footnote, epilogue, appendix, endnote, references

- ● Write summaries reflecting understanding of graphic features: labels, headings, subheadings, sidebars, legends

- ■ Write about how the information, illustrations, and other graphics provide an integrated set of ideas

- ■ Write about how graphics and text are carefully placed in a nonfiction text to effectively communicate ideas

- ■ Notice artistry in illustrations

- ■ Write about the characteristics (medium, style) of the work of some illustrators

- ■ Write about how illustrations and graphics help communicate the writer's message

Style and Language

- ■ Recognize and write about humor in nonfiction texts

- ■ Notice and write about elements of the writer's craft: word choice, use of literary elements

- ■ Appreciate and write about the value of embedded primary and secondary sources within a text

- ■ Notice and record language that reveals the author's attitude (tone) toward the character, subject, or topic: seriousness, humor, respect, affection

- ■ Write and think critically about a writer's word choice

● Thinking *Within* the Text　　◆ Thinking *Beyond* the Text　　■ Thinking *About* the Text

Writing

Writing Continuum

The classroom, from prekindergarten through middle school, is a place where students learn the many ways that writing plays a role in their lives. They learn to write by writing and noticing the decisions writers make. They learn to write by engaging in the writing process with the expert help of the teacher and with the support of their peers.

Writing is multifaceted in that it orchestrates thinking, language, and mechanics. The writing process can be described as a series of steps (getting an idea, drafting, revising, editing, and publishing), but it is in fact a recursive process in which all of these things happen not in a linear way but as a dynamic process, always in motion. Writers constantly apply and reapply everything they know to successive attempts. They move forward, back up, redo, have sudden insights; but with opportunity and teaching they build effective—even powerful—writing systems over time.

Writing is a basic tool for learning as well as for communicating with others. In our schools, students are expected to write in every subject area. We want them to become individuals who can use many types of writing for a wide range of purposes and audiences throughout their lives. Elsewhere we have written that "the writing terrain spreads out in many directions, real and imaginary, and encompasses in-depth intellectual investigations of biology, geology, history, anthropology, and other fields" (Fountas and Pinnell 2001b, 423).

Students need to develop a basic knowledge of the writing process and to know how to vary the process for different genres and purposes. Preschoolers can "make books" by telling a story through drawings even before they can read or write! All students like using blank books to make a variety of books of their own. Even young students can produce simple publications; as they write year after year, they engage in the same basic process but at more sophisticated levels. Their range becomes broader and their publications more complex.

Demonstration: Almost every genre listed in the continuum is first demonstrated in a read aloud or with examples of *shared, interactive,* or *modeled writing.* Young students will have a shared or group experience in all the genres they are eventually expected to produce independently. Even young students can have this important experience through shared, interactive, or modeled writing:

▶ In *shared writing,* the teacher and students compose a text together. The teacher is the scribe. Often, especially with very young students and sometimes with older students, the teacher works on a chart displayed on an easel. Students contribute each word of the composition and reread it many times. Sometimes the teacher asks younger students to say the word slowly as they think how a word is spelled. At other times the teacher (with student input) writes the composition on the chart quickly. The text becomes a model, example, or reference for student writing and discussion.

▶ *Interactive writing* is identical to and proceeds in the same way as shared writing, with one exception: Occasionally the teacher, while making teaching points that help students attend to various features of letters and words, will invite a student to come up to the easel and contribute a letter, word, or part of a word. This process is especially helpful to beginning readers because their contributions to the actual writing have high instructional value. For student contribution, the teacher selects a word or word part that is "just acquired or nearly known" by the student. The teacher writes the words students can write easily and the words that are too difficult. After students have developed a large writing vocabulary and systems for spelling words, you would shift to using shared writing most of the time. At this point in time, the process of students' contributing writing has little instructional value and is very time consuming. Your time is better spent on getting students' ideas down quickly and guiding the process. Also, students will be producing a great deal of writing as independent work. This shift happens by about the end of second grade. But remember that the process of shared writing is always interactive in the sense that it is based on a high level of student participation and talk.

» *Modeled writing* may be used at every grade level. Here, the teacher demonstrates the process of writing in a particular genre, sometimes thinking aloud to reveal what is going on as he makes purposeful writing decisions. The teacher may have prepared the piece of writing (or thought through the demonstration) prior to class but talks through the process with the students.

Mentors: A major component in learning to write in a particular genre is to apprentice with other writers. Writers learn to write from studying the craft of other writers. If students experience several books by a particular author and illustrator, they soon learn what is special about a book by that author or illustrator. They start to notice topics, characteristics of illustrations, types of stories, and language. They may record or remember words and language in order to borrow it. As they grow more sophisticated, they notice what writers do to make their writing effective and begin to use texts by those mentors as models when planning, revising, and publishing writing. They notice purpose, topic, and genre choice and begin to make those choices for themselves.

Students may even participate in formal study of authors or illustrators to learn about their craft—how they portray characters, use dialogue, and organize information. Graphics and illustrations offer many examples to young writers relative to illustrating their work clearly. Very sophisticated readers and writers are still learning from mentor texts as they seek examples of the treatment of themes or ideas, create dialogue and show character development, and prepare persuasive or critical pieces. Through the process of taking on all of the understandings listed in this continuum, the students realize that published authors can be their mentors.

English Language Learners: Additional complexity is introduced into the process of becoming a writer if the student is an English language learner. The expectations for each grade level of the continuum are the same for students whose first language is English and for those who are learning English as a second language. The expectations for *instruction,* however, are different.

English language learners will need a greater level of support as they expand their control of oral English and, alongside it, written English. Start where students are, but give them rich opportunities to hear written language read aloud and to talk about concepts and ideas before they are expected to write about them.

As you work with this continuum, you will find that some of the expectations—especially those related to the syntax of language, vocabulary, and grammar and usage—are very difficult for English language learners to reach. And this will be quite different for individuals of all ages. It depends on the time and opportunity they have had to learn English. They will reach these goals if they have a nurturing language environment. But at the present, it is important to accept what they say, engage them in conversations, and help them expand their use of language. When you ask them to dictate language, converse to see how much you can expand to use English syntax. You may decide to record language exactly as they speak or to make shifts that help them expand knowledge of English language. This is a delicate process that is different for every learner. At the bottom line, the message the students read after dictation or in shared writing must be one that they can read with teacher support.

Shared/interactive writing is an effective tool for helping English language learners begin to compose and construct written text. By composing text collaboratively, with the teacher as scribe to guide the structure and control conventions, students can create their own exemplar texts. Shared/interactive writing offers group support and strong models. As students reread the interactive writing, they internalize conventional English syntactic patterns, relevant vocabulary, and the features of the genre.

In individual conferences, teachers can help English language learners rehearse what they want to write and help them expand their ideas. As a teacher, see through the quality of those ideas rather than being blinded by grammar or vocabulary. They need to keep expanding thinking as they learn conventions. Also, include frequent experiences with shared and performance reading, which involves students in rereading and thinking about the meaning of familiar texts.

The Writing Continuum: This writing continuum is presented in a one-year span, the goals ideally to be achieved by the end of the grade. Since learning to write is akin to a spiral, you will see many of the same goals repeated across the grades. However, students will be working toward these goals in increasingly sophisticated ways.

In this continuum, we describe writing in four major areas: purpose and genre; craft; conventions; and process. These four areas of learning apply to all students, prekindergarten through grade eight.

Writing is a complex process. As you can see from Figure I-1, each element is closely related to another. In the center, you see writing described as a processing system. Writing and reading are complementary processes; learning in one helps learning in the other. Surrounding the central circle, the terms *purpose* and *audience* reflect the way writers begin with a purpose and with awareness of a particular audience as they think about *genre*. They select a genre—such as functional, narrative, informational, persuasive, poetic, or hybrid—according to purpose, audience, and the meaning of the piece. Writers consider genre, craft, and conventions simultaneously as they write, although one aspect may have dominance in any part of the process. All of these elements are in the service of *communicating meaning*. Writers use aspects of *craft* such as organization, idea development, language use, word choice, and voice. And they use *conventions* such as grammar and usage, capitalization, punctuation, spelling, and handwriting or wordprocessing. (Note that *text layout* relates to both craft and conventions.) The recursive process of writing is illustrated by the terms describing actions in the outside circle: *planning and rehearsing, drawing, drafting and revising, editing and proofreading,* and *publishing,* along with the outcome for students, *viewing self as a writer.* All of these areas of learning are constantly under development across years of schooling.

WRITING

FIGURE I-1 *A Processing System for Writing*

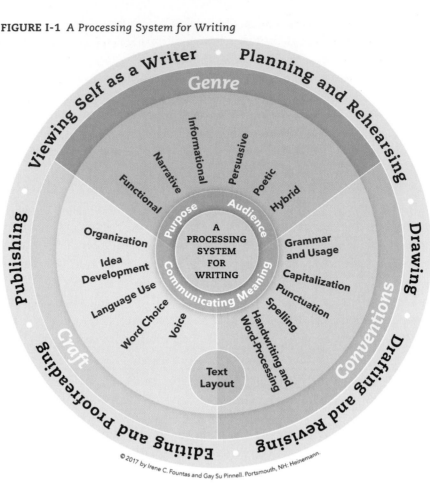

Purpose and Genre

When writers write, they may have a purpose in mind and select the genre accordingly. They may want to tell a story that will communicate a larger meaning; to inform or entertain; to persuade people to take action on an issue that is important to them. It is important to recognize that effective writers do not write in a genre just to practice it. They choose the genre that will best convey the meaning they intend. Of course, teachers introduce new genres to students so that they can learn to write in those genres, but the ultimate goal is to establish a repertoire of genres from which writers can select. It is important to establish the desire to write in a genre by making it interesting and enjoyable. For instructional purposes, we have described traditional genres within each purpose category, even as we recognize that several genres or forms might be used to support a given purpose—an informational friendly letter, for example, or a functional poem.

In the PreK–8 continuum on writing, we categorize genres under six major areas: functional writing, narrative writing, informational writing, persuasive writing, poetic writing, and hybrids. It is important to note that the literary genres of fiction and nonfiction *flow across* these areas, although some texts—functional, for example—fall almost completely into one or the other. We consider these six areas to be of vital concern for teachers of writing. These categories bring a focus to writing instruction across the grades, and they contain the genres that students will need to use skillfully in their academic work and in the professions.

Nonfiction writing, in particular, has become more interesting and engaging, going beyond reports and "textbook-like" pieces to texts that reflect all aspects of the writer's craft. We want students to learn from mentor texts how to produce interesting nonfiction that focuses on a topic or one aspect of a topic. Students learn how to use resources to be sure they have accurate information and how to sustain focus. Through engaging nonfiction writing, students can learn how to inform, but also to argue a point and to persuade, abilities that can serve them well in life!

For each genre within these categories, we have two important sets of information: Understanding the Genre, which reflects key understandings particular to the genre (what students need to *know* about the genre); and Writing in the Genre, which refers to the way the student demonstrates understanding by taking on the various kinds of writing within the genre (what students *do* with the genre). Also for each genre, we list sample forms of writing that can, among others, be part of the writing curriculum.

Functional Texts

As adults, we use a large range of functional texts every day, ranging from very simple communications to sophisticated letters. The genres that follow are categorized as functional.

Friendly letters. Notes, cards, invitations, email, and friendly letters are written communications that require the writer to provide particular kinds of information and to write in a tone and form that is appropriate.

Formal letters. Business letters and editorials are formal documents written with a particular purpose. They get right to the point, exclude extraneous details, and have required parts.

Lists and procedures. Lists are planning tools that help people accomplish daily tasks; they are also the building blocks of more complicated texts, such as poems and informational pieces. Procedures, like how-to texts and directions, require student writers to think through and clearly explain the steps in a process.

Test writing. Test writing is required in academia. Students must learn that some writing is for the expressed purpose of showing someone else how much you know. They need to analyze a test for the expectations and write to the point.

Writing about reading. Writing about reading, too, is required in school to reflect students' thinking within, beyond, and about a text they have read. Almost any genre or form can be used to respond to a text. We have provided a complete separate continuum for this important area of literacy (see Writing About Reading continuum).

Narrative Texts

A narrative is a text that is told like a story with a beginning, a series of events, and an ending. For fiction, typical narrative structure involves the introduction of characters and setting, a story problem, a series of events, and resolution of the problem. Usually there is a "high point" or "climax" in which the problem is resolved, and shortly after that the story ends. Nonfiction texts, too, can be told in chronological order, so they are classified as narratives. These texts include biographical texts (biography, autobiography, and memoir) and narrative nonfiction, for example, an account of a time in history.

Narratives are usually told in time order, but they may become very complex. For example, using mentor texts as examples, students may take on variations in narrative structure such as flashbacks, flash forwards, stories-within-stories; they may change from first-person narrative to third-person narrative; they may change narrators completely.

In this continuum, we include five types of narrative text—one fiction and four nonfiction. For each type, we list important understandings and identify specific goals related to writing in that genre.

Fiction. A short story is a form of fiction about an event in the life of a main character (or several) and supporting characters. Short fiction is carefully crafted both to entertain and to communicate emotions and messages. Because it is short, the number of events will be limited, but the writer can still communicate character change of some kind, for example, a "lesson" that the character learns. We want students to learn that good fiction reveals something about life, connects with readers, and communicates the deeper meanings of a theme.

Short stories can be written in any fiction genre: *realistic fiction, historical fiction, fantasy* (including science fiction and material written in the style of traditional literature). Students may retell their own version of an animal fantasy or may write new endings or sequels to texts they have read. Your students are learning some elements of the craft of fiction as they write personal memory stories; they can move to write stories about people or animals in imitation of the mentor texts they are hearing read aloud or reading. As they grow more sophisticated, students can undertake aspects of the craft of fiction, such as working on the lead, revealing characters, showing characters' feelings and characters' changes, and the development of plot.

Memoir. Children begin by writing personal narratives or personal memory stories, and these evolve into memoir and from there to other kinds of biographical texts. A memoir is typically a short piece of writing in which a person shares an intense memory. Usually, a memoir involves creating sensory images, communicating feelings, and evoking emotions.

We want students to learn the craft and conventions of memoir by writing about their own lives. We wouldn't call these personal memory stories formal memoirs, but even very young students can begin by sketching, telling, and writing simple stories—in chronological order—about their families, friends, and pets. It is important for students to understand from the beginning that they are writing about what they know. In doing so, they will learn to observe their worlds closely, looking for examples that will be true to life. Memoir is important as a foundation for all kinds of writing. For example, students learn to write clear sentences, to use strong adjectives and verbs, and to stay away from unimportant details and redundant information. Students develop the ability to write fiction by telling these stories from experience.

Throughout schooling, students continue to write memoir, learning from mentor texts and becoming more sophisticated. They learn to write about "small moments" that capture strong feelings or significant experiences. They begin to understand the more formal notion of memoir as a brief, often intense memory of an event or person. A memoir has an element of reflection and teaches the reader a larger meaning.

Biography. A biography is the true story of a person's life written by another person. It is usually presented in chronological order and tells the person's whole life, but the structure may vary, to focus on one aspect of a person's life.

Younger writers can tell simple stories about family members or friends, moving over several years toward fully documented biographical sketches or profiles of role models or public figures, contemporary or historical. In all cases, the biographer selects a subject for stated reasons, selects events, and tells the story in a way that reveals the writer's perspective to the audience. Writers of biography need to work to present an unbiased account; however, the stance of the writer will be evident.

Writers use craft to make the biography interesting. It may be fictionalized for interest and readability, but the writer must understand and differentiate between what is real and documented (through credible sources like personal interviews, documents, and other written texts) and what the writer has added to create interest. At some point, students might also write texts that could be called "fictionalized biography," in which almost everything is documented and added material is *likely,* or "biographical fiction," in which even more fictional material is added, giving the entire narrative a somewhat speculative nature.

Autobiography. An autobiography is the true story of a person's life written by that same person. It is usually presented in chronological order, although that may vary. The writer of an autobiography is inherently biased! But he or she is also obligated to tell the truth. Young students work toward autobiography as they write personal memory stories and memoir.

Narrative nonfiction. Narrative nonfiction is a piece of informational writing that is organized in chronological order. It is different from a fiction narrative in that it doesn't have a central problem that is resolved at some point in a plot. It does communicate accurate information in a narrative structure.

Informational Texts

In the category of informational writing, we include expository texts, speeches, feature articles, reports, and essays. All of these forms of informational writing usually use expository text structure. In general, information is organized into categories, and the categories are ordered logically to make sense to readers, to inform them, and sometimes to persuade them. (Persuasive writing, or argument, is so important that we place it in a category by itself.)

Expository texts. Throughout schooling and beyond, the ability to write expository nonfiction is important. In writing about a topic, students should use many aspects of the writer's craft— an interesting "lead," clear statements, the use of examples, and a good organization. Nonfiction writers use underlying structures such as description, cause and effect, chronological sequence, temporal sequence, categorization, problem and solution, and question and answer. (Here, we are talking not about a narrative but the insertion of temporal sequence into a text that, overall, is organized into categories.)

Younger writers can write "facts" or "observations" centered on a single topic and then organized and presented in a meaningful way. For example, just placing "like" information together on a page is a big step toward writing effective short expository nonfiction. As students learn more in the content areas, they get interested in a topic, conduct research to find more about it, and then write a piece. Expository nonfiction can take several forms.

Speeches. Students can prepare presentations and speeches that they will then make to a known audience. Even if they only outline the speech or prepare slides, they will use writing to create the organizing structure. Alternatively, students can write the entire speech and read it aloud.

Feature articles. A feature article focuses on one aspect of a topic. The article is clearly organized and reflects all of the aspects of craft that characterize good expository writing. In addition, there is emphasis on engaging readers and keeping them interested in the topic. For example, the writer works on an interesting lead and uses clear and interesting examples. The writer may use graphics to communicate information and photographs to enhance the text and make it interesting.

Reports. In school and in many jobs students may have after schooling, individuals are required to write clear, and sometimes convincing, reports. A report should offer facts and examples that are authentic and support each point made by the writer. Students in elementary school are often required to write reports of experimentation or of research on a topic. These may be simple in the lower grades, but students in the upper grades learn to document the sources of their information and to use elements such as footnotes, endnotes, and bibliographies.

Essays. An essay is a highly sophisticated, short literary composition in which the writer clearly states a point of view. The essay may be analytical, critical, or persuasive. The ability to compose an essay is based on many years not only of writing but also of engaging in critical thinking. Essays are appropriate in the upper elementary grades and in middle school, and, of course, they are required of students in high school and college.

Persuasive Texts

We have placed persuasive writing here as an additional category because of the particular demands it makes of the writer. Argument and persuasive writing seek to convince the reader to think in a certain way, and, ultimately, to act in a certain way.

When the purpose is to convince the audience, added challenge confronts the writer. Not only must the writing be clear, well-organized, and interesting, but also it must speak directly to the audience. Argument and persuasion have the audience in mind.

All of the genres listed under expository nonfiction can take the form of persuasion and argument, and the writing is expected to meet the criteria for high quality in each. One difference might be that the writer does not attempt to be unbiased in persuasion and argument. In other words, you can write a speech or a feature article to inform the audience in an unbiased way; *or* you can write a speech to persuade the audience to agree with your opinion. The difference in purpose affects selection of information to include, word choice, voice, etc.

Persuasion and argument are closely related, but there is a slight difference.

▶ Persuasion seeks to *convince* the audience of a point of view and to prompt a ways of thinking (an opinion) or an action. Persuasive writing may appeal to the emotions and can be largely based on opinions. The writer may use "loaded" words; sometimes the persuasive writing is based solely on the credibility of the writer. The writer may tell a biased point of view from his own experiences, or include "stories" that may or may not be totally factual, or include facts but ignore contradictory facts.

▶ Argument, on the other hand, must have a solid base of evidence. A written argument must have a series of logically organized points, each of which is supported with credible evidence. An argument includes counterarguments and the evidence to disconfirm them. The audience is convinced because of the logic and the evidence—not just on the basis of emotion.

These differences are slight but important. It is obvious that persuasion and argument are very challenging forms of writing. Students learn about these forms by experiencing them, in interactive read-aloud and in their own reading. They begin to express their opinions in oral language, backing up their opinions with evidence.

In their writing about reading (see *Writing About Reading,* pages 161–222), students may write critically about the texts they read and back their statements with evidence from the text. They may write letters to the editor of newspapers or journals using persuasion or argument. An essay has an element of argument; and many speeches do as well.

Poetic Texts

Young writers need to learn to understand poetry as a special genre for communicating meaning and describing feelings and sensory images. There are many different forms of poetry: traditional rhymes, songs, and verses; free verse; lyric poetry; narrative poetry; limericks; cinquains; concrete poetry; haiku; "found" poetry; list poems; and formula poems. Very young children enjoy rhymes and songs, but as they experience more they learn that poetry does not have to rhyme. It involves selecting words carefully to communicate emotions and to create images. Once students have a well-established understanding of free verse, you can introduce them to a variety of other forms through mentor texts. Before writing poetry, students need to hear poems read aloud and read poems aloud themselves. This exposure gives students the feel of poetry and lets them gradually internalize the forms it can take. They learn to observe the world closely and to experiment with words and phrases so that they begin to produce poetic language.

Hybrids

Hybrid texts, those that combine more than one genre into a coherent whole, serve any purpose the writer chooses. They may engage, inform, persuade, or serve a functional purpose. We have included these at the upper levels only. At their simplest—embedding a friendly letter into an ongoing narrative, for example—they may be manageable for the fluent middle-grade writer. More complex forms—parallel explanation and narrative, for example—require deft perspective and style changes that can be managed only by advanced writers. It is important for writers to study and produce these hybrid texts, learning to embed texts like directions, maps, recipes, charts, etc. They will be asked to read them on tests; writing helps them to understand the combined genres.

Craft

The previous section describes the product of writing—what students are expected to produce as an outcome. Getting to that product is an educational process and requires attention to skills and strategies in the next three sections: craft, conventions, and the process of writing.

All of the previous genres involve crafting an effective piece of writing that is clearly organized and contains well-developed ideas. The writer must use language appropriate for the genre, including the specific words selected. We want younger students to consider word choice carefully so that the piece conveys precise meaning. Older students will have larger vocabularies, but they can also use tools like a thesaurus. But we don't want them to insert "big words" or any kind of words just for the sake of doing it. That will make their writing contrived rather than authentic.

Above all, the writing must have *voice*—it must reveal the person behind the writing. That means the writing takes on characteristics that reveal the writer's unique style. Students can write with voice if they are expressing feelings or telling about events or topics that are important to them. The writing shows their passion. Voice develops throughout a writer's career, and it is revealed in the way the writer uses every aspect of craft—sentence structure, word choice, language, and punctuation.

The craft section of the continuum states goals for each area. These goals apply in general to all genres, though some elements of craft are more relevant to some genres than to others. We include the following:

Organization
This section addresses the way the writer arranges the information or structures the narrative. It includes the structure of the whole text—beginnings and endings and the arrangement of ideas. Fiction writers use literary elements such as exposition of the characters, setting, and plot, a series of events, and plot resolution. Nonfiction writers use either narrative or expository structure and underlying structures, such as description, compare and contrast, cause and effect, problem and solution, and sequence.

Idea Development
Idea development focuses on the way the writer presents and supports the main ideas and themes of the text.

Language Use
This section describes goals for the way the writer uses sentences, phrases, and expressions to describe events, actions, or information.

Word Choice
Word choice attends to the particular words the writer selects to convey meaning.

Voice
Voice is the individual's unique style as a writer. It conveys the writer's feelings and passion in a story or topic.

Conventions

Knowing and observing the conventions of writing make it possible to communicate ideas clearly. Substance must be there and so must craft, but without correct spelling, conventional grammar, and punctuation, it will be difficult to get people to value the writing. Of course, great writers often violate some of these conventions, especially in fiction, but they do so for an artistic purpose. The first eight years of school are the time to establish a firm grasp of the conventions of writing, including:

Text Layout
Young children must learn the basics of writing words left to right across the page with spaces between them. But even sophisticated writers must develop the ability to use layout in a way that contributes to and enhances meaning, especially when graphics are included.

Grammar and Usage The grammar (syntax) of written English language is more formal than spoken language. There are rules for how sentences are put together, how parts of speech are used, how verb tense is made consistent, and how paragraphs are formed. All languages have a grammar, and English grammar is even more difficult for English language learners than vocabulary. But they want to be effective users of English grammar, and mentor texts and writing are important in the process of learning. We provide a detailed grammar continuum in Appendix: Grammar, Usage, and Mechanics.

Capitalization The appropriate use of capital letters makes texts more readable and signals proper nouns and specialized functions (titles, for example).

Punctuation Punctuation adds meaning to the text, makes it more readable, and signals to the reader the writer's intentions in terms of using meaningful phrases. Punctuation is also highly related to grammar.

Spelling Conventional spelling is critical to the presentation of a piece of writing, both in appearance and meaning.

Handwriting and Word-Processing The writer's handwriting must be legible. Effective handwriting also increases writing fluency and ease, so the writer can give more attention to the message. For the same reasons, it is important for students to develop rapid, efficient keyboarding skills. In fact, in today's world, keyboarding skills go a long way in compensating for less-than-good handwriting.

Learning these conventions is a challenging and complex task, one accomplished over many years. We do not want students to devote so much time and energy to conventions that they become fearful writers or do not develop voice. We do want conventions to be an important part of the editing process.

Writing Process

Students learn to write by writing—by engaging in all of the component processes many times. The writing process is recursive; the same processes are used over and over and some simultaneously as they become more sophisticated. And the components take place roughly in order, but at any point in the process the writer can and will use any or all of the components. In this continuum, we describe four key phases in the process: planning and rehearsing, drafting and revising, editing and proofreading, and publishing. In addition, we've included two overarching categories that pervade the entire process: sketching and drawing and viewing self as a writer.

Planning and Rehearsing

This phrase involves gathering information, trying out ideas, and thinking about some critical aspects of the text, such as purpose and audience, before beginning to write. Of course, a writer will often stop during drafting and gather more information or rethink the purpose after discussing it with others. This area includes curriculum goals for:

Purpose. Writers have a clear purpose for writing the text, and this purpose influences genre selection and organization.

Audience. Writers think of the audience, which may be known or unknown. It is important even for younger students to think of the audience as all readers of the text—not just the teacher.

Oral language. Writers can generate ideas and try out their ideas through conversation with others.

Gathering seeds. An important writer's tool is a notebook in which they can collect ideas, experiment, sketch, diagram, and freewrite. Writers use notebooks as a resource for ideas, formats, and techniques.

Content, topic, theme. Writers carefully select the content or topic of the piece with interest, purpose, and theme in mind.

Inquiry and research. In preparation for writing informational texts and biography, writers will often spend an extended time gathering information. This is also true when an individual is writing historical fiction or developing a plot in an unfamiliar setting.

Genre/form. With audience in mind, as well as content or purpose, writers select the genre for the piece and the particular form of the genre.

Drawing

Whether used to capture ideas, store quick images to aid recall, visually arrange ideas to clarify structure or information in a draft, or enhance the effectiveness of a published work, sketching and drawing support the entire writing process. Goals in this section apply to all phases of the writing process.

Drafting and Revising

A writer may produce an initial draft and then revise it to make it more effective, but most writers revise while drafting and sometimes also draft more material after revising. There are several ways to draft and revise a text, and all of these may be used any time during the process. Students use them throughout the grades, and these include:

Producing a draft. Writers write an initial draft, getting ideas down quickly.

Rereading. Writers reread to remember what has been written, to assess clarity, and to revise.

Adding information. Writers add ideas, details, words, phrases, sentences, paragraphs, or dialogue to a piece of writing to make it more effective.

Deleting information. Writers delete redundancy, unimportant information, and extraneous details to make the piece clearer.

Reorganizing information. Writers move information around to make the piece more logical or more interesting.

Changing text. Writers identify vague parts and provide specificity; work on transitions; or changes words, phrases, and sentences.

Using tools and techniques. Writers acquire a repertoire of tools and techniques for drafting and revising a text.

Understanding the process. Writers actively work on drafting and revising and use other writers as mentors and peer reviewers.

Editing and Proofreading

Once the content and organization are in place, students may wish to polish select-ed drafts to prepare them for publication. The editing and proofreading phase focuses on the form of the composition.

Editing for conventions. Over the years, as students acquire knowledge of the conven-tions, we can expect them to use that knowledge in editing their writing.

Using tools. Students also need to learn the tools that will help them in editing—for example, the dictionary, a thesaurus, and technology.

Understanding the process. Students learn when, how, and why to elicit editing help.

Publishing

Writers may produce many final drafts that are shared with their peers, but sometimes they also publish pieces of writing. These pieces will have received a final edit and will include all the elements of a published work, including a cover with all necessary information, typed and laid-out text, and graphics as appropriate. For younger students publishing may simply mean a stapled book. Publishing can be defined in a variety of ways. It may mean publishing for a known audience—the class or the school. Or, occasionally it means publishing to an unknown audience—for example, a newsletter, a website, or blog. For some students, publishing simply means reading a piece to peers to celebrate the writing rather than taking a great deal of time to type it and make it into a formally prepared piece. Taking this final step is important for young writers because it gives them a sense of accomplishment and gives them an opportunity to share their talent with a wider audience. Over time, as students build up many final drafts and published pieces, they can reflect on their own development as writers.

Viewing Self as a Writer

Finally, we need to think of our students as lifelong writers. Developing as a writer means more than producing piece after piece and gradually improving. We want our students to make writing a part of their lives—to see themselves as writers who are constantly observing the world and gathering ideas and information for their writing. They use writing for a variety of real purposes and audiences. They need to become independent, self-motivated writers, consciously entering into their own learning and development and, in the process, expanding the ability to know themselves and their world. Most of all, they need to be able to seek out mentors so they can continue to expand their understandings of the possibilities of this craft. In the last section of the continuum, we list goals in this area.

Using the Writing Continuum

We have described the components of the grade-by-grade Writing continuum as well as the organization. You can use the continuum as a planning document and a way of assessing progress. As with all of the continua, keep in mind that the behaviors described here represent goals for a year of instruction.

Selecting Purpose, Genre, and Form

Writing

Most writing for preschool children is generated through dictated writing or very simple shared or interactive writing. The teacher may guide children to tell about their own experiences or to retell something from a story. Sometimes teachers label pictures or children's drawings as a demonstration of writing. Preschool children's independent writing consists largely of drawing or painting accompanied by the use of whatever they have noticed about writing. They may write their names (or parts of them); they may use non-letter-like or letter-like forms mixed with some known letters. They may use the letters they know over and over in strings. Even if children are only pretending to write, we can tell a great deal about their growing knowledge of and interest in written language by observing how they use the space or create forms on the page. From their attempts we can observe that they are beginning to distinguish between pictures and print. You may want to invite children to talk about their drawings (stories or just labels). If the child requests it, you may write a simple sentence or two that the child dictates, but it is important not to write on the child's paper. If the child wants it, write on a sticky note. Many children can remember and "read" their own sentences even if you cannot.

FUNCTIONAL WRITING
(Purpose–to perform a practical task)

LABEL

▶ **Understanding the Genre**

- Understand that a writer or illustrator can add a label to help readers understand a drawing or photograph
- Understand that a label provides important information

▶ **Writing in the Genre**

- Begin to label drawings with approximated writing
- Participate actively in suggesting labels during shared reading and writing

FRIENDLY LETTER

▶ **Understanding the Genre**

- Understand that people use writing to communicate with each other
- Understand letters or notes as written communication among people
- Understand that written communication can be used for different purposes: e.g., to give information, to invite, to give thanks
- Understand that a friendly letter can be written in various forms: e.g., note, card, letter, invitation, email
- Understand that people include their names (and the name or names of one or more recipients) in a friendly letter
- Understand that an invitation must include specific information

▶ **Writing in the Genre**

- Participate actively in writing notes, letters, invitations, etc., through shared and interactive writing
- Use shared or approximated writing to write to a known audience (classmates, family)

- Actively participate in suggesting information to include in writing during shared or interactive writing
- Add illustrations or decorations to written messages
- Create a friendly letter in approximated form (note, card, letter, invitation, email)

PROCEDURAL TEXT

▶ **Understanding the Genre**

- Understand that a procedural text helps people know how to do something
- Understand that a procedural text can be written in various forms: e.g., list, directions with steps
- Understand that a procedural text often shows one item under another item and often includes a number or letter for each item
- Understand that pictures can help readers understand information or how to do something
- Understand that captions can be written under pictures to give people more information

▶ **Writing in the Genre**

- Actively participate in group writing of lists to help remember how to do something
- Suggest items for lists
- Actively participate in suggesting the order of items in a list
- Add drawings to lists
- Make a list for an authentic purpose

WRITING ABOUT READING

- See *Writing About Reading,* pages 161–222.

Selecting Purpose, Genre, and Form (cont.)

Writing

NARRATIVE WRITING (Purpose–to tell a story)

MEMOIR (PERSONAL MEMORY STORY)

▶ **Understanding the Genre**

- Understand that you can talk, draw, and write about things that have happened to you
- Understand that when you talk about or write about something from your own life, you often use the words *I* or *we*
- Understand that you tell the things that happened in order so your readers will understand the personal memory story
- Understand that a personal memory story should be interesting to your listeners or readers

▶ **Writing in the Genre**

- Draw a picture and tell a story about it
- Draw a sequence of related pictures and tell about them
- Draw pictures in a simple book, sometimes including approximated writing, and tell a story in sequence about them
- Tell, draw, or approximate writing about stories they have heard or read
- Tell, draw, or approximate writing to tell about a personal experience
- Use some words orally that indicate passage of time: e.g., *then, again, after*
- Talk about one's feelings while telling a story of an experience
- Begin to use some features of narrative texts (drawings matching text, titles, page numbers, speech bubbles or thought bubbles) with teacher help

INFORMATIONAL WRITING
(Purpose–to explain or give facts about a topic)

FACTUAL TEXT

▶ **Understanding the Genre**

- Understand that you can write to tell what you know about something
- Understand that a writer (and illustrator) wants to tell others information
- Begin to notice how the writers of nonfiction texts show facts (labeling, making clear drawings, showing pictures)

▶ **Writing in the Genre**

- Participate actively in shared or interactive writing of a factual text
- Make a drawing of an object or process and approximate writing or talking about it
- Make a series of drawings showing an object or process and approximate writing or talking about it
- Use a short book with related ideas to talk or approximate writing about a topic
- Show awareness of audience when drawing and approximating writing about a topic
- Begin to use some features of informational text (page numbers, titles, labeled drawings) with teacher help

POETIC WRITING (Purpose–to express feelings, sensory images, ideas, or stories)

POETRY

▶ **Understanding the Genre**

- Understand poetry (as well as songs and rhymes) as a pleasurable way to express feelings, to tell how something looks or feels, or to tell a story
- Understand that a writer (or illustrator) can represent a song or rhyme in writing
- Notice interesting words (words for sounds, figurative words, unusual words) when reading poetry in a shared way
- Notice rhyming words when reading poetry in a shared way
- Begin to notice how space and lines are used in poems, songs, and rhymes
- Understand that a poem can be serious or funny

▶ **Writing in the Genre**

- Actively participate in shared writing of a poem, song, or rhyme
- Illustrate poems with drawings
- Begin to intentionally use space in a way that represents poetry
- Talk about how something looks, smells, tastes, feels, or sounds
- Notice and enjoy rhyme and humor

WRITING

Selecting Goals Behaviors and Understandings to Notice, Teach, and Support

Writing

CRAFT

ORGANIZATION

▶ Text Structure

- Actively participate in shared or interactive writing about a topic or theme
- Use approximated writing and pictures to make a short book that tells a story or has information about a topic or theme
- Tell a story for dictation that has a beginning, middle, and end
- Begin to write the title and one's own name as the author on the cover of a story

▶ Beginnings, Endings, Titles

- Suggest a beginning and an ending for a piece of shared or interactive writing
- Use approximated writing to write either a beginning or an ending of a piece of writing
- Suggest a title for a piece of shared or interactive writing

▶ Presentation of Ideas

- Tell about an experience or topic in a way that can be written by the teacher
- Present ideas in a logical sequence
- Provide some supportive ideas for bigger ideas in talking about a topic or theme
- Suggest logically related ideas in group story or topic writing

IDEA DEVELOPMENT

- Provide details that support main topics or ideas during shared or interactive writing
- Begin to be aware of the difference between writing facts "about" something and telling a story
- Write and/or draw about one topic on a page
- Begin to realize that every page in a book is related to the same thing (story, topic)

LANGUAGE USE

- Begin to be aware that the language of books is different in some ways from talk
- Show evidence of awareness of the language of books when talking about or retelling a story for dictation or shared or interactive writing
- Realize that what you say (oral language) can be put into writing
- Use one's own oral language to dictate a story, a label, or other writing

WORD CHOICE

- Show awareness of new words encountered in interactive read-aloud or conversation
- Use new words when talking about a drawing
- Use new words when telling a story or talking about an informational topic

VOICE

- Begin to develop interesting ways of talking about personal experiences

Hawa

My Day

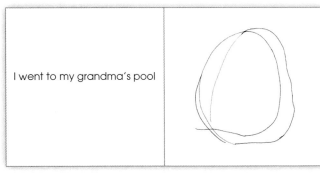

I went to my grandma's pool

I swam in my grandma's pool.

I picked apples in the park

A prekindergartener's story about visiting her grandma

Selecting Goals Behaviors and Understandings to Notice, Teach, and Support *(cont.)*

Writing

- Begin to tell a story from a particular perspective
- Express opinions about a theme or topic
- Participate actively in shared or interactive writing about what is known or remembered

CONVENTIONS

For additional information about grammar and usage and spelling, see Appendix: Grammar, Usage, and Mechanics.

TEXT LAYOUT

- Begin to understand that print is laid out in certain ways and that the lines and spaces are important
- Begin to understand that print is placed from top to bottom on a page
- Separate print (or approximated print) from pictures
- Begin to write words, letters, or approximated letters in clusters to show the look of words
- Show awareness of layout and use of space when copying print
- Show awareness of left-to-right directionality during shared reading and shared or interactive writing
- Identify spaces between words in a piece of shared or interactive writing

GRAMMAR AND USAGE

▶ Parts of Speech

- Use nouns and verbs in agreement most of the time when suggesting ideas for shared or interactive writing or producing language for dictation
- Use prepositional phrases when suggesting ideas for shared or interactive writing or producing language for dictation

▶ Tense

- Use past tense to describe events when suggesting ideas for shared or interactive writing or producing language for dictation: e.g., *I went . . .*
- Use present tense when producing language for dictation: e.g., *I like . . .*
- Begin to use future tense when producing language for dictation: e.g., *I will go . . .*

▶ Sentence Structure

- Use simple but conventional sentence structure when suggesting ideas for shared or interactive writing
- Dictate simple but conventional sentence

SPELLING

- Write in scribbles or random strings
- Repeat some scribble shape over and over
- Mix in some letter-like symbols when writing in scribbles
- Write name conventionally (all capital letters or capital letter and lowercase)
- Use known letters from name to make repeated patterns on a page
- Understand that your name is a word
- Begin to be aware that a word is always spelled the same
- Use own knowledge of own speech to connect sounds to letters or words
- Write one or more words in approximated form: e.g., one's name, *lv* (*love*), *m* (*mom*)
- Construct temporary phonetic spellings with some relationship to the conventional spelling (sound or letter)

HANDWRITING AND WORD-PROCESSING

- Use hand to hold pencil and paper
- Hold pencil or marker with satisfactory grip
- Hold pencil or marker efficiently to begin to approximate writing or write a few letters
- Move pencil only in desired direction
- Begin to understand that writers start on the left (or close to the left) side of a piece of paper and move to the right
- Begin to understand that writers make decisions about the placement of pictures and print
- Write with a preferred hand
- Locate letters or symbols on a keyboard and understand how to press them to make something happen on a screen and/or to make letters appear
- Use simple programs on the computer with adult help
- Begin to understand word boundaries and that words have space between them

I got ice cream and it fell down

Then we went home

Selecting Goals Behaviors and Understandings to Notice, Teach, and Support *(cont.)*

Writing

WRITING PROCESS

PLANNING AND REHEARSING

▶ Purpose

- Choose to draw and write for a specific purpose
- Engage in drawing or writing as exploration and discovery processes that also integrate some planning
- Begin to adjust drawing and dictated messages according to the purpose
- Choose paper for writing
- Draw and write (or approximate writing), extracting ideas from particular environments: e.g., restaurants, house, pets, home, shops, doctor's office
- Actively contribute to shared or interactive writing around a topic or theme
- Write name on drawing and writing

▶ Audience

- Become aware of the people who will read the writing/drawing or might like to see it and what they will want to know
- Actively seek an audience for sharing writing and drawing
- Write or draw with an understanding that it is meant to be read by others

▶ Oral Language

- Generate and expand ideas through talk with peers and the teacher
- Look for ideas and topics in personal experiences, shared through talk
- Use storytelling to generate and rehearse language that may be written later
- Tell a story in chronological order
- Rehearse language for informational writing by retelling experiences using chronological order, describing what is seen, or repeating procedural steps in order

▶ Gathering Seeds/Resources/Experimenting with Writing

- Talk about ideas for writing and drawing
- Understand how writers get ideas: e.g., telling about things that have happened, telling about what they know
- Record information in drawing and approximated writing
- Use drawings as a source for ideas for writing

▶ Content, Topic, Theme

- Observe carefully (objects, animals, people, places, actions) before writing about them
- Select topics for writing and drawing

▶ Inquiry/Research/Exploration

- Use drawings to tell a series of ideas learned through inquiry about a topic
- Use drawings to add information or revise thinking

- Ask questions about a topic
- Remember important information about a topic and contribute ideas to shared or interactive writing
- Remember important labels for drawings and dictate or write them using letters or approximate spellings

DRAFTING AND REVISING

▶ Understanding the Process

- Understand the role of a talk with the teacher to help in drawing and writing
- Understand that writers can share their writing with others
- Understand that writers can add to their drawings or approximated writings
- Actively participate in adding to or changing shared or interactive writing
- Understand that a writer can create drawings or write like other writers and illustrators

▶ Producing a Draft

- Convey a message in print
- Draw and approximate writing about a continuous message on a simple topic

▶ Rereading

- Share drawing and writing with others
- Talk about, draw, and approximate writing to produce a piece
- Talk about the drawings or writing in a consistent way each time it is shared
- Look carefully at a drawing to see if details should be added

▶ Adding Information

- Add details to a drawing to show the full meaning
- Add additional details in dictated or approximated writing to expand on a topic
- Add speech bubbles or thought bubbles to a picture to use dialogue or to show thoughts

▶ Deleting Information

- Delete or cover parts of a drawing that do not fit

▶ Changing a Text

- Cross out to change a text
- Understand that a writer can change a text or drawing to make it clearer or more interesting to readers
- Participate in group decisions about changing a text

▶ Using Tools and Techniques

- Add pages to a book or booklet with the help of an adult
- Begin to use classroom resources such as an ABC or name chart

Selecting Goals Behaviors and Understandings to Notice, Teach, and Support *(cont.)*

Writing

EDITING AND PROOFREADING

▶ **Understanding the Process**

- Understand that writers try to make their writing and drawings interesting and informative
- Understand that making letters and using space makes writing easier to read
- Understand that when you write or draw something you can change it

▶ **Editing for Conventions**

- Understand that a teacher may point out something in shared or interactive writing that needs to be changed
- Notice as a teacher points out correct letter formation in group writing

PUBLISHING

- Produce approximated writing to accompany drawing
- Create approximated writing and illustrations that work together to express meaning
- Create illustrations as an integral part of the composing process
- Create illustrations (often in collaboration with others) to enhance a piece of group writing (shared or interactive)
- When finished with a piece of writing and drawing, talk about it to others

DRAWING

- Use drawing as a way to plan for writing
- Use drawing and other art media to represent ideas and information
- Add or remove details to revise drawing

VIEWING SELF AS A WRITER

- Take on approximated writing independently
- Understand how writing and drawing are related
- Demonstrate confidence in attempts at drawing and writing
- Have ideas to tell, write, draw about
- Select favorite drawings and writings from a collection
- Produce a quantity of drawing and approximated writing within the time available: e.g., one per day
- Keep working independently rather than waiting for a teacher to help
- Make attempts to solve problems
- Try out techniques other writers and illustrators have used

WRITING

Selecting Purpose, Genre, and Form

Writing

At the beginning of the year, most writing for kindergarteners consists of shared or interactive writing and their own approximated attempts. Quickly, they learn to use everything they know—their names, a few known words, and known letters—to generate their own pieces of writing. They use drawing extensively to express their ideas and support their thinking. By the end of the year, we can observe them using space to define words, writing left to right and top to bottom on pages, matching print with drawings in a meaningful way, spelling many words conventionally, and composing messages and stories. Conversation with teachers and peers supports the process.

FUNCTIONAL WRITING
(Purpose–to perform a practical task)

LABEL

▶ **Understanding the Genre**

- Understand that a writer or illustrator can add a label to help readers understand a drawing or photograph
- Understand that a label provides important information

▶ **Writing in the Genre**

- Write a label for an object in the classroom
- Add words to pictures
- Create a label for an illustration that accompanies a written piece
- Make a label book as one type of book

FRIENDLY LETTER

▶ **Understanding the Genre**

- Understand that written communication can be used for different purposes: e.g., to give information, to invite, to give thanks
- Understand that a friendly letter can be written in various forms: e.g., note, card, letter, invitation, email
- Understand that the sender and the receiver must be clearly shown
- Understand that an invitation must include specific information
- Understand how to learn about writing notes, cards, and invitations by noticing the characteristics of examples

▶ **Writing in the Genre**

- Write with a specific purpose in mind
- Write to a known audience or a specific reader
- Write notes, cards, invitations, and emails to others
- Include important information in the communication
- Write language that seems like talking

PROCEDURAL TEXT

▶ **Understanding the Genre**

- Understand that a procedural text helps people know how to do something
- Understand that a procedural text can be written in various forms: e.g., list, directions with steps (how-to)
- Understand that a procedural text often shows one item under another item and may include a number or letter for each item
- Understand that pictures can accompany the writing to help readers understand the information
- Understand that a caption can be written under a picture to give people more information
- Understand lists are a helpful way to organize information

▶ **Writing in the Genre**

- Use drawings in the process of drafting, revising, or publishing procedural writing
- Write captions under pictures
- Use lists to plan activities or support memory
- Place items in the list that are appropriate for its purpose or category
- Make lists in the appropriate form with one item under another

WRITING ABOUT READING

- See *Writing About Reading,* pages 147-208.

NARRATIVE WRITING *(Purpose–to tell a story)*

MEMOIR (PERSONAL MEMORY STORY)

▶ **Understanding the Genre**

- Understand that writers may tell stories from their own lives
- Understand that a story from your life is usually written in first person (using *I* and *we*)
- Understand that the writer can look back or think about the memory or experience and share thoughts and feelings about it
- Understand that a personal memory story should be one that is important to the writer

▶ **Writing in the Genre**

- Draw a picture or a series of pictures and tell or write about them
- Use simple words that show the passage of time (*then, after*)
- Explain one's thoughts and feelings about an experience or event
- Think of topics, events, or experiences from own life that are interesting to write about
- Write an engaging beginning and a satisfying ending to a story
- Understand that a story can be a "small moment" (description of a brief but memorable experience)

Selecting Purpose, Genre, and Form (cont.)

Writing

- Provide some descriptive details to make the story more interesting
- Use dialogue as appropriate to add to the meaning of the story
- Develop voice as a writer through telling own stories or memories from one's own life
- Usually write in first person to achieve a strong voice
- Tell a story across several pages in order to develop the story or idea
- Tell events in order that they occurred in a personal narrative
- Notice craft decisions that the author or illustrator has made and try out some of these decisions in one's own writing with teacher support

INFORMATIONAL WRITING
(Purpose–to explain or give facts about a topic)

FACTUAL TEXT

▶ **Understanding the Genre**

- Understand how to write a factual text from listening to mentor texts read aloud and discussing them
- Understand that a writer of a factual text uses words and illustrations to make it interesting to readers
- Understand that writers of nonfiction (factual) texts have many ways to show facts: e.g., labels, drawings, photos

▶ **Writing the Genre**

- Make a drawing or series of drawings of objects or processes and talk or write about them
- Write books or short pieces that are enjoyable to read and at the same time give information to readers about a topic
- Use features (e.g., page numbers, title, labeled pictures, table of contents, or others) to guide the reader
- Think about the readers (audience) when writing on a topic
- Select interesting information to include in a piece of writing
- Write a book with all pages and ideas related to the same topic or set of facts

POETIC WRITING *(Purpose–to express feelings, sensory images, ideas, or stories)*

POETRY

▶ **Understanding the Genre**

- Understand poetry as a way to communicate in sensory images about everyday life
- Understand poetry as a way to communicate about and describe thoughts and feelings
- Notice specific words when reading poetry and sometimes use them in talk or writing
- Understand that print and space look different in poems and attempt these layouts in approximating the writing of poems
- Understand that a writer can use familiar poems as mentor texts
- Understand that poems can be created from other kinds of texts
- Understand that poems may look and sound different from one another

- Understand that poems do not have to rhyme
- Notice language that "sounds like" a poem (rhythmic, descriptive, or sensory language)

▶ **Writing in the Genre**

- Approximate the use of line breaks and white space when writing poems
- Place words on the page to look like a poem
- Use language to describe how something looks, smells, tastes, feels, or sounds
- Select and write some words that convey feelings or images
- Closely observe the world (animals, objects, people) to get ideas for poems

Selecting Goals Behaviors and Understandings to Notice, Teach, and Support

Writing

CRAFT

ORGANIZATION

▶ Text Structure

- Make decisions about where in a text to place features such as photographs and drawings
- Create a picture book as one form of writing
- Include facts and details in informational writing
- Put together the related details on a topic in a text
- Write a nonfiction or fiction narrative that is ordered chronologically
- Write a story or informational book that has a beginning, a series of things happening, and an ending or an introductory and summary sentence
- Write a title and author's name on the cover of a story or book
- Write an author page at the beginning or end of a book that gives information about the author (picture, writing)
- Dedicate a story to someone and write dedication on the cover, on the title page or copyright page, or on a page of its own

▶ Beginnings, Endings, Titles

- Use a variety of beginnings through drawing and/or writing to engage the reader
- Use an ending that is interesting or leaves the reader satisfied
- Select an appropriate title for a poem, story, or informational book

▶ Presentation of Ideas

- Tell about experiences or topics in a way that others can understand
- Tell one part, idea, or group of ideas on each page of a book
- Present ideas in logical sequence
- Introduce ideas followed by some supportive details and examples
- Use time appropriately as an organizing tool

IDEA DEVELOPMENT

- Provide supportive description or details to explain the important ideas
- Write and/or draw about one idea on a page
- Communicate clearly the main points intended for readers to understand
- Tell a story with a problem, at least one episode, a solution, and an ending
- Begin to understand the difference between telling a story and telling facts about something

LANGUAGE USE

- Begin to be aware that the language of books is different in some ways from talk
- Use known oral language in writing even if unsure how to spell some words
- Understand that the writer is using language to communicate meaning
- Show evidence of using language from storybooks and informational books that have been read aloud
- Realize that what you say (oral language) can be put into writing
- Use one's own oral language to dictate a story, a label, or other writing

WORD CHOICE

- Learn new words from reading and listening and trying them out in writing
- Use vocabulary appropriate for the topic

A kindergartener's memoir about a dog he loves

Selecting Goals Behaviors and Understandings to Notice, Teach, and Support *(cont.)*

Writing

VOICE

- Tell a story or give information in an interesting way
- Write about personal experiences in a way one would talk about it
- Express thoughts and feelings about a topic
- Express opinions about a theme or topic
- Write and draw about what is known and remembered
- Write in an expressive way (similar to oral language)
- Share one's thoughts and feelings about a topic

CONVENTIONS

For additional information about grammar and usage, capitalization, punctuation, and spelling, see Appendix: Grammar, Usage, and Mechanics.

TEXT LAYOUT

- Use spaces between words to help readers understand the writing
- Place words in lines, starting left to right, top to bottom
- Place titles and headings in the appropriate place on a page
- Understand that layout of print and illustrations is important in conveying the meaning of a text
- Understand that print and pictures can be placed in a variety of places on the page within a book

GRAMMAR AND USAGE

▶ Parts of Speech

- Use nouns, pronouns, adjectives, verbs, prepositions, and conjunctions
- Use prepositional phrases: e.g., *to the bus, on the bus*

▶ Tense

- Use past tense to describe events when suggesting ideas for shared or interactive writing or producing language for dictation
- Use present tense when producing language for dictation: e.g., *I like . . .*
- Use future tense when producing language for dictation: e.g., *I will go . . .*

▶ Sentence Structure

- Use conventional sentence structure (noun + verb)

CAPITALIZATION

- Demonstrate knowledge of the use of upper- and lowercase letters of the alphabet
- Locate a capital letter at the beginning of a sentence during shared or interactive writing or in a piece of dictated writing
- Notice capital letters in names
- Write one's own name with a capital letter at the beginning
- Show awareness of the position of capital letters at the beginning of some words
- Use a capital letter at the beginning of a familiar proper noun

PUNCTUATION

- Notice the use of punctuation marks in books and try them out in one's own writing
- Use periods, exclamation marks, and question marks as end marks
- Read one's writing aloud and think where punctuation would go

Selecting Goals Behaviors and Understandings to Notice, Teach, and Support *(cont.)*

Writing

CONVENTIONS *(continued)*

SPELLING

- Say words slowly to hear a sound and write a letter that represents it
- Spell approximately twenty-five high-frequency words conventionally
- Use knowledge of phonogram patterns to generate multisyllable words
- Attempt unknown words through sound analysis
- Write some words with consonant letters appropriate for sounds in words (beginning and ending)
- Write a letter for easy-to-hear vowel sounds
- Understand that letters represent sounds
- Construct temporary phonetic spellings that are mostly readable
- Use conventional symbols to write words
- Use simple resources to help in spelling words or check on spelling (word walls, personal word lists)

HANDWRITING AND WORD-PROCESSING

- Hold pen or pencil with satisfactory grip
- Use a preferred hand consistently for writing
- Locate letter keys on a computer keyboard to type simple messages
- Access and use simple programs on the computer (easy word-processing, games)
- Write letters in groups to form words
- Understand word boundaries and leave space between words most of the time
- Write left to right in lines
- Return to the left margin to start a new line
- Write letters to represent meaning and put them together in some words with standard spelling and some temporary spelling with recognizable letter-sound representations
- Form upper- and lowercase letters efficiently in manuscript print
- Form upper- and lowercase letters proportionately in manuscript print

WRITING PROCESS

PLANNING AND REHEARSING

▶ Purpose

- Draw and write for a specific purpose
- Think about the purpose for writing each text
- Think about how the purpose affects the kind of writing
- Choose paper to match desired organization and the genre
- Draw and write, extracting ideas from particular environments: e.g., restaurants, house, shops, doctor's office
- Actively contribute to shared or interactive writing around a topic or theme
- Write name and date on writing
- Choose the type of text to fit the purpose: e.g., poem, factual book, alphabet book, photo book, label book, story with pictures
- Write to inform the audience and also to engage or interest others

▶ Audience

- Think about the people who will read the writing or might like to read it and what they will want to know
- Actively seek an audience for sharing writing and drawing
- Include important information and details in the drawing or writing that the audience needs to know
- Write with an understanding that it is meant to be read by others

▶ Oral Language

- Generate and expand ideas through talk with peers and teacher
- Look for ideas and topics in personal experiences, shared through talk
- Use storytelling to generate and rehearse language that may be written later
- Tell stories in chronological order
- Rehearse language for informational writing by retelling experiences using chronological order, describing what they know, or repeating procedural steps in order

▶ Gathering Seeds/Resources/Experimenting with Writing

- Dictate ideas or topics for writing
- Contribute to group writing (shared or interactive) with ideas or topics
- Understand that writers gather information for their writing: e.g., objects, books, photos, sticky notes, etc.
- Record information in words or a drawing
- Use a drawing to share or remember thinking

▶ Content, Topic, Theme

- Observe carefully before writing about a person, animal, object, place, action
- Select a topic for informational writing and drawing
- Select information or facts that will support the topic
- Select details and events to tell the story

▶ Inquiry/Research/Exploration

- Use drawings to tell about a topic or tell a story
- Ask questions and gather information on a topic
- Remember important information about a topic in order to write about it
- Participate actively in experiences and recall information that contributes to writing and drawing
- Remember important labels for drawings

DRAFTING AND REVISING

▶ Understanding the Process

- Understand that it is helpful to talk about your writing with another person (teacher)
- Understand that writers get help from other writers
- Understand that writers can change writing in response to teacher or peer feedback

Selecting Goals Behaviors and Understandings to Notice, Teach, and Support *(cont.)*

Writing

- Understand that writers can learn how to write from other writers
- Understand revision as a means for making written messages stronger and clearer to readers

▶ Producing a Draft

- Draw or write a continuous message on a simple topic
- Use words and drawings to compose and revise writing

▶ Rereading

- Reread writing each day (and during writing on the same day) before continuing to write
- Reread writing to be sure the meaning is clear
- Reread writing to be sure there are no missing words or information
- Review a drawing to revise by adding (or deleting) information

▶ Adding Information

- Add details to a drawing to give more information to the reader and to make the writing more interesting
- Add dialogue in speech bubbles or thoughts in thought bubbles to provide information or provide narration
- Add words, phrases, or sentences to make the writing more interesting or exciting for readers
- Add words, phrases, or sentences to provide more information to readers

▶ Deleting Information

- Delete text to better express meaning and make more logical
- Delete words or sentences that do not make sense
- Delete pages when information is not needed

▶ Changing a Text

- Cross out to change a text
- Participate in group decisions about changing a shared writing text

▶ Reorganizing Information

- Rearrange and revise writing to better express meaning or make the text more logical (reorder drawings, reorder pages, cut and paste)
- Reorganize and revise the writing to better express the writer's meaning or make the text more logical

▶ Using Tools and Techniques

- Add letters, words, phrases, or sentences using a caret, a strip of paper, or sticky note
- Add pages to a book or booklet
- Remove pages from a book or booklet
- Cross out words or sentences with pencil or marker

EDITING AND PROOFREADING

▶ Understanding the Process

- Understand that writers try to make their writing and drawings interesting and informative
- Understand that a writer uses what is known to spell words

- Understand that the better the spelling and space between words, the easier it is for the reader to read it

▶ Editing for Conventions

- Check and correct letter formation or orientation
- Edit for spelling errors by making another attempt
- Notice words that do not look right and spell by saying them slowly to represent as much of the word as possible
- Recognize that the teacher may be final editor

PUBLISHING

- Produce approximated writing to accompany drawing
- Create illustrations and writing that work together to express the meaning
- Create illustrations as an integral part of the composing process
- Share a text with peers by reading it aloud to the class
- Create illustrations (often in collaboration with others) to enhance a piece of group writing (shared or interactive)
- When finished with a piece of writing, talk about it to others
- Select a poem, story, or informational book to publish in a variety of appropriate ways: e.g., typed/printed, framed and mounted or otherwise displayed
- Use labels and captions on drawings that are displayed

DRAWING

- Understand that when both writing and drawing are on a page, they are mutually supportive, with each extending the other
- Use sketches and drawing to plan, draft, revise, and publish writing
- Use drawings to represent people, places, things, and ideas
- Add to or remove details from drawings to plan, draft, revise work
- Create drawings that employ careful attention to color or detail
- Create drawings that are related to the written text and increase readers' understanding and enjoyment

VIEWING SELF AS A WRITER

- Take on both approximated and conventional writing independently
- Understand how writing and drawing are related
- Demonstrate confidence in attempts at drawing and writing
- Have ideas to tell, write, draw about
- Think of what to work on next as a writer
- Select best pieces of writing from own collection
- Self-evaluate writing and talk about what is good about it and what techniques were used
- Produce a quantity of writing within the time available: e.g., one or two pages per day
- Keep working independently rather than waiting for a teacher to help
- Make attempts to solve problems
- Try out techniques other writers and illustrators used
- Take risks as a writer
- Talk about oneself as a writer

WRITING

Selecting Purpose, Genre, and Form

Writing

Most first graders will begin the year with a repertoire of known words and some experience in drawing and writing to express their ideas. Some may be only beginning to realize the functions of print. They will benefit from rich demonstrations of writing through shared and interactive writing for a variety of purposes. First graders will also benefit from writing workshop with a daily minilesson, independent writing, individual confering with the teacher, and sharing with peers. By the end of the year, they will demonstrate writing narratives, informational texts, a variety of functional texts, and some poetic texts. They will demonstrate the use of conventions in terms of lines, spaces, many correctly spelled words, and many good attempts at more complex words. Opportunities to draw will extend their thinking.

FUNCTIONAL WRITING
(Purpose—to perform a practical task)

LABEL

▶ **Understanding the Genre**

- Understand that a writer or illustrator can add a label to help readers
- Understand that a label can add important information

▶ **Writing in the Genre**

- Write a label for an object in the classroom
- Add words to pictures
- Create a label for an illustration that accompanies a written piece
- Make a label book as one type of book

FRIENDLY LETTER

▶ **Understanding the Genre**

- Understand that written communication can be used for different purposes: e.g., to give information, to invite, to give thanks
- Understand that a friendly letter can be written in various forms: e.g., note, card, letter, invitation, email
- Understand that the sender and the receiver must be clearly shown
- Understand that an invitation must include specific information
- Understand how to learn about writing notes, cards, and invitations by noticing the characteristics of examples

▶ **Writing in the Genre**

- Write with a specific purpose in mind
- Write to a known audience or a specific reader
- Write notes, cards, invitations, and emails to others
- Include important information in the communication
- Write with a friendly tone (conversational language)

PROCEDURAL TEXT

▶ **Understanding the Genre**

- Understand that a procedural text helps people know how to do something
- Understand that a procedural text can be written in various forms: e.g., list, directions with steps (how-to)

- Understand that a procedural text often shows one item under another item and may include a number for each item
- Understand that a procedural text often includes a list of what is needed to do the procedure
- Understand that pictures can accompany the writing to help readers understand the information

▶ **Writing in the Genre**

- Use drawings in the process of drafting, revising, or publishing procedural writing
- Write captions under pictures
- Use lists to plan activities or support memory
- Place items in the list that are appropriate for its purpose or category
- Make lists in the appropriate form with one item under another
- Write sequential directions in procedural or how-to books

WRITING ABOUT READING

- See *Writing About Reading,* pages 147–208.

NARRATIVE WRITING *(Purpose—to tell a story)*

MEMOIR (PERSONAL MEMORY STORY)

▶ **Understanding the Genre**

- Understand that writers may tell stories from their own lives
- Understand that a story from your life is usually written in first person (using *I* and *we*)
- Understand that the writer can look back or think about the memory or experience and share thoughts and feelings about it
- Understand that a personal memory story should be one that is important to the writer
- Understand how to craft a personal memory story or narrative from mentor texts

▶ **Writing in the Genre**

- Draw a picture or a series of pictures and tell or write about them
- Use simple words that show the passage of time (*then, after*)
- Explain one's thoughts and feelings about an experience or event
- Think of topics, events, or experiences from own life that are interesting to write about
- Write an engaging beginning and a satisfying ending to a story

Selecting Purpose, Genre, and Form (cont.)

Writing

- Understand that a story can be a "small moment" (description of a brief but memorable experience)
- Provide some descriptive details to make the story more interesting
- Use dialogue as appropriate to add to the meaning of the story
- Develop voice as a writer through telling own stories or memories from own life
- Usually write in first person to achieve a strong voice
- Tell a story across several pages in order to develop the story or idea
- Tell events in order that they occurred in personal narratives
- Notice craft decisions that the author or illustrator has made and try out some of these decisions in one's own writing with teacher support

INFORMATIONAL WRITING
(Purpose–to explain or give facts about a topic)

EXPOSITORY TEXT

▶ **Understanding the Genre**

- Understand that a writer may work to get readers interested in a topic
- Understand how to write a factual text from listening to mentor texts read aloud and discussing them
- Understand that a writer of a factual text uses words and illustrations to make it interesting to readers
- Understand that writers of nonfiction texts have many ways to show facts: e.g., labels, drawings, photos

▶ **Writing in the Genre**

- Use illustrations and book and print features (e.g., labeled pictures, diagrams, table of contents, headings, sidebars, page numbers) to guide the reader
- Write books and short pieces of writing that are enjoyable to read and at the same time give information to readers about the same topic
- Think about the readers (audience) and what they need to know
- Select interesting information to include in a piece of writing

POETIC WRITING *(Purpose–to express feelings, sensory images, ideas, or stories)*

POETRY

▶ **Understanding the Genre**

- Understand poetry as a way to communicate in sensory images about everyday life
- Understand poetry as a way to communicate about and describe thoughts and feelings
- Understand the importance of specific word choice in poetry and sometimes use these words in talk and writing
- Understand that print and space look different in poems and attempt these layouts in approximating the writing of poems
- Understand that a writer can use poems as mentor texts
- Understand that poems can be created from other kinds of texts
- Understand that poems may look and sound different from one another

- Understand that poems do not have to rhyme
- Recognize poetic language (rhythm, descriptive words that evoke senses, some rhyme)

▶ **Writing in the Genre**

- Closely observe the world (animals, objects, people) to get ideas for poems
- Write poems that convey feelings or images
- Use language to describe how something looks, smells, tastes, feels, or sounds
- Place words on a page to look like a poem
- Use line breaks and white space when writing poems
- Write poems from other kinds of texts (story, informational text)
- Sometimes borrow specific words or phrases from writing and make them into a poem

WRITING

Selecting Purpose, Genre, and Form (cont.)

Writing

Turtel hunting

Jesse

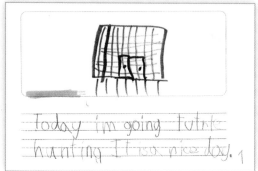

Today im going tutnt hunting If is a nice day. 1

I went to get a life Jacit so did my cosins and— 2

am. Then I went to the doke. My grand Po was un— 3

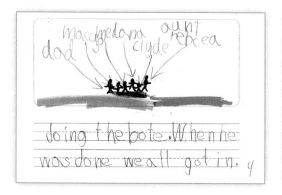

doing the bote. When he was done we all got in. 4

My dad startdd rowing. we moved throw the 5

cove. When we were by the big log. We sowe a 6

tutul !!!!! We all took a net and— 7

A first grader's memoir

Selecting Purpose, Genre, and Form *(cont.)*

Writing

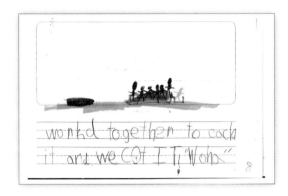

worked together to coch
it and we COT I T "Wohs"

8

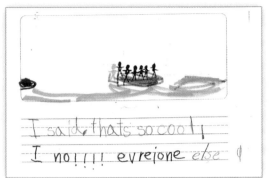

I said, thats so cool,
I no!!!! evreione else

9

said. Lets bring it back
to the lodge I said.

10

Good ide said my
Aunt. We slowly moved

11

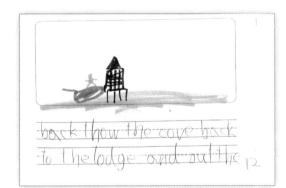

back threw the cove back
to the lodge and put the

12

turtul in the turtul cage.
We shoud name leb and

13

Grandpa Steve. then let
it go. "Bye turtel wee!"

14

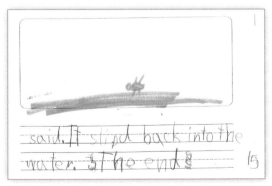

said. It stried back into the
water. The end

15

WRITING

Selecting Goals Behaviors and Understandings to Notice, Teach, and Support

Writing

CRAFT

ORGANIZATION

▶ **Text Structure**

- Make decisions about where in a text to place illustrations such as photographs, drawings, diagrams, maps
- Create a picture book as one form of writing
- Include facts and details in informational writing
- Put together the related details on a topic in a text
- Write a nonfiction or fiction narrative that is ordered chronologically
- Write a story that has a beginning, a series of things happening, and an ending or an informational text that has introductory and summary sentences
- Write a title and the author's name on the cover of a story or book
- Write an author page at the beginning or end of a book that tells details about the author (picture, writing)
- Dedicate a story to someone and write the dedication on the inside of the cover, on the title page or copyright page, or on a page of its own

▶ **Beginnings, Ending, Titles**

- Use a variety of beginnings to engage the reader
- Use an ending that is interesting, leaves the reader satisfied, or gets the reader to think more about a story or topic
- Select an appropriate title for a poem, story, or informational book

▶ **Presentation of Ideas**

- Tell about experiences or topics in a way that others can understand
- Tell one part, idea, or group of ideas on each page of a book
- Present ideas in a logical sequence
- Introduce ideas followed by some supportive details and examples
- Use time appropriately as an organizing tool
- Show steps in enough details that a reader can follow a sequence

IDEA DEVELOPMENT

- Provide supportive description, details, or examples to explain the important ideas in shared or interactive writing
- Understand how information helps the reader learn about a topic
- Write and/or draw about one topic on a page or across several pages of a book, including one category of information related to a main topic on every page
- Gather and internalize information and then write in one's own words
- Communicate clearly the main points intended for readers to understand
- Write a story with a problem, several episodes, a solution, and an ending
- Develop ideas differently when writing a story and when writing facts about something

LANGUAGE USE

- Be aware that the language of books is different in some ways from talk
- Use known oral vocabulary in writing even if unsure how to spell some words
- Understand the writer is using language to communicate meaning
- Show evidence of using language from storybooks and informational books that have been read aloud
- Write a piece relying on one's knowledge of oral language
- Learn ways of using language and constructing texts from other writers (reading books and hearing them read aloud) and apply understandings to one's own writing

WORD CHOICE

- Learn new words from reading and listening and trying them out in writing
- Use vocabulary appropriate for the topic
- Vary word choice to create interesting description and dialogue
- Use some common (simple) connectives (transitional words) for relating ideas and showing meaning through nonfiction texts (*and, but, so, because, before, after*)

VOICE

- Tell a story or give information in an interesting way
- Write about personal experiences in the way one would talk about it
- Express thoughts and feelings about a topic
- Express opinions about a theme or topic
- Write and draw about what is known and remembered
- Write in an expressive way (similar to oral language)
- Show enthusiasm and energy for the topic
- Read writing aloud to help think critically about voice

CONVENTIONS

For additional information about grammar and usage, capitalization, punctuation, and spelling, see Appendix: Grammar, Usage, and Mechanics.

TEXT LAYOUT

- Use spaces between words
- Place words in lines, starting left to right, top to bottom
- Place titles and headings in the appropriate place on a page
- Understand that layout of print and illustrations is important in conveying the meaning of a text
- Begin to incorporate illustrations and organizational tools in nonfiction texts: e.g., drawing or photograph with caption or label, map, diagram; table of contents, heading, sidebar
- Use the size of print to convey meaning in printed text

Selecting Goals Behaviors and Understandings to Notice, Teach, and Support *(cont.)*

Writing

- Understand that print and pictures can be placed in a variety of places on the page within a book
- Use underlining and bold print to convey meaning
- Use indentation or spacing to set off paragraphs

GRAMMAR AND USAGE

▶ Parts of Speech

- Use nouns, pronouns, adjectives, verbs, adverbs, prepositions, and conjunctions
- Use prepositional phrases: e.g., *to the bus, on the bus*
- Use modifiers: e.g., <u>red</u> dress; ran <u>fast</u>

▶ Tense

- Write in past tense: e.g., *he asked a question*
- Write in present tense: e.g., *he asks a question*
- Write in future tense: e.g., *he will ask a question*

▶ Sentence Structure

- Use conventional sentence structure (noun + verb)
- Suggest conventionally structured experiences in shared writing

CAPITALIZATION

- Demonstrate knowledge of the use of upper- and lowercase letters of the alphabet
- Show awareness of the position of capital letters at the beginning of some words
- Use uppercase letters in a title
- Use a capital letter for the first word of a sentence
- Use a capital letter at the beginning of a familiar proper noun

PUNCTUATION

- Notice the use of punctuation marks in books and try them out in one's own writing
- Use periods, exclamation marks, and question marks as end marks
- Read one's writing aloud and think where punctuation would go

SPELLING

- Say words slowly to hear a sound and write a letter that represents it
- Spell approximately one hundred high-frequency words conventionally and reflect spelling in final drafts
- Say words to break them into syllables to spell them
- Use phonogram patterns to generate words
- Attempt unknown words through sound analysis
- Attempt unknown words using known word parts and letter-sound knowledge
- Write some words with consonant letters appropriate for sounds in words (beginning and ending)
- Represent several sounds, including beginning and ending
- Write a letter for easy-to-hear vowel sounds
- Construct phonetic spellings that are readable

- Use conventional symbols to write words
- Use simple resources to help in spelling words or check on spelling (word walls, personal word lists)
- Use some inflectional endings such as *s* and *ing*
- Spell words with regular consonant-sound relationships and with regular short-vowel patterns correctly
- Include a vowel in each word
- Represent consonant blends and digraphs with letter clusters in words
- Begin to develop a sense of when a word does not "look right"

HANDWRITING AND WORD-PROCESSING

- Hold pen or pencil with satisfactory grip
- Use a preferred hand consistently for writing
- Locate letter keys on a computer keyboard to type simple messages
- Access and use simple programs on the computer (easy word-processing, games)
- Write letters in groups to form words
- Leave appropriate space between words
- Write left to right in lines
- Return to the left margin to start a new line
- Write letters and words that can be easily read
- Form upper- and lowercase letters efficiently in manuscript print
- Form upper- and lowercase letters proportionately in manuscript print

WRITING PROCESS

PLANNING AND REHEARSING

▶ Purpose

- Draw and write for a specific purpose
- Think about the purpose for writing each text
- Consider how the purpose affects the kind of writing
- Choose paper to match the organization of the text: e.g., booklets, pages, single pages with space for illustrations
- Draw and write, extracting ideas from particular environments: e.g., restaurants, houses, shops, doctor's offices
- Actively contribute to shared or interactive writing around a topic or theme
- Write name and date on writing
- Choose the form of text to fit the purpose: e.g., poem, ABC book, photo book, label book, story with pictures
- Write to inform the audience and also to engage or interest others

▶ Audience

- Think about the people who will read the writing or might like to read it and what they will want to know
- Actively seek an audience for sharing writing and drawing
- Include important information and details in the drawing or writing that the audience needs to know
- Write with an understanding that it is meant to be read by others

WRITING

Selecting Goals Behaviors and Understandings to Notice, Teach, and Support *(cont.)*

Writing

WRITING PROCESS *(continued)*

PLANNING AND REHEARSING *(continued)*

▶ **Oral Language**

- Generate and expand ideas through talk with peers and teacher
- Look for ideas and topics in personal experiences, shared through talk
- Use storytelling to generate and rehearse language that may be written later
- Tell stories in chronological order
- Rehearse language for informational writing by retelling experiences using chronological order, describing what they know, or repeating procedural steps in order

▶ **Gathering Seeds/Resources/Experimenting with Writing**

- Generate ideas or topics for writing
- Contribute to group writing (shared or interactive) with ideas or topics
- Gather information for writing: e.g., objects, books, photos, sticky notes, etc.
- Record information in words or a drawing
- Use a drawing to share or remember thinking

▶ **Content, Topic, Theme**

- Observe carefully before writing about a person, animal, object, place, action
- Select one's own topic for informational writing and state what is important about the topic
- Select information that will support the topic
- Select details and events to tell the story
- Choose topics that one knows about, cares about, or wants to learn about
- Choose a topic that is interesting to the writer
- Tell about a topic in an interesting way
- Stay focused on a topic
- Give a story or informational piece a title

▶ **Inquiry/Research/Exploration**

- Observe carefully to detect and describe change (growth, change over time in plants or animals, chemical changes in food), and talk about observations
- Observe in the environment to notice details or changes
- Use drawings to show how something looks, how something works, or the process or change
- Sometimes label drawings
- Talk about drawings from observation
- Actively contribute to shared or interactive writing to report the results of investigation
- Ask questions and gather information on a topic
- Remember important information about a topic in order to write about it

- Participate actively in experiences and recall information that contributes to writing and drawing (using notebooks and artifacts)
- Remember important labels for drawings
- Take notes or make sketches to help in remembering information

▶ **Genre/Forms**

- Select from a variety of forms the kind of text that will fit the purpose: e.g., poems, stories with pictures, books with words and illustrations; books with illustrations only; ABC books; label books; poetry collections; question and answer books

DRAFTING AND REVISING

▶ **Understanding the Process**

- Understand the role of talk in helping writers
- Understand that writers get help from other writers
- Understand that writers can change writing in response to teacher or peer feedback
- Understand revision as a means for making written messages stronger and clearer to readers

▶ **Producing a Draft**

- Write a continuous message on a simple topic
- Use drawings to add information to, elaborate on, or increase readers' enjoyment and understanding
- Use words and drawings to compose and revise writing

▶ **Rereading**

- Reread writing each day (and during writing on the same day) before continuing to write
- Reread writing to be sure the meaning is clear
- Reread writing to be sure there are no missing words or information
- Review a drawing to revise by adding or deleting information

▶ **Adding Information**

- Add thoughts in thought bubbles or dialogue in speech bubbles or quotation marks to provide information or provide narration
- Add descriptive words (adjectives, adverbs) and phrases to help readers visualize and understand events, actions, processes, or topics
- Add words, phrases, or sentences to make the writing more interesting or exciting for readers
- Add words, phrases, or sentences to provide more information to readers
- Add words, phrases, or sentences to clarify meaning for readers

▶ **Deleting Information**

- Delete text to better express meaning and make more logical
- Delete words or sentences that do not make sense or don't fit the topic
- Delete pages when information is not needed
- Delete extra words or sentences

Selecting Goals Behaviors and Understandings to Notice, Teach, and Support *(cont.)*

Writing

▶ Changing a Text

- Mark parts that are not clear and provide more information
- Participate in group discussions about shared writing texts

▶ Reorganizing Information

- Rearrange and revise writing to better express meaning or make the text more logical (reorder drawings, reorder pages, cut and paste)
- Reorganize and revise the writing to better express the writer's meaning or make the text more logical
- Reorder pages by laying them out and reassembling them

▶ Using Tools and Techniques

- Add letters, words, phrases, or sentences using a caret, a strip of paper, or sticky note
- Add pages to a book or booklet
- Remove pages from a book or booklet
- Cross out words or sentences with pencil or marker
- Use a number to identify place to add information and an additional paper with numbers to write the information for insertion

EDITING AND PROOFREADING

▶ Understanding the Process

- Understand that writers try to make their writing and drawings interesting and informative
- Understand that a writer uses what is known to spell words
- Understand that the more accurate the spelling and the clearer the space between words, the easier it is for the reader to read it

▶ Editing for Conventions

- Check and correct letter formation or orientation
- Edit for spelling errors by making another attempt
- Notice words that do not look right and spell by saying them slowly to represent as much of the word as possible
- Edit for the conventional spelling of known words
- Recognize that the teacher may be the final editor who will make the edits the writer has not yet learned how to do prior to publishing

▶ Using Tools

- Use beginning reference tools: e.g., word walls or personal word collections or dictionaries

PUBLISHING

- Produce writing to explain, label, or otherwise accompany drawing
- Create illustrations and writing that work together to express the meaning
- Create illustrations as an integral part of the composing process
- Create illustrations (often in collaboration with others) to enhance a piece of shared writing
- Share a text with peers by reading it aloud to the class
- When finished with a piece of writing, talk about it to others
- Put several stories or poems together in a book

- Select a poem, story, or informational book to publish in a variety of appropriate ways: e.g., typed/printed, framed and mounted or otherwise displayed
- Use labels and captions on drawings that are displayed
- When preparing a piece for publication, use simple resources to check spelling as appropriate to the age (word walls, personal word lists)

DRAWING

- Understand that when both writing and drawing are on a page, they are mutually supportive, with each extending the other
- Use drawing to plan, draft, revise, or publishing writing
- Use drawings to represent people, places, things, and ideas
- Add or remove details to drawings to revise information
- Create drawings that employ careful attention to color or detail
- Create drawings that are related to the written text and increase readers' understanding and enjoyment

VIEWING SELF AS A WRITER

- Take on both approximated and conventional writing independently
- Understand how writing and drawing are related
- Demonstrate confidence in attempts at drawing and writing
- Have a list or notebook with topics and ideas for writing
- Think of what to work on next as a writer
- Select best pieces of writing from own collection
- Self-evaluate writing and talk about what is good about it and what techniques were used
- Produce a quantity of writing within the time available: e.g., one or two pages per day
- Keep working independently rather than waiting for a teacher to help
- Make attempts to solve problems
- Try out techniques other writers and illustrators have used
- Take risks as a writer
- Talk about oneself as a writer

WRITING

Selecting Purpose, Genre, and Form

Writing

Most second graders will have learned to produce simple narratives and other genres through composing and writing. They will continue to benefit from using drawing to extend their thinking and express their ideas. By the end of the year they will demonstrate the use of some literary language as well as the structure of narratives (exposition of problem and solution). Many texts they write will be personal memory stories. They will also be able to produce organized, factual texts. Using mentor texts will help them to refine their writing and make it more interesting. They will be able to write many words using conventional spelling and produce more complex sentences.

FUNCTIONAL WRITING
(Purpose–to perform a practical task)

FRIENDLY LETTER

▶ **Understanding the Genre**

- Understand that written communication can be used for different purposes: e.g., to give information, to invite, to give thanks
- Understand that a friendly letter can be written in various forms: e.g., note, card, letter, invitation, email
- Understand that the sender and the receiver must be clearly shown
- Understand that a note or card should include short greetings and relevant information
- Understand that an invitation must include specific information about the time and place of the event
- Understand that a friendly letter is more formal than an email, note, or card
- Understand that a friendly letter has parts (date, salutation, closing signature, and sometimes *P.S.*)
- Understand how to learn about writing notes, cards, invitations, emails, and friendly letters by noticing the characteristics of examples

▶ **Writing in the Genre**

- Write a card, note, invitation, or friendly letter with the purpose in mind
- Write notes, cards, invitations, and email for a variety of purposes
- Write to a known audience or a specific reader
- Address the audience appropriately
- Include important information in the communication
- Write a friendly letter with all parts

PROCEDURAL TEXT

▶ **Understanding the Genre**

- Understand that a procedural text helps people know how to do something
- Understand that a procedural text can be written in various forms: e.g., list, directions with steps (how-to)
- Understand that a procedural text often shows one item under another item and may include a number or letter for each item
- Understand that lists are a functional way to organize information
- Understand that a procedural text often includes a list of what is needed to do the procedure

- Understand how drawings can help the reader understand information
- Understand how to craft procedural writing from mentor texts

▶ **Writing in the Genre**

- Write captions under pictures
- Use a list to plan an activity or support memory
- Use a list to develop writing in various genres and forms
- Make a list with items that are appropriate for the purpose of the list
- Make a list in the appropriate form with one item under another
- Use number words or transition words
- Write steps of a procedure with appropriate sequence and explicitness
- Include a picture to illustrate a step in a procedure
- Write a procedural how-to book

TEST WRITING

▶ **Understanding the Genre**

- Understand that test writing often requires writing about an assigned topic
- Understand that test writing may involve creating expository texts or persuasive texts
- Understand that some test writing serves the purpose of demonstrating what a person knows or can do as a writer
- Understand that test writing often requires writing about something real

▶ **Writing in the Genre**

- Analyze the prompt to understand the purpose, audience, and genre that is appropriate for the writing
- Read and internalize the criteria for an acceptable response
- Write focused responses to questions and to prompts
- Write concisely and to the direction of the question or prompt
- Elaborate on important points
- Exclude extraneous details
- Incorporate one's knowledge of craft in shaping responses

WRITING ABOUT READING

- See *Writing About Reading,* pages 161–222

Selecting Purpose, Genre, and Form (cont.)

Writing

NARRATIVE WRITING (Purpose–to tell a story)

FICTION

▶ Understanding the Genre

- Understand that fiction genres include realistic fiction, traditional literature (folktale, tall tale, fairy tale, fable), and fantasy
- Understand that fiction can be written in various forms: e.g., narratives of several pages, picture books, wordless picture books, poems, songs, plays, letters
- Understand that a fiction text may involve one or more events in the life of a main character
- Understand that a writer uses various elements of fiction (e.g., setting, plot with problem and solution, characters) in a fiction text
- Understand that writers can learn to craft fiction by using mentor texts as models
- Use the terms *fiction, folktale, tall tale, fairy tale,* and *fable* to describe the genre

▶ Writing in the Genre

- Write a simple fiction story, either realistic or fantasy
- Describe characters by how they look and what they do
- Describe the setting with appropriate detail

MEMOIR

▶ Understanding the Genre

- Understand that writers may tell stories from their own lives
- Understand that a story from your life is usually written in first person (using *I* and *we*)
- Understand that a memoir is a biographical text in which a writer reflects on a memorable experience, time, place, or person
- Understand that a factual text may use literary techniques (interesting words, description, illustrations) to engage and entertain readers as it gives them factual information
- Understand that the writer can look back or think about the memory or experience and share thoughts and feelings about it
- Understand that a personal memory story should be one that is important to the writer
- Understand how to craft a memoir or a personal memory story from mentor texts

▶ Writing in the Genre

- Select a meaningful topic
- Usually write in first person to achieve a strong voice
- Write an engaging beginning and a satisfying ending to a story
- Select "small moments" or experiences and share thinking and feelings about them

- Describe a setting and how it is related to the writer's experiences
- Use words that show the passage of time
- Tell details about the most important moments in a story or experience while eliminating unimportant details
- Write in a way that shows the significance of the story
- Reveal something important about self or about life
- Describe characters by what they do, say, and think and what others say about them
- Use dialogue as appropriate to add to the meaning of the story
- Use some literary language that is different from oral language

INFORMATIONAL WRITING
(Purpose–to explain or give facts about a topic)

EXPOSITORY TEXT

▶ Understanding the Genre

- Understand that to write a factual text, the writer needs to become very knowledgeable about a topic
- Understand that the writer may work to get readers interested in a topic
- Understand that a factual text may use literary techniques (interesting words, description, photos, graphics, drawings with labels) to engage and entertain readers as it gives them factual information
- Understand how to write a factual text from mentor texts

▶ Writing in the Genre

- Use illustrations and book and print features (e.g., labeled pictures, diagrams, table of contents, headings, sidebars, page numbers) to guide the reader
- Write a piece that is interesting and enjoyable to read
- Write about a topic keeping the audience and their interests involved
- Provide interesting details that develop a topic
- Introduce information in categories
- Provide supporting details in each category
- Use some vocabulary specific to the topic
- Provide information that teaches readers about a topic
- Sometimes use a narrative structure to help readers understand information and interest them in a topic

WRITING

Selecting Purpose, Genre, and Form *(cont.)*

Writing

POETIC WRITING *(Purpose—to express feelings, sensory images, ideas, or stories)*

POETRY

▶ Understanding the Genre

- Understand poetry as a way to communicate about and describe feelings, sensory images, ideas, or stories
- Understand that a writer can create different types of poems: e.g., rhyming poems, unrhyming poems
- Understand the importance of specific word choice in poetry
- Understand that a poem can be created from other kinds of texts
- Understand that poems may look and sound different from one another
- Understand the way print and space work in poems
- Understand that poems take a variety of visual shapes on a page
- Understand that poems do not have to rhyme

▶ Writing in the Genre

- Closely observe the world (animals, objects, people) to get ideas for poems
- Write poems that convey feelings or images
- Place words on a page to look like a poem
- Use language to describe how something looks, smells, tastes, feels, or sounds
- Use line breaks and white space when writing poems
- Write poems from other kinds of texts (story, informational text)
- Sometimes borrow specific words or phrases from writing and make them into a poem

A second grader's book about how to travel

Selecting Goals Behaviors and Understandings to Notice, Teach, and Support

Writing

CRAFT

ORGANIZATION

▶ Text Structure

- Make decisions about where in a text to place features such as photographs with legends, insets, sidebars, and graphics
- Create a picture book as one kind of writing
- Write a fiction or nonfiction narrative that is ordered chronologically
- Write a story that has a beginning, a series of things happening, and an ending or an informational text that has introductory and summary sentences
- Understand that an informational text is ordered by logic (sequences, ideas related to each other)
- Write an author page at the beginning or end of a book to give information about the author
- Dedicate a story to someone and write the dedication inside the cover, on the title page or copyright page, or on a page of its own

▶ Beginnings, Endings, Titles

- Use a variety of beginnings to engage the reader
- Use a variety of endings to engage and satisfy the reader
- Use a variety of beginning, middle, and ending structures appropriate to the genre
- Select an appropriate title for a poem
- Generate multiple titles for the piece and select the one that best fits the content of an informational piece or the plot or characterization in a narrative

▶ Presentation of Ideas

- Tell one part, idea, or group of ideas on each page of a book
- Present ideas in a logical sequence
- Organize information according to purpose
- Show major topics by using headings
- Use headings, a table of contents, and other features to help the reader find information and understand how facts are related
- Introduce ideas followed by supportive details and examples
- Use time appropriately as an organizing tool
- Show steps in enough detail that a reader can follow a sequence
- Bring a piece to closure through an ending or summary statement
- Order the writing in ways that are characteristic to the genre (narrative or informational)
- Use illustrations (e.g., drawings, photographs, diagrams) to provide information
- Use some vocabulary specific to the topic or content

IDEA DEVELOPMENT

- Understand the difference between developing a narrative (or plot) and giving information about a topic in categories
- Understand how information helps the reader learn about a topic

- Gather and internalize information and then write in one's own words
- Write and/or draw about one idea on a page or across several pages of a book
- Communicate clearly the main points intended for readers to understand
- Arrange information in a logical way so that ideas build on one another
- Structure a narrative and sustain writing to develop it logically

LANGUAGE USE

- Understand that what you say (oral language) can be put into writing
- Be aware that the language of books is different in some ways from talk
- Use known oral vocabulary in writing even if unsure how to spell some words
- Understand the writer is using language to communicate meaning
- Show evidence of using language from storybooks and informational books that have been read aloud
- Learn ways of using language and constructing texts from other writers (reading books and hearing them read aloud) and apply understandings to one's own writing
- Borrow a word, phrase, or a sentence from another writer
- Use memorable words or phrases
- Show through language instead of telling
- Use examples to make meaning clear to readers
- Begin to develop a sense of the language of different genres

WORD CHOICE

- Learn new words from reading and try them out in writing
- Use vocabulary appropriate for the topic
- Vary word choice to create interesting description and dialogue
- Show ability to vary the text by choosing alternative words (e.g., alternatives for *said*) when appropriate
- Use common (simple) connectives (transitional words) for relating ideas and showing meaning through nonfiction texts (*and, but, so, because, before, after*)

VOICE

- Write about personal experiences as one speaks
- Write in an expressive way but also recognize how language in a book would sound
- Write in a way that speaks directly to the reader
- Show enthusiasm and energy for the topic
- Use punctuation to make the text clear, effective, and interesting, and to support voice
- Read writing aloud to help think critically about voice

WRITING

Selecting Goals Behaviors and Understandings to Notice, Teach, and Support *(cont.)*

Writing

CONVENTIONS

For additional information about grammar and usage, capitalization, punctuation, and spelling, see Appendix: Grammar, Usage, and Mechanics.

TEXT LAYOUT

- Arrange print on the page to support the text's meaning and to help the reader notice important information
- Understand that layout of print and illustrations is important in conveying the meaning of a text
- Understand how to use layout, spacing, and size of print to create titles, headings, and subheadings
- Use underlining and bold print to convey meaning
- Incorporate nonfiction text features (captions, labels, insets, sidebars, table of contents) into writing
- Use the size of print to convey meaning in printed text
- Use indentation or spacing to set off paragraphs

GRAMMAR AND USAGE

▶ **Parts of Speech**

- Use nouns and pronouns correctly so that they agree (in gender, number, case): e.g., *Mike, he*
- Use adjectives, adverbs, and prepositions correctly

▶ **Tense**

- Write in past tense: e.g., *he walked fast yesterday*
- Write in present tense: e.g., *he walks fast*
- Write in future tense: e.g., *he will walk fast tomorrow*

▶ **Sentence Structure**

- Write complete sentences (subject and predicate)
- Use a range of types of sentences: e.g., declarative, interrogative, imperative, exclamatory

▶ **Paragraphing**

- Understand that each page of a student's book focuses on one idea
- Understand and use paragraph structure (indented or block) to organize sentences that focus on one idea

CAPITALIZATION

- Use a capital letter for the first word, the last word, and most other words in a title
- Use a capital letter for the first word of a sentence
- Use capital letters for the names of people, places, days, months, cities, states

PUNCTUATION

- Use periods, exclamation marks, and question marks as end marks
- Read one's writing aloud and think where punctuation would go

- Understand and use ellipses to show pause or anticipation, often before something surprising
- Use quotation marks to show simple dialogue or to show what someone said
- Use apostrophes in contractions and many possessives
- Use commas to separate items in a series

SPELLING

- Correctly spell approximately two hundred familiar high-frequency words, words with regular letter-sound relationships (including consonant blends and digraphs and some vowel patterns), and commonly used endings and reflect spelling in final drafts
- Take apart multisyllable words to spell the parts accurately or close to accurately
- Use simple resources to help in spelling words or check on spelling (word walls, personal word lists)
- Use basic rules for adding inflectional endings to words (drop *e*, double letter)
- Use simple and some complex plurals
- Spell simple possessives
- Spell most contractions
- Spell words that have been studied (spelling words)
- Write easy compound words accurately
- Spell correctly many one-syllable words that have vowel and *r*
- Begin to develop a sense of when a word does not "look right"

HANDWRITING AND WORD-PROCESSING

- Form upper- and lowercase letters efficiently and proportionately in manuscript print
- Begin to develop efficient keyboarding skills
- Make changes on the screen to revise and edit, and publish documents

WRITING PROCESS

PLANNING AND REHEARSING

▶ **Purpose**

- Write for a specific purpose: e.g., to inform, entertain, persuade, reflect, instruct, retell, maintain relationships, plan
- Understand how the purpose of the writing influences the selection of genre
- Select the genre for the writing based on the purpose
- Tell whether a piece of writing is functional, narrative, informational, or poetic

▶ **Audience**

- Write with specific readers or audience in mind
- Understand that writing is shaped by the writer's purpose and understanding of the audience
- Plan and organize information for the intended readers
- Understand audience as all readers rather than just the teacher

Selecting Goals Behaviors and Understandings to Notice, Teach, and Support *(cont.)*

Writing

▶ Oral Language

- Generate and expand ideas through talk with peers and teacher
- Look for ideas and topics in personal experiences, shared through talk
- Use talk and storytelling to generate and rehearse language that may be written later
- Tell stories in chronological order
- Explore relevant questions in talking about a topic
- When rehearsing language for an informational piece, use vocabulary specific to the topic
- When rehearsing language for narrative writing, use action and content words appropriate for the story

▶ Gathering Seeds/Resources/Experimenting with Writing

- Dictate ideas/topics for writing
- Contribute to group writing ideas/topics (shared or interactive)
- Use a writer's notebook or booklet as a tool for collecting ideas, experimenting, planning, sketching, or drafting
- Reread a writer's notebook to select and develop a topic
- Use sketching, webs, lists, and freewriting to think about, plan for, and try out writing
- Try out beginnings

▶ Content, Topic, Theme

- Observe carefully events, people, settings, and other aspects of the world to gather information on a topic
- Select own topics for informational writing and state what is important about the topic
- Select information that will support the topic
- Choose topics that one knows about, cares about, or wants to learn about
- Choose topics that are interesting to the writer
- Tell about a topic in an interesting way
- Stay focused on a topic
- Get ideas from other books and writers about how to approach a topic
- Communicate the significance of the topic to an audience
- Decide what is most important about the topic or story
- Select details that will support a topic or story
- Give a story, poem, or informational piece a title

▶ Inquiry/Research/Exploration

- Observe carefully to describe and compare animals, plants, objects, people, and talk about observations
- Observe carefully to detect and describe change (growth, change over time in plants or animals, chemical changes in food), and talk about observations
- Observe in the environment to notice details or changes
- Use drawings with labels to show how something looks, how something works, or the process or change
- Sometimes label drawings

- Talk about drawings from observation
- Actively contribute to shared or interactive writing to report the results of investigation
- Form questions to answer about a topic
- Select the most important information about a topic or story
- Participate actively in experiences and recall information that contributes to writing and drawing (using notebooks and artifacts)
- Remember important labels for drawings
- Take notes or make sketches to help in remembering or generating information
- Gather information (with teacher assistance) about a topic from books or other print and media resources while preparing to write about it

▶ Genre/Forms

- Select the genre for the writing based on the purpose: e.g., friendly letter, procedural text; fiction, memoir; expository text; poetry
- Select from a variety of forms: e.g., notes, cards, letters, invitations, email; books with illustrations and words, alphabet books, label books, question and answer books, illustration-only books; poems
- Understand that illustrations play different roles in a text: e.g., increase reader's enjoyment, add information, show sequence or step-by-step process

DRAFTING AND REVISING
▶ Understanding the Process

- Understand the role of the writer, teacher, or peer writer in conference
- Understand that other writers can be helpful in the process
- Change writing in response to peer or teacher feedback
- Understand revision as a means for making written messages stronger and clearer to readers

▶ Producing a Draft

- Write a continuous message on a simple topic
- Use drawings to add information to, elaborate on, or increase readers' enjoyment and understanding
- Write a draft or a discovery draft (writing fast and as much as possible on a topic)
- Understand the importance of the lead in a story or nonfiction piece
- Bring the piece to closure with an ending or final statement
- Establish an initiating event and follow a series of events in a narrative
- Present ideas in logical order across a nonfiction piece

▶ Rereading

- Reread each day before writing more
- Reread and revise the draft or rewrite a section to clarify meaning
- Reread the writing to be sure there are no missing words or information
- Identify the statement (and sometimes restatement) of the main idea of a piece
- Identify the most exciting part of a story

WRITING

Selecting Goals Behaviors and Understandings to Notice, Teach, and Support *(cont.)*

Writing

WRITING PROCESS *(continued)*

DRAFTING AND REVISING *(continued)*

▶ Adding Information

- Add ideas in thought bubbles or dialogue in quotation marks or speech bubbles to provide information, provide narration, or show thoughts and feelings
- Add descriptive words (adjectives, adverbs) and phrases to help readers visualize and understand events, actions, processes, or topics
- Add words, phrases, or sentences to make the writing more interesting or exciting for readers
- Add words, phrases, or sentences to provide more information to readers
- Add word, phrases, or sentences to clarify meaning for readers

▶ Deleting Information

- Delete text to better express meaning and make the text more logical
- Delete words or sentences that do not make sense or do not fit the topic or message
- Delete pages when information is not needed
- Take out unnecessary words, phrases, or sentences that are repetitive or do not add to the meaning

▶ Changing a Text

- Change words to make the writing more interesting
- Identify vague parts or confusing ideas and provide specificity

▶ Reorganizing Information

- Rearrange and revise writing to better express meaning or make the text more logical: e.g., reorder drawings, reorder pages, cut and paste
- Reorder pages by laying them out and reassembling them

▶ Using Tools and Techniques

- Add words, letters, phrases, or sentences using a variety of techniques: e.g., caret, sticky notes, spider's legs, numbered items on a separate page
- Use a number to identify place to add information and an additional paper with numbers to write the information to insert
- Delete words, phrases, or sentences from a text (crossing out or using word-processing) to make the meaning clearer
- Reorder the information in a text to make the meaning clearer by cutting apart, cutting and pasting, laying out pages, using word-processing

EDITING AND PROOFREADING

▶ Understanding the Process

- Understand that a writer uses what is known to spell words
- Understand that the more accurate the spelling and the clearer the space between words, the easier it is for the reader to read it
- Know how to use an editing and proofreading checklist

▶ Editing for Conventions

- Check and correct letter formation
- Edit for spelling errors by circling words that do not look right and spelling them another way
- Edit for the conventional spelling of known words
- Understand that the teacher will be final spelling editor for the published piece after the student has used everything known
- Edit for capitalization
- Edit for end punctuation
- Edit for sentence sense

▶ Using Tools

- Use beginning reference tools: e.g., word walls, personal word lists, or word cards to assist in word choice or checking spelling
- Use spell check, accepting or rejecting changes as needed

PUBLISHING

- Produce writing to explain, label, or otherwise accompany drawing
- Create illustrations and writing that work together to express the meaning
- Include graphics or illustrations as appropriate to the text
- Create illustrations (often in collaboration with others) to enhance a piece of shared writing
- Share a text with peers by reading it aloud to the class
- Put several stories or poems together in a book
- Select a poem, story, or informational book to publish in a variety of appropriate ways: e.g., typed/printed, framed and mounted or otherwise displayed
- Use labels and captions on drawings that are displayed
- In anticipation of an audience, add book and print features to the text during the publishing process: e.g., illustrations and other graphics, cover spread, title, dedication, table of contents, about the author piece
- Attend to layout of text in final publication
- Understand publishing as the sharing of a piece of writing with a purpose and an audience in mind

DRAWING

- Understand that when both writing and drawing are on a page, they are mutually supportive, with each extending the other
- Use drawings and sketches to represent people, places, things, and ideas in the composing, revising, and publishing process
- Use sketching to support memory and help in planning
- Use drawing to capture details important to a topic
- Provide important information in illustrations
- Add labels or sentences to drawings as needed to explain them
- Add details to drawings to add information or increase interest
- Create drawings that employ careful attention to color or detail
- Create drawings that are related to the written text and increase readers' understanding and enjoyment

Selecting Goals Behaviors and Understandings to Notice, Teach, and Support *(cont.)*

Writing

VIEWING SELF AS A WRITER

- Take on both approximated and conventional writing independently
- Have a list or notebook with topics and ideas for writing
- Select best pieces of writing from one's own collection and give reasons for the selections
- Self-evaluate writing and talk about what is good about it and what techniques were used
- Produce a reasonable quantity of writing within the time available
- Write with independent initiative and investment
- Attend to the language and craft of other writers (mentor texts) in order to learn more as a writer
- Attend to the nuances of illustrations and how they enhance a text in order to try them out for oneself
- Take risks as a writer
- Write in a variety of genres across the year
- Understand writing as a vehicle to communicate something the writer thinks
- Discuss what is being worked on as a writer
- Talk about oneself as a writer
- Seek feedback on writing
- Be willing to work at the craft of writing, incorporating new learning from instruction
- Compare previous to revised writing and notice and talk about the differences
- State what was learned from each piece of writing
- Write with fluency and ease
- Notice what makes writing effective and name the craft or technique
- Mark the most important part of a piece of one's own or others' writing

Selecting Purpose, Genre, and Form

Writing

Through immersion in new types of texts, third-grade students learn the characteristics of effective writing in various genres. Their ability to craft pieces expands as they write with voice and more skill in their presentation of ideas. They experience new tools and techniques in the writing process and apply a greater range of conventions.

FUNCTIONAL WRITING
(Purpose–to perform a practical task)

FRIENDLY LETTER

▶ **Understanding the Genre**

- Understand that written communication can be used for different purposes: e.g., to give information, to invite, to give thanks
- Understand that a friendly letter can be written in various forms: e.g., note, card, letter, invitation, email
- Understand that the sender and the receiver must be clearly shown
- Understand that a note or card should include short greetings and relevant information
- Understand that an invitation must include specific information about the time and place of the event
- Understand that a friendly letter is more formal than an email, note, or card
- Understand that a friendly letter has parts (date, salutation, closing signature, and sometimes *P.S.*)
- Understand how to learn about writing notes, cards, invitations, emails, and friendly letters by noticing the characteristics of examples

▶ **Writing in the Genre**

- Write a card, note, invitation, or friendly letter with a specific purpose in mind
- Write notes, cards, invitations, and email for a variety of purposes
- Write to a known audience or a specific reader
- Address the audience appropriately
- Include important information in the communication
- Write a friendly letter with all parts

PROCEDURAL TEXT

▶ **Understanding the Genre**

- Understand that a procedural text helps people know how to do something
- Understand that a procedural text can be written in various forms: e.g., list, directions with steps (how-to)
- Understand that a procedural text often shows one item under another item and may include a number or letter for each item
- Understand that a list is a functional way to organize information
- Understand that a procedural text often includes a list of what is needed to do a procedure
- Understand how to craft procedural writing from mentor texts

▶ **Writing in the Genre**

- Use a list to plan an activity or support memory
- Use a list to develop writing in various genres and forms
- Make a list with items that are appropriate for the purpose of the list
- Make a list in the appropriate form with one item under another
- Use number words or transition words
- Write steps of a procedure with appropriate sequence and explicitness
- Write a procedural how-to book with drawings to illustrate a process

TEST WRITING

▶ **Understanding the Genre**

- Understand that test writing often requires writing about an assigned topic
- Understand that test writing may involve creating expository texts or persuasive texts
- Understand that some test writing serves the purpose of demonstrating what a person knows or can do as a writer
- Understand that test writing can take various forms: e.g., short constructed response (sometimes called *short answer*), extended constructed response (or *essay*)
- Understand that test writing often requires writing about something real
- Understand that test writing involves analyzing what is expected of the writer and then planning and writing a response that reflects it
- Understand test writing as a response carefully tailored to meet precise instructions
- Use the terms *test writing, short constructed response,* and *extended constructed response* to describe this type of functional writing

▶ **Writing in the Genre**

- Analyze the prompt to understand the purpose, audience, and genre that is appropriate for the writing
- Read and internalize the criteria for an acceptable response
- Write focused responses to questions and to prompts
- Write concisely and to the direction of the question or prompt
- Elaborate on important points
- Exclude extraneous details
- Incorporate one's knowledge of craft in shaping responses

WRITING ABOUT READING

- See *Writing About Reading,* pages 147–208.

Selecting Purpose, Genre, and Form (cont.)

Writing

NARRATIVE WRITING *(Purpose–to tell a story)*

FICTION

▶ Understanding the Genre

- Understand that fiction genres include realistic fiction, traditional literature (folktale, tall tale, fairy tale, fable), and fantasy
- Understand that fiction can be written in various forms: e.g., narrative text, picture books, wordless picture books, poems, songs, plays, letters
- Understand that an additional purpose of a fiction text is to explore a theme or teach a lesson
- Understand that a fiction text may involve one or more events in the life of a main character
- Understand that a writer uses various elements of fiction (e.g., setting, plot with problem and solution, characters) in a fiction text
- Understand that writers can learn to craft fiction by using mentor texts as models
- Use the terms *realistic fiction, folktale, tall tale, fairy tale,* and *fable* to describe the genre

▶ Writing in the Genre

- Write a simple fiction story, either realistic or fantasy
- Describe the setting with appropriate detail
- Develop an interesting story with believable characters and a realistic plot
- Show the problem of the story and how one or more characters respond to it
- Describe characters by how they look and what they do
- Show rather than tell how characters feel

MEMOIR

▶ Understanding the Genre

- Understand that writers may tell stories from their own lives
- Understand that a story from your life is usually written in first person (using *I* and *we*)
- Understand that a memoir is a biographical text in which a writer reflects on a memorable experience, place, time, or person
- Understand that a factual text may use literary techniques (interesting words and language, descriptions that appeal to the senses, illustrations) to engage and entertain readers as it gives them factual information
- Understand that the writer can look back or think about the memory or experience and share thoughts and feelings about it
- Understand that a personal memory story should be one that is important to the writer
- Understand how to craft a memoir or a personal memory story from mentor texts

▶ Writing in the Genre

- Select a meaningful topic
- Usually write in first person to achieve a strong voice
- Write an engaging beginning and a satisfying ending to a story
- Select "small moments" or experiences and share thinking and feelings about them
- Describe a setting and how it is related to the writer's experiences
- Use words that show the passage of time
- Tell details about the most important moments in a story or experience while eliminating unimportant details
- Write in a way that shows the significance of the story
- Reveal something important about self or about life
- Describe people by what they do, say, and think and what others say about them
- Use dialogue as appropriate to add to the meaning of the story
- Use some literary language that is different from oral language

INFORMATIONAL WRITING
(Purpose–to explain or give facts about a topic)

EXPOSITORY TEXT

▶ Understanding the Genre

- Understand that a writer creates an expository text for readers to learn about a topic
- Understand that to write an expository text, the writer needs to become very knowledgeable about a topic
- Understand that the writer may work to get readers interested in a topic
- Understand that a factual text may use literary techniques (interesting language, description, comparison, photos, graphics, drawings with labels) to engage and entertain readers as it gives them factual information
- Understand that a writer can learn how to write an expository text from mentor texts

▶ Writing in the Genre

- Use illustrations and book and print features (e.g., labeled pictures, diagrams, table of contents, headings, sidebars, page numbers) to guide the reader
- Write a piece that is interesting and enjoyable to read
- Write about a topic, keeping the audience and their interests involved
- Provide information that teaches or informs readers about a topic
- Introduce information in categories and provide interesting supporting details in each category that develops a topic
- Use some vocabulary specific to the topic

WRITING

Selecting Purpose, Genre, and Form (cont.)

Writing

POETIC WRITING (Purpose–to express feelings, sensory images, ideas, or stories)

POETRY

▶ Understanding the Genre

- Understand poetry as a unique way to communicate about and describe feelings, sensory images, ideas, or stories
- Understand that a writer can create different types of poems: e.g., rhyming poems, unrhyming poems
- Understand the importance of specific word choice in poetry
- Understand the difference between ordinary language and poetic language
- Understand that a poem can be created from other kinds of texts
- Understand that poems may look and sound different from one another
- Understand the way print and space work in poems
- Understand that poems take a variety of visual shapes on a page
- Understand that poems do not have to rhyme

▶ Writing in the Genre

- Closely observe the world (animals, objects, people) to get ideas for poems
- Write poems that convey feelings or images
- Use language to describe how something looks, smells, tastes, feels, or sounds
- Use poetic language to communicate meaning
- Remove extra words to clarify the meaning and make the writing more powerful
- Use line breaks and white space when writing poems
- Place words on a page to look like a poem
- Write a variety of poems
- Write poems from other kinds of texts (story, informational text)
- Sometimes borrow specific words or phrases from writing and make them into a poem

The Little Beach
By Rebecca Melhado

Salty sand
soft as a cloud
slowly shifting
to and fro
to and fro

Ocean rocking
bobbing rowboats
pulling sand
in and out
in and out

Seagulls crying
screaming loudly
swirling, twisting
getting ready to steal...
someone's lunch!

A third grader's poem

Selecting Goals Behaviors and Understandings to Notice, Teach, and Support

Writing

CRAFT

ORGANIZATION

▶ Text Structure

- Make decisions about where in a text to place features such as photographs with legends, insets, sidebars, and graphics
- Write fiction and nonfiction narratives that are ordered chronologically
- Write stories and informational books that have a beginning, a series of things happening, and an ending or introductory and summary sentences
- Write an informational text using expository structure that is ordered by logic: e.g., sequences, ideas related to each other, categories of related information
- Begin to use underlying structural patterns to present different kinds of information in nonfiction: e.g., description, temporal sequence, question and answer, cause and effect, chronological sequence, compare and contrast, problem and solution

▶ Beginnings, Endings, Titles

- Use a variety of beginnings to engage the reader
- Use a variety of endings to engage and satisfy the reader
- Use a variety of beginning, middle, and ending structures appropriate to the genre
- Select an appropriate title for a poem, story, or informational book
- Generate multiple titles for the piece and select the one that best fits the content of an informational piece or the plot or characterization in a narrative

▶ Presentation of Ideas

- Tell one part, idea, event, or group of ideas on each page of a book
- Present ideas clearly and in a logical sequence
- Organize information according to purpose and genre
- Introduce ideas followed by supportive details and examples
- Use time appropriately as an organizing tool
- Show steps in enough detail that a reader can follow a sequence
- Bring a piece to closure through an ending or summary statement
- Use headings, a table of contents, and other features to help the reader find information and understand how facts are related
- Use illustrations (diagrams, graphics, photos, charts) to provide information
- Use vocabulary specific to the topic or content

IDEA DEVELOPMENT

- Understand the difference between developing a narrative (or plot) and giving information using description, cause and effect, compare and contrast, or problem and solution
- Introduce, develop, and conclude the topic or story
- Structure a narrative and sustain writing to develop it logically
- Develop a logical plot by creating a story problem and addressing it over multiple events until it is resolved

- Understand how information helps the reader learn about a topic
- Gather and internalize information and then write it in own words
- Communicate clearly the main points intended for the reader to understand
- Arrange information in a logical way so that ideas build on one another

LANGUAGE USE

- Understand that the writer is using language to communicate meaning
- Show evidence of using language from story books and informational books that have been read aloud
- Learn ways of using language and constructing texts from other writers (reading books and hearing them read aloud) and apply understandings to one's own writing
- Continue to learn from other writers by borrowing ways with words, phrases, and sentences
- Use memorable words or phrases
- Use language to show instead of tell
- Use examples to make meaning clear
- Begin to use particular language typical of different genres
- Use variety in sentence structure
- Use language to create sensory images
- Use a variety of transitions and connections: e.g., words, phrases, sentences, and paragraphs

WORD CHOICE

- Learn new words from reading and try them out in writing
- Use vocabulary appropriate for the topic
- Use range of descriptive words to enhance meaning
- Vary word choice to create interesting description and dialogue
- Show ability to vary the text by choosing alternative words: e.g., *replied* for *said*
- Use common (simple) connectives and some sophisticated connectives (words that link ideas and clarify meaning) that are used in written texts but do not appear often in everyday oral language: e.g., *although, however, therefore, though, unless, whenever*

VOICE

- Write about personal experiences with voice
- Write in an expressive way but also recognize how language in a book would sound
- Write in a way that speaks directly to the reader
- Show enthusiasm and energy for the topic
- Write in a way that shows care and commitment to the topic
- Use engaging titles and language
- Use punctuation to make the text clear, effective, and interesting, and to support voice
- Read writing aloud to help think critically about voice

Selecting Goals Behaviors and Understandings to Notice, Teach, and Support *(cont.)*

Writing

CONVENTIONS

For additional information about grammar and usage, capitalization, punctuation, and spelling, see Appendix: Grammar, Usage, and Mechanics.

TEXT LAYOUT

- Arrange print on the page to support the text's meaning and to help the reader notice important information
- Use layout of print and illustrations to convey the meaning of a text
- Use layout, spacing, and size of print to create titles and headings
- Incorporate book and print features (e.g., labeled pictures, diagrams, table of contents, headings, sidebars, page numbers) into nonfiction writing
- Use the size of print to convey meaning in printed text
- Use underlining, italics, and bold print to convey a specific meaning
- Use underlining for words in titles
- Use indentation or spacing to set off paragraphs

GRAMMAR AND USAGE

▶ **Parts of Speech**

- Use nouns and pronouns correctly so that they agree (in gender, number, case): e.g., *Mike, he*
- Recognize and use the eight parts of speech of the English language in an accepted, standard way
- Use subject-verb agreement: e.g., *blanket is; blankets are*

▶ **Tense**

- Write in past tense: e.g., *he walked fast yesterday*
- Write in present tense: e.g., *he walks fast*
- Write in future tense: e.g., *he will walk fast tomorrow*

▶ **Sentence Structure**

- Write complete sentences (subject and predicate)
- Use a range of types of sentences: e.g., declarative, interrogative, imperative, exclamatory
- Use conventional structure for both simple and compound sentences
- Write some sentences with embedded clauses (complex) and dialogue
- Write uninterrupted dialogue in conventional structure

▶ **Paragraphing**

- Understand and use paragraph structure (indented or block) to organize sentences that focus on one idea
- Understand and use paragraphs to show speaker change in dialogue

CAPITALIZATION

- Use capitals to start the first, last, and most other words in a title
- Use a capital letter for the first word of a sentence
- Use capital letters appropriately to capitalize days, months, city and state names, and specific places
- Use capitals for names of people and places
- Use all capital letters for a heading for emphasis
- Use capitals for the first word in a greeting in a letter
- Use capital letters correctly in uninterrupted dialogue

PUNCTUATION

- Consistently use periods, exclamation marks, and question marks as end marks in a conventional way
- Read one's writing aloud and think where punctuation would go
- Understand and use ellipses to show pause or anticipation, often before something surprising
- Understand and use quotation marks to indicate simple dialogue to show the exact words someone said
- Use correct punctuation of uninterrupted dialogue
- Use apostrophes correctly in contractions and possessives
- Use commas correctly to separate items in a series
- Break words at the syllables at the end of a line using a hyphen

SPELLING

- Correctly spell approximately 300 familiar high-frequency words, words with regular letter-sound relationships (including consonant blends and digraphs and some vowel patterns), and commonly used endings and reflect spelling in final drafts
- Use knowledge of syllables and phonogram patterns to generate multisyllable words
- Take apart multisyllables to spell the parts accurately or almost accurately
- Use reference tools to check on spelling when editing final draft (dictionary, digital resources)
- Use basic rules for adding inflectional endings to words (drop *e*, double letter)
- Spell simple and some complex plurals
- Spell most possessives (singular and plural)
- Spell most contractions
- Spell words that have been studied (spelling words)
- Write many compound words accurately
- Spell correctly many one and two syllable words that have vowel and *r*
- Write common abbreviations correctly
- Monitor own spelling by noticing when a word does not "look right" and should be checked

HANDWRITING AND WORD-PROCESSING

- Write fluently in both manuscript and cursive handwriting with appropriate spacing
- Use efficient keyboarding skills
- Make changes on the screen to revise and edit, and publish documents
- Use word-processor to plan, draft, revise, edit, and publish
- Use word-processing with understanding of how to produce and vary text (layout, font, special techniques) according to purpose, audience, etc.

Selecting Goals Behaviors and Understandings to Notice, Teach, and Support *(cont.)*

Writing

WRITING PROCESS

PLANNING AND REHEARSING

▶ **Purpose**

- Write for a specific purpose: e.g., to inform, entertain, persuade, reflect, instruct, retell, maintain relationships, plan
- Understand how the purpose of the writing influences the selection of genre
- Select the genre for the writing based on the purpose
- Tell whether a piece of writing is functional, narrative, informational, or poetic
- Have clear goals and understand how the goals will affect the writing

▶ **Audience**

- Write with specific readers or audience in mind
- Understand that writing is shaped by the writer's purpose and understanding of the audience
- Plan and organize information for the intended readers
- Understand audience as all readers rather than just the teacher

▶ **Oral Language**

- Generate and expand ideas through talk with peers and teacher
- Look for ideas and topics in personal experiences, shared through talk
- Use talk and storytelling to generate and rehearse language that may be written later
- Explore relevant questions in talking about a topic
- When rehearsing language for an informational piece, use vocabulary specific to the topic
- When rehearsing language for a narrative writing, use action and content words appropriate for the story

▶ **Gathering Seeds/Resources/Experimenting with Writing**

- Use a writer's notebook or booklet as a tool for collecting ideas, experimenting, planning, sketching, or drafting
- Reread a writer's notebook to select topics: e.g., select small moments that can be expanded
- Use sketching, webs, lists, and freewriting to think about, plan for, and try out writing
- Make diagrams to assist in planning
- Try out new writing techniques
- Make notes about crafting ideas
- Choose a setting and describe in details that evoke a particular mood

▶ **Content, Topic, Theme**

- Observe carefully events, people, settings, and other aspects of the world to gather information on a topic
- Select own topics for informational writing and state what is important about the topic

- Select information that will support the topic
- Choose topics that one knows about, cares about, or wants to learn about
- Choose topics that are interesting to the writer
- Tell about a topic in an interesting way
- Stay focused on a topic
- Get ideas from other books and writers about how to approach a topic
- Communicate the significance of the topic to an audience
- Decide what is most important about the topic or story
- Use resources (print and online) to get information on a topic
- Select details that will support a topic or story
- Select title that fits the content to publish or complete as final draft

▶ **Inquiry/Research/Exploration**

- Make scientific observations, use notes and sketches to document them, and talk with others about connections and patterns
- Form questions about a topic
- Select the most important information
- Participate actively in experiences and recall information that contributes to writing and drawing (using notebooks and artifacts)
- Remember important labels for drawings
- Take notes or make sketches to help in remembering or generating information
- Gather information (with teacher assistance) about a topic from books or other print and media resources while preparing to write about it
- Understand that a writer gains ideas from other writers but should credit the other writers and/or put these ideas in one's own words

▶ **Genre/Forms**

- Select the genre for the writing based on the purpose: e.g., friendly letter, procedural text; realistic fiction, traditional literature (folktale, tall tale, fairy tale, fable), fantasy; biography, autobiography, memoir; expository text; poetry
- Choose a form for the writing: e.g., notes, cards, letters, invitations, email, lists, directions with steps (how-to); narrative texts, picture books, wordless picture books, poems, songs, plays, letters
- Understand that illustrations play different roles in a text: e.g., increase reader's enjoyment, add information, show sequence

DRAFTING AND REVISING

▶ **Understanding the Process**

- Understand the role of the writer, teacher, or peer writer in conference
- Understand that other writers can be helpful in the process
- Change writing in response to peer or teacher feedback
- Know how to use an editing and proofreading checklist
- Understand revision as a means for making written messages stronger and clearer to readers

WRITING

Selecting Goals Behaviors and Understandings to Notice, Teach, and Support *(cont.)*

Writing

WRITING PROCESS *(continued)*

DRAFTING AND REVISING *(continued)*

▶ **Producing a Draft**

- Write a continuous message on a simple topic
- Use drawings to add information to, elaborate on, or increase readers' enjoyment and understanding
- Produce a piece with several parts that resemble paragraphs
- Write a draft or discovery draft (writing fast and as much as possible on a topic)
- Understand the importance of the lead in a story or nonfiction piece
- Bring the piece to closure with an ending or final statement
- Establish an initiating event and follow with a series of events in a narrative
- Present ideas in logical order across the piece
- Organize and present information in paragraphs in a way that demonstrates clear understanding of their structure to group ideas
- Show steps or phrases in time order when incorporating temporal or chronological sequence into a nonfiction text

▶ **Rereading**

- Reread each day before writing more
- Reread and revise the draft or rewrite sections to clarify meaning
- Reread the text to be sure there are no missing words or information
- Identify language in the story that shows character change (or learning a lesson in a memoir)
- Identify the statement (and sometimes restatement) of the main idea of a piece
- Identify the most exciting part of a story
- Reread a piece asking self, "Have I made clear what I want readers to understand?"

▶ **Adding Information**

- Add ideas in thought bubbles or dialogue in quotation marks or speech bubbles to provide information, provide narration, or show thoughts and feelings
- Add descriptive words (adjectives, adverbs) and phrases to help readers visualize and understand events, actions, processes, or topics
- Add words, phrases, or sentences to make the writing more interesting or exciting for readers
- Add words, phrases, or sentences to provide more information to readers
- Add word, phrases, or sentences to clarify meaning for readers
- After reflection and rereading, add substantial pieces of text (paragraphs, pages) to provide further explanation, clarify points, add interest, or support points

▶ **Deleting Information**

- Delete text to better express meaning and make more logical
- Delete words or sentences that do make sense or do not fit the topic or message

- Delete pages when information is not needed
- Take out unnecessary words, phrases, or sentences that are repetitive or do not add to the meaning

▶ **Changing a Text**

- Change words to make the writing more interesting
- Identify vague parts and provide specificity

▶ **Reorganizing Information**

- Rearrange and revise writing to better express meaning or make the text more logical: e.g., reorder drawings, reorder pages, cut and paste
- Reorganize and revise the writing to better express the writer's meaning or make the text more logical
- Reorder pages by laying them out and reassembling them

▶ **Using Tools and Techniques**

- Add words, letters, phrases, or sentences using a variety of techniques: e.g., caret, sticky notes, spider's legs, numbered items on a separate page, word-processing
- Use a number to identify place to add information and an additional paper with numbers to write the information to insert
- Delete words, phrases, or sentences from a text (crossing out or using word-processing) to make the meaning clearer
- Reorder the information in a text to make the meaning clearer by cutting apart, cutting and pasting, laying out pages, using word-processing

EDITING AND PROOFREADING

▶ **Understanding the Process**

- Understand that a writer uses what is known to spell words
- Understand that the more accurate the spelling and the clearer the space between words, the easier it is for the reader to read it
- Know how to use an editing and proofreading checklist

▶ **Editing for Conventions**

- Check and correct letter formation
- Edit for spelling errors by circling words that do not look right and spelling them another way
- Edit for the conventional spelling of known words
- Understand that the teacher will be final spelling editor for the published piece after the student has used everything known
- Edit for capitalization, punctuation, and sentence sense

▶ **Using Tools**

- Use beginning reference tools: e.g., personal word lists, thesaurus to assist in word choice or checking spelling
- Use spell check, accepting or rejecting changes as needed

PUBLISHING

- Produce writing to explain, label, or otherwise accompany drawing
- Create illustrations and writing that work together to express the meaning

Selecting Goals Behaviors and Understandings to Notice, Teach, and Support *(cont.)*

Writing

- Include graphics or illustrations as appropriate to the text
- Share a text with peers by reading it aloud to the class
- Put several stories or poems together
- Select a poem, story, or informational book to publish in a variety of appropriate ways: e.g., typed/printed, framed and mounted or otherwise displayed
- Add cover spread with title and author information
- In anticipation of an audience, add book and print features during the publishing process: e.g., illustrations and other graphics, cover spread, title, dedication, table of contents, about the author piece
- Attend to layout of text in final publication
- Understand publishing as the sharing of a piece of writing with a purpose and an audience in mind
- Begin to understand the importance of citing sources of information

DRAWING

- Understand that when both writing and drawing are on a page, they are mutually supportive, with each extending the other
- Use drawings and sketches to represent people, places, things, and ideas in the composing, revising, and publishing process
- Create drawings that are related to the written text and increase readers' understanding and enjoyment
- Use sketching to support memory and help in planning
- Use drawing to capture detail that is important to a topic
- Provide important information in the illustrations
- Add labels or sentences to drawings as needed to explain them
- Add details to drawings to add information or increase interest
- Create drawings that employ careful attention to color or detail
- Understand the difference between drawing and sketching and use them to support planning, revising, and publishing the writing process
- Use sketching to create quick representations of images, usually an outline in pencil or pen

VIEWING SELF AS A WRITER

- Have topics and ideas for writing in a list or notebook
- Select best pieces of writing from own collection and give reasons for the selections
- Self-evaluate writing and talk about what is good about it and what techniques were used
- Produce a reasonable quantity of writing within the time available
- Write routinely over extended timeframes and shorter timeframes from a range of discipline-specific tasks, purposes, and audiences
- Write with independent initiative and investment
- Attend to the language and craft of other writers in order to learn more as a writer
- Attend to the nuances of illustrations and how they enhance a text in order to try them out for oneself
- Take risks as a writer
- Write in a variety of genres across the year

- Understand writing as a vehicle to communicate something the writer thinks
- Show ability in a conference to discuss what is being worked on as a writer
- Talk about oneself as a writer
- Seek feedback on writing
- Be willing to work at the craft of writing, incorporating new learning from instruction
- Compare previous writing to revised writing and notice and talk about the differences
- State what was learned from each piece of writing
- Articulate goals as a writer
- Write with fluency and ease
- Notice what makes writing effective and name the craft or technique
- Mark the most important part of a piece of one's own or others' writing

Selecting Purpose, Genre, and Form

Writing

Fourth graders write for a variety of purposes. Their writing shows explicit understanding of the purposes and characteristics of the genre. Expository nonfiction and formal letters become new and important genres. They expand their understanding of persuasive writing and learn more about how to craft it. By year end, they are using craft and convention elements, and tools such as the writer's notebook with confidence.

FUNCTIONAL WRITING
(Purpose–to perform a practical task)

FRIENDLY LETTER

▶ **Understanding the Genre**

- Understand that written communication can be used for different purposes: e.g., to give information, to invite, to give thanks
- Understand that a friendly letter can be written in various forms: e.g., note, card, letter, invitation, email
- Understand that an invitation requires specific information
- Understand that a friendly letter is more formal than an email, note, or card
- Understand that a friendly letter has parts (date, salutation, closing signature, and sometimes *P.S.*)
- Understand how to learn about writing notes, cards, invitations, emails, and friendly letters by noticing the characteristics of examples
- Understand that while email is a quick form of communication, it is a written document and care should be taken with word choice and content
- Use the terms *note, card, letter, invitation,* and *email* to describe the forms

▶ **Writing in the Genre**

- Write a note, card, friendly letter, invitation, or email with a specific purpose in mind
- Write to a known audience or a specific reader
- Address the audience appropriately
- Vary level of formality appropriate to purpose and audience
- Include important information in the communication
- Write a friendly letter with all parts
- Write a letter to an author that demonstrates appreciation for a text the individual has written
- Write a letter to an illustrator that demonstrates appreciation for the details and style of illustrations

FORMAL LETTER

▶ **Understanding the Genre**

- Understand that a formal letter can be written in various forms: e.g., business letter
- Understand that a business letter is a formal document with a particular purpose
- Understand that a business letter has parts: e.g., date, inside address, formal salutation followed by a colon, body organized into paragraphs, closing, signature and title of sender, and sometimes notification of a copy or enclosure

- Understand that a writer can learn to write effective business letters by studying the characteristics of examples
- Use the term *business letter* to describe the form

▶ **Writing in the Genre**

- Write to a specified audience that may be an individual or an organization or group
- Address the audience appropriately
- Include important information and exclude unnecessary details
- Organize the body into paragraphs
- Understand the component parts of a business letter and how to lay them out on a page
- Write formal letters

PROCEDURAL TEXT

▶ **Understanding the Genre**

- Understand that a procedural text helps people know how to do something
- Understand that a procedural text can be written in various forms: e.g., list, sequential directions (how-to)
- Understand that a procedural text often shows one item under another item and may include a number or letter for each item
- Understand that a list is a functional way to organize information and can be used as a planning tool
- Understand that a procedural text often includes a list of what is needed to do a procedure
- Understand how to craft procedural writing from mentor texts

▶ **Writing in the Genre**

- Use a list to plan an activity or support memory
- Use a list to develop writing in various genres and forms
- Write steps of a procedure with appropriate sequence and explicitness, using number words or transition words
- Write clear directions, guides, and "how-to" texts with illustrations (drawings or graphics)

TEST WRITING

▶ **Understanding the Genre**

- Understand that test writing often requires writing about an assigned topic
- Understand that test writing may involve creating expository texts or persuasive texts
- Understand that some test writing serves the purpose of demonstrating what a person knows or can do as a writer

Selecting Purpose, Genre, and Form *(cont.)*

Writing

- Understand that test writing can take various forms: e.g., short constructed response (sometimes called *short answer*), extended constructed response (or *essay*)
- Understand that test writing often requires writing about something real
- Understand that test writing involves analyzing what is expected of the writer, and then planning and writing a response that fits the criteria
- Understand test writing as a response carefully tailored to meet precise instructions
- Understand that test writing often requires taking a position, developing a clear argument, and providing evidence for points
- Understand that test writing often requires inferring and explaining the motives of a character or person
- Learn how to write on tests by studying examples of short constructed responses and extended constructed responses
- Use the terms *test writing, short constructed response,* and *extended constructed response* to describe this type of functional writing

▶ Writing in the Genre

- Analyze prompts to determine purpose, audience, and genre (e.g., expository text, persuasive text) that is appropriate
- Read and internalize the criteria for an acceptable response
- Write focused responses to questions and to prompts
- Write concisely and to the direction of the question or prompt
- Reflect on bigger ideas and make or defend a claim that is substantiated
- Respond to a text in a way that reflects analytic or aesthetic thinking
- Restate a claim with further evidence
- State a point of view and provide evidence
- Elaborate on important points
- Exclude extraneous details
- Incorporate one's knowledge of craft in shaping responses
- Proofread carefully for spelling and conventions

WRITING ABOUT READING

- See *Writing About Reading,* pages 147–208.

NARRATIVE WRITING *(Purpose—to tell a story)*

FICTION

▶ Understanding the Genre

- Understand that fiction genres include realistic fiction, historical fiction, traditional literature (folktale, tall tale, fairy tale, fable), and fantasy
- Understand that fiction can be written in various forms: e.g., narrative text, picture books, wordless picture books, poems, songs, plays, letters, short stories, diary or journal entries
- Understand that an additional purpose of a fiction text is to explore a theme or teach a lesson

- Understand that a fiction text may involve one or more events in the life of a main character
- Understand that a writer uses various elements of fiction (e.g., setting, plot with problem and solution, characters) in a fiction text
- Understand the structure of narrative, including lead or beginning, introduction of characters, setting, problem, series of events, resolution of problem, and ending
- Understand that the setting of fiction may be current or historical
- Understand that writers can learn to craft fiction by using mentor texts as models
- Use the terms *realistic fiction, historical fiction, folktale, tall tale, fairy tale, fable, myth, legend, fantasy,* and *science fiction* to describe the genre

▶ Writing in the Genre

- Write a fiction story, either realistic or fantasy
- With fantasy, include imaginative character, setting, and plot elements
- Begin with a compelling lead to capture reader's attention
- Describe the setting with appropriate detail
- Develop a plot that includes tension and one or more scenes
- Show the problem of the story and how one or more characters respond to it
- Describe characters by how they look, what they do, say, and think, and what others say about them
- Show rather than tell how characters feel
- Take a point of view by writing in first or third person
- Write a believable and satisfying ending to the story

BIOGRAPHY, AUTOBIOGRAPHY, MEMOIR, AND NARRATIVE NONFICTION

▶ Understanding the Genre

- Understand that narrative nonfiction genres include biography, autobiography, memoir, and narrative nonfiction (a nonfiction text that is told chronologically)
- Understand that biographical texts can be written in various forms: e.g., biographical sketches, autobiographical sketches, personal narratives, poems, songs, plays, letters, diary or journal entries
- Understand biography as a true account of a person's life
- Understand autobiography as a true account of a person's life written and narrated by that person
- Understand that a biography or an autobiography can be about the person's whole life or a part of it
- Understand that the writer of a biography or autobiography needs to select the most important events in a person's life
- Establish the significance of events and personal decisions made by the subject of a biography or autobiography
- Understand memoir or personal narrative as a brief, often intense, memory of or reflection on a person, time, or event
- Understand that a memoir can be composed of a series of vignettes

Selecting Purpose, Genre, and Form (cont.)

Writing

NARRATIVE WRITING (Purpose–to tell a story) (continued)

BIOGRAPHY, AUTOBIOGRAPHY, MEMOIR, AND NARRATIVE NONFICTION (continued)

▶ **Understanding the Genre** (continued)

- Understand that a biography, autobiography, or memoir may have characteristics of fiction (e.g., setting, conflict, characters, dialogue, and resolution) even though the events are true or that it can be completely factual
- Understand the difference between true biography and fictionalized biography
- Write various kinds of biographical texts by studying mentor texts
- Understand that a narrative nonfiction text includes selected important events and turning points
- Understand that a narrative nonfiction text often includes an underlying structural pattern such as cause and effect or problem and solution
- Understand that a narrative nonfiction text indicates passing of time using words (e.g., *then, after a time*), dates and periods of time, and ages of people
- Understand that the setting may be important in a narrative nonfiction text
- Understand that a narrative nonfiction text includes people that are real
- Understand that a narrative nonfiction text often includes quotes of a person's exact words
- Understand that a narrative nonfiction text should include only true events and people and may require research
- Use the terms *biography, biographical sketch, autobiography, autobiographical sketch, personal narrative, memoir, poem, song, play, letter, diary entry,* and *journal entry* to describe the genre and forms

▶ **Writing in the Genre**

- Choose a subject and state a reason for the selection
- Select important events and turning points to include and exclude extraneous events and details
- Select and write personal experiences as "small moments" and share thinking and feelings about them
- Use small moments or experiences to communicate a bigger message
- Reveal something important about self or about life
- Create a series of vignettes that together communicate a bigger message
- Use words that show the passage of time
- Tell events in chronological order or use another structural pattern: e.g., description, temporal sequence, question and answer, cause and effect, compare and contrast, problem and solution, categorization
- Describe and develop a setting and explain how it is related to the writer's experiences
- Describe the subject's important decisions and a turning point in the narrative

- Describe the subject by what she did or said as well as others' opinions
- Show the significance of the subject
- Show how the subject changes
- Describe people by how they look, what they do, say, and think, and what others say about them
- Use dialogue as appropriate to add to the meaning of the narrative
- Experiment with literary language (powerful nouns and verbs, figurative language)
- Write an ending that fits the piece
- Show cause and effect and/or problem and solution as appropriate in writing narrative nonfiction
- Include quotes from real people in a narrative nonfiction text and place them in quotation marks

INFORMATIONAL WRITING (Purpose–to explain or give facts about a topic)

EXPOSITORY TEXT

▶ **Understanding the Genre**

- Understand that a writer creates an expository text for readers to learn about a topic
- Understand that to write an expository text, the writer needs to become very knowledgeable about a topic
- Understand that an expository text may require research and will require organization
- Understand that an expository text can be written in various forms: e.g., essay, report, news article, feature article
- Understand than an essay is a short composition used to explain a topic and/or give the writer's point of view about a topic
- Understand the basic structure of an essay: e.g., introduction, body, conclusion
- Understand that a report is a formal presentation of a topic
- Understand that a report may include several categories of information about a single topic
- Understand that a report has an introductory section, followed by more information in categories or sections
- Understand that a feature article usually focuses on one aspect of a topic
- Understand that a feature article begins with a lead paragraph, with more detailed information in subsequent paragraphs, and a conclusion
- Understand that a feature article reveals the writer's point of view about the topic or subject
- Understand that a factual text may use literary language and literary techniques to engage and entertain readers as it gives them factual information
- Understand that a writer can learn how to write various forms of expository text from mentor texts
- Use the terms *expository text, essay, report, news article,* and *feature article* to describe the genre and forms

Selecting Purpose, Genre, and Form (cont.)

Writing

▶ **Writing in the Genre**

- Use illustrations and book and print features (e.g., labeled pictures, diagrams, table of contents, headings, subheadings, sidebars, boxes of facts set off from other text, page numbers) to guide the reader
- Write a piece that is interesting and enjoyable to read
- Write about a topic, keeping in mind the audience and their interests and likely background knowledge
- Provide information that teaches or informs readers about a topic
- Write an effective lead paragraph and conclusion
- Organize information using categorization or another underlying structural pattern: e.g., description, temporal sequence, question and answer, cause and effect, chronological sequence, compare and contrast, problem and solution
- Provide interesting supporting details that develop a topic
- Include facts, figures, statistics, examples, and anecdotes when appropriate
- Use quotes from experts (written texts, speeches, or interviews) when appropriate
- Use some vocabulary specific to the topic
- Use literary language to make topic interesting to readers

PERSUASIVE WRITING (*Purpose–to persuade*)

PERSUASIVE TEXT

▶ **Understanding the Genre**

- Understand that argument or persuasive texts can be written in various forms: e.g., editorial, letter to the editor, essay
- Understand that the purpose of persuasion or argument may be to convince the reader to take the writer's point of view, take some action, or improve some aspect of the world
- Understand that an editorial is a formal text with a public audience
- Understand that a letter to the editor is formal text with a public audience: e.g., the editor of a publication and its readers
- Understand that a letter to the editor has parts: e.g., date, formal salutation, body organized into paragraphs, closing, signature and title of sender
- Understand than an essay is a formal text often written for a teacher or a test
- Understand the importance of supporting each idea or argument with facts, reasons, or examples
- Use the terms *persuasive text, argument, editorial, letter to the editor,* and *essay* to describe the genre and forms
- Understand that a writer can learn to write various forms of argument and persuasion by studying the characteristics of examples in mentor texts

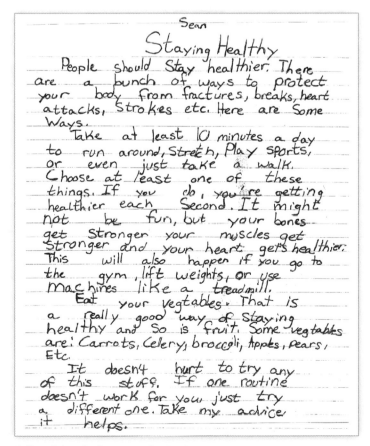

A fourth grader's persuasive text

Selecting Purpose, Genre, and Form (cont.)

Writing

PERSUASIVE WRITING (Purpose–to persuade) (continued)

PERSUASIVE TEXT

▶ **Writing in the Genre**

- Write an editorial, a letter to the editor, or an essay
- Address the audience appropriately according to the form
- Choose topics from stories or everyday observations
- Begin with a title or opening that tells the reader what is being argued or explained and end with a conclusion
- Provide a series of clear arguments with reasons to support the argument
- Include important information and exclude unnecessary details
- Use opinions supported by facts
- Provide "expert testimony" or quotes to support argument
- Organize the body of the text into paragraphs
- Include illustrations, charts, or diagrams as necessary

POETIC WRITING (Purpose–to express feelings, sensory images, ideas, or stories)

POETRY

▶ **Understanding the Genre**

- Understand poetry as a unique way to communicate about and describe feelings, sensory images, ideas, or stories
- Understand that a writer can create different types of poems: e.g., limerick, haiku, concrete poem
- Understand the importance of specific word choice in poetry
- Understand the difference between poetic language and ordinary language
- Notice the beat or rhythm of a poem and its relation to line breaks
- Understand the way print works in poems and demonstrate the use in reading and writing them on a page using white space and line breaks

- Understand that poems take a variety of shapes
- Understand that poems do not have to rhyme
- Use the terms *poem, limerick, haiku,* and *concrete poem* to describe poetry
- Understand that a writer can learn to write a variety of poems from studying mentor texts

▶ **Writing in the Genre**

- Observe closely to select topics or content and write with detail
- Use words to convey images
- Use words to convey strong feelings
- Write with detail and create images
- Select topics that are significant and help readers see in a new way
- Select topics that have strong meaning
- Use white space and line breaks to communicate the meaning and tone of the poem
- Understand the role of line breaks, white space for pause, breath, or emphasis
- Shape words on a page to look like a poem
- Remove extra words to clarify the meaning and make the writing more powerful
- Use repetition, refrain, rhythm, and other poetic techniques
- Use words to show not tell
- Write a variety of types of poems
- Write a poetic text in response to another poem, reflecting the same style, topic, mood, or voice
- Write a poetic text in response to prose text, either narrative or informational
- Choose a title that communicates the meaning of a poem

Selecting Goals Behaviors and Understandings to Notice, Teach, and Support

Writing

CRAFT

ORGANIZATION

▶ Text Structure

- Use organization in writing that is related to purpose and genre (letters, essays)
- Make decisions about where in a text to place features such as photographs with legends, insets, sidebars, and graphics
- Write fictional narratives with characters involved in a plot, events ordered by time
- Write fiction and nonfiction narratives that are ordered chronologically
- Use underlying structural patterns to present different kinds of information in nonfiction: e.g., description, temporal sequence, question and answer, cause and effect, chronological sequence, compare and contrast, problem and solution, categorization

▶ Beginnings, Endings, Titles

- Begin with a purposeful and engaging lead
- Use a variety of beginnings and endings to engage the reader
- Bring a piece to closure with a concluding statement
- End a narrative with a problem solution and a satisfying conclusion
- Understand that narratives can begin at the beginning, middle, or end
- End an informational piece with a thoughtful or enlightening conclusion
- Select an appropriate title for a poem, story, or informational book
- Generate multiple titles for the piece and select the one that best fits the content of an informational piece or the plot or characterization in a narrative

▶ Presentation of Ideas

- Tell one part, idea, event, or group of ideas on each page of a book
- Present ideas clearly and in a logical sequence
- Organize information according to purpose and genre
- Show topics and subtopics by using headings and subheadings
- Use paragraphs to organize ideas
- Use well-crafted transitions to support the pace and flow of the writing
- Introduce ideas with facts, details, examples, and explanations from multiple authorities
- Introduce ideas followed by supportive details and examples
- Use time appropriately as an organizing tool
- Show steps in enough detail that a reader can follow a sequence
- Bring a piece to closure through an ending or summary statement
- Use headings, subheadings, a table of contents, and other features to help the reader find information and understand how facts are related in expository writing
- Use graphics (diagrams, illustrations, photos, charts) to provide information
- Use vocabulary specific to the topic or content

IDEA DEVELOPMENT

- Understand the difference between developing a narrative (or plot) and giving information using description, cause and effect, compare and contrast, problem and solution, or categorization
- Introduce, develop, and conclude the topic or story
- Hold the reader's attention with clear, focused content
- Structure a narrative and sustain writing to develop it logically
- Develop a logical plot by creating a story problem and addressing it over multiple events until it is resolved
- Understand how information helps the reader learn about a topic
- Gather and internalize information and then write it in own words
- Engage the reader with ideas that show strong knowledge of the topic
- Communicate clearly the main points intended for the reader to understand
- Arrange information in a logical way so that ideas build on one another
- Provide details that are accurate, relevant, interesting, and vivid

LANGUAGE USE

- Understand that the writer is using language to communicate meaning
- Show evidence of using language from story books and informational books that have been read aloud
- Learn ways of using language and constructing texts from other writers (reading books and hearing them read aloud) and apply understandings to one's own writing
- Continue to learn from other writers by borrowing ways with words, phrases, and sentences
- Use memorable words or phrases
- Vary language and style as appropriate to audience and purpose
- Use language to show instead of tell
- Use language to give directions
- Find and write language to explain abstract concepts and ideas
- Use language to clearly state main ideas and supporting details
- Use examples to make meaning clear
- Begin to use particular language typical of different genres
- Use language to create sensory images
- Use language to elicit feelings
- Use figurative language (e.g., simile, metaphor, personification) to make comparisons
- Use variety in sentence structure and sentence length
- Use concrete sensory details and descriptive language to develop plot (tension and problem resolution) and setting in memoir, biography, and fiction
- Use descriptive language and dialogue to present characters/subjects who appear in narratives (memoir, biography, and fiction) and informational writing
- Use language to show feelings of characters
- Use dialogue and action to draw readers into the story
- Select a point of view with which to tell a story

WRITING

Selecting Goals Behaviors and Understandings to Notice, Teach, and Support *(cont.)*

Writing

CRAFT *(continued)*

LANGUAGE USE *(continued)*

- Use language to establish a point of view
- Understand the differences between first and third person
- Write in both first and third person and understand the differences in effect so as to choose appropriately
- Arrange simple and complex sentences for an easy flow and sentence transition
- Vary sentence length to create feeling or mood
- Use a variety of transitions and connections: e.g., words, phrases, sentences, and paragraphs

WORD CHOICE

- Learn new words from reading and try them out in writing
- Use vocabulary appropriate for the topic
- Choose the best words to fit the writer's purpose and meaning
- Choose words with the audience in mind
- Use range of descriptive words to enhance meaning
- Vary word choice to create interesting description and dialogue
- Select words to make meanings memorable
- Use strong nouns and verbs
- Use colorful modifiers and style as appropriate to audience and purpose
- Use words that convey an intended mood or effect
- Show ability to vary the text by choosing alternative words: e.g., *replied* for *said*
- Learn and use content words typical of disciplinary language: e.g., science, history, math, social studies
- Where needed, use academic language in an appropriate way to write about topics in various disciplines
- Use common (simple) connectives and some sophisticated connectives (words that link ideas and clarify meaning) that are used in written texts but do not appear often in everyday oral language: e.g., *although, however, therefore, though, unless, whenever*

VOICE

- Write about personal experiences with voice
- Write in an expressive way but also recognize how language in a book would sound
- Write in a way that speaks directly to the reader
- Show enthusiasm and energy for the topic
- Write in a way that shows care and commitment to the topic
- Use engaging titles and language
- Include details that add to the voice
- Use dialogue selectively to communicate voice
- Use punctuation to make the text clear, effective, interesting, and to support voice
- Produce narrative writing that is engaging, honest, and reveals the person behind the writing
- Produce expository writing that reveals the stance of the writer toward the topic
- Produce persuasive writing including argument with logical evidence to support ideas and to counter opposing argument
- Read writing aloud to help think critically about voice

CONVENTIONS

For additional information about grammar and usage, capitalization, punctuation, and spelling, see Appendix: Grammar, Usage, and Mechanics.

TEXT LAYOUT

- Arrange print on the page to support the text's meaning and to help the reader notice important information
- Use layout of print and illustrations to convey the meaning of a text
- Use layout of print and illustrations (e.g., drawings, photos, maps, diagrams) to convey the meaning in a nonfiction text
- Use layout, spacing, and size of print to create titles, headings, and subheadings
- Incorporate book and print features (e.g., labeled pictures, diagrams, table of contents, headings, subheadings, sidebars, page numbers) into nonfiction writing
- Use the size of print to convey meaning in printed text
- Use underlining, italics, and bold print to convey a specific meaning
- Use underlining for words in titles
- Use indentation or spacing to set off paragraphs

GRAMMAR AND USAGE

▶ **Parts of Speech**

- Use nouns and pronouns correctly so that they agree (in gender, number, case): e.g., *Mike, he*
- Recognize and use the eight parts of speech of the English language in an accepted, standard way
- Use subject-verb agreement: e.g., *astronaut is; astronauts are*
- Use objective and nominative case pronouns in an accepted, standard way: e.g., *me, him, her; I, he, she*
- Use indefinite and relative pronouns correctly: e.g., *everyone, both; that, who, whose*
- Correctly use verbs that are often misused: e.g., *lie/lay; rise/raise*

▶ **Tense**

- Use the same tense for two or more actions happening at the same time: e.g., *I poured the milk into the bowl and called the kitten's name*
- Use different tenses to show two or more actions happening at different times: e.g., *the kitten laps up the milk I poured an hour ago*
- Write sentences in present, past, future, present perfect, and past perfect tenses as needed to express meaning

Selecting Goals Behaviors and Understandings to Notice, Teach, and Support *(cont.)*

Writing

▶ Sentence Structure

- Write complete sentences (subject and predicate)
- Use a range of types of sentences: e.g., declarative, interrogative, imperative, exclamatory
- Use conventional sentence structure for simple sentences, compound sentences, and complex sentences with embedded clauses
- Sometimes vary sentence structure and length for reasons of craft
- Place phrases in sentences
- Place clauses in sentences
- Write sentences in past, present, future, present perfect, and past perfect tenses as fits intended meaning and purpose
- Write uninterrupted dialogue in conventional structures

▶ Paragraphing

- Understand and use paragraph structure (indented or block) to organize sentences that focus on one idea
- Create transitions between paragraphs to show the progression of ideas
- Understand and use paragraphs to show speaker change in dialogue

CAPITALIZATION

- Use a capital letter in the first word of a sentence
- Use capital letters appropriately for the first letter in days, months, holidays, city and state names, and titles of books
- Use capital letters correctly in dialogue
- Use capitalization for specialized functions (emphasis, key information, voice)
- Use more complex capitalization with increasing accuracy, such as in abbreviations and with quotation marks in split dialogue

PUNCTUATION

- Consistently use periods, exclamation marks, and question marks as end marks in a conventional way
- Read one's writing aloud and think about where to place punctuation
- Understand and use ellipses to show pause or anticipation, often before something surprising
- Use dashes correctly to indicate a longer pause or slow down the reading to emphasize particular information
- Use commas and quotation marks correctly in writing interrupted and uninterrupted dialogue as well as to show a verbatim quote
- Use apostrophes correctly in contractions and possessives
- Use commas correctly to separate an introductory clause or items in a series
- Use commas and parentheses correctly to set off parenthetical information
- Divide words correctly at the syllable break and at the end of a line using a hyphen
- Use colons correctly to introduce a list of items or a long, formal statement or quotation
- Use brackets to separate a different idea or kind of information
- Use indentation correctly to identify paragraphs

- Notice the role of punctuation in the craft of writing
- Try out new ways of using punctuation
- Study mentor texts to learn the role of punctuation in adding voice to writing

SPELLING

- Spell approximately 500 familiar high-frequency words, a wide range of plurals, and base words with inflectional endings and reflect spelling in final drafts
- Use a range of spelling strategies to take apart and spell multisyllable words (word parts, connections to known words, complex sound-to-letter cluster relationships)
- Use reference tools to check on spelling when editing final draft (dictionary, digital resources)
- Spell complex plurals correctly: e.g., *knife/knives, woman/women, sheep/sheep*
- Spell a full range of contractions, plurals, possessives, and compound words
- Spell words that have been studied (spelling words)
- Spell correctly two- or three-syllable words that have vowel and *r*
- Be aware of the spelling of common suffixes (e.g., *-ion, -ment, -ly*)
- Use difficult homophones (e.g., *their, there*) correctly
- Monitor own spelling by noticing when a word does not "look right" and should be checked

HANDWRITING AND WORD-PROCESSING

- Write fluently and legibly in cursive handwriting with appropriate spacing
- Use efficient keyboarding skills to create drafts, revise, edit, and publish
- Use word-processor to get ideas down, revise, edit, and publish
- Use word-processing with understanding of how to produce and vary text (layout, font, special techniques) according to purpose, audience, etc.
- Show familiarity with computer and word-processing terminology
- Create website entries and articles with appropriate text layout, graphics, and access to information through searching
- Make wide use of computer skills in presenting text

WRITING PROCESS

PLANNING AND REHEARSING

▶ Purpose

- Write for a specific purpose: e.g., to inform, entertain, persuade, reflect, instruct, retell, maintain relationships, plan
- Understand how the purpose of the writing influences the selection of genre
- Select the genre for the writing based on the purpose
- Tell whether a piece of writing is functional, narrative, informational, or poetic
- Have clear goals and understand how the goals will affect the writing

Selecting Goals Behaviors and Understandings to Notice, Teach, and Support *(cont.)*

Writing

WRITING PROCESS *(continued)*

PLANNING AND REHEARSING *(continued)*

▶ **Audience**

- Write with specific readers or audience in mind
- Understand that writing is shaped by the writer's purpose and understanding of the audience
- Plan and organize information for the intended readers
- Understand audience as all readers rather than just the teacher

▶ **Oral Language**

- Generate and expand ideas through talk with peers and teacher
- Look for ideas and topics in personal experiences, shared through talk
- Use talk and storytelling to generate and rehearse language that may be written later
- Explore relevant questions in talking about a topic
- When rehearsing language for an informational piece, use vocabulary specific to the topic
- When rehearsing language for a narrative writing, use action and content words appropriate for the story

▶ **Gathering Seeds/Resources/Experimenting with Writing**

- Use a writer's notebook or booklet as a tool for collecting ideas, experimenting, planning, sketching, or drafting
- Reread a writer's notebook to select topics: e.g., select small moments that can be expanded
- Use sketching, webs, lists, and freewriting to think about, plan for, and try out writing
- Gather a variety of entries (e.g., character map, timeline, sketches, observations, freewrites, drafts, lists) in a writer's notebook
- Think through a topic, focus, organization, and audience
- Try out titles, different headings and endings, develop setting and characters in a writer's notebook
- Use notebooks to plan, gather, and rehearse for future published writing
- Make a plan for an essay that makes a claim and contains supporting evidence
- Choose helpful tools: e.g., webs, T-charts, sketches, charts, diagrams, lists, outlines, flowcharts
- Choose a setting and describe in details that evoke a particular mood

▶ **Content, Topic, Theme**

- Observe carefully events, people, settings, and other aspects of the world to gather information on a topic
- Select information that will support the topic
- Choose topics that one knows about, cares about, or wants to learn about

- Choose topics that are interesting to the writer
- Tell about a topic in an interesting way
- Stay focused on a topic to produce a well-organized piece of writing that is long enough to fully explain the points (e.g., facts, arguments) the writer wants to make
- Get ideas from other books and writers about how to approach a topic: e.g., organization, point of view, layout
- Communicate the significance of the topic to an audience
- Show the audience (by stating or providing important information) what is important about the topic
- Use resources (print and online) to get information on a topic
- Select details that will support a topic or story
- Select title that fits the content to publish or complete as final draft
- Develop a clear, main idea around which a piece of writing will be planned
- Use the organizing features of electronic text (e.g., bulletin boards, databases, keyword searches, email addresses) to locate information
- Understand a range of genres and forms and select from them according to topic and purpose and audience

▶ **Inquiry/Research/Exploration**

- Make scientific observations, use notes and sketches to document them, and talk with others about connections and patterns
- Form questions to explore and locate sources for information about a topic, characters, or setting
- Select and include only the information that is appropriate to the topic and to the category
- Use notes to record and organize information
- Conduct research to gather information in planning a writing project: e.g., live interviews, Internet, artifacts, articles, books
- Create categories of information
- Determine when research is necessary to cover a nonfiction topic adequately
- Search for appropriate information from multiple sources: e.g., books and other print materials, websites, interview
- Understand the concept of plagiarism
- Understand that a writer gains ideas from other writers but should credit the other writers and/or put those ideas into one's own words
- Understand that a writer may quote another writer by placing the exact words in quotes and referencing the source
- Record sources of information for citation

▶ **Genre/Forms**

- Select the genre for the writing based on the purpose: e.g., friendly letter, formal letter, procedural text; realistic fiction, historical fiction, traditional literature (folktale, tall tale, fairy tale, fable), and fantasy; biography, autobiography, memoir, narrative nonfiction; expository text; persuasive text; poetry

Selecting Goals Behaviors and Understandings to Notice, Teach, and Support *(cont.)*

Writing

- Choose a form for the writing: e.g., notes, cards, letters, invitations, email, lists, directions with steps (how-to); narrative texts, picture books, wordless picture books, poems, songs, plays, letters, short stories, diary and journal entries, biographical and autobiographical sketches, personal narratives; essays, reports, news and feature articles; editorials, letters to the editor
- Understand that illustrations play different roles in a text: e.g., increase reader's enjoyment, add information, show sequence

DRAFTING AND REVISING

▶ Understanding the Process

- Understand the role of the writer, teacher, or peer writer in conference
- Change writing in response to peer or teacher feedback
- Know how to use an editing and proofreading checklist
- Understand revision as a means for making written messages stronger and clearer to readers
- Use writers as mentors in making revisions and revisions while drafting (recursive process)

▶ Producing a Draft

- Write a continuous message, sometimes organized into categories that are related to a larger topic or idea
- Use drawings to add information to, elaborate on, or increase readers' enjoyment and understanding
- Write a draft or discovery draft (writing fast and as much as possible on a topic)
- Understand the importance of the lead in a story or nonfiction piece
- Revise the lead to find the most interesting and engaging language
- Bring the piece to closure with an effective summary, parting idea, or satisfying ending
- Establish an initiating event and follow with a series of events in a narrative
- Present ideas in logical order across the piece
- Maintain central idea or focus across paragraphs
- Organize and present information in paragraphs in a way that demonstrates clear understanding of their structure to group ideas
- Show steps or phrases in time order when incorporating temporal or chronological sequence into a nonfiction text
- Establish a situation, plot or problem, and point of view in fiction drafts
- Provide insight as to why an incident or event is memorable
- When writing a biography, memoir, or fiction story, establish important decisions (made by the central character or subject) and the outcomes of those decisions
- Generate multiple titles to help think about the focus of the piece
- Select a title that fits the content

▶ Rereading

- Reread writing to think about what to write next
- Reread writing to rethink and make changes
- Reread and revise the discovery draft or rewrite sections to clarify meaning
- Reread the text to be sure there are no missing words or information
- Identify language in the story that shows character change (or learning a lesson in a memoir)
- Identify the statement (and sometimes restatement) of the main idea of a piece
- Identify the most exciting part of a story
- Reread a piece asking self, "Have I made clear what I want readers to understand?"
- Reread writing to check for clarity and purpose
- Identify information that may confuse the reader
- Identify information that may be related to the topic
- Identify information that either distracts from or does not contribute to the central purpose and message

▶ Adding Information

- Add ideas in thought bubbles or dialogue in quotation marks or speech bubbles to provide information, provide narration, or show thoughts and feelings
- Add descriptive words (adjectives, adverbs) and phrases to help readers visualize and understand events, actions, processes, or topics
- Add words, phrases, or sentences to make the writing more interesting or exciting for readers
- Add words, phrases, or sentences to provide more information to readers
- Add word, phrases, or sentences to clarify meaning for readers
- After reflection and rereading, add substantial pieces of text (paragraphs, pages) to provide further explanation, clarify points, add interest, or support points
- Add details or examples to make the piece clearer or more interesting
- Add transitional words and phrases to clarify meaning and make the writing smoother
- Reread and change or add words to ensure that meaning is clear
- Add descriptive words and details to writing or drawings
- Use footnotes to add information

▶ Deleting Information

- Delete text to better express meaning and make more logical
- Delete words or sentences that do not make sense or do not fit the topic or message
- Delete pages or paragraphs when information is not needed
- Identify redundant words, phrases, or sentences and remove if they do not serve a purpose or enhance the voice
- Reread and cross out words to ensure that meaning is clear

WRITING

Selecting Goals Behaviors and Understandings to Notice, Teach, and Support *(cont.)*

Writing

WRITING PROCESS *(continued)*

DRAFTING AND REVISING *(continued)*

▶ **Changing a Text**

- Identify vague parts and provide specificity
- Vary word choice to make the piece more interesting
- Work on transitions to achieve better flow
- Reshape writing to make the text into a different genre: e.g., personal narrative to poem

▶ **Reorganizing Information**

- Rearrange and revise writing to better express meaning or make the text more logical (reorder drawings, reorder pages, cut and paste)
- Reorganize and revise the writing to better express the writer's meaning or make the text more logical
- Reorder pages or paragraphs by laying them out and reassembling them

▶ **Using Tools and Techniques**

- Add words, letters, phrases, or sentences using a variety of techniques: e.g., caret, sticky notes, spider's legs, numbered items on a separate page, word-processing
- Use a number to identify place to add information and an additional paper with numbers to write the information to insert
- Delete words, phrases, or sentences from a text (crossing out or using word-processing) to make the meaning clearer
- Reorder the information in a text to make the meaning clearer by cutting apart, cutting and pasting, laying out pages, using word-processing

EDITING AND PROOFREADING

▶ **Understanding the Process**

- Understand that a writer uses what is known to spell words
- Know how to use an editing and proofreading checklist
- Understand that a writer (after using what is known) can ask another person to do a final edit
- Understand the limitations of spell check and grammar check on the computer
- Understand how to use tools to self-evaluate writing and assist the writer in copyediting

▶ **Editing for Conventions**

- Check and correct letter formation
- Edit for the conventional spelling of known words
- Edit for spelling errors by circling words that do not look right and spelling them another way
- Understand that the teacher will be final spelling editor for the published piece after the student has used everything known
- Edit for capitalization and punctuation
- Edit for grammar and sentence sense
- Edit for word suitability and precise meaning

- Determine where new paragraphs should begin
- Check and correct spacing and layout
- Prepare final draft with self-edit and submit (teacher edit prior to publishing)

▶ **Using Tools**

- Use reference tools to check on spelling and meaning
- Use a thesaurus to search for more interesting words
- Use spell check, accepting or rejecting changes as needed
- Use grammar check, accepting or rejecting changes as needed

PUBLISHING

- Produce writing to explain, label, or otherwise accompany drawing
- Create illustrations and writing that work together to express the meaning
- Create illustrations or other art for pieces that are in final form
- Share a text with peers by reading it aloud to the class
- Put several stories or poems together in a book
- Select a poem, story, or informational book to publish in a variety of appropriate ways: e.g., typed/printed, framed and mounted or otherwise displayed
- Add cover spread with title and author information
- In anticipation of an audience, add book and print features during the publishing process: e.g., illustrations and other graphics, cover spread, title, dedication, table of contents, about the author piece, headings, subheadings
- Attend to layout of text in final publication
- Understand publishing as the sharing of a piece of writing with a purpose and an audience in mind
- Understand the importance of citing sources of information and some conventions for citations

DRAWING

- Understand that when both writing and drawing are on a page, they are mutually supportive, with each extending the other
- Use sketches or drawings to represent people, places, and things, and also to communicate mood and abstract ideas as appropriate to the genre and form
- Create drawings that are related to the written text and increase readers' understanding and enjoyment
- Use sketching to support memory and help in planning
- Use sketching to capture detail that is important to a topic
- Provide important information in the illustrations
- Add detail to drawings to add information or increase interest
- Create drawings that employ careful attention to color or detail
- Understand the difference between drawing and sketching and use them to support the writing process
- Use sketching to create quick representations of images, usually an outline in pencil or pen

Selecting Goals Behaviors and Understandings to Notice, Teach, and Support *(cont.)*

Writing

- Sometimes use diagrams or other graphics to support the process and/or add meaning
- Sketch and draw with a sense of relative size and perspective
- Use the terms *sketching* and *drawing* to refer to these processes and forms

VIEWING SELF AS A WRITER

- Have topics and ideas for writing in a list or notebook
- Select examples of best writing in all genres attempted
- Self-evaluate writing and talk about what is good about it and what techniques were used
- Self-evaluate pieces of writing in light of what is known about a genre
- Produce a reasonable quantity of writing within the time available
- Write routinely over extended timeframes and shorter timeframes from a range of discipline-specific tasks, purposes, and audiences
- Write with independent initiative and investment
- Attend to the nuances of illustrations and how they enhance a text in order to try them out for oneself
- Take risks as a writer
- Write in a variety of genres across the year
- Understand writing as a vehicle to communicate something the writer thinks
- Show ability in a conference to discuss what is being worked on as a writer
- Seek feedback on writing
- Be willing to work at the craft of writing, incorporating new learning from instruction
- Compare previous writing to revised writing and notice and talk about the differences
- State what was learned from each piece of writing
- Articulate goals as a writer
- Write with fluency and ease
- Notice what makes writing effective and name the craft or technique
- Show interest in and work at crafting good writing, incorporating new learning from instruction
- Suggest possible revisions to peers
- Mark the most important part of a piece of one's own or others' writing

Selecting Purpose, Genre, and Form

Writing

By year end, grade five writers can select purpose and genre for a wide range of writing, including hybrid texts, with more skill. They know many mentor texts they can use as resources. They continue to expand their ability to write argument and persuasion effectively. They also select writers to apprentice with and use their writer's notebook for useful inquiry and planning.

FUNCTIONAL WRITING
(Purpose–to perform a practical task)

FORMAL LETTER

▶ Understanding the Genre

- Understand that a formal letter can be written in various forms: e.g., business letter
- Understand that a business letter is a formal document with a particular purpose
- Understand that a business letter has parts: e.g., date, inside address, formal salutation followed by a colon, body organized into paragraphs, closing, signature and title of sender, and sometimes notification of a copy or enclosure
- Understand that a writer can learn to write effective business letters by studying the characteristics of examples
- Use the term *business letter* to describe the form

▶ Writing in the Genre

- Write to a specified audience that may be an individual or an organization or group
- Address the audience appropriately
- Include important information and exclude unnecessary details
- Organize the body into paragraphs
- Understand the component parts of a business letter and how to lay them out on a page
- Write formal letters

PROCEDURAL TEXT

▶ Understanding the Genre

- Understand that a procedural text helps people know how to do something
- Understand that a procedural text can be written in various forms: e.g., list, sequential directions (how-to)
- Understand that a procedural text often shows one item under another item and may include a number or letter for each item
- Understand that a list is a functional way to organize information and can be used as a planning tool
- Understand that a procedural text often includes a list of what is needed to do a procedure
- Understand how to craft procedural writing from mentor texts

▶ Writing in the Genre

- Use a list to plan an activity or support memory
- Use a list to develop writing in various genres and forms

- Write steps of a procedure with appropriate sequence and explicitness, using number words or transition words
- Write clear directions, guides, and "how-to" texts

TEST WRITING

▶ Understanding the Genre

- Understand that test writing often requires writing about an assigned topic
- Understand that test writing may involve creating expository texts or persuasive texts
- Understand that some test writing serves the purpose of demonstrating what a person knows or can do as a writer
- Understand that test writing can take various forms: e.g., short constructed response (sometimes called *short answer*), extended constructed response (or *essay*)
- Understand that test writing often requires writing about something real
- Understand that test writing involves analyzing what is expected of the writer, and then planning and writing a response that fits the criteria
- Understand test writing as a response carefully tailored to meet precise instructions
- Understand that test writing often requires taking a position, developing a clear argument, and providing evidence for points
- Understand that test writing often requires inferring and explaining the motives of a character or person
- Understand that test writing sometimes requires taking a perspective that may come from a different time or setting than the reader
- Learn how to write on tests by studying examples of short constructed responses and extended constructed responses
- Use the terms *test writing, short constructed response,* and *extended constructed response* to describe this type of functional writing

▶ Writing in the Genre

- Analyze prompts to determine purpose, audience, and genre (e.g., expository text, persuasive text) that is appropriate
- Read and internalize the criteria for an acceptable response
- Write focused responses to questions and to prompts
- Write concisely and to the direction of the question or prompt
- Reflect on bigger ideas and make or defend a claim that is substantiated
- Respond to a text in a way that reflects analytic or aesthetic thinking
- Restate a claim with further evidence
- State a point of view and provide evidence

Selecting Purpose, Genre, and Form (cont.)

Writing

- State a point of view of another individual
- Elaborate on important points
- Exclude extraneous details
- Incorporate one's knowledge of craft in shaping responses
- Proofread carefully for spelling and conventions

WRITING ABOUT READING

- See *Writing About Reading,* pages 147–208.

NARRATIVE WRITING (Purpose–to tell a story)

FICTION

▶ Understanding the Genre

- Understand that fiction genres include realistic fiction, historical fiction, traditional literature (folktale, tall tale, fairy tale, fable, myth, legend, ballad), and fantasy (including science fiction)
- Understand that fiction can be written in various forms: e.g., narrative text, picture books, wordless picture books, poems, songs, plays, letters, short stories, diary or journal entries, narrative poetry
- Understand that an additional purpose of a fiction text is to explore a theme or teach a lesson
- Understand that a fiction text may involve one or more events in the life of a main character
- Understand that a writer uses various elements of fiction (e.g., setting, plot with problem and solution, characters) in a fiction text
- Understand the structure of narrative, including lead or beginning, introduction of characters, setting, problem, series of events, resolution of problem, and ending
- Understand that the setting of fiction may be current or historical
- Understand that writers can learn to craft fiction by using mentor texts as models
- Use the terms *realistic fiction, historical fiction, folktale, tall tale, fairy tale, fable, myth, legend, epic, ballad, fantasy,* and *science fiction* to describe the genre

▶ Writing in the Genre

- Write a fiction story, either realistic or fantasy
- With fantasy, include imaginative character, setting, and plot elements
- Begin with a compelling lead to capture reader's attention
- Describe the setting with appropriate detail
- Develop a plot that includes tension and one or more scenes
- Show the problem of the story and how one or more characters responds to it
- Assure that the events and setting for historical fiction are accurate
- Describe characters by how they look, what they do, say, and think, and what others say about them
- Show rather than tell how characters feel
- Take a point of view by writing in first or third person
- Write a believable and satisfying ending to the story

BIOGRAPHY, AUTOBIOGRAPHY, MEMOIR, AND NARRATIVE NONFICTION

▶ Understanding the Genre

- Understand that narrative nonfiction genres include biography, autobiography, and memoir, and narrative nonfiction
- Understand that biographical texts can be written in various forms: e.g., biographical sketches, autobiographical sketches, personal narratives, poems, songs, plays, photo essays, speeches, letters, diary or journal entries
- Understand biography as a true account of a person's life
- Understand autobiography as a true account of a person's life written and narrated by that person
- Understand that a biography or an autobiography can be about the person's whole life or a part of it
- Understand that the writer of a biography or autobiography needs to select the most important events in a person's life
- Establish the significance of events and personal decisions made by the subject of a biography or autobiography
- Understand memoir or personal narrative as a brief, often intense, memory of or reflection on a person, time, or event
- Understand that a memoir has significance in the writer's life and usually shows something significant to others
- Understand that a memoir can be composed of a series of vignettes
- Understand that a biography, autobiography, or memoir may have characteristics of fiction (e.g., setting, conflict, characters, dialogue, and resolution) even though the events are true or that it can be completely factual
- Understand the difference between true biography and fictionalized biography
- Write various kinds of biographical texts by studying mentor texts
- Understand that a narrative nonfiction text includes selected important events and turning points
- Understand that a narrative nonfiction text often includes an underlying structural pattern such as cause and effect or problem and solution
- Understand that a narrative nonfiction text indicates passing of time using words (e.g., *then, after a time*), dates and periods of time, and ages of people
- Understand that the setting may be important in a narrative nonfiction text
- Understand that a narrative nonfiction text includes people that are real
- Understand that a narrative nonfiction text often includes quotes of a person's exact words
- Understand that a narrative nonfiction text should include only true events and people and may require research
- Use the terms *biography, biographical sketch, autobiography, autobiographical sketch, personal narrative, memoir, narrative nonfiction, poem, song, play, letter, diary entry, journal entry, photo essay,* and *speech*

Selecting Purpose, Genre, and Form (cont.)

Writing

NARRATIVE WRITING (Purpose–to tell a story) (continued)

BIOGRAPHY, AUTOBIOGRAPHY, MEMOIR, AND NARRATIVE NONFICTION (continued)

▶ **Writing in the Genre**

- Choose a subject and state a reason for the selection
- **Write an engaging lead that captures interest and that may foreshadow the content**
- Select important events and turning points to include and exclude extraneous events and details
- Select and write personal experiences as "small moments" and share thinking and feelings about them
- Use small moments or experiences to communicate a bigger message
- Reveal something important about self or about life
- Create a series of vignettes that together communicate a bigger message
- Use words that show the passage of time in a variety of ways
- Tell events in chronological order or use another structural pattern: e.g., description, temporal sequence, question and answer, cause and effect, compare and contrast, problem and solution, categorization
- Describe and develop a setting and explain how it is related to the writer's experiences
- Describe the subject's important decisions and a turning point in the narrative
- Describe the subject by what she did or said as well as others' opinions
- Show the significance of the subject
- Show how the subject changes
- Describe people by how they look, what they do, say, and think, and what others say about them
- Use dialogue as appropriate to add to the meaning of the narrative
- Experiment with literary language (powerful nouns and verbs, figurative language)
- Write an ending that fits the piece
- **Select important events and turning points to include in narrative nonfiction**
- Show cause and effect and/or problem and solution as appropriate in writing narrative nonfiction
- Include quotes from real people in a narrative nonfiction text and place them in quotation marks with appropriate references

INFORMATIONAL WRITING
(Purpose–to explain or give facts about a topic)

EXPOSITORY TEXT

▶ **Understanding the Genre**

- Understand that a writer creates an expository text for readers to learn about a topic

- Understand that to write an expository text, the writer needs to become very knowledgeable about a topic
- Understand that an expository text may require research and will require organization
- **Understand that an expository text can be written in various forms: e.g., essay, report, feature article, photo essay, speech**
- Understand than an essay is a short composition used to explain a topic and/or give the writer's point of view about a topic
- Understand the basic structure of an essay: e.g., introduction, body, conclusion
- Understand that a report is a formal presentation of a topic
- Understand that a report may include several categories of information about a single topic
- Understand that a report has an introductory section, followed by more information in categories or sections
- Understand that a feature article usually focuses on one aspect of a topic
- Understand that a feature article begins with a lead paragraph, with more detailed information in subsequent paragraphs, and a conclusion
- Understand that a feature article reveals the writer's point of view about–and often his or her fascination with–the topic or subject
- Understand that a speech is a formal text written to be delivered orally to a public audience
- Understand that a factual text may use literary language and literary techniques to engage and entertain readers as it gives them factual information
- Understand that a writer can learn how to write various forms of expository text from mentor texts
- **Use the terms *expository text, essay, report, news article, feature article, photo essay,* and *speech* to describe the genre and forms**

▶ **Writing in the Genre**

- Use illustrations and book and print features (e.g., labeled pictures, diagrams, table of contents, headings, subheadings, sidebars, boxes of facts set off from other text, page numbers) to guide the reader
- Write a piece that is interesting and enjoyable to read
- Write about a topic that is interesting and substantive and to which the writer is committed, keeping in mind the audience and their interests and likely background knowledge
- Provide information that teaches or informs readers about a topic
- **Write an engaging lead and first section that orient the reader and provide an introduction to the topic**
- Organize information using categorization or another underlying structural pattern: e.g., description, temporal sequence, question and answer, cause and effect, chronological sequence, compare and contrast, problem and solution
- Provide interesting supporting details that develop a topic
- Include facts, figures, statistics, examples, and anecdotes when appropriate

Selecting Purpose, Genre, and Form *(cont.)*

Writing

- Use quotes from experts (written texts, speeches, or interviews) when appropriate
- Credit sources of information as appropriate
- Use some vocabulary specific to the topic
- Use literary language to make topic interesting to readers
- Reveal the writer's convictions about the topic through a unique voice
- Write multiple paragraphs with smooth transitions
- Write an effective conclusion

PERSUASIVE WRITING *(Purpose—to persuade)*

PERSUASIVE TEXT

▶ **Understanding the Genre**

- Understand that argument and persuasive texts can be written in various forms: e.g., editorial, letter to the editor, essay, speech
- Understand that the purpose of a persuasive text or argument may be to convince the reader to take the writer's point of view on an issue, to take some action, to critique society, or to improve some aspect of the world
- Understand that an editorial is a formal text with a public audience
- Understand that a letter to the editor is formal text with a public audience: e.g., the editor of a publication and its readers
- Understand that a letter to the editor has parts: e.g., date, formal salutation, body organized into paragraphs, closing, signature and title of sender
- Understand than an essay is a formal text often written for a teacher or a test
- Understand that a speech is a formal text written to be delivered orally with the intent of persuading an audience to believe or do something
- Understand the importance of supporting each idea or argument with facts, reasons, or examples
- Use the terms *argument, persuasive text, editorial, letter to the editor, essay,* and *speech* to describe the genre and forms
- Understand that a writer can learn to write various forms of argument or persuasion by studying the characteristics of examples in mentor texts

▶ **Writing in the Genre**

- Write an editorial, a letter to the editor, or an essay
- Address the audience appropriately according to the form
- Choose topics from stories or everyday observations
- Begin with a title or opening that tells the reader what is being argued or explained and conclude with a summary
- Provide a series of clear arguments with reasons to support the argument
- Include important information and exclude unnecessary details
- Use opinions supported by facts
- Provide "expert testimony" or quotes to support argument
- Organize the body of the text into paragraphs

- Write well-crafted sentences that express the writer's convictions
- Write a logical, thoughtful ending
- Include illustrations, charts, or diagrams as necessary

POETIC WRITING *(Purpose—to express feelings, sensory images, ideas, or stories)*

POETRY

▶ **Understanding the Genre**

- Understand poetry as a unique way to communicate about and describe feelings, sensory images, ideas, or stories
- Understand that a writer can create different types of poems: e.g., narrative poem, limerick, haiku, concrete poem
- Understand the importance of specific word choice in poetry
- Understand the difference between poetic language and ordinary language
- Notice the beat or rhythm of a poem and its relation to line breaks
- Understand the way print works in poems and demonstrate the use in reading and writing them on a page using white space and line breaks
- Understand that poems take a variety of shapes
- Understand that poems do not have to rhyme
- Use the terms *poem, narrative poem, limerick, haiku,* and *concrete poem* to describe specific types of poetry
- Understand that a writer can learn to write a variety of poems from studying mentor texts

▶ **Writing in the Genre**

- Observe closely to select topics or content and write with detail
- Use words to convey images and strong feelings
- Use figurative language and other literary devices such as alliteration, onomatopoeia, simile, metaphor, and personification
- Select topics that are significant and help readers see in a new way
- Select topics that have strong meaning
- Use white space and line breaks to communicate the meaning and tone of the poem
- Understand the role of line breaks, white space for pause, breath, or emphasis
- Shape words on a page to look like a poem
- Remove extra words to clarify the meaning and make the writing more powerful
- Use repetition, refrain, rhythm, and other poetic techniques
- Use words to show not tell
- Write a variety of types of poems
- Write a poetic text in response to another poem, reflecting the same style, topic, mood, or voice
- Write a poetic text in response to prose text, either narrative or informational
- Choose a title that communicates the meaning of a poem

WRITING

Selecting Purpose, Genre, and Form (cont.)

Writing

HYBRID WRITING

HYBRID TEXT

▶ **Understanding the Genre**

- Understand that a hybrid text mixes two or more genres
- Understand that a hybrid text blends two genres in order to communicate information in different ways: e.g., through prose narrative, poem, and list
- Understand that a writer uses more than one genre to increase engagement or make the text come alive
- Understand that the genres in the text must be integrated into a harmonious whole that communicates a message
- Use the term *hybrid* text to describe the genre
- Understand that a writer can learn how to write hybrid texts by studying mentor texts

▶ **Writing in the Genre**

- Select different genres with a clear purpose in mind
- Write pieces of the text in different genres according to purpose
- Integrate the genres to create a coherent whole
- Transition smoothly from one tense to another
- Transition smoothly from writing in one person to writing in another (for example, from first person to third person)
- Guide the reader so that the transitions between genres are accessible

---

Julio the Bear
By: Chris Han

Last month I found a bear at recess! It was a cute little bear. I took it home, got yelled at, the usual thing that happens when you bring home a baby bear. It was a hard thing taking care of a bear. Now that it's out in the wild, I'm not taking a bear home anymore. Done that, been there, don't want to go back.

It was usual day at Annandale Terrace Elementary School. The sun was out, people talking loudly, yep. I was out on the field near the kickball area. All of a sudden, THUMP. "What the-…Holy Toledo!" A 2 foot baby bear just thumped my on the head. I ran away from the bear, which didn't work really well since it was faster than me. I got tired after 1 minute of running; the teachers patrolling at recess should look out better. I figured I better stop, I was going to die anyway. I dropped to the ground to accept my faith. I felt coldness on my cheek; he must be ready to bite my head off. I opened my eyes, he was licking my cheek! He wasn't half bad at all. I decided to keep him for a while. I lined up and waited for school to end.

At dismissal, I ran out to the filed. I found the bear, and petted him for a while. "I guess I'll call you Julio." Finally I got back to my senses, WHAT ARE MY PARENTS GOING TO SAY! But that only lasted for a second, I brought him home anyway. When I entered the door, I left Julio on the porch. Julio thumped me to make me think straight. Oh

gosh, my parents are home. "What is this…?" My mom said surprised. It's Julio." I replied nervously. "What's with the bear?!" My mom yelled. "Um mom…Let's discuss in the house." After a couple minutes of "discussion", we came to a conclusion. I could keep him for a day. (He wasn't that big anyway.).

I brought him to my room wondering what to do with him. I took a nap with him; he's so cuddly, like a teddy bear! We played catch, he broke my ball. We played basketball, he broke that too. I decided balls aren't a good idea. We started to wrestle; we rolled down the hill, and rolled in a mud puddle. When mom called us inside to eat, she commanded us to take a bath. It was fun washing a bear while you in it. It's like washing a dog. I fed Julio some of my steak. After dinner we got sleepy since I haven't played this much before. The next day, I gave Julio some of my eggs and toast. I decided to walk to school to spend as much time as Julio as a can before I let him go. A lot of people stared at us while walking to Annandale Terrace. When I was around school grounds, I let him go in the forest. I hugged him and he thumped me. I'll miss his thumps. I waited for him to go till I couldn't see him again.

It was fun having Julio around, just like a baby brother. I had the best time with Julio around. If I haven't found him, I would probably be bored lying in my bed with nothing to do. Julio was kind of like best friend. The kind where he jokes around with you knowing you don't mean them. Taking care of him wasn't even that hard. I wish he could've stayed longer.

A fifth grader's story about an unusual pet

Selecting Goals Behaviors and Understandings to Notice, Teach, and Support

Writing

CRAFT

ORGANIZATION

▶ Text Structure

- Use organization in writing that is related to purpose and genre (letters, essays)
- Make decisions about where in a text to place features such as photographs with legends, insets, sidebars, and graphics
- Write fictional narratives with characters involved in a plot, events ordered by time
- Write fiction and nonfiction narratives that are ordered chronologically
- Use underlying structural patterns to present different kinds of information in nonfiction: e.g., description, temporal sequence, question and answer, cause and effect, chronological sequence, compare and contrast, problem and solution, categorization

▶ Beginnings, Ending, Titles

- Begin with a purposeful and engaging lead
- Begin a narrative at the beginning, middle, or end
- Use a variety of beginnings and endings to engage the reader
- End a narrative with problem resolution and a satisfying conclusion
- Understand that narratives can begin at the beginning, middle, or end
- End an informational piece with a thoughtful or enlightening conclusion
- Select an appropriate title for a poem, story, or informational book
- Generate multiple titles for the piece and select the one that best fits the content of an informational piece or the plot or characterization in a narrative

▶ Presentation of Ideas

- Tell one part, idea, event, or group of ideas on each page of a book
- Present ideas clearly and in a logical sequence or categories
- Organize information according to purpose and genre
- Show topics and subtopics by using headings and subheadings
- Use paragraphs to organize ideas
- Use well-crafted transitions to support the pace and flow of the writing
- Introduce ideas with facts, details, examples, and explanations from multiple authorities
- Introduce ideas followed by supportive details and examples
- Use time appropriately as an organizing tool
- Show steps in enough detail that a reader can follow a sequence
- Bring a piece to closure through an ending or summary statement
- Use headings, subheadings, a table of contents, and other features to help the reader find information and understand how facts are related in expository writing
- Use graphics (diagrams, illustrations, photos, charts) to provide information
- Use vocabulary specific to the topic or content

IDEA DEVELOPMENT

- Understand the difference between developing a narrative (or plot) and giving information using description, cause and effect, compare and contrast, problem and solution, or categorization
- Introduce, develop, and conclude the topic or story
- Hold the reader's attention with clear, focused content
- Structure a narrative and sustain writing to develop it logically
- Develop a logical plot by creating a story problem and addressing it over multiple events until it is resolved
- Understand how information helps the reader learn about a topic
- Gather and internalize information and then write it in own words
- Engage the reader with ideas that show strong knowledge of the topic
- Communicate clearly the main points intended for the reader to understand
- Arrange information in a logical way so that ideas build on one another
- Provide supporting details that are accurate, relevant, interesting, and vivid

LANGUAGE USE

- Understand that the writer is using language to communicate meaning
- Show evidence of using language from story books and informational books that have been read aloud
- Learn ways of using language and constructing texts from other writers (reading books and hearing them read aloud) and apply understandings to one's own writing
- Continue to learn from other writers by borrowing ways with words, phrases, and sentences
- Use memorable words or phrases
- Vary language and style as appropriate to audience and purpose
- Use language to show instead of tell
- Use language to give directions
- Find and write language to explain abstract concepts and ideas
- Use language to clearly state main ideas and supporting details
- Use examples to make meaning clear
- Use particular language typical of different genres
- Use language to develop arguments and support with evidence
- Use language to create sensory images
- Use language to elicit feelings
- Use figurative language (e.g., simile, metaphor, personification) to make comparisons
- Use variety in sentence structure and sentence length
- Use concrete sensory details and descriptive language to develop plot (tension and problem resolution) and setting in memoir, biography, and fiction
- Use descriptive language and dialogue to present characters/subjects who appear in narratives (memoir, biography, and fiction) and informational writing
- Use language to show feelings of characters

Selecting Goals Behaviors and Understandings to Notice, Teach, and Support *(cont.)*

Writing

CRAFT *(continued)*

LANGUAGE USE *(continued)*

- Use dialogue and action to draw readers into the story
- Select a point of view with which to tell a story
- Use language to establish a point of view
- Understand the differences between first and third person
- Write in both first and third person and understand the differences in effect so as to choose appropriately
- Arrange simple and complex sentences for an easy flow and sentence transition
- Vary sentence length to create feeling or mood and communicate meaning
- Use repeated language for particular purposes
- Use a variety of transitions and connections: e.g., words, phrases, sentences, and paragraphs
- Use linking words and phrases to connect opinion and reasons
- Use language with efficiency while writing: e.g., trimming words, combining sentences

WORD CHOICE

- Learn new words from reading and try them out in writing
- Use vocabulary appropriate for the topic
- Choose the best words to fit the writer's purpose and meaning
- Choose words with the audience in mind
- Use range of descriptive words to enhance meaning
- Vary word choice to create interesting description and dialogue
- Select words to make meanings memorable
- Use strong nouns and verbs
- Use colorful modifiers and style as appropriate to audience and purpose
- Use words that convey an intended mood or effect
- Show ability to vary the text by choosing alternative words: e.g., *replied, cried, exclaimed, muttered, whispered, barked, sneered, whined* for *said*
- Learn and use content words typical of disciplinary language: e.g., science, history, math, social studies
- Where needed, use academic language in an appropriate way to write about topics in various disciplines
- Use common (simple) connectives and some sophisticated connectives (words that link ideas and clarify meaning) that are used in written texts but do not appear often in everyday oral language: e.g., *although, however, therefore, though, unless, whenever*

VOICE

- Write about personal experiences with voice
- Write in an expressive way but also recognize how language in a book would sound
- Write in a way that speaks directly to the reader
- Show enthusiasm and energy for the topic
- Write in a way that shows care and commitment to the topic
- Write with voice as well as begin to develop literary voice
- Use engaging titles and language
- Include details that add to the voice
- Use dialogue selectively to communicate voice
- Use punctuation to make the text clear, effective, interesting, and to support voice
- Produce narrative writing that is engaging, honest, and reveals the person behind the writing
- Produce expository writing that reveals the stance of the writer toward the topic
- Produce persuasive writing including argument with logical evidence to support ideas and to counter opposing argument
- Read writing aloud to help think critically about voice

CONVENTIONS

For additional information about grammar and usage, capitalization, punctuation, and spelling, see Appendix: Grammar, Usage, and Mechanics.

TEXT LAYOUT

- Arrange print on the page to support the text's meaning and to help the reader notice important information
- Use layout of print and illustrations to convey the meaning of a text
- Use layout of print and illustrations (e.g., drawings, photos, maps, diagrams) to convey the meaning in a nonfiction text
- Use layout, spacing, and size of print to create titles, headings, and subheadings
- Incorporate book and print features (e.g., labeled pictures, diagrams, table of contents, headings, subheadings, sidebars, page numbers) into nonfiction writing
- Use the size of print to convey meaning in printed text
- Use underlining, italics, and bold print to convey a specific meaning
- Use underlining for words in titles
- Use indentation or spacing to set off paragraphs

GRAMMAR AND USAGE

▶ **Parts of Speech**

- Recognize and use the eight parts of speech of the English language in an accepted, standard way
- Use subject-verb agreement: e.g., *astronaut is; astronauts are*
- Use objective and nominative case pronouns in an accepted, standard way: e.g., *me, him, her; I, he, she*
- Use indefinite and relative pronouns correctly: e.g., *everyone, both; that, who, whose*
- Correctly use verbs that are often misused: e.g., *lie/lay; rise/raise*

Selecting Goals Behaviors and Understandings to Notice, Teach, and Support *(cont.)*

Writing

▶ Tense

- Use the same tense for two or more actions happening at the same time: e.g., *I poured the milk into the bowl and called the kitten's name*
- Use different tenses to show two or more actions happening at different times: e.g., *the kitten laps up the milk I poured an hour ago*
- Write sentences in present, past, future, present perfect, and past perfect tenses as needed to express meaning

▶ Sentence Structure

- Write complete sentences (subject and predicate)
- Use a range of types of sentences: e.g., declarative, interrogative, imperative, exclamatory
- Use conventional sentence structure for simple sentences, compound sentences, and complex sentences with embedded clauses
- Sometimes vary sentence structure and length for reasons of craft
- Place phrases in sentences
- Place clauses in sentences
- Write sentences in past, present, future, present perfect, and past perfect tenses as fits intended meaning and purpose
- Write dialogue in conventional structures

▶ Paragraphing

- Understand and use paragraph structure (indented or block) to organize sentences that focus on one idea
- Create transitions between paragraphs to show the progression of ideas
- Understand and use paragraphs to show speaker change in dialogue

CAPITALIZATION

- Use a capital letter in the first word of a sentence
- Use capital letters appropriately for the first letter in days, months, holidays, city and state names, and in titles
- Use capital letters correctly in dialogue
- Use capitalization for specialized functions (emphasis, key information, voice)
- Use more complex capitalization with increasing accuracy, such as in abbreviations and with quotation marks in split dialogue

PUNCTUATION

- Consistently use periods, exclamation marks, and question marks as end marks in a conventional way
- Read one's writing aloud and think about where to place punctuation
- Understand and use ellipses to show pause or anticipation, often before something surprising
- Use dashes correctly to indicate a longer pause or slow down the reading to emphasize particular information
- Use commas and quotation marks correctly in writing uninterrupted and interrupted dialogue as well as to show a verbatim quote
- Use apostrophes correctly in contractions and possessives
- Use commas correctly to separate an introductory clause or items in a series, or to set off a person's name in direct address

- Use commas and parentheses correctly to separate parenthetical information
- Divide words correctly at the syllable break and at the end of a line using a hyphen
- Use colons correctly to introduce a list of items or a long, formal statement or quotation
- Use semicolons correctly to separate independent clauses that are closely related in thought but are not joined by a conjunction
- Use brackets to separate a different idea or kind of information
- Use indentation to identify paragraphs
- Notice the role of punctuation in the craft of writing
- Try out new ways of using punctuation
- Study mentor texts to learn the role of punctuation in adding voice to writing

SPELLING

- Spell over 500 familiar high-frequency words, a wide range of plurals, and base words with inflectional endings and reflect spelling in final drafts
- Use a range of spelling strategies to take apart and spell multisyllable words (word parts, connections to known words, complex sound-to-letter cluster relationships)
- Use reference tools to check on spelling when editing final draft (dictionary, digital resources)
- Spell complex plurals correctly: e.g., *knife/knives, woman/women, sheep/sheep*
- Spell a full range of contractions, plurals, possessives, and compound words
- Spell words that have been studied (spelling words)
- Spell multisyllable words that have vowel and *r*
- Be aware of the spelling of common suffixes: e.g., *-ion, -ment, -ly*
- Use difficult homophones (*their, there*) correctly
- Monitor own spelling by noticing when a word does not "look right" and should be checked

HANDWRITING AND WORD-PROCESSING

- Write fluently and legibly in cursive handwriting with appropriate spacing
- Use efficient keyboarding skills to create drafts, revise, edit, and publish
- Use word-processor to get ideas down, revise, edit, and publish
- Use word-processing with understanding of how to produce and vary text (layout, font, special techniques) according to purpose, audience, etc.
- Show familiarity with computer and word-processing terminology
- Create website entries and articles with appropriate text layout, graphics, and access to information through searching
- Make wide use of computer skills in presenting text

Selecting Goals Behaviors and Understandings to Notice, Teach, and Support *(cont.)*

Writing

WRITING PROCESS

PLANNING AND REHEARSING

▶ Purpose

- Write for a specific main purpose and sometimes also for one or more secondary purposes: e.g., to inform; to explain or give facts about a topic; to instruct; to entertain; to tell or retell a story; to express feelings, sensory images, ideas, or stories; to persuade; to perform a practical task; to reflect; to plan; to maintain relationships
- Understand how the purpose of the writing influences the selection of genre
- Select the genre for the writing based on the purpose
- Tell whether a piece of writing is functional, narrative, informational, or poetic
- Have clear goals and understand how the goals will affect the writing

▶ Audience

- Write with specific readers or audience in mind
- Understand that writing is shaped by the writer's purpose and understanding of the audience
- Plan and organize information for the intended readers
- Understand audience as all readers rather than just the teacher

▶ Oral Language

- Generate and expand ideas through talk with peers and teacher
- Look for ideas and topics in personal experiences, shared through talk
- Use talk and storytelling to generate and rehearse language that may be written later
- Explore relevant questions in talking about a topic
- When rehearsing language for an informational piece, use vocabulary specific to the topic
- When rehearsing language for a narrative writing, use action and content words appropriate for the story

▶ Gathering Seeds/Resources/Experimenting with Writing

- Use a writer's notebook or booklet as a tool for collecting ideas, experimenting, planning, sketching, or drafting
- Reread a writer's notebook to select topics: e.g., select small moments that can be expanded
- Use sketching, webs, lists, and freewriting to think about, plan for, and try out writing
- Gather a variety of entries (e.g., character map, timeline, sketches, observations, freewrites, drafts, lists) in a writer's notebook
- Think through a topic, focus, organization, and audience
- Try out titles, different headings and endings, develop setting and characters in a writer's notebook
- Use notebooks to plan, gather, and rehearse for future published writing
- Plan for a story by living inside the story, gaining insight into characters so that the story can be written as it happens

- Make a plan for an essay that makes a claim and contains supporting evidence
- Choose helpful tools: e.g., webs, T-charts, sketches, charts, diagrams, lists, outlines, flowcharts
- Choose a setting and describe in details that evoke a particular mood or tone

▶ Content, Topic, Theme

- Observe carefully events, people, settings, and other aspects of the world to gather information on a topic
- Select information that will support the topic
- Choose topics that one knows about, cares about, or wants to learn about
- Choose topics that are interesting to the writer
- Tell about a topic in an interesting way
- Stay focused on a topic to produce a well-organized piece of writing that is long enough to fully explain the points (e.g., facts, arguments) the writer wants to make
- Get ideas from other books and writers about how to approach a topic: e.g., organization, point of view, layout
- Communicate the significance of the topic to an audience
- Show the audience (by stating or providing important information) what is important about the topic
- Use texts (print and online) to get information on a topic
- Select details that will support a topic or story
- Select title that fits the content to publish or complete as final draft
- Develop a clear, main idea around which a piece of writing will be planned
- Use the organizing features of electronic text (e.g., bulletin boards, databases, keyword searches, email addresses) to locate information
- Understand a range of genres and forms and select from them according to topic and purpose and audience

▶ Inquiry/Research/Exploration

- Make scientific observations, use notes and sketches to document them, and talk with others about patterns, connections, and discoveries
- Form questions to explore and locate sources for information about a topic, characters, or setting
- Select and include only the information that is appropriate to the topic and to the category
- Use notes to record and organize information
- Conduct research to gather information in planning a writing project: e.g., live interviews, Internet, artifacts, articles, books
- Create categories of information
- Determine when research is necessary to cover a nonfiction topic adequately
- Search for appropriate information from multiple sources: e.g., books and other print materials, websites, interview
- Understand the concept of plagiarism
- Understand that a writer gains ideas from other writers but should credit the other writers and/or put these ideas into one's own words

Selecting Goals Behaviors and Understandings to Notice, Teach, and Support *(cont.)*

Writing

- Record sources of information for citation
- Understand that a writer may quote another writer by placing the exact words in quotes and referencing the source

▶ **Genre/Forms**

- Select the genre for the writing based on the purpose: e.g., formal letter, procedural text; realistic fiction, historical fiction, traditional literature (folktale, tall tale, fairy tale, fable, myth, legend, epic, ballad), and fantasy (including science fiction); biography, autobiography, memoir, narrative nonfiction; expository text; persuasive text; poetry; hybrid text
- Choose a form for the writing: e.g., notes, cards, letters, invitations, email, lists, directions with steps (how-to); picture books, wordless picture books, poems, songs, plays, letters, short stories, diary and journal entries, narrative poetry, biographical and autobiographical sketches, personal narratives; essays, reports, news and feature articles, photo essays, speeches; editorials, letters to the editor

DRAFTING AND REVISING

▶ Understanding the Process

- Understand the role of the writer, teacher, or peer writer in conference
- Change writing in response to peer or teacher feedback
- Know how to use an editing and proofreading checklist
- Understand revision as a means for making written messages stronger and clearer to readers
- Understand that a writer rereads and revises while drafting (recursive process) and they keep doing it over and over with new pieces of writing
- Name, understand the purpose of, try out, and internalize crafting techniques
- Use writers as mentors in making revisions and revisions while drafting (recursive process)
- Use mentor texts in making revisions and publishing

▶ Producing a Draft

- Write a continuous message, sometimes organized into categories that are related to a larger topic or idea
- Use drawings to add information to, elaborate on, or increase readers' enjoyment and understanding
- Write a draft or discovery draft (writing fast and as much as possible on a topic)
- Understand the importance of the lead in a story or nonfiction piece
- Begin to develop a style for drafting: e.g., from slow, deliberate drafting with ongoing revision, to fast writing of ideas for revision later
- Revise the lead to find the most interesting and engaging language
- Bring the piece to closure with an effective summary, parting idea, or satisfying ending
- Establish an initiating event and follow with a series of events in a narrative
- Present ideas in logical order across the piece
- Maintain central idea or focus across paragraphs

- Produce a series of coherent paragraphs that present information logically and lead readers through the nonfiction piece or story
- Show steps or phases in time order when incorporating temporal or chronological sequence into a nonfiction text
- Establish a situation, plot or problem, and point of view in fiction drafts
- Provide insight as to why an incident or event is memorable
- When writing a biography, memoir, or fiction story, establish important decisions (made by the central character or subject) and the outcomes of those decisions
- Generate multiple titles to help think about the focus of the piece
- Select a title that fits the content

▶ Rereading

- Reread writing to think about what to write next
- Reread writing to rethink and make changes
- Reread and revise the discovery draft or rewrite sections to clarify meaning
- Reread the text to be sure there are no missing words or information
- Identify language in the story that shows character change (or learning a lesson in a memoir)
- Identify the statement (and sometimes restatement) of the main idea of a piece
- Identify the turning point of a story and/or the most exciting part of a story
- Reread writing to check for clarity and purpose
- Identify information that may be related to the topic
- Identify information that either distracts from or does not contribute to the central purpose and message

▶ Adding Information

- Add ideas in thought bubbles or dialogue in quotation marks or speech bubbles to provide information, provide narration, or show thoughts and feelings
- Add descriptive words (adjectives, adverbs) and phrases to help readers visualize and understand events, actions, processes, or topics
- Add words, phrases, or sentences to make the writing more interesting or exciting for readers
- Add words, phrases, or sentences to provide more information to readers
- Add word, phrases, or sentences to clarify meaning for readers
- After reflection and rereading, add substantial pieces of text (paragraphs, pages) to provide further explanation, clarify points, add interest, or support points
- Add details or examples to make the piece clearer or more interesting
- Add transitional words and phrases to clarify meaning and make the writing smoother
- Reread and change or add words to ensure that meaning is clear
- Add descriptive words and details to writing or drawings to enhance meaning, not simply to add information
- Add information in footnotes or endnotes

WRITING

Selecting Goals Behaviors and Understandings to Notice, Teach, and Support *(cont.)*

Writing

WRITING PROCESS *(continued)*

DRAFTING AND REVISING *(continued)*

▶ Deleting Information

- Delete text to better express meaning and make more logical
- Delete words or sentences that do not make sense or do not fit the topic or message
- Delete pages or paragraphs when information is not needed
- Identify redundant words, phrases, or sentences or paragraphs and remove if they do not serve a purpose or enhance the voice
- Reread and cross out words to ensure that meaning is clear

▶ Changing a Text

- Identify vague parts and provide specificity
- Vary word choice to make the piece more interesting
- Work on transitions to achieve better flow
- Reshape writing to make the text into a different genre: e.g., personal narrative to poem

▶ Reorganizing Information

- Rearrange and revise writing to better express meaning or make the text more logical (reorder drawings, reorder pages, cut and paste)
- Reorganize and revise the writing to better express the writer's meaning or make the text more logical
- Reorder pages or paragraphs by laying them out and reassembling them

▶ Using Tools and Techniques

- Add words, letters, phrases, or sentences using a variety of techniques: e.g., caret, sticky notes, spider's legs, numbered items on a separate page, word-processing
- Use a number to identify place to add information and an additional paper with numbers to write the information to insert
- Delete words, phrases, or sentences from a text (crossing out or using word-processing) to make the meaning clearer
- Reorder the information in a text to make the meaning clearer by cutting apart, cutting and pasting, laying out pages, using word-processing

EDITING AND PROOFREADING

▶ Understanding the Process

- Understand that a writer uses what is known to spell words
- Know how to use an editing and proofreading checklist
- Understand that a writer (after using what is known) can ask another person to do a final edit
- Understand the limitations of spell check and grammar check on the computer
- Understand how to use tools to self-evaluate writing and assist the writer in copyediting

▶ Editing for Conventions

- Check and correct letter formation
- Edit for the conventional spelling of known words
- Edit for spelling errors by circling words that do not look right and spelling them another way
- Understand that the teacher will be final spelling editor for the published piece after the student has used everything known
- Edit for capitalization and punctuation
- Edit for grammar and sentence sense
- Edit for word suitability and precise meaning
- Determine where new paragraphs should begin
- Check and correct spacing and layout
- Integrate quotations and citations into written text in a way that maintains the coherence and flow of the writing
- Prepare final draft with self-edit and submit (teacher edit prior to publishing)

▶ Using Tools

- Use reference tools to check on spelling and meaning
- Use a thesaurus to search for more interesting words
- Use spell check, accepting or rejecting changes as needed
- Use grammar check, accepting or rejecting changes as needed

PUBLISHING

- Produce writing to explain, label, or otherwise accompany drawing
- Create illustrations and writing that work together to express the meaning
- Create illustrations or other art for pieces that are in final form
- Share a text with peers by reading it aloud to the class
- Put several stories or poems together
- Select a poem, story, or informational book to publish in a variety of appropriate ways: e.g., typed/printed, framed and mounted or otherwise displayed
- Add cover spread with title and author information
- In anticipation of an audience, add book and print features during the publishing process: e.g., illustrations and other graphics, cover spread, title, dedication, table of contents, about the author piece, headings, subheadings
- Attend to layout of text in final publication
- Understand publishing as the sharing of a piece of writing with a purpose and an audience in mind
- Understand the importance of citing sources of information and some conventions for citation
- Add bibliography of sources where needed

Selecting Goals Behaviors and Understandings to Notice, Teach, and Support *(cont.)*

Writing

DRAWING

- Understand that when both writing and drawing are on a page, they are mutually supportive, with each extending the other
- Use sketches or drawings to represent people, places, and things, and also to communicate mood and abstract ideas as appropriate to the genre and form
- Create drawings that are related to the written text and increase readers' understanding and enjoyment
- Use sketching to support memory and help in planning
- Use sketching to capture detail that is important to a topic
- Provide important information in the illustrations
- Add detail to drawings to add information or increase interest
- Create drawings that employ careful attention to color or detail
- Understand the difference between drawing and sketching and use them to support the writing process
- Use sketching to create quick representations of images, usually an outline in pencil or pen
- Use sketches to create drawings in published pieces
- Use diagrams or other graphics to support the process and/or add meaning
- Sketch and draw with a sense of relative size and perspective
- Use the terms *sketching* and *drawing* to refer to these processes and forms

VIEWING SELF AS A WRITER

- Have topics and ideas for writing in a list or notebook
- Select examples of best writing in all genres attempted
- Self-evaluate writing and talk about what is good about it and what techniques were used
- Self-evaluate pieces of writing in light of what is known about a genre
- Produce a reasonable quantity of writing within the time available
- Write routinely over extended timeframes and shorter timeframes from a range of discipline-specific tasks, purposes, and audiences
- Write with independent initiative and investment
- Attend to the nuances of illustrations and how they enhance a text in order to try them out for oneself
- Take risks as a writer
- Write in a variety of genres across the year
- Understand writing as a vehicle to communicate something the writer thinks
- Discuss in the writing conference what one is working on as a writer
- Seek feedback on writing
- Be willing to work at the craft of writing, incorporating new learning from instruction
- Compare previous writing to revised writing and notice and talk about the differences
- State what was learned from each piece of writing
- Articulate goals as a writer
- Write with fluency and ease

- Notice what makes writing effective and name the craft or technique
- Show interest in and work at crafting good writing, applying what has been learned about crafting in each piece
- Suggest possible revisions to peers
- Understand that all revision is governed by the writer's decision-making of what will communicate meaning to the reader
- Mark the most important part of a piece of one's own or others' writing

Selecting Purpose, Genre, and Form

Writing

Sixth graders use writing across all genres to accomplish many purposes. They demonstrate independence in conceptualization and producing pieces. They have learned how conventions apply to the writer's craft, and though they use mentor texts well, they produce unique pieces that reflect their personality and interests. Sixth graders tackle complex genres such as essays and argument. They are able to self-evaluate and take more risks as writers.

FUNCTIONAL WRITING
(Purpose—to perform a practical task)

FORMAL LETTER

▶ **Understanding the Genre**

- Understand that a formal letter can be written in various forms: e.g., business letter
- Understand that a business letter is a formal document with a particular purpose
- Understand that a business letter has parts: e.g., date, inside address, formal salutation followed by a colon, body organized into paragraphs, closing, signature and title of sender, and sometimes notification of a copy or enclosure
- Understand that a writer can learn to write effective business letters by studying the characteristics of examples
- Use the term *business letter* to describe the form

▶ **Writing in the Genre**

- Write to a specified audience that may be an individual or an organization or group
- Address the audience appropriately
- Include important information and exclude unnecessary details
- Organize the body into paragraphs
- Understand the component parts of a business letter and how to lay them out on a page
- Write formal letters

TEST WRITING

▶ **Understanding the Genre**

- Understand that test writing often requires writing about an assigned topic
- Understand that test writing may involve creating expository texts or persuasive texts
- Understand that some test writing serves the purpose of demonstrating what a person knows or can do as a writer
- Understand that test writing can take various forms: e.g., short constructed response (sometimes called *short answer*), extended constructed response (or *essay*)
- Understand that test writing often requires writing about something real
- Understand that test writing involves analyzing what is expected of the writer, and then planning and writing a response that fits the criteria
- Understand test writing as a response carefully tailored to meet precise instructions

- Understand that test writing often requires taking a position, developing a clear argument, and providing evidence for points
- Understand that test writing often requires inferring and explaining the motives of a character or person
- Understand that test writing sometimes requires taking a perspective that may come from a different time or setting than the reader
- Learn how to write on tests by studying examples of short constructed responses and extended constructed responses
- Use the terms *test writing, short constructed response,* and *extended constructed response* to describe this type of functional writing

▶ **Writing in the Genre**

- Analyze prompts to determine purpose, audience, and genre (e.g., expository text, persuasive text) that is appropriate
- Read and internalize the criteria for an acceptable response
- Write focused responses to questions and to prompts
- Write concisely and to the direction of the question or prompt
- Reflect on bigger ideas and make or defend a claim that is substantiated
- Respond to a text in a way that reflects analytic or aesthetic thinking
- Restate a claim with further evidence
- State alternate points of view and critically analyze the evidence of each
- Elaborate on important points
- Incorporate one's knowledge of craft in shaping responses
- Proofread carefully for spelling and conventions

WRITING ABOUT READING

- See *Writing About Reading,* pages 147–208.

NARRATIVE WRITING *(Purpose—to tell a story)*

FICTION

▶ **Understanding the Genre**

- Understand that fiction genres include realistic fiction, historical fiction, traditional literature (folktale, tall tale, fairy tale, fable, myth, legend, ballad), and fantasy (including science fiction)
- Understand that fiction can be written in various forms: e.g., picture books, wordless picture books, poems, songs, plays, letters, short stories, diary or journal entries, narrative poetry, lyrical poetry, free verse, ballads
- Understand that an additional purpose of a fiction text is to explore a theme or teach a lesson
- Understand that a fiction text may involve one or more events in the life of a main character

Selecting Purpose, Genre, and Form *(cont.)*

Writing

- Understand that a writer uses various elements of fiction (e.g., setting, plot with problem and solution, characters) in a fiction text
- Understand that the setting of fiction may be current, historical, or imaginary
- Understand the structure of narrative, including lead or beginning, introduction of characters, setting, problem, series of events, resolution of problem, and ending
- Understand that a work of fiction may use time flexibly to begin after the end, at the end, in the middle, or at the beginning
- Understand that a fiction writer may use imagery or figurative language
- Understand that a fiction writer may use irony or satire
- Understand that writers can learn to craft fiction by using mentor texts as models
- Use the terms *realistic fiction, historical fiction, folktale, tall tale, fairy tale, fable, myth, legend, epic, ballad, fantasy,* and *science fiction* to describe the genre

▶ **Writing in the Genre**

- Write a fiction story, either realistic or fantasy
- With fantasy, include imaginative character, setting, and plot elements
- With fantasy, develop a consistent imaginary world
- Begin with a compelling lead to capture reader's attention
- Describe the setting with appropriate detail
- Develop a plot that is believable and engaging to readers
- Show the problem of the story and how one or more characters responds to it
- Move the plot along with action
- Show readers how the setting is important to the problem of the story
- Assure that the events and setting for historical fiction are accurate
- Describe and develop believable characters by showing how they look, what they do, say, and think, and what others say about them
- Show rather than tell how characters feel
- Show one or more characters' points of view by writing in first or third person
- Use dialogue skillfully in ways that show character traits and feelings
- Write a believable and satisfying ending to the story
- Experiment with literary features and devices such as imagery, figurative language, symbolism, irony, and satire

BIOGRAPHY, AUTOBIOGRAPHY, MEMOIR, AND NARRATIVE NONFICTION

▶ **Understanding the Genre**

- Understand that narrative nonfiction genres include biography, autobiography, and memoir, and narrative nonfiction
- Understand that biographical texts can be written in various forms: e.g., biographical sketches, autobiographical sketches, personal narratives, poems, songs, plays, photo essays, speeches, letters, diary or journal entries

- Understand biography as a true account of a person's life
- Understand autobiography as a true account of a person's life written and narrated by that person
- Understand that a biography or an autobiography can be about the person's whole life or a part of it
- Understand that biographers select their subjects to show their importance and impact
- Understand that a biographer reveals his or her own stance toward the subject by selection of information and by the way it is described
- Understand the need for a biographer to report all important information in an effort to take an unbiased view
- Understand the need to document evidence and cite sources
- Understand that a biography or autobiography may begin at any point in the story of a person's life
- Establish the significance of events and personal decisions made by the subject of a biography or autobiography
- Understand memoir or personal narrative as a brief, often intense, memory of or reflection on a person, time, or event
- Understand that a memoir has significance in the writer's life and usually shows something significant to others
- Understand that a memoir can be composed of a series of vignettes
- Understand that a biography, autobiography, or memoir may have characteristics of fiction (e.g., setting, conflict, characters, dialogue, and resolution) even though the events are true or that it can be completely factual
- Understand that a memoir can be written in first, second, or third person, although it is usually in first person
- Understand the difference between true biography and fictionalized biography
- Write various kinds of biographical texts by studying mentor texts
- Understand that a narrative nonfiction text includes selected important events and turning points
- Understand that a narrative nonfiction text often includes an underlying structural pattern such as cause and effect or problem and solution
- Understand that a narrative nonfiction text indicates passing of time using words (e.g., *then, after a time*), dates and periods of time, and ages of people
- Understand that the setting may be important in a narrative nonfiction text
- Understand that a narrative nonfiction text includes people that are real
- Understand that a narrative nonfiction text often includes quotes of a person's exact words
- Understand that a narrative nonfiction text should include only true events and people and may require research
- Use the terms *biography, biographical sketch, autobiography, autobiographical sketch, personal narrative, memoir, narrative nonfiction, poem, song, play, letter, diary entry, journal entry, photo essay, speech, lyrical poetry, free verse,* and *ballad*

Selecting Purpose, Genre, and Form *(cont.)*

Writing

BIOGRAPHY, AUTOBIOGRAPHY, MEMOIR, AND NARRATIVE NONFICTION *(continued)*

▶ Writing in the Genre

- Choose a subject and state a reason for the selection
- Write an engaging lead that captures interest and that may foreshadow the content
- Create interest in the subject by selecting and reporting information in an engaging way
- Select important events to include and exclude extraneous events and details
- Reveal the writer's point of view by giving the reasons for omitting significant parts of the subject's life: e.g., focusing on childhood or on the presidential years only
- Select and write personal experiences as "small moments" and share thinking and feelings about them
- Reveal something important about self or about life
- Create a series of vignettes that together communicate a bigger message
- Tell events in chronological order or use another structural pattern: e.g., description, temporal sequence, question and answer, cause and effect, compare and contrast, problem and solution, categorization
- Describe and develop a setting and explain how it is related to the writer's experiences
- Describe the subject's important decisions, and show how those decisions influenced his or her life or the lives of others
- Describe the subject by what she did or said as well as others' opinions
- Show how the subject changes
- Reveal the subject's feelings by describing actions or using quotations
- Describe people by how they look, what they do, say, and think, and what others say about them
- Use dialogue as appropriate to add to the meaning of the narrative, but understand that adding any undocumented information fictionalizes a biographical text to an extent
- Experiment with literary language (powerful nouns and verbs, figurative language)
- Write with imagery so that the reader understands the feelings of the writer or others
- Write an ending that fits the piece
- Select important events and turning points to include in narrative nonfiction
- Show cause and effect and/or problem and solution as appropriate in writing narrative nonfiction
- Include quotes from real people in a narrative nonfiction text and place them in quotation marks with appropriate references

EXPOSITORY TEXT

▶ Understanding the Genre

- Understand that a writer creates an expository text for readers to learn about a topic
- Understand that to write an expository text, the writer needs to become very knowledgeable about a topic
- Understand that an expository text may require research and will require organization
- Understand that an expository text can be written in various forms: e.g., essay, report, news article, feature article, photo essay, speech
- Understand than an essay is a short composition used to explain a topic and/or give the writer's point of view about a topic
- Understand the basic structure of an essay: e.g., introduction, body, conclusion
- Understand that an essay can be used to analyze one or more pieces of literature (see *Writing About Reading*, pages 161-222)
- Understand that a report is a formal presentation of a topic
- Understand that a report may include several categories of information about a single topic
- Understand that a report has an introductory section, followed by more information in categories or sections
- Understand that a feature article usually focuses on one aspect of a topic
- Understand that a feature article begins with a lead paragraph, with more detailed information in subsequent paragraphs, and a conclusion
- Understand that a feature article reveals the writer's point of view about–and often his or her fascination with–the topic or subject
- Understand that a speech is a formal text written to be delivered orally to a public audience
- Understand that a factual text may use literary language and literary techniques to engage and entertain readers as it gives them factual information
- Understand that a writer can learn how to write various forms of expository text from mentor texts
- Use the terms *expository text, essay, report, news article, feature article, photo essay,* and *speech* to describe the genre and forms

▶ Writing in the Genre

- Use illustrations and book and print features (e.g., labeled pictures, diagrams, table of contents, headings, subheadings, sidebars, boxes of facts set off from other text, page numbers) to guide the reader
- Write a piece that is interesting and enjoyable to read
- Write about a topic that is interesting and substantive and to which the writer is committed, keeping in mind the audience and their interests and likely background knowledge
- Provide information that teaches or informs readers about a topic
- Write with a wider audience in mind

Selecting Purpose, Genre, and Form (cont.)

Writing

- Help readers think in new ways about a subject or topic
- Write an engaging lead and first section that orient the reader and provide an introduction to the topic
- Organize information using categorization or another underlying structural pattern: e.g., description, temporal sequence, question and answer, cause and effect, chronological sequence, compare and contrast, problem and solution
- Provide interesting supporting details that develop a topic
- Include facts, figures, statistics, examples, and anecdotes when appropriate
- Use quotes from experts (written texts, speeches, or interviews) when appropriate
- Credit sources of information as appropriate
- Use some vocabulary specific to the topic
- Use literary language to make topic interesting to readers
- Reveal the writer's convictions about the topic through a unique voice
- Write multiple paragraphs with smooth transitions
- Write an effective conclusion

PERSUASIVE WRITING *(Purpose—to persuade)*

PERSUASIVE TEXT

▶ **Understanding the Genre**

- Understand that argument and persuasive texts can be written in various forms: e.g., editorial, letter to the editor, essay, speech
- Understand that the purpose of a persuasive text or argument may be to convince the reader to take the writer's point of view on an issue, to take some action, to critique society, or to improve some aspect of the world
- Understand that an editorial is a formal text with a public audience
- Understand that a letter to the editor is formal text with a public audience: e.g., the editor of a publication and its readers
- Understand that a letter to the editor has parts: e.g., date, formal salutation, body organized into paragraphs, closing, signature and title of sender
- Understand than an essay is a formal text often written for a teacher or a test
- Understand that a speech is a formal text written to be delivered orally with the intent of persuading the audience to believe or do something
- Understand the importance of supporting each idea or argument with facts, reasons, or examples
- Use the terms *argument, persuasive text, editorial, letter to the editor, essay,* and *speech* to describe the genre and forms
- Understand that a writer can learn to write various forms of argument or persuasion by studying the characteristics of examples in mentor texts

▶ **Writing in the Genre**

- Write an editorial, a letter to the editor, a speech, or an essay
- Address the audience appropriately according to the form

- Choose topics from stories or everyday observations
- Begin with a title or opening that tells the reader what is being argued or explained—a clearly stated thesis
- Provide a series of clear arguments with reasons to support the argument
- Include important information and exclude unnecessary details
- Use opinions supported by facts
- Provide "expert testimony" or quotes to support argument
- Organize the body of the text into paragraphs
- Write well-crafted sentences that express the writer's convictions
- Write a logical, thoughtful ending
- Include illustrations, charts, or diagrams as necessary

POETIC WRITING *(Purpose—to express feelings, sensory images, ideas, or stories)*

POETRY

▶ **Understanding the Genre**

- Understand poetry as a unique way to communicate about and describe feelings, sensory images, ideas, or stories
- Understand that a writer can create different types of poems: e.g., free verse, lyrical poem, narrative poem, ballad, limerick, haiku, concrete poem
- Understand the difference between poetic language and ordinary language
- Understand that poetry is a spare way of communicating deep meaning
- Notice the beat or rhythm of a poem and its relation to line breaks
- Understand the way print works in poems and demonstrate the use in reading and writing them on a page using white space and line breaks
- Understand that poetry often includes sensory images and symbolism
- Understand that different types of poems can be used to convey different moods
- Understand that different types of poems appeal to readers in different ways
- Use the terms *poem, free verse, lyrical poem, narrative poem, ballad, limerick, haiku,* and *concrete poem* to describe specific types of poetry
- Understand that a writer can learn to write a variety of poems from studying mentor texts

▶ **Writing in the Genre**

- Observe closely to select topics or content and write with detail
- Collect language and images as a basis for writing poetry
- Use words to convey images and strong feelings
- Use figurative language and other literary devices such as alliteration, onomatopoeia, simile, metaphor, personification, and symbolism
- Select topics that are significant and help readers see in a new way
- Select topics that have strong meaning

Selecting Purpose, Genre, and Form *(cont.)*

Writing

POETIC WRITING *(Purpose–to express feelings, sensory images, ideas, or stories) (continued)*

POETRY *(continued)*

▶ **Writing in the Genre** *(continued)*

- Use white space and line breaks to communicate the meaning and tone of the poem
- Understand the role of line breaks, white space for pause, breath, or emphasis
- Remove extra words to clarify the meaning and make the writing more powerful
- Use repetition, refrain, rhythm, and other poetic techniques
- Use words to show not tell
- Write a variety of types of poems according to purpose, topic, and meaning
- Write a poetic text in response to another poem, reflecting the same style, topic, mood, or voice
- Write a poetic text in response to prose text, either narrative or informational
- Choose a title that communicates the meaning of a poem
- Write a strong ending to a poem

HYBRID WRITING

HYBRID TEXT

▶ **Understanding the Genre**

- Understand that a hybrid text mixes two or more genres
- Understand that a hybrid text blends two genres in order to communicate information in different ways: e.g., through prose narrative, poem, and list
- Understand that a writer uses more than one genre to increase engagement or make the text come alive
- Understand that the genres in the text must be integrated into a harmonious whole that communicates a message
- Use the term *hybrid* text to describe the genre
- Understand that a writer can learn how to write hybrid texts by studying mentor texts

▶ **Writing in the Genre**

- Select different genres with a clear purpose in mind
- Write pieces of the text in different genres according to purpose
- Integrate the genres to create a coherent whole
- Transition smoothly from one tense to another
- Transition smoothly from writing in one person to writing in another (for example, from first person to third person)
- Guide the reader so that the transitions between genres are accessible

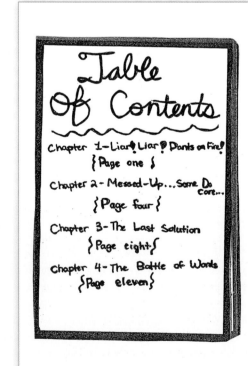

A sixth grader's fiction book

Selecting Goals Behaviors and Understandings to Notice, Teach, and Support

Writing

CRAFT

ORGANIZATION

▶ **Text Structure**

- Organize information to fit purpose: e.g., functional, narrative, informational, persuasive, poetic
- Make decisions about where in a text to place features such as photographs with legends, insets, sidebars, and graphics
- Write fictional narratives with characters involved in a plot, events ordered by time
- Write fiction and nonfiction narratives that are ordered chronologically
- Use underlying structural patterns to present different kinds of information in nonfiction: e.g., description, temporal sequence, question and answer, cause and effect, chronological sequence, compare and contrast, problem and solution, categorization
- Vary structural patterns to add interest to a piece

▶ **Beginnings, Ending, Titles**

- Decide whether a piece is unbiased or persuasive and use the decision to influence the lead and the development of ideas
- Begin with a purposeful and engaging lead that sets the tone for the piece
- Begin a narrative at the beginning, middle, or end
- Use a variety of beginnings and endings to engage the reader
- Engage readers' interest by presenting a problem, conflict, interesting person, or surprising information
- Bring a narrative text to a satisfying problem resolution and concluding scene
- End an informational text with a thoughtful or enlightening conclusion
- Bring the piece to closure, to a logical conclusion, through an ending or summary statement
- Select an appropriate title for a poem, story, or informational book
- Generate multiple title for the piece and select the one that best fits the content of an informational piece or the plot or characterization in a narrative

▶ **Presentation of Ideas**

- Order the writing in ways that are characteristic to the purpose and genre
- Put important ideas together to communicate about a topic (categories)
- Clearly show topics and subtopics and indicate them with headings and subheadings in expository writing
- Present reports that are clearly organized with introduction, facts and details to illustrate the important ideas, logical conclusions, and underlying structural patterns
- Introduce ideas followed by supportive details and examples
- Use time appropriately as an organizing tool
- Support ideas with facts, details, examples, and explanations from multiple authorities

- Use well-crafted paragraphs to organize ideas
- Establish a main or controlling idea that provides perspective on the topic
- Write arguments to support claims with clear reasons and relevant evidence
- Build tension by slowing down or speeding up scenes
- Use well-crafted transitions to support the pace and flow of the writing
- Show steps in enough detail that a reader can follow a sequence
- Bring a piece to closure through an ending or summary statement
- Use language to foreshadow the ending
- Write informative texts to examine a topic and convey ideas through the selection, organization, and analysis of relevant content
- Use graphics (diagrams, illustrations, photos, charts) to provide information
- Use vocabulary specific to the topic or content

IDEA DEVELOPMENT

- Understand the difference between developing a narrative (or plot) and giving information using description, cause and effect, compare and contrast, problem and solution, or categorization
- Introduce, develop, and conclude the topic or story
- Hold the reader's attention with clear, focused content
- Structure a narrative and sustain writing to develop it logically
- Develop a logical plot by creating a story problem and addressing it over multiple events until it is resolved
- Understand how information helps the reader learn about a topic
- Gather and internalize information and then write it in own words
- Engage the reader with ideas that show strong knowledge of the topic
- Communicate clearly the main points intended for the reader to understand
- Arrange information in a logical way so that ideas build on one another
- Provide supporting details that are accurate, relevant, interesting, and vivid

LANGUAGE USE

- Understand that the writer is using language to communicate meaning
- Show evidence of using language from story books and informational books that have been read aloud
- Learn ways of using language and constructing texts from other writers (reading books and hearing them read aloud) and apply understandings to one's own writing
- Continue to learn from other writers by borrowing ways with words, phrases, and sentences
- Use memorable words or phrases
- Vary language and style as appropriate to audience and purpose
- Use language to show instead of tell
- Use language to give directions
- Find and write language to explain abstract concepts and ideas

Selecting Goals Behaviors and Understandings to Notice, Teach, and Support *(cont.)*

Writing

CRAFT *(continued)*

LANGUAGE USE *(continued)*

- Use language to clearly state main ideas and supporting details
- Use examples to make meaning clear
- Use particular language typical of different genres
- Use language to develop arguments and support with evidence
- Use language to create sensory images
- Use figurative language (e.g., simile, metaphor, personification) to make comparisons
- Use variety in sentence structure and sentence length
- Use concrete sensory details and descriptive language to develop plot (tension and problem resolution) and setting in memoir, biography, and fiction
- Use descriptive language and dialogue to present characters/subjects who appear in narratives (memoir, biography, and fiction) and informational writing
- Use language to show feelings of characters or elicit feelings from readers
- Use dialogue and action to draw readers into the story
- Select a point of view with which to tell a story
- Use language to establish a point of view
- Understand the differences between first and third person
- Write in both first and third person and understand the differences in effect so as to choose appropriately
- Write in second person when talking directly to the reader to inform or persuade
- Arrange simple and complex sentences for an easy flow and sentence transition
- Vary sentence length to create feeling or mood and communicate meaning
- Use repetition of a word, phrase, or sentence for effect
- Use phrases or sentences that are striking and memorable
- Use a variety of transitions and connections: e.g., words, phrases, sentences, and paragraphs
- Use linking words and phrases to connect opinion and reasons
- Use language with efficiency while writing: e.g., trimming words, combining sentences

WORD CHOICE

- Learn new words from reading and try them out in writing
- Use vocabulary appropriate for the topic
- Choose the best words to fit the writer's purpose and meaning
- Choose words with the audience in mind
- Use range of descriptive words to enhance meaning
- Vary word choice to create interesting description and dialogue
- Select words to make meanings memorable
- Use strong nouns and verbs
- Use colorful modifiers and style as appropriate to audience and purpose

- Use words that convey an intended mood or effect
- Show ability to vary the text by choosing alternative words: e.g., *replied, taunted, agreed, affirmed, urged, volunteered* for *said*
- Learn and use content words typical of disciplinary language: e.g., science, history, math, social studies
- Where needed, use academic language in an appropriate way to write about topics in various disciplines
- Use common (simple) connectives and some sophisticated connectives (words that link ideas and clarify meaning) that are used in written texts but do not appear often in everyday oral language: e.g., *although, however, therefore, though, unless, whenever*

VOICE

- Write about personal experiences with voice
- Write in an expressive way but also recognize how language in a book would sound
- Write in a way that speaks directly to the reader
- Show enthusiasm and energy for the topic
- Write in a way that shows care and commitment to the topic
- Write with voice as well as begin to develop literary voice
- State information in a unique or unusual way
- Use engaging titles and language
- Include details that add to the voice
- Use dialogue selectively to communicate voice
- Use punctuation to make the text clear, effective, interesting, and to support voice
- Produce narrative writing that is engaging and honest, and reveals the person behind the writing
- Produce expository writing that reveals the stance of the writer toward the topic
- Produce persuasive writing including argument with logical evidence to support ideas and to counter opposing argument
- Read writing aloud to help think critically about voice

CONVENTIONS

For additional information about grammar and usage, capitalization, punctuation, and spelling, see Appendix: Grammar, Usage, and Mechanics.

TEXT LAYOUT

- Indicate the importance of information through layout and print characteristics
- Use layout of print and illustrations (e.g., drawings, photos, maps, diagrams) to convey the meaning in a nonfiction text
- Indicate the structure of the text through variety in layout and print characteristics, including titles, headings, and subheadings
- Incorporate book and print features (e.g., labeled pictures, diagrams, table of contents, headings, subheadings, sidebars, page numbers) into nonfiction writing

Selecting Goals Behaviors and Understandings to Notice, Teach, and Support *(cont.)*

Writing

- Use a wide range of print characteristics to communicate meaning: e.g., white space, layout, italics, bold, font size and style, icons, underlining
- Use indentation or spacing to set off paragraphs

GRAMMAR AND USAGE

▶ Parts of Speech

- Recognize and use the eight parts of speech of the English language in an accepted, standard way
- Use subject-verb agreement: e.g., *astronaut is; astronauts are*
- Use objective and nominative case pronouns in an accepted, standard way: e.g., *me, him, her; I, he, she*
- Use indefinite and relative pronouns correctly: e.g., *everyone, both; that, who, whose*
- Correctly use verbs that are often misused: e.g., *lie/lay; rise/raise*

▶ Tense

- Use the same tense for two or more actions happening at the same time: e.g., *I poured the milk into the bowl and called the kitten's name*
- Use different tenses to show two or more actions happening at different times: e.g., *the kitten laps up the milk I poured an hour ago*
- Write sentences in present, past, future, present perfect, and past perfect tenses as needed to express meaning

▶ Sentence Structure

- Write complete sentences (subject and predicate)
- Use a range of types of sentences: e.g., declarative, interrogative, imperative, exclamatory
- Use conventional sentence structure and punctuation for simple sentences, compound sentences, and complex sentences with embedded clauses
- Sometimes vary sentence structure and length for reasons of craft
- Place phrases and clauses in sentences
- Write sentences in past, present, future, present perfect, and past perfect tenses as fits intended meaning and purpose
- Write dialogue in conventional structures

▶ Paragraphing

- Understand and use paragraph structure (indented or block) to organize sentences that focus on one idea
- Create transitions between paragraphs to show to progression of ideas
- Understand and use paragraphs to show speaker change in dialogue

CAPITALIZATION

- Use a capital letter in the first word of a sentence
- Use capital letters for proper nouns
- Use capital letters appropriately for the first letter in days, months, holidays, city and state names, and in titles and headings
- Use capital letters correctly in dialogue

- Use capitalization for specialized functions (emphasis, key information, voice)
- Use more complex capitalization with increasing accuracy, such as in abbreviations and with quotation marks in split dialogue

PUNCTUATION

- Consistently use periods, exclamation marks, and question marks as end marks in a conventional way
- Read one's writing aloud and think about where to place punctuation
- Understand and use ellipses to show pause or anticipation, often before something surprising
- Use dashes correctly to indicate a longer pause or slow down the reading to emphasize particular information
- Use commas and quotation marks correctly in writing uninterrupted and interrupted dialogue as well as to show a verbatim quote
- Use apostrophes correctly in contractions and possessives
- Use commas correctly to separate an introductory clause or items in a series, or to set off a person's name in direct address
- Use commas and parentheses correctly to separate parenthetical information
- Divide words correctly at the syllable break and at the end of a line using a hyphen
- Use colons correctly to introduce a list of items or a long, formal statement or quotation
- Use semicolons correctly to separate independent clauses that are closely related in thought but are not joined by a conjunction
- Use brackets to separate a different idea or kind of information
- Use indentation to identify paragraphs
- Appropriately punctuate headings, sidebars, and titles
- Notice the role of punctuation in the craft of writing
- Try out new ways of using punctuation
- Study mentor texts to learn the role of punctuation in adding voice to writing
- Use appropriate punctuation in references, footnotes, and endnotes

SPELLING

- Spell a large number (approximately 750 to 1,000) of high-frequency words, a wide range of plurals, and base words with inflectional endings and reflect spelling in final drafts
- Use a range of spelling strategies to take apart and spell multisyllable words (word parts, connections to known words, complex sound-to-letter cluster relationships)
- Use reference tools to check on spelling when editing final draft (dictionary, digital resources)
- Spell complex plurals correctly: e.g., *knife/knives, woman/women, sheep/sheep*
- Spell a full range of contractions, plurals, possessives, and compound words
- Spell words that have been studied (spelling words)
- Spell multisyllable words that have vowel and *r*
- Be aware of the spelling of common suffixes: e.g., *-ion, -ment, -ly*

Selecting Goals Behaviors and Understandings to Notice, Teach, and Support *(cont.)*

Writing

CONVENTIONS *(continued)*

SPELLING *(continued)*

- Use difficult homophones correctly: e.g., *principle/principal, council/counsel*
- Use word origin to assist in spelling and expanding writing vocabulary
- Understand that many English words come from another language and have Greek or Latin roots
- Notice alternative spellings of some words from other cultures
- Notice how the spelling of some words has changed over time
- Monitor own spelling by noticing when a word does not "look right" and should be checked

HANDWRITING AND WORD-PROCESSING

- Write fluently and legibly in cursive handwriting with appropriate spacing
- Use efficient keyboarding skills to create drafts, revise, edit, and publish
- Use word-processor to get ideas down, revise, edit, and publish
- Use word-processing with understanding of how to produce and vary text (layout, font, special techniques) according to purpose, audience, etc.
- Show familiarity with computer and word-processing terminology
- Create website entries and articles with appropriate text layout, graphics, and access to information through searching
- Make wide use of computer skills in presenting text: e.g., text, tables, graphics, multimedia

WRITING PROCESS

PLANNING AND REHEARSING

▶ Purpose

- Write for a specific main purpose and sometimes also for one or more secondary purposes: e.g., to inform; to explain or give facts about a topic; to instruct; to entertain; to tell or retell a story; to express feelings, sensory images, ideas, or stories; to persuade; to perform a practical task; to reflect; to plan; to maintain relationships
- Understand how the purpose of the writing influences the selection of genre
- Select the genre for the writing based on the purpose
- Tell whether a piece of writing is functional, narrative, informational, or poetic
- Have clear goals and understand how the goals will affect the writing

▶ Audience

- Write with specific readers or audience in mind
- Understand that writing is shaped by the writer's purpose and understanding of the audience
- Plan and organize information for the intended readers
- Understand audience as all readers rather than just the teacher
- Consider a varied audience when planning the piece
- Identify and write for an audience that is not personally known

▶ Oral Language

- Generate and expand ideas through talk with peers and teacher
- Look for ideas and topics in personal experiences, shared through talk
- Use talk and storytelling to generate and rehearse language that may be written later
- Explore relevant questions in talking about a topic
- When rehearsing language for an informational piece, use vocabulary specific to the topic
- When rehearsing language for a narrative writing, use action and content words appropriate for the story
- Experiment with language that is particular to a setting: e.g., archaic words, the sounds of accents in spoken language, words or language structures other than English

▶ Gathering Seeds/Resources/Experimenting with Writing

- Use a writer's notebook or booklet as a tool for collecting ideas, experimenting, planning, sketching, or drafting
- Reread a writer's notebook to select topics: e.g., select small moments that can be expanded
- Use sketching, webs, lists, and freewriting to think about, plan for, and try out writing
- Gather a variety of entries (e.g., character map, timeline, sketches, observations, freewrites, drafts, lists) in a writer's notebook
- Think through a topic, focus, organization, and audience
- Think through an informational topic to plan organization and treatment of the topic
- Try out titles, different headings and endings, develop setting and characters in a writer's notebook
- Use notebooks to plan, gather, and rehearse for future published writing
- Plan for a story by living inside the story, gaining insight into characters so that the story can be written as it happens
- Make a plan for an essay that makes a claim and contains supporting evidence
- Choose helpful tools: e.g., webs, T-charts, sketches, charts, diagrams, lists, outlines, flowcharts

Selecting Goals Behaviors and Understandings to Notice, Teach, and Support *(cont.)*

Writing

- Choose a setting and describe in details that evoke a particular mood or tone
- Gather relevant information from multiple print and digital sources, using search terms effectively
- Assess the credibility of each source using search terms effectively

▶ Content, Topic, Theme

- Observe carefully events, people, settings, and other aspects of the world to gather information on a topic
- Select information that will support the topic
- Choose topics that the writer knows about, cares about, or wants to learn about
- Choose topics that are interesting to the writer
- Tell about a topic in an interesting way
- Stay focused on a topic to produce a well-organized piece of writing that is long enough to fully explain the points (e.g., facts, arguments) the writer wants to make
- Get ideas from other books and writers about how to approach a topic: e.g., organization, point of view, layout
- Communicate the significance of the topic to an audience
- Show the audience (by stating or providing important information) what is important about the topic
- Use texts (print and online) to get information on a topic
- Select details that will support a topic or story
- Select title that fits the content to publish or complete as final draft
- Develop a clear, main idea around which a piece of writing will be planned
- Use the organizing features of electronic text (e.g., bulletin boards, databases, keyword searches, email addresses) to locate information
- Understand a range of genres and forms and select from them according to topic and purpose and audience

▶ Inquiry/Research/Exploration

- Make scientific observations, use notes and sketches to document them, and talk with others about patterns, connections, and discoveries
- Form questions to explore and locate sources for information about a topic, characters, or setting
- Select and include only the information that is appropriate to the topic and to the category
- Take and use notes to record and organize information
- Conduct research to gather information in planning a writing project: e.g., live interviews, Internet, artifacts, articles, books
- Create categories of information and organize categories into larger sections
- Determine when research is necessary to cover a nonfiction topic adequately

- Search for appropriate information from multiple sources: e.g., books and other print materials, websites, interview
- Draw evidence from literary or informational texts to support analysis, reflection, and research
- Document sources while gathering information so that it will be easy to provide references
- Understand that a writer gains ideas from other writers but should credit the other writers and/or put these ideas into one's own words
- Understand the concept of plagiarism and avoid it by citing sources for quotations and information used
- Understand that a writer may quote another writer or speaker by placing the exact words in quotes and referencing the source accurately
- Understand that in a research report a writer documents information with references for sources

▶ Genre/Forms

- Select the genre for the writing based on the purpose: e.g., formal letter, procedural text; realistic fiction, historical fiction, traditional literature (folktale, tall tale, fairy tale, fable, myth, legend, epic, ballad), and fantasy (including science fiction); biography, autobiography, memoir; expository text; persuasive text; poetry; hybrid text
- Choose a form for the writing: e.g., notes, cards, letters, invitations, email, lists, directions with steps (how-to); picture books, wordless picture books, poems, songs, plays, letters, short stories, diary and journal entries, narrative poetry, lyrical poetry, free verse, ballads, biographical and autobiographical sketches, personal narratives; essays, reports, news and feature articles, photo essays, speeches; editorials, letters to the editor

DRAFTING AND REVISING

▶ Understanding the Process

- Understand the role of the writer, teacher, or peer writer in conference
- Change writing in response to peer or teacher feedback
- Know how to use an editing and proofreading checklist
- Understand revision as a means for making written messages stronger and clearer to readers
- Understand that all revision is governed by the writer's decision of what will communicate meaning to the reader
- Understand that a writer rereads and revises while drafting (recursive process) and keeps doing it over and over with new pieces of writing
- Write successive drafts to show substantive revisions
- Name, understand the purpose of, try out, and internalize crafting techniques
- Use writers as mentors in making revisions and revisions while drafting (recursive process)
- Emulate the writing of other good writers by thinking of or examining mentor texts during the drafting and revision processes

Selecting Goals Behaviors and Understandings to Notice, Teach, and Support *(cont.)*

Writing

WRITING PROCESS *(continued)*

DRAFTING AND REVISING *(continued)*

▶ **Producing a Draft**

- Write a well-organized article focused on a topic
- Use drawings to add information to, elaborate on, or increase readers' enjoyment and understanding
- Write a draft or discovery draft (writing fast and as much as possible on a topic)
- Understand the importance of the lead of a fiction or nonfiction text
- Begin to develop a style for drafting: e.g., from slow, deliberate drafting with ongoing revision, to fast writing of ideas for revision later
- Revise the lead to find the most interesting and engaging language
- Bring the piece to closure with an effective summary, parting idea, or satisfying ending
- Establish an initiating event and follow with a series of events in a narrative
- Present ideas in logical order across the piece
- Maintain central idea or focus across paragraphs
- Produce a series of coherent paragraphs that present information logically and lead readers through the nonfiction piece or story
- Show steps or phases in time order when incorporating temporal or chronological sequence into a nonfiction text
- Establish a situation, plot or problem, and point of view in fiction drafts
- Provide insight as to why an incident or event is memorable
- When writing a biography, memoir, or fiction story, establish important decisions (made by the central character or subject) and the outcomes of those decisions
- Generate multiple titles to help think about the focus of the piece
- Select a title that fits the content

▶ **Rereading**

- Reread writing to think about what to write next
- Reread writing to rethink and make changes
- Reread and revise the discovery draft or rewrite sections to clarify meaning
- Reread the text to be sure there are no missing words or information
- Identify language in the story that shows character change (or learning a lesson in a memoir)
- Identify the statement (and sometimes restatement) of the main idea of a piece
- Identify the turning point of a story and/or the most exciting part of a story
- Reread writing to check for clarity and purpose
- Identify language that does not contribute to the central purpose or message

▶ **Adding Information**

- Add ideas in thought bubbles or dialogue in quotation marks or speech bubbles to provide information, provide narration, or show thoughts and feelings
- Add descriptive words (adjectives, adverbs) and phrases to help readers visualize and understand events, actions, processes, or topics
- Add words, phrases, or sentences to make the writing more interesting or exciting for readers
- Add words, phrases, or sentences to provide more information to readers
- Add word, phrases, or sentences to clarify meaning for readers
- After reflection and rereading, add substantial pieces of text (paragraphs, pages) to provide further explanation, clarify points, add interest, or support points
- Add details or examples to make the piece clearer or more interesting
- Add transitional words and phrases to clarify meaning and make the writing smoother
- Reread and change or add words to ensure that meaning is clear
- Add descriptive words and details to increase imagery or enhance meaning, not simply to add information
- Add words, phrases, sentences, and paragraphs to add excitement to a narrative
- Add information in footnotes or endnotes

▶ **Deleting Information**

- Delete text to better express meaning and make more logical
- Delete words, sentences, paragraphs, or pages that do not make sense, or add necessary information or ideas
- Identify redundant words, phrases, or sentences and remove if they do not serve a purpose or enhance the voice
- Reread and cross out words to ensure that meaning is clear
- Delete information (e.g., unnecessary details, description, examples) that clutters up the writing and obscures the central meaning

▶ **Changing a Text**

- Identify vague parts and change the language or content to be more precise
- Vary word choice to make the piece more interesting
- Work on transitions to achieve better flow
- Reshape writing to make the text into a different genre: e.g., personal narrative to poem
- Embed genres within the text to create hybrid text

▶ **Reorganizing Information**

- Rearrange and revise writing to better express meaning or make the text more logical (reorder drawings, reorder pages, cut and paste)
- Reorganize and revise the writing to better express the writer's meaning or make the text more logical
- Move information to increase suspense or move the action
- Move information to the front or end of the text for greater impact on the reader
- Reorder pages or paragraphs by laying them out and reassembling them

Selecting Goals Behaviors and Understandings to Notice, Teach, and Support *(cont.)*

Writing

▶ Using Tools and Techniques

- Add words, letters, phrases, or sentences using a variety of techniques: e.g., caret, sticky notes, spider's legs, numbered items on a separate page, word-processing
- Use a number to identify place to add information and an additional paper with numbers to write the information to insert
- Delete words, phrases, or sentences from a text (crossing out or using word-processing) to make the meaning clearer
- Reorder the information in a text to make the meaning clearer by cutting apart, cutting and pasting, laying out pages, using word-processing
- Use standard symbols for revising and editing

EDITING AND PROOFREADING

▶ Understanding the Process

- Understand that a writer uses what is known to spell words
- Know how to use an editing and proofreading checklist
- Understand that a writer (after using what is known) can ask another person to do a final edit
- Understand the limitations of spell check and grammar check on the computer
- Understand how to use tools to self-evaluate writing and assist the writer in copyediting
- Know the function of an editor and respond to suggestions without defensiveness

▶ Editing for Conventions

- Check and correct letter formation
- Edit for the conventional spelling of known words
- Edit for spelling errors by circling words that do not look right and spelling them another way
- Understand that the teacher will be final spelling editor for the published piece after the student has used everything known
- Edit for capitalization and punctuation
- Edit for grammar and sentence sense
- Edit for word suitability and precise meaning
- Edit for cadence (rhythm, modulation, appealing quality) of sentences
- Determine where new paragraphs should begin
- Check and correct spacing and layout using layout skillfully to communicate meaning
- Integrate quotations and citations into written text in a way that maintains the coherence and flow of the writing
- Prepare final draft with self-edit and submit (teacher edit prior to publishing)

▶ Using Tools

- Use reference tools to check on spelling and meaning
- Use a thesaurus to search for more interesting words
- Use spell check, accepting or rejecting changes as needed

- Use grammar check, accepting or rejecting changes as needed
- Make corrections in response to editing marks by the teacher or other writers

PUBLISHING

- Produce writing to explain, label, or otherwise accompany drawing
- Create illustrations and writing that work together to express the meaning
- Create illustrations or other art for pieces that are in final form
- Share a text with peers by reading it aloud to the class
- Put several stories or poems together
- Select a poem, story, or informational book to publish in a variety of appropriate ways: e.g., typed/printed, framed and mounted or otherwise displayed
- Add cover spread with title and author information
- In anticipation of an audience, add book and print features during the publishing process: e.g., illustrations and other graphics, cover spread, title, dedication, table of contents, about the author piece, headings, subheadings
- Attend to layout of text in final publication
- Understand publishing as the sharing of a piece of writing with a purpose and an audience in mind
- Understand the importance of citing sources of information and conventions for citation
- Add bibliography of sources where needed
- Add abstract or short summary where needed

DRAWING

- Understand that when both writing and drawing are on a page, they are mutually supportive, with each extending the other
- Use sketches or drawings to represent people, places, and things, and also to communicate mood and abstract ideas as appropriate to the genre and form
- Create drawings that are related to the written text and increase readers' understanding and enjoyment
- Use sketching to support memory and help in planning
- Use sketching to capture detail that is important to a topic
- Provide important information in the illustrations
- Add detail to drawings to add information or increase interest
- Create drawings that employ careful attention to color or detail
- Understand the difference between drawing and sketching and use them to support the writing process
- Use sketching to create quick representations of images, usually an outline in pencil or pen
- Use sketches to create drawings in published pieces
- Use diagrams or other graphics to support the process and/or add meaning
- Sketch and draw with a sense of relative size and perspective
- Use the terms *sketching* and *drawing* to refer to these processes and forms

Selecting Goals Behaviors and Understandings to Notice, Teach, and Support (cont.)

Writing

WRITING PROCESS (continued)

VIEWING SELF AS A WRITER

- Have topics and ideas for writing in a list or notebook
- Select examples of best writing in all genres attempted
- Self-evaluate writing and talk about what is good about it and what techniques were used
- Self-evaluate pieces of writing in light of what is known about a genre
- Be productive as a writer, writing a specified quantity within a designated time period: e.g., average of one piece each week
- Write routinely over extended timeframes and shorter timeframes from a range of discipline-specific tasks, purposes, and audiences
- Write with independent initiative and investment
- Attend to the nuances of illustrations and how they enhance a text in order to try them out for oneself
- Take risks as a writer
- Write in a variety of genres across the year
- Understand writing as a vehicle to communicate something the writer thinks
- Discuss in the writing conference what one is working on as a writer
- Seek feedback on writing
- Be willing to work at the craft of writing, incorporating new learning from instruction
- Compare previous writing to revised writing and notice and talk about the differences
- State what was learned from each piece of writing
- Articulate goals and plan for improving writing
- Write with fluency and ease
- Name the qualities or techniques of good writing, and work to acquire them
- Show interest in and work at crafting good writing, applying what has been learned about crafting in each piece
- Provide editing and revision help to peers
- Understand that all revision is governed by the writer's decision making of what will communicate meaning to the reader
- Mark the most important part of a piece of one's own or others' writing

Selecting Purpose, Genre, and Form

Writing

As they use writing for a variety of authentic purposes, middle school writers develop a deep understanding of writing for many purposes and audiences. They select mentor texts and construct hybrid texts and multimedia presentations with authority and skill. They demonstrate proficiency in writing challenging genres such as reports, literary essays, editorials, and argument. They can use written language in many formal ways. The behaviors and understandings also apply well to their developing skill as high school writers.

FUNCTIONAL WRITING
(Purpose–to perform a practical task)

FORMAL LETTER

▶ **Understanding the Genre**

- Understand that a formal letter can be written in various forms: e.g., business letter
- Understand that a business letter is a formal document with a particular purpose
- Understand that a business letter has parts: e.g., date, inside address, formal salutation followed by a colon, body organized into paragraphs, closing, signature and title of sender, and sometimes notification of a copy or enclosure
- Understand that a writer can learn to write effective business letters by studying the characteristics of examples
- Use the term *business letter* to describe the form

▶ **Writing in the Genre**

- Write to a specified audience that may be an individual or an organization or group
- Address the audience appropriately
- Include important information and exclude unnecessary details
- Organize the body into paragraphs
- Understand the component parts of a business letter and how to lay them out on a page
- Write formal letters

TEST WRITING

▶ **Understanding the Genre**

- Understand that test writing often requires writing about an assigned topic
- Understand that test writing may involve creating expository texts or persuasive texts
- Understand that some test writing serves the purpose of demonstrating what a person knows or can do as a writer
- Understand that test writing involves analyzing expectations
- Understand that test writing can take various forms: e.g., short constructed response (sometimes called *short answer*), extended constructed response (or *essay*)
- Understand that test writing often requires writing about something real
- Understand that test writing involves analyzing what is expected of the writer, and then planning and writing a response that fits the criteria

- Understand test writing as a response carefully tailored to meet precise instructions
- Understand that test writing often requires taking a position, developing a clear argument, and providing evidence for points
- Understand that test writing often requires inferring and explaining the motives of a character or person
- Understand that test writing sometimes requires taking the perspective of a particular individual (historical figure, fictional character)
- Learn how to write on tests by studying examples of short constructed responses and extended constructed responses
- Use the terms *test writing, short constructed response,* and *extended constructed response* to describe this type of functional writing

▶ **Writing in the Genre**

- Analyze prompts to determine purpose, audience, and genre (e.g., expository text, persuasive text) that is appropriate
- Read and internalize the criteria for an acceptable response
- Write focused responses to questions and to prompts
- Write concisely and to the direction of the question or prompt
- Reflect on bigger ideas and make or defend a claim that is substantiated
- Respond to a text in a way that reflects analytic or aesthetic thinking
- Restate a claim with further evidence
- State alternate points of view and critically analyze the evidence of each
- Elaborate on important points
- Incorporate one's knowledge of craft in shaping responses
- Proofread carefully for spelling and conventions

WRITING ABOUT READING

- See *Writing About Reading,* pages 147–208.

NARRATIVE WRITING *(Purpose–To tell a story)*

FICTION

▶ **Understanding the Genre**

- Understand that fiction genres include realistic fiction, historical fiction, traditional literature (folktale, tall tale, fairy tale, fable, myth, legend, epic, ballad), and fantasy (including science fiction)
- Understand that fiction can be written in various forms: e.g., picture books, wordless picture books, poems, songs, plays, letters, short stories, diary or journal entries, narrative poetry, lyrical poetry, free verse, ballads

Selecting Purpose, Genre, and Form (cont.)

Writing

NARRATIVE WRITING (Purpose–to tell a story) (continued)

FICTION (continued)

▶ **Understanding the Genre** (continued)

- Understand that an additional purpose of a fiction text is to explore a theme or teach a lesson
- Understand that a fiction text may involve one or more events in the life of a main character
- Understand that a writer uses various elements of fiction (e.g., setting, plot with problem and solution, characters) in a fiction text
- Understand that the setting of fiction may be current, historical, or imaginary
- Understand that the plot of a fiction text may have a straightforward structure: e.g., beginning, several episodes, problem, solution, and ending
- Understand that the plot of a fiction text may have variations in narrative structure (e.g., flashback, story-within-a-story, flash-forward, time-lapse) and may begin at the beginning, in the middle, at the end, or after the end of a story
- Understand that a fiction writer may use a variety of language and literary features: e.g., imagery, descriptive and figurative language, symbolism, mood, tone, irony or satire, one or more points of view, dialogue
- Understand that a fiction text involves events in the life of one or more characters
- Understand that a fiction text may present and explore one or more messages or themes
- Understand that writers can learn to craft fiction by using mentor texts as models
- Use the terms *realistic fiction, historical fiction, folktale, tall tale, fairy tale, fable, myth, legend, epic, ballad, fantasy,* and *science fiction* to describe the genre

▶ **Writing in the Genre**

- Write a fiction story, either realistic or fantasy
- With fantasy, include imaginative character, setting, and plot elements
- With fantasy, develop a consistent imaginary world
- Use elements of fantasy and/or science to write a story
- Begin with a compelling lead to capture reader's attention
- Describe the setting with appropriate detail and reveal its relevance to the plot through the events and dialogue
- Develop a plot that that is believable and engaging to readers, including a conflict, several episodes, a resolution, and an ending
- Show the problem of the story and how one or more characters responds to it
- Move the plot along with action
- Show readers how the setting is important to the problem of the story
- Assure that the events and setting for historical fiction are accurate
- Describe and develop believable and appealing characters

- Show characters' motivations and feelings by describing how they look, what they do, say, and think, as well as what others say about them
- Use an appropriate, effective point of view: e.g., first person, third person
- Use dialogue skillfully in ways that show character traits and feelings
- Write a believable and satisfying ending to the story, whatever the genre
- Experiment with literary features and devices such as imagery, figurative language, symbolism, irony, and satire

BIOGRAPHY, AUTOBIOGRAPHY, MEMOIR, AND NARRATIVE NONFICTION

▶ **Understanding the Genre**

- Understand that narrative nonfiction genres include biography, autobiography, and memoir, and narrative nonfiction
- Understand that biographical texts can be written in various forms: e.g., biographical sketches, autobiographical sketches, personal narratives, poems, songs, plays, photo essays, speeches, letters, diary or journal entries
- Understand biography as a true account of a person's life
- Understand autobiography as a true account of a person's life written and narrated by that person
- Understand that a biography or an autobiography can be about the person's whole life or a part of it
- Understand that biographers select their subjects to show their importance and impact
- Understand that a biographer reveals his or her own stance toward the subject by selection of information and by the way it is described
- Understand the need for a biographer to report all important information in an effort to take an unbiased view
- Understand the need to document evidence and cite sources
- Understand that a biography or autobiography may begin at any point in the story of a person's life
- Establish the significance of events and personal decisions made by the subject of a biography or autobiography
- Understand memoir or personal narrative as a brief, often intense, memory of or reflection on a person, time, or event
- Understand that a memoir has significance in the writer's life and usually shows something significant to others
- Understand that a memoir can be composed of a series of vignettes
- Understand that a biography, autobiography, or memoir may have characteristics of fiction (e.g., setting, conflict, characters, dialogue, and resolution) even though the events are true or that it can be completely factual
- Understand that a memoir can be written in first, second, or third person, although it is usually in first person
- Understand the difference between true biography and fictionalized biography
- Write various kinds of biographical texts by studying mentor texts
- Understand that a narrative nonfiction text includes selected important events and turning points

Selecting Purpose, Genre, and Form (cont.)

Writing

- Understand that a narrative nonfiction text often includes an underlying structural pattern such as cause and effect or problem and solution
- Understand that a narrative nonfiction text indicates passing of time using words (e.g., *then, after a time*), dates and periods of time, and ages of people
- Understand that the setting may be important in a narrative nonfiction text
- Understand that a narrative nonfiction text includes people that are real
- Understand that a narrative nonfiction text often includes quotes of a person's exact words
- Understand that a narrative nonfiction text should include only true events and people and may require research
- Use the terms *biography, biographical sketch, autobiography, autobiographical sketch, personal narrative, memoir, narrative nonfiction, poem, song, play, letter, diary entry, journal entry, photo essay, speech, lyrical poetry, free verse,* and *ballad*

▶ Writing in the Genre

- Choose a subject and state a reason for the selection
- Write an engaging lead that captures interest and that may foreshadow the content
- Create interest in the subject by selecting and reporting information in an engaging way
- Select important events to include and exclude extraneous events and details
- Reveal the writer's point of view by giving the reasons for omitting significant parts of the subject's life: e.g., focusing on childhood or on the presidential years only
- Select and write personal experiences as "small moments" and share thinking and feelings about them
- Reveal something important about self or about life
- Create a series of vignettes that together communicate a bigger message
- Tell events in chronological order or use another structural pattern: e.g., description, temporal sequence, question and answer, cause and effect, compare and contrast, problem and solution, categorization
- Describe and develop a setting and explain how it is related to the writer's experiences
- Describe the subject's important decisions, and show how those decisions influenced his or her life or the lives of others
- Describe the subject by what she did or said as well as others' opinions
- Show how the subject changes
- Reveal the subject's feelings by describing actions or using quotations
- Describe people by how they look, what they do, say, and think, and what others say about them
- Use dialogue as appropriate to add to make the subject "come to life," but understand that adding any undocumented information fictionalizes a biographical text to an extent

- Experiment with literary language (powerful nouns and verbs, figurative language)
- Write with imagery so that the reader understands the feelings of the writer or others
- Write an ending that fits the piece
- Select important events and turning points to include in narrative nonfiction
- Show cause and effect and/or problem and solution as appropriate in writing narrative nonfiction
- Show the passing of time in a variety of ways
- Describe the setting if needed in a narrative nonfiction text
- Include quotes from real people in a narrative nonfiction text and place them in quotation marks with appropriate references

INFORMATIONAL WRITING
(Purpose—to explain or give facts about a topic)

EXPOSITORY TEXT

▶ Understanding the Genre

- Understand that a writer creates an expository text for readers to learn about a topic
- Understand that to write an expository text, the writer needs to become very knowledgeable about a topic
- Understand that an expository text may require research and will require organization
- Understand that a writer may reveal purposes and beliefs even if they are not stated explicitly in an expository text
- Understand that an expository text can be written in various forms: e.g., essay, report, news article, feature article, photo essay, speech
- Understand than an essay is a short composition used to explain a topic and/or give the writer's point of view about a topic
- Understand the basic structure of an essay: e.g., introduction, body, conclusion
- Understand that an essay can be used to analyze one or more pieces of literature (see *Writing About Reading,* pages 161-222)
- Understand that a report is a formal presentation of a topic
- Understand that a report may include several categories of information about a single topic
- Understand that a report has an introductory section, followed by more information in categories or sections
- Understand that a feature article usually focuses on one aspect of a topic
- Understand that a feature article begins with a lead paragraph, with more detailed information in subsequent paragraphs, and a conclusion
- Understand that a feature article reveals the writer's point of view about—and often his or her fascination with or passion for—the topic or subject
- Understand that a speech is a formal text written to be delivered orally to a public audience

Selecting Purpose, Genre, and Form (cont.)

Writing

INFORMATIONAL WRITING
(Purpose–to explain or give facts about a topic) (continued)

EXPOSITORY TEXT *(continued)*

▶ **Understanding the Genre** *(continued)*

- Understand that a factual text may use literary language and literary techniques to engage and entertain readers as it gives them factual information
- Understand that a writer can learn how to write various forms of expository text from mentor texts
- Use the terms *expository text, essay, report, news article, feature article, photo essay,* and *speech* to describe the genre and forms

▶ **Writing in the Genre**

- Use illustrations and book and print features (e.g., labeled pictures, diagrams, table of contents, headings, subheadings, sidebars, boxes of facts set off from other text, page numbers) to guide the reader
- Write a piece that is interesting and enjoyable to read
- Write about a topic that is interesting and substantive and to which the writer is committed, keeping in mind the audience and their interests and likely background knowledge

---

Book Review of *The Diary of Anne Frank*

Anne Frank,
The Diary of a Young Girl

During the Holocaust over 11,000,000 people died. Six million of those killed were Jews. Others who were victims of Adolph Hitler's horrid wrath included Catholics, Gypsies, homosexuals, and people of African Origin. <u>Anne Frank, the Diary of Young Girl</u> is a sad, yet true, account of one Jewish girl's life in hiding from the Nazis and their power.

In the year 1942 Anne's family, which consisted of her, her sister, Margot, her mother, Edith, and her father, Otto, moved into 263 Prisengracht Road, in Amsterdam, Holland, in the hopes that they could stay alive and together during the war. With them was the Van Dann family and a man named Albert Dussel. The eight of them lived in fear of the fact that one day the SS men could push aside the bookshelf that separated their home from the outside world, and send them off to a concentration camp. Sadly, on August 4, 1944 their worst nightmares became a reality. SS Sgt. Karl Silberbauer entered the Annex, and took them to one of the SS headquarters, where they sent the different family members to Auschwitz where all of them besides Otto Frank lost their lives. This book tells the story of their time in hiding from Anne's very own eyes and ears. Anne talks about a side of the war that you hardly ever hear of. It shows a true account of what one girl thought while she was in hiding, and how with each passing day her hope could strengthen, weaken, or possibly die.

In my opinion this book is an extremely sad, but touching story. The feeling that Anne is able to convey through her journal is unbelievable. Anne was a humble girl who was always optimistic, and that alone seemed to be more inspiration than anything else in this book. To me the book showed a side of the Holocaust that could not have been expressed in 1,000,000 museums. The book was real, it was not a vision of what most probably was true, it was the hard core truth. It taught me about what someone would have to give up to try to stay alive, and how in most situations that person's attempts would fail. It also taught me about the bravery of those who risked their lives to save those in danger. I would recommend this book to anybody who wants to learn about the holocaust, and is not afraid of the terror that went on during the six years between the beginning of the war in 1939, and the liberation of the work and concentration camps in 1945. This book has touched many people in this world, and today one of those people is me. We can never take back the millions who were lost during the Holocaust, but we can help prevent such terrors from happening again. It could be as simple as not letting people talk cruelly about others behind their backs, or not assuming that just because you dislike one person you will not like everybody else around them. This book has opened my eyes to a new side of this world's history and I will never forget what I have learned from it.

A middle school student's book review

- Provide information that teaches or informs readers about a topic
- Write with a wider audience in mind
- Help readers think in new ways about a subject or topic
- Write an engaging lead and first section that orient the reader and provide an introduction to the topic
- Organize information using categorization or another underlying structural pattern: e.g., description, temporal sequence, question and answer, cause and effect, chronological sequence, compare and contrast, problem and solution
- Provide interesting supporting details that develop a topic
- Include facts, figures, statistics, examples, and anecdotes when appropriate
- Use quotes from experts (written texts, speeches, or interviews) when appropriate
- Credit sources of information as appropriate
- Avoid bias and/or present perspectives and counterperspectives on a topic
- Be aware of purpose and stance in relation to a topic
- Use some vocabulary specific to the topic
- Use literary language to make topic interesting to readers
  - Reveal the writer's convictions about the topic through a unique voice
  - Write multiple paragraphs with smooth transitions
  - Write an effective conclusion

PERSUASIVE WRITING *(Purpose–to persuade)*

PERSUASIVE TEXT

▶ **Understanding the Genre**

- Understand that argument and persuasion can be written in various forms: e.g., editorial, letter to the editor, essay, speech
- Understand that the purpose of a persuasive text or argument may be to convince the reader to take the writer's point of view on an issue, to take some action, to critique society, or to improve some aspect of the world
- Understand that an editorial is a formal text with a public audience
- Understand that a letter to the editor is formal text with a public audience: e.g., the editor of a publication and its readers
- Understand that a letter to the editor has parts: e.g., date, formal salutation, body organized into paragraphs, closing, signature and title of sender
- Understand than an essay is a formal text often written for a teacher or a test
- Understand that a speech is a formal text written to be delivered orally with the intent of persuading an audience to believe or do something
- Understand the importance of supporting each idea or argument with facts, reasons, or examples

Selecting Purpose, Genre, and Form *(cont.)*

Writing

- Use the terms *argument, persuasive text, editorial, letter to the editor, essay,* and *speech* to describe the genre and forms
- Understand that a writer can learn to write various forms of persuasive text by studying the characteristics of examples in mentor texts
- Understand the difference between argument and persuasion

▶ Writing in the Genre

- Write an editorial, a letter to the editor, a speech, or an essay
- Address the audience appropriately according to the form
- Choose topics from stories or everyday observations
- Begin with a title or opening that tells the reader what is being argued or explained–a clearly stated thesis
- Provide a series of clear arguments with reasons to support the argument
- Include important information and exclude unnecessary details
- Use opinions supported by facts
- Provide "expert testimony" or quotes to support argument
- Organize the body of the text into paragraphs
- Write well-crafted sentences that express the writer's convictions
- Write a logical, thoughtful ending
- Include illustrations, charts, or diagrams as necessary

POETIC WRITING *(Purpose–to express feelings, sensory images, ideas, or stories)*

POETRY

▶ Understanding the Genre

- Understand poetry as a unique way to communicate about and describe feelings, sensory images, ideas, or stories
- Understand that a writer can create different types of poems: e.g., free verse, lyrical poem, narrative poem, ballad, epic, saga, limerick, haiku, concrete poem
- Understand the difference between poetic language and ordinary language
- Understand that poetry is a spare way of communicating deep meaning
- Notice the beat or rhythm of a poem and its relation to line breaks
- Understand the way print works in poems and demonstrate the use in reading and writing them on a page using white space and line breaks
- Understand that poetry often includes sensory images and symbolism
- Understand that different types of poems can be used to convey different moods
- Understand that different types of poems appeal to readers in different ways
- Use the terms *poem, free verse, lyrical poem, narrative poem, ballad, epic, saga, limerick, haiku,* and *concrete poem* to describe specific types of poetry
- Understand that a writer can learn to write a variety of poems from studying mentor texts

▶ Writing in the Genre

- Observe closely to select topics or content and write with detail
- Collect language and images as a basis for writing poetry
- Use words to convey images and strong feelings
- Use figurative language and other literary devices such as alliteration, onomatopoeia, simile, metaphor, personification, and symbolism
- Select topics that are significant and help readers see in a new way
- Select topics that have strong meaning
- Use white space and line breaks to communicate the meaning and tone of the poem
- Understand the role of line breaks, white space for pause, breath, or emphasis
- Remove extra words to clarify the meaning and make the writing more powerful
- Use repetition, refrain, rhythm, and other poetic techniques
- Use words to show not tell
- Write a variety of types of poems according to purpose, topic, and meaning
- Write a poetic text in response to another poem, reflecting the same style, topic, mood, or voice
- Write a poetic text in response to prose text, either narrative or informational
- Choose a title that communicates the meaning of a poem
- Write a strong ending to a poem

HYBRID WRITING

HYBRID TEXT

▶ Understanding the Genre

- Understand that a hybrid text mixes two or more genres
- Understand that a hybrid text blends two genres in order to communicate information in different ways: e.g., through prose narrative, poem, and list
- Understand that a writer uses more than one genre to increase engagement or make the text come alive
- Understand that the genres in the text must be integrated into a harmonious whole that communicates a message
- Use the term *hybrid* text to describe the genre
- Understand that a writer can learn to write hybrid texts by studying mentor texts

▶ Writing in the Genre

- Experiment with embedding genres within a text
- Select different genres with a clear purpose in mind
- Write pieces of the text in different genres according to purpose
- Integrate the genres to create a coherent whole
- Transition smoothly from one tense to another
- Transition smoothly from writing in one person to writing in another (for example, from first person to third person)
- Guide the reader so that the transitions between genres are accessible

Selecting Goals Behaviors and Understandings to Notice, Teach, and Support

Writing

CRAFT

ORGANIZATION

▶ Text Structure

- Organize information to fit purpose: e.g., functional, narrative, informational, persuasive, poetic
- Make decisions about where in a text to place features such as photographs with legends, insets, sidebars, and graphics
- Write fictional narratives with characters involved in a plot, events ordered by time
- Write fiction and nonfiction narratives that are ordered chronologically
- Use underlying structural patterns to present different kinds of information in nonfiction: e.g., description, temporal sequence, question and answer, cause and effect, chronological sequence, compare and contrast, problem and solution, categorization
- Vary structural patterns to add interest to a piece

▶ Beginnings, Ending, Titles

- Decide whether a piece is unbiased or persuasive and use the decision to influence the lead and the development of ideas
- Begin with a purposeful and engaging lead that sets the tone for the piece
- Begin a narrative at the beginning, middle, or end
- Use a variety of beginnings and endings to engage the reader
- Engage readers' interest by presenting a problem, conflict, interesting person, or surprising information
- Bring a narrative text to a satisfying problem resolution and concluding scene
- End an informational text with a thoughtful or enlightening conclusion
- Bring the piece to closure, to a logical conclusion, through an ending or summary statement
- Select an appropriate title for a poem, story, or informational book
- Generate multiple titles for the piece and select the one that best fits the content of an informational piece or the plot or characterization in a narrative

▶ Presentation of Ideas

- Order the writing in ways that are characteristic to the purpose and genre
- Put important ideas together to communicate about a topic (categories)
- Clearly show topics and subtopics and indicate them with headings and subheadings in expository writing
- Present reports that are clearly organized with introduction, facts and details to illustrate the important ideas, logical conclusions, and underlying structural patterns
- Introduce ideas followed by supportive details and examples
- Use time appropriately as an organizing tool
- Support ideas with facts, details, examples, and explanations from multiple authorities

- Use well-crafted paragraphs to organize ideas
- Establish a main or controlling idea that provides perspective on the topic
- Write arguments to support claims with clear reasons and relevant evidence
- Build tension by slowing down or speeding up scenes
- Use well-crafted transitions to support the pace and flow of the writing
- Show steps in enough detail that a reader can follow a sequence
- Bring a piece to closure through an ending or summary statement
- Use language to foreshadow the ending
- Write informative texts to examine a topic and convey ideas through the selection, organization, and analysis of relevant content
- Use graphics (diagrams, illustrations, photos, charts) to provide information
- Use vocabulary specific to the topic or content

IDEA DEVELOPMENT

- Understand the difference between developing a narrative (or plot) and giving information using description, cause and effect, compare and contrast, problem and solution, or categorization
- Introduce, develop, and conclude the topic or story
- Hold the reader's attention with clear, focused content
- Structure a narrative and sustain writing to develop it logically
- Develop a logical plot by creating a story problem and addressing it over multiple events until it is resolved
- Understand how information helps the reader learn about a topic
- Gather and internalize information and then write it in own words
- Engage the reader with ideas that show strong knowledge of the topic
- Arrange information in a logical way so that ideas build on one another
- Communicate clearly the main points intended for the reader to understand
- Provide supporting details that are accurate, relevant, interesting, and vivid

LANGUAGE USE

- Understand that the writer is using language to communicate meaning
- Show evidence of using language from story books and informational books that have been read aloud
- Learn ways of using language and constructing texts from other writers (reading books and hearing them read aloud) and apply understandings to one's own writing
- Continue to learn from other writers by borrowing ways with words, phrases, and sentences
- Use memorable words or phrases
- Vary language and style as appropriate to audience and purpose
- Use language to show instead of tell
- Use language to give directions
- Find and write language to explain abstract concepts and ideas

Selecting Goals Behaviors and Understandings to Notice, Teach, and Support *(cont.)*

Writing

- Use language to clearly state main ideas and supporting details
- Use examples to make meaning clear
- Use particular language typical of different genres
- Use language to develop arguments and support with evidence
- Use language to create sensory images
- Use figurative language (e.g., simile, metaphor, personification) to make comparisons
- Experiment with using language for satire
- Use variety in sentence structure and sentence length
- Use concrete sensory details and descriptive language to develop plot (tension and problem resolution) and setting in memoir, biography, and fiction
- Use descriptive language and dialogue to present characters/subjects who appear in narratives (memoir, biography, and fiction) and informational writing
- Use sound devices such as alliteration or onomatopoeia
- Use language to show feelings of characters or elicit feelings from readers
- Use dialogue and action to draw readers into the story
- Select a point of view with which to tell a story
- Use language to establish a point of view
- Understand the differences between first and third person
- Write in both first and third person and understand the differences in effect so as to choose appropriately
- Write in second person when talking directly to the reader to inform or persuade
- Arrange simple and complex sentences for an easy flow and sentence transition
- Vary sentence length to create feeling or mood and communicate meaning
- Take risks in grammar to achieve an intended effect
- Use repetition of a word, phrase, or sentence for effect
- Use phrases or sentences that are striking and memorable
- Use a variety of transitions and connections: e.g., words, phrases, sentences, and paragraphs
- Use linking words and phrases to connect opinion and reasons
- Use language with efficiency while writing: e.g., trimming words, combining sentences

WORD CHOICE

- Learn new words from reading and try them out in writing
- Use vocabulary appropriate for the topic
- Choose the best words to fit the writer's purpose and meaning
- Choose words with the audience in mind
- Use range of descriptive words to enhance meaning
- Vary word choice to create interesting description and dialogue
- Select words to make meanings memorable
- Use strong nouns and verbs
- Use colorful modifiers and style as appropriate to audience and purpose
- Use words that convey an intended mood or effect
- Show ability to vary the text by choosing alternative words: e.g., *suggested, retorted, vowed, wailed, speculated, sputtered*
- Learn and use content words typical of disciplinary language: e.g., science, history, math, social studies
- Where needed, use academic language in an appropriate way to write about topics in various disciplines
- Use sophisticated connectives used mostly in written texts and some academic connectives that are used in the academic discipline and do not usually appear in oral language: e.g., *alternatively, consequently, despite, conversely, eventually, finally, in contrast, initially, likewise, nevertheless, nonetheless, previously, specifically, ultimately, whereas, whereby*

VOICE

- Write about personal experiences with voice
- Write in an expressive way but also recognize how language in a book would sound
- Write in a way that speaks directly to the reader
- Write texts that have energy
- Write in a way that shows care and commitment to the topic
- Write with voice as well as begin to develop literary voice
- State information in a unique or unusual way
- Engage in self-reflection to reveal the writer's unique perspective
- Write with a cadence that demonstrates the individualistic style of the writer
- Use engaging titles and language
- Include details that add to the voice
- Use dialogue selectively to communicate voice
- Share thoughts, feelings, inner conflict, and convictions through inner dialogue Use punctuation to make the text clear, effective, interesting, and to support voice
- Produce narrative writing that is engaging and honest, and reveals the person behind the writing
- Produce expository writing that reveals the stance of the writer toward the topic
- Produce persuasive writing including argument with logical evidence to support ideas and to counter opposing argument
- Read writing aloud to help think critically about voice

Selecting Goals Behaviors and Understandings to Notice, Teach, and Support *(cont.)*

Writing

CONVENTIONS

For additional information about grammar and usage, capitalization, punctuation, and spelling, see Appendix: Grammar, Usage, and Mechanics.

TEXT LAYOUT

- Indicate the importance of information through layout and print characteristics
- Use layout of print and illustrations (e.g., drawings, photos, maps, diagrams) to convey the meaning in a nonfiction text
- Indicate or support the structure of the text through variety in layout and print characteristics, including titles, headings, and subheadings
- Incorporate book and print features (e.g., labeled pictures, diagrams, table of contents, headings, subheadings, sidebars, page numbers) into nonfiction writing
- Use a full range of print characteristics to communicate meaning: e.g., white space, layout, italics, bold, font size and style, icons, underlining
- Use indentation or spacing to set off paragraphs

GRAMMAR AND USAGE

▶ Parts of Speech

- Recognize and use the eight parts of speech of the English language in an accepted, standard way
- Use subject-verb agreement: e.g., *astronaut is; astronauts are*
- Use objective and nominative case pronouns in an accepted, standard way: e.g., *me, him, her; I, he, she*
- Use indefinite and relative pronouns correctly: e.g., *everyone, both; that, who, whose*
- Correctly use verbs that are often misused: e.g., *lie/lay; rise/raise*

▶ Tense

- Use the same tense for two or more actions happening at the same time: e.g., *I poured the milk into the bowl and called the kitten's name*
- Use different tenses to show two or more actions happening at different times: e.g., *the kitten laps up the milk I poured an hour ago*
- Write sentences in present, past, future, present perfect, and past perfect tenses as needed to express meaning

▶ Sentence Structure

- Write complete sentences (subject and predicate)
- Use a range of types of sentences: e.g., declarative, interrogative, imperative, exclamatory
- Use conventional sentence structure and punctuation for simple sentences, compound sentences, and complex sentences with embedded clauses
- Sometimes vary sentence structure and length for reasons of craft
- Place phrases and clauses in sentences
- Write sentences in past, present, future, present perfect, and past perfect tenses as fits intended meaning and purpose

- Sometimes vary sentence structure and length for reasons of craft, including the creation of meaning through sentences and sometimes fragments of sentences, that are related in complex ways
- Write dialogue in conventional structures

▶ Paragraphing

- Understand and use paragraph structure (indented or block) to organize sentences that focus on one idea
- Create transitions between paragraphs to show to progression of ideas
- Understand and use paragraphs to show speaker change in dialogue

CAPITALIZATION

- Use a capital letter in the first word of a sentence
- Use capital letters for proper nouns
- Use capital letters appropriately for the first letter in days, months, holidays, city and state names, and in titles and headings
- Use capital letters correctly in dialogue
- Use capitalization for specialized functions (emphasis, key information, voice)
- Use more complex capitalization with increasing accuracy, such as in abbreviations and with quotation marks in split dialogue

PUNCTUATION

- Consistently use periods, exclamation marks, and question marks as end marks in a conventional way
- Read one's writing aloud and think about where to place punctuation
- Understand and use ellipses to show pause or anticipation, often before something surprising
- Use dashes correctly to indicate a longer pause or slow down the reading to emphasize particular information
- Use commas and quotation marks correctly in writing uninterrupted and interrupted dialogue or to enclose the exact words of a direct quote (with reference)
- Use apostrophes correctly in contractions and possessives
- Use commas correctly to separate an introductory clause or items in a series, or to set off a person's name in direct address
- Use commas and parentheses correctly to separate parenthetical information
- Divide words correctly at the syllable break and at the end of a line using a hyphen
- Use colons correctly to introduce a list of items or a long, formal statement or quotation
- Use semicolons correctly to separate independent clauses that are closely related in thought but are not joined by a conjunction
- Use brackets to separate a different idea or kind of information
- Use indentation to identify paragraphs
- Appropriately punctuate headings, sidebars, and titles
- Notice the role of punctuation in the craft of writing
- Try out new ways of using punctuation

Selecting Goals Behaviors and Understandings to Notice, Teach, and Support *(cont.)*

Writing

- Make purposeful choices for punctuation to reveal the intended meaning
- Study mentor texts to learn the role of punctuation in adding voice to writing
- Use appropriate punctuation in references, footnotes, and endnotes

SPELLING

- Spell a large number of high-frequency words (approximately 1,000 to 3,000), a wide range of plurals, and base words with inflectional endings and reflect spelling in final drafts
- Use a range of spelling strategies to take apart and spell multisyllable words (word parts, connections to known words, complex sound-to-letter cluster relationships)
- Use reference tools to check on spelling when editing final draft (dictionary, digital resources)
- Spell complex plurals correctly: e.g., *knife/knives, woman/women, sheep/sheep*
- Spell a full range of contractions, plurals, possessives, and compound words
- Spell words that have been studied (spelling words)
- Spell multisyllable words that have vowel and *r*
- Be aware of the spelling of common suffixes: e.g., *-ion, -ment, -ly*
- Use difficult homophones correctly: e.g., *principle/principal, council/counsel*
- Use word origin to assist in spelling and expanding writing vocabulary
- Understand that many English words come from another language and have Greek or Latin roots
- Notice alternative spellings of some words from other cultures
- Notice how the spelling of some words has changed over time
- Monitor own spelling by noticing when a word does not "look right" and should be checked

HANDWRITING AND WORD-PROCESSING

- Write fluently and legibly in cursive handwriting with appropriate spacing
- Use efficient keyboarding skills to create drafts, revise, edit, and publish
- Use word-processor to get ideas down, revise, edit, and publish
- Use word-processing with understanding of how to produce and vary text (layout, font, special techniques) according to purpose, audience, etc.
- Show familiarity with computer and word-processing terminology
- Create website entries and articles with appropriate text layout, graphics, and access to information through searching
- Make wide use of computer skills in presenting text: e.g., text, tables, graphics, multimedia

WRITING PROCESS

PLANNING AND REHEARSING

▶ Purpose

- Write for a specific main purpose and sometimes also for one or more secondary purposes: e.g., to inform; to explain or give facts about a topic; to instruct; to entertain; to tell or retell a story; to express feelings, sensory images, ideas, or stories; to persuade; to perform a practical task; to reflect; to plan; to maintain relationships
- Understand how the purpose of the writing influences the selection of genre
- Select the genre for the writing based on the purpose
- Tell whether a piece of writing is functional, narrative, informational, or poetic
- Have clear goals and understand how the goals will affect the writing

▶ Audience

- Write with specific readers or audience in mind
- Understand that writing is shaped by the writer's purpose and understanding of the audience
- Plan and organize information for the intended readers
- Understand audience as all readers rather than just the teacher
- Consider a varied audience when planning the piece
- Identify and write for an audience that is not personally known

▶ Oral Language

- Generate and expand ideas through talk with peers and teacher
- Look for ideas and topics in personal experiences, shared through talk
- Use talk and storytelling to generate and rehearse language that may be written later
- Explore relevant questions in talking about a topic
- When rehearsing language for an informational piece, use vocabulary specific to the topic
- When rehearsing language for a narrative writing, use action and content words appropriate for the story
- Experiment with language that is particular to a setting: e.g., archaic words, the sounds of accents in spoken language, words or language structures other than English

▶ Gathering Seeds/Resources/Experimenting with Writing

- Use a writer's notebook or booklet as a tool for collecting ideas, experimenting, planning, sketching, or drafting
- Reread a writer's notebook to select topics: e.g., select small moments that can be expanded
- Use sketching, webs, lists, and freewriting to think about, plan for, and try out writing
- Gather a variety of entries (e.g., character map, timeline, sketches, observations, freewrites, drafts, lists) in a writer's notebook
- Think through a topic, focus, organization, and audience

Selecting Goals Behaviors and Understandings to Notice, Teach, and Support *(cont.)*

Writing

WRITING PROCESS *(continued)*

PLANNING AND REHEARSING *(continued)*

▶ **Gathering Seeds/Resources/Experimenting with Writing** *(continued)*

- Think through an informational topic to plan organization and treatment of the topic
- Try out titles, different heads and endings, develop setting and characters in a writer's notebook
- Use notebooks to plan, gather, and rehearse for future published writing
- Plan for a story by living inside the story, gaining insight into characters so that the story can be written as it happens
- Make a plan for an essay that makes a claim and contains supporting evidence
- Choose helpful tools: e.g., webs, T-charts, sketches, charts, diagrams, lists, outlines, flowcharts
- Choose a setting and describe in details that evoke a particular mood or tone
- Gather relevant information from multiple print and digital sources, using search terms effectively
- Assess the credibility of each source using search terms effectively

▶ **Content, Topic, Theme**

- Observe carefully events, people, settings, and other aspects of the world to gather information on a topic
- Select information that will support the topic
- Choose topics that the writer knows about, cares about, or wants to learn about
- Choose topics that are interesting to the writer
- Tell about a topic in an interesting way
- Stay focused on a topic to produce a well-organized piece of writing that is long enough to fully explain the points (e.g., facts, arguments) the writer wants to make
- Get ideas from other books and writers about how to approach a topic: e.g., organization, point of view, layout
- Communicate the significance of the topic to an audience
- Show the audience (by stating or providing important information) what is important about the topic
- Use texts (print and online) to get information on a topic
- Select details that will support a topic or story
- Select title that fits the content to publish or complete as final draft
- Develop a clear, main idea around which a piece of writing will be planned
- Use the organizing features of electronic text (e.g., bulletin boards, databases, keyword searches, email addresses) to locate information
- Understand a range of genres and forms and select from them according to topic and purpose and audience

▶ **Inquiry/Research/Exploration**

- Make scientific observations, use notes and sketches to document them, and talk with others about patterns, connections, and discoveries
- Form questions to explore and locate sources for information about a topic, characters, or setting
- Select and include only the information that is appropriate to the topic and to the category
- Take and use notes to record and organize information
- Conduct research to gather information in planning a writing project: e.g., live interviews, Internet, artifacts, articles, books
- Create categories of information and organize categories into larger sections
- Determine when research is necessary to cover a nonfiction topic adequately
- Search for appropriate information from multiple sources: e.g., books and other print materials, websites, interview
- Evaluate sources for validity and point of view
- Draw evidence from literary or informational texts to support analysis, reflection, and research
- Document sources while gathering information so that it will be easy to provide references
- Understand that a writer gains ideas from other writers but should credit the other writers and/or put these ideas into one's own words
- Understand the concept of plagiarism and avoid it by citing sources for quotations and information used
- Understand that a writer may quote another writer or speaker by placing the exact words in quotes and referencing the source accurately
- Understand that in a research report a writer documents information with references for the sources and that there are prescribed forms for preparing reference lists, bibliographies, footnotes, and endnotes

▶ **Genre/Forms**

- Select the genre for the writing based on the purpose: e.g., formal letter, procedural text; realistic fiction, historical fiction, traditional literature (folktale, tall tale, fairy tale, fable, myth, legend, epic, ballad), and fantasy (including science fiction); biography, autobiography, memoir; expository text; persuasive text; poetry; hybrid text
- Choose a form for the writing: e.g., notes, cards, letters, invitations, email, lists, directions with steps (how-to); picture books, wordless picture books, poems, songs, plays, letters, short stories, diary and journal entries, narrative poetry, lyrical poetry, free verse, ballads, epics/sagas, biographical and autobiographical sketches, personal narratives; essays, reports, news and feature articles, photo essays, speeches; editorials, letters to the editor

Selecting Goals Behaviors and Understandings to Notice, Teach, and Support *(cont.)*

Writing

DRAFTING AND REVISING

▶ Understanding the Process

- Understand the role of the writer, teacher, or peer writer in conference
- Change writing in response to peer or teacher feedback
- Know how to use an editing and proofreading checklist
- Understand revision as a means for making written messages stronger and clearer to readers
- Understand that all revision is governed by the writer's decision of what will communicate meaning to the reader
- Understand that a writer rereads and revises while drafting (recursive process) and keeps doing it over and over with new pieces of writing
- Write successive drafts to show substantive revisions
- Name, understand the purpose of, try out, and internalize crafting techniques
- Use writers as mentors in making revisions and revisions while drafting (recursive process)
- Emulate the writing of other good writers by thinking of or examining mentor texts during the drafting and revision processes

▶ Producing a Draft

- Write a well-organized article focused on a central topic
- Use drawings to add information to, elaborate on, or increase readers' enjoyment and understanding
- Write a draft or discovery draft (writing fast and as much as possible on a topic)
- Understand the importance of the lead of a fiction or nonfiction text
- Begin to develop a style for drafting: e.g., from slow, deliberate drafting with ongoing revision, to fast writing of ideas for revision later
- Revise the lead to find the most interesting and engaging language
- Bring the piece to closure with an effective summary, parting idea, or satisfying ending
- Establish an initiating event and follow with a series of events in a narrative
- Present ideas in logical order across the piece
- Maintain central idea or focus across paragraphs
- Produce a series of coherent paragraphs that present information logically and lead readers through the nonfiction piece or story
- Show steps or phases in time order when incorporating temporal or chronological sequence into a nonfiction text
- Establish a situation, plot or problem, and point of view in fiction drafts
- Provide insight as to why an incident or event is memorable
- When writing a biography, memoir, or fiction story, establish important decisions (made by the central character or subject) and the outcomes of those decisions
- Establish multiple-paragraph pieces and longer texts when appropriate

- Generate multiple titles to help think about the focus of the piece
- Select a title that fits the content

▶ Rereading

- Reread writing to think about what to write next
- Reread writing to rethink and make changes
- Reread and revise the discovery draft or rewrite sections to clarify meaning
- Reread the text to be sure there are no missing words or information
- Identify language in the story that shows character change (or learning a lesson in a memoir)
- Identify the statement (and sometimes restatement) of the main idea of a piece
- Identify the turning point of a story and/or the most exciting part of a story
- Reread writing to check for clarity and purpose
- Identify language that does not contribute to the central purpose or message

▶ Adding Information

- Add ideas in thought bubbles or dialogue in quotation marks or speech bubbles to provide information, provide narration, or show thoughts and feelings
- Add descriptive words (adjectives, adverbs) and phrases to help readers visualize and understand events, actions, processes, or topics
- Add words, phrases, or sentences to make the writing more interesting or exciting for readers
- Add words, phrases, or sentences to provide more information to readers
- Add word, phrases, or sentences to clarify meaning for readers
- After reflection and rereading, add substantial pieces of text (paragraphs, pages) to provide further explanation, clarify points, add interest, or support points
- Add details or examples to make the piece clearer or more interesting
- Add transitional words and phrases to clarify meaning and make the writing smoother
- Reread and change or add words to ensure that meaning is clear
- Add descriptive words and details to increase imagery or enhance meaning, not simply to add information
- Add words, phrases, sentences, and paragraphs to add excitement to a narrative
- Add information in footnotes or endnotes

▶ Deleting Information

- Delete text to better express meaning and make more logical
- Delete words, sentences, paragraphs, or pages that do not make sense, or add necessary information or ideas
- Identify redundant words, phrases, or sentences and remove if they do not serve a purpose or enhance the voice
- Reread and cross out words to ensure that meaning is clear
- Delete information (e.g., unnecessary details, description, examples) that clutters up the writing and obscures the central meaning

WRITING

Selecting Goals Behaviors and Understandings to Notice, Teach, and Support *(cont.)*

Writing

WRITING PROCESS *(continued)*

DRAFTING AND REVISING *(continued)*

▶ **Changing a Text**

- Identify vague parts and change the language or content to be more precise
- Vary word choice to make the piece more interesting
- Work on transitions to achieve better flow
- Reshape writing to make the text into a different genre: e.g., personal narrative to poem
- Embed genres within the text to create hybrid text

▶ **Reorganizing Information**

- Rearrange and revise writing to better express meaning or make the text more logical (reorder drawings, reorder pages, cut and paste)
- Reorganize and revise the writing to better express the writer's meaning or make the text more logical
- Move information to increase suspense or move the action
- Move information to the front or end of the text for greater impact on the reader
- Reorder pages or paragraphs by laying them out and reassembling them

▶ **Using Tools and Techniques**

- Add words, letters, phrases, or sentences using a variety of techniques: e.g., caret, sticky notes, spider's legs, numbered items on a separate page, word-processing
- Use a number to identify place to add information and an additional paper with numbers to write the information to insert
- Delete words, phrases, or sentences from a text (crossing out or using word-processing) to make the meaning clearer
- Reorder the information in a text to make the meaning clearer by cutting apart, cutting and pasting, laying out pages, using word-processing
- Use standard symbols for revising and editing

EDITING AND PROOFREADING

▶ **Understanding the Process**

- Understand that a writer uses what is known to spell words
- Know how to use an editing and proofreading checklist
- Understand that a writer (after using what is known) can ask another person to do a final edit
- Understand the limitations of spell check and grammar check on the computer
- Understand how to use tools to self-evaluate writing and assist the writer in copyediting
- Know the function of an editor and respond to suggestions without defensiveness

▶ **Editing for Conventions**

- Check and correct letter formation
- Edit for the conventional spelling of known words
- Edit for spelling errors by circling words that do not look right and spelling them another way
- Understand that the teacher will be final spelling editor for the published piece after the student has used everything known
- Edit for capitalization and punctuation
- Edit for grammar and sentence sense
- Edit for word suitability and precise meaning
- Edit for cadence (rhythm, modulation, appealing quality) of sentences
- Determine where new paragraphs should begin
- Check and correct spacing and layout using layout skillfully to communicate meaning
- Integrate quotations and citations into written text in a way that maintains the coherence and flow of the writing
- Prepare final draft with self-edit and submit (teacher edit prior to publishing)

▶ **Using Tools**

- Use reference tools to check on spelling and meaning
- Use a thesaurus to search for more interesting words
- Use spell check, accepting or rejecting changes as needed
- Use grammar check, accepting or rejecting changes as needed
- Make corrections in response to editing marks by the teacher or other writers

PUBLISHING

- Produce writing to explain, label, or otherwise accompany drawing
- Create illustrations and writing that work together to express the meaning
- Create illustrations or other art for pieces that are in final form
- Share a text with peers by reading it aloud to the class
- Put several stories or poems together
- Select a poem, story, or informational book to publish in a variety of appropriate ways: e.g., typed/printed, framed and mounted or otherwise displayed
- Add cover spread with title and author information
- In anticipation of an audience, add book and print features during the publishing process: e.g., illustrations and other graphics, cover spread, title, dedication, table of contents, about the author piece, headings, subheadings
- Attend to layout of text in final publication
- Understand publishing as the sharing of a piece of writing with a purpose and an audience in mind
- Understand the importance of citing sources of information and conventions for citation
- Add bibliography of sources where needed
- Add abstract or short summary where needed

Selecting Goals Behaviors and Understandings to Notice, Teach, and Support *(cont.)*

Writing

DRAWING

- Understand that when both writing and drawing are on a page, they are mutually supportive, with each extending the other
- Use sketches or drawings to represent people, places, and things, and also to communicate mood and abstract ideas as appropriate to the genre and form
- Create drawings that are related to the written text and increase readers' understanding and enjoyment
- Use sketching to support memory and help in planning
- Use sketching to capture detail that is important to a topic
- Provide important information in the illustrations
- Add detail to drawings to add information or increase interest
- Create drawings that employ careful attention to color or detail
- Understand the difference between drawing and sketching and use them to support the writing process
- Use sketching to create quick representations of images, usually an outline in pencil or pen
- Use sketches to create drawings in published pieces
- Use diagrams or other graphics to support the process and/or add meaning
- Sketch and draw with a sense of relative size and perspective
- Use the terms *sketching* and *drawing* to refer to these processes and forms

VIEWING SELF AS A WRITER

- Have topics and ideas for writing in a list or notebook
- Select examples of best writing in all genres attempted
- Self-evaluate writing and talk about what is good about it and what techniques were used
- Self-evaluate pieces of writing in light of what is known about a genre
- Be productive as a writer, writing a specified quantity within a designated time period: e.g., average of one piece each week
- Write routinely over extended timeframes and shorter timeframes from a range of discipline-specific tasks, purposes, and audiences
- Write with independent initiative and investment
- Attend to the nuances of illustrations and how they enhance a text in order to try them out for oneself
- Take risks as a writer
- Write in a variety of genres across the year
- Attempt to write in new or unfamiliar genres: e.g., satire/parody
- Understand writing as a vehicle to communicate something the writer thinks
- Discuss with others what one is working on as a writer
- Seek feedback on writing
- Be willing to work at the craft of writing, incorporating new learning from instruction
- Compare previous writing to revised writing and notice and talk about the differences

- State what was learned from each piece of writing
- Articulate goals and plan for improving writing
- Write with fluency and ease
- Name the qualities or techniques of good writing, and work to acquire them
- Show interest in and work at crafting good writing, applying what has been learned about crafting in each piece
- Provide editing and revision help to peers
- Understand that all revision is governed by the writer's decision making of what will communicate meaning to the reader
- Mark the most important part of a piece of one's own or others' writing

Oral and Visual Communication

Oral and Visual Communication Continuum

Language is a child's most powerful learning tool. Within all of the instructional contexts that are part of a comprehensive language and literacy curriculum, learning is mediated by oral language. There are numerous references to oral language in every continuum presented in this book. Students reveal their thinking about texts through discussion with others. Their talk is essential to writing. They learn how words work through listening to, talking about, and working with them. By listening to texts read aloud, they internalize language that they will use as they talk and write. They learn language by using it for a variety of purposes and audiences. So, in a sense, oral communication is not only an integral part of every component of the curriculum but a building block toward future communication. It represents the students' thinking. We need to intentionally develop the kind of oral language competencies that students need to take them into the future.

We have created this continuum to focus on the broader area of *communication* beyond the printed word. We cannot now know exactly the kinds of communication skills that will be important in 2020 and beyond, but we can equip our students with the foundational competencies in listening, speaking, reading, writing, and technology that will allow them to take advantage of new opportunities for communication. In this continuum, we examine critical curriculum goals in two areas: listening and speaking, and presentation.

Command of language is important for every child's future. At the same time, we recognize that *language use is at the heart of every child's culture*. The ways children learn to use language in the home and extended family will also be important to them throughout their lives. As teachers, it's our role to respect the home language (and the customs that surround it) and encourage students to sustain it. School should be an *expansion* of the student's language repertoire, not a *correction*. As you use this continuum, be mindful of what you know about the language groups and cultures from which your students come. In some cultures, for example, it is not considered desirable for young children to speak a great deal in the presence of adults. In others, it may be considered rude to look directly at the adult who is speaking. Children may have learned different ways of storytelling or of responding to questions. Some children may simply be more comfortable with drawing than with a verbal response, especially if they are just beginning to learn English. There may be expectations listed here that are not appropriate for some of the children you teach; and, if so, just ignore them. Your overarching goal is to create a community within which students feel safe and respected and to invite them to express their thinking in many ways.

Listening and Speaking

Students learn by listening and responding to others. Interaction is key to gaining a deeper understanding of texts. Students need the kind of interactive skills that make good dialogue, collaboration, and problem-solving possible; they also need to develop the ability to sustain a deeper and more extended discussion of academic content. This area includes:

▶ *Listening and Understanding.* Students spend a good deal of time in school listening to explanations and directions. They learn by active listening, so it is important that they develop a habit of listening with attention and remembering details. Also, it is important that they listen actively to texts read aloud. Through listening during daily interactive read-aloud lessons, students have the opportunity to internalize the syntactic patterns of written language, to learn how texts work, and to expand vocabulary and content knowledge. You will find specific information related to vocabulary development in the Phonics, Spelling, and Word Study continuum (see Word Meaning/Vocabulary).

▶ *Social Interaction.* Social interaction is basic to success on the job as well as a happy personal life. Through conversation, people bond with each other, collaborate, and get things done. In the elementary and middle school, students develop their ability to interact with others in positive, constructive ways. They learn the social conventions that make productive dialogue work, and they learn to work within a community.

▶ *Extended Discussion.* In content areas, social interaction extends to inquiry around important ideas and social issues. Discussion is central to learning in all areas, but it is critical to the development of reading comprehension. Through extended discussion, students expand their understanding of texts that they have read or heard read aloud. They develop the ability to remember the necessary details of texts and to think beyond and about them. Extended discussion requires knowledge and skill. Students need to be able to sustain a thread of discussion and to listen and respond to others. They need to learn such conventions as getting a turn in the discussion and building on each other's ideas. Even young students can begin to learn how to sustain a text discussion, and their ability grows across the years.

▶ *Content.* It also matters what students talk about. Their ideas must be substantive, and they are best developed through collaborative inquiry. They build concepts and ideas as they talk with others while learning. They need to be able to explain and describe their thinking, make predictions and inferences, and back up their talk with evidence from personal experience and/or texts. Through daily discussion over the years, they learn the art of argument.

▶ *Cultural Sensitivity.* Today's students come to our classrooms from all over the world. Whatever your goals, they cannot be achieved unless students feel welcome and safe. As you work with this continuum, be sensitive to the areas that might be in conflict with the home cultures from which your students come. The more information you can gain about the students' home and neighborhood cultures, the more effective you will be in creating a classroom community where each student's contributions are valued. Be selective in the goals you aim for and in the way you work toward them. For example, some students might need a longer period of silence and observation before participating; some might need to "rehearse" their remarks or hear many models before joining in. You'll want to accept varying pronunciations and attempts at syntax. A gentle, friendly invitation is a good way to go.

ORAL AND VISUAL COMMUNICATION

Growing competence in listening, social interaction, extended discussion, and content will help students use language as a tool for learning across the curriculum.

Presentation

The ability to speak effectively to a group—small or large—is an enormous advantage to an individual. Many students are afraid of speaking to a group, largely because of inexperience or even a bad experience. We see performance as a basic competence that needs to be developed across the years. Even young students can talk to the class about their own lives or their writing; they can prepare illustrations to support their communication. As students move into the upper elementary grades, they have many technological tools that enable them to combine media. We describe a continuum of learning in six areas related to presentation: voice, conventions, organization, word choice, ideas and content, and media.

> *Voice.* Here, *voice* refers to the speaker's personal style. We have all watched gifted speakers who captivate their audience. While we are not expecting every student to become a public speaker, we do hope that each student can develop ways of speaking that will capture the interest and attention of those listening. Speakers learn how to begin in a way that engages the audience and to use voice modulation and gesture in interesting ways.

> *Conventions.* Certain conventions are basic to making effective presentations. For example, the speaker needs to enunciate words clearly, talk at an appropriate volume, and use an effective pace—not too slow and not too fast. Looking directly at the audience and making eye contact is also helpful. With practice, these conventions can become automatic, freeing the speaker to concentrate on the ideas he is expressing.

> *Organization.* An effective presentation is well planned and organized. The speaker can organize information in various ways—problem and solution or cause and effect, for example. Effective presentations are concise and clear rather than unfocused and random. The speaker needs to keep the audience in mind when planning the organizational structure of a particular presentation.

> *Word Choice.* Effective speakers choose their words carefully both to make an impact on the audience and to communicate meaning clearly. Speakers often need to use specific words related to the content area they are covering, and they may need to define these words for the audience. Speakers can also use more literary language to increase listeners' interest. They choose their words with the audience in mind; more formal language may be needed in a professional presentation than in an everyday conversation or a discussion.

> *Ideas and Content.* The substance of a presentation is important. Technique is wasted if the ideas and content are not substantive. Effective speakers demonstrate their understanding through the information they have chosen to present. They know how to establish an argument, use persuasive strategies, provide examples, and cite relevant evidence.

> *Media.* The use of different kinds of visual displays generally enhances oral presentations, although media can sometimes be overused. For the youngest children, the use of media may include pictures, drawings, or posters, though that is changing quickly. As their presentations grow more sophisticated, students can make use of a wide array of electronic resources in order to create multimedia presentations. Speakers can even present information in other ways; for example, by creating

interactive, nonlinear websites that members of the audience can explore on their own. Today's technology allows presenters to share their knowledge of a topic in different ways.

Communication

The territory of communication is multifaceted and involves a wide range of competencies. Language is at once an individual's most important learning tool and the vehicle for presenting to the world. Through language, people form the critical emotional relationships that shape their lives, they make their way to success in school and in careers, and they reveal themselves to others and build social relationships. Because students spend so much time in schools, the experience we provide has a major influence on their development of oral language skills. The classroom can provide opportunities to use oral language to the maximum, to talk with others about texts, expressing feelings and insights, and to engage in inquiry and present the results to peers. Not every student will become a dynamic oral presenter, but each can learn to cogently express ideas based on reading and research. Think of oral language as a long continuum from the early years of school to the time when students are required to demonstrate their knowledge publicly (the first public being their classmates). Language is the way we negotiate our world. While the primary development of language is in the home, school plays a vital part in using language as a tool for learning and in expanding language to wider communication.

Using the Oral and Visual Communication Continuum

The Oral and Visual Communication continuum lists behaviors and understandings to notice, teach, and support in two main areas: (1) Listening and Speaking; and (2) Presentation. Like the Writing continuum, no texts are listed because the students themselves are producing the texts—oral, written, and visual. Use this continuum in connection with the Writing continuum; often students will need to make outlines or notes for presentation, and sometimes they will write them as speeches. But most of the time, oral and written communication is a highly creative process that involves many ways of presenting one's ideas to others. The goals listed here can help you observe students' interactions and make decisions about how to help them become more effective in small and large group situations. If students have daily opportunities to present their ideas to others in a safe and supportive environment, they will grow in confidence and verbal ability.

ORAL AND VISUAL COMMUNICATION

Selecting Goals Behaviors and Understandings to Notice, Teach, and Support

Oral and Visual Communication

LISTENING AND SPEAKING

▶ **Listening and Understanding**

- Listen with active attention to texts that are read aloud
- Listen with attention and understanding to simple and clear directions
- Remember and follow simple directions with one or two steps
- Ask questions when directions are not clearly understood
- Look at the speaker when being spoken to
- Listen actively to others as they read or speak
- Compare personal knowledge and experiences with what is heard
- Listen with attention and understanding to oral reading of stories, poems, songs, and informational texts
- Ask questions about the stories, poems, songs, and informational texts that are read aloud

▶ **Social Interactions**

- Speak at an appropriate volume
- Adjust speaking volume for different contexts
- Use courteous terms such as *please* and *thank you*
- Engage in conversation during play
- Enter a conversation appropriately
- Refrain from speaking over others
- Sustain a conversation with others: e.g., teachers, family, peers
- Take turns when speaking with others
- Engage in dramatic dialogue in play or role-playing contexts

▶ **Extended Discussion**

- Understand and use words related to familiar common experiences and topics
- Follow a topic and add to discussion
- Listen to and respond to the statements of others
- Form clear questions to get information
- Actively participate in the give and take of conversation
- Use some specific vocabulary (e.g., title, cover, author) in conversations about books
- Notice and learn new words related to topics of inquiry in the classroom

- Act out stories with or without props
- Engage in dramatic play

▶ **Content**

- Describe people and places in a story
- Share knowledge of story structure by telling what happened
- Predict future events in a story and tell why
- Begin to verbalize reasons for problems, events, and actions in stories
- Begin to understand the concept of cause and effect
- Discuss what is already known about a topic
- Report what is known or learned about in an informational text
- Talk about how people, places, and events are alike and different
- Express opinions and tell why
- Recognize that others have feelings different from one's own
- Ask questions, demonstrating curiosity
- Join in on songs, rhymes, and chants

PRESENTATION

▶ **Voice**

- Talk about a topic with enthusiasm
- Tell stories in an interesting way
- Speak with confidence

▶ **Conventions**

- Speak at appropriate volume to be heard, but not too loudly
- Look at the audience (or other person) while speaking
- Speak at an appropriate rate to be understood

▶ **Organization**

- Tell personal experiences in an understandable sequence
- Present information or ideas in an understandable way

▶ **Word Choice**

- Understand and use words related to familiar experiences and topics
- Use some language from stories when retelling them
- Use some descriptive words

▶ **Ideas and Content**

- Tell stories from personal experience
- Retell stories from texts
- Recite songs and short poems

Selecting Goals Behaviors and Understandings to Notice, Teach, and Support

Oral and Visual Communication

LISTENING AND SPEAKING

▶ Listening and Understanding

- Listen with active attention to texts that are read aloud
- Listen with attention and understanding to directions
- Remember and follow simple directions with two to three steps
- Ask questions when directions are not clearly understood
- Look at the speaker when being spoken to
- Listen actively to others read or talk about their writing and give feedback
- Compare personal knowledge and experiences with what is heard
- Listen to and speak to a partner about a given idea, and make a connection to the partner's idea
- Listen with attention and understanding to oral reading of stories, poems, songs, and informational texts
- Ask questions about the stories, poems, songs, and informational texts that are read aloud
- Ask questions to clarify unknown words heard while actively listening

▶ Social Interactions

- Speak at an appropriate volume
- Adjust speaking volume for different contexts
- Use courteous conversational conventions: e.g., *please, thank you,* greetings
- Engage in conversation during play
- Enter a conversation appropriately
- Refrain from speaking over others
- Sustain a conversation with others: e.g., teachers, family, peers
- Take turns when speaking
- Engage in dramatic dialogue in play or role-playing contexts

▶ Extended Discussion

- Understand and use words related to familiar common experiences and topics
- Follow a topic and add to discussion
- Listen to and respond to the statements of others
- Form clear questions to get information

- Actively participate in the give and take of conversation
- Use some specific vocabulary (e.g., title, cover, author) in conversations about books
- Notice and learn new words related to topics of inquiry in the classroom
- Act out stories with or without props
- Engage in dramatic play
- Engage actively in conversational routines: e.g., turn and talk in pairs, triads

▶ Content

- Explain and describe people, events, places, and things in a story
- Share knowledge of story structure telling what happened, mostly in order
- Predict future events in a story and tell why
- Begin to verbalize reasons for problems, events, and actions in stories
- Discuss cause-and-effect relationships
- Offer solutions and explanations for story problems
- Discuss what is already known about a topic
- Report what is known or learned about in an informational text
- Describe similarities and differences among people, places, events, and things
- Express opinions and tell why
- Express and reflect on their own feelings and recognize that others' feelings might be different
- Ask many questions, demonstrating curiosity
- Initiate and join in on songs, rhymes, and chants
- Show interest in the meaning of words

PRESENTATION

▶ Voice

- Talk about a topic with enthusiasm
- Tell stories in an interesting way
- Speak with confidence

▶ Conventions

- Speak at appropriate volume to be heard, but not too loud
- Look at the audience (or other person) while speaking
- Speak at an appropriate rate to be understood

▶ Organization

- Have an audience in mind before starting to speak
- Tell personal experiences in a logical sequence
- Present information or ideas in a logical sequence
- Speak to one topic at a time, and stay on topic
- Demonstrate knowledge of story structure

▶ Word Choice

- Understand and use words related to familiar experiences and topics
- Use language from stories when retelling
- Use descriptive words

▶ Ideas and Content

- Tell stories from personal experience
- Retell familiar stories or stories from texts
- Recite short poems and songs
- Share knowledge about a simple, familiar topic

▶ Media

- Sometimes share pictures or artifacts about a known topic
- Perform plays and puppet shows that involve speaking as a character

Selecting Goals Behaviors and Understandings to Notice, Teach, and Support

Oral and Visual Communication

ORAL AND VISUAL COMMUNICATION

LISTENING AND SPEAKING

▶ Listening and Understanding

- Listen with active attention to texts that are read aloud
- Listen with attention and understanding to directions
- Remember and follow directions with multiple steps
- Ask questions when directions are not clearly understood
- Look at the speaker when being spoken to
- Listen actively to others read or talk about their writing and give feedback
- Compare personal knowledge and experiences with what is heard
- Listen to and speak to a partner about a given idea, and make a connection to the partner's idea
- Listen with attention and understanding to oral reading of stories, poems, and informational texts
- Ask and answer questions about stories, poems, songs, and informational texts that are read aloud
- Ask questions to clarify unknown words heard while actively listening
- Provide at least one reason for agreement with an idea or opinion

▶ Social Interactions

- Speak at an appropriate volume
- Adjust speaking volume for different contexts
- Use courteous conversational conventions: e.g., *please, thank you,* greetings
- Engage in conversation during play
- Enter a conversation appropriately
- Refrain from speaking over others
- Sustain a conversation with others: e.g., teachers, family, peers
- Take turns when speaking
- Engage in dramatic dialogue in play or role-playing contexts
- Demonstrate respectful listening behaviors

▶ Extended Discussion

- Understand and use words related to familiar common experiences and topics
- Follow a topic and add to discussion with comments on the same topic

- Listen to and respond to the statements of others
- Form clear questions to get information
- Actively participate in the give and take of conversation
- Use grade level-appropriate vocabulary in conversations about books
- Notice and learn new words related to topics of inquiry in the classroom
- Act out stories with or without props
- Engage actively in conversational routines: e.g., turn and talk
- Listen and respond to a partner by agreeing or disagreeing and explaining reasons

▶ Content

- Explain and describe people, events, places, and things in a story
- Share knowledge of story structure by telling what happened, mostly in order
- Predict future events in a story and tell why
- Recall stories including events, characters, problems
- Begin to verbalize reasons for problems, events, and actions in stories
- Discuss cause-and-effect relationships
- Express opinions and explain reasoning
- Offer solutions and explanations for story problems
- Use background knowledge from experience or reading to identify new information
- Discuss what is already known about a topic and how it is known
- Report what is known or learned about in an informational text
- Describe similarities and differences among people, places, events, and things
- Express and reflect on their own feelings and recognize the feelings of others
- Ask many questions, demonstrating curiosity
- Initiate and join in on songs, rhymes, and chants
- Show interest in the meaning of words

PRESENTATION

▶ Voice

- Talk about a topic with enthusiasm
- Tell stories in an interesting way
- Speak with confidence

▶ Conventions

- Speak at appropriate volume to be heard, but not too loud
- Look at the audience (or other person) while speaking
- Speak at an appropriate rate to be understood
- Answer questions asked by the audience

▶ Organization

- Have a topic, story, or response in mind before starting to speak
- Tell personal experiences in a logical sequence
- Present ideas and information in a logical sequence
- Speak to one topic at a time, and stay on topic
- Demonstrate knowledge of story structure

▶ Word Choice

- Understand and use words related to familiar experiences and topics
- Use language from stories when retelling
- Use descriptive words

▶ Ideas and Content

- Tell stories from personal experience
- Retell familiar stories or stories from texts
- Recite short poems and songs
- Make brief oral reports that demonstrate understanding of a simple, familiar topic

▶ Media

- Use props, images, or illustrations to extend the meaning of a presentation
- Perform plays and puppet shows that involve speaking as a character

Selecting Goals Behaviors and Understandings to Notice, Teach, and Support

Oral and Visual Communication

LISTENING AND SPEAKING

▶ Listening and Understanding

- Listen with active attention to texts that are read aloud
- Listen to, remember, and follow directions with multiple steps
- Ask questions when directions are not clearly understood
- Look at the speaker when being spoken to
- Listen actively to others read or talk about their writing and give feedback
- Compare personal knowledge and experiences with what is heard
- Listen to and speak to a partner about a given idea, and make a connection to the partner's idea
- Listen with attention and understanding to oral reading of stories, poems, and informational texts
- Listen with attention during instruction, and respond with statements and questions
- Ask clarifying questions when listening to texts read aloud, or to presentations by teachers and other students
- Ask questions to clarify unknown words heard while actively listening
- Recall and state ideas from oral reading and presentations
- Provide more than one reason for agreement with an idea or opinion
- Understand and interpret information presented through audio/visual media

▶ Social Interactions

- Speak at an appropriate volume
- Adjust speaking volume for different contexts
- Use conventions of respectful conversation
- Enter a conversation appropriately
- Refrain from speaking over others
- Sustain a conversation with a variety of audiences
- Take turns when speaking
- Demonstrate respectful listening behaviors

▶ Extended Discussion

- Follow a topic and add to discussion with comments on the same topic
- Listen, respond, and build on the statements of others

- Ask questions for clarification or to gain information
- Actively participate in the give and take of conversation
- Use grade level-appropriate vocabulary in conversations about books
- Notice and learn new words related to topics of inquiry in the classroom
- Engage actively in conversational routines: e.g., turn and talk
- Ask follow-up questions during partner, small-group, and whole-class discussion
- Relate or compare one's own knowledge and experience with information from others
- Listen and respond to a partner by agreeing, disagreeing, or adding on and explaining reasons

▶ Content

- Explain and describe people, events, places, and things in a story
- Share knowledge of story structure by describing setting, characters, events, or endings
- Predict future events in a story and explain reasons
- Recall stories including events, characters, problems
- Verbalize reasons for problems, events, and actions in stories
- Discuss cause-and-effect relationships
- Express opinions and support with evidence
- Offer solutions and explanations for story problems
- Use background knowledge from experience or reading to identify new information
- Discuss what is already known about a topic and how it is known
- Describe similarities and differences among people, places, events, and things
- Express and reflect on their own feelings and recognize the feelings of others
- Use language to talk about the messages in texts
- Show interest in the meaning of words and work actively to learn and use them

PRESENTATION

▶ Voice

- Speak about a topic with enthusiasm
- Tell stories and present information in an interesting way
- Show confidence when presenting
- Vary speaking voice for emphasis

▶ Conventions

- Speak at appropriate volume to be heard when addressing large and small groups
- Look at the audience (or other person) while talking
- Speak at an appropriate rate to be understood
- Enunciate words clearly enough to be understood with regional or other accents acceptable
- Enunciate words clearly in their own languages as well as in English
- Answer questions asked by the audience
- Pronounce most words in a standard way (with variations based on child's home language or regional dialect)
- Use intonation and word stress to emphasize important ideas
- Vary language according to purpose

▶ Organization

- Have a topic, story, or response in mind before starting to speak
- Have an audience in mind before starting to speak
- Maintain a clear focus on the important or main ideas
- Present ideas and information in a logical sequence
- Speak to one topic at a time, and stay on topic
- Demonstrate knowledge of story structure
- Have a clear beginning and conclusion
- Have a plan or notes to support the presentation

Selecting Goals Behaviors and Understandings to Notice, Teach, and Support *(cont.)*

Oral and Visual Communication

PRESENTATION *(continued)*

▶ **Word Choice**

- Understand and use words related to familiar experiences and topics
- Use language from stories and informational texts when retelling or making a report
- Use descriptive words that are grade-level appropriate
- Use language appropriate for oral presentations

▶ **Ideas and Content**

- Tell stories from personal experiences
- Retell familiar stories or stories from texts
- Recite short poems and songs
- Make brief oral reports that demonstrate understanding of a topic
- Engage in role play of characters or events encountered in stories
- Demonstrate understanding of a topic by providing relevant facts and details

▶ **Media**

- Use props, illustrations, images, or other digital media to enhance a presentation
- Perform plays and puppet shows that involve speaking as a character
- Identify and acknowledge sources of information included in presentations

Selecting Goals Behaviors and Understandings to Notice, Teach, and Support

Oral and Visual Communication

LISTENING AND SPEAKING

▶ Listening and Understanding

- Listen with active attention to texts that are read aloud
- Listen to, remember, and follow directions with multiple steps
- Listen actively to others read, or talk about their writing, and give feedback
- Compare personal knowledge and experiences with what is heard
- Listen to and speak to a partner about a given idea, and make a connection to the partner's idea
- Listen with attention and understanding to oral reading of stories, poems, and informational texts
- Listen with attention during instruction, and respond with statements and questions
- Ask clarifying questions when listening to texts read aloud or to presentations by teachers and other students
- Ask questions to clarify unknown words heard while actively listening
- Recall and state ideas from oral reading and presentations
- Provide more than one reason for agreement with an idea or opinion
- Understand and interpret information presented through audio/visual media

▶ Social Interactions

- Speak at an appropriate volume
- Adjust speaking volume for different contexts
- Use conventions of respectful conversation
- Enter a conversation appropriately
- Refrain from speaking over others
- Sustain a conversation with a variety of audiences
- Demonstrate respectful listening behaviors
- Use turn-taking with courtesy in small-group discussion
- Use appropriate conventions in small-group discussion (e.g., "I agree with _____ because . . ."; "I'd like to change the subject . . .")

▶ Extended Discussion

- Follow a topic and add to a discussion with comments on the same topic

- Listen, respond, and build on the statements of others
- Ask questions for clarification or to gain information
- Actively participate in the give and take of conversation
- Use grade level-appropriate vocabulary in conversations about books
- Notice and learn new words related to topics of inquiry in the classroom
- Engage actively in conversational routines: e.g., turn and talk
- Ask follow-up questions during partner, small-group, and whole-class discussion
- Relate or compare one's own knowledge and experience with information from others
- Listen and respond to a partner by agreeing, disagreeing or adding on, and explaining reasons
- Restate points that have been made and extend or elaborate upon them

▶ Content

- Recognize and discuss people, events, places, and things in a text
- Share knowledge of story structure by describing setting, characters, events, or endings
- Make predictions based on evidence
- Recall stories including events, characters, problems
- Discuss reasons for problems, events, and actions in stories
- Discuss cause-and-effect relationships
- Express opinions and support with evidence
- Offer solutions and explanations for story problems
- Use background experience or reading to identify new information
- Discuss what is already known about a topic and how it is known
- Describe similarities and differences among people, places, events, and things
- Express and reflect on their own feelings and recognize the feelings of others
- Use language to talk about the messages in texts
- Show interest in the meaning of words and work actively to learn and use them

PRESENTATION

▶ Voice

- Speak about a topic with enthusiasm
- Tell stories and present information in an interesting way
- Show confidence when presenting
- Vary speaking voice for emphasis

▶ Conventions

- Speak at appropriate volume to be heard when addressing large and small groups
- Look at the audience (or other person) while talking
- Speak at an appropriate rate to be understood
- Enunciate words clearly enough to be understood by a small group or the class (with regional and other accents being acceptable)
- Enunciate words clearly in their own languages as well as English
- Answer questions asked by the audience
- Pronounce most words in a standard way (with variations based on student's home language or regional dialect)
- Use intonation and word stress to emphasize important ideas
- Vary language according to purpose
- Use mostly conventional grammar (depending on individual opportunities over time)
- Stand with good posture

▶ Organization

- Have a topic, story, or response in mind before starting to speak
- Have an audience in mind before starting to speak
- Maintain a clear focus on the important or main ideas
- Present ideas and information in a logical sequence
- Speak to one topic at a time, and stay on topic
- Demonstrate knowledge of story structure
- Have a clear beginning and conclusion
- Have a plan or notes to support the presentation

ORAL AND VISUAL COMMUNICATION

Selecting Goals Behaviors and Understandings to Notice, Teach, and Support *(cont.)*

Oral and Visual Communication

ORAL AND VISUAL COMMUNICATION

PRESENTATION *(continued)*

▶ **Word Choice**

- Understand and use words related to familiar experiences and topics as well as content and technical terms from academic disciplines
- Use language from stories and informational texts when retelling or making a report
- Use descriptive words that are grade-level appropriate
- Use language appropriate to oral presentations

▶ **Ideas and Content**

- Recite short poems and songs
- Make brief oral reports that demonstrate understanding of a topic
- Engage in role play of characters or events encountered in stories
- Demonstrate understanding of a topic by providing relevant facts and details

▶ **Media**

- Use graphics (e.g., charts, illustrations, or other digital media) as appropriate to communicate meaning or to enhance a presentation
- Identify and acknowledge sources of information included in presentations
- Read aloud own writing and discuss with others
- Perform readers' theater scripts or poems with expression

Selecting Goals Behaviors and Understandings to Notice, Teach, and Support

Oral and Visual Communication

LISTENING AND SPEAKING

▶ Listening and Understanding

- Listen with active attention to texts that are read aloud
- Listen to, remember, and follow directions with multiple steps
- Listen actively to others read, or talk about their writing, and give feedback
- Listen to and speak to a partner about a given idea, and make a connection to the partner's idea
- Listen with attention and understanding to oral reading of stories, poems, and informational texts
- Listen with attention during instruction, and respond with statements and questions
- Ask clarifying questions when listening to texts read aloud or to presentations by teachers and other students
- Ask questions to clarify unknown words heard while actively listening
- Provide several reasons for agreement with an idea or opinion
- Understand and interpret information presented through audio/visual media
- Analyze how a speaker uses evidence and examples effectively
- Summarize ideas from oral reading or presentation

▶ Social Interactions

- Speak at an appropriate volume
- Adjust speaking volume for different contexts
- Use conventions of respectful conversation
- Enter a conversation appropriately
- Refrain from speaking over others
- Sustain a conversation with a variety of audiences
- Actively participate in conversation by listening and looking at the person speaking
- Use turn-taking with courtesy in small-group discussion
- Use appropriate conventions in small-group discussion (e.g., "I agree with _____ because . . ."; "I'd like to change the subject . . .")

- Use conventional techniques that encourage others to talk: e.g., "What do you think?" "Do you agree? Why or why not?"
- Respond to others' ideas before changing the subject
- Understand and use language for the purpose of humor: e.g., jokes, riddles, puns
- Use nonpejorative and inclusive language: e.g., nonsexist, nonracist, unbiased
- Understand the role of nonverbal language and use it effectively
- Use tone and gesture in an appropriate way

▶ Extended Discussion

- Follow a topic and add to a discussion with comments on the same topic
- Build on the talk of others by making statements related to the speaker's topic and by responding to cues
- Ask questions for clarification or to gain information.
- Actively participate in conversation during whole- and small-group discussion.
- Use grade level-appropriate vocabulary in conversations about books
- Learn new words related to topics of inquiry in the classroom
- Engage actively in conversational routines: e.g., turn and talk
- Ask follow-up questions during partner, small-group, and whole-class discussion
- Relate or compare one's own knowledge and experience with information from others
- Listen and respond to a partner by agreeing, disagreeing or adding on, and explaining reasons
- Restate points that have been made and extend or elaborate upon them
- Play the role of group leader when needed
- Evaluate one's own part in a group discussion as well as the effectiveness of the group
- Facilitate a group discussion by ensuring that everyone has a chance to speak

- Use respectful turn-taking conventions
- Suggest new lines of discussion when appropriate
- Recall information, big ideas, or points made by others
- Sustain a discussion by staying on the main topic and requesting or signaling a change of topic

▶ Content

- Recognize and discuss people, events, places, and things in a text
- Share knowledge of story structure by describing setting, characters, events, or endings
- Make predictions based on evidence
- Recall stories including events, characters, problems
- Discuss reasons for problems, events, and actions
- Discuss cause-and-effect relationships
- Express opinions and support arguments with evidence
- State and discuss problem and solutions
- Use background knowledge from experience or reading to identify new information
- Discuss what is already known about a topic and how it is known
- Compare and contrast people, places, events, and things
- Express and reflect on their own feelings and recognize the feelings of others
- Demonstrate understanding of deeper messages in texts
- Show interest in the meaning of words and work actively to learn and use them
- Use descriptive language when discussing a topic or idea
- Demonstrate understanding of the subtle differences in the meaning of words: e.g., *bright, glowing*
- Identify and understand figurative meanings of words when they are used as similes and metaphors
- Identify the connotation and denotation of words

Selecting Goals Behaviors and Understandings to Notice, Teach, and Support *(cont.)*

Oral and Visual Communication

ORAL AND VISUAL COMMUNICATION

PRESENTATION

▶ Voice

- Communicate interest in and enthusiasm about a topic
- Present information in ways that engage listeners' attention
- Show confidence when presenting
- Use expression, tone, word stress, and pitch for emphasis
- Use effective introductions in oral presentations to capture attention
- Pause effectively to enhance interest and emphasize points
- Use personal interpretation and style when reading aloud

▶ Conventions

- Speak with appropriate volume for audience size and location
- Speak directly to the audience, making eye contact with individuals
- Speak at an appropriate rate to be understood
- Enunciate words clearly enough to be understood by a small group or the class (with regional and other accents being acceptable)
- Answer questions asked by the audience
- Make an effort to pronounce names and non-English words correctly
- Vary the use of language for different kinds of presentations: e.g., dramatic, narrative, reports
- Use mostly conventional grammar and pronunciation of words (depending on individual opportunities over time)
- Stand with good posture

▶ Organization

- Have an audience in mind before starting to speak
- Maintain a clear focus on the important or main ideas
- Present ideas and information in a logical sequence
- Have a clear introduction, body, and conclusion to your topic
- Choose clear examples that are related to the topic

- Use underlying structural patterns common for expository topics: e.g., description, cause and effect, chronological sequence, temporal sequence, compare and contrast, problem and solution
- Have a plan or notes to support the presentation

▶ Word Choice

- Understand and use words related to familiar experiences and topics as well as some content and technical terms from academic disciplines
- Use language from stories and informational texts when retelling stories or making a report
- Use language appropriate for oral presentations
- Define technical words within a presentation to help the audience to understand their meanings
- Vary word choice to be specific and precise while keeping the audience in mind
- Use figurative language to create visual images where appropriate

▶ Ideas and Content

- Recite poems or tell stories with effective use of intonation and word stress to emphasize important ideas, engage listeners' interest, and show character traits
- Make oral reports that demonstrate understanding of a topic
- Engage in role play of characters or events encountered in stories
- Demonstrate understanding of a topic by providing relevant facts and details
- Add evaluative comments, making clear that opinion is being stated (e.g., "I think . . ."), and provide evidence
- Make persuasive presentations that establish a clear argument and support the argument with evidence

▶ Media

- Use graphics (e.g., diagrams, illustrations, slideshows, other digital media) to communicate meaning or to enhance a presentation
- Identify and acknowledge sources of information included in presentations
- Read aloud and discuss own writing with others

- Integrate technology tools (e.g., slideshows, video, audio) into multimedia presentations
- Perform readers' theater scripts or poems with expression

Selecting Goals Behaviors and Understandings to Notice, Teach, and Support

Oral and Visual Communication

LISTENING AND SPEAKING

▶ Listening and Understanding

- Identify own purpose for listening
- Listen with active attention to texts that are read aloud
- Listen actively to others read, or talk about their writing, and give feedback
- Listen to and speak to a partner about a given idea, make a connection to the partner's idea
- Listen with attention and understanding to oral reading of stories, poems, and informational texts
- Listen with attention during instruction, and respond with statements and questions
- Ask clarifying questions when listening to texts read aloud or to presentations by teachers and other students
- Ask questions to clarify unknown words heard while actively listening
- Identify essential information for note-taking
- Provide several reasons for agreement with an idea or opinion
- Understand and interpret information presented in audio/visual media
- Analyze how a speaker uses evidence and examples effectively
- Summarize ideas from oral reading or presentation

▶ Social Interactions

- Listen respectfully and responsibly
- Respect the age, gender, position, and cultural traditions of the speaker
- Speak at an appropriate volume
- Adjust speaking volume for different contexts.
- Use conventions of respectful conversation
- Enter a conversation appropriately
- Refrain from speaking over others
- Sustain a conversation with a variety of audiences
- Actively participate in conversation by listening and looking at the person speaking
- Demonstrate balance in conversation by taking turns
- Use conventional techniques that encourage others to talk (e.g., "What do you think?" "Do you agree? Why or Why not?")

- Respond to others' ideas before changing the subject
- Understand and use language for the purpose of humor (e.g., jokes, riddles, puns)
- Use nonpejorative and inclusive language (e.g., nonsexist, nonracist, unbiased)
- Understand the role of nonverbal language and use it effectively
- Use tone and gesture in an appropriate way

▶ Extended Discussion

- Follow a topic and add to a discussion with comments on the same topic
- Build on the talk of others by making statements related to the speaker's topic and by responding to cues.
- Monitor own understanding of others' comments and ask for clarification and elaboration
- Actively participate in conversation during whole- and small-group discussion
- Use grade level-appropriate vocabulary in conversations about books
- Learn new words related to topics of inquiry in the classroom
- Engage actively in conversational routines (e.g., turn and talk)
- Ask follow-up questions during partner, small-group and whole-class discussion
- Relate or compare one's own knowledge and experience with information from others
- Listen and respond to a partner by agreeing, disagreeing or adding on, and explain reasons
- Restate points that have been made and extend or elaborate upon them
- Demonstrate effectiveness as a group leader
- Evaluate one's own part in a group discussion as well as the effectiveness of the group
- Facilitate a group discussion by ensuring that everyone has a chance to speak
- Use respectful turn-taking conventions
- Suggest new lines of discussion when appropriate
- Recall, restate, or paraphrase information, big ideas, or points made by others
- Sustain a discussion by staying on the main topic and requesting or signaling a change of topic
- Negotiate issues without conflict or anger

▶ Content

- Recognize and discuss people, events, places and things in a text
- Share knowledge of story structure by describing setting, characters, events or endings
- Make predictions based on evidence
- Discuss reasons for problems, events, and actions
- Recall stories including events, characters, problems
- Report interesting and/or new information from background experience or reading
- Discuss cause-and-effect relationships
- Express opinions and support with evidence and logical reasoning
- State and discuss problem and solutions
- Discuss what is already known about a topic and how it is known
- Compare and contrast people, places, events, and things
- Express and reflect on their own feelings and recognize the feelings of others
- Demonstrate understanding of deeper messages in texts
- Demonstrate knowledge of content area subjects
- Show interest in the meaning of words and work actively to learn and use them
- Use descriptive language when discussing a topic or idea
- Demonstrate understanding of the subtle differences in the meaning of words (e.g., *motive*, *intent*)
- Identify and understand new meanings of words when they are used as similes and metaphors
- Identify the connotation and denotation of words
- Understand the meaning of idioms

Selecting Goals Behaviors and Understandings to Notice, Teach, and Support *(cont.)*

Oral and Visual Communication

PRESENTATION

▶ Voice

- Communicate interest in and enthusiasm about a topic
- Present information in ways that engage listeners' attention
- Speak with confidence and in a relaxed manner
- Use expression, tone, word stress and pitch for emphasis
- Use effective introductions in oral presentations to capture attention
- Use effective closings in oral presentations to summarize information, persuade, or stimulate thinking
- Pause effectively to enhance interest and emphasize points
- Use personal interpretation and style when speaking

▶ Conventions

- Speak with appropriate volume for audience size and location
- Speak directly to the audience, making eye contact with individuals
- Speak at an appropriate rate to be understood
- Enunciate words clearly enough to be understood by a small group or the class (with regional and other accents being acceptable)
- Answer questions asked by the audience
- Pronounce names and non-English words correctly
- Vary the use of language for different kinds of presentations (e.g., dramatic, narrative, reports)
- Use mostly conventional grammar and pronunciation of words (depending on individual opportunities over time)
- Stand with good posture
- Use hand gestures appropriately

▶ Organization

- Have an audience in mind before starting to speak
- Maintain a clear focus on the important or main ideas
- Present ideas and information in a concise manner with a logical sequence

- Have a clear introduction, body, and conclusion to your topic
- Choose clear examples that are related to the topic
- Use structures common to expository topics (e.g., compare and contrast, description, cause and effect, problem and solution, chronological and temporal sequence)
- Prepare a plan or notes to support the presentation

▶ Word Choice

- Understand and use words related to familiar experiences and topics as well as content and technical terms from academic disciplines
- Use language from books and informational texts when presenting
- Use language appropriate for oral presentations
- Define technical words within a presentation to help the audience to understand their meaning
- Vary word choice to be specific and precise while keeping the audience in mind
- Use figurative language to create visual images where appropriate
- Be aware of using words with connotative meaning relative to social values and stereotypes

▶ Ideas and Content

- Deliver oral reports that demonstrate understanding of a topic
- Recite poems or tell stories with effective use of intonation and word stress to emphasize important ideas, engage listeners' interest, and show character traits
- Engage in role play of characters or events encountered in texts
- Demonstrate understanding of a topic by providing relevant facts and details
- Add evaluative comments, making clear that opinion is being stated (e.g., "I think . . .") and provide evidence
- Make persuasive presentations that establish a clear argument and support it with evidence

▶ Media

- Use graphics (e.g., diagrams, illustrations, or other digital media) to communicate meaning or enhance a presentation
- Identify and acknowledge sources of information included in presentations
- Read aloud and discuss own writing with others
- Integrate technology tools (e.g., *slideshows*, video, audio) in multimedia presentations

Selecting Goals Behaviors and Understandings to Notice, Teach, and Support

Oral and Visual Communication

LISTENING AND SPEAKING

▶ Listening and Understanding

- Identify own purpose for listening
- Listen with active attention to texts that are read aloud
- Listen actively to others read or talk about their writing and give feedback
- Listen to and speak to a partner about a given idea, and make a connection to the partner's idea
- Listen with attention and understanding to oral reading of stories, poems, and informational texts
- Listen with attention during instruction, and respond with statements and questions
- Ask clarifying questions when listening to texts read aloud or to presentations by teachers and other students
- Ask questions to clarify unknown words heard while actively listening
- Identify essential information for note-taking
- Provide several reasons for agreement with an idea or opinion
- Analyze how a speaker uses evidence and examples effectively
- Summarize ideas from oral reading or presentation
- Critically analyze the credibility of the speaker or media message
- Critique presentations for logic, presentation of evidence for arguments, subtexts, and inclusion or exclusion of information
- Recognize faulty reasoning and bias in presentations and media messages
- Identify, analyze, and critique persuasive techniques
- Understand dialect and its relationship to meaning

▶ Social Interactions

- Listen respectfully and responsibly
- Respect the age, gender, position, and cultural traditions of the speaker
- Speak at an appropriate volume
- Adjust speaking volume for different contexts
- Use conventions of respectful conversation
- Enter a conversation appropriately
- Refrain from speaking over others

- Sustain a conversation with a variety of audiences
- Actively participate in conversation by listening and looking at the person speaking
- Demonstrate balance in conversation by taking turns
- Use conventional techniques that encourage others to talk: e.g., "What do you think?" "Do you agree? Why or why not?"
- Respond to others' ideas before changing the subject
- Understand and use language for the purpose of humor: e.g., jokes, riddles, puns
- Use nonpejorative and inclusive language: e.g., nonsexist, nonracist, unbiased
- Understand the role of nonverbal language and use it effectively
- Use tone and gesture in an appropriate way

▶ Extended Discussion

- Follow a topic and add to a discussion with comments on the same topic
- Build on the talk of others by making statements related to the speaker's topic and by responding to cues
- Monitor own understanding of others' comments and ask for clarification and elaboration
- Actively participate in conversation during whole- and small-group discussion.
- Use grade level-appropriate vocabulary in conversations about texts
- Learn new words related to topics of inquiry in the classroom
- Engage actively in conversational routines: e.g., turn and talk
- Ask follow-up questions during partner, small-group, and whole-class discussion
- Relate or compare one's own knowledge and experience with information from others
- Listen and respond to a partner by agreeing, disagreeing or adding on, and explaining reasons
- Demonstrate effectiveness as a group leader
- Evaluate one's own part in a group discussion as well as the effectiveness of the group
- Facilitate a group discussion by ensuring that everyone has a chance to speak
- Use respectful turn-taking conventions

- Suggest new lines of discussion when appropriate
- Recall, restate, or paraphrase information, big ideas, or points made by others
- Sustain a discussion by staying on the main topic and requesting or signaling a change of topic
- Negotiate issues without conflict or anger
- Listen and respond, taking an alternative perspective
- Remember others' comments and consider one's own thinking in relation to those comments
- Anticipate disagreement and use language to promote collaborative discussion
- Recognize disagreement and use language to help reach agreement or maintain equanimity among group members
- Deal with mature themes and difficult issues in a thoughtful and serious way
- Use language to express independent, critical thinking

▶ Content

- Recognize and discuss people, events, places, and things in a text
- Make predictions based on evidence
- State and discuss problems, events, actions, and solutions
- Discuss cause-and-effect relationships
- Express opinions and support them with evidence and logical reasoning
- Discuss what is already known about a topic and how it is known
- Compare and contrast people, places, events, and things
- Express and reflect on their own feelings and recognize the feelings of others
- Demonstrate understanding of deeper messages in texts
- Demonstrate knowledge of content area subjects
- Show interest in the meaning of words and work actively to learn and use them
- Use descriptive language when discussing a topic or idea
- Demonstrate understanding of similes, metaphors, idioms, and word connotations

Selecting Goals Behaviors and Understandings to Notice, Teach, and Support *(cont.)*

Oral and Visual Communication

PRESENTATION

▶ **Voice**

- Communicate interest in and enthusiasm about a topic
- Present information in ways that engage listeners' attention
- Speak with confidence and in a relaxed manner
- Use expression, tone, word stress, and pitch for emphasis
- Use effective introductions in oral presentations to capture attention
- Use effective closings in oral presentations to summarize information, persuade, or stimulate thinking
- Pause effectively to enhance interest and emphasize points
- Use personal interpretation and style when speaking
- Where appropriate, use dramatic devices such as volume increase or decrease and pauses to engage listeners

▶ **Conventions**

- Speak with appropriate volume for audience size and location
- Speak directly to the audience, making eye contact with individuals
- Speak at an appropriate rate to be understood
- Enunciate words clearly enough to be understood by a group (with regional and other dialects being acceptable)
- Answer questions asked by the audience
- Pronounce names and non-English words correctly
- Vary the use of language for different kinds of presentations: e.g., dramatic, narrative, reports
- Use mostly conventional grammar and pronunciation of words (depending on individual opportunities over time)
- Stand with good posture
- Use hand gestures appropriately
- Demonstrate effective body language while speaking

▶ **Organization**

- Have an audience in mind before planning the presentation

- Maintain a clear focus on the important or main ideas
- Present ideas and information in a concise manner with a logical sequence
- Sequence ideas, examples, and evidence in a way that shows their relationship
- Have a clear introduction, body, and conclusion to your topic
- Demonstrate awareness of the knowledge base and interests of the audience
- Choose clear examples that are related to the topic
- Use underlying structural patterns common for expository topics: e.g., description, cause and effect, chronological sequence, temporal sequence, compare and contrast, problem and solution
- Select genre of oral presentation with audience in mind
- Prepare a plan or notes to support the presentation

▶ **Word Choice**

- Understand and use words related to familiar experiences and topics as well as many content and technical terms from academic disciplines
- Use language from books and informational texts when presenting
- Use language appropriate for oral presentations
- Define technical words within a presentation to help the audience understand their meaning
- Vary word choice to be specific and precise while keeping audience in mind
- Use figurative language to create visual images where appropriate
- Use specific vocabulary to argue, draw contrasts, and indicate agreement and disagreement
- Be aware of using words with connotative meaning relative to social values and stereotypes

▶ **Ideas and Content**

- Recite poems or tell stories with effective use of intonation and word stress to emphasize important ideas, engage listeners' interest, and show character traits
- Deliver oral reports that demonstrate understanding of a topic

- Make expository presentations that report research or explore a topic thoroughly
- Deliver both formal and informal presentations, and vary content, language, and style appropriately
- Demonstrate understanding of a topic by providing facts, statistics, examples, anecdotes, and quotations
- Add evaluative comments, making clear that opinion is being stated (e.g., "I think . . ."), and provide evidence
- Make persuasive presentations that establish a clear argument and support it with evidence
- Use persuasive strategies: e.g., examples that appeal to emotions
- Address counterarguments and listener bias
- Recognize and address opposing points of view on an issue or topic
- Include multiple primary and secondary sources to support points
- Differentiate between evidence based on facts and evidence based on opinion
- Establish an argument at the beginning of a presentation
- Use effective presentation devices: e.g., examples, case studies, analogies
- Involve audience members by asking them questions or engaging them in an activity
- Use feedback from others when planning presentations

▶ **Media**

- Use graphics (e.g., diagrams, illustrations, or other digital media) to communicate meaning or to enhance a presentation
- Identify and acknowledge sources of information included in presentations
- Read aloud and discuss own writing with others
- Integrate technology tools (e.g., slideshows, video, audio) in multimedia presentations

Selecting Goals Behaviors and Understandings to Notice, Teach, and Support

Oral and Visual Communication

LISTENING AND SPEAKING

▶ Listening and Understanding

- Identify own purpose for listening
- Listen with active attention to texts that are read aloud
- Listen actively to others read or talk about their writing and give feedback
- Listen to and speak to a partner about a given idea, and make a connection to the partner's idea
- Listen with attention and understanding to oral reading of stories, poems, and informational texts
- Listen with attention during instruction, and respond with statements and questions
- Listen with attention during oral presentations, and recognize a speaker's purpose and point of view
- Ask questions to clarify unknown words heard while actively listening
- Identify essential information for note-taking
- Provide several reasons for agreement with an idea or opinion
- Summarize ideas from oral reading or presentation
- Critically analyze the credibility of the speaker or media message
- Critique presentations for logic or presentation of evidence for arguments, subtexts, and inclusion or exclusion of information
- Recognize faulty reasoning and bias in presentations and media messages
- Identify, analyze, and critique persuasive techniques
- Understand dialect and its relationship to meaning

▶ Social Interactions

- Listen respectfully and responsibly
- Respect the age, gender, position, and cultural traditions of the speaker
- Speak at an appropriate volume
- Adjust speaking volume for different contexts
- Use conventions of respectful conversation
- Enter a conversation appropriately
- Refrain from speaking over others
- Sustain a conversation with a variety of audiences

- Speak with peers and adults to establish, maintain, and enhance personal relationships at home, in school, and in the community
- Actively participate in conversation by listening and looking at the person speaking
- Demonstrate balance in conversation by taking turns
- Use conventional techniques that encourage others to talk: e.g., "What do you think?" "Do you agree? Why or why not?"
- Respond to others' ideas before changing the subject
- Understand and use language for the purpose of humor: e.g., jokes, riddles, puns
- Use nonpejorative and inclusive language: e.g., nonsexist, nonracist, unbiased
- Understand the role of nonverbal language and use it effectively
- Use tone and gesture in an appropriate way

▶ Extended Discussion

- Follow the topic and add to a discussion with comments on the same topic
- Build on the talk of others by making statements related to the speaker's topic and by responding to cues
- Monitor own understanding of others' comments and ask for clarification and elaboration
- Actively participate in conversation during whole- and small-group discussion
- Use grade level-appropriate vocabulary in conversations about texts
- Learn new words related to topics of inquiry in the classroom
- Engage actively in conversational routines: e.g., turn and talk
- Ask follow-up questions during partner, small-group, and whole-class discussion
- Relate or compare one's own knowledge and experience with information from others
- Listen and respond to a partner by agreeing, disagreeing or adding on, and explaining reasons
- Demonstrate effectiveness as a group leader
- Evaluate one's own part in a group discussion as well as the effectiveness of the group
- Facilitate a group discussion by ensuring that everyone has a chance to speak
- Use respectful turn-taking conventions

- Suggest new lines of discussion when appropriate
- Recall, restate, or paraphrase information, big ideas, or points made by others
- Sustain a discussion, staying on the main topic and requesting or signaling a change of topic
- Negotiate issues without conflict or anger
- Listen and respond, taking an alternative perspective
- Remember others' comments and consider one's own thinking in relation to them
- Anticipate disagreement and use language to promote collaborative discussion
- Recognize disagreement and use language to help reach agreement or maintain equanimity
- Deal with mature themes and difficult issues in a thoughtful and serious way
- Use language to express independent, critical thinking

▶ Content

- Recognize and discuss people, events, places, and things in a text
- Make predictions based on evidence
- State and discuss problems, events, actions, and solutions
- Discuss cause-and-effect relationships
- Express opinions and support them with evidence and logical reasoning
- Discuss what is already known about a topic and how it is known
- Use descriptive language when talking about people and places
- Compare and contrast people, places, events, and things
- Express and reflect on feelings of self and others
- Demonstrate understanding of deeper messages in texts
- Demonstrate knowledge of content area subjects
- Articulate and reflect on their own feelings and recognize the feelings of others
- Show interest in the meaning of words and work actively to learn and use them
- Use descriptive language when discussing a topic or idea
- Demonstrate understanding of similes, metaphors, idioms, and word connotations

Selecting Goals Behaviors and Understandings to Notice, Teach, and Support *(cont.)*

Oral and Visual Communication

PRESENTATION

▶ Voice

- Communicate interest in and enthusiasm about a topic
- Present information in ways that engage listeners' attention
- Speak with confidence and in a relaxed manner
- Use expression, tone, word stress, and pitch for emphasis
- Use effective introductions in oral presentations to capture attention
- Use effective closings in oral presentations to summarize information, persuade, or stimulate thinking
- Pause effectively to enhance interest and emphasize points
- Use personal interpretation and style when speaking
- Where appropriate, use dramatic devices such as volume increase or decrease and pauses to engage listeners

▶ Conventions

- Speak with appropriate volume for audience size and location
- Speak directly to the audience, making eye contact with individuals
- Speak at an appropriate rate to be understood
- Enunciate words clearly enough to be understood by a group (with regional and other dialects being acceptable)
- Answer questions asked by the audience
- Pronounce names and non-English words correctly
- Vary the use of language for different kinds of presentations: e.g., dramatic, narrative, reports
- Use mostly conventional grammar and pronunciation of words (depending on individual opportunities over time)
- Stand with good posture
- Use hand gestures appropriately
- Demonstrate effective body language while speaking

▶ Organization

- Have an audience in mind before planning the presentation
- Maintain a clear focus on the important or main ideas
- Present ideas and information in a concise manner with a logical sequence
- Sequence ideas, examples, and evidence in a way that shows their relationship
- Have a clear introduction, body, and conclusion to your topic
- Demonstrate awareness of the knowledge base and interests of the audience
- Use underlying structural patterns common for expository topics: e.g., description, cause and effect, chronological sequence, temporal sequence, compare and contrast, problem and solution
- Select genre of oral presentation with audience in mind
- Prepare a plan or notes to support the presentation

▶ Word Choice

- Understand and use words related to familiar experiences and topics as well as many content and technical terms from academic disciplines
- Use language from books and informational texts when presenting
- Use language appropriate for oral presentations
- Define technical words within a presentation to help the audience to understand their meaning
- Vary word choice to be specific and precise while keeping the audience in mind
- Use figurative language to create visual images where appropriate
- Use specific vocabulary to argue, draw contrasts, and indicate agreement and disagreement
- Be aware of using words with connotative meaning relative to social values and stereotypes
- Use words in a satirical or ironical way to create an impact or humor (where appropriate)

▶ Ideas and Content

- Recite poems or tell stories with effective use of intonation and word stress to emphasize important ideas, engage listeners' interest, and show character traits
- Deliver oral reports that demonstrate understanding of a topic
- Make expository presentations that report research or explore a topic thoroughly
- Deliver both formal and informal presentations and vary content, language, and style appropriately
- Demonstrate understanding of a topic by providing facts, statistics, examples, anecdotes, and quotations
- Add evaluative comments, making clear that opinion is being stated (e.g., "I think . . ."), and provide evidence
- Make persuasive presentations that establish a clear argument and support it with evidence
- Support the argument with relevant evidence
- Use persuasive strategies: e.g., examples that appeal to emotions
- Address counterarguments and listener bias
- Recognize and address opposing points of view on an issue or topic
- Include multiple primary and secondary sources to support points
- Credit sources of information and opinions accurately in presentations and handouts
- Differentiate between evidence based on facts and evidence based on opinion
- Establish an argument at the beginning of a presentation
- Use effective presentation devices: e.g., examples, case studies, analogies
- Involve audience members by asking them questions or engaging them in an activity
- Use feedback from others when planning presentations

▶ Media

- Use graphics (e.g., diagrams, illustrations, or other digital media) to communicate meaning or to enhance a presentation
- Identify and acknowledge sources of information included in presentations
- Read aloud and discuss own writing with others
- Integrate technology tools (e.g., slideshows, video, audio) in multimedia presentations

Technological Communication

Technological Communication Continuum

The human ability to use language creates society and makes all achievements and all relationships possible. This powerful tool—communication—is greatly extended through technology. Communication is possible today in ways that did not exist even a few years ago. And technology is changing so rapidly, it is hard for school districts to keep up with the latest advances. Today students can be connected audibly and visibly to other people, including students like themselves in all parts of the world. The reach is almost unlimited. We have rapid communication through keyboards and voice-to-speech programs; students are daily involved in chatting with individuals far distant. They can access people from the past at the click of a key or mouse; news and information are (literally) at their fingertips. While there are dangers, and schools should certainly set limits and be cautious, the possibilities are amazing. The learning now bursts outside the classroom walls, and technology is the vehicle.

Learning how to use technology for clear and precise communication is an absolute necessity in today's society. From basic computer functions to the more complex tasks of comprehending and creating digital texts, often it seems that students are much more sophisticated than their teachers in this area of literacy learning. Indeed, the very existence of today's technology greatly expands the definition of what it means to be literate. Yet, we need to give careful attention to what students know and are able to do as they utilize their technological skills in the interest of becoming more literate.

▶ *Computer Literacy.* At a functional level, students need to understand how and why to use computers, tablets, and other digital devices to create documents, find information, and communicate with others. We want them to be comfortable with electronic conversations and learning groups; to use rapid and efficient keyboarding for word processing; to create websites, blogs, and multimedia presentations; and to use the Internet as a tool for gathering information. When used properly, spelling and grammar checkers, cutting and pasting, and access to digital images have made creating well-written and well-designed final drafts easier than ever. At the same time, it is important that even our youngest students begin to understand that using technology and the Internet requires both a different set of literacy skills as well as particular attention to their own ethical and responsible behavior.

▶ *Online Reading and Information Literacy.* In addition to traditional forms of print, both paper and electronic, nonprint media from radio, television, and the Internet have become the most frequent sources for learning about the world. Providing opportunities for students to understand, explore, and document the use of these various media has become a critical part of a literacy curriculum. When they are online, texts have the ability to change constantly, both in terms of content and design, and this requires that students develop new comprehending strategies. From basic web searching and documentation in the early grades to more sophisticated database research, citation management, and integration of multiple sources of information at the upper grades, reading online texts and developing information literacy skills have become key components of our students' overall literacy development. They need to develop strong abilities in critically evaluating the accuracy of content and the sources of information.

▸ *Composing and Publishing Digital Texts.* As our concept of writing broadens to include the processes of composing images, websites, presentations, and audio and visual media, students now have a number of ways to communicate their messages to a wider variety of audiences. Students can integrate what they have learned about how to comprehend online texts in order to develop their own texts. Moreover, electronic tools such as digital cameras, graphic editors, and presentation software all have the potential to enhance students' communication. At the same time, students need to be aware of how to manage and cite their sources, as well as how to incorporate materials, especially copyrighted materials, from these sources in an appropriate and ethical manner.

A note of caution: Student use of digital communication tools must be carefully monitored. Use approved websites and teach students about appropriate behavior. Your school district will undoubtedly have policies and firewalls to protect students and teachers. At the same time, you will find digital communication a wonderful way to stay in touch with your students and their families. You can respond to their writing, to their notes about reading, and to their questions. You can share their assignments with parents, answers questions, and make quick progress reports.

Today, digital communication has become a core component of our students' literacy learning. We need our students to be as effective in comprehending and creating oral, visual, and technological media as they are with comprehending and creating traditional print texts. In turn, they can rely on multiple forms of media to read and write about their individual and professional interests, as well as to be informed, engaged, and thoughtful citizens.

Using the Technological Communication Continuum

The Technological Communication continuum presents behaviors and understandings to notice, teach, and support and are listed in two categories: (1) Digital and Media Literacy; and (2) Communication and Publishing. Like the Writing About Reading and Writing continua, no text characteristics are specified because students will be creating them; but you can infer the kind of formal and informal texts that are involved in the actions described. Also, items are not sorted by thinking within, beyond, and about the text. Publications created through technology are both similar to and much more complex than those that students create through writing. The goals on this continuum can be integrated with all of the goals for reading, writing, and writing about reading. But you will notice that along with learning technological literacy, students are also learning about ethical and moral behavior, which in many ways cannot be separated from literacy learning.

TECHNOLOGICAL
COMMUNICATION

Selecting Goals Behaviors and Understandings to Notice, Teach, and Support

Technological Communication

DIGITAL AND MEDIA LITERACY

- Understand the basic control and navigation strategies such as on/off, volume, screen orientation, accessing the keyboard, and simple mouse or touch movements
- With guidance, launch, use, and close appropriate software, apps, and websites
- With guidance, ask questions and search for information using approved websites, e-books, and apps

COMMUNICATION AND PUBLISHING

- Use simple software and apps to express ideas using digital media such as drawings, audio, and video
- Create simple multimedia products or e-books with support
- Use e-mail to send messages to classmates, families, and the teacher
- Scan and send original pictures via e-mail

Selecting Goals Behaviors and Understandings to Notice, Teach, and Support

Technological Communication

DIGITAL AND MEDIA LITERACY

- Understand the basic control and navigation strategies such as on/off, volume, screen orientation, accessing the keyboard, and simple mouse or touch movements
- Launch, use, and close appropriate software, apps, and websites
- With guidance, access digital equipment, software, apps that require a personal password
- Use approved digital resources such as websites, e-books, and apps to engage in simple searches to discover and gather information
- Understand that ideas and information can be conveyed through different media, such as text, drawings, photos, video, and audio

COMMUNICATION AND PUBLISHING

- Use simple software and apps to express ideas using text and other digital media such as drawings, audio, and video
- Create simple multimedia products or e-books with support
- Share ideas with an authentic audience through blogs, videoconferencing, and other online tools with support
- Use e-mail to send messages to classmates, families, and the teacher
- Scan and send original pictures via e-mail

TECHNOLOGICAL
COMMUNICATION

Selecting Goals Behaviors and Understandings to Notice, Teach, and Support

Technological Communication

DIGITAL AND MEDIA LITERACY

- Increase efficiency by knowing the location of letters, numbers, and special keys and characters on keyboard
- Launch, use, and close appropriate software, apps, and websites
- Access software, apps, and websites that require a personal password
- Use approved digital resources such as websites, e-books, and apps to engage in simple searches to discover and gather information
- Understand that ideas and information can be conveyed through different media, such as text, drawings, photos, video, and audio
- Gather and talk about information from approved websites, e-books, apps, and software using a variety of methods including downloading a file or copying/pasting text and images, and citing sources
- Understand the general characteristics of digital citizenship and responsible use of technology, which includes carefully thinking about one's online identity, what personal information should not be shared, respecting others, knowing the difference between one's work and the work of others

COMMUNICATION AND PUBLISHING

- Use software, apps, and online tools, to express ideas, tell a story, craft a persuasive argument, or write a poem using text and other digital media such as drawings, images, audio, and video
- Share ideas with an authentic audience through blogs, videoconferencing, and other online tools with support
- Share work with peers and make changes based on their suggestions
- Use artifacts to create simple documents, multimedia products, or e-books
- Use e-mail to send messages and other artifacts (such as photos, videos, or scans of original artwork)

Selecting Goals Behaviors and Understandings to Notice, Teach, and Support

Technological Communication

DIGITAL AND MEDIA LITERACY

- Increase efficiency by knowing the location of letters, numbers, and special keys and characters on keyboard
- Launch, use, and close appropriate software, apps, and websites
- Access software, apps, and websites that require a personal password
- Use approved digital resources such as websites, e-books, and apps to engage in simple searches to discover and gather information
- Understand that ideas and information can be conveyed through different media, such as text, drawings, photos, video, and audio
- Gather and talk about information from approved websites, e-books, apps, and software using a variety of methods including downloading a file or copying/pasting text and images, and citing sources
- Understand the general characteristics of digital citizenship and responsible use of technology, which includes carefully thinking about one's online identity, what personal information should not be shared, respecting others, knowing the difference between one's work and the work of others

COMMUNICATION AND PUBLISHING

- Use software, apps, and online tools, to express ideas, tell a story, craft a persuasive argument, or write a poem using text and other digital media such as drawings, images, audio, and video
- Share ideas with an authentic audience through blogs, videoconferencing, and other online tools with support
- Share work with peers and make changes based on their suggestions
- Use artifacts to create a simple documents, multimedia products, or e-books
- Use e-mail to send messages and other artifacts (such as photos, videos, or scans of original artwork)

Selecting Goals Behaviors and Understandings to Notice, Teach, and Support

Technological Communication

DIGITAL AND MEDIA LITERACY

- Increase keyboard fluency and automaticity through writing and online exploration
- Improve productivity through the use of advanced features found in software, apps, and online tools, such as spell check, image or draw tools in an authoring app, or the bookmark tool in an online browser
- Use approved digital resources such as websites, databases, e-books, and apps to locate, evaluate, and analyze content
- Use a variety of search strategies to increase the effectiveness of your search including key words, search engine filters, and symbols like quotation marks and plus/minus
- Gather information from approved websites, e-books, apps, and software using a variety of methods including downloading file or copying/pasting text and images, and citing sources
- Understand the characteristics of digital citizenship and responsible use of technology, which includes carefully thinking about one's online identity, what personal information should not be shared, respecting others, protecting others by reporting abuses, knowing the difference between your work and the work of others, citing sources, and the respectful and proper use of technology

COMMUNICATION AND PUBLISHING

- Use software, apps, and online tools to express ideas, write an opinion piece, or a poem using text and other digital media such as drawings, images, audio, and video
- Observe the differences between online environments that allow for collaboration and the cocreation of content and those that are limited to one-way communication
- Share ideas with an authentic audience through blogs, videoconferencing, and other online tools with support
- Share work for teacher and peer feedback using editing tools such as comments, highlighting, audio notes, and make revisions based on their suggestions
- Use artifacts to publish in a variety of formats including a simple document, multimedia product, or e-books
- Use e-mail for a wide variety of purposes
- Understand characteristics of different online environments used to publish for an authentic audience such as school websites, classroom blog and wikis, as well as publishing an e-book for ereaders on computers or mobile devices
- Communicate to and with an authentic audience through blogs, videoconferencing, and other online tools with support. Communication can include conversations with experts and/or students from other schools in your district, state, country, and around the world

TECHNOLOGICAL COMMUNICATION

Selecting Goals Behaviors and Understandings to Notice, Teach, and Support

Technological Communication

| **DIGITAL AND MEDIA LITERACY** | **COMMUNICATION AND PUBLISHING** |

DIGITAL AND MEDIA LITERACY

- Increase keyboard fluency and automaticity through writing and online exploration, and use shortcuts or hand gestures to increase navigation efficiency
- Improve productivity through the use of advanced features found in software, apps, and online tools, such as spell check, image or draw tools in an authoring app, or the bookmark tool in an online browser
- Use a variety of digital resources such as websites, public and subscription-based databases, e-books, and apps to locate, evaluate, and analyze literary and informational content
- Use different search strategies to increase the effectiveness of your searches including key words, search engine filters, and symbols
- Locate websites that fit one's needs and purpose
- Identify the purpose of a website
- Determine when a website was last updated
- Determine whether a website presents one perspective or multiple perspectives
- Identify the names of one or more website authors
- Understand the difference between a website author's name and the organization to which the author is connected
- Be alert to an author's point of view, examine for bias, and validate the author's authority on the topic
- Gather information from websites, e-books, apps, and software using a variety of methods including downloading files or copying/pasting text and images, citing sources for each artifact collected
- Understand the characteristics of digital citizenship and the responsible use of technology, which includes thinking about one's online identity, what personal information should not be shared, respecting others, understanding cyberbullying and the role of a helpful bystander, protecting others and reporting abuses, and citing sources
- Engage in synchronous and asynchronous learning activities that include discussion forum, chat, document sharing, and resource exploration

COMMUNICATION AND PUBLISHING

- Use software and apps to express ideas, write an opinion piece, or a poem using text and other digital media such as drawings, images, audio, and video
- Observe the opportunities that exist in online environments that allow for collaboration and the co-creation of content and those that are limited to one-way communication
- Share ideas with an authentic audience through blogs, videoconferencing, and other online tools with support
- Share work for teacher and peer feedback using editing tools such as comments, highlighting, audio notes, and make revisions based on their suggestions
- Use e-mail for a wide variety of purposes
- Recognize that different audiences require different degrees of formality when communicating with tools such as e-mail, social networking, discussion forums, and blogs
- Understand characteristics of different online environments used to publish for an authentic audience such as school websites, classroom blog, wikis, and social networks, as well as publishing e-books on computers or mobile devices
- Communicate to and with an authentic audience through blogs, videoconferencing, and other online tools with support. Communication can include conversations with experts and/or students from other schools in your district, state, country, and around the world
- Create visuals to enhance written work, such as graphic organizers, charts, tables, drawings, images. Use spreadsheet or survey tools to help organize and generate alternative visual representations of data
- Design or use templates to create newsletters, brochures, web pages, or presentations. Experiment with a combination of software, apps, and online tools to improve the quality of your product and its ability to reach different audiences

Selecting Goals Behaviors and Understandings to Notice, Teach, and Support

Technological Communication

| DIGITAL AND MEDIA LITERACY | COMMUNICATION AND PUBLISHING |

DIGITAL AND MEDIA LITERACY

- Increase keyboard fluency and automaticity through writing and online exploration, and use keyboarding shortcuts or hand gestures to increase navigation efficiency
- Improve productivity through the use and integration of advanced features found in software, apps, and online tools, such as spell check, image or draw tools in an authoring app, or the bookmark tool in an online browser
- Use a variety of digital resources such as websites, public and subscription-based databases, e-books, and apps to locate, evaluate, and analyze literary and informational content
- Use different strategies to increase the effectiveness of your searches including key words, advanced search engine filters, and symbols
- Develop curation strategies to gather and organize information about a topic using online tools like social bookmarking, search engine alerts, and content or subject-based blogs
- Locate websites that fit one's needs and purpose
- Identify the purpose of a website
- Determine when a website was last updated
- Determine whether a website presents one perspective or multiple perspectives
- Identify the names of one or more website authors
- Understand the difference between a website author's name and the organization to which the author is connected
- Be alert to an author's point of view, examine for bias, and validate their authority on the topic through multiple sources
- Gather information from websites, e-books, apps, and software using a variety of methods including downloading files or copying/pasting text and images, citing sources for each artifact collected
- Understand the characteristics of digital citizenship and the responsible use of technology, which includes thinking about one's online identity, what personal information should not be shared, respecting others, understanding cyberbullying and the role of a helpful bystander, protecting others and reporting abuses, and citing sources
- Engage in synchronous and asynchronous learning activities that include discussion forum, chat, document sharing, survey tools, and resource exploration

COMMUNICATION AND PUBLISHING

- Use software and apps to express ideas, write an opinion piece, or a poem using text and other digital media such as drawings, images, audio, and video
- Observe the opportunities that exist in online environments that allow for collaboration and the co-creation of content and those that are limited to one-way communication
- Share ideas with an authentic audience through blogs, videoconferencing, and other online tools
- Share work for teacher and peer feedback using editing tools such as comments, highlighting, audio notes, and make revisions based on their suggestions
- Demonstrate that different audiences require different degrees of formality when communicating with tools such as e-mail, social networking, discussion forums, and blogs
- Understand the characteristics of different online environments used to publish for an authentic audience such as school websites, classroom blog, wikis, and social networks, as well as publishing e-books on computers or mobile devices
- Communicate to and with an authentic audience through blogs, videoconferencing, and other online tools with support. Communication can include conversations with experts and/or students from other schools in your district, state, country, and around the world
- Create visuals to enhance written work, such as graphic organizers, charts, tables, drawings, and images. Use spreadsheet or survey tools to help organize and generate alternative visual representations of data
- Design or use templates to create newsletters, brochures, web pages, or presentations. Experiment with a combination of software, apps, and online tools to improve the quality of your product and its ability to reach different audiences

TECHNOLOGICAL COMMUNICATION

Selecting Goals Behaviors and Understandings to Notice, Teach, and Support

Technological Communication

DIGITAL AND MEDIA LITERACY

- Increase keyboard fluency and automaticity through writing and online exploration, and use keyboarding shortcuts, hand gestures, or voice to increase navigation efficiency
- Improve productivity and quality of work through the use and integration of a variety of software, apps, and online tools
- Understand cloud computing and its relationship to file management, data storage, and privacy considerations
- Use a variety of digital resources such as websites, public and subscription-based databases, e-books, and apps to locate, evaluate, and analyze literary and informational content
- Use different strategies to increase the effectiveness of your searches including key words, advanced search engine filters, and symbols
- Develop curation strategies to gather and organize information about a topic using online tools like social bookmarking, search engine alerts, content or subject-based blogs, and social media aggregators that draw from blogs and other online resources categorized by content area
- Locate websites that fit one's needs and purpose
- Identify the purpose of a website
- Determine when a website was last updated
- Determine whether a website presents one perspective or multiple perspectives
- Identify the names of one or more website authors
- Understand the difference between a website author's name and the organization to which the author is connected
- Consider information about a website author, as well as the author's credentials and affiliations, to determine level of expertise
- Identify the author's view of a topic, including any evidence of bias, and how it may affect words and images on the website
- Determine the reliability of a website based on analysis of author expertise, accuracy of information, validity of sources, scientific evidence, etc.
- Gather information from websites, e-books, apps, and software using a variety of methods including downloading files or copy/paste text and images, highlighting and notes features embedded in social bookmarking tools, and citing sources for each artifact collected using word processing, social bookmarking, or citation management tools
- Examine and think critically about the different strategies used by the media (TV, movies, news, video, multimedia blogs) and other content providers to engage and influence
- Understand the characteristics of digital citizenship and the responsible use of technology, which includes building a positive online identity, knowing what personal information should not be shared, respecting others, understanding cyberbullying and engaging in the role of a helpful bystander, protecting others, reporting abuses, and understanding copyright
- Engage in synchronous and asynchronous learning activities that include discussion forum, chat, document sharing, survey tools, and resource exploration

COMMUNICATION AND PUBLISHING

- Use software and apps to express ideas, write an opinion piece, or a poem using text and other digital media such as drawings, images, audio, and video
- Observe the opportunities that exist in online environments that allow for collaboration and the co-creation of content and those that are limited to one-way communication
- Share ideas with an authentic audience through blogs, videoconferencing, and other online tools
- Share work for teacher and peer feedback using editing tools such as comments, highlighting, audio notes, and make revisions based on their suggestions
- Demonstrate that different audiences require different degrees of formality when communicating with tools such as e-mail, social networking, discussion forums, and blogs
- Understand the characteristics of different online environments used to publish for an authentic audience such as school websites, classroom blog, wikis, and social networks, as well as publishing e-books on computers or mobile devices
- Communicate to and with an authentic audience through blogs, video conferencing, and other online tools with support. Communication can include conversations with experts and/or students from other schools in your district, state, country, and around the world
- Create visuals to enhance written work, such as graphic organizers, charts, tables, drawings, and images. Use spreadsheet or survey tools to help organize and generate alternative visual representations of data
- Design or use templates to create newsletters, brochures, web pages, or presentations. Experiment with a combination of software, apps, and online tools to improve the quality of your product and its ability to reach different audiences

Selecting Goals Behaviors and Understandings to Notice, Teach, and Support

Technological Communication

DIGITAL AND MEDIA LITERACY

- Increase keyboard fluency and automaticity through writing and online exploration, and use keyboarding shortcuts, hand gestures, or voice to increase navigation efficiency
- Improve productivity and quality of work through the use and integration of a variety of software, apps, and online tools
- Understand cloud computing and its relationship to file management, data storage, and privacy considerations
- Use a variety of digital resources such as websites, public and subscription-based databases, e-books, and apps to locate, evaluate, and analyze literary and informational content
- Use different strategies to increase the effectiveness of your searches by including key words, advanced search engine filters, and symbols
- Develop curation strategies to gather and organize information about a topic using online tools like social bookmarking, search engine alerts, content or subject-based blogs, and social media aggregators that draw from blogs and other online resources categorized by content area
- Locate websites that fit one's needs and purpose
- Identify the purpose of a website
- Determine when a website was last updated
- Determine whether a website presents one perspective or multiple perspectives
- Identify the names of one or more website authors
- Understand the difference between a website author's name and the organization to which the author is connected
- Consider information about a website author, as well as the author's credentials and affiliations, to determine level of expertise
- Identify the author's view of a topic, including any evidence of bias, and how it may affect words and images on the website
- Determine the reliability of a website based on analysis of author expertise, accuracy of information, validity of sources, scientific evidence, etc.
- Gather information from websites, e-books, apps, and software using a variety of methods including downloading files or copy/paste text and images, highlighting and notes features embedded in social bookmarking tools, and citing sources for each artifact collected using word processing, social bookmarking, or citation management tools
- Examine and think critically the different strategies used by the media (TV, movies, news, video, multimedia blogs) and other content providers to engage and influence
- Understand the characteristics of digital citizenship and the responsible use of technology, which includes building a positive online identity, knowing what personal information should not be shared, respecting others, understanding cyberbullying and engaging in the role of a helpful bystander, protecting others, reporting abuses, and understanding copyright
- Engage in synchronous and asynchronous learning activities that include discussion forum, chat, document sharing, survey tools, and resource exploration

COMMUNICATION AND PUBLISHING

- Use software and apps to express ideas, write an opinion piece, or a poem using text and other digital media such as drawings, images, audio, and video
- Communicate with others using e-mail or other forms of digital communication like voice and videoconferencing tools
- Observe the opportunities that exist in online environments that allow for collaboration and the co-creation of content and those that are limited to one-way communication
- Share ideas with an authentic audience through blogs, videoconferencing, and other online tools
- Share work for teacher and peer feedback using editing tools such as comments, highlighting, audio notes, and make revisions based on their suggestions
- Demonstrate that different audiences require different degrees of formality when engaged in online communication; this understanding can be demonstrated using different communication tools, such as e-mail, social networking, discussion forums, and blogs
- Understand the characteristics of different online environments used for publishing to an authentic audience such as school websites, classroom blog, wikis, social networks, cable media outlets, as well as publishing an e-book for ereaders on computers or mobile devices
- Communicate to and with an authentic audience through blogs, video conferencing, and other online tools with support. Communication can include conversations with experts and/or students from other schools in your district, state, country, and around the world
- Create visuals to enhance written work, such as graphic organizers, charts, tables, drawings, and images. Use spreadsheet or survey tools to help organize and generate alternative visual representations of the data
- Design or use templates to create newsletters, brochures, web pages, presentations, infographic, or video shorts. Experiment with a combination of software, apps, and online tools to improve the quality of your product and its ability to reach different audiences

TECHNOLOGICAL COMMUNICATION

Phonics, Spelling, and Word Study

Phonics, Spelling, and Word Study Continuum

This continuum of learning for phonics, spelling, and word study is derived from three decades of work with teachers and students as well as reading research (of others and our own) on how children learn about sounds, letters, and words over time. Our work is based on the premise that students not only need to acquire phonics and word analysis understandings, but also they need to apply these understandings daily to reading and writing continuous text. We believe that *it is essential* for all readers and writers to have a wide range of word-solving strategies—possibly hundreds—they can use rapidly, flexibly, and in a largely unconscious way as they move through a text, maintaining a focus on meaning.

We have previously published *Phonics Lessons* and *Word Study Lessons* (Fountas and Pinnell, Heinemann 2003, Fountas and Pinnell, Heinemann 2004). These lessons are based on a detailed continuum specifying principles that learners develop over time. In this book, we present these same understandings in two different ways: as a grade-by-grade continuum and as word work in guided reading. All of the principles are based on the six areas of learning that are appropriate for grades PreK–8 and that we have previously described and summarize here. For further information on the behaviors and understandings in this continuum, see our publications:

> ▶ *Word Matters: Teaching Phonics and Spelling in the Reading/Writing Classroom*
>
> ▶ *Interactive Writing: How Language and Literacy Come Together, Grades K, 1, 2*
>
> ▶ *Guided Reading: Responsive Teaching Across the Grades*, Second Edition
>
> ▶ *Phonics Lessons: Letters, Words, and How They Work, Grades K, 1, 2*
>
> ▶ *Word Study Lessons: Phonics, Spelling, and Vocabulary, Grade 3*

Grade-by-Grade Continuum

The grade-by-grade Phonics, Spelling, and Word Study continuum presents a general guide to the kinds of understandings students will need to acquire by the end of each grade. These understandings are related to the texts that they are expected to read at the appropriate levels. In presenting this grade-by-grade continuum, *we are not* suggesting that students should be held back because they do not know specific details about letters, sounds, and words. Instead, we are suggesting that specific teaching will be needed to support learners. The continuum can support instruction and extra services.

Word Work for Guided Reading

The Guided Reading continuum contains additional information about phonics, spelling, and word study. Here we have selected important understandings about letters, sounds, and words for the word work you include within guided reading at a particular text level. At the end of the guided-reading lesson, you can include a few minutes of work with letters or words to help readers develop fluency and flexibility in noticing parts of words and taking them apart. You invite students to notice features, parts, or patterns and then give them opportunities to work with them, developing speed and flexibility in looking, saying, breaking, and making. Students may use magnetic letters to make words and take them apart or write on individual whiteboards. The word-solving principles in the Guided Reading continuum are stated in terms of the text levels. They describe the actions proficient readers need to develop in relation to the text demands. Use your knowledge of the students' strengths in word solving in texts, and visit the grade-by-grade learning continuum to select learning goals for your whole-class minilessons, application of principles, and group share.

Nine Areas of Learning

Each grade level lists principles over which students will have developed control by the end of the school year. Across grades PreK–8, the principles are organized into nine broad categories of learning. These are related to the levels of text that students are expected to read upon completing that grade. (They are also related to writing in that students use letter-sound relationships, spelling patterns, and word structure as they spell words while writing meaningful messages. You will find much evidence of learning about phonics as you examine their writing.) Some of the areas apply to all grades, while others phase out as students gain full control of them. The nine areas of learning follow. Notice that the first three apply only to grades prekindergarten to grade one.

Early Literacy Concepts

Even before they can read, students begin to develop some awareness of how written language works. For example, early understandings about literacy include knowing that

- print and pictures are different but are connected;
- you read the print, not the pictures;
- you turn pages to read and look at the left page first;
- you read left to right and then go back to the left to start a new line;
- words are groups of letters with a space on either side;
- there is a difference between a word and a letter;
- there are uppercase (or capital) and lowercase letters;
- a letter is always the same, and you look at the parts to identify it;
- the first word in a sentence is on the left, and the last word is before the ending punctuation mark;
- the first letter in a word is on the left, and the last letter is right before the space (or ending punctuation).

More of the understandings above are stated in the PreK–2 continuum.

Many students enter kindergarten with good knowledge of early literacy concepts. If they do not, explicit and systematic instruction, along with immersion in engaging and pleasurable experiences with books, can help them become oriented quickly. While most of these early literacy concepts are not considered phonics, they are basic to the child's understanding of print and should be acquired early.

Phonological Awareness

A key to becoming literate is the ability to hear the sounds in words. Hearing individual sounds allows the learner to connect sounds to letters. Students respond to the sounds of language in a very natural way. They love rhyme, repetition, and rhythm. Young students naturally enjoy and remember nursery rhymes and songs because of the way they sound. This general response to the sounds of language is called *phonological awareness*. As students become more aware of language, they notice sounds in a more detailed way. *Phonemic awareness* involves recognizing the *individual* sounds in words and, eventually, being able to identify, isolate, and manipulate them. Students with phonemic awareness have an advantage in that being able to hear the sounds allows them to connect specific sounds with letters.

Letter Knowledge

Letter knowledge refers to what students need to know about the graphic characters in our alphabet—how the letters look, how to distinguish one from another, how to detect them within continuous text, and how to use them in words. A finite set of twenty-six letters, a capital and a lowercase form of each, is used to indicate all the sounds of the English language (forty-four phonemes). The sounds in the language change as dialect, articulation, and other speech factors vary, but all must be connected to letters. Learners will also encounter alternative forms of some letters (*a* and ɑ, for example) and will eventually learn to recognize letters in cursive writing. Children need to learn the names and purposes of letters, as well as their distinguishing features (the small differences that help you separate a *d* from an *a,* for example). When they can identify letters, they can associate them with sounds, and the alphabetic principle is mastered.

Letter-Sound Relationships

Even after prekindergarten to grade two, students continue to learn about letters and sounds including the complex relationships that exist in English. The sounds of oral language are related in both simple and complex ways to the twenty-six letters of the alphabet. Learning the connections between letters and sounds is basic to understanding written language. Students tend to learn the regular connections between letters and sounds (*b* for the first sound in *bat*) first. But they must also learn that often letters appear together—for example, it is efficient to think of the two sounds at the beginning of *black* together. Sometimes a single sound like /*ch*/ is represented by two letters; sometimes a group of letters represents one sound, as in *eigh* for /*a*/. Students learn to look for and recognize these letter combinations as units, which makes their word solving more efficient.

Spelling Patterns

Efficient word solvers look for and find patterns in the way words are constructed. Knowing spelling patterns helps students notice and use larger parts of words, thus making word solving faster and easier. Patterns are also helpful to students in writing words because they can quickly produce the patterns rather than work laboriously with individual sounds and letters. One way to look at word patterns is to examine the way simple words and syllables are put together. In the consonant-vowel-consonant (CVC) pattern, the vowel is usually a short (terse) sound, as in *tap*. In the consonant-vowel-consonant-silent *e* (CVC*e*) pattern, the vowel usually has a long (lax) sound. You will not be using this technical language with students, but they can learn to compare words with these patterns.

Phonograms are spelling patterns that represent the sounds of *rimes* (the last parts of words or syllables within words). In "school language," they are sometimes called *word families*. Some examples of rimes are *-at, -am,* and *-ot.* When you add the *onset* (first part of the word or syllable) to a phonogram like *-ot,* you can make *pot, plot,* or *slot.* A word like *ransom* has two onsets (*r-* and *s-*) and two rimes *-an* and *-om*). You will not need to teach every phonogram as a separate item. Once students understand that there are patterns, know many examples, and learn how to look for patterns, they will quickly discover more for themselves.

High-Frequency Words

Knowing a core of high-frequency words is a valuable resource for students as they build their reading and writing processing systems. We can also call these *high-utility* words because they appear often and can sometimes be used to help in solving other words. Automatically recognizing high-frequency words allows students to concentrate on understanding and on solving new words. In general, students first learn simple high-frequency words and in the process develop efficient systems for learning more words; the process accelerates. Students continuously add to the core of high-frequency words they know. Lessons devoted to high-frequency words can develop automaticity and help students look more carefully at the features of words.

Word Meaning and Vocabulary

The term *vocabulary* refers to the words one knows in oral or written language. For comprehension and coherence, students need to know the meaning of the words in the texts they read and write. It is important for them to constantly expand their listening, speaking, reading, and writing vocabularies and to develop more complex understandings of words they already know (for example, words may have multiple meanings or be used figuratively). Expanding vocabulary means developing categories of words: labels, concept words, synonyms, antonyms, homonyms, and all parts of speech. The meaning of a word often varies with the context; accuracy in spelling frequently requires knowing the meaning if you want to write the word. Pronouncing words accurately is also related to knowing word meanings. Knowing many synonyms and antonyms will help students build more powerful systems for connecting and categorizing words. Most important— reading comprehension is highly dependent on understanding the meaning of words.

Word Structure

Words are built according to rules. Looking at the structure of words will help students learn how words are related to one another and how they can be changed by adding letters, letter clusters, and larger word parts. Readers who can break down words into syllables and notice categories of word parts can also apply word-solving strategies efficiently.

An *affix* is a letter or letters added before a word (in which case it's called a *prefix*) or after a word (in which case it's called a *suffix*) to change its function and meaning. A *base word* is a complete word that may also function as a word part with affixes. A *root word* is the part that may have Greek or Latin origins (such as *phon* in *telephone*). It does not necessarily stand alone as a word. It will not be necessary for young students to make these distinctions when they are beginning to learn about simple affixes, but noticing these word parts will help students read and understand words as well as spell them correctly. Word parts that are added to base words signal meaning. For example, they may signal relationships (*tall, taller, tallest*) or time (*work, worked; carry, carried*). Principles related to word structure include understanding the meaning and structure of compound words, contractions, plurals, and possessives.

Word-Solving Actions

Word solving is related to all of the categories of learning previously described, but we have created an additional category devoted specifically to word solving that focuses on the strategic moves readers and writers make when they use their knowledge of the language system while reading and writing continuous text. These strategies are "in-the-head" actions that are invisible, although we can often infer them from overt behaviors. The principles listed in this section represent readers' and writers' ability to use all the information in the continuum.

Using the Phonics, Spelling, and Word Study Continuum

Word solving is basic to the complex act of reading. When readers can employ a flexible range of strategies for solving words rapidly and efficiently, attention is freed for comprehension. Word solving is fundamental to fluent, phrased reading.

We place the behaviors and understandings included in the Phonics, Spelling, and Word Study continuum mainly in the "thinking within the text" category in the twelve systems for strategic actions. At the bottom line, readers must read the words at a high level of accuracy in order to do the kind of thinking necessary to understand the literal meaning of the text. In addition, this continuum focuses on word meanings, or vocabulary. Vocabulary development is an important factor in understanding the meaning of a text and has long been recognized as playing an important role in reading comprehension. As with other continua, keep in mind that the behaviors listed here represent goals for a year of instruction.

You can use the grade-by-grade phonics continuum as an overall map when you plan your school year. It is useful for planning phonics and vocabulary minilessons, which will support student's word solving in reading, as well as for planning spelling lessons, which will support students' writing. For a detailed description of competency lessons for teaching and specific assessments, see the four volumes: *Phonics Lessons: Letters, Words, and How They Work (Grades K, 1, and 2)* and *Word Study Lessons: Phonics, Spelling, and Vocabulary (Grade 3)* (Fountas and Pinnell, Heinemann 2004). In addition, this continuum will serve as a good resource in teaching word study strategies during shared and guided reading lessons.

Describing the complexity of learning across these nine areas and over many years requires a great deal of detailed work. The continuum presented here is organized grade by grade for convenient reference. You can find great detail in another volume, *The Fountas and Pinnell Comprehensive Phonics, Spelling, and Word Study Guide* (2017). In this volume, you will find behaviors and principles related to each of the nine areas. For each behavior or principle, many examples of words and word parts are listed. You will also find one or more examples of instructional language that will help you understand the idea or behavior or communicate it clearly to students. Then, a series of dots identifies the typical time period (early, middle, or late across each year of schooling from PreK to grades 6–8) within which students are developing those understandings. This volume shows how, over time, learning builds on learning. It is designed to help you think analytically about this complicated area of learning and be more precise in your planning and teaching for phonics, spelling, and word study.

Selecting Goals Behaviors and Understandings to Notice, Teach, and Support

Phonics, Spelling, and Word Study

EARLY LITERACY CONCEPTS

- Distinguish and talk about the differences between pictures and print
- Understand that you look at the print when reading
- Understand and talk about the purpose of print in writing
- Understand the concept of a letter
- Begin to understand the concept of a word
- Recognize and point to one's name
- Use left-to-right directionality to read print in a shared way with others
- Use letters from one's name to represent it or to "write" a message
- Begin to understand the concepts of first and last in written language
- Match one spoken word with one group of letters on very short lines of print when reading in a shared way with others
- Use one's name to learn about words and to make connections to words

PHONOLOGICAL AWARENESS

▶ Rhyming Words

- Hear and say rhyming words: e.g., *new, blue*
- Hear and connect rhyming words: e.g., *fly, high, buy, sky*
- Hear and generate rhyming words: e.g., *a bug in a ___ (hug, jug, mug, rug)*

▶ Syllables

- Hear, say, and clap syllables: e.g., *farm, be/fore*

LETTER KNOWLEDGE

▶ Identifying Letters

- Recognize and point to the distinctive features of letter forms
- Recognize some letters and state their names, especially those letters in children's names

▶ Recognizing Letters in Words and Sentences

- Recognize and name letters in the environment (signs, labels, etc.)
- Understand and talk about the fact that words are formed with letters
- Recognize and name some letters in words

SPELLING PATTERNS

▶ Phonogram Patterns

- Recognize and talk about the fact that some letters appear often together in many words

WORD-SOLVING ACTIONS

▶ Using What Is Known to Solve Words

- Recognize and find names
- Use the initial letter in a name to make connections to other words: e.g., *Max, Maria, make*
- Use the letters in names to make connections to other words: e.g., *Dan, money, run*

▶ Analyzing Words to Solve Them

- Say a word slowly to hear any sound

Selecting Goals Behaviors and Understandings to Notice, Teach, and Support

Phonics, Spelling, and Word Study

EARLY LITERACY CONCEPTS

- Distinguish and talk about the differences between pictures and print
- Understand and talk about the purpose of print in reading
- Understand and talk about the purpose of print in writing
- Understand and talk about the concept of a letter
- Understand and talk about the concept of a word
- Recognize and point to one's name
- Use left-to-right directionality to read one to four lines of print
- Use letters from one's name to represent it or to write a message
- Write one's first name with all letters in acurate sequence
- Construct one's name accurately with magnetic letters or letter cards
- Understand and talk about the concepts of first and last In written language
- Understand and demonstrate that one spoken word matches one group of letters
- Locate the first and last letters of words in continuous text
- Understand and talk about the concept of a book
- Use one's name to learn about words and to make connections to words and to other names

PHONOLOGICAL AWARENESS

▶ Rhyming Words

- Hear and say rhyming words: e.g., *new, blue*
- Hear and connect rhyming words: e.g., *fly, high, buy, sky*
- Hear and generate rhyming words: e.g., *a bug in a ___ (hug, jug, mug, rug)*

▶ Words

- Hear and recognize word boundaries
- Divide sentences into words: e.g., *I - like - to - play*

▶ Syllables

- Hear, say, and clap syllables: e.g., *farm, be/fore, a/ni/mal*
- Blend syllables: e.g., *let/ter, letter*

▶ Onsets and Rimes

- Hear and divide onsets and rimes: e.g., *m-en, bl-ack*
- Blend onsets with rimes: e.g., *d-og, dog*

▶ Phonemes

- Hear and say two phonemes (sounds) in a word: e.g., /a/ /t/
- Divide a word into phonemes: e.g., *no,* /n/ /ō/
- Hear and say three phonemes in a word: e.g., /r/ /u/ /n/
- Hear and say the beginning phoneme in a word: e.g., *sun,* /s/
- Hear and say the ending phoneme in a word: e.g., *bed,* /d/
- Hear and say the same beginning phoneme in words: e.g., *run, red,* /r/
- Hear and say the same ending phoneme in words: e.g., *win, fun,* /n/
- Blend two or three phonemes in a word: e.g., /l/ /o/ /t/, *lot*
- Add a phoneme to the beginning of a word: e.g., /s/ + *it = sit*
- Change the beginning phoneme to make a new word: e.g., *not, hot* (change /n/ to /h/)
- Change the ending phoneme to make a new word: e.g., *his, him,* (change /s/ to /m/)
- Hear and say the middle phoneme in a word with three phonemes: e.g., *fit,* /i/
- Hear and say the same middle phoneme in words: e.g., *cat, ran,* /a/

LETTER KNOWLEDGE

▶ Identifying Letters

- Recognize and point to the distinctive features of letter forms
- Recognize letters and state their names
- Recognize and point to uppercase letters and lowercase letters: e.g., *B, b*
- Distinguish and talk about the differences between the uppercase and lowercase forms of a letter
- Categorize letters by features
- Recognize and talk about the order of the alphabet

▶ Recognizing Letters in Words and Sentences

- Recognize and name letters in the environment (signs, labels, etc.)
- Understand and talk about the fact that words are formed with letters
- Recognize and name letters in words
- Recognize and talk about the sequence of letters in a word
- Recognize and name letters in words in continuous text
- Begin to make connections among words by recognizing the position of a letter: e.g., *was, we; good, said; just, put*

▶ Forming Letters

- Use efficient and consistent motions to form letters in manuscript print with writing tools

LETTER-SOUND RELATIONSHIPS

▶ Consonants

- Understand and talk about the fact that some letters represent consonant sounds: e.g., the letter *b* stands for the first sound in *boy*
- Recognize and use beginning consonant sounds and the letters that represent them: *b, c, d, f, g, h, j, k, l, m, n, p, qu, r, s, t, v, w, y, z*
- Recognize, point to, and say the same beginning consonant sound and the letter that represents the sound: e.g., *bay, bee*

▶ Vowels

- Understand and talk about the fact that some letters represent vowel sounds

Selecting Goals Behaviors and Understandings to Notice, Teach, and Support *(cont.)*

Phonics, Spelling, and Word Study

SPELLING PATTERNS

▶ **Phonogram Patterns**

- Recognize and talk about the fact that words, in general, have letter patterns that can appear in many words
- Recognize and use the consonant-vowel-consonant (CVC) pattern: e.g., *cap, get, pig, got, but*
- Recognize and use more common phonograms with a VC pattern: *-ab, -ad, -ag, -am, -an, -ap, -at, -aw, -ay; -ed, -en, -et, -ew; -id, -ig, -im, -in, -ip, -it; -ob, -od, -og, -op, -ot, -ow* (as in *show* or as in *cow*); *-ub, -ug, -um, -un, -ut*
- Recognize and use some phonograms with a vowel-consonant-silent *e* (VCe) pattern: *-ace, -ade, -ake*

HIGH-FREQUENCY WORDS

- Recognize and use high-frequency words with one, two, or three letters: e.g., *a, I, in, is, of, to, and, the*
- Read and write approximately twenty-five high-frequency words
- Locate and read high-frequency words in continuous text

WORD MEANING/ VOCABULARY

▶ **Concept Words**

- Recognize and use concept words: e.g., color names, number words, days of the week, months of the year, seasons

WORD STRUCTURE

▶ **Syllables**

- Understand and talk about the concept of a syllable
- Hear, say, clap, and identify syllables in one- or two- syllable words: e.g., *big, frog, gold; lit/tle, mon/key, sil/ver*

WORD-SOLVING ACTIONS

▶ **Using What Is Known to Solve Words**

- Recognize and find names

- Use the initial letter in a name to make connections to other words: e.g., *M̲ax, M̲aria, m̲ake, ho̲me, from̲*
- Use the letters in names to make connections to other words: e.g., *Da̲n, mo̲n̲ey, ru̲n̲*
- Use the initial letter in a name to read and write other words: e.g., *T̲om, t̲oy, t̲own, s̲t̲op, ca̲t*
- Use the letters in names to read and write other words: e.g., *Me̲g, be̲g̲an, bi̲g*
- Use known words to monitor word-solving accuracy
- Recognize and read known words quickly
- Use knowledge of letter-sound relationships to monitor word-solving accuracy
- Identify words that start the same and use them to solve unknown words: e.g., *b̲at, b̲ell*

▶ **Analyzing Words to Solve Them**

- Say a word slowly to hear the initial sound in the word
- Say a word slowly to hear the final sound in the word

▶ **Changing, Adding, or Removing Parts to Solve Words**

- Change the beginning sound or sounds to make and solve a new word: e.g., *he/me* (change /h/ to /m/), *more/shore* (change /m/ to /sh/), *bright/might* (change /b/ /r/ to /m/)

▶ **Spelling Strategies**

- Spell known words quickly
- Make a first attempt to spell an unknown word
- Use known words to help spell an unknown word
- Use letter-sound relationships to help spell an unknown word

Selecting Goals Behaviors and Understandings to Notice, Teach, and Support

Phonics, Spelling, and Word Study

EARLY LITERACY CONCEPTS

- Understand and talk about the concept of a letter
- Understand and talk about the concept of a word
- Locate the first and last letters of words in continuous text
- Understand and talk about the concept of a sentence
- Understand and talk about the concept of a book
- Use one's name to learn about words and to make connections to words
- Demonstrate word-by-word matching left to right with return sweep on four or more lines of print

PHONOLOGICAL AWARENESS

▶ Rhyming Words

- Hear and say rhyming words: e.g., *new, blue*
- Hear and connect rhyming words: e.g., *fly, high, buy, sky*
- Hear and generate rhyming words: e.g., *a bug in a ___ (hug, jug, mug, rug)*

▶ Syllables

- Hear, say, and clap syllables: e.g., *farm, be/fore, a/ni/mal*
- Blend syllables: e.g., *let/ter, letter*
- Divide words into syllables: e.g., *never, nev/er*
- Delete a syllable from a word: e.g., *a/round, round; be/hind, be*

▶ Onsets and Rimes

- Hear and divide onsets and rimes: e.g., *m-en, bl-ack*
- Blend onsets with rimes: e.g., *d-og, dog*

▶ Phonemes

- Hear and say two phonemes (sounds) in a word: e.g., /a/ /t/
- Divide a word into phonemes: e.g., *no*, /n/ /ō/
- Hear and say three phonemes in a word: e.g., /r/ /u/ /n/
- Hear and say the beginning phoneme in a word: e.g., *sun*, /s/

- Hear and say the ending phoneme in a word: e.g., *bed*, /d/
- Hear and say the same beginning phoneme in words: e.g., *run, red*, /r/
- Hear and say the same ending phoneme in words: e.g., *win, fun*, /n/
- Blend two or three phonemes in a word: e.g., /l/ /o/ /t/, *lot*
- Add a phoneme to the beginning of a word: e.g., /s/ + *it = sit*
- Change the beginning phoneme to make a new word: e.g., *not, hot* (change /n/ to /h/)
- Change the ending phoneme to make a new word: e.g., *his, him*, (change /s/ to /m/)
- Hear and say the middle phoneme in a word with three phonemes: e.g., *fit*, /i/
- Hear and say the same middle phoneme in words: e.g., *cat, ran*, /a/
- Hear and say four or more phonemes in a word in sequence: e.g., /s/ /p/ /e/ /n/ /d/
- Blend three or four phonemes in a word: e.g., /n/ /e/ /s/ /t/, *nest*
- Delete the beginning phoneme of a word: e.g., *can, an* (delete /k/)
- Delete the ending phoneme of a word: e.g., *wind, win* (delete /d/)
- Add a phoneme to the end of a word: e.g., *an* + /d/ = *and*
- Change the middle phoneme in a word with three phonemes to make a new word: e.g., *hit, hat*, (change /i/ to /a/)

LETTER KNOWLEDGE

▶ Identifying Letters

- Recognize and point to the distinctive features of letter forms
- Recognize letters and state their names
- Recognize and point to uppercase letters and lowercase letters: e.g., *B, b*
- Distinguish and talk about the differences between the uppercase and lowercase forms of a letter
- Categorize letters by features
- Recognize and talk about the order of the alphabet
- Recognize and talk about the fact that letters can be consonants or vowels

▶ Recognizing Letters in Words and Sentences

- Understand and talk about the fact that words are formed with letters
- Recognize and name letters in words
- Recognize and talk about the sequence of letters in a word
- Recognize and name letters in words in continuous text
- Understand that a word is always spelled the same way
- Make connections among words by recognizing the position of a letter: e.g., *was, we; good, said; just, put*

▶ Forming Letters

- Use efficient and consistent motions to form letters in manuscript print with writing tools

LETTER-SOUND RELATIONSHIPS

▶ Consonants

- Understand and talk about the fact that some letters represent consonant sounds: e.g., the letter *b* stands for the first sound in *boy*
- Recognize and use beginning consonant sounds and the letters that represent them: *b, c, d, f, g, h, j, k, l, m, n, p, qu, r, s, t, v, w, y, z*
- Recognize, point to, and say the same beginning consonant sound and the letter that represents the sound: e.g., *bag, bee*
- Recognize and use ending consonant sounds and the letters that represent them: *b, d, f, g, k, l, m, n, p, r, s, t, v, z*
- Recognize and use medial consonant sounds and the letters that represent them: *b, c, d, e, f, g, h, j, k, l, m, n, p, qu, r, s, t, v, w, x, y, z*
- Recognize and use ending consonant sounds sometimes represented by double consonant letters: *off, hill, dress, buzz*
- Recognize and say consonant clusters that blend two or three consonant sounds (onsets): *bl, cl, fl, gl, pl, sl, br, cr, dr, fr, gr, pr, tr, sc, sk, sm, sn, sp, st, sw, tw, qu; scr, spl, spr, squ, str*
- Recognize and use two consonant letters that represent one sound at the beginning of a word: e.g., *change, phone, shall, thirty, where*

Selecting Goals Behaviors and Understandings to Notice, Teach, and Support *(cont.)*

Phonics, Spelling, and Word Study

LETTER-SOUND RELATIONSHIPS *(continued)*

▶ Consonants *(continued)*

- Recognize and use two consonant letters that represent one sound in the middle of a word: e.g., ex*ch*ange, ne*ph*ew, fi*sh*es, some*th*ing, every*wh*ere, si*ng*er
- Recognize and use consonant letters that represent two or more different sounds at the beginning of a word: *c*ar, *c*ity; *g*et, *g*ym; *th*ink, *th*ey; *ch*air, *ch*orus, *ch*oir, *ch*ef
- Recognize and use consonant letters that represent two or more different sounds at the end of a word: clini*c*, spi*c*e; hu*g*, ca*g*e; ri*ch*, stoma*ch*; ba*th*, smoo*th*
- Recognize and use consonant clusters (blends) at the end of a word: *ct, ft, ld, lf, lp, lt, mp, nd, nk, nt, pt, sk, sp, st*

▶ Vowels

- Understand and talk about the fact that some letters represent vowel sounds
- Hear and identify short vowel sounds in words and the letters that represent them
- Recognize and use short vowel sounds at the beginning of words: e.g., *at, every, into, onto, up*
- Recognize and use short vowel sounds in the middle of words (CVC): e.g., *hat, bed, wind, stop, run*
- Hear and identify long vowel sounds in words and the letters that represent them
- Recognize and use long vowel sounds in words with silent *e* (CVC*e*): e.g., *late, Pete, pine, robe, cube*
- Contrast short and long vowel sounds in words: e.g., *at/ate, pet/Pete, bit/bite, hop/hope, cut/cute*
- Recognize and use *y* as a vowel sound: e.g., *happy, sky*

▶ Letter-Sound Representations

- Understand and talk about how to use the computer keyboard
- Understand and talk about how to use capital letters correctly

SPELLING PATTERNS

▶ Phonogram Patterns

- Recognize and talk about the fact that words, in general, have letter patterns that can appear in many words
- Recognize and use the consonant-vowel-consonant (CVC) pattern: e.g., *cap, get, pig, got, but*
- Recognize and use more common phonograms with a VC pattern: *-ab, -ad, -ag, -am, -an, -ap, -at, -aw, -ay; -ed, -en, -et, -ew; -id, -ig, -im, -in, -ip, -it; -ob, -od, -og, -op, -ot, -ow* (as in *show* or as in *cow*); *-ub, -ug, -um, -un, -ut*
- Recognize and use phonograms with a vowel-consonant-silent *e* (VC*e*) pattern: *-ace, -ade, -ake, -ale, -ame, -ane, -ape, -ate, -ave; -ice, -ide, -ile, -ine, -ite, -ive; -oke, -ose*

▶ Vowel Phonogram Patterns in Single-Syllable Words

- Recognize and use phonogram patterns with a short vowel sound in single-syllable words: e.g., *-ab, -ack, -ad, -ag, -am, -an, -and, -ap, -at; -ed, -ell, -en, -end, -et; -id, -ig, -ill, -in, -ing, -ip, -it; -ob, -ock, -og, -op, -ot; -ub, -uck, -ug, -un, -up, -ut*

HIGH-FREQUENCY WORDS

- Recognize and use high-frequency words with one, two, or three letters: e.g., *a, I, in, is, of, to, and, the*
- Locate and read high-frequency words in continuous text
- Recognize and use high-frequency words with three or more letters: e.g., *you, was, for, are, that, with, they, this*
- Read and write approximately one hundred high-frequency words
- Develop and use strategies for acquiring a large core of high-frequency words

WORD MEANING/ VOCABULARY

▶ Concept Words

- Recognize and use concept words: e.g., color names, number words, days of the week, months of the year, seasons

▶ Related Words

- Recognize and talk about the fact that words can be related in many ways:
  - ◆ sound: e.g., *hear/here*
  - ◆ spelling: e.g., *bite/kite*
  - ◆ category: e.g., *hat/coat, mother/father*
- Recognize and use synonyms (words that have almost the same meaning): e.g., *high/tall*
- Recognize and use antonyms (words that have opposite meanings): e.g., *cold/hot*

WORD STRUCTURE

▶ Syllables

- Understand and talk about the concept of a syllable
- Hear, say, clap, and identify syllables in one- or two- syllable words: e.g., *big, frog; lit/tle, mon/key*

▶ Compound Words

- Recognize and use common compound words: e.g., *into, sometimes, something, without*

▶ Contractions

- Understand and talk about the concept of a contraction
- Recognize and use contractions with *not*: e.g., *can't, don't*
- Recognize and use contractions with *am* and *are*: *I'm; we're*
- Recognize and use contractions with *is* or *has*: e.g., *he's, she's, it's*
- Recognize and use contractions with *will*: e.g., *I'll, we'll, you'll, he'll, she'll*

▶ Plurals

- Understand and talk about the fact that a noun can refer to more than one person, place, or thing: e.g., *fathers, towns, toys*
- Recognize and use plurals that add *-s*: e.g., *books, cars, dogs, farms, mothers, zoos*
- Recognize and use plurals that add *-es* to words that end with the letters *ch, sh, s, x,* or *z*: e.g., *dishes, boxes*

Selecting Goals Behaviors and Understandings to Notice, Teach, and Support *(cont.)*

Phonics, Spelling, and Word Study

▶ Suffixes: Inflectional Endings

- ■ Recognize and use the ending *-s* when making a verb agree with its subject: e.g., *cats run/cat runs; they jump/she jumps, dogs play/dog plays*
- ■ Understand and talk about the fact that the ending *-ed* when forming the past tense of a verb can represent several different sounds: e.g., *closed, added, walked*

WORD-SOLVING ACTIONS

▶ Using What Is Known to Solve Words

- ■ Recognize and find names
- ■ Use the initial letter in a name to make connections to other words: e.g., *Max, Maria, make, home, from*
- ■ Use the letters in names to make connections to other words: e.g., *Dan, money, run*
- ■ Use the initial letter in a name to read and write other words: e.g., *Tom, toy, town, stop, cat*
- ■ Use the letters in names to read and write other words: e.g., *Meg, began, big*
- ■ Identify rhyming words and use them to solve unknown words: e.g., *down/clown/drown*
- ■ Use known words to monitor word-solving accuracy
- ■ Recognize and read known words quickly
- ■ Use knowledge of letter-sound relationships to monitor word-solving accuracy
- ■ Identify words that start the same and use them to solve unknown words: e.g., *bat, bell*
- ■ Use onsets and rimes in known words to read and write other words with the same parts: e.g., *thr-ow, thr-ee; thr-ow, gr-ow*
- ■ Identify words that end the same and use them to solve unknown words: e.g., *chin, main*
- ■ Identify words that have the same letter pattern and use them to solve an unknown word: e.g., *hat/sat, light/night*
- ■ Use known word parts (some are words) to solve unknown larger words: e.g., *in/into, can/canvas; us, crust*

▶ Analyzing Words to Solve Them

- ■ Say a word slowly to hear the initial sound in the word
- ■ Say a word slowly to hear the final sound in the word
- ■ Say a word slowly to hear the sounds in sequence
- ■ Recognize the sequence of letters and the sequence of sounds to read a word or word part
- ■ Recognize and use onsets and rimes to read words: e.g., *b-ag, bag; gr-in, grin; pl-ate, plate*

▶ Changing, Adding, or Removing Parts to Solve Words

- ■ Change the beginning sound or sounds to make and solve a new word: e.g., *he/me* (change /h/ to /m/), *more/shore* (change /m/ to /sh/), *bright/might* (change /b/ /r/ to /m/)
- ■ Change the ending sound or sounds to make and solve a new word: e.g., *in/it* (change /n/ to /t/), *them/then* (change /m/ to /n/), *rest/red* (change /s/ /t/ to /d/)

▶ Taking Words Apart to Solve Them

- ■ Take apart a compound word to read two smaller words: e.g., *birthday, birth, day; everywhere, every, where; sidewalk, side, walk*

▶ Using Strategies to Solve Words and Determine Their Meanings

- ■ Use connections between or among words that mean the same or almost the same to solve an unknown word: e.g., *damp, wet*
- ■ Use connections between or among words that mean the opposite or almost the opposite to solve an unknown word: e.g., *stale, fresh*

▶ Spelling Strategies

- ■ Spell known words quickly
- ■ Make a first attempt to spell an unknown word
- ■ Use known words to help spell an unknown word
- ■ Use letter-sound relationships to help spell an unknown word
- ■ Use phonogram patterns and letter patterns to help spell a word

Selecting Goals Behaviors and Understandings to Notice, Teach, and Support

Phonics, Spelling, and Word Study

LETTER-SOUND RELATIONSHIPS

▶ Consonants

- Recognize and use ending consonant sounds and the letters that represent them: *b, d, f, g, k, l, m, n, p, r, s, t, v, z*
- Recognize and use medial consonant sounds and the letters that represent them: *b, c, d, e, f, g, h, j, k, l, m, n, p, qu, r, s, t, v, w, x, y, z*
- Recognize and use ending consonant sounds sometimes represented by double consonant letters: *off, hill, dress, buzz*
- Recognize and say consonant clusters that blend two or three consonant sounds (onsets): *bl, cl, fl, gl, pl, sl, br, cr, dr, fr, gr, pr, tr, sc, sk, sm, sn, sp, st, sw, tw, qu; scr, spl, spr, squ, str*
- Recognize and use two consonant letters that represent one sound at the beginning of a word: e.g., *change, phone, shall, thirty, where*
- Recognize and use two consonant letters that usually represent one sound at the end of a word: e.g., *branch, rock, song, dash, both*
- Recognize and use two consonant letters that represent one sound in the middle of a word: e.g., *exchange, nephew, fishes, something, everywhere, singer*
- Recognize and use middle consonant sounds sometimes represented by double consonant letters: *puddle, bigger, swimmer, dropped*
- Recognize and use consonant letters that represent two or more different sounds at the beginning of a word: *car, city; get, gym; think, they; chair, chorus, choir, chef*
- Recognize and use consonant letters that represent two or more different sounds at the end of a word: *clinic, spice; hug, cage; rich, stomach; bath, smooth*
- Recognize and use consonant letters that represent two or more different sounds in the middle of a word: *cyclone, nicest; bugle, magic; inches, school, machine; mouthwash, feather*

- Recognize and use consonant clusters (blends) at the end of a word: *ct, ft, ld, lf, lp, lt, mp, nd, nk, nt, pt, sk, sp, st*
- Recognize and use less frequent consonant digraphs at the beginning or end of a word: *gh, ph (e.g., rough, phone, telegraph)*
- Recognize and use consonant letters that represent no sound: *lamb, scene, sign, rhyme, know, calm, island, listen, wrap*
- Understand and talk about the fact that some consonant sounds can be represented by several different letters or letter clusters: e.g., *kayak, picnic, truck, stomach, antique; thief, stiff, cough, graph*

▶ Vowels

- Hear and identify long vowel sounds in words and the letters that represent them
- Recognize and use long vowel sounds in words with silent *e* (CVCe): e.g., *late, Pete, pine, robe, cube*
- Contrast short and long vowel sounds in words: e.g., *at/ate, pet/Pete, bit/bite, hop/hope, cut/cute*
- Recognize and use *y* as a vowel sound: e.g., *happy, sky*
- Recognize and use letter combinations that represent long vowel sounds: e.g., *chain, play, neat, meet, pie, light, roast, toe, row, blue, fruit, new*
- Recognize and use letter combinations that represent unique vowel sounds: *oi as in oil; oy as in boy; ou as in house; ow as in cow*
- Recognize and use a letter or letter combinations that represent the /o̅/ vowel sound (as in *saw*): e.g., *autumn, paw, soft, taught, bought, talk*
- Recognize and use vowel sounds with *r*: e.g., *chair, care, pear; car; year, pioneer, here; her, first, hurt, learn; corn, more, floor, roar, pour; cure*
- Recognize and use vowel sounds in closed syllables (CVC): *hab/it, lem/on, fig/ure, rob/in, pub/lic*
- Recognize and use vowel sounds in open syllables (CVC): *ba/by, e/ven, pi/lot, ho/tel, hu/man*

▶ Letter-Sound Representations

- Understand and talk about how to use the computer keyboard
- Understand and talk about how to use capital letters correctly

SPELLING PATTERNS

▶ Phonogram Patterns

- Recognize and use more common phonograms with a VC pattern: *-ab, -ad, -ag, -am, -an, -ap, -at, -aw, -ay; -ed, -en, -et, -ew; -id, -ig, -im, -in, -ip, -it; -ob, -od, -og, -op, -ot, -ow (as in show or as in cow); -ub, -ug, -um, -un, -ut*
- Recognize and use less common phonograms with a VC pattern: *-ax; -eg, -em, -ep, -ex, -ey; -ib, -ix; -on, -ox, -oy; -ud, -up, -us*
- Recognize and use phonograms with a vowel-consonant-silent e (VCe) pattern: *-ace, -ade, -ake, -ale, -ame, -ane, -ape, -ate, -ave; -ice, -ide, -ile, -ine, -ite, -ive; -oke, -ose*
- Recognize and use phonograms that end with a double consonant (VCC): e.g., *-all, -ass; -ell, -ess; -ill; -uff*
- Recognize and use phonograms with a double vowel (VVC): *-eed, -eek, -eel, -eem, -een, -eep, -eer, -eet; -ood, -oof, -ook, -ool, -oom, -oon, -oop, -oor, -oot*
- Recognize and use some phonograms with ending consonant clusters (VCC): e.g., *ack, -ank, -ash, -est, -ick, -ing, -ink, -ock, -uck, -ump, -unk*
- Recognize and use some phonograms with vowel combinations (VVC): e.g., *-ail, -ain, -eat*

▶ Vowel Phonogram Patterns in Single-Syllable Words

- Recognize and use phonogram patterns with a short vowel sound in single-syllable words: e.g., *-ab, -ack, -ad, -ag, -am, -amp, -an, -ank, -ap, -at; -ell, -end, -ent, -est, -et; -ick, -ill, -in, -ing, -ink, -ip, -it; -ob, -ock, -og, -op, -ot; -ub, -ug, -ump, -unk, -ut*
- Recognize and use phonogram patterns with a long vowel sound in single-syllable words: e.g., *-ace, -ade, -ail, -ain, -ake, -ame, -ane, -ate, -ave, -ay, -aze; -ead, -eak, -eal, -eam, -ear, -eat, -ee, -eed, -eek, -eel, -eep, -eet, -ice, -ide, -ies, -ight, -ime, -ind, -ine, -ite, -ive, -y; -oat, -oke, -old, -one, -ope, -ow; -ue*

Selecting Goals Behaviors and Understandings to Notice, Teach, and Support *(cont.)*

Phonics, Spelling, and Word Study

- Recognize and use phonogram patterns with the /ü/ vowel sound (as in *moon*) in single-syllable words: *-ew, -o, -oo, -ood, -oof, -ool, -oom, -oon, -oop, -oot, -oup*

- Recognize and use phonogram patterns with the /u˙ / vowel sound (as in *book*) in single-syllable words: *-ood, -ook, -oot, -ull, -ush*

- Recognize and use phonogram patterns with the /o˙ / vowel sound (as in *saw*) in single-syllable words: e.g., *-alk, -all, -alt, -aw, -awl, -awn, -ong, -oss, -ost, -oth*

- Recognize and use phonogram patterns with vowels and *r* in single-syllable words: e.g., *-air, -ar, -ard, -are, -ark, -arm, -arn, -arp, -art, -ear, -eer, -ir, -ird, -irt, -oor, -ord, -ore, -orn, -ort, -our, -ur, -urn*

▶ Assorted Patterns in Multisyllable Words

- Understand and talk about the fact that some words have a double consonant: e.g., *pebble, hidden, earmuff, jiggle, yellow, fulfill, happy, messy, express, bottle, boycott*

HIGH-FREQUENCY WORDS

- Locate and read high-frequency words in continuous text

- Recognize and use high-frequency words with three or more letters: e.g., *you, was, for, are, that, with, they, this*

- Recognize and use longer high-frequency words, some with more than one syllable: e.g., *after, around, before, their, there, these, very, which*

- Read and write approximately two hundred high-frequency words

- Develop and use strategies for acquiring a large core of high-frequency words

WORD MEANING/ VOCABULARY

▶ Concept Words

- Recognize and use concept words that can have sets and subsets: e.g., *food: fruit (apple, pear), vegetable (carrot, pea)*

▶ Related Words

- Recognize and talk about the fact that words can be related in many ways: e.g.,
  - ◆ sound: e.g., *hear/here*
  - ◆ spelling: e.g., *bite/kite*
  - ◆ category: e.g., *hat/coat, mother/father*

- Recognize and use synonyms (words that have almost the same meaning): e.g., *high/tall*

- Recognize and use antonyms (words that have opposite meanings): e.g., *cold/hot*

- Recognize and use homophones (words that have the same sound, different spellings, and different meanings): e.g., *blew/blue*

- Recognize and use homographs (words that have the same spelling, different meanings and origins, and may have different pronunciations): e.g., *duck, present*

- Recognize and use words with multiple meanings: e.g., *cover*

▶ Combined and Created Words

- Recognize and use compound words: e.g., *blueberry, snowstorm*

- Recognize and use compound words with common parts: e.g., *doghouse, housekeeper, schoolhouse; beside, inside, sidewalk*

WORD STRUCTURE

▶ Syllables

- Understand and talk about the concept of a syllable

- Hear, say, clap, and identify syllables in one- or two- syllable words: e.g., *big, frog, gold; lit/tle, mon/key, sil/ver*

- Understand and talk about the fact that each syllable contains one vowel sound

- Recognize and use syllables in words with double consonants: e.g., *ap/ple, bot/tle*

- Hear, say, clap, and identify syllables in words with three or more syllables: e.g., *an/oth/er, bi/cy/cle, el/e/va/tor*

▶ Compound Words

- Recognize and use common compound words: e.g., *cannot, into, maybe, myself, sometimes, something, today, without, yourself*

- Recognize and use other compound words: e.g., *airport, birthday, blueberry, flashlight, highway, homesick, peanut, railroad, sidewalk, snowstorm*

- Recognize and use compound words that have frequently used component words: e.g., *anybody, anymore, anyone, anything, anytime, anyway, anywhere*

- Recognize and use compound words that have common parts: e.g., *bookcase, bookmark, bookshelf, notebook, scrapbook, textbook*

▶ Contractions

- Understand and talk about the concept of a contraction

- Recognize and use contractions with *not*: e.g., *aren't, can't, couldn't, didn't, doesn't, don't, hadn't, hasn't, haven't, isn't, wasn't*

- Recognize and use contractions with *am* and *are*: *I'm; we're, you're, they're*

- Recognize and use contractions with *is* or *has*: e.g., *he's, she's, it's; that's, there's, what's*

- Recognize and use contractions with *will*: e.g., *I'll, we'll, you'll, he'll, she'll, it'll, they'll*

- Recognize and use contractions with *have*: e.g., *I've, we've, you've, they've*

▶ Plurals

- Recognize and use plurals that add *-es* to words that end with the letters *ch, sh, s, x,* or *z*: e.g., *branches, dishes, boxes*

- Recognize and use plurals that add *-s* to words that end with a vowel and *y*: e.g., *boys, chimneys, holidays*

- Recognize and use plurals that add *-es* to words that end with a consonant and *y* after changing the *y* to *i*: e.g., *countries*

▶ Possessives

- Recognize and use possessives that add an apostrophe and *s* to singular nouns (including proper nouns) to show ownership: e.g., *boy's popcorn, Pat's neck, town's library, whale's eyes*

Selecting Goals Behaviors and Understandings to Notice, Teach, and Support *(cont.)*

Phonics, Spelling, and Word Study

WORD STRUCTURE *(continued)*

▶ Suffixes

- Understand and talk about the concept of a suffix

- Understand and talk about the fact that several basic rules govern the spelling of words with suffixes:

  - ◆ For many words, there are no spelling changes when adding a suffix: e.g., *run/runs, bright/brighter/brightest, teach/teacher*

  - ◆ For words that end with silent *e,* usually drop the *e* when adding a suffix that begins with a vowel, but usually keep the *e* when adding a suffix that begins with a consonant: e.g., *live/living* but *live/lives*

  - ◆ For one-syllable words that end with a single vowel and one consonant, usually double the final consonant when adding a suffix that begins with a vowel, but usually do not double the final consonant when adding a suffix that begins with a consonant: e.g., *grin/grinning* but *grin/grins, sad/sadder/saddest*

▶ Suffixes: Inflectional Endings

- Recognize and use the ending *-es* when making a verb agree with its subject: e.g., *they miss/she misses; children splash/child splashes; they cry/he cries*

- Recognize and use the ending *-ing* when forming the present participle of a verb: e.g., *help/helping, live/living, grin/grinning, visit/visiting*

- Recognize and use the ending *-ed* when forming the past tense of a verb: e.g., *help/helped, live/lived, grin/grinned, visit/visited*

- Understand and talk about the fact that the ending *-ed* when forming the past tense of a verb can represent several different sounds: e.g., *closed, added, walked*

▶ Suffixes: Comparative Endings

- Recognize and use the suffixes *-er* and *-est* to show comparison: e.g., *bright/brighter/brightest, sad/sadder/saddest*

▶ Suffixes: Noun Suffixes

- Recognize and use the suffixes *-er, -or, -ar,* and *-ist,* which name a person or thing that does something, to form a noun:

  - ◆ er: e.g., *teach/teacher, bake/baker, carry/carrier*

  - ◆ -or: e.g., *visit/visitor, edit/editor*

  - ◆ -ar: e.g., *beg/beggar*

  - ◆ -ist: e.g., *art/artist*

▶ Abbreviations

- Recognize and use common abbreviations and understand the full form of the words they shorten: e.g.,

  - ◆ titles, names, degrees and professional terms: *Mr.* (*Mister,* title for a man), *Ms.* (title for a woman), *Mrs.* (title for a married woman), *Miss* (title for a girl or an unmarried woman), *Dr.* (*Doctor*)

  - ◆ days of week and months: *Mon.* (*Monday*), *Tues., Wed., Thurs., Fri., Sat., Sun.; Jan.* (*January*), *Feb., Mar., Apr., Aug., Sept., Oct., Nov., Dec.*

  - ◆ addresses and geographical terms: *St.* (*Street*), *Ave.* (*Avenue*), *Rd.* (*Road*), *Apt.* (*Apartment*), *Blvd.* (*Boulevard*), *CA* or *Calif.* (*California*), *U.S.* or *US* (*United States*); *Mt.* (*Mountain*), *E* (*East*), *N, W, S*

  - ◆ times and dates: *a.m.* or *am* (the time from midnight to noon), *p.m.* or *pm* (the time from noon to midnight)

  - ◆ measurements: *in.* (*inch* or *inches*), *ft.* (*foot* or *feet*), *yd.* (*yard* or *yards*), *mi.* (*mile* or *miles*), *lb.* (*pound* or *pounds*), *oz.* (*ounce* or *ounces*)

WORD-SOLVING ACTIONS

▶ Using What Is Known to Solve Words

- Identify rhyming words and use them to solve unknown words: e.g., *down/clown/drown*

- Use known words to monitor word-solving accuracy

- Recognize and read known words quickly

- Use knowledge of letter-sound relationships to monitor word-solving accuracy

- Use onsets and rimes in known words to read and write other words with the same parts: e.g., *thr-ow, thr-ee; thr-ow, gr-ow*

- Identify words that end the same and use them to solve unknown words: e.g., *chin, main*

- Identify words that have the same letter pattern and use them to solve an unknown word: e.g., *hat/sat, light/night*

- Use known word parts (some are words) to solve unknown larger words: e.g., *in/into, can/canvas*

▶ Analyzing Words to Solve Them

- Say a word slowly to hear the sounds in sequence

- Recognize the sequence of letters and the sequence of sounds to read a word or word part

- Recognize and use onsets and rimes to read words: e.g., *b-ag, bag; gr-in, grin*

▶ Changing, Adding, or Removing Parts to Solve Words

- Change the beginning sound or sounds to make and solve a new word: e.g., *he/me* (change /h/ to /m/), *more/shore* (change /m/ to /sh/), *bright/might* (change /b/ /r/ to /m/)

- Change the ending sound or sounds to make and solve a new word: e.g., *in/it* (change /n/ to /t/), *them/then* (change /m/ to /n/), *rest/red* (change /s/ /t/ to /d/)

- Change a middle sound to make and solve a new word: e.g., *big/bag* (change /i/ to /a/), *fill/fell* (change /i/ to /e/)

- Change an onset or rime to read or write other words: e.g., *br-ing, th-ing* (change *br* to *th*), *br-ing, br-own* (change *ing* to *own*)

- Add a letter to the beginning or end of a word to read and write other words: e.g., *in/win; ten/tent*

- Add a consonant cluster or a consonant digraph to the beginning or end of a word to read and write other words: e.g., *an/plan, in/thin; go/gold*

- Remove a letter from the beginning or end of a word to read and write other words: e.g., *sit/it, his/is; bark/bar*

- Remove a consonant cluster or a consonant digraph from the beginning or end of a word to read and write other words: e.g., *plan/an, thin/in; gold/go*

- Remove the inflectional ending from a base word to read and write other words: e.g., *sits/sit, jumping/jump, player/play, wished/wish*

Selecting Goals Behaviors and Understandings to Notice, Teach, and Support *(cont.)*

Phonics, Spelling, and Word Study

▶ Taking Words Apart to Solve Them

- Take apart a compound word to read two smaller words: e.g., *birthday, birth, day; everywhere, every, where; sidewalk, side, walk*
- Break a word into syllables to decode manageable units: e.g., *re/mem/ber, be/fore*

▶ Using Strategies to Solve Words and Determine Their Meanings

- Use connections between or among words that mean the same or almost the same to solve an unknown word: e.g., *damp, wet*
- Use connections between or among words that mean the opposite or almost the opposite to solve an unknown word: e.g., *stale, fresh*

▶ Using Reference Tools to Solve and Find Information About Words

- Use alphabetical order to locate information about words in a variety of reference tools
- Use a glossary to solve and find information about words
- Use a dictionary to solve and find information about words

▶ Spelling Strategies

- Spell known words quickly
- Make a first attempt to spell an unknown word
- Use known words to help spell an unknown word
- Use letter-sound relationships to help spell an unknown word
- Use phonogram patterns and letter patterns to help spell a word
- Use sound and letter sequence to help spell a word
- Use syllables to help spell a word
- Use the spelling of the smaller words within a compound word to help spell a compound word
- Use a spelling routine to help spell a word
- Use a mnemonic device to help spell a word: e.g., *fri<u>end</u>s to the <u>end</u>, a <u>bear</u> bit my <u>ear</u>*
- Ask for help when all known spelling strategies have been tried

Selecting Goals Behaviors and Understandings to Notice, Teach, and Support

Phonics, Spelling, and Word Study

LETTER KNOWLEDGE

▶ Forming Letters

- Use efficient and consistent motions to form letters in cursive writing with writing tools

LETTER-SOUND RELATIONSHIPS

▶ Consonants

- Recognize and say consonant clusters that blend two or three consonant sounds (onsets): *bl, cl, fl, gl, pl, sl, br, cr, dr, fr, gr, pr, tr, sc, sk, sm, sn, sp, st, sw, tw, qu; scr, spl, spr, squ, str*
- Recognize and use two consonant letters that represent one sound at the beginning of a word: e.g., *change, phone, shall, thirty, where*
- Recognize and use two consonant letters that usually represent one sound at the end of a word: e.g., *branch, rock, song, dash, both*
- Recognize and use two consonant letters that represent one sound in the middle of a word: e.g., *fishes, something, everywhere, singer*
- Recognize and use middle consonant sounds sometimes represented by double consonant letters: *rubber, coffee, announce, dropped, arrive, lesson, buzzing*
- Recognize and use consonant letters that represent two or more different sounds at the beginning of a word: *car, city; get, gym; think, they; chair, chorus, choir, chef*
- Recognize and use consonant letters that represent two or more different sounds at the end of a word: *clinic, spice; hug, cage; rich, stomach; bath, smooth*
- Recognize and use consonant letters that represent two or more different sounds in the middle of a word: *cyclone, nicest; bugle, magic; inches, school, machine; mouthwash, feather*
- Recognize and use consonant clusters (blends) at the end of a word: *ct, ft, ld, lf, lp, lt, mp, nd, nk, nt, pt, sk, sp, st*
- Recognize and use less frequent consonant digraphs at the beginning or end of a word: *gh, ph* (e.g., *rough, phone, telegraph*)
- Recognize and use consonant letters that represent no sound: *lamb, scene, sign, rhyme, know, calm, island, listen, wrap*

- Understand and talk about the fact that some consonant sounds can be represented by several different letters or letter clusters: e.g., *kayak, picnic, truck, stomach, thief, stiff, cough, graph*

▶ Vowels

- Recognize and use *y* as a vowel sound: e.g., *happy, sky*
- Recognize and use letter combinations that represent long vowel sounds: e.g., *chain, play, neat, meet, pie, light, roast, toe, row, blue, fruit, new*
- Recognize and use letter combinations that represent unique vowel sounds: *oi* as in *oil; oy* as in *boy; ou* as in *house; ow* as in *cow*
- Recognize and use a letter or letter combinations that represent the /o˙/ vowel sound (as in *saw*): e.g., *autumn, paw, soft, taught, bought, talk*
- Recognize and use letter combinations that represent two different vowel sounds: e.g., *meat, break; they, key; tie, piece; spoon, book; snow, cow*
- Recognize and use vowel sounds with *r:* e.g., *chair, care, pear; car; year, pioneer, here; her, first, hurt, learn; corn, more, floor, roar, pour; cure*
- Recognize and use vowel sounds in closed syllables (CVC): *hab/it, lem/on, fig/ure, rob/in, pub/lic*
- Recognize and use vowel sounds in open syllables (CVC): *ba/by, e/ven, pi/lot, ho/tel, hu/man*

▶ Letter-Sound Representations

- Understand and talk about how to use the computer keyboard
- Understand and talk about how to use capital letters correctly
- Understand and talk about how to form cursive letters correctly, efficiently, and fluently

SPELLING PATTERNS

▶ Phonogram Patterns

- Recognize and use less common phonograms with a VC pattern: *-ax; -eg, -em, -ep, -ex, -ey; -ib, -ix; -on, -ox, -oy; -ud, -up, -us*

- Recognize and use phonograms with a vowel-consonant-silent *e* (VCe) pattern: *-ace, -ade, -ake, -ale, -ame, -ane, -ape, -ate, -ave; -ice, -ide, -ile, -ine, -ite, -ive; -oke, -ose*
- Recognize and use phonograms that end with a double consonant (VCC): e.g., *-all, -ass; -ell, -ess; -ill; -uff*
- Recognize and use phonograms with a double vowel (VVC): *-eed, -eek, -eel, -eem, -een, -eep, -eer, -eet; -ood, -oof, -ook, -ool, -oom, -oon, -oop, -oor, -oot*
- Recognize and use phonograms with ending consonant clusters (VCC): e.g., *ack, -act, -aft, -amp, -and, -ang, -ank, -ant, -ash, -ask, -ast, -ath; -eck, -elt, -end, -ent, -ept, -est; -ick, -ift, -imp, -ing, -ink, -int, -ish, -isk, -ist; -ock, -omp, -ond; -uck, -umb, -ump, -ung, -unk, -unt, -ush, -ust*
- Recognize and use phonograms with vowel combinations (VVC): e.g., *-aid, -ail, -ain, -ait; -ead, -eak, -eal, -eam, -ean, -eap, -ear, -eat; -ied, -ief, -ies; -oak, -oat, -oil, -our, -out*

▶ Vowel Phonogram Patterns in Single-Syllable Words

- Recognize and use phonogram patterns with a short vowel sound in single-syllable words: e.g., *-ab, -ack, -ad, -ag, -am, -amp, -an, -ank, -ap, -at; -ell, -end, -ent, -est, -et; -ick, -ill, -in, -ing, -ink, -ip, -it; -ob, -ock, -og, -op, -ot; -ub, -ug, -ump, -unk, -ut*
- Recognize and use phonogram patterns with a long vowel sound in single-syllable words: e.g., *-ace, -ade, -ail, -air, -ake, -ame, -ane, -ate, -ave, -ay, -aze; -ead, -eak, -eal, -eam, -ear, -eat, -ee, -eed, -eek, -eel, -eep, -eet; -ice, -ide, -ies, -ight, -ime, -ind, -ine, -ite, -ive, -y; -oat, -oke, -old, -one, -ope, -ow; -ue*
- Recognize and use phonogram patterns with the /ü/ vowel sound (as in *moon*) in single-syllable words: *-ew, -o, -oo, -ood, -oof, -ool, -oom, -oon, -oop, -oot, -oup*
- Recognize and use phonogram patterns with the /u˙/ vowel sound (as in *book*) in single-syllable words: *-ood, -ook, -oot, -ull, -ush*
- Recognize and use phonogram patterns with the /o˙/ vowel sound (as in *saw*) in single-syllable words: e.g., *-alk, -all, -alt, -aw, -awl, -awn, -ong, -oss, -ost, -oth*

Selecting Goals Behaviors and Understandings to Notice, Teach, and Support *(cont.)*

Phonics, Spelling, and Word Study

- Recognize and use phonogram patterns with vowels and *r* in single-syllable words: e.g., *-air, -ar, -ard, -are, -ark, -arm, -arn, -arp, -art, -ear, -eer, -ir, -ird, -irt, -oor, -ord, -ore, -orn, -ort, -our, -ur, -urn*
- Recognize and use phonogram patterns with the /ou/ vowel sound (as in *cow*) in single-syllable words: e.g., *-oud, -our, -out, -ow, -owl, -own*
- Recognize and use phonogram patterns with the /oi/ vowel sound (as in *boy*) in single-syllable words: e.g., *-oil, -oin, -oy*

▶ Assorted Patterns in Multisyllable Words

- Understand and talk about the fact that some words have a double consonant: e.g., *pebble, hidden, earmuff, jiggle, yellow, fulfill, happy, messy, express, bottle, boycott*
- Understand and talk about the fact that some words have a pattern with a double consonant that represents two sounds: e.g., *success, accident*
- Recognize and use frequently appearing syllable patterns in multisyllable words: e.g., <u>a</u>lone, <u>be</u>fore, <u>en</u>ter, <u>im</u>itate, <u>in</u>crease, <u>re</u>peat, <u>un</u>happy; trou<u>ble</u>, other, pur<u>ple</u>, alread<u>y</u>

▶ Vowel Phonogram Patterns in Multisyllable Words

- Recognize and use short vowel phonograms that appear in multisyllable words: e.g., *-ab, -ack, -act, -ad, -ag, -am, -an, -ank, -ap, -at; -ell, -end, -ent, -est, -et; -ick, -ill, -in, -ing, -ip, -it; -ob, -ock, -og, -op, -ot; -ub, -ug, -unk, -ut*
- Recognize and use long vowel phonograms that appear in multisyllable words: e.g., *-ace, -ade, -ail, -ake, -ame, -ane, -ate, -ay, -aze; -ead, -eal, -eam, -ear, -eat, -ee, -eed, -eel, -eep, -eet; -ice, -ide, -ies, -ight, -ime, -ind, -ine, -ite, -ive, -y; -oat, -oke, -old, -one, -ope, -ow; -ue*

HIGH-FREQUENCY WORDS

- Locate and read high-frequency words in continuous text
- Recognize and use longer high-frequency words, some with more than one syllable: e.g., *after, around, before, their, there, these, very, which*

- Develop and use strategies for acquiring a large core of high-frequency words
- Read and write approximately five hundred high-frequency words

WORD MEANING/ VOCABULARY

▶ Concept Words

- Recognize and use concept words that can have sets and subsets: e.g., *food: fruit (apple, pear), vegetable (carrot, pea)*

▶ Related Words

- Recognize and talk about the fact that words can be related in many ways: e.g.,
  - ◆ sound: e.g., *hear/here, weather/whether*
  - ◆ spelling: e.g., *bite/kite*
  - ◆ category: e.g., *hat/coat, mother/father*
- Recognize and use synonyms (words that have almost the same meaning): e.g., *mistake/error, high/tall*
- Recognize and use antonyms (words that have opposite meanings): e.g., *cold/hot, appear/vanish*
- Recognize and use homophones (words that have the same sound, different spellings, and different meanings): e.g., *blew/blue*
- Recognize and use homographs (words that have the same spelling, different meanings and origins, and may have different pronunciations): e.g., *content, duck, present*
- Recognize and use words with multiple meanings: e.g., *cover, organ*

▶ Combined and Created Words

- Recognize and use compound words: e.g., *blueberry, overhead, snowstorm*
- Recognize and use compound words with common parts: e.g., *dog<u>house</u>, <u>house</u>keeper, school<u>house</u>; be<u>side</u>, in<u>side</u>, <u>side</u>walk*

▶ Figurative Uses of Words

- Recognize and use onomatopoetic words: e.g., *buzz, hiss, plop, quack, thump, whack, zoom*

▶ Parts of Words

- Understand and discuss the concept of prefixes and recognize their use in determining the meaning of some English words: e.g., *ad-, ant-, anti-, bi-, circu-, com-, con-, contra-, contro-, counter-, dec-, dis-, em-, en-, ex-, in-, inter-, intra-, mal-, mis-, mon-, mono-, multi-, non-, oct-, pent-, per-, poly-, pre-, quadr-, re-, sub-, super-, trans-, tri-, un-, uni-*

▶ Word Origins

- Develop interest in vocabulary by recognizing and appreciating aspects of words and by "collecting" and discussing interesting word and using them in conversation

WORD STRUCTURE

▶ Syllables

- Recognize and use syllables in words with double consonants: e.g., *ap/ple, bot/tle, tun/nel*
- Hear, say, clap, and identify syllables in words with three or more syllables: e.g., *an/oth/er, bi/cy/cle, fish/er/man, el/e/va/tor, un/u/su/al*
- Recognize and use open syllables–syllables that end with a single vowel, which usually represents a long vowel sound: e.g., *o/pen, pi/lot, ti/ger*
- Recognize and use closed syllables– syllables that end with a consonant and usually have a short vowel sound: e.g., *can/dle, fif/teen*
- Recognize and use *r*-influenced syllables– syllables that contain one or two vowels followed by the letter *r*: e.g., *a/part/ment, for/get, four/teen*
- Recognize and use vowel combination syllables–syllables that contain two or more letters together that represent one vowel sound: e.g., *be/tween, en/joy*
- Recognize and use VCe syllables–syllables that contain a (long) vowel followed by a consonant and then silent *e*: e.g., *be/side, eve/ning, in/vite, lone/ly*
- Recognize and use consonant + *le* syllables–syllables that contain a consonant followed by the letters *le*: e.g., *a/ble, ea/gle*
- Recognize and use syllables in words with the VCCV pattern (syllable juncture): e.g., *ber/ry, both/er*

Selecting Goals Behaviors and Understandings to Notice, Teach, and Support (cont.)

Phonics, Spelling, and Word Study

WORD STRUCTURE (continued)

▶ **Syllables** (continued)

- Recognize and use syllables in words with the VCCCV pattern (syllable juncture): e.g., *emp/ty, hun/dred*
- Recognize and use syllables in words with the VV pattern: e.g., *gi/ant*

▶ **Compound Words**

- Recognize and use many compound words: e.g., *airport, birthday, blueberry, flashlight, highway, homesick, peanut, railroad, sidewalk, snowstorm*
- Recognize and use compound words that have frequently used words: e.g., *everybody, everyday, everyone, everything, everywhere; somebody, someday, somehow, someone, someplace, something, sometime, somewhat, somewhere*
- Recognize and use compound words that have common parts: e.g., *countdown, download, downstairs, downtown, facedown, sundown; campfire, firefighter, firehouse, fireplace, firewood, wildfire*

▶ **Contractions**

- Recognize and use contractions with *not*: e.g., *aren't, can't, couldn't, didn't, doesn't, don't, hadn't, hasn't, haven't, isn't, wasn't, weren't, wouldn't*
- Recognize and use contractions with *am* and *are*: *I'm; we're, you're, they're*
- Recognize and use contractions with *is* or *has*: e.g., *he's, she's, it's; that's, there's, what's*
- Recognize and use contractions with *will*: e.g., *I'll, we'll, you'll, he'll, she'll, it'll, they'll*
- Recognize and use contractions with *have*: e.g., *I've, we've, you've, they've*

▶ **Plurals**

- Recognize and use plurals that add *-es* to words that end with the letters *ch, sh, s, x,* or *z*: e.g., *branches, dishes, classes, boxes*
- Recognize and use plurals that add *-s* to words that end with a vowel and *y*: e.g., *boys, chimneys, holidays*
- Recognize and use plurals that add *-es* to words that end with a consonant and *y* after changing the *y* to *i*: e.g., *countries, jellies*

- Recognize and use plurals that add *-es* to words after changing the final *f* or *fe* to *v*: e.g., *knives, scarves, wolves*
- Recognize and use irregular plurals that change the spelling of the word: e.g., *goose/geese, mouse/mice, ox/oxen, woman/women*
- Recognize and use irregular plurals that are the same as the singular form of the word: e.g., *deer, moose, salmon, sheep*
- Recognize and use plurals that add *-s* to words that end with *o*: e.g., *pianos*
- Recognize and use plurals that add *-es* to words that end with a consonant and *o*: e.g., *heroes*

▶ **Possessives**

- Recognize and use possessives that add an apostrophe and *s* to singular nouns (including proper nouns) that end with *s* to show ownership: e.g., *princess's closet, Texas's flag*

▶ **Suffixes**

- Understand and talk about the concept of a suffix
- Understand and talk about the fact that several basic rules govern the spelling of words with suffixes: e.g.,
  - ◆ For many words, there are no spelling changes when adding a suffix: e.g., *run/runs, bright/brighter/ brightest, final/finally, teach/teacher*
  - ◆ For words that end with silent *e*, usually drop the *e* when adding a suffix that begins with a vowel, but usually keep the *e* when adding a suffix that begins with a consonant: e.g., *live/living* but *live/lives, fierce/fiercer/fiercest, please/pleasant* but *grace/graceful*
  - ◆ For one-syllable words that end with a single vowel and one consonant, usually double the final consonant when adding a suffix that begins with a vowel, but usually do not double the final consonant when adding a suffix that begins with a consonant: e.g., *grin/grinning* but *grin/grins, sad/sadder/saddest, flat/flatten, beg/beggar* but *fit/fitness*
  - ◆ For multisyllable words with an unaccented final syllable that ends with a single vowel and one consonant, usually do not double the final consonant when adding a suffix: e.g., *visit/visited*

- ◆ For words that end with a consonant and *y*, usually change the *y* to *i* and add the suffix, but for words that end with a vowel and *y*, usually keep the *y* and add the suffix: e.g, *copy/copied* but *enjoy/enjoyed*

▶ **Suffixes: Inflectional Endings**

- Recognize and use the ending *-es* when making a verb agree with its subject: e.g., *they miss/she misses; children splash/child splashes; boys search/boy searches, they cry/ he cries*
- Recognize and use the ending *-ing* when forming the present participle of a verb: e.g., *help/helping, live/living, grin/grinning, visit/visiting, copy/copying, enjoy/enjoying, mix/mixing*
- Recognize and use the ending *-ed* when forming the past tense of a verb: e.g., *help/helped, live/lived, grin/grinned, visit/visited, copy/copied, enjoy/enjoyed, mix/mixed*
- Understand and talk about the fact that the ending *-ed* when forming the past tense of a verb can represent several different sounds: e.g., *closed, added, walked*

▶ **Suffixes: Comparative Endings**

- Recognize and use the suffixes *-er* and *-est* to show comparison: e.g., *bright/brighter/ brightest, fierce/fiercer/fiercest, sad/sadder/ saddest*

▶ **Suffixes: Adjective and Adverb Suffixes**

- Recognize and use the suffix *-ly,* meaning "in a specific manner, period of time, or order," to form an adverb: e.g., *live/lively, sad/sadly, easy/easily*

▶ **Suffixes: Noun Suffixes**

- Recognize and use the suffixes *-er, -or, -ar,* and *-ist,* which name a person or thing that does something, to form a noun: e.g.,
  - ◆ -er: e.g., *teach/teacher, bake/baker, drum/ drummer, carry/carrier*
  - ◆ -or: e.g., *visit/visitor, edit/editor*
  - ◆ -ar: e.g., *beg/beggar*
  - ◆ -ist: e.g., *art/artist, piano/pianist*

Selecting Goals Behaviors and Understandings to Notice, Teach, and Support *(cont.)*

Phonics, Spelling, and Word Study

▶ Prefixes

- Understand and discuss the concept of a prefix
- Recognize and use the prefix *re-*, meaning "again": e.g., *remake, repay, refresh*
- Recognize and use prefixes that mean "not": e.g.,
  - ◆ un- *(unfair, unkind)*
  - ◆ in- *(invisible)*
  - ◆ dis- *(disappear)*
  - ◆ non- *(nonsense, nonfiction, nonstop)*
- Recognize and use prefixes that mean "bad, badly" or "wrong, wrongly": e.g.,
  - ◆ mis- *(mistake)*
  - ◆ mal- *(malfunction)*
- Recognize and use prefixes that refer to sequence: e.g., pre-, meaning "before" *(preheat)*
- Recognize and use prefixes that indicate amount, extent, or location: e.g.,
  - ◆ sub- *(subway)*
  - ◆ super- *(supermarket)*

▶ Abbreviations

- Recognize and use common abbreviations and understand the full form of the words they shorten: e.g.,
  - ◆ titles, names, degrees, and professional terms: *Mr. (Mister,* title for a man), *Ms.* (title for a woman), *Mrs.* (title for a married woman), *Miss* (title for a girl or an unmarried woman), *Dr. (Doctor)*
  - ◆ days of week and months: *Mon. (Monday), Tues., Wed., Thurs., Fri., Sat., Sun.; Jan. (January), Feb., Mar., Apr., Aug., Sept., Oct., Nov., Dec.*
  - ◆ addresses and geographical terms: *St. (Street), Ave. (Avenue), Rd. (Road), Apt. (Apartment), Blvd. (Boulevard), CA* or *Calif. (California), U.S.* or *US (United States); Mt. (Mountain), E (East), N, W, S*
  - ◆ times and dates: *a.m.* or *am (the time from midnight to noon), p.m.* or *pm (the time from noon to midnight)*
  - ◆ measurements: *in. (inch* or *inches), ft. (foot* or *feet), yd. (yard* or *yards), mi. (mile* or *miles), lb. (pound* or *pounds), oz. (ounce* or *ounces), c* or *c. (cup* or *cups), pt. (pint* or *pints), qt. (quart* or *quarts), gal. (gallon* or *gallons)*

WORD-SOLVING ACTIONS

▶ Using What Is Known to Solve Words

- Recognize and read known words quickly
- Use knowledge of letter-sound relationships to monitor word-solving accuracy
- Use onsets and rimes in known words to read and write other words with the same parts: e.g., *thr-ow, thr-ee; thr-ow, gr-ow*
- Identify words that have the same letter pattern and use them to solve an unknown word: e.g., *hat/sat, light/night, curious/ furious*
- Use known word parts (some are words) to solve unknown larger words: e.g., *in/into, can/canvas*

▶ Analyzing Words to Solve Them

- Recognize the sequence of letters and the sequence of sounds to read a word or word part
- Recognize and use onsets and rimes to read words: e.g., *b-ag, bag; gr-in, grin; pl-ate, plate*

▶ Changing, Adding, or Removing Parts to Solve Words

- Change a middle sound to make and solve a new word: e.g., *big/bag* (change /i/ to /a/), *fill/fell* (change /i/ to /e/), *bank/bunk* (change /a/ to /u/)
- Change an onset or rime to read or write other words: e.g., *br-ing, th-ing* (change *br* to *th*), *br-ing, br-own* (change *ing* to *own*)
- Add a letter to the beginning or end of a word to read and write other words: e.g., *in/win; ten/tent*
- Add a consonant cluster or a consonant digraph to the beginning or end of a word to read and write other words: e.g., *an/plan, in/thin; go/gold*
- Remove a letter from the beginning or end of a word to read and write other words: e.g., *sit/it, his/is; bark/bar*
- Remove a consonant cluster or a consonant digraph from the beginning or end of a word to read and write other words: e.g., *plan/an, thin/in; gold/go*

▶ Taking Words Apart to Solve Them

- Take apart a compound word to read two smaller words: e.g., *birthday, birth, day; everywhere, every, where; sidewalk, side, walk*
- Break a word into syllables to decode manageable units: e.g., *re/mem/ber, hos/pi/tal, be/fore*

▶ Using Strategies to Solve Words and Determine Their Meanings

- Use connections between or among words that mean the same or almost the same to solve an unknown word: e.g., *damp, wet*
- Use connections between or among words that mean the opposite or almost the opposite to solve an unknown word: e.g., *stale, fresh*

▶ Using Reference Tools to Solve and Find Information About Words

- Use a glossary to solve and find information about words
- Use a dictionary to solve and find information about words

▶ Spelling Strategies

- Spell known words quickly
- Make a first attempt to spell an unknown word
- Use letter-sound relationships to help spell an unknown word
- Use phonogram patterns and letter patterns to help spell a word
- Use sound and letter sequence to help spell a word
- Use syllables to help spell a word
- Use the spelling of the smaller words within a compound word to help spell a compound word
- Use a spelling routine to help spell a word
- Use a mnemonic device to help spell a word: e.g., *friends to the end, a bear bit my ear*
- Use a dictionary to confirm or correct the spelling of a word
- Ask for help when all known spelling strategies have been tried

PHONICS, SPELLING, AND WORD STUDY

Selecting Goals Behaviors and Understandings to Notice, Teach, and Support

Phonics, Spelling, and Word Study

LETTER-SOUND RELATIONSHIPS

▶ Consonants

- Recognize and use two consonant letters that usually represent one sound at the end of a word: e.g., bran<u>ch</u>, ro<u>ck</u>, so<u>ng</u>, da<u>sh</u>, bo<u>th</u>

- Recognize and use two consonant letters that represent one sound in the middle of a word: e.g., ex<u>ch</u>ange, nep<u>h</u>ew, fi<u>sh</u>es, some<u>th</u>ing, every<u>wh</u>ere, si<u>ng</u>er

- Recognize and use middle consonant sounds sometimes represented by double consonant letters: ru<u>bb</u>er, a<u>cc</u>ording, pu<u>dd</u>le, co<u>ff</u>ee, bi<u>gg</u>er, co<u>ll</u>ect, swi<u>mm</u>er, a<u>nn</u>ounce, dro<u>pp</u>ed, a<u>rr</u>ive, le<u>ss</u>on, a<u>tt</u>ic, bu<u>zz</u>ing

- Recognize and use consonant letters that represent two or more different sounds at the beginning of a word: <u>c</u>ar, <u>c</u>ity; <u>g</u>et, <u>g</u>ym; <u>th</u>ink, <u>th</u>ey; <u>ch</u>air, <u>ch</u>orus, <u>ch</u>oir, <u>ch</u>ef

- Recognize and use consonant letters that represent two or more different sounds at the end of a word: clini<u>c</u>, spi<u>ce</u>; hu<u>g</u>, ca<u>ge</u>; ri<u>ch</u>, stoma<u>ch</u>; ba<u>th</u>, smoo<u>th</u>

- Recognize and use consonant letters that represent two or more different sounds in the middle of a word: cy<u>c</u>lone, ni<u>c</u>est; bu<u>g</u>le, ma<u>g</u>ic; in<u>ch</u>es, s<u>ch</u>ool, ma<u>ch</u>ine; mou<u>th</u>wash, fea<u>th</u>er

- Recognize and use less frequent consonant digraphs at the beginning or end of a word: gh, ph (e.g., rou<u>gh</u>, <u>ph</u>one, telegra<u>ph</u>)

- Recognize and use consonant letters that represent no sound: lam<u>b</u>, <u>sc</u>ene, si<u>g</u>n, rhyme, <u>k</u>now, ca<u>l</u>m, i<u>s</u>land, li<u>s</u>ten, <u>w</u>rap

- Understand and talk about the fact that some consonant sounds can be represented by several different letters or letter clusters: e.g., kaya<u>k</u>, picni<u>c</u>, tru<u>ck</u>, stoma<u>ch</u>, <u>th</u>ief, sti<u>ff</u>, cou<u>gh</u>, gra<u>ph</u>

▶ Vowels

- Recognize and use letter combinations that represent long vowel sounds: e.g., ch<u>ai</u>n, pl<u>ay</u>, n<u>ea</u>t, m<u>ee</u>t, p<u>ie</u>, l<u>igh</u>t, r<u>oa</u>st, t<u>oe</u>, r<u>ow</u>, bl<u>ue</u>, fr<u>ui</u>t, n<u>ew</u>

- Recognize and use letter combinations that represent unique vowel sounds: oi as in oil; oy as in boy; ou as in house; ow as in cow

- Recognize and use a letter or letter combinations that represent the /o˙/ vowel sound (as in saw): e.g., <u>au</u>tumn, p<u>aw</u>, s<u>o</u>ft, t<u>augh</u>t, b<u>ough</u>t, t<u>a</u>lk

- Recognize and use letter combinations that represent two different vowel sounds: e.g., m<u>ea</u>t, br<u>ea</u>k; th<u>ey</u>, k<u>ey</u>; t<u>ie</u>, p<u>ie</u>ce; sp<u>oo</u>n, b<u>oo</u>k; sn<u>ow</u>, c<u>ow</u>

- Recognize and use vowel sounds with r: e.g., chair, care, pear; car; year, pioneer, here; her, first, hurt, learn; corn, more, floor, roar, pour; cure

- Recognize and use vowel sounds in closed syllables (CVC): hab/it, lem/on, fig/ure, rob/in, pub/lic

- Recognize and use vowel sounds in open syllables (CVC): ba/by, e/ven, pi/lot, ho/tel, hu/man

▶ Letter-Sound Representations

- Understand and talk about how to use the computer keyboard

- Understand and talk about how to use capital letters correctly

- Understand and talk about how to form cursive letters correctly, efficiently, and fluently

SPELLING PATTERNS

▶ Phonogram Patterns

- Recognize and use phonograms with vowel combinations (VVC): e.g., -aid, -ail, -ain, -ait; -ead, -eak, -eal, -eam, -ean, -eap, -ear, -eat; -ied, -ief, -ies; -oak, -oat, -oil, -our, -out

- Recognize and use more difficult phonogram patterns in single- syllable words: e.g.,
  - ◆ VVCC (e.g., p<u>ain</u>t, f<u>aul</u>t, r<u>eac</u>h, b<u>eas</u>t, sp<u>eec</u>h, t<u>ooth</u>, w<u>oul</u>d, s<u>oun</u>d, s<u>outh</u>)
  - ◆ VVCe (e.g., pr<u>ais</u>e, w<u>eav</u>e, sn<u>eez</u>e, n<u>ois</u>e, l<u>oos</u>e, m<u>ous</u>e)
  - ◆ VCCe (e.g., d<u>anc</u>e, p<u>ast</u>e, j<u>udg</u>e)
  - ◆ VCCC (e.g., r<u>anc</u>h, p<u>atc</u>h, b<u>enc</u>h, l<u>unc</u>h)
  - ◆ VVCCe (e.g., p<u>ounc</u>e)
  - ◆ VVCCC (e.g., c<u>augh</u>t, h<u>eal</u>th, w<u>eigh</u>t)

▶ Vowel Phonogram Patterns in Single-Syllable Words

- Recognize and use phonogram patterns with the /o˙/ vowel sound (as in saw) in single-syllable words: e.g., -alk, -all, -alt, -aw, -awl, -awn, -ong, -oss, -ost, -oth

- Recognize and use phonogram patterns with vowels and r in single-syllable words: e.g., -air, -ar, -ard, -are, -ark, -arm, -arn, -arp, -art, -ear, -eer, -ir, -ird, -irt, -oor, -ord, -ore, -orn, -ort, -our, -ur, -urn

▶ Assorted Patterns in Multisyllable Words

- Understand and talk about the fact that some words have a double consonant: e.g., hidden, earmuff, yellow, happy, messy, express, bottle

- Understand and talk about the fact that some words have a pattern with a double consonant that represents two sounds: e.g., success, accident

- Recognize and use frequently appearing syllable patterns in multisyllable words: e.g., <u>a</u>lone, <u>be</u>fore, <u>en</u>ter, <u>i</u>mitate, <u>in</u>crease, <u>re</u>peat, <u>un</u>happy; trou<u>ble</u>, oth<u>er</u>, pur<u>ple</u>, alrea<u>dy</u>

▶ Vowel Phonogram Patterns in Multisyllable Words

- Recognize and use short vowel phonograms that appear in multisyllable words: e.g., -ab, -ack, -act, -ad, -ag, -am, -an, -ank, -ap, -at; -ell, -end, -ent, -est, -et; -ick, -ill, -in, -ing, -ip, -it; -ob, -ock, -og, -op, -ot; -ub, -ug, -unk, -ut

- Recognize and use long vowel phonograms that appear in multisyllable words: e.g., -ace, -ade, -ail, -ake, -ame, -ane, -ate, -ay, -aze; -ead, -eal, -eam, -ear, -eat, -ee, -eed, -eel, -eep, -eet; -ice, -ide, -ies, -ight, -ime, -ind, -ine, -ite, -ive, -y; -oat, -oke, -old, -one, -ope, -ow; -ue

- Recognize and use unique vowel phonograms that appear in multisyllable words: e.g., -oint, -oy, -ound, -own

- Recognize and use other vowel phonograms that appear in multisyllable words: e.g., -alk, -all, -alt, -aught, -ault, -aw, -awn, -ong, -ought; -ood, -ook, -oot; -oo, -ood, -oof, -ool, -oom, -oon, -oose, -ew; -ead

Selecting Goals Behaviors and Understandings to Notice, Teach, and Support *(cont.)*

Phonics, Spelling, and Word Study

HIGH-FREQUENCY WORDS

- Develop and use strategies for acquiring a large core of high-frequency words
- Read and write approximately five hundred high-frequency words
- Recognize commonly misspelled words and rewrite them correctly

WORD MEANING/ VOCABULARY

▶ Concept Words

- Recognize and use concept words that can have sets and subsets: e.g., *food: fruit (apple, pear), vegetable (carrot, pea)*

▶ Related Words

- Recognize and talk about the fact that words can be related in many ways: e.g.,
  - ◆ sound: e.g., *hear/here, weather/whether*
  - ◆ spelling: e.g., *bite/kite*
  - ◆ category: e.g., *hat/coat, mother/father*
- Recognize and use synonyms (words that have almost the same meaning): e.g., *mistake/error, high/tall*
- Recognize and use antonyms (words that have opposite meanings): e.g., *cold/hot, appear/vanish*
- Recognize and use homophones (words that have the same sound, different spellings, and different meanings): e.g., *blew/blue, higher/hire*
- Recognize and use homographs (words that have the same spelling, different meanings and origins, and may have different pronunciations): e.g., *content, duck, present, pupil*
- Recognize and use words with multiple meanings: e.g., *cover, degree, organ*

▶ Combined and Created Words

- Recognize and use compound words: e.g., *blueberry, overhead, snowstorm*
- Recognize and use compound words with common parts: e.g., *doghouse, housekeeper, schoolhouse; beside, inside, sidewalk; waterfall, watermelon, waterproof*
- Recognize and use portmanteau words, which come from blending two distinct words: e.g., *motel (motor hotel)*

- Recognize and use clipped words, which come from shortening words: e.g., *lab (laboratory), phone (telephone), photo (photograph)*
- Recognize and use acronyms, which come from combining the initial letter or letters of multiword names or phrases: e.g., *radar (radio detecting and ranging), scuba (self-contained underwater breathing apparatus)*

▶ Figurative Uses of Words

- Recognize and use onomatopoetic words: e.g., *buzz, hiss, plop, quack, thump, whack, zoom*
- Recognize and discuss the fact that some words have literal and figurative meanings: e.g.,
  - ◆ *cold*–"less warm than usual"; "unfriendly"
  - ◆ *shark*–"a large, usually ferocious fish that lives in warm seas"; "a dishonest person who preys on others"
  - ◆ *fork*–"a tool with a handle and two or more long, pointed parts at one end"; "anything shaped like a fork, or any branching"
- Recognize and use similes to make a comparison: e.g.,
  - ◆ *The child's lovely eyes shone like a pair of moons in the evening sky.*
  - ◆ *The police officer's mood seemed as light as an autumn breeze.*
- Recognize and use metaphors to make a comparison: e.g.,
  - ◆ *My heart became a block of ice.*
  - ◆ *He glimpsed the silver lace of frost on the window.*
  - ◆ *She is a sparkling star.*
- Recognize and discuss the fact that commonly used idioms have meanings different from the meanings of the separate words: e.g., *go fly a kite, hold your tongue, on the fence, hit the nail on the head, hit the road, sweat bullets*

▶ Parts of Words

- Understand and discuss the concept of prefixes and recognize their use in determining the meaning of some English words: e.g., *ad-, ant-, ante-, anti-, bi-, circu-, com-, con-, contra-, contro-, counter-, dec-, dis-, em-, en-, ex-, fore-, in-, inter-, intra-, mal-, mis-, mon-, mono-, multi-, non-, oct-, pent-, per-, poly-, post-, pre-, quadr-, re-, sub-, super-, trans-, tri-, un-, uni-*
- Understand and discuss the concept of suffixes and recognize their use in determining the meaning of some English words: e.g., *-able, -al, -ance, -ant, -ar, -arium, -ed, -ence, -ent, -er, -es, -est, -ful, -ial, -ian, -ible, -ic, -ical, -ing, -ion, -ious, -ish, -ist, -ity, -less, -ly, -ment, -ness, -or, -orium, -ous, -s, -sion, -tion, -y*

▶ Word Origins

- Develop interest in vocabulary by recognizing and appreciating aspects of words and by "collecting" and discussing interesting word and using them in conversation
- Understand and discuss the fact that cognates are words in different languages that have similar meanings and spellings because they have related origins: e.g., English *alphabet*, French *alphabet*, Italian *alfabeto*, German *Alphabet*
- Understand and discuss the fact that English words or terms are derived from many different sources, such as other languages, technology, names, trademarked products, and social practices: e.g., *tortilla, parliament, harmonica, khaki, algebra; blog, hashtag, hyperlink; sandwich, valentine, hamburger; xerox, jeep, Band-Aid, Kleenex; fist bump, social media, takeout*
- Understand and discuss the concept of Latin roots and recognize their use in determining the meanings of some English words: e.g., *aqua, aud, bene, cap, centr, clos, clud, clus, corp, cred, dict, duc, duct, dur, equa, equi, fac, fer, fic, fin, firm, flect, flex, form, fract, frag, grad, gress, hab, hib, ject, join, junct, loc, luc, lum, man, mem, min, miss, mit, mob, mot, mov, ped, pel, pend, pens, pon, pop, port, pos, prim, prin, pub, puls, quer, ques, quir, quis, rupt, scribe, script, sens, sent, sign, sist, sol, son, spec, sta, stat, stit, stru, struct, tain, tempo, ten, tent, tin, terr, tract, val, ven, vent, ver, vers, vert, vid, vis, voc, vok*

PHONICS, SPELLING, AND WORD STUDY

Selecting Goals Behaviors and Understandings to Notice, Teach, and Support (cont.)

Phonics, Spelling, and Word Study

WORD MEANING/ VOCABULARY (continued)

▶ Word Origins (continued)

- Understand and discuss the concept of Greek roots and recognize their use in determining the meaning of some English words: e.g., *aer, arch, aster, astr, astro, bio, chron, cycl, dem, geo, gram, graph, hydr, hydro, log, mega, meter, micro, ology, phon, photo, pod, pol, poli, polis, scop, scope, tele, therm*

WORD STRUCTURE

▶ Syllables

- Hear, say, clap, and identify syllables in words with three or more syllables: e.g., *fish/er/man, par/a/graph; el/e/va/tor, un/u/su/al, wat/er/mel/on*

- Recognize and use open syllables–syllables that end with a single vowel, which usually represents a long vowel sound: e.g., *o/pen, pi/lot, ti/ger*

- Recognize and use closed syllables–syllables that end with a consonant and usually have a short vowel sound: e.g., *can/dle, fif/teen, mod/ern*

- Recognize and use *r*-influenced syllables–syllables that contain one or two vowels followed by the letter *r*: e.g., *a/part/ment, dirt/y, for/get, four/teen, gar/bage, prair/ie*

- Recognize and use vowel combination syllables–syllables that contain two or more letters together that represent one vowel sound: e.g., *be/tween, en/joy, mid/night*

- Recognize and use VCe syllables–syllables that contain a (long) vowel followed by a consonant and then silent *e*: e.g., *be/side, eve/ning, in/vite, lone/ly, stam/pede, state/ment*

- Recognize and use consonant + *le* syllables–syllables that contain a consonant followed by the letters *le*: e.g., *a/ble, ea/gle, scram/ble, tem/ple*

- Recognize and use syllables in words with the VCCV pattern (syllable juncture): e.g., *ber/ry, both/er, dis/may, hel/met*

- Recognize and use syllables in words with the VCCCV pattern (syllable juncture): e.g., *emp/ty, hun/dred, king/dom, mon/ster*

- Recognize and use syllables in words with the VV pattern: e.g., *gi/ant, ru/in*

▶ Compound Words

- Recognize and use compound words that have frequently used component words: e.g., *somebody, someday, somehow, someone, someplace, something, sometime, somewhat, somewhere*

- Recognize and use compound words that have common parts: e.g., *campfire, firefighter, firehouse, fireplace, firewood, wildfire*

▶ Contractions

- Recognize and use contractions with *have*: e.g., *I've, we've, you've, they've*

- Recognize and use contractions with *had* or *would*: e.g., *I'd, we'd, you'd, he'd, she'd, they'd*

▶ Plurals

- Recognize and use plurals that add *-es* to words that end with a consonant and *y* after changing the *y* to *i*: e.g., *countries, jellies, rubies*

- Recognize and use plurals that add *-es* to words after changing the final *f* or *fe* to *v*: e.g., *knives, scarves, wolves*

- Recognize and use irregular plurals that change the spelling of the word: e.g., *goose/ geese, mouse/mice, ox/oxen, woman/women*

- Recognize and use irregular plurals that are the same as the singular form of the word: e.g., *deer, moose, salmon, sheep*

- Recognize and use plurals that add *-s* to words that end with *o*: e.g., *pianos, rodeos*

- Recognize and use plurals that add *-es* to words that end with a consonant and *o*: e.g., *echoes, heroes*

▶ Possessives

- Recognize and use possessives that add an apostrophe and *s* to singular nouns (including proper nouns) that end with *s* to show ownership: e.g., *princess's closet, Texas's flag, harness's buckle*

- Recognize and use possessives that add an apostrophe to plural nouns that end with *s* to show ownership: e.g., *girls' disappointment, woodpeckers' clatter*

- Recognize and use possessives that add an apostrophe and *s* to irregular plural nouns to show ownership: e.g., *oxen's strength, women's jackets*

▶ Suffixes

- Understand and talk about the concept of a suffix

- Understand and talk about the fact that several basic rules govern the spelling of words with suffixes: e.g.,

  - ◆ For many words, there are no spelling changes when adding a suffix: e.g., *run/runs, bright/brighter/brightest, final/finally, teach/teacher*

  - ◆ For words that end with silent *e*, usually drop the *e* when adding a suffix that begins with a vowel, but usually keep the *e* when adding a suffix that begins with a consonant: e.g., *live/living* but *live/lives, fierce/fiercer/fiercest, please/pleasant* but *grace/graceful*

  - ◆ For one-syllable words that end with a single vowel and one consonant, usually double the final consonant when adding a suffix that begins with a vowel, but usually do not double the final consonant when adding a suffix that begins with a consonant: e.g., *grin/grinning* but *grin/ grins, sad/sadder/saddest, flat/flatten, beg/beggar* but *fit/fitness*

  - ◆ For multisyllable words with an unaccented final syllable that ends with a single vowel and one consonant, usually do not double the final consonant when adding a suffix: e.g., *visit/visited, slender/ slenderer, develop/developer*

  - ◆ For words that end with a consonant and *y*, usually change the *y* to *i* and add the suffix, but for words that end with a vowel and *y*, usually keep the *y* and add the suffix: e.g, *copy/copied* but *enjoy/enjoyed*

▶ Suffixes: Inflectional Endings

- Recognize and use the ending *-ing* with multisyllable verbs with an accented last syllable when forming the present participle of a verb: e.g., *remind/reminding, enjoy/enjoying*

Selecting Goals Behaviors and Understandings to Notice, Teach, and Support *(cont.)*

Phonics, Spelling, and Word Study

- Recognize and use the ending *-ed* with multisyllable verbs with an accented last syllable when forming the past tense of a verb: e.g., *remind/reminded, enjoy/enjoyed*
- Recognize and use the ending *-ing* with multisyllable verbs with an accent not on the last syllable when forming the present participle of a verb: e.g., *locate/locating, enjoy/enjoying*
- Recognize and use the ending *-ed* with multisyllable verbs with an accent not on the last syllable when forming the past tense of a verb: e.g., *locate/located, enjoy/enjoyed*

▶ Suffixes: Comparative Endings

- Recognize and use the suffixes *-er* and *-est* to show comparison: e.g., *bright/brighter/ brightest, fierce/fiercer/fiercest, sad/sadder/ saddest, slender/slenderer/slenderest, crazy/ crazier/craziest*

▶ Suffixes: Adjective and Adverb Suffixes

- Recognize and use the suffix *-ly*, meaning "in a specific manner, period of time, or order," to form an adverb: e.g., *live/lively, sad/sadly, easy/easily*
- Recognize and use the suffix *-y*, meaning "having or containing," to form an adjective: e.g., *dirt/dirty, ache/achy, knot/knotty, velvet/velvety*
- Recognize and use the suffix *-ish*, meaning "like," "somewhat," or "relating to," to form an adjective: e.g., *self/selfish, blue/bluish, big/biggish, woman/womanish, baby/babyish, boy/boyish*
- Recognize and use the suffixes *-able* and *-ible*, meaning "capable of," to form an adjective:
  - ◆ Add *-able* to base words: e.g., *afford/ affordable, hit/hittable, credit/creditable*
  - ◆ Add *-ible* to word roots: e.g., *terr/terrible*
- Recognize and use the suffixes *-ful*, meaning "full of," and *-less*, meaning "without," to form an adjective: e.g.,
  - ◆ -ful: e.g., *fear/fearful, care/careful, forget/forgetful, pocket/pocketful, pity/pitiful, joy/joyful*
  - ◆ -less: e.g., *fear/fearless, care/careless, pity/pitiless, joy/joyless*

- Recognize and use the suffixes *-ant* and *-ent*, meaning "characterized by" or "inclined to," to form an adjective:
  - ◆ -ant: e.g., *import/important, rely/reliant*
  - ◆ -ent: e.g., *insist/insistent, urge/urgent, differ/different*

▶ Suffixes: Noun Suffixes

- Recognize and use the suffixes *-er, -or, -ar,* and *-ist,* which name a person or thing that does something, to form a noun: e.g.,
  - ◆ -er: e.g., *teach/teacher, bake/baker, drum/drummer, develop/developer, carry/carrier, picnic/picnicker*
  - ◆ -or: e.g., *visit/visitor, bet/bettor, edit/editor*
  - ◆ -ar: e.g., *beg/beggar*
  - ◆ -ist: e.g., *art/artist, type/typist, drug/ druggist, piano/pianist*
- Recognize and use the suffix *-ness*, meaning "state or quality of being," to form a noun: e.g., *kind/kindness, close/closeness, fit/ fitness*
- Recognize and use the suffixes *-ion, -tion,* and *-sion,* to show the quality or state of something by changing a verb to a noun: e.g.,
  - ◆ -ion: e.g., *discuss/discussion, protect/ protection*
  - ◆ -tion: e.g., *introduce/introduction*
  - ◆ -sion: e.g., *decide/decision*

▶ Prefixes

- Understand and discuss the concept of a prefix
- Recognize and use the prefix *re-*, meaning "again": e.g., *remake, repay, refresh*
- Recognize and use prefixes that mean "not": e.g.,
  - ◆ un- (*unfair, unkind*)
  - ◆ in- (*invisible*)
  - ◆ dis- (*disappear*)
  - ◆ non- (*nonsense, nonfiction, nonstop*)
- Recognize and use prefixes that mean "bad, badly" or "wrong, wrongly": e.g.,
  - ◆ mis- (*mistake*)
  - ◆ mal- (*malfunction*)
- Recognize and use prefixes that refer to sequence: e.g.,
  - ◆ pre-, meaning "before" (*preheat*)
  - ◆ fore-, meaning "before," "earlier," or "in front" (*forehead*)

- Recognize and use prefixes that indicate amount, extent, or location: e.g.,
  - ◆ sub- (*subway*)
  - ◆ super- (*supermarket*)
- Recognize and use number-related prefixes: e.g., *uniform, bicycle, triangle, octopus*
- Recognize and use prefixes that mean "out" or "without" or "in, into, or within": e.g.,
  - ◆ ex- (*explode*)

▶ Abbreviations

- Recognize and use common abbreviations and understand the full form of the words they shorten: e.g.,
  - ◆ titles, names, degrees, and professional terms: *Mr. (Mister,* title for a man), *Ms.* (title for a woman), *Mrs.* (title for a married woman), *Miss* (title for a girl or an unmarried woman), *Dr. (Doctor)*
  - ◆ days of week and months: *Mon. (Monday), Tues., Wed., Thurs., Fri., Sat., Sun.; Jan. (January), Feb., Mar., Apr., Aug., Sept., Oct., Nov., Dec.*
  - ◆ addresses and geographical terms: *St. (Street), Ave. (Avenue), Rd. (Road), Apt. (Apartment), Blvd. (Boulevard), CA* or *Calif. (California), U.S.* or *US (United States); Mt. (Mountain), E (East), N, W, S*
  - ◆ times and dates: *a.m.* or *am (the time from midnight to noon), p.m.* or *pm (the time from noon to midnight)*
  - ◆ measurements: *in. (inch* or *inches), ft. (foot* or *feet), yd. (yard* or *yards), mi. (mile* or *miles), lb. (pound* or *pounds), oz. (ounce* or *ounces), c* or *c. (cup* or *cups), pt. (pint* or *pints), qt. (quart* or *quarts), gal. (gallon* or *gallons), cu.* or *cu (cubic), sq. (square), mph* or *m.p.h. (miles per hour)*

PHONICS, SPELLING, AND WORD STUDY

Selecting Goals Behaviors and Understandings to Notice, Teach, and Support *(cont.)*

Phonics, Spelling, and Word Study

WORD STRUCTURE *(continued)*

▸ Roots

- Recognize and use word roots from Latin or Greek:
  - ◆ Latin–e.g., *aqua, aud, bene, cap, centr, clos, clud, clus, corp, cred, dict, duc, duct, dur, equa, equi, fac, fer, fic, fin, firm, flect, flex, form, fract, frag, grad, gress, hab, hib, ject, join, junct, loc, luc, lum, man, mem, min, miss, mit, mob, mot, mov, ped, pel, pend, pens, pon, pop, port, pos, prim, prin, pub, puls, quer, ques, quir, quis, rupt, scribe, script, sens, sent, sign, sist, sol, son, spec, sta, stat, stit, stru, struct, tain, tempo, ten, tent, tin, terr, tract, val, ven, vent, ver, vers, vert, vid, vis, voc, vok*
  - ◆ Greek–e.g., *aer, arch, aster, astr, astro, bio, chron, cycl, dem, geo, gram, graph, hydr, hydro, log, mega, meter, micro, ology, phon, photo, pod, pol, poli, polis, scop, scope, tele, therm*

WORD-SOLVING ACTIONS

▸ Using What Is Known to Solve Words

- Identify words that have the same letter pattern and use them to solve an unknown word: e.g., *hat/sat, light/night, crumb/thumb, curious/furious*
- Use known word parts (some are words) to solve unknown larger words: e.g., *in/into, can/canvas; us, crust*

▸ Taking Words Apart to Solve Them

- Break a word into syllables to decode manageable units: e.g., *re/mem/ber, hos/pi/tal, be/fore, de/part/ment*

▸ Using Strategies to Solve Words and Determine Their Meanings

- Use connections between or among words that mean the same or almost the same to solve an unknown word: e.g., *damp, wet*
- Use connections between or among words that mean the opposite or almost the opposite to solve an unknown word: e.g., *stale, fresh*
- Recognize and use word parts to solve an unknown word and understand its meaning: e.g., *conference*–prefix *con-* ("with or together"), Latin root *fer* ("to bring" or "to carry"), suffix *-ence* ("state of" or "quality of")

- Recognize and use connections between or among related words that have the same word root or base word to solve unknown words: e.g., *support/supports/supported/supportive/unsupportive*
- Recognize and use a word's origin to solve an unknown word and understand its form and meaning
- Recognize and use Latin roots to solve an unknown word and determine its meaning: e.g., the Latin root *cred*, meaning "believe," in the word *credible*, meaning "capable of being believed" or "believable"
- Recognize and use Greek roots to solve an unknown word and determine its meaning: e.g., the Greek root *graph*, meaning "write," in the word *autograph*, meaning "the writing of one's name"

▸ Using Reference Tools to Solve and Find Information About Words

- Use a glossary to solve and find information about words
- Use a dictionary to solve and find information about words

▸ Spelling Strategies

- Make a first attempt to spell an unknown word
- Use phonogram patterns and letter patterns to help spell a word
- Use sound and letter sequence to help spell a word
- Use syllables to help spell a word
- Use the spelling of the smaller words within a compound word to help spell a compound word
- Use a spelling routine to help spell a word
- Use a mnemonic device to help spell a word: e.g., *fri**end**s to the **end**, a **bear** bit my **ear***
- Use a dictionary to confirm or correct the spelling of a word
- Use word origins to understand and remember the spelling of some words: e.g., *beret, chalet, champagne, lasagna, coyote, mosquito*
- Use an electronic program to check your spelling
- Ask for help when all known spelling strategies have been tried

Selecting Goals Behaviors and Understandings to Notice, Teach, and Support

Phonics, Spelling, and Word Study

LETTER-SOUND RELATIONSHIPS

▶ Consonants

- Recognize and use consonant letters that represent two or more different sounds at the beginning of a word: <u>c</u>ar, <u>c</u>ity; <u>g</u>et, <u>g</u>ym; <u>th</u>ink, <u>th</u>ey; <u>ch</u>air, <u>ch</u>orus, <u>ch</u>oir, <u>ch</u>ef

- Recognize and use consonant letters that represent two or more different sounds at the end of a word: clini<u>c</u>, spi<u>c</u>e; hu<u>g</u>, ca<u>g</u>e; ri<u>ch</u>, stoma<u>ch</u>; ba<u>th</u>, smoo<u>th</u>

- Recognize and use consonant letters that represent two or more different sounds in the middle of a word: <u>c</u>yclone, ni<u>c</u>est; bu<u>g</u>le, ma<u>g</u>ic; in<u>ch</u>es, <u>sch</u>ool, ma<u>ch</u>ine; mou<u>th</u>wash, fea<u>th</u>er

- Understand and talk about the fact that some consonant sounds can be represented by several different letters or letter clusters: e.g., kaya<u>k</u>, pi<u>c</u>ni<u>c</u>, tru<u>ck</u>, stoma<u>ch</u>, <u>th</u>ief, sti<u>ff</u>, cou<u>gh</u>, <u>gr</u>a<u>ph</u>

SPELLING PATTERNS

▶ Phonogram Patterns

- Recognize and use more difficult phonogram patterns in single-syllable words: e.g.,
  - ◆ VVCC (e.g., <u>paint</u>, <u>fault</u>, <u>reach</u>, <u>beast</u>, <u>speech</u>, <u>tooth</u>, <u>pouch</u>, <u>would</u>, <u>sound</u>, <u>south</u>)
  - ◆ VVCe (e.g., <u>praise</u>, <u>weave</u>, <u>sneeze</u>, <u>noise</u>, <u>loose</u>, <u>mouse</u>)
  - ◆ VCCe (e.g., <u>dance</u>, <u>paste</u>, <u>wedge</u>, <u>judge</u>)
  - ◆ VCCC (e.g., <u>ranch</u>, <u>patch</u>, <u>bench</u>, <u>ditch</u>, <u>lunch</u>)
  - ◆ VVCCe (e.g., <u>pounce</u>)
  - ◆ VVCCC (e.g., <u>caught</u>, <u>launch</u>, <u>health</u>, <u>weight</u>, <u>sought</u>)

▶ Assorted Patterns in Multisyllable Words

- Understand and talk about the fact that some words have a double consonant: e.g., pebble, hidden, earmuff, jiggle, yellow, happy, messy, express, bottle

- Understand and talk about the fact that some words have a pattern with a double consonant that represents two sounds: e.g., success, accident

- Recognize and use frequently appearing syllable patterns in multisyllable words: e.g., <u>alone</u>, <u>before</u>, <u>enter</u>, <u>im</u>itate, <u>increase</u>, <u>repeat</u>, <u>unhappy</u>; trou<u>ble</u>, other, <u>purple</u>, already

▶ Vowel Phonogram Patterns in Multisyllable Words

- Recognize and use short vowel phonograms that appear in multisyllable words: e.g., -ab, -ack, -act, -ad, -ag, -am, -an, -ank, -ap, -at; -ell, -end, -ent, -est, -et; -ick, -ill, -in, -ing, -ip, -it; -ob, -ock, -og, -op, -ot; -ub, -ug, -unk, -ut

- Recognize and use long vowel phonograms that appear in multisyllable words: e.g., -ace, -ade, -ail, -ake, -ame, -ane, -ate, -ay, -aze; -ead, -eal, -eam, -ear, -eat, -ee, -eed, -eel, -eep, -eet; -ice, -ide, -ies, -ight, -ime, -ind, -ine, -ite, -ive, -y; -oat, -oke, -old, -one, -ope, -ow; -ue

- Recognize and use unique vowel phonograms that appear in multisyllable words: e.g., -oint, -oy, -ound, -own

- Recognize and use other vowel phonograms that appear in multisyllable words: e.g., -alk, -all, -alt, -aught, -ault, -aw, -awn, -ong, -ought; -ood, -ook, -oot; -oo, -ood, -oof, -ool, -oom, -oon, -oose, -ew; -ead

HIGH-FREQUENCY WORDS

- Recognize commonly misspelled words and rewrite them correctly

- Continue to use a flexible range of strategies to acquire a large core of high-frequency words

WORD MEANING/ VOCABULARY

▶ Related Words

- Recognize and talk about the fact that words can be related in many ways: e.g.,
  - ◆ sound: e.g., hear/here, weather/whether
  - ◆ spelling: e.g., bite/kite, increase/release
  - ◆ category: e.g., hat/coat, mother/father

- Recognize and use synonyms (words that have almost the same meaning): e.g., mistake/error, high/tall, desperately/frantically

- Recognize and use antonyms (words that have opposite meanings): e.g., cold/hot, appear/vanish

- Recognize and use homophones (words that have the same sound, different spellings, and different meanings): e.g., blew/blue, higher/hire, patience/patients

- Recognize and use homographs (words that have the same spelling, different meanings and origins, and may have different pronunciations): e.g., content, duck, present, pupil, temple

- Recognize and use words with multiple meanings: e.g., cover, credit, degree, organ

- Understand the concept of analogies to determine relationships among words: e.g.,
  - ◆ synonyms–alert : aware : elevate : raise
  - ◆ antonyms–feeble : strong : durable : flimsy
  - ◆ homophones–hoard : horde : cereal : serial
  - ◆ object/use–catalog : advertise : goggles : protect
  - ◆ part/whole–chapter : book : musician : orchestra
  - ◆ cause/effect–comedy : laughter : drought : famine
  - ◆ member/category–celery : vegetable : plumber : occupation
  - ◆ denotation/connotation–inexpensive : cheap : thin : scrawny

▶ Combined and Created Words

- Recognize and use portmanteau words, which come from blending two distinct words: e.g., motel (motor hotel), smash (smack mash), smog (smoke fog)

- Recognize and use clipped words, which come from shortening words: e.g., lab (laboratory), phone (telephone), photo (photograph)

- Recognize and use acronyms, which come from combining the initial letter or letters of multiword names or phrases: e.g., radar (<u>ra</u>dio <u>d</u>etecting <u>a</u>nd <u>r</u>anging), scuba (<u>s</u>elf-<u>c</u>ontained <u>u</u>nderwater <u>b</u>reathing <u>a</u>pparatus)

- Recognize and discuss the fact that palindromes are words that are spelled the same in either direction: e.g., gag, kayak, noon

Selecting Goals Behaviors and Understandings to Notice, Teach, and Support *(cont.)*

Phonics, Spelling, and Word Study

WORD MEANING/ VOCABULARY *(continued)*

▶ Figurative Uses of Words

- Recognize and use onomatopoetic words: e.g., *buzz, hiss, plop, quack, thump, whack, zoom*

- Recognize and discuss the fact that some words have literal and figurative meanings: e.g.,

  - *cold*–"less warm than usual"; "unfriendly"

  - *shark*–"a large, usually ferocious fish that lives in warm seas"; "a dishonest person who preys on others"

  - *fork*–"a tool with a handle and two or more long, pointed parts at one end"; "anything shaped like a fork, or any branching"

- Recognize and use similes to make a comparison: e.g.,

  - *The child's lovely eyes shone like a pair of moons in the evening sky.*

  - *The police officer's mood seemed as light as an autumn breeze.*

- Recognize and use metaphors to make a comparison: e.g.,

  - *My heart became a block of ice.*

  - *He glimpsed the silver lace of frost on the window.*

  - *She is a sparkling star.*

- Recognize and discuss the fact that commonly used idioms have meanings different from the meanings of the separate words: e.g., *go fly a kite, hold your tongue, on the fence, hit the nail on the head, hit the road, sweat bullets*

▶ Parts of Words

- Understand and discuss the concept of prefixes and recognize their use in determining the meaning of some English words: e.g., *ad-, ant-, ante-, anti-, bi-, circu-, com-, con-, contra-, contro-, counter-, dec-, dis-, em-, en-, ex-, fore-, in-, inter-, intra-, mal-, mis-, mon-, mono-, multi-, non-, oct-, pent-, per-, poly-, post-, pre-, quadr-, re-, sub-, super-, trans-, tri-, un-, uni-*

- Understand and discuss the concept of suffixes and recognize their use in determining the meaning of some English words: e.g., *-able, -al, -ance, -ant, -ar, -arium, -ed, -ence, -ent, -er, -es, -est, -ful, -ial, -ian, -ible, -ic, -ical, -ing, -ion, -ious, -ish, -ist, -ity, -less, -ly, -ment, -ness, -or, -orium, -ous, -s, -sion, -tion, -y*

▶ Word Origins

- Develop interest in vocabulary by recognizing and appreciating aspects of words and by "collecting" and discussing interesting word and using them in conversation

- Understand and discuss the fact that cognates are words in different languages that have similar meanings and spellings because they have related origins: e.g., English *alphabet*, French *alphabet*, Italian *alfabeto*, German *Alphabet*

- Understand and discuss the fact that English words or terms are derived from many different sources, such as other languages, technology, names, trademarked products, and social practices: e.g., *tortilla, parliament, harmonica, khaki, algebra; blog, hashtag, hyperlink; sandwich, valentine, hamburger; xerox, jeep, Band-Aid, Kleenex; fist bump, social media, takeout*

- Understand and discuss the concept of Latin roots and recognize their use in determining the meanings of some English words: e.g., *aqua, aud, bene, cap, centr, clos, clud, clus, corp, cred, dict, duc, duct, dur, equa, equi, fac, fer, fic, fin, firm, flect, flex, form, fract, frag, grad, gress, hab, hib, ject, join, junct, loc, luc, lum, man, mem, min, miss, mit, mob, mot, mov, ped, pel, pend, pens, pon, pop, port, pos, prim, prin, pub, puls, quer, ques, quir, quis, rupt, scribe, script, sens, sent, sign, sist, sol, son, spec, sta, stat, stit, stru, struct, tain, tempo, ten, tent, tin, terr, tract, val, ven, vent, ver, vers, vert, vid, vis, voc, vok*

- Understand and discuss the concept of Greek roots and recognize their use in determining the meaning of some English words: e.g., *aer, arch, aster, astr, astro, bio, chron, cycl, dem, geo, gram, graph, hydr, hydro, log, mega, meter, micro, ology, phon, photo, pod, pol, poli, polis, scop, scope, tele, therm*

- Recognize and use prefixes, suffixes, and word roots that have Greek and Latin origins to understand word meaning: e.g., *incredible–in-* ("not"), Latin *cred* ("believe") and *-ible* ("capable of"); *antibiotic–anti-* ("opposite" or "against"), Greek *bio* ("life") and *-ic* ("related to")

- Recognize and discuss the fact that words in different languages or in the same language may have a common origin: e.g., *escribir* (Spanish "to write"), *describe*, and *script* derive from Latin *scribere*, "to write"

WORD STRUCTURE

▶ Syllables

- Recognize and use consonant + *le* syllables–syllables that contain a consonant followed by the letters *le*: e.g., *a/ble, ea/gle, scram/ble, tem/ple*

- Recognize and use syllables in words with the VCCV pattern (syllable juncture): e.g., *ber/ry, both/er, dis/may, hel/met*

- Recognize and use syllables in words with the VCCCV pattern (syllable juncture): e.g., *emp/ty, hun/dred, king/dom, mon/ster*

- Recognize and use syllables in words with the VV pattern: e.g., *gi/ant, ru/in, sci/ence*

▶ Contractions

- Recognize and use contractions with *had* or *would*: e.g., *I'd, we'd, you'd, he'd, she'd, they'd; there'd, who'd*

- Recognize and discuss multiple contractions with *not* and *have* (almost solely in oral language): e.g., *mustn't've, shouldn't've, wouldn't've*

▶ Plurals

- Recognize and use irregular plurals that change the spelling of the word: e.g., *goose/ geese, mouse/mice, ox/oxen, woman/women*

- Recognize and use irregular plurals that are the same as the singular form of the word: e.g., *deer, moose, salmon, sheep*

- Recognize and use irregular plurals that are formed by changing the final letters of the base word: e.g., *cactus, cacti*

Selecting Goals Behaviors and Understandings to Notice, Teach, and Support *(cont.)*

Phonics, Spelling, and Word Study

▶ **Possessives**

■ Recognize and use possessives that add an apostrophe to plural nouns that end with *s* to show ownership: e.g., *girls' disappointment, woodpeckers' clatter*

■ Recognize and use possessives that add an apostrophe and *s* to irregular plural nouns to show ownership: e.g., *oxen's strength, women's jackets*

▶ **Suffixes**

■ Understand and talk about the concept of a suffix

■ Understand and talk about the fact that several basic rules govern the spelling of words with suffixes: e.g.,

◆ For many words, there are no spelling changes when adding a suffix: e.g., *run/runs, bright/brighter/brightest, final/finally, teach/teacher*

◆ For words that end with silent *e,* usually drop the *e* when adding a suffix that begins with a vowel, but usually keep the *e* when adding a suffix that begins with a consonant: e.g., *live/living* but *live/lives, fierce/fiercer/fiercest, please/pleasant* but *grace/graceful, bake/baker* but *aware/awareness*

◆ For one-syllable words that end with a single vowel and one consonant, usually double the final consonant when adding a suffix that begins with a vowel, but usually do not double the final consonant when adding a suffix that begins with a consonant: e.g., *grin/grinning* but *grin/grins, sad/sadder/saddest, flat/flatten, pet/petted* but *sin/sinful, beg/beggar* but *fit/fitness*

◆ For multisyllable words with an accented final syllable that ends with a single vowel and one consonant, follow the rules for one-syllable words: *excel/excellent, admit/admittance*

◆ For multisyllable words with an unaccented final syllable that ends with a single vowel and one consonant, usually do not double the final consonant when adding a suffix: e.g., *visit/visited, slender/slenderer, civil/civilize, limit/limitless, develop/developer*

◆ For words that end with a consonant and *y,* usually change the *y* to *i* and add the suffix, but for words that end with a vowel and *y,* usually keep the *y* and add the suffix: e.g, *copy/copied* but *enjoy/enjoyed, identify/identifiable* but *pay/payable, carry/carrier* but *employ/employer*

▶ **Suffixes: Inflectional Endings**

■ Recognize and use the ending *-ing* with multisyllable verbs with an accented last syllable when forming the present participle of a verb: e.g., *remind/reminding, rely/relying, enjoy/enjoying*

■ Recognize and use the ending *-ed* with multisyllable verbs with an accented last syllable when forming the past tense of a verb: e.g., *remind/reminded, rely/relied, enjoy/enjoyed*

■ Recognize and use the ending *-ing* with multisyllable verbs with an accent not on the last syllable when forming the present participle of a verb: e.g., *locate/locating, differ/differing, rely/relying, enjoy/enjoying*

■ Recognize and use the ending *-ed* with multisyllable verbs with an accent not on the last syllable when forming the past tense of a verb: e.g., *locate/located, differ/differed, rely/relied, enjoy/enjoyed*

▶ **Suffixes: Adjective and Adverb Suffixes**

■ Recognize and use the suffix *-ly,* meaning "in a specific manner, period of time, or order," to form an adverb: e.g., *live/lively, sad/sadly, easy/easily, automatic/automatically*

■ Recognize and use the suffixes *-able* and *-ible,* meaning "capable of," to form an adjective: e.g.,

◆ Add *-able* to base words: e.g., *afford/affordable, hit/hittable, credit/creditable*

◆ Add *-ible* to word roots: e.g., *terr/terrible, vis/visible, sens/sensible*

■ Recognize and use the suffixes *-ful,* meaning "full of," and *-less,* meaning "without," to form an adjective: e.g.,

◆ -ful: e.g., *fear/fearful, care/careful, sin/sinful, forget/forgetful, pocket/pocketful, pity/pitiful, joy/joyful*

◆ -less: e.g., *fear/fearless, care/careless, limit/limitless, pity/pitiless, joy/joyless*

■ Recognize and use the suffixes *-ant* and *-ent,* meaning "characterized by" or "inclined to," to form an adjective: e.g.,

◆ -ant: e.g., *import/important, ignore/ignorant, rely/reliant*

◆ -ent: e.g., *insist/insistent, urge/urgent, excel/excellent, differ/different*

■ Recognize and use the suffixes *-ous* and *-ious,* meaning "full of," "like," or "having the quality of," to form an adjective: e.g.,

◆ -ous: e.g., *humor/humorous, adventure/adventurous, fury/furious, joy/joyous, courage/courageous*

◆ -ious: e.g., *grace/gracious*

■ Recognize and use the suffixes *-al, -ial, -ian, -ic,* and *-ical,* meaning "like," "related to," or "suitable for," to form an adjective: e.g.,

◆ -al: e.g., *globe/global, refer/referral, ceremony/ceremonial*

◆ -ial: e.g., *part/partial, editor/editorial, spec/special*

◆ -ian: e.g., *civil/civilian, reptile/reptilian*

◆ -ic: e.g., *hero/heroic, magnet/magnetic*

◆ -ical: e.g., *myth/mythical, type/typical, biography/biographical*

▶ **Suffixes: Noun Suffixes**

■ Recognize and use the suffix *-ness,* meaning "state or quality of being," to form a noun: e.g., *kind/kindness, close/closeness, fit/fitness, bitter/bitterness, dizzy/dizziness*

■ Recognize and use the suffixes *-ion, -tion,* and *-sion,* to show the quality or state of something by changing a verb to a noun: e.g.,

◆ -ion: e.g., *adopt/adoption, discuss/discussion, revise/revision, create/creation, protect/protection*

◆ -tion: e.g., *introduce/introduction*

◆ -sion: e.g., *extend/extension, decide/decision*

■ Recognize and use the suffix *-ment,* meaning "act of," "condition of being," or "product of," to form a noun: e.g., *punish/punishment, measure/measurement* but *argue/argument*

■ Recognize and use the suffix *-ity,* meaning "state or condition of being," to form a noun: e.g., *major/majority, dense/density*

Selecting Goals Behaviors and Understandings to Notice, Teach, and Support (cont.)

Phonics, Spelling, and Word Study

WORD STRUCTURE (continued)

▶ Suffixes: Noun Suffixes (continued)

■ Recognize and use the suffixes -ant and -ent, meaning "someone or something that performs an action," to form a noun: e.g.,

- -ant: e.g., assist/assistant, inhabit/inhabitant
- -ent: e.g., correspond/correspondent

■ Recognize and use the suffixes -ance and -ence, meaning "state of" or "quality of," to form a noun: e.g.,

- -ance: e.g., attend/attendance, rely/reliance
- -ence: e.g., exist/existence

■ Recognize and use the suffixes that mean "act or process of," "state of," "result of," "amount or collection of," or "something that" to form a noun: e.g.,

- -age: e.g., short/shortage, use/usage
- -ure: e.g., moist/moisture

▶ Prefixes

■ Understand and discuss the concept of a prefix

■ Recognize and use the prefix re-, meaning "again": e.g., remake, repay, reassure, refresh

■ Recognize and use prefixes that mean "not": e.g.,

- un- (unfair, unkind, unaware)
- in- (invisible, incredible)
- dis- (disappear, dislike, disobey, disagree)
- non- (nonsense, nonfiction, nonstop)

■ Recognize and use prefixes that mean "bad, badly" or "wrong, wrongly": e.g.,

- mis- (mistake, mislead)
- mal- (malfunction)

■ Recognize and use prefixes that refer to sequence: e.g.,

- pre-, meaning "before" (preheat, predict)
- fore-, meaning "before," "earlier," or "in front" (forehead, foresee)

■ Recognize and use prefixes that indicate amount, extent, or location: e.g.,

- sub- (subway, submarine)
- super- (supermarket, supernatural)

■ Recognize and use number-related prefixes: e.g., uniform, bicycle, triangle, quadrangle, pentagon, octopus, century

■ Recognize and use prefixes that mean "out" or "without" or "in, into, or within": e.g.,

- ex- (explode, export, exclude)
- in- (inspect, include)

■ Recognize and use prefixes that mean "around," "across," "beyond," or "through": e.g.,

- circu-, circum- (circular)
- peri- (period)
- trans- (transport)
- per- (permit)

■ Recognize and use prefixes that change form depending on the first letter of the word root or base word (assimilated prefixes): e.g.,

- ad- meaning "to or toward" (adjoin)
  - ac- (account)
  - af- (affect)
  - al- (allow)
  - an- (announce)
  - ap- (approach)
  - ar- (arrest)
  - at- (attempt)
- sub- meaning "under or lower" or "smaller" (subtract)
  - suc- (success)
  - suf- (suffix)
  - sug- (suggestion)
  - sup- (suppose)
  - sur- (surround)
  - sus- (suspect)
- ob- meaning "to," "toward," or "against" (observe)
  - of- (offer)
  - op- (oppose)
- com- meaning "with or together" (companion)
  - con- (connect)
  - cor- (correspond)
- ex- meaning "out," "without," "from," or "away" (exclaim)
  - ef- (effort)
  - e- (erase)

▶ Abbreviations

■ Recognize and use common abbreviations and understand the full form of the words they shorten: e.g.,

- titles, names, degrees, and professional terms: Mr. (Mister, title for a man), Ms. (title for a woman), Mrs. (title for a married woman), Miss (title for a girl or an unmarried woman), Dr. (Doctor)
- days of week and months: Mon. (Monday), Tues., Wed., Thurs., Fri., Sat., Sun.; Jan. (January), Feb., Mar., Apr., Aug., Sept., Oct., Nov., Dec.
- addresses and geographical terms: St. (Street), Ave. (Avenue), Rd. (Road), Apt. (Apartment), Blvd. (Boulevard), CA or Calif. (California), U.S. or US (United States); Mt. (Mountain), E (East), N, W, S
- times and dates: a.m. or am (the time from midnight to noon), p.m. or pm (the time from noon to midnight)
- measurements: in. (inch or inches), ft. (foot or feet), yd. (yard or yards), mi. (mile or miles), lb. (pound or pounds), oz. (ounce or ounces), c or c. (cup or cups), pt. (pint or pints), qt. (quart or quarts), gal. (gallon or gallons), cu. or cu (cubic), sq. (square), mph or m.p.h. (miles per hour)

▶ Roots

■ Recognize and use word roots from Latin or Greek: e.g.,

- Latin–e.g., aqua, aud, bene, cap, centr, clos, clud, clus, corp, cred, dict, duc, duct, dur, equa, equi, fac, fer, fic, fin, firm, flect, flex, form, fract, frag, grad, gress, hab, hib, ject, join, junct, loc, luc, lum, man, mem, min, miss, mit, mob, mot, mov, ped, pel, pend, pens, pon, pop, port, pos, prim, prin, pub, puls, quer, ques, quir, quis, rupt, scribe, script, sens, sent, sign, sist, sol, son, spec, sta, stat, stit, stru, struct, tain, tempo, ten, tent, tin, terr, tract, val, ven, vent, ver, vers, vert, vid, vis, voc, vok
- Greek–e.g., aer, arch, aster, astr, astro, bio, chron, cycl, dem, geo, gram, graph, hydr, hydro, log, mega, meter, micro, ology, phon, photo, pod, pol, poli, polis, scop, scope, tele, therm

Selecting Goals Behaviors and Understandings to Notice, Teach, and Support *(cont.)*

Phonics, Spelling, and Word Study

WORD-SOLVING ACTIONS

▶ Using What Is Known to Solve Words

- Identify words that have the same letter pattern and use them to solve an unknown word: e.g., *hat/sat, light/night, crumb/thumb, curious/furious*
- Use known word parts (some are words) to solve unknown larger words: e.g., <u>in</u>/<u>into</u>, <u>can</u>/<u>canvas</u>; <u>us</u>, <u>crust</u>

▶ Taking Words Apart to Solve Them

- Break a word into syllables to decode manageable units: e.g., *re/mem/ber, hos/pi/tal, be/fore, de/part/ment*

▶ Using Strategies to Solve Words and Determine Their Meanings

- Use connections between or among words that mean the same or almost the same to solve an unknown word: e.g., *damp, wet*
- Use connections between or among words that mean the opposite or almost the opposite to solve an unknown word: e.g., *stale, fresh*
- Recognize and use word parts to solve an unknown word and understand its meaning: e.g., *conference*–prefix *con-* ("with or together"), Latin root *fer* ("to bring" or "to carry"), suffix *-ence* ("state of" or "quality of")
- Recognize and use connections between or among related words that have the same word root or base word to solve unknown words: e.g., *support/supports/supported/supportive/unsupportive*
- Recognize and use a word's origin to solve an unknown word and understand its form and meaning
- Recognize and use Latin roots to solve an unknown word and determine its meaning: e.g., the Latin root *cred,* meaning "believe," in the word *credible,* meaning "capable of being believed" or "believable"
- Recognize and use Greek roots to solve an unknown word and determine its meaning: e.g., the Greek root *graph,* meaning "write," in the word *autograph,* meaning "the writing of one's name"

▶ Using Reference Tools to Solve and Find Information About Words

- Use a glossary to solve and find information about words
- Use a dictionary to solve and find information about words
- Recognize and use different types of dictionaries (e.g., medical, foreign language, geographical, visual, reverse, thesaurus) to solve and find information about words

▶ Spelling Strategies

- Make a first attempt to spell an unknown word
- Use phonogram patterns and letter patterns to help spell a word
- Use sound and letter sequence to help spell a word (including many multisyllable words)
- Use syllables to help spell a word
- Use the spelling of the smaller words within a compound word to help spell a compound word
- Use a spelling routine to help spell a word
- Use a mnemonic device to help spell a word: e.g., *fri<u>end</u>s to the <u>end</u>, a <u>bear</u> bit my <u>ear</u>*
- Use a dictionary to confirm or correct the spelling of a word
- Use word origins to understand and remember the spelling of some words: e.g., *beret, chalet, champagne, lasagna, coyote, mosquito*
- Use an electronic program to check your spelling
- Ask for help when all known spelling strategies have been tried

Selecting Goals Behaviors and Understandings to Notice, Teach, and Support

Phonics, Spelling, and Word Study

LETTER-SOUND RELATIONSHIPS

▶ Consonants

- Recognize and use consonant letters that represent two or more different sounds at the beginning of a word: e.g., _car, city; get, gym; think, they; chair, chorus, choir, chef_

- Recognize and use consonant letters that represent two or more different sounds at the end of a word: _clinic, spice; hug, cage; rich, stomach; bath, smooth_

- Recognize and use consonant letters that represent two or more different sounds in the middle of a word: _cyclone, nicest; bugle, magic; inches, school, machine; mouthwash, feather_

- Understand and talk about the fact that some consonant sounds can be represented by several different letters or letter clusters: e.g., _kayak, picnic, truck, stomach, thief, stiff, cough, graph_

SPELLING PATTERNS

▶ Vowel Phonogram Patterns in Multisyllable Words

- Recognize and use vowel phonograms that appear in multisyllable words: e.g., _-alk, -all, -alt, -aught, -ault, -aw, -awn, -ong, -ought; -ood, -ook, -oot; -oo, -ood, -oof, -ool, -oom, -oon, -oose, -ew; -ead_

HIGH-FREQUENCY WORDS

- Recognize commonly misspelled words and rewrite them correctly

WORD MEANING/ VOCABULARY

▶ Related Words

- Recognize and use synonyms (words that have almost the same meaning): e.g., _mistake/error, destroy/demolish, high/tall, desperately/frantically_

- Recognize and use antonyms (words that have opposite meanings): e.g., _cold/hot, appear/vanish, abundant/scarce, fantasy/reality_

- Recognize and use homophones (words that have the same sound, different spellings, and different meanings): e.g., _blew/blue, higher/hire, patience/patients_

- Recognize and use homographs (words that have the same spelling, different meanings and origins, and may have different pronunciations): e.g., _content, duck, invalid, present, pupil, temple_

- Recognize and use words with multiple meanings: e.g., _cover, credit, degree, monitor, organ_

- Understand the concept of analogies to determine relationships among words: e.g.,
  - synonyms–_alert : aware : elevate : raise_
  - antonyms–_feeble : strong : durable : flimsy_
  - homophones–_hoard : horde : cereal : serial_
  - object/use–_catalog : advertise : goggles : protect_
  - part/whole–_chapter : book : musician : orchestra_
  - cause/effect–_comedy : laughter : drought : famine_
  - member/category–_celery : vegetable : plumber : occupation_
  - denotation/connotation–_inexpensive : cheap : thin : scrawny_

▶ Combined and Created Words

- Recognize and use portmanteau words, which come from blending two distinct words: e.g., _motel (motor hotel), smash (smack mash), smog (smoke fog)_

- Recognize and use clipped words, which come from shortening words: e.g., _ad (advertisement), lab (laboratory), phone (telephone), photo (photograph)_

- Recognize and use acronyms, which come from combining the initial letter or letters of multiword names or phrases: e.g., _NATO (North Atlantic Treaty Organization), radar (radio detecting and ranging), scuba (self-contained underwater breathing apparatus)_

- Recognize and discuss the fact that palindromes are words that are spelled the same in either direction: e.g., _gag, kayak, noon_

▶ Figurative Uses of Words

- Recognize and discuss the fact that some words have literal and figurative meanings: e.g.,
  - _cold_–"less warm than usual"; "unfriendly"
  - _shark_–"a large, usually ferocious fish that lives in warm seas"; "a dishonest person who preys on others"
  - _fork_–"a tool with a handle and two or more long, pointed parts at one end"; "anything shaped like a fork, or any branching"

- Recognize and use similes to make a comparison: e.g.,
  - _The child's lovely eyes shone like a pair of moons in the evening sky._
  - _The police officer's mood seemed as light as an autumn breeze._

- Recognize and use metaphors to make a comparison: e.g.,
  - _My heart became a block of ice._
  - _He glimpsed the silver lace of frost on the window._
  - _She is a sparkling star._

- Recognize and discuss the fact that commonly used idioms have meanings different from the meanings of the separate words: e.g., _go fly a kite, hold your tongue, on the fence, hit the nail on the head, hit the road, sweat bullets_

- Recognize, say, and talk about words that are jumbled for humorous effect: e.g.,
  - spoonerisms–_a lack of pies_ for _a pack of lies_
  - malapropisms–_the very pineapple of politeness_ for _the very pinnacle of politeness_

▶ Parts of Words

- Understand and discuss the concept of prefixes and recognize their use in determining the meaning of some English words: e.g., _ad-, ant-, ante-, anti-, bi-, circu-, com-, con-, contra-, contro-, counter-, dec-, dis-, em-, en-, ex-, fore-, in-, inter-, intra-, mal-, mis-, mon-, mono-, multi-, non-, oct-, pent-, per-, poly-, post-, pre-, quadr-, re-, sub-, super-, trans-, tri-, un-, uni-_

Selecting Goals Behaviors and Understandings to Notice, Teach, and Support (cont.)

Phonics, Spelling, and Word Study

- Understand and discuss the concept of suffixes and recognize their use in determining the meaning of some English words: e.g., *-able, -al, -ance, -ant, -ar, -arium, -ed, -ence, -ent, -er, -es, -est, -ful, -ial, -ian, -ible, -ic, -ical, -ing, -ion, -ious, -ish, -ist, -ity, -less, -ly, -ment, -ness, -or, -orium, -ous, -s, -sion, -tion, -y*

▶ Word Origins

- Develop interest in vocabulary by recognizing and appreciating aspects of words and by "collecting" and discussing interesting word and using them in conversation

- Understand and discuss the fact that cognates are words in different languages that have similar meanings and spellings because they have related origins: e.g., English *alphabet*, French *alphabet*, Italian *alfabeto*, German *Alphabet*

- Understand and discuss the fact that English words or terms are derived from many different sources, such as other languages, technology, names, trademarked products, and social practices: e.g., *tortilla, parliament, harmonica, khaki, algebra; blog, hashtag, hyperlink; sandwich, valentine, hamburger; xerox, jeep, Band-Aid, Kleenex; fist bump, social media, takeout*

- Understand and discuss the concept of Latin roots and recognize their use in determining the meanings of some English words: e.g., *aqua, aud, bene, cap, centr, clos, clud, clus, corp, cred, dict, duc, duct, dur, equa, equi, fac, fer, fic, fin, firm, flect, flex, form, fract, frag, grad, gress, hab, hib, ject, join, junct, loc, luc, lum, man, mem, min, miss, mit, mob, mot, mov, ped, pel, pend, pens, pon, pop, port, pos, prim, prin, pub, puls, quer, ques, quir, quis, rupt, scribe, script, sens, sent, sign, sist, sol, son, spec, sta, stat, stit, stru, struct, tain, tempo, ten, tent, tin, terr, tract, val, ven, vent, ver, vers, vert, vid, vis, voc, vok*

- Understand and discuss the concept of Greek roots and recognize their use in determining the meaning of some English words: e.g., *aer, arch, aster, astr, astro, bio, chron, cycl, dem, geo, gram, graph, hydr, hydro, log, mega, meter, micro, ology, phon, photo, pod, pol, poli, polis, scop, scope, tele, therm*

- Recognize and use prefixes, suffixes, and word roots that have Greek and Latin origins to understand word meaning: e.g., *incredible–in-* ("not"), Latin *cred* ("believe") and *-ible* ("capable of"); *antibiotic–anti-* ("opposite" or "against"), Greek *bio* ("life") and *-ic* ("related to")

- Recognize and discuss the fact that words in different languages or in the same language may have a common origin: e.g., *escribir* (Spanish "to write"), *describe*, and *script* derive from Latin *scribere*, "to write"

WORD STRUCTURE

▶ Contractions

- Recognize and discuss multiple contractions with *not* and *have* (almost solely in oral language): e.g., *mustn't've, shouldn't've, wouldn't've*

▶ Plurals

- Recognize and use irregular plurals that are formed by changing the final letters of the base word: e.g., *crisis, crises; medium, media; cactus, cacti*

▶ Possessives

- Recognize and use possessives that add an apostrophe to plural nouns that end with *s* to show ownership: e.g., *girls' disappointment, woodpeckers' clatter*

- Recognize and use possessives that add an apostrophe and *s* to irregular plural nouns to show ownership: e.g., *oxen's strength, women's jackets*

▶ Suffixes

- Understand and talk about the concept of a suffix

- Understand and talk about the fact that several basic rules govern the spelling of words with suffixes: e.g.,

  - ◆ For many words, there are no spelling changes when adding a suffix: e.g., *run/runs, bright/brighter/ brightest, moist/moisten, final/finally, teach/teacher*

  - ◆ For words that end with silent *e*, usually drop the *e* when adding a suffix that begins with a vowel, but usually keep the *e* when adding a suffix that begins with a consonant: e.g., *live/living* but *live/lives, fierce/fiercer/fiercest, please/pleasant* but *grace/graceful, bake/baker* but *aware/awareness*

  - ◆ For one-syllable words that end with a single vowel and one consonant, usually double the final consonant when adding a suffix that begins with a vowel, but usually do not double the final consonant when adding a suffix that begins with a consonant: e.g., *grin/grinning* but *grin/grins, sad/sadder/saddest, flat/flatten, pet/petted* but *sin/sinful, beg/beggar* but *fit/fitness*

  - ◆ For multisyllable words with an accented final syllable that ends with a single vowel and one consonant, follow the rules for one-syllable words: *excel/excellent, admit/admittance*

  - ◆ For multisyllable words with an unaccented final syllable that ends with a single vowel and one consonant, usually do not double the final consonant when adding a suffix: e.g., *visit/visited, slender/slenderer, civil/civilize, limit/limitless, develop/developer*

  - ◆ For words that end with a consonant and *y*, usually change the *y* to *i* and add the suffix, but for words that end with a vowel and *y*, usually keep the *y* and add the suffix: e.g, *copy/copied* but *enjoy/enjoyed, identify/identifiable* but *pay/payable, carry/carrier* but *employ/employer*

▶ Suffixes: Inflectional Endings

- Recognize and use the ending *-ing* with multisyllable verbs with an accented last syllable when forming the present participle of a verb: e.g., *remind/reminding, decline/declining, rely/relying, enjoy/enjoying*

- Recognize and use the ending *-ed* with multisyllable verbs with an accented last syllable when forming the past tense of a verb: e.g., *remind/reminded, decline/declined, rely/relied, enjoy/enjoyed*

- Recognize and use the ending *-ing* with multisyllable verbs with an accent not on the last syllable when forming the present participle of a verb: e.g., *locate/locating, differ/differing, rely/relying, enjoy/enjoying, panic/panicking*

- Recognize and use the ending *-ed* with multisyllable verbs with an accent not on the last syllable when forming the past tense of a verb: e.g., *cherish/cherished, locate/located, differ/differed, rely/relied, enjoy/enjoyed, panic/panicked*

Selecting Goals Behaviors and Understandings to Notice, Teach, and Support *(cont.)*

Phonics, Spelling, and Word Study

WORD STRUCTURE *(continued)*

▶ Suffixes: Verb Suffixes

- Recognize and use the suffix *-en*, meaning "to make or become" or "to give or gain," to form a verb: e.g., *moist/moisten, haste/hasten, flat/flatten*

- Recognize and use the suffix *-ize*, meaning "to make or become," to form a verb: e.g., *equal/equalize, civil/civilize*

▶ Suffixes: Adjective and Adverb Suffixes

- Recognize and use the suffix *-ly*, meaning "in a specific manner, period of time, or order," to form an adverb: e.g., *frequent/frequently, live/lively, sad/sadly, easy/easily, automatic/automatically*

- Recognize and use the suffixes *-able* and *-ible*, meaning "capable of," to form an adjective: e.g.,
  - Add *-able* to base words: e.g., *afford/affordable, hit/hittable, commit/committable, credit/creditable, identify/identifiable*
  - Add *-ible* to word roots: e.g., *terr/terrible, vis/visible, sens/sensible*

- Recognize and use the suffixes *-ful*, meaning "full of," and *-less*, meaning "without," to form an adjective: e.g.,
  - *-ful*: e.g., *fear/fearful, care/careful, sin/sinful, forget/forgetful, pocket/pocketful, pity/pitiful, joy/joyful*
  - *-less*: e.g., *fear/fearless, care/careless, limit/limitless, pity/pitiless, joy/joyless*

- Recognize and use the suffixes *-ant* and *-ent*, meaning "characterized by" or "inclined to," to form an adjective: e.g.,
  - *-ant*: e.g., *import/important, ignore/ignorant, rely/reliant*
  - *-ent*: e.g., *insist/insistent, urge/urgent, excel/excellent, differ/different*

- Recognize and use the suffixes *-ous* and *-ious*, meaning "full of," "like," or "having the quality of," to form an adjective: e.g.,
  - *-ous*: e.g., *humor/humorous, adventure/adventurous, fury/furious, joy/joyous, courage/courageous*
  - *-ious*: e.g., *grace/gracious*

- Recognize and use the suffixes *-al, -ial, -ian, -ic,* and *-ical,* meaning "like," "related to," or "suitable for," to form an adjective: e.g.,
  - *-al*: e.g., *globe/global, refer/referral, ceremony/ceremonial, loc/local*
  - *-ial*: e.g., *part/partial, editor/editorial, spec/special*
  - *-ian*: e.g., *civil/civilian, reptile/reptilian, grammar/grammarian*
  - *-ic*: e.g., *hero/heroic, athlete/athletic, magnet/magnetic*
  - *-ical*: e.g., *myth/mythical, type/typical, biography/biographical*

▶ Suffixes: Noun Suffixes

- Recognize and use the suffix *-ness*, meaning "state or quality of being," to form a noun: e.g., *kind/kindness, close/closeness, fit/fitness, bitter/bitterness, dizzy/dizziness*

- Recognize and use the suffixes *-ion, -tion,* and *-sion,* to show the quality or state of something by changing a verb to a noun: e.g.,
  - *-ion*: e.g., *adopt/adoption, discuss/discussion, revise/revision, create/creation, protect/protection*
  - *-tion*: e.g., *introduce/introduction*
  - *-sion*: e.g., *extend/extension, decide/decision*

- Recognize and use the suffix *-ment*, meaning "act of," "condition of being," or "product of," to form a noun: e.g., *punish/punishment, measure/measurement* but *argue/argument, employ/employment*

- Recognize and use the suffix *-ity*, meaning "state or condition of being," to form a noun: e.g., *major/majority, dense/density*

- Recognize and use the suffixes *-ant* and *-ent,* meaning "someone or something that performs an action," to form a noun: e.g.,
  - *-ant*: e.g., *assist/assistant, inhabit/inhabitant, occupy/occupant*
  - *-ent*: e.g., *correspond/correspondent*

- Recognize and use the suffixes *-ance* and *-ence,* meaning "state of" or "quality of," to form a noun: e.g.,
  - *-ance*: e.g., *attend/attendance, rely/reliance, annoy/annoyance*
  - *-ence*: e.g., *exist/existence*

- Recognize and use the suffixes that mean "act or process of," "state of," "result of," "amount or collection of," or "something that" to form a noun: e.g.,
  - *-age*: e.g., *short/shortage, use/usage, bag/baggage, marry/marriage*
  - *-ure*: e.g., *moist/moisture*

▶ Prefixes

- Understand and discuss the concept of a prefix

- Recognize and use the prefix *re-*, meaning "again": e.g., *remake, repay, reassure, refresh*

- Recognize and use prefixes that mean "not": e.g.,
  - *un-* (*unfair, unkind, unaware*)
  - *in-* (*invisible, incredible, insane*)
  - *dis-* (*disappear, dislike, disobey, disagree*)
  - *non-* (*nonsense, nonfiction, nonstop*)

- Recognize and use prefixes that mean "bad, badly" or "wrong, wrongly": e.g.,
  - *mis-* (*mistake, mislead*)
  - *mal-* (*malfunction*)

- Recognize and use prefixes that refer to sequence: e.g.,
  - *pre-*, meaning "before" (*preheat, predict, prescribe*)
  - *fore-*, meaning "before," "earlier," or "in front" (*forehead, foresee, foretell*)
  - *pro-*, meaning "before" or "forward" (*proclaim, promotion*)

- Recognize and use prefixes that indicate amount, extent, or location: e.g.,
  - *sub-* (*subway, submarine*)
  - *super-* (*supermarket, superpower, supernatural*)

- Recognize and use number-related prefixes: e.g., *uniform, bicycle, triangle, quadrangle, pentagon, octopus, century*

- Recognize and use prefixes that mean "with or together" or "between or among": e.g.,
  - *com-* (*compose*)
  - *con-* (*construct*)

- Recognize and use prefixes that mean "out" or "without" or "in, into, or within": e.g.,
  - *ex-* (*explode, export, exclude*)
  - *in-* (*inspect, include*)

Selecting Goals Behaviors and Understandings to Notice, Teach, and Support *(cont.)*

Phonics, Spelling, and Word Study

■ Recognize and use prefixes that mean "make" or "put in or put on": e.g.,

◆ en- *(enclose, enable)*

■ Recognize and use prefixes that mean "around," "across," or "beyond," or "through": e.g.,

◆ circu-, circum- *(circular)*

◆ peri- *(period)*

◆ trans- *(transport)*

◆ per- *(permit)*

■ Recognize and use prefixes that change form depending on the first letter of the word root or base word (assimilated prefixes): e.g.,

◆ ad- meaning "to or toward" *(adjoin, adhere)*

 ◆ ac- *(account)*

 ◆ af- *(affect)*

 ◆ al- *(allow)*

 ◆ an- *(announce)*

 ◆ ap- *(approach, approve)*

 ◆ ar- *(arrest, arrival)*

 ◆ as- *(assign, assure)*

 ◆ at- *(attempt)*

◆ sub- meaning "under or lower" or "smaller" *(subtract, submarine)*

 ◆ suc- *(success)*

 ◆ suf- *(suffix)*

 ◆ sug- *(suggestion)*

 ◆ sup- *(suppose)*

 ◆ sur- *(surround, surrender)*

 ◆ sus- *(suspect, suspend)*

◆ ob- meaning "to," "toward," or "against" *(observe, obstruct)*

 ◆ oc- *(occupy, occur)*

 ◆ of- *(offer, offend)*

 ◆ op- *(oppose)*

◆ com- meaning "with or together" *(companion, compact)*

 ◆ con- *(connect)*

 ◆ cor- *(correspond)*

◆ ex- meaning "out," "without," "from," or "away" *(exclaim, exchange)*

 ◆ ef- *(effort)*

 ◆ e- *(erase)*

▶ Abbreviations

■ Recognize and use common abbreviations and understand the full form of the words they shorten: e.g.,

◆ titles, names, degrees, and professional terms: *Mr.* (*Mister,* title for a man), *Ms.* (title for a woman), *Mrs.* (title for a married woman), *Miss* (title for a girl or an unmarried woman), *Dr.* (*Doctor*), *Sgt.* (*Sergeant*); *Jr.* (*Junior*), *Sr.* (*Senior*); *MD* or *M.D.* (*Doctor of Medicine*), *PhD* or *Ph.D.* (*Doctor of Philosophy*), *RN* or *R.N.* (*Registered Nurse*)

◆ days of week and months: *Mon.* (*Monday*), *Tues., Wed., Thurs., Fri., Sat., Sun.; Jan.* (*January*), *Feb., Mar., Apr., Aug., Sept., Oct., Nov., Dec.*

◆ addresses and geographical terms: *St.* (*Street*), *Ave.* (*Avenue*), *Rd.* (*Road*), *Apt.* (*Apartment*), *Blvd.* (*Boulevard*), *CA* or *Calif.* (*California*), *U.S.* or *US* (*United States*); *Mt.* (*Mountain*), *E* (*East*), *N, W, S*

◆ scholarly references: *etc.* (*et cetera*), *e.g.* (*for example*), *i.e.* (*that is*), *p.* (*page*), *pp.* (*pages*), *ed.* (*edition* or *editor*), *vol.* (*volume*), *fig.* (*figure*)

◆ times and dates: *a.m.* or *am* (*the time from midnight to noon*), *p.m.* or *pm* (*the time from noon to midnight*)

◆ measurements: *in.* (*inch* or *inches*), *ft.* (*foot* or *feet*), *yd.* (*yard* or *yards*), *mi.* (*mile* or *miles*), *lb.* (*pound* or *pounds*), *oz.* (*ounce* or *ounces*), *c* or *c.* (*cup* or *cups*), *pt.* (*pint* or *pints*), *qt.* (*quart* or *quarts*), *gal.* (*gallon* or *gallons*), *cu.* or *cu* (*cubic*), *sq.* (*square*), *mph* or *m.p.h.* (*miles per hour*); *mm* (*millimeter* or *millimeters*), *mg* (*milligram* or *milligrams*), *ml* (*milliliter* or *milliliters*), *cm* (*centimeter* or *centimeters*), *km* (*kilometer* or *kilometers*)

◆ businesses and organizations: *Co.* (*Company*), *Corp.* (*Corporation*), *Inc.* (*Incorporated*), *Ltd.* (*Limited*), *Assoc.* or *Assn.* (*Association*), *dept.* (*department*), *asst.* or *Asst.* (*assistant*), *pd.* (*paid*)

▶ Roots

■ Recognize and use word roots from Latin or Greek: e.g.,

◆ Latin—e.g., *aqua, aud, bene, cap, centr, clos, clud, clus, corp, cred, dict, duc, duct, dur, equa, equi, fac, fer, fic, fin, firm, flect, flex, form, fract, frag, grad, gress, hab, hib, ject, join, junct, loc, luc, lum, man, mem, min, miss, mit, mob, mot, mov, ped, pel, pend, pens, pon, pop, port, pos, prim, prin, pub, puls, quer, ques, quir, q uis, rupt, scribe, script, sens, sent, sign, sist, sol, son, spec, sta, stat, stit, stru, struct, tain, tempo, ten, tent, tin, terr, tract, val, ven, vent, ver, vers, vert, vid, vis, voc, vok*

◆ Greek—e.g., *aer, arch, aster, astr, astro, bio, chron, cycl, dem, geo, gram, graph, hydr, hydro, log, mega, meter, micro, ology, phon, photo, pod, pol, poli, polis, scop, scope, tele, therm*

WORD-SOLVING ACTIONS

▶ Taking Words Apart to Solve Them

■ Break a word into syllables to decode manageable units: e.g., *re/mem/ber, hos/pi/tal, be/fore, de/part/ment*

▶ Using Strategies to Solve Words and Determine Their Meanings

■ Recognize and use word parts to solve an unknown word and understand its meaning: e.g., *conference*–prefix *con-* ("with or together"), Latin root *fer* ("to bring" or "to carry"), suffix *-ence* ("state of" or "quality of")

■ Recognize and use connections between or among related words that have the same word root or base word to solve unknown words: e.g., *support/supports/supported/supportive/unsupportive*

■ Recognize and use a word's origin to solve an unknown word and understand its form and meaning

■ Recognize and use Latin roots to solve an unknown word and determine its meaning: e.g., the Latin root *cred*, meaning "believe," in the word *credible*, meaning "capable of being believed" or "believable"

■ Recognize and use Greek roots to solve an unknown word and determine its meaning: e.g., the Greek root *graph*, meaning "write," in the word *autograph*, meaning "the writing of one's name"

Selecting Goals Behaviors and Understandings to Notice, Teach, and Support *(cont.)*

Phonics, Spelling, and Word Study

WORD-SOLVING ACTIONS
(continued)

▶ **Using Reference Tools to Solve and Find Information About Words**

- Use a glossary to solve and find information about words
- Use a dictionary to solve and find information about words
- Recognize and use different types of dictionaries (e.g., medical, foreign language, geographical, visual, reverse, thesaurus) to solve and find information about words

▶ **Spelling Strategies**

- Make a first attempt to spell an unknown word
- Use phonogram patterns and letter patterns to help spell a word including phonograms in multisyllable words
- Use sound and letter sequence to help spell a word
- Use syllables to help spell a word
- Use the spelling of the smaller words within a compound word to help spell a compound word
- Use a spelling routine to help spell a word
- Use a mnemonic device to help spell a word: e.g., *fri<u>end</u>s to the <u>end</u>, a <u>bear</u> bit my <u>ear</u>*
- Use a dictionary to confirm or correct the spelling of a word
- Use word origins to understand and remember the spelling of some words: e.g., *beret, chalet, champagne, lasagna, coyote, mosquito*
- Use an electronic program to check your spelling
- Ask for help when all known spelling strategies have been tried

Selecting Goals Behaviors and Understandings to Notice, Teach, and Support

Phonics, Spelling, and Word Study

SPELLING PATTERNS

▶ Vowel Phonogram Patterns in Multisyllable Words

- Recognize and use vowel phonograms that appear in multisyllable words: e.g., -alk, -all, -alt, -aught, -ault, -aw, -awn, -ong, -ought; -ood, -ook, -oot; -oo, -ood, -oof, -ool, -oom, -oon, -oose, -ew; -ead

HIGH-FREQUENCY WORDS

- Recognize commonly misspelled words and rewrite them correctly

WORD MEANING/ VOCABULARY

▶ Related Words

- Recognize and use synonyms (words that have almost the same meaning): e.g., *mistake/error, destroy/demolish, high/tall, desperately/frantically*

- Recognize and use antonyms (words that have opposite meanings): e.g., *cold/hot, appear/vanish, abundant/scarce, fantasy/ reality*

- Recognize and use homophones (words that have the same sound, different spellings, and different meanings): e.g., *blew/blue, choral/coral, higher/hire, patience/patients*

- Recognize and use homographs (words that have the same spelling, different meanings and origins, and may have different pronunciations): e.g., *content, duck, flounder, invalid, present, pupil, sewer, temple*

- Recognize and use words with multiple meanings: e.g., *cover, credit, degree, monitor, novel, organ*

- Understand the concept of analogies to determine relationships among words: e.g.,
  - synonyms–*alert : aware : elevate : raise*
  - antonyms–*feeble : strong : durable : flimsy*
  - homophones–*hoard : horde : cereal : serial*
  - object/use–*catalog : advertise : goggles : protect*
  - part/whole–*chapter : book : musician : orchestra*
  - cause/effect–*comedy : laughter : drought : famine*

  - member/category–*celery : vegetable : plumber : occupation*
  - denotation/connotation–*inexpensive : cheap : thin : scrawny*

▶ Combined and Created Words

- Recognize and use portmanteau words, which come from blending two distinct words: e.g., *motel (motor hotel), smash (smack mash), smog (smoke fog)*

- Recognize and use clipped words, which come from shortening words: e.g., *ad (advertisement), dorm (dormitory), lab (laboratory), phone (telephone), photo (photograph)*

- Recognize and use acronyms, which come from combining the initial letter or letters of multiword names or phrases: e.g., *NATO (North Atlantic Treaty Organization), radar (radio detecting and ranging), scuba (self-contained underwater breathing apparatus)*

- Recognize and discuss the fact that palindromes are words that are spelled the same in either direction: e.g., *gag, kayak*

▶ Figurative Uses of Words

- Recognize and discuss the fact that some words have literal and figurative meanings: e.g.,
  - *cold*–"less warm than usual"; "unfriendly"
  - *shark*–"a large, usually ferocious fish that lives in warm seas"; "a dishonest person who preys on others"
  - *fork*–"a tool with a handle and two or more long, pointed parts at one end"; "anything shaped like a fork, or any branching"

- Recognize and use similes to make a comparison: e.g.,
  - *The child's lovely eyes shone like a pair of moons in the evening sky.*

- Recognize and use metaphors to make a comparison: e.g.,
  - *My heart became a block of ice.*

- Recognize, say, and discuss the fact that commonly used idioms have meanings different from the meanings of the separate words: e.g., *go fly a kite, hold your tongue, on the fence, hit the nail on the head, hit the road, sweat bullets*

- Recognize, say, and talk about words that are jumbled for humorous effect: e.g.,
  - spoonerisms–*a lack of pies* for *a pack of lies*
  - malapropisms–*the very pineapple of politeness* for *the very pinnacle of politeness*

▶ Parts of Words

- Understand and discuss the concept of prefixes and recognize their use in determining the meaning of some English words: e.g., *ad-, ant-, ante-, anti-, bi-, circu-, com-, con-, contra-, contro-, counter-, dec-, dis-, em-, en-, ex-, fore-, in-, inter-, intra-, mal-, mis-, mon-, mono-, multi-, non-, oct-, pent-, per-, poly-, post-, pre-, quadr-, re-, sub-, super-, trans-, tri-, un-, uni-*

- Understand and discuss the concept of suffixes and recognize their use in determining the meaning of some English words: e.g., *-able, -al, -ance, -ant, -ar, -arium, -ed, -ence, -ent, -er, -es, -est, ful, ial, ian, -ible, -ic, -ical, -ing, -ion, -ious, -ish, -ist, -ity, -less, -ly, -ment, -ness, -or, -orium, -ous, -s, -sion, -tion, -y*

▶ Word Origins

- Develop interest in vocabulary by recognizing and appreciating aspects of words and by "collecting" and discussing interesting word and using them in conversation

- Understand and discuss the fact that cognates are words in different languages that have similar meanings and spellings because they have related origins: e.g., English *alphabet*, French *alphabet*, Italian *alfabeto*, German *Alphabet*

- Understand and discuss the fact that English words or terms are derived from many different sources, such as other languages, technology, names, trademarked products, and social practices: e.g., *tortilla, parliament, harmonica, khaki, algebra; blog, hashtag, hyperlink; sandwich, valentine, hamburger; xerox, jeep, Band-Aid, Kleenex; fist bump, social media, takeout*

Selecting Goals Behaviors and Understandings to Notice, Teach, and Support (cont.)

Phonics, Spelling, and Word Study

WORD MEANING/ VOCABULARY (continued)

▶ Word Origins (continued)

- Understand and discuss the concept of Latin roots and recognize their use in determining the meanings of some English words: e.g., *aqua, aud, bene, cap, centr, clos, clud, clus, corp, cred, dict, duc, duct, dur, equa, equi, fac, fer, fic, fin, firm, flect, flex, form, fract, frag, grad, gress, hab, hib, ject, join, junct, loc, luc, lum, man, mem, min, miss, mit, mob, mot, mov, ped, pel, pend, pens, pon, pop, port, pos, prim, prin, pub, puls, quer, ques, quir, quis, rupt, scribe, script, sens, sent, sign, sist, sol, son, spec, sta, stat, stit, stru, struct, tain, tempo, ten, tent, tin, terr, tract, val, ven, vent, ver, vers, vert, vid, vis, voc, vok*

- Understand and discuss the concept of Greek roots and recognize their use in determining the meaning of some English words: e.g., *aer, arch, aster, astr, astro, bio, chron, cycl, dem, geo, gram, graph, hydr, hydro, log, mega, meter, micro, ology, phon, photo, pod, pol, poli, polis, scop, scope, tele, therm*

- Recognize and use prefixes, suffixes, and word roots that have Greek and Latin origins to understand word meaning: e.g., *incredible–in-* ("not"), Latin *cred* ("believe") and *-ible* ("capable of"); *antibiotic–anti-* ("opposite" or "against"), Greek *bio* ("life") and *-ic* ("related to")

- Recognize and discuss the fact that words in different languages or in the same language may have a common origin: e.g., *escribir* (Spanish "to write"), *describe*, and *script* derive from Latin *scribere*, "to write"

WORD STRUCTURE

▶ Contractions

- Recognize and discuss multiple contractions with *not* and *have* (almost solely in oral language): e.g., *mustn't've, shouldn't've, wouldn't've*

▶ Plurals

- Recognize and use irregular plurals that are formed by changing the final letters of the base word: e.g., *crisis, crises; medium, media; cactus, cacti*

▶ Suffixes

- Understand and talk about the concept of a suffix

- Understand and talk about the fact that several basic rules govern the spelling of words with suffixes: e.g.,

  ◆ For many words, there are no spelling changes when adding a suffix: e.g., *run/runs, bright/brighter/ brightest, moist/moisten, final/finally, teach/teacher*

  ◆ For words that end with silent *e*, usually drop the *e* when adding a suffix that begins with a vowel, but usually keep the *e* when adding a suffix that begins with a consonant: e.g., *live/living* but *live/lives, fierce/fiercer/fiercest, sterile/sterilize, please/pleasant* but *grace/graceful, bake/baker* but *aware/awareness*

  ◆ For one-syllable words that end with a single vowel and one consonant, usually double the final consonant when adding a suffix that begins with a vowel, but usually do not double the final consonant when adding a suffix that begins with a consonant: e.g., *grin/grinning* but *grin/grins, sad/sadder/saddest, flat/flatten, pet/petted* but *sin/sinful, beg/beggar* but *fit/fitness*

  ◆ For multisyllable words with an accented final syllable that ends with a single vowel and one consonant, follow the rules for one-syllable words: *remit/remitting* but *remit/remits, excel/excellent, admit/admittance, commit/commitment*

  ◆ For multisyllable words with an unaccented final syllable that ends with a single vowel and one consonant, usually do not double the final consonant when adding a suffix: e.g., *visit/visited, slender/slenderer, civil/civilize, vigil/vigilant, limit/limitless, develop/developer*

  ◆ For words that end with a consonant and *y*, usually change the *y* to *i* and add the suffix, but for words that end with a vowel and *y*, usually keep the *y* and add the suffix: e.g, *copy/copied* but *enjoy/enjoyed, crazy/crazier/craziest* but *coy/coyer/coyest, identify/identifiable* but *pay/payable, carry/carrier* but *employ/employer*

▶ Suffixes: Inflectional Endings

- Recognize and use the ending *-ing* with multisyllable verbs with an accented last syllable when forming the present participle of a verb: e.g., *remind/reminding, decline/ declining, remit/remitting, rely/relying, enjoy/enjoying*

- Recognize and use the ending *-ed* with multisyllable verbs with an accented last syllable when forming the past tense of a verb: e.g., *remind/reminded, decline/declined, remit/remitted, rely/relied, enjoy/enjoyed*

- Recognize and use the ending *-ing* with multisyllable verbs with an accent not on the last syllable when forming the present participle of a verb: e.g., *cherish/cherishing, locate/locating, differ/differing, rely/relying, enjoy/enjoying, panic/panicking*

- Recognize and use the ending *-ed* with multisyllable verbs with an accent not on the last syllable when forming the past tense of a verb: e.g., *cherish/cherished, locate/located, differ/differed, rely/relied, enjoy/enjoyed, panic/panicked*

▶ Suffixes: Verb Suffixes

- Recognize and use the suffix *-en*, meaning "to make or become" or "to give or gain," to form a verb: e.g., *moist/moisten, haste/ hasten, flat/flatten*

- Recognize and use the suffix *-ize*, meaning "to make or become," to form a verb: e.g., *equal/equalize, sterile/sterilize, civil/civilize, apology/apologize, bapt/baptize*

▶ Suffixes: Adjective and Adverb Suffixes

- Recognize and use the suffix *-ly*, meaning "in a specific manner, period of time, or order," to form an adverb: e.g., *frequent/ frequently, live/lively, sad/sadly, livid/lividly, easy/easily, notable/notably, automatic/ automatically*

Selecting Goals Behaviors and Understandings to Notice, Teach, and Support *(cont.)*

Phonics, Spelling, and Word Study

- Recognize and use the suffixes *-able* and *-ible*, meaning "capable of," to form an adjective: e.g.,
  - Add *-able* to base words: e.g., *afford/affordable, enforce/enforceable, hit/hittable, commit/committable, credit/creditable, identify/identifiable, portray/portrayable*
  - Add *-ible* to word roots: e.g., *terr/terrible, vis/visible, sens/sensible, flex/flexible, aud/audible*

- Recognize and use the suffixes *-ful*, meaning "full of," and *-less*, meaning "without," to form an adjective: e.g.,
  - *-ful*: e.g., *fear/fearful, care/careful, sin/sinful, forget/forgetful, pocket/pocketful, pity/pitiful, joy/joyful*
  - *-less*: e.g., *fear/fearless, care/careless, brim/brimless, limit/limitless, pity/pitiless, joy/joyless*

- Recognize and use the suffixes *-ant* and *-ent*, meaning "characterized by" or "inclined to," to form an adjective: e.g.,
  - *-ant*: e.g., *import/important, ignore/ignorant, vigil/vigilant, rely/reliant, buoy/buoyant*
  - *-ent*: e.g., *insist/insistent, urge/urgent, excel/excellent, differ/different*

- Recognize and use the suffixes *-ous* and *-ious*, meaning "full of," "like," or "having the quality of," to form an adjective: e.g.,
  - *-ous*: e.g., *humor/humorous, adventure/adventurous, fury/furious, joy/joyous, courage/courageous*
  - *-ious*: e.g., *grace/gracious, prestige/prestigious*

- Recognize and use the suffixes *-al, -ial, -ian, -ic,* and *-ical*, meaning "like," "related to," or "suitable for," to form an adjective: e.g.,
  - *-al*: e.g., *emotion/emotional, globe/global, refer/referral, clinic/clinical, ceremony/ceremonial, loc/local*
  - *-ial*: e.g., *part/partial, finance/financial, editor/editorial, spec/special*
  - *-ian*: e.g., *civil/civilian, reptile/reptilian, grammar/grammarian*
  - *-ic*: e.g., *hero/heroic, athlete/athletic, magnet/magnetic, chron/chronic*
  - *-ical*: e.g., *myth/mythical, type/typical, biography/biographical, log/logical*

- Recognize and use the suffixes *-ative, -itive,* and *-ive*, meaning "inclined to," to form an adjective: e.g.,
  - *-ative*: e.g., *affirm/affirmative, conserve/conservative, interpret/interpretative, authority/authoritative, tent/tentative*
  - *-itive*: e.g., *add/additive, compete/competitive, sens/sensitive*
  - *-ive*: e.g., *act/active, impulse/impulsive, pens/pensive*

▶ Suffixes: Noun Suffixes

- Recognize and use the suffix *-ness*, meaning "state or quality of being," to form a noun: e.g., *kind/kindness, close/closeness, fit/fitness, bitter/bitterness, dizzy/dizziness*

- Recognize and use the suffixes *-ion, -tion,* and *-sion*, to show the quality or state of something by changing a verb to a noun: e.g.,
  - *-ion*: e.g., *adopt/adoption, commune/communion; discuss/discussion, revise/revision, create/creation, protect/protection*
  - *-tion*: e.g., *introduce/introduction*
  - *-sion*: e.g., *extend/extension, decide/decision*

- Recognize and use the suffix *-ment*, meaning "act of," "condition of being," or "product of," to form a noun: e.g., *punish/punishment, measure/measurement* but *argue/argument, commit/commitment, merry/merriment, employ/employment*

- Recognize and use the suffix *-ity*, meaning "state or condition of being," to form a noun: e.g., *major/majority, dense/density, elastic/elasticity, complex/complexity*

- Recognize and use the suffixes *-ant* and *-ent*, meaning "someone or something that performs an action," to form a noun: e.g.,
  - *-ant*: e.g., *assist/assistant, pollute/pollutant, inhabit/inhabitant, occupy/occupant*
  - *-ent*: e.g., *correspond/correspondent, reside/resident*

- Recognize and use the suffixes *-ance* and *-ence*, meaning "state of" or "quality of," to form a noun: e.g.,
  - *-ance*: e.g., *attend/attendance, endure/endurance, admit/admittance, rely/reliance, annoy/annoyance*
  - *-ence*: e.g., *exist/existence, coincide/coincidence, excel/excellence*

- Recognize and use the suffixes that mean "act or process of," "state of," "result of," "amount or collection of," or "something that" to form a noun: e.g.,
  - *-age*: e.g., *short/shortage, use/usage, bag/baggage, marry/marriage*
  - *-ure*: e.g., *moist/moisture, legislate/legislature, fract/fracture*

- Recognize and use the suffixes *-arium* and *-orium*, meaning "a place for," to form a noun: e.g.,
  - *-arium*: e.g., *planetarium, solarium*
  - *-orium*: e.g., *auditorium, emporium*

▶ Prefixes

- Understand and discuss the concept of a prefix

- Recognize and use the prefix *re-*, meaning "again": e.g., *remake, repay, reassure, refresh*

- Recognize and use prefixes that mean "not": e.g.,
  - *un-* (*unfair, unkind, unaware, unravel*)
  - *in-* (*invisible, incredible, insane, infinite*)
  - *dis-* (*disappear, dislike, disobey, disagree*)
  - *non-* (*nonsense, nonfiction, nonstop, nonviolent*)

- Recognize and use prefixes that mean "bad, badly" or "wrong, wrongly": e.g.,
  - *mis-* (*mistake, mislead, misfortune*)
  - *mal-* (*malform, malfunction, malpractice*)

- Recognize and use prefixes that refer to sequence: e.g.,
  - *pre-*, meaning "before" (*preheat, precaution, predict, prescribe*)
  - *fore-*, meaning "before," "earlier," or "in front" (*forefather, forehead, foresee, foretell*)
  - *pro-*, meaning "before" or "forward" (*proactive, proclaim, promotion*)
  - *ante-*, meaning "before" (*antedate, anteroom, antechamber, antecedent*)
  - *post-*, meaning "after" (*postdate, postpone, postwar, postscript*)

- Recognize and use prefixes that indicate amount, extent, or location: e.g.,
  - *sub-* (*subway, submarine, subsoil, subset*)
  - *super-* (*supermarket, superpower, superscript, supernatural*)

Selecting Goals Behaviors and Understandings to Notice, Teach, and Support *(cont.)*

Phonics, Spelling, and Word Study

WORD STRUCTURE *(continued)*

▶ Prefixes *(continued)*

- Recognize and use number-related prefixes: e.g., *uniform, monarch, monogram, bicycle, triangle, quadrangle, pentagon, octopus, decade, century, hemisphere, semicircle, multicolor, polyrhythmic*

- Recognize and use prefixes that mean "with or together" or "between or among": e.g.,
  - ◆ com- *(compile, compose, compress)*
  - ◆ con- *(construct, confer, conform)*
  - ◆ inter- *(interact, interchange, interlock)*

- Recognize and use prefixes that mean "out" or "without" or "in, into, or within": e.g.,
  - ◆ ex- *(explode, export, exclude)*
  - ◆ in- *(inspect, include, inflate)*
  - ◆ intra- *(intracompany, intrastate, intravenous)*

- Recognize and use prefixes that mean "make" or "put in or put on": e.g.,
  - ◆ em- *(empower, embed, embark)*
  - ◆ en- *(enclose, enable, entangle)*

- Recognize and use prefixes that mean "around," "across," or "beyond," or "through": e.g.,
  - ◆ circu-, circum- *(circular, circuit, circumference)*
  - ◆ peri- *(periscope, perimeter, period)*
  - ◆ trans- *(transport, transaction, transatlantic)*
  - ◆ per- *(permit, perspiration, persist)*

- Recognize and use prefixes that mean "opposite," or "against": e.g.,
  - ◆ ant-, anti- *(antonym, antacid, antifreeze, antisocial)*
  - ◆ contra-, contro- *(contradict, contraband, controversy, controversial)*
  - ◆ counter- *(counterclockwise, counterpart)*

- Recognize and use the prefix *de-*, which means "opposite," "down or lower," or "take away or remove": e.g., *decentralize, depress, descend, defrost*

- Recognize and use prefixes that change form depending on the first letter of the word root or base word (assimilated prefixes): e.g.,
  - ◆ in- meaning "not" or "in, into, or within" *(invisibility, inability)*
    - ◆ il- *(illegal, illegible)*
    - ◆ im- *(immigrant, immortal)*
    - ◆ ir- *(irregular, irresponsible)*
  - ◆ ad- meaning "to or toward" *(adjoin, adhere)*
    - ◆ ac- *(account, acclaim)*
    - ◆ af- *(affect, affirm)*
    - ◆ ag- *(aggressive, aggravate)*
    - ◆ al- *(allow, allot)*
    - ◆ an- *(announce, annex)*
    - ◆ ap- *(approach, approve)*
    - ◆ ar- *(arrest, arrival)*
    - ◆ as- *(assign, assure)*
    - ◆ at- *(attempt, attraction)*
  - ◆ sub- meaning "under or lower" or "smaller" *(subtract, submarine)*
    - ◆ suc- *(success, succession)*
    - ◆ suf- *(suffix, sufficient)*
    - ◆ sug- *(suggestion)*
    - ◆ sum- *(summon)*
    - ◆ sup- *(suppose, suppress)*
    - ◆ sur- *(surround, surrender)*
    - ◆ sus- *(suspect, suspend)*
  - ◆ ob- meaning "to," "toward," or "against" *(observe, obstruct)*
    - ◆ oc- *(occupy, occur)*
    - ◆ of- *(offer, offend)*
    - ◆ op- *(oppose, oppress)*
    - ◆ o- *(omit)*
  - ◆ com- meaning "with or together" *(companion, compact)*
    - ◆ col- *(collide, collapse)*
    - ◆ con- *(connect, connotation)*
    - ◆ cor- *(correspond, corrode)*
    - ◆ co- *(coordinate, coworker)*
  - ◆ ex- meaning "out," "without," "from," or "away" *(exclaim, exchange)*
    - ◆ ef- *(effort, effective)*
    - ◆ e- *(elapse, erase)*

▶ Abbreviations

- Recognize and use common abbreviations and understand the full form of the words they shorten: e.g.,
  - ◆ titles, names, degrees, and professional terms: *Mr.* (*Mister*, title for a man), *Ms.* (title for a woman), *Mrs.* (title for a married woman), *Miss* (title for a girl or an unmarried woman), *Dr.* (*Doctor*), *Sgt.* (*Sergeant*); *Jr.* (*Junior*), *Sr.* (*Senior*); *MD* or *M.D.* (*Doctor of Medicine*), *PhD* or *Ph.D.* (*Doctor of Philosophy*), *RN* or *R.N.* (*Registered Nurse*)
  - ◆ days of week and months: *Mon.* (*Monday*), *Tues., Wed., Thurs., Fri., Sat., Sun.; Jan.* (*January*), *Feb., Mar., Apr., Aug., Sept., Oct., Nov., Dec.*
  - ◆ addresses and geographical terms: *St.* (*Street*), *Ave.* (*Avenue*), *Rd.* (*Road*), *Apt.* (*Apartment*), *Blvd.* (*Boulevard*), *CA* or *Calif.* (*California*), *U.S.* or *US* (*United States*); *Mt.* (*Mountain*), *E* (*East*), *N, W, S*
  - ◆ scholarly references: *etc.* (*et cetera*), *e.g.* (*for example*), *i.e.* (*that is*), *p.* (*page*), *pp.* (*pages*), *ed.* (*edition* or *editor*), *vol.* (*volume*), *fig.* (*figure*)
  - ◆ times and dates: *a.m.* or *am* (*the time from midnight to noon*), *p.m.* or *pm* (*the time from noon to midnight*); *BCE* or *b.c.e.* (*before the Common Era*), *CE* or *c.e.* (*of the Common Era*)
  - ◆ measurements: *in.* (*inch* or *inches*), *ft.* (*foot* or *feet*), *yd.* (*yard* or *yards*), *mi.* (*mile* or *miles*), *lb.* (*pound* or *pounds*), *oz.* (*ounce* or *ounces*), *c* or *c.* (*cup* or *cups*), *pt.* (*pint* or *pints*), *qt.* (*quart* or *quarts*), *gal.* (*gallon* or *gallons*), *cu.* or *cu* (*cubic*), *sq.* (*square*), *mph* or *m.p.h.* (*miles per hour*); *mm* (*millimeter* or *millimeters*), *mg* (*milligram* or *milligrams*), *ml* (*milliliter* or *milliliters*), *cm* (*centimeter* or *centimeters*), *km* (*kilometer* or *kilometers*)
  - ◆ businesses and organizations: *Co.* (*Company*), *Corp.* (*Corporation*), *Inc.* (*Incorporated*), *Ltd.* (*Limited*), *Assoc.* or *Assn.* (*Association*), *dept.* (*department*), *asst.* or *Asst.* (*assistant*), *pd.* (*paid*)

Selecting Goals Behaviors and Understandings to Notice, Teach, and Support *(cont.)*

Phonics, Spelling, and Word Study

▶ Roots

■ Recognize and use word roots from Latin or Greek: e.g.,

  ◆ Latin–e.g., *aqua, aud, bene, cap, centr, clos, clud, clus, corp, cred, dict, duc, duct, dur, equa, equi, fac, fer, fic, fin, firm, flect, flex, form, fract, frag, grad, gress, hab, hib, ject, join, junct, loc, luc, lum, man, mem, min, miss, mit, mob, mot, mov, ped, pel, pend, pens, pon, pop, port, pos, prim, prin, pub, puls, quer, ques, quir, q uis, rupt, scribe, script, sens, sent, sign, sist, sol, son, spec, sta, stat, stit, stru, struct, tain, tempo, ten, tent, tin, terr, tract, val, ven, vent, ver, vers, vert, vid, vis, voc, vok*

  ◆ Greek–e.g., *aer, arch, aster, astr, astro, bio, chron, cycl, dem, geo, gram, graph, hydr, hydro, log, mega, meter, micro, ology, phon, photo, pod, pol, poli, polis, scop, scope, tele, therm*

WORD-SOLVING ACTIONS

▶ Taking Words Apart to Solve Them

■ Break a word into syllables to decode manageable units: e.g., *re/mem/ber, hos/pi/tal, be/fore, de/part/ment*

▶ Using Strategies to Solve Words and Determine Their Meanings

■ Recognize and use word parts to solve an unknown word and understand its meaning: e.g., *conference*–prefix *con-* ("with or together"), Latin root *fer* ("to bring" or "to carry"), suffix *-ence* ("state of" or "quality of")

■ Recognize and use connections between or among related words that have the same word root or base word to solve unknown words: e.g., *support/supports/supported/ supportive/unsupportive*

■ Recognize and use a word's origin to solve an unknown word and understand its form and meaning

■ Recognize and use Latin roots to solve an unknown word and determine its meaning: e.g., the Latin root *cred,* meaning "believe," in the word *credible,* meaning "capable of being believed" or "believable"

■ Recognize and use Greek roots to solve an unknown word and determine its meaning: e.g., the Greek root *graph,* meaning "write," in the word *autograph,* meaning "the writing of one's name"

▶ Using Reference Tools to Solve and Find Information About Words

■ Use a glossary to solve and find information about words

■ Use a dictionary to solve and find information about words

■ Recognize and use different types of dictionaries (e.g., medical, foreign language, geographical, visual, reverse, thesaurus) to solve and find information about words

▶ Spelling Strategies

■ Make a first attempt to spell an unknown word

■ Use phonogram patterns and letter patterns to help spell a word including phonograms in long and/or technical multisyllable words

■ Use sound and letter sequence to help spell a word

■ Use syllables to help spell a word

■ Use the spelling of the smaller words within a compound word to help spell a compound word

■ Use a spelling routine to help spell a word

■ Use a mnemonic device to help spell a word: e.g., *fri<u>end</u>s to the <u>end</u>, a b<u>ear</u> bit my <u>ear</u>*

■ Use a dictionary to confirm or correct the spelling of a word

■ Use word origins to understand and remember the spelling of some words: e.g., *beret, chalet, champagne, lasagna, coyote, mosquito*

■ Use an electronic program to check your spelling

■ Ask for help when all known spelling strategies have been tried

Guided Reading

Guided Reading Continuum

The following level-by-level continuum contains detailed descriptions of ways proficient readers are expected to think *within, beyond,* and *about* the texts they are processing at each level on the text gradient. For a description of the gradient, see *Guided Reading: Responsive Teaching Across the Grades,* Second Edition. We have produced the A–Z continuum to assist teachers who are using a gradient of texts to teach guided reading lessons or other small-group lessons. You will see the gradient again in Figure I–1. (Download full-size color copy at *www.fountasandpinnell.com.*) You will also see the approximate instructional-level expectations for reading by level. We view these as reasonable expectations, but your school or district may want to adjust the goals to fit your own.

We suggest that you use a benchmark assessment system to determine each student's instructional reading level. To learn about the *Benchmark Assessment System* that correlates directly to our A–Z levels, see *www.fountasandpinnell.com.*

Guided reading is a highly effective form of small-group instruction. Based on assessment, the teacher brings together a group of readers who are similar enough in their reading development that they can be taught together. They read independently at about the same level and can take on a more challenging new text selected by the teacher. The

FIGURE I–1 *Text Gradient and Instructional Level Expectations*

F&P TEXT LEVEL GRADIENT™

FOUNTAS & PINNELL LEVELS	GRADE-LEVEL GOALS
A B C D	Kindergarten
E F G H	Grade One
I J K	
L M	Grade Two
N O P	Grade Three
Q R	Grade Four
S T U	Grade Five
V W X	Grade Six
Y Z	Grade Seven–Eight
Z+	High School/Adult

Fountas & Pinnell
INSTRUCTIONAL LEVEL EXPECTATIONS FOR READING

	Beginning of Year (Aug.–Sept.)	1st Interval of Year (Nov.–Dec.)	2nd Interval of Year (Feb.–Mar.)	End of Year (May–June)
Grade K	C	D	E	
	B	C	D	
	A	B	C	
				Below C
Grade 1	E	G	I	K
	D	F	H	J
	C	E	G	I
	Below C	Below E	Below G	Below I
Grade 2	K	L	M	N
	J	K	L	M
	I	J	K	L
	Below I	Below J	Below K	Below L
Grade 3	N	O	P	Q
	M	N	O	P
	L	M	N	O
	Below L	Below M	Below N	Below O
Grade 4	Q	R	S	T
	P	Q	R	S
	O	P	Q	R
	Below O	Below P	Below Q	Below R
Grade 5	T	U	V	W
	S	T	U	V
	R	S	T	U
	Below R	Below S	Below T	Below U
Grade 6	W	X	Y	Z
	V	W	X	Y
	U	V	W	X
	Below U	Below V	Below W	Below X
Grades 7–8	Z	Z	Z	Z
	Y	Y	Z	Z
	X	X	Y	Y
	Below X	Below X	Below Y	Below Y

KEY

Exceeds Expectations

Meets Expectations

Approaches Expectations: Needs Short-Term Intervention

Does Not Meet Expectations: Needs Intensive Intervention

The Instructional Level Expectations for Reading chart is intended to provide general guidelines for grade level goals, which should be adjusted based on school/district requirements and professional teacher judgement.

Heinemann
DEDICATED TO TEACHERS

© Fountas, Irene C. & Pinnell, Gay Su and Heinemann, Portsmouth NH, 2012.

10/26/16

Fountas & Pinnell LITERACY™

teacher supports the reading in a way that enables students to read the more challenging text with effective processing, thus expanding their reading powers. They learn how to problem-solve efficiently by reading a text that is not too easy, nor too hard. The framework of a guided reading lesson is detailed in Figure I–2. For a full description of guided reading, see *Guided Reading: Responsive Teaching Across the Grades*, Second Edition.

General Aspects of the Guided Reading Continuum

As you use the continuum, there are several important points to keep in mind.

1. *The cognitive actions that readers employ while processing print are essentially the same across levels. Readers are simply applying them to successively more demanding levels of text, and they are always growing in complexity.* Beginning readers are sorting out the complex concepts related to using print (left-to-right directionality, voice-print match, the relationships between spoken and written language), so their processing is slower and their overt behaviors show us how they are working on print. They are reading texts with familiar topics and very simple, natural language, yet even these texts demand that they understand story lines, think about characters, and engage in more complex thinking such as making predictions.

For higher-level readers, much of the processing is unconscious and unobservable. These readers automatically and effortlessly solve large numbers of words, tracking print across complex sentences that they process without explicit attention to the in-the-head actions that are happening. While reading, they focus on the meaning of the text and engage in complex thinking processes (for example, inferring what the writer is implying but not saying, critically examining the ideas in the text, or noticing aspects of the writer's craft). Yet at times, higher-level readers will need to closely examine a word to solve it or reread it to tease out the meaning of especially complex sentence structures.

All readers are simultaneously employing a wide range of systems of strategic actions while processing print (see Figure I–3, page 404 and inside front cover). The twelve systems of strategic actions include:

- *Searching for and using information.* Beginning readers will overtly search for information in the letters and words, the pictures, or the sentence structure; they also use their own background knowledge.

- *Self-monitoring their reading for accuracy and understanding and self-correcting when necessary.* Beginning readers will overtly display evidence of monitoring and self-correcting while higher-level readers keep this evidence "underground"; but all readers monitor or check on themselves as they read.

- *Solving the words using a flexible range of strategies.* Early readers are just beginning to acquire ways of looking at words, and they work with a few signposts and word features (simple letter-sound relationships and word parts). High-level readers employ a broad and flexible range of word-solving strategies that are largely unconscious, freeing attention for deep thinking.

- *Sustaining fluent, phrased reading.* At early levels (A, B), readers will be working to match one spoken word to one written word and will be pointing crisply at each word to assist the eye and voice in this process; however, at level C, when

GUIDED READING

FIGURE I–2 *Framework for Guided Reading*

STRUCTURE OF A GUIDED READING LESSON

Element	Potential Teaching Moves to Support Reading with Accuracy, Comprehension, and Fluency
Introduction to the Text	• Activate and/or provide needed background knowledge. • Invite students to share thinking. • Enable students to hear and sometimes say new language structures. • Have students say and sometimes locate specific words in the text. • Help students make connections to present knowledge of texts, content, and experiences. • Reveal the structure of the text. • Use new vocabulary words in conversation to reveal meaning. • Prompt students to make predictions based on the information revealed so far. • Draw attention to the writer's craft to support analysis. • Draw attention to accuracy or authenticity of the text–writer's credentials, references, or presentation of evidence as appropriate. • Draw attention to illustrations–pictures, charts, graphs, maps, cutaways–and the information they present.
Reading the Text	• Teach for, prompt for, or reinforce the effective use of systems of strategic actions (including searching for and using information, monitoring and self-correcting, solving words, and fluency.) • Clear up confusions as needed.
Discussing the Text	• Gather evidence of comprehension by observing what students say about the text. • Invite students to pose questions and clarify their understandings. • Help students learn to discuss the meaning of the text together. • Extend students' expression of understandings through questioning, summarizing, restating, and adding to their comments.

Teaching for Processing Strategies	• Revisit the text to demonstrate or reinforce any aspect of reading, including all systems of strategic actions:
	  • Searching for and using information • Predicting
	  • Monitoring and self-correcting • Making connections
	  • Solving words • Synthesizing
	  • Maintaining fluency • Inferring
	  • Adjusting reading (purpose and genre) • Analyzing
	  • Summarizing (remembering information) • Critiquing
	• Provide explicit demonstrations of strategic actions using any part of the text that has just been read.

Word Work	• Based on patterns of your students' needs as evidenced in your observations, teach any aspect of word analysis that is needed–letters, letter-sound relationships, breaking words apart, noticing base words and affixes, using root meaning, connecting words, using analogy. • Have students manipulate words using magnetic letters or use white boards or pencil and paper to have students make, take apart, or write words with efficiency and flexibility.
Extending the Meaning (optional)	• Use writing about reading, drawing about reading, or extended talk to reflect on or explore any aspect of understanding the text.

GUIDED READING

dialogue is first presented, they will begin to make their reading sound like talking. As the finger is withdrawn and the eyes take over the process at subsequent levels, students will read increasingly complex texts with appropriate rate, word stress, phrasing, and pausing in a smoothly operating system. In and of itself, fluency is not a stage or level of reading. Readers apply strategies in an integrated way to achieve fluent reading at every level after the early behaviors are in place.

▶ *Adjusting reading in order to process a variety of texts.* At all levels, readers may slow down to problem-solve words or complex language and resume a normal pace, although at higher levels this process is mostly unobservable. Readers make adjustments as they search for information; they may reread, search graphics or illustrations, go back to specific references in the text, or use specific readers' tools. At all levels, readers also adjust expectations and ways of reading according to purpose, genre, and previous reading experiences. At early levels, readers have only beginning experiences to draw on; but at more advanced levels, they have rich resources in terms of the knowledge of genre (see Fountas and Pinnell, 2006, 159 ff). Proficient readers are highly flexible, responding in many ways simultaneously.

▶ *Remembering information in summary form.* Summarizing implies the selection and reorganization of important information. Readers constantly summarize information as they read a text, thus forming prior knowledge with which to understand the rest of the text; they also remember this summary information long after reading.

▶ *Making predictions.* At all levels, readers constantly make and confirm or disconfirm predictions. Usually, these predictions are implicit rather than voiced, and they add not only to understanding but also to enjoyment of a text. All readers predict based on the information in the text and their own background knowledge, with more advanced readers bringing a rich foundation of knowledge, including how many genres and types of text are organized and crafted.

▶ *Making connections.* At all levels, readers use their prior knowledge as well as their personal experiences and knowledge of other texts to interpret a text. As they expand their reading experience, they have more information to help them understand every text. At the most advanced levels, readers are required to understand mature and complex ideas and themes that are in most cases beyond their personal experience; yet they can empathize with the human condition, drawing from previous reading.

▶ *Synthesizing new information.* At all levels, readers gain new information from the texts they read, although readers who are just beginning to construct a reading process are processing texts on very familiar topics. As they move through successive levels of text, readers encounter much new information, which they incorporate into their own background knowledge. As a result of reading, they learn and change, and this happens through both fiction and nonfiction.

▶ *Reading "between the lines" to infer what is not explicitly stated in the text.* To some degree, all texts require inference. At very simple levels, readers may infer characters' feelings (surprised, happy, sad) or traits (lazy, greedy). But at high levels, readers need to infer constantly to understand both fiction and nonfiction texts. They understand what the writer implies but does not state directly.

▶ *Thinking analytically about a text to notice how it is constructed or how the writer has crafted language.* Thinking analytically about a text means reflecting on it, holding it up for examination, and drawing some conclusions about it.

GUIDED READING

FIGURE I–3 *Systems of Strategic Actions*

SYSTEMS OF STRATEGIC ACTIONS FOR PROCESSING WRITTEN TEXTS		
WAYS OF THINKING	**THINKING *WITHIN* THE TEXT**	**Searching for and Using Information**	Searching for and using all kinds of information in a text
		Monitoring and Self-Correcting	Checking on whether reading sounds right, looks right, and makes sense
		Solving Words	Using a range of strategies to take words apart and understand what words mean while reading continuous text
		Maintaining Fluency	Integrating sources of information in a smoothly operating process that results in expressive, phrased reading
		Adjusting	Reading in different ways as appropriate to purpose for reading and type of text
		Summarizing	Putting together and carrying important information forward while reading and disregarding irrelevant information
	THINKING *BEYOND* THE TEXT	**Predicting**	Anticipating what will follow while reading continuous text
		Making Connections • personal • world • texts	Searching for and using connections to knowledge that readers have gained through their personal experiences, learning about the world, and reading other texts that enhance the understanding of the text
		Synthesizing	Putting together information from the text and from the reader's own background knowledge in order to create new understandings
		Inferring	Going beyond the literal meaning of a text to think about what is not there but is implied by the writer
	THINKING *ABOUT* THE TEXT	**Analyzing**	Examining elements of a text to know more about how it is constructed
		Critiquing	Evaluating a text based on the reader's personal, world, or text knowledge

GUIDED READING

Readers at early levels may comment that the text was funny or exciting; they do not, however, engage in a great deal of analysis, which could be artificial and detract from enjoying the text. More advanced readers will notice more about how the writer (and illustrator when appropriate) has organized the text and crafted the language.

▸ *Thinking critically about a text.* Thinking critically about a text involves complex ways of evaluating it. Beginning readers may simply say what they like or dislike about a text, sometimes being specific about why; but increasingly advanced readers engage in higher-level thinking as they evaluate the quality or authenticity of a text and this kind of analysis often enhances enjoyment.

2. *Readers are always meeting greater demands at every level because the texts are increasingly challenging.* The categories for these demands may be similar, but the specific challenges are constantly increasing. For example, at many of the lower levels of text, readers are challenged to use phonogram patterns (or consonant clusters and vowel patterns) to solve one-syllable words. At upper levels, they are challenged to use these same patterns in multisyllable words. In addition, readers must learn to use word endings as they take apart words. Word endings change words and add meaning. At lower levels, readers are attending to endings such as *-s, -ed,* and *-ing,* but as words become increasingly complex at successive levels, they will encounter endings such as *-ment, -ent, -ant, -ible,* and *-able.*

At all levels, readers must identify characters and follow plots; but at lower levels, characters are one-dimensional and plots are a simple series of events. Across the levels, however, readers encounter multiple characters that are highly complex and change over time. Plots have more episodes; subplots are full of complexity. Across the levels there is greater demand for inference and analysis. Over time, students learn to use academic language to talk about texts.

3. *Readers' knowledge of genres expands over time but also grows in depth within genres.* For some texts at very low levels, it is difficult to determine genre. For example, a simple repetitive text may focus on a single topic, such as fruit, with a child presenting an example of a different type of fruit on each page. The pages could be in just about any order, except that there is often some kind of conclusion at the end. Such a text is organized in a structure that is characteristic of non-fiction, which helps beginning readers understand information presented in categories, but it is technically fiction because the narrator is not real. At this level, however, it is not important for students to identify pure genre categories, but simply to experience and learn about a variety of ways to organize texts.

Moving across the levels of the gradient, however, examples of genres become more precise and varied. At early levels, students read examples of fiction (usually realistic fiction, traditional literature, and simple fantasy) and simple informational texts on single topics. Across the levels, nonfiction texts become more and more complex, offering information on a variety of topics, as well as a range of underlying structures for presentation (description; comparison and contrast; cause and effect; temporal sequence; and problem and solution). These underlying structures appear at all levels after the very beginning ones, but they are combined in increasingly complex ways. Students also learn and use academic language for talking about the genres of text and their characteristics.

4. *At each level, the content load of texts becomes heavier, requiring an increased amount of background knowledge.* Content knowledge is a key factor in understanding texts; it includes vocabulary and concepts. Beginning texts are necessarily structured to take advantage of familiar content that most young students know; yet, even some very simple texts may require knowledge of some labels (for example, *zoo animals*) that may be unfamiliar to the students you teach. Success at successive levels will depend not only on study in the content areas but on wide reading of texts that expand the individual's vocabulary and content knowledge.

5. *At each level, the themes and ideas are more mature, requiring readers to consider perspectives and understand cultures beyond their own.* Students can connect simple themes and ideas to their own lives, but even at beginning levels they find that their experiences are stretched by realistic stories, simple fantasy, and traditional tales. At levels of increasing complexity, readers are challenged to understand and empathize with characters (and the subjects of biography) who lived in past times or in distant places and who have very different experiences and perspectives from the readers' own. At higher levels, fantasy requires that readers understand completely imaginary worlds. As they meet greater demands across the levels, they must depend on previous reading, as well as on discussions of the themes and ideas.

6. *The specific descriptions of thinking within, beyond, and about text do not change dramatically from level to level.* As you look at the continuum of text features along the gradient A to Z, you will see only small changes level to level. The gradient represents a gradual increase in the demands of text, but you must always remember that the same feature may appear but readers will experience a slightly more difficult example of it. Similarly, the expectations for readers' thinking change gradually over time as they develop from kindergarten through grade eight. If you look at the demands across two or three levels you will notice only a few changes in expectations. But if you contrast levels like the following, you will find some very clear differences.

- ▶ Level A with Level D
- ▶ Level E with Level H
- ▶ Level I with Level N
- ▶ Level L with Level P
- ▶ Level R with Level U
- ▶ Level V with Level Z

The continuum does not represent neat "stages" of learning. Readers vary in what they give attention to and enjoy. And they are all different from each other. The continuum represents progress over time, and if you examine the expectations in the ranges suggested, you get a picture of the remarkable growth our students make from prekindergarten through grade eight.

Using the Guided Reading Continuum

The guided reading continuum for grades K–8 is organized by level, A to Z. Each level has several sections.

Section 1: Characteristics of Readers

The first section of each continuum provides a brief description of what you may find to be generally true of readers at the particular level. Remember that all readers are individuals and that individuals vary widely. It is impossible to create a description that is true of all readers for whom a level is appropriate for independent reading or instruction. In fact, it is inappropriate to refer to any individual as "a level ___ reader"! We level *books,* not *readers.* But it is helpful to keep in mind the general expectations of readers at a level so that books may be well selected and appropriate support may be given to individuals and groups.

Section 2: Selecting Texts for Guided Reading Lessons

This section provides detailed descriptions of text characteristics at each level, A–Z. It is organized into ten categories as shown in Figure I–4.

Studying the text characteristics of books at a given level will provide a good inventory of the challenges readers will meet across that level. Remember that there are a great variety of texts within each level, and that these characteristics apply to what is *generally true* for texts at the level. For the individual text, some factors may be more important than others in making demands on the readers. Examining these texts factors relative to the books you select for guided reading will help in planning introductions that help readers meet the demands of more challenging texts and process them effectively.

Section 3: Demands of the Text—Ways of Thinking

The heart of the guided reading continuum is a description of the expectations for readers at the level. The descriptions are organized into three larger categories and twelve subcategories, as shown in Figure I–3.

As you work with readers at each level, examine the specific descriptions within categories.

- *Planning an introduction to a text.* Examine the categories to determine what might be challenging for readers. Frame the introduction to help them engage in particular thinking processes.

- *Guiding interactions with individual readers.* Observe reading behaviors and support students to problem-solve at difficulty. Draw their attention to what they need to know through demonstrating, prompting, or reinforcing actions.

- *Discussing the meaning of a text after reading the whole text or a part of it.* Invite readers to comment on various aspects of the text and to build on one another's points. Refer to the continuum as you think about the evidence of understanding they are demonstrating through conversation. Guide the discussion when appropriate to help them engage in new ways of thinking.

- *Revisiting the text to do some specific teaching.* Demonstrate effective ways of operating on a text in a way that will help readers learn how to do something as readers that they can apply to other texts. The teaching may focus on any area of the systems of strategic actions.

FIGURE I–4 *Ten Characteristics of Texts for Guided Reading*

TEN CHARACTERISTICS OF TEXTS FOR GUIDED READING

Genre	*Genre* is the type of text and refers to a system by which fiction and nonfiction texts are classified. Form is the particular format in which a genre may be presented. Forms and genres have characteristic features.
Text Structure	*Structure* is the way the text is organized and presented. The structure of most fiction and biographical texts is narrative, arranged primarily in chronological sequence. Factual texts are organized categorically or topically and may have sections with headings. Writers of factual texts use several underlying structural patterns to provide information to readers. The most important are description; chronological sequence; comparison and contrast; cause and effect; and problem and solution. The presence of these structures, especially in combination, can increase the challenge for readers.
Content	*Content* refers to the subject matter of the text–the facts and concepts that are important to understand. In fiction, content may be related to the setting or to the kinds of problems characters have. In factual texts, content refers to the topic of focus. Content is considered in relation to the prior experience of readers.
Themes and Ideas	*Themes and ideas* are the larger messages that are communicated by the writer. Ideas may be concrete and accessible or complex and abstract. A text may have multiple themes or a main theme and several supporting themes. A text may have a main idea and several messages.
Language and Literary Features	*Language and literary features* make a text enjoyable and satisfying to readers. Written language is qualitatively different from spoken language. Fiction writers use dialogue, figurative language, and other kinds of literary structures such as character, setting, and plot. Factual writers use description and technical language. Contemporary nonfiction writers use literary writing to make texts engaging, and they often present argument. In hybrid texts you may find a wide range of literary language.
Sentence Complexity	*Sentence complexity* refers to the way words are arranged in order in sentences with punctuation. Meaning is mapped onto the syntax of language. Texts with simpler, more natural sentences are easier to process. Sentences with embedded and conjoined clauses make a text more difficult.
Vocabulary	*Vocabulary* refers to words and their meanings. The more known vocabulary words in a text, the easier it will be. The individual's reading and writing vocabularies refer to words that she understands and can also read or write. Simple words that exist in the oral vocabulary (Tier 1) are the easiest. Tier 2 words are those that appear more often in writing and in the talk of mature language users. Tier 3 words are those used in academic disciplines.
Words	*Words* are the groups of letters arranged in print that readers must recognize and solve. The challenge in a text partly depends on the number and the difficulty of the words that the reader must solve by recognizing them or decoding them. Having a great many of the same high-frequency words makes texts more accessible for beginning readers. Multisyllable words make a text more difficult.
Illustrations	*Illustrations* include the drawings, paintings, or photographs that accompany the text and add meaning and enjoyment. In factual texts, illustrations also include graphics that provide a great deal of information that readers must integrate with the text. Illustrations are an integral part of a high-quality text. Increasingly, fiction texts are including a range of graphics, including labels, sidebars, photos and legends, charts, and graphs. After grade one, texts may include graphic texts that communicate information or a story in a sequence of pictures and words.
Book and Print Features	*Book and print features* are the physical aspects of the text–what readers cope with in terms of length, size, and layout. Book and print features also include organizational tools like a table of contents, headings and subheadings, and sidebars; text resources like a glossary, pronunciation guide, and index; and a variety of graphic features in graphic texts that communicate how the text is read. Some features outside the body of the text (for example, endpapers, title page, dedication, front and back covers, and dust jacket or book flap) are called the peritext. All of these features hold meaning and aesthetic appeal for proficient readers.

GUIDED READING

▶ *Engaging readers in "hands-on" word work to support ease and flexibility in word solving.* You can use this continuum to help you notice what readers know and need to know in terms of word analysis and meaning.

▶ *Extending the meaning of the text.* Plan writing, drawing, or deeper discussion that will support students in engaging in deeper ways of thinking about texts. (See the Writing About Reading continuum for examples.)

Section 4: Planning Word Work for Guided Reading

In thinking-within-the-text section at each level, a separate section provides suggestions for phonics and word work. Guided reading is intended to be used as one component of an integrated literacy framework that also includes specific lessons on phonics, spelling, and word study. The details of that curriculum—for lessons and independent activities—are presented in the phonics, spelling, and word study continuum and expanded in *Phonics Lessons* and *Word Study Lessons,* K–3 (Fountas and Pinnell 2003, 2004). These lessons are systematic, sequenced, and multilevel in the activities used to help students apply principles, usually as whole-class activities. The goals embedded in guided reading apply the principles during text reading where phonics and word study instruction is most effective.

As they read texts, individuals are always applying phonics and word study principles, and across the gradient they do so on more and more complex words. Word solving includes not only decoding but deriving the meaning of words, as indicated in the Solving Words category in the first row of Figure I–3.

In addition, an important component of a guided reading lesson is some brief but focused attention to words and how they work. This quick word work should address the students' needs in visual processing. The goal is to build their fluency and flexibility in taking words apart. In this section, you will find a list of suggestions to help you select word study activities that will enable you to tailor instruction on words to the specific demands of the level of text. Make principles related to word solving visible to students through the following types of activities:

▶ Invite students to work with letters or words using magnetic letters on a vertical board or on the table. Magnetic letters are particularly helpful when demonstrating how to take words apart or change words. Have students make words, change words, and take apart words.

▶ Invite students to notice aspects of letters or words using a white board, chalkboard, or magnetic letters that all students can see.

▶ Have students use individual small white boards (or chalkboards) to write and change words to demonstrate the principles. (Each student can have a small eraser or an old sock on one hand so that changes can be made quickly.) Use erasable markers on white boards.

▶ Give students individual word cards for instant word recognition.

▶ Ask students to sort word cards into categories or match words to illustrate a principle.

▶ Make word webs to illustrate the connections and relationships between words.

As you plan, conduct, and reflect on guided reading lessons at the various levels, move to the appropriate level and note what your students already know and do well and what they need to be able to do so that your introduction, interactions, and teaching points can be more specific to their needs at any given point in time.

Readers at Level

At level A, readers are just beginning to learn how print works and to construct the alphabetic principle—that is, to understand that there are relationships between sounds and letters. They learn to look (aided by the finger) across one line of print and to look left to right across words. They learn to search for and use information from pictures and to use simple language structures to read very simple sentences. Readers differentiate print from pictures and begin to notice the distinctive features of letters, attaching names to them. They begin to read one-line sentences with simple words and on familiar topics. They learn to match one spoken word with one word in print. As they read, they acquire some easy high-frequency words that they can read in every context, and they begin to notice and use visual signposts in many words. They use known words and awareness of print to notice mismatches and begin to self-monitor. Reading and rereading these very simple texts helps them gain gradual control of ways to look at and work with print. At the same time, they take meaning from pictures and construct stories. They relate meaningful information from nonfiction texts and connect it to things they know.

Selecting Texts Characteristics of Texts at **Level A**

GENRE

▶ **Fiction**

- Realistic fiction
- Simple fables
- Simple animal fantasy

▶ **Nonfiction**

- Simple factual texts

FORMS

- Some series books
- Picture books

TEXT STRUCTURE

- Very simple narratives carried by pictures

CONTENT

- Content interesting to and relevant for young children
- Familiar, easy content: e.g., family and home, play, pets, animals, school, food, community, friends, daily activities, the human body, weather, seasons, transportation, toys
- All content directly and explicitly supported by picture information
- Humor that is easy to grasp: e.g., silly characters, funny situations

THEMES AND IDEAS

- Themes reflecting everyday life: e.g., friendship, family relationships, self, nature
- Clear, simple ideas easy to identify
- Ideas close to children's experience: e.g., sharing with others, caring for others, doing your job, helping your family, taking care of self, staying healthy, caring for your world, having fun, noticing your world

LANGUAGE AND LITERARY FEATURES

- Simple language patterns that are close to oral language
- Repeating language patterns
- Familiar settings close to children's experience
- Mostly nameless, simple characters that do not change
- A few simple elements of fantasy: e.g., talking animals

SENTENCE COMPLEXITY

- Short, predictable sentences (usually three to six words) that are close to oral language
- Simple sentences (subject and predicate, no embedded phrases or clauses)
- Subject preceding verb in most sentences
- A few sentences with adjectives

VOCABULARY

- A few words that are new to children but easy to understand in context
- Some simple words for sounds (onomatopoetic)
- All words that are in common oral vocabulary for young children (Tier 1)
- Concept words illustrated by pictures
- A few very simple adjectives describing people, places, or things

WORDS

- Mostly one-, two-, and three-syllable words fully supported by the pictures
- Some simple plurals using -s or -es
- Repeated use of a few easy high-frequency words: e.g., *is, it, I, am, the, here, look*
- A few verbs with inflectional endings: e.g., -s, -ing
- Many words with easy, predictable letter-sound relationships (decodable)
- Words with easy spelling patterns (VC, CVC, CVCe)

The dog is running.

4

5

ILLUSTRATIONS

- Clear illustrations that fully support meaning
- Illustrations that match print very closely
- Illustrations that add meaning to the text
- Illustrations that support each page of text
- Very simple illustrations with no distracting detail
- Consistent layout of illustrations and print
- Clear separation of illustrations and print
- A few labeled photographs

BOOK AND PRINT FEATURES

LENGTH

- Short, usually sixteen pages (eight pages of print)
- Print separate from pictures on alternating pages
- Typically fewer than fifty words per book

PRINT AND LAYOUT

- Print in large, plain font
- Print always on white or very pale background
- One line of text on each page
- Sentences beginning on the left
- Consistent placement of print
- Most texts double or triple spaces between lines
- Exaggerated spaces between words
- Print clearly separated from pictures

PUNCTUATION

- Period only punctuation in most texts

Selecting Goals Behaviors and Understandings to Notice, Teach, and Support

THINKING *WITHIN* THE TEXT

SEARCHING FOR AND USING INFORMATION

- Read left to right across one line of print
- Match word by word over one line of print, with all sentences beginning on the left
- Coordinate eyes and point to search for and use visual information in print
- Reread to search for and use information from language structure or meaning
- Search for and use information from pictures that match the print closely, have few distracting details, and clearly support meaning
- Use consistent layout of illustrations and print to search for and use information
- Use clear separation of illustrations and print to search for and use information
- Use language patterns close to oral language to search for and use information
- Use repeating language patterns to search for and use information
- Use simple sentence structures (subject and predicate with no embedded phrases or clauses) to search for and use information
- Sustain searching for information over a short text (usually sixteen pages with one line of print on each of the alternating pages and typically fewer than fifty words)
- Notice and use punctuation marks (periods)
- Notice and use capital and lowercase letters
- Use the illustrations to search for and use information
- Use labels on photographs to search for and use information
- Use understanding of familiar, easy content to search for and use information: e.g., family and home, play, pets, animals, school, food, community, friends, daily activities, the human body, weather, seasons, seasons, transportation, toys
- Understand that the illustrations closely and explicitly support the content and use them to search for and use information
- Identify a sound and link it to a letter

MONITORING AND SELF-CORRECTING

- Show evidence of close attention to print
- Use voice-print match to self-monitor and self-correct
- Reread the sentence to problem-solve, self-correct, or confirm
- Recognize a letter and use meaning to self-monitor and self-correct
- Use language structure to self-monitor and self-correct
- Use visual features of words to self-monitor and self-correct
- Use recognition of high-frequency words to self-monitor and self-correct
- Use known words to self-monitor and self-correct
- Use illustrations as a resource to self-monitor and self-correct
- Use understanding of how the story works (narrative structure) to self-monitor and self-correct
- Cross check one source of information with another (voice-print match) to self-correct

SOLVING WORDS

▶ Reading Words

- Recognize words in clear, plain font that are on a white or very light background
- Recognize a few high-frequency words quickly and easily
- Recognize one-, two-, and some three-syllable words fully supported by the pictures
- Read some simple regular plurals formed with the endings -*s* or -*es* that are fully supported by pictures and language structure
- Read words that are repeated within the same text: e.g., *is, it, I, am*
- Read a few verbs with inflectional endings (e.g., -*s, -ing*) fully supported by pictures and language structure
- Read a few words with very easy, predictable letter-sound relationships (decodable)
- Read some words with easy spelling patterns with the support of pictures and language (VC, CVC, CVC*e*)
- Say a word and predict its first letter
- Say a word slowly to hear and identify the first sound and connect that sound to a letter
- Locate easy high-frequency words in a text
- Notice visual features of a word and use them to locate or read the word

Selecting Goals Behaviors and Understandings to Notice, Teach, and Support *(cont.)*

THINKING *WITHIN* THE TEXT *(continued)*

▶ Vocabulary

- Understand the meaning of a few words that are new but easy to understand in the context of the text and with picture support
- Expand understanding of the meaning of words by connection with the pictures and/or understanding the context: e.g., *zoo, farm*
- Read and understand a few simple words that stand for sounds (onomatopoetic words)
- Understand vocabulary words that are in common oral vocabulary for emergent readers (Tier 1)
- Understand the meaning of simple regular plurals formed with the endings *-s* or *-es*
- Understand a few simple adjectives describing people, places, or things
- Understand words that indicate characters: e.g., a few easy-to-read names, family members
- Understand words that show action: e.g., *play, ride, ran*
- Understand words like *I* and *me* that may indicate the narrator of a text
- Recognize and understand labels for familiar objects, animals, people, the human body, weather, daily activities

MAINTAINING FLUENCY

- Sustain momentum through the entire short text
- Point crisply and read at a steady rate, slowly enough to match voice to print but without long pauses
- Notice the period and pause after it
- Drop the voice at a period
- Stress words that are in bold

ADJUSTING

- Slow down to problem-solve words and resume reading with momentum
- Understand that a nonfiction book gives facts
- Notice and read a label on a photograph or illustration

SUMMARIZING

- Remember information while reading to understand the meaning of the text
- Talk about important information after reading
- Remember and talk about the important events or ideas in a simple text
- Remember and talk about clear, simple ideas that are easy to identify

Selecting Goals Behaviors and Understandings to Notice, Teach, and Support *(cont.)*

THINKING *BEYOND* THE TEXT

PREDICTING

◆ Use knowledge of language structure to anticipate the text

◆ Make predictions based on information in pictures that closely match the text

◆ Predict the ending of a story based on reading the beginning and middle

◆ Make predictions based on knowledge of the events of everyday life: e.g., family, cooking, play, pets, school, food, community, friends

◆ Make predictions based on personal experiences and knowledge: e.g., family and home, play, pets, animals, school, food, community, friends, daily activities, the human body, weather, seasons, transportation, toys

MAKING CONNECTIONS

◆ Make connections between personal experience and a text

◆ Make connections among books in a series

◆ Identify recurring characters or settings when applicable

◆ Make connections between background knowledge of familiar content and the content in the text

◆ Make connections among texts on the same topic or with the same content

SYNTHESIZING

◆ Talk about what is known about the topic before reading the text

◆ Talk about what is learned from reading the text

◆ Talk about any new labels for content that are learned from the text

INFERRING

◆ Infer meaning of story or content from pictures that add meaning to the text

◆ Make inferences about where the story takes place to help understand it

◆ Talk about the pictures, revealing interpretation of a problem or of characters' feelings

◆ Infer humor that is easy to grasp: e.g., silly characters, funny situations

◆ Infer ideas about familiar content: e.g., friendships, family relationships, self, nature

Selecting Goals Behaviors and Understandings to Notice, Teach, and Support *(cont.)*

THINKING *ABOUT* THE TEXT

ANALYZING

- Understand how the ideas and information in a book are related to each other
- Understand how the events, content, and ideas in a text are related to the title
- Recognize that a text can be imagined (fiction) or can give information (nonfiction)
- Recognize settings that are familiar: e.g., home, school, neighborhood
- Recognize and follow a chronological sequence of events
- Recognize that there are characters in a story
- Recognize that a story can have animals that act like people
- Use language and pictures to talk about a text (title, beginning, ending)

- Recognize that a text can have true information
- Understand that a nonfiction book gives facts or tells how to do something
- Recognize that a process happens in time order
- Use some specific language to talk about texts: e.g., *front cover, back cover, page, page number, author, illustrator, illustration, photograph, title*

CRITIQUING

- Share opinions about a text
- Share opinions about an illustration

Planning for Letter and Word Work After Guided Reading

Using your recent observations of the readers' ability to take words apart quickly and efficiently while reading text, plan for one to three minutes of active engagement of students' attention to letters, sounds, and words. Prioritize the readers' noticing of print features and active hands-on use of magnetic letters, a white board, word cards, or pencil and paper to promote fluency and flexibility in visual processing.

Examples:

- Recognize a few easy high-frequency words quickly (for example, *a, an, I, go, it*)
- Make a few easy high-frequency words (*is, it, I, am, can, the*)
- Write a few easy high-frequency words (*and, is, on, to*)
- Recognize a few easy CVC words (*can, get, big, not, run*)
- Make and break apart a few easy CVC words (*can, get, big, not, run*)

- Write a few easy CVC words (*can, get, big, not, run*)
- Clap the syllables in one- and two-syllable words (from pictures)
- Match or sort pictures by beginning or ending sounds (*car, cake; house, dress*)
- Match or sort pictures by rhyming sounds at the end (*man, fan, can*)
- Match or sort letters by a variety of features—uppercase or lowercase; tall or short; with or without long straight lines, short straight lines, circles, tails, tunnels

- Search for and locate letters by name quickly
- Match or sort lowercase and uppercase letters (*a* and *A*, *d* and *D*)
- Read the Alphabet Linking Chart in different ways—singing, by letter names, pictures and words, all vowels, all consonants, letters only, backwards order, every other letter

LEVEL **A**

Readers at Level

At level B, readers are learning how print works, establishing control of left-to-right directionality across words and across lines of print. They firm up voice-print match while reading texts with two or more lines of print. Readers may recognize and use repeating language patterns in texts that have very simple stories and focus on a single idea, and they will learn more about the distinctive features of letters and the connections between sounds and letters. It is very important that they consistently self-monitor their reading, attempt to self-correct as they notice mismatches, and check one source of information against another. Readers begin to notice and use visual signposts and expand their core of simple high-frequency words. At the same time, they take meaning from pictures and use it to help them understand stories. They relate meaningful information from nonfiction texts and connect it to things they know.

Selecting Texts Characteristics of Texts at Level B

GENRE

▶ **Fiction**
- Realistic fiction
- Simple fables
- Simple animal fantasy

▶ **Nonfiction**
- Simple factual texts

FORMS
- Some series books
- Picture books

TEXT STRUCTURE
- Very simple narratives carried by pictures

CONTENT
- Content interesting to and relevant for young children
- Familiar, easy content: e.g., family and home, play, pets, animals, school, food, community, friends, daily activities, the human body, weather, seasons, transportation, toys
- All content directly and explicitly supported by picture information
- Humor that is easy to grasp: e.g., silly characters, funny situations

THEMES AND IDEAS
- Themes reflecting everyday life: e.g., friendship, family relationships, self, nature
- Clear, simple ideas easy to identify

- Ideas close to children's experience: e.g., sharing with others, caring for others, doing your job, helping your family, taking care of self, staying healthy, caring for your world, having fun, noticing your world

LANGUAGE AND LITERARY FEATURES
- Simple language patterns that are close to oral language
- Repeating language patterns
- Familiar settings close to children's experience
- Mostly nameless, simple characters that do not change
- Occasional use of a few words of dialogue, often in a speech bubble, or of unspoken thoughts shown in a thought bubble
- A few simple elements of fantasy: e.g., talking animals

SENTENCE COMPLEXITY
- Short, predictable sentences (usually five to ten words) that are close to oral language
- Simple sentences (subject and predicate, no embedded phrases or clauses)
- Subject preceding verb in most sentences
- A few sentences with adjectives
- A few sentences with dialogue, usually a speech bubble or one or two words, or with unspoken thoughts shown in a thought bubble

VOCABULARY
- A few words that are new to children but easy to understand in context
- Words for sounds (onomatopoetic)
- All words that are in common oral vocabulary for young children (Tier 1)
- Concept words illustrated by pictures
- A few very simple adjectives describing people, places, or things

WORDS
- Mostly one-, two-, and three-syllable words fully supported by the pictures
- Some simple plurals using -s or -es
- Repeated use of a few easy high-frequency words: e.g., and, to, up, the here, look, is, it, me
- A few verbs with inflectional endings: e.g., -s, -ing
- Many words with easy, predictable letter-sound relationships (decodable)
- Words with easy spelling patterns (VC, CVC, CVCe)

ILLUSTRATIONS
- Clear illustrations that fully support meaning
- Illustrations that match print very closely
- Illustrations that add meaning to the text
- Illustrations that support each page of text
- Very simple illustrations with no distracting detail
- Consistent layout of illustrations and print
- Clear separation of illustrations and print
- A few labeled photographs or illustrations

We like to row
at camp.

6

7

BOOK AND PRINT FEATURES

LENGTH

- Short, usually sixteen pages (eight pages of print)
- Print separate from pictures on alternating pages
- Typically fewer than eighty words per book (40–80)

PRINT AND LAYOUT

- Print in large, plain font
- Print always on white or very pale background
- Two to three lines of text on each page
- Sentences beginning on the left
- Sentences turn over one or more lines
- Consistent placement of print
- Most texts double or triple spaces between lines
- Exaggerated spaces between words
- Print clearly separated from pictures

PUNCTUATION

- Period only punctuation in most texts
- Some use of question marks, commas, and quotation marks

Selecting Goals Behaviors and Understandings to Notice, Teach, and Support

THINKING *WITHIN* THE TEXT

SEARCHING FOR AND USING INFORMATION

- Read left to right across two or three lines of print
- Match word by word over two or three lines of print, with all sentences beginning on the left
- Coordinate eyes and pointing to search for and use visual information in print
- Use return sweep to read the second or third line of print on a page
- Reread to search for and use information from language structure or meaning
- Search for and use information from pictures that match the print closely, have few distracting details, and clearly support meaning
- Use clear separation of illustrations and print to search for and use information
- Use consistent layout of illustrations and print to search for and use information
- Use language patterns close to oral language to search for and use information
- Use repeating language patterns to search for and use information
- Use simple sentence structures (subject and predicate with no embedded phrases or clauses) to search for and use information
- Sustain searching for information over a short text (usually sixteen pages with two to three lines of print on alternate pages and fewer than eighty words)
- Notice and use punctuation marks (periods, question marks, commas, quotation marks)
- Notice and use capital and lowercase letters
- Search for and understand information in a few words of dialogue, often in a speech bubble, or unspoken thoughts shown in a thought bubble
- Use the illustrations to search for and use information
- Use labels on photographs or illustrations to search for and use information
- Use understanding of familiar, easy content to search for and use information: e.g., family and home, play, pets, animals, school, food, community, friends, daily activities, the human body, weather, seasons, transportation, toys
- Understand that the illustrations closely and explicitly support the content and use them to search and use information
- Identify a sound and link it to a letter

MONITORING AND SELF-CORRECTING

- Show evidence of close attention to print
- Use voice-print match to self-monitor and self-correct
- Reread the sentence to problem-solve, self-correct, or confirm
- Recognize a letter and use meaning to self-monitor and self-correct
- Use language structure to self-monitor and self-correct
- Use visual features of words to self-monitor and self-correct
- Use recognition of high-frequency words to self-monitor and self-correct
- Use known words to self-monitor and self-correct
- Cross-check one kind of information against another to monitor and self-correct reading (i.e., cross-checking meaning with visual information)
- Use illustrations as a resource to self-monitor and self-correct
- Use understanding of how the book works to self-monitor and self-correct

SOLVING WORDS

▶ **Reading Words**

- Recognize words in clear, plain font that are on a white or very light background
- Recognize a few high-frequency words quickly and easily
- Recognize one-, two-, and some three-syllable words fully supported by the pictures
- Read some simple regular plurals formed with the endings -s or -es fully supported by pictures and language structure
- Read words that are repeated within the same text: e.g., *is, it, I, am*
- Read a few verbs with inflectional endings (e.g., -s, -ing) that are fully supported by pictures and language structure
- Read a few words with very easy, predictable letter-sound relationships (decodable)
- Read some words with easy spelling patterns with the support of pictures and language (VC, CVC, CVCe)
- Say a word and predict its first letter
- Say a word slowly to hear and identify the first sound and connect that sound to a letter

Selecting Goals Behaviors and Understandings to Notice, Teach, and Support *(cont.)*

THINKING *WITHIN* THE TEXT *(continued)*

- Locate easy high-frequency words in a text
- Notice visual features of a word and use them to locate or read the word

▶ Vocabulary

- Understand the meaning of a few words that are new but easy to understand in the context of the text and with picture support
- Expand understanding of the meaning of words by connection with the pictures and/or understanding the context: e.g., *zoo, farm*
- Read and understand a few simple words that stand for sounds (onomatopoetic words)
- Understand vocabulary words that are in common oral vocabulary for early emergent readers (Tier 1)
- Understand the meaning of simple regular plurals formed with the endings *-s* or *-es*
- Understand a few simple adjectives describing people, places, or things
- Understand words that indicate characters: e.g., a few easy-to-read names, family members
- Understand words that show action: e.g., *play, ride, ran*
- Understand words like *I* and *me* that may indicate the narrator of a text
- Understand the meaning of simple words used to assign dialogue: e.g., *said*
- Recognize and understand labels for familiar objects, animals, people, the human body, weather, daily activities

MAINTAINING FLUENCY

- Sustain momentum through an entire short text
- Point crisply and read at a steady rate, slowly enough to match voice to print but without long pauses
- Notice the period and stop after it
- Drop the voice at a period
- Take a short breath after a comma
- Stress words that are in bold
- Read dialogue indicated by quotation marks with expression

ADJUSTING

- Slow down to problem-solve words and resume reading with momentum
- Understand that a text is fiction and that a story has a beginning, middle, and end
- Understand that a nonfiction book gives facts
- Notice and read labels on photographs or illustrations

SUMMARIZING

- Remember information while reading to understand the meaning of the text
- Talk about important information after reading the text
- Remember and talk about the important events in a simple story
- Remember and talk about clear, simple ideas that are easy to identify

LEVEL **B**

Selecting Goals Behaviors and Understandings to Notice, Teach, and Support *(cont.)*

THINKING *BEYOND* THE TEXT

PREDICTING

- Use knowledge of language structure to anticipate the text
- Make predictions based on information in pictures that closely match the text
- Predict the ending of a story based on reading the beginning and middle
- Make predictions based on knowledge of the events of everyday life: e.g., family, cooking, play, pets, school, food, community, friends
- Make predictions based on personal experiences and knowledge: e.g., family and home, play, pets, animals, school, food, community, friends, daily activities, the human body, weather, seasons, transportation, toys

MAKING CONNECTIONS

- Make connections between personal experience and texts
- Make connections among books in a series
- Identify recurring characters or settings when applicable
- Make connections between background knowledge of familiar content and the content in the text
- Make connections among texts on the same topic or with the same content

SYNTHESIZING

- Talk about what is known about the topic before reading the text
- Talk about what is learned from reading the text
- Talk about any new labels for content that are learned from the text

INFERRING

- Infer meaning of story or content from pictures that add meaning to the text
- Make inferences about where the story takes place to help understand it
- Talk about characters' feelings inferred from pictures of the story
- Talk about the pictures, revealing interpretation of a problem or of characters' feelings
- Infer humor that is easy to grasp: e.g., silly characters, funny situations
- Infer ideas about familiar content: e.g., friendships, family relationships, self, nature, food, health, community

THINKING *ABOUT* THE TEXT

ANALYZING

- Understand how the ideas and information in a book are related to each other
- Understand how the events, content, and ideas in a text are related to the title
- Recognize that a text can be imagined (fiction) or it can give information (nonfiction)
- Recognize settings that are familiar: e.g., home, school, neighborhood
- Recognize and follow a chronological sequence of events
- Recognize that there are characters (people or animals in a story)
- Recognize that a story can have animals that act like people

- Use language and pictures to talk about a text (title, beginning, ending)
- Recognize that a text can have true information (factual text)
- Understand that a nonfiction book gives facts or tells how to do something
- Recognize that a process happens in time order
- Use some specific language to talk about texts: e.g., *front cover, back cover, page, page number, author, illustrator, illustration, photograph, title*

CRITIQUING

- Share opinions about a text
- Share opinions about an illustration

Selecting Goals Behaviors and Understandings to Notice, Teach, and Support *(cont.)*

Planning for Letter and Word Work After Guided Reading

Using your recent observations of the readers' ability to take words apart quickly and efficiently while reading text, plan for one to three minutes of active engagement of students' attention to letters, sounds, and words. Prioritize the readers' noticing of print features and active hands-on use of magnetic letters, a white board, word cards, or pencil and paper to promote fluency and flexibility in visual processing.

Examples:

- Recognize a few easy high-frequency words quickly (for example, *at, like, of, so, you*)
- Make and break apart a few easy high frequency words (*do, my, she, up*)
- Write a few easy high-frequency words (*the, here, look, is, it, me*)
- Recognize a few CVC words (*dad, red, did, hot, sun*)
- Make and break apart a few CVC words (*can, dad, red, did, hot, sun*)
- Write a few CVC words (*can, dad, red, did, hot, sun*)

- Clap the syllables in one- and two-syllable words (from pictures)
- Match or sort pictures by beginning or ending sounds (*ball, bear, baby; bus, dress, horse*)
- Match or sort pictures by rhyming sounds at the end (*book, look, took*)
- Listen for and identify each sound in a few words using sound boxes
- Match or sort letters by a variety of features quickly—uppercase or lowercase; tall or short; with or without long straight lines, short straight lines, circles, tails, tunnels

- Recognize letters by name and locate them in words quickly
- Match or sort lowercase and uppercase letters quickly (*b* and *B*, *e* and *E*)
- Read the Alphabet Linking Chart in different ways—singing, by letter names, pictures and words, all vowels, all consonants, letters only, backwards order, every other letter

GUIDED READING

Readers at Level

At level C, readers encounter simple stories and familiar topics; most texts have two to five lines of print on each page. Readers smoothly and automatically move left to right across words and across lines of print, sweeping back to the left margin for each new line and reading print on both left and right pages. Reading becomes smooth, allowing for some expression, and the eyes take over the process of matching the spoken word to the printed word. Readers move away from needing to point and they begin to read in phrases. Readers notice quotation marks and reflect dialogue with the voice. At this level, readers consistently monitor their reading and cross-check one source of information against another. They continue to develop a core of high-frequency words that they recognize quickly and easily, sometimes using multiple sources. Overt self-correction reveals readers' growing control of the ability to process print. Readers use text and pictures to construct the meaning of stories and nonfiction texts. They infer meaning from pictures and connect the meaning of texts to their own experiences. They are able to distinguish stories from factual texts.

Selecting Texts Characteristics of Texts at **Level C**

GENRE

▶ **Fiction**

- Realistic fiction
- Simple retellings of folktales
- Simple fables
- Simple animal fantasy

▶ **Nonfiction**

- Simple factual texts
- Some easy procedural texts

FORMS

- Some series books
- Picture books

TEXT STRUCTURE

- Very simple narratives with beginning, middle, several episodes, and end
- Narrative texts with repetitive episodes
- Texts with repetition of more than one event and language pattern
- Texts with underlying structural patterns: simple description, temporal sequence (nonfiction)

CONTENT

- Content interesting to and relevant for young children
- Familiar, easy content: e.g., family and home, play, pets, animals, school, food, community, friends, daily activities, the human body, weather, seasons, transportation, toys
- Most content directly and explicitly supported by picture information

- Humor that is easy to grasp: e.g., silly characters, funny situations
- A few stories with content familiar to children through prior experiences with storytelling, media, and hearing books read: e.g., folktales and fantasy

THEMES AND IDEAS

- Themes reflecting everyday life: e.g., relationships with family and others, self, nature, similarities and differences, work and play
- Clear, simple ideas easy to identify
- Ideas close to children's experience: e.g., sharing with others, caring for others, doing your job, helping your family, taking care of self, staying healthy, caring for your world, having fun, noticing your world, working and playing with others, learning new things

LANGUAGE AND LITERARY FEATURES

- Simple language patterns that are close to oral language
- Repeating language patterns
- Familiar settings close to children's experience
- Simple plot with problem and solution
- Simple characters that do not change and often have names
- Occasional use of a few words of dialogue, often in a speech bubble, or of unspoken thoughts shown in a thought bubble
- Simple dialogue and dialogue with pronouns (assigned by *said* in many texts)

- A few simple elements of fantasy: e.g., talking animals
- Very simple procedural language

SENTENCE COMPLEXITY

- Short sentences, usually five to ten words
- More than one sentence pattern repeated in the same book
- Simple sentences with subject and predicate
- Some sentences with clauses or phrases
- Subject preceding verb in most sentences
- Some sentences that are questions
- Sentences with adjectives and prepositional phrases
- Some sentences with dialogue

VOCABULARY

- A few words that are new to children but easy to understand in context
- Words for sounds (onomatopoetic)
- All words that are in common oral vocabulary for young children (Tier 1)
- Concept words illustrated by pictures
- Many simple adjectives describing people, places, or things

WORDS

- Mostly one-, two-, and three-syllable words fully supported by the pictures
- Some simple plurals using *-s* or *-es*
- Repeated use of a few easy high-frequency words: e.g., *and, to, up, said, the, here, look, is, it, me, he*

Here is a penguin.

The penguin uses its feet

to hold on to its egg!

14

15

- Verbs with inflectional endings: e.g., *-s, -ing, -ed*
- Many words with easy, predictable letter-sound relationships (decodable)
- Words with easy spelling patterns (VC, CVC, CVCe)
- Some words with apostrophes: e.g., simple contractions and possessives

ILLUSTRATIONS

- Clear illustrations that fully support meaning
- Illustrations that match print very closely
- Illustrations that add meaning to the text
- Illustrations on every page or page spread
- Very simple illustrations with no distracting detail
- Consistent layout of illustrations and print
- Clear separation of illustrations and print
- A few labeled photographs or illustrations

BOOK AND PRINT FEATURES

LENGTH

- Short, usually sixteen pages (eight pages of print)
- Print separate from pictures on alternating pages
- Typically fewer than 100 words per book (50–100)

PRINT AND LAYOUT

- Print in large, plain font
- Print always on white or very pale background
- Two to five lines of text on each page
- Sentences beginning on the left
- Sentences turn over one or more lines
- Consistent placement of print
- Most texts with double or triple spaces between lines
- Exaggerated spaces between words
- Print clearly separated from pictures
- Many texts with layout supporting phrasing

PUNCTUATION

- Use of period, comma, question mark, exclamation mark, and quotation marks
- Ellipses in some texts to indicate that the sentence finishes on the next page

Selecting Goals Behaviors and Understandings to Notice, Teach, and Support

SEARCHING FOR AND USING INFORMATION

- Read left to right across two or three lines of print
- Match word by word over two or three lines of print, with all sentences beginning on the left
- Coordinate eyes and pointing to search for and use visual information in print
- Use return sweep to read the second, third, or fourth line of print on a page
- Reread to search for and use information from language structure or meaning
- Search for and use information from pictures that match the print closely, have few distracting details, and clearly support meaning
- Use clear separation of illustrations and print to search for and use information
- Use consistent layout of illustrations and print to search for and use information
- Use language patterns close to oral language to search for and use information
- Use repeating language patterns to search for and use information
- Use simple sentence structures (subject and predicate with some a few embedded phrases and clauses) to search for and use information
- Sustain searching for information over a short text (usually sixteen pages with two to five lines of print on each page and fewer than 100 words)
- Notice and use punctuation marks (period, comma, quotation marks, exclamation mark, question mark in most texts)
- Notice and use capital and lowercase letters
- Search for and understand information in simple dialogue, dialogue with pronouns (usually assigned by *said*), and some split dialogue
- Use illustrations to search for and use information
- Use labels on photographs to search for and use information
- Use understanding of familiar, easy content to search for and use information: e.g., family and home, play, pets, animals, school, food, community, friends, daily activities, the human body, weather, seasons, transportation, toys
- Understand that the pictures closely and explicitly support the content and use them to search and use information
- Identify a sound and link it to a letter

MONITORING AND SELF-CORRECTING

- Show evidence of close attention to print
- Use voice-print match to self-monitor and self-correct
- Reread the sentence to problem-solve, self-correct, or confirm
- Recognize a letter and use meaning to self-monitor and self-correct
- Use language structure to self-monitor and self-correct
- Use visual features of words to self-monitor and self-correct
- Use recognition of high-frequency words to self-monitor and self-correct
- Use known words to self-monitor and self-correct
- Cross-check one kind of information against another to monitor and self-correct reading (i.e., cross-checking meaning with visual information)
- Cross-check using more than one source (visual information and pictures)
- Use pictures as a resource to self-monitor and self-correct
- Use understanding of how the book works to self-monitor and self-correct
- Use content knowledge of a simple topic to self-monitor and self-correct

SOLVING WORDS

▶ **Reading Words**

- Recognize words in clear, plain font that are on a plain white or very light background
- Recognize a few high-frequency words quickly and easily
- Recognize one-, two-, and some three-syllable words fully supported by the pictures
- Read some simple regular plurals formed with the endings *-s* or *-es* fully supported by pictures and language structure
- Read words that are repeated within the same text: e.g., *is, it, I, am*
- Read a few verbs with inflectional endings (e.g., *-s, -ing*) that are fully supported by pictures and language structure
- Read a few words with apostrophes: e.g., simple contractions and possessives

Selecting Goals Behaviors and Understandings to Notice, Teach, and Support *(cont.)*

THINKING *WITHIN* THE TEXT *(continued)*

- Read a few words with very easy, predictable, and decodable letter-sound relationships
- Read some words with easy spelling patterns with the support of pictures and language (VC, CVC, CVCe)
- Say a word and predict its first letter
- Say a word slowly to hear and identify the first sound and connect that sound to a letter
- Locate easy high-frequency words in a text
- Notice visual features of a word and use them to locate or read the word

▸ Vocabulary

- Understand the meaning of a few words that are new but easy to understand in the context of the text and with picture support
- Expand understanding of the meaning of words by connection with the pictures and/or understanding the context: e.g., *zoo, farm*
- Read and understand a few simple words that stand for sounds (onomatopoetic words)
- Understand vocabulary words that are in common oral vocabulary for emergent readers (Tier 1)
- Understand the meaning of simple regular plurals formed with the endings *-s* or *-es*
- Understand a few simple adjectives describing people, places, or things
- Understand words that indicate characters: e.g., a few easy-to-read names, family members
- Understand words that show the action of the plot: e.g., *play, ride, ran*
- Understand words such as *I* and *me* that may indicate the narrator of a text
- Understand the meaning of simple words that assign dialogue: e.g., *said, asked*
- Recognize and understand labels for familiar objects, animals, people, the human body, weather, daily activities

MAINTAINING FLUENCY

- Sustain momentum through an entire short text
- Read mostly without pointing but with correct voice-print match
- Read at a steady rate, slow enough to match voice to print but without long pauses usually with no pointing
- Begin to read in phrased units
- Notice periods, quotation marks, commas, exclamation marks, and question marks, and begin to reflect them with the voice through intonation and pausing
- Begin to demonstrate stress on words in a way that shows attention to meaning
- Stress words that are in bold
- Reread to notice the language or meaning
- Show recognition of dialogue with some phrasing even when in varying structures: e.g., *said Mom* and *Mom said*

ADJUSTING

- Slow down to problem-solve words and resume reading with momentum
- Understand that a text is fiction and that a story has a beginning, middle, several episodes, and end
- Understand that a nonfiction book gives facts
- Notice labels on photographs

SUMMARIZING

- Remember important information while reading to understand the meaning of the text
- Talk about the important information after reading
- Remember and talk about the important events in a simple story
- Remember and talk about clear, simple ideas that are easy to identify

Selecting Goals Behaviors and Understandings to Notice, Teach, and Support *(cont.)*

THINKING *BEYOND* THE TEXT

PREDICTING

- ◆ Use knowledge of language structure to anticipate the text
- ◆ Make predictions based on information in pictures that closely match the text
- ◆ Predict the ending of a story based on reading the beginning and middle
- ◆ Make predictions based on knowledge of the events of everyday life e.g., family, cooking, play, pets, school, food, community, friends
- ◆ Make predictions based on personal experiences and knowledge: e.g., family and home, play, pets, animals, school, food, community, friends, daily activities, the human body, weather, seasons, transportation, toys

MAKING CONNECTIONS

- ◆ Make connections between personal experience and a text
- ◆ Make connections among books in a series
- ◆ Identify recurring characters or settings when applicable
- ◆ Make connections between background knowledge of familiar content and the content in the text
- ◆ Make connections among texts on the same topic or with the same content

SYNTHESIZING

- ◆ Talk about what is known about the topic before reading the text
- ◆ Talk about what is learned from reading the text
- ◆ Talk about any new labels for content that are learned from the text

INFERRING

- ◆ Infer meaning of story or content from pictures that add meaning to the text
- ◆ Make inferences about where the story takes place (as shown in pictures) to help understand it
- ◆ Talk about characters' feelings inferred from pictures of the story
- ◆ Talk about the pictures, revealing interpretation of a problem or of characters' feelings
- ◆ Infer humor that is easy to grasp: e.g., silly characters, funny situations
- ◆ Infer ideas about familiar content: e.g., friendships, family relationships, self, nature, food, health, community

Selecting Goals Behaviors and Understandings to Notice, Teach, and Support *(cont.)*

THINKING *ABOUT* THE TEXT

ANALYZING

- Understand how the ideas and information in a book are related to each other
- Understand how the events, content, and ideas in a text are related to the title
- Recognize that a text can be imagined (fiction) or it can give information (nonfiction)
- Recognize settings that are familiar: e.g., home, school, neighborhood
- Recognize and follow a chronological sequence of events
- Recognize that there are characters (people or animals in a story)
- Recognize that a text can have animals that act like people
- Use language and pictures to talk about a text (title, beginning, several episodes, ending)
- Recognize that a text can have true information (factual text)
- Understand that a nonfiction book gives facts or tells how to do something

- Recognize that a process happens in time order
- Use some specific language to talk about literary features: e.g., *beginning, ending, problem, character*
- Use some specific language to talk about book and print features: e.g., *front cover, back cover, page, author, illustrator, illustration, photograph, title, label*

CRITIQUING

- Share opinions about a text
- Share opinions about an illustration or photograph

Planning for Letter and Word Work After Guided Reading

Using your recent observations of the readers' ability to take words apart quickly and efficiently while reading text, plan for one to three minutes of active engagement of students' attention to letters, sounds, and words. Prioritize the readers' noticing of print features and active hands-on use of magnetic letters, a white board, word cards, or pencil and paper to promote fluency and flexibility in visual processing.

Examples:

- Recognize a few easy high-frequency words (for example, *all, for, if, one, put*)
- Make and break apart several easy high-frequency words (*look, then, the, so, him, his*)
- Write several easy high-frequency words (*be, day, don't, not*)
- Recognize several CVC words (*bag, yes, fit, got, fun*)
- Make, break apart, or write several CVC words (*bag, yes, fit, got, fun*)

- Hear and divide CVC words into onsets and rimes (*b-ag, y-es, f-it, g-ot, f-un*)
- Say and clap the syllables in one- and two-syllable words (from pictures)
- Match or sort words with rhyming sounds at the end (using pictures)
- Listen for and identify each sound in a few words using sound boxes
- Match or sort pictures with letters by beginning or ending sounds (*goat, garden, girl; run, balloon, fireman*)

- Locate a word by recognizing the first letter and its sound
- Say a word slowly and write the letter or letters related to each sound
- Sort letters by a variety of features quickly—uppercase or lowercase; tall or short, with or without long straight lines, short straight lines, circles, tails, tunnels
- Read the Alphabet Linking Chart in different ways—singing, by letter names, pictures and words, all vowels, all consonants, letters only, backwards order, every other letter

Readers at Level

At level D, readers process and understand simple fiction and fantasy stories and easy informational texts. They can track print with their eyes over two to six lines per page without pointing, and they can process texts with more varied and more complex language patterns. They notice and use a range of punctuation and read dialogue, reflecting the meaning through phrasing, intonation, and appropriate word stress. Readers can solve many easy, regular two-syllable words—usually words with inflectional endings such as *ing* and simple compound words. Pointing may occasionally be used at difficulty, but readers drop the finger when they are confident and are reading easily. The core of known high-frequency words is expanding. Readers consistently monitor their reading, cross-check one source of information with another, and often use multiple sources of information. Readers use text and pictures to construct the meaning of stories and nonfiction texts. They infer meaning from pictures and connect the meaning of texts to their own experiences. At level D, readers process and understand simple and some split dialogue.

Selecting Texts Characteristics of Texts at **Level D**

GENRE

▶ **Fiction**
- Realistic fiction
- Simple retellings of folktales
- Simple fables
- Simple animal fantasy

▶ **Nonfiction**
- Simple factual texts
- Some easy procedural texts

FORMS
- Some series books
- Picture books
- Readers' theater scripts

TEXT STRUCTURE
- Simple narrative with several episodes
- Narrative texts with repetitive episodes
- Variation in narrative structure: e.g., cumulative tales, circular stories
- Texts with underlying structural patterns: description, temporal sequence, question and answer (nonfiction)

CONTENT
- Content interesting to and relevant for young children
- Familiar, easy content: e.g., family and home, play, pets, animals, school, food, community, friends, daily activities, the human body, weather, seasons, transportation, toys

- High level of support provided by picture information
- A few stories with content familiar to children through prior experiences with storytelling, media, and hearing books read: e.g., folktales and fantasy

THEMES AND IDEAS
- Themes reflecting everyday life: e.g., imagination, courage, fears, friendship, family relationships, self, home, nature, growing, behavior, community, first responsibilities, diversity, feelings
- Clear, simple ideas easy to identify
- Ideas close to children's experience: e.g., sharing with others, caring for others, doing your job, helping your family, taking care of self, staying healthy, caring for your world, having fun, noticing your world, working and playing with others, learning new things
- Humor that is easy to grasp: e.g., silly characters, funny situations

LANGUAGE AND LITERARY FEATURES
- Simple language patterns that are close to oral language
- Some repeating language patterns
- Familiar settings close to children's experience
- Simple sequence of events (often repeated)
- Simple plot with problem and solution
- Characters that do not change and often have names

- Some dialogue in speech bubbles or unspoken thoughts shown in thought bubbles
- Simple dialogue and dialogue with pronouns (assigned by *said* in many texts)
- Some use of split dialogue
- A few simple elements of fantasy: e.g., talking animals
- Very simple procedural language

SENTENCE COMPLEXITY
- Short sentences, usually five to ten words
- Several sentence patterns repeated in the same book
- Variety of language structures
- Simple sentences with subject and predicate
- Some sentences with clauses or phrases
- Subject preceding verb in most sentences
- Some sentences that are questions
- Sentences with adjectives, adverbs, and prepositional phrases
- A few sentences beginning with phrases
- Sentences with dialogue

VOCABULARY
- A few words that are new to children but easy to understand in context
- Words for sounds (onomatopoetic)
- Almost all words that are in common oral vocabulary for young children (Tier 1)
- Concept words illustrated by pictures
- Some variation in words used to assign dialogue: e.g., *said, asked*

Elephant jumped.
Her bananas fell
to the ground.

4

5

- Many simple adjectives describing people, places, or things
- A few adverbs describing action
- Simple connectives (words, phrases that clarify relationships and ideas): e.g., *and, but, so, before, after*

WORDS

- Mostly one-, two-, and three-syllable words with high picture support
- Simple plurals using *-s* or *-es*
- Repeated use of more than twenty-five easy high-frequency words
- Verbs with inflectional endings: e.g., *-s, -ing, -ed*
- Many words with easy, predictable letter-sound relationships (decodable)
- Words with easy spelling patterns (VC, CVC, CVC*e*)
- Some words with apostrophes: e.g., simple contractions and possessives
- Simple (common) connectives

ILLUSTRATIONS

- Illustrations of the important story action, content, and ideas in the text
- Illustrations that add meaning to the text

- Illustrations on every page or page spread
- Illustrations with details that add interest but do not distract from focusing on meaning
- Illustrations that add humor
- Some variety of layout in illustrations and print
- Clear separation of illustrations and print
- Labeled photographs and drawings

BOOK AND PRINT FEATURES

LENGTH

- Short, usually sixteen pages
- Typically fewer than 150 words per book (100–150)

PRINT AND LAYOUT

- Print in large, plain font
- Print always on white or very pale background
- Mostly two to six lines of text on each page
- Sentences beginning on the left
- Sentences turn over one or more lines
- Consistent placement of print
- Most texts with double or triple spaces between lines
- Exaggerated spaces between words

- Print clearly separated from pictures
- Many texts with layout supporting phrasing

PUNCTUATION

- Use of period, comma, question mark, exclamation mark, and quotation marks
- Ellipses in some texts to indicate that the sentence finishes on the next page

LEVEL

D

Selecting Goals Behaviors and Understandings to Notice, Teach, and Support

THINKING *WITHIN* THE TEXT

SEARCHING FOR AND USING INFORMATION

- Read left to right across three to six lines of print
- Match word by word over three to six lines of print, with all sentences beginning on the left
- Coordinate eyes and pointing to search for and use visual information in print
- Use return sweep to read several lines of print after the first line
- Reread to search for and use information from language structure or meaning
- Search for and use information from pictures that match the print closely, have few distracting details, and clearly support meaning
- Use clear separation of illustrations and print to search for and use information
- Use consistent layout of illustrations and print to search for and use information
- Use language patterns close to oral language to search for and use information
- Recognize more than one repeating language pattern in a text and use to search for information
- Use simple sentence structures (subject and predicate with some embedded phrases and clauses) to search for and use information
- Sustain searching for information over a short text (usually sixteen pages with two to six lines of print on each page and fewer than 150 words)
- Search for and use information that appears in beginning and ending phrases
- Notice and use punctuation marks (period, comma, question mark, exclamation mark, and quotation marks in most texts)
- Notice and use capital and lowercase letters
- Search for and understand information in simple dialogue (sometimes in speech bubbles), unspoken thoughts in thought bubbles, dialogue with pronouns (often assigned by *said*), and split dialogue
- Search for information in a text that has no repeating language patterns
- Use the chronological order of a simple story to search for and use information
- Use details in the illustrations to search for and use information
- Use labels on photographs to search for and use information
- Use background understanding of familiar, easy content to search for and use information: e.g., family and home, play, pets, animals, school, food, community, friends, daily activities, the human body, weather, seasons, transportation, toys
- Understand that the pictures closely and explicitly support the content and use them to search for and use information

MONITORING AND SELF-CORRECTING

- Show evidence of close attention to print
- Use voice-print match to self-monitor and self-correct over three to six lines of print
- Reread the sentence to problem-solve, self-correct, or confirm
- Use language structure to self-monitor and self-correct
- Use visual features of words to self-monitor and self-correct
- Use recognition of high-frequency words to self-monitor and self-correct
- Reread the sentence to problem-solve, self-correct, or confirm
- Consistently cross-check one kind of information against another to monitor and self-correct reading (i.e., cross-checking meaning with visual information)
- Cross-check using more than one source (visual information and pictures)
- Use two or more sources of information (meaning, language structure, visual information) to self-monitor and self-correct
- Drop finger pointing when confident in reading a text but occasionally bring it back to monitor or confirm when encountering difficulty
- Use pictures as a resource to self-monitor and self-correct
- Use understanding of how the book works to self-monitor and self-correct
- Use understanding of characters to self-monitor and self-correct
- Use understanding of dialogue to self-monitor and self-correct
- Use content knowledge of a simple topic to self-monitor and self-correct
- Use knowledge from pictures to self-monitor and self-correct

SOLVING WORDS

▶ **Reading Words**

- Recognize words in clear, plain font that are on a white or very light background
- Recognize more than twenty-five high-frequency words quickly and easily
- Recognize one-, two-, and some three-syllable words fully supported by the pictures
- Read some simple regular plurals formed with the endings *-s* or *-es* that are fully supported by pictures and language structure
- Read words that are repeated within the same text: e.g., *am, like, we, this, look, said, here, my, she, come*
- Read verbs with inflectional endings (e.g., *-s, -ing, -ed*) fully supported by pictures and language structure
- Read words with very easy, predictable, and decodable letter-sound relationships

Selecting Goals Behaviors and Understandings to Notice, Teach, and Support *(cont.)*

THINKING *WITHIN* THE TEXT *(continued)*

- Read words with easy spelling patterns with the support of pictures and language (VC, CVC, CVC*e*)
- Say a word and predict its first letter
- Locate easy high-frequency words in a text: e.g., *and, to, up, said, with*
- Notice visual features of a word and use them to locate or read the word
- Read some words containing apostrophes (simple contractions and possessives)
- Read simple words that assign dialogue: e.g., *said, asked*
- Read simple connectives

▶ Vocabulary

- Understand the meaning of some words that are new but easy to understand in the context of the text and with picture support
- Expand understanding of the meaning of words by connection with the pictures and/or understanding the context: e.g., *zoo, farm, circus*
- Read and understand a few simple words that stand for sounds (onomatopoetic words)
- Understand vocabulary words that are in common oral vocabulary for early readers (Tier 1)
- Understand the meaning of simple regular plurals formed with the endings *-s* or *-es*
- Understand a few simple adjectives describing people, places, or things
- Understand simple contractions using an apostrophe and letters from the word *not*
- Understand words with an apostrophe indicating possession
- Understand some words that require the use of multiple sources of information (background knowledge, pictures, visual information)
- Understand words that indicate characters: e.g., easy-to-read names, family members, community members such as teachers
- Understand words that show the action of the plot: e.g., verbs such as *is, go, run, ran, like, ride, can*
- Understand words such as *I, me,* and *we* that may indicate the narrator of a text
- Understand the meaning of simple words that assign dialogue: e.g., *said, asked*
- Read and understand the meaning of simple connectives
- Recognize and understand labels for familiar objects, animals, people, the human body, weather, daily activities, simple processes such as cooking or growing plants
- Use details in illustrations to understand new vocabulary

MAINTAINING FLUENCY

- Sustain momentum through an entire short text
- Read mostly without pointing but with correct voice-print match
- Notice periods, quotation marks, commas, exclamation marks, and question marks, and begin to reflect them with the voice through intonation and pausing
- Read with phrasing
- Demonstrate stress on words in a way that shows attention to meaning
- Stress words that are in bold
- Reread to notice the language or meaning
- Show recognition of dialogue with some phrasing even when in varying structures: e.g., *said Mom* and *Mom said*
- Recognize and use ellipses in some texts to show that a sentence finishes on the next page

ADJUSTING

- Slow down to problem-solve words and resume reading with momentum
- Recognize that a text is fiction and tells a story with a beginning, middle, several episodes, and end
- Understand that a nonfiction book gives facts
- Notice labels on photographs and use them to understand the words in the text
- Adjust reading to notice information in photographs
- Adjust to accommodate some variety in layout of illustrations and print

SUMMARIZING

- Remember important information while reading to understand the meaning of the text
- Talk about the important information after reading
- Remember the order of events in a simple story and talk about them after reading
- Summarize the problem in a simple story and talk about the solution
- Remember and talk about clear, simple ideas that are easy to identify
- Understand when sequence is important (e.g., cooking, planting) and talk about events or steps in order

LEVEL **D**

Selecting Goals Behaviors and Understandings to Notice, Teach, and Support *(cont.)*

GUIDED READING

THINKING *BEYOND* THE TEXT

PREDICTING

◆ Use varied language structures to anticipate the text

◆ Make predictions based on information in pictures that closely match the text

◆ Predict the ending of a story based on reading the beginning and middle

◆ Make predictions based on knowledge of the events of everyday life: e.g., family, cooking, play, pets, school, food, community, friends

◆ Make predictions based on understanding a simple sequence of events with a problem and outcome

◆ Make predictions based on personal experiences and knowledge: e.g., family and home, play, pets, animals, school, food, community, friends, daily activities, the human body, weather, seasons, transportations, toys

◆ Make predictions based on a temporal sequence: e.g., plants growing, eggs hatching, weather changing, food cooking

MAKING CONNECTIONS

◆ Make connections between personal experience and a text

◆ Make connections among books in a series

◆ Use background knowledge to understand settings: e.g., home, school, park, community

◆ Identify recurring characters or settings when applicable

◆ Bring background knowledge of traditional literature to recognize common characters and events in a folktale

◆ Use background knowledge to understand settings close to children's experience: e.g., home, school, park, community, and (if applicable) beach and snow

◆ Make connections between background knowledge of familiar content and the content in the text

◆ Make connections among texts on the same topic or with the same content

◆ Access background knowledge to understand simple processes: e.g., ice melting, food cooking, building an object

SYNTHESIZING

◆ Talk about what is known about the topic before reading the text

◆ Talk about the text, showing understanding of events or topic

◆ Talk about the events of a simple plot

◆ Talk about what is learned about characters and problems in a story

◆ Talk about any new labels for content that are learned from the text

◆ Identify new knowledge gained when reading a text

INFERRING

◆ Infer meaning of story or content from pictures that add meaning to the text

◆ Make inferences about where the story takes place (as shown in pictures) to help understand it

◆ Talk about characters' feelings based on inference from pictures and text, especially dialogue

◆ Talk about the pictures, revealing interpretation of a problem or of characters' feelings

◆ Infer humor that is easy to grasp: e.g., silly characters, funny situations

◆ Infer some obvious character traits from the story and pictures: e.g., kind, brave, funny

◆ Infer ideas about familiar content: e.g., friendships, family relationships, self, nature, food, health, community

◆ Infer simple processes by noticing the steps: cooking, water freezing, plants growing

Selecting Goals Behaviors and Understandings to Notice, Teach, and Support *(cont.)*

THINKING *ABOUT* THE TEXT

ANALYZING

- Understand how the ideas and information in a book are related to each other
- Understand how the events, content, and ideas in a text are related to the title
- Recognize that a text can be imagined (fiction) or it can give information (nonfiction)
- Understand that a story can be like real life or can be something that could not be true in real life (fantasy)
- Recognize settings that are familiar: e.g., home, school, neighborhood
- Recognize and follow a chronological sequence of events
- Identify a simple story problem and how it is resolved
- Recognize and understand variety in narrative structure: e.g., cumulative tale, circular story
- Recognize that there are characters (people or animals in a story)
- Recognize characters that are typical of animal fantasy or traditional literature
- Notice that illustrations add to important story action
- Use language and pictures to talk about a text (title, beginning, several episodes, ending)

- Recognize that a text can have true information
- Understand that a nonfiction book gives facts or tells how to do something
- Recognize that a process happens in time order
- Understand that illustrations and photographs add to the ideas and information in a text
- Use some specific language to talk about types of texts: e.g., *family, friends, and school story*
- Use some specific language to talk about literary features: e.g., *beginning, ending, problem, character*
- Use some specific language to talk about book and print features: e.g., *front cover, back cover, page, author, illustrator, illustration, photograph, title, label*

CRITIQUING

- Share opinions about a text
- Share opinions about an illustration or photograph
- Have favorite books and say why

Planning for Letter and Word Work After Guided Reading

Using your recent observations of the readers' ability to take words apart quickly and efficiently while reading text, plan for one to three minutes of active engagement of students' attention to letters, sounds, and words. Prioritize the readers' noticing of print features and active hands-on use of magnetic letters, a white board, word cards, or pencil and paper to promote fluency and flexibility in visual processing.

Examples:

- Recognize a few easy high-frequency words quickly (for example, *as, by, came, get, had, her, his, out*)
- Make or write high-frequency words quickly (*make, this, but, come, him, his*)
- Review making and breaking apart high-frequency words from previous levels
- Recognize and break apart several CVC words easily and quickly (*man, pet, hit, box, cut*)
- Make, break apart, or write several CVC words quickly (*man, pet, hit, box, cut*)
- Hear and divide CVC words into onsets and rimes (*m an, p et, h it, b ox, c ut*)

- Add *-s* to a singular noun to make a plural noun and read it (*dog/dogs*)
- Say and clap the syllables in one-, two-, and three-syllable words (from pictures)
- Listen for and identify each sound in a few words using sound boxes
- Change the beginning phoneme of a word to make a different one-syllable word (*day, may*)
- Change the ending phoneme of a word to make a different one-syllable word (*men, met*)

- Match pictures with letters by beginning or ending sounds (*farm, flower, frog; book, milk, park*)
- Sort letters quickly by a variety of features–uppercase or lowercase; tall or short; with or without long straight lines, short straight lines, circles, tails
- Read the Alphabet Linking Chart in different ways–singing, by letter names, pictures and words, all vowels, all consonants, letters only, backwards order, every other letter

GUIDED READING

LEVEL **D**

Readers at Level E

At level E, readers encounter texts that usually have up to eight lines of print on most pages. They are flexible enough to process texts with varied placement of print and a wide range of punctuation. Texts have more complex stories and require more attention to understand, but other processes, for example, tracking print, are becoming automatic for readers. They take apart longer words with inflectional endings and read some sentences that carry over two to three lines or even across two pages. Readers rely much more on the print as the illustrations, while supportive, are not sufficient to predict the story. Left-to-right directionality and voice-print match are automatic and effortless, and oral reading demonstrates fluency and phrasing with appropriate stress on words. They read without pointing, bringing in the finger only occasionally at difficulty. Readers recognize a large number of high-frequency words and easily solve words with regular letter-sound relationships as well as a few irregular words. At level E in fiction, readers follow simple plots, read dialogue, understand a story problem, and notice when the problem is solved. They understand that stories can be make-believe. In nonfiction, they explore familiar topics but begin to learn some new content (for example, something interesting about an animal). They make consistent use of the meaning in pictures.

Selecting Texts Characteristics of Texts at **Level E**

GENRE

▶ **Fiction**
- Realistic fiction
- Simple retellings of folktales
- Simple fables
- Simple animal fantasy

▶ **Nonfiction**
- Variety of expository texts on easy topics
- Procedural texts

FORMS
- Some series books
- Picture books
- Simple plays
- Readers' theater scripts

TEXT STRUCTURE
- Simple narratives with beginning, series of episodes, and ending
- Narrative texts with repetitive episodes
- Variation in narrative structure: e.g., cumulative tales, circular stories
- Underlying structural patterns: description, temporal sequence, chronological sequence, question and answer (nonfiction)

CONTENT
- Content interesting to and relevant for young children
- Familiar, easy content: e.g., family and home, play, pets, animals, school, food, community, friends, daily activities, the human body, weather, seasons, transportation, toys
- High level of support provided by picture information
- A few stories with content familiar to children through prior experiences with storytelling, media, and hearing books read: e.g., folktales and fantasy
- Some content that goes beyond children's immediate experience

THEMES AND IDEAS
- Concrete themes close to children's experience: e.g., imagination, courage, fears, friendship, family relationships, self, home, nature, growing, behavior, community, first responsibilities, diversity, belonging, peer relationships, feelings
- Clear, simple ideas easy to identify
- Ideas close to children's experience: e.g., sharing with others, caring for others, doing your job, helping your family, taking care of self, staying healthy, caring for your world, empathizing with others, problem solving, valuing differences, expressing feelings
- Humor that is easy to understand

LANGUAGE AND LITERARY FEATURES
- Simple language patterns that are close to oral language
- A few repeating or alternating language patterns
- Texts with familiar settings close to children's experience
- Simple sequence of events (sometimes repeated)
- Simple plot with problem and solution
- Characters that do not change, most with names
- Simple dialogue and dialogue with pronouns (assigned by *said* in many texts)
- Frequent use of split dialogue
- A few simple elements of fantasy: e.g., talking animals
- Very simple procedural language

SENTENCE COMPLEXITY
- Some longer sentences with more than ten words
- Simple sentences with subject and predicate
- Variety of language structures
- Sentences with clauses or phrases
- Sentences that are questions
- Sentences with adjectives, adverbs, and prepositional phrases
- Sentences beginning with phrases
- Sentences with dialogue

The coconut rolls
in the waves.

The coconut won't stay
in the waves
for very long.

6

7

VOCABULARY

- A few words that are new to children but easy to understand in context
- Words for sounds (onomatopoetic)
- Almost all words that are in common oral vocabulary for young children (Tier 1)
- Concept words illustrated by pictures
- Some variation in words used to assign dialogue: e.g., *said, asked*
- Many simple adjectives describing people, places, or things
- Adverbs describing action
- Simple connectives (words, phrases that clarify relationships and ideas): e.g., *and, but, so, before, after*

WORDS

- Mostly one-, two-, and three-syllable words with high picture support
- Simple plurals using *-s* or *-es*
- A variety of high-frequency words (50+)
- Verbs with inflectional endings: e.g., *-s, -ing, -ed*
- Many words with easy, predictable letter-sound relationships (decodable)
- Words with easy spelling patterns (VC, CVC, CVV, CVC*e*, CVVC, VC*e*)
- Simple contractions: e.g., words formed with *am, not,* and *is*
- Simple possessives: e.g., *cat's nose*
- Simple (common) connectives

ILLUSTRATIONS

- Illustrations of the important story action, content, and ideas in the text
- Illustrations that add meaning to the text
- Illustrations with details that add interest but do not distract from focusing on meaning
- Illustrations that add humor
- Illustrations on every page or page spread
- Some variety of layout in illustrations and print
- Clear separation of illustrations and print
- Labeled photographs and drawings

BOOK AND PRINT FEATURES

LENGTH

- Short, usually sixteen pages
- Typically fewer than 250 words per book (150–250)

PRINT AND LAYOUT

- Print in large, plain font
- Print always on white or very pale background
- Mostly two to eight lines of text on each page
- Sentences beginning on the left
- Sentences turn over one or more lines
- Some limited variation in print placement
- Most texts with double or triple spaces between lines
- Exaggerated spaces between words
- Print clearly separated from pictures
- Many texts with layout supporting phrasing

PUNCTUATION

- Use of period, comma, question mark, exclamation mark, and quotation marks
- Ellipses in some texts to indicate that the sentence finishes on the next page

LEVEL
E

Selecting Goals Behaviors and Understandings to Notice, Teach, and Support

THINKING *WITHIN* THE TEXT

SEARCHING FOR AND USING INFORMATION

- Read left to right across three to eight lines of print
- Match word by word over three to eight lines of print, with all sentences beginning on the left
- Use return sweep to read several lines of print after the first line
- Reread to search for and use information from language structure or meaning
- Search for and use information from pictures that match the print closely, have few distracting details, and clearly support meaning
- Use clear separation of illustrations and print to search for and use information
- Use consistent layout of illustrations and print to search for and use information
- Use language patterns close to oral language to search for and use information
- Recognize more than one repeating language pattern in a text and use to search for information
- Use simple sentence structures (subject and predicate with some embedded phrases and clauses) to search for and use information
- Sustain searching for information over a short text (usually sixteen pages with two to eight lines of print on each page and typically fewer than 250 words)
- Search for and use information that appears in beginning and ending phrases or clauses
- Notice and use punctuation marks (period, comma, question mark, exclamation mark, and quotation marks in most texts)
- Search for information in sentences with clauses or phrases
- Search for information in simple sentences (both statements and questions)
- Search for and understand information in simple dialogue, dialogue with pronouns (often assigned by *said*), split dialogue, and some long stretches of dialogue
- Search for information in a text that has no repeating language patterns
- Use the chronological order of a simple story to search for and use information
- Use details in the illustrations (sometimes with speech bubbles or thought bubbles) to search for and use information
- Use labels on photographs or illustrations to search for and use information
- Use background understanding of familiar, easy content to search for and use information: e.g., family and home, play, pets, animals, school, food, community, friends, daily activities, the human body, weather, seasons, seasons, transportation, toys
- Understand that the pictures closely and explicitly support the content and use them to search and use information

MONITORING AND SELF-CORRECTING

- Show evidence of close attention to visual features of words
- Use voice-print match to self-monitor and self-correct over three to eight lines of print
- Reread a sentence to problem-solve, self-correct, or confirm
- Self-correct close to the point of error (repeating to beginning of paragraph or sentence)
- Use visual features of words to self-monitor and self-correct
- Use recognition of high-frequency words to self-monitor and self-correct
- Use known words to self-monitor and self-correct
- Use some repeating language patterns to search for and use information
- Consistently cross-check one kind of information against another to monitor and self-correct reading (i.e., cross-checking meaning with visual information)
- Use multiple sources of information (visual information in print, meaning/pictures, language structure) to monitor and self-correct
- Bring back finger pointing occasionally as needed to monitor or confirm when encountering difficulty
- Use pictures as a resource to self-monitor and self-correct
- Use understanding of how the book works (narrative structure) to self-monitor and self-correct
- Use understanding of characters to self-monitor and self-correct
- Use understanding of dialogue to self-monitor and self-correct
- Use content knowledge of a simple topic to self-monitor and self-correct
- Use information from pictures to self-monitor and self-correct

SOLVING WORDS

▶ **Reading Words**

- Recognize words in clear, plain font that are on a plain white or very light background
- Recognize fifty or more high-frequency words quickly and easily
- Recognize one-, two-, and some three-syllable words mostly supported by the pictures
- Read some simple regular plurals formed with the endings *-s* or *-es* that are fully supported by pictures and language structure
- Read verbs with inflectional endings (e.g., *-s, -ing, -ed*) fully supported by pictures and language structure
- Read words with very easy, predictable, and decodable letter-sound relationships
- Read some words with easy spelling patterns with the support of pictures and language (VC, CVC, CVC*e*, CVV, CVVC, VC*e*)
- Say a word and predict its first letter(s)
- Locate high-frequency words and other important words in a text

Selecting Goals Behaviors and Understandings to Notice, Teach, and Support *(cont.)*

THINKING *WITHIN* THE TEXT *(continued)*

- Say a word slowly to identify the sounds in a word (beginning, ending, middle)
- Notice visual features of a word and use them to locate or read the word
- Read some simple contractions and possessive nouns (words with apostrophes)
- Read simple words that assign dialogue: e.g., *said, asked*
- Read simple connectives

▶ Vocabulary

- Understand the meaning of some words that are new but easy to understand in the context of the text and with picture support
- Expand understanding of the meaning of words by connection with the pictures and/or understanding the context
- Read and understand words that stand for sounds (onomatopoetic words)
- Understand vocabulary words that are in common oral vocabulary for early readers (Tier 1)
- Understand the meaning of simple regular plurals formed with the endings *-s* or *-es*
- Understand the meaning of simple adjectives describing people, places, or things
- Understand simple contractions using an apostrophe and one or more letters from words such as *not, am, are, is, has,* and *will*
- Understand words with an apostrophe indicating possession
- Understand some words that require the use of multiple sources of information (background knowledge, pictures, visual information)
- Understand words that indicate characters: e.g., easy-to-read names, family members, community members such as teachers
- Understand words such as *I, me,* and *we* that may indicate the narrator of a text
- Understand the meaning of simple words that assign dialogue: e.g., *said, asked*
- Read and understand the meaning of simple connectives
- Recognize and understand labels for familiar objects, animals, people, the human body, weather, daily activities, simple processes such as cooking or growing plants
- Use details in illustrations or photographs to understand new vocabulary

MAINTAINING FLUENCY

- Sustain momentum through an entire short text
- Read without pointing but with correct voice-print match
- Notice periods, quotation marks, commas, exclamation marks, and question marks, and begin to reflect them with the voice through intonation and pausing
- Read with phrasing usually with a layout designed to support phrasing
- Demonstrate stress on words in a way that shows attention to meaning
- Stress words that are in bold
- Reread to notice the language or meaning
- Show recognition of dialogue with some phrasing even when in varying structures: e.g., *said Mom* and *Mom said*
- Recognize and use ellipses in some texts to indicate when a sentence finishes on the next page

ADJUSTING

- Slow down to problem-solve words and resume reading with momentum
- Recognize that a text is fiction and tells a story that has a beginning, middle, series of episodes, and end
- Understand that a nonfiction book gives facts
- Notice labels on photographs and use them to understand the words in the text
- Adjust reading to notice information in photographs
- Adjust to accommodate some variety in layout of illustrations and print
- Adjust reading to reflect a series of steps in an easy procedural book

SUMMARIZING

- Remember important information while reading to understand the meaning of the text
- Talk about the important information after reading
- Remember the order of events in a simple story and talk about them after reading
- Summarize the problem in a simple story and talk about the solution
- Remember and talk about clear, simple ideas that are easy to identify
- Understand when sequence is important (e.g., cooking, planting) and talk about events or steps in order

Selecting Goals Behaviors and Understandings to Notice, Teach, and Support *(cont.)*

GUIDED READING

THINKING *BEYOND* THE TEXT

PREDICTING

- ◆ Use varied language structures to anticipate the text
- ◆ Make predictions based on information in pictures that closely match the text
- ◆ Make predictions based on knowledge and personal experience
- ◆ Predict the ending of a story based on reading the beginning and middle
- ◆ Make predictions based on knowledge of the events of everyday life: e.g., family, cooking, play, pets, school, food, community, friends
- ◆ Make predictions based on a temporal sequence: e.g., plants growing, eggs hatching, weather changing, food cooking

MAKING CONNECTIONS

- ◆ Make connections between personal experience and a text
- ◆ Make connections among books in a series
- ◆ Use background knowledge to understand settings: e.g., home, school, park, community
- ◆ Identify recurring characters or settings when applicable
- ◆ Bring background knowledge of traditional literature to recognize common characters and events in a folktale
- ◆ Use background knowledge to understand settings close to children's experience: e.g., home, school, park, community, and (if applicable) beach and snow
- ◆ Make connections between background knowledge of familiar content and the content in the text
- ◆ Make connections among texts on the same topic or with the same content
- ◆ Access background knowledge to understand simple processes: e.g., ice melting, food cooking, building an object

SYNTHESIZING

- ◆ Talk about what is known about the topic before reading the text
- ◆ Talk about the text, showing understanding of events or topic
- ◆ Talk about the events of a simple plot
- ◆ Talk about what is learned about characters and problems in a story
- ◆ Talk about any new labels for content that are learned from the text
- ◆ Identify new knowledge gained when reading texts

INFERRING

- ◆ Infer meaning of story or content from pictures that add meaning to the text
- ◆ Make inferences about where the story takes place (as shown in pictures) to help understand it
- ◆ Talk about characters' feelings based on inference from pictures and text, especially dialogue
- ◆ Talk about the pictures, revealing interpretation of a problem or of characters' feelings
- ◆ Infer humor that is easy to grasp: e.g., silly characters, funny situations
- ◆ Infer some obvious character traits from the story and pictures: e.g., kind, brave, funny
- ◆ Infer ideas about familiar content
- ◆ Infer simple processes by noticing the steps: cooking, water freezing, plants growing

LEVEL E

Selecting Goals Behaviors and Understandings to Notice, Teach, and Support *(cont.)*

THINKING *ABOUT* THE TEXT

ANALYZING

- Understand how the ideas and information in a book are related to each other
- Understand how the events, content, and ideas in a text are related to the title
- Recognize that a text can be imagined (fiction) or it can give information (nonfiction)
- Understand that a story can be like real life or can be something that could not be true in real life (fantasy)
- Recognize settings that are familiar: e.g., home, school, neighborhood
- Recognize and follow a chronological sequence of events
- Identify a simple story problem and how it is resolved
- Recognize and understand variety in narrative structure: e.g., cumulative tale, circular story
- Recognize that there are characters (people or animals in a story)
- Recognize characters that are typical of animal fantasy or traditional literature
- Notice a writer's use of humorous words or onomatopoetic words and talk about how they add to the action
- Notice that illustrations add to important story action
- Recognize that a text can have true information

- Understand that a nonfiction book gives facts or tells how to do something
- Recognize that a process happens in time order
- Recognize very simple procedural language (directions)
- Understand that illustrations and photographs add to the ideas and information in a text
- Use some specific language to talk about types of texts: e.g., *fiction; family, friends, and school story; nonfiction; informational text; informational book; factual text*
- Use some beginning academic language to talk about forms: e.g., *series book*
- Use some beginning academic language to talk about literary features: e.g., *beginning, ending, problem, character*
- Use some specific language to talk about book and print features: e.g., *front cover, back cover, page, author, illustrator, illustration, photograph, title, label, drawing*

CRITIQUING

- Share opinions about a text
- Share opinions about an illustration or photograph
- Have favorite books and say why

Planning for Letter and Word Work After Guided Reading

Using your recent observations of the readers' ability to take words apart quickly and efficiently while reading text, plan for one to three minutes of active engagement of students' attention to letters, sounds, and words. Prioritize the readers' noticing of print features and active hands-on use of magnetic letters, a white board, word cards, or pencil and paper to promote fluency and flexibility in visual processing.

Examples:

- Recognize many easy high-frequency words (for example, *but, did, little, now, our, said, that, us*)
- Make, break apart, or write many high-frequency words (for example, *away, been, have, into, very, was, your*)
- Review high-frequency words from previous levels
- Make, break apart, or write words using VC (*if*), CVC (*hen*), and CVCe (*take*) patterns
- Build and break apart words quickly with magnetic letters

- Add *-s* or *-es* to a singular noun to make a plural noun (*basket/baskets, lunch/lunches*)
- Break apart one-syllable words that begin with a consonant or a consonant cluster into onsets and rimes (*bl-ack, st-ep, f-ish, st-op, j-ust*)
- Listen for and identify each sound in a few words using sound boxes
- Change the beginning phoneme to make a new word, and change the ending phoneme to make a new word (*not, hot; his, him*)

- Change the middle phoneme in a word with three phonemes to make a new word (*bag, big*)
- Say a word slowly and write the letter or letters related to each sound
- Sort letters quickly by a variety of features–uppercase or lowercase; tall or short; with or without long straight lines, short straight lines, circles, tails
- Read the Consonant Cluster Linking Chart in different ways–all words, backwards order, every other box

GUIDED READING

Readers at Level **F**

At level F, readers are building implicit knowledge of the characteristics of different genres of texts. They can read stretches of both simple and split dialogue. They quickly and automatically recognize a large number of high-frequency words and use letter/sound information to take apart simple regular words as well as some multisyllable words while reading. They recognize and use inflectional endings, plurals, contractions, and possessives. They can also process and understand syntax that largely reflects patterns particular to written language. In fiction, readers begin to encounter dialogue among multiple characters in stories with multiple episodes. In informational texts, they learn new facts about topics. They read without pointing and with appropriate rate, pausing, phrasing, intonation, and word stress. Level F presents texts with dialogue, some of it unassigned. In fiction, readers follow simple plots, identify and understand a story problem, and search for meaning in the text and in pictures. Characters may "learn a lesson" in a story, and readers can notice character attributes and infer feelings. In nonfiction, they explore familiar topics but continue to learn some new content (for example, names of animals and/or something interesting about them). They notice recurring characters when they read books in a series.

Selecting Texts Characteristics of Texts at **Level F**

GENRE

▶ **Fiction**

- Realistic fiction
- Simple retellings of folktales
- Simple fables
- Simple animal fantasy

▶ **Nonfiction**

- Variety of expository texts on easy topics
- Procedural texts

FORMS

- Some series books
- Picture books
- Simple plays
- Readers' theater scripts

TEXT STRUCTURE

- Simple narratives with beginning, series of episodes, and ending
- Narrative texts with repetitive episodes
- Variation in narrative structure: e.g., cumulative tales, circular stories
- Underlying structural patterns: description, temporal sequence, chronological sequence, question and answer

CONTENT

- Content interesting to and relevant for young children
- Familiar, easy content: e.g., family and home, play, pets, animals, school, food, community, friends, daily activities, the human body, weather, seasons, transportation, toys
- Moderate level of support provided by picture information
- A few stories with content familiar to children through prior experiences with storytelling, media, and hearing books read: e.g., folktales and fantasy
- Some content that goes beyond children's immediate experience

THEMES AND IDEAS

- Concrete themes close to children's experience: e.g., imagination, courage, fears, friendship, family relationships, self, home, nature, growing, behavior, community, first responsibilities, diversity, belonging, peer relationships, feelings
- Clear, simple ideas easy to identify
- Ideas close to children's experience: e.g., sharing with others, caring for others, doing your job, helping your family, taking care of self, staying healthy, caring for your world, empathizing with others, problem solving, valuing differences, expressing feelings
- Humor that is easy to understand

LANGUAGE AND LITERARY FEATURES

- A few repeating or alternating language patterns
- Texts with familiar settings close to children's experience
- Simple sequence of events
- Plot with conflict and resolution
- Characters that do not change
- Most characters with names
- Dialogue with pronouns, and split dialogue
- Dialogue usually assigned to speaker
- A few instances of unassigned dialogue
- Dialogue among multiple characters
- A few elements of fantasy: e.g., talking animals
- Procedural language

SENTENCE COMPLEXITY

- Some longer sentences with more than ten words
- Sentences with subject and predicate, both statements and questions
- Variation in placement of subject, verb, adjectives, and adverbs
- Sentences with clauses or phrases
- Sentences with adjectives, adverbs, and prepositional phrases
- Sentences beginning with phrases
- Sentences with dialogue

Brother said, "Stand on your head, Grandpa. Those hiccups will stop." Grandpa stood on his head. But he still had the hiccups.

8

9

VOCABULARY

- A few words that are new to children but easy to understand in context
- Words for sounds (onomatopoetic)
- Almost all words that are in common oral vocabulary for young children (Tier 1)
- Concept words illustrated by pictures
- Some variation in words used to assign dialogue: e.g., *said, asked, cried*
- Many simple adjectives describing people, places, or things
- Adverbs describing action
- Simple connectives (words, phrases that clarify relationships and ideas): e.g., *and, but, so, before, after*

WORDS

- Mostly one-, two-, and three-syllable words with high picture support
- Simple plurals using *-s* or *-es*
- Some irregular plurals: e.g., *mice*
- A variety of high-frequency words (50+)
- Verbs with inflectional endings: e.g., *-s, -ing, -ed*
- Many words with easy, predictable letter-sound relationships (decodable)
- Words with easy spelling patterns (VC, CVC, CVV, CVCe, CVVC, VCe)

- Simple contractions: e.g., words formed with *am, not,* and *is*
- Simple possessives: e.g., *cat's nose*
- Simple (common) connectives

ILLUSTRATIONS

- Illustrations of the important story action, content, and ideas in the text
- Illustrations that add meaning and humor to the text
- Illustrations with details that add interest but are not distracting
- Illustrations on every page or page spread
- Some variety of layout in illustrations and print
- Clear separation of illustrations and print
- Labeled photographs and drawings

BOOK AND PRINT FEATURES

LENGTH

- Short, usually sixteen pages
- Typically fewer than 300 words per book (150–300)

PRINT AND LAYOUT

- Print in large, plain font
- Print always on white or very pale background

- Mostly three to eight lines of text per page
- Sentences beginning on the left
- Sentences turn over one or more lines
- Some limited variation in print placement
- Most texts with double or triple spaces between lines
- Clear spaces between words
- Print clearly separated from pictures
- Many texts with layout supporting phrasing

PUNCTUATION

- Use of period, comma, question mark, exclamation mark, and quotation marks
- Ellipses in some texts to indicate that the sentence finishes on the next page

LEVEL **F**

Selecting Goals Behaviors and Understandings to Notice, Teach, and Support

THINKING *WITHIN* THE TEXT

SEARCHING FOR AND USING INFORMATION

- Sustain searching for information over a short text (usually sixteen pages with three to eight lines of print on each page and fewer than 300 words)
- Use background understanding of familiar, easy content to search for and use information: e.g., family and home, play, pets, animals, school, food, community, friends, daily activities, the human body, weather, seasons, seasons, transportation, toys
- Reread to search for and use information from language structure or meaning
- Use simple sentence structures (subject and predicate with some embedded phrases and clauses) to search for and use information
- Search for and use information that appears in beginning and ending phrases or clauses
- Search for information in simple sentences (both statements and questions)
- Search for information in sentences with variation in placement of subject, verb, adjectives, and adverbs
- Search for and understand information in simple dialogue, dialogue with pronouns, split dialogue, assigned or unassigned dialogue, dialogue among multiple characters, and some long stretches of dialogue
- Use the chronological order of a simple story to search for and use information
- Notice and use punctuation marks (period, comma, question mark, exclamation mark, and quotation marks in most texts)
- Search for and use information from pictures that match the print closely, have few distracting details, and clearly support meaning
- Understand that the pictures closely and explicitly support the content and use pictures to search and use information
- Use labels or captions on photographs or graphics to search for information
- Use details in the illustrations to search for and use information

MONITORING AND SELF-CORRECTING

- Sometimes reread the sentence or phrase to problem-solve, self-correct, or confirm
- Self-correct close to the point of error
- Use visual features of words to self-monitor and self-correct
- Use recognition of high-frequency words and other known words to self-monitor and self-correct

- Use multiple sources of information (visual information in print, meaning/pictures, language structure) to monitor and self-correct
- Read without pointing except occasionally at point of difficulty
- Use pictures as a resource to self-monitor and self-correct
- Use understanding of how the book works (narrative structure) to self-monitor and self-correct
- Use understanding of characters to self-monitor and self-correct
- Use understanding of dialogue to self-monitor and self-correct
- Use content knowledge of a simple topic to self-monitor and self-correct
- Use information from pictures to self-monitor and self-correct

SOLVING WORDS

▶ Reading Words

- Recognize words in clear, plain font that are on a plain white or very light background
- Recognize fifty or more high-frequency words quickly and easily
- Recognize one-, two-, and some three-syllable words fully supported by the pictures
- Read some simple plurals using -s or -es that are fully supported by pictures and language structure
- Read verbs with the inflectional ending -s, fully supported by pictures and language structure: e.g., *helps*
- Read present participles of verbs with the inflectional ending -*ing,* fully supported by pictures and language structure: e.g., *helping*
- Read past participles of verbs with the inflectional ending -*ed,* fully supported by pictures and language structure: e.g., *helped*
- Read some words with easy spelling patterns with the support of pictures and language (VC, CVC, CVC*e,* CVV, CVVC, VC*e*)
- Say a word and predict its first letter(s)
- Locate high-frequency words and other important words in a text
- Say a word slowly to identify sounds in the word (beginning, ending, middle)
- Notice visual features of a word and use them to locate or read the word
- Read simple contractions: e.g., words formed with *not, am, are, is, has,* and *will*
- Read possessives: e.g., *a cat's nose*
- Read simple words that assign dialogue: e.g., *said, asked, cried*
- Read simple connectives

Selecting Goals Behaviors and Understandings to Notice, Teach, and Support *(cont.)*

THINKING *WITHIN* THE TEXT *(continued)*

▶ Vocabulary

- Understand the meaning of some words that are new but easy to understand in the context of the text and with picture support
- Expand understanding of the meaning of words by connection with the pictures and/or understanding the context
- Read and understand words that stand for sounds (onomatopoetic words)
- Understand vocabulary words that are in common oral vocabulary for early readers (Tier 1)
- Understand the meaning of simple regular plurals formed with the endings *-s* or *-es*
- Understand the meaning of simple adjectives describing people, places, or things
- Understand the meaning of simple contractions using an apostrophe and one or more letters from words such as *not, am, are, is, has,* and *will*
- Understand words with an apostrophe indicating possession
- Understand some words that require the use of multiple sources of information (background knowledge, pictures, visual information)
- Understand words that indicate characters: e.g., easy-to-read names, family members, community members such as teachers
- Understand words such as *I, me,* and *we* that may indicate the narrator of a text
- Understand the meaning of words that assign dialogue: e.g., *said, asked, cried*
- Understand the meaning and function of simple connectives
- Recognize and understand labels for familiar objects: e.g., animals, people, the human body, weather, daily activities, simple processes such as cooking or growing plants
- Use details in illustrations to understand new vocabulary

MAINTAINING FLUENCY

- Sustain momentum through an entire short text
- Notice periods, quotation marks, commas, exclamation marks, and question marks, and begin to reflect them with the voice through intonation and pausing
- Read with phrasing, usually guided by a text with layout designed to support phrasing

- Demonstrate stress on words in a way that shows attention to meaning
- Stress words that are in bold
- Adjust reading to show awareness of sentence variety: i.e., placement of subject, verb, adjectives, and adverbs
- Reread to notice the language or meaning
- Show recognition of dialogue with phrasing
- Recognize and use ellipses in some texts indicating that a sentence finishes on the next page

ADJUSTING

- Slow down to problem-solve words and resume reading with momentum
- Recognize that a text is fiction and tells a story that has a beginning, middle, series of episodes, and end
- Understand that a nonfiction book tells facts
- Notice labels on photographs and use them to understand the words in the text
- Adjust reading to notice information in a photograph
- Adjust to accommodate some variety in layout of illustrations and print
- Adjust reading to reflect a series of steps in an easy procedural book

SUMMARIZING

- Remember important information while reading to understand the meaning of the text
- Talk about the important information after reading
- Remember the order of events in a simple story and talk about them after reading
- Summarize the problem in a simple story and talk about the solution
- Include characters (by name) when telling what happens in a story
- Remember and talk about clear, simple ideas that are easy to identify
- Understand when sequence is important (e.g., cooking, planting) and talk about events or steps in order

Selecting Goals Behaviors and Understandings to Notice, Teach, and Support *(cont.)*

THINKING *BEYOND* THE TEXT

PREDICTING

- Use sentences with varied placement of subject, verb, adjectives, and adverbs to anticipate the text
- Make predictions based on information in pictures
- ◆ Make predictions based on knowledge, personal experience, and experience with texts
- Predict the ending of a story based on reading the beginning and middle
- Make predictions based on understanding a narrative structure
- Make predictions based on a temporal sequence: e.g., plants growing, eggs hatching, weather changing, food cooking

MAKING CONNECTIONS

- Make connections between personal experience and a text
- Make connections among books in a series
- Use background knowledge to understand settings: e.g., home, school, park, community
- Identify recurring characters or settings when applicable
- Use background knowledge of traditional literature to recognize common characters and events in a folktale
- Use background knowledge to understand settings close to children's experience: e.g., home, school, park, community, and (if applicable) beach and snow
- Make connections between background knowledge of familiar content and the content in the text
- Make connections among texts on the same topic or with the same content
- Access background knowledge to understand simple processes: e.g., ice melting, food cooking, building an object

SYNTHESIZING

- Talk about what is known about the topic before reading the text
- Talk about the text, showing understanding of events or topic
- Talk about the events of a simple plot
- Talk about what is learned about characters and problems in a story
- Talk about any new labels for content that are learned from the text
- Identify new knowledge gained when reading a text

INFERRING

- Infer meaning of story or content from pictures that add meaning to the text
- Make inferences about where the story takes place (as shown in pictures) to help understand it
- Talk about characters' feelings based on inferences from pictures and text, especially dialogue
- Talk about the pictures, revealing interpretation of a problem or of characters' feelings
- Infer humor that is easy to grasp: e.g., humorous characters and story problems
- Infer some obvious character traits from the story and pictures: e.g., kind, brave, funny
- Infer ideas about familiar content
- Infer simple processes by noticing the steps: e.g., cooking, water freezing, plants growing

Selecting Goals Behaviors and Understandings to Notice, Teach, and Support *(cont.)*

THINKING **ABOUT** THE TEXT

ANALYZING

- Understand how the ideas and information in a book are related to each other
- Understand how the events, content, and ideas in a text are related to the title
- Recognize that a text can be imagined (fiction) or it can give information (nonfiction)
- Understand that a story can be like real life or can be something that could not be true in real life (fantasy)
- Recognize settings that are familiar: e.g., home, school, neighborhood
- Recognize and follow a chronological sequence of events
- Identify a simple story problem and how it is resolved
- Recognize and understand variety in narrative structure: e.g., cumulative tale, circular story
- Recognize that the people and animals in a story are called characters
- Recognize characters that are typical of animal fantasy or traditional literature
- Notice a writer's use of humorous words or onomatopoetic words and talk about how they add to the action
- Notice that illustrations add to important story action

- Recognize that a text can have true information
- Understand that a nonfiction book gives facts or tells how to do something
- Recognize that a process happens in time order
- Recognize very simple procedural language (directions)
- Understand that illustrations or photographs add to the ideas and information in a text
- Use some specific language to talk about genres and special types of texts: e.g., *fiction; family, friends, and school story; nonfiction; informational text; informational book; factual text*
- Use beginning academic language to talk about forms: e.g., *series book*
- Use beginning academic language to talk about literary features: e.g., *beginning, ending, problem, character*
- Use some specific language to talk about book and print features: e.g., *front cover, back cover, page, author, illustrator, illustration, photograph, title, label, drawing*

CRITIQUING

- Share opinions about a text
- Share opinions about an illustration or photograph
- Have favorite books and say why

Planning for Letter and Word Work After Guided Reading

Using your recent observations of the readers' ability to take words apart quickly and efficiently while reading text, plan for one to three minutes of active engagement of students' attention to letters, sounds, and words. Prioritize the readers' noticing of print features and active hands-on use of magnetic letters, a white board, word cards, or pencil and paper to promote fluency and flexibility in visual processing.

Examples:

- Recognize many easy high-frequency words (for example, *after, got, here, saw, then, this, who*)
- Write many high-frequency words quickly (*from, man, play, there, what, with*)
- Review high-frequency words from previous levels
- Recognize and use contractions with *not* (*can't, don't*), *am* (*I'm*), and *are* (*we're, you're*)
- Add -*s* or -*es* to a singular noun to make a plural noun (*kitten/kittens, dress/dresses*)
- Add an inflectional ending to a word to make a new word (*help/helping, help/helped*)
- Read, make, break apart, write, or sort words with a consonant cluster that blends two or three consonant sounds (<u>bl</u>ack, <u>gr</u>ass; <u>spr</u>ing, <u>str</u>eet)

- Recognize, make, or break apart words that begin with a consonant digraph (<u>ch</u>ange, <u>ph</u>one, <u>sh</u>all, <u>th</u>irty, <u>wh</u>ere)
- Break apart one-syllable words that begin with a consonant, a consonant cluster, or a consonant digraph into onsets and rimes (*c-at, sl-ed, ch-ip, bl-ock, l-unch*)
- Read, make, or break apart words on a white board that contain double consonant letters at the end or in the middle (*hill, better*)
- Recognize, make, break apart, or write words with a CVC pattern and a short vowel sound (*sat*) and words with a VCe pattern and a long vowel sound (*cake*)
- Recognize, make, break apart, or write words with a VVC pattern including a double vowel (*deer; good, room*)

- Listen for and identify each sound in a few words using sound boxes
- Change one or more letters—a consonant, a consonant cluster, a consonant digraph, or a vowel—at the beginning, middle, or end of a word to make a new word (*cat/bat, bat/bet, bet/best, best/chest*)
- Sort letters quickly by a variety of features—uppercase or lowercase; tall or short; with or without long straight lines, short straight lines, circles, tails
- Read the Consonant Cluster Linking Chart in different ways—all words, backwards order, every other box

GUIDED READING

Readers at Level **G**

At level G, readers encounter a wide range of texts and continue to internalize knowledge of the characteristics of genres. They are still reading texts with three to eight lines of print per page, but print size may be slightly smaller and there are more words on a page. With early reading behaviors completely under control and quick and automatic recognition of a large number of high-frequency words, readers have attention to give to slightly more complex story lines and ideas. They can notice character attributes and infer their feelings. Characters do not develop or change much, but they often learn a lesson. Readers are able to use a range of word-solving strategies (letter-sound information, making connections between or among words, and using word parts) while attending to meaning. They read texts with some content-specific words, but most texts have only a few challenging vocabulary words. In their oral reading they demonstrate (without pointing) appropriate rate, phrasing, intonation, and word stress. At Level G children read fiction texts with multiple characters and a series of episodes, many of which are repetitive in nature. They read both assigned and unassigned dialogue, follow straightforward plots, and identify a problem and its resolution. Nonfiction texts at level G present familiar topics, but readers expand the number of content words they know. Readers are beginning to use academic language to talk about texts.

Selecting Texts Characteristics of Texts at **Level G**

GENRE

▶ **Fiction**

- Realistic fiction
- Traditional literature (mostly folktales, fables)
- Animal fantasy

▶ **Nonfiction**

- Variety of expository texts on easy topics
- Procedural texts

FORMS

- Some series books
- Picture books
- Simple plays
- Readers' theater scripts

TEXT STRUCTURE

- Narrative texts with straightforward structure (beginning, series of episodes, and ending) but more episodes included
- Narrative texts with repetitive episodes
- Variation in narrative structure: e.g., cumulative tales, circular stories
- Underlying structural patterns: description, temporal sequence, chronological sequence, question and answer (nonfiction)

CONTENT

- Content interesting to and relevant for young children
- Familiar content: e.g., family and home, play, pets, animals, school, food, community, friends, daily activities, the human body, weather, seasons, transportation, toys
- Moderate level of support provided by picture information
- A few stories with content familiar to children through prior experiences with storytelling, media, and hearing books read: e.g., folktales and fantasy
- Some content that goes beyond children's immediate experience

THEMES AND IDEAS

- Concrete themes close to children's experience: e.g., imagination, courage, fears, friendship, family relationships, self, home, nature, growing, behavior, community, first responsibilities, diversity, belonging, peer relationships, feelings
- Clear, simple ideas easy to identify
- Ideas close to children's experience: e.g., sharing with others, caring for others, doing your job, helping your family, taking care of self, staying healthy, caring for your world, empathizing with others, problem solving, valuing differences, expressing feelings
- Humor that is easy to understand

LANGUAGE AND LITERARY FEATURES

- Some texts with settings that are not typical of many children's experience
- Simple sequence of events
- Plot with conflict and resolution
- Characters that do not change and some revealed over a series of books
- Most characters with names
- Dialogue among multiple characters, dialogue with pronouns, and split dialogue
- Dialogue usually assigned to speaker, with some unassigned dialogue
- Some long stretches of dialogue
- A few simple elements of fantasy: e.g., talking animals
- Language that speaks directly to the reader
- Procedural language
- Language used to make comparisons

SENTENCE COMPLEXITY

- Some longer sentences with more than ten words
- Statements and questions
- Variation in placement of subject, verb, adjectives, and adverbs
- Sentences with clauses or phrases
- Sentences with adjectives, adverbs, and prepositional phrases

Monster trucks don't look like other trucks. They have bigger wheels.

Some of them have eyes and horns. Some of them have teeth and a tail.

tail

horns

eye

teeth

- Many sentences beginning with phrases
- Some sentences beginning with subordinate (dependent) clauses
- A few compound sentences joined by *and*
- Some complex sentences with variety in order of clauses
- Sentences with dialogue

VOCABULARY

- A few words that are new to children but easy to understand in context
- Words for sounds (onomatopoetic)
- Almost all words that are in common oral vocabulary for young children (Tier 1)
- Some content-specific words requiring use of context for understanding introduced, explained, and illustrated in the text
- Some variation in words used to assign dialogue: e.g., *said, asked, cried*
- Many adjectives describing people, places, or things
- Adverbs describing action
- Simple connectives (words, phrases that clarify relationships and ideas): e.g., *and, but, so, before, after*

WORDS

- One-, two-, and three-syllable words with moderate picture support
- Simple plurals using *-s* or *-es* and some irregular plurals: e.g., *mice*
- A variety of high-frequency words (100+)
- Verbs with inflectional endings: e.g., *-s, -ing, -ed*
- Many words with easy, predictable letter-sound relationships (decodable)
- Words with easy spelling patterns (VC, CVC, CVV, CVC*e*, CVVC, VC*e*)
- Simple contractions: e.g., words formed with *am, not,* and *is*
- Simple possessives: e.g., *cat's nose*
- Simple (common) connectives

ILLUSTRATIONS

- Illustrations of the important story action, content, and ideas in the text
- Illustrations that enhance and extend meaning in the text and sometimes add humor
- Illustrations with details that add interest
- Illustrations on every page or page spread
- Variety of layout in illustrations and print
- Clear separation of illustrations and print with labels or captions photographs and drawings

BOOK AND PRINT FEATURES

LENGTH

- Short, usually sixteen pages
- Typically fewer than 300 words per book (200–300)

PRINT AND LAYOUT

- Print in clear font on pale background, sometimes with "knockout" (white on black)
- Mostly texts three to eight lines of text per page
- Sentences beginning on the left and turning over several lines
- Some limited variation in print placement
- Most texts with double or triple spaces between lines
- Clear spaces between words
- Print clearly separated from pictures
- Many texts with layout supporting phrasing

PUNCTUATION

- Use of period, comma, question mark, exclamation mark, and quotation marks
- Ellipses in some texts to indicate that the sentence finishes on the next page

Selecting Goals Behaviors and Understandings to Notice, Teach, and Support

SEARCHING FOR AND USING INFORMATION

- Sustain searching for information over a short text (usually sixteen pages with three to eight lines of print on each page and fewer than 300 words)
- Use background understanding of familiar, easy content to search for and use information
- Reread to search for and use information from multiple sources
- Use sentence structures (subject and predicate with some embedded phrases and clauses) to search for and use information
- Search for and use information that appears in beginning and ending phrases or clauses
- Search for information in sentences (both statements and questions) with phrases or clauses (some subordinate)
- Search for information in sentences with variation in placement of subject, verb, adjectives, and adverbs
- Search for and understand information presented in a variety of ways: e.g., simple dialogue, dialogue with pronouns, split dialogue, assigned and sometimes unassigned dialogue, dialogue among multiple characters, and some long stretches of dialogue
- Use the chronological order of a simple story to search for and use information
- Notice and use punctuation marks (period, comma, question mark, exclamation mark, and quotation marks)
- Search for and use information from pictures or graphics
- Use labels or captions on photographs and drawings to search for and use information
- Use details in the illustrations to search for and use information

MONITORING AND SELF-CORRECTING

- Sometimes reread the sentence or phrase to problem-solve, self-correct, or confirm
- Self-correct close to the point of error
- Use visual features of words to self-monitor and self-correct
- Use recognition of high-frequency words and other known words to self-monitor and self-correct
- Use multiple sources of information (visual information in print, meaning/pictures, language structure) to monitor and self-correct
- Read without pointing
- Use understanding of how the book works (narrative structure) to self-monitor and self-correct

- Use understanding of characters to self-monitor and self-correct
- Use understanding of dialogue to self-monitor and self-correct
- Use content knowledge of a simple topic to self-monitor and self-correct

SOLVING WORDS

▶ Reading Words

- Recognize words in clear, plain font that are on a plain white or very light background
- Recognize 100+ high-frequency words quickly and easily
- Recognize one-, two-, and three-syllable words with moderate picture support
- Read a range of regular and irregular plurals that are fully supported by pictures and language structure
- Read verbs with the inflectional ending *-s,* fully supported by pictures and language structure: e.g., *helps*
- Read present participles of verbs with the inflectional ending *-ing,* fully supported by pictures and language structure: e.g., *helping*
- Read past participles of verbs with the inflectional ending *-ed,* fully supported by pictures and language structure: e.g., *helped*
- Read some words with easy spelling patterns with the support of pictures and language (VC, CVC, CVC*e,* CVV, CVVC, VC*e*)
- Use word parts to solve some two-syllable or three-syllable words
- Locate high-frequency words and other important words in a text
- Say a word slowly to identify sounds in the word (beginning, ending, middle)
- Notice visual features of a word and use them to locate or read the word
- Read a range of contractions: e.g., words formed with *not, am, are, is, has,* and *will*
- Read possessives: e.g., *a cat's nose*
- Read words that assign dialogue: e.g., *said, asked, cried, yelled*

▶ Vocabulary

- Understand the meaning of some words that are new but easy to understand in the context of the text and with picture support
- Understand some content-specific words introduced, explained, and illustrated in context

GUIDED READING

LEVEL **G**

Selecting Goals Behaviors and Understandings to Notice, Teach, and Support *(cont.)*

THINKING *WITHIN* THE TEXT *(continued)*

- Expand understanding of the meaning of words by connection with the pictures and/or understanding the context
- Read and understand words that stand for sounds (onomatopoetic words)
- Understand vocabulary words that are in common oral vocabulary for early readers (Tier 1)
- Understand the meaning of simple regular plurals formed with the endings -s or -es
- Understand the meaning of simple adjectives describing people, places, or things
- Understand the meaning of contractions using an apostrophe and one or more letters from words such as *not, am, are, is, has,* and *will*
- Understand words with an apostrophe indicating possession
- Understand some words that require the use of multiple sources of information (background knowledge, pictures, visual information)
- Understand words that indicate characters: e.g., easy-to-read names, family members, community members such as teachers
- Understand that words such as *I, me,* and *we* may signal the narrator of a text
- Understand the meaning of a variety of words that assign dialogue
- Recognize and understand labels for familiar objects, animals, people, the human body, weather, daily activities, simple processes such as cooking or growing plants

MAINTAINING FLUENCY

- Sustain momentum through an entire short text
- Notice periods, quotation marks, commas, exclamation marks, and question marks, and reflect them with the voice through intonation and pausing
- Demonstrate stress on words in a way that shows attention to meaning
- Stress words that are in bold
- Adjust reading to show awareness of sentence variety: i.e., placement of subject, verb, adjectives, and adverbs
- Reread to notice the language or meaning
- Show recognition of dialogue with phrasing
- Recognize and use ellipses in some texts to indicate when a sentence finishes on the next page

ADJUSTING

- Slow down to problem-solve words and resume reading with momentum
- Adjust reading to accommodate compound sentences and sentences with a variety in order of clauses
- Recognize that a text is fiction and tells a story that has a beginning, middle, series of episodes, and end
- Understand that a nonfiction book tells facts
- Notice labels or captions on photographs and drawings and use them to understand the words in the text
- Adjust reading to notice information in a photograph or drawing
- Adjust to accommodate some variety in layout of illustrations and print
- Adjust reading to reflect a series of steps in an easy procedural book

SUMMARIZING

- Remember important information while reading to understand the meaning of the text
- Talk about the important information after reading
- Remember the order of events in a simple story and talk about events after reading
- Summarize the problem in a simple story and talk about the solution
- Include characters (by name) when telling what happens in a story
- Remember and talk about clear, simple ideas that are easy to identify
- Understand when sequence is important (e.g., cooking, planting) and talk about events or steps in order

Selecting Goals Behaviors and Understandings to Notice, Teach, and Support *(cont.)*

THINKING *BEYOND* THE TEXT

PREDICTING

- ◆ Use sentences with varied placement of subject, verb, adjectives, and adverbs to anticipate the text
- ◆ Make predictions based on information in pictures
- ◆ Make predictions based on knowledge, personal experience, and experience with texts
- ◆ Predict the ending of a story based on reading the beginning and middle
- ◆ Make predictions based on understanding a narrative structure
- ◆ Make predictions based on a temporal sequence: e.g., plants growing, eggs hatching, weather changing, food cooking

MAKING CONNECTIONS

- ◆ Make connections between personal experience and a text
- ◆ Make connections among books in a series
- ◆ Use background knowledge to understand settings: e.g., home, school, park, community
- ◆ Identify recurring characters or settings when applicable
- ◆ Use background knowledge of traditional literature to recognize common characters and events in a folktale
- ◆ Use background knowledge to understand settings close to children's experience: e.g., home, school, park, community, and (if applicable) beach and snow
- ◆ Make connections between background knowledge of familiar content and the content in the text
- ◆ Make connections among texts on the same topic or with the same content
- ◆ Access background knowledge to understand simple processes: e.g., ice melting, food cooking, building an object

SYNTHESIZING

- ◆ Talk about what is known about the topic before reading the text
- ◆ Talk about the text, showing understanding of events or topic
- ◆ Talk about the events of a simple plot
- ◆ Talk about what is learned about characters and problems in a story
- ◆ Talk about any new labels for content that are learned from the text
- ◆ Identify new knowledge gained when reading a text

INFERRING

- ◆ Infer meaning of story or content from pictures that add meaning to the text
- ◆ Notice aspects of the setting from the text and pictures and make inferences to help understand the story
- ◆ Talk about characters' feelings based on inferences from pictures and text, especially dialogue
- ◆ Talk about the pictures, revealing interpretation of a problem or of characters' feelings
- ◆ Infer humor that is easy to grasp: e.g., humorous characters and story problems
- ◆ Infer some obvious character traits from the story and pictures: e.g., kind, brave, funny
- ◆ Infer ideas about familiar content
- ◆ Infer simple temporal sequences by noticing the steps: e.g., cooking, water freezing, plants growing

Selecting Goals Behaviors and Understandings to Notice, Teach, and Support *(cont.)*

THINKING *ABOUT* THE TEXT

ANALYZING

- Recognize that a text can be imagined (fiction) or it can give information (nonfiction)
- Understand that a story can be like real life or can be something that could not be true in real life (fantasy)
- Recognize characters that are typical of animal fantasy or traditional literature
- Recognize that a text can have true information
- Understand that a nonfiction book gives facts or tells how to do something
- Understand how the ideas and information in a book are related to each other
- Recognize and follow chronological sequence of events
- Recognize and understand variety in narrative structure: e.g., cumulative tale, circular story
- Recognize that a process happens in time order
- Recognize repetitive episodes in a text
- Understand how the events, content, and ideas in a text are related to the title
- Recognize settings that are familiar: e.g., home, school, neighborhood
- Identify a simple story problem and how it is resolved
- Recognize that the people and animals in a story are called characters

- Notice a writer's use of humorous words or onomatopoetic words and talk about how they add to the action
- Recognize procedural language (directions)
- Recognize language that speaks directly to the reader: e.g., *you, your*
- Notice that illustrations add to important story action
- Think analytically about graphics (diagrams) and how they show information
- Understand that illustrations or photographs add to the ideas and information in a text
- Use academic language to talk about genres and special types of texts: e.g., *fiction; family, friends, and school story; nonfiction; informational text; informational book; factual text*
- Use academic language to talk about forms: e.g., *series book*
- Use academic language to talk about literary features: e.g., *beginning, ending, problem, character*
- Use some specific language to talk about book and print features: e.g., *front cover, back cover, page, author, illustrator, illustration, photograph, title, label, drawing*

CRITIQUING

- Share opinions about a text and give rationales and examples
- Share opinions about an illustration or photograph
- Have favorite books and say why

Planning for Word Work After Guided Reading

Using your recent observations of the readers' ability to take words apart quickly and efficiently while reading text, plan for one to three minutes of active engagement of students' attention to letters, sounds, and words. Prioritize the readers' noticing of print features and active hands-on use of magnetic letters, a white board, word cards, or pencil and paper to promote fluency and flexibility in visual processing.

Examples:

- Recognize many high-frequency words (for example, *around, before, could, friend, they, two, went, where*)
- Review high-frequency words from previous levels
- Recognize and use contractions with *is* (*he's, it's, where's*) and *has* (*she's, there's, what's*)
- Add *-es* to a singular noun to make a plural noun (*lunch/lunches*)
- Add an inflectional ending to a word to make a new word (*ask/asking, asked; live/living, lived; stop/stopping, stopped*)
- Listen for and identify each sound in a few words using sound boxes

- Change the beginning sound or sounds to make a new word (*man/than*–change /m/ to /th/; *by/fly*–change /b/ to /f/ /l/)
- Change the ending sound or sounds to make a new word (*dog/dolls*–change /g/ to /l/ /z/)
- Change a middle sound to make a new word (*big/bag*–change /i/ to /a/)
- Recognize, make, and break apart words that begin with an initial consonant, a consonant cluster, or a consonant digraph (*m̲ilk; t̲ruck, s̲pring; t̲hink, s̲how*)
- Recognize, make, and break apart words with double consonant letters in the middle (*le̲tter, happ̲y*)

- Read, make, break apart, and write words with a CVC pattern and a short vowel sound (*let*) and words with a VCe pattern and a long vowel sound (*make*)
- Recognize, make, and break apart words that contain phonograms with a double vowel pattern (*feet, balloon*)
- Solve words using letter-sound analysis from left to right (*s-t-e-p*)
- Sort letters quickly by a variety of features–uppercase or lowercase; tall or short; with or without long straight lines, short straight lines, circles, tails
- Read the Consonant Cluster Linking Chart in a variety of ways

Readers at Level

At level H, readers encounter challenges similar to Level G, but the language and vocabulary are even more complex and the stories are longer and more literary. Readers process a great deal of dialogue and reflect it through appropriate word stress and phrasing in oral reading. In fiction, they will find that plots and characters are more elaborated but are still simple and straightforward. They notice attributes of characters and infer feelings and motives. Characters do not change much, but they may learn a lesson. Nonfiction challenges readers with topics that may offer some information beyond their current knowledge, and readers may encounter vocabulary words connected to content that is new. They solve multisyllable words (many with inflectional endings), plurals, contractions, and possessives. Automatically reading a large number of high-frequency words, they can meet the demands for more in-depth thinking and also solve words with complex spelling patterns. In order to achieve efficient and smooth processing, readers begin to do more silent reading. In oral reading, they demonstrate (without pointing) appropriate rate, phrasing, intonation, and word stress. Readers use academic language to talk about texts.

Selecting Texts Characteristics of Texts at **Level H**

GENRE

▶ **Fiction**
- Realistic fiction
- Traditional literature (mostly folktales, fables)
- Animal fantasy

▶ **Nonfiction**
- Expository texts
- Procedural texts

FORMS
- Some series books
- Picture books
- Simple plays
- Readers' theater scripts

TEXT STRUCTURE
- Narrative texts with straightforward structure (beginning, series of episodes, and ending) but more episodes included
- Narrative texts with multiple episodes, some episodes similar
- Variation in narrative: e.g., cumulative tales, circular stories
- Underlying structural patterns: description, temporal sequence, chronological sequence, question and answer (nonfiction)

CONTENT
- Content interesting to and relevant for young children
- Familiar content: e.g., family and home, play, pets, animals, school, food, community, friends, daily activities, the human body, weather, seasons, transportation, machines
- Moderate level of support provided by picture information
- More content that goes beyond children's immediate experience: e.g., different environments and communities, animals of the world
- Some stories with content familiar to children through prior experiences with storytelling, media, and hearing books read: e.g., folktales and fantasy

THEMES AND IDEAS
- Concrete themes close to children's experience: e.g., imagination, courage, fears, friendship, family relationships, self, home, nature, growing, behavior, community, first responsibilities, diversity, belonging, peer relationships, feelings
- Clear, simple ideas easy to identify and understand
- Ideas close to children's experience: e.g., sharing with others, caring for others, doing your job, helping your family, taking care of self, staying healthy, caring for your world, empathizing with others, problem solving, valuing differences, expressing feelings)
- Humor that is easy to understand

LANGUAGE AND LITERARY FEATURES
- Some texts with settings that are not typical of many children's experiences
- Plot with conflict and resolution
- Plot that includes multiple episodes
- Characters with names
- Characters that change very little but may do some learning, and some characters revealed over a series of books
- Variety in presentation of dialogue: e.g., dialogue among multiple characters, dialogue with pronouns, split dialogue, direct dialogue
- Dialogue usually assigned to speaker, with some unassigned
- Some long stretches of dialogue
- A few simple elements of fantasy: e.g., talking animals
- Procedural language
- Language used to make comparisons
- Some descriptive language

SENTENCE COMPLEXITY
- Some longer sentences with more than fifteen words
- Statements and questions
- Variation in placement of subject, verb, adjectives, and adverbs
- Some sentences with clauses or phrases
- Sentences and clauses that are questions

"We iced the cupcakes,"
said Rabbit.
"Now what can we do?"

Bear wrote, "Take out the trash."

"It seems **very** strange
to take out the trash!" Rabbit said.
"But we'll do it for you, Bear."

10

Rabbit and the little snakes
took the trash out of the can
and put it on the floor.

Bear couldn't stand it any longer.

11

- Sentences with adjectives, adverbs, and prepositional phrases
- Many sentences beginning with phrases
- Some sentences beginning with subordinate (dependent) clauses
- A few compound sentences joined by *and*
- Some complex sentences with variety in order of clauses

VOCABULARY

- Most vocabulary words known by children through oral language, listening to stories, or reading
- Almost all words that are in common oral vocabulary for younger children (Tier 1)
- A few words that appear in the vocabulary of mature language users (Tier 2)
- Some content-specific words introduced, explained, and illustrated in the text requiring use of context for understanding
- Some variation in words used to assign dialogue: e.g., *said, asked, cried, yelled*
- Many adjectives describing people, places, or things
- Adverbs describing action
- Simple connectives (words, phrases that clarify relationships and ideas): e.g., *and, but, so, before, after*

WORDS

- One-, two-, and three-syllable words with moderate picture support
- Simple plurals using *-s* or *-es* and some irregular plurals: e.g., *sheep*
- A variety of high-frequency words (100+)
- Verbs with inflectional endings: e.g., *-s, -ing, -ed*
- Many words with easy, predictable letter-sound relationships (decodable)
- Words with easy spelling patterns (VC, CVC, CVV, CVC*e*, CVVC, VC*e*)
- Simple contractions: e.g., words formed with *am, not,* and *is*
- Simple possessives: e.g., *cat's nose*
- Compound words
- Simple connectives

ILLUSTRATIONS

- Illustrations of the important story action, content, and ideas in the text
- Illustrations that enhance and extend meaning in the text
- Illustrations with details that add interest and sometimes humor
- Illustrations on every page or page spread
- Variety of layout in illustrations and print
- Clear separation of illustrations and print
- Some simple illustrations in a variety of forms: e.g., photo and/or drawing with label or caption, diagram

BOOK AND PRINT FEATURES

LENGTH

- Short, usually sixteen pages
- Typically less than 350 words per book (200–350)

PRINT AND LAYOUT

- Print in clear font on pale background, sometimes with "knockout" (white on black)
- Mostly three to eight lines of text per page
- Sentences beginning on the left and turning over several lines
- Some limited variation in print placement
- Most texts with double or triple spaces between lines
- Clear spaces between words
- Print clearly separated from pictures
- Many texts with layout supporting phrasing

PUNCTUATION

- Use of period, comma, question mark, exclamation mark, and quotation marks
- Ellipses in some texts to indicate that the sentence finishes on the next page

Selecting Goals Behaviors and Understandings to Notice, Teach, and Support

THINKING *WITHIN* THE TEXT

SEARCHING FOR AND USING INFORMATION

- Sustain searching for information over a short text (usually sixteen pages with three to eight lines of print on each page and fewer than 350 words)
- Use some organizational tools and text resources to search for information: e.g., title, headings
- Use background understanding of familiar, easy content to search for and use information
- Reread to search for and use information from multiple sources
- Use sentence structures (subject and predicate with some embedded phrases and clauses) to search for and use information
- Search for and use information that appears in beginning and ending phrases or clauses
- Search for information in sentences (both statements and questions) with clauses or phrases
- Search for information in sentences with variation in placement of subject, verb, adjectives, and adverbs
- Search for and understand information presented in a variety of ways: e.g., simple dialogue, dialogue with pronouns, split dialogue, assigned and sometimes unassigned dialogue, dialogue among multiple characters, some long stretches of dialogue, direct dialogue
- Use the chronological order of a simple story to search for and use information
- Notice and use (period, comma, question mark, exclamation mark, and quotation marks)
- Search for and use information from pictures or graphics
- Use labels or captions on photographs and drawings to search for and use information
- Use details in the illustrations to search for and use information

MONITORING AND SELF-CORRECTING

- Sometimes reread the sentence or phrase to problem-solve, self-correct, or confirm
- Self-correct close to the point of error
- Use visual features of words to self-monitor and self-correct
- Use recognition of high-frequency words and other known words to self-monitor and self-correct

- Use multiple sources of information (visual information in print, meaning/pictures, language structure) to monitor and self-correct
- Show evidence of close attention to visual features of words
- Read without pointing
- Use awareness of narrative structure and of character attributes to self-monitor and self-correct
- Use understanding of dialogue to self-monitor and self-correct
- Use content knowledge of a simple topic to self-monitor and self-correct

SOLVING WORDS

▶ Reading Words

- Recognize words in clear, plain font that are on a plain white or very light background
- Recognize 100+ high-frequency words quickly and easily
- Recognize one-, two-, and three-syllable words with moderate picture support
- Read a range of regular and irregular plurals that are fully supported by pictures and language structure
- Read verbs with inflectional endings fully supported by pictures and language structure
- Read present participles of verbs with the inflectional ending *-ing,* fully supported by pictures and language structure: e.g., *helping*
- Read past participles of verbs with the inflectional ending *-ed,* fully supported by pictures and language structure: e.g., *helped*
- Read some words with easy spelling patterns with the support of pictures and language (VC, CVC, CVC*e,* CVV, CVVC, VC*e*)
- Use word parts to solve some two-syllable or three-syllable words
- Locate high-frequency words and other important words in a text
- Say a word slowly to identify sounds in the word
- Read a range of contractions: e.g., words formed with *not, am, are, is, has,* and *will*
- Read possessives: e.g., *a cat's nose*
- Read a variety of words that assign dialogue
- Read many compound words: e.g., *into, bedroom, playground*

Selecting Goals Behaviors and Understandings to Notice, Teach, and Support *(cont.)*

THINKING *WITHIN* THE TEXT *(continued)*

▶ Vocabulary

- Understand the meaning of some words that are new but easy to understand in the context of the text and with picture support
- Expand understanding of the meaning of words by connection with the pictures and/or understanding the context
- Understand some content-specific words introduced, explained, and illustrated in context
- Read and understand words that stand for sounds (onomatopoetic words)
- Understand vocabulary words that are in common oral vocabulary for early readers (Tier 1)
- Understand the meaning of a few words that appear in the vocabulary of mature language users (Tier 2)
- Understand the meaning of simple regular plurals formed with the endings *-s* or *-es*
- Understand the meaning of simple adjectives describing people, places, or things
- Understand the meaning of present participles and past participles of verbs with the inflectional endings *-ing* and *-ed*: e.g., *am looking, have looked*
- Understand the meaning of contractions using an apostrophe and one or more letters from words such as *not, am, are, is, has,* and *will*
- Understand words with an apostrophe indicating possession
- Understand some words that require the use of multiple sources of information (background knowledge, pictures, visual information)
- Understand words that indicate characters: e.g., easy-to-read names, family members, community members such as teachers
- Understand that words such as *I, me,* and *we* may signal the narrator of a text
- Understand the meaning of a variety of words that assign dialogue
- Recognize and understand labels for familiar objects, animals, people, the human body, weather, daily activities, simple processes such as cooking or growing plants
- Use details in illustrations to understand new vocabulary
- Understand the meaning and function of simple connectives

MAINTAINING FLUENCY

- Notice periods, quotation marks, commas, exclamation marks, and question marks, and reflect them with the voice through intonation and pausing
- Demonstrate stress on words in a way that shows attention to meaning and stress words in bold
- Adjust reading to show awareness of sentence variety: i.e., placement of subject, verb, adjectives, and adverbs
- Reread to notice the language or meaning
- Recognize dialogue with phrasing, word stress, and intonation

ADJUSTING

- Slow down to problem-solve words and resume reading with momentum
- Adjust reading to accommodate compound sentences and sentences with variety in order of clauses
- Recognize that a text is fiction and tells a story that has a beginning, middle, series of episodes, and end
- Understand that a nonfiction book tells facts
- Notice labels or captions on photographs and drawings and use them to understand the words in the text
- Adjust reading to notice information in a photograph or drawing
- Adjust to accommodate some variety in layout of illustrations and print
- Adjust reading to reflect a series of steps in an easy procedural book

SUMMARIZING

- Remember important information while reading to understand the meaning of the text
- Talk about the important information after reading
- Summarize the story including plot events, problem, resolution, and characters
- Summarize information in the text, selecting the information that is important
- Tell information about a temporal sequence in time order

Selecting Goals Behaviors and Understandings to Notice, Teach, and Support *(cont.)*

THINKING *BEYOND* THE TEXT

PREDICTING

- ◆ Use sentences with varied placement of subject, verb, adjectives, and adverbs, variety in placement of clauses, and some compound sentences to anticipate the text
- ◆ Make predictions based on information in pictures
- ◆ Make predictions based on personal knowledge and experience with texts
- ◆ Predict the ending of a story based on reading the beginning and middle
- ◆ Predict outcomes or endings based on repeating episodes in the plot
- ◆ Make predictions based on understanding of narrative structure
- ◆ Make predictions based on knowledge from personal experiences and from reading: e.g., food, cooking, pets, animals of the world, health and the human body, different environments and communities, machines
- ◆ Make predictions based on knowledge of underlying text structures: e.g., description, temporal sequence, question and answer, chronological sequence
- ◆ Make predictions based on a temporal sequence: e.g., plants growing, eggs hatching, making something, the water cycle

MAKING CONNECTIONS

- ◆ Make connections between personal experience and a text
- ◆ Make connections among books in a series
- ◆ Use background knowledge to understand settings
- ◆ Use background knowledge of traditional literature to recognize common characters and events in a folktale
- ◆ Make connections between background knowledge of familiar content and the content in the text
- ◆ Make connections among texts on the same topic or with similar content
- ◆ Access background knowledge to understand description or temporal sequence

SYNTHESIZING

- ◆ Talk about what the reader knows about the topic before reading the text, and identify new knowledge gained from reading
- ◆ Talk about the text, showing understanding of events, topic, or content
- ◆ Talk about what is learned from the characters, the problem, and the resolution of the problem

INFERRING

- ◆ Infer meaning of story or content from pictures that add meaning to the text
- ◆ Notice aspects of the setting from the text and pictures and make inferences to help understand the story
- ◆ Talk about characters' feelings based on inferences from pictures and text, especially dialogue
- ◆ Talk about the pictures, revealing interpretation of a problem or of characters' feelings
- ◆ Infer obvious humor: e.g., humorous characters, language, and story problems
- ◆ Infer some obvious character traits from the story and pictures
- ◆ Infer ideas about familiar content
- ◆ Infer temporal sequences and notice the steps

GUIDED READING

LEVEL

Selecting Goals Behaviors and Understandings to Notice, Teach, and Support *(cont.)*

THINKING *ABOUT* THE TEXT

ANALYZING

- Recognize that a text can be imagined (fiction) or it can give information (nonfiction)
- Understand that a story can be like real life or can be something that could not be true in real life (fantasy)
- Recognize characters that are typical of animal fantasy or traditional literature
- Recognize that a text can have true information
- Understand that a nonfiction book gives facts tells how to do something
- Understand how the ideas and information in a book are related to each other
- Recognize and follow a chronological sequence of events
- Recognize and understand variety in narrative structure: e.g., cumulative tale, circular story
- Recognize that a process happens in time order
- Recognize repetitive episodes in a text
- Recognize a writer's use of underlying text structures: e.g., description, temporal sequence, question and answer, chronological sequence
- Understand how the events, content, and ideas in a text are related to the title
- Recognize settings that are familiar
- Identify a story problem and how it is resolved

- Recognize that the people and animals in a story are called characters
- Notice a writer's use of humorous words or onomatopoetic words and talk about how they add to the action
- Recognize procedural language (directions)
- Recognize language that speaks directly to the reader: e.g., *you, your*
- Notice that illustrations add to important story action
- Think analytically about graphics (diagrams)
- Understand that illustrations or photographs add to the ideas and information in a text
- Use academic language to talk about genres and special types of texts: e.g., *fiction; family, friends, and school story; folktale; nonfiction; informational text; informational book; factual text*
- Use academic language to talk about forms: e.g., *series book, play*
- Use academic language to talk about literary features: e.g., *beginning, ending, problem, character*
- Use some specific language to talk about book and print features: e.g., *front cover, back cover, page, author, illustrator, illustration, photograph, title, label, drawing, heading*

CRITIQUING

- Share opinions about a text and give rationales and examples
- Share opinions about an illustration or photograph
- Have favorite books and say why

Planning for Word Work After Guided Reading

Using your recent observations of the readers' ability to take words apart quickly and efficiently while reading text, plan for one to three minutes of active engagement of students' attention to letters, sounds, and words. Prioritize the readers' noticing of print features and active hands-on use of magnetic letters, a white board, word cards, or pencil and paper to promote fluency and flexibility in visual processing.

Examples:

- Recognize and write many high-frequency words (for example, *just, mother, over, too, were, when, will*)
- Review high-frequency words from previous levels
- Recognize and use contractions with *will* (*I'll, we'll, that'll*)
- Add *-es* to a singular noun to make a plural noun (*wish/wishes*)
- Add an apostrophe and an *s* to a singular noun to show ownership (*dog's bone, Emma's pencil*)
- Add an inflectional ending to a word to make a new word (*call/calling, called; please/pleasing, pleased*)

- Change the beginning sound or sounds to make a new word (*day/stay*–change /d/ to /st/)
- Change the ending sound or sounds to make a new word (*hen/help*–change /n/ to /l/ /p/)
- Change a middle sound to make a new word (*let/lot*–change /e/ to /aw/)
- Recognize and identify each letter in a few words using letter boxes
- Recognize, make, and break apart words that begin with an initial consonant, a consonant cluster, or a consonant digraph (*night; brown, spring; thank, shoe*)
- Recognize, make, and break apart words with double consonant letters in the middle (*letter, hurry*)

- Read, make, break apart, and write words with a CVC pattern and a short vowel sound (*hat*) and words with a VCe pattern and a long vowel sound (*game*)
- Recognize, make, and break apart words that contain phonograms with a double vowel pattern (*soon, green*)
- Solve words using letter-sound analysis from left to right (*s-t-r-ee-t*)
- Sort letters quickly by a variety of features–uppercase or lowercase; tall or short; with or without long straight lines, short straight lines, circles, tails
- Read the Consonant Cluster Chart in a variety of ways

GUIDED READING

LEVEL **H**

Readers at Level

At level I, readers process texts that are mostly short (sixteen pages), as well as a few easy illustrated chapter books (forty to sixty pages) that require them to sustain attention and memory over time. They encounter compound sentences and some other long sentences of more than fifteen words that contain prepositional phrases, adjectives, adverbs, and clauses. Readers can effectively process these complex sentences and, in addition, automatically recognize a large number of words. Readers use word-solving strategies for complex spelling patterns, multisyllable words, plurals, contractions, possessives, and many words with inflectional endings. They read many texts silently, following the text with their eyes and without pointing. In oral reading, they reflect appropriate rate, word stress, intonation, phrasing, and pausing. Readers process texts with multiple characters and episodes. In fiction texts they can identify the setting, the story problem, and how it is resolved. They can identify character attributes and feelings and detect change (although at this level characters are not fully developed). They learn new content from nonfiction texts and notice when a writer uses underlying structures such as description, temporal sequence, question and answer, and chronological sequence. Readers use academic language to talk about texts.

Selecting Texts Characteristics of Texts at **Level I**

GENRE

▶ **Fiction**

- Realistic fiction
- Traditional literature (folktale, fairy tale, fable)
- Animal fantasy

▶ **Nonfiction**

- Expository texts
- Simple narrative nonfiction
- Procedural texts

FORMS

- Some series books
- Picture books
- Beginning chapter books with illustrations
- Simple plays
- Readers' theater scripts

TEXT STRUCTURE

- Narrative texts with straightforward structure (beginning, series of episodes, and an ending)
- Narrative texts with multiple episodes, with episodes that may be more elaborate, and with less repetition of similar episodes
- Some books with very short chapters, each with narrative structure
- Variation in narrative: e.g., cumulative tales, circular stories

- Underlying structural patterns: description, temporal sequence, chronological sequence, question and answer (nonfiction)

CONTENT

- Content interesting to and relevant for young readers
- Familiar content: e.g., family and home, play, pets, animals, school, food, community, friends, daily activities, the human body, weather, seasons, transportation, machines
- Moderate level of support provided by picture information
- More content that goes beyond students' immediate experience: e.g., different environments and communities, animals of the world
- Some stories with content familiar to students through prior experiences with storytelling, media, and hearing books read: e.g., folktales and fantasy

THEMES AND IDEAS

- Concrete themes close to students' experience: e.g., imagination, courage, fears, friendship, family relationships, self, home, nature, growing, behavior, community, first responsibilities, diversity, belonging, peer relationships, feelings
- Clear, simple ideas easy to identify and understand

- Ideas close to students' experience: e.g., sharing with others, caring for others, doing your job, helping your family, taking care of self, staying healthy, caring for your world, empathizing with others, problem solving, valuing differences, expressing feelings

LANGUAGE AND LITERARY FEATURES

- Some texts with settings that are not typical of many children's experiences
- Plot with conflict and resolution
- Plot that includes multiple episodes
- Characters with names
- Characters that change very little but may do some learning, and some characters revealed over a series of books
- Variety in presentation of dialogue: e.g., dialogue among multiple characters, dialogue with pronouns, split dialogue, direct dialogue
- Dialogue usually assigned to speaker, with some unassigned
- Some long stretches of dialogue
- Elements of fantasy: e.g., talking animals or inanimate objects
- Basic motifs of traditional literature and modern fantasy: e.g., struggle between good and evil, magic, fantastic or magical objects, wishes, trickery, transformations
- Procedural language
- Language used to make comparisons
- Some descriptive language

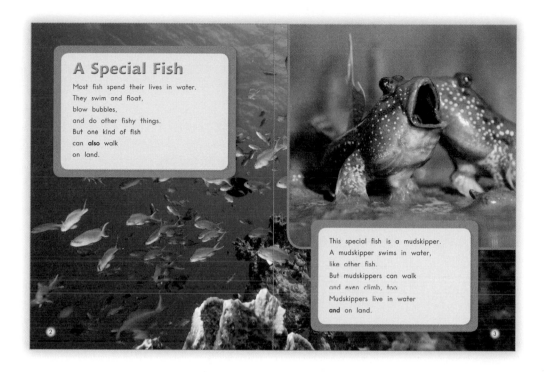

A Special Fish

Most fish spend their lives in water.
They swim and float,
blow bubbles,
and do other fishy things.
But one kind of fish
can **also** walk
on land.

This special fish is a mudskipper.
A mudskipper swims in water,
like other fish.
But mudskippers can walk
and even climb, too.
Mudskippers live in water
and on land.

SENTENCE COMPLEXITY

- Some longer sentences with more than fifteen words
- Statements and questions
- Variation in placement of subject, verb, adjectives, and adverbs
- Some sentences with clauses or phrases
- Sentences with adjectives, adverbs, and prepositional phrases
- Many sentences beginning with phrases
- Some sentences beginning with subordinate (dependent) clauses
- A few compound sentences joined by conjunctions
- Some complex sentences with variety in order of clauses

VOCABULARY

- Most vocabulary words known by children through oral language, listening to stories, or reading
- Most words that are in common oral vocabulary for younger children (Tier 1)
- A few words that appear in the vocabulary of mature language users (Tier 2)
- Some content-specific words introduced, explained, and illustrated in the text requiring use of context for understanding
- Variation in words used to assign dialogue: e.g., *said, asked, cried, yelled*
- Many adjectives describing people, places, or things

- Adverbs describing actions
- Simple connectives (words, phrases that clarify relationships and ideas): e.g., *and, but, so, before, after*

WORDS

- Mostly one-, two-, and three-syllable words with moderate picture support
- Simple plurals using -s or -es and some irregular plurals: e.g., *sheep*
- A variety of high-frequency words (100+)
- Verbs with inflectional endings: e.g., *-s, -ing, -ed*
- Words with easy spelling patterns (VC, CVC, CVV, CVCe, CVVC, VCe, VCC)
- Contractions, possessives, and compound words

ILLUSTRATIONS

- Illustrations of the important content and ideas in the text
- Illustrations that enhance and extend meaning in the text
- Illustrations with details that add interest and sometimes humor
- Illustrations that support interpretation, enhance enjoyment, or set mood but that are not necessary for understanding
- Many short texts with illustrations on every page or page spread
- Some texts with minimal illustrations

- Variety of layout in illustrations and print
- Simple illustrations in a variety of forms: e.g., photo and/or drawing with label or caption, diagram, map

BOOK AND PRINT FEATURES

LENGTH

- Short, usually sixteen pages
- Typically less than 500 words per book (200–500)

PRINT AND LAYOUT

- Print in clear font on pale background, sometimes with "knockout" (white on black)
- Mostly three to eight lines of text per page
- Sentences beginning on the left and turning over several lines
- Some limited variation in print placement
- Most texts with double or triple spaces between lines
- Clear spaces between words
- Print clearly separated from pictures
- Captions under pictures that provide important information

PUNCTUATION

- Use of period, comma, question mark, exclamation mark, and quotation marks
- Ellipses in some texts to indicate that the sentence finishes on the next page

ORGANIZATIONAL TOOLS

- Title, heading

Selecting Goals Behaviors and Understandings to Notice, Teach, and Support

SEARCHING FOR AND USING INFORMATION

- Sustain searching for information over a short text (eight to sixteen pages) and/or over an easy illustrated chapter book (forty to sixty pages)
- Use organizational tools to search for information: e.g., title, some headings
- Use background understanding of familiar, easy content to search for and use information
- Reread to search for and use information from language structure or meaning from multiple sources
- Use sentence structures (subject and predicate with some embedded phrases and clauses) to search for and use information
- Search for and use information that appears in beginning and ending phrases or clauses
- Search for information in sentences with clauses or phrases
- Search for information in sentences with variation in placement of subject, verb, adjectives, and adverbs
- Search for and understand information presented in a variety of ways: e.g., simple dialogue, dialogue with pronouns, split dialogue, assigned and sometimes unassigned dialogue, dialogue among multiple characters, some long stretches of dialogue, direct dialogue
- Use the chronological order of a simple story to search for and use information
- Notice and use punctuation marks (period, comma, question mark, exclamation mark, and quotation marks in many texts)
- Search for and use information from pictures or graphics
- Use labels or captions on photographs and drawings to search for and use information
- Use details in the illustrations to search for and use information

MONITORING AND SELF-CORRECTING

- Sometimes reread a word or phrase to self-monitor or self-correct
- Self-correct close to the point of error
- Use visual features of words to self-monitor and self-correct
- Use recognition of high-frequency words and other known words to self-monitor and self-correct

- Use multiple sources of information (visual information in print, meaning/pictures, language structure) to monitor and self-correct
- Show evidence of close attention to visual features of words
- Read without pointing
- Use awareness of narrative structure and of character attributes to self-monitor and self-correct
- Use understanding of dialogue to self-monitor and self-correct
- Use content knowledge of a simple topic to self-monitor and self-correct

SOLVING WORDS

▶ **Reading Words**

- Recognize words in clear, plain font that are on a plain white or very light background
- Recognize 100+ high-frequency words quickly and easily
- Recognize one-, two-, and three-syllable words with moderate picture support
- Read a range of regular and irregular plurals that are supported by language structure
- Read verbs in all tenses with inflectional endings that are supported by language structure
- Read some words with easy spelling patterns with the support of pictures and language (VC, CVC, CVC*e*, CVV, CVVC, VC*e*)
- Use word parts to solve some two-syllable or three-syllable words
- Locate high-frequency words and other important words in a text
- Say a word slowly to identify sounds in the word
- Read a range of contractions: e.g., words formed with *not, am, are, is, has,* and *will*
- Read a range of possessives: e.g., *a cat's nose, its, dogs' tails*
- Read many words that assign dialogue: e.g., *said, asked, cried, shouted, muttered*
- Read simple compound words: e.g., *into, sometimes*
- Read a variety of compound words and connect those with common parts

Selecting Goals Behaviors and Understandings to Notice, Teach, and Support *(cont.)*

THINKING *WITHIN* THE TEXT *(continued)*

▶ Vocabulary

- Understand the meaning of some words that are new but easy to understand in the context of the text, some with low picture support
- Expand understanding of the meaning of words by connection with the pictures and/or understanding the context
- Understand some content-specific words introduced, explained, and illustrated in context
- Read and understand words that stand for sounds (onomatopoetic words)
- Understand vocabulary words that are in common oral vocabulary for early readers (Tier 1)
- Understand the meaning of some words that appear in the vocabulary of mature language users (Tier 2)
- Understand the meaning of simple regular plurals formed with the endings *-s* or *-es*
- Understand the meaning of simple adjectives describing people, places, or things
- Understand the meaning of present participles and past participles of verbs with the inflectional endings *-ing* and *-ed*: e.g., *is looking, have looked*
- Understand the meaning of contractions using an apostrophe and one or more letters from words such as *not, am, are, is, has,* and *will*
- Understand words with an apostrophe indicating possession
- Understand some words that require the use of multiple sources of information (background knowledge, pictures, visual information)
- Understand words that indicate characters: e.g., easy-to-read names, family members, community members such as teachers
- Understand that words such as *I, me,* and *we* may signal the narrator of a text
- Understand the meaning of a variety of simple words that assign dialogue
- Recognize and understand labels for familiar objects, animals, people, the human body, weather, daily activities, simple processes such as cooking or growing plants
- Use details in illustrations to understand new vocabulary
- Understand the meaning and function of simple connectives

MAINTAINING FLUENCY

- Sustain momentum through an entire short text or a beginning chapter book, making significant progress daily
- Notice periods, quotation marks, commas, exclamation marks, and question marks, and begin to reflect them with the voice through intonation and pausing
- Demonstrate stress on words in a way that shows attention to meaning and stress words in bold
- Adjust reading to show awareness of sentence variety: i.e., placement of subject, verb, adjectives, and adverbs
- Reread to notice the language or meaning
- Recognize dialogue with phrasing, word stress, and intonation

ADJUSTING

- Slow down to problem-solve words and resume reading with momentum
- Adjust reading to accommodate compound sentences and sentences with a variety in order of clauses
- Recognize that a text is fiction and tells a story that has a beginning, middle, series of episodes, and end
- Understand that a nonfiction book tells facts
- Notice labels or captions on photographs and drawings and use them to understand the words in the text
- Adjust reading to notice information in a photograph or drawing
- Adjust to accommodate some variety in layout of illustrations and print
- Adjust reading to reflect a series of steps in an easy procedural book

SUMMARIZING

- Remember important information while reading to understand the meaning of the text
- Talk about the important information after reading
- Summarize the story including plot events, problem, resolution, and characters
- Summarize information in the text, selecting the information that is important
- Tell information about a temporal sequence in time order

Selecting Goals Behaviors and Understandings to Notice, Teach, and Support *(cont.)*

THINKING *BEYOND* THE TEXT

PREDICTING

- Use sentences with varied placement of subject, verb, adjectives, and adverbs, variety in placement of clauses, and some compound sentences to anticipate the text
- Make predictions based on information in pictures
- Make predictions based on personal knowledge and experience with texts
- Predict the ending of a story based on reading the beginning and middle
- Predict outcomes or endings based on repeating episodes in the plot
- Make predictions based on understanding of narrative structure
- Make predictions based on knowledge from personal experiences and from reading: e.g., food, cooking, pets, animals of the world, health and the human body, different environments and communities, machines
- Make predictions based on knowledge of underlying text structures: e.g., description, temporal sequence, question and answer, chronological sequence
- Make predictions based on a temporal sequence: e.g., plants growing, eggs hatching, making something, the water cycle

MAKING CONNECTIONS

- Make connections between personal experience and a text
- Make connections among books in a series
- Use background knowledge to understand settings
- Make connections between a text and an illustration that supports interpretation, enhances enjoyment, or sets mood
- Use background knowledge of traditional literature to recognize common characters and events in a folktale

- Make connections between background knowledge of familiar content and the content in the text
- Make connections among texts on the same topic or with similar content
- Access background knowledge to understand description or temporal sequence

SYNTHESIZING

- Talk about what the reader knows about the topic before reading the text and identify new knowledge gained from reading
- Talk about the text, showing understanding of events, topic, or content
- Talk about what is learned from the characters, the problem, and the resolution of the problem

INFERRING

- Infer meaning of story or content from pictures that add meaning to the text
- Notice aspects of the setting from the text and pictures and make inferences to help understand the story
- Talk about characters' feelings based on inferences from pictures and text, especially dialogue
- Talk about the pictures, revealing interpretation of a problem or of characters' feelings
- Infer obvious humor: e.g., humorous characters, language, and story problems
- Infer some obvious character traits from the story and pictures
- Infer ideas about familiar content
- Infer temporal sequences and notice the steps

THINKING *ABOUT* THE TEXT

ANALYZING

- Recognize that a text can be imagined (fiction) or it can give information (nonfiction)
- Understand that a story can be like real life or can be something that could not be true in real life (fantasy)
- Recognize characters that are typical of animal fantasy or traditional literature
- Recognize that a text can have true information
- Understand that a nonfiction book gives facts or tells how to do something
- Understand how the ideas and information in a book are related to each other

- Recognize and follow chronological sequence of events
- Recognize and understand variety in narrative structure: e.g., cumulative tale, circular story
- Recognize that a process happens in time order
- Recognize repetitive episodes in a text
- Recognize a writer's use of underlying text structures: e.g., description, temporal sequence, question and answer, chronological sequence
- Understand how the events, content, and ideas in a text are related to the title
- Recognize settings that are familiar
- Identify a story problem and how it is resolved

Selecting Goals Behaviors and Understandings to Notice, Teach, and Support *(cont.)*

THINKING *ABOUT* THE TEXT *(continued)*

- Talk about the characters in a story and how the writer shows what they are like
- Notice a writer's use of humorous words or onomatopoetic words and talk about how they add to the action
- Recognize very simple procedural language (directions)
- Recognize language that speaks directly to the reader: e.g., *you, your*
- Notice that illustrations add to important story action
- Think analytically about graphics (e.g., diagrams, maps)
- Understand that illustrations or photographs add to the ideas and information in a text
- Recognize that a text can have minimal illustrations
- Use some academic language to talk about genres: e.g., *fiction; family, friends, and school story; folktale; nonfiction; informational text; informational book; factual text*

- Use some academic language to talk about forms: e.g., *series book, play*
- Use some academic language to talk about literary features: e.g., *beginning, ending, problem, character*
- Use some specific language to talk about book and print features: e.g., *front cover, back cover, page, author, illustrator, illustration, photograph, title, label, drawing, heading, caption*

CRITIQUING

- Share opinions about a text and give rationales and examples
- Share opinions about an illustration or photograph
- Have favorite books and say why

Planning for Word Work After Guided Reading

Using your recent observations of the readers' ability to take words apart quickly and efficiently while reading text, plan for one to three minutes of active engagement of students' attention to letters, sounds, and words. Prioritize the readers' noticing of print features and active hands-on use of magnetic letters, a white board, word cards, or pencil and paper to promote fluency and flexibility in visual processing.

Examples:

- Recognize and write many high-frequency words
- Review high-frequency words from previous levels
- Take apart a compound word (*without, with, out*)
- Take apart a two-syllable word (*oth-er, ap-ple*)
- Recognize and use contractions with *have* (*I've, you've, should've*)
- Add *-es* to a singular noun to make a plural noun (*box/boxes*)
- Recognize and use irregular plurals that change the spelling of the word (*child/children, foot/feet*)
- Add an apostrophe and an *s* to a singular noun to show ownership (*kitten's nose, Juan's turtle*)

- Add an inflectional ending to a word to make a new word (*fix/fixing, fixed; skate/skating, skated*)
- Change the beginning sound or sounds to make a new word (*light/night*–change /l/ to /n/; *flew/new*–change /f/ /l/ to /n/)
- Change the ending sound or sounds to make a new word (*wet/went*–change /t/ to /n/ /t/)
- Change a middle sound to make a new word (*sat/sit*–change /a/ to /i/)
- Recognize and identify each letter in a few words using letter boxes
- Recognize, make, and break apart words that begin with an initial consonant, a consonant cluster, or a consonant digraph (*t̲ail; p̲rize; s̲how, t̲hing*)

- Recognize, make, and break apart words with double consonant letters in the middle (*pre̲t̲ty, ra̲b̲bit*)
- Read, write, make, and break apart words with a consonant cluster that blends two or three consonant sounds (*s̲tory, s̲treet*)
- Read, make, write, and break apart one-syllable words with a variety of phonogram patterns (*dog, fine, hand, near*)
- Recognize, make, and break apart words that contain phonograms with a double vowel pattern (*bee, look, door*)
- Recognize and use homophones–words that have the same sound, different spellings, and different meanings (*no, know*)
- Sort words in a variety of ways

Readers at Level

At level J, readers process a variety of texts, including short informational texts on familiar topics, short fiction texts, and longer illustrated narratives that have short chapters. They learn new content from informational texts and search for information in a variety of graphics. They adjust their reading strategies to process a range of fiction texts and informational texts including simple biographies. Readers are able to discuss the attributes and motives of characters and, where appropriate, the setting in which the action takes place. At level J there is only minimal character development. Readers process an increased number of longer and more complex sentences (those with more than fifteen words containing prepositional phrases, adjectives, adverbs, clauses, and both compound and complex sentences). Readers are able to automatically recognize a large number of words, and they can quickly apply word-solving strategies to multisyllable words with inflectional endings and suffixes. They can read a wide range of plurals, contractions, and possessives. In oral reading, they reflect appropriate rate, word stress, intonation, phrasing, and pausing (recognizing and using a range of punctuation). They read silently during independent reading and during individual reading opportunities during guided reading lessons. Readers continue to develop awareness of the characteristics of genres and can discuss them; they use academic language to talk about fiction and nonfiction texts.

Selecting Texts Characteristics of Texts at **Level J**

GENRE

▶ **Fiction**

- Realistic fiction
- Traditional literature (folktale, fairy tale, fable)
- Animal fantasy

▶ **Nonfiction**

- Expository nonfiction
- Narrative nonfiction
- Some simple biographies on familiar subjects
- Procedural texts

FORMS

- Some series books
- Picture books
- Beginning chapter books with illustrations
- Simple plays
- Readers' theater scripts
- Letters, journal entries

TEXT STRUCTURE

- Narrative texts with straightforward structure (beginning, series of episodes, and an ending)
- Narrative texts with multiple episodes, with episodes that may be more elaborate, and with less repetition of similar episodes

- Some books with very short chapters, each with narrative structure
- Some embedded forms (e.g., letters, directions) within narrative and expository structures
- Variation in narrative: e.g., cumulative tales, circular stories
- Some books with chapters connected to a single plot
- Nonfiction books divided into sections
- Underlying structural patterns: description, temporal sequence, chronological sequence, question and answer (nonfiction)

CONTENT

- Content interesting to and relevant for young readers
- Familiar content: e.g., family and home, play, pets, animals, school, food, community, friends, daily activities, the human body, weather, seasons, transportation, machines
- Moderate level of support provided by picture information
- More content that goes beyond students' immediate experience: e.g., different environments and communities, animals of the world

- Some stories with content familiar to students through prior experiences with storytelling, media, and hearing books read: e.g., folktales and fantasy
- Some content that requires accessing prior knowledge

THEMES AND IDEAS

- Concrete themes close to students' experience: e.g., imagination, courage, fears, friendship, family relationships, self, home, nature, growing, behavior, community, first responsibilities, diversity, belonging, peer relationships, feelings
- Clear, simple ideas easy to identify and understand
- Ideas close to students' experience: e.g., sharing with others, caring for others, doing your job, helping your family, taking care of self, staying healthy, caring for your world, empathizing with others, problem solving, valuing differences, expressing feelings

LANGUAGE AND LITERARY FEATURES

- Some texts with settings that are not typical of many students' experiences
- Some settings that are distant in time and geography
- Plot with conflict and resolution
- Plot that includes multiple episodes

Sasha kept walking
until she saw a woman
and a crying child.

"My boy is very hungry,"
the woman told Sasha.
"But I have nothing to feed him."

8

Sasha felt bad for the hungry child,
and she gave her bread to the woman.

"This will fill his belly," Sasha said.

"Thank you," said the woman.
"Please take this pencil as a gift.
It isn't much,
but it's all that I have to give."

9

- Characters with names
- Characters that change very little but may do some learning
- Clear evidence of character attributes
- Characters that are revealed over a series of books
- Variety in presentation of dialogue: e.g., dialogue among multiple characters, dialogue with pronouns, split dialogue, direct dialogue
- Unassigned dialogue
- Some long stretches of dialogue
- Elements of fantasy: e.g., talking animals or inanimate objects
- Basic motifs of traditional literature and modern fantasy: e.g., struggle between good and evil, magic, fantastic or magical objects, wishes, trickery, transformations
- Literary language typical of traditional literature: e.g., *long ago and far away*
- Procedural language
- Language used to make comparisons
- Descriptive language
- Language that speaks directly to the reader

SENTENCE COMPLEXITY

- Some longer sentences with more than fifteen words
- Variation in placement of subject, verb, adjectives, and adverbs
- Sentences with clauses or phrases
- Sentences with multiple adjectives, adverbs, and prepositional phrases
- Sentences with nouns, verbs, adjectives, and adverbs in a series, divided by commas
- Many sentences beginning with phrases
- Some sentences beginning with subordinate (dependent) clauses
- Sentences with simple common connectives: e.g., but, because
- Some complex sentences with variety in order of clauses

VOCABULARY

- Most vocabulary words known by children through oral language, listening to stories, or reading
- Most words that are in common oral vocabulary for younger students (Tier 1)
- Some words that appear in the vocabulary of mature language users (Tier 2)

- Some content-specific words introduced, explained, and illustrated in the text requiring use of context for understanding
- Wide variation in words used to assign dialogue
- Many adjectives describing people, places, or things
- Adverbs that describe actions
- Many common connectives (words, phrases that clarify relationships and ideas): e.g., *and, but, so, before, after*

WORDS

- Mostly one-, two-, three-, and four-syllable words with some picture support
- Full range of plurals signaled by language structure
- A variety of high-frequency words (150+)
- A wide variety of words with inflectional endings
- Words with easy spelling patterns (VC, CVC, CVV, CVCe, CVVC, VCe, VCC)
- Contractions, possessives, and compound words
- Common (simple) connectives

Selecting Texts Characteristics of Texts at Level **J** *(cont.)*

ILLUSTRATIONS

- Illustrations of the important content and ideas in the text
- Illustrations that enhance and extend meaning in the text
- Illustrations with details that add interest
- Illustrations that support interpretation, enhance enjoyment, or set mood but that are not necessary for understanding
- Many short texts with illustrations on every page or page spread
- Some texts with minimal illustrations
- Variety of layout in illustrations and print
- More than one kind of graphic on a page spread
- Simple illustrations in a variety of forms: e.g., photo and/or drawing with label or caption, diagram, map

BOOK AND PRINT FEATURES

LENGTH

- Usually sixteen to thirty-two pages
- Typically less than 700 words per book (250-700)
- Some books divided into chapters
- Some books divided into sections

PRINT AND LAYOUT

- Many lines of print on a page (approximately three to twelve lines in short texts)
- Some sentences starting in the middle of a line
- Variety in placement of print and pictures, reflecting different genres
- Most texts with double or triple spaces between lines
- Captions under pictures that provide important information
- Print placed in sidebars and graphics that provide important information

PUNCTUATION

- Period, comma, question mark, exclamation mark, and quotation marks in most texts
- Ellipses in some texts to indicate that the sentence finishes on the next page

ORGANIZATIONAL TOOLS

- Title, table of contents, chapter title, heading, sidebar

ORGANIZATIONAL TOOLS

- Title, table of contents, chapter title, heading, sidebar

TEXT RESOURCES

- Dedication

Selecting Goals Behaviors and Understandings to Notice, Teach, and Support

SEARCHING FOR AND USING INFORMATION

- Sustain searching for information over a short text (sixteen to thirty-two pages) and/or over an easy illustrated chapter book (forty to sixty pages)
- Use organizational tools to search for information: e.g., title, table of contents, chapter title, heading
- Read texts with some sentences starting in the middle of a line after punctuation
- Use background understanding of familiar, easy content to search for and use information
- Reread to search for and use information from language structure or meaning from multiple sources
- Search for and use information in texts with variety in placement of the body text, sidebars, and graphics
- Search for information in sentences with nouns, verbs, adjectives, or adverbs in a series divided by commas
- Search for and use information that appears in beginning and ending phrases or clauses
- Search for and understand information presented in a variety of ways: e.g., simple dialogue, dialogue with pronouns, split dialogue, assigned and sometimes unassigned dialogue, dialogue among multiple characters, some long stretches of dialogue, direct dialogue
- Search for and understand information over some long stretches of dialogue with multiple characters talking
- Search for information in simple sentences that may be statements or questions
- Use the chronological order of a simple story to search for and use information
- Search for information across chapters connected to a single plot
- Notice and use punctuation marks (period, comma, question mark, exclamation mark, and quotation marks in most texts)
- Search for and use information from pictures or graphics
- Use details in the pictures to search for and use information

MONITORING AND SELF-CORRECTING

- Sometimes reread a word or phrase to self-monitor or self-correct
- Self-correct close to the point of error
- Use visual features of words to self-monitor and self-correct
- Use recognition of known words to self-monitor and self-correct
- Use multiple sources of information (visual information in print, meaning/pictures, graphics, language structure) to monitor and self-correct
- Show evidence of close attention to visual features of words
- Read without pointing
- Use awareness of narrative structure and of character attributes to self-monitor and self-correct
- Use understanding of dialogue to self-monitor and self-correct
- Use content knowledge of a simple topic to self-monitor and self-correct

SOLVING WORDS

▶ Reading Words

- Recognize 200+ high-frequency words quickly and easily
- Recognize two-, three-, and four-syllable words with some picture support
- Read plurals using -s and -es, most supported by pictures and language structure
- Read a range of regular and irregular plurals that are supported by language structure
- Read verbs in all tenses with inflectional endings that are supported by language structure
- Read some words with easy spelling patterns supported by pictures and language (VC, CVC, CVCe, CVV, CVVC, VCe, VCC)
- Use word parts to solve multisyllable words
- Locate important new words in a text
- Read contractions, possessives, compound words, and simple connectives
- Connect compound words that have the same parts
- Read a wide range of words that assign dialogue
- Notice parts of words and connect them to other words to solve them
- Solve words rapidly while processing continuous text and with minimum overt self-correction

Selecting Goals Behaviors and Understandings to Notice, Teach, and Support *(cont.)*

THINKING *WITHIN* THE TEXT *(continued)*

VOCABULARY

- Understand the meaning of some words that are new but easy to understand in the context of the text, some with low picture support
- Understand some content-specific words introduced, explained, and illustrated in context
- Add to oral vocabulary through reading
- Understand many words that are in common oral vocabulary for early readers (Tier 1)
- Understand some words that appear in the language of mature language users and in written texts (Tier 2)
- Understand the meaning of a range of regular and irregular plurals
- Understand the meaning of adjectives describing nouns or pronouns
- Understand the meaning of adverbs that describe verbs
- Understand the meaning of a range of verbs in all tenses with inflectional endings
- Understand the meaning of contractions and possessives
- Understand some words that require the use of multiple sources of information (background knowledge, pictures, visual information)
- Understand the function and meaning of common connectives
- Understand words such as *I, me,* and *we* that may signal the narrator of a text
- Understand the meaning of a range of words that assign dialogue
- Recognize and understand labels for familiar objects, animals, people, the human body, weather, daily activities, procedures, some scientific processes
- Use details in illustrations to understand new vocabulary
- Use a glossary to learn or check the meaning of words

MAINTAINING FLUENCY

- Read both orally and silently at a rate that reflects fluent processing but also maintains comprehension and accuracy
- Sustain momentum through an entire short text or a beginning chapter book, making significant progress daily
- Notice periods, quotation marks, commas, exclamation marks, and question marks, and begin to reflect them with the voice through intonation and pausing
- Read orally with appropriate phrasing, pausing, intonation, word stress, and rate

- Adjust reading to show awareness or sentence variety: i.e., placement of parts of speech, phrases, and clauses
- Stress words that are in bold or italics
- Reread to notice the language or meaning
- Recognize and read expressively a variety of dialogue, some unassigned
- Reflect numbered and bulleted lists with the voice when reading orally

ADJUSTING

- Slow down to problem-solve words and resume reading with momentum
- Adjust reading to accommodate compound sentences and sentences with a variety in order of clauses
- Adjust to accommodate embedded forms (e.g., letters, journal entries) within narrative and expository texts
- Adjust to read parts in a readers' theater script or play
- Recognize that a text is fiction and tells a story that has a beginning, middle, series of episodes, and end
- Understand that a nonfiction book tells facts
- Understand that when you read a biography, you are reading the story of a person's life
- Notice labels or captions on photographs and drawings and use them to understand the words in the text
- Adjust reading to accommodate varied placement of text body, photographs and drawings with labels or captions, sidebars, and graphics
- Adjust reading to reflect a series of steps in a procedural text

SUMMARIZING

- Remember important information while reading to understand the meaning of the text
- Talk about important information in organized summary form after reading
- Summarize the story including plot events, problem, resolution, and characters
- Summarize information in the text, selecting the information that is important
- Summarize temporal sequence in time order
- Summarize simple narrative nonfiction or biography in time order

Selecting Goals Behaviors and Understandings to Notice, Teach, and Support *(cont.)*

THINKING *BEYOND* THE TEXT

PREDICTING

- Use sentences with varied placement of subject, verb, adjectives, and adverbs, variety in placement of clauses, and some compound sentences to anticipate the text
- Make predictions based on information in illustrations and graphics
- Make predictions based on background knowledge and experience in reading texts
- Predict events of the plot, behavior of characters, and the ending of a story based on understanding of the setting, problem, and characters
- Make predictions based on understanding of narrative structure
- Make predictions based on knowledge from personal experiences and from reading: e.g., food, cooking, pets, animals of the world, health and the human body, community, the environment, machines
- Make predictions based on knowledge of underlying text structures: e.g., description, temporal sequence, question and answer, chronological sequence
- Make predictions based on a temporal sequence: e.g., plants growing, eggs hatching, making something, the water cycle

MAKING CONNECTIONS

- Make connections between personal experience and texts
- Use prior knowledge to understand the content in a nonfiction text
- Make connections among books in a series
- Use background knowledge to understand settings
- Make connections between a text and an illustration that supports interpretation, enhances enjoyment, or sets mood
- Use background knowledge of traditional literature to recognize common characters and events in a folktale
- Use background knowledge (from experience and reading) to understand settings in stories
- Make connections among texts on the same topic or with similar content
- Access background knowledge to understand description or temporal sequence

SYNTHESIZING

- Talk about what the reader knows about the topic before reading the text and identify new knowledge gained from reading
- Talk about the text, showing understanding of events, topic, or content
- Talk about what is learned from the characters, the problem, and the resolution of the problem

INFERRING

- Infer meaning of story or content from pictures that add meaning to the text
- Notice aspects of the setting from the text and pictures and make inferences about setting to help understand the story
- Talk about characters' feelings based on inferences from pictures and text, especially dialogue
- Talk about the pictures, revealing interpretation of a problem or of characters' feelings
- Infer obvious humor: e.g., humorous characters, language, and story problems
- Infer ideas about familiar content
- Infer temporal sequences and reasons for each step

GUIDED READING

LEVEL **J**

Selecting Goals Behaviors and Understandings to Notice, Teach, and Support *(cont.)*

THINKING ***ABOUT*** THE TEXT

ANALYZING

- Distinguish between realistic fiction and fantasy
- Recognize characters that are typical of animal fantasy or traditional literature
- Understand what distinguishes nonfiction from fiction
- Recognize a writer's use of embedded forms (e.g., letters, journal entries, emails) within narrative or expository texts
- Recognize when a writer uses temporal (time) order to describe a process
- Recognize that a text can have true information
- Understand how the ideas and information in a book are related to each other
- Recognize and follow chronological sequence of events
- Recognize and understand variety in narrative structure: e.g., cumulative tale, circular story
- Recognize a writer's use of underlying text structures: e.g., description, temporal sequence, question and answer, chronological sequence
- Understand how the events, content, and ideas in a text are related to the title
- Recognize settings that are familiar, as well as some settings distant in time and geography
- Identify a central story problem in a text with multiple episodes
- Notice the evidence a writer provides to show character attributes
- Notice a writer's use of humorous words or onomatopoetic words and talk about how they add to the action
- Recognize very simple procedural language: e.g., directions
- Recognize language that speaks directly to the reader: e.g., *you, your*

- Notice and follow unassigned dialogue
- Notice and understand literary language that is typical of traditional literature: e.g., *A long time ago there lived*
- Notice how a writer uses common connectives (e.g., *but, because*) to clarify relationships between ideas
- Notice that illustrations add to important story action
- Notice and understand how the graphics and sidebars complement the body of the text
- Understand that illustrations or photographs add to the ideas and information in a text
- Use some academic language to talk about genres: e.g., *fiction; family, friends, and school story; folktale; animal story; humorous story; nonfiction; informational text; informational book; factual text*
- Use some academic language to talk about forms: e.g., *series book, play*
- Use some academic language to talk about literary features: e.g., *beginning, ending, problem, character, time and place, question and answer*
- Use some specific language to talk about book and print features: e.g., *front cover, back cover, page, author, illustrator, illustration, photograph, title, label, drawing, heading, caption, table of contents, chapter, chapter title, dedication, sidebar*

CRITIQUING

- Share opinions about a text and give rationales and examples
- Share opinions about an illustration or photograph
- Have favorite books, writers, and illustrators, and describe their qualities

Selecting Goals Behaviors and Understandings to Notice, Teach, and Support *(cont.)*

Planning for Word Work After Guided Reading

Using your recent observations of the readers' ability to take words apart quickly and efficiently while reading text, plan for one to three minutes of active engagement of students' attention to letters, sounds, and words. Prioritize the readers' noticing of print features and active hands-on use of magnetic letters, a white board, word cards, or pencil and paper to promote fluency and flexibility in visual processing.

Examples:

- Recognize and write many high-frequency words
- Review high-frequency words from previous levels
- Take apart compound words and notice parts that appear in many compound words: e.g., *somebody, someone, sometime, someday*
- Take apart a two-syllable word (*wom-an, squir-rel*)
- Recognize and use contractions with *had* or *would* (*I'd, we'd, you'd, he'd, she'd, they'd, who'd*)

- Add *-s* or *-es* to a singular noun to make a plural noun (*clown/clowns; circus/circuses*)
- Change *y* to *i* and add *-es* to a singular noun to make a plural noun (*penny/pennies*)
- Add an inflectional ending to a word to make a new word (*snow/snowing, snowed; trick/tricking, tricked*)
- Recognize and identify each letter in a few words using letter boxes
- Read, make, break apart, and write one-syllable words with a variety of phonogram patterns (*hot, made, old, rain*) including the use of *y* as a vowel (*by, my*)

- Recognize, make, and break apart words that contain phonograms with a double vowel pattern (*room, took*)
- Solve words using letter-sound analysis from left to right (*n-o-th-i-ng*)
- Recognize and use homophones–words that have the same sound, different spellings, and different meanings (*nose, knows*)
- Sort words in a variety of ways

Readers at Level

At level K, readers process a wide range of genres (realistic fiction, animal fantasy, traditional literature, some simple biographies, expository nonfiction, and other informational texts). They read many illustrated chapter books (including some series books). Most fiction texts have multiple episodes related to a single plot, but the demand on the reader's memory is higher than at previous levels. They read about characters that change very little but are at the same time more complex; and readers encounter some literary language. Readers process a great deal of dialogue, some of it unassigned, and are challenged to read stories based on concepts that are distant in time and geography and reflect diverse cultures. Readers solve many content-specific words and some technical words in informational texts. They encounter new information and ideas in nonfiction texts and learn from them. They automatically recognize a large number of words and quickly apply word-solving strategies to multisyllable words with inflectional endings, and to words with suffixes and prefixes. They can read a wide range of plurals, contractions, and possessives. They read silently in independent reading, but when reading orally they demonstrate all aspects of fluent reading. Readers continue to develop awareness of the characteristics of genres and can discuss them. Their ability to use academic language is expanding.

Selecting Texts Characteristics to Texts at **Level K**

GENRE

▶ Fiction

- Realistic fiction
- Traditional literature (folktale, fairy tale, fable)
- Animal fantasy

▶ Nonfiction

- Expository nonfiction
- Narrative nonfiction
- Some simple biographies on familiar subjects
- Procedural texts

FORMS

- Series books
- Picture books
- Beginning chapter books with illustrations
- Plays
- Readers' theater scripts
- Some graphic texts
- Letters, journal entries

TEXT STRUCTURE

- Narrative texts with straightforward structure (beginning, series of episodes, and an ending)
- Narrative texts with multiple episodes, with episodes that may be more elaborate, and with less repetition of similar episodes
- Some books with very short chapters, each with narrative structure

- Some embedded forms (e.g., letters, directions) within narrative and expository structures
- Variation in narrative: e.g., cumulative tales, circular stories
- Some books with chapters connected to a single plot
- Nonfiction books divided into sections
- Underlying structural patterns: description, temporal sequence, chronological sequence, question and answer

CONTENT

- Content interesting to and relevant for readers
- Continued presence of familiar content
- Varied levels of support provided by picture information
- More content that goes beyond students' immediate experience: e.g., different environments and communities, animals of the world
- Some stories with content familiar to students through prior experiences with storytelling, media, and hearing books read aloud
- Some content that requires accessing prior knowledge
- Some content that requires the reader to search for information in graphics: e.g., maps, charts, diagrams, illustrated drawings, labeled photographs

THEMES AND IDEAS

- Concrete themes close to students' experience: e.g., imagination, courage, fears, friendship, family relationships, self, home, nature, growing, behavior, community, first responsibilities, diversity, belonging, peer relationships, feelings
- Some books with multiple ideas, easy to understand
- Ideas close to students' experience: e.g., sharing with others, caring for others, doing your job, helping your family, taking care of self, staying healthy, caring for your world, empathizing with others, problem solving, valuing differences, expressing feelings, learning about life's challenges

LANGUAGE AND LITERARY FEATURES

- Some texts with settings that are not typical of many students' experiences
- Some settings that are distant in time and geography
- Settings that are important to comprehension of the fiction narrative or biography
- Plot with conflict and resolution
- Plot that includes multiple episodes
- Main characters and supporting characters
- Characters that may learn simple lessons but not essentially change
- Characters that are revealed over a series of events, chapters, or book series

Wildlife Crossings

Many people want to help
animals cross roads.
They can't teach animals
to look both ways.
But people can build wildlife crossings
for animals to use.
Wildlife crossings are places
where animals can cross the road safely.

The animals can walk over the road
or under the road.
They don't have to walk *on* the road at all.
The animals won't be hurt by cars.

tunnel

bridge

160

6

7

- Variety in presentation of dialogue: e.g., dialogue among multiple characters, dialogue with pronouns, split dialogue, direct dialogue
- Unassigned dialogue
- Some long stretches of dialogue
- Most texts written in first- or third-person narrative, with a few in second person
- Most texts told from a single point of view
- Elements of fantasy: e.g., talking animals or inanimate objects
- Basic motifs of traditional literature and modern fantasy: e.g., struggle between good and evil, magic, fantastic or magical objects, wishes, trickery, transformations
- Literary language typical of traditional literature: e.g., *long ago and far away*
- Some figurative language: e.g., metaphor, simile
- Procedural language
- Language used to make comparisons
- Descriptive language
- Language used to show chronological order and temporal sequence
- Language that speaks directly to the reader

SENTENCE COMPLEXITY

- Some longer sentences with more than fifteen words
- Variation in placement of subject, verb, adjectives, and adverbs
- Sentences with clauses or phrases
- Sentences with multiple adjectives, adverbs, and prepositional phrases
- Sentences with nouns, verbs, adjectives, and adverbs in a series, divided by commas
- Many sentences beginning with phrases and subordinate (dependent) clauses
- Sentences with simple (common) connectives
- Some complex sentences with variety in order of clauses
- Occasional use of parenthetical material embedded in sentences

VOCABULARY

- Some vocabulary words acquired by students through reading or listening to stories or nonfiction read aloud
- Most words that are in common oral vocabulary for the age group (Tier 1)
- Some words that appear in the vocabulary of mature language users (Tier 2)

- Many content-specific words introduced, explained, and illustrated in the text, requiring use of context for understanding
- Wide variation in words used to assign dialogue or speech
- Many adjectives describing people, places, or things
- Adverbs that describe actions
- Words with multiple meanings
- New vocabulary that requires strategic action to understand: e.g., derive meaning from context
- Many common connectives (words, phrases that clarify relationships and ideas): e.g., *and, but, so, before, after*

WORDS

- One-, two-, three-, and four-syllable words
- Full range of plurals signalled by language structure
- A variety of high-frequency words (200+)
- A wide variety of verbs with inflectional endings
- Adjectives with the comparative endings *-er, -est*
- Many multisyllable words with some complex letter-sound relationships

LEVEL **K**

Selecting Texts Characteristics of Texts at **Level K** (*cont.*)

WORDS (*continued*)

- Words with easy spelling patterns (VC, CVC, CVV, CVC*e*, CVVC, VC*e*, VCC)
- Wide range of contractions and possessives
- Full range of compound words
- Common (simple) connectives

ILLUSTRATIONS

- Illustrations of the important content and ideas in the text
- Illustrations that enhance and extend meaning in the text
- Illustrations with details that add interest
- Illustrations that support interpretation, enhance enjoyment, or set mood, but are not necessary for understanding
- Many short texts with illustrations on every page or page spread
- Some texts with minimal illustrations
- Variety of layout in illustrations and print
- More than one kind of graphic on a page spread
- A few books with black-and-white illustrations
- Some graphic texts in which illustrations carry much of the meaning
- Some short chapter books with an illustration every three of four pages
- Simple illustrations in a variety of forms: e.g., photo and/or drawing with label or caption, diagram, map

BOOK AND PRINT FEATURES

LENGTH

- Usually sixteen to thirty-two pages
- Wide variation in number of words (350–700)
- Some books divided into chapters
- Some books divided into sections

PRINT AND LAYOUT

- Variety in font size
- Variety in print and background color
- Many lines of print on a page (approximately three to twelve lines in short texts)
- Sentences starting middle of a line
- Variety in placement of print and pictures, reflecting different genres
- Information shown in a variety of picture and print combinations in graphic texts

- Captions under pictures that provide important information
- Print placed in sidebars and graphics that provide important information

PUNCTUATION

- Period, comma, question mark, exclamation mark, and quotation marks in most texts
- Ellipses in some texts to indicate that the sentence finishes on the next page

ORGANIZATIONAL TOOLS

- Title, table of contents, chapter title, heading, sidebar

TEXT RESOURCES

- Dedication, author's note, glossary

Selecting Goals Behaviors and Understandings to Notice, Teach, and Support

THINKING *WITHIN* THE TEXT

SEARCHING FOR AND USING INFORMATION

- Sustain searching for information over a short text (usually under thirty-two pages) and/or over an easy illustrated chapter book
- Use organizational tools and text resources to search for information: e.g., title, table of contents, chapter title, heading, sidebar, glossary
- Read texts with some sentences starting in the middle of a line after punctuation
- Reread to search for and use information from multiple sources
- Search for and use information in texts with variety in placement of the body of a text, sidebars, and graphics
- Search for information in sentences with nouns, verbs, adjectives, or adverbs in a series divided by commas
- Search for information in sentences with multiple clauses or phrases
- Search for and understand information presented in a variety of ways: e.g., simple dialogue, dialogue with pronouns, split dialogue, assigned and sometimes unassigned dialogue, dialogue among multiple characters, some long stretches of dialogue, direct dialogue
- Search for and understand information over some long stretches of dialogue with multiple characters talking
- Search for and use information from previous books when reading a series
- Use organizational tools to search for information: e.g., title, table of contents, chapter title, heading, sidebar
- Use text resources to search for information: e.g., author's note, glossary
- Use background knowledge to search for and understand information about settings
- Use the chronological order within multiple episodes to search for and use information
- Search for information across chapters connected to a single plot
- Notice and use punctuation marks: e.g., period, comma, question mark, exclamation mark, quotation marks
- Search for and use information from a wide variety of illustrations or graphics

MONITORING AND SELF-CORRECTING

- Sometimes reread a word or phrase to self-monitor or self-correct
- Self-correct close to the point of error
- Use multiple sources of information (visual information in print, meaning/pictures, graphics, language structure) to monitor and self-correct
- Use visual features of words to self-monitor and self-correct
- Use recognition of known words to self-monitor and self-correct
- Use awareness of narrative structure and of character attributes to self-monitor and self-correct

- Use understanding of dialogue to self-monitor and self-correct
- Use content knowledge of a simple topic to self-monitor and self-correct

SOLVING WORDS

▶ Reading Words

- Recognize a large number of high-frequency words quickly and automatically
- Recognize multisyllable words or take them apart by syllables to solve them
- Read plurals using *-s* and *-es,* most supported by pictures and language structure
- Read a range of regular and irregular plurals that are supported by language structure
- Read words that show comparison with the suffixes *-er* and *-est*
- Read verbs of all tenses with inflectional endings
- Use word parts to solve words
- Notice phonogram patterns and use them to solve multisyllable words
- Read a wide range of contractions, possessives, compound words, and simple connectives
- Read a wide range of words that assign dialogue
- Notice parts of words and connect them to other words to solve them
- Solve words rapidly while processing continuous text and with minimum overt self-correction

▶ Vocabulary

- Derive the meaning of a new word from words around it in the sentence or paragraph
- Expand meaning of a word by connecting it to other words
- Add to oral vocabulary through reading
- Connect words to synonyms and antonyms to expand understanding
- Understand many words that are in common oral vocabulary for the age group (Tier 1)
- Understand words that appear in the language of mature users and in written texts (Tier 2)
- Understand the meaning of a range of regular and irregular plurals
- Understand that some words have multiple meanings
- Understand many words that have multiple meanings and identify the specific meaning that applies in a sentence or paragraph
- Understand the meaning of verbs in all tenses
- Understand the meaning of a wide range of contractions and possessives

Selecting Goals Behaviors and Understandings to Notice, Teach, and Support *(cont.)*

THINKING *WITHIN* THE TEXT *(continued)*

SOLVING WORDS *(continued)*

▶ **Vocabulary** *(continued)*

- Understand words that require the use of multiple sources of information (background knowledge, pictures, visual information)
- Understand the function and meaning of common (simple) connectives
- Understand that words such as *I, me,* and *we* that may signal the narrator of a text
- Understand the meaning of a variety of words that assign dialogue: e.g., *said, asked, cried, shouted, answered, whispered*
- Understand the meaning of verbs that show the action in a story, adjectives that describe characters or setting, and adverbs that describe the action
- Understand some content-specific words introduced, explained, and illustrated in context
- Use details in illustrations to understand new vocabulary
- Use a glossary to learn or check the meaning of words
- Understand key words in graphics such as maps, diagrams, and charts

MAINTAINING FLUENCY

- Read both orally and silently at a rate that reflects fluent processing but also maintains comprehension and accuracy
- Sustain momentum through short texts and some beginning chapter books, making significant progress each day
- Notice periods, quotation marks, commas, exclamation marks, and question marks and begin to reflect them with the voice through intonation and pausing
- Read orally with appropriate phrasing, pausing, intonation, word stress, and rate
- Read silently at a satisfactory rate
- Stress words that are in bold or italics
- Reread to notice the language or meaning
- Recognize and read expressively a variety of dialogue, some unassigned
- Read parts in a script with expression
- Reflect numbered and bulleted lists with the voice when reading orally

ADJUSTING

- Slow down to problem-solve words and resume reading with momentum
- Adjust reading to show awareness or sentence variety (i.e., placement of parts of speech, phrases, and clauses)
- Adjust reading to accommodate compound sentences and sentences with a variety in order of clauses
- Adjust to accommodate embedded forms (e.g., letters) within narrative and expository texts
- Adjust reading to process a graphic text
- Recognize that a text is fiction and tells a story that has a beginning, middle, problem, series of episodes, and end
- Adjust to read parts in a readers' theater script or a play
- Understand that a nonfiction book tells facts
- Understand that when you read a biography, you are reading the story of a person's life
- Notice labels or captions on photographs and drawings and use them to understand the words in the text
- Adjust reading to accommodate varied placement of text body, photographs and drawings with labels or captions, sidebars, and graphics
- Adjust reading to reflect a series of steps in a procedural text

SUMMARIZING

- Remember important information while reading to understand the meaning of the text
- Talk about the important information in organized summary form after reading
- Summarize the story including plot events, problem, resolution, and characters
- Summarize information in the text, selecting the information that is important
- Summarize a temporal sequence in time order
- Summarize simple narrative nonfiction or biography in time order

Selecting Goals Behaviors and Understandings to Notice, Teach, and Support *(cont.)*

THINKING *BEYOND* THE TEXT

PREDICTING

- Use knowledge of grammatical structure (clauses, phrases) to anticipate the text
- Make predictions based on the meaning of the text, with or without picture support
- Make predictions based on knowledge and experience
- Make predictions throughout a text based on the organizational structure (narrative, expository)
- Predict events of the plot, behavior of characters, and the ending of a story based on understanding of the setting, problem, and characters
- Make predictions based on knowledge of the genres of realistic fiction, animal fantasy, traditional literature
- Make predictions based on knowledge from personal experiences and from reading: e.g., food, cooking, pets, animals of the world, health and the human body, community, the environment, machines
- Make predictions based on knowledge of underlying text structures: e.g., description, temporal sequence, question and answer, chronological sequence
- Make predictions based on a temporal sequence: e.g., plants growing, eggs hatching, making something, the water cycle

MAKING CONNECTIONS

- Make connections between personal experience and texts
- Make connections among books in a series
- Use background knowledge to understand settings
- Make connections among texts of the same genre
- Use background knowledge of traditional literature to recognize common characters and events in a folktale
- Make connections between the events in chapters that are connected to a single plot
- Use background knowledge (from experience and reading) to understand settings in stories
- Access background knowledge acquired from reading to understand the content of a text

- Make connections among texts on the same topic or with similar content
- Access background knowledge to understand description or temporal sequence

SYNTHESIZING

- Talk about what the reader knows about the topic before reading the text and identify new knowledge gained from reading
- Talk about the text showing understanding of events, topic, or content
- Talk about what is learned from the characters, the problem, and the resolution of the problem

INFERRING

- Infer meaning of story or content from pictures that add meaning to the text
- Notice aspects of the setting from the text and pictures and make inferences to help understand the story
- Talk about the pictures, revealing interpretation of a problem or of characters' feelings
- Notice and understand humor in a text
- Infer information about characters, setting, plot, and action from graphic texts, in which illustrations carry much of the meaning
- Infer ideas about familiar content
- Infer temporal sequences and notice the reasons for each step
- Understand and infer the importance of the setting of a biography that may be distant in time and geography from students' own knowledge

Selecting Goals Behaviors and Understandings to Notice, Teach, and Support *(cont.)*

THINKING *ABOUT* THE TEXT

ANALYZING

- Distinguish between fiction and nonfiction and articulate the characteristic differences
- Understand and describe characteristics of fiction genres, including realistic fiction, traditional literature (folktale, fairy tale, fable), and fantasy
- Understand that a story can be like real life or can be something that could not be true in real life (fantasy)
- Recognize characters that are typical of animal fantasy or traditional literature
- Recognize that a text can have true information
- Understand that a nonfiction book gives facts or tells how to do something
- Understand and describe the characteristics of nonfiction genres: e.g., expository text, simple narrative nonfiction, biography, and procedural text
- Understand that a biography is the story of a person's life and is usually told in chronological order
- Understand the unique characteristics of graphic texts
- Understand how the ideas and information in a book are related to each other
- Recognize a writer's use of embedded forms (e.g., letters) within narrative or expository texts
- Recognize and follow chronological sequence of events
- Recognize and understand variety in narrative structure: e.g., cumulative tale, circular story
- Recognize that a process happens in time order
- Recognize a writer's use of underlying text structures: e.g., description, temporal sequence, question and answer
- Understand how the events, content, and ideas in a text are related to the title
- Recognize settings that are familiar as well as some distant in time and geography
- Understand how a setting is important to the plot and the characters' perspectives
- Identify a central story problem in a text with multiple episodes
- Understand the role of supporting characters in a story
- Notice the evidence a writer provides to show character attributes
- Understand the perspective from which a story is told and talk about why a writer selected it
- Understand first-person and third-person narrative
- Notice and follow unassigned dialogue

- Notice a writer's use of humorous words or onomatopoetic words and talk about how they add to the action
- Recognize very simple procedural language: e.g., directions
- Recognize when the writer uses second person (speaks directly to the reader): e.g., *you, your*
- Notice language used to show chronological order
- Notice a writer's use of figurative language (metaphor, simile)
- Notice how a writer uses simple connectives (*because, before, after*) to clarify relationships between ideas
- Notice how a writer uses more sophisticated connectives that are not typically used in oral language: e.g., *meanwhile*
- Notice parenthetical material set off by commas or parentheses
- Notice that illustrations add to important story action
- Understand that illustrations carry the dialogue and action in graphic texts
- Notice and understand how the graphics and sidebars complement the body of the text
- Understand that illustrations or photographs add to the ideas and information in a text
- Use some academic language to talk about genres: e.g., *fiction; family, friends, and school story; folktale; animal story; humorous story; nonfiction; informational text; informational book; factual text; how-to book*
- Use some academic language to talk about forms: e.g., *series book, play, chapter book, letter*
- Use some academic language to talk about literary features: e.g., *beginning, ending, problem, character, time and place, question and answer, main character, character change, message, dialogue, topic*
- Use some specific language to talk about book and print features: e.g., *front cover, back cover, page, author, illustrator, illustration, photograph, title, label, drawing, heading, caption, table of contents, chapter, chapter title, dedication, sidebar, glossary, map, diagram, author's note, illustrator's note, section*

CRITIQUING

- Share opinions about a text and give rationales and examples
- Share opinions about an illustration or photograph
- Give an opinion about the believability of plot or characters
- Talk critically about what a writer does to make a topic interesting or important
- Talk about why the subject of a biography is important or sets an example for others

Selecting Goals Behaviors and Understandings to Notice, Teach, and Support *(cont.)*

Planning for Word Work After Guided Reading

Using your recent observations of the readers' ability to take words apart quickly and efficiently while reading text, plan for one to three minutes of active engagement of students' attention to letters, sounds, and words. Prioritize the readers' noticing of print features and active hands-on use of magnetic letters, a white board, word cards, or pencil and paper to promote fluency and flexibility in visual processing.

Examples:

- Recognize and write many high-frequency words
- Review high-frequency words from previous levels
- Take apart compound words and notice how the parts contribute to meaning
- Take apart compound words and notice parts that appear in many compound words: e.g., *somebody, someone, sometime, someday, today*
- Recognize and use contractions with *not, am, are, is, has, will, have, had,* and *would*
- Add *-s* or *-es* to a singular noun to make a plural noun (*farmer/farmers; branch/branches*)
- Change *y* to *i* and add *-es* to a singular noun to make a plural noun (*berry/berries*)

- Add an inflectional ending to a word to make a new word (*finish/finishing, finished; skate/skating, skated*)
- Add the suffix *-er* or or the suffix *-est* to a word to show comparison (*dark/darker/darkest; clean/cleaner/cleanest*)
- Add the suffix *er* to a word to form a noun that names a person or thing that does something (*teach, teacher*)
- Recognize, make, and break apart words that end with a consonant cluster or a consonant digraph (*ba<u>nd</u>, ba<u>ng</u>, ba<u>nk</u>, he<u>lp</u>, hims<u>elf</u>; eno<u>ugh</u>, kno<u>ck</u>, mou<u>th</u>*)
- Recognize and use words with consonant letters that have no sound (*lam<u>b</u>, li<u>gh</u>t, si<u>gn</u>*)
- Contrast short and long vowel sounds in words (*bit/bite, hop/hope*)
- Recognize and use vowel sounds with *r* (*chair, care, card, corn, floor*)

- Recognize, make, and break apart words that contain phonograms with a double vowel pattern (*deep, wood*)
- Break apart two-syllable words by syllable (*care/ful, din/ner*)
- Hear, say, clap, and identify syllables in words with three or more syllables (*an/oth/er, bi/cy/cle, bas/ket/ball, be/gin/ning*)
- Solve words using letter-sound analysis from left to right (*h-u-n-t-er*)
- Recognize and use homophones (words with the same pronunciation, different spellings, and different meanings) (*their, there; blue, blew*)
- Recognize and use homographs (words with the same spelling, different meanings and origins, and may have different pronunciations) (*read, present*)
- Sort words based on any word feature

Readers at Level

At level L, readers process easy chapter books including some series books, with more sophisticated characters and few illustrations, as well as short informational and fiction books. They adjust their reading to process a range of genres including realistic fiction, several special types of fiction (mystery, sports), traditional literature (folktale, fairy tale, fable), fantasy, and informational texts (biography and memoir), as well as hybrid texts. Readers understand that books can have chapters with multiple episodes related to a single plot. They learn some new content through reading and are required to bring more prior knowledge to the process; but the content is usually accessible through the text and illustrations. At this level, readers begin to recognize themes across texts (courage, community, peer relationships), and they understand some abstract ideas (empathizing with others, valuing differences). They encounter characters that learn and change and that are revealed through descriptions of what they say, think, and do, as well as by what others say and think about them. They process complex sentences with embedded clauses and figurative and poetic language. They recognize and/or flexibly solve a large number of words, including plurals, contractions, possessives, many multisyllable words, many content-specific words, and some technical words. They read silently in independent reading; in oral reading, they demonstrate all aspects of smooth, fluent processing. Readers continue to expand their knowledge of the characteristics of genre and can discuss them. Academic language is expanding.

Selecting Texts Characteristics of Texts at **Level L**

GENRE

▶ Fiction

- Realistic fiction
- Traditional literature (folktale, fairy tale, fable)
- Fantasy
- Special types of fiction: e.g., mystery, adventure story, sports story

▶ Nonfiction

- Expository nonfiction
- Narrative nonfiction
- Biography (mostly well-known subjects)
- Memoir (mostly well-known subjects)
- Procedural texts

FORMS

- Series books
- Picture books
- Beginning chapter books with illustrations
- Plays
- Readers' theater scripts
- Graphic texts
- Letters, journal entries

TEXT STRUCTURE

- Narrative texts with straightforward structure (beginning, series of episodes, and ending) but more episodes included
- Narrative texts with multiple episodes that may be more elaborated
- Some books with very short chapters, each with narrative structure
- Some embedded forms (e.g., letters, directions) within narrative and expository structures
- Variation in narrative: e.g., cumulative tales, circular stories
- Some books with chapters connected to a single plot
- Nonfiction books divided into sections
- Underlying structural patterns: description, temporal sequence, chronological sequence, comparison and contrast, question and answer

CONTENT

- Content interesting to and relevant for the reader
- Continued presence of familiar content with more content that goes beyond students' immediate experience: e.g., different environments and communities, animals of the world

- Varied levels of support provided by picture information
- Some stories with content familiar to students through prior experiences with storytelling, media, and hearing books read aloud
- Some content that requires accessing prior knowledge
- Some content that requires the reader to search for information in graphics: e.g., maps, charts, diagrams, illustrated drawings, labeled photographs

THEMES AND IDEAS

- Concrete themes close to students' experience: e.g., imagination, courage, fears, friendship, family relationships, self, home, nature, growing, behavior, community, first responsibilities, diversity, belonging, peer relationships, feelings
- Some books with multiple ideas, easy to understand
- Ideas close to children's experience: e.g., caring for others, doing your job, helping your family, taking care of self, staying healthy, caring for your world, empathizing with others, problem solving, valuing differences, learning about life's challenges

LEVEL **L**

Emma came out a few minutes later. She was last to get in the car.

Mom looked puzzled. She said, "It's warm, Emma. Why are you wearing your coat?"

"It's not THAT warm," said Emma.

"Oh yes, it is," said Grace.

"And your coat looks weird, bumpy or something," said Mom.

"It's not THAT bumpy," said Emma.

"Some bumps are moving," said Grace.

"They're not moving THAT much!" cried Emma.

"They're squealing too," said Grace.

"They're not squealing THAT much," said Emma.

Mom looked in the mirror. "Emma, bumps don't squeal."

"Some bumps do," said Emma.

LANGUAGE AND LITERARY FEATURES

- Some texts with settings that are not typical of many students' experiences
- Some settings that are distant in time and geography
- Settings that are important to comprehension of the fiction narrative or biography
- Plot with conflict and resolution
- Plot that includes multiple episodes
- Main characters and supporting characters
- Characters that learn and change, with reasons for character change explicit and obvious
- Characters revealed by what they say, think, and do and by what others say and think about them
- Characters revealed over a series of events, chapters, or book series

- Variety in presentation of dialogue: e.g., dialogue among multiple characters, dialogue with pronouns, split dialogue, direct dialogue, including unassigned dialogue and long stretches of dialogue
- Most texts written in first- or third-person narrative, with some procedural texts in second person
- Basic motifs of traditional literature and modern fantasy: e.g., struggle between good and evil, fantastic or magical objects, wishes, trickery, transformations
- Literary language typical of traditional literature: e.g., *long ago and far away*
- Some figurative language: e.g., metaphor, simile
- Poetic language
- Procedural language
- Language used to make comparisons
- Use of expressive language in dialogue
- Descriptive language
- Language used to show chronological order and temporal sequence
- Language that speaks directly to the reader

SENTENCE COMPLEXITY

- Some longer sentences with more than fifteen words and many clauses and phrases
- Variation in placement of subject, verb, adjectives, and adverbs
- Sentences with multiple adjectives, adverbs, and prepositional phrases
- Sentences with nouns, verbs, adjectives, and adverbs in a series, divided by commas
- Many sentences beginning with phrases and subordinate (dependent) clauses
- Sentences with simple (common) connectives
- Some complex sentences with variety in order of clauses
- Occasional use of parenthetical material embedded in sentences

Selecting Texts Characteristics of Texts at **Level L** (*cont.*)

VOCABULARY

- Some vocabulary words that are acquired by students through reading or listening to stories or nonfiction read aloud
- Most words that are in common oral vocabulary for the age group (Tier 1)
- Some words that appear in the vocabulary of mature language users (Tier 2)
- Many content-specific words introduced, explained, and illustrated in the text requiring the use of context for understanding
- Wide variation in words used to assign dialogue or speech
- Many adjectives describing people, places, or things
- Adverbs that describe actions
- Words with multiple meanings
- New vocabulary that requires strategic action to understand: e.g., derive meaning from context
- Many common connectives (words, phrases that clarify relationships and ideas): e.g., *and, but, so, because, before, after*

WORDS

- Many multisyllable words, some technical or scientific
- Full range of plurals signaled by language structure
- A variety of high-frequency words (200+)
- A wide variety of verbs with inflectional endings
- Adjectives with the comparative endings *-er, -est*
- Nouns formed with verbs and the suffix *-er*: e.g., *teacher, baker*
- Many multisyllable words with complex letter-sound relationships
- Words with easy spelling patterns (VC, CVC, CVV, CVC*e*, CVVC, VC*e*, VCC)
- Wide range of contractions and possessives
- Full range of compound words
- Base words with affixes (prefixes and suffixes)
- Common (simple) connectives

ILLUSTRATIONS

- Illustrations of the important content and ideas in the text
- Illustrations that enhance and extend meaning in the text
- Illustrations with details that add interest
- Illustrations that support interpretation, enhance enjoyment, or set mood, but are not necessary for understanding
- Many short texts with illustrations on every page or page spread
- Some texts with minimal illustrations
- Variety of layout in illustrations and print
- More than one kind of graphic on a page spread
- A few books with black-and-white illustrations
- Some graphic texts in which illustrations carry much of the meaning
- Some short chapter books with illustrations every three or four pages
- Simple illustrations in a variety of forms: e.g., photo and/or drawing with label or caption, diagram, map

BOOK AND PRINT FEATURES

LENGTH

- Wide variation in length (mostly shorter than forty-eight pages)
- Wide variation in number of words (350–1000)
- Some books divided into chapters
- Some book divided into sections

PRINT AND LAYOUT

- Variety in font size
- Variety in print and background color
- Many lines of print on a page (five to twenty-four lines)
- Sentences beginning where previous sentence ends
- Variety in placement of print and pictures, reflecting different genres
- Most texts single spaced but with clear space between lines
- Information shown in a variety of picture and print combinations in graphic texts
- Captions under pictures that provide important information
- Print placed in sidebars and graphics that provide important information

PUNCTUATION

- Period, comma, question mark, exclamation mark, and quotation marks in most texts
- Ellipses in some texts to indicate that the sentence finishes on the next page

ORGANIZATIONAL TOOLS

- Title, table of contents, chapter title, heading, sidebar

TEXT RESOURCES

- Dedication, author's note, glossary

Selecting Goals Behaviors and Understandings to Notice, Teach, and Support

SEARCHING FOR AND USING INFORMATION

- Sustain searching for information over a text (usually under forty-eight pages) and/or over in a short chapter book
- Reread occasionally to search for and use information from multiple sources
- Search for and use information from previous books when reading a series
- Use background knowledge to search for and understand information about settings
- Use organizational tools to search for information: e.g., title, table of contents, chapter title, heading, sidebar
- Use text resources to search for information: e.g., author's note, pronunciation guide, glossary
- Search for information in sentences with multiple clauses or phrases
- Search for information in sentences with variation in placement of subject, verb, adjectives, and adverbs
- Search for information in sentences with nouns, verbs, adjectives, or adverbs in a series, divided by commas
- Search for and understand information presented in a variety of ways: e.g., simple dialogue, dialogue with pronouns, split dialogue, assigned and sometimes unassigned dialogue, dialogue among multiple characters, some long stretches of dialogue, direct dialogue
- Search for and understand information over some long stretches of dialogue with multiple characters talking
- Use the chronological order within multiple episodes to search for and use information
- Search for information across chapters connected to a single plot
- Search for and use information in texts with variety in placement of the body of a text, sidebars, and graphics
- Notice and use punctuation marks: e.g., period, comma, question mark, exclamation mark, quotation marks
- Search for and use information from a wide variety of illustrations or graphics

MONITORING AND SELF-CORRECTING

- Reread a word or phrase occasionally to monitor or self-correct
- Self-correct close to the point of error
- Use multiple sources of information (visual information in print, meaning/pictures, graphics, language structure) to monitor and self-correct
- Self-monitor and self-correct using visual features of words
- Self-monitor and self-correct using recognition of known words
- Use awareness of narrative structure and of character attributes to self-monitor and self-correct
- Use understanding of dialogue to self-monitor and self-correct
- Use content knowledge of a simple topic to self-monitor and self-correct

SOLVING WORDS

▶ Reading Words

- Recognize a large number of high-frequency words quickly and automatically
- Recognize multisyllable words or take them apart by syllables to solve them
- Read plurals using -s and -es, most supported by pictures and language structure
- Read a range of regular and irregular plurals that are supported by language structure
- Read words that show comparison with the suffixes -er and -est
- Read verbs of all tenses with inflectional endings
- Use letter-sound relationships to read words of one or more syllables
- Notice phonogram patterns and use them to solve multisyllable words
- Use many different kinds of word parts to solve words
- Read a wide range of contractions, possessives, and compound words
- Read a variety of words that assign dialogue
- Notice parts of words and connect them to other words to solve them
- Solve words rapidly while processing continuous text and with minimum overt self-correction
- Read many words with affixes (prefixes and suffixes)

▶ Vocabulary

- Expand meaning of a word by connecting it to other words
- Derive the meaning of a new word from context
- Add to oral vocabulary through reading
- Connect words to synonyms and antonyms to expand understanding
- Understand many words that are in common oral vocabulary for the age group (Tier 1)
- Understand words that appear in the language of mature users and in written texts (Tier 2)
- Understand the meaning of regular and irregular plurals
- Understand that some words have multiple meanings
- Understand many words that have multiple meanings and identify the specific meaning that applies in a sentence or paragraph
- Understand the meaning of comparatives
- Understand the meaning of verbs that become nouns using -er and -ing (gerund)
- Understand the meaning of verbs in all tenses
- Understand the meaning of a wide range of contractions and possessives

Selecting Goals Behaviors and Understandings to Notice, Teach, and Support *(cont.)*

GUIDED READING

THINKING *WITHIN* THE TEXT *(continued)*

SOLVING WORDS *(continued)*

▶ Vocabulary *(continued)*

- Understand words that require the use of multiple sources of information (i.e., background knowledge, pictures, visual information)
- Understand the meaning and function of common (simple) connectives
- Identify base words and understand prefixes and suffixes that add or change meaning or function
- Understand that words such as *I, me,* and *we* that may signal the narrator of a text
- Understand a variety of words that assign dialogue
- Understand the meaning of verbs that show the action in a story, adjectives that describe characters or setting, and adverbs that describe the action
- Understand some content-specific words introduced, explained, and illustrated in context
- Use details in illustrations to understand new vocabulary
- Use a glossary to learn or check the meaning of words
- Understand key words in graphics such as maps, diagrams, and charts

MAINTAINING FLUENCY

- Read orally with appropriate phrasing, pausing, intonation, word stress, and rate
- Read both orally and silently at a rate that reflects fluent processing but also maintains comprehension and accuracy
- Sustain momentum through short texts and some beginning chapter books, making significant progress each day
- Notice periods, quotation marks, commas, exclamation marks, and question marks and reflect them with the voice through intonation and pausing
- Read silently at a satisfactory rate
- Stress words that are in bold or italics
- Recognize and read expressively a variety of dialogue, some unassigned
- Read parts in a script with expression
- Reflect numbered and bulleted lists with the voice when reading orally

ADJUSTING

- Slow down to problem-solve words and resume reading with momentum
- Adjust reading to show awareness of sentence variety (i.e., placement of parts of speech, phrases, and clauses)
- Adjust reading to accommodate compound sentences and sentences with a variety in order of clauses
- Adjust to accommodate embedded forms (e.g., letters) within narrative and expository texts
- Adjust expectations to process different parts of a simple hybrid text
- Adjust reading to process a graphic text
- Adjust to recognize and use characteristics of special types of fiction such as mystery, adventure story, sports story
- Adjust to read parts in a readers' theater script or a play
- Understand that a nonfiction book tells facts
- Understand that when you read a biography, you are reading the story of a person's life
- Notice labels or captions on photographs and drawings and use them to understand the words in the text
- Adjust reading to accommodate varied placement of text body, photographs and drawings with labels or captions, sidebars, and graphics
- Adjust reading to reflect a series of steps in a procedural text

SUMMARIZING

- Remember important information while reading to understand the meaning of the text
- Talk about the important information in organized summary form after reading
- Summarize the story including plot events, problem, resolution, and characters
- Summarize information in the text, selecting the information that is important
- Summarize temporal sequence in time order
- Summarize narrative nonfiction or biography in time order

Selecting Goals Behaviors and Understandings to Notice, Teach, and Support *(cont.)*

THINKING *BEYOND* THE TEXT

PREDICTING

- Use knowledge of grammatical structure (clauses, phrases) to anticipate the text
- Make predictions based on the meaning of the text, with or without picture support
- Make predictions based on knowledge and experience
- Make predictions throughout a text based on the organizational structure (narrative, expository)
- Predict events of the plot, behavior of characters, and the ending of a story based on understanding of the setting, problem, and characters
- Make predictions based on knowledge of fiction genres: e.g., realistic fiction, traditional literature, fantasy, hybrid text
- Make predictions based on knowledge from personal experiences and from reading: e.g., food, cooking, pets, animals of the world, health and the human body, community, the environment, machines
- Make predictions based on knowledge of nonfiction genres: e.g., expository text, simple narrative nonfiction, biography, memoir, procedural text, hybrid text
- Make predictions based on knowledge of underlying text structures: e.g., description, temporal sequence, question and answer, chronological sequence
- Make predictions based on a temporal sequence: e.g., plants growing, eggs hatching, making something, the water cycle

MAKING CONNECTIONS

- Make connections between personal experience and texts
- Make connections among books in a series
- Use background knowledge to understand settings
- Make connections among texts of the same genre
- Use background knowledge of traditional literature to recognize common characters and events
- Make connections between the events in chapters that are connected to a single plot
- Use background knowledge (from experience and reading) to understand settings in stories
- Access background knowledge acquired from reading to understand the content of a text
- Make connections among texts on the same topic or with similar content
- Access background knowledge to understand description or temporal sequence

SYNTHESIZING

- Talk about what the reader knows about the topic before reading the text and identify new knowledge gained from reading
- Talk about the text showing understanding of events, topic, or content
- Talk about what is learned from the characters, the problem, and the resolution of the problem

INFERRING

- Make inferences about setting to help in understanding the story
- Infer character traits, feelings, and motivations from what characters say, think, or do and what others say or think about them
- Talk about the pictures, revealing interpretation of a problem or of characters' feelings
- Notice and understand humor in a text
- Recognize and understand traits in complex characters that change
- Infer reasons for character change
- Infer information about characters, setting, plot, and action from graphic texts, in which illustrations carry much of the meaning
- Infer ideas about familiar content
- Infer temporal sequences and the reasons for each step
- Understand and infer the importance of the setting of a biography that may be distant in time and geography from students' own knowledge

Selecting Goals Behaviors and Understandings to Notice, Teach, and Support *(cont.)*

THINKING *ABOUT* THE TEXT

ANALYZING

- Distinguish between fiction and nonfiction and articulate the characteristic differences
- Understand and describe characteristics of fiction genres, including realistic fiction, traditional literature (folktale, fairy tale, fable, myth), fantasy, and hybrid text
- Distinguish between realistic fiction and fantasy
- Understand that there may be different genres in each of the larger categories of fiction and nonfiction
- Identify and understand characteristics of special types of fiction: e.g., mystery; adventure story; animal story; family, friends, and school story
- Recognize characters that are typical of fantasy or traditional literature
- Understand and describe the characteristics of nonfiction genres: e.g., expository text, simple narrative nonfiction, biography, memoir, procedural text, and hybrid text
- Understand that a biography is the story of a person's life and is usually told in chronological order
- Understand the unique characteristics of graphic texts
- Understand that the information and ideas in a text are related to each other, and notice how the author presents this
- Recognize a writer's use of embedded forms (e.g., letters) within narrative or expository texts
- Recognize and follow chronological sequence of events
- Recognize and understand variety in narrative structure
- Understand first- and third-person narrative
- Recognize when a writer uses temporal (time) order to describe a process
- Recognize a writer's use of underlying text structures: e.g., description, temporal sequence, question and answer, chronological sequence, comparison and contrast
- Think analytically about the significance of a title
- Recognize settings that are familiar as well as some distant in time and geography
- Understand how a setting is important to the plot and the characters' perspectives
- Identify a central story problem in a text with multiple episodes
- Understand the role of supporting characters in a story
- Notice the evidence a writer provides to show character attributes and motives as well as characters' changes
- Understand the perspective from which a story is told and talk about why a writer selected it
- Notice language used to show chronological order

- Notice a writer's use of figurative language (metaphor, simile, onomatopoeia)
- Notice how a writer uses common (simple) connectives (e.g., *because, before, after*) to clarify relationships between ideas
- Notice parenthetical material set off by commas or parentheses
- Notice and follow unassigned dialogue
- Notice a fiction writer's use of poetic and expressive language in dialogue
- Notice a writer's use of humorous words or onomatopoetic words and talk about how they add to the action
- Recognize very simple procedural language: e.g., directions
- Recognize when the writer uses second person (speaks directly to the reader): e.g., *you, your*
- Understand that illustrations carry the dialogue and action in graphic texts
- Notice that illustrations add to important story action
- Notice and understand how the graphics and sidebars complement the body of the text
- Understand that illustrations or photographs add to the ideas and information in a text
- Use some academic language to talk about genres: e.g., *fiction; family, friends, and school story; folktale; animal story; humorous story; nonfiction; informational text; informational book; factual text; how-to book*
- Use some academic language to talk about forms: e.g., *series book, play, chapter book, letter*
- Use some academic language to talk about literary features: e.g., *beginning, ending, problem, character, time and place, question and answer, main character, character change, message, dialogue, topic, events*
- Use some specific language to talk about book and print features: e.g., *front cover, back cover, page, author, illustrator, illustration, photograph, title, label, drawing, heading, caption, table of contents, chapter, chapter title, dedication, sidebar, glossary, map, diagram, author's note, illustrator's note, section*

CRITIQUING

- Share opinions about a text and give rationales and examples
- Share opinions about an illustration or photograph
- Give an opinion about the believability of plot or characters
- Talk critically about what a writer does to make a topic interesting or important
- Talk about why the subject of a biography is important or sets an example for others

Selecting Goals Behaviors and Understandings to Notice, Teach, and Support *(cont.)*

Planning for Word Work After Guided Reading

Using your recent observations of the readers' ability to take words apart quickly and efficiently while reading text, plan for one to three minutes of active engagement of students' attention to letters, sounds, and words. Prioritize the readers' noticing of print features and active hands-on use of magnetic letters, a white board, word cards, or pencil and paper to promote fluency and flexibility in visual processing.

Examples:

- Take apart compound words and notice how the parts contribute to meaning and notice parts that appear in many compound words: e.g., *somebody, someone, sometime, someday, today*
- Recognize and use contractions with *not, am, are, is, has, will, have, had,* and *would*
- Add *-s* or *-es* to a singular noun to make a plural noun (*evening/evenings; princess/princesses*)
- Change *y* to *i* and add *-es* to a singular noun to make a plural noun (*library/libraries*)
- Add an inflectional ending to a word to make a new word (*print/printing, printed; smile/smiling, smiled*)
- Add the suffix *-er* or or the suffix *-est* to a word to show comparison (*full/ fuller/ fullest; great/ greater/greatest*)

- Add the suffix *–er* to a word to form a noun that names a person or thing that does something (*bake, baker; kick, kicker dance, dancer*)
- Recognize, make, and break apart words that end with a consonant cluster or a consonant digraph (*sou<u>nd</u>, tru<u>nk</u>, wor<u>ld</u>; spla<u>sh</u>, throu<u>gh</u>, o'clo<u>ck</u>, fini<u>sh</u>*)
- Recognize and use words with consonant letters that have no sound (<u>k</u>now, ei<u>gh</u>t, lis<u>t</u>en)
- Recognize, make, and break apart words that contain phonograms with a double vowel pattern (*week, tooth*)
- Recognize and use vowel sounds with *r* (*hardly, important, terrible*)
- Recognize letter patterns that look the same but represent different vowel sounds (*d<u>ea</u>r, b<u>ea</u>r*) as well as letter patterns that look different but represent the same vowel sound (*s<u>ai</u>d, b<u>e</u>d*)

- Break apart multisyllable words by syllable (*cor-ner, hap-pen, eve-ry-where*)
- Hear, say, clap, and identify syllables in words with three or more syllables (*eve/ry/where, li/brar/y, won/der/ful*)
- Solve words using letter-sound analysis from left to right (*s-pl-a-sh*)
- Recognize and use homophones (words with the same pronunciation, different spellings, and different meanings) (*through, threw; dear, deer*)
- Recognize and use homographs (words with the same spelling, different meanings and origins, and may have different pronunciations) (*bear, hide*)
- Sort words based on any word features

Readers at Level

At level M, readers know the characteristics of a range of genres: several types of realistic fiction, traditional literature, fantasy, a range of informational texts, and hybrid texts. Some texts are chapter books, and readers are becoming interested in special forms, such as longer series books, poems, plays, and graphic texts. Fiction narratives are straightforward but have elaborate plots with many episodes and multiple characters that show some change over time. They read short nonfiction texts, mostly on single topics, and are able to identify and use underlying structural patterns (description, cause and effect, chronological sequence, temporal sequence, categorization, comparison and contrast, problem and solution, question and answer). They can process sentences of varying complexity that may contain prepositional phrases, introductory clauses, and lists of nouns, verbs, or adjectives. Readers solve words smoothly and automatically in both silent and oral reading, and they can read and understand descriptive words, some complex content-specific words, and some technical words. They read silently and independently. In oral reading, they demonstrate all aspects of smooth, fluent processing. Readers continue to expand their knowledge of the characteristics of genre and can discuss them. Use of academic language is expanding.

Selecting Texts Characteristics of Texts at **Level M**

GENRE

▶ **Fiction**

- Realistic fiction
- Traditional literature (folktale, fairy tale, fable)
- Fantasy
- Special types of fiction: e.g., mystery; adventure story; sports story; animal story; family, friends, and school story; humorous story

▶ **Nonfiction**

- Expository nonfiction
- Narrative nonfiction
- Biography
- Memoir
- Procedural texts

FORMS

- Series books
- Picture books
- Beginning chapter books with illustrations
- Readers' theater scripts
- Graphic texts
- Letters, journal entries

TEXT STRUCTURE

- Narrative texts with straightforward structure (beginning, series of episodes, and ending) but more episodes included
- Narrative texts with multiple episodes that may be more elaborated
- Some books with very short chapters, each with narrative structure
- Some embedded forms (e.g., letters, directions) within narrative and expository structures
- Variation in narrative: e.g., cumulative tales, circular stories
- Some books with chapters connected to a single plot
- Nonfiction books divided into sections
- Underlying structural patterns: description, cause and effect, chronological sequence, temporal sequence, comparison and contrast, question and answer

CONTENT

- Content interesting to and relevant for the reader
- Continued presence of familiar content with more content that goes beyond students' immediate experience: e.g., different environments and communities; animals of the world; healthy eating and nutrition; muscular, skeletal, and nervous systems

- Varied levels of support provided by picture information
- Some content familiar to students through prior experiences with reading texts
- Some content that requires accessing prior knowledge
- Some content that requires the reader to search for information in graphics: e.g., maps, charts, diagrams, illustrated drawings, labeled photographs

THEMES AND IDEAS

- Concrete themes close to students' experience: e.g., imagination, courage, fears, friendship, family relationships, self, home, nature, growing, behavior, community, first responsibilities, diversity, belonging, peer relationships, feelings
- Some books with multiple ideas, easy to understand
- Ideas close to students' experience: e.g., caring for others, doing your job, helping your family, taking care of self, staying healthy, caring for your world, empathizing with others, problem solving, valuing differences, learning about life's challenges

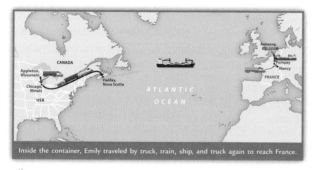

"France, Wisconsin?" Nick asked. "I've never heard of it."

"No," Mrs. Herndon said. "All the way across the ocean. In the *country* of France."

Everyone had questions. How had Emily traveled so far? How had she survived? No one knew.

Now the Herndons worried about the biggest question of all. How would Emily get home? A plane ticket from France to Wisconsin cost a lot of money!

Inside the container, Emily traveled by truck, train, ship, and truck again to reach France.

12

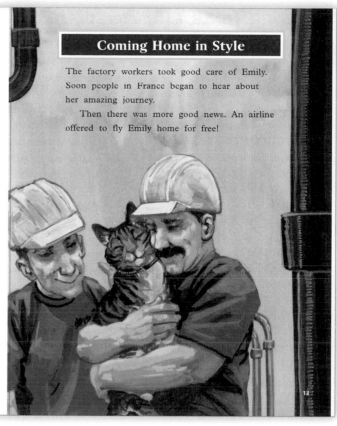

Coming Home in Style

The factory workers took good care of Emily. Soon people in France began to hear about her amazing journey.

Then there was more good news. An airline offered to fly Emily home for free!

13

LANGUAGE AND LITERARY FEATURES

- Some texts with settings that are not typical of many students' experiences
- Some settings that are distant in time and geography
- Settings that are important to comprehension of the fiction narrative or biography
- Plot with conflict and resolution
- Plot that includes multiple episodes
- Main characters and supporting characters
- Characters that learn and change, with reasons for character change explicit and obvious
- Characters revealed by what they say, think, and do and by what others say and think about them
- Characters revealed over a series of events, chapters, or book series

- Variety in presentation of dialogue: e.g., dialogue among multiple characters, dialogue with pronouns, split dialogue, direct dialogue, including unassigned dialogue and long stretches of dialogue
- Most texts written in first- or third-person narrative, with some procedural texts in second person
- Basic motifs of traditional literature and modern fantasy: e.g., struggle between good and evil, fantastic or magical objects, wishes, trickery, transformations
- Literary language typical of traditional literature: e.g. *long ago and far away*
- Some figurative language: e.g., metaphor, simile
- Poetic language
- Procedural language
- Language used to make comparisons
- Use of expressive language in dialogue
- Descriptive language
- Language used to show chronological order and temporal sequence
- Language that speaks directly to the reader

SENTENCE COMPLEXITY

- Some longer sentences with more than fifteen words and many clauses and phrases
- Variation in placement of subject, verb, adjectives, and adverbs
- Many sentences with embedded clauses or phrases
- Sentences with multiple adjectives, adverbs, and prepositional phrases
- Sentences with nouns, verbs, adjectives, and adverbs in a series, divided by commas
- Many sentences beginning with phrases or subordinate (dependent) clauses
- Sentences with simple, common connectives: e.g., *unless, until*
- Some complex sentences with variety in order of clauses
- Occasional use of parenthetical material embedded in sentences

Selecting Goals Behaviors and Understandings to Notice, Teach, and Support *(cont.)*

THINKING *WITHIN* THE TEXT *(continued)*

SOLVING WORDS *(continued)*

▶ **Vocabulary** *(continued)*

- Understand words that require the use of multiple sources of information (i.e., background knowledge, pictures, visual information)
- Understand the meaning and function of common (simple) connectives
- Identify base words and understand prefixes and suffixes that add or change meaning or function
- Understand that words such as *I, me,* and *we* that may signal the narrator of a text
- Understand a variety of words that assign dialogue
- Understand the meaning of verbs that show the action in a story, adjectives that describe characters or setting, and adverbs that describe the action
- Understand some content-specific words introduced, explained, and illustrated in context
- Use details in illustrations to understand new vocabulary
- Use a glossary to learn or check the meaning of words
- Understand key words in graphics such as maps, diagrams, and charts

MAINTAINING FLUENCY

- Read orally with appropriate phrasing, pausing, intonation, word stress, and rate
- Read both orally and silently at a rate that reflects fluent processing but also maintains comprehension and accuracy
- Sustain momentum through short texts and some short chapter books, making significant progress daily
- Notice periods, quotation marks, commas, exclamation marks, and question marks and begin to reflect them with the voice through intonation and pausing
- Read silently at a satisfactory rate
- Stress words that are in bold or italics
- Recognize and read expressively a variety of dialogue, some unassigned
- Read parts in a script with expression
- Reflect numbered and bulleted lists with the voice when reading orally

ADJUSTING

- Slow down to problem-solve words and resume reading with momentum
- Adjust reading to show awareness of sentence variety (i.e., placement of parts of speech, phrases, and clauses)
- Adjust reading to accommodate compound sentences and sentences with a variety in order of clauses
- Adjust to accommodate embedded forms (e.g., letters) within narrative and expository texts
- Adjust expectations to process different parts of a hybrid text
- Adjust reading to process a graphic text
- Recognize that a text is fiction and tells a story that has a beginning, problem, series of events, and end
- Adjust to recognize and use characteristics of special types of fiction such as mystery; adventure story; animal story; family, friends, and school story
- Adjust to read parts in a readers' theater script or a play
- Understand that when you read a biography, you are reading the story of a person's life
- Notice labels or captions on photographs and drawings and use them to understand the words in the text
- Adjust reading to accommodate varied placement of text body, photographs and drawings with labels or captions, sidebars, and graphics
- Adjust reading to reflect a series of steps in a procedural text

SUMMARIZING

- Remember important information while reading to understand the meaning of the text
- Talk about the important information in organized summary form after reading
- Summarize the story including plot events, problem, resolution, and characters
- Summarize information in the text, selecting the information that is important
- Summarize temporal sequence in time order
- Summarize narrative nonfiction or biography in time order

GUIDED READING

LEVEL **M**

Selecting Goals Behaviors and Understandings to Notice, Teach, and Support *(cont.)*

THINKING *BEYOND* THE TEXT

PREDICTING

- Use knowledge of grammatical structure and experience with written language to anticipate the text
- Make predictions based on knowledge, personal experience, study in the content areas, and other reading
- Make predictions throughout a text based on the organizational structure (narrative, expository)
- Predict the ending of a story based on knowledge of how plots work and understanding of settings, characters, and the story problem
- Make predictions based on knowledge of a variety of everyday events
- Predict the plot and characters of a sequel to a known book
- Make predictions based on knowledge of fiction genres: e.g., realistic fiction, traditional literature, fantasy, hybrid text
- Make predictions based on knowledge from personal experiences and from reading: e.g., food; cooking; pets; animals of the world; healthy eating and nutrition; muscular, skeletal, and nervous systems
- Make predictions based on knowledge of nonfiction genres: e.g., expository text, simple narrative nonfiction, biography, memoir, procedural text, hybrid text
- Make predictions based on knowledge of underlying text structures: e.g., description, cause and effect, chronological sequence, temporal sequence, comparison and contrast, question and answer
- Make predictions based on a temporal sequence: e.g., plants growing, eggs hatching, making something, the water cycle

MAKING CONNECTIONS

- Make connections between personal experience and texts
- Make connections among books in a series
- Use background knowledge to understand settings
- Make connections among texts of the same genre
- Use background knowledge of traditional literature to recognize common characters and events
- Make connections between the events in chapters that are connected to a single plot
- Use background knowledge (from experience and reading) to understand settings in stories

- Access background knowledge acquired from reading to understand the content of a text
- Make connections among texts on the same topic or with similar content
- Access background knowledge to understand description or temporal sequence
- Make connections to other areas of study: e.g., science, social studies

SYNTHESIZING

- Talk about what the reader knows about the topic before reading the text and identify new knowledge gained from reading
- Talk about the text showing understanding of events, topic, or content
- Talk about the lessons the story teaches
- Talk about what is learned from the characters, the problem, and the resolution of the problem

INFERRING

- Infer temporal sequences and the reasons for each step
- Notice and understand humor in a text
- Make inferences about setting to help in understanding the story
- Understand and infer the importance of the setting of a biography that may be distant in time and geography from students' own knowledge
- Infer character traits, feelings, and motivations from what characters say, think, or do and what others say or think about them
- Recognize and understand traits in complex characters that change
- Infer reasons for character change
- Talk about the pictures, revealing interpretation of a problem or of characters' feelings
- Infer information about characters, setting, plot, and action from graphic texts, in which illustrations carry much of the meaning
- Infer ideas about familiar content

GUIDED READING

LEVEL
M

Selecting Goals Behaviors and Understandings to Notice, Teach, and Support *(cont.)*

GUIDED READING

THINKING *ABOUT* THE TEXT

ANALYZING

- Distinguish between fiction and nonfiction and articulate the characteristic differences
- Understand the unique characteristics of graphic texts
- Understand and describe characteristics of fiction genres, including realistic fiction, traditional literature (folktale, fairy tale, fable, myth), fantasy, and hybrid text
- Notice elements and basic motifs of fantasy: e.g., the supernatural, imaginary and otherworldly creatures, gods and goddesses, talking animals, struggle between good and evil, magic, fantastic or magical objects, wishes, trickery, transformations
- Distinguish between realistic fiction and fantasy
- Understand that there may be different genres in each of the larger categories of fiction and nonfiction
- Identify and understand characteristics of special types of fiction: e.g., mystery; adventure story; animal story; family, friends, and school story
- Recognize and understand variety in narrative structure
- Recognize that a text can have true information
- Understand that a nonfiction book gives facts or tells how to do something
- Understand and describe the characteristics of nonfiction genres: e.g., expository text, simple narrative nonfiction, biography, memoir, procedural text, and hybrid text
- Understand that a biography is the story of a person's life and is usually told in chronological order
- Understand that the information and ideas in a text are related to each other, and notice how the author presents this
- Recognize a writer's use of embedded forms (e.g., letters) within narrative or expository texts
- Recognize and follow chronological sequence of events
- Identify a central story problem in a text with multiple episodes
- Understand first- and third-person narrative
- Understand that a nonfiction book may be procedural (i.e., "how-to")
- Understand that a nonfiction book may have "how-to" procedures embedded within it
- Recognize when a writer uses temporal (time) order to describe a process
- Recognize a writer's use of underlying text structures: e.g., description, cause and effect, chronological sequence, temporal sequence, comparison and contrast, question and answer
- Think analytically about the significance of a title
- Recognize settings that are familiar as well as some distant in time and geography
- Understand how a setting is important to the plot and the characters' perspectives
- Recognize characters that are typical of fantasy or traditional literature
- Understand the role of supporting characters in a story

- Notice the evidence a writer provides to show character attributes and motives as well as characters' changes
- Understand the perspective from which a story is told and talk about why a writer selected it
- Notice language used to show chronological order
- Notice a writer's use of figurative language (metaphor, simile, onomatopoeia)
- Notice how a writer uses common (simple) connectives (e.g., *because, before, after*) to clarify relationships between ideas
- Notice parenthetical material set off by commas or parentheses
- Notice and follow unassigned dialogue in fiction
- Notice a fiction writer's use of poetic and expressive language in dialogue
- Notice a writer's use of humorous words or onomatopoetic words and talk about how they add to the action
- Recognize very simple procedural language: e.g., directions
- Recognize when the writer uses second person (speaks directly to the reader): e.g., *you, your*
- Understand that illustrations carry the dialogue and action in graphic texts
- Notice how illustrations add to important story action
- Notice and understand how the graphics and sidebars complement the body of the text
- Understand that illustrations or photographs add to the ideas and information in a text
- Use some academic language to talk about genres: e.g., *fiction; family, friends, and school story; folktale; animal story; humorous story; nonfiction; informational text; informational book; factual text; how-to book*
- Use some academic language to talk about forms: e.g., *series book, play, chapter book, letter*
- Use some academic language to talk about literary features: e.g., *beginning, ending, problem, character, time and place, question and answer, main character, character change, message, dialogue, topic, events, solution*
- Use some specific language to talk about book and print features: e.g., *front cover, back cover, page, author, illustrator, illustration, photograph, title, label, drawing, heading, caption, table of contents, chapter, chapter title, dedication, sidebar, glossary, map, diagram, author's note, illustrator's note, section*

CRITIQUING

- Share opinions about a text and give rationales and examples
- Share opinions about an illustration or photograph
- Give an opinion about the believability of plot or characters
- Talk critically about what a writer does to make a topic interesting or important
- Talk about why the subject of a biography is important or sets an example for others

LEVEL

M

Selecting Goals Behaviors and Understandings to Notice, Teach, and Support *(cont.)*

Planning for Word Work After Guided Reading

Using your recent observations of the readers' ability to take words apart quickly and efficiently while reading text, plan for one to three minutes of active engagement of students' attention to letters, sounds, and words. Prioritize the readers' noticing of print features and active hands-on use of magnetic letters, a white board, word cards, or pencil and paper to promote fluency and flexibility in visual processing.

Examples:

- Take apart compound words and notice how the parts contribute to meaning and notice parts that appear in many compound words: e.g., *somebody, someone, sometime, someday, today*

- Recognize and use contractions with *not, am, are, is, has, will, have, had,* and *would*

- Add *-s* or *-es* to a singular noun to make a plural noun (*village/villages; fox/foxes*)

- Change *y* to *i* and add *-es* to a singular noun to make a plural noun (*family/ families*)

- Add the suffix *-er* to a word to form a noun that names a person or thing that does something (*dance, dancer; sing, singer*)

- Take apart words with a variety of endings (*tables/table; seeming, seemed/seem; roundest, rounder/round; rancher/ranch*)

- Recognize and break apart words with some prefixes (<u>re</u>turn, <u>un</u>happy, <u>in</u>side, <u>dis</u>cover, <u>non</u>stop)

- Work flexibly with a base word, adding or taking away one or more affixes to make a new word (*write/<u>writing</u>/<u>rewrite</u>*)

- Recognize and break apart words with an open syllable and a long vowel sound (*o/pen, ti/ger*) and a closed syllable with a short vowel sound (*can/dle, din/ner, pop/corn*)

- Take apart two-syllable words by syllable (*quick-ly, rac-coon*)

- Hear, say, clap, and identify syllables in words with three or more syllables (*tel/e/phone, sud/den/ly, re/mem/ber*)

- Solve words using letter-sound analysis from left to right (*v-i-ll-a-g-e*)

- Recognize and use homophones (*hay, hey; poor, pour*) and homographs (*band, count, leave*)

- Sort words based on any word features

LEVEL **M**

Readers at Level

At level N, readers will process a wide range of fiction and nonfiction genres in a variety of forms including picture books, series books, chapter books (some with sequels), poems, plays, and graphic texts. Fiction narratives are straightforward but have plots with many episodes and multiple characters who develop and change over time. They take on historical fiction, which offers special challenges in terms of setting. Readers become interested in reading special types of fiction such as mysteries, sports stories, and books about school. They develop preferences as readers. Some nonfiction texts provide information in categories on several related topics, and readers can identify and use underlying structures (description, cause and effect, chronological sequence, temporal sequence, categorization, comparison and contrast, problem and solution, question and answer). They continue to read silently at a good rate and automatically use a wide range of word-solving actions while focusing on meaning. In oral reading, they continue to read with phrasing, fluency, and appropriate word stress in a way that reflects meaning and recognizes punctuation. Readers slow down to solve words or search for information and then resume normal pace; there is little overt problem solving. They can process sentences that are complex, with prepositional phrases, introductory clauses, and lists of nouns, verbs, or adjectives. They can read and understand descriptive words, some complex content-specific words, and some technical words. Length of text is no longer a critical factor as students are beginning to read texts that vary greatly. Word solving is smooth and automatic in both silent and oral reading. Readers continue to expand knowledge of the characteristics of genre and can articulate them. Academic vocabulary expands.

Selecting Texts Characteristics of Texts at **Level N**

GENRE

▶ Fiction

- Realistic fiction
- Historical fiction
- Traditional literature (folktale, fairy tale, fable)
- Fantasy
- Hybrid texts
- Special types of fiction: e.g., mystery; adventure story; sports story; animal story; family, friends, and school story; humorous story

▶ Nonfiction

- Expository nonfiction
- Narrative nonfiction
- Biography
- Memoir
- Procedural texts
- Hybrid texts

FORMS

- Series books
- Picture books
- Beginning chapter books with illustrations
- Chapter books with sequels
- Plays
- Readers' theater scripts
- Graphic texts
- Letters, journal entries

TEXT STRUCTURE

- Narrative texts with straightforward structure (beginning, series of episodes, and ending) but more episodes included
- Narrative texts with multiple episodes that may be more elaborated
- Some books with very short chapters, each with narrative structure
- Some embedded forms (e.g., letters, directions) within narrative and expository structures
- Some books with chapters connected to a single plot
- Some collections of short stories related to an overarching theme
- Nonfiction books divided into sections
- Underlying structural patterns: description, cause and effect, chronological sequence, temporal sequence, comparison and contrast, question and answer

CONTENT

- Content interesting to and relevant for the reader
- A balance of familiar and new content
- Much content that goes beyond students' immediate experience
- Some books with little or no picture support for content: e.g., chapter book
- Some content that requires accessing prior knowledge
- Content that requires the reader to take on perspectives from diverse cultures and bring cultural knowledge to understanding
- Some content that requires the reader to search for information in graphics: e.g., maps, charts, diagrams, illustrated drawings, labeled photographs

THEMES AND IDEAS

- Many light, humorous stories
- Some texts with deeper meanings about content familiar to most readers
- Texts with deeper meanings applicable to important human problems and social issues

It was early September, and still the weather was nothing but heat. Splashing and laughter came from the lake. Deena crossed the driveway, hoping it would be cooler in the house.

The gravel was sharp underfoot. Deena looked for sandier places to step and—gah! She screamed and yanked her foot away from the moving rock.

No, not a rock. It was a dusty-dry baby snapper the size of Deena's big toe.

The shell was bumpy with ridges, and the whole turtle was a sad, dusty gray, even its thin little tail. Deena backed away.

The turtle didn't move. She had scared it with her jump and yell. It just sat there, baking in its hot shell.

- Some abstract themes that require inferential thinking
- Some challenging themes: e.g., the environment, human relationships, family problems

LANGUAGE AND LITERARY FEATURES

- Some texts with settings that are not typical of many students' experiences
- Some settings that are distant in time and geography
- Settings that are important to comprehension of the fiction narrative or biography
- Plot with conflict and resolution
- Plot that includes multiple episodes
- Main characters and supporting characters
- Multidimensional characters
- Characters revealed by what they say, think, and do and by what others say and think about them

- Characters revealed over a series of events, chapters, or book series
- Variety in presentation of dialogue: e.g., dialogue among multiple characters, dialogue with pronouns, split dialogue, direct dialogue, including unassigned dialogue and long stretches of dialogue
- Most texts written in first- or third-person narrative, with some procedural texts in second person
- Basic motifs of traditional literature and modern fantasy: e.g., struggle between good and evil, fantastic or magical objects, wishes, trickery, transformations
- Literary language typical of traditional literature: e.g., *long ago and far away*
- Some figurative language: e.g., metaphor, simile
- Poetic language
- Procedural language
- Language used to make comparisons
- Use of expressive language in dialogue

- Descriptive language
- Language used to show chronological order and temporal sequence
- Some persuasive language
- Language that speaks directly to the reader

SENTENCE COMPLEXITY

- Some longer sentences with more than twenty words and many phrases and clauses
- Variation in sentence length and structure
- Sentences with a wide variety of parts of speech
- Variation in placement of subject, verb, adjectives, and adverbs
- Sentences with multiple adjectives, adverbs, and prepositional phrases
- Many sentences beginning with phrases or subordinate (dependent) clauses
- Sentences with simple, common connectives: e.g., *therefore, so, although*
- Some complex sentences with variety in order of clauses

Selecting Goals Behaviors and Understandings to Notice, Teach, and Support *(cont.)*

THINKING *WITHIN* THE TEXT *(continued)*

SOLVING WORDS *(continued)*

▶ **Vocabulary** *(continued)*

- Understand that a word with an apostrophe may indicate possession or a contraction
- Understand words that require the use of multiple sources of information (i.e., background knowledge, pictures, visual information)
- Understand the meaning and function of common (simple) connectives: e.g., *but, because, then, unless, until, so*
- Identify base words and understand prefixes and suffixes that add or change meaning or function
- Understand that some words have connotative meanings that are essential to understanding the text
- Understand that words such as *I, me,* and *we* may signal the narrator of a text
- Understand the meaning of a wide range of words that assign dialogue
- Understand the meaning of verbs that show the action in a story, adjectives that describe characters or setting, and adverbs that describe the action
- Understand some content-specific words introduced, explained, and illustrated in context
- Use details in illustrations to understand new vocabulary
- Use a glossary to learn the meaning of words
- Understand key words in graphics such as maps, diagrams, and charts

MAINTAINING FLUENCY

- Read orally with appropriate phrasing, pausing, intonation, word stress, and rate
- Read silently at a slightly faster rate than when reading orally while maintaining comprehension and accuracy
- Sustain momentum through short texts and some short chapter books, making significant progress daily
- Notice periods, quotation marks, commas, exclamation marks, and question marks and begin to reflect them with the voice through intonation and pausing
- Stress words that are in bold, italics, or varied font
- Recognize and read expressively a variety of dialogue, some unassigned
- Read parts in a script with expression
- Reflect numbered and bulleted lists with the voice when reading orally

ADJUSTING

- Slow down to problem-solve words and resume reading with momentum
- Adjust oral reading to show awareness of sentence variety (i.e., placement of parts of speech, phrases, and clauses)
- Adjust reading to accommodate compound sentences and sentences with a variety in order of clauses
- Adjust to accommodate embedded forms (e.g., letters) within narrative and expository texts
- Adjust expectations to process different parts of a hybrid text
- Adjust reading to process a graphic text
- Adjust reading to recognize the purpose and characteristics of genre
- Adjust to recognize and use characteristics of special types of fiction such as mystery; adventure story; animal story; family, friends, and school story
- Adjust to read parts in a readers' theater script or a play
- Notice labels or captions on photographs and drawings and use them to understand the words in the text
- Adjust reading to accommodate varied placement of text body, photographs and drawings with labels or captions, sidebars, and graphics

SUMMARIZING

- Remember important information while reading to understand the meaning of the text
- Talk about the important information in organized summary form after reading
- Summarize the story including characters, story problem, events of the plot, and resolution of the plot (fiction)
- Summarize information in the text, selecting the information that is important (nonfiction)
- Summarize temporal sequence in time order
- Summarize narrative nonfiction or biography in time order

Selecting Goals Behaviors and Understandings to Notice, Teach, and Support *(cont.)*

THINKING *BEYOND* THE TEXT

PREDICTING

- Use knowledge of grammatical structure and experience with written language to anticipate the text
- Make predictions based on personal experience and content knowledge built through reading
- Make predictions throughout a text based on the organizational structure (narrative, expository)
- Predict the ending of a story based on knowledge of how plots work and understanding of settings, characters, and the story problem
- Make predictions based on knowledge of fiction genres: realistic fiction, historical fiction, traditional literature, fantasy, hybrid text
- Predict the plot and characters of a sequel to a known book
- Make predictions based on knowledge of nonfiction genres: e.g., expository text, simple narrative nonfiction, biography, memoir, procedural text, hybrid text
- Make predictions based on knowledge of underlying text structures: e.g., description, cause and effect, chronological sequence, temporal sequence, comparison and contrast, question and answer
- Make predictions based on a temporal sequence: e.g., plants growing, eggs hatching, making something, food preparation and delivery, the water cycle

MAKING CONNECTIONS

- Make connections between personal experience and texts
- Make connections among books in a series
- Use background knowledge to understand settings
- Make connections among texts of the same genre
- Use background knowledge of traditional literature to recognize common characters and events
- Use background knowledge to understand settings in stories
- Access background knowledge acquired from reading to understand the content of a text
- Make connections among texts on the same topic or with similar content
- Access background knowledge to understand description or temporal sequence
- Make connections to other areas of study: e.g., science, social studies

SYNTHESIZING

- Talk about what the reader knows about the topic before reading the text and identify new knowledge gained from reading
- Talk about the text showing understanding of events, topic, or content
- Talk about the lessons the story teaches
- Talk about what is learned from the characters, the problem, and the resolution of the problem
- Talk about what is learned about other cultures from characters or settings
- Synthesize new content from texts
- Take on perspectives from diverse cultures and bring cultural knowledge to understanding a text

INFERRING

- Infer temporal sequences and the reasons for each step
- Notice and understand humor in a text
- Make inferences about setting to help in understanding the story
- Understand and infer the importance of the setting of a biography that may be distant in time and geography from students' own knowledge
- Infer character traits, feelings, and motivations from what characters say, think, or do and what others say or think about them
- Recognize and understand traits in complex characters that change
- Infer reasons for character change
- Infer multiple dimensions of characters
- Infer some abstract themes and ideas
- Infer the overarching theme(s) in a collection of short stories
- Infer the writer's message(s) in a text
- Infer the larger message in a text (i.e., what we can learn from it beyond the facts)
- Talk about the pictures, revealing interpretation of a problem or of characters' feelings
- Infer information about characters, setting, plot, and action from graphic texts, in which illustrations carry much of the meaning
- Make inferences from texts that have few or no pictures
- Infer the meaning of a range of graphics that require reader interpretation and are essential to comprehending the text

GUIDED READING

Selecting Goals Behaviors and Understandings to Notice, Teach, and Support *(cont.)*

THINKING *ABOUT* THE TEXT

ANALYZING

- Distinguish between fiction and nonfiction and articulate the characteristic differences
- Understand the unique characteristics of graphic texts
- Distinguish between fiction or nonfiction, and articulate the differences between the two
- Understand and describe characteristics of fiction genres, including realistic fiction, historical fiction, traditional literature (folktale, fairy tale, fable, myth), fantasy, and hybrid text
- Notice elements and basic motifs of fantasy: e.g., the supernatural, imaginary and otherworldly creatures, talking animals, struggle between good and evil, magic, fantastic or magical objects, wishes, trickery, transformations
- Distinguish between realistic fiction and fantasy
- Understand that there may be different genres in each of the larger categories of fiction and nonfiction
- Identify and understand characteristics of special types of fiction: e.g., mystery; adventure story; animal story; family, friends, and school story
- Recognize characters that are typical of fantasy or traditional literature
- Understand and describe the characteristics of nonfiction genres: e.g., expository text, simple narrative nonfiction, biography, memoir, procedural text, and hybrid text
- Understand that a biography is the story of a person's life and is usually told in chronological order
- Understand that the information and ideas in a text are related to each other, and notice how the author presents this
- Recognize a writer's use of embedded forms (e.g., letters) within narrative or expository texts
- Recognize and follow chronological sequence of events
- Recognize and understand variety in narrative structure
- Understand the use of first person or third person in fiction narratives
- Understand the use of second person in nonfiction texts
- Understand that a nonfiction book may be procedural (i.e., "how-to")
- Understand that a nonfiction book may have "how-to" procedures embedded within it
- Recognize when a writer uses temporal (time) order to describe a process
- Recognize a writer's use of underlying text structures: e.g., description, cause and effect, chronological sequence, temporal sequence, comparison and contrast, question and answer
- Infer the writer's purpose in choosing a topic or telling a story
- Think analytically about the significance of a title
- Recognize settings that are familiar as well as some distant in time and geography

- Understand how a setting is important to the plot and the characters' perspectives
- Identify a central story problem in a text with multiple episodes
- Understand the role of supporting characters in a story
- Notice the evidence a writer provides to show character attributes and motives as well as characters' changes
- Understand the perspective from which a story is told and talk about why a writer selected it
- Notice how a fiction writer creates suspense
- Notice language used to show chronological order
- Notice a writer's use of figurative language (metaphor, simile, onomatopoeia)
- Notice how a writer uses common (simple) connectives (e.g., *because, before, after*) to clarify relationships between ideas
- Notice parenthetical material set off by commas or parentheses
- Notice and follow unassigned dialogue
- Notice a writer's use of humorous words or onomatopoetic words and talk about how they add to the action
- Understand that illustrations carry the dialogue and action in graphic texts
- Notice a fiction writer's use of poetic and expressive language in dialogue
- Notice how illustrations add to important story action
- Notice and understand how the graphics and sidebars complement the body of the text
- Understand that illustrations or photographs add to the ideas and information in a text
- Use some academic language to talk about genres: e.g., *fiction; family, friends, and school story; folktale; animal story; humorous story; fairy tale; fable; tall tale; realistic fiction; mystery; adventure story; sports story; nonfiction; informational text; informational book; factual text; how-to book; biography*
- Use some academic language to talk about forms: e.g., *series book, play, chapter book, comics, letter*
- Use some academic language to talk about literary features: e.g., *beginning, ending, problem, character, question and answer, main character, character change, message, dialogue, topic, events, solution, setting, description, time order, problem and solution, comparison and contrast, main idea*
- Use some specific language to talk about book and print features: e.g., *front cover, back cover, page, author, illustrator, illustration, photograph, title, label, drawing, heading, caption, table of contents, chapter, chapter title, dedication, sidebar, glossary, map, diagram, infographic, author's note, illustrator's note, section, book jacket, acknowledgments, subheading, text, pronunciation guide*

LEVEL
N

Selecting Goals Behaviors and Understandings to Notice, Teach, and Support *(cont.)*

THINKING *ABOUT* THE TEXT *(continued)*

CRITIQUING

- Share opinions about a text and give rationales and examples
- Share opinions about an illustration or photograph
- Give an opinion about the believability of a plot or characters
- State specifically what makes a plot or character believable

- Talk critically about what a writer does to make a topic interesting or important
- Talk about why the subject of a biography is important or sets an example for others
- Describe what the illustrations and graphics add to a text

Planning for Word Work After Guided Reading

Using your recent observations of the readers' ability to take words apart quickly and efficiently while reading text, plan for one to three minutes of active engagement of students' attention to letters, sounds, and words. Prioritize the readers' noticing of print features and active hands-on use of magnetic letters, a white board, word cards, or pencil and paper to promote fluency and flexibility in visual processing.

Examples:

- Recognize and use contractions with *not, am, are, is, has, will, have, had,* and *would*
- Make a full range of plural nouns, including regular plurals that require spelling changes and irregular plurals (*arrow/arrows; church/churches; cherry/ cherries; tooth/teeth*)
- Take apart words with a variety of endings (*calendars/calendar; chewing, chewed/ chew; neatest, neater/neat*) and discuss how various endings change a word's meaning or function

- Recognize and break apart words with prefixes (*unusual, intend, disappear, mistake, pretend*)
- Work flexibly with a base word, adding or taking away one or more affixes to make a new word (*fasten/unfasten/ fastened*)
- Break apart two-syllable words by syllable (*in/quire, treas/ure*)
- Recognize and break apart words with an open syllable with a long vowel sound (*mo/ment, pi/lot, o/cean*) and a closed syllable with a short vowel sound (*giv/en, han/dle, man/age*)

- Identify syllables in words with three or more syllables (*ad/ven/ture, au/to/mo/bile, prob/a/bly*)
- Solve words using letter-sound analysis from left to right (*r-e-m-e-m-b-er*)
- Recognize and use homophones (*beat, beet; heel, he'll; sail, sale*) and homographs (*lean, steep, wake*)
- Sort words based on any word features

Readers at Level

At level O, readers can identify the characteristics of a growing number of genres. They read both chapter books and shorter fiction and nonfiction texts. Fiction narratives are straightforward but have plots with multiple episodes and characters who develop and change over time. They are reading a wide range of genres and gaining depth within genres. They enjoy series books and special types of fiction texts such as mystery and sports stories. Readers may also encounter hybrid texts that combine more than one genre in a coherent whole. Some nonfiction texts provide information in categories on several related topics, and readers can identify and use underlying structures (description, cause and effect, chronological sequence, temporal sequence, categorization, comparison and contrast, problem and solution, question and answer). They can process sentences that are complex, contain prepositional phrases, introductory clauses, and lists of nouns, verbs, or adjectives. They solve new vocabulary words, some defined in the text and others to be derived from context or reference tools. Word solving is smooth and automatic in both silent and oral reading. Oral reading demonstrates fluency in all dimensions. They can read and understand descriptive words, some complex content-specific words, common connectives, and some technical words. Length is no longer a critical factor as texts vary widely. They read silently with little overt problem solving. They continue to expand academic vocabulary that they understand and can use.

Selecting Texts Characteristics Texts at **Level O**

GENRE

▶ Fiction

- Realistic fiction
- Historical fiction
- Traditional literature (folktale, fairy tale, fable)
- Fantasy
- Hybrid texts
- Special types of fiction: e.g., mystery; adventure story; sports story; animal story; family, friends, and school story; humorous story

▶ Nonfiction

- Expository nonfiction
- Narrative nonfiction
- Biography
- Autobiography
- Memoir
- Procedural texts
- Hybrid texts

FORMS

- Series books
- Picture books
- Beginning chapter books with illustrations
- Chapter books with sequels
- Plays

- Readers' theater scripts
- Graphic texts
- Letters, journal entries

TEXT STRUCTURE

- Narrative texts with straightforward structure (beginning, series of episodes, and ending) but more episodes included
- Narrative texts with multiple episodes that may be more elaborated
- Some books with very short chapters, each with narrative structure
- Some embedded forms (e.g., letters, directions, journal entries, emails) within narrative and expository structures
- Some books with chapters connected to a single plot
- Some collections of short stories related to an overarching theme
- Nonfiction books divided into sections, some with subsections
- Underlying structural patterns: description, cause and effect, chronological sequence, temporal sequence, comparison and contrast, question and answer

CONTENT

- Content interesting to and relevant for the reader
- A balance of familiar and new content

- Much content that goes beyond students' immediate experience
- Some books with little or no picture support for content: e.g., chapter book
- Some content that requires accessing prior knowledge
- Content that requires the reader to take on perspectives from diverse cultures and bring cultural knowledge to understanding
- Much content that requires the reader to search for information in graphics: e.g., maps, charts, diagrams, illustrated drawings, labeled photographs

THEMES AND IDEAS

- Many light, humorous stories
- Some texts with deeper meaning about content familiar to most readers
- Texts with deeper meanings applicable to important human problems and social issues
- Some abstract themes that require inferential thinking
- Some challenging themes: e.g., the environment, human relationships, people from many cultures

Daily Alta California.

SAN FRANCISCO, CALIFORNIA   TUESDAY, FEBRUARY 7, 1888.

"I did only my simple duty, and as any other teacher would have done... I tried to take care of my children."

February 1888

Many people died in the storm, which was covered by newspapers around the country. Reporters also wrote many stories about Minnie Freeman's bravery. Minnie said she wasn't a hero. She just did what she had to do. From across the country, people sent her gifts, including a gold watch and chain. There were 16 rubies on it, one for each of the students she kept safe from the storm.

14

15

LANGUAGE AND LITERARY FEATURES

- Some texts with settings that are not typical of many students' experiences
- Some settings that are distant in time and geography
- Settings that are important to comprehension of the fiction narrative or biography
- Plot with conflict and resolution
- Plot that includes multiple episodes
- Main characters and supporting characters
- Multidimensional characters
- Characters revealed by what they say, think, and do and by what others say and think about them
- Characters that develop as the result of events of the plot
- Characters revealed over a series of events, chapters, or book series
- Some texts that reveal the perspectives of more than one character
- Variety in presentation of dialogue: e.g., dialogue among multiple characters, dialogue with pronouns, split dialogue, direct dialogue, including unassigned dialogue and long stretches of dialogue

- Most texts written in first- or third-person narrative, with some procedural texts in second person
- Basic motifs of traditional literature and modern fantasy: e.g., struggle between good and evil, fantastic or magical objects, wishes, trickery, transformations
- Literary language typical of traditional literature: e.g., *long ago and far away*
- Some figurative language: e.g., metaphor, simile
- Poetic language
- Language that creates suspense
- Procedural language
- Language used to make comparisons
- Use of expressive language in dialogue
- Descriptive language
- Language used to show chronological order and temporal sequence
- Some persuasive language
- Language that speaks directly to the reader

SENTENCE COMPLEXITY

- Some longer sentences with more than twenty words and many phrases and clauses
- Variation in sentence length and structure

- Sentences with a wide variety of parts of speech
- Variation in placement of subject, verb, adjectives, and adverbs
- Sentences with multiple adjectives, adverbs, and prepositional phrases
- Many sentences beginning with phrases or subordinate (dependent) clauses
- Sentences with more common (simple) connectives
- Variety in order of clauses
- Occasional use of parenthetical material embedded in sentences
- Sentences with a wide variety of punctuation based on complexity

VOCABULARY

- Some vocabulary words that are acquired by students through reading or listening to stories or nonfiction read aloud
- Most words that are in common oral vocabulary for the age group (Tier 1)
- Some words that appear in the vocabulary of mature language users (Tier 2)
- Occasional use of words particular to a discipline (Tier 3)

LEVEL **O**

Selecting Goals Behaviors and Understandings to Notice, Teach, and Support *(cont.)*

THINKING *WITHIN* THE TEXT *(continued)*

SOLVING WORDS *(continued)*

▶ Vocabulary

- Derive the meaning of a new word from the context of the sentence, the paragraph, or the whole text
- Expand meaning of a word by connecting it to other words
- Add to vocabulary through reading
- Connect words to synonyms and antonyms to expand understanding
- Understand a large number of words that are in common oral vocabulary for the age group (Tier 1)
- Understand some words that appear in the language of mature users and in written texts (Tier 2)
- Understand some words particular to academic disciplines (Tier 3)
- Understand the meaning and function in sentences of all parts of speech
- Understand the meaning of regular and irregular plurals
- Understand many words that have multiple meanings and identify the specific meaning that applies in a sentence or paragraph
- Understand words that require the use of multiple sources of information (i.e., background knowledge, pictures, visual information)
- Understand the meaning and function of common (simple) connectives
- Identify base words and understand prefixes and suffixes that add or change meaning, function, or tense
- Understand denotative, connotative, figurative meaning of words
- Understand that words such as *I, me,* and *we* that may indicate the narrator of a text
- Understand the connotative meanings of words necessary to make inferences, including words used to assign dialogue: e.g., *said, asked, cried, shouted, answered, whispered, replied, yelled, moaned*
- Understand the connotative meanings of descriptive adjectives, verbs, and adverbs
- Understand and acquire content-specific words that require the use of strategic actions (i.e., using definitions within the body of a text, the glossary or other reference tools)
- Understand key words in graphics such as maps, diagrams, and charts

MAINTAINING FLUENCY

- Read silently at a slightly faster rate than when reading orally while maintaining comprehension and accuracy
- Sustain momentum through short texts and some short chapter books, making significant progress each day
- Notice periods, quotation marks, commas, exclamation marks, and question marks and begin to reflect them with the voice through intonation and pausing
- Read orally with appropriate phrasing, pausing, intonation, word stress, and rate

- Stress words that are in bold, italics, or varied font
- Recognize and read expressively a variety of dialogue, some unassigned
- Read parts in a script with expression
- Reflect numbered and bulleted lists with the voice when reading orally

ADJUSTING

- Slow down to problem-solve or search for information and resume reading with momentum
- Adjust reading to accommodate compound sentences and sentences with a variety in order of clauses
- Adjust reading to recognize the purpose and characteristics of the genre of a text
- Adjust to accommodate embedded forms (e.g., letters, journal entries) within narrative and expository texts
- Adjust expectations to process different parts of a hybrid text
- Adjust reading to process a graphic text
- Adjust reading to recognize and use characteristics of fiction genres: e.g., realistic fiction, historical fiction, traditional literature, fantasy, hybrid text
- Adjust to recognize and use characteristics of special types of fiction such as mystery; adventure story; animal story; family, friends, and school story
- Adjust to read parts in a readers' theater script or a play
- Adjust reading to recognize nonfiction genres: e.g., expository nonfiction, narrative nonfiction, biography, autobiography, memoir, procedural text, hybrid text
- Adjust reading to reflect a series of steps in procedural texts
- Adjust reading to accommodate varied placement of text body, photographs with captions, sidebars, and graphics

SUMMARIZING

- Summarize important parts of a text (i.e., chapters or sections)
- Summarize the story including characters, story problem, events of the plot, and resolution of the plot (fiction)
- Summarize the important information in the text in a clear and logical way without extraneous detail (nonfiction)
- Summarize narrative nonfiction, biography, or a temporal sequence in time order
- Sometimes use graphics to summarize a text: e.g., timeline or diagram of a chronological or temporal process

Selecting Goals Behaviors and Understandings to Notice, Teach, and Support *(cont.)*

THINKING *BEYOND* THE TEXT

PREDICTING

- ◆ Use knowledge of grammatical structure and experience with written language to anticipate the text
- ◆ Make predictions based on personal experience and content knowledge
- ◆ Make predictions based on previous reading experiences
- ◆ Make predictions throughout a text based on the organizational structure (narrative, expository)
- ◆ Predict the ending of a story based on knowledge of how plots work and understanding of settings, characters, and the story problem
- ◆ Make predictions based on knowledge of fiction genres: e.g., realistic fiction, historical fiction, traditional literature, fantasy, and hybrid text
- ◆ Predict potential solutions to the problem in the story
- ◆ Use previous reading of a book in a series to predict types of characters and plots in a sequel or another book in the series
- ◆ Make predictions based on knowledge of nonfiction genres: e.g., expository nonfiction, narrative nonfiction, biography, autobiography, memoir, procedural text, hybrid text
- ◆ Make predictions using the logical organization or structure of the text
- ◆ Make predictions based on knowledge of underlying text structures: e.g., description, cause and effect, chronological sequence, temporal sequence, comparison and contrast, question and answer

MAKING CONNECTIONS

- ◆ Make connections between personal experience and texts
- ◆ Make connections among books in a series
- ◆ Use background knowledge to understand settings
- ◆ Make connections among texts of the same genre
- ◆ Use background knowledge of traditional literature to recognize common characters and events
- ◆ Make connections between the events in chapters that are connected to a single plot
- ◆ Use background knowledge to understand settings in stories
- ◆ Access background knowledge acquired from reading to understand the content of a text
- ◆ Make connections among texts on the same topic or with similar content
- ◆ Access background knowledge to understand description or temporal sequence
- ◆ Make connections to other areas of study: e.g., science; social studies

SYNTHESIZING

- ◆ Compare previous understandings with the new understandings the text provides
- ◆ Identify interesting, new, or surprising information in a text
- ◆ Express new ways of thinking based on engagement with the text
- ◆ Talk about the lessons the story teaches
- ◆ Talk about new ways of thinking resulting from vicarious experiences in reading fiction
- ◆ Talk about new understanding of different cultures, places, and times in history
- ◆ Synthesize new content from texts
- ◆ Take on perspectives from diverse cultures and bring cultural knowledge to understanding a text

INFERRING

- ◆ Infer temporal sequences and the reasons for each step
- ◆ Make inferences about setting to help in understanding the story
- ◆ Infer character traits, feelings, and motivations from what characters say, think, or do and what others say or think about them
- ◆ Infer the traits of characters that are complex and change
- ◆ Infer character development from evidence in behavior as well as reasons for change
- ◆ Understand and infer the importance of the setting of a biography that may be distant in time and geography from students' own knowledge
- ◆ Understand the problems of challenging situations: e.g., war, the environment
- ◆ Infer some abstract themes and ideas
- ◆ Make inferences from print narrative alone (no pictures)
- ◆ Infer the larger message in a text (i.e., what we can learn from it beyond the facts)
- ◆ Infer information from the pictures that add meaning to the text
- ◆ Talk about the pictures, revealing interpretation of a problem or of characters' feelings
- ◆ Use illustrations to infer characters' feelings
- ◆ Infer information about characters, setting, plot, and action from graphic texts, in which illustrations carry much of the meaning
- ◆ Infer the meaning of a range of graphics that require reader interpretation and are essential to comprehending the text
- ◆ Infer important information from familiar content as well as topics more distant from students' typical experience: e.g., different parts of the world, history, science

LEVEL **O**

Selecting Goals Behaviors and Understandings to Notice, Teach, and Support *(cont.)*

THINKING *ABOUT* THE TEXT

ANALYZING

- Distinguish between fiction or nonfiction and articulate the differences between the two
- Understand and describe characteristics of fiction genres, including realistic fiction, historical fiction, traditional literature (folktale, fairy tale, fable, myth), fantasy, and hybrid text
- Notice elements and basic motifs of fantasy: e.g., the supernatural, imaginary and otherworldly creatures, talking animals, struggle between good and evil, magic, fantastic or magical objects, wishes, trickery, transformations
- Understand the difference between realistic and historical fiction (events that could happen in the real world) and fantasy
- Identify and understand characteristics of special types of fiction: e.g., mystery; adventure story; animal story; family, friends, and school story
- Recognize characters that are typical of fantasy or traditional literature
- Understand and describe the characteristics of nonfiction genres, including expository nonfiction, narrative nonfiction, biography, autobiography, memoir, procedural text, and hybrid text
- Understand that a biography is the story of a person's life and is usually told in chronological order
- Notice that a biography is built around significant events, problems to overcome, and the subject's decisions
- Understand that the information and ideas in a text are related to each other and notice how the author presents this
- Recognize a writer's use of embedded forms (e.g., letters, journal entries) within narrative or expository texts
- Recognize and follow chronological sequence of events
- Recognize and understand variety in narrative structure
- Understand the use of first person or third person in fiction narratives
- Understand the use of second person in nonfiction texts
- Understand that a nonfiction book may be procedural (i.e., "how-to")
- Understand that a nonfiction book may have "how-to" procedures embedded within it
- Recognize a writer's use of temporal sequence to describe a process and chronological sequence to describe an event in time order
- Recognize a writer's use of problem and solution
- Recognize a writer's use of compare and contrast
- Notice that a writer organizes a text into categories and subcategories
- Think analytically about the significance of a title
- Infer the writer's purpose in choosing a topic or telling a story

- Recognize settings that are familiar as well as some distant in time and geography
- Understand how a setting is important to the plot and the characters' perspectives
- Identify a central story problem in a text with multiple episodes
- Relate character development to the events of the plot
- Understand the role of supporting characters in a story
- Notice the evidence a writer provides to show character attributes and motives as well as characters' changes
- Understand the perspective from which a story is told and talk about why a writer selected it
- Notice and follow unassigned dialogue
- Notice how a fiction writer creates suspense
- Notice language used to show chronological order
- Notice a writer's use of figurative language
- Notice a writer's use of simple connectives to show how ideas are related in a text: e.g., *unless, until, because*
- Notice parenthetical material set off by commas or parentheses
- Notice a fiction writer's use of italics to indicate unspoken thought
- Notice a fiction writer's use of poetic and expressive language in dialogue
- Notice a writer's use of humorous words or onomatopoetic words and talk about how they add to the action
- Notice literary language typical of traditional literature: e.g., *a long time ago there lived, long ago and far away, once there lived*
- Notice when a fiction or nonfiction writer uses the second person to talk directly to the reader
- Understand that illustrations carry the dialogue and action in graphic texts
- Notice that illustrations add to the reader's understanding of the characters, the action, and the feeling of the story
- Notice how illustrations add to important story action
- Recognize how illustrations enhance the meaning of a text
- Notice how the writer uses graphics to convey information that complements the body of the text
- Understand that illustrations or photographs add to the ideas and information in a text
- Use some academic language to talk about genres: e.g., *fiction; family, friends, and school story; folktale; animal story; humorous story; fairy tale; fable; tall tale; realistic fiction; mystery; adventure story; sports story; nonfiction; informational text; informational book; factual text; how-to book; biography; autobiography*
- Use some academic language to talk about forms: e.g., *series book, play, chapter book, comics, letter*

Selecting Goals Behaviors and Understandings to Notice, Teach, and Support *(cont.)*

THINKING *ABOUT* THE TEXT *(continued)*

- Use some academic language to talk about literary features: e.g., *beginning, ending, problem, character, question and answer, main character, character change, message, dialogue, topic, events, solution, setting, description, time order, problem and solution, comparison and contrast, main idea*
- Use some specific language to talk about book and print features: e.g., *front cover, back cover, page, author, illustrator, illustration, photograph, title, label, drawing, heading, caption, table of contents, chapter, chapter title, dedication, sidebar, glossary, map, diagram, infographic, author's note, illustrator's note, section, book jacket, acknowledgments, subheading, text, pronunciation guide*

CRITIQUING

- Share opinions about a text and give rationales and examples
- Share opinions about an illustration or photograph
- Give an opinion about the believability of plot, character actions, or the resolution of a problem
- State specifically what makes a plot or character believable
- Talk critically about what a writer does to make a topic interesting or important
- Talk about why the subject of a biography is important or sets an example for others
- Describe what the illustrations and graphics add to a text

Planning for Word Work After Guided Reading

Using your recent observations of the readers' ability to take words apart quickly and efficiently while reading text, plan for one to three minutes of active engagement of students' attention to letters, sounds, and words. Prioritize the readers' noticing of print features and active hands-on use of magnetic letters, a white board, word cards, or pencil and paper to promote fluency and flexibility in visual processing.

Examples:

- Recognize and use contractions with *not, am, are, is, has, will, have, had,* and *would*
- Make a full range of plural nouns, including regular plurals that require spelling changes and irregular plurals (*forest/forests; harness/harnesses; jelly/jellies; knife/knives*)
- Take apart words with a variety of endings (*beast/beasts; combing, combed/comb; plainest, plainer/plain*) and discuss how various endings change a word's meaning or function

- Recognize and break apart words with prefixes (<u>un</u>less, <u>in</u>stead, <u>dis</u>cover, <u>mis</u>chief, <u>pre</u>pare)
- Work flexibly with a base word, adding or taking away one or more affixes to make a new word (*snap/<u>un</u>snap/snap<u>ped</u>*)
- Recognize and break apart words with vowel sounds with *r* (*chair, care; jar; year, here; her, dirt, purple, learn; more, floor, roar, pour; curious*)
- Make word ladders by changing letters and/or word parts
- Break apart two-syllable words by syllable (*sec/ond, whis/per*)

- Recognize and break apart words with an open syllable and use a long vowel sound (*la/zy, mo/tor, u/nite*) and a closed syllable with a short vowel sound (*bun/dle, cab/in, sig/nal*)
- Identify syllables in words with three or more syllables (*A/mer/i/can, cal/en/dar, co/co/nut*)
- Recognize and use homophones (*ant, aunt; in, inn; night, knight*) and homographs (*bow, base, brush*)
- Recognize and use base words and affixes to derive word meaning
- Sort words based on any word features

Readers at Level

At level P, readers can identify the characteristics of a growing number of genres, including biographies, persuasive texts, and hybrid texts that blend more than one genre in a coherent whole. They read fiction and nonfiction texts in a wide range of forms including chapter books, chapter books with sequels, picture books, and series books. Fiction narratives are straightforward but have plots with multiple episodes building toward problem resolution. Problems in fiction texts present internal conflict. Characters develop and change over time. Readers are able to understand abstract and mature themes and take on diverse perspectives and issues related to race, language, and culture. Some nonfiction texts provide information in categories on several related topics, many of which are well beyond readers' typical experience. Readers can identify and use underlying structures (description, cause and effect, chronological sequence, temporal sequence, categorization, comparison and contrast, problem and solution, question and answer). They can process sentences that are complex and contain prepositional phrases, introductory clauses, and lists of nouns, verbs, or adjectives. They solve new vocabulary words, some defined in the text and others to be derived from context or reference tools. Word solving is smooth and automatic in both silent and oral reading. They can read and understand descriptive words, some complex content- specific words, common connectives, and some technical words. They read silently; in oral reading, they demonstrate all aspects of smooth, fluent processing with little overt problem solving. They continue to expand the academic vocabulary that they understand and can use.

Selecting Texts Characteristics of Texts at **Level P**

GENRE

▶ **Fiction**

- Realistic fiction
- Historical fiction
- Traditional literature (folktale, fairy tale, fable)
- Fantasy
- Hybrid texts
- Special types of fiction: e.g., mystery; adventure story; sports story; animal story; family, friends, and school story; humorous story

▶ **Nonfiction**

- Expository nonfiction
- Narrative nonfiction
- Biography
- Autobiography
- Memoir
- Procedural texts
- Persuasive texts
- Hybrid texts

FORMS

- Series books
- Picture books
- Chapter books with some illustrations
- Chapter books with sequels

- Plays
- Readers' theater scripts
- Graphic texts
- Letters, journal entries

TEXT STRUCTURE

- Narrative texts with straightforward structure (beginning, series of episodes, and ending) but more episodes included
- Narrative texts with multiple episodes that may be more elaborated
- Some books with very short chapters, each with narrative structure
- Some embedded forms (e.g., letters, directions, journal entries, emails) within narrative and expository structures
- Some books with chapters connected to a single plot
- Some collections of short stories related to an overarching theme
- Nonfiction books divided into sections, some with subsections
- Underlying structural patterns: description, cause and effect, chronological sequence, temporal sequence, categorization, comparison and contrast, problem and solution, question and answer

CONTENT

- Content interesting to and relevant for the reader
- A balance of familiar and new content
- Much content that goes beyond students' immediate experience
- Some books with little or no picture support for content: e.g., chapter book
- Some content that requires accessing prior knowledge
- Content that requires the reader to take on perspectives from diverse cultures and bring cultural knowledge to understanding
- Much content that requires the reader to search for information in graphics: e.g., maps, charts, diagrams, illustrated drawings, labeled photographs

THEMES AND IDEAS

- Some texts with deeper meaning about content familiar to most readers but not fully explained
- Ideas and themes that require a perspective not familiar to the reader
- Texts with deeper meanings applicable to important human problems and social issues

He explained to Winnie, "A damsel in distress is a lady who needs help." Then he shouted to the lady, "Never fear, dear lady! I will save you!" And he began to climb the tower.

6

The tower was high, and Sir Gladwin's armor was heavy, but he kept climbing. He got the lady over his shoulder. She was very light. Perhaps she had not eaten for days! He carried her down and sat her under a tree.

"You will be all right now," he told her. "I will stop in the next town and send help."

The poor lady was so upset she never said a word.

7

- Many ideas and themes that require understanding of cultural diversity
- Some texts with abstract themes that require inferential thinking
- Some challenging themes: e.g., war, the environment

LANGUAGE AND LITERARY FEATURES

- Some texts with settings that are not typical of many students' experiences
- Some settings that are distant in time and geography
- Settings that are important to comprehension of the fiction narrative or biography
- Plot with conflict and resolution
- Plot that includes multiple episodes
- Main characters and supporting characters
- Multidimensional characters

- Characters revealed by what they say, think, and do and by what others say and think about them
- Characters that develop as the result of events of the plot
- Characters revealed over a series of events, chapters, or book series
- Some texts that reveal the perspectives of more than one character
- Variety in presentation of dialogue: e.g., dialogue among multiple characters, dialogue with pronouns, split dialogue, direct dialogue, including unassigned dialogue and long stretches of dialogue
- Most texts written in first- or third-person narrative, with some procedural texts in second person
- Basic motifs of traditional literature and modern fantasy: e.g., struggle between good and evil, fantastic or magical objects, wishes, trickery, transformations

- Literary language typical of traditional literature: e.g., *long ago and far away*
- Some figurative language: e.g., metaphor, simile
- Poetic language
- Language that creates suspense
- Language and events that convey an emotional atmosphere (mood) in a text, affecting how the reader feels: e.g., tension, sadness, happiness, curiosity
- Procedural language
- Language used to make comparisons
- Use of expressive language in dialogue
- Descriptive language
- Language used to show chronological order and temporal sequence
- Some persuasive language
- Language that speaks directly to the reader

GUIDED READING

Selecting Goals Behaviors and Understandings to Notice, Teach, and Support *(cont.)*

THINKING *WITHIN* THE TEXT *(continued)*

SOLVING WORDS *(continued)*

▶ **Vocabulary**

- Derive the meaning of a new word from the context of the sentence, the paragraph, or the whole text
- Expand meaning of a word by connecting it to other words
- Add actively to vocabulary through learning new words from reading
- Connect words to synonyms and antonyms to expand understanding
- Understand a large body of words that are in common oral vocabulary for the age group (Tier 1)
- Understand many words that appear in the language of mature users and in written texts (Tier 2)
- Understand some words particular to academic disciplines (Tier 3)
- Understand the meaning and function in sentences of all parts of speech
- Understand the meaning of regular and irregular plurals
- Understand many words that have multiple meanings and identify the specific meaning that applies in a sentence or paragraph
- Understand words that require the use of multiple sources of information (i.e., background knowledge, pictures, visual information)
- Understand the meaning and function of common connectives
- Identify base words and understand prefixes and suffixes that add or change meaning, function, or tense
- Understand denotative, connotative, and figurative meaning of words
- Understand the connotative meanings of words that contribute to the mood of the text
- Understand that in graphic texts, information about words is in the illustrations, and also that many unusual words appear in graphic texts (i.e., onomatopoetic)
- Understand the connotative meanings of words necessary to make inferences, including words used to assign dialogue: e.g., *said, asked, cried, shouted, answered, whispered, replied, yelled, moaned*
- Understand the connotative meanings of descriptive adjectives, verbs, and adverbs
- Understand and acquire content-specific words that require the use of strategic actions (i.e., using definitions within the body of a text, the glossary or other reference tools)
- Understand key words in graphics such as maps, diagrams, and charts

MAINTAINING FLUENCY

- Read silently at a slightly faster rate than when reading orally while maintaining comprehension and accuracy
- Sustain momentum through short texts and some short chapter books, making significant progress each day

- Notice periods, quotation marks, commas, exclamation marks, and question marks and reflect them with the voice through intonation and pausing
- Read orally with appropriate phrasing, pausing, intonation, word stress, and rate
- Stress words that are in bold, italics, or varied font
- Recognize and read expressively a variety of dialogue, some unassigned
- Read parts in a script with expression
- Reflect numbered and bulleted lists with the voice when reading orally

ADJUSTING

- Slow down to problem-solve or search for information and resume reading with momentum
- Adjust reading to accommodate compound sentences and sentences with a variety in order of clauses
- Adjust oral reading to show awareness of sentence variety (i.e., placement of parts of speech, phrases, and clauses)
- Adjust reading to recognize the purpose and characteristics of fiction and nonfiction genres and of special types of fiction texts like mystery
- Adjust to accommodate embedded forms (e.g., letters, journal entries) within narrative and expository texts
- Adjust expectations to process different parts of a hybrid text
- Adjust reading to process a graphic text
- Adjust to read parts in a readers' theater script or a play
- Adjust reading to reflect a series of steps in procedural texts
- Adjust reading to accommodate varied placement of text body, photographs with captions, sidebars, and graphics
- Adjust reading to reflect a series of steps in a procedural text
- Adjust reading to recognize the tone of a persuasive text

SUMMARIZING

- Talk about the text after reading, including important information in organized summary form
- Summarize important parts of a text (i.e., chapters or sections)
- Summarize the story including characters, story problem, events of the plot, and resolution of the plot
- Summarize the important information in the text in a clear and logical way without extraneous detail
- Summarize narrative nonfiction, biography, or a temporal sequence in time order
- Sometimes use graphics to summarize a text: e.g., timeline or diagram of a chronological or temporal process

Selecting Goals Behaviors and Understandings to Notice, Teach, and Support *(cont.)*

THINKING *BEYOND* THE TEXT

PREDICTING

- Use knowledge of grammatical structure and experience with written language to anticipate the text
- Make predictions based on knowledge and experience
- Make predictions based on previous reading experiences
- Make predictions throughout a text based on the organizational structure (narrative, expository)
- Predict the ending of a story based on knowledge of how plots work and understanding of settings, characters, and the story problem
- Make predictions based on knowledge of fiction genres: e.g., realistic fiction, historical fiction, traditional literature, fantasy, and hybrid text
- Predict potential solutions to the problem in the story
- Use previous reading of a book in a series to predict types of characters and plots in a sequel or another book in the series
- Make predictions based on knowledge of nonfiction genres: e.g., expository nonfiction, narrative nonfiction, biography, autobiography, memoir, procedural text, persuasive text, hybrid text
- Make predictions using the logical organization or structure of the text
- Make predictions based on knowledge of underlying text structures: e.g., description, cause and effect, chronological sequence, temporal sequence, comparison and contrast, problem and solution, question and answer

MAKING CONNECTIONS

- Make connections between personal experience and texts
- Make connections among books in a series
- Use background knowledge to understand settings
- Make connections among texts of the same genre
- Use background knowledge of traditional literature to recognize common characters and events
- Make connections between the events in chapters that are connected to a single plot
- When reading chapter books, make connections between previous events of the plot and what is happening at another point in the text
- Use background knowledge to understand settings in stories
- Access background knowledge acquired from reading to understand the content of a text
- Make connections among texts on the same topic or with similar content
- Access background knowledge to understand description or temporal sequence
- Make connections to other areas of study: e.g., history, geography, culture

SYNTHESIZING

- Compare previous understandings with the new understandings the text provides
- Identify interesting, new, or surprising information in a text
- Express new ways of thinking based on engagement with the text
- Talk about the lessons the story teaches
- Talk about new ways of thinking from vicarious experiences in reading fiction
- Talk about new understanding of different cultures, places, and times in history
- Synthesize new content from texts
- Take on perspectives from diverse cultures and bring cultural knowledge to understanding a text

INFERRING

- Make inferences about setting to help in understanding the story
- Infer character traits, feelings, and motivations from what characters say, think, or do and what others say or think about them
- Infer the traits of characters that are complex and change
- Infer character development from evidence in behavior as well as reasons for change
- Infer complex relationships between and among characters by noticing evidence in their responses to each other
- Understand and infer the importance of the setting of a biography that may be distant in time and geography from students' own knowledge
- Understand the problems of challenging situations: e.g., war, the environment, society's problems such as poverty, war
- Infer some abstract themes and ideas
- Make inferences from print narrative alone (no pictures)
- Infer the larger message in a text (i.e., what we can learn from it beyond the facts)
- Infer information from the pictures that add meaning to the text
- Talk about the pictures, revealing interpretation of a problem or of characters' feelings
- Use illustrations to infer characters' feelings
- Infer information about characters, setting, plot, and action from graphic texts, in which illustrations carry much of the meaning
- Infer the meaning of a range of graphics that require reader interpretation and are essential to comprehending the text
- Understand the connotative meanings of words as used in the language
- Understand the connotative meanings of words that contribute to the mood of the text
- Infer important information from familiar content as well as topics more distant from students' typical experience: e.g., different parts of the world, history, science

Selecting Goals Behaviors and Understandings to Notice, Teach, and Support (*cont.*)

THINKING *ABOUT* THE TEXT

ANALYZING

- Distinguish between fiction and nonfiction and articulate the differences between the two
- Understand that a graphic text may represent any fiction or nonfiction genre
- Understand and describe characteristics of fiction genres, including realistic fiction, historical fiction, traditional literature (folktale, fairy tale, fable, myth), fantasy, and hybrid text
- Notice elements and basic motifs of fantasy: e.g., the supernatural, imaginary and otherworldly creatures, gods and goddesses, talking animals, struggle between good and evil, magic, fantastic or magical objects, wishes, trickery, transformations
- Understand the difference between realistic and historical fiction (events that could happen in the real world) and fantasy
- Identify and understand characteristics of special types of fiction: e.g., mystery; adventure story; animal story; family, friends, and school story
- Understand and describe the characteristics of nonfiction genres, including expository nonfiction, narrative nonfiction, biography, autobiography, memoir, procedural text, persuasive text, and hybrid text
- Understand that a biography is the story of a person's life and is usually told in chronological order
- Notice that a biography is built around significant events, problems to overcome, and the subject's decisions
- Understand that the information and ideas in a text are related to each other and notice how the author presents this
- Recognize a writer's use of embedded forms (e.g., letters, journal entries) within narrative or expository texts
- Recognize and understand variety in narrative structure
- Understand the role of supporting characters in a story
- Understand the use of first person or third person in fiction narratives
- Understand the use of second person in nonfiction texts
- Understand that a nonfiction book may be procedural (i.e., "how-to")
- Understand that a nonfiction book may have "how-to" procedures embedded within it
- Notice that a writer organizes a text into categories and subcategories
- Recognize a writer's use of underlying text structures: e.g., description, cause and effect, chronological sequence, temporal sequence, comparison and contrast, problem and solution, question and answer
- Think analytically about the significance of a title
- Infer the writer's purpose in choosing a topic or telling a story
- Recognize settings that are familiar as well as some distant in time and geography
- Understand how a setting is important to the plot and the characters' perspectives

- Identify a central story problem in a text with multiple episodes
- Relate character development to the events of the plot
- Notice the evidence a writer provides to show character attributes and motives as well as characters' changes
- Understand the perspective from which a story is told and talk about why a writer selected it
- Notice how a fiction writer creates suspense
- Notice and think analytically about a writer's use of argument or persuasion
- Notice language used to show chronological order
- Notice a writer's use of figurative language
- Notice a writer's use of simple connectives to show how ideas are related in a text: e.g., *unless, until, because, finally*
- Notice parenthetical material set off by commas or parentheses
- Notice a fiction writer's use of italics to indicate unspoken thought
- Notice a fiction writer's use of poetic and expressive language in dialogue
- Notice a writer's use of humorous words or onomatopoetic words and talk about how they add to the action
- Notice literary language typical of traditional literature: e.g., *a long time ago there lived, long ago and far away, once there lived*
- Notice when the writer uses the second person to talk directly to the reader
- Understand that illustrations carry the dialogue and action in graphic texts
- Notice how illustrations add to the reader's understanding of the characters, the action, and the feeling of the story
- Recognize how illustrations enhance the meaning of a text
- Notice how the writer uses graphics to convey information that complements the body of the text
- Understand that illustrations or photographs add to the ideas and information in a text
- Use some academic language to talk about genres: e.g., *fiction; family, friends, and school story; folktale; animal story; humorous story; fairy tale; fable; tall tale; realistic fiction; mystery; adventure story; sports story; nonfiction; informational text; informational book; factual text; how-to book; biography; autobiography*
- Use some academic language to talk about forms: e.g., *series book, play, chapter book, comics, graphic text, letter*
- Use some academic language to talk about literary features: e.g., *beginning, ending, problem, character, question and answer, main character, character change, message, dialogue, topic, events, solution, setting, description, time order, problem and solution, comparison and contrast, main idea*
- Use some specific language to talk about book and print features: e.g., *front cover, back cover, page, author, illustrator, illustration, photograph, title, label, drawing, heading, caption, table of contents, chapter, chapter title, dedication, sidebar, glossary, map, diagram, infographic, author's note, illustrator's note, section, book jacket, acknowledgments, subheading, text, pronunciation guide*

Selecting Goals Behaviors and Understandings to Notice, Teach, and Support *(cont.)*

THINKING *ABOUT* THE TEXT *(continued)*

CRITIQUING

- Share opinions about a text and give rationales and examples
- Share opinions about an illustration or photograph
- Evaluate the quality of illustrations or graphics
- Describe what the illustrations and graphics add to a text
- Assess how graphics add to the quality of the text or provide additional information
- Give an opinion about the believability of plot, character actions, or the resolution of a problem
- State specifically what makes a plot or character believable

- Share opinions of characters and talk about how they could have made different decisions or behaved differently
- Assess whether a text is authentic and consistent with life experience
- Assess whether a text is authentic and consistent with reader's background knowledge
- Evaluate aspects of a text that add to enjoyment or interest: e.g., humorous characters or surprising information
- Talk critically about what a writer does to make a topic interesting or important
- Talk about why the subject of a biography is important or sets an example for others

Planning for Word Work After Guided Reading

Using your recent observations of the readers' ability to take words apart quickly and efficiently while reading text, plan for one to three minutes of active engagement of students' attention to letters, sounds, and words. Prioritize the readers' noticing of print features and active hands-on use of magnetic letters, a white board, word cards, or pencil and paper to promote fluency and flexibility in visual processing.

Examples:

- Recognize and use contractions with *not, am, are, is, has, will, have, had,* and *would*
- Make a full range of plural nouns, including regular plurals that require spelling changes and irregular plurals (*plow/plows; address/addresses; army/ armies; child/children*)
- Recognize and solve words in which one consonant sound is represented by several different letters or letter clusters (*awake, picnic, truck; thief, stiff*)

- Work flexibly with a base word, adding or taking away one or more affixes to make a new word (*arrange/prearrange/ arrangement*)
- Break apart two-, three-, and four-syllable words by syllable (*re/ward, his/tor/y, eve/ry/bod/y*)
- Make word ladders by changing letters and/or word parts

- Recognize and break apart words with an open syllable and a long vowel sound (*si/lent, cho/sen*) and a closed syllable with a short vowel sound (*gath/er, met/al, sim/ple*)
- Recognize and use homophones (*die, dye; fir, fur; I'd, eyed*) and homographs (*club, content, skip*)
- Sort words based on any word features

GUIDED READING

LEVEL **P**

Readers at Level

At level Q, readers automatically read and understand a wide range of genres, including science fiction and other more complex fantasy works, biography, autobiography, and memoir, and hybrid texts that blend more than one genre in a coherent whole. They read fiction and nonfiction texts in various forms including letters and diaries and journal entries, photo essays and news articles, and short stories, as well as chapter books, series books, picture books, and graphic texts. Fiction narratives are usually straightforward but have elaborate plots and some variation. There are many complex characters who develop and change over time. Readers understand perspectives different from their own as well as settings and people far distant in time and space. They can process sentences that are complex, contain prepositional phrases, introductory clauses, and lists of nouns, verbs, or adjectives; and they solve new vocabulary words, some defined in the text and others to be derived from context or reference tools. They recognize and understand common connectives as well as some sophisticated connectives. Most reading is silent, but fluency and phrasing in oral reading are well established. Readers are challenged by many longer descriptive words and by content-specific and technical words that require using embedded definitions, background knowledge, and understanding of text features such as sidebars, glossaries, and references. They can take apart multisyllable words and use a full range of word-solving skills. They read and understand texts in a variety of layouts as well as fonts and print characteristics and consistently search for information in illustrations and increasingly complex graphics. Readers continue to expand the academic vocabulary that they understand and can use.

Selecting Texts Characteristics of Texts at **Level Q**

GENRE

▶ **Fiction**

- Realistic fiction
- Historical fiction
- Traditional literature (folktale, fairy tale, fable)
- More complex fantasy including science fiction
- Hybrid texts
- Special types of fiction: e.g., mystery; adventure story; sports story; animal story; family, friends, and school story; humorous story

▶ **Nonfiction**

- Expository nonfiction
- Narrative nonfiction
- Biography
- Autobiography
- Memoir
- Procedural texts
- Persuasive texts
- Hybrid texts

FORMS

- Series books
- Picture books
- Chapter books
- Chapter books with sequels
- Plays
- Readers' theater scripts
- Graphic texts
- Letters, diaries, journal entries
- Short stories
- Photo essays and news articles

TEXT STRUCTURE

- Narrative texts with straightforward structure and multiple episodes that may be more elaborated
- Embedded forms (e.g., letters, directions, journal entries, emails) within narrative and expository structures
- Variations in structure: e.g., story-within-a-story, simple flashback
- Books with chapters connected to a single plot
- Some collections of short stories related to an overarching theme
- Nonfiction books divided into sections, and some with subsections
- Underlying structural patterns: description, cause and effect, chronological sequence, temporal sequence, comparison and contrast, problem and solution, question and answer

CONTENT

- Content interesting to and relevant for the reader
- Some books with little or no picture support for content: e.g., chapter books
- Much content that requires accessing prior knowledge
- Content that requires the reader to take on perspectives from diverse cultures and bring cultural knowledge to understanding
- Most texts with new content that will engage and interest readers and expand knowledge: e.g., travel, experience with other cultures, adventures in science, survival
- Settings in some texts that require content knowledge of disciplines: e.g., history, geography, culture, language
- Most content that goes beyond students' immediate experience

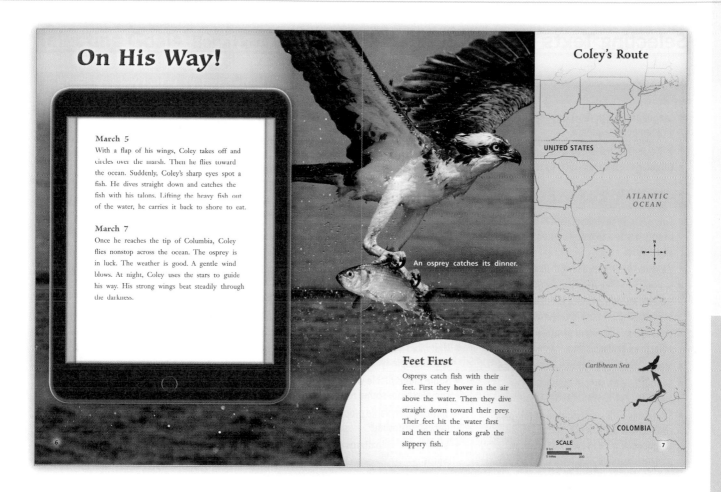

On His Way!

March 5

With a flap of his wings, Coley takes off and circles over the marsh. Then he flies toward the ocean. Suddenly, Coley's sharp eyes spot a fish. He dives straight down and catches the fish with his talons. Lifting the heavy fish out of the water, he carries it back to shore to eat.

March 7

Once he reaches the tip of Columbia, Coley flies nonstop across the ocean. The osprey is in luck. The weather is good. A gentle wind blows. At night, Coley uses the stars to guide his way. His strong wings beat steadily through the darkness.

An osprey catches its dinner.

Feet First

Ospreys catch fish with their feet. First they **hover** in the air above the water. Then they dive straight down toward their prey. Their feet hit the water first and then their talons grab the slippery fish.

Coley's Route

UNITED STATES

ATLANTIC OCEAN

Caribbean Sea

COLOMBIA

SCALE

■ Much content that requires the reader to search for information in graphics: e.g., maps, charts, diagrams, illustrated drawings, labeled photographs

THEMES AND IDEAS

■ Some texts with deeper meaning about content familiar to most readers but not fully explained

■ Themes and ideas that require a perspective not familiar to the reader

■ Complex ideas on many different topics that require real or vicarious experience (through reading) for understanding

■ Texts with deeper meanings applicable to important human problems and social issues

■ Many ideas and themes that require understanding of cultural diversity

■ Some texts with abstract themes that require inferential thinking

■ Some challenging themes: e.g., war, the environment, racism

LANGUAGE AND LITERARY FEATURES

■ Settings that are distant in time and geography

■ Settings that are important to comprehension of the fiction narrative or biography

■ Variety in narrative plot structure: e.g., story-within-a-story, simple flashback

■ Plot that includes multiple episodes

■ Main characters and supporting characters

■ Multidimensional characters

■ Characters revealed by what they say, think, and do and by what others say and think about them

■ Characters revealed over a series of events, chapters, or book series

■ Characters that develop as the result of events of the plot

■ Reasons for character change that are complex and require inference

■ Some texts that reveal the perspectives of more than one character

■ Variety in presentation of dialogue: e.g., dialogue among multiple characters, dialogue with pronouns, split dialogue, direct dialogue, including unassigned dialogue and long stretches of dialogue

■ Most texts written in first- or third-person narrative, with some procedural texts in second person

■ Basic motifs of traditional literature and modern fantasy: e.g., struggle between good and evil, fantastic or magical objects, wishes, trickery, transformations

■ Literary language typical of traditional literature: e.g., *long ago and far away*

■ Some figurative language: e.g., metaphor, simile

■ Poetic language

■ Language that creates suspense

■ Language and events that convey an emotional atmosphere (mood) in a text, affecting how the reader feels: e.g., tension, sadness, happiness, curiosity

■ Procedural language

■ Language used to make comparisons

■ Use of expressive language in dialogue

■ Descriptive language

Selecting Goals Behaviors and Understandings to Notice, Teach, and Support *(cont.)*

SOLVING WORDS *(continued)*

- Solve words by identifying base words and affixes (prefixes and suffixes)
- Read hyphenated words divided across lines and across pages
- Demonstrate flexibility in using different strategies for solving words

▶ Vocabulary

- Derive the meaning of new words and expand meaning of known words using flexible strategies: e.g., context in a sentence; connections to other words; synonyms and antonyms; word parts; base words and affixes; word function in a sentence
- Actively and consistently add to vocabulary through reading
- Connect words to synonyms and antonyms to expand understanding
- Understand a large body of words that are in common oral vocabulary for students at the grade (Tier 1)
- Understand many words that appear in the language of mature users and in written texts (Tier 2)
- Understand some words particular to academic disciplines (Tier 3)
- Understand the meaning and function in sentences of all parts of speech
- Understand the meaning of regular and irregular plurals
- Understand many words that have multiple meanings and identify the specific meaning that applies in a sentence or paragraph
- Understand words that require the use of multiple sources of information (i.e., background knowledge, pictures, visual information)
- Understand the meaning and function of common (simple) connectives that occur in oral language and some sophisticated (complex) connectives that are more typical of written language
- Identify base words and understand prefixes and suffixes that add or change meaning, function, or tense
- Understand denotative, connotative, idiomatic, and figurative meaning of words
- Understand the connotative meanings of words that contribute to the mood of the text
- Understand that in graphic texts, information about words is in the illustrations, and also that many unusual words appear in graphic texts (i.e. onomatopoetic)
- Understand the connotative meanings of words necessary to make inferences, including words used to assign dialogue: e.g., *said, asked, cried, shouted, answered, whispered, replied, yelled, moaned*

- Understand the connotative meanings of descriptive adjectives, verbs, and adverbs, and use them to make inferences about characters
- Derive the meanings of technical words and author-created words in science fiction
- Understand and acquire content-specific words that require the use of strategic actions (i.e., using definitions within the body of a text, the glossary or other reference tools)
- Understand key words in graphics such as maps, diagrams, and charts

MAINTAINING FLUENCY

- Read silently at a slightly faster rate than when reading orally while maintaining comprehension and accuracy
- Sustain momentum through short texts and some short chapter books or books of short stories, making significant progress each day
- Notice periods, commas, question marks, exclamation marks, parentheses, quotation marks, dashes, and ellipses and begin to reflect them with the voice through intonation and pausing
- Read orally with appropriate phrasing, pausing, intonation, word stress, and rate
- Stress words that are in bold, italics, or varied font
- Recognize and read expressively a variety of dialogue, some unassigned
- Read parts in a script with expression
- Show in the voice when words in a text (sometimes shown in italics) reflect unspoken thought
- Reflect numbered and bulleted lists with the voice when reading orally

ADJUSTING

- Slow down to problem-solve or search for information and resume reading with momentum
- Adjust reading to accommodate compound sentences and sentences with a variety in order of clauses
- Adjust oral reading to show awareness of sentence variety (i.e., placement of parts of speech, phrases, and clauses)
- Adjust reading to recognize the purpose and characteristics of fiction and nonfiction genres and of special types of fiction texts like mystery

GUIDED READING

Selecting Goals Behaviors and Understandings to Notice, Teach, and Support *(cont.)*

THINKING *WITHIN* THE TEXT *(continued)*

- Adjust to accommodate embedded forms (e.g., letters, diaries, journal entries) within narrative and expository texts
- Adjust expectations to process different parts of a hybrid text
- Adjust reading to process a graphic text
- Adjust reading to understand that a text can be a collection of short stories related to an overarching theme
- Adjust to read parts in a readers' theater script or a play
- Adjust reading to reflect a series of steps in procedural texts
- Adjust reading to accommodate varied placement of text body, photographs with captions, sidebars, and graphics
- Adjust reading to reflect a series of steps in a procedural text
- Adjust reading to recognize a persuasive text

SUMMARIZING

- Summarize important parts of a text (i.e., chapters or sections)
- Summarize the story including characters, story problem, events of the plot, and resolution of the plot (fiction)
- Summarize the important information in the text in a clear and logical way without extraneous detail (nonfiction)
- Summarize narrative nonfiction, biography, or a temporal sequence in time order
- Summarize a writer's argument or main idea
- Sometimes use graphics to summarize a text: e.g., timeline or diagram of a chronological or temporal process

THINKING *BEYOND* THE TEXT

PREDICTING

- Make predictions based on personal experience and content knowledge
- Make predictions based on previous reading experiences
- Make predictions throughout a text based on the organizational structure (narrative, expository)
- Justify predictions with evidence from the text
- Predict the ending of a story based on knowledge of how plots work and understanding of settings, characters, and the story problem
- Make predictions based on knowledge of a variety of everyday events
- Make predictions based on knowledge of fiction genres: e.g., realistic fiction, historical fiction, traditional literature, fantasy including science fiction, and hybrid text

- Make predictions based on knowledge of special types of fiction: e.g., mystery; adventure story; animal story; family, friends, and school story
- Predict potential solutions to the problem in the story
- Use previous reading of a book in a series to predict types of characters and plots in a sequel or another book in the series
- Make predictions based on knowledge of nonfiction genres: e.g., expository nonfiction, narrative nonfiction, biography, autobiography, memoir, procedural text, persuasive text, hybrid text
- Make predictions based on knowledge of special forms: e.g., letters, diaries, journal entries; photo essays, news articles
- Make predictions using the logical organization of the text
- Make predictions based on knowledge of underlying text structures: e.g., description, cause and effect, chronological sequence, temporal sequence, comparison and contrast, problem and solution, question and answer

Selecting Goals Behaviors and Understandings to Notice, Teach, and Support *(cont.)*

THINKING *BEYOND* THE TEXT *(continued)*

MAKING CONNECTIONS

- Make connections among personal experiences, historical or current events, and texts
- Connect texts to the problems of society
- Make connections among books in a series
- Use knowledge from one text to understand content in another text
- Make many different kinds of connections among texts: e.g., author, illustrator, content, genre, topic, theme or message, events, problem, characters, language and style
- State explicitly the nature of connections: e.g., topic, theme, message, characters, genre, writer, style
- Make connections between previous events of the plot and what is happening at another point in the text when reading chapter books
- Use background knowledge of traditional literature to recognize common characters and events
- Make connections between the events in chapters that are connected to a single plot
- Use background knowledge to understand settings in stories
- Access background knowledge acquired from reading to understand the content of a text
- Make different kinds of connections among texts: e.g., content, graphics, main idea or message, text structure

SYNTHESIZING

- Compare previous understandings with the new understandings the text provides
- Identify interesting, new, or surprising information in a text
- Express new ways of thinking based on engagement with the text
- Provide evidence from the text to support statements describing new learning
- Talk about the lessons the story teaches
- Talk about new ways of thinking from vicarious experiences in reading fiction
- Talk about new understanding of different cultures, places, and times in history
- Synthesize new content from a text and describe it to others with evidence from the text
- Take on perspectives from diverse cultures and bring cultural knowledge to understanding a text

INFERRING

- Make inferences about setting to help in understanding the story
- Understand and infer the importance of the setting of a biography that may be distant in time and geography from students' own knowledge
- Infer character traits, feelings, and motivations from what characters say, think, or do and what others say or think about them
- Infer character development from evidence in behavior as well as reasons for change
- Infer complex relationships between and among characters by noticing evidence in their responses to each other
- Understand the problems of challenging situations: e.g., war, the environment
- Infer some abstract themes and ideas
- Infer the overarching theme(s) in a collection of short stories
- Infer the writer's message(s) in a text
- Infer the larger message in a text (i.e., what we can learn from it beyond the facts)
- Infer information from the pictures that add meaning to the text
- Talk about the pictures, revealing interpretation of a problem or of characters' feelings
- Use illustrations to infer characters' feelings
- Infer information about characters, setting, plot, and action from graphic texts, in which illustrations carry much of the meaning
- Make inferences from print narrative alone (no pictures)
- Infer the meaning of a range of graphics that require reader interpretation and are essential to comprehending the text
- Understand the connotative meanings of words that contribute to the mood and meaning of the text
- Infer important information from familiar content as well as topics more distant from students' typical experience: e.g., history, geography, culture, language

Selecting Goals Behaviors and Understandings to Notice, Teach, and Support *(cont.)*

THINKING *ABOUT* THE TEXT

ANALYZING

- Understand that a graphic text may represent any fiction or nonfiction genre
- Distinguish between fiction and nonfiction and understand the unique characteristics of both, including graphic texts
- Understand and describe characteristics of fiction genres, including realistic fiction, historical fiction, traditional literature (folktale, fairy tale, fable, myth), fantasy, and hybrid text
- Notice elements and basic motifs of fantasy: e.g., the supernatural, imaginary and otherworldly creatures, gods and goddesses, talking animals, struggle between good and evil, magic, fantastic or magical objects, wishes, trickery, transformations
- Understand the difference between realistic and historical fiction (events that could happen in the real world) and fantasy
- Identify and understand characteristics of special types of fiction: e.g., mystery; adventure story; animal story; family, friends, and school story
- Understand and describe the characteristics of nonfiction genres, including expository nonfiction, narrative nonfiction, biography, autobiography, memoir, procedural text, persuasive text, and hybrid text
- Understand that a biography is the story of a person's life and is usually told in chronological order
- Notice that a biography is built around significant events, problems to overcome, and the subject's decisions
- Notice the format of a photo essay and understand the purpose
- Understand that a nonfiction writer may use argument or persuasion
- Understand that the information and ideas in a text are related to each other and notice how the author presents this
- Recognize a writer's use of embedded forms (e.g., letters, journal entries) within narrative or expository texts
- Understand that a nonfiction book may be procedural (i.e., "how-to")
- Understand that a nonfiction book may have "how-to" procedures embedded within it
- Notice that a writer organizes a text into categories and subcategories
- Recognize a writer's use of underlying text structures: e.g., description, cause and effect, chronological sequence, temporal sequence, comparison and contrast, problem and solution, question and answer
- Think analytically about the significance of a title
- Infer the writer's purpose in choosing a topic or telling a story

- Recognize settings that are familiar as well as some distant in time and geography
- Understand how a setting is important to the plot and the characters' perspectives
- Notice characteristics of setting in fantasy that involve magic and/or an imaginary world
- Identify a central story problem in a text with multiple episodes
- Recognize and understand variation in plot structure: story-within-a-story, flashback
- Relate character development to the events of the plot
- Understand the role of supporting characters in a story
- Notice the evidence a writer provides to show character attributes and motives as well as characters' changes
- Understand the perspective from which a story is told and talk about why a writer selected it
- Understand first- and third-person narrative
- Notice a fiction writer's use of italics to indicate unspoken thought
- Notice how a fiction writer creates suspense
- Notice language used to show chronological order
- Notice a writer's use of figurative language
- Notice a writer's use of common or simple (e.g., *because, after*) and more complex or sophisticated connectives (e.g., *therefore, however, meanwhile, moreover, otherwise*) to show how ideas are related in a text
- Notice parenthetical material set off by commas or parentheses
- Notice a fiction writer's use of poetic and expressive language in dialogue
- Notice a writer's use of humorous words or onomatopoetic words and talk about how they add to the action
- Notice literary language typical of traditional literature: e.g., *a long time ago there lived, long ago and far away, once there lived*
- Notice and think analytically about a writer's use of argument or persuasion
- Recognize procedural language: e.g., directions
- Notice when the writer uses the second person to talk directly to the reader
- Understand that illustrations carry the dialogue and action in graphic texts
- Notice how illustrations add to the reader's understanding of the characters, the action, and the feeling of the story
- Recognize how illustrations enhance the meaning of a text

Selecting Goals Behaviors and Understandings to Notice, Teach, and Support *(cont.)*

THINKING *ABOUT* THE TEXT *(continued)*

ANALYZING *(continued)*

- Notice how the writer uses graphics to convey information that complements the body of the text
- Understand that illustrations or photographs add to the ideas and information in a text
- Use some academic language to talk about genres: e.g., *fiction; family, friends, and school story; folktale; animal story; humorous story; fairy tale; fable; tall tale; realistic fiction; mystery; adventure story; sports story; historical fiction; fantasy; nonfiction; informational text; informational book; factual text; how-to book; biography; autobiography; narrative nonfiction; memoir; procedural text; persuasive text, hybrid text*
- Use some academic language to talk about forms: e.g., *series book, play, chapter book, comics, graphic text, letter, sequel, short story, diary entry, journal entry, news article, feature article*
- Use some academic language to talk about literary features: e.g., *beginning, ending, character, question and answer, main character, character change, message, dialogue, topic, events, setting, description, time order, problem and solution, comparison and contrast, main idea, flashback, conflict, resolution, theme, descriptive language, simile, cause and effect, categorization, persuasive language*
- Use some specific language to talk about book and print features: e.g., *front cover, back cover, page, author, illustrator, illustration, photograph, title, label, drawing, heading, caption, table of contents, chapter, chapter title, dedication, sidebar, glossary, map, diagram, infographic, author's note, illustrator's note, section, book jacket, acknowledgments, subheading, text, pronunciation guide*

CRITIQUING

- Share opinions about a text and give rationales and examples
- Share opinions about an illustration or photograph
- Evaluate the quality of illustrations or graphics
- Describe what the illustrations and graphics add to a text
- Assess how graphics add to the quality of the text or provide additional information
- Give an opinion about the believability of plot, character actions, or the resolution of a problem
- State specifically what makes a plot or character believable
- Share opinions of characters and talk about how they could have made different decisions or behaved differently
- Assess whether a text is authentic and consistent with life experience
- Assess whether a text is authentic and consistent with reader's background knowledge of content
- Distinguish between fact and opinion
- Evaluate aspects of a text that add to enjoyment or interest: e.g., humorous characters or surprising information
- Express tastes and preferences in reading and support choices with descriptions and examples of literary elements: e.g., genre, setting, plot, theme, character, style and language
- Talk critically about what a writer does to make a topic interesting or important
- Talk about why the subject of a biography is important or sets an example for others
- Notice the author's qualifications to write on a topic

Selecting Goals Behaviors and Understandings to Notice, Teach, and Support *(cont.)*

Planning for Word Work After Guided Reading

Using your recent observations of the readers' ability to take words apart quickly and efficiently while reading text, plan for one to three minutes of active engagement of students' attention to letters, sounds, and words. Prioritize the readers' noticing of print features and active hands-on use of magnetic letters, a white board, word cards, or pencil and paper to promote fluency and flexibility in visual processing.

Examples:

- Recognize and use contractions with *not, am, are, is, has, will, have, had,* and *would*
- Make a full range of plural nouns, including regular plurals that require spelling changes and irregular plurals (*astronaut/astronauts; mattress/mattresses; buggy/buggies; calf/calves*)
- Recognize and solve words in which one consonant sound is represented by several different letters or letter clusters (*kaya<u>k</u>, atti<u>c</u>, trac<u>k</u>, stoma<u>ch</u>; mischie<u>f</u>, pu<u>ff</u>, rou<u>gh</u>*)

- Work flexibly with a base word, adding or taking away one or more affixes to make a new word (*direct/<u>mis</u>direct/direct<u>ion</u>*)
- Recognize and use words with vowel sounds with *r* (*stairs, bare; argue; fear, steer; were, dirt, purple, learn; born, according, soar, four; curious*)
- Break apart two-, three-, and four-syllable words by syllable (*glis/ten, mag/a/zine, a/rith/me/tic*)

- Make word ladders by changing letters and/or word parts
- Read, make, and break apart words with an open syllable and a long vowel sound (*ba/con, free/dom, si/ren*) and a closed syllable with a short vowel sound (*hon/est, cab/bage, slen/der*)
- Recognize and use homophones (*steal, steel; braid, brayed; mist, missed*) and homographs (*does, train, spell*)
- Sort words based on any word features

Readers at Level

At level R, readers automatically read and understand a very wide range of genres, including a variety of special types of realistic and historical fiction, biographical texts, narrative and expository nonfiction, persuasive texts, and hybrid texts that blend more than one genre in a coherent whole. They read short and longer forms. Fiction narratives are straightforward but have complex problems with many episodes and multidimensional characters who develop and change over time. They experience some variation in narrative structure (for example, flashbacks or change in narrators). As readers, they encounter perspectives different from their own as well as settings and people far distant in time and space. They can process sentences (some with more than twenty words) that contain prepositional phrases, introductory clauses, and lists of nouns, verbs, or adjectives. They solve new vocabulary words, some defined in the text and others unexplained. Most reading is silent, but all dimensions of fluency in oral reading are well established. Readers are challenged by many longer descriptive words and by content specific and technical words that require using embedded definitions, background knowledge, and understanding of text features such as headings, subheadings, and call-outs. They can take apart multi-syllable words and use a full range of word-solving skills. They read and understand texts in a variety of layouts as well as fonts and print characteristics and consistently search for information in illustrations and increasingly complex graphics.

Selecting Texts Characteristics of Texts at **Level R**

GENRE

▶ **Fiction**
- Realistic fiction
- Historical fiction
- Traditional literature (folktale, fairy tale, fable)
- More complex fantasy including science fiction
- Hybrid texts
- Special types of fiction: e.g., mystery; adventure story; sports story; animal story; family, friends, and school story; humorous story

▶ **Nonfiction**
- Expository nonfiction
- Narrative nonfiction
- Biography
- Autobiography
- Memoir
- Procedural texts
- Persuasive texts
- Hybrid texts

FORMS
- Series books
- Picture books
- Chapter books

- Chapter books with sequels
- Plays
- Readers' theater scripts
- Graphic texts
- Letters, diaries, journal entries
- Short stories
- Photo essays and news articles

TEXT STRUCTURE

- Narrative texts with straightforward structure and multiple episodes that may be more elaborated
- Embedded forms (e.g., letters, directions, journal entries, emails) within narrative and expository structures
- Variations in structure: e.g., story-within-a-story, simple flashback
- Books with chapters connected to a single plot
- Some collections of short stories related to an overarching theme
- Nonfiction books divided into sections, and some with subsections
- Underlying structural patterns: description, cause and effect, chronological sequence, temporal sequence, comparison and contrast, problem and solution, question and answer

CONTENT

- Content interesting to and relevant for the reader
- Some books with little or no picture support for content: e.g., chapter books
- Much content that requires accessing prior knowledge
- Content that requires the reader to take on perspectives from diverse cultures and bring cultural knowledge to understanding
- Most texts with new content that will engage and interest readers and expand knowledge: e.g., travel, experience with other cultures, adventures in science, survival
- Settings in some texts that require content knowledge of disciplines: e.g., history, geography, culture, language
- Most content that goes beyond students' immediate experience
- Much content that requires the reader to search for information in graphics: e.g., maps, charts, diagrams, illustrated drawings, labeled photographs

Isabel imagined telling her mother she couldn't find the jacket. She imagined the yelling, the punishments. Maybe she wouldn't even be able to play soccer anymore.

"Shouldn't you turn the jacket in? To lost and found?" she asked, her voice slightly wobbly. She stared at the girl's face. She saw defiance. And underneath that, something else. Something she recognized. Fear.

The girl had been staring at Isabel, too. "Hey," she said. She had a thoughtful look on her face, as though she was trying to work something out.

"Hey. Is this *your* jacket?"

14   15

THEMES AND IDEAS

- Some texts with deeper meaning about content familiar to most readers but not fully explained
- Themes and ideas that require a perspective not familiar to the reader
- Complex ideas on many different topics that require real or vicarious experience (through reading) for understanding
- Texts with deeper meanings applicable to important human problems and social issues
- Many ideas and themes that require understanding of cultural diversity
- Some texts with abstract themes that require inferential thinking
- Some challenging themes: e.g., war, the environment

LANGUAGE AND LITERARY FEATURES

- Settings that are distant in time and geography
- Settings in fantasy that require the reader to accept elements of another world that could not exist in the real world
- Settings that are important to comprehension of the fiction narrative or biography
- Variety in narrative plot structure: e.g., story-within-a-story, simple flashback
- Main characters and supporting characters
- Multidimensional characters
- Characters revealed by what they say, think, and do and by what others say and think about them
- Characters revealed over a series of events, chapters, or book series
- Reasons for character change that are complex and require inference
- Some texts that reveal the perspectives of more than one character
- Variety in presentation of dialogue: e.g., dialogue among multiple characters, dialogue with pronouns, split dialogue, direct dialogue, including unassigned dialogue and long stretches of dialogue
- Some chains of unassigned dialogue for which speakers must be inferred
- Most texts written in first- or third-person narrative, with some procedural texts in second person
- Basic motifs of traditional literature and modern fantasy: e.g., struggle between good and evil, fantastic or magical objects, wishes, trickery, transformations
- Literary language typical of traditional literature: e.g., *long ago and far away*
- Figurative language: e.g., metaphor, simile
- Poetic language
- Language that creates suspense
- Language and events that convey an emotional atmosphere (mood) in a text, affecting how the reader feels: e.g., tension, sadness, happiness, curiosity
- Procedural language
- Language used to make comparisons
- Descriptive language
- Language used to show chronological order and temporal sequence
- Some persuasive language
- Language that speaks directly to the reader

Selecting Texts Characteristics of Texts at **Level R** *(cont.)*

SENTENCE COMPLEXITY

- Some longer sentences with more than twenty words and many embedded phrases and clauses
- Variation in sentence length and structure
- Sentences with a wide variety of parts of speech, including multiple adjectives, adverbs, and prepositional phrases
- Variation in placement of subject, verb, adjectives, and adverbs
- Many sentences beginning with phrases
- Sentences with simple connectives or subordinate (dependent) clauses
- Sentences with sophisticated or complex connectives that are not typical of oral language: e.g., *however, therefore, meanwhile, moreover, otherwise*
- Use of parenthetical material embedded in sentences

VOCABULARY

- Vocabulary words that are generally acquired by students through reading or listening to stories or nonfiction read aloud
- Many words that appear in the vocabulary of mature language users (Tier 2)
- Some words particular to a discipline (Tier 3)
- Wide variation in words used to assign dialogue
- Many words with multiple meanings
- Many words with figurative meaning
- Some idioms
- New vocabulary requiring strategic action to understand: e.g., derive meaning from context, use reference tools, notice morphology, use word roots, use analogy
- Some words with connotative meanings that are essential to understanding the text
- Many common connectives (words, phrases that clarify relationships and ideas and that are used frequently in oral language): e.g., *and, but, so, because, before, after*
- A few sophisticated (complex) connectives (words, phrases that link ideas and clarify meaning and that are used in written texts but do not appear often in everyday oral language): e.g., *although, however, meantime, meanwhile moreover, otherwise, unless, therefore, though, unless, until, whenever, yet*

WORDS

- Many multisyllable words, some technical or scientific
- Full range of plurals
- Unlimited number of high-frequency words with multiple syllables
- Some multisyllable words with some complex letter-sound relationships
- Some multisyllable proper nouns that are difficult to decode
- Wide range of contractions and possessives
- Full range of compound words
- Base words with affixes (prefixes and suffixes)
- Some words divided (hyphenated) across lines
- Common connectives and some sophisticated connectives

ILLUSTRATIONS

- Illustrations that enhance and extend meaning in the text
- Many short texts that have illustrations on every page or every few pages
- Some short chapter books with only a few illustrations
- Some texts with minimal illustrations
- Variety of layout in illustrations and print
- A few books with black-and-white illustrations
- Some complex, nuanced illustrations that communicate mood and meaning (literal, figurative, symbolic) to match or extend the text
- Graphics that require reader interpretation and are essential for comprehending informational text
- More than one kind of graphics on a page spread
- A range of graphics that provide information that matches and extends the text: e.g., photograph and drawing with label and/or caption; diagram, cutaway; map with legend or key, scale; infographic

BOOK AND PRINT FEATURES

LENGTH

- Wide variation in length (mostly shorter than forty-eight pages)
- Wide variation in number of words (700–2,500)

- Some books divided into chapters
- Books divided into sections and subsections

PRINT AND LAYOUT

- Mostly small but readable font size
- Variety in print and background color
- Many lines of print on a page (to about thirty-four lines)
- Sentences beginning where previous sentence ends
- Variety in print placement, reflecting different genres
- Many texts single spaced but with clear space between lines
- Italics indicating unspoken thought in some texts
- Information shown in a variety of picture and print combinations in graphic texts
- Captions under pictures that provide important information
- Print and illustrations integrated in most texts, with print wrapping around pictures
- Print placed in sidebars and graphics that provide important information

PUNCTUATION

- Period, comma, question mark, exclamation mark, parentheses, quotation marks, hyphen, dash, and ellipses in most texts

ORGANIZATIONAL TOOLS

- Title, table of contents, chapter title, heading, subheading, sidebar

TEXT RESOURCES

- Dedication, acknowledgments, author's note, pronunciation guide, glossary

Selecting Goals Behaviors and Understandings to Notice, Teach, and Support

THINKING *WITHIN* THE TEXT

SEARCHING FOR AND USING INFORMATION

- Sustain searching for information over a text (usually under forty-eight pages) and/or in a chapter book with as many as 2,500 + words
- Search for information across chapters connected to a single plot
- Search for information and language that states or implies the larger message(s) of the text
- Search for information in texts where print wraps around sidebars, pictures, and other graphics
- Use background knowledge to search for and understand information about settings, geographical areas, history, economics
- Use organizational tools to search for information: e.g., title, table of contents, chapter title, heading, subheading, sidebar, call-out
- Use text resources to search for information: e.g., acknowledgments, author's note, pronunciation guide, glossary
- Sustain searching over some longer sentences with more than twenty words, and multiple clauses and phrases
- Search for information in sentences that vary in length, structure, and punctuation based on text complexity
- Search for information in sentences with variation in placement of subject, verb, adjectives, and adverbs
- Search for information in sentences with nouns, verbs, adjectives, and adverbs in a series, divided by commas
- Search for and understand information presented in a variety of ways: e.g., simple dialogue, dialogue with pronouns, split dialogue, assigned and sometimes unassigned dialogue, dialogue among multiple characters, some long stretches of dialogue, direct dialogue
- Search for and understand information over some long stretches of dialogue with multiple characters talking
- Use the chronological order within multiple episodes to search for and use information
- Notice and use punctuation marks: e.g., period, comma, question mark, exclamation mark, parentheses, quotation marks, hyphen, dash, ellipses
- Search for and use information from a wide variety of illustrations or graphics
- Search for and use information in texts with variety in placement of the body of a text, sidebars, and graphics
- Search for information in a variety of graphics (photos, drawings with labels and captions, diagrams, maps)

MONITORING AND SELF-CORRECTING

- Use multiple sources of information (visual information in print, meaning/pictures, graphics, language structure) to monitor and self-correct
- Self-correct covertly prior to or after error, with little overt self-correction
- Closely monitor understanding of texts using knowledge of a wide range of fiction genres: e.g., realistic fiction, historical fiction, traditional literature (folktale, fairy tale, fable, myth, legend, epic, ballad), fantasy including science fiction, hybrid text
- Closely monitor understanding of texts using knowledge of a wide range of forms: e.g., poems, plays, graphic texts, letters, diaries, journal entries, short stories
- Use understanding of plot, setting, and character to monitor and correct reading
- Use awareness of narrative structure and the attributes of multidimensional characters that change to self-monitor and self-correct
- Use content knowledge of the topic of a text to self-monitor and self-correct
- Use knowledge of nonfiction genres to monitor understanding of a text: e.g., expository nonfiction, narrative nonfiction, biography, autobiography, memoir, procedural text, persuasive text
- Use information from graphics (e.g., maps, diagrams, charts, photos, illustrations) to self-monitor reading

SOLVING WORDS

▶ Reading Words

- Recognize a large number of high-frequency words and other multisyllable words rapidly and automatically
- Solve multisyllable words by taking them apart using syllables
- Read the full range of regular and irregular plurals
- Identify spelling patterns within multisyllable words to solve them
- Read some multisyllable words with complex letter-sound relationships
- Read a wide range of contractions, possessives, compound words, adjectives, adverbs, comparatives, common and complex connectives
- Notice parts of words and connect them to other words to solve them

Selecting Goals Behaviors and Understandings to Notice, Teach, and Support *(cont.)*

THINKING *WITHIN* THE TEXT *(continued)*

SOLVING WORDS *(continued)*

▶ Reading Words *(continued)*

- Solve words rapidly while processing continuous text and with minimum overt self-correction
- Read some multisyllable proper nouns that are difficult to decode and use text resources like pronunciation guide as needed
- Solve words by identifying base words and affixes (prefixes and suffixes)
- Read hyphenated words divided across lines and across pages
- Demonstrate flexibility in using many different strategies for solving words

▶ Vocabulary

- Derive the meaning of new words and expand meaning of known words using flexible strategies: e.g., context in a sentence; connections to other words; synonyms and antonyms; word parts; base words and affixes; word function in a sentence
- Actively and consistently add to vocabulary through reading
- Connect words to synonyms and antonyms to expand understanding
- Understand a large body of words that are in common oral vocabulary (Tier 1)
- Understand many words that appear in the language of mature users and in written texts (Tier 2)
- Understand some words particular to academic disciplines (Tier 3)
- Understand the meaning and function in sentences of all parts of speech
- Understand the meaning of regular and irregular plurals
- Understand many words that have multiple meanings and identify the specific meaning that applies in a sentence or paragraph
- Understand words that require the use of multiple sources of information (i.e., background knowledge, pictures, visual information)
- Understand the meaning and function of common (simple) connectives that occur in oral language and some sophisticated (complex) connectives that are more typical of written language
- Identify base words and understand prefixes and suffixes that add or change meaning, function, or tense
- Understand denotative, connotative, idiomatic, and figurative meaning of words

- Understand the connotative or figurative meanings of words that contribute to the mood of the text, including words that assign dialogue: e.g., *whispered, snarled*
- Understand that in graphic texts, information about words is in the illustrations, and also that many unusual words appear in graphic texts (i.e., onomatopoetic)
- Understand the connotative meanings of descriptive adjectives, verbs, and adverbs, and use them to make inferences about characters
- Derive the meanings of technical words and author-created words in science fiction
- Understand and acquire content-specific words that require the use of strategic actions (i.e., using definitions within the body of a text, the glossary or other reference tools)
- Understand key words in graphics such as maps, diagrams, and charts

MAINTAINING FLUENCY

- Read silently at a slightly faster rate than when reading orally while maintaining comprehension and accuracy
- Demonstrate the ability to skim and scan while reading silently to search for information quickly
- Sustain momentum through short texts and some short chapter books or books of short stories, making significant progress each day
- Notice periods, commas, question marks, exclamation marks, parentheses, quotation marks, dashes, and ellipses and reflect them with the voice through intonation and pausing
- Read orally with appropriate phrasing, pausing, intonation, word stress, and rate
- Stress words that are in bold, italics, or varied font
- Recognize and read expressively a variety of dialogue, some unassigned
- Read parts in a script with expression
- Show in the voice when words in a text (sometimes shown in italics) reflect unspoken thought
- Reflect numbered and bulleted lists with the voice when reading orally

GUIDED READING

LEVEL **R**

Selecting Goals Behaviors and Understandings to Notice, Teach, and Support *(cont.)*

THINKING *WITHIN* THE TEXT *(continued)*

ADJUSTING

- Slow down to problem-solve or search for information and resume reading with momentum
- Adjust reading to accommodate compound sentences and sentences with a variety in order of clauses
- Adjust reading to recognize the purpose and characteristics of fiction and nonfiction genres and of special types of fiction texts like mystery
- Adjust to accommodate embedded forms (e.g., letters, diaries, journal entries) within narrative and expository texts
- Adjust expectations to read a simple hybrid text
- Adjust reading to process a graphic text
- Adjust reading to understand that a text can be a collection of short stories related to an overarching theme
- Adjust reading to recognize variations in narrative structure: e.g., story-within-a-story, simple flashback
- Adjust reading to reflect a series of steps in procedural texts
- Adjust reading to accommodate varied placement of text body, photographs with captions, sidebars, and graphics
- Adjust reading to recognize a persuasive text

SUMMARIZING

- Summarize important parts of a text (i.e., chapters or sections)
- Summarize a story including important aspects of setting, plot (events, problem, climax, resolution), characters, theme or lesson (fiction)
- Summarize the important information in the text in a clear and logical way without extraneous detail (nonfiction)
- Summarize narrative nonfiction, biography, or a temporal sequence in time order
- Summarize a writer's argument or main idea
- Sometimes use graphics to summarize a text: e.g., timeline or diagram of a chronological or temporal process

Selecting Goals Behaviors and Understandings to Notice, Teach, and Support *(cont.)*

THINKING *BEYOND* THE TEXT

PREDICTING

- Make predictions based on personal experience and content knowledge
- Make predictions based on previous reading experiences
- Make predictions throughout a text based on the organizational structure (narrative, expository)
- Justify predictions with evidence from the text
- Predict the ending of a story based on knowledge of how plots work and understanding of settings, characters, and the story problem
- Make predictions based on knowledge of a variety of everyday events
- Make predictions based on knowledge of fiction genres: e.g., realistic fiction, historical fiction, traditional literature, fantasy including science fiction, and hybrid text
- Make predictions based on knowledge of special types of fiction: e.g., mystery; adventure story; animal story; family, friends, and school story
- Predict potential solutions to the problem in the story
- Use previous reading of a book in a series to predict types of characters and plots in a sequel or another book in the series
- Make predictions based on knowledge from personal experiences and from reading: e.g., food production, environment, nature, problems of society, survival of a species
- Make predictions based on knowledge of nonfiction genres: e.g., expository nonfiction, narrative nonfiction, biography, autobiography, memoir, procedural text, persuasive text, hybrid text
- Make predictions based on knowledge of special forms: e.g., letters, diaries, journal entries; photo essays, news articles
- Make predictions using the logical organization of the text
- Make predictions based on knowledge of underlying text structures: e.g., description, cause and effect, chronological sequence, temporal sequence, comparison and contrast, problem and solution, question and answer

MAKING CONNECTIONS

- Make connections among personal experiences, historical or current events, and texts
- Use knowledge from one text to understand content in another text
- Make many different kinds of connections among texts: e.g., author, illustrator, content, genre, topic, theme or message, events, problem, characters, language and style

- Make different kinds of connections among texts: e.g., content, graphics, main idea or message, text structure
- State explicitly the nature of connections: e.g., topic, theme, message, characters, genre, writer, style
- Use background knowledge of traditional literature to recognize common characters and events
- Make connections between the events in chapters that are connected to a single plot
- Use background knowledge to understand settings in stories
- Make connections with the human traits and problems that are shared among people of many different cultures
- Access background knowledge acquired from reading to understand the content of texts
- Make connections between previous events of the plot and what is happening at another point in the text when reading chapter books
- Access background knowledge to understand descriptions of temporal sequence

SYNTHESIZING

- Compare previous understandings with the new understandings the text provides
- Identify interesting, new, or surprising information in a text
- Express new ways of thinking based on engagement with the text
- Provide evidence from the text to support statements describing new learning
- Talk about the lessons the story teaches
- Talk about new ways of thinking from vicarious experiences in reading fiction
- Talk about new understanding of different cultures, places, and times in history
- Synthesize new content from texts and describe it to others with evidence from the text
- Take on perspectives from diverse cultures and bring cultural knowledge to understanding a text

Selecting Goals Behaviors and Understandings to Notice, Teach, and Support *(cont.)*

THINKING *BEYOND* THE TEXT *(continued)*

INFERRING

- Infer phases or steps in temporal processes
- Make inferences about setting to help in understanding the story
- Understand and infer the importance of the setting of a biography that may be distant in time and geography from students' own knowledge
- Infer character traits, feelings, and motivations from what characters say, think, or do and what others say or think about them
- Infer the causes for character traits and for problems that a character experiences
- Infer traits of multidimensional characters that have both good and bad traits and have choices to make
- Infer character development from evidence in behavior as well as reasons for change
- Infer complex relationships between and among characters by noticing evidence in their responses to each other
- Understand the problems of challenging situations: e.g., war, the environment
- Infer some abstract themes and ideas

- Infer messages of a text and discuss how they are applicable to people's lives
- Infer the overarching theme(s) in a collection of short stories
- Infer the larger message in a text (i.e., what can be learned from it beyond the facts)
- Infer information from the pictures that add meaning to the text
- Talk about the pictures, revealing interpretation of a problem or of characters' feelings
- Use illustrations to infer characters' feelings
- Infer information about characters, setting, plot, and action from graphic texts, in which illustrations carry much of the meaning
- Make inferences from print narrative alone (no pictures)
- Infer the meaning of a range of graphics that require reader interpretation and are essential to comprehending the text
- Understand the connotative meanings of words that contribute to the mood and meaning of the text
- Infer important information from familiar content as well as topics more distant from students' typical experience: e.g., different parts of the world, history, science

Selecting Goals Behaviors and Understandings to Notice, Teach, and Support *(cont.)*

THINKING *ABOUT* THE TEXT

ANALYZING

- Understand that a graphic text may represent any fiction or nonfiction genre
- Understand the unique characteristics of fiction and nonfiction graphic texts
- Understand and describe characteristics of fiction genres, including realistic fiction, historical fiction, traditional literature (folktale, fairy tale, fable, myth, legend, epic, ballad), fantasy, and hybrid text
- Notice elements and basic motifs of fantasy: e.g., the supernatural, imaginary and otherworldly creatures, gods and goddesses, talking animals, struggle between good and evil, magic, fantastic or magical objects, wishes, trickery, transformations
- Understand the difference between realistic and historical fiction (events that could happen in the real world) and fantasy
- Identify and understand characteristics of special types of fiction: e.g., mystery; adventure story; animal story; family, friends, and school story
- Understand and describe the characteristics of nonfiction genres, including expository nonfiction, narrative nonfiction, biography, autobiography, memoir, procedural text, persuasive text, and hybrid text
- Understand that a biography is the story of a person's life and is usually told in chronological order
- Notice that a biography is built around significant events, problems to overcome, and the subject's decisions
- Understand that the information and ideas in a text are related to each other and notice how the author presents this
- Recognize a writer's use of embedded forms (e.g., letters, journal entries) within narrative or expository texts
- Understand first- and third-person narrative
- Understand that a nonfiction book may be procedural (i.e., "how-to")
- Understand that a nonfiction book may have "how-to" procedures embedded within it
- Recognize a writer's use of underlying text structures: e.g., description, cause and effect, chronological sequence, temporal sequence, comparison and contrast, problem and solution, question and answer
- Notice that a writer organizes a text into categories and subcategories
- Think analytically about the significance of a title
- Recognize settings that are familiar as well as some distant in time and geography
- Understand how a setting is important to the plot and the characters' perspectives
- Notice characteristics of setting in fantasy that involve magic and/or an imaginary world

- Identify a central story problem in a text with multiple episodes
- Recognize and understand variation in plot structure: story-within-a-story, flashback
- Relate character development to the events of the plot
- Understand the role of supporting characters in a story
- Notice the evidence a writer provides to show character attributes and motives as well as characters' changes
- Understand the perspective from which a story is told and talk about why a writer selected it
- Notice how a fiction writer creates and sustains suspense
- Notice language used to show chronological order
- Notice a writer's use of figurative language
- Notice a writer's use of simple and more sophisticated connectives to show how ideas are related in a text
- Notice parenthetical material set off by commas or parentheses
- Notice a fiction writer's use of italics to indicate unspoken thought
- Notice a fiction writer's use of poetic and expressive language in dialogue
- Notice a writer's use of humorous words or onomatopoetic words and talk about how they add to the action
- Notice literary language typical of traditional literature: e.g., *a long time ago there lived, long ago and far away, once there lived*
- Notice and think analytically about a writer's use of argument or persuasion
- Notice when the writer uses the second person to talk directly to the reader
- Understand that illustrations carry the dialogue and action in graphic texts
- Notice that illustrations add to the reader's understanding of the characters, the action, and the feeling of the story
- Recognize how illustrations enhance the meaning of a text
- Notice the format of a photo essay and understand the purpose
- Notice how the writer uses graphics to convey information that complements the body of the text
- Understand that illustrations or photographs add to the ideas and information in a text
- Use some academic language to talk about genres: e.g., *fiction; family, friends, and school story; folktale; animal story; humorous story; fairy tale; fable; tall tale; realistic fiction; mystery; adventure story; sports story; historical fiction; fantasy; nonfiction; informational text; informational book; factual text; how-to book; biography; autobiography; narrative nonfiction; memoir; procedural text; persuasive text, hybrid text*
- Use some academic language to talk about forms: e.g., *series book, play, chapter book, comics, graphic text, letter, sequel, short story, diary entry, journal entry, news article, feature article*

Selecting Goals Behaviors and Understandings to Notice, Teach, and Support *(cont.)*

THINKING *ABOUT* THE TEXT *(continued)*

- Use some academic language to talk about literary features: e.g., *beginning, ending, character, question and answer, main character, character change, message, dialogue, topic, events, setting, description, time order, problem and solution, comparison and contrast, main idea, flashback, conflict, resolution, theme, descriptive language, simile, cause and effect, categorization, persuasive language*
- Use some specific language to talk about book and print features: e.g., *front cover, back cover, page, author, illustrator, illustration, photograph, title, label, drawing, heading, caption, table of contents, chapter, chapter title, dedication, sidebar, glossary, map, diagram, infographic, author's note, illustrator's note, section, book jacket, acknowledgments, subheading, text, pronunciation guide*

CRITIQUING

- Share opinions about a text and give rationales and examples
- Evaluate the quality of illustrations or graphics and share opinions
- Describe what the illustrations and graphics add to a text
- Assess how graphics add to the quality of the text or provide additional information

- Give an opinion about the believability of plot, character actions, or the resolution of a problem
- State specifically what makes a plot or character believable
- Share opinions of characters and talk about how they could have made different decisions or behaved differently
- Assess whether a text is authentic and consistent with life experience
- Assess whether a text is authentic and consistent with reader's background knowledge
- Distinguish between fact and opinion
- Evaluate aspects of a text that add to enjoyment or interest: e.g., humorous characters or surprising information
- Express tastes and preferences in reading and support choices with descriptions and examples of literary elements: e.g., genre, setting, plot, theme, character, style and language
- Talk critically about what a writer does to make a topic interesting or important
- Talk about why the subject of a biography is important or sets an example for others
- Notice the author's qualifications to write on a topic

Planning for Word Work After Guided Reading

Using your recent observations of the readers' ability to take words apart quickly and efficiently while reading text, plan for one to three minutes of active engagement of students' attention to letters, sounds, and words. Prioritize the readers' noticing of print features and active hands-on use of magnetic letters, a white board, word cards, or pencil and paper to promote fluency and flexibility in visual processing.

Examples:

- Make a full range of plural nouns, including regular plurals that require spelling changes and irregular plurals (*character/characters; wilderness/wildernesses; supply/supplies; self/selves*)
- Recognize and solve words in which one consonant sound is represented by several different letters or letter clusters (*speak, arithmetic, thick; if, stuff, tough*)

- Work flexibly with a base word, changing letters or adding or taking away one or more affixes to make a new word (*plum/plug/plugged/unplug*)
- Break apart two-, three-, and four-syllable words quickly by syllable (*help/ful, neigh/bor/hood, par/tic/u/lar*)
- Make word ladders by changing letters and/or word parts

- Read, make, and break apart words with an open syllable and a long vowel sound (*ca/ble, fi/nal, mo/tion*) and a closed syllable with a short vowel sound (*pep/per, plan/et, rob/in*)
- Recognize and use homophones (*caught, cot; creak, creek; main, mane*) and homographs (*dock, pit, firm*)
- Sort words based on any word features

Readers at Level

At level S, readers are able to articulate characteristics of genre for a wide range of fiction and nonfiction texts, including realistic and historical fiction, biographical texts, narrative and expository nonfiction, as well as hybrids. They notice text structure and use it as a support for understanding stories and content. They also have developed favorite genres and types of texts, for example, adventure or mystery. Texts range in length from feature articles to longer chapter books. Most fiction narratives are straightforward but some have variations in the narrative structure. Settings challenge readers to understand perspectives far from their own experience; through reading, they learn about other cultures, languages, and histories. They can process sentences (some with more than twenty words) that contain prepositional phrases, introductory clauses, and lists of nouns, verbs, or adjectives. They solve new vocabulary words, some defined in the text and others unexplained. Most reading is silent, but all dimensions of fluency in oral reading are well established. Readers are challenged by many longer descriptive words and by content specific and technical words that require using embedded definitions, background knowledge, and understanding of text features such as headings, subheadings, and call-outs. They can take apart multisyllable words and use a full range of word-solving skills. They read and understand texts in a variety of layouts as well as fonts and print characteristics and consistently search for information in illustrations and increasingly complex graphics. Readers make connections across texts, inferring larger meanings. Readers' use of academic language continues to grow.

Selecting Texts Characteristics of Texts at **Level S**

GENRE

▶ Fiction

- Realistic fiction
- Historical fiction
- Traditional literature (folktale, fairy tale, fable)
- More complex fantasy including science fiction
- Hybrid texts
- Special types of fiction: e.g., mystery; adventure story; sports story; animal story; family, friends, and school story; humorous story

▶ Nonfiction

- Expository nonfiction
- Narrative nonfiction
- Biography
- Autobiography
- Memoir
- Procedural texts
- Persuasive texts
- Hybrid texts

FORMS

- Series books
- Picture books
- Chapter books

- Chapter books with sequels
- Plays
- Readers' theater scripts
- Graphic texts
- Letters, diaries, and journal entries
- Short stories
- Photo essays and news articles

TEXT STRUCTURE

- Narrative texts with straightforward structure and multiple episodes that may be more elaborated
- Embedded forms (e.g., letters, directions, journal entries, emails) within narrative and expository structures
- Variations in structure: e.g., story-within-a-story, simple flashback
- Books with chapters connected to a single plot
- Collections of short stories related to an overarching theme
- Texts that change perspective and/or narrator within the larger narrative
- Nonfiction books divided into sections, and some with subsections

- Underlying structural patterns: description, cause and effect, chronological sequence, temporal sequence, categorization, comparison and contrast, problem and solution, question and answer

CONTENT

- Content interesting to and relevant for the reader
- Some books with little or no picture support for content: e.g., chapter books
- Much content that requires accessing prior knowledge
- Content that requires the reader to take on perspectives from diverse cultures and bring cultural knowledge to understanding
- Most texts with new content that will engage and interest readers and expand knowledge: e.g., travel, experience with other cultures, adventures in science, survival
- Settings in some texts that require content knowledge of disciplines: e.g., history, geography, culture, language
- Most content that goes beyond students' immediate experience

GUIDED READING

Eek! Bats!

When local residents learned that an enormous bat colony was growing under the bridge, some of them panicked. Horror movies and spooky stories had given bats a bad name, and folks were scared.

Some people were afraid the bats would come after them aggressively, flying into their hair or invading their homes. Some believed the bats would bite them or their children, or their pets, and infect them with **rabies**. Rabies is a serious illness that can be fatal to animals and people.

Alarming headlines began to appear in the local papers. "BATS SINK TEETH INTO AUSTIN," said one. "MASS FEAR IN THE AIR AS BATS INVADE CITY," screamed another. Frightened residents started petitions calling for the bats to be exterminated. At the very least, they wanted the bat colony to be forced outside the city limits. One group even suggested using a blowtorch to burn the bats out of their roosting spot under the bridge!

Because people didn't have accurate information about bats, their fears took over. While a few local **conservationists** called for the bat colony to be protected, the majority of citizens loudly demanded that city officials get rid of it.

This fake movie poster from Austin in the 1980s portrayed the bridge bats as dangerous monsters.

Scary headlines added to people's fears.

8   9

- Much content that requires the reader to search for information in graphics: e.g., maps, charts, diagrams, illustrated drawings, labeled photographs

THEMES AND IDEAS

- Some texts with deeper meaning about content familiar to most readers but not fully explained
- Themes and ideas that require a perspective not familiar to the reader
- Complex ideas on many different topics that require real or vicarious experience (through reading) for understanding
- Texts with deeper meanings applicable to important human problems and social issues
- Many ideas and themes that require understanding of cultural diversity
- Some texts with abstract themes that require inferential thinking
- Some challenging themes: e.g., war, the environment

LANGUAGE AND LITERARY FEATURES

- Settings that are distant in time and geography
- Settings in fantasy that require the reader to accept elements of another world that could not exist in the real world
- Settings that are important to comprehension of the fiction narrative or biography
- Variety in narrative plot structure: e.g., story-within-a-story, simple flashback
- Main characters and supporting characters
- Multidimensional characters
- Characters revealed by what they say, think, and do and by what others say and think about them
- Characters revealed over a series of events, chapters, or book series
- Reasons for character change that are complex and require inference
- Some texts that reveal the perspectives of more than one character

- Variety in presentation of dialogue: e.g., dialogue among multiple characters, dialogue with pronouns, split dialogue, direct dialogue, including unassigned dialogue and long stretches of dialogue
- Some chains of unassigned dialogue for which speakers must be inferred
- Most texts written in first or third person narrative, with some procedural texts in second person
- Basic motifs of traditional literature and modern fantasy: e.g., struggle between good and evil, fantastic or magical objects, wishes, trickery, transformations
- Moral lesson near the end of the story (sometimes explicitly stated)
- Literary language typical of traditional literature: e.g., *long ago and far away*
- Figurative language: e.g., metaphor, simile
- Poetic language
- Language that creates suspense
- Language and events that convey an emotional atmosphere (mood) in a text, affecting how the reader feels: e.g., tension, sadness, happiness, curiosity

LEVEL **S**

Selecting Goals Behaviors and Understandings to Notice, Teach, and Support *(cont.)*

SOLVING WORDS *(continued)*

▶ Vocabulary

- Derive the meaning of new words and expand meaning of known words using flexible strategies: e.g., context in a sentence; connections to other words; synonyms and antonyms; word parts; base words and affixes; word function in a sentence
- Actively and consistently add to vocabulary through reading
- Connect words to synonyms and antonyms to expand understanding
- Understand a large body of words that are in common oral vocabulary (Tier 1)
- Understand some words that appear in the language of mature users and in written texts (Tier 2)
- Understand some words particular to academic disciplines (Tier 3)
- Understand the meaning and function of all parts of speech
- Understand the meaning of regular and irregular plurals
- Understand many words that have multiple meanings and identify the specific meaning that applies in a sentence or paragraph
- Understand words that require the use of multiple sources of information (i.e., background knowledge, pictures, visual information)
- Understand the meaning and function of common (simple) connectives that occur in oral language and some sophisticated (complex) connectives that are more typical of written language
- Identify base words and understand prefixes and suffixes that add or change meaning, function, or tense
- Understand denotative, connotative, idiomatic, and figurative meaning of words
- Understand the connotative or figurative meanings of words that contribute to the mood of the text including words that assign dialogue; e.g., *whispered, snarled*
- Add actively to vocabulary through learning new words from reading
- Understand that in graphic texts, information about words is in the illustrations, and also that many unusual words appear in graphic texts (i.e., onomatopoetic)
- Understand the connotative meanings of descriptive adjectives, verbs, and adverbs, and use them to make inferences about characters
- Derive the meanings of technical words and author-created words in science fiction
- Understand and acquire content-specific words that require the use of strategic actions (i.e., using definitions within the body of a text, the glossary or other reference tools)
- Understand key words in graphics such as maps, diagrams, and charts

MAINTAINING FLUENCY

- Read orally with appropriate phrasing, pausing, intonation, word stress, and rate
- Read silently at a slightly faster rate than when reading orally while maintaining comprehension and accuracy
- Demonstrate the ability to skim and scan while reading silently to search for information quickly
- Sustain momentum through short texts and some short chapter books or books of short stories, making significant progress daily
- Notice periods, commas, question marks, exclamation marks, parentheses, quotation marks, dashes, and ellipses and begin to reflect them with the voice through intonation and pausing
- Stress words that are in bold, italics, or varied font
- Recognize and read expressively a variety of dialogue, some unassigned
- Read parts in a script with demonstration of all dimensions of fluency
- Show in the voice when words in a text (sometimes shown in italics) reflect unspoken thought
- Orally read novels in verse reflecting the meaning and rhythm with the voice
- Reflect numbered and bulleted lists with the voice when reading orally

ADJUSTING

- Slow down to problem-solve or search for information and resume reading with momentum
- Adjust reading to accommodate compound sentences and sentences with a variety in order of clauses
- Adjust reading to recognize the purpose and characteristics of fiction and nonfiction genres and of special types of fiction texts like mystery
- Adjust to accommodate embedded forms (e.g., letters, diaries, journal entries) within narrative and expository texts
- Adjust expectations to read a simple hybrid text
- Adjust reading to process a graphic text
- Adjust reading to understand that a text can be a collection of short stories related to an overarching theme
- Adjust to read parts in a readers' theater script or a play
- Adjust reading to understand that a text can be a collection of short stories related to an overarching theme

LEVEL
S

Selecting Goals Behaviors and Understandings to Notice, Teach, and Support *(cont.)*

THINKING *WITHIN* THE TEXT *(continued)*

- Adjust reading to recognize variations in narrative structure: e.g., story-within-a-story, simple flashback
- Adjust reading to follow texts that change perspective and/or narrator within the larger narrative
- Adjust reading to reflect a series of steps in procedural texts
- Adjust reading to accommodate varied placement of text body, photographs with captions, sidebars, and graphics
- Adjust reading to reflect a series of steps in a procedural text
- Adjust reading to recognize a persuasive text

SUMMARIZING

- Summarize important parts of a text (i.e., chapters or sections)
- Summarize a story including important aspects of setting, plot (events, problem, climax, resolution), characters, theme or lesson (fiction)
- Summarize the important information in the text in a clear and logical way without extraneous detail (nonfiction)
- Summarize narrative nonfiction, biography, or a temporal sequence in time order
- Summarize a writer's argument or main idea
- Sometimes use graphics to summarize a text: e.g., timeline or diagram of a chronological or temporal process

THINKING *BEYOND* THE TEXT

PREDICTING

- Make predictions based on personal experience and content knowledge
- Make predictions throughout a text based on the organizational structure (narrative, expository)
- Justify predictions with evidence from the text
- Predict the ending of a story based on knowledge of how plots work and understanding of settings, characters, and the story problem
- Make predictions based on knowledge of fiction genres: e.g., realistic fiction, historical fiction, traditional literature, fantasy including science fiction, and hybrid text
- Make predictions based on knowledge of special types of fiction: e.g., mystery; adventure story; animal story; family, friends, and school story
- Predict potential solutions to the problem in the story
- Use previous reading of a book in a series to predict types of characters and plots in a sequel or another book in the series
- Make predictions based on knowledge from personal experiences and from reading: e.g., food production, environment, nature, problems of society, survival of a species
- Make predictions based on knowledge of nonfiction genres: e.g., expository nonfiction, narrative nonfiction, biography, autobiography, memoir, procedural text, persuasive text, hybrid text
- Make predictions based on knowledge of special forms: e.g., letters, diaries, and journal entries; photo essays, news articles
- Make predictions based on knowledge of underlying text structures: e.g., description, cause and effect, chronological sequence, temporal sequence, categorization, comparison and contrast, problem and solution, question and answer

MAKING CONNECTIONS

- Make connections among personal experiences, historical or current events, and texts
- Use knowledge from one text to understand content in another text
- Make many different kinds of connections among texts: e.g., author, illustrator, content, genre, topic, theme or message, events, problem, characters, language and style
- Make different kinds of connections among texts: e.g., content, graphics, main idea or message, text structure
- State explicitly the nature of connections: e.g., topic, theme, message, characters, genre, writer, style
- Make connections between students' lives and the content that are particularly appropriate for adolescents
- Use background knowledge of traditional literature to recognize common characters and events
- Use background knowledge of past events to understand historical fiction
- Make connections between the events in chapters that are connected to a single plot
- Use background knowledge or content area study to understand settings in both historical and realistic fiction stories
- Make connections with the human traits and problems that are shared among people of many different cultures
- Use background knowledge to understand settings in stories
- Access background knowledge acquired from reading to understand the content of texts
- When reading chapter books, make connections between previous events of the plot and what is happening at another point in the text
- Access background knowledge to understand descriptions of temporal sequence

LEVEL **S**

Selecting Goals Behaviors and Understandings to Notice, Teach, and Support *(cont.)*

THINKING ***BEYOND*** THE TEXT *(continued)*

SYNTHESIZING

- Talk about what the reader knows about the topic before reading the text and identify new knowledge gained from reading
- Compare previous understandings with the new understandings the text provides
- Identify interesting, new, or surprising information in a text
- Express new ways of thinking based on engagement with the text
- Provide evidence from the text to support statements describing new learning
- Describe changing perspective as a story unfolds
- Talk about new ways of thinking from vicarious experiences in reading fiction
- Talk about new understanding of different cultures, places, and times in history
- Synthesize new content from texts and describe it to others with evidence from the text
- Take on perspectives from diverse cultures and bring cultural knowledge to understanding a text

INFERRING

- Make inferences about setting to help in understanding the story
- Understand and infer the importance of the setting of a biography that may be distant in time and geography from students' own knowledge
- Infer character traits, feelings, and motivations from what characters say, think, or do and what others say or think about them
- Infer the causes for character traits and for problems that a character experiences
- Infer traits of multidimensional characters that have both good and bad traits and have choices to make
- Infer complex relationships between and among characters by noticing evidence in their responses to each other
- Compare inferences with those of other readers and consider alternative interpretations of characters' motives and the writer's message

- Infer potential solutions to the story problem and find evidence to support them
- Understand the problems of challenging situations: e.g., war, the environment
- Infer some abstract themes and ideas
- Infer messages of a text and discuss how they are applicable to people's lives
- Infer universal human themes and issues that affect human problems across the world
- Infer the overarching theme(s) in a collection of short stories
- Infer the larger message in a text (i.e., what can be learned from it beyond the facts)
- Infer information from the pictures that add meaning to the text
- Talk about the pictures, revealing interpretation of a problem or of characters' feelings
- Use illustrations to infer characters' feelings
- Infer information about characters, setting, plot, and action from graphic texts, in which illustrations carry much of the meaning
- Make inferences from print narrative alone (no pictures)
- Infer the meaning of a range of graphics that require reader interpretation and are essential to comprehending the text
- Understand the connotative meanings of words that contribute to the mood and meaning of the text
- Infer beliefs, customs, and perspectives of people who live in other cultures
- Infer beliefs, customs, and perspectives of people who live in the near and distant past
- Infer attitudes that may be new or contrary to readers' current beliefs
- Infer what life might be like and what people might believe and do at a time in the future
- Infer important information from familiar content as well as topics more distant from students' typical experience: e.g., different parts of the world, history, science

Selecting Goals Behaviors and Understandings to Notice, Teach, and Support *(cont.)*

THINKING *ABOUT* THE TEXT

ANALYZING

- Understand that a graphic text may represent any fiction or nonfiction genre
- Understand the unique characteristics of fiction and nonfiction graphic texts
- Understand and describe characteristics of fiction genres, including realistic fiction, historical fiction, traditional literature (folktale, fairy tale, fable, myth, legend, epic, ballad), fantasy, and hybrid text
- Notice elements and basic motifs of fantasy: e.g., the supernatural, imaginary and otherworldly creatures, gods and goddesses, talking animals, struggle between good and evil, magic, fantastic or magical objects, wishes, trickery, transformations
- Understand the difference between realistic and historical fiction (events that could happen in the real world) and fantasy
- Identify and understand characteristics of special types of fiction: e.g., mystery; adventure story; animal story; family, friends, and school story
- Understand and describe the characteristics of nonfiction genres, including expository nonfiction, narrative nonfiction, biography, autobiography, memoir, procedural text, persuasive text, and hybrid text
- Understand that a biography is the story of a person's life and is usually told in chronological order
- Notice that a biography is built around significant events, problems to overcome, and the subject's decisions
- Understand that a nonfiction book may be procedural (i.e., "how-to")
- Understand that a nonfiction book may have "how-to" procedures embedded within it
- Understand that the information and ideas in a text are related to each other and notice how the author presents this
- Recognize a writer's use of embedded forms (e.g., letters, journal entries) within narrative or expository texts
- Recognize and understand variation in plot structure: story-within-a-story, flashback
- Understand first-, third-, and second-person narrative

- Recognize a writer's use of underlying text structures: e.g., description, cause and effect, chronological sequence, temporal sequence, categorization, comparison and contrast, problem and solution, question and answer
- Notice that a writer organizes a text into categories and subcategories
- Think analytically about the significance of a title
- Notice aspects of the writer's craft: e.g., style, syntax, use of one or more narrators
- Recognize settings that are familiar as well as some distant in time and geography
- Understand how a setting is important to the plot and the characters' perspectives
- Notice characteristics of setting in fantasy that involve magic and/or an imaginary world
- Identify a central story problem in a text with multiple episodes
- Notice when a text has a moral lesson close to the end of the story
- Relate character development to the events of the plot
- Understand the role of supporting characters in a story
- Notice the evidence a writer provides to show character attributes and motives as well as characters' changes
- Understand the perspective from which a story is told and talk about why a writer selected it
- Notice a change of perspective and/or narrator within the larger text and hypothesize why the writer has presented the text in this way
- Notice how a fiction writer creates and sustains suspense
- Notice language used to show chronological order
- Notice a writer's use of figurative language and discuss how it adds to the meaning or enjoyment of a text
- Notice a writer's use of common and more sophisticated connectives to show how ideas are related in a text
- Notice a fiction writer's use of italics to indicate unspoken thought
- Notice a fiction writer's use of poetic and expressive language in dialogue
- Notice a writer's use of humorous words or onomatopoetic words and talk about how they add to the action

Selecting Goals Behaviors and Understandings to Notice, Teach, and Support *(cont.)*

THINKING *ABOUT* THE TEXT *(continued)*

ANALYZING *(continued)*

- Notice literary language typical of traditional literature: e.g., *a long time ago there lived, long ago and far away, once there lived*
- Notice and think analytically about a writer's use of argument or persuasion
- Notice when the writer uses the second person to talk directly to the reader
- Understand that illustrations carry the dialogue and action in graphic texts
- Notice that illustrations add to the reader's understanding of the characters, the action, and the feeling or mood of the story
- Recognize how illustrations enhance the meaning of a text
- Notice the format of a photo essay and understand the purpose
- Notice how the writer uses graphics to convey information that complements the body of the text
- Understand that illustrations or photographs add to the ideas and information in a text

- After reading several books by an author, discuss style, use of language, typical content
- Use some academic language to talk about genres: e.g., *fiction; family, friends, and school story; folktale; animal story; humorous story; fairy tale; fable; tall tale; realistic fiction; mystery; adventure story; sports story; historical fiction; fantasy; nonfiction; informational text; informational book; factual text; how-to book; biography; autobiography; narrative nonfiction; memoir; procedural text; persuasive text, hybrid text*
- Use some academic language to talk about forms: e.g., *series book, play, chapter book, comics, graphic text, letter, sequel, short story, diary entry, journal entry, news article, feature article*
- Use some academic language to talk about literary features: e.g., *beginning, ending, character, question and answer, main character, character change, message, dialogue, topic, events, setting, description, time order, problem and solution, comparison and contrast, main idea, flashback, conflict, resolution, theme, descriptive language, simile, cause and effect, categorization, persuasive language*

- Use some specific language to talk about book and print features: e.g., *front cover, back cover, page, author, illustrator, illustration, photograph, title, label, drawing, heading, caption, table of contents, chapter, chapter title, dedication, sidebar, glossary, map, diagram, infographic, author's note, illustrator's note, section, book jacket, acknowledgments, subheading, text, pronunciation guide, chart, graph, timeline, index*

CRITIQUING

- Share opinions about an illustration or photograph
- Evaluate the quality of illustrations or graphics
- Assess how graphics add to the quality of the text or provide additional information
- Give an opinion about the believability of plot, character actions, or the resolution of a problem
- Assess whether a text is authentic and consistent with life experience
- State specifically what makes a plot or character believable
- Share opinions of characters and talk about how they could have made different decisions or behaved differently
- Assess whether a text is authentic and consistent with reader's background knowledge
- Express tastes and preferences in reading and support choices with descriptions and examples of literary elements: e.g., *genre, setting, plot, theme, character, style and language*
- Share opinions about a text and give rationales and examples
- Evaluate aspects of a text that add to enjoyment or interest: e.g., humorous characters or surprising information
- Evaluate the text in terms of readers' own experiences as preadolescents
- Talk critically about what a writer does to make a topic interesting or important
- Talk about why the subject of a biography is important or sets an example for others
- Notice the author's qualifications to write on a topic
- Distinguish between fact and opinion

Selecting Goals Behaviors and Understandings to Notice, Teach, and Support *(cont.)*

Planning for Word Work After Guided Reading

Using your recent observations of the readers' ability to take words apart quickly and efficiently while reading text, plan for one to three minutes of active engagement of students' attention to letters, sounds, and words. Prioritize the readers' noticing of print features and active hands-on use of magnetic letters, a white board, word cards, or pencil and paper to promote fluency and flexibility in visual processing.

Examples:

- Make a full range of plural nouns, including regular plurals that require spelling changes and irregular plurals (*experiment/experiments; mistress/mistresses; glossary/glossaries; goose/geese*)
- Recognize and solve words in which one consonant sound is represented by several different letters or letter clusters (*squeak, panic, wreck; wharf, giraffe, enough*)

- Work flexibly with a base word, changing letters or adding or taking away one or more affixes to make a new word (*sell/seal/sealing/unseal*)
- Break apart multisyllable words by syllable (*base/ment, coy/o/te, de/part/ment, a/quar/i/um, par/tic/u/lar*)
- Make word ladders by changing letters and/or word parts

- Break apart words with an open syllable and a long vowel sound (*fa/vor, bee/tle, fro/zen*) and a closed syllable with a short vowel sound (*lan/tern, mid/night, pol/ish*)
- Recognize and use homophones (*aye, I; weighed, wade; caller, collar*) and homographs (*pupil, port, pant*)
- Sort words based on any word features

Readers at Level

At level T, readers will process a very wide range of genres, and many texts will be longer with many lines of print on each page, requiring readers to sustain attention to remember information and connect ideas over an extended period of time (as much as a week or more). Readers use genre features to support comprehension, and they recognize the characteristics of a wide range of genres. Complex fantasy, as well as myths, legends, epics, ballads, and symbolism, offer added challenge. Readers understand perspectives different from their own, as well as settings and characters far distant in time or geography. Most reading is silent; all dimensions of fluency in oral reading are well established. Readers are challenged by many longer descriptive words and by content-specific and technical words that require using embedded definitions, background knowledge, and reference tools. Readers understand text features such as copyright information, author's notes, and indexes. They can take apart long multisyllable words and use a full range of word-solving strategies. They can read a wide range of declarative, imperative, exclamatory, and interrogative sentences. They search for and use information in an integrated way, using complex graphics and texts that present content requiring background knowledge. Readers make connections across texts by themes and ideas, topics, and writing styles. They notice elements of the writer's craft and can analyze texts, recognizing literary techniques such as simple symbolism and the use of underlying text structures (e.g., problem and solution). Readers continue to expand in their understanding and use of academic language.

Selecting Texts Characteristics of Texts at **Level T**

GENRE

▶ Fiction

- Realistic fiction
- Historical fiction
- Traditional literature (folktale, myth, legend)
- More complex fantasy including science fiction
- Hybrid texts
- Special types of fiction: e.g., mystery; adventure story; sports story; animal story; family, friends, and school story; humorous story

▶ Nonfiction

- Expository nonfiction
- Narrative nonfiction
- Biography
- Autobiography
- Memoir
- Procedural texts
- Persuasive texts
- Hybrid texts

FORMS

- Series books
- Picture books
- Chapter books
- Chapter books with sequels
- Plays
- Readers' theater scripts
- Graphic texts
- Letters, diaries, and journal entries
- Short stories
- Photo essays and news articles

TEXT STRUCTURE

- Texts with multiple episodes that are elaborated with many details
- Embedded forms (e.g., letters, directions, journal entries, emails) within narrative and expository structures
- Variations in structure: e.g., story-within-a-story, flashback, flash-forward, time-lapse
- Books with chapters connected to a single plot
- Texts with circular plot
- Texts with parallel plots
- Some longer texts with main plot and subplots
- Some complex plots with multiple story lines
- Collections of short stories related to an overarching theme
- Texts that change perspective and/or narrator within the larger narrative

- Nonfiction books divided into sections, and some with subsections
- Underlying structural patterns: description, cause and effect, chronological sequence, temporal sequence, categorization, comparison and contrast, problem and solution, question and answer

CONTENT

- Content interesting to and relevant for the reader
- Some books with little or no picture support for content: e.g., chapter books
- Much content that requires accessing prior knowledge
- Content that invites critical thinking to judge authenticity and accuracy
- Content that requires the reader to take on perspectives from diverse cultures and bring cultural knowledge to understanding
- Most texts with new content that will engage and interest readers and expand knowledge: e.g., travel, experience with other cultures, adventures in science, survival
- Content that goes beyond students' immediate experience

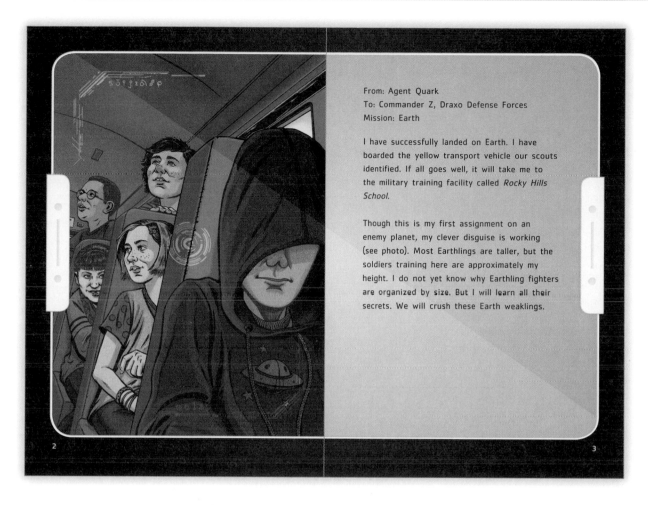

From: Agent Quark
To: Commander Z, Draxo Defense Forces
Mission: Earth

I have successfully landed on Earth. I have boarded the yellow transport vehicle our scouts identified. If all goes well, it will take me to the military training facility called *Rocky Hills School.*

Though this is my first assignment on an enemy planet, my clever disguise is working (see photo). Most Earthlings are taller, but the soldiers training here are approximately my height. I do not yet know why Earthling fighters are organized by size. But I will learn all their secrets. We will crush these Earth weaklings.

- Settings in some texts that require content knowledge of disciplines: e.g., history, geography, culture, language
- Much content that requires the reader to search for information in graphics: e.g., maps, charts, diagrams, illustrated drawings, labeled photographs

THEMES AND IDEAS

- Texts with themes and ideas that involve the problems of preadolescents
- Themes and ideas that require a perspective not familiar to the reader
- Complex ideas on many different topics that require real or vicarious experience (through reading) for understanding
- Texts with deeper meanings applicable to important human problems and social issues: e.g., hardship, war, racism, economic struggle, the environment
- Many ideas and themes that require understanding of cultural diversity
- Some texts with abstract themes that require inferential thinking
- Themes that evoke alternative interpretations

LANGUAGE AND LITERARY FEATURES

- Settings that are distant in time and geography
- Settings in fantasy that require the reader to accept elements of another world that could not exist in the real world
- Settings that are important to comprehension of the fiction narrative or biography
- Variety in narrative plot structure: e.g., story-within-a-story, simple flashback
- Main characters and supporting characters
- Multidimensional characters
- Characters revealed by what they say, think, and do and by what others say and think about them
- Characters revealed over a series of events, chapters, or book series
- Reasons for character change that are complex and require inference
- Some texts that reveal the perspectives of more than one character

- Variety in presentation of dialogue: e.g., dialogue among multiple characters, dialogue with pronouns, split dialogue, direct dialogue, including unassigned dialogue and long stretches of dialogue
- Some chains of unassigned dialogue for which speakers must be inferred
- Most texts written in first- or third-person narrative, with some procedural texts in second person
- Basic motifs of traditional literature and modern fantasy: e.g., struggle between good and evil, fantastic or magical objects, wishes, trickery, transformations
- Moral lesson near the end of the story (sometimes explicitly stated)
- Literary language typical of traditional literature: e.g., *long ago and far away*
- Poetic language and figurative language: e.g., metaphor, simile
- Language and events that convey an emotional atmosphere (mood) in a text, affecting how the reader feels: e.g., tension, suspense, sadness, happiness, curiosity
- Use of symbolism

Selecting Texts Characteristics of Texts at **Level T** (cont.)

LANGUAGE AND LITERARY FEATURES (continued)

- Some colloquial language in dialogue that reflects characters' personalities and/or setting
- Procedural language
- Language used to make comparisons
- Descriptive language
- Language used to show chronological order and temporal sequence
- Persuasive language

SENTENCE COMPLEXITY

- Wide range of declarative, imperative, exclamatory, or interrogative sentences
- Variation in sentence length and structure
- Sentences with a wide variety of parts of speech, including multiple adjectives, adverbs, and prepositional phrases
- Sentences with common connectives and many sophisticated connectives
- Frequent use of parenthetical material embedded in sentences

VOCABULARY

- Many words that appear in the vocabulary of mature language users (Tier 2)
- Many words particular to a discipline (Tier 3)
- Wide variation in words used to assign dialogue
- Many words with multiple meanings
- Many words with figurative meaning
- Frequent use of idioms
- New vocabulary requiring strategic action to understand: e.g., derive meaning from context, use reference tools, notice morphology, use word roots, use analogy
- Words with connotative meanings that are essential to understanding the text
- Many common connectives (words, phrases that clarify relationships and ideas and that are used frequently in oral language): e.g., *and, but, so, because, before, after*
- Sophisticated (complex) connectives (words, phrases that link ideas and clarify meaning and that are used in written texts but do not appear often in everyday oral language): e.g., *although, however, meantime, meanwhile moreover, otherwise, unless, therefore, though, unless, until, whenever, yet*

- Some words from regional or historical dialects
- Some words (including slang) used informally by particular groups of people
- Some words from languages other than English
- Some archaic words

WORDS

- Many multisyllable words, some technical or scientific
- Full range of plurals
- Unlimited number of high-frequency words with multiple syllables
- Multisyllable words with some complex letter-sound relationships
- Multisyllable proper nouns that are difficult to decode
- Wide range of contractions and possessives
- Full range of compound words
- Base words with affixes (prefixes and suffixes)
- Some words divided (hyphenated) across lines
- Common connectives and sophisticated connectives

ILLUSTRATIONS

- Illustrations that enhance and extend meaning in the text
- Short texts that have illustrations on every page or every few pages
- Texts with illustrations every three or four pages
- Short chapter books with only a few illustrations and some longer books
- Some texts with no illustrations other than decorative elements such as vignettes
- Variety of layout in illustrations and print
- A few books with black-and-white illustrations
- Some complex, nuanced illustrations that communicate mood and meaning (literal, figurative, symbolic) to match or extend the text
- Graphics that require reader interpretation and are essential for comprehending informational text
- More than one kind of graphics on a page spread

- A range of graphics that provide information that matches and extends the text: e.g., photograph and drawing with label and/or caption; diagram, cutaway; map with legend or key, scale; infographic; chart; graph; timeline

BOOK AND PRINT FEATURES

LENGTH

- Wide variation in length (mostly shorter than forty-eight pages)
- Wide variation in number of words (2,000+)
- Some books divided into chapters
- Books divided into sections and subsections

PRINT AND LAYOUT

- Mostly small but readable font size
- Variety in print and background color
- Variety in print placement, reflecting different genres
- Italics indicating unspoken thought in some texts
- Information shown in a variety of picture and print combinations in graphic texts
- Captions under pictures that provide important information
- Print and illustrations integrated in most texts, with print wrapping around pictures
- Print placed in sidebars and graphics that provide important information

PUNCTUATION

- Period, comma, question mark, exclamation mark, parentheses, quotation marks, hyphen, dash, and ellipses in most texts

ORGANIZATIONAL TOOLS

- Title, table of contents, chapter title, heading, subheading, sidebar

TEXT RESOURCES

- Dedication, acknowledgments, author's note, pronunciation guide, glossary, index, foreword, footnote, endnote, epilogue, appendix, references

Selecting Goals Behaviors and Understandings to Notice, Teach, and Support

THINKING *WITHIN* THE TEXT

SEARCHING FOR AND USING INFORMATION

- Sustain searching over some longer sentences with more than twenty words and multiple clauses and phrases
- Sustain searching over short texts (under forty-eight pages) and some books that are divided into chapters and may have more than 2,500 words
- Search for information and language that states or implies the larger message(s) of the text
- Search for information in texts with many features: e.g., body text, sidebars, and graphics
- Use background knowledge to search for and understand information about settings, geographical areas, history, economics
- Use organizational tools to search for information: e.g., title, table of contents, chapter title, heading, subheading, sidebar, callout
- Use text resources to search for information: e.g., acknowledgments, author's note, pronunciation guide, glossary, references, index
- Search for information in sentences that vary in length, structure, and punctuation based on complexity
- Search for information in sentences with nouns, verbs, adjectives, and adverbs in a series, divided by commas
- Search for and understand information presented in a variety of ways: e.g., simple dialogue, dialogue with pronouns, split dialogue, assigned and sometimes unassigned dialogue, dialogue among multiple characters, some long stretches of dialogue, direct dialogue
- Use the chronological order within multiple episodes to search for and use information when reading short stories and chapter books
- Search for information in a variety of narrative structures: e.g., story-within-a-story (framed narrative); flashback, flash-forward, time-lapse (fractured narrative); circular narrative; multiple or parallel plots
- Notice and use punctuation marks: e.g., period, comma, question mark, exclamation mark, parentheses, quotation marks, hyphen, dash, ellipses
- Search for and use information from a wide variety of illustrations or graphics
- Search for and use information in texts with variety in placement of the body text, sidebars, and graphics

MONITORING AND SELF-CORRECTING

- Self-monitor reading using multiple sources of information: i.e., background knowledge, syntax, word meaning, word structure, awareness of text structure, meaning of the whole text, graphics, layout, genre
- Read with very little overt self-correction

- Self-correct covertly prior to or after error, and show very little overt self-correction
- Closely monitor understanding of texts using knowledge of a wide range of fiction genres: e.g., realistic fiction, historical fiction, traditional literature (folktale, fairy tale, fable, myth, legend, epic, ballad), fantasy including science fiction, hybrid text
- Closely monitor understanding of texts using knowledge of a wide range of forms: e.g., poems, plays, graphic texts, letters, diaries, journal entries, short stories
- Use understanding of literary elements (e.g., plot, main and supporting characters, setting, narrative structure) to monitor and correct reading
- Use awareness of the attributes of multidimensional characters to self-monitor and self-correct
- Use content knowledge of the topic of a text to self-monitor and self-correct
- Use knowledge of nonfiction genres to monitor understanding of a text: e.g., expository nonfiction, narrative nonfiction, biography, autobiography, memoir, procedural text, persuasive text
- Use information from graphics (e.g., maps, diagrams, charts, photos, illustrations) to self-monitor reading

SOLVING WORDS

▶ Reading Words

- Recognize a large number of high-frequency words and multisyllable words rapidly and automatically
- Use a wide range of strategies for solving multisyllable words: e.g., using syllables, recognizing spelling patterns within words, using complex letter-sound relationships, noticing base words and affixes, using the context of the text, or using text resources
- Solve words by identifying simple, complex, and modified or shortened word parts within multisyllable words
- Read multisyllable words with complex letter-sound relationships
- Read all parts of speech as well as possessives and contractions
- Solve words rapidly while processing continuous text and with minimum overt self-correction
- Read proper nouns, words from other languages, and technical words from academic disciplines that are difficult to decode and use text resources like a pronunciation guide as needed
- Solve words by identifying base words and affixes (prefixes and suffixes)
- Employ word-solving strategies in a flexible way

GUIDED READING

LEVEL **T**

Selecting Goals Behaviors and Understandings to Notice, Teach, and Support *(cont.)*

PREDICTING

◆ Make predictions based on personal experience, previous reading, and content area study

◆ Make predictions throughout a text based on the organizational structure (i.e., narrative; expository)

◆ Justify predictions with evidence from the text

◆ Make predictions based on the panels in a graphic text

◆ Predict the ending of a story based on understanding of different kinds of narrative structure and understanding of setting, plot, and characters

◆ Make predictions based on knowledge of the purposes and unique characteristics of fiction and nonfiction genres as well as special types of fiction texts

◆ Predict potential solutions to the problem in the story and discuss the likelihood of alternatives

◆ Use previous reading of a book in a series to predict types of characters and plots in a sequel or another book in the series

◆ Make predictions based on plot structure: e.g., predict connections between characters and events in a text with circular plot, parallel plots, main plot and subplot

◆ Make predictions based on knowledge of special forms: e.g., letters, diaries, and journal entries; photo essays, news articles

◆ Make predictions based on knowledge of underlying text structures: e.g., description, cause and effect, chronological sequence, temporal sequence, categorization, comparison and contrast, problem and solution, question and answer

MAKING CONNECTIONS

◆ Make connections between texts and personal experience, content learned in past reading, and disciplinary knowledge

◆ Use knowledge from one text to understand content, setting, or problems in another

◆ Make many different kinds of connections among texts: e.g., author, illustrator, content, genre, topic, theme or message, events, problem, characters, language, graphics, text structure, writing style

◆ State explicitly the nature of connections: e.g., topic, theme, message, characters, genre, writer, style

◆ Make connections between students' lives and the content that are particularly appropriate for adolescents

◆ Use multiple sources of information to confirm or disprove predictions, including text and illustrations

◆ Make connections between fiction and nonfiction texts that have the same setting: e.g., geographic locations, periods in history

◆ Use background knowledge of past events to understand historical fiction

◆ Use disciplinary knowledge to understand setting in realistic and historical fiction texts

◆ Use previous reading of nonfiction to understand the events in historical fiction

◆ Make connections with the human traits and problems that are shared among people of many different cultures

◆ Use scientific knowledge to understand fantasy and science fiction

◆ Use background knowledge of traditional literature to recognize common characters and events in fantasy

◆ Use disciplinary knowledge to understand content and concepts in a text

SYNTHESIZING

◆ Identify familiar and new content and ideas gained while reading a text

◆ Mentally form categories of related information and revise them as new information is acquired across texts

◆ Integrate new information and ideas to consciously create new understandings

◆ Explicitly state new knowledge, ideas, and attitudes built from reading fiction and nonfiction texts

◆ Provide evidence from the text to support statements describing new learning

◆ Build new knowledge across texts that are connected by topic, content, theme, or message

◆ Describe changing perspective as more of a story unfolds

◆ Talk about lessons learned from a character's experience and behavior in a text

◆ Apply new perspectives acquired from vicarious experiences in a fiction text to live their own lives

◆ Talk about new ways of thinking that spring from vicarious experiences in reading a fiction text

◆ Apply perspective learned from reading fiction to issues and problems that face preadolescents: e.g., peer pressure, social relationships, bullying, maturation

◆ Talk about new understanding of different cultures, places, and times in history

◆ Synthesize new facts, perspectives, or conceptual frameworks from texts and describe these to others using evidence from the text

◆ Take on perspectives from diverse cultures and bring cultural knowledge to understanding a text

Selecting Goals Behaviors and Understandings to Notice, Teach, and Support *(cont.)*

THINKING *BEYOND* THE TEXT *(continued)*

INFERRING

- Make inferences about setting to help in understanding the story
- Infer the impact of the setting on the subject of a biography and the motives or reasons for the subject's decisions
- Infer feelings and motives of multiple characters across complex plots with some subplots, circular plots, parallel plots
- Infer feelings and motives of multiple characters across circular or parallel plots
- Infer the causes for character traits and for problems that the character experiences
- Infer traits of multidimensional characters that have both good and bad traits and have choices to make
- Infer character development from evidence in behavior as well as reasons for change
- Infer complex relationships between and among characters by noticing evidence in their responses to each other and thoughts about each other
- Infer potential solutions to the story problem and find evidence to support them
- Infer the writer's messages in some texts that have serious and mature topics and themes: e.g., war, racism, family problems, bullying
- Infer themes, ideas, and characters' feelings from the panels in graphic texts
- Infer some abstract ideas and themes that reflect the writer's message or main idea in a text
- Infer the meaning of some simple symbolism
- Infer a writer's beliefs or biases
- Infer how messages are important to people's lives today
- Infer attitudes that may be new or contrary to readers' current beliefs

- Infer universal human themes and issues that affect human problems across the world
- Infer the overarching theme(s) in a collection of short stories
- Compare inferences with those of other readers and consider alternative interpretations of characters' motives and the writer's message
- Infer the larger message in a text (i.e., what can be learned from it beyond the facts)
- Infer information from illustrations, photographs, drawings, and graphics that add meaning to the text
- Infer information about characters, setting, plot, and action from graphic texts, in which illustrations carry much of the meaning
- Make inferences from print narrative alone (no pictures)
- Infer emotions conveyed by pictures
- Infer the mood of the text from the characteristics of the illustrations
- Infer the meaning of a range of graphics that require reader interpretation and are essential to comprehending the text
- Infer the significance of design and other features of the peritext
- Understand the connotative meanings of words that contribute to the mood of the text
- Infer beliefs, customs, and perspectives of people who live in other cultures
- Infer beliefs, customs, and perspectives of people who live in the near and distant past
- Infer what life might be like and what people might believe and do at a time in the future
- Infer important information from familiar content as well as topics more distant from students' typical experience: e.g., different parts of the world, history, science

GUIDED READING

Selecting Goals   Behaviors and Understandings to Notice, Teach, and Support *(cont.)*

THINKING *ABOUT* THE TEXT

ANALYZING

- Understand that there may be different genres and special forms in each of the larger categories of fiction and nonfiction
- Understand that a graphic text may represent any fiction or nonfiction genre
- Identify fictional and factual components in a hybrid text
- Discuss a writer's purpose in selecting a particular genre, topic, subject, or type of narrative structure
- Understand and describe characteristics of fiction genres, including realistic fiction, historical fiction, traditional literature (folktale, fairy tale, fable, myth, legend), fantasy, and hybrid text
- Notice elements and basic motifs of fantasy: e.g., the supernatural, imaginary and otherworldly creatures, gods and goddesses, talking animals, struggle between good and evil, magic, fantastic or magical objects, wishes, trickery, transformations
- Identify and understand characteristics of special types of fiction: e.g., mystery; adventure story; animal story; family, friends, and school story
- Understand that fiction genres may be combined within one text
- Understand the difference between realism and fantasy across fiction texts
- Notice characteristics of settings in fantasy that require believing in magic and/or an imaginary world
- Understand and describe the characteristics of nonfiction genres, including expository nonfiction, narrative nonfiction, biography, autobiography, memoir, procedural text, persuasive text, and hybrid text
- Understand that nonfiction genres may be combined within one text
- Notice that a biography is built around significant events, problems to overcome, and the subject's decisions
- Understand that a procedural nonfiction book may have "how-to" procedures embedded within it
- Understand that a nonfiction writer may use argument in a persuasive text
- Understand that the information and ideas in a text are related to each other and notice how the author presents this
- Recognize a writer's use of embedded forms (e.g., letters, directions, journal entries) within narrative and expository text structures
- Recognize and understand variety in narrative structure: e.g., circular plot, parallel plots, main plot and subplot(s), story-within-a-story, flashback, flash-forward, time-lapse
- Recognize a writer's use of underlying text structures: e.g., description, cause and effect, chronological sequence, temporal sequence, categorization, comparison and contrast, problem and solution, question and answer
- Notice and understand expository text structure (categorized information) and the use of narrative structure for biographical texts and other types of narrative nonfiction

- Think analytically about the significance of a title
- Notice aspects of the writer's craft: e.g., style, syntax, use of one or more narrators
- After reading several books by an author, discuss style, use of language, typical content
- Understand the characteristics of settings (cultural, physical, historical) and the way they affect characters' attitudes and decisions
- Think analytically about the significance of the setting and its importance to the plot
- Notice parallel and circular plots
- Identify the central story problem or conflict in a text with multiple episodes or parallel plots
- Notice when a text has a moral lesson close to the end of the story
- Notice how a writer reveals main and supporting characters by what they do, think, or say, and by what others say about them or how others respond to them
- Analyze the roles of supporting characters and how they are important (or unimportant) in the story and in the development of main character(s)
- Analyze a text to think about the perspective from which the story is told and notice when that perspective changes
- Notice how a fiction writer creates, sustains, and releases suspense
- Notice language used to show chronological and temporal order
- Notice a writer's use of figurative language and state how it specifically adds to the meaning or enjoyment of a text
- Notice a writer's use of both common and sophisticated connectives as well as some academic connectives
- Notice parenthetical material set off by commas or parentheses
- Understand that a writer selects first-, third-, or second-person point of view to tell a story and also may use several points of view in the same story
- Notice a fiction writer's use of poetic and expressive language in dialogue
- Notice literary language typical of traditional literature: e.g., *a long time ago there lived, long ago and far away, once there lived*
- Notice a writer's use of humorous words or onomatopoetic words and talk about how they add to the action
- Notice the logic and structure of a writer's argument
- Notice how a writer uses language in a persuasive way
- Notice how the writer/illustrator selects and places photos in a way that tells a story or communicates a larger meaning in a photo essay
- Understand that illustrations carry the dialogue and action in a graphic text
- Understand how illustrations and text work together to enhance meaning and communicate the mood of the text

Selecting Goals Behaviors and Understandings to Notice, Teach, and Support *(cont.)*

THINKING *ABOUT* THE TEXT *(continued)*

ANALYZING *(continued)*

- Use some academic language to talk about genres: e.g., *fiction; family, friends, and school story; folktale; animal story; humorous story; fairy tale; fable; tall tale; realistic fiction; mystery; adventure story; sports story; historical fiction; fantasy; traditional literature; myth; legend; science fiction; nonfiction; informational text; informational book; factual text; how-to book; biography; autobiography; narrative nonfiction; memoir; procedural text; persuasive text, hybrid text; expository text*

- Use some academic language to talk about forms: e.g., *series book, play, chapter book, comics, graphic text, letter, sequel, short story, diary entry, journal entry, news article, feature article*

- Use some academic language to talk about literary features: e.g., *beginning, ending, character, question and answer, main character, message, dialogue, topic, events, setting, description, problem and solution, comparison and contrast, main idea, flashback, conflict, resolution, theme, descriptive language, simile, cause and effect, categorization, persuasive language, plot, character development, supporting character, point of view, figurative language, metaphor, temporal sequence, chronological sequence, subject, argument*

- Use some specific language to talk about book and print features: e.g., *front cover, back cover, page, author, illustrator, illustration, photograph, title, label, drawing, heading, caption, table of contents, chapter, chapter title, dedication, sidebar, glossary, map, diagram, infographic, author's note, illustrator's note, section, book jacket, acknowledgments, subheading, text, pronunciation guide, chart, graph, timeline, index, foreword, cutaway, footnote, epilogue, endnote, appendix, references*

CRITIQUING

- Evaluate the quality of illustrations or graphics and share opinions
- Assess how graphics add to the quality of the text or provide additional information
- Give an opinion about the believability of plot, character actions, or resolution
- State specifically what makes a plot or character believable
- Share opinions of characters and talk about how they could have made different decisions or behaved differently
- Assess whether a text is authentic and consistent with life experience
- Notice the references and assurances the writer provides to authenticate a text
- Distinguish between primary and secondary sources and think critically about the authenticity of a text
- Distinguish between fact and opinion
- Agree or disagree with a writer's arguments and give rationales for opinions
- Share opinions about a written text and/or about illustrations and give rationales and examples
- Evaluate aspects of a text that add to enjoyment: e.g., humorous character or surprising information
- Express tastes and preferences in reading and support choices with descriptions and examples of literary elements: e.g., genre, setting, plot, theme, character, style, and language
- Evaluate the authenticity of a text in terms of readers' own experiences as preadolescents (or adolescents)
- Talk critically about what a writer does to make a topic interesting or important
- Talk about why the subject of a biography is important or sets an example for others

Planning for Word Work After Guided Reading

Using your recent observations of the readers' ability to take words apart quickly and efficiently while reading text, plan for one to three minutes of active engagement of students' attention to letters, sounds, and words. Prioritize the readers' noticing of print features and active hands-on use of magnetic letters, a white board, word cards, or pencil and paper to promote fluency and flexibility in visual processing.

Examples:

- Make a full range of plural nouns, including regular plurals that require spelling changes and irregular plurals (*autograph/autographs; goddess/ goddesses; ceremony/ceremonies; ox/oxen*)

- Work flexibly with a base word, changing letters or adding or taking away one or more affixes to make a new word (*advice/ advise/advising/misadvise*)

- Recognize and use word roots (Greek and Latin) to take apart and determine the meanings of some English words (*geo*, meaning "the earth," and *graph*, meaning "the write," in *geography*, "study of the earth's surface, climate, continents, countries, peoples, natural resources, industries, and products")

- Sort words based on any word features

- Break apart multisyllable words quickly by syllable (*a/dopt, ben/e/fit, de/ter/mine, dec/la/ra/tion, i/mag/i/nar/y*)

- Recognize and break apart words with an open syllable and a long vowel sound (*a/gent, ce/dar, no/ble*) and a closed syllable with a short vowel sound (*nap/kin, bon/fire, clum/sy*)

- Recognize and use homophones (*aisle, isle, I'll; alter, altar; but, butt*) and homographs (*dove, keen, fawn*)

Readers at Level

At level U, readers will process the full range of genres, and texts will be longer, requiring readers to sustain attention and remember information, and connect ideas over many days of reading. They automatically adjust to different genres and use genre characteristics to support comprehension. They can articulate the unique characteristics of many genres. Complex or "high" fantasy as well as myths, legends, epics, ballads, and symbolism offer added challenge. Readers understand perspectives different from their own, and understand settings and characters far distance in time or geography. Some content requires readers to call on emotional and social maturity for understanding. They expand their ability to detect bias, and are able to critique texts in terms of believability and authenticity. Most reading is silent; in oral reading, all dimensions of fluency are well established. Readers are challenged by many longer descriptive words, by content-specific and technical words, and by idioms, words, and phrases from languages other than English. They can take apart long multisyllable words and use a full range of word-solving strategies. They use and understand disciplinary vocabulary. They search for and use information in an integrated way, using complex graphics and texts that present content requiring background knowledge. Readers connect themes, big ideas, messages, writing styles, topics, and other elements across texts. They notice different aspects of the writer's craft, and they can reflect analytic thinking in their talk. They use academic language easily as they talk about texts, and academic language is always expanding. They begin to take on the very complex thinking that satire and parody require.

Selecting Texts Characteristics of Texts at **Level U**

GENRE

▶ Fiction

- Realistic fiction
- Historical fiction
- Traditional literature (folktale, myth, legend)
- Complex fantasy and science fiction
- Hybrid texts
- Special types of fiction: e.g., mystery; adventure story; sports story; animal story; family, friends, and school story; humorous story

▶ Nonfiction

- Expository nonfiction
- Narrative nonfiction
- Biography
- Autobiography
- Memoir
- Procedural texts
- Persuasive texts
- Hybrid texts

FORMS

- Series books
- Picture books
- Chapter books
- Chapter books with sequels

- Plays
- Readers' theater scripts
- Graphic texts
- Letters, diaries, and journal entries
- Short stories
- Photo essays and news articles

TEXT STRUCTURE

- Texts with multiple episodes that are elaborated with many details
- Embedded forms (e.g., letters, directions, journal entries, emails) within narrative and expository structures
- Variations in structure: e.g., story-within-a-story, flashback, flash-forward, time-lapse
- Books with chapters connected to a single plot
- Texts with circular plot or parallel plots
- Longer texts with main plot and subplots
- Complex plots with multiple story lines
- Collections of short stories related to an overarching theme
- Texts that change perspective and/or narrator within the larger narrative
- Nonfiction books divided into sections, and some with subsections

- Underlying structural patterns: description, cause and effect, chronological sequence, temporal sequence, categorization, comparison and contrast, problem and solution, question and answer

CONTENT

- Content interesting to and relevant for the reader
- Some books with little or no picture support for content: e.g., chapter books
- Much content that requires accessing prior knowledge
- Content that invites critical thinking to judge authenticity and accuracy
- Content that requires the reader to take on perspectives from diverse cultures and bring cultural knowledge to understanding
- Most texts with new content that will engage and interest readers and expand knowledge: e.g., travel, experience with other cultures, adventures in science, survival
- Settings in some texts that require content knowledge of disciplines: e.g., history, geography, culture, language
- Content that requires emotional and social maturity to understand

LEVEL
U

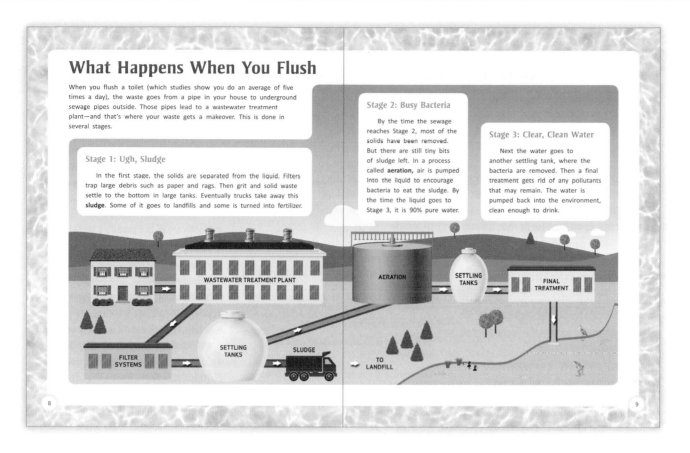

What Happens When You Flush

When you flush a toilet (which studies show you do an average of five times a day), the waste goes from a pipe in your house to underground sewage pipes outside. Those pipes lead to a wastewater treatment plant—and that's where your waste gets a makeover. This is done in several stages.

Stage 1: Ugh, Sludge

In the first stage, the solids are separated from the liquid. Filters trap large debris such as paper and rags. Then grit and solid waste settle to the bottom in large tanks. Eventually trucks take away this **sludge**. Some of it goes to landfills and some is turned into fertilizer.

Stage 2: Busy Bacteria

By the time the sewage reaches Stage 2, most of the solids have been removed. But there are still tiny bits of sludge left. In a process called **aeration**, air is pumped into the liquid to encourage bacteria to eat the sludge. By the time the liquid goes to Stage 3, it is 90% pure water.

Stage 3: Clear, Clean Water

Next the water goes to another settling tank, where the bacteria are removed. Then a final treatment gets rid of any pollutants that may remain. The water is pumped back into the environment, clean enough to drink.

WASTEWATER TREATMENT PLANT

AERATION

SETTLING TANKS

FINAL TREATMENT

FILTER SYSTEMS

SETTLING TANKS

SLUDGE

TO LANDFILL

8

9

- Most content goes beyond students' immediate experience
- Much content that requires the reader to search for information in graphics: e.g., maps, charts, diagrams, illustrated drawings, labeled photographs

THEMES AND IDEAS

- Texts with themes and ideas that involve the problems of preadolescents
- Themes and ideas that require a perspective not familiar to the reader
- Complex ideas on many different topics that require real or vicarious experience (through reading) for understanding
- Texts with deeper meanings applicable to important human problems and social issues: e.g., hardship, war, racism, economic struggle, the environment
- Many ideas and themes that require understanding of cultural diversity
- Some texts with abstract themes that require inferential thinking
- Themes that evoke alternative interpretations

LANGUAGE AND LITERARY FEATURES

- Settings that are distant in time and geography
- Settings in fantasy that require the reader to accept elements of another world that could not exist in the real world
- Settings that are important to comprehension of the fiction narrative or biography
- Variety in narrative plot structure: e.g., story-within-a-story, simple flashback
- Main characters and supporting characters
- Multidimensional characters
- Characters revealed by what they say, think, and do and by what others say and think about them
- Characters revealed over a series of events, chapters, or book series
- Reasons for character change that are complex and require inference
- Some texts that reveal the perspectives of more than one character
- Variety in presentation of dialogue: e.g., dialogue among multiple characters, dialogue with pronouns, split dialogue, direct dialogue, including unassigned dialogue and long stretches of dialogue

- Some chains of unassigned dialogue for which speakers must be inferred
- Most texts written in first- or third-person narrative, with some procedural texts in second person
- Basic motifs of traditional literature and modern fantasy: e.g., struggle between good and evil, fantastic or magical objects, wishes, trickery, transformations
- Moral lesson near the end of the story (sometimes explicitly stated)
- Literary language typical of traditional literature: e.g., *long ago and far away*
- Poetic language and figurative language: e.g., metaphor, simile
- Language and events that convey an emotional atmosphere (mood) in a text, affecting how the reader feels: e.g., tension, suspense, sadness, happiness, curiosity
- Use of symbolism
- Some colloquial language in dialogue that reflects characters' personalities and/or setting
- Procedural language
- Language used to make comparisons
- Descriptive language
- Language used to show chronological order and temporal sequence
- Persuasive language and argument

Selecting Goals Behaviors and Understandings to Notice, Teach, and Support *(cont.)*

SOLVING WORDS *(continued)*

▶ Vocabulary

- Derive the meaning of new words and expand meaning of known words using flexible strategies: e.g., context in a sentence; connections to other words; synonyms and antonyms; word parts; base words and affixes; word function in a sentence; text resources

- Actively and consistently add to vocabulary through reading

- Understand many words that appear in writing and in the vocabulary of mature language users (Tier 2)

- Understand some words particular to academic disciplines (Tier 3)

- Understand the meaning and function of all parts of speech

- Understand how a writer uses words in a text to indicate perspective or point of view: i.e., first person, second person, third person

- Understand many words that have multiple meanings and identify the specific meaning that applies in a sentence or paragraph

- Understand the meaning and function of common connectives that occur in oral language and many sophisticated (complex) connectives that are more typical of written language

- Understand the meaning and function of academic connectives that appear in written texts but are seldom used in everyday oral language

- Understand denotative, connotative, idiomatic, and figurative meaning of words

- Understand the connotative and figurative meanings of words that contribute to the mood of the text, including words that assign dialogue: e.g., *whispered, snarled, sighed*

- Understand that in graphic texts, information about words is in the illustrations, and also that many unusual words appear in graphic texts

- Understand words used in regional or historical dialects

- Understand the connotative meanings of descriptive adjectives, verbs, and adverbs, and use to make inferences about characters

- Derive the meanings of technical words and author-created words in science fiction

- Understand words used informally by particular groups of people: e.g., slang, dialect

- Understand some words from languages other than English

- Understand the meanings of some archaic words

- Understand the meanings of some words used satirically

- Understand and acquire a large number of content-specific words that require the use of strategic actions (i.e., conceptual understanding of content, definitions within the body of a text, a glossary, or other text resources)

- Understand key words in graphics such as maps, diagrams, and charts

MAINTAINING FLUENCY

- Read orally in a way that demonstrates all dimensions of fluency (pausing, phrasing, intonation, word stress, rate)

- Read silently at a faster rate than when reading orally and also maintaining comprehension

- Demonstrate the ability to skim and scan while reading silently to search for information quickly

- In oral reading, show recognition of a wide range of declarative, imperative, exclamatory, or interrogative sentences

- Sustain momentum while reading a wide variety of texts, many that are long

- Notice periods, commas, question marks, exclamation marks, parentheses, quotation marks, dashes, and ellipses and begin to reflect them with the voice through intonation and pausing

- Stress words that are in bold, italics, or varied font

- Recognize and read expressively a variety of dialogue, some unassigned

- Read parts in a script with demonstration of all dimensions of fluency

- Show in the voice when words in a text (sometimes shown in italics) reflect unspoken thought

- Orally read novels in verse reflecting the meaning and rhythm with the voice

- Reflect numbered and bulleted lists with the voice when reading orally

- Use the voice to reflect disciplinary content in different ways: e.g., historical account vs. scientific argument

Selecting Goals Behaviors and Understandings to Notice, Teach, and Support *(cont.)*

THINKING *WITHIN* THE TEXT *(continued)*

ADJUSTING

- Adjust reading to recognize a wide range of declarative, imperative, exclamatory, or interrogative sentences, many that are very complex
- Adjust reading to recognize a hybrid text or a text with embedded forms such as letters, diaries, journal entries, and other authentic documents
- Adjust reading to form expectations based on purposes and characteristics of fiction and nonfiction genres as well as special forms of fiction texts
- Adjust reading to meet the special demands of a graphic text
- Slow down to search for or reflect on information or to enjoy language and resume reading with momentum
- Adjust reading to accommodate a wide variety of complex sentences with embedded phrases and clauses as well as parenthetical information
- Adjust to accommodate embedded forms (e.g., letters, diaries, journal entries, and other authentic documents) within narrative and expository texts
- Adjust expectations with regard to the multiple genres in a hybrid text
- Adjust reading to understand that a text can be a collection of short stories related to an overarching theme
- Adjust reading to meet the unique demands of graphic texts
- Adjust to read parts in a readers' theater script or a play
- Adjust reading to recognize variations in narrative structure: e.g., story-within-a-story, flashback, flash-forward, time-lapse

- Adjust reading to follow texts that change perspective and/or narrator within the larger narrative
- Adjust to read speeches reflecting the point of view of the speaker
- Adjust reading to recognize forms: e.g., poems; plays; graphic texts, letters, diaries and journal entries; photo essays and news articles
- Adjust to recognize the use of argument in a persuasive text
- Adjust reading to accommodate varied placement of body text, photographs with captions, sidebars, and graphics
- Adjust reading to reflect a series of steps in a procedural text

SUMMARIZING

- Present a concise, organized oral summary that includes all important information
- Present an organized oral summary of a section or chapter of a text
- Present an organized oral summary that includes setting (if important), significant plot events including climax and resolution, main characters and supporting characters, character change (where significant), and the theme or lesson (fiction)
- Present a logically organized oral summary that includes important information expressing the main idea or larger message and reflects the overall structure (expository or narrative) as well as important underlying text structures: e.g., description, cause and effect, chronological sequence, temporal sequence, categorization, comparison and contrast, problem and solution, question and answer (nonfiction)

GUIDED READING

LEVEL
U

Selecting Goals Behaviors and Understandings to Notice, Teach, and Support *(cont.)*

THINKING *BEYOND* THE TEXT

PREDICTING

- Make predictions based on personal experience, previous reading, and content area study
- Make predictions throughout a text based on the organizational structure (i.e., narrative; expository)
- Justify predictions with evidence from the text
- Make predictions based on the panels in a graphic text
- Predict the ending of a story based on understanding of different kinds of narrative structure and understanding of setting, plot, and characters
- Make predictions based on knowledge of the characteristics of fiction and nonfiction genres, as well as an understanding of and experience reading different types of fiction texts such as mystery or survival stories
- Predict potential solutions to the problem in the story and discuss the likelihood of alternatives
- Use previous reading of a book in a series to predict types of characters and plots in a sequel or another book in the series
- Make predictions based on plot structure: e.g., predict connections between characters and events in a text with circular plot, parallel plots, main plot and subplot
- Make predictions based on knowledge of special forms: e.g., letters, diaries, and journal entries; photo essays and news articles
- Make predictions based on knowledge of underlying text structures: e.g., description, cause and effect, chronological sequence, temporal sequence, categorization, comparison and contrast, problem and solution, question and answer

MAKING CONNECTIONS

- Make connections between texts and personal experience, content learned in past reading, and disciplinary knowledge
- Use knowledge from one text to understand content, setting, or problems in another
- Make many different kinds of connections among texts: e.g., author, illustrator, content, genre, topic, theme or message, events, problem, characters, language, writing style, text structure, graphics
- State explicitly the nature of connections: e.g., topic, theme, message, characters, genre, writer, style
- Make connections between students' lives and the content that are particularly appropriate for adolescents
- Use multiple sources of information to confirm or disprove predictions, including text and illustrations
- Make connections between fiction and nonfiction texts that have the same setting: e.g., geographic locations, periods in history
- Use background knowledge of past events to understand historical fiction
- Use disciplinary knowledge to understand setting in realistic and historical fiction texts

- Use previous reading of nonfiction to understand the events in historical fiction
- Make connections with the human traits and problems that are shared among people of many different cultures
- Use scientific knowledge to understand fantasy including science fiction
- Use background knowledge of traditional literature to recognize common characters and events in fantasy
- Use disciplinary knowledge to understand content and concepts in a text

SYNTHESIZING

- Identify familiar and new content and ideas gained while reading a text
- Mentally form categories of related information and revise them as new information is acquired across texts
- Integrate new information and ideas to consciously create new understandings
- Explicitly state new knowledge, ideas, and attitudes built from reading fiction and nonfiction texts
- Provide evidence from the text to support statements describing new learning
- Build new knowledge across texts that are connected by topic, content, theme, or message
- Describe changing perspective as more of a story unfolds
- Talk about lessons learned from a character's experience and behavior in a text
- Apply new perspectives acquired from vicarious experiences while reading a fiction text to live their own lives
- Talk about new ways of thinking that spring from vicarious experiences while reading a fiction text
- Apply perspective learned from reading fiction to issues and problems that face preadolescents: e.g., peer pressure, social relationships, bullying, maturation
- Talk about new understanding of different cultures, places, and times in history
- Synthesize new facts, perspectives, or conceptual frameworks from texts and describe these to others using evidence from the text
- Take on perspectives from diverse cultures and bring cultural knowledge to understanding a text

INFERRING

- Make inferences about setting to help in understanding the story
- Infer the impact of the setting on the subject of a biography and the motives or reasons for the subject's decisions
- Infer feelings and motives of multiple characters across complex plots with some subplots
- Infer feelings and motives of multiple characters across circular or parallel plots

The Fountas & Pinnell Literacy Continuum, Grades PreK–8

Selecting Goals Behaviors and Understandings to Notice, Teach, and Support *(cont.)*

THINKING *BEYOND* THE TEXT *(continued)*

- Infer the causes for character traits and for problems that the character experiences
- Infer traits of multidimensional characters that have both good and bad traits and have choices to make
- Infer character development from evidence in behavior as well as reasons for change
- Infer complex relationships between and among characters by noticing evidence in their responses to each other and thoughts about each other
- Infer potential solutions to the story problem and find evidence to support them
- Infer the writer's messages in some texts that have serious and mature topics and themes: e.g., war, racism, family problems, bullying
- Infer themes, ideas, and characters' feelings from the panels in graphic texts
- Infer some abstract ideas and themes that reflect the writer's message or main idea in a text
- Infer a writer's beliefs or biases
- Infer how messages are important to people's lives today
- Infer attitudes that may be new or contrary to readers' current beliefs
- Infer universal human themes and issues that affect human problems across the world
- Infer the overarching theme(s) in a collection of short stories
- Compare inferences with those of other readers and consider alternative interpretations of characters' motives and the writer's message

- Infer the larger message in a text (i.e., what can be learned from it beyond the facts)
- Infer information from illustrations, photographs, drawings, and graphics that add meaning to the text
- Infer information about characters, setting, plot, and action from graphic texts, in which illustrations carry much of the meaning
- Make inferences from print narrative alone (no pictures)
- Infer the meaning of a range of graphics that require reader interpretation and are essential to comprehending the text
- Infer the significance of design and other features of the peritext
- Infer the meaning of some simple symbolism
- Infer the meanings of words used ironically or satirically
- Understand the connotative meanings of words that contribute to the mood of the text
- Infer the mood of the text from the writer's use of language and the characteristics of the illustrations
- Infer beliefs, customs, and perspectives of people who live in other cultures
- Infer beliefs, customs, and perspectives of people who live in the near and distant past
- Infer what life might be like and what people might believe and do at a time in the future
- Infer important information from familiar content as well as topics more distant from students' typical experience: e.g., different parts of the world, history, science

THINKING *ABOUT* THE TEXT

ANALYZING

- Understand that there may be different genres and special forms in each of the larger categories of fiction and nonfiction
- Understand that a graphic text may represent any fiction or nonfiction genre
- Identify fictional and factual components in a hybrid text
- Discuss a writer's purpose in selecting a particular genre, topic, subject, or type of narrative structure
- Understand and describe characteristics of fiction genres, including realistic fiction, historical fiction, traditional literature (folktale, fairy tale, fable, myth, legend), fantasy, and hybrid text
- Notice elements and basic motifs of fantasy: e.g., the supernatural, imaginary and otherworldly creatures, gods and goddesses, talking animals, struggle between good and evil, magic, fantastic or magical objects, wishes, trickery, transformations
- Identify and understand characteristics of special types of fiction: e.g., mystery; adventure story; animal story; family, friends, and school story

- Understand that fiction genres may be combined within one text
- Understand the difference between realism and fantasy across fiction texts
- Understand and describe the characteristics of nonfiction genres, including expository nonfiction, narrative nonfiction, biography, autobiography, memoir, procedural text, persuasive text, and hybrid text
- Understand that nonfiction genres may be combined within one text
- Notice that a biography is built around significant events, problems to overcome, and the subject's decisions
- Understand that the information and ideas in a text are related to each other and notice how the author presents this
- Recognize a writer's use of embedded forms (e.g., letters, directions, journal entries) within narrative and expository text structures
- Recognize and understand variety in narrative structure: e.g., circular plot, parallel plots, main plot and subplot(s), story-within-a-story, flashback, flash-forward, time-lapse

Selecting Goals Behaviors and Understandings to Notice, Teach, and Support *(cont.)*

THINKING *ABOUT* THE TEXT *(continued)*

ANALYZING *(continued)*

- Understand that a procedural nonfiction book may have "how-to" procedures embedded within it
- Recognize a writer's use of underlying text structures: e.g., description, cause and effect, chronological sequence, temporal sequence, categorization, comparison and contrast, problem and solution, question and answer
- Notice and understand expository text structure (categorized information) and the use of narrative structure for biographical texts and other types of narrative nonfiction
- Think analytically about the significance of a title and notice symbolism or multiple meanings
- Notice aspects of the writer's craft: e.g., style, syntax, use of one or more narrators
- Notice characteristics of settings in fantasy that require believing in magic and/or an imaginary world
- Understand the characteristics of settings (cultural, physical, historical) and the way they affect characters' attitudes and decisions
- Think analytically about the significance of the setting and its importance to the plot
- Identify the central story problem or conflict in a text with multiple episodes or parallel plots
- Notice when a text has a moral lesson close to the end of the story
- Notice how a writer reveals main and supporting characters by what they do, think, or say, and by what others say about them or how others respond to them
- Analyze the roles of supporting characters and how they are important (or unimportant) in the story and in the development of main character(s)
- Analyze a text to think about the perspective from which the story is told and notice when that perspective changes
- Notice language used to show chronological and temporal order
- Notice a writer's use of language and state how it specifically adds to the meaning, quality, and mood of a text
- Notice a writer's use of figurative language and state how it specifically adds to the meaning or enjoyment of a text
- Notice a writer's use of both common and sophisticated connectives as well as some academic connectives
- Notice a writer's use of non-sentences for literary effect
- After reading several books by an author, discuss style, use of language, typical content
- Understand that a writer selects first-, third-, or second-person point of view to tell a story and also may use several points of view in the same story

- Notice a writer's use of figurative language and state how it specifically adds to the meaning or enjoyment of a text
- Notice a writer's use of poetic and expressive language in dialogue
- Notice how a writer creates, sustains, and releases suspense
- Notice literary language typical of traditional literature: e.g., *a long time ago there lived, long ago and far away, once there lived*
- Notice a writer's use of humorous words or onomatopoetic words and talk about how they add to the action
- Understand that a nonfiction writer may use argument in a persuasive text
- Notice the logic and structure of a writer's argument
- Notice how a writer uses language in a persuasive way
- Notice how the writer/illustrator selects and places photos in a way that tells a story or communicates a larger meaning in a photo essay
- Understand that illustrations carry the dialogue and action in a graphic text
- Understand how illustrations and text work together to enhance meaning and communicate the mood of the text
- Use academic language to talk about genres: e.g., *fiction; family, friends, and school story; folktale; animal story; humorous story; fairy tale; fable; tall tale; realistic fiction; mystery; adventure story; sports story; historical fiction; fantasy; traditional literature; myth; legend; science fiction; nonfiction; informational text; informational book; factual text; how-to book; biography; autobiography; narrative nonfiction; memoir; procedural text; persuasive text, hybrid text; expository text*
- Use academic language to talk about forms: e.g., *series book, play, chapter book, comics, graphic text, letter, sequel, short story, diary entry, journal entry, news article, feature article*
- Use academic language to talk about literary features: e.g., *beginning, ending, character, question and answer, main character, message, dialogue, topic, events, setting, description, problem and solution, comparison and contrast, main idea, flashback, conflict, resolution, theme, descriptive language, simile, cause and effect, categorization, persuasive language, plot, character development, supporting character, point of view, figurative language, metaphor, temporal sequence, chronological sequence, subject, argument*
- Use specific language to talk about book and print features: e.g., *front cover, back cover, page, author, illustrator, illustration, photograph, title, label, drawing, heading, caption, table of contents, chapter, chapter title, dedication, sidebar, glossary, map, diagram, infographic, author's note, illustrator's note, section, book jacket, acknowledgments, subheading, text, pronunciation guide, chart, graph, timeline, index, foreword, cutaway, footnote, epilogue, endnote, appendix, references*

Selecting Goals Behaviors and Understandings to Notice, Teach, and Support *(cont.)*

THINKING *ABOUT* THE TEXT *(continued)*

CRITIQUING

- Evaluate the quality of illustrations or graphics and share opinions
- Assess how graphics add to the quality of the text or provide additional information
- Think critically about characters and their actions, and share opinions
- Assess whether a text is authentic from their reading both fiction and nonfiction
- Notice the references and assurances the writer provides to authenticate a text
- Distinguish between primary and secondary sources and think critically about the authenticity of a text
- Distinguish between fact and opinion
- Agree or disagree with a writer's arguments and give rationales for opinions

- Share opinions about a written text and/or about illustrations and give rationales and examples
- Evaluate aspects of a text that add to enjoyment: e.g., humorous character or surprising information
- Express tastes and preferences in reading and support choices with descriptions and examples of literary elements: e.g., genre, setting, plot, theme, character, style, and language
- Evaluate the authenticity of a text in terms of readers' own experiences as preadolescents (or adolescents)
- Think critically about how a writer does (or does not) make a topic interesting and engaging, and share opinions
- Think critically about the quality of a text and how well it exemplifies its genre, and share opinions
- Talk about why the subject of a biography is important or sets an example for others

Planning for Word Work After Guided Reading

Using your recent observations of the readers' ability to take words apart quickly and efficiently while reading text, plan for one to three minutes of active engagement of students' attention to letters, sounds, and words. Prioritize the readers' noticing of print features and active hands-on use of magnetic letters, a white board, word cards, or pencil and paper to promote fluency and flexibility in visual processing.

Examples:

- Make a full range of plural nouns, including regular plurals that require spelling changes and irregular plurals (*revolution/revolutions; recess/recesses; emergency/emergencies; cactus/cacti*)
- Work flexibly with a base word, changing letters or adding or taking away one or more affixes to make a new word (*mash/mask/masked/unmask*)
- Recognize and use word roots (Greek and Latin) to take apart and determine the meanings of some English words (*mem,* meaning "mindful," in *memory,* "ability to remember or keep in the mind")

- Recognize and use words that have similar meanings because they have the same root (*port* meaning "to carry": *porter* meaning "person employed to carry loads or baggage," *portable* meaning "easily carried")`
- Sort words based on any word features
- Break apart multisyllable words by syllable (*nim/ble, pho/no/graph, sit/u/a/tion, u/ni/ver/si/ty*)

- Recognize and break words with an open syllable and a long vowel sound (*e/vil, ho/ly, hu/mor*) and a closed syllable with a short vowel sound (*ran/som, ref/uge, prof/it*)
- Recognize and use homophones (*capitol, capital; vain, vein; steak, stake*) and homographs (*sole, squash, temple*)

Readers at Level

At level V, readers are challenged by highly sophisticated genres such as high fantasy, myths, and legends. Texts vary a great deal in length; many read complex feature articles on a variety of nonfiction topics; they read many examples of argument and may also process speeches (current or historical) that reveal the speaker's attitudes and views. Readers understand perspectives different from their own, including settings and characters far distant in time or geography. Most reading is silent; all dimensions of fluency are well established in oral reading. In addition, readers can be very expressive when they present poetry or readers' theater. Readers are challenged by many longer descriptive words, by content-specific and technical words, and by idioms, words, and phrases from languages other than English. They can take apart multisyllable words and use a full range of word-solving strategies. They search for and use information in an integrated way, using complex graphics and texts that present content requiring background knowledge. They use and understand disciplinary vocabulary as well as academic vocabulary to talk about texts. Readers make a rich array of connections across fiction and nonfiction texts—themes, overarching big ideas, insights into social responsibility, elements of the writer's craft. They continue to grow in the academic vocabulary they control.

Selecting Texts Characteristics of Texts at **Level V**

GENRE

▶ Fiction

- Realistic fiction
- Historical fiction
- Traditional literature (folktale, myth, legend)
- High fantasy and science fiction
- Hybrid texts
- Special types of fiction: e.g., mystery; adventure story; sports story; animal story; family, friends, and school story; humorous story

▶ Nonfiction

- Expository nonfiction
- Narrative nonfiction
- Biography
- Autobiography
- Memoir
- Procedural texts
- Persuasive texts
- Hybrid texts

FORMS

- Series books
- Picture books
- Chapter books
- Chapter books with sequels
- Plays
- Readers' theater scripts
- Graphic texts

- Letters, diaries, and journal entries
- Short stories
- Photo essays and news articles
- Speeches

TEXT STRUCTURE

- Texts with multiple episodes that are elaborated with many details
- Embedded forms (e.g., letters, directions, journal entries, emails) within narrative and expository structures
- Variations in structure: e.g., story-within-a-story, flashback, flash-forward, time-lapse
- Fiction books with chapters connected to a single plot
- Texts with circular plot or parallel plots
- Longer texts with main plot and subplots
- Complex plots with multiple story lines
- Collections of short stories related to an overarching theme
- Texts that change perspective and/or narrator within the larger narrative
- Nonfiction books divided into sections, and some with subsections
- Underlying structural patterns: description, cause and effect, chronological sequence, temporal sequence, categorization, comparison and contrast, problem and solution, question and answer

CONTENT

- Content interesting to and relevant for the reader
- Some books with little or no picture support for content: e.g., chapter books
- Much content that requires accessing prior knowledge
- Content that invites critical thinking to judge authenticity and accuracy
- Content that requires the reader to take on perspectives from diverse cultures and bring cultural knowledge to understanding
- Most texts with new content that will engage and interest readers and expand knowledge: e.g., travel, experience with other cultures, adventures in science, survival
- Some content that requires emotional and social maturity to understand
- Complex content that requires analysis and study to understand
- Content that goes beyond students' immediate experience
- Texts that require content knowledge of disciplines: e.g., history, geography, culture, language, sciences, arts, math concepts
- Much content that requires the reader to search for information in graphics: e.g., maps, charts, diagrams, illustrated drawings, labeled photographs

Pop!

I jumped.

"What was that?" Sissy asked, big-eyed.

I secured the bottom lock. "Uh... probably just a car. It must've backfired." I wanted to open the door and look outside in the worst way. Instead I turned the deadbolt tight.

Pop!

I pushed my fingers against the hard metal of the lock. I liked how cold and solid it felt, and I reminded myself I was not scared.

"Sissy! No!"

One second of inattention, that's all it took. Sissy had run to the heavy drapes covering the front window. Well, not really drapes—blankets. Because they were cheaper, Mom said. Thicker, is what I thought.

I grabbed my sister and pulled her back from the window.

6

7

THEMES AND IDEAS

- Texts with themes and ideas that involve the problems of preadolescents and adolescents
- Themes and ideas that require a perspective not familiar to the reader
- Complex ideas on many different topics that require real or vicarious experience (through reading) for understanding
- Texts with deeper meanings applicable to important human problems and social issues: e.g., hardship, war, racism, economic struggle, the environment
- Many ideas and themes that require understanding of cultural diversity
- Some texts with abstract themes that require inferential thinking
- Themes that evoke alternative interpretations

LANGUAGE AND LITERARY FEATURES

- Settings that are distant in time and geography
- Settings in fantasy that require the reader to accept elements of another world that could not exist in the real world
- Settings that are important to comprehension of the fiction narrative or biography
- Variety in narrative plot structure: e.g., story-within-a-story, simple flashback
- Main characters and supporting characters
- Multidimensional characters
- Characters revealed by what they say, think, and do and by what others say and think about them
- Characters revealed over a series of events, chapters, or book series

- Reasons for character change that are complex and require inference
- Some texts that reveal the perspectives of more than one character
- Variety in presentation of dialogue: e.g., dialogue among multiple characters, dialogue with pronouns, split dialogue, direct dialogue, including unassigned dialogue and long stretches of dialogue
- Some chains of unassigned dialogue for which speakers must be inferred
- Most texts written in first- or third-person narrative, with some procedural texts in second person
- Basic motifs of traditional literature and modern fantasy: e.g., struggle between good and evil, fantastic or magical objects, wishes, trickery, transformations

Selecting Texts Characteristics of Texts at **Level V** (cont.)

LANGUAGE AND LITERARY FEATURES (continued)

- Moral lesson near the end of the story (sometimes explicitly stated)
- Literary language typical of traditional literature: e.g., *long ago and far away*
- Poetic language and figurative language: e.g., metaphor, simile
- Language and events that convey an emotional atmosphere (mood) in a text, affecting how the reader feels: e.g., tension, suspense, sadness, happiness, curiosity
- Use of symbolism
- Some colloquial language in dialogue that reflects characters' personalities and/or setting
- Procedural language
- Language used to make comparisons
- Descriptive language
- Language used to show chronological order and temporal sequence
- Persuasive language and argument
- Language that reveals the author's attitude or feelings toward a subject or topic (the tone that is reflected in the style of writing): e.g., lighthearted, ironic, earnest, affectionate, formal, sarcastic, angry

SENTENCE COMPLEXITY

- Wide range of declarative, imperative, exclamatory, or interrogative sentences
- Variation in sentence length and structure, with multiple embedded phrases and clauses
- Sentences with a wide variety of parts of speech, including multiple adjectives, adverbs, and prepositional phrases
- Sentences with common connectives and sophisticated connectives
- Some sentences with academic connectives
- Long sentences joined by semicolons or colons
- Frequent use of parenthetical material embedded in sentences
- Some non-sentences for literary effect

VOCABULARY

- Most words that appear in the vocabulary of mature language users (Tier 2)
- Many words particular to a discipline (Tier 3)
- Wide variation in words used to assign dialogue
- Many words with multiple meanings
- Many words with figurative meaning
- Frequent use of idioms
- New vocabulary requiring strategic action to understand: e.g., derive meaning from context, use reference tools, notice morphology, use word roots, use analogy
- Words with connotative meanings that are essential to understanding the text
- Common connectives that link ideas and clarify meaning and are typical of oral speech, as well as many sophisticated connectives that do not appear often in everyday oral language: e.g., *although, however, meantime, meanwhile moreover, otherwise, unless, therefore, though, unless, until, whenever, yet*
- Some academic connectives that link ideas and clarify meaning and that appear in written texts but are seldom used in everyday oral language: e.g., *conversely, eventually, finally, in contrast, initially, likewise, nevertheless, nonetheless, previously, specifically, ultimately, whereas, whereby*
- Words used ironically
- Some words from regional or historical dialects
- Some words (including slang) used informally by particular groups of people
- Some words from languages other than English
- Some archaic words

WORDS

- Many multisyllable words, some technical or scientific
- Full range of plurals
- Unlimited number of high-frequency words with multiple syllables
- Multisyllable words with some complex letter-sound relationships
- Multisyllable proper nouns that are difficult to decode

- Words that offer decoding challenges because they are archaic, come from regional dialect, or are from languages other than English
- Wide range of contractions and possessives
- Full range of compound words
- Base words with affixes (prefixes and suffixes)
- Common, sophisticated, and academic connectives

ILLUSTRATIONS

- Illustrations that enhance and extend meaning in the text
- Short texts that have illustrations on every page or every few pages
- Texts with illustrations every three or four pages
- Short chapter books with only a few illustrations and some longer books
- Texts with no illustrations other than decorative elements such as vignettes
- Variety of layout in illustrations and print
- A few books with black-and-white illustrations
- Some complex, nuanced illustrations that communicate mood and meaning (literal, figurative, symbolic) to match or extend the text
- Graphics that require reader interpretation and are essential for comprehending informational text
- More than one kind of graphics on a page spread
- A range of graphics that provides information that matches and extends the text: e.g., photograph and drawing with label and/or caption; diagram, cutaway; map with legend or key, scale; infographic; chart; graph; timeline

BOOK AND PRINT FEATURES

LENGTH

- Wide variation in length (mostly shorter than forty-eight pages)
- Wide variation in number of words (2,000+)
- Some books divided into chapters
- Books divided into sections and subsections

GUIDED READING

LEVEL
V

Selecting Texts Characteristics of Texts at **Level V** *(cont.)*

PRINT AND LAYOUT

- Mostly small but readable font size
- Variety in print and background color
- Variety in print placement, reflecting different genres
- Italics indicating unspoken thought in some texts
- Information shown in a variety of picture and print combinations in graphic texts
- Captions under pictures that provide important information
- Print and illustrations integrated in most texts, with print wrapping around pictures
- Print placed in sidebars and graphics that provide important information

PUNCTUATION

- Period, comma, question mark, exclamation mark, semicolon, colon, parentheses, quotation marks, hyphen, dash, and ellipses in most texts

ORGANIZATIONAL TOOLS

- Title, table of contents, chapter title, heading, subheading, sidebar

TEXT RESOURCES

- Dedication, acknowledgments, author's note, pronunciation guide, glossary, index, foreword, footnote, endnote, epilogue, appendix, references
- Texts with design features that add to the aesthetic appeal of the whole (peritext)
- Texts with design features that enhance meaning, communicate culture, or create mood (peritext)

Selecting Goals Behaviors and Understandings to Notice, Teach, and Support *(cont.)*

THINKING *ABOUT* THE TEXT *(continued)*

ANALYZING *(continued)*

- Analyze a text to think about the perspective from which the story is told and notice when that perspective changes
- Notice how a writer creates, sustains, and releases suspense
- Analyze complex messages and ideas in a text
- Notice language used to show chronological and temporal order
- Reflect on a writer's use of words with connotative meanings, and discuss what it conveys to the reader
- Notice a writer's use of figurative language and state how it specifically adds to the meaning or enjoyment of a text
- Notice a writer's use of language and state how it specifically adds to the meaning, quality, and mood of a text
- Notice and interpret language that reveals the writer's attitude and communicates the tone of a text
- Notice a writer's use of both common and sophisticated connectives as well as some academic connectives
- Discuss why a writer might insert parenthetical information into a sentence
- Locate language in a text that reveals setting, problem, character traits, character change, theme, symbolic meanings, narrator, mood, tone
- Understand that a writer selects first-, third-, or second-person point of view to tell a story and also may use several points of view in the same story
- Notice a writer's use of poetic and expressive language in dialogue
- Notice literary language typical of traditional literature: e.g., *a long time ago there lived, long ago and far away, once there lived*
- Notice a writer's use of humorous words or onomatopoetic words and talk about how they add to the action
- Understand that a nonfiction writer may use argument in a persuasive text
- Notice how a writer uses language in a persuasive way

- Notice how the writer/illustrator selects and places photos in a way that tells a story or communicates a larger meaning in a photo essay
- Understand that illustrations carry the dialogue and action in a graphic text
- Understand how illustrations and text work together to enhance meaning and communicate the mood of the text
- Use academic language to talk about genres: e.g., *fiction; family, friends, and school story; folktale; animal story; humorous story; fairy tale; fable; tall tale; realistic fiction; mystery; adventure story; sports story; historical fiction; fantasy; traditional literature; myth; legend; science fiction; nonfiction; informational text; informational book; factual text; how-to book; biography; autobiography; narrative nonfiction; memoir; procedural text; persuasive text, hybrid text; expository text*
- Use academic language to talk about forms: e.g., *series book, play, chapter book, comics, graphic text, letter, sequel, short story, diary entry, journal entry, news article, feature article*
- Use academic language to talk about literary features: e.g., *beginning, ending, character, question and answer, main character, message, dialogue, topic, events, setting, description, problem and solution, comparison and contrast, main idea, flashback, conflict, resolution, theme, descriptive language, simile, cause and effect, categorization, persuasive language, plot, character development, supporting character, point of view, figurative language, metaphor, temporal sequence, chronological sequence, subject, argument, subplot*
- Use specific language to talk about book and print features: e.g., *front cover, back cover, page, author, illustrator, illustration, photograph, title, label, drawing, heading, caption, table of contents, chapter, chapter title, dedication, sidebar, glossary, map, diagram, infographic, author's note, illustrator's note, section, book jacket, acknowledgments, subheading, text, pronunciation guide, chart, graph, timeline, index, foreword, cutaway, footnote, epilogue, endnote, appendix, references, prologue, bibliography*

Selecting Goals Behaviors and Understandings to Notice, Teach, and Support *(cont.)*

THINKING *ABOUT* THE TEXT *(continued)*

CRITIQUING

- Critique a writer's argument in terms of whether it is logical and well supported
- Evaluate the quality of illustrations or graphics and share opinions
- Assess how graphics add to the quality of the text or provide additional information
- Think critically about characters and their actions, and share opinions
- Assess whether a text is authentic in relation to information from their reading both fiction and nonfiction
- Notice the references and assurances the writer provides to authenticate a text
- Distinguish between primary and secondary sources and think critically about the authenticity of a text
- Distinguish between fact and opinion
- Agree or disagree with a writer's arguments and give rationales for opinions
- Share opinions about a written text and/or illustrations and give rationales and examples

- Evaluate aspects of a text that add to enjoyment: e.g., humorous character or surprising information
- Express tastes and preferences in reading and support choices with descriptions and examples of literary elements: e.g., genre, setting, plot, theme, character, style, and language
- Evaluate the authenticity of a text in terms of readers' own experiences as preadolescents and adolescents
- Think critically about how a writer does (or does not) make a topic interesting and engaging, and share opinions
- Think critically about the quality of a text and how well it exemplifies its genre, and share opinions
- Think critically about the subject of a biography, discussing the achievements, admirable traits, and flaws of the individual
- Talk about why the subject of a biography is important or sets an example for others
- Notice persuasion and think critically about factors such as bias and unsupported statements

Planning for Word Work After Guided Reading

Using your recent observations of the readers' ability to take words apart quickly and efficiently while reading text, plan for one to three minutes of active engagement of students' attention to letters, sounds, and words. Prioritize the readers' noticing of print features and active hands-on use of magnetic letters, a white board, word cards, or pencil and paper to promote fluency and flexibility in visual processing.

Examples:

- Make a full range of plural nouns, including regular plurals that require spelling changes and irregular plurals (*flake/flakes; kindness/kindnesses; ray/rays; bully/bullies; ox/oxen*)
- Work flexibly with a base word, changing letters or adding or taking away one or more affixes to make a new word (*crane/crank/crank<u>ing</u>/<u>un</u>cranking*) and discussing changes in meaning or function
- Sort words to put together words with the same base, words with the same prefix, words with the same suffix
- Make word ladders by changing base words, prefixes, or suffixes

- Recognize and use word roots (Greek and Latin) to take apart and determine the meanings of some English words (*aud*, meaning "hear," in *audience*, "a group of people gathered to hear or see something")
- Recognize and use words that have similar meanings because they have the same root (*fer* meaning "carry": <u>*ferry*</u> meaning "to carry people, vehicles, and goods across a narrow stretch of water," *trans<u>fer</u>* meaning "to move from one person or place to another")
- Make word webs by centering on a base word or word root and thinking of the words related to it

- Break apart multisyllable words by syllable (*chis/el, a/ban/don, a/bil/i/ty, pro/nun/ci/a/tion*)
- Sort words by any word feature
- Have an "open sort" where students notice characteristics of words and ask other students to determine the feature they used for sorting
- Recognize and use an open syllable with a long vowel sound (*la/bor, fe/ver, po/lo*) and a closed syllable with a short vowel sound (*ban/jo, grid/dle, con/crete*)
- Recognize and use homophones (*read, reed; aisle, isle; rode, road*) and homographs (*arch, bluff*)

Readers at Level

At level W, readers process the full range of genres. They automatically and skillfully adjust strategic actions according the needs presented by certain genres. Also, they understand the human condition and problems as they meet them again and again in texts. High fantasy, myths, and legends offer added challenge and require readers to identify classical motifs such as "the hero's quest." Biographies offer a range of individuals who may not be previously known to readers and may not be admirable. Readers will encounter mature themes that expand their knowledge of social issues. In addition, readers will encounter advanced literary elements and devices, such as author's tone, mood, symbolism, and irony. Readers use high-level academic language to talk about texts. Themes are multidimensional and may be understood on several levels. Most reading is silent; all dimensions of fluency in oral reading are well established. In addition, students are able to read aloud with expressiveness after practice (for example, in readers' theater). Readers are challenged by a heavy load of content-specific and technical words that require using embedded definitions, background knowledge, and a wide variety of text features. Readers use disciplinary and academic language. They search for and use information in an integrated way, using complex graphics and texts that present content requiring background knowledge. Many texts require knowledge of historical events and may contain language that is archaic or from regional dialects or languages other than English. Control of academic language continues to expand.

Selecting Texts Characteristics of Texts at **Level W**

GENRE

▶ **Fiction**

- Realistic fiction
- Historical fiction
- Traditional literature (folktale, myth, legend)
- High fantasy and science fiction
- Hybrid texts
- Special types of fiction: e.g., mystery; adventure story; sports story; animal story; family, friends, and school story; humorous story

▶ **Nonfiction**

- Expository nonfiction
- Narrative nonfiction
- Biography
- Autobiography
- Memoir
- Procedural texts
- Persuasive texts
- Hybrid texts

FORMS

- Series books
- Picture books
- Chapter books
- Chapter books with sequels
- Plays
- Readers' theater scripts

- Graphic texts
- Letters, diaries, and journal entries
- Short stories
- Photo essays and news articles
- Speeches

TEXT STRUCTURE

- Texts with multiple episodes that are elaborated with many details
- Embedded forms (e.g., letters, directions, journal entries, emails) within narrative and expository structures
- Variations in structure: e.g., story-within-a-story, flashback, flash-forward, time-lapse
- Fiction books with chapters connected to a single plot
- Texts with circular plot or parallel plots
- Longer texts with main plot and subplots
- Complex plots with multiple story lines
- Collections of short stories related to an overarching theme
- Texts with a change in perspective and/or narrator signaled by new chapter, section, or paragraph; language or literary feature (e.g., verb tense, imagery, setting); or print features (e.g., font, print placement)
- Nonfiction books divided into sections, and some with subsections

- Underlying structural patterns: description, cause and effect, chronological sequence, temporal sequence, categorization, comparison and contrast, problem and solution, question and answer

CONTENT

- Content interesting to and relevant for the reader
- Many books with little or no picture support for content: e.g., chapter books
- Much content that requires accessing prior knowledge
- Content that invites critical thinking to judge authenticity and accuracy
- Content that requires the reader to take on perspectives from diverse cultures and bring cultural knowledge to understanding
- Most texts have new content that will engage and interest readers and expand knowledge: e.g., travel, experience with other cultures, adventures in science, survival
- Some content that requires emotional and social maturity to understand
- Complex content that requires analysis and study to understand
- Most content goes beyond students' immediate experience

Shiny memories from Chihuly's childhood fill the studio.
Marbles that rolled and clinked.
Japanese fishing floats, washed up on beaches.
Now Chihuly wants the orbs to be big, bigger,
as big as they can be.
He stacks them up,
and spreads them about,
rolling shooters suspended in a moment.

Chihuly's glass
cannot stay on the table or shelf.
Chihuly's glass
sprouts from snow, from rock,
dangles from the ceiling,
shimmers at the bottom of a swimming pool.
Chihuly hangs glass from bridges,
castles, canals.
Perches it in gardens,
and floats it down rivers.

shooter (SHOO-ter) a marble used to knock other marbles in and out of a circle

12

13

- Texts that require content knowledge of disciplines: e.g., history, geography, culture, language, sciences, arts, math concepts
- Much content that requires the reader to search for information in graphics: e.g., maps, charts, diagrams, illustrated drawings, labeled photographs

THEMES AND IDEAS

- Many texts with themes and ideas that involve societal issues important to adolescents: e.g., family, growing up, sexuality
- Themes and ideas that require a perspective not familiar to the reader
- Complex ideas on many different topics that require real or vicarious experience (through reading) for understanding
- Texts with deeper meanings applicable to important human problems and social issues: e.g., hardship, war, racism, economic struggle, social class, the environment

- Wide range of challenging themes and ideas that build social awareness and reveal insights into the human condition
- Many ideas and themes that require understanding of cultural diversity
- Texts with abstract themes that require inferential thinking
- Texts that present multiple themes that may be understood in many layers
- Themes that evoke alternative interpretations

LANGUAGE AND LITERARY FEATURES

- Settings that are distant in time and geography
- Settings in fantasy that require the reader to accept elements of another world that could not exist in the real world
- Settings that are important to comprehension of the fiction narrative or biography

- Variety in narrative plot structure: e.g., story-within-a-story, simple flashback
- Main characters and supporting characters
- Multidimensional characters
- Characters revealed by what they say, think, and do and by what others say and think about them
- Characters revealed over a series of events, chapters, or book series
- Reasons for character change that are complex and require inference
- Some texts that reveal the perspectives of more than one character
- "Round" characters that have a complex range of good and bad attributes and that change during the course of the plot, and "flat" characters that do not change but may play an important role in the plot
- Variety in presentation of dialogue: e.g., dialogue among multiple characters, dialogue with pronouns, split dialogue, direct dialogue, including unassigned dialogue and long stretches of dialogue

GUIDED READING

LEVEL
W

Selecting Texts Characteristics of Texts at **Level W** *(cont.)*

LANGUAGE AND LITERARY FEATURES *(continued)*

- Some chains of unassigned dialogue for which speakers must be inferred
- Most texts written in first- or third-person narrative, with some procedural texts in second person
- Basic motifs of traditional literature and modern fantasy: e.g., struggle between good and evil, fantastic or magical objects, wishes, trickery, transformations
- Moral lesson near the end of the story (sometimes explicitly stated)
- Literary language typical of traditional literature: e.g., *long ago and far away*
- Poetic language and figurative language: e.g., metaphor, simile
- Language and events that convey an emotional atmosphere (mood) in a text, affecting how the reader feels: e.g., tension, suspense, sadness, happiness, curiosity
- Use of symbolism
- Some colloquial language in dialogue that reflects characters' personalities and/or setting
- Procedural language
- Language used to make comparisons
- Descriptive language
- Language used to show chronological order and temporal sequence
- Persuasive language and argument
- Language that reveals the author's attitude or feelings toward a subject or topic (the tone that is reflected in the style of writing): e.g., lighthearted, ironic, earnest, affectionate, formal, sarcastic, angry

SENTENCE COMPLEXITY

- Wide range of declarative, imperative, exclamatory, or interrogative sentences
- Variation in sentence length and structure
- Sentences with a wide variety of parts of speech, including multiple adjectives, adverbs, and prepositional phrases
- Sentences with common, sophisticated, and academic connectives
- Long sentences joined by semicolons or colons
- Frequent use of parenthetical material embedded in sentences
- Some non-sentences for literary effect

VOCABULARY

- Most words that appear in the vocabulary of mature language users (Tier 2)
- Many words particular to a discipline (Tier 3)
- Wide variation in words used to assign dialogue
- Many words with multiple meanings
- Many words with figurative meaning
- Frequent use of idioms
- New vocabulary requiring strategic action to understand: e.g., derive meaning from context, use reference tools, notice morphology, use word roots, use analogy
- Words with connotative meanings that are essential to understanding the text
- Common connectives that link ideas and clarify meaning and are typical of oral speech, as well as many sophisticated connectives that do not appear often in everyday oral language: e.g., *although, however, meantime, meanwhile moreover, otherwise, therefore, though, unless, until, whenever, yet*
- Some academic connectives that link ideas and clarify meaning and that appear in written texts but are seldom used in everyday oral language: e.g., *conversely, eventually, finally, in contrast, initially, likewise, nevertheless, nonetheless, previously, specifically, ultimately, whereas, whereby*
- Words used ironically
- Some words from regional or historical dialects
- Words (including slang) used informally by particular groups of people
- Words from languages other than English
- Some archaic words

WORDS

- A large number of multisyllable words, many technical or scientific
- Full range of plurals
- Unlimited number of high-frequency words with multiple syllables
- Multisyllable words with some complex letter-sound relationships
- Multisyllable proper nouns that are difficult to decode

- Words that offer decoding challenges because they are archaic, come from regional dialect, or are from languages other than English
- Wide range of contractions and possessives
- Full range of compound words
- Base words with affixes (prefixes and suffixes)
- Common, sophisticated, and academic connectives

ILLUSTRATIONS

- Illustrations that enhance and extend meaning in the text
- Short texts that have illustrations on every page or every few pages
- Texts with illustrations every three or four pages
- Texts with no illustrations other than decorative elements such as vignettes
- Variety of layout in illustrations and print
- A few books with black-and-white illustrations
- Graphic texts that provide a great deal of information in the illustrations
- Some complex, nuanced illustrations that communicate mood and meaning (literal, figurative, symbolic) to match or extend the text
- Graphics that require reader interpretation and are essential for comprehending informational text
- Several kinds of graphics on a single page spread
- A range of graphics that provide information that matches and extends the text: e.g., photograph and drawing with label and/or caption; diagram, cutaway; map with legend or key, scale; infographic; chart; graph; timeline

BOOK AND PRINT FEATURES

LENGTH

- Wide variation in length (mostly shorter than forty-eight pages)
- Wide variation in number of words (2,000+)
- Some books divided into chapters
- Books divided into sections and subsections

PRINT AND LAYOUT

- Mostly small but readable font size
- Variety in print and background color

Selecting Texts Characteristics of Texts at **Level W** (cont.)

- Variety in print placement, reflecting different genres
- Italics indicating unspoken thought in some texts
- Information shown in a variety of picture and print combinations in graphic texts
- Captions under pictures that provide important information
- Print and illustrations integrated in most texts, with print wrapping around pictures
- Print placed in sidebars and graphics that provide important information
- Some archaic print in historical texts

PUNCTUATION

- Period, comma, question mark, exclamation mark, semicolon, colon, parentheses, quotation marks, hyphen, dash, and ellipses in most texts

ORGANIZATIONAL TOOLS

- Title, table of contents, chapter title, heading, subheading, sidebar

TEXT RESOURCES

- Dedication, acknowledgments, author's note, pronunciation guide, glossary, index, foreword, footnote, endnote, epilogue, appendix, references
- Texts with design features that add to the aesthetic appeal of the whole (peritext)
- Texts with design features that enhance meaning, communicate culture, or create mood (peritext)

GUIDED READING

LEVEL **W**

Selecting Goals Behaviors and Understandings to Notice, Teach, and Support

THINKING *WITHIN* THE TEXT

SEARCHING FOR AND USING INFORMATION

- Sustain searching for information texts with wide variety in length
- Sustain searching over long and highly complex sentences that include multiple phrases, clauses, and lists, and the full range of punctuation marks
- Search for information in texts with multiple features and very dense print
- Search for information in complex texts that rely on academic discourse
- Search for information in texts that use academic vocabulary and present highly complex concepts
- Search for and use information to understand multiple plots, perspectives, and themes in a single text
- Search for information and language that states or implies the larger message(s) of the text
- Use background knowledge to search for and understand disciplinary information
- Use organizational tools to search for information: e.g., title, table of contents, chapter title, heading, subheading, sidebar, callout
- Use text resources to search for information: e.g., acknowledgments, author's note, pronunciation guide, glossary, references, index
- Search for information in sentences that vary in length, structure, and punctuation based on text complexity
- Search for information in sentences with variation in placement of subject, verb, adjectives, and adverbs
- Search for information in dialogue presented in a variety of ways: e.g., assigned and unassigned, split dialogue, direct dialogue
- Search for information in a strategic way, using knowledge of text structure and readers' tools
- Use knowledge of linear narrative structure (chronological order) within multiple episodes to search for and use information
- Use knowledge of variations in narrative structure to search for and use information e.g., story-within-a-story (framed narrative); flashback and flashforward (fractured narrative); circular narrative; multiple or parallel plots
- Search for information in a variety of narrative structures: e.g., story-within-a-story (framed narrative); flashback and flash-forward (fractured narrative); circular narrative; multiple or parallel plots
- Notice and use punctuation marks: e.g., period, comma, question mark, exclamation mark, semicolon, colon, parentheses, quotation marks, hyphen, dash, ellipses
- When needed, reread to search for and use information from the body text, sidebars, insets, and graphics
- Search for and use information in texts with variety in placement of the body text, sidebars, and graphics

MONITORING AND SELF-CORRECTING

- Self-monitor reading using multiple sources of information: i.e., background knowledge, syntax, word meaning, word structure, awareness of text structure, meaning of the whole text, graphics, layout, design
- Self-correct covertly prior to or after error and showing little overt self-correction
- Closely monitor understanding of texts using knowledge of a wide range of genres and forms: e.g., realistic, historical, high fantasy, science fiction, myths, and legends, poetry, plays
- Use understandings of literary elements (e.g., plot, main and supporting characters, setting, narrative structure) to monitor and correct reading
- Use awareness of narrative structure and of character attributes (many of which may be multidimensional and change) to self-monitor and self-correct
- Use content knowledge of the topic of a text to self-monitor and self-correct
- Use knowledge of nonfiction genres to monitor understanding of a text: e.g., expository nonfiction, narrative nonfiction, biography, autobiography, memoir, procedural text, persuasive text
- Use knowledge of a range of academic disciplines to monitor understandings of conceptual ideas that cross disciplines
- Monitor understanding using knowledge of disciplinary vocabulary
- Use information from graphics (e.g., maps, diagrams, charts, photos, illustrations) to self-monitor reading

SOLVING WORDS

▶ Reading Words

- Recognize a large number of many different kinds of words rapidly and automatically and continue to add to number of known words
- Use a wide range of strategies for solving multisyllable words: e.g., using syllables, recognizing spelling patterns within words, using complex letter-sound relationships, noticing base words and affixes, using the context of the text, or using text resources
- Solve words by identifying simple, complex, and modified or shortened word parts within multisyllable words
- Read multisyllable words with complex letter-sound relationships
- Read all parts of speech as well as possessives and contractions
- Solve words rapidly while processing continuous text and with minimum overt self-correction
- Read proper nouns, words from other languages, and technical words from academic disciplines that are difficult to decode and use text resources like a pronunciation guide as needed

LEVEL **W**

Selecting Goals Behaviors and Understandings to Notice, Teach, and Support *(cont.)*

THINKING *WITHIN* THE TEXT *(continued)*

- Solve words by identifying base words and affixes (prefixes and suffixes)
- Solve words that offer decoding challenges because they are archaic, come from regional dialect, or are from languages other than English
- Employ word-solving strategies in a flexible way
- Read common, sophisticated, and academic connectives

▶ Vocabulary

- Derive the meaning of new words and expand meaning of known words using flexible strategies: e.g., context in a sentence; connections to other words; synonyms and antonyms; word parts; base words and affixes; word function in a sentence; text resources
- Actively and consistently add to vocabulary through reading
- Understand many words that appear in writing and in the vocabulary of mature language users (Tier 2)
- Understand words particular to academic disciplines (Tier 3)
- Understand the meaning and function in sentences of all parts of speech
- Understand how a writer uses words in a text to indicate perspective or point of view: i.e., first person, second person, third person
- Understand many words that have multiple meanings and identify the specific meaning that applies in a sentence or paragraph
- Understand the meaning and function of common connectives that occur in oral language and many sophisticated (complex) connectives that are more typical of written language
- Understand the meaning and function of academic connectives that appear in written texts but are seldom used in everyday oral language
- Understand denotative, connotative, idiomatic, and figurative meanings of words
- Understand the connotative and figurative meanings of words that contribute to the mood of the text, including words that assign dialogue: e.g., *sighed, whispered*
- Understand the connotative meanings of words that contribute to the tone of the text
- Understand that in graphic texts, information about words is in the illustrations, and also that many unusual words appear in graphic texts
- Understand words used in regional or historical dialects
- Understand the connotative meanings of descriptive adjectives, verbs, and adverbs, and use to make inferences about characters
- Derive the meanings of technical words and author-created words in science fiction

- Understand words used informally by particular groups of people: e.g., slang, dialect
- Understand some words from languages other than English
- Understand the meanings of some archaic words
- Understand the meanings of some words used satirically
- Understand and acquire a large number of content-specific words that require the use of strategic actions (i.e., conceptual understanding of content, definitions within the body of a text, a glossary, or other text resources)
- Understand key words in graphics such as maps, diagrams, and charts

MAINTAINING FLUENCY

- Read orally in a way that demonstrates all dimensions of fluency (pausing, phrasing, intonation, word stress, rate)
- Read silently at a rapid rate (much faster than oral reading) while maintaining comprehension
- Demonstrate the ability to skim and scan while reading silently to search for information quickly
- Engage in silent reading at a rate fast enough to process a large amount of text with comprehension
- In oral reading, show recognition of a wide range of declarative, imperative, exclamatory, or interrogative sentences
- Sustain momentum while reading a wide variety of texts, many that are long
- Notice periods, commas, question marks, exclamation marks, parentheses, quotation marks, dashes, and ellipses and begin to reflect them with the voice through intonation and pausing
- Recognize and read expressively a variety of dialogue, some unassigned
- Read parts in a script with demonstration of all dimensions of fluency
- Show in the voice when words in a text (sometimes shown in italics) reflect unspoken thought
- Orally read novels in verse reflecting the meaning and rhythm with the voice
- Reflect numbered and bulleted lists with the voice when reading orally
- Use the voice to reflect disciplinary content in different ways: e.g., historical account vs. scientific argument
- Read speeches in a way that reflects the original speaker's intent
- When reading aloud, show in the voice when a writer means something different than the words alone indicate

GUIDED READING

Selecting Goals Behaviors and Understandings to Notice, Teach, and Support *(cont.)*

THINKING *WITHIN* THE TEXT *(continued)*

ADJUSTING

- Adjust reading to recognize a wide range of declarative, imperative, exclamatory, or interrogative sentences, many that are very complex
- Adjust reading to recognize a hybrid text or a text with embedded forms such as letters, diaries, journal entries, and other authentic documents
- Adjust reading to form expectations based on purposes and characteristics of fiction and nonfiction genres as well as special forms such as graphic texts
- Adjust reading to meet the special demands of a graphic text
- Slow down to search for or reflect on information or to enjoy language and resume reading with momentum
- Adjust reading to accommodate a wide variety of complex sentences with embedded phrases and clauses as well as parenthetical information
- Adjust to accommodate embedded forms (e.g., letters, diaries, journal entries, and other authentic documents) within narrative and expository texts
- Adjust expectations with regard to the multiple genres in a hybrid text
- Adjust reading to understand that a text can be a collection of short stories related to an overarching theme
- Adjust reading to recognize and use characteristics of special types of fiction such as mystery; adventure story; animal story; family, friends, and school story; satire/parody
- Adjust to read parts in a readers' theater script or a play, including longer stretches of dialogue and occasional use of monologue
- Adjust reading to recognize variations in narrative structure: e.g., story-within-a-story, flashback, flash-forward, time-lapse
- Adjust reading to process texts with multiple or parallel plots, each with its own cast of characters
- Adjust reading to follow texts that change perspective and/or narrator within the larger narrative

- Adjust reading to recognize nonfiction genres: e.g., expository nonfiction, narrative nonfiction, biography, autobiography, memoir, procedural text, persuasive text, hybrid text
- Adjust reading to recognize forms: e.g., poems; plays; graphic texts; letters, diaries and journal entries; photo essays and news articles; speeches (and similar persuasive texts such as brief debate excerpts and position papers)
- Adjust to recognize the use of complex forms of argument in a persuasive text
- Adjust reading to accommodate varied placement of body text, photographs with captions, sidebars, and graphics
- Adjust reading to reflect a series of steps in a procedural text

SUMMARIZING

- Present a concise, organized oral summary that includes all important information
- Summarize a selected section of a text that is significant to understanding characters, the plot, or the message
- Present an organized oral summary that includes setting (if important), significant plot events including climax and resolution, main characters and supporting characters, character change (where significant), and one or more themes (fiction)
- Present a logically organized oral summary that includes important information expressing the main idea or larger message and reflects the overall structure (expository or narrative) as well as important underlying text structures: e.g., description, cause and effect, chronological sequence, temporal sequence, categorization, comparison and contrast, problem and solution, question and answer (nonfiction)
- Present a review of a text that includes all important information noted above and that also identifies particular elements of style and/or literary quality

Selecting Goals Behaviors and Understandings to Notice, Teach, and Support *(cont.)*

THINKING *BEYOND* THE TEXT

PREDICTING

- Make predictions based on personal experience typical of preadolescents and adolescents
- Make and continually revise predictions based on background or disciplinary knowledge of text structure in fiction and nonfiction
- Make and continually revise predictions based on disciplinary knowledge that is necessary to understand fiction and nonfiction texts
- Make predictions throughout a text based on text structure (all forms of narrative and expository text structure)
- Justify predictions with evidence from the text
- Make predictions based on the panels in graphic texts
- Make predictions based on the unique features of graphic texts
- Use multiple sources of information to confirm or disconfirm predictions, including text and illustrations
- Predict the ending of a story based on understanding of different kinds of narrative structure and understanding of setting, plot, and characters
- Make predictions based on knowledge of the characteristics of fiction and nonfiction genres, as well as an understanding of and experience reading different types of fiction texts such as mystery or survival stories
- Make predictions based on plot structure: e.g., predict connections between characters and events in a text with circular plot, parallel plots, main plot and subplot
- Make predictions based on knowledge of special forms: e.g., letters, diaries, and journal entries; photo essays, news articles; speeches
- Make predictions based on knowledge of underlying text structures: e.g., description, cause and effect, chronological sequence, temporal sequence, categorization, comparison and contrast, problem and solution, question and answer

MAKING CONNECTIONS

- Make connections between texts and personal experience, content learned in past reading, and disciplinary knowledge
- Connect the content and problems in fiction and nonfiction texts to current and historical social issues and global problems
- Make many different kinds of connections among texts: e.g., content, genre, theme, author, illustrator, characters or subject of a biography, style, message, text structure, graphics
- State explicitly the nature of connections: e.g., topic, theme, message, characters, genre, writer, style, mood, tone

- Make connections between their lives and content and plots that are particularly appropriate for preadolescents
- Use disciplinary knowledge (history, geography, culture, language) to understand settings, events, and characters in realistic and historical fiction texts
- Use previous reading of nonfiction to understand the events in historical fiction
- Make connections with the human traits and problems that are shared among people of many different cultures
- Use disciplinary knowledge (science) to understand fantasy including science fiction
- Use background knowledge of traditional literature to recognize common characters and events in fantasy
- Apply understandings of elements and basic motifs of fantasy to comprehend texts: e.g., the supernatural, imaginary and otherworldly creatures, gods and goddesses, talking animals, struggle between good and evil, magic, fantastic or magical objects, wishes, trickery, transformations
- Connect symbols to the ideas or emotions they represent
- Use disciplinary knowledge to understand content and concepts in a text
- Make connections among fiction and nonfiction to make history more vivid and understandable

SYNTHESIZING

- Develop social awareness and new insights into the human condition from reading texts
- Mentally form categories of related information and revise them as new information is acquired across texts
- Integrate new information and ideas to consciously create new understandings
- Explicitly state new knowledge, ideas, and attitudes built from reading fiction and nonfiction texts
- Build new knowledge across texts that are connected by topic, content, theme, or message
- Describe changing perspective as more of a story unfolds in both short stories and texts with chapters
- Talk about lessons learned from a character's experience and behavior in a text
- Apply new perspectives acquired from vicarious experiences while reading a fiction text to live their own lives
- Talk about new ways of thinking that spring from vicarious experiences while reading a fiction text

GUIDED READING

Selecting Goals Behaviors and Understandings to Notice, Teach, and Support *(cont.)*

THINKING *BEYOND* THE TEXT *(continued)*

SYNTHESIZING *(continued)*

◆ Apply perspective learned from reading fiction to issues and problems that face preadolescents or adolescents: e.g., peer pressure, social relationships, bullying, maturation, career choices, life decisions

◆ Talk about new understanding of different cultures, places, and times in history

◆ Synthesize new facts, perspectives, or conceptual frameworks from texts and describe these to others using evidence from the text

◆ Take on perspectives from diverse cultures and bring cultural knowledge to understanding a text

◆ Expand knowledge of the language and the structure of academic disciplines through reading

◆ Use inquiry to build knowledge of a topic through reading more than one written source

INFERRING

◆ Infer information from all elements of a text (body, sidebars, illustrations, graphics, appendices, etc.)

◆ Infer the meaning of some symbolism

◆ Make inferences about setting to help in understanding the story

◆ Infer the impact of the setting on the subject of a biography and the motives or reasons for the subject's decisions

◆ Identify round characters and infer the traits and development of those characters in a text

◆ Identify flat characters and infer the unchanging traits of those characters in a text

◆ Infer feelings and motives of multiple characters across complex plots with some subplots

◆ Infer character traits, feelings, and motivations from what characters say, think, or do and what others say or think about them

◆ Infer complex relationships between and among characters by noticing evidence in their responses to each other

◆ Compare inferences with those of other readers and consider alternative interpretations of characters' motives and the writer's message

◆ Infer potential solutions to a story problem and find supporting evidence in the text

◆ Infer symbolic meanings in a text

◆ Infer humor in a text

◆ Infer themes, ideas, and characters' feelings from the panels in graphic texts

◆ Infer some abstract ideas and themes that reflect the writer's message or main idea in a text

◆ Infer a writer's biases and underlying beliefs

◆ Infer the deeper meaning of satire or parody

◆ Infer the underlying meaning of language used satirically

◆ Infer the individual, situation, or problem that is the subject of a satire or parody

◆ Infer attitudes that may be new or contrary to readers' current beliefs

◆ Infer multiple themes or messages in a text that may be understood in many layers

◆ Infer how the messages and themes in fiction texts are applicable to today's life

◆ Infer universal human themes and issues that affect human problems across the world

◆ Infer the overarching theme(s) in a collection of short stories

◆ Infer the attitude of a biographer toward a subject

◆ Infer the purpose of a writer of a biography, autobiography, or memoir

◆ Infer the larger message in a text (i.e., what can be learned from it beyond the facts)

◆ Infer hidden or explicit messages in a persuasive text

◆ Infer the writer's messages in some texts that have serious and mature topics and challenging themes and ideas: e.g., war, racism, family problems, bullying

◆ Infer information about characters, setting, plot, and action from graphic texts, in which illustrations carry much of the meaning

◆ Infer the significance of design and other features of the peritext

◆ Infer the meaning of a range of graphics that require reader interpretation and are essential to comprehending the text

◆ Infer the meanings of words used ironically or satirically

◆ Use the writer's language to infer the mood and tone of a text

◆ Infer beliefs, customs, and perspectives of people who live in other cultures

◆ Infer beliefs, customs, and perspectives of people who live in the near and distant past

◆ Infer what life might be like and what people might believe and do at a time in the future

◆ Infer important information from familiar content as well as topics more distant from students' typical experience: e.g., different parts of the world, history, science

◆ Use disciplinary knowledge to infer the important information in a text

Selecting Goals Behaviors and Understandings to Notice, Teach, and Support *(cont.)*

THINKING *ABOUT* THE TEXT

ANALYZING

- Understand that there may be different genres and special forms in each of the larger categories of fiction and nonfiction
- Understand that a graphic text may represent any fiction or nonfiction genre
- Understand that the divisions between genres are not always clear, and identify fiction and nonfiction genres in a hybrid text
- Discuss a writer's purpose in selecting a particular genre, topic, subject, or type of narrative structure
- Notice elements and basic motifs of fantasy: e.g., the supernatural, imaginary and otherworldly creatures, gods and goddesses, talking animals, struggle between good and evil, magic, fantastic or magical objects, wishes, trickery, transformations
- Identify and understand characteristics of special types of fiction: e.g., mystery; adventure story; animal story; family, friends, and school story
- Understand that fiction genres may be combined within one text
- Understand the difference between realism and fantasy across fiction texts
- Understand and describe the characteristics of nonfiction genres, including expository nonfiction, narrative nonfiction, biography, autobiography, memoir, procedural text, persuasive text, and hybrid text
- Understand that nonfiction genres may be combined within one text
- Notice that a biography is built around significant events, problems to overcome, and the subject's decisions
- Understand that the information and ideas in a text are related to each other and notice how the author presents this
- Recognize a writer's use of embedded forms (e.g., letters, directions, journal entries) within narrative and expository text structures
- Recognize and understand variety in narrative structure: e.g., circular plot, parallel plots, main plot and subplot(s), story-within-a-story, flashback, flash-forward, time-lapse
- Recognize a writer's use of underlying text structures: e.g., description, cause and effect, chronological sequence, temporal sequence, categorization, comparison and contrast, problem and solution, question and answer
- Notice and understand expository text structure (categorized information) and the use of narrative structure for biographical texts and other types of narrative nonfiction
- Notice the logic and structure of a writer's argument
- Think analytically about the significance of a title and notice symbolism or multiple meanings
- Notice aspects of the writer's craft: e.g., style, syntax, use of one or more narrators
- Notice characteristics of settings in fantasy that require believing in magic and/or an imaginary world
- Understand the characteristics of settings (cultural, physical, historical) and the way they affect characters' attitudes and decisions

- Think analytically about the significance of the setting and its importance to the plot
- Identify the central story problem or conflict in a text with multiple episodes or parallel plots
- Notice when a text includes a moral lesson (sometimes implied and sometimes explicit) close to the end of the story
- Identify and differentiate between internal conflict and external conflict
- Notice how a writer reveals main and supporting characters by what they do, think, or say, and by what others say about them or how others respond to them
- Identify round characters (those who change and develop) and flat characters (those who do not change) in a text
- Analyze the roles of supporting characters and how they are important (or unimportant) in the story and in the development of main character(s)
- Analyze a text to think about the perspective from which the story is told and notice when that perspective changes
- Notice a writer's use of monologue and soliloquy (typically in a play) as well as extended dialogue to reveal a character's thoughts
- Notice how a writer creates, sustains, and releases suspense
- Notice language used to show chronological and temporal order
- Reflect on a writer's use of words with connotative meanings, and discuss what it conveys to the reader
- Notice a writer's use of language and state how it specifically adds to the meaning, quality, and mood of a text
- Notice a writer's use of figurative language and state how it specifically adds to the meaning or enjoyment of a text
- Notice and interpret language that reveals the writer's attitude and communicates the tone of a text
- Notice a writer's use of both common and sophisticated connectives as well as some academic connectives
- Discuss why a writer might insert parenthetical information into a sentence
- Notice a writer's use of non-sentences for literary effect
- After reading several books by an author, discuss style, use of language, typical content
- Recognize and compare writing styles, making connections within multiple works of a single writer as well as making connections between works by different writers
- Locate language in a text that reveals setting, problem, character traits, character change, theme, symbolic meanings, narrator, mood, tone
- Notice how a writer uses language to help readers experience what characters are feeling
- Understand that a writer selects first-, third-, or second-person point of view to tell a story and also may use several points of view in the same story
- Notice a writer's use of poetic and expressive language in dialogue

Selecting Goals Behaviors and Understandings to Notice, Teach, and Support *(cont.)*

THINKING ***ABOUT*** THE TEXT *(continued)*

ANALYZING *(continued)*

- Notice a writer's use of irony and the language that typifies it
- Notice literary language typical of traditional literature: e.g., *a long time ago there lived, long ago and far away, once there lived*
- Notice a writer's use of humorous words or onomatopoetic words and talk about how they add to the action
- Understand that a nonfiction writer may use argument in a persuasive text
- Notice how a writer uses language in a persuasive way
- Notice and discuss how characteristics of the peritext enhance meaning, symbolize culture, create mood, or help readers interpret the text
- Understand that illustrations carry the dialogue and action in a graphic text
- Understand how illustrations and text work together to enhance meaning and communicate the mood of the text
- Understand and describe characteristics of fiction genres, including realistic fiction, historical fiction, traditional literature (folktale, fairy tale, fable, myth, legend), fantasy, and hybrid text
- Notice how the writer/illustrator selects and places photos in a way that tells a story or communicates a larger meaning in a photo essay
- Use academic language to talk about genres: e.g., *fiction; family, friends, and school story; folktale; animal story; humorous story; fairy tale; fable; tall tale; realistic fiction; mystery; adventure story; sports story; historical fiction; fantasy; traditional literature; myth; legend; science fiction; nonfiction; informational text; informational book; factual text; how-to book; biography; autobiography; narrative nonfiction; memoir; procedural text; persuasive text, hybrid text; expository text*

- Use academic language to talk about forms: e.g., *series book, play, chapter book, comics, graphic text, letter, sequel, short story, diary entry, journal entry, news article, feature article*
- Use some academic language to talk about literary features: e.g., *beginning, ending, character, question and answer, main character, message, dialogue, topic, events, setting, description, problem and solution, comparison and contrast, main idea, flashback, conflict, resolution, theme, descriptive language, simile, cause and effect, categorization, persuasive language, plot, character development, supporting character, point of view, figurative language, metaphor, temporal sequence, chronological sequence, subject, argument, subplot, flash-forward, time-lapse, story-within-a-story, symbol, symbolism, first-person narrative, third-person narrative, second-person narrative, mood*
- Use specific language to talk about book and print features: e.g., *front cover, back cover, page, author, illustrator, illustration, photograph, title, label, drawing, heading, caption, frame, panel, table of contents, chapter, chapter title, dedication, sidebar, glossary, map, diagram, infographic, author's note, illustrator's note, section, book jacket, acknowledgments, subheading, text, pronunciation guide, chart, graph, timeline, index, foreword, cutaway, footnote, epilogue, endnote, appendix, references, prologue, bibliography*

LEVEL W

Selecting Goals Behaviors and Understandings to Notice, Teach, and Support *(cont.)*

THINKING *ABOUT* THE TEXT *(continued)*

CRITIQUING

- Critique a writer's argument in terms of whether it is logical and well supported
- Evaluate the quality of illustrations or graphics and share opinions
- Assess how graphics add to the quality of the text or provide additional information
- Think critically about characters and their actions, and share opinions
- Assess whether a text is authentic in relation to information from their reading both fiction and nonfiction
- Notice the references and assurances the writer provides to authenticate a text
- Distinguish between primary and secondary sources and think critically about the authenticity of a text
- Distinguish between fact and opinion
- Agree or disagree with a writer's arguments and give rationales for opinions
- Share opinions about a written text and/or illustrations and give rationales and examples
- Evaluate aspects of a text that add to enjoyment: e.g., humorous character or surprising information

- Express tastes and preferences in reading and support choices with descriptions and examples of literary elements: e.g., genre, setting, plot, theme, character, style, and language
- Evaluate the authenticity of a text in terms of readers' own experiences as preadolescents and adolescents
- Think critically about how a writer does (or does not) make a topic interesting and engaging, and share opinions
- Think critically about the quality of a text and how well it exemplifies its genre, and share opinions
- Think critically about the subject of a biography, discussing the achievements, admirable traits, and flaws of the individual
- Talk about why the subject of a biography is important or sets an example for others
- Critique a biography in terms of the relative importance and/or value of its chosen subject
- Critique the presentation of the subject of a biography, noting bias
- Think critically about the writing of an autobiography or memoir to detect error or bias
- Notice persuasion and think critically about factors such as bias and unsupported statements

Planning for Word Work After Guided Reading

Using your recent observations of the readers' ability to take words apart quickly and efficiently while reading text, plan for one to three minutes of active engagement of students' attention to letters, sounds, and words. Prioritize the readers' noticing of print features and active hands-on use of magnetic letters, a white board, word cards, or pencil and paper to promote fluency and flexibility in visual processing.

Examples:

- Make a full range of plural nouns, including regular plurals that require spelling changes and irregular plurals (*banquet/banquets; couch/couches; essay/ essays; bounty/bounties; axis/axes*)
- Work flexibly with a base word, changing letters or adding or taking away one or more affixes to make a new word (*assume/ assure/assuring/reassuring*) and discussing changes in meaning or function
- Sort words to put together words with the same base, words with the same prefix, words with the same suffix
- Make word ladders by changing base words, prefixes, or suffixes

- Recognize and use word roots (Greek and Latin) to take apart and determine the meanings of some English words (*cred,* meaning "believe," in *credit,* "believe in the truth of something")
- Recognize and use words that have similar meanings because they have the same root (*man* meaning "hand": *manual* meaning "of the hands," *manuscript* meaning "a handwritten or keyboarded book or article")
- Make word webs by centering on a base word or word root and thinking of the words related to it

- Break apart multisyllable words by syllable (*pon/der, can/di/date, e/vap/o/rate, de/ter/mi/na/tion*)
- Sort words by any word feature
- Have an "open sort" where students notice characteristics of words and ask other students to determine the feature they used for sorting
- Recognize and use an open syllable with a long vowel sound (*ha/zel, o/dor, ri/val*) and a closed syllable with a short vowel sound (*beck/on, men/ace, cal/i/co*)
- Recognize and use homophones (*bad, bade; lain, lane; duel, dual*) and homographs (*bass, flush*)

Readers at Level

At level X, readers are challenged by a wide variety of fiction and nonfiction texts from which they derive disciplinary knowledge. The range of special types of fiction expands to include horror and romance stories. While you would not use these types in guided reading, your students will be sampling this wide range in their outside reading. In guided reading it is important that texts engage adolescent readers and at the same time increase their understanding of what it means to be human. Texts help them explore the world—past, present, and future—and become global citizens. They are able to process and understand a wide range of texts across all genres. Many texts are long and have complex sentences and paragraphs as well as many multisyllable words, and readers are expected to understand and respond to mature themes such as sexuality, abuse, poverty, and war. Complex fantasy, myths, and legends offer added challenge by requiring readers to recognize classical motifs such as "the hero's quest" and to identify moral issues. In addition, readers encounter literary language used to convey irony. Themes and characters are multidimensional, may be understood on several levels, and are developed in complex ways. Some texts may include archaic language or regional dialect. Biographies offer a range of subjects who may or may not be admirable, requiring critical thinking on the part of readers. Readers are challenged by a heavy load of content-specific and technical words that require using embedded definitions, background knowledge, and reference tools. Readers search for and use information including complex graphics and texts that present content requiring background knowledge in an integrated way. Readers have developed knowledge of content, including scientific information and historical events, and they apply prior understandings in a critical way when reading fiction and nonfiction texts. Most reading is silent; all dimensions of fluency are well established in oral reading. They understand and use disciplinary and academic vocabulary. Readers continue to extend control of the adademic language they can use.

Selecting Texts Characteristics for of Texts at **Level X**

GENRE

▶ Fiction

- Realistic fiction
- Historical fiction
- Traditional literature (folktale, myth, legend)
- High fantasy and science fiction
- Hybrid texts
- Special types of fiction: e.g., mystery; adventure story; sports story; animal story; family, friends, and school story; humorous story; horror story; romance story

▶ Nonfiction

- Expository nonfiction
- Narrative nonfiction
- Biography
- Autobiography
- Memoir
- Procedural texts
- Persuasive texts
- Hybrid texts

FORMS

- Series books
- Picture books
- Chapter books
- Chapter books with sequels
- Plays
- Readers' theater scripts
- Graphic texts
- Letters, diaries, and journal entries
- Short stories
- Photo essays and news articles
- Speeches

TEXT STRUCTURE

- Texts with multiple episodes that are elaborated with many details
- Embedded forms (e.g., letters, directions, journal entries, emails) within narrative and expository structures
- Variations in structure: e.g., story-within-a-story, flashback, flash-forward, time-lapse
- Fiction texts with chapters connected to a single plot

- Texts with circular plot or parallel plots
- Longer texts with main plot and subplots
- Complex plots with multiple story lines
- Collections of short stories related to an overarching theme
- Texts with a change in perspective and/or narrator signaled by new chapter, section, or paragraph; language or literary feature (e.g., verb tense, imagery, setting); or print features (e.g., font, print placement)
- Nonfiction books divided into sections, and some with subsections
- Underlying structural patterns: description, cause and effect, chronological sequence, temporal sequence, categorization, comparison and contrast, problem and solution, question and answer

CONTENT

- Content interesting to and relevant for the reader
- Many books with little or no picture support for content: e.g., chapter books

The Monster's Tale

The next morning, Mary took up her pen and started writing. "It was on a dreary night of November…" the story began.

In her story, an ambitious young man, Victor Frankenstein, believes he's discovered the secret of life. He plans to turn a collection of dead people's body parts into a living human being. Victor means well, but he doesn't think things through. When the stitched-together body comes to life as a huge, hideous monster, Victor runs away, frightened by what he's done.

The abandoned monster is gentle at first. He wanders around trying to make friends, but he inspires only fear. People attack him, and he turns violent. Angry at Victor for creating his miserable life, he kills Victor's brother, best friend, and bride. In the end, Victor tracks the monster to the North Pole, but dies before he can kill him. The monster sails off on an ice raft, also prepared to die.

8 / 9

GUIDED READING

- Much content that requires accessing prior knowledge
- Content that invites critical thinking to judge authenticity and accuracy
- Content that requires the reader to take on perspectives from diverse cultures and bring cultural knowledge to understanding
- Most texts have new content that will engage and interest readers and expand knowledge: e.g., travel, experience with other cultures, adventures in science, survival
- Some content that requires emotional and social maturity to understand
- Complex content that requires analysis and study to understand
- Content that goes beyond students' immediate experience
- Texts that require content knowledge of disciplines: e.g., history, geography, culture, language, sciences, arts, math concepts
- Much content that requires the reader to search for information in graphics: e.g., maps, charts, diagrams, illustrated drawings, labeled photographs

THEMES AND IDEAS

- Many texts with themes and ideas that involve societal issues important to adolescents: e.g., family, growing up, sexuality, world issues, death
- Themes and ideas that require a perspective not familiar to the reader
- Complex ideas on many different topics that require real or vicarious experience (through reading) for understanding
- Texts with deeper meanings applicable to important human problems and social issues: e.g., hardship, war, racism, economic struggle, social class, the environment
- Wide range of challenging themes and ideas that build social awareness and reveal insights into the human condition
- Many ideas and themes that require understanding of cultural diversity
- Texts with abstract themes that require inferential thinking
- Texts that present multiple themes that may be understood in many layers
- Themes that evoke alternative interpretations

LANGUAGE AND LITERARY FEATURES

- Settings that are distant in time and geography
- Settings in fantasy that require the reader to accept elements of another world that could not exist in the real world
- Settings that are important to comprehension of the fiction narrative or biography
- Variety in narrative plot structure: e.g., story-within-a-story, simple flashback
- Some texts with multiple plots, each with its own set of main and supporting characters
- Main characters and supporting characters
- Multidimensional characters
- Characters revealed by what they say, think, and do and by what others say and think about them
- Characters revealed over a series of events, chapters, or book series
- Reasons for character change that are complex and require inference
- Some texts that reveal the perspectives of more than one character

LEVEL **X**

Selecting Texts Characteristics of Texts at **Level X** (cont.)

LANGUAGE AND LITERARY FEATURES (continued)

- "Round" characters that have a complex range of good and bad attributes and that change during the course of the plot, and "flat" characters that do not change but may play an important role in the plot
- Variety in presentation of dialogue: e.g., dialogue among multiple characters, dialogue with pronouns, split dialogue, direct dialogue, including unassigned dialogue and long stretches of dialogue
- Some chains of unassigned dialogue for which speakers must be inferred
- Most texts written in first- or third-person narrative, with some procedural texts in second person
- Basic motifs of traditional literature and modern fantasy: e.g., struggle between good and evil, fantastic or magical objects, wishes, trickery, transformations
- Moral lesson near the end of the story (sometimes explicitly stated)
- Literary language typical of traditional literature: e.g., *long ago and far away*
- Descriptive, poetic, and figurative language: e.g., imagery, metaphor, simile, personification, allegory, hyperbole
- Language and events that convey an emotional atmosphere (mood) in a text, affecting how the reader feels: e.g., tension, suspense, sadness, happiness, curiosity
- Use of symbolism
- Some colloquial language in dialogue that reflects characters' personalities and/or setting
- Procedural language
- Language used to make comparisons
- Descriptive language
- Language used to show chronological order and temporal sequence
- Persuasive language and argument
- Language that reveals the author's attitude or feelings toward a subject or topic (the tone that is reflected in the style of writing): e.g., lighthearted, ironic, earnest, affectionate, formal, sarcastic, angry
- Some texts with dense presentation of facts and ideas

SENTENCE COMPLEXITY

- Wide range of declarative, imperative, exclamatory, or interrogative sentences
- Variation in sentence length and structure
- Sentences with a wide variety of parts of speech, including multiple adjectives, adverbs, and prepositional phrases
- Sentences with common, sophisticated, and academic connectives
- Long, very complex sentences joined by semicolons or colons
- Frequent use of parenthetical material embedded in sentences
- Some non-sentences for literary effect

VOCABULARY

- Most words that appear in the vocabulary of mature language users (Tier 2)
- Many words particular to a discipline (Tier 3)
- Wide variation in words used to assign dialogue
- Words with multiple meanings
- Words with figurative meaning
- Frequent use of idioms
- New vocabulary requiring strategic action to understand: e.g., derive meaning from context, use reference tools, notice morphology, use word roots, use analogy
- Words with connotative meanings that are essential to understanding the text
- Common connectives that link ideas and clarify meaning and are typical of oral speech, as well as many sophisticated connectives that do not appear often in everyday oral language: e.g., *although, however, meantime, meanwhile moreover, otherwise, therefore, though, unless, until, whenever, yet*
- Some academic connectives that link ideas and clarify meaning and that appear in written texts but are seldom used in everyday oral language: e.g., *conversely, eventually, finally, in contrast, initially, likewise, nevertheless, nonetheless, previously, specifically, ultimately, whereas, whereby*
- Some words used ironically
- Some words from regional or historical dialects

- Words (including slang) used informally by particular groups of people
- Words from languages other than English
- Some archaic words

WORDS

- A large number of multisyllable words, many technical or scientific
- Full range of plurals
- Unlimited number of high-frequency words with multiple syllables
- Multisyllable words with some complex letter-sound relationships
- Multisyllable proper nouns that are difficult to decode
- Words that offer decoding challenges because they are archaic, come from regional dialect, or are from languages other than English
- Wide range of contractions and possessives
- Full range of compound words
- Base words with multiple affixes (prefixes and suffixes)
- Common, sophisticated, and academic connectives

ILLUSTRATIONS

- Illustrations that enhance and extend meaning in the text
- Short texts that have illustrations on every page or every few pages
- Texts with illustrations every three or four pages
- Texts with no illustrations other than decorative elements such as vignettes
- Variety of layout in illustrations and print
- Books with black-and-white illustrations
- Graphic texts that provide a great deal of information in the illustrations
- Some complex, nuanced illustrations that communicate mood and meaning (literal, figurative, symbolic) to match or extend the text
- Graphics that require reader interpretation and are essential for comprehending informational text
- Several kinds of graphics on a single page spread

Selecting Texts Characteristics of Texts at **Level X** *(cont.)*

- A range of graphics that provide information that matches and extends the text: e.g., photograph and drawing with label and/or caption; diagram, cutaway; map with legend or key, scale; infographic; chart; graph; timeline

BOOK AND PRINT FEATURES

LENGTH

- Wide variation in length (short texts about forty-eight pages)
- Wide variation in number of words (2,000+)
- Some books divided into chapters
- Books divided into sections and subsections

PRINT AND LAYOUT

- Mostly small but readable font size
- Variety in print and background color
- Variety in print placement, reflecting different genres
- Italics indicating unspoken thought in some texts
- Information shown in a variety of picture and print combinations in graphic texts
- Captions under pictures that provide important information
- Print and illustrations integrated in most texts, with print wrapping around pictures
- Print placed in sidebars and graphics that provide important information
- Some archaic print in historical texts

PUNCTUATION

- Period, comma, question mark, exclamation mark, semicolon, colon, parentheses, quotation marks, hyphen, dash, and ellipses in most texts

ORGANIZATIONAL TOOLS

- Title, table of contents, chapter title, heading, subheading, sidebar

TEXT RESOURCES

- Dedication, acknowledgments, author's note, pronunciation guide, glossary, index, foreword, footnote, endnote, epilogue, appendix, references
- Texts with design features that add to the aesthetic appeal of the whole (peritext)
- Texts with design features that enhance meaning, communicate culture, create mood (peritext), or have symbolic meaning

Selecting Goals Behaviors and Understandings to Notice, Teach, and Support

THINKING *WITHIN* THE TEXT

SEARCHING FOR AND USING INFORMATION

- Sustain searching for information texts with wide variety in length
- Sustain searching over long and highly complex sentences that include multiple phrases, clauses, and lists, and the full range of punctuation marks
- Search for information in dense texts that use academic vocabulary and present highly complex concepts
- Search for information in texts with multiple features and very dense print
- Search for information in complex texts that rely on academic discourse
- Search for and use information to understand multiple plots, perspectives, and themes in a single text
- Search for information and language that states or implies the larger message(s) of the text
- Use background knowledge to search for and understand disciplinary information
- Use organizational tools to search for information: e.g., title, table of contents, chapter title, heading, subheading, sidebar, callout
- Use text resources to search for information: e.g., acknowledgments, author's note, pronunciation guide, glossary, references, index
- Search for information in sentences that vary in length, structure, and punctuation based on text complexity
- Search for information in sentences with variation in placement of subject, verb, adjectives, and adverbs
- Search for information in dialogue presented in a variety of ways: e.g., assigned and unassigned, split dialogue, direct dialogue
- Search for information in a strategic way, using knowledge of text structure and readers' tools
- Use knowledge of linear narrative structure (chronological order) within multiple episodes to search for and use information
- Use knowledge of variations in narrative structure to search for and use information e.g., story-within-a-story (framed narrative); flashback and flashforward (fractured narrative); circular narrative; multiple or parallel plots
- Search for information in a variety of narrative structures: e.g., story-within-a-story (framed narrative); flashback and flash-forward (fractured narrative); circular narrative; multiple or parallel plots
- Notice and use punctuation marks: e.g., period, comma, question mark, exclamation mark, semicolon, colon, parentheses, quotation marks, hyphen, dash, ellipses
- When needed, reread to search for and use information from the body text, sidebars, insets, and graphics
- Search for and use information in texts with variety in placement of the body text, sidebars, and graphics

MONITORING AND SELF-CORRECTING

- Self-monitor reading using multiple sources of information: i.e., background knowledge, syntax, word meaning, word structure, awareness of text structure, meaning of the whole text, graphics layout, design
- Self-correct covertly prior to or after error and show little overt self-correction
- Closely monitor understanding of texts using knowledge of a wide range of genres and forms: e.g., realistic, historical, high fantasy, science fiction, myths, and legends, poetry, plays
- Use understandings of literary elements (e.g., plot, main and supporting characters, setting, narrative structure) to monitor and correct reading
- Use awareness of narrative structure and of character attributes (many of which may be multidimensional and change) to self-monitor and self-correct
- Use content knowledge of the topic of a text to self-monitor and self-correct
- Use knowledge of nonfiction genres to monitor understanding of a text: e.g., expository nonfiction, narrative nonfiction, biography, autobiography, memoir, procedural text, persuasive text
- Use disciplinary knowledge to monitor understanding of texts that are dense with information and ideas
- Use knowledge of a range of academic disciplines to monitor understandings of conceptual ideas that cross disciplines
- Monitor understanding using knowledge of disciplinary vocabulary
- Use information from graphics (e.g., maps, diagrams, charts, photos, illustrations) to self-monitor reading

SOLVING WORDS

▶ Reading Words

- Recognize a large number of many different kinds of words rapidly and automatically and continue to add to a large number of known words
- Use a wide range of strategies for solving multisyllable words: e.g., using syllables, recognizing spelling patterns within words, using complex letter-sound relationships, noticing base words and affixes, using the context of the text, or using text resources
- Solve words by identifying simple, complex, and modified or shortened word parts within multisyllable words
- Read multisyllable words with complex letter-sound relationships
- Solve words rapidly while processing continuous text and with minimum overt self-correction

Selecting Goals Behaviors and Understandings to Notice, Teach, and Support *(cont.)*

THINKING *WITHIN* THE TEXT *(continued)*

- Read proper nouns, words from other languages, and technical words from academic disciplines that are difficult to decode and use text resources like a pronunciation guide as needed
- Solve words by identifying base words and affixes (prefixes and suffixes)
- Solve words that offer decoding challenges because they are archaic, come from regional dialect, or are from languages other than English
- Employ word-solving strategies in a flexible way
- Read common, sophisticated, and academic connectives

▶ Vocabulary

- Derive the meaning of new words and expand meaning of known words using flexible strategies: e.g., context in a sentence; connections to other words; synonyms and antonyms; word parts; base words and affixes; word function in a sentence; text resources
- Actively and consistently add to vocabulary through reading
- Understand many words commonly used in oral language (Tier 1) and many words that appear in writing and in the vocabulary of mature language users (Tier 2)
- Understand many words particular to academic disciplines (Tier 3)
- Understand the meaning and function of all parts of speech
- Understand how a writer uses words in a text to indicate perspective or point of view: i.e., first person, second person, third person
- Understand many words that have multiple meanings and identify the specific meaning that applies in a sentence or paragraph
- Understand the meaning and function of common connectives that occur in oral language and many sophisticated (complex) connectives that are more typical of written language
- Understand the meaning and function of academic connectives that appear in written texts but are seldom used in everyday oral language
- Understand denotative, connotative, idiomatic, and figurative meanings of words
- Understand the connotative and figurative meanings of words that contribute to the mood of the text, including words that assign dialogue: e.g., *sighed, whispered*
- Understand the connotative meanings of words that contribute to the tone of the text
- Understand that in graphic texts, information about words is in the illustrations, and also that many unusual words appear in graphic texts
- Understand words used in regional or historical dialects
- Understand the connotative meanings of descriptive adjectives, verbs, and adverbs, and use to make inferences about characters
- Derive the meanings of technical words and author-created words in science fiction

- Understand words used informally by particular groups of people: e.g., slang, dialect
- Understand some words from languages other than English
- Understand the meanings of some archaic words
- Understand the meanings of some words used satirically
- Understand and acquire a large number of content-specific words that require the use of strategic actions (i.e., conceptual understanding of content, definitions within the body of a text, a glossary, or other text resources)
- Understand key words in graphics such as maps, diagrams, and charts

MAINTAINING FLUENCY

- Read orally in a way that demonstrates all dimensions of fluency (pausing, phrasing, intonation, word stress, rate)
- Read silently at a rapid rate (much faster than oral reading) while maintaining comprehension
- Demonstrate the ability to skim and scan while reading silently to search for information quickly
- Engage in silent reading at a rate fast enough to process a large amount of text with comprehension
- In oral reading, show recognition of a wide range of declarative, imperative, exclamatory, or interrogative sentences
- Sustain momentum while reading a wide variety of texts, many that are long
- Notice periods, commas, question marks, exclamation marks, parentheses, quotation marks, dashes, and ellipses and begin to reflect them with the voice through intonation and pausing
- Recognize and read expressively a variety of dialogue, some unassigned
- Read parts in a script with demonstration of all dimensions of fluency
- Show in the voice when words in a text (sometimes shown in italics) reflect unspoken thought
- Orally read novels in verse reflecting the meaning and rhythm with the voice
- Reflect numbered and bulleted lists with the voice when reading orally
- Use the voice to reflect disciplinary content in different ways: e.g., historical account vs. scientific argument
- Read speeches in a way that reflects the original speaker's intent
- When reading aloud, show in the voice when a writer means something different than the words alone indicate
- When reading orally, show in the voice when a writer uses subtle literary devices like irony

LEVEL
X

Selecting Goals Behaviors and Understandings to Notice, Teach, and Support *(cont.)*

THINKING *WITHIN* THE TEXT *(continued)*

ADJUSTING

- Adjust reading to recognize a wide range of declarative, imperative, exclamatory, or interrogative sentences, many that are very complex
- Adjust reading to recognize a hybrid text or a text with embedded forms such as letters, diaries, journal entries, and other authentic documents
- Adjust reading to form expectations based on purposes and characteristics of fiction and nonfiction genres as well as special forms such as graphic texts
- Adjust reading to meet the special demands of a graphic text
- Slow down to search for or reflect on information or to enjoy language and resume reading with momentum
- Adjust reading to accommodate a wide variety of complex sentences with embedded phrases and clauses as well as parenthetical information
- Adjust to accommodate embedded forms (e.g., letters, diaries, journal entries, and other authentic documents) within narrative and expository texts
- Adjust expectations with regard to the multiple genres in a hybrid text
- Adjust reading to understand that a text can be a collection of short stories related to an overarching theme
- Adjust reading to recognize and use characteristics of special types of fiction such as mystery; adventure story; animal story; family, friends, and school story; satire/parody; horror story; romance
- Adjust to read parts in a script, including longer stretches of dialogue and occasional use of monologue
- Adjust reading to recognize variations in narrative structure: e.g., story-within-a-story, flashback, flash-forward, time-lapse
- Adjust reading to process texts with multiple or parallel plots, each with its own cast of characters
- Adjust reading to follow texts that change perspective and/or narrator within the larger narrative
- Adjust reading to recognize nonfiction genres: e.g., expository nonfiction, narrative nonfiction, biography, autobiography, memoir, procedural text, persuasive text, hybrid text

- Adjust reading to recognize forms: e.g., poems; plays; graphic texts; letters, diaries and journal entries; photo essays and news articles; speeches (and similar persuasive texts such as brief debate excerpts and position papers)
- Adjust to recognize the use of complex forms of argument in a persuasive text
- Adjust reading to accommodate varied placement of body text, photographs with captions, sidebars, and graphics
- Adjust reading to reflect a series of steps in a procedural text
- Adjust reading to process a text with dense presentation of facts and ideas

SUMMARIZING

- Present a concise, organized oral summary that includes all important information
- Summarize a selected section of a text that is significant to understanding characters, the plot, or the message
- Summarize important parts of a text (chapters or sections) in a way that addresses specific questions or clarifies the larger meaning of the text
- Present an organized oral summary that includes setting (if important), significant plot events including climax and resolution, main characters and supporting characters, character change (where significant), and one or more themes (fiction)
- Present a logically organized oral summary that includes important information expressing the main idea or larger message and reflects the overall structure (expository or narrative) as well as important underlying text structures: e.g., description, cause and effect, chronological sequence, temporal sequence, categorization, comparison and contrast, problem and solution, question and answer (nonfiction)
- Present a review of a text that includes all important information noted above and that also identifies particular elements of style and/or literary quality

LEVEL **X**

Selecting Goals Behaviors and Understandings to Notice, Teach, and Support *(cont.)*

THINKING *BEYOND* THE TEXT

PREDICTING

- Make predictions based on personal experience typical of preadolescents and adolescents
- Make and continually revise predictions based on previous reading and content area study
- Continually revise predictions based on knowledge of text structure in fiction and nonfiction
- Continually revise predictions based on disciplinary knowledge that is necessary to understand fiction and nonfiction texts
- Make predictions throughout a text based on text structure (all forms of narrative and expository text structure)
- Justify predictions with evidence from the text
- Make predictions based on the panels in graphic texts
- Make predictions based on the unique features of graphic texts
- Use multiple sources of information to confirm or disconfirm predictions, including text and illustrations
- Predict the ending of a story based on understanding of different kinds of narrative structure and understanding of setting, plot, and characters
- Make predictions based on knowledge of the characteristics of fiction and nonfiction genres, as well as an understanding of and experience reading different types of fiction texts such as mystery or survival stories
- Make predictions based on plot structure: e.g., predict connections between characters and events in a text with circular plot, parallel plots, main plot and subplot
- Make predictions based on knowledge of special forms: e.g., letters, diaries, and journal entries; photo essays and news articles; speeches
- Make predictions based on knowledge of underlying text structures: e.g., description, cause and effect, chronological sequence, temporal sequence, categorization, comparison and contrast, problem and solution, question and answer

MAKING CONNECTIONS

- Make connections between texts and personal experience, content learned in past reading, and disciplinary knowledge
- Connect the content and problems in fiction and nonfiction texts to current and historical social issues and global problems
- Make many different kinds of connections among texts: e.g., content, genre, theme, author, illustrator, characters or subject of a biography, style, message
- State explicitly the nature of connections: e.g., topic, theme, message, characters, genre, writer, style, mood, tone
- Make connections between their lives and content and plots that are particularly appropriate to preadolescents and adolescents

- Use disciplinary knowledge (history, geography, culture, language) to understand settings, events, and characters in realistic and historical fiction texts
- Use previous reading of nonfiction to understand the events in historical fiction
- Make connections with the human traits and problems that are shared among people of many different cultures
- Use disciplinary knowledge (science) to understand fantasy including science fiction
- Use background knowledge of traditional literature to recognize common characters and events in fantasy
- Apply understandings of elements and basic motifs of fantasy to comprehend fantasy and science fiction
- Connect symbols to the ideas or emotions they represent
- Use disciplinary knowledge to understand content and concepts in a text
- Use disciplinary knowledge from the natural sciences and social sciences to understand the content in a wide variety of texts
- Make connections among fiction and nonfiction to make history more vivid and understandable
- Build disciplinary knowledge by making connections across disciplines through wide reading of texts

SYNTHESIZING

- Develop social awareness and new insights into the human condition from reading texts
- Mentally form categories of related information and revise them as new information is acquired across texts
- Integrate new information and ideas to consciously create new understandings
- Explicitly state new knowledge, ideas, and attitudes built from reading fiction and nonfiction texts
- Build new knowledge across texts that are connected by topic, content, theme, or message
- Use texts in many genres (e.g., realistic fiction, historical fiction, traditional literature) to gain new insights into cultures and historical times that cannot be accessed directly
- Describe changing perspective as more of a story unfolds in both short stories and texts with chapters
- Talk about lessons learned from a character's experience and behavior in a text
- Apply new perspectives acquired from vicarious experiences while reading a fiction text to live their own lives
- Talk about new ways of thinking that spring from vicarious experiences while reading a fiction text

GUIDED READING

LEVEL
X

Selecting Goals Behaviors and Understandings to Notice, Teach, and Support *(cont.)*

THINKING *BEYOND* THE TEXT *(continued)*

SYNTHESIZING *(continued)*

- Apply perspective learned from reading fiction to issues and problems that face preadolescents and adolescents: e.g., peer pressure, social relationships, bullying, maturation, career choices, life decisions
- Talk about new understanding of different cultures, places, and times in history
- Synthesize new facts, perspectives, or conceptual frameworks from texts and describe these to others using evidence from the text
- Take on perspectives from diverse cultures and bring cultural knowledge to understanding a text
- Expand knowledge of the language and the structure of academic disciplines through reading
- Use inquiry to build knowledge of a topic through reading more than one written source (including primary and secondary sources)

INFERRING

- Infer the meaning of some symbolism
- Make inferences about setting to help in understanding the story
- Infer the impact of the setting on the subject of a biography and the motives or reasons for the subject's decisions
- Identify round characters and infer the traits and development of those characters in a text
- Identify flat characters and infer the unchanging traits of those characters in a text
- Infer feelings and motives of multiple characters across complex plots with some subplots
- Infer character traits, feelings, and motivations from what characters say, think, or do and what others say or think about them
- Infer complex relationships between and among characters by noticing evidence in their responses to each other
- Compare inferences with those of other readers and consider alternative interpretations of characters' motives and the writer's message
- Infer potential solutions to a story problem and find supporting evidence in the text
- Distinguish multiple plots in a text, each with its own set of main and supporting characters, and infer relationships among those characters
- Infer symbolic meanings in a text
- Infer humor in a text
- Infer themes, ideas, and characters' feelings from the panels in graphic texts

- Infer some abstract ideas and themes that reflect the writer's message or main idea in a text
- Infer a writer's biases and underlying beliefs
- Infer multiple themes or messages in a text that may be understood in many layers
- Infer how the messages and themes in fiction texts are applicable to today's life
- Infer universal human themes and issues that affect human problems across the world
- Infer the overarching theme(s) in a collection of short stories
- Infer the attitude of a biographer toward a subject
- Infer the purpose of a writer of a biography, autobiography, or memoir
- Infer the larger message in a nonfiction text (i.e., what can be learned from it beyond the facts)
- Infer hidden or explicit messages in a persuasive text
- Infer the writer's messages in some texts that have serious and mature topics and challenging themes and ideas: e.g., war, racism, family problems, bullying
- Infer information from all elements of a text (body, sidebars, illustrations, graphics, appendices, etc.)
- Infer information about characters, setting, plot, and action from graphic texts, in which illustrations carry much of the meaning
- Infer the meaning of a range of graphics that require reader interpretation and are essential to comprehending the text
- Infer the significance of design and other features of the peritext
- Infer the meanings of words used ironically
- Use the writer's language to infer the mood and tone of a text
- Infer beliefs, customs, and perspectives of people who live in other cultures
- Infer beliefs, customs, and perspectives of people who live in the near and distant past
- Infer what life might be like and what people might believe and do at a time in the future
- Infer attitudes that may be new or contrary to readers' current beliefs
- Infer important information from familiar content as well as topics more distant from students' typical experience: e.g., different parts of the world, history, science
- Use disciplinary knowledge to infer the important information in a text

Selecting Goals Behaviors and Understandings to Notice, Teach, and Support *(cont.)*

THINKING *ABOUT* THE TEXT

ANALYZING

- Understand that there may be different genres and special forms in each of the larger categories of fiction and nonfiction
- Understand that a graphic text may represent any fiction or nonfiction genre
- Understand that the divisions between genres are not always clear, and identify fiction and nonfiction genres in a hybrid text
- Discuss a writer's purpose in selecting a particular genre, topic, subject, or type of narrative structure
- Recognize a writer's selection of genre and text structure for different purposes and audiences
- Understand and describe characteristics of fiction genres, including realistic fiction, historical fiction, traditional literature (folktale, fairy tale, fable, myth, legend), fantasy, and hybrid text
- Notice elements and basic motifs of fantasy: e.g., the supernatural, imaginary and otherworldly creatures, gods and goddesses, talking animals, struggle between good and evil, magic, fantastic or magical objects, wishes, trickery, transformations
- Analyze fantasy to determine elements and basic motifs
- Identify and understand characteristics of special types of fiction: e.g., mystery; adventure story; animal story; family, friends, and school story
- Understand that fiction genres may be combined within one text
- Understand the difference between realism and fantasy across fiction texts
- Understand and describe the characteristics of nonfiction genres, including expository nonfiction, narrative nonfiction, biography, autobiography, memoir, procedural text, persuasive text, and hybrid text
- Understand that nonfiction genres may be combined within one text
- Notice that a biography is built around significant events, problems to overcome, and the subject's decisions
- Understand that the information and ideas in a text are related to each other and notice how the author presents this
- Recognize a writer's use of embedded forms (e.g., letters, directions, journal entries) within narrative and expository text structures
- Recognize and understand variety in narrative structure: e.g., circular plot, parallel plots, main plot and subplot(s), story-within-a-story, flashback, flash-forward, time-lapse

- Recognize a writer's use of underlying text structures: e.g., description, cause and effect, chronological sequence, temporal sequence, categorization, comparison and contrast, problem and solution, question and answer
- Notice and understand expository text structure (categorized information) and the use of narrative structure for biographical texts and other types of narrative nonfiction
- Notice the logic and structure of a writer's argument
- Think analytically about the significance of a title and notice symbolism or multiple meanings
- Notice aspects of the writer's craft: e.g., style, syntax, use of one or more narrators
- Identify and understand a writer's use of literary devices such as contradiction, paradox, and allusion
- Notice characteristics of settings in fantasy that require believing in magic and/or an imaginary world
- Understand the characteristics of settings (cultural, physical, historical) and the way they affect characters' attitudes and decisions
- Think analytically about the significance of the setting and its importance to the plot
- Identify the central story problem or conflict in a text with multiple episodes or parallel plots
- Recognize and understand multiple plots, each with its own set of main and supporting characters, in a text
- Notice when a text includes a moral test (sometimes implied and sometimes explicit) close to the end of the story
- Identify and differentiate between internal conflict and external conflict
- Notice how a writer reveals main and supporting characters by what they do, think, or say, and by what others say about them or how others respond to them
- Identify round characters (those who change and develop) and flat characters (those who do not change) in a text
- Analyze the roles of supporting characters and how they are important (or unimportant) in the story and in the development of main character(s)
- Analyze a text to think about the perspective from which the story is told and notice when that perspective changes
- Notice how a writer creates, sustains, and releases suspense
- Notice language used to show chronological and temporal order

GUIDED READING

LEVEL **X**

Selecting Goals Behaviors and Understandings to Notice, Teach, and Support *(cont.)*

ANALYZING *(continued)*

- Reflect on a writer's use of words with connotative meanings, and discuss what it conveys to the reader
- Notice a writer's use of language and state how it specifically adds to the meaning, quality, and mood of a text
- Notice a writer's use of figurative language and state how it specifically adds to the meaning or enjoyment of a text
- Notice and interpret language that reveals the writer's attitude and communicates the tone of a text
- Notice a writer's use of both common and sophisticated connectives as well as some academic connectives
- Discuss why a writer might insert parenthetical information into a sentence
- Notice a writer's use of non-sentences for literary effect
- After reading several books by an author, discuss style, use of language, typical content
- Recognize and compare writing styles, making connections within multiple works of a single writer as well as making connections between works by different writers
- Locate language in a text that reveals setting, problem, character traits, character change, theme, symbolic meanings, narrator, mood, tone
- Notice how a writer uses language to help readers experience what characters are feeling
- Understand that a writer selects first-, second-, or third-person point of view to tell a story
- Notice a writer's use of figurative language (including metaphor, simile, personification, extended metaphor, and allegory) and state how it specifically adds to the meaning or enjoyment of a text
- Notice a writer's use of poetic and expressive language in dialogue
- Notice a writer's use of monologue and soliloquy (typically in a play) as well as extended dialogue to reveal a character's thoughts
- Notice a writer's use of irony and the language that typifies it
- Notice literary language typical of traditional literature: e.g., *a long time ago there lived, long ago and far away, once there lived*
- Notice a writer's use of humorous words or onomatopoetic words and talk about how they add to the action
- Understand that a nonfiction writer may use argument in a persuasive text
- Notice how a writer uses language in a persuasive way
- Understand that illustrations carry the dialogue and action in a graphic text
- Understand how illustrations and text work together to enhance meaning and communicate the mood of the text
- Notice how the writer/illustrator selects and places photos in a way that tells a story or communicates a larger meaning in a photo essay

- Notice and discuss how characteristics of the peritext enhance meaning, symbolize culture, create mood, or help readers interpret the text
- Use academic language to talk about genres: e.g., *fiction; family, friends, and school story; folktale; animal story; humorous story; fairy tale; fable; tall tale; realistic fiction; mystery; adventure story; sports story; historical fiction; fantasy; traditional literature; myth; legend; science fiction; nonfiction; informational text; informational book; factual text; how-to book; biography; autobiography; narrative nonfiction; memoir; procedural text; persuasive text, hybrid text; expository text*
- Use academic language to talk about forms: e.g., *series book, play, chapter book, comics, graphic text, letter, sequel, short story, diary entry, journal entry, news article, feature article*
- Use academic language to talk about literary features: e.g., *beginning, ending, character, question and answer, main character, message, dialogue, topic, events, setting, description, problem and solution, comparison and contrast, main idea, flashback, conflict, resolution, theme, descriptive language, simile, cause and effect, categorization, persuasive language, plot, character development, supporting character, point of view, figurative language, metaphor, temporal sequence, chronological sequence, subject, argument, subplot, flash-forward, time-lapse, story-within-a-story, symbol, symbolism, first-person narrative, third-person narrative, second-person narrative, mood*
- Use specific language to talk about book and print features: e.g., *front cover, back cover, page, author, illustrator, illustration, photograph, title, label, drawing, heading, caption, frame, panel, table of contents, chapter, chapter title, dedication, sidebar, glossary, map, diagram, infographic, author's note, illustrator's note, section, book jacket, acknowledgments, subheading, text, pronunciation guide, chart, graph, timeline, index, foreword, cutaway, footnote, epilogue, endnote, appendix, references, prologue, bibliography*

CRITIQUING

- Critique a writer's argument in terms of whether it is logical and well supported
- Evaluate the quality of illustrations or graphics and share opinions
- Assess how graphics add to the quality of the text or provide additional information
- Evaluate the authenticity of a text in terms of readers' own experiences as preadolescents and adolescents
- Use other information (from research, reading, etc.) to evaluate the authenticity of a text
- Assess whether a text is authentic in relation to students' life experiences as well as information from their reading both fiction and nonfiction

Selecting Goals Behaviors and Understandings to Notice, Teach, and Support *(cont.)*

THINKING *ABOUT* THE TEXT *(continued)*

- Notice the references and assurances the writer provides to authenticate a text
- Distinguish between primary and secondary sources and think critically about the authenticity of a text
- Distinguish between fact and opinion
- Agree or disagree with a writer's arguments and give rationales for opinions
- Share opinions about a text and give rationales and examples
- Evaluate aspects of a text that add to enjoyment: e.g., humorous character or surprising information
- Express preferences with specific references to characteristics of fiction and nonfiction genres
- Express tastes and preferences in reading and support choices with descriptions and examples of literary elements: e.g., genre, setting, plot, theme, character, style, and language

- Think critically about how a writer does (or does not) make a topic interesting and engaging, and share opinions
- Think critically about the quality of a text and how well it exemplifies its genre, and share opinions
- Think critically about characters and their actions, and share opinions
- Think critically about the subject of a biography, discussing the achievements, admirable traits, and flaws of the individual
- Talk about why the subject of a biography is important or sets an example for others
- Critique a biography in terms of the relative importance and/or value of its chosen subject
- Critique the presentation of the subject of a biography, noting bias
- Think critically about the writing of an autobiography or memoir to detect error or bias
- Notice persuasion and think critically about factors such as bias and unsupported statements

Planning for Word Work After Guided Reading

Using your recent observations of the readers' ability to take words apart quickly and efficiently while reading text, plan for one to three minutes of active engagement of students' attention to letters, sounds, and words. Prioritize the readers' noticing of print features and active hands-on use of magnetic letters, a white board, word cards, or pencil and paper to promote fluency and flexibility in visual processing.

Examples:

- Make a full range of plural nouns, including regular plurals that require spelling changes and irregular plurals (*decoration/decorations; latch/latches; duchess/duchesses; grizzly/grizzlies; crisis/crises*)
- Work flexibly with a base word, changing letters or adding or taking away one or more affixes to make a new word (*injury/injure/reinjure/reinjured*) and discussing changes in meaning or function
- Sort words to put together words with the same base, words with the same prefix, words with the same suffix
- Make word ladders by changing base words, prefixes, or suffixes

- Recognize and use word roots (Greek and Latin) to take apart and determine the meanings of some English words (*form*, meaning "a shape," in *formation*, "process of making or shaping something")
- Recognize and use words that have similar meanings because they have the same root (*grad* meaning "to step": *grade* meaning "degree in rank, quality, or value," *graduate* meaning "to finish a course of study at a school and be given a paper saying so")
- Make word webs by centering on a base word or word root and thinking of the words related to it

- Break apart multisyllable words by syllable (*ward/robe, sig/na/ture, lit/er/a/ture, re/spon/si/bil/i/ty*)
- Sort words by any word feature
- Have an "open sort" where students notice characteristics of words and ask other students to determine the feature they used for sorting
- Recognize and use an open syllable with a long vowel sound (*lo/cate, ma/jor, di/et*) and a closed syllable with a short vowel sound (*bis/cuit, med/dle, bil/lion*)
- Recognize and use homophones (*baron, barren; might, mite; beach, beech*) and homographs (*lark, punch*)

Readers at Level

At level Y, readers encounter the same challenges as at level X, but there is increased demand for students to bring disciplinary knowledge to their reading and to understand literary qualities. Understanding texts will require analytic thinking. Readers will need to use sophisticated understanding of text structure and of the elements of literature to think deeply about texts. They will encounter ambiguity and need to work it out; messages are complex and have significant implications for society. Readers recognize subtle symbolism and humor. Stories present difficult human problems and circumstances. Characters are neither "good" nor "bad" but show the complexity of human personality. Readers engage in texts to learn more about themselves and to think about their lives and others'. Deep comprehension at these levels means getting inside the writer's craft. Readers are challenged by nearly the full range of genres. Many texts are long and have complex sentences and paragraphs as well as many multisyllable words, and readers are expected to understand and respond to mature themes such as sexuality, abuse, poverty, and war. Complex fantasy, myths, and legends offer added challenge by requiring readers to recognize classical motifs such as "the hero's quest" and to identify moral issues. In addition, readers encounter literary language used to convey irony. Themes and characters are multidimensional, may be understood on several levels, and are developed in complex ways. Some texts may include archaic language or regional dialect. In nonfiction, readers are challenged by a heavy load of content-specific and technical words that require using embedded definitions, disciplinary knowledge, and reference tools. Readers search for and use information including complex graphics and texts that present content requiring background knowledge in an integrated way. In particular, readers at this level should think critically about the quality and authenticity of a text, evaluate arguments, and detect bias. Most reading is silent; all dimensions of fluency are well established in oral reading. Readers understand and use disciplinary and academic vocabulary. In addition, readers are actively adding to their understanding of disciplinary knowledge.

Selecting Texts Characteristics of Texts at **Level Y**

GENRE

▶ **Fiction**

- Realistic fiction
- Historical fiction
- Traditional literature (folktale, myth, legend)
- High fantasy and science fiction
- Hybrid texts
- Special types of fiction: e.g., mystery; adventure story; sports story; animal story; family, friends, and school story; humorous story; horror story; romance story

▶ **Nonfiction**

- Expository nonfiction
- Narrative nonfiction
- Biography
- Autobiography
- Memoir
- Procedural texts
- Persuasive texts
- Hybrid texts

FORMS

- Series books
- Picture books
- Chapter books
- Chapter books with sequels
- Plays
- Readers' theater scripts
- Graphic texts
- Letters, diaries, and journal entries
- Short stories
- Photo essays and news articles
- Speeches

TEXT STRUCTURE

- Texts with multiple episodes that are elaborated with many details
- Embedded forms (e.g., letters, directions, journal entries, emails) within narrative and expository structures
- Variations in structure: e.g., story-within-a-story, flashback, flash-forward, time-lapse

- Fiction books with chapters connected to a single plot
- Texts with circular plot or parallel plots
- Longer texts with main plot and subplots
- Complex plots with multiple story lines
- Collections of short stories related to an overarching theme
- Texts with a change in perspective and/or narrator signaled by new chapter, section, or paragraph; language or literary feature (e.g., verb tense, imagery, setting); or print features (e.g., font, print placement)
- Nonfiction books divided into sections, and some with subsections
- Underlying structural patterns: description, cause and effect, chronological sequence, temporal sequence, categorization, comparison and contrast, problem and solution, question and answer

From Body to Mummy

After the embalmers perfected their method, mummification became very popular in Egypt. Everyone wanted their loved ones to live on after death. With so many customers, the embalmers needed a system to help them handle all the bodies. Here's how some scientists think it worked.

Immediately after death, embalmers took the body to **Ibu** (ee-boo), which means "Place of Washing." There, probably in an open-sided tent near the Nile River, the body was carefully washed in a salty mixture of water and natron.

Next, the body was moved to the "House of Mummification," or **Per-Nefer** (pair-neff-uhr), to be cleaned out and dried. To drain all the fluids, the body was first placed on its back on a slanted table.

The embalmers started their work by removing the brain. They didn't want to damage the head, so they inserted a hooked instrument into one nostril and swirled the hook inside the skull. Then they used a long-handled spoon to scoop out the brain matter. The Egyptians didn't believe the brain was worth anything, so they just threw it away.

STEP ONE: Ibu
At **Ibu** the body was thoroughly washed. It is likely that this took place near the Nile, but far from any town, so townspeople didn't have to smell the bodies.

STEP TWO: Per-Nefer
At **Per-Nefer** the brain and other organs were removed from the body, and the body was dried in natron so that it would not rot. The body was left to dry for more than a month.

STEP THREE: Wabet
At **Wabet** the body was shaped, rubbed with sweet-smelling oils, and wrapped in cloth.

Mummification Step by Step

10 11

CONTENT

- Content interesting to and relevant for the reader
- Many books with little or no picture support for content: e.g., chapter books
- Much content that requires accessing prior knowledge
- Content that invites critical thinking to judge authenticity and accuracy
- Content that requires the reader to take on perspectives from diverse cultures and bring cultural knowledge to understanding
- Most texts have new content that will engage and interest readers and expand knowledge: e.g., travel, experience with other cultures, adventures in science, survival
- Content that requires emotional and social maturity to understand
- Complex content that requires analysis and study to understand
- Content that goes beyond students' immediate experience
- Texts that require content knowledge of disciplines: e.g., history, geography, culture, language, sciences, arts, math concepts
- Content that requires the reader to search for information in graphics: e.g., maps, charts, diagrams, illustrated drawings, labeled photographs

THEMES AND IDEAS

- Many texts with themes and ideas that involve societal issues important to adolescents: e.g., family, growing up, sexuality, world issues, death and illness, poverty
- Themes and ideas that require a perspective not familiar to the reader
- Complex ideas on many different topics that require real or vicarious experience (through reading) for understanding
- Texts with deeper meanings applicable to important human problems and social issues: e.g., hardship, war, racism, economic struggle, social class, the environment
- Wide range of challenging themes and ideas that build social awareness and reveal insights into the human condition
- Many ideas and themes that require understanding of cultural diversity
- Texts with abstract themes that require inferential thinking
- Texts that present multiple themes that may be understood in many layers
- Themes that evoke alternative interpretations

LANGUAGE AND LITERARY FEATURES

- Settings that are distant in time and geography
- Settings in fantasy that require the reader to accept elements of another world that could not exist in the real world
- Settings that are important to comprehension of the fiction narrative or biography
- Variety in narrative plot structure: e.g., story-within-a-story, simple flashback

Selecting Texts Characteristics of Texts at **Level Y** (cont.)

LANGUAGE AND LITERARY FEATURES (continued)

- Some texts with multiple plots, each with its own set of main and supporting characters
- Main characters and supporting characters
- Multidimensional characters
- Characters revealed by what they say, think, and do and by what others say and think about them
- Characters revealed over a series of events, chapters, or book series
- Reasons for character change that are complex and require inference
- Some texts that reveal the perspectives of more than one character
- "Round" characters that have a complex range of good and bad attributes and that change during the course of the plot, and "flat" characters that do not change but may play an important role in the plot
- Variety in presentation of dialogue: e.g., dialogue among multiple characters, dialogue with pronouns, split dialogue, direct dialogue, including unassigned dialogue and long stretches of dialogue
- Some chains of unassigned dialogue for which speakers must be inferred
- Most texts written in first- or third-person narrative, with some procedural texts in second person
- Basic motifs of traditional literature and modern fantasy: e.g., struggle between good and evil, fantastic or magical objects, wishes, trickery, transformations
- Moral lesson near the end of the story (sometimes explicitly stated)
- Literary language typical of traditional literature: e.g., *long ago and far away*
- Descriptive, poetic, and figurative language: e.g., imagery, metaphor, simile, personification, allegory, hyperbole
- Language and events that convey an emotional atmosphere (mood) in a text, affecting how the reader feels: e.g., tension, suspense, sadness, happiness, curiosity
- Use of symbolism
- Some colloquial language in dialogue that reflects characters' personalities and/or setting
- Procedural language
- Language used to make comparisons
- Descriptive language

- Language used to show chronological order and temporal sequence
- Persuasive language and argument
- Language that reveals the author's attitude or feelings toward a subject or topic (the tone that is reflected in the style of writing): e.g., lighthearted, ironic, earnest, affectionate, formal, sarcastic, angry
- Some texts with dense presentation of facts and ideas

SENTENCE COMPLEXITY

- Some longer sentences with more than twenty words
- Wide range of declarative, imperative, exclamatory, or interrogative sentences
- Variation in sentence length and structure
- Sentences with a wide variety of parts of speech, including multiple adjectives, adverbs, and prepositional phrases
- Sentences with common, sophisticated, and academic connectives
- Long, very complex sentences joined by semicolons or colons
- Frequent use of parenthetical material embedded in sentences
- Some non-sentences for literary effect

VOCABULARY

- Most words that appear in the vocabulary of mature language users (Tier 2)
- Many words particular to a discipline (Tier 3)
- Wide variation in words used to assign dialogue
- Many words with multiple meanings
- Many words with figurative meaning
- Frequent use of idioms
- New vocabulary requiring strategic action to understand: e.g., derive meaning from context, use reference tools, notice morphology, use word roots, use analogy
- Words with connotative meanings that are essential to understanding the text
- Common connectives that link ideas and clarify meaning and are typical of oral speech, as well as many sophisticated connectives that do not appear often in everyday oral language: e.g., *although, however, meantime, meanwhile, moreover, otherwise, therefore, though, unless, until, whenever, yet*

- Some academic connectives that link ideas and clarify meaning and that appear in written texts but are seldom used in everyday oral language: e.g., *conversely, eventually, finally, in contrast, initially, likewise, nevertheless, nonetheless, previously, specifically, ultimately, whereas, whereby*
- Some words used ironically
- Some words from regional or historical dialects
- Words (including slang) used informally by particular groups of people
- Words from languages other than English
- Some archaic words

WORDS

- A large number of multisyllable words, many technical or scientific
- Full range of plurals
- Unlimited number of high-frequency words with multiple syllables
- Many words with easy, predictable letter-sound relationships (decodable)
- Many multisyllable words with some complex letter-sound relationships
- Some multisyllable proper nouns that are difficult to decode
- Words that offer decoding challenges because they are archaic, come from regional dialect, or are from languages other than English
- Wide range of contractions and possessives
- Full range of compound words
- Base words with multiple affixes (prefixes and suffixes)
- Common, sophisticated, and academic connectives

ILLUSTRATIONS

- Illustrations that enhance and extend meaning in the text
- Texts with illustrations every three or four pages
- Texts with no illustrations other than decorative elements such as vignettes
- Variety of layout in illustrations and print
- Books with variation in color to communicate mood: e.g., sepia, black-and-white, color

Selecting Texts Characteristics of Texts at **Level Y** *(cont.)*

- Graphic texts that provide a great deal of information in the illustrations
- Some complex, nuanced illustrations that communicate mood and meaning (literal, figurative, symbolic) to match or extend the text
- Graphics that require reader interpretation and are essential for comprehending informational text
- Several kinds of graphics on a single page spread
- A range of graphics that provide information that matches and extends the text: e.g., photograph and drawing with label and/or caption; diagram, cutaway; map with legend or key, scale; infographic; chart; graph; timeline

BOOK AND PRINT FEATURES

LENGTH

- Wide variation in length (mostly shorter than forty-eight pages)
- Wide variation in number of words (2,000+)
- Some books divided into chapters
- Books divided into sections and subsections

PRINT AND LAYOUT

- Variety in print and background color
- Variety in print placement, reflecting different genres
- Italics indicating unspoken thought in some texts
- Information shown in a variety of picture and print combinations in graphic texts
- Captions under pictures that provide important information
- Print and illustrations integrated in most texts, with print wrapping around pictures
- Print placed in sidebars and graphics that provide important information
- Some archaic print in historical texts

PUNCTUATION

- Period, comma, question mark, exclamation mark, semicolon, colon, parentheses, quotation marks, hyphen, dash, and ellipses in most texts

ORGANIZATIONAL TOOLS

- Title, table of contents, chapter title, heading, subheading, sidebar

TEXT RESOURCES

- Dedication, acknowledgments, author's note, pronunciation guide, glossary, index, foreword, footnote, endnote, epilogue, appendix, references
- Texts with design features that add to the aesthetic appeal of the whole (peritext)
- Texts with design features that enhance meaning, communicate culture, create mood (peritext), or have symbolic meaning

Selecting Goals Behaviors and Understandings to Notice, Teach, and Support

THINKING *WITHIN* THE TEXT

SEARCHING FOR AND USING INFORMATION

- When needed, reread to search for and use information from the body text, sidebars, insets, and graphics
- Sustain searching for information texts with wide variety in length
- Sustain searching over long and highly complex sentences that include multiple phrases, clauses, and lists, and the full range of punctuation marks
- Search for information in dense texts that use academic vocabulary and present highly complex concepts
- Search for information in texts with multiple features and very dense print
- Search for and use information in texts that have multiple features, very dense print, and complex graphics and that reveal multiple facets of a disciplinary topic
- Search for information in complex texts that rely on academic discourse
- Search for and use information to understand multiple plots, perspectives, and themes in a single text
- Search for information and language that states or implies the larger message(s) of the text
- Use background knowledge to search for and understand disciplinary information
- Use disciplinary vocabulary and understanding of text structure in academic disciplines to search for and use information
- Use organizational tools to search for information: e.g., title, table of contents, chapter title, heading, subheading, sidebar, callout
- Use text resources to search for information: e.g., acknowledgments, author's note, pronunciation guide, glossary, references, index
- Search for information in sentences that vary in length, structure, and punctuation based on text complexity
- Search for information in sentences with variation in placement of subject, verb, adjectives, and adverbs
- Search for information in dialogue presented in a variety of ways: e.g., assigned and unassigned, split dialogue, direct dialogue
- Search for information in a strategic way, using knowledge of text structure and readers' tools
- Use knowledge of linear narrative structure (chronological order) within multiple episodes to search for and use information
- Use knowledge of variations in narrative structure to search for and use information: e.g., story-within-a-story (framed narrative); flashback and flash-forward (fractured narrative); circular narrative; multiple or parallel plots
- Search for information in a variety of narrative structures: e.g., story-within-a-story (framed narrative); flashback and flash-forward (fractured narrative); circular narrative; multiple or parallel plots
- Notice and use punctuation marks: e.g., period, comma, question mark, exclamation mark, semicolon, colon, parentheses, quotation marks, hyphen, dash, ellipses
- Search for and use information in texts with variety in placement of the body text, sidebars, and graphics

MONITORING AND SELF-CORRECTING

- Self-monitor reading using multiple sources of information: i.e., background knowledge, syntax, word meaning, word structure, awareness of text structure, meaning of the whole text, graphics, layout, design
- Continue to monitor accuracy, self-correcting rarely (only when necessary for making sense of a text)
- Monitor comprehension closely so understanding is always assured
- Closely monitor understanding of texts using knowledge of a wide range of genres and forms: e.g., realistic, historical, high fantasy, science fiction, myths, legends, poetry, plays
- Use understandings of literary elements (e.g., plot, main and supporting characters, setting, narrative structure) to monitor and correct reading
- Use awareness of narrative structure and of character attributes (many of which may be multidimensional and change) to self-monitor and self-correct
- Use knowledge of genres to monitor understanding of a text: e.g., expository nonfiction, narrative nonfiction, biography, autobiography, memoir, procedural text, persuasive text
- Use disciplinary knowledge to monitor understanding of texts that are dense with information and ideas
- Use knowledge of a range of academic disciplines to monitor understandings of conceptual ideas that cross disciplines
- Monitor understanding using knowledge of disciplinary vocabulary
- Use information from graphics (e.g., maps, diagrams, charts, photos, illustrations) to self-monitor reading

SOLVING WORDS

▶ Reading Words

- Access a very large reading vocabulary and, without conscious effort, keep attention on the meaning and language of the text
- In the infrequent instance that word solving is required, use a wide range of strategies for solving multisyllable words: e.g., using syllables, recognizing spelling patterns within words, using complex letter-sound relationships, noticing base words and affixes, using the context of the text, or using text resources
- Solve words by identifying simple, complex, and modified or shortened word parts within multisyllable words
- Read multisyllable words, many that incorporate words or word parts from languages other than English
- Solve words rapidly while processing continuous text and with minimum overt self-correction
- Read proper nouns, words from other languages, and technical words from academic disciplines that are difficult to decode and use text resources like a pronunciation guide as needed
- Solve words by identifying base words and affixes (prefixes and suffixes)

Selecting Goals Behaviors and Understandings to Notice, Teach, and Support *(cont.)*

THINKING *WITHIN* THE TEXT *(continued)*

- Solve words that offer decoding challenges because they are archaic, come from regional dialect, or are from languages other than English
- Read common, sophisticated, and academic connectives

▶ Vocabulary

- Employ the use of a wide range of text resources (e.g., glossary) and reference tools (e.g., dictionaries, textbooks) to probe the meaning and history of words as an area of inquiry
- Derive the meaning of new words and expand meaning of known words using flexible strategies: e.g., context in a sentence; connections to other words; synonyms and antonyms; word parts; base words and affixes; word function in a sentence; text resources
- Understand a wide range of Tier 2 words (those that appear frequently in writing) as well as Tier 3 words (those used in academic disciplines)
- Continue to derive the meaning of a large number of words that are specific to academic disciplines (Tier 3) and add them to the reading vocabulary
- Understand disciplinary vocabulary that occurs with frequency and is used primarily within the context of learning in the discipline (Tier 3)
- Understand the meaning and function in sentences of all parts of speech
- Understand how a writer uses words in a text to indicate perspective or point of view: i.e., first person, second person, third person
- Understand many words that have multiple meanings and identify the specific meaning that applies in a sentence or paragraph
- Understand the meaning and function of common connectives that occur in oral language and many sophisticated (complex) connectives that are more typical of written language
- Understand the meaning and function of academic connectives that appear in written texts but are seldom used in everyday oral language
- Understand denotative, connotative, idiomatic, and figurative meanings of words
- Understand the connotative and figurative meanings of words that contribute to the mood of the text, including words that assign dialogue: e.g., *sighed, whispered*
- Understand the connotative meanings of words that contribute to the tone of the text
- Understand that in graphic texts, information about words is in the illustrations, and also that many unusual words appear in graphic texts
- Understand words used in regional or historical dialects
- Understand the connotative meaning of words (descriptive adjectives, verbs, adverbs) necessary to communicate nuances of characters' behavior
- Derive the meaning of technical words and author-created words in science fiction

- Derive the meaning of author-created words designed to communicate nuances of setting, character attributes, and action in some fantasy and science fiction texts
- Understand words used informally by particular groups of people: e.g., slang, dialect
- Understand words, phrases, idioms, and expressions from languages other than English
- Understand a range of archaic words designed to communicate nuances of setting and character attributes
- Understand why a fiction writer would use a word in a satirical or ironic way
- Recognize ambiguous use of words whose meanings may be subject to interpretation
- Understand and acquire a large number of content-specific words that require the use of strategic actions (i.e., conceptual understanding of content, definitions within the body of a text, glossary, or other reference tool)
- Understand key words in graphics such as maps, diagrams, and charts

MAINTAINING FLUENCY

- Read orally in a way that demonstrates all dimensions of fluency (pausing, phrasing, intonation, word stress, rate)
- Read silently at a rapid rate (much faster than oral reading) while maintaining comprehension
- Demonstrate the ability to skim and scan while reading silently to search for information quickly
- Engage in silent reading at a rate fast enough to process a large amount of text with comprehension
- In oral reading, show recognition of a wide range of declarative, imperative, exclamatory, or interrogative sentences
- Sustain momentum while reading a wide variety of texts, many that are long
- Notice periods, commas, question marks, exclamation marks, parentheses, quotation marks, dashes, and ellipses and begin to reflect them with the voice through intonation and pausing
- Read speeches in a way that reflects the original speaker's intent
- When reading aloud, show in the voice when a writer means something different than the words alone indicate
- When reading orally, show in the voice when a writer uses subtle literary devices like irony
- Recognize and read expressively a variety of dialogue, some unassigned
- Read parts in a script with demonstration of all dimensions of fluency
- Show in the voice when words in a text (sometimes shown in italics) reflect unspoken thought
- Orally read novels in verse reflecting the meaning and rhythm with the voice

GUIDED READING

Selecting Goals Behaviors and Understandings to Notice, Teach, and Support *(cont.)*

MAINTAINING FLUENCY *(continued)*

- Read fiction and poetry in a dramatic and expressive way as appropriate for an audience
- Reflect numbered and bulleted lists with the voice when reading orally
- Use the voice to reflect disciplinary content in different ways: e.g., historical account vs. scientific argument

ADJUSTING

- Adjust reading to recognize a wide range of declarative, imperative, exclamatory, or interrogative sentences, many that are very complex
- Adjust reading to recognize a hybrid text or a text with embedded forms such as letters, diaries, journal entries, and other authentic documents
- Adjust reading to form expectations based on purposes and characteristics of fiction and nonfiction genres as well as special forms such as complex graphic texts
- Adjust reading to meet the special demands of a graphic text
- Slow down to search for or reflect on information or to enjoy language and resume reading with momentum
- Adjust reading to accommodate a wide variety of complex sentences with embedded phrases and clauses as well as parenthetical information
- Adjust to accommodate embedded forms (e.g., letters, diaries, journal entries, and other authentic documents) within narrative and expository texts
- Adjust expectations with regard to the multiple genres in a hybrid text
- Adjust reading to recognize and use characteristics of special types of fiction such as mystery; adventure story; animal story; family, friends, and school story; satire/parody; horror story; romance
- Adjust to read parts in a script, including longer stretches of dialogue and occasional use of monologue or soliloquy
- Adjust reading to recognize variations in narrative structure: e.g., story-within-a-story, flashback, flash-forward, time-lapse
- Adjust reading to process texts with multiple or parallel plots, each with its own cast of characters
- Adjust reading to follow texts that change perspective and/or narrator within the larger narrative
- Adjust reading to recognize nonfiction genres: e.g., expository nonfiction, narrative nonfiction, biography, autobiography, memoir, procedural text, persuasive text, hybrid text

- Adjust reading to recognize forms: e.g., poems; plays; graphic texts; letters, diaries and journal entries; photo essays and news articles; speeches (and similar persuasive texts such as brief debate excerpts and position papers)
- Adjust to recognize the use of complex forms of argument in a persuasive text including editorials, propaganda, and advertising
- Adjust reading to process very dense texts with body text and many graphic features
- Adjust reading to reflect a series of steps in a procedural text
- Adjust reading to process a text with dense presentation of facts and ideas

SUMMARIZING

- Present a concise, organized oral summary that includes all important information
- Present an oral summary that consists of important information and, where important, offers an opinion with evidence
- Summarize a selected section of a text that is significant to understanding characters, the plot, or the message
- Summarize important parts of a text (chapters or sections) in a way that addresses specific questions or clarifies the larger meaning of the text
- Present an organized oral summary that includes setting (if important), significant plot events including climax and resolution, main characters and supporting characters, character change (where significant), and one or more themes (fiction)
- Present a logically organized oral summary that includes important information expressing the main idea or larger message and reflects the overall structure (expository or narrative) as well as important underlying text structures: e.g., description, cause and effect, chronological sequence, temporal sequence, categorization, comparison and contrast, problem and solution, question and answer (nonfiction)
- Present an organized oral summary that includes all of the important information (as indicated above) and also offers evidence of the authenticity of a text
- Present a review of a text that includes all important information noted above and that also identifies particular elements of style and/or literary quality

Selecting Goals Behaviors and Understandings to Notice, Teach, and Support *(cont.)*

THINKING ***BEYOND*** THE TEXT

PREDICTING

◆ Make predictions based on current understanding of human behavior and emotions gained from personal experience and from vicarious experiences in reading fiction and nonfiction texts

◆ Make predictions based on background or disciplinary knowledge in the social sciences and natural sciences

◆ Make predictions based on broad knowledge of literary works: e.g., genres, special types, text structures, purposes

◆ Make predictions based on the panels in graphic texts

◆ Justify predictions with evidence from the text

◆ Justify predictions with evidence from understanding of human experience and/or disciplinary and literary knowledge

◆ Predict the ending of a story based on understanding of different kinds of narrative structure and understanding of setting, plot, and characters

◆ Make predictions based on knowledge of the characteristics of fiction and nonfiction genres, as well as an understanding of and experience reading different types of fiction texts such as mystery or survival stories

◆ Understand that there are many variations in narrative plot structure

◆ Make predictions based on plot structure: e.g., predict connections between characters and events in a text with circular plot, parallel plots, main plot and subplot

◆ Make predictions about the action of the plot, problem resolution, and character behavior in complex texts

◆ Use content knowledge in the natural and social disciplines to interpret the information in texts and use it to predict the meaning of further content

◆ Make predictions based on knowledge of special forms: e.g., letters, diaries, and journal entries; photo essays and news articles; speeches

◆ Make predictions based on knowledge of underlying text structures: e.g., description, cause and effect, chronological sequence, temporal sequence, categorization, comparison and contrast, problem and solution, question and answer

MAKING CONNECTIONS

◆ Connect disciplinary knowledge from the natural and social sciences to the content of fiction and nonfiction texts

◆ Connect the content and problems in fiction and nonfiction texts to current and historical social issues and global problems

◆ Make many different kinds of connections among texts: e.g., content, genre, theme, author, illustrator, characters or subject of a biography, style, message

◆ State explicitly the nature of connections: e.g., topic, theme, message, characters or subjects, genre, author, style, mood, tone, illustrator

◆ Connect texts to their own lives and to content and plots that are particularly important to preadolescents and adolescents

◆ Use disciplinary knowledge from the natural and social sciences to understand settings, plots, and characters in both historical and realistic fiction

◆ Use disciplinary knowledge (science and technology) to understand science fiction

◆ Make connections with the human traits and problems that are shared among people of many different cultures

◆ Apply understandings of elements and basic motifs of fantasy to comprehend fantasy and science fiction

◆ Use disciplinary knowledge from the natural sciences to understand the problems and settings in all fiction texts

◆ Connect symbols to the ideas or emotions they represent

◆ Connect problems and characters in fiction texts to global issues and problems faced by human beings

◆ Make connections between disciplinary knowledge of the natural and social sciences and the content of texts

◆ Use disciplinary knowledge from the natural and social sciences to understand the content in a wide variety of texts

◆ Make connections between knowledge of the characteristics and structures of nonfiction genres (narrative and expository, persuasive, procedural, biographical) and the structures actually encountered in texts

◆ Use inquiry to connect texts by topic, genre, and structure

◆ Build disciplinary knowledge by making connections across disciplines through wide reading of nonfiction

SYNTHESIZING

◆ Use fiction and nonfiction texts to develop new insights into the human condition and form social attitudes, opinions, and moral views on current and historical social issues

◆ Create mental categories or representations of bodies of knowledge; access and continually revise categories or representations as new information is encountered in a variety of texts

◆ Explicitly state new knowledge, ideas, and attitudes built from reading fiction and nonfiction texts and provide evidence from the texts

◆ Build new knowledge across fiction and nonfiction texts that are connected in topic, content, or theme

◆ Use texts in many genres (e.g., realistic fiction, historical fiction, traditional literature) to gain new insights into cultures and historical times that cannot be accessed directly

◆ Express changes in ideas, attitudes, or values developed as a result of reading all genres of fiction texts

◆ Apply perspective learned from reading fiction to issues and problems that face adolescents and young adults in society: e.g., peer pressure, social relationships, bullying, maturation, career choices, life decisions

◆ Recognize familiar and new information and categories of information when encountered in texts

Selecting Goals Behaviors and Understandings to Notice, Teach, and Support *(cont.)*

SYNTHESIZING *(continued)*

◆ Recognize perspectives and belief systems that are contrary to one's own and make decisions about changing perspectives and beliefs in response

◆ Recognize new information in arguments in persuasive texts and make decisions about changing beliefs or attitudes in response

◆ Continue to expand knowledge of the language and structure of academic and scientific disciplines through reading

◆ Expand knowledge of academic vocabulary through reading

◆ Use inquiry to build knowledge of a topic through reading more than one written source (primary and secondary)

INFERRING

◆ Infer comparisons being made by an author in an extended metaphor or allegory

◆ Infer information about characters, setting, plot, and action from graphic texts, in which illustrations carry much of the meaning

◆ Make inferences about setting to help in understanding the story

◆ Infer the significance of the setting in a biographical text

◆ Infer a character's thoughts and feelings as revealed in a monologue or soliloquy, usually in a play

◆ Identify round characters and infer the traits and development of those characters in a text

◆ Identify flat characters and infer the unchanging traits of those characters in a text

◆ Infer feelings and motives of multiple characters across complex plots with some subplots

◆ Infer character traits, feelings, and motivations from what characters say, think, or do and what others say or think about them

◆ Infer complex relationships between and among characters by noticing evidence in their responses to each other

◆ Compare inferences with those of other readers and consider alternative interpretations of characters' motives and the writer's message

◆ Infer potential solutions to a story problem and find supporting evidence in the text

◆ Distinguish multiple plots in a text, each with its own set of main and supporting characters, and infer relationships among those characters

◆ Infer symbolic meanings in a text

◆ Infer themes, ideas, and characters' feelings from the panels in graphic texts

◆ Infer abstract ideas and themes that have relevance to human problems globally

◆ Infer the writer's biases and underlying beliefs

◆ Infer attitudes that may be new or contrary to readers' current beliefs

◆ Infer multiple themes or messages in a text that may be understood in many layers

◆ Infer how the messages and themes in fiction texts are applicable to today's life

◆ Infer universal human themes and issues that affect human problems across the world

◆ Infer the overarching theme(s) in a collection of short stories

◆ Infer the purpose of a writer of a memoir or autobiography

◆ Infer the attitude of a biographer toward a subject

◆ Infer hidden or explicit messages in a persuasive text

◆ Infer the writer's message (some subtly implied) in texts that include serious and mature subject matter: e.g., hardship, war, racism, economic struggle, social class, the environment

◆ Infer information from all elements of a text: e.g., body, sidebars, illustrations, graphics, various text resources, decorative or informative illustrations and/or print outside the body of the text (peritext)

◆ Infer the significance of design and other features of the peritext

◆ Use the writer's language to infer the mood and tone of a text

◆ Infer the meaning or meanings of an allusion in a text

◆ Infer humor in a text

◆ Infer beliefs, customs, and perspectives of people who live in other cultures

◆ Infer beliefs, customs, and perspectives of people who live in the near and distant past

◆ Infer what life might be like and what people might believe and do at a time in the future

◆ Infer the significance of, and the interrelationships between, global problems that have implications for the quality of life, the survival of species, or the future

◆ Infer the larger messages in a nonfiction text: i.e., whatever can be learned beyond the facts

◆ Use disciplinary knowledge from the natural or social sciences to infer the significance of information in a text

Selecting Goals Behaviors and Understandings to Notice, Teach, and Support *(cont.)*

THINKING *ABOUT* THE TEXT

ANALYZING

- Understand that there may be different genres and special forms in each of the larger categories of fiction and nonfiction
- Understand that a graphic text may represent any fiction or nonfiction genre
- Understand that the divisions between genres are not always clear, and identify fiction and nonfiction genres in a hybrid text
- Understand and describe characteristics of fiction genres, including realistic fiction, historical fiction, traditional literature (folktale, fairy tale, fable, myth, legend), fantasy, and hybrid text
- Notice elements and basic motifs of fantasy: e.g., the supernatural, imaginary and otherworldly creatures, gods and goddesses, talking animals, struggle between good and evil, magic, fantastic or magical objects, wishes, trickery, transformations
- Analyze fantasy to determine elements and basic motifs
- Identify and understand characteristics of special types of fiction: e.g., mystery; adventure story; animal story; family, friends, and school story
- Understand that fiction genres may be combined within one text
- Understand the difference between realism and fantasy across fiction texts
- Understand and describe the characteristics of nonfiction genres, including expository nonfiction, narrative nonfiction, biography, autobiography, memoir, procedural text, persuasive text, and hybrid text
- Understand that nonfiction genres may be combined within one text
- Notice that a biography is built around significant events, problems to overcome, and the subject's decisions
- Understand that the information and ideas in a text are related to each other and notice how the author presents this
- Recognize a writer's use of embedded forms (e.g., letters, directions, journal entries) within narrative and expository text structures
- Recognize how a writer uses exposition (information provided to the reader about setting, characters, etc.)
- Recognize a writer's use of underlying text structures: e.g., description, cause and effect, chronological sequence, temporal sequence, categorization, comparison and contrast, problem and solution, question and answer
- Notice and understand expository text structure (categorized information) and the use of narrative structure for biographical texts and other types of narrative nonfiction
- Notice the logic and structure of a writer's argument
- Think analytically about the significance of a title and notice symbolism or multiple meanings
- Recognize a writer's selection of genre and text structure for different purposes and audiences
- Think analytically about the significance of literary elements in a text
- Identify and understand a writer's use of literary devices such as contradiction, paradox, and allusion
- Notice when a text includes a moral lesson (sometimes implied and sometimes explicit) close to the end of the story
- Identify and differentiate between internal conflict and external conflict
- Analyze a text to think about the perspective from which the story is told and notice when that perspective changes
- Notice how a writer creates, sustains, and releases suspense
- Notice characteristics of settings in fantasy that require believing in magic and/or an imaginary world
- Understand the characteristics of settings (cultural, physical, historical) and the way they affect characters' attitudes and decisions
- Notice how a writer reveals main and supporting characters by what they do, think, or say, and by what others say about them or how others respond to them
- Identify round characters (those who change and develop) and flat characters (those who do not change) in a text
- Analyze the roles of supporting characters and how they are important (or unimportant) in the story and in the development of main character(s)
- Identify the central story problem or conflict in a text with multiple episodes or parallel plots
- Recognize and understand variety in narrative structure: e.g., circular plot, parallel plots, main plot and subplot(s), story-within-a-story, flashback, flash-forward, time-lapse
- Recognize and understand multiple plots, each with its own set of main and supporting characters, in a text
- Reflect on a writer's use of words with connotative meanings, and discuss what it conveys to the reader
- Notice a writer's use of language and state how it specifically adds to the meaning, quality, and mood of a text
- Notice a writer's use of figurative language and state how it specifically adds to the meaning or enjoyment of a text
- Notice and interpret language that reveals the writer's attitude and communicates the tone of a text
- Notice a writer's use of both common and sophisticated connectives as well as some academic connectives
- Discuss a writer's purpose in selecting a particular genre, topic, subject, or type of narrative structure
- Notice aspects of the writer's craft: e.g., style, syntax, use of one or more narrators
- Reflect analytically about a writer's word choice in terms of connotations

Selecting Goals Behaviors and Understandings to Notice, Teach, and Support *(cont.)*

THINKING *ABOUT* THE TEXT *(continued)*

ANALYZING *(continued)*

- Notice a writer's use of non-sentences for literary effect
- Recognize and compare writing styles, making connections within multiple works of a single writer as well as making connections between works by different writers
- Locate language in a text that reveals setting, problem, character traits, character change, theme, symbolic meanings, narrator, mood, tone
- Notice how a writer uses language to help readers experience what characters are feeling
- Understand that a writer selects first-, second-, or third-person point of view to tell a story
- Notice a writer's use of figurative language (including metaphor, simile, personification, extended metaphor, and allegory) and state how it specifically adds to the meaning or enjoyment of a text
- Notice a writer's use of poetic and expressive language in dialogue
- Notice a writer's use of monologue and soliloquy (typically in a play) as well as extended dialogue to reveal a character's thoughts
- Notice a writer's use of irony and the language that typifies it
- Notice literary language typical of traditional literature: e.g., *a long time ago there lived, long ago and far away, once there lived*
- Notice a writer's use of humorous words or onomatopoetic words and talk about how they add to the action
- Understand that a nonfiction writer may use argument in a persuasive text
- Notice how a writer uses language in a persuasive way
- Notice language used to show chronological and temporal order
- Understand how illustrations and text work together to enhance meaning and communicate the mood of the text
- Notice how the writer/illustrator selects and places photos in a way that tells a story or communicates a larger meaning in a photo essay
- Notice and discuss how characteristics of the peritext enhance meaning, symbolize culture, create mood, or help readers interpret the text
- Use academic language to talk about genres: e.g., *fiction; family, friends, and school story; folktale; animal story; humorous story; fairy tale; fable; tall tale; realistic fiction; mystery; adventure story; sports story; historical fiction; fantasy; traditional literature; myth; legend; science fiction; nonfiction; informational text; informational book; factual text; how-to book; biography; autobiography; narrative nonfiction; memoir; procedural text; persuasive text, hybrid text; expository text*

- Use academic language to talk about forms: e.g., *series book, play, chapter book, comics, graphic text, letter, sequel, short story, diary entry, journal entry, news article, feature article*
- Use academic language to talk about literary features: e.g., *beginning, ending, character, question and answer, main character, message, dialogue, topic, events, setting, description, problem and solution, comparison and contrast, main idea, flashback, conflict, resolution, theme, descriptive language, simile, cause and effect, categorization, persuasive language, plot, character development, supporting character, point of view, figurative language, metaphor, temporal sequence, chronological sequence, subject, argument, subplot, flash-forward, time-lapse, story-within-a-story, symbol, symbolism, first-person narrative, third-person narrative, secnd-person narrative, mood*
- Use specific language to talk about book and print features: e.g., *front cover, back cover, page, author, illustrator, illustration, photograph, title, label, drawing, heading, caption, frame, panel, table of contents, chapter, chapter title, dedication, sidebar, glossary, map, diagram, infographic, author's note, illustrator's note, section, book jacket, acknowledgments, subheading, text, pronunciation guide, chart, graph, timeline, index, foreword, cutaway, footnote, epilogue, endnote, appendix, references, prologue, bibliography*

CRITIQUING

- Evaluate the overall quality of a text (e.g., illustrations or graphics, quality of writing, format/structure) and share opinions
- Critique a piece of literature by breaking it into component parts and evaluating how they fit together to accomplish the writer's purpose or communicate a message
- Critique the plot of a piece of literature to evaluate it in terms of believability and logic
- Critique the choice of setting and how it affects the theme and the mood of the story
- Critique the writer's creation of characters, how they face challenges, and how they develop in terms of believability, logic, and role in communicating the message
- Critique the writer's theme and message in terms of value and credibility
- Critique a text in a way that expresses the student's own opinions and impressions (as opposed to merely summarizing)
- Critique the use of graphics, sidebars, and body text, and discuss how they add to the quality of a text and/or help readers understand the topic

Selecting Goals Behaviors and Understandings to Notice, Teach, and Support *(cont.)*

THINKING *ABOUT* THE TEXT *(continued)*

- Use other information (from research, reading, etc.) to evaluate the authenticity of a text
- Compare content, topic, or events across several sources and use information to critique individual texts or groups of texts
- Notice the references and assurances the writer provides to authenticate a text
- Distinguish between primary and secondary sources and think critically about the authenticity of a text
- Agree or disagree with a writer's arguments and give rationales for opinions
- Express personal opinions about aspects of the text that make it engaging or interesting and provide examples and evidence from the text to justify
- Express tastes and preferences in reading and support choices with descriptions and examples of literary elements: e.g., plot, setting, language, characterization

- Express preferences with specific references to characteristics of fiction and nonfiction genres
- Think critically about the quality of a text and how well it exemplifies its genre, and share opinions
- Critique the selection of subject for a biography as worthwhile or important
- Think critically about the subject of a biography, discussing the achievements, admirable traits, and flaws of the individual
- Think critically about the writer's tone to examine a text for bias
- Critique the presentation of content and/or the subject of biography to uncover bias, distortion of fact, or omission of important information
- Think critically about the writing in a memoir or autobiography to detect error or bias
- Critique the text in terms of its relevance to today's social issues and problems affecting people: families, society, the future, quality of life, protection of the environment

Planning for Word Work After Guided Reading

Using your recent observations of the readers' ability to take words apart quickly and efficiently while reading text, plan for one to three minutes of active engagement of students' attention to letters, sounds, and words. Prioritize the readers' noticing of print features and active hands-on use of magnetic letters, a white board, word cards, or pencil and paper to promote fluency and flexibility in visual processing.

Examples:

- Make a full range of plural nouns, including regular plurals that require spelling changes and irregular plurals (*pheasant/pheasants; fortress/fortresses; galley/galleys; personality/personalities; die/dice*)
- Work flexibly with a base word, changing letters or adding or taking away one or more affixes to make a new word (*soot/sort/resort/resorting*) and discussing changes in meaning or function
- Sort words to put together words with the same base, words with the same prefix, words with the same suffix
- Make word ladders by changing base words, prefixes, or suffixes

- Recognize and use word roots (Greek and Latin) to take apart and determine the meanings of some English words (*dem*, meaning "people," in *democratic*, "of or like a government that is run by the people who live under it")
- Recognize and use words that have similar meanings because they have the same root (*therm* meaning "heat": *thermometer* meaning "device for measuring temperature," *thermostat* meaning "automatic device for controlling temperature")
- Make word webs by centering on a base word or word root and thinking of the words related to it

- Break apart multisyllable words by syllable (*va/cant, u/ten/sil, spec/i/men, veg/e/ta/tion*)
- Sort words by any word feature
- Have an "open sort" where students notice characteristics of words and ask other students to determine the feature they used for sorting
- Recognize and use an open syllable with a long vowel sound (*fa/ble, ti/dy, le/gal*) and a closed syllable with a short vowel sound (*mel/on, bish/op, nes/tle*)
- Recognize and use homophones (*rap, wrap; brewed, brood; bussed, bust*) and homographs (*pelt, peer*)

Readers at Level

Level Z is the most complex at which you would work with students in guided reading groups. The themes are mature, focusing on difficult human problems and relationships. Settings may involve war, tragedy, sexuality, natural disaster, poverty, racism, and violent behavior; but they are not so extreme that you couldn't use them at school. (Texts with very mature themes that would be inappropriate for classroom use are leveled at Z+ and Z++.) As with other complex levels, readers are challenged by the full range of fiction and nonfiction genres. Complex fantasy, myths, and legends offer added challenge by requiring readers to recognize classical motifs such as "the hero's quest" and to identify moral issues. In addition, readers encounter abstract, special types of fiction, such as satire, and literary language used to convey irony. Themes and characters are multidimensional, may be understood on several levels, and are developed in complex ways. Some texts may include archaic language or regional dialect. In nonfiction, readers are challenged by a heavy load of information in the academic disciplines. All texts at this level require critical thinking to understand. Readers should think critically about authenticity and bias. Readers search for and use information including complex graphics and texts that present content requiring background knowledge in an integrated way. Most reading is silent; all dimensions of fluency are well established in oral reading. Readers understand and use disciplinary and academic vocabulary. In addition, readers are actively adding to their understanding of disciplinary knowledge.

Selecting Texts Characteristics of Texts at **Level Z**

GENRE

▶ Fiction

- Realistic fiction
- Historical fiction
- Traditional literature: e.g., folktale, myth, legend, epic, ballad
- High fantasy and science fiction
- Hybrid texts
- Special types of fiction: e.g., mystery; adventure story; sports story; animal story; family, friends, and school story; humorous story; satire/parody; horror story; romance story

▶ Nonfiction

- Expository nonfiction
- Narrative nonfiction
- Biography
- Autobiography
- Memoir
- Procedural texts
- Persuasive texts
- Hybrid texts

FORMS

- Series books
- Picture books
- Chapter books
- Chapter books with sequels
- Plays
- Readers' theater scripts
- Graphic texts
- Short stories
- Letter, diary, and journal entry
- Photo essays and news articles
- Speeches

TEXT STRUCTURE

- Texts with multiple episodes that are elaborated with many details
- Embedded forms (e.g., letters, directions, journal entries, emails) within narrative and expository structures
- Variations in structure: e.g., story-within-a-story, flashback, flash-forward, time-lapse
- Fiction books with chapters connected to a single plot
- Longer texts with main plot and subplots
- Complex plots with multiple story lines
- Some collections of short stories related to an overarching theme

- Texts with a change in perspective and/or narrator signaled by new chapter, section, or paragraph; language or literary feature (e.g., verb tense, imagery, setting); or print features (e.g., font, print placement)
- Nonfiction books divided into sections, and some with subsections

CONTENT

- Content interesting to and relevant for the reader
- Many books with little or no picture support for content: e.g., chapter books
- Much content that requires accessing prior knowledge
- Content that invites critical thinking to judge authenticity and accuracy
- Content that requires the reader to take on perspectives from diverse cultures and bring cultural knowledge to understanding
- Texts with new content that will engage and interest readers and expand knowledge: e.g., travel, experience with other cultures, adventures in science, survival
- Settings that require content knowledge of disciplines: e.g., history, geography, culture, language
- Content that requires emotional and social maturity to understand

- Complex content that requires analysis and study to understand
- Content that goes beyond students' immediate experience
- Texts that require content knowledge of disciplines: e.g., history, geography, culture, language, sciences, arts, math concepts
- Content that requires the reader to search for information in graphics: e.g., maps, charts, diagrams, illustrated drawings, labeled photographs

THEMES AND IDEAS

- Many texts with themes and ideas that involve societal issues important to adolescents: e.g., family, growing up, sexuality, world issues, death and illness, poverty
- Themes and ideas that require a perspective not familiar to the reader

- Complex ideas on many different topics that require real or vicarious experience (through reading) for understanding
- Texts with deeper meanings applicable to important human problems and social issues: e.g., hardship, war, racism, economic struggle, social class, the environment
- Wide range of challenging themes and ideas that build social awareness and reveal insights into the human condition
- Many ideas and themes that require understanding of cultural diversity
- Texts that present mature issues such as sexuality, murder, abuse, nuclear war, drug addiction
- Texts with abstract themes that require inferential thinking
- Texts that present multiple themes that may be understood in many layers
- Themes that evoke alternative interpretations

LANGUAGE AND LITERARY FEATURES

- Settings that are distant in time and geography
- Settings in fantasy that require the reader to accept elements of another world that could not exist in the real world
- Settings that are important to comprehension of the fiction narrative or biography
- Variety in narrative plot structure: e.g., story-within-a-story, simple flashback
- Some texts with multiple plots, each with its own set of main and supporting characters
- Main characters and supporting characters
- Multidimensional characters
- Characters revealed by what they say, think, and do and by what others say and think about them
- Characters revealed over a series of events, chapters, or book series

Selecting Texts Characteristics of Texts at **Level Z** *(cont.)*

LANGUAGE AND LITERARY FEATURES *(continued)*

- Reasons for character change that are complex and require inference
- Some texts that reveal the perspectives of more than one character
- "Round" characters that have a complex range of good and bad attributes and that change during the course of the plot, and "flat" characters that do not change but may play an important role in the plot
- Variety in presentation of dialogue: e.g., dialogue among multiple characters, dialogue with pronouns, split dialogue, direct dialogue, including unassigned dialogue and long stretches of dialogue
- Some chains of unassigned dialogue for which speakers must be inferred
- Most texts written in first- or third-person narrative, with some procedural texts in second person
- Basic motifs of traditional literature and modern fantasy: e.g., struggle between good and evil, the hero's quest, fantastic or magical objects, wishes, trickery, transformations, secondary or alternative worlds
- Moral lesson near the end of the story (sometimes explicitly stated)
- Literary language typical of traditional literature and modern fantasy: e.g., *long ago and far away*
- Descriptive, poetic, and figurative language: e.g., imagery, metaphor, simile, personification, allegory, hyperbole
- Language and events that convey an emotional atmosphere (mood) in a text, affecting how the reader feels: e.g., tension, suspense, sadness, happiness, curiosity
- Use of symbolism
- Some colloquial language in dialogue that reflects characters' personalities and/or setting
- Procedural language
- Language used to make comparisons
- Descriptive language
- Language used to show chronological order and temporal sequence
- Persuasive language and argument

- Language that reveals the author's attitude or feelings toward a subject or topic (the tone that is reflected in the style of writing): e.g., lighthearted, ironic, earnest, affectionate, formal, sarcastic, angry
- Some texts with dense presentation of facts and ideas

SENTENCE COMPLEXITY

- Some longer sentences with more than twenty words
- Wide range of declarative, imperative, exclamatory, or interrogative sentences
- Variation in sentence length and structure
- Sentences with a wide variety of parts of speech, including multiple adjectives, adverbs, and prepositional phrases
- Sentences with common, sophisticated, and academic connectives
- Long, very complex sentences joined by semicolons or colons
- Frequent use of parenthetical material embedded in sentences
- Some non-sentences for literary effect

VOCABULARY

- Many words that appear in the vocabulary of mature language users (Tier 2)
- Many words particular to a discipline (Tier 3)
- Wide variation in words used to assign dialogue
- Many words with multiple meanings
- Many words with figurative meaning
- Frequent use of idioms
- New vocabulary requiring strategic action to understand: e.g., derive meaning from context, use reference tools, notice morphology, use word roots, use analogy
- Words with connotative meanings that are essential to understanding the text
- Common connectives that link ideas and clarify meaning and are typical of oral speech, as well as many sophisticated connectives that do not appear often in everyday oral language: e.g., *although, however, meantime, meanwhile moreover, otherwise, unless, therefore, though, unless, until, whenever, yet*

- Some academic connectives that link ideas and clarify meaning and that appear in written texts but are seldom used in everyday oral language: e.g., *conversely, eventually, finally, in contrast, initially, likewise, nevertheless, nonetheless, previously, specifically, ultimately, whereas, whereby*
- Some words used ironically or satirically
- Some words from regional or historical dialects
- Words (including slang) used informally by particular groups of people
- Words from languages other than English
- Some archaic words

WORDS

- A large number of multisyllable words, many technical or scientific
- Full range of plurals
- Unlimited number of high-frequency words with multiple syllables
- Many words with easy, predictable letter-sound relationships (decodable)
- Many multisyllable words with some complex letter-sound relationships
- Some multisyllable proper nouns that are difficult to decode
- Words that offer decoding challenges because they are archaic, come from regional dialect, or are from languages other than English
- Wide range of contractions and possessives
- Full range of compound words
- Base words with multiple affixes (prefixes and suffixes)
- Common, sophisticated, and academic connectives

ILLUSTRATIONS

- Illustrations that enhance and extend meaning in the text
- Texts with illustrations every three or four pages
- Many texts with no illustrations other than decorative elements (vignette) and some with a few black-and-white illustrations
- Variety of layout in illustrations and print
- More than one kind of graphics on a page spread

Selecting Texts Characteristics of Texts at **Level Z** (cont.)

- Books with variation in color to communicate mood: e.g., sepia, black-and-white, color
- Graphic texts that provide a great deal of information in the illustrations
- Some complex, nuanced illustrations that communicate mood and meaning (literal, figurative, symbolic) to match or extend the text
- Graphics that require reader interpretation and are essential for comprehending informational text
- A range of graphics that provide information that matches and extends the text: e.g., photograph and drawing with label and/or caption; diagram, cutaway; map with legend or key, scale; infographic; chart; graph; timeline

BOOK AND PRINT FEATURES

LENGTH

- Wide variation in length (mostly shorter than forty-eight pages)
- Wide variation in number of words (2,000+)
- Some books divided into chapters
- Books divided into sections and subsections

PRINT AND LAYOUT

- Variety in print and background color
- Variety in print placement, reflecting different genres
- Italics indicating unspoken thought in some texts
- Information shown in a variety of picture and print combinations in graphic texts
- Captions under pictures that provide important information
- Print and illustrations integrated in most texts, with print wrapping around pictures
- Print placed in sidebars and graphics that provide important information
- Some archaic print in historical texts

PUNCTUATION

- Period, comma, question mark, exclamation mark, semicolon, colon, parentheses, quotation marks, hyphen, dash, and ellipses in most texts

ORGANIZATIONAL TOOLS

- Title, table of contents, chapter title, heading, subheading, sidebar

TEXT RESOURCES

- Dedication, acknowledgments, author's note, pronunciation guide, glossary, index, foreword, footnote, endnote, epilogue, appendix, references
- Texts with design features that add to the aesthetic appeal of the whole (peritext)
- Texts with design features that enhance meaning, communicate culture, create mood (peritext), or have symbolic meaning

GUIDED READING

LEVEL **Z**

Selecting Goals Behaviors and Understandings to Notice, Teach, and Support

THINKING *WITHIN* THE TEXT

SEARCHING FOR AND USING INFORMATION

- When needed, reread to search for and use information from the body text, sidebars, insets, and graphics
- Sustain searching for information texts with wide variety in length
- Sustain searching over long and highly complex sentences that include multiple phrases, clauses, and lists, and the full range of punctuation marks
- Search for information in dense texts that use academic vocabulary and present highly complex concepts
- Search for information in texts with multiple features and very dense print
- Search for and use information in texts that have multiple features, very dense print, and complex graphics and that reveal multiple facets of a disciplinary topic
- Search for information in complex texts that rely on academic discourse
- Search for and use information to understand multiple plots, perspectives, and themes in a single text
- Search for information and language that states or implies the larger message(s) of the text
- Use background knowledge to search for and understand disciplinary information
- Use disciplinary vocabulary and understanding of text structure in academic disciplines to search for and use information
- Use organizational tools to search for information: e.g., title, table of contents, chapter title, heading, subheading, sidebar, callout
- Use text resources to search for information: e.g., acknowledgments, author's note, pronunciation guide, glossary, references, index
- Search for information in sentences that vary in length, structure, and punctuation based on text complexity
- Search for information in sentences with variation in placement of subject, verb, adjectives, and adverbs
- Search for information in dialogue presented in a variety of ways: e.g., assigned and unassigned, split dialogue, direct dialogue
- Search for information in a strategic way, using knowledge of text structure and readers' tools
- Use knowledge of linear narrative structure (chronological order) within multiple episodes to search for and use information
- Use knowledge of variations in narrative structure to search for and use information e.g., story-within-a-story (framed narrative); flashback and flash-forward (fractured narrative); circular narrative; multiple or parallel plots
- Search for information in a variety of narrative structures: e.g., story-within-a-story (framed narrative); flashback and flash-forward (fractured narrative); circular narrative; multiple or parallel plots
- Notice and use punctuation marks: e.g., period, comma, question mark, exclamation mark, semicolon, colon, parentheses, quotation marks, hyphen, dash, ellipses
- Search for and use information in texts with variety in placement of the body text, sidebars, and graphics

MONITORING AND SELF-CORRECTING

- Self-monitor reading using multiple sources of information: i.e., background knowledge, syntax, word meaning, word structure, awareness of text structure, meaning of the whole text, graphics, layout, design
- Continue to monitor accuracy, self-correcting rarely (only when necessary for making sense of a text)
- Monitor comprehension closely so understanding is always assured
- Closely monitor understanding of texts using knowledge of a wide range of genres and forms: e.g., realistic, historical, high fantasy, science fiction, myths, and legends, poetry, plays
- Use understandings of literary elements (e.g., plot, main and supporting characters, setting, narrative structure) to monitor and correct reading
- Use awareness of narrative structure and of character attributes (many of which may be multidimensional and change) to self-monitor and self-correct
- Use knowledge of nonfiction genres to monitor understanding of a text: e.g., expository nonfiction, narrative nonfiction, biography, autobiography, memoir, procedural text, persuasive text
- Use disciplinary knowledge to monitor understanding of texts that are dense with information and ideas
- Use knowledge of a range of academic disciplines to monitor understandings of conceptual ideas that cross disciplines
- Monitor understanding using knowledge of disciplinary vocabulary
- Use information from graphics (e.g., maps, diagrams, charts, photos, illustrations) to self-monitor reading

SOLVING WORDS

▶ Reading Words

- Access a very large reading vocabulary and, without conscious effort, keep attention on the meaning and language of the text
- In the infrequent instance that word solving is required, use a wide range of strategies for solving multisyllable words: e.g., using syllables, recognizing spelling patterns within words, using complex letter-sound relationships, noticing base words and affixes, using the context of the text, or using text resources
- Solve words by identifying simple, complex, and modified or shortened word parts within multisyllable words
- Read multisyllable words, many that incorporate words or word parts from languages other than English
- Solve words rapidly while processing continuous text and with minimum overt self-correction
- Read proper nouns, words from other languages, and technical words from academic disciplines that are difficult to decode and use text resources like a pronunciation guide as needed
- Solve words by identifying base words and affixes (prefixes and suffixes)

Selecting Goals Behaviors and Understandings to Notice, Teach, and Support *(cont.)*

THINKING *WITHIN* THE TEXT *(continued)*

- ▪ Solve words that offer decoding challenges because they are archaic, come from regional dialect, or are from languages other than English
- Read common, sophisticated, and academic connectives

▶ Vocabulary

- Employ the use of a wide range of text resources (e.g., glossary) and reference tools (e.g., dictionaries, textbooks) to probe the meaning and history of words as an area of inquiry
- Derive the meaning of new words and expand meaning of known words using flexible strategies: e.g., context in a sentence; connections to other words; synonyms and antonyms; word parts; base words and affixes; word function in a sentence; text resources
- Understand a wide range of Tier 2 words (those that appear frequently in writing) as well as Tier 3 words (those used in academic disciplines)
- Continue to derive the meaning of a large number of words that are specific to academic disciplines (Tier 3) and add them to the reading vocabulary
- Understand disciplinary vocabulary that occurs with frequency and is used primarily within the context of learning in the discipline (Tier 3)
- Understand the meaning and function in sentences of all parts of speech
- Understand how a writer uses words in a text to indicate perspective or point of view: i.e., first person, second person, third person
- Understand many words that have multiple meanings and identify the specific meaning that applies in a sentence or paragraph
- Understand the meaning and function of common connectives that occur in oral language and many sophisticated (complex) connectives that are more typical of written language
- Understand the meaning and function of academic connectives that appear in written texts but are seldom used in everyday oral language
- Add actively to vocabulary through learning new words from reading
- Understand denotative, connotative, idiomatic, and figurative meanings of words
- Understand the connotative and figurative meanings of words that contribute to the mood of the text, including words that assign dialogue: e.g., *sighed, whispered*
- Understand the connotative meanings of words that contribute to the tone of the text
- Understand that in graphic texts, information about words is in the illustrations, and also that many unusual words appear in graphic texts
- Understand words used in regional or historical dialects
- Understand the connotative meaning of words (descriptive adjectives, verbs, adverbs) necessary to communicate nuances of characters' behavior
- Derive the meaning of technical words and author-created words in science fiction

- Derive the meaning of author-created words designed to communicate nuances of setting, character attributes, and action in some fantasy and science fiction texts
- Understand words used informally by particular groups of people: e.g., slang, dialect
- Understand words, phrases, idioms, and expressions from languages other than English
- Understand a range of archaic words designed to communicate nuances of setting and character attributes
- Understand why a fiction writer would use a word in a satirical or ironic way
- Recognize ambiguous use of words whose meanings may be subject to interpretation
- Understand and acquire a large number of content-specific words that require the use of strategic actions (i.e., conceptual understanding of content, definitions within the body of a text, glossary, or other reference tool)
- Understand key words in graphics such as maps, diagrams, and charts

MAINTAINING FLUENCY

- Read orally in a way that demonstrates all dimensions of fluency (pausing, phrasing, intonation, word stress, rate)
- Read silently at a rapid rate (much faster than oral reading) while maintaining comprehension
- Demonstrate the ability to skim and scan while reading silently to search for information quickly
- Engage in silent reading at a rate fast enough to process a large amount of text with comprehension
- In oral reading, show recognition of a wide range of declarative, imperative, exclamatory, or interrogative sentences
- Sustain momentum while reading a wide variety of texts, many that are long
- Notice periods, commas, question marks, exclamation marks, parentheses, quotation marks, dashes, and ellipses and begin to reflect them with the voice through intonation and pausing
- Read speeches in a way that reflects the original speaker's intent
- When reading aloud, show in the voice when a writer means something different than the words alone indicate
- When reading orally, show in the voice when a writer uses subtle literary devices like irony, satire, or parody
- Recognize and read expressively a variety of dialogue, some unassigned
- Read parts in a script with demonstration of all dimensions of fluency
- Show in the voice when words in a text (sometimes shown in italics) reflect unspoken thought
- Orally read novels in verse reflecting the meaning and rhythm with the voice

GUIDED READING

Selecting Goals Behaviors and Understandings to Notice, Teach, and Support *(cont.)*

MAINTAINING FLUENCY *(continued)*

- Read fiction and poetry in a dramatic and expressive way as appropriate for an audience
- Reflect numbered and bulleted lists with the voice when reading orally
- Use the voice to reflect disciplinary content in different ways: e.g., historical account vs. scientific argument

ADJUSTING

- Adjust reading to recognize a wide range of declarative, imperative, exclamatory, or interrogative sentences, many that are very complex
- Adjust reading to recognize a hybrid text or a text with embedded forms such as letters, diaries, journal entries, and other authentic documents
- Adjust reading to form expectations based on purposes and characteristics of fiction and nonfiction genres as well as special forms such as complex graphic texts
- Adjust reading to meet the special demands of a graphic text
- Slow down to search for or reflect on information or to enjoy language and resume reading with momentum
- Adjust reading to accommodate a wide variety of complex sentences with embedded phrases and clauses as well as parenthetical information
- Adjust to accommodate embedded forms (e.g., letters, diaries, journal entries, and other authentic documents) within narrative and expository texts
- Adjust expectations with regard to the multiple genres in a hybrid text
- Adjust reading to recognize and use characteristics of fiction genres and forms: e.g., realistic fiction, historical fiction, simple and some high fantasy, traditional literature, science fiction, embedded letters, diaries, and journal entries
- Adjust reading to process complex graphic texts
- Adjust to read parts in a script, including longer stretches of dialogue and occasional use of monologue or soliloquy
- Adjust reading to recognize variations in narrative structure: e.g., story-within-a-story, flashback, flash-forward, time-lapse
- Adjust reading to process texts with multiple or parallel plots, each with its own cast of characters
- Adjust reading to follow texts that change perspective and/or narrator within the larger narrative

- Adjust reading to recognize nonfiction genres: e.g., expository nonfiction, narrative nonfiction, biography, autobiography, memoir, procedural text, persuasive text, hybrid text
- Adjust reading to recognize forms: e.g., poems; plays; graphic texts; letters, diaries and journal entries; photo essays and news articles; speeches (and similar persuasive texts such as brief debate excerpts and position papers)
- Adjust to recognize the use of complex forms of argument in a persuasive text including editorials, propaganda, and advertising
- Adjust reading to process very dense texts with body text and many graphic features
- Adjust reading to reflect a series of steps in a procedural text
- Adjust reading to process a text with dense presentation of facts and ideas

SUMMARIZING

- Present a concise, organized oral summary that includes all important information
- Present an oral summary that consists of important information and, where important, offers an opinion with evidence
- Summarize a selected section of a text that is significant to understanding characters, the plot, or the message
- Summarize important parts of a text (chapters or sections) in a way that addresses specific questions or clarifies the larger meaning of the text
- Present an organized oral summary that includes setting (if important), significant plot events including climax and resolution, main characters and supporting characters, character change (where significant), and one or more themes (fiction)
- Present a logically organized oral summary that includes important information expressing the main idea or larger message and reflects the overall structure (expository or narrative) as well as important underlying text structures: e.g., description, cause and effect, chronological sequence, temporal sequence, categorization, comparison and contrast, problem and solution, question and answer (nonfiction)
- Present an organized oral summary that includes all of the important information (as indicated above) and also offers evidence of the authenticity of a text
- Present a review of a text that includes all important information noted above and that also identifies particular elements of style and/or literary quality

Selecting Goals Behaviors and Understandings to Notice, Teach, and Support *(cont.)*

THINKING *BEYOND* THE TEXT

PREDICTING

- ◆ Make predictions based on current understanding of human behavior and emotions gained from personal experience and from vicarious experiences in reading fiction and nonfiction texts
- ◆ Make predictions based on background or disciplinary knowledge in the social sciences and natural sciences
- ◆ Make predictions based on broad knowledge of literary works: e.g., genres, special types, text structures, purposes
- ◆ Make predictions based on the panels in graphic texts
- ◆ Justify predictions with evidence from the text
- ◆ Justify predictions with evidence from understanding of human experience and/or disciplinary and literary knowledge
- ◆ Predict the ending of a story based on understanding of different kinds of narrative structure and understanding of setting, plot, and characters
- ◆ Make predictions based on knowledge of challenging types of texts such as satire and parody
- ◆ Make predictions based on knowledge of the characteristics of fiction and nonfiction genres, as well as an understanding of and experience reading different types of fiction texts such as mystery or survival stories
- ◆ Understand that there are many variations in narrative plot structure
- ◆ Make predictions based on plot structure: e.g., predict connections between characters and events in a text with circular plot, parallel plots, main plot and subplot
- ◆ Make predictions about the action of the plot, problem resolution, and character behavior in complex texts
- ◆ Use content knowledge in the natural and social disciplines to interpret the information in texts and use it to predict the meaning of further content
- ◆ Make predictions based on knowledge of special forms: e.g., letters, diaries, and journal entries; photo essays and news articles; speeches
- ◆ Make predictions based on knowledge of underlying text structures: e.g., description, cause and effect, chronological sequence, temporal sequence, categorization, comparison and contrast, problem and solution, question and answer

MAKING CONNECTIONS

- ◆ Connect disciplinary knowledge from the natural and social sciences to the content of fiction and nonfiction texts
- ◆ Connect the content and problems in fiction and nonfiction texts to current and historical social issues and global problems
- ◆ Make many different kinds of connections among texts: e.g., content, genre, theme, author, illustrator, characters or subject of a biography, style, message
- ◆ State explicitly the nature of connections: e.g., topic, theme, message, characters or subjects, genre, author, style, mood, tone, illustrator

- ◆ Connect texts to their own lives and to content and plots that are particularly important to preadolescents and adolescents
- ◆ Use disciplinary knowledge from the natural and social sciences to understand settings, plots, and characters in both historical and realistic fiction
- ◆ Use disciplinary knowledge (science and technology) to understand science fiction
- ◆ Make connections with the human traits and problems that are shared among people of many different cultures
- ◆ Apply understandings of elements and basic motifs of fantasy to comprehend fantasy and science fiction
- ◆ Use disciplinary knowledge from the natural sciences to understand the problems and settings in all fiction texts
- ◆ Connect symbols to the ideas or emotions they represent
- ◆ Connect problems and characters in texts to global issues and problems faced by human beings
- ◆ Make connections between disciplinary knowledge of the natural and social sciences and the content of texts
- ◆ Use disciplinary knowledge from the natural and social sciences to understand the content in a wide variety of texts
- ◆ Make connections between knowledge of the characteristics and structures of nonfiction genres (narrative and expository, persuasive, procedural, biographical) and the structures actually encountered in texts
- ◆ Use inquiry to connect texts by topic, genre, and structure
- ◆ Build disciplinary knowledge by making connections across disciplines through wide reading of nonfiction

SYNTHESIZING

- ◆ Use fiction and nonfiction texts to develop new insights into the human condition and form social attitudes, opinions, and moral views on current and historical social issues
- ◆ Create mental categories or representations of bodies of knowledge; access and continually revise categories or representations as new information is encountered in a variety of texts
- ◆ Explicitly state new knowledge, ideas, and attitudes built from reading fiction and nonfiction texts and provide evidence from the texts
- ◆ Build new knowledge across fiction and nonfiction texts that are connected in topic, content, or theme
- ◆ Use texts in many genres (e.g., realistic fiction, historical fiction, traditional literature) to gain new insights into cultures and historical times that cannot be accessed directly
- ◆ Express changes in ideas, attitudes, or values developed as a result of reading all genres of fiction texts
- ◆ Apply perspective learned from reading fiction to issues and problems that face adolescents and young adults in society: e.g., peer pressure, social relationships, bullying, maturation, career choices, life decisions

Selecting Goals Behaviors and Understandings to Notice, Teach, and Support *(cont.)*

THINKING *BEYOND* THE TEXT *(continued)*

SYNTHESIZING *(continued)*

- Recognize familiar and new information and categories of information when encountered in texts
- Recognize perspectives and belief systems that are contrary to one's own and make decisions about changing perspectives and beliefs in response
- Recognize new information in arguments in persuasive texts and make decisions about changing beliefs or attitudes in response
- Continue to expand knowledge of the language and structure of academic and scientific disciplines through reading
- Expand knowledge of academic vocabulary through reading
- Use inquiry to build knowledge of a topic through reading more than one written source (primary and secondary)

INFERRING

- Infer the humor in satire or parody
- Infer comparisons being made by an author in an extended metaphor or allegory
- Infer information about characters, setting, plot, and action from graphic texts, in which illustrations carry much of the meaning
- Make inferences about setting to help in understanding the story
- Infer beliefs, customs, and perspectives of people who live in other cultures
- Infer the significance of the setting in a biographical text
- Infer a character's thoughts and feelings as revealed in a monologue or soliloquy
- Identify round characters and infer the traits and development of those characters in a text
- Identify flat characters and infer the unchanging traits of those characters in a text
- Infer feelings and motives of multiple characters across complex plots with some subplots
- Infer character traits, feelings, and motivations from what characters say, think, or do and what others say or think about them
- Infer complex relationships between and among characters by noticing evidence in their responses to each other
- Compare inferences with those of other readers and consider alternative interpretations of characters' motives and the writer's message
- Infer the individual, situation, or problem that is the subject of a satire or parody
- Infer symbolic meanings in a text
- Infer themes, ideas, and characters' feelings from the panels in graphic texts

- Infer abstract ideas and themes that have relevance to human problems globally
- Infer the writer's biases and underlying beliefs
- Infer the deeper meaning of satire or parody
- Distinguish multiple plots in a text, each with its own set of main and supporting characters, and infer relationships among those characters
- Infer multiple themes or messages in a text that may be understood in many layers
- Infer how the messages and themes in fiction texts are applicable to today's life
- Infer universal human themes and issues that affect human problems across the world
- Infer the overarching theme(s) in a collection of short stories
- Infer the purpose of a writer of a memoir or autobiography
- Infer the attitude of a biographer toward a subject
- Infer hidden or explicit messages in a persuasive text
- Infer the larger messages in a nonfiction text: i.e., whatever can be learned beyond the facts
- Infer the writer's message (some subtly implied) in texts that include serious and mature subject matter: e.g., hardship, war, racism, economic struggle, social class, the environment
- Infer information from all elements of a text: e.g., body, sidebars, illustrations, graphics, various text resources, decorative or informative illustrations and/or print outside the body of the text (peritext)
- Infer the meaning or meanings of an allusion in a text
- Use the writer's language to infer the mood and tone of a text
- Infer the underlying meaning of language used satirically
- Infer humor in a text
- Infer beliefs, customs, and perspectives of people who live in the near and distant past
- Infer what life might be like and what people might believe and do at a time in the future
- Infer attitudes that may be new or contrary to readers' current beliefs
- Infer potential solutions to a story problem and find supporting evidence in the text
- Infer the significance of, and the interrelationships between, global problems that have implications for the quality of life, the survival of species, or the future
- Use disciplinary knowledge from the natural or social sciences to infer the significance of information in a text
- Infer the significance of design and other features of the peritext

Selecting Goals Behaviors and Understandings to Notice, Teach, and Support *(cont.)*

THINKING *ABOUT* THE TEXT

ANALYZING

- Understand that there may be different genres and special forms in each of the larger categories of fiction and nonfiction
- Understand that a graphic text may represent any fiction or nonfiction genre
- Understand that the divisions between genres are not always clear, and identify fiction and nonfiction genres in a hybrid text
- Understand and describe characteristics of fiction genres, including realistic fiction, historical fiction, traditional literature (folktale, fairy tale, fable, myth, legend, epic, ballad), fantasy, and hybrid text
- Notice elements and basic motifs of fantasy: e.g., the supernatural, imaginary and otherworldly creatures, gods and goddesses, talking animals, struggle between good and evil, magic, fantastic or magical objects, wishes, trickery, transformations
- Analyze fantasy to determine elements and basic motifs
- Identify and understand characteristics of special types of fiction: e.g., mystery; adventure story; animal story; family, friends, and school story; satire/parody
- Notice satire and parody and begin to understand deeper meanings in relation to what is being satirized or parodied
- Understand that fiction genres may be combined within one text
- Understand the difference between realism and fantasy across fiction texts
- Have a deep understanding of the characteristics of fiction genres and use this information to analyze a text
- Understand and describe the characteristics of nonfiction genres, including expository nonfiction, narrative nonfiction, biography, autobiography, memoir, procedural text, persuasive text, and hybrid text
- Understand that nonfiction genres may be combined within one text
- Have a deep understanding of the characteristics of nonfiction genres and use this information to analyze texts
- Understand that the information and ideas in a text are related to each other and notice how the author presents this
- Recognize a writer's use of embedded forms (e.g., letters, directions, journal entries) within narrative and expository text structures
- Recognize how a writer uses exposition (information provided to the reader about setting, characters, etc.)
- Recognize a writer's use of underlying text structures: e.g., description, cause and effect, chronological sequence, temporal sequence, categorization, comparison and contrast, problem and solution, question and answer
- Notice and understand expository text structure (categorized information) and the use of narrative structure for biographical texts and other types of narrative nonfiction
- Notice the logic and structure of a writer's argument
- Think analytically about the significance of a title and notice symbolism or multiple meanings
- Recognize a writer's selection of genre and text structure for different purposes and audiences

- Identify and understand a writer's use of literary devices such as contradiction, paradox, and allusion
- Understand a writer's purpose and meaning in writing satire or parody
- Notice the humor in satire and parody and understand its role in persuasion
- Notice when a text includes a moral test (sometimes implied and sometimes explicit) close to the end of the story
- Identify and differentiate between internal conflict and external conflict
- Analyze a text to think about the perspective from which the story is told and notice when that perspective changes
- Notice how a writer creates, sustains, and releases suspense
- Notice and identify the writer's purpose in using literary devices such as foreshadowing, variety of conflict, irony (verbal, situational, dramatic), symbolism, tone, imagery
- Determine a writer's messages through an examination of the themes that appear in his or her works: e.g., human confrontation with nature, lack of humanity, rebellion, struggle for understanding, different types of conflict, struggle for justice, family conflict, pain of love or loss, competition in society, clash between civilizations and non-civilizations, destiny or fate
- Apply analytic thinking to understand very mature topics and themes
- Apply analytic thinking to understand very mature topics and ideas
- Notice characteristics of settings in fantasy that require believing in magic and/or an imaginary world
- Understand the characteristics of settings (cultural, physical, historical) and the way they affect characters' attitudes and decisions
- Notice how a writer reveals main and supporting characters by what they do, think, or say, and by what others say about them or how others respond to them
- Identify round characters (those who change and develop) and flat characters (those who do not change) in a text
- Analyze the roles of supporting characters and how they are important (or unimportant) in the story and in the development of main character(s)
- Understand that the writer may express a theme through the feelings of a main character, characters' thoughts, dialogue, character development, action, or events
- Think analytically about the significance of literary elements in a text
- Identify the central story problem or conflict in a text with multiple episodes or parallel plots
- Recognize and understand variety in narrative structure: e.g., circular plot, parallel plots, main plot and subplot(s), story-within-a-story, flashback, flash-forward, time-lapse
- Recognize and understand multiple plots, each with its own set of main and supporting characters, in a text
- Reflect on a writer's use of words with connotative meanings, and discuss what it conveys to the reader

Selecting Goals Behaviors and Understandings to Notice, Teach, and Support *(cont.)*

THINKING *ABOUT* THE TEXT *(continued)*

ANALYZING *(continued)*

- Notice a writer's use of language and state how it specifically adds to the meaning, quality, and mood of a text
- Notice a writer's use of figurative language and state how it specifically adds to the meaning or enjoyment of a text
- Notice and interpret language that reveals the writer's attitude and communicates the tone of a text
- Notice a writer's use of both common and sophisticated connectives as well as some academic connectives
- Discuss a writer's purpose in selecting a particular genre, topic, subject, or type of narrative structure
- Notice aspects of the writer's craft: e.g., style, syntax, use of one or more narrators
- Reflect analytically about a writer's word choice in terms of connotations
- Notice a writer's use of non-sentences for literary effect
- Recognize and compare writing styles, making connections within multiple works of a single writer as well as making connections between works by different writers
- Notice a writer's use of satirical language
- Locate language in a text that reveals setting, problem, character traits, character change, theme, symbolic meanings, narrator, mood, tone
- Notice how a writer uses language to help readers experience what characters are feeling
- Understand that a writer selects first-, second-, or third-person point of view to tell a story
- Notice a writer's use of figurative language (including metaphor, simile, personification, extended metaphor and allegory) and state how it specifically adds to the meaning or enjoyment of a text
- Notice a writer's use of poetic and expressive language in dialogue
- Notice a writer's use of monologue and soliloquy (typically in a play) as well as extended dialogue to reveal a character's thoughts
- Notice a writer's use of irony and the language that typifies it
- Notice literary language typical of traditional literature: e.g., *a long time ago there lived, long ago and far away, once there lived*
- Notice a writer's use of humorous words or onomatopoetic words and talk about how they add to the action
- Understand that a nonfiction writer may use argument in a persuasive text
- Notice how a writer uses language to persuade in a variety of persuasive texts and contexts (e.g., argument, essay, advertising, propaganda)
- Notice language used to show chronological and temporal order
- Understand how illustrations and text work together to enhance meaning and communicate the mood of the text
- Notice how the writer/illustrator selects and places photos in a way that tells a story or communicates a larger meaning in a photo essay

- Notice and discuss how characteristics of the peritext enhance meaning, symbolize culture, create mood, or help readers interpret the text
- Use academic language to talk about genres: e.g., *fiction; family, friends, and school story; folktale; animal story; humorous story; fairy tale; fable; tall tale; realistic fiction; mystery; adventure story; sports story; historical fiction; fantasy; traditional literature; myth; legend; ballad; science fiction; epic; satire/parody; nonfiction; informational text; informational book; factual text; how-to book; biography; autobiography; narrative nonfiction; memoir; procedural text; persuasive text, hybrid text; expository text*
- Use academic language to talk about forms: e.g., *series book, play, chapter book, comics, graphic text, letter, sequel, short story, diary entry, journal entry, news article, feature article, saga*
- Use academic language to talk about literary features: e.g., *beginning, ending, character, question and answer, main character, message, dialogue, topic, events, setting, description, problem and solution, comparison and contrast, main idea, flashback, conflict, resolution, theme, descriptive language, simile, cause and effect, categorization, persuasive language, plot, character development, supporting character, point of view, figurative language, metaphor, temporal sequence, chronological sequence, subject, argument, subplot, flash-forward, time-lapse, story-within-a-story, symbol, symbolism, first-person narrative, third-person narrative, second-person narrative, mood, episode, climax, rising action, falling action, circular plot, parallel plots, protagonist, antagonist, tone, irony, round and flat characters, personification*
- Use specific language to talk about book and print features: e.g., *front cover, back cover, page, author, illustrator, illustration, photograph, title, label, drawing, heading, caption, frame, panel, table of contents, chapter, chapter title, dedication, sidebar, glossary, map, diagram, infographic, author's note, illustrator's note, section, book jacket, acknowledgments, subheading, text, pronunciation guide, chart, graph, timeline, index, foreword, cutaway, footnote, epilogue, endnote, appendix, references, prologue, bibliography*

CRITIQUING

- Evaluate the overall quality of a text (e.g., illustrations or graphics, quality of writing, format/structure) and share opinions
- Critique a piece of literature by breaking it into component parts and evaluating how they fit together to accomplish the writer's purpose or communicate a message
- Critique the plot of a piece of literature to evaluate it in terms of believability and logic
- Critique the choice of setting and how it affects the theme and the mood of the story
- Critique the writer's creation of characters, how they face challenges, and how they develop in terms of believability, logic, and role in communicating the message
- Critique the writer's theme and message in terms of value and credibility

Selecting Goals   Behaviors and Understandings to Notice, Teach, and Support *(cont.)*

THINKING *ABOUT* THE TEXT *(continued)*

- Critique a text using several dimensions: strength and reasonableness of arguments, degree of bias, documentation of facts, qualifications of writer, impact of style and presentation
- Critique the use of graphics, sidebars, and body text, and discuss how they add to the quality of a text and/or help readers understand the topic
- Use other information (from research, reading, etc.) to evaluate the authenticity of a text
- Compare content, topic, or events across several sources and use information to critique individual texts or groups of texts
- Notice the references and assurances the writer provides to authenticate a text
- Distinguish between primary and secondary sources and think critically about the authenticity of a text
- Agree or disagree with a writer's arguments and give rationales for opinions
- Express personal opinions about aspects of the text that make it engaging or interesting and provide examples and evidence from the text to justify
- Express tastes and preferences in reading and support choices with descriptions and examples of literary elements: e.g., plot, setting, language, characterization

- Express preferences with specific references to characteristics of fiction and nonfiction genres
- Critique a text in a way that expresses the student's own opinions and impressions (as opposed to merely summarizing)
- Think critically about the quality of a fiction text and how well it exemplifies its genre, and share opinions
- Critique the selection of subject for a biography as worthwhile or important
- Think critically about the subject of a biography, discussing the achievements, admirable traits, and flaws of the individual
- Think critically about the writer's tone to examine a text for bias
- Critique the presentation of content and/or the subject of biography to uncover bias, distortion of fact, or omission of important information
- Think critically about the writing in a memoir or autobiography to detect error or bias
- Critique the text in terms of its relevance to today's social issues and problems affecting people: families, society, the future, quality of life, protection of the environment

Planning for Word Work After Guided Reading

Using your recent observations of the readers' ability to take words apart quickly and efficiently while reading text, plan for one to three minutes of active engagement of students' attention to letters, sounds, and words. Prioritize the readers' noticing of print features and active hands-on use of magnetic letters, a white board, word cards, or pencil and paper to promote fluency and flexibility in visual processing.

Examples:

- Make a full range of plural nouns, including regular plurals that require spelling changes and irregular plurals (*annoyance/annoyances; ambush/ ambushes; alloy/alloys; directory/ directories; radius/radii*)
- Work flexibly with a base word, changing letters or adding or taking away one or more affixes to make a new word (*scald/ scaly/nonscaly/scalier*) and discussing changes in meaning or function
- Sort words to put together words with the same base, words with the same prefix, words with the same suffix

- Make word ladders by changing base words, prefixes, or suffixes
- Recognize and use word roots (Greek and Latin) to take apart and determine the meanings of some English words (*bio*, meaning "life," in *biology*, "the scientific study of living things")
- Recognize and use words that have similar meanings because they have the same root (*ver* meaning "true": *verdict* meaning "the decision of a jury," *verify* meaning "to prove to be true")
- Make word webs by centering on a base word or word root and thinking of the words related to it

- Break apart multisyllable words by syllable (*frig/id, re/mem/brance, tes/ti/mo/ny, dis/a/gree/a/ble*)
- Sort words by any word feature
- Have an "open sort" where students notice characteristics of words and ask other students to determine the feature they used for sorting
- Recognize and use an open syllable with a long vowel sound (*la/den, cli/max, slo/gan*) and a closed syllable with a short vowel sound (*liv/id, bom/bard, shut/ter*)
- Recognize and use homophones (*gait, gate; packed, pact; hoard, horde*) and homographs (*keen, quarry*)

GUIDED READING

Grammar, Usage, and Mechanics

Grammar, Usage, and Mechanics Continuum

All you have to do to realize that the English language varies widely in form and use is to watch television for about two hours, changing channels frequently. Perhaps because of television and movies, and now social media, wide access to every geographical area of the world has greatly increased tolerance and value for different dialects, sentence patterns, idioms, expressions. We enjoy listening to different patterns of speech from people in all walks of life. One thing has not changed, however: Power is associated with language grammar and use.

Two social markers have survived all of the liberating changes of the last century. These markers—speech and literacy—are required if the individual is to have access to the highest levels of power. And, of these two, literacy is the lesser! Our speech immediately signals to others our level of education and implies knowledge and expertise. (There is actually no relationship between proper grammar, intelligence, and skill—but it seems that way.) The bottom line is that when people enter the world of work and/or higher education, there is a big payoff in being able to speak with what in the past was called "proper grammar" or "standard grammar.' It's the way language is used by newscasters, executives, salespeople, advertisers, politicians, teachers, doctors, lawyers, and others, at least in public life.

A set of underlying "rules" governs the use of language, and that is true of every language and every dialect or register of every language. A dialect is a form of a language that is specific to a geographic region or to a particular group of people. The rules refer to features of phonology (pronunciation), the syntax or grammar of a language, the vocabulary, and other features of language. A register is a variety of a language used in a particular setting or for a particular purpose. We all have a number of registers, meaning that we speak differently with our close friends in social situations than we might while teaching a class or giving a speech. All of this variation shows just how amazing language is and what a huge body of knowledge all speakers have.

So what we try to do in school is to help students broaden or expand their use of language. Our purpose is not to communicate to them that their own language (which members of their own family speak) is "bad" and that standard English is somehow "good." One descriptive phrase that many teachers we know find helpful is "like they say it in books." Our real purpose is to help each student grow in the development of a formal register that will serve him well in academic and work situations. They can continue to use their other registers with friends and at home, but now they have a greater range.

We have included the information in this appendix as a resource for teachers so that they have a vision of the characteristics of that formal register. Over the time students spend with us in grades pre-K to 8, we work hard to support language, knowledge of how formal English "works," and the ability to present oneself as skillful speaker of the language. We recognize that some careers do not require control of formal English—but a great many do. In addition, the formal use of English is highly advantageous in social situations. We want to increase student choices and access—not limit them.

Linguistic Competence—More Than Good Grammar

We wish to acknowledge that using formal, rule-governed English does not equal linguistic competence, which among many skills includes excellent communication, use of the imagination, ability to express one's thinking articulately, and the ability to listen before responding. You can speak in accordance with all the rules of grammar and still say nothing worthwhile and/or still have difficulty communicating your point. (All you have to do, again, is watch television for two hours and you will find plenty of examples!) You can use formal grammar and write poorly. You can use "nonstandard" grammar and communicate vividly, richly, and convincingly. So, while we are emphasizing formal language usage here, we do so within a rich language program that involves large amounts of meaningful talk, reading, and writing that will help students know *what* to say (or have something to say).

Immersing, Teaching, Supporting—Not "Correcting"

The information in this appendix is provided to support your work in helping students expand their knowledge of how language is used. This chart can be a resource as you teach in the following ways:

- Interact with students, providing a model of formal grammar and usage. *(Nothing is more powerful in language learning than engaging with other speakers of the language.)*

- Read to students, providing models not only of formal grammar and usage but also of excellent writing. *(Students will begin to take on the language of books very early.)*

- Have conversations with students about their writing, giving advice on conventions. *(Writing slows down and makes visible the way words are put together in sentences and sentences in paragraphs. Students learn how nouns, verbs, and other parts of speech fit together. They can move them around and reform sentences. They can choose new words.)*

- Engage students in close reading of a text so that they look carefully at the way a writer uses language. *(This makes the models come alive. Language is more visible.)*

- Invite students to engage in talk that is grounded in texts. *(They gain power over the language as they discuss it. They find examples to support their points. They take on the language of the text.)*

- Help students develop their own oral speaking powers through presentation, readers' theater, and speeches. *(When you prepare for a presentation, you take special care with the language. You ask for feedback, and you change the language to communicate better. Students begin to sense a need for formal speaking.)*

All of the above are far more powerful and effective than "correcting" a student's oral language immediately, particularly before an audience of peers, which simply discourages further speaking. Only by speaking can a student take on formal English patterns. We want to create the *desire* to expand use of language.

What About Grammar Lessons?

A very traditional approach to teaching standard usage is to assign students to exercises—often using worksheets—which they have to fill out with correct verb tense selection, plural forms, etc. While you may occasionally want to teach a minilesson on some kind of usage that almost all students need to learn, isolated grammar lessons are probably the least effective way to expand your students' speech and writing. They need to talk and write about *something*; hearing models of English read, reading closely, and talking and writing about reading are more meaningful and effective. Using models is also more likely to assure that students transfer the new learning about usage into their own talk and writing.

One of the problems is that whole-class grammar lessons are inefficient. Some students will already know the new structures, and for others, the structures are too hard. Also, it is not very helpful for students to memorize lists of rules. They need to be able to apply the rules and, eventually, to know them implicitly.

If you want to teach a short grammar lesson, relate it to a book you have read or some shared writing that you and the students are doing together. Pointing out how language works (for example, noun and verb agreement or use of adjectives) is teaching grammar on a text that has meaning for students. In guided reading, you can help students with some tricky language structure as you introduce the book, and they can even "rehearse" the language so that they become accustomed to the pattern and the rhythm. Knowing what "sounds right" goes a long way in learning formal grammar, and that will take years for many students.

What About English Language Learners?

We suspect this question came to your mind immediately when you saw the title of this appendix. While every classroom consists of a diverse group of language users, the presence of English language learners introduces special challenges and opportunities.

First, we have to recognize that they are very different from each other, so we have diversity within diverse groups! ELLs vary according to

- the languages spoken in their homes;
- the amount of time they have been speaking English;
- whether they are literate in the first language;
- the number of opportunities they have to enter into conversation with English speakers;
- the models of English they are exposed to.

In general, the research on ELLs suggests that there are some general phases in the acquisition of English (see *Guided Reading: Responsive Teaching Across the Grades, Second Edition*). They move from "beginning, which may involve silence or one-word answers, to "early" with the use of key words to participate, and simple sentences in about six to eighteen months. From there, it takes about two to five more years to become "advanced" users of English. So, these ELLs are not only learning English but also expanding the ways they use English and probably developing a variety of English registers. What a complex task!

These learners need a very rich language experience, including many safe contexts in which to try speak English. Interactive read-aloud, shared reading, book clubs, and guided reading all offer opportunity for text-based talk. Provide maximum opportunities for interaction; make it possible for students to share; but do it in an invitational way. You will see your students taking on the body of knowledge shown in this chart, but they will need time and opportunity. Meanwhile, your listening to them and responding in a meaningful way, showing that you value the meaning of what they have to say, will be the best encouragement they can get.

When Should They Know What?

This chart represents a body of knowledge and understandings that students acquire in highly diverse ways. When they all come in with such a variety of language knowledge, we would not want to prescribe when *all* students should acquire a particular structure. What matters is that all are gaining control over standard English language structures. Some general principles are:

- Simpler concepts will be learned before complex ones.
- Learning is continuous and cumulative.
- Language use becomes increasingly complex because concepts build on one another.
- Learning depends on opportunity.
- Learners need to hear examples of language use within meaningful situations before they can engage in formal study of them.
- Successful acquisition of language use depends on much more than direct instruction.

In general, items on the chart are grouped from simple to more complex—although we caution that this may not work as a learning sequence for all students.

Using the Grammar, Usage, and Mechanics Chart

This chart is not intended to be a curriculum for instruction in formal grammar. The primary, intermediate, and middle-school designations for each bullet are approximated and will vary a great deal by individual. Each learner is constantly revising her ability to use language in sophisticated ways. It's important to remember that a language learner can speak with highly standardized and sophisticated grammar *without being able to recite the exact "rules."* As you look at this chart, you will see many examples of grammatical language that you use in talking and writing but might not be able to label. That's because these rules are *unconsciously* held even though they are used just about every minute of the day. Speakers internalize this system of rules through use. This chart details rules of usage based on the appropriate time we would see speakers *using* them—not when we would expect them to recite the rules. They may never explicitly know all the rules. So, when you ask a reader a question like "does it sound right?" you mean something quite complex. You are asking the reader to consider the language in light of what he presently "knows" implicitly. It's the internal sense you want to help students develop and so it is a good thing for you to have a reference tool. The best way to help speakers expand their repertoire of standard usage is to immerse them in language by

- hearing it read aloud;
- using oral language that is grounded in texts;
- engaging in wide reading of their choice (remembering that all texts provide a demonstration of standard English usage);
- writing about reading;
- giving them opportunities to write for varied purposes and audiences.

You can use this chart as a resource across instructional contexts. As well, in other continua you will find reference in briefer form to students' understanding of and use of conventions of language usage. The understanding and use of language is integrated into what students discuss and write.

Sometimes it has been so long since our own linguistic studies that, while we use language in a formal way, we have to search for the exact language to describe it. All of the items in a category may not come readily to mind. So the chart can be used for quick reference. It places the information in one place. Use it to

- develop your understandings of the language;
- guide your observations of student language use in talk and writing;
- help you notice learning and growth;
- give you some language with which to talk about language structure as appropriate to the age group;
- suggest areas of learning in shared reading;
- guide your text introductions in guided reading;
- inform your conferences with students in writing;
- suggest a focus in shared writing;
- suggest valuable language structures for shared reading;
- suggest some "friendly" language for each behavior that can be used for explanation or instruction (see "Instructional Language").

The instructional language provides a clear statement of the behavior or principle. You may need to shape it if you want to use it in an explicit way with students. Remember that there are only some behaviors and principles that students need to be able to talk about explicitly.

GRAMMAR, USAGE, AND MECHANICS

BEHAVIOR	INSTRUCTIONAL LANGUAGE	GRADE LEVEL		
		PRIMARY	INTERMEDIATE	MIDDLE SCHOOL
Parts of Speech				
1 Recognize and use the eight parts of speech of the English language.	*Words have different functions in a sentence.* *The eight parts of speech are names for words with eight different functions.* *The parts of speech are noun, pronoun, adjective, verb, adverb, preposition, conjunction, and interjection.*		•	•
2 Recognize and use nouns: • names of persons: e.g., *woman, Emily Dickinson* • names of places: e.g., *city, Chicago* • names of things: e.g., *automobile, Chevrolet; stallion, Flame; theater, Radio City Music Hall* • names of ideas: e.g., *honesty.*	*A noun is a word used to name a person, place, thing, or idea.* *A common noun is the general name for a person, place, thing, or idea.* *A proper noun is the formal name of a particular person, place, or thing. A proper noun begins with a capital letter.*	•	•	•
3 Recognize and use pronouns (simpler will be learned before more complex): • personal: e.g., *I, you, he, she, it, we, you, they (nominative case); me, you, her, him, it, us, you, them (objective case); my, mine, your, yours, his, her, hers, its, our, ours, your, yours, their, theirs (possessive case)* • relative: e.g., *that, which, who, whom, whose* • Interrogative: *what, which, who, whom, whose* • demonstrative: *that, these, this, those* • indefinite: e.g., *all, another, any, anybody, anyone, anything, both, each, either, everybody, everyone, everything, few, many, more, most, much, neither, nobody, none, no one, nothing, one, other, several, some, somebody, someone, something* • reflexive and intensive: *myself, yourself, himself, herself, itself, ourselves, yourselves, themselves.* • reflexive and intensive: *myself, ourselves; yourself, yourselves; himself, herself, itself, themselves.*	*A pronoun is a word used in place of one or more nouns.* *Sometimes a pronoun replaces one or more pronouns.*	•	•	•
4 Recognize and use adjectives: • that describe what something is like: e.g., <u>green</u> eyes, <u>large</u> tree, <u>talented</u> singer, <u>Shakespeare</u> play • that identify something: e.g., <u>the</u> flower, <u>this</u> book, <u>those</u> dogs, <u>his</u> opinion, <u>Italian</u> sausage • that quantify something: e.g., <u>a</u> story, <u>an</u> egg, <u>eleven</u> candles, <u>several</u> bikes, <u>no</u> money.	*An adjective is a word used to change the meaning of a noun or a pronoun by making it more specific.* *Adjectives tell what kind, which one, or how many or how much.* *Sometimes a noun is used as an adjective. A proper adjective is formed from a proper noun and begins with a capital letter.* *Some words can be used as pronouns or adjectives. The word's function in a sentence determines which part of speech it is. An adjective modifies a noun or pronoun, whereas a pronoun takes the place of a noun.*	•	•	•

GRAMMAR, USAGE, AND MECHANICS

BEHAVIOR	INSTRUCTIONAL LANGUAGE	GRADE LEVEL		
		PRIMARY	INTERMEDIATE	MIDDLE SCHOOL
Parts of Speech (continued)				
5 Recognize and use verbs: • that express a physical or mental action: e.g., *make, pulled, will remember* • that express the condition or the state of being of a person, place, thing, or idea: e.g., *is, remained, will seem.*	A verb is a word used to help to make a statement. A verb tells about an action or a condition or state of being.	•	•	•
6 Recognize and use adverbs: • that describe how something is done: e.g., *chewed <u>slowly</u>, replies <u>sincerely</u>* • that identify when something happens: e.g., *will arrive <u>tomorrow</u>, <u>finally</u> awoke* • that describe where something happens: e.g., *spilled <u>everywhere</u>, fell <u>backward</u>* • that specify the degree of something: e.g., *<u>completely</u> happy, sprinted <u>very</u> fast.*	An adverb is a word used to change the meaning of a verb, an adjective, or another adverb by making it more specific. Most adverbs tell how, when, where, how much, or how often the action of the verb is done. Sometimes an adverb changes the meaning of an adjective or another adverb by telling how much or how often about that adjective or adverb.	•	•	•
7 Recognize and use prepositions: e.g., • *about, above, across, after, against, along, among, around, as, at, before, behind, below, beneath, beside, besides, between, beyond, but, by, down, during, except, for, from, in, inside, into, like, near, of, off, on, onto, out, outside, over, past, since, through, throughout, to, toward, under, underneath, until, up, upon, with, within, without* • *(compound) according to, along with, apart from, aside from, as of, because of, by means of, in addition to, in front of, in place of, in spite of, instead of, next to, on account of, out of.*	A preposition is a word used to show the relationship between a noun or pronoun and another word in a sentence. A compound preposition is a group of words that acts as a preposition. A preposition always introduces a phrase. The noun or pronoun at the end of the phrase is the object of the preposition. Many words can be used as prepositions or adverbs. The word's function in a sentence determines which part of speech it is. An adverb can stand on its own, whereas a preposition always introduces a phrase.		•	•
8 Recognize and use conjunctions: • coordinating—e.g., *and, but, for, nor, or, so, yet* • subordinating—e.g., *after, although, as, as far as, as if, as long as, as much as, as soon as, as though, as well as, because, before, considering (that), even though, how, if, in order that, provided, since, so long as, so that, than, that, though, unless, until, when, whenever, where, wherever, whether, while, why* • correlative—e.g., *both . . . and, either . . . or, neither . . . nor, not only . . . but (also), whether . . . or.*	A conjunction is a word used to join words or groups of words. Sometimes a conjunction joins two words. Sometimes a conjunction joins groups of words or parts of a sentence. A coordinating conjunction connects words or groups of words used in the same way. A subordinating conjunction begins a subordinate clause and joins it to an independent clause. Correlative conjunctions are pairs of conjunctions that connect words or groups of words used in the same way.		•	•
9 Recognize and use interjections: e.g., *Ah, Hey, My goodness, Oh, Ouch, Well, What, Wow.*	An interjection is a word used to express sudden strong feeling or excitement. Interjections are usually followed by an exclamation point. An interjection has no grammatical relation to other words in the sentence.		•	•

GRAMMAR, USAGE, AND MECHANICS

BEHAVIOR	INSTRUCTIONAL LANGUAGE	GRADE LEVEL		
		PRIMARY	INTERMEDIATE	MIDDLE SCHOOL
Verb Tense				
10 Recognize and use common verb tenses: • present: e.g., *walks, walk* • past: e.g., *walked* • future: e.g., *will walk* • present perfect: e.g., *has walked, have walked* • past perfect: e.g., *had walked* • future perfect: e.g., *will have walked.*	*The form of a verb shows the time of the action or state of being. This is the verb's tense.* *The simple tenses are present, past, and future.* *The present tense shows actions that happen or states of being that exist in the present.* *The past tense shows actions or states of being that began and ended in the past.* *The future tense shows actions or states of being that will happen or exist in the future.* *The perfect tenses are present perfect, past perfect, and future perfect.* *The present perfect tense shows actions or states of being that began in the past and continue in the present.* *The past perfect tense shows actions or states of being that ended before another past action began.* *The future perfect tense shows actions or states of being that will have have ended before another action or state of being begins in the future.*	•	•	•
11 Recognize and use the past tense of regular verbs, which add *-ed* to the end of a base word: e.g., *helped, asked, played; liked, lived; stopped, fitted; cried, tried.*	*Many verbs keep the same basic form with the ending -ed to show actions in the past. These are regular verbs.* *Use basic rules to spell words with suffixes correctly.*	•	•	•
12 Recognize and use the past tense of irregular verbs, which do not use the suffix *-ed*: e.g., *come/came, eat/ate, fall/fell, grow/grew, teach/taught.*	*The basic form of some verbs changes to show actions in the past. These are irregular verbs.*	•	•	•
Agreement				
13 Recognize and use subject-verb agreement: • singular subject and singular verb: e.g., *A word has meaning.* • plural subject and plural verb: e.g., *Words have meaning.*	*A subject is either singular or plural in number.* *A singular subject refers to one person, place, thing, or idea.* *A plural subject refers to more than one person, place, thing, or idea.* *A verb is either singular or plural in number.* *A verb and its subject agree, or match, in number.* *Singular verbs are used with singular subjects. Plural verbs are used with plural subjects.*		•	•

GRAMMAR, USAGE, AND MECHANICS

BEHAVIOR	INSTRUCTIONAL LANGUAGE	GRADE LEVEL		
		PRIMARY	INTERMEDIATE	MIDDLE SCHOOL
Agreement *(continued)*				
14 Recognize and use pronoun-antecedent agreement: e.g., • singular, feminine: e.g., <u>Jane</u> believed that <u>she</u> was right. • singular, masculine: e.g., The <u>boy</u> considered <u>his</u> options. • singular, neuter: e.g., The <u>tree</u> lost <u>its</u> leaves in the storm. • plural: e.g., The <u>dogs</u> licked <u>their</u> lips.	*Sometimes a pronoun refers to another word in a sentence.* *A pronoun agrees, or matches, in number with the word to which it refers.* *A singular pronoun agrees in gender with the word to which it refers.*		•	•
Sentences				
15 Recognize the subject and the predicate as the two basic parts of a sentence.	*A sentence is a group of words that expresses a complete thought and contains two basic parts–a subject and a predicate.* *The simple subject of a sentence is usually a noun or a pronoun. The subject does or is whatever the verb says.* *The simple predicate of a sentence is a verb. The predicate usually shows what the subject does or is.* *In most sentences, the subject comes before the predicate.*		•	•
16 Recognize complements and understand their functions in sentences: e.g., • direct object: e.g., I bought a <u>gift</u>. • indirect object: e.g., I bought <u>you</u> a gift. • predicate noun: e.g., The gift is a <u>surprise</u>. • predicate adjective: e.g., The gift is <u>enormous</u>.	*Complements are part of the predicate. A compliment is a word or a group of words that completes the meaning of the verb.* *Many sentences have complements, but some sentences have none. There are four types of complements.* *A direct object answers the question "what?" after an action verb and names the person or thing receiving the action.* *An indirect object usually appears before a direct object and tells to whom or for whom the action of a verb is done.* *A predicate noun (or predicate nominative) follows a linking verb and renames the subject.* *A predicate adjective follows a linking verb and describes the subject.*		•	•
17 Recognize and use the four types of sentences: • declarative: e.g., You gave me the book. • interrogative: e.g., Did you give me the book? • imperative: e.g., Please give me the book. • exclamatory: e.g., Wow, you gave me the book!	*There are four types of sentences. Each type has a different purpose.* *A declarative sentence makes a statement.* *An interrogative sentence asks a direct question.* *An imperative sentence makes a request or gives a command.* *An exclamatory sentence expresses strong feeling or excitement.*		•	•

GRAMMAR, USAGE, AND MECHANICS

BEHAVIOR	INSTRUCTIONAL LANGUAGE	GRADE LEVEL		
		PRIMARY	**INTERMEDIATE**	**MIDDLE SCHOOL**

Sentences *(continued)*

	BEHAVIOR	INSTRUCTIONAL LANGUAGE	PRIMARY	INTERMEDIATE	MIDDLE SCHOOL
18	Recognize and use phrases and understand their functions in sentences: • prepositional: e.g., *I walk to school <u>in the morning</u>.* • adjective: e.g., *The man <u>with the green hat</u> is my father.* (modifying "man") • adverb: e.g., *I walk <u>to school</u> in the morning.* (modifying "walked")	*A phrase is a group of related words in a sentence.* *A phrase does not contain a verb and its subject.* *A phrase is used as a single part of speech in a sentence.* *A prepositional phrase includes a preposition, a noun or pronoun called the "object of the preposition," and any words that modify that object.* *An adjective phrase is a prepositional phrase that modifies a noun or a pronoun.* *An adverb phrase is a prepositional phrase that modifies a verb, an adjective, or adverb.*			•
19	Recognize and use clauses, and understand their functions in sentences: • independent clause: e.g., *<u>A tree is a large plant</u> that has a woody trunk, branches, and leaves.* • subordinate clause: e.g., *A tree is a large plant <u>that has a woody trunk, branches, and leaves</u>.* • subordinate clause used as an adjective: e.g., *She loves books <u>that take place in Spain</u>.* (modifying "books") • subordinate clause used as an adverb: e.g., *He first strummed a guitar <u>when he was seven years old</u>.* (modifying "strummed") • subordinate clause used as a noun: e.g., *<u>What this team needs now</u> is a victory.* (subject of the verb "is")	*A clause is a group of words that contains a verb and its subject and is used as part of a sentence.* *An independent clause expresses a complete thought and can stand by itself as a sentence.* *A subordinate clause does not express a complete thought and cannot stand by itself as a sentence.* *An adjective clause is a subordinate clause that modifies a noun or a pronoun.* *An adverb clause a subordinate clause that modifies a verb, an adjective, or adverb.* *A noun clause is a subordinate clause used as a noun.*			•
20	Recognize and use sentences with various structures: • simple: e.g., *I adore vegetables.* • compound: e.g., *<u>I adore vegetables</u>, and <u>I also love flowers</u>.* • complex: e.g., *<u>I love flowers that blossom in winter</u>.* • compound-complex: e.g., *<u>I adore vegetables</u>, and <u>I also love flowers that blossom in winter</u>.*	*Sentences can be classified according to their structure.* *A simple sentence has one independent clause.* *A compound sentence has two or more independent clauses.* *A complex sentence has one independent clause and one or more subordinate clauses.* *A compound-complex sentence two or more independent clauses and one or more subordinate clauses.*		•	•
21	Use complete sentences and avoid common sentence problems in writing: • sentence fragment: e.g., *That I wanted to go to the ballgame.* • run-on sentence: e.g., *The telephone rang, no one answered.*	*It is important in writing to use complete sentences and to avoid common sentence problems such as sentence fragments and run-on sentences.* *A sentence fragment is a phrase or subordinate clause that is capitalized and punctuated mistakenly as if it is a complete sentence.* *A run-on sentence is two independent clauses put together with incorrect punctuation.*		•	•

GRAMMAR, USAGE, AND MECHANICS

BEHAVIOR	INSTRUCTIONAL LANGUAGE	GRADE LEVEL		
		PRIMARY	INTERMEDIATE	MIDDLE SCHOOL
Sentences *(continued)*				
22 Recognize, understand the function of, and use simple connectives: • adding ideas or showing similarity: e.g., *also, and, and so, too* • showing difference: e.g., *but* • showing time or sequence: e.g., *after, before, first, second* • showing space or place: e.g., *above, around, below, down, near, under, up* • showing causes, results, or conditions: e.g., *because.*	*Connectives are conjunctions, prepositions, and adverbs that link ideas and clarify the relationship between those ideas.* *Simple connectives are used frequently in oral language and in written language.*	•	•	•
23 Recognize and use sophisticated connectives: • adding ideas or showing similarity: e.g., *along with, another, as far as, as if, as though, as much as, as well, as well as, as with, besides, both . . . and, either . . . or, equally, further, furthermore, in addition, in addition to, let alone, like, likewise, moreover, nor, not only . . . but also, or, then, whether . . . or, with* • showing difference: e.g., *against, although, apart from, aside from, even so, even though, except, however, in place of, in spite of, instead, instead of, nevertheless, nonetheless, on the other hand, otherwise, rather, still, than, though, unlike, unless, without, yet* <div align="right">*(Continues)*</div>	*Connectives are conjunctions, prepositions, and adverbs that link ideas and clarify the relationship between those ideas.* *Sophisticated connectives can appear in oral language but are more likely associated with written language.*		•	•

GRAMMAR, USAGE, AND MECHANICS

BEHAVIOR	INSTRUCTIONAL LANGUAGE	GRADE LEVEL		
		PRIMARY	INTERMEDIATE	MIDDLE SCHOOL

Sentences (continued)

23	*(Continued)* Recognize and use sophisticated connectives: • showing time or sequence: e.g., *afterward(s), as, as long as, as of, as soon as, at last, at once, at this moment, at this point, during, finally, from here on, from now on, gradually, in the beginning, in the end, in the meantime, last, last of all, lastly, later, meanwhile, next, next to, now, of, presently, previously, since, soon, then, thereafter, to begin with, ultimately, until, when, whenever, while* • showing space or place: e.g., *across, along, among, anywhere, at, before, beyond, behind, beneath, beside, between, beyond, by, directly ahead, elsewhere, everywhere, from, here, in, in front of, in the background, inside, into, nearby, next, next to, off, on, on the other side, onto, opposite, out, out of, outside, over, past, there, through, throughout, to, toward, underneath, upon, where, wherever, within* • showing causes, results, or conditions: e.g., *about, according to, as a result, as long as, by, consequently, considering, for, for this reason, hence, how, if, in that case, provided, since, so, so as, so long as, so that, that, then, therefore, thus, under the circumstances, unless, whether, why* Recognize and use sophisticated connectives: • giving example or illustration: e.g., *as you can see, for example, for instance, for one thing, in fact, in the same way, such as* • summarizing or reporting: e.g., *as you can see, finally, on the whole, therefore.*	*Connectives are conjunctions, prepositions, and adverbs that link ideas and clarify the relationship between those ideas.* *Sophisticated connectives can appear in oral language but are more likely associated with written language.*		•	•

GRAMMAR, USAGE, AND MECHANICS

	BEHAVIOR	INSTRUCTIONAL LANGUAGE	GRADE LEVEL		
			PRIMARY	INTERMEDIATE	MIDDLE SCHOOL

Sentences *(continued)*

	BEHAVIOR	INSTRUCTIONAL LANGUAGE	PRIMARY	INTERMEDIATE	MIDDLE SCHOOL
24	Recognize and use academic connectives: • adding ideas or showing similarity: e.g., *additionally, in the same way/manner, neither . . . nor, of equal importance, similarly* • showing difference: e.g., *alternatively, by contrast, conversely, despite, in contrast, in other respects, on the contrary, whereas* • showing time or sequence: e.g., *at length, hence, subsequently* • showing space or place: e.g., *adjacent to, lastly* • showing causes, results, or conditions: e.g., *accordingly, as a consequence, by means of, in order that, on account of, whereby* • giving example or illustration: e.g., *as exemplified by, as seen in, as shown by, in the case of* • summarizing or reporting: e.g., *in conclusion, in short, in summary, to repeat, to sum up.*	*Connectives are conjunctions and adverbs that link ideas and clarify the relationship between those ideas.* *Academic connectives can appear in oral language but are used primarily in written language.*		•	•

Modifiers

	BEHAVIOR	INSTRUCTIONAL LANGUAGE	PRIMARY	INTERMEDIATE	MIDDLE SCHOOL
25	Recognize and use the three forms of comparison with adjectives and adverbs: e.g., • *tall/taller/tallest, soon/sooner/soonest (one-syllable adjectives and adverbs)* • *brittle/brittler/brittlest, lively/livelier/livliest; restless, more restless, most restless, sweetly, more sweetly, most sweetly (two-syllable adjectives and adverbs)* • *treacherous, more treacherous, most treacherous, incredibly, more incredibly, most incredibly (adjectives and adverbs with more than two syllables).*	*Adjectives and adverbs have three forms to show the three levels or degrees of comparison–positive, comparative, and superlative.* *The positive form is the adjective or adverb itself.* *For most one-syllable adjectives and adverbs, form the comparative and the superlative by adding -er or -est to the base word.* *For some two-syllable adjectives and adverbs, form the comparative and the superlative by adding -er or -est to the base word. For other two-syllable adjectives and adverbs, form the comparative and the superlative by using the words* more/less *and* most/least *before the modifier.* *For adjectives and adverbs with more than two syllables, form the comparative and the superlative by using the words* more/less *and* most/least.		•	•

Mechanics

	BEHAVIOR	INSTRUCTIONAL LANGUAGE	PRIMARY	INTERMEDIATE	MIDDLE SCHOOL
26	Understand the functions of capital letters and use capitalization correctly.	*Use a capital letter for the first word of a sentence.* *Use a capital letter for a proper noun.* *Use a capital letter for a proper adjective.* *Use a capital letter for the titles of people, books, periodicals, stories, poems, plays, films, television programs, works of art, and musical compositions.*	•	•	•

GRAMMAR, USAGE, AND MECHANICS

BEHAVIOR	INSTRUCTIONAL LANGUAGE	GRADE LEVEL		
		PRIMARY	INTERMEDIATE	MIDDLE SCHOOL
Mechanics *(continued)*				
27 Understand the functions of marks of punctuation and use punctuation correctly.	*There are three end marks—period, question mark, and exclamation mark.*	•	•	•
	Use a period at the end of a statement and sometimes at the end of a command or request.			
	Use a question mark at the end of a direct question.			
	Use an exclamation mark at the end of an exclamation and sometimes at the end of a command or request.			
	Use a comma to join independent clauses along with a conjunction, and to separate items in a series, introductory elements, interrupters, and nonessential clauses and phrases.			
	Use a semicolon to separate independent clauses that are closely related in thought but are not joined by a conjunction.			
	Use a dash to show an abrupt break in thought and to separate additional information.			
	Use parentheses to enclose additional information.			
	Use a colon to introduce a list of items or a long, formal statement or quotation.			
	Use quotation marks to enclose a person's exact words.			
	Use an apostrophe to form a possessive noun and to show where a letter or letters have been omitted in a contraction.			
	Use a hyphen to divide a word at the end of a line.			

Glossary

Glossary

abbreviation Shortened form of a word that uses some of the letters: e.g., *Mr., etc., NY.*

academic language The language needed to be successful in schools and in other scholarly settings. Academic language is often used in classroom lessons, assignments, presentations, and books. Another term for academic language is *academic vocabulary.*

accented syllable A syllable that is given emphasis in pronunciation. See also *syllable, stress.*

acronym A word formed by combining the initial letter or letters of a group of words: e.g., *radar = radio detecting and ranging.*

adjective suffix A suffix put at the end of a word root or base word to form an adjective. See also *suffix.*

adjusting (as a strategic action) Reading in different ways as appropriate to the purpose for reading and type of text.

adventure / adventure story A contemporary realistic or historical fiction or fantasy text that presents a series of exciting or suspenseful events, often involving a main character taking a journey and overcoming danger and risk.

adverb suffix A suffix put at the end of a word root or base word to form an adverb. See also *suffix.*

affix A letter or group of letters added to the beginning or ending of a base or root word to change its meaning or function (a *prefix* or a *suffix*).

allegory A narrative with symbolic meaning, often personifying abstract ideas, told to teach or explain something.

alliteration The repetition of identical or similar initial consonant sounds in consecutive or nearby words or syllables.

alphabet book / ABC book A book that helps children develop the concept and sequence of the alphabet by pairing alphabet letters with pictures of people, animals, or objects with labels related to the letters.

alphabet linking chart A chart containing upper- and lowercase letters of the alphabet paired with pictures representing words beginning with each letter (*a, apple*).

alphabetic principle The concept that there is a relationship between the spoken sounds in oral language and the graphic forms in written language.

analogy The resemblance of a known word to an unknown word that helps you solve the unknown word's meaning. Often an analogy shows the relationship between two pairs of words.

analyzing (as a strategic action) Examining the elements of a text in order to know more about how it is constructed, and noticing aspects of the writer's craft.

animal fantasy A modern fantasy text geared to a very young audience in which animals act like people and encounter human problems.

animal story A contemporary realistic or historical fiction or fantasy text that involves animals and that often focuses on the relationships between humans and animals.

antonym A word that has the opposite meaning from another word: e.g., *cold* versus *hot.*

archaic word A word that is part of the language of the past and has specialized uses in language today.

assessment A means for gathering information or data that reveals what learners control, partially control, or do not yet control consistently.

assonance The repetition of identical or similar vowel sounds in stressed syllables in words that usually end with different consonant sounds.

autobiography A biographical text in which the story of a real person's life is written and narrated by that person. Autobiography is usually told in chronological sequence but may be in another order.

automaticity Rapid, accurate, fluent word decoding without conscious effort or attention.

ballad A type of traditional poem or tale, often recited or sung, and usually telling a story important to a particular region or culture. First handed down orally and later in writing, ballads usually feature a hero whose deeds and attributes have grown and become exaggerated over time.

base word A word in its simplest form, which can be modified by adding affixes: e.g., *read; reread, reading.* A base word has meaning, can stand on its own, and is easily apparent in the language. Compare to *word root.*

behavior An observable action.

biography A biographical text in which the story of a real person's life is written and narrated by another person. Biography is usually told in chronological sequence but may be in another order.

blend To combine sounds or word parts.

bold / boldface Type that is heavier and darker than usual, often used for emphasis.

book and print features The physical attributes of a text: e.g., font, layout, length.

callout A nonfiction text feature, such as a definition, a quote, or an important concept, that is highlighted by being set to one side of a text or enlarged within the body of the text.

capitalization The use of capital letters, usually the first letter in a word, as a convention of written language (for example, for proper names and to begin sentences).

categorization A structural pattern used especially in nonfiction texts to present information in logical categories (and subcategories) of related material.

cause and effect A structural pattern used especially in nonfiction texts, often to propose the reasons or explanations for how and why something occurs.

chapter book A form of early reading text that is divided into chapters, each of which narrates an episode in the whole.

choral reading Reading aloud in unison with a group.

chronological sequence A structural pattern used especially in nonfiction texts to describe a series of events in the order they happened in time.

circular story A fiction story in which a sense of completeness or closure results from the way the end of a piece returns to subject matter, wording, or phrasing found at the beginning of the story.

clipped word A word formed from shortening another word: e.g., *ad (advertisement).*

closed syllable A syllable that ends in a consonant: e.g., *lem*-on.

cognates Words that appear in different languages with very similar spellings and meanings.

comparative ending A suffix (e.g., *-er, -est*) put at the end of a base word to show comparison between or among two or more things.

compare and contrast A structural pattern used especially in nonfiction texts to compare two ideas, events, or phenomena by showing how they are alike and how they are different.

compound word A word made of two or more smaller words or morphemes: e.g., *play ground.* The meaning of a compound word can be a combination of the meanings of the words it is made of or can be unrelated to the meanings of the combined units.

concept book A book organized to develop an understanding of an abstract or generic idea or categorization.

concept word A word that represents an abstract idea or name. Categories of concept words include color names, number words, days of the week, months of the year, seasons, and so on.

concrete poetry A poem with words (and sometimes punctuation) arranged to represent a visual picture of the idea the poem is conveying.

conflict In a fiction text, a central problem within the plot that is resolved near the end of the story. In literature, characters

GLOSSARY

are usually in conflict with nature, with other people, with society as a whole, or with themselves. Another term for conflict is *problem*.

connective A word or phrase that clarifies relationships and ideas in language. Simple connectives appear often in both oral and written language: e.g., *and, but, because.* Sophisticated connectives are used in written texts but do not appear often in everyday oral language: e.g., *although, however, yet.* Academic connectives appear in written texts but are seldom used in oral language: e.g., *in contrast, nonetheless, whereas.*

connotation The emotional meaning or association a word carries beyond its strict dictionary definition.

consonant A speech sound made by partial or complete closure of the airflow that causes friction at one or more points in the breath channel. The consonant sounds are represented by the letters *b, c, d, f, g, h, j, k, l, m, n, p, qu, r, s, t, v, w, y,* and *z.*

consonant blend Two or more consonant letters that often appear together in words and represent sounds that are smoothly joined, although each of the sounds can be heard in the word: e.g., *trim.*

consonant cluster A sequence of two or three consonant letters: e.g., *trim, chair.*

consonant cluster linking chart A chart of common consonant clusters paired with pictures representing words beginning with each: e.g., *bl, block.*

consonant digraph Two consonant letters that appear together and represent a single sound that is different from the sound of either letter: e.g., she*ll.*

content (as a text characteristic) The subject matter of a text.

contraction A shortened form of one or more words. A letter or letters are left out, and an apostrophe takes the place of the missing letter or letters.

conventions In writing, formal usage that has become customary in written language. Grammar and usage, capitalization, punctuation, spelling, and handwriting and word-processing are categories of writing conventions.

counting book A book in which the structure depends on a numerical progression.

critiquing (as a strategic action) Evaluating a text based on the reader's personal, world, or text knowledge, and thinking critically about the ideas in the text.

cumulative tale A folktale in which story events are repeated with each new episode, giving them a rhythmic quality.

cursive A form of handwriting in which letters are connected.

decoding Using letter-sound relationships to translate a word from a series of symbols to a unit of meaning.

description A structural pattern used especially in nonfiction texts to provide sensory and emotional details so that readers can determine how something looks, moves, tastes, smells, or feels.

dialect A regional variety of a language. In most languages, including English and Spanish, dialects are mutually intelligible; the differences are actually minor.

dialogue Spoken words, usually set off with quotation marks in text. Dialogue is an element of a writer's style.

diary A record of events and observations written in the first person and kept regularly in sequential, dated entries.

diction Clear pronunciation and enunciation in speech.

dimension A trait, characteristic, or attribute of a character in fiction.

directionality The orientation of print (in the English language, from left to right).

distinctive letter features Visual features that make each letter of the alphabet different from every other letter.

draft An early version of a writer's composition.

drafting and revising The process of getting ideas down on paper and shaping them to convey the writer's message.

drawing In writing, creating a rough image (i.e., a sketch) or a finished image (i.e., a drawing) of a person, place, thing, or idea to capture, work with, and render the writer's ideas.

early literacy concepts Very early understandings related to how written language or print is organized and used—how it works.

editing and proofreading The process of polishing the final draft of a written composition to prepare it for publication.

editorial A form of persuasive nonfiction text in which the purpose is to state and defend an opinion, usually by an editor of a magazine, newspaper, or other media source.

endpapers The sheets of heavy paper at the front and back of a hardback book that join the book block to the hardback binding. Endpapers are sometimes printed with text, maps, or design.

English language learner A person whose native language is not English and who is acquiring English as an additional language.

epic A traditional tale or long narrative poem, first handed down orally and later in writing. Usually an epic involves a journey and a set of tasks or tests in which the hero triumphs. Generally the nature of the deeds and attributes of the hero have grown and become exaggerated over time.

essay An analytic or interpretive piece of expository writing with a focused point of view, or a persuasive text that provides a body of information related to a social or scientific issue.

exaggeration An overstatement intended to go beyond the truth to make something seem greater than it is.

expository text / expository nonfiction A nonfiction text that gives the reader information about a topic.

Expository texts use a variety of underlying text structures such as description, temporal sequence, categorization, compare and contrast, problem and solution, and question and answer. Forms of expository text include reports, news articles, and feature articles.

fable A folktale that demonstrates a useful truth and teaches a lesson. Usually including personified animals or natural elements such as the sun, fables appear to be simple but often convey abstract ideas.

factual text See *informational text.*

fairy tale A folktale about real problems but also involving magic and magical creatures. Also called "wonder tales," fairy tales have been handed down through oral language over the years.

family, friends, and school story A contemporary realistic text focused on the everyday experiences of children of a variety of ages, including relationships with family and friends and experiences at school.

fantasy A fiction text that contains elements that are highly unreal. Fantasy as a category of fiction includes genres such as animal fantasy, fantasy, and science fiction.

feature article A form of expository text that presents information organized around a central theme or idea, or one particular aspect of a topic.

fiction Invented, imaginative prose or poetry that tells a story. Along with nonfiction, fiction is one of two basic genres of literature.

figurative language Language that compares two objects or ideas to allow the reader to see something more clearly or understand something in a new way. An element of a writer's style, figurative language changes or goes beyond literal meaning. See also *simile, metaphor, personification.*

fluency In reading, this term names the ability to read continuous text with good momentum, phrasing, appropriate pausing, intonation, and stress. In word solving, this term names the ability to solve words with speed, accuracy, and flexibility.

folktale A traditional fiction text about a people or "folk," originally handed down orally from generation to generation. Folktales are usually simple tales and often involve talking animals.

font In printed text, the collection of type (letters) in a particular style.

form A kind of text that is characterized by particular elements. Short story, for example, is a form of fiction writing.

formal letter In writing, a functional nonfiction text usually addressed to a stranger, in which the form (for example, a business letter) follows specific conventions.

fractured fairy tale A retelling of a familiar fairy tale with characters, setting, or plot events changed, often for comic effect.

free verse A type of poetry with irregular meter. Free verse may include rhyme, alliteration, and other poetic sound devices.

friendly letter In writing, a functional nonfiction text usually addressed to friends and family that may take the form of notes, letters, invitations, or email.

functional text A nonfiction text intended to accomplish a practical task. Examples of functional texts include letters, lists, test writing, and writing about reading.

gathering seeds Collecting ideas, snippets of language, descriptions, and sketches for potential use in written composition.

genre A kind of category of text or artistic work or a class of artistic endeavor (including music, drama, and studio arts) that has a characteristic form or technique.

grammar Complex rules by which people can generate an unlimited number of phrases, sentences, and longer texts in that language. *Conventional grammar* refers to the accepted grammatical conventions in a society.

grapheme A letter or cluster of letters representing a single sound, or phoneme: e.g., *a*, *eigh*, *ay*.

graphic feature In fiction texts, graphic features are usually illustrations. In nonfiction texts, graphic features include photographs, paintings and drawings, charts, diagrams, tables and graphs, maps, and timelines.

graphic text A form of text with comic strips or other illustrations on every page. In fiction, a story line continues across the text; illustrations, which depict moment-to-moment actions and emotions, are usually accompanied by dialogue in speech balloons and occasional narrative description of actions. In nonfiction, factual information is presented in categories or sequence.

graphophonic relationship The relationship between the oral sounds of the language and the written letters or clusters of letters. See also *semantic system*, *syntactic system*.

Greek root A word root that comes from Greek. Many English words contain Greek roots. See also *word root*.

guide words The words at the top of a dictionary page to indicate the first and last word on the page.

haiku An ancient Japanese form of non-rhyming poetry that creates a mental picture and makes a concise emotional statement.

have a try To write a word, notice that it doesn't look quite right, try it two or three other ways, and decide which construction looks right; to make an attempt and self-check.

high fantasy A long, complex modern fantasy text characterized by the motifs of traditional literature—the hero, the hero's quest, the struggle between good and evil. High fantasy involves stories that take place in an alternative world alongside the real world, or where our world does not exist.

high-frequency words Words that occur often in the spoken and written language.

historical fiction A fiction text that takes place in a realistically (and often factually) portrayed setting of a past era. Compare to *realistic fiction*.

homograph One of two or more words spelled alike but different in meaning, derivation, or pronunciation: e.g., the *bat* flew away, he swung the *bat*; take a *bow*, *bow* and arrow.

homonym One of two or more words spelled and pronounced alike but different in meaning: e.g., we had *quail* for dinner; I would *quail* in fear. A homonym is a type of homograph.

homophone One of two or more words pronounced alike but different in spelling and meaning: e.g., *meat*, *meet*; *bear*, *bare*.

horror / horror story A fiction text in which events evoke a feeling of dread in both the characters and the reader. Horror stories often involve elements of fantasy, but they may also fit into the category of realism.

humorous story A realistic fiction text that is full of fun and meant to entertain.

hybrid / hybrid text A text that includes at least one nonfiction genre and at least one fiction genre blended in a coherent whole.

idea development In writing, the craft of presenting and elaborating the ideas and themes of a text.

idiom A phrase with meaning that cannot be derived from the conjoined meanings of its elements: e.g., *raining cats and dogs*.

illustration Graphic representation of important content (for example, art, photos, maps, graphs, charts) in a fiction or nonfiction text.

imagery The use of language—descriptions, comparisons, and figures of speech—that helps the mind form sensory impressions. Imagery is an element of a writer's style.

inferring (as a strategic action) Going beyond the literal meaning of a text and thinking about what is not stated but is implied by the writer.

inflectional ending A suffix added to a base word to show tense, plurality, possession, or comparison: e.g., dark-*er*.

infographic An illustration—often in the form of a chart, graph, or map—that includes brief text and that presents and analyzes data about a topic in a visually striking way.

informational text A nonfiction text in which a purpose is to inform or give facts about a topic. Informational texts include the following genres—biography, autobiography, memoir, and narrative nonfiction, as well as expository texts, procedural texts, and persuasive texts.

interactive read-aloud A teaching context in which students are actively listening and responding to an oral reading of a text.

interactive writing A teaching context in which the teacher and students cooperatively plan, compose, and write a group text; both teacher and students act as scribes (in turn).

intonation The rise and fall in pitch of the voice in speech to convey meaning.

irony The use of words to express the opposite of the literal meaning.

italic / italics A type style that is characterized by slanting letters.

journal See *diary*.

label A written word or phrase that names the content of an illustration.

label book A picture book consisting of illustrations with brief identifying text.

language and literary features (as text characteristics) Qualities particular to written language that are qualitatively different from those associated with spoken language: e.g., dialogue, setting, description, mood.

language structure See *syntax*.

language use The craft of using sentences, phrases, and expressions to describe events, actions, or information.

Latin root A word root that comes from Latin. Many English words contain Latin roots. See also *word root*.

layout The way the print and illustrations are arranged on a page.

legend In relation to genre, this term names a traditional tale, first handed down orally and later in writing, that tells about a noteworthy person or event. Legends are believed to have some root in history, but the accuracy of the events and people they describe is not always verifiable. In relation to book and print features, this term names a key on a map or chart that explains what symbols stand for.

letter See *friendly letter* and *formal letter*.

letter combination Two or more letters that appear together and represent vowel sounds in words: e.g, *ea* in *meat*, *igh* in *sight*.

letter knowledge The ability to recognize and label the graphic symbols of language.

letters Graphic symbols representing the sounds in a language. Each letter has particular distinctive features and may be identified by letter name or sound.

letter-sound relationships The correspondence of letter(s) and sound(s) in written or spoken language.

lexicon Words that make up language.

limerick A type of rhyming verse, usually surprising and humorous and frequently nonsensical.

lists and procedures Functional writing that includes simple lists and how-to texts.

literary devices Techniques used by a writer to convey or enhance the story, such as figures of speech, imagery, symbolism, and point of view.

literary nonfiction A nonfiction text that employs literary techniques, such as figurative language, to present information in engaging ways.

log A form of chronological, written record, usually of a journey.

long vowel The elongated vowel sound that is the same as the name of the vowel. It is sometimes represented by two or more letters: e.g., *cake, eight, mail*. Another term for long vowel is *lax vowel*.

lowercase letter A small letter form that is usually different from its corresponding capital or uppercase form.

lyrical poetry A songlike type of poetry that has rhythm and sometimes rhyme and is memorable for sensory images and description.

main idea The central underlying idea, concept, or message that the author conveys in a nonfiction text. Compare to *theme, message*.

maintaining fluency (as a strategic action) Integrating sources of information in a smoothly operating process that results in expressive, phrased reading.

making connections (as a strategic action) Searching for and using connections to knowledge gained through personal experiences, learning about the world, and reading other texts.

malapropism The replacement of a word with another word that sounds similar but has a different meaning, creating a humorous effect. Compare to *spoonerism*.

media Channels of communication for information or entertainment. Newspapers and books are print media; television and the Internet are electronic media.

memoir A biographical text in which a writer takes a reflective stance in looking back on a particular time or person. Usually written in the first person, memoirs are often briefer and more intense accounts of a memory or set of memories than the accounts found in biographies and autobiographies.

mentor texts Books or other texts that serve as examples of excellent writing. Mentor texts are read and reread to provide models for literature discussion and student writing.

message An important idea that an author conveys in a fiction or nonfiction text. See also *main idea, theme*.

metaphor A type of figurative language that describes one thing by comparing it to another unlike thing without using the word *like* or *as*. Compare to *simile*.

modeled writing An instructional technique in which a teacher demonstrates the process of composing a particular genre, making the process explicit for students.

monitoring and self-correcting (as a strategic action) Checking whether the reading sounds right, looks right, and makes sense, and solving problems when it doesn't.

monologue A long speech given by one person in a group.

mood Language and events that convey an emotional atmosphere in a text, affecting how the reader feels. An element of a writer's style, mood is established by details, imagery, figurative language, and setting. Compare to *tone*.

morpheme The smallest unit of meaning in a language. Morphemes may be free or bound. For example, *run* is a unit of meaning that can stand alone (a free morpheme). In *runs* and *running*, the added *-s* and *-ing* are also units of meaning. They cannot stand alone but add meaning to the free morpheme. The *-s* and *-ing* are examples of bound morphemes.

morphemic strategies Ways of solving words by discovering meaning through the combination of significant word parts or morphemes: e.g., *happy, happiest; run, runner, running*.

morphological system Rules by which morphemes (building blocks of vocabulary) fit together into meaningful words, phrases, and sentences.

morphology The combination of morphemes (building blocks of meaning) to form words; the rules by which words are formed from free and bound morphemes—for example, root words, prefixes, and suffixes.

multiple-meaning word A word that means something different depending on the way it is used: e.g., *run—home run, run in your stocking, run down the street, a run of bad luck*.

multisyllable word A word that contains more than one syllable.

mystery / mystery story A special type of realistic or historical fiction or fantasy text that deals with the solution of a crime or the unraveling of secrets.

myth A traditional narrative text, often based in part on historical events, that explains human behavior and natural events or phenomena such as seasons and the sky.

narrative nonfiction A nonfiction text that tells a story using a narrative structure and literary language to make a topic interesting and appealing to readers.

narrative poetry A type of poetry with rhyme and rhythm that relates an event or episode.

narrative text A fiction or nonfiction text that uses a narrative structure and tells a story.

narrative text structure A method of organizing a text. A simple narrative structure follows a traditional sequence that includes a beginning, a problem, a series of events, a resolution of the problem, and an ending. Alternative narrative structures may include devices such as flashback or flash-forward to change the sequence of events or allow for multiple narrators. See also *organization, text structure,* and *nonnarrative text structure.*

news article A form of expository text that presents factual information about one or more events.

nonfiction Prose or poetry that provides factual information.

According to their structures, nonfiction texts can be organized into the categories of narrative and nonnarrative. Along with fiction, nonfiction is one of the two basic genres of literature.

nonnarrative text structure A method of organizing a text. Nonnarrative structures are used especially in three genres of nonfiction—expository texts, procedural texts, and persuasive texts. In nonnarrative nonfiction texts, underlying structural patterns include description, cause and effect, chronological sequence, temporal sequence, categorization, compare and contrast, problem and solution, and question and answer. See also *organization, text structure,* and *narrative text structure.*

noun suffix A suffix put at the end of a word root or base word to form a noun. See also *suffix.*

novella A fiction text that is shorter than a novel but longer than a short story.

nursery rhyme A short rhyme for children, usually telling a story.

onomatopoeia The representation of sound with words.

onset In a syllable, the part (consonant, consonant cluster, or consonant digraph) that comes before the vowel: e.g., the *cr* in *cream.* See also *rime.*

onset-rime segmentation The identification and separation of the onset (first part) and rime (last part, containing the vowel) in a word: e.g., *dr-ip.*

open syllable A syllable that ends in a vowel sound: e.g., *ho*-tel.

organization The arrangement of ideas in a text according to a logical structure, either narrative or nonnarrative. Another term for organization is *text structure.*

organizational tools Book and print features that help to organize a text: e.g., table of contents, section title, sidebar.

orthographic awareness The knowledge of the visual features of written language, including distinctive features of letters as well as spelling patterns in words.

orthography The representation of the sounds of a language with the proper letters according to standard usage (spelling).

palindrome A word that is spelled the same in either direction: e.g., *noon.*

parody A literary text in which the style of an author or an author's work is imitated for humorous effect.

performance reading An instructional context in which the students read orally to perform for others; they may read in unison or take parts. Shared reading, choral reading, and readers' theater are kinds of performance reading.

peritext Decorative or informative illustrations and/or print outside the body of the text. Elements of the peritext add to the aesthetic appeal and may have cultural significance or symbolic meaning.

personal narrative A brief text, usually autobiographical and written in the first person, that

GLOSSARY

tells about one event in the writer's life.

personification A figure of speech in which an animal is spoken of or portrayed as if it were a person, or in which a lifeless thing or idea is spoken of or portrayed as a living thing. Personification is a type of figurative language.

persuasive text A nonfiction text intended to convince the reader of the validity of a set of ideas—usually a particular point of view.

phoneme The smallest unit of sound in spoken language. There are forty-four units of speech sounds in English.

phoneme addition To add a beginning or ending sound to a word: e.g., /h/ + *and*; *an* + /t/.

phoneme blending To identify individual sounds and then to put them together smoothly to make a word: e.g., /k//a//t/ = *cat*.

phoneme deletion To omit a beginning, middle, or ending sound of a word: e.g., /k//a//s//k/ - /k/ = *ask*.

phoneme-grapheme correspondence The relationship between the sounds (phonemes) and letters (graphemes) of a language.

phoneme isolation The identification of an individual sound—beginning, middle, or end—in a word.

phoneme manipulation The movement of sounds from one place in a word to another.

phoneme reversal The exchange of the first and last sounds of a word to make a different word.

phoneme substitution The replacement of the beginning, middle, or ending sound of a word with a new sound.

phonemic (or phoneme) awareness The ability to hear individual sounds in words and to identify particular sounds.

phonemic strategies Ways of solving words that use how words sound and relationships between letters and letter clusters and phonemes in those words.

phonetics The scientific study of speech sounds—how the sounds are made vocally and the relation of speech sounds to the total language process.

phonics The knowledge of letter-sound relationships and how they are used in reading and writing. Teaching phonics refers to helping children acquire this body of knowledge about the oral and written language systems; additionally, teaching phonics helps children use phonics knowledge as part of a reading and writing process. Phonics instruction uses a small portion of the body of knowledge that makes up phonetics.

phonogram A phonetic element represented by graphic characters or symbols. In word recognition, words containing a graphic sequence composed of a vowel grapheme and an ending consonant grapheme (such as *an* or *it*) are sometimes called a word family.

phonological awareness The awareness of words, rhyming words, onsets and rimes, syllables, and individual sounds (phonemes).

phonological system The sounds of the language and how they work together in ways that are meaningful to the speakers of the language.

photo essay A form of nonfiction text in which meaning is carried by a series of photographs with no text or very spare text.

picture book A form of illustrated fiction or nonfiction text in which pictures work with the text to tell a story or provide information.

planning and rehearsing The process of collecting, working with, and selecting ideas for a written composition.

play A form of dramatic text written to be performed rather than just read. A play will include references to characters, scenery, and action, as well as stage directions, and usually consists of scripted (written) dialogue between characters. Plays can be realistic fiction, historical fiction, or fantasy, and they might also include elements of special types of fiction such as mystery or romance.

plot The events, actions, conflict, and resolution of a story presented in a certain order in a fiction text. A simple plot progresses chronologically from start to end, whereas more complex plots may shift back and forth in time.

plural Of, relating to, or constituting more than one.

poetic text A fiction or nonfiction text intended to express feelings, sensory images, ideas, or stories.

poetry Compact, metrical writing characterized by imagination and artistry and imbued with intense meaning. Along with prose, poetry is one of the two broad categories into which all literature can be divided.

point of view The angle, or perspective, from which a fiction story is told, usually the first person (the narrator is a character in the story) or the third person (an unnamed narrator is not a character in the story).

portmanteau word A word made from blending two distinct words and meanings; e.g., *smoke + fog = smog.*

possessive Grammatical form used to show ownership; e.g., *John's, his.*

predicting (as a strategic action) Using what is known to think about what will follow while reading continuous text.

prefix A group of letters placed in front of a base word to change its meaning: e.g., *pre*plan.

principle In phonics, a generalization or a sound-spelling relationship that is predictable.

problem See *conflict.*

problem and solution A structural pattern used especially in nonfiction texts to define a problem and clearly propose a solution. This pattern is often used in persuasive and expository texts.

procedural text A nonfiction text that explains how to do something. Procedural texts are almost always organized in temporal sequence and take the form of directions (or "how-to" texts) or descriptions of a process.

propaganda One-sided speaking or writing deliberately used to influence the thoughts and actions of someone in alignment with specific ideas or views.

prose The ordinary form of spoken or written language in sentences and paragraphs and without the metrical structure of poetry. Along with poetry, prose is one of the two broad categories into which all literature can be divided. Prose includes two basic genres, fiction and nonfiction.

publishing The process of making the final draft of a written composition public.

punctuation Marks used in written text to clarify meaning and separate structural units. The comma and the period are common punctuation marks.

purpose A writer's overall intention in creating a text, or a reader's overall intention in reading a text. To tell a story is one example of a writer's purpose, and to be entertained is one example of a reader's purpose.

question and answer A structural pattern used especially in nonfiction texts to organize information in a series of questions with responses. Questions-and-answer texts may be based on a verbal or written interview, or on frequently arising or logical questions about a topic.

***r*-controlled vowel sound** The modified or *r*-influenced sound of a vowel when it is followed by *r* in a syllable: e.g., *hurt.*

Reader's Notebook A notebook or folder of bound pages in which students write about their reading. The Reader's Notebook is used to keep a record of texts read and to express thinking. It may have several different sections to serve a variety of purposes.

readers' theater A performance of literature—i.e., a story, a play, or poetry—read aloud expressively by one or more persons rather than acted.

realistic fiction A fiction text that takes place in contemporary or modern times about believable characters involved in events that could happen. Contemporary realistic fiction usually presents modern problems that are typical for the characters, and it may highlight social issues. Compare with *historical fiction.*

related words Words that are related because of sound, spelling, category, or meaning. See also *synonym, antonym, homophone, homograph, analogy.*

report A form of expository text that synthesizes information from several sources in order to inform the reader about some general principles.

resolution / solution The point in the plot of a fiction story when the main conflict is solved.

rhyme The repetition of vowel and consonant sounds in the stressed syllables of words in verse, especially at the ends of lines.

rhythm The regular or ordered repetition of stressed and unstressed syllables in poetry, other writing, or speech.

rime In a syllable, the ending part containing the letters that represent the vowel sound and the consonant letters that follow: i.e., dr-*eam*. See also *onset*.

romance A special type of contemporary realistic or historical fiction text focused on the development of romantic (and sometimes sexual) attraction between characters.

root word See *word root*.

run-on sentence Two or more independent clauses that do not form a complete sentence because they are not joined correctly by punctuation and/or by a conjunction.

saga A long, sophisticated traditional tale or narrative poem.

satire Formerly, a fiction text that uses sarcasm and irony to portray and ridicule human failures. Like comedy, tragedy, and epic, satire was once a widely produced genre; it now appears in different forms or embedded within other genres.

schwa The sound of the middle vowel in an unstressed syllable (the *e* in *happen* and the sound between the *k* and *l* in *freckle*).

science fiction A modern fantasy text that involves technology, futuristic scenarios, and real or imagined scientific phenomena.

searching for and using information (as a strategic action) Looking for and thinking about all kinds of content in order to make sense of a text while reading.

segment To divide into parts: e.g., *to/ma/to*.

self-correcting Noticing when reading doesn't make sense, sound right, or look right, and fixing it when it doesn't.

semantic system The system by which speakers of a language communicate meaning through language. See also *graphophonic relationship, syntactic system*.

sentence complexity (as a text characteristic) The complexity of the structure or syntax of a sentence. Addition of phrases and clauses to simple sentences increases complexity.

sentence fragment A group of words written as a sentence but lacking some element—usually a subject or a verb—that would allow it to stand independently as a complete sentence.

sequel A form of literary work, typically a fiction text, that continues a story begun in a previous book. The central character usually remains the same, and new secondary characters may be introduced. Books with sequels are generally meant to be read in order.

series / series book A set of books that are connected by the same character(s) or setting. Each book in a series stands alone, and often books may be read in any order.

sets and subsets In relation to concept words, words that represent big ideas or items and words that represent related smaller ideas or items.

shared reading An instructional context in which the teacher involves a group of students in the reading of a particular big book in order to introduce aspects of literacy (such as print conventions), develop reading strategies (such as decoding or predicting), and teach vocabulary.

shared writing An instructional context in which the teacher involves a group of students in the composing of a coherent text together. The teacher writes while scaffolding children's language and ideas.

short story A form of prose fiction that is focused on human experience as it is revealed in a series of interrelated events. Shorter and less complex structurally than novellas and novels, short stories use most of the same literary elements that are found in those forms.

short vowel A brief-duration sound represented by a vowel letter: e.g., the lal in *cat*.

Short Write A sentence or paragraph that students write at intervals while reading a text. Students may use sticky notes, note paper, or their Reader's Notebooks to write about what they are thinking, feeling, or visualizing as they read. They may also note personal connections to the text.

silent *e* The final *e* in a spelling pattern that usually signals a long vowel sound in the word and that does not represent a sound itself: e.g., *make*.

simile A type of figurative language that describes one thing by comparing it to another unlike thing using the word *like* or *as*. Compare to *metaphor*.

solving words (as a strategic action) Using a range of strategies to take words apart and understand their meaning(s).

sources of information The various cues in a written text that combine to make meaning (for example, syntax, meaning, and the physical shape and arrangement of type).

speech A form of expository, procedural, or persuasive text written to be spoken orally to an audience.

speech bubble A shape, often rounded, containing the words a character or person says in a cartoon or other text. Another term for *speech bubble* is *speech balloon*.

spelling patterns Beginning letters (onsets) and common phonograms (rimes), which form the basis for the English syllable. Knowing these patterns, a student can build countless words.

split dialogue Written dialogue in which a "*said* phrase" divides the speaker's words: e.g., "Come on," said Mom. "Let's go home."

spoonerism The switching of the first letters of words in a phrase, creating a humorous effect. Compare to *malapropism*.

sports story A contemporary realistic or historical fiction text focused on athletes and sports.

story-within-a-story A structural device occasionally used in fiction texts to present a shorter, self-contained narrative within the context of the longer primary narrative. See also *plot*.

strategic action Any one of many simultaneous, coordinated thinking activities that go on in a reader's head. See *thinking within, beyond, and about the text*.

stress The emphasis given to some syllables or words in pronunciation. See also *accented syllable*.

style The way a writer chooses and arranges words to create a meaningful text. Aspects of style include sentence length, word choice, and the use of figurative language and symbolism.

suffix A group of letters added at the end of a base word or word root to change its function or meaning: e.g., hand*ful*, hope*less*.

summarizing (as a strategic action) Putting together and remembering important information, disregarding irrelevant information, while reading.

syllabication The division of words into syllables.

syllable A minimal unit of sequential speech sounds composed of a vowel sound or a consonant-vowel combination. A syllable always contains a vowel or vowel-like speech sound: e.g., *pen/ny*.

synonym One of two or more words that have different sounds but the same meaning: e.g., *high, tall*.

syntactic awareness The knowledge of grammatical patterns or structures.

syntactic system Rules that govern the ways in which morphemes and words work together in sentence patterns. This system is not the same as proper grammar, which refers to the accepted grammatical conventions. See also *graphophonic relationship*, *semantic system*.

syntax The way sentences are formed with words and phrases and the grammatical rules that govern their formation.

synthesizing (as a strategic action) Combining new information or ideas from reading text with existing knowledge to create new understandings.

tall tale A folktale that revolves around a central legendary character with extraordinary physical features or abilities. Tall tales are characterized by much exaggeration.

temporal sequence An underlying structural pattern used especially in nonfiction texts to describe the sequence in which something always or usually occurs, such as the steps in a process.

test writing A type of functional writing in which students are prompted to write a short constructed response (sometimes called *short answer*) or an extended constructed response (or *essay*).

text structure The overall architecture or organization of a piece of writing. Another term for text structure is *organization*. See also *narrative text structure* and *nonnarrative text structure*.

theme The central underlying idea, concept, or message that the author conveys in a fiction text. Compare to *main idea*.

thinking within, beyond, and about the text Three ways of thinking about a text while reading. Thinking within the text involves efficiently and effectively understanding what's on the page, the author's literal message. Thinking beyond the text requires making inferences and putting text ideas together in different ways to construct the text's meaning. In thinking about the text, readers analyze and critique the author's craft.

thought bubble A shape, often rounded, containing the words (or sometimes an image that suggests one or more words) a character or person thinks in a cartoon or other text. Another term for *thought bubble* is *thought balloon*.

tone An expression of the author's attitude or feelings toward a subject reflected in the style of writing. Compare to *mood*.

tools As text characteristics, parts of a text designed to help the reader access or better understand it (table of contents, glossary, headings). In writing, references that support the writing process (dictionary, thesaurus).

topic The subject of a piece of writing.

traditional literature Stories passed down in oral or written form through history. An integral part of world culture, traditional literature includes folktales, tall tales, fairy tales, fables, myths, legends, epics, and ballads.

underlying structural pattern See *nonnarrative text structure*.

understandings Basic concepts that are critical to comprehending a particular area of content.

uppercase letter A large letter form that is usually different from its corresponding lowercase form. Another term for *uppercase letter* is *capital letter*.

verb suffix A suffix put at the end of a word root or base word to form a verb. See also *suffix*.

viewing self as writer Having attitudes and using practices that support a student's becoming a lifelong writer.

visual strategies Ways of solving words that use knowledge of how words look, including the clusters and patterns of the letters in words.

vocabulary Words and their meanings. See also *word meaning / vocabulary*.

voice The unique way that a writer uses language to convey ideas.

vowel A speech sound or phoneme made without stoppage of or friction in the airflow. The vowel sounds are represented by *a, e, i, o, u,* and sometimes *y*.

vowel combination See *letter combination*.

word A unit of meaning in language.

word analysis To break apart words into parts or individual sounds in order to parse them.

word boundaries The white space that appears before the first letter and after the last letter of a word and that defines the letter or letters as a word. It is important for young readers to learn to recognize word boundaries.

word-by-word matching Usually applied to a beginning reader's ability to match one spoken word with one printed word while reading and pointing. In older readers, the eyes take over the process.

word choice In writing, the craft of choosing words to convey precise meaning.

word family A term often used to designate words that are connected by phonograms or rimes (e.g., *hot, not, pot, shot*). A word family can also be a series of words connected by meaning (e.g., *baseless, baseline, baseboard*).

word meaning / vocabulary *Word meaning* refers to the commonly accepted meaning of a word in oral or written language. *Vocabulary* often refers to the words one knows in oral or written language.

word origins The ancestry of a word in English and other languages.

word root A word part, usually from another language, that carries the essential meaning of and is the basis for an English word: e.g., *flect, reflect*. Most word roots cannot stand on their own as English words. Some word roots can be combined with affixes to create English words. Compare to *base word*. See also *Greek root, Latin root*.

word structure The parts that make up a word.

wordless picture book A form in which a story is told exclusively with pictures.

words (as a text characteristic) Decodability of words in a text; phonetic and structural features of words.

word-solving actions The strategies a reader uses to recognize words and understand their meaning(s).

writer's notebook A written log of potential writing topics or ideas that a writer would like to explore; a place to keep the writer's experimentations with writing styles.

References

References

Fountas, Irene C., and Gay Su Pinnell. 2017, 2011, 2008. *Fountas & Pinnell Benchmark Assessment Systems 1 and 2.* Portsmouth, NH: Heinemann.

Use this system to determine reading levels, gain specific information about reader's strengths and needs, and document progress over time.

———. 2017. *Guided Reading: Responsive Teaching Across the Grades,* Second Edition. Portsmouth, NH: Heinemann.

Use this book for help with teaching guided reading lessons. Learn how to select and introduce texts, teach during and after reading, and assess student progress.

———. 2015, 2014, 2009. *Leveled Literacy Intervention.* Orange System (Levels A–C, Kindergarten); Green System (Levels A–J, Grade 1); Blue System (Levels C–N, Grade 2); Red System (Levels L–Q, Grade 3); Gold System (Levels O–T, Grade 4); Purple System (Levels R–W, Grade 5); Teal System (Levels U–Z, Grade 6). Portsmouth, NH: Heinemann.

You can use these systems to align classroom teaching and intervention services. Leveled Literacy Intervention (LLI) *includes the professional book,* When Readers Struggle: Teaching That Works; *a program guide, lesson guides, a technology package, and fiction and nonfiction student books. The Lesson Guides provide specific help in implementing several lesson frameworks. The Guided Reading continuum is an integral part of lesson plans. The Orange system provides 110 lessons to be used with 110 different titles; Green includes 130 lessons and titles; Blue includes 120 lessons and titles; Red includes 192 lessons and 144 titles; Gold includes 192 lessons and 144 titles; Purple includes 204 lessons and 144 titles; and Teal includes 204 lessons and 144 titles. Each LLI system provides a complete range of resources, including children's books to support children who are struggling.*

———. 2014. *Fountas & Pinnell Select Collections.* Portsmouth, NH: Heinemann.

———. 2014. *Fountas & Pinnell Select Genre Sets.* Portsmouth, NH: Heinemann.

Use the PM Readers Collections and Genre Sets organized according to their F&P Text Level Gradient™ within your classroom. Fountas & Pinnell Select Collections K–3 provides the classroom with books suitable for independent, guided, and take-home reading.

———. 2013. "*Benchmark Assessment System 1* App." iTunes App Store. Portsmouth, NH: Heinemann.

———. 2013. "*Benchmark Assessment System 2* App." iTunes App Store. Portsmouth, NH: Heinemann.

———. 2013. "Fountas & Pinnell Universal Reading Record App." iTunes App Store. Portsmouth, NH: Heinemann.

These three Reading Record apps can be used as an efficient alternative to taking a reading record on paper. The Reading Record apps records the following student information: oral reading rate and accuracy rate, self-correction ratio rate, fluency score, and comprehension score. Use the apps to time the conference, calculate reading rates and ratios, save the record as a PDF, and sync the data to the Online Data Management System.

———. 2013. "*Leveled Literacy Intervention Blue* App." iTunes App Store. Portsmouth, NH: Heinemann.

———. 2013. "*Leveled Literacy Intervention Green* App." iTunes App Store. Portsmouth, NH: Heinemann.

———. 2013. "*Leveled Literacy Intervention Gold* App." iTunes App Store. Portsmouth, NH: Heinemann.

———. 2013. "*Leveled Literacy Intervention Orange* App." iTunes App Store. Portsmouth, NH: Heinemann.

———. 2013. "*Leveled Literacy Intervention Purple* App." iTunes App Store. Portsmouth, NH: Heinemann.

———. 2013. "*Leveled Literacy Intervention Red* App." iTunes App Store. Portsmouth, NH: Heinemann.

———. 2013. "*Leveled Literacy Intervention Teal* App." iTunes App Store. Portsmouth, NH: Heinemann.

Use the apps above for each Leveled Literacy Intervention *system, each app providing the teacher with all of the Reading Records and texts specific to each system. Use the apps to complete Reading Records among your students in a paperless format, time the conference, calculate reading rates and ratios, save the record as a PDF, and sync the data to the Online Data Management System.*

———. 2013, 2011. *Reader's Notebook, K–2, 2–4, 4–8.* Portsmouth, NH: Heinemann.

Use the Reader's Notebook *to encourage reflection, inquiry, critical thinking, and dialogue about reading. The* Reader's Notebook *can be used to help students account for what they read through drawing and writing as they explore and convey their understanding.*

———. 2013. "*Sistema de evaluacion de la lectura* App." iTunes App Store. Portsmouth, NH: Heinemann.

Use this Reading Record App with your Spanish-speaking English language learners. This paperless Reading Record App, similar to the English version, records the following student information: oral reading rate and accuracy rate, self-correction ratio rate, fluency score, and comprehension score. Use the apps to time the conference, calculate reading rates and ratios, save the record as a PDF, and sync the data to the Online Data Management System.

———. 2013, 2009, 2006. *The Fountas & Pinnell Leveled Book List, K–8, Volumes 1 & 2.* Portsmouth, NH: Heinemann.

Use these books and the leveled books website, www.FountasandPinnellLeveledBooks.com, with your studies of the Guided Reading continuum to analyze the characteristics of texts and select just-the-right book to use for guided reading.

———. 2013, 2009. *The Fountas & Pinnell Prompting Guide Part 1 for Oral Reading and Early Writing, Spanish Edition.* Portsmouth, NH: Heinemann.

———. 2012, 2009. *The Fountas & Pinnell Prompting Guide Part 1 for Oral Reading and Early Writing.* Portsmouth, NH: Heinemann.

———. 2012, 2009. *The Fountas & Pinnell Prompting Guide Part 2 for Comprehension: Thinking, Talking, and Writing.* Portsmouth, NH: Heinemann.

———. 2012, 2009. *The Fountas & Pinnell Prompting Guide Part 2 for Comprehension: Thinking, Talking, and Writing, Spanish Edition.* Portsmouth, NH: Heinemann.

The two tools listed above provide specific suggestions for language that you can use to teach, prompt for, and reinforce effective reading behaviors.

———. 2012. *The Fountas & Pinnell Genre Prompting Guide for Fiction.* Portsmouth, NH: Heinemann.

———. 2012. *The Fountas & Pinnell Genre Prompting Guide for Nonfiction, Poetry, and Test Taking, K–8.* Portsmouth, NH: Heinemann.

The Genre Prompting Guides *above are used to help guide students' inquiry toward explicit understandings of the characteristics of genres. Each prompting guide contains precise language for teaching readers how to focus their thinking and understanding of genres through inquiry.*

———. 2012. *Genre Study: Teaching with Fiction and Nonfiction Books.* Portsmouth, NH: Heinemann.

Use this professional resource with students to embark on an exploration into the study of genre.

———. 2012. *The Fountas & Pinnell Genre Quick Guide, K–8*. Portsmouth, NH: Heinemann.

This spiral-bound companion to Genre Study: Teaching with Fiction and Nonfiction Books *is designed to help you actively engage students in the exploration of texts so that they can notice and name genre characteristics and construct working definitions that guide their thinking as readers and writers.*

———. 2009. "Fountas & Pinnell Online Data Management Systems, Version 2." Portsmouth, NH: Heinemann.

Use the Fountas & Pinnell Online Data Management Systems to manage all of your assessment data.

———. 2008. *The Fountas & Pinnell Prompting Guides 1, 2, and Spanish Editions*. Portsmouth, NH: Heinemann. eBook.

The Prompting Guide eBook apps, available in English and Spanish, are suitable to use as ready-reference tools while working with students in several instructional contexts.

———. 2006. *Leveled Books, K–8 Matching Texts to Readers for Effective Teaching*. Portsmouth, NH: Heinemann.

Use this book and the leveled books website, www.FountasandPinnellLeveledBooks.com, with your studies of the Guided Reading continuum to analyze the characteristics of texts and select just-the-right book to use for guided reading.

———. 2006. *Teaching for Comprehending and Fluency: Thinking, Talking, and Writing About Reading, K–8*. Portsmouth, NH: Heinemann.

Use this book in your studies of the interactive read-aloud and literature discussions, shared and performance reading, and Guided Reading continuum to skillfully teach meaning making and fluency within any instructional context.

———. 2005. *Guided Reading: Essential Elements, The Skillful Teacher* (videotapes). Portsmouth, NH: Heinemann.

Use these videotapes with your studies in the Interactive Read-Aloud and Literature Discussion and Guided Reading continua. In the first part, "Essential Elements," watch guided reading lessons as they unfold to see how teachers introduce a text, support students as they read orally and silently, discuss text meaning, use "teaching points" to reinforce effective reading strategies, revisit the text to extend meaning, and conduct word work as needed. In part two, "The Skillful Teacher," observe the planning and organizing behind guided reading and learn how to meet the needs of individual readers. You'll discover how to group students, select books, plan book introductions, support word solving, teach comprehension strategies, develop fluency, and take running records.

———. 2005, 2001. *The Primary Literacy Video Collection: Guided Reading, Word Study, and Classroom Management*. Portsmouth, NH: Heinemann.

View these videos to see examples of classroom teaching and to learn how to create, organize, and manage a classroom environment that encourages and supports independent literacy learning.

———. 2004. *Word Study Lessons: Phonics, Spelling, and Vocabulary (Grade 3)*. Portsmouth, NH: firsthand.

Use this book with your studies of the Guided Reading continuum to choose the lessons that align with your students' needs.

———. 2001. *Guiding Readers and Writers: Teaching Comprehension, Genre, and Content Literacy*. Portsmouth, NH: Heinemann.

Use this book to explore and learn about the essential components of a quality upper-elementary literacy program.

McCarrier, Andrea, Gay Su Pinnell, and Irene C. Fountas. 2000. *Interactive Writing: How Language and Literacy Come Together, K–2.* Portsmouth, NH: Heinemann.

Use Interactive Writing *to support children's critical understanding of the writing process. In a step-by-step format, this book demonstrates how teachers can use interactive writing to teach a range of foundational literacy skills by sharing the pen with young writers.*

Pinnell, Gay Su, and Irene C. Fountas. 2011. *Literacy Beginnings: A Prekindergarten Handbook.* Portsmouth, NH: Heinemann.

A guide for supporting emerging readers, writers, and language users through play and exploration.

———. 2009. *When Readers Struggle: Teaching That Works.* Portsmouth, NH: Heinemann.

Use this volume to help you design and implement effective intervention programs for children in grades K–3 who have difficulty learning to read and write.

———. 2004, 2003. *Phonics Lessons: Letters, Words, and How They Work (Grades K, 1, and 2).* Portsmouth, NH: firsthand.

———. 2004, 2003. *Word Study Lessons: Phonics, Spelling, and Vocabulary (Grade 3).* Portsmouth, NH: Heinemann.

Use Phonics Lessons *and* Word Study Lessons *with your studies of the Phonics, Spelling, and Word Study and Guided Reading continua to choose the lessons that align with your students' needs.*

———. 2004. *Sing a Song of Poetry, Grades K, 1, and 2.* Portsmouth, NH: Heinemann.

Use these companions to the Phonics Lessons *series to utilize poetry to its full advantage to expand children's oral language capabilities, develop phonological awareness, and teach about the intricacies of print.*

———. 1998. *Word Matters: Teaching Phonics and Spelling in the Reading/Writing Classroom.* Portsmouth, NH: Heinemann.

This book will help you design and teach for effective word-solving strategies.